String Trimmer and Blower

SERVICE MANUAL ■ 3RD EDITION

P.O. Box 12901 ■ Overland Park, KS 66282-2901
Phone: 800-262-1954 Fax: 800-633-6219
www.clymer.com

Library of Congress Catalog Card Number 98-73995

February, 2003
July, 2004
March, 2008

This book can be recycled. Please remove cover.

Cover photo courtesy of:
Echo, Inc.

String Trimmer and Blower

SERVICE MANUAL ■ 3RD EDITION

String Trimmer and Blower Manufacturers

- Alpina
- Black & Decker
- Bunton
- John Deere
- Dolmar
- Echo
- Elliot
- Green Machine
- Hoffco
- Homelite
- Husqvarna
- IDC
- Jonsered
- Kaaz
- Lawn Boy
- Makita
- Maruyama
- McCulloch
- Olympyk
- Pioneer/Partner
- Poulan
- Redmax
- Robin
- Ryan
- Ryobi
- Sears
- Shindaiwa
- SMC
- Snapper
- Solo
- Stihl
- Tanaka (TAS)
- Toro
- TML (Trail)
- Wards
- Weed Eater
- Western Auto
- Windmill
- Yard Pro
- Yazoo

String Trimmer and Blower Gasoline Engines

- Alphina
- John Deere
- Dolmar
- Echo
- Efco
- Fuji-Robin
- Homelite
- Husqvarna
- IDC
- Jonsered
- Kawasaki
- Kioritz
- Komatsu
- McCulloch
- Mitsubishi
- Piston Powered Products
- Poulan
- Sachs-Dolmar
- Shindaiwa
- Stihl
- Tanaka (TAS)
- Tecumseh
- TML (Trail)
- Toro

Publisher Shawn Etheridge

EDITORIAL

Managing Editor
James Grooms

Editor
Steven Thomas

Associate Editors
Rick Arens

Group Production Manager
Dylan Goodwin

Production Manager
Greg Araujo

Senior Production Editor
Darin Watson

Production Editors
Holly McComas
Adriane Roberts
Taylor Wright

Production Designer
Jason Hale

Technical Illustrators
Matt Hall
Bob Meyer

MARKETING/SALES AND ADMINISTRATION

Sales Managers
Justin Henton
Matt Tusken

Marketing and Sales Representative
Erin Gribbin

Director, Operation–Books
Ron Rogers

Customer Service Manager
Terri Cannon

Customer Service Account Specialist
Courtney Hollars

Customer Service Representatives
Dinah Bunnell
April LeBlond

Warehouse & Inventory Manager
Leah Hicks

Penton Media

P.O. Box 12901, Overland Park, KS 66282-2901 • 800-262-1954 • 913-967-1719

More information available at *clymer.com*

CONTENTS

GENERAL MAINTENANCE, SERVICE AND REPAIR

TRIMMER SERVICE SECTIONS

BLOWER SERVICE SECTION

DUAL DIMENSIONS

This service manual provides specifications in both the U.S. Customary and Metric (SI) systems of measurement. The first specification is given in the measuring system perceived by us to be the preferred system when servicing a particular component, while the second specification (given in parenthesis) is the converted measurement. For instance, a specification of "0.011 inch (0.28 mm)" would indicate that we feel the preferred measurement, in this instance, is the U.S. system of measurement and the metric equivalent of 0.011 inch is 0.28 mm.

GENERAL MAINTENANCE AND REPAIR

TRIMMER INFORMATION

Line trimmers and brush cutters are manufactured for every use from the smallest home lawn to large scale commercial landscaping and grounds-care operation.

The drive may be electrical from rechargeable batteries, from 110 volt AC current delivered through an extension cable or by a two-stroke air-cooled gasoline engine.

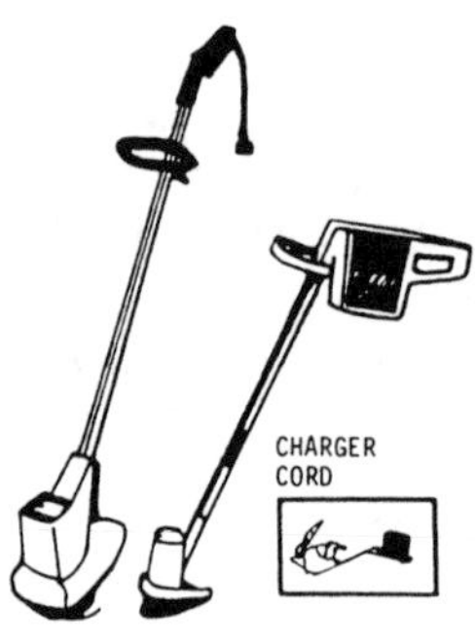

Battery powered trimmers are fine for light trimming, but can't handle heavy grass, weeds or brush. Most models must be recharged after about 45 minutes of operation. A full recharging may require 15 to 24 hours.

Electrical units operating on 110 volt AC current may have more power reserve than battery powered units, however, extension cord length should not exceed 100 feet even when using 14 gage or larger wire.

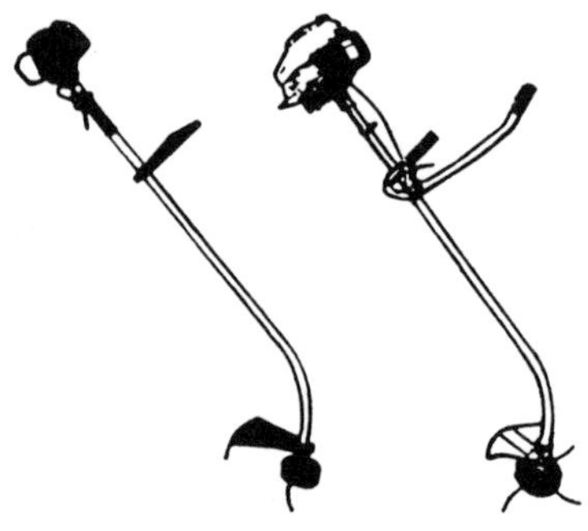

Gasoline engine powered trimmers may be used virtually anywhere that an operator can walk, but usually require more maintenance than a similar electrical unit.

Monofilament spin trimmers use spinning monofilament line (or lines) that is 0.050 to 0.130 inch in diameter. It's not fishing line, which requires high-tensile strength compared with trimmer line that must resist bending against plants. Spinning monofilament line actually breaks off plants rather than cutting them, much like breaking a plant by striking the stem with a stick.

Depending on head design, trimmers may have one, two, three, or even four lines extended for cutting at the same time. As the line wears back or breaks off, more line may be extended manually or automatically. Manual models require trimmer engine to be stopped. Loosening a lock knob or screw and rotating a housing advances new line. On semi-automatic trimmer heads, line is advanced by tapping the trimmer head on the ground with engine running at full rpm while others require quick adjustment of throttle speed. A cutoff blade on the trimmer shield prevents automatic extenders from letting out too much line, which would then overload the trimmer and reduce cutting efficiency. The motor or engine must be stopped before line is manually extended on other trimmers.

Tall, tough weeds require a weed blade that can replace the monofilament head on some heavier gasoline-powered trimmers. Some of the strongest heavy-duty units can be equipped with brush or saw blade for cutting saplings, brush and low, small tree limbs. Only trimmers designed for such use should be equipped with weed or brush blades. To avoid trimmer damage and possibly serious accidents, only the recommended weed or brush blades should be used. A blade that is too large overloads the trimmer, and the speed of some trimmers is too fast for safe blade operation.

On some power trimmers, the cutting head is attached directly to the output shaft of the engine or motor that is mounted at the lower end of the machine. This eliminates the driveshaft, bearings, etc., required if the power source is attached at the upper end of the trimmer.

A lower engine location exposes the engine to more dust, dirt and debris than is found at the upper position. Placing the engine at the cutting head also shifts most of the weight to that position and operator must support the weight while cutting, increasing operator fatigue.

Trimmers with engine at the upper end expose the operator to more engine noise and heat, but weight of such trimmers is better balanced and the engine is easier to keep clean. Trimmers with a curved shaft drive the cutting head directly from the engine through a flexible shaft. This provides a simple, economical drive.

Straight shaft trimmers have a set of bevel gears in a case atop the cutting head which changes direction of power flow and can change head speed in rela-

tion to engine speed if desired. The lower, straight shaft makes it easier to trim farther under low tree limbs, fences and other obstacles.

On some trimmers, a centrifugal clutch (similar to those on chain saws) engages the trimmer head when the engine is accelerated and is disengaged when engine speed is reduced. This improves trimmer safety and makes it easier to start the engine by not having to spin the trimmer head or blade also.

A trimmer that "feels fine" in the store may feel very heavy after long use in the hot sun. Both total weight and balance of a trimmer can affect how fast the operator becomes tired. For instance, some smaller gas trimmers weigh less than 8 pounds while bigger models weigh 25 pounds or more. (Electric models weigh approximately 2 to 10 pounds.)

Smaller trimmers may require more time to complete a given task, but operators with moderate strength may be able to use a smaller trimmer with fewer rest breaks and finish in about the same time as they would when using a trimmer that's too big.

Weed and brush blade should never be used without a shoulder harness on models fully supported by the operator. An approved shoulder harness will be designed to prevent the trimmer head from accidentally swinging back and possibly injuring the operator if the blade kicks against a solid object or if the operator slips. A correctly-adjusted shoulder harness also reduces fatigue and makes trimmer operation much easier.

The cutting head can be removed easily from some trimmers and replaced by other attachments. A blower attachment can remove leaves and grass clippings from sidewalks, driveways, etc. A power edger provides a neat appearance between lawns and sidewalks, driveways or other paved areas. And, a power hoe can weed gardens or flower beds and loosen soil for better infiltration of moisture.

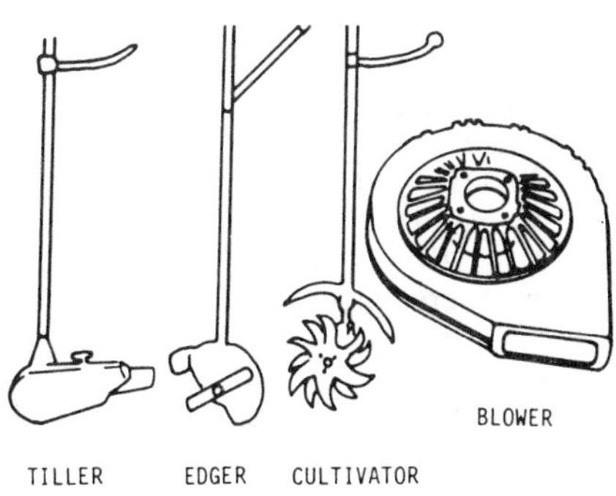

Such attachments eliminate the need to buy separate power units for each tool and, thus, can save considerable money. However, they are usually best for smaller lawns and gardens, particularly if two or more attachments must be used simultaneously.

OPERATING SAFETY

Edger and trimmers are cutting tools and must be operated with great care to reduce the chance of injury. Dangers include electrical shock, burning, muscle strain and being hit by projectile thrown by rotating unit. The operator should exercise caution and observe the following checklist.

Observe the following check list **in addition to STANDARD SAFETY PRACTICES.**

1. Remove debris from working area.
2. Keep people and animals well away from working area. (At least 20 feet from trimmer.)
3. Maintain proper balance and footing at all times. Don't overreach.
4. Be extremely careful of kick back, especially when using a hard blade cutter.
5. Cut only with discharge aimed at a safe direction, away from operator, windows, etc.
6. Use weed and brush blades only on edger/trimmers designed for their use. If the operator carries the full weight of the unit, an attached harness designed to prevent accidental injury to operator must be used.

If the edger/trimmer is powered by a gasoline engine, check fuel requirement before filling tank. The engines of spin trimmers which are carried by the operator, are lubricated by oil which should be mixed with the gasoline before filling tank. Overheating, rapid wear and serious damage will result if tank of 2 stroke engines requiring gasoline and oil mix is filled with only gasoline. Recommended ratio of oil to fuel is often marked on cap of fuel tank, but operator's manual should be checked for recommended type and amount oil.

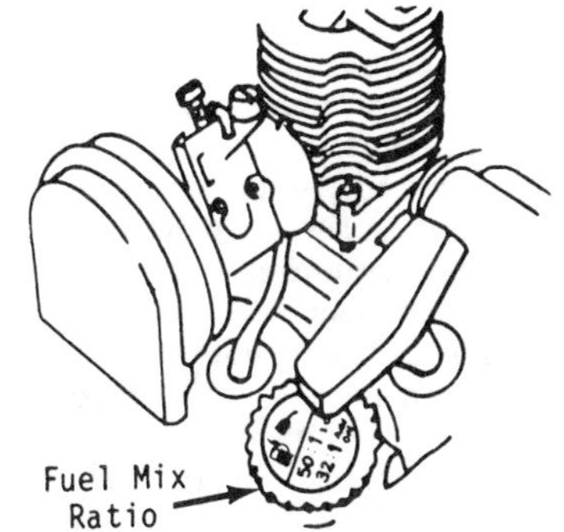

SETTING UP THE UNIT

Key to setting up and operating is the direction of rotation at the cutter. Cutting should only occur in the segment of the cutting plane that will discharge cuttings away from the operator or to the side. The cutter of some models rotates clockwise while the cutter of others turns counter-clockwise.

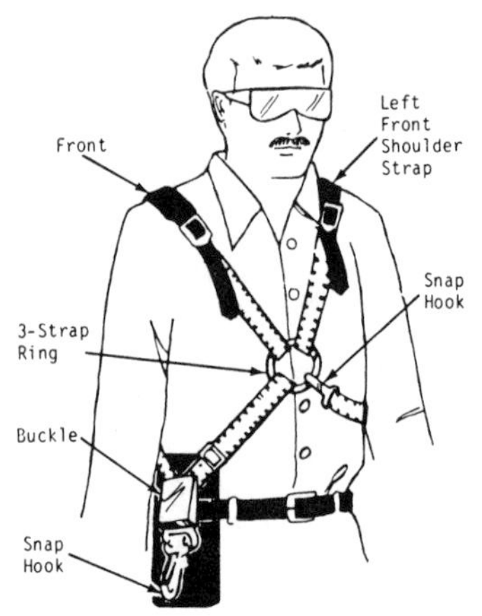

On models so equipped, put the shoulder harness on and adjust size to the user's body. Adjust position of hip guard so that suspension hook will be correct height for easy control of edger/trimmer. The harness plates on back and chest should be level. Make final adjustment so that pressure is even on both shoulders.

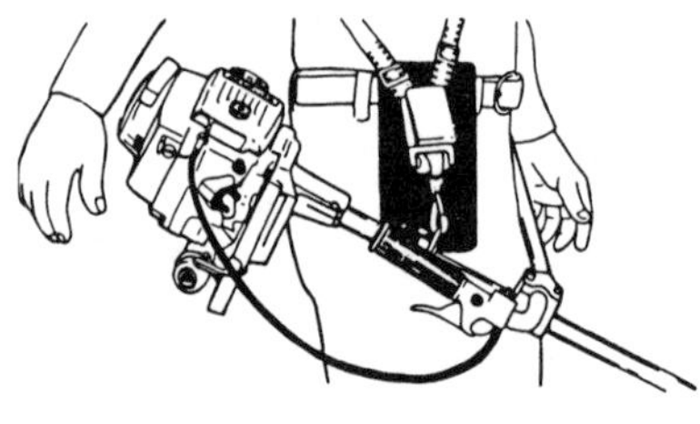

Trimmer should hang freely in front when operator stands squarely with feet about shoulder distance apart. Change balance by moving the hook eye on the drive shaft tube. When fuel tank is empty, trimmer head should float slightly above ground.

Adjust handle bar position for comfortable convenient operation while edger/trimmer is hanging from shoulder strap or harness.

Adjust for trim **mowing**, by positioning the cutting head horizontal, parallel to the ground. Adjust for **trimming** around trees, sidewalks, driveways, curbs, lawn furniture, etc., by turning the cutting head at about 30 degree angle from horizontal. Adjust for **edging** by positioning cutting head vertical (90 degrees from surface to be trimmed).

Adjusting the cutting angle should be accomplished by turning the cutting head or by relocating the handle. Forcibly holding the unit at an uncomfortable angle is only suggested if a change is for a very short time.

On gasoline powered models, fill fuel tank with correct type or mixture of fuel as specified by manufacturer.

Vibration, heat and noise of the operating unit may increase fatigue, decrease operator control and impair hearing. Nonslip gloves, properly adjusted shoulder strap (or harness), ear protection and appropriate protective clothing will help reduce the danger to the operator.

On all models, inspect area to cut and remove all debris that may clog or damage cutting head and all debris which could be damaged or thrown by cutter. Wire, string, rope, vines and cords can wrap around rotating head causing damage or possible injury. Rocks, cans, bottles, sticks and similar items can be thrown by cutter causing damage to property or injury to humans or animals.

STARTING ENGINE

DANGER: Before starting the edger/trimmer, make sure that all other people and animals are at least 20 feet away and that all parts are in place and tight.

On gasoline powered models, lay the edger/trimmer down on flat, clear area away from tall grass or brush. Operate primer or choke, move ignition switch to "ON" position; then, open fuel shut-off valve and open fuel tank cap vent. Squeeze and hold throttle trigger to ½ speed position, hold trimmer to ground as convenient and pull rewind starter

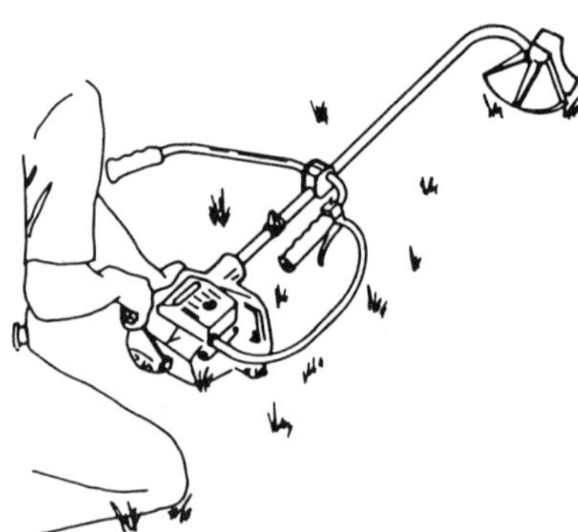

handle smartly. Do not let cord snap back because starter may be damaged.

On models with primer, it may be necessary to operate primer to keep engine running after first starting. On 2 stroke engines wilth choke, push choke in, then attempt to start after engine has tried to start.

On all models, engine should warm enough to idle smoothly without operating primer or with choke open soon after starting. If equipped with automatic clutch, cutting head should not rotate at idle speed.

MOWING

Trim mowing is very much like having a very narrow rotary lawn mower for places where a regular mower is too wide. String trimmers are also used to mow areas too rough for a standard rotary mower, such as some rocky places.

Cut only in segment of the cutting plane that is away from the operator as indicated by the shaded area in the illustration. Discharge will then be away from operator. When mowing, the cutting head must be kept parallel to the ground. The cut height of the grass should be maintained as if cut with a regular mower. Smooth even cutting will be im-

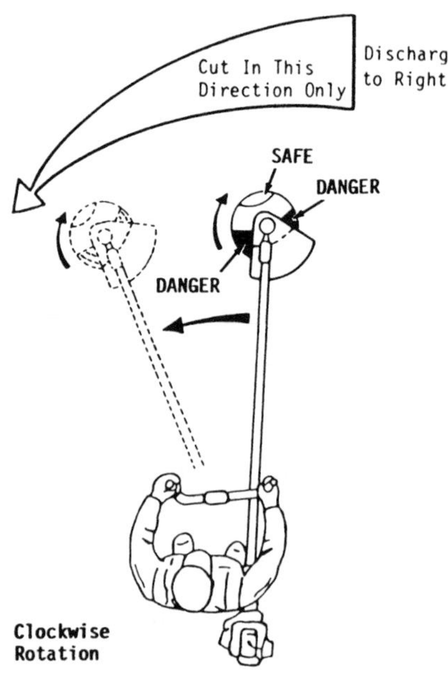

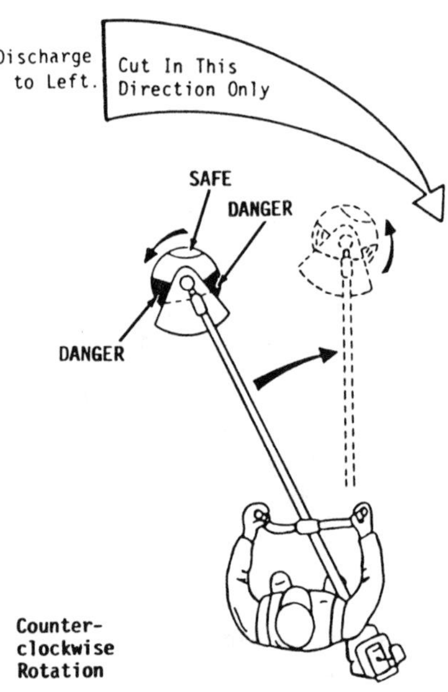

possible if cutting head is angled while attempting to mow.

TRIMMING

The cutting head should be about 30 degrees to the horizontal when trimming around sidewalks, driveways, curbs, lawn furniture, etc. The lower edge should be next to the sidewalk, etc., and should taper upward to the regular cut height of the grass.

WARNING: Always cut so that discharge is away from operator. Never operate with discharge toward feet or legs.

It is possible to forcibly hold the trimmer at the 30 degree angle; however, operator fatigue is increased unnecessarily and safety is compromised. Handle, hook eye or cutting head angles are easily adjusted so that correct 30 degree angle is the natural, easy position of trimmer.

Adjust angle so that the cutting plane is higher on discharge side. Confine cutting to the segment of the cutting plane away from operator so that discharge will be away from operator.

CAUTION: Be careful when trimming around objects such as small pipes, rods or fencing. Trimmer string will wrap around small objects and damage end of trimmer string.

String that is frayed from use is more gentle for trimming around trees and plants than line that has been recently extended and cut. Be careful not to damage bark of trees while trimming.

SCALPING

It's sometimes desirable to remove all grass from certain areas. This scalping is accomplished in much the same way as trimming, except much closer.

Adjust the cutting head so that cutting plane is about 30 degrees from horizontal and discharge is away from operator. Adjust handle, hook eye or cutting head as required so that trimmer will easily assume the desired angle naturally.

Confine cutting to the segment of the cutting plane so that discharge will be away from operator.

Begin scalping area around object, by first cutting perimeter. After establishing outer limits, scalp inside by working in direction necessary to discharge grass toward perimeter.

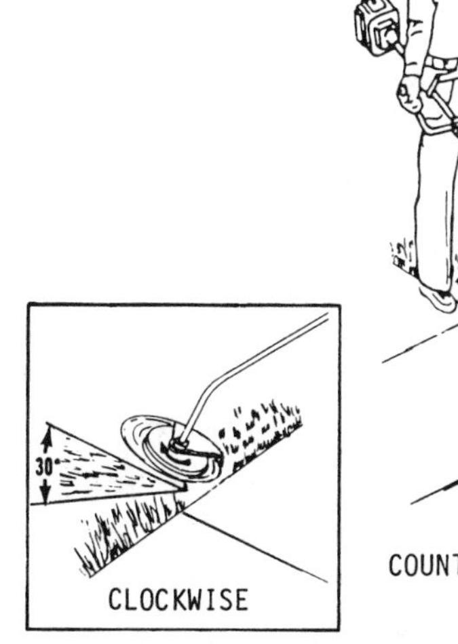

When cutting next to trees or plants, frayed ends of trimmer string will be more gentle than if the line is recently extended and cut. Trees can be damaged or killed if bark is removed from circumference of tree.

CAUTION: Be careful when cutting around objects such as pipes or rods. Trimmer string may wrap around small objects which can't be moved and are too strong to be cut.

EDGING

The cutter head should be turned so that cutting plane is vertical, perpendicular to part being edged and so that discharge is toward front away from operator.

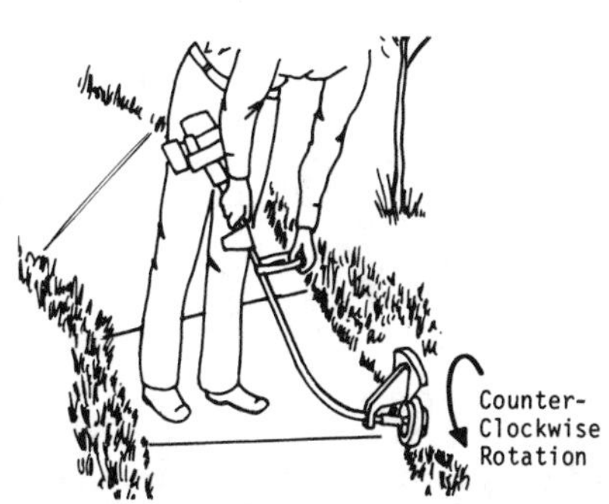

DANGER: Cut grass, dirt, stones, etc., will be discharged violently when edging, because of the position of the cutting head. Always wear protective glasses or goggles when operating edger. Be especially cautious of the discharge and make sure other people, animals, automobiles, etc., will not be affected by discharge.

Adjust position of handle, hook eye or cutting head angle so that edger is in a natural easy position for comfortable control.

WEED, BRUSH AND CLEARING BLADES

Some edgers and trimmers can be equipped with hard plastic or metal blades for cutting weeds, brush or small trees.

WARNING: Rigid blades should be used only on units supported by wheels or suspended from operator by a harness.

Monofilament string trimmers are designed for safe, easy operation while cutting light grass. Blades may be available to replace the string cutting head; however, make sure that replacement blade is for specific model and is recommended by the manufacturer.

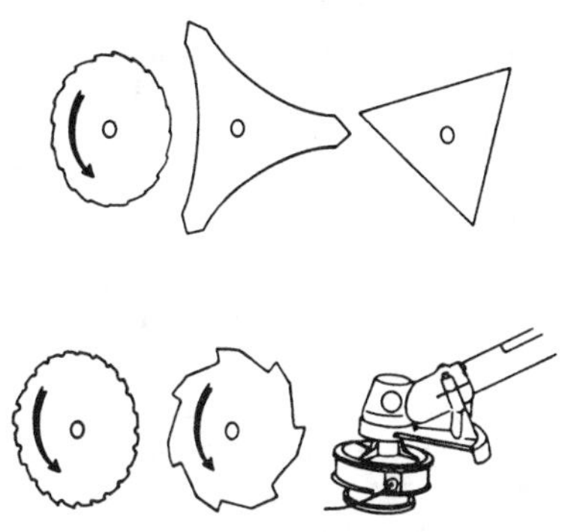

DANGER: Be careful of kick back. Harnesses are designed to minimize danger of injury, but be extremely careful to maintain control at all times when using rigid blades.

Cutting blades that are hard are more dangerous to use than a monofilament string, even though general operation is similar. Blades may be metal or hard plastic, but the rigid design is used to force the cutting edge through the object to be cut. If the object can't be moved or cut by the blade, something else will happen, often with undesirable results. Three results are: The blade breaks apart; The blade stops turning; The cutting head kicks back pushing blade away from object to be cut. Even when used properly, rigid blades impose heavy shock loads to the blade and drive. Stop engine and check condition of blade frequently. Never operate unit if condition of blade, any part of drive or control is cracked, broken or slipping.

DANGER: Always stop engine before inspecting condition or removing debris from around blade. NEVER depend upon clutch to keep blade from turning while engine is running.

Consult dealer for tools and instructions for sharpening blade. Install new blade if condition is questioned. The cost of a new blade is much less costly than injury.

Blades with 3 to 8 widely spaced large teeth or cutter bars are available for some models. This blade is designed for cutting larger grass/weeds and may be made of either ridged plastic or metal. Install blade with sharp cutting edge toward direction of rotation.

DANGER: Kick back is able to occur more easily with wide tooth spacing. Do not swing cutter into hard to cut areas. Check area to be cut carefully and remove or mark anything that would impair cutting or trip operator.

These blades are highly effective for cutting large unrestricted areas, but violent kick back is likely to occur if used near fences, walls or similar firm objects. Blades with more than three teeth are not recommended for use around objects which could cause kick back, but blade can sometimes be installed upside down to reduce kick back. Remove and install blade correctly, with sharp cutting edge toward direction of rotation as soon as practical.

Circular saw blades and clearing blades made especially for specific models can be used to cut brush, including small trees. This type of blade should be used only at ground level; never overhead.

Install blade with sharp cutting edge toward direction of rotation for normal cutting.

WARNING: Blade and drive parts will be damaged by hitting blade against trees, rocks or other solid objects.

Always cut by moving the cutting head, twisting your whole body opposite the rotation of the cutting head. Do not just swing the unit with your arms and hands. Do not cut during the return swing. Cuts should be a series of wedge shaped arcs as shown.

Work stops are provided on some models for cutting larger (but still small) trees. The heavier stop is usually at the rear and is preferred. Do not attempt to cut with work on opposite side of stop.

BASIC OPERATING CHECK LIST

Electric Powered Edger/Trimmers

Check for proper line length or blade for sharpness and condition before use. Stop, disconnect extension cord and check condition frequently during use.

Check cooling air filters for cleanliness and condition before using. Stop and clean cooling air filter frequently, especially when operating in dirty conditions.

Lubricate as recommended by manufacturer. Most use permanently lubricated bearings and require no lubrication; however some require periodic oiling.

Check for proper length extension cord to reach all areas without exceeding safe limit. Attach extension cord and check for operation.

Notice any irregularities during operation, especially vibration or speed. Check for blade or line damage and overheating.

Remove and clean cooling air filter at the end of each working day. Install new filter if damaged.

Clean all accumulated grass, dirt and other debris from motor and cutter.

Inspect cutting blade or line and service if required. Rigid blades can be sharpened. Consult dealer for sharpening tools and instruction.

Gasoline Powered Edger/Trimmers

Check for proper line length or blade for sharpness and condition before use. Stop engine and check condition frequently during use, especially if engine speed increases or unit begins to vibrate.

Check cooling air passages for cleanliness. Grass and dirt should have been cleaned after use, but regardless, don't start off with unit dirty. Also, birds or insects may have built nests in cooling passages since last use.

Check for sufficient amount of fuel to finish anticipated work that day. Be sure that fuel for models requiring gasoline and oil blend is mixed in proper ratio.

Clean around fuel filler cap before removing cap for filling.

Fill fuel tank with required type of gasoline and oil mix. Always leave some room for expansion in tank. Some manufacturers suggest ¾ full.

Start engine and check for proper engine operation. Accelerate and check operation of clutch (if so equipped) and cutter. If binding, overloading or vibration is evident, stop, and repair cause.

At the end of each working day, clean air passages, clean engine air filter and sharpen blade, if equipped with rigid blade.

Fill gear box with approved lubricant at end of each working day. Lithium grease is used for most models with gear box at lower end of drive shaft.

After each 20 hours of operation, remove, clean and lubricate drive shaft, then reinstall, reversing ends to equalize wear.

BLOWER OPERATION

TYPES

Blowers are classified as either backpack blowers or hand-held blowers. Backpack models have a blower power assembly in a unit that is carried on the back of the operator. A flexible blower or vacuum tube extends from the blower to be directed by the operator. Hand-held units have a power unit that is carried in the operator's hand and a rigid blower or vacuum tube attached to the blower.

Two major advantages of the hand-held blower are ease of use and compact design. But these benefits are offset by a requirement for light weight, which may mean less power, to lessen operator fatigue. Backpack blowers offer greater operator comfort, more power and greater versatility, but are generally heavier and more complex than hand-held units.

Some blowers are capable of operating as a vacuum by attaching or reconfiguring tubing. Blowers also can function as sprayers or misters, either using gravity or a pump to supply the solution to the spray head.

OPERATING SAFELY

Blowers are designed to move objects using air as the moving force. Air can be propelled by a blower to approximately 120 mph, sufficient speed to harm people and damage property. The operator should observe the following safety points as well as accepted safety procedures related to the operation of gasoline powered equipment:

• Do not operate blower in an enclosed or poorly ventilated area.
• Do not point blower towards people, animals or objects, such as cars and buildings that may be damaged.
• Do not blow debris to a location that may create a hazard or hide a potential hazard.
• Do not operate blower in a potential fire hazard area unless the unit is equipped with fire-prevention devices that function properly, *i.e.*, a spark arrestor.

The operator should wear proper clothing, safety eyewear, ear plugs and dust mask.

Before using a backpack blower, the operator should check the fit of the backpack and perform adjustments as needed to obtain a comfortable position. This should be done with the engine stopped. Be sure there is no loose clothing that can contact the muffler or be sucked into the impeller. (If operator has long hair, be sure it cannot reach impeller.)

STARTING ENGINE

DANGER: Start blower engine away from refueling area and away from bystanders.

To start blower, position unit squarely on ground with blower hose pointing in a safe direction. Open fuel valve and close choke. If so equipped, set fast-idle button or latch. If so equipped, operate primer button. Move ignition switch to "ON" position and operate rewind starter smoothly but rapidly. Do not fully extend starter rope or allow rope to snap back into starter, otherwise starter may be damaged.

When engine is cold, it may be necessary to operate primer or leave the choke on until the engine is sufficiently warm to run with a normal mixture. Disengage the fast-idle device when the engine will idle at normal idle speed. Turn off choke when engine will idle smoothly at normal idle speed and accelerate cleanly without hesitation from idle to full throttle.

The engine will usually start easily if started shortly after the engine was stopped. If the engine was stopped while hot and sits for an extended period, the fuel may have percolated from the fuel passages. It may be necessary to operate the choke for a short period to get fuel to the engine, but do not overchoke or flooding will occur.

Each model requires certain techniques to start a cold or hot engine easily. These techniques usually are learned only by operation of the equipment.

ROUTINE MAINTENANCE

Three key elements for good maintenance are:

1. Keep the electric motor or gasoline engine cool.
2. Keep dirt and debris out of the rotating parts, especially engine parts.
3. Keep parts lubricated.

Attention to these items will result in equipment that will perform when needed for its designed service life.

COOLING SYSTEM

The electric motor or gasoline engine used to power the trimmers, brush cutters and blowers in this manual are cooled by air passing by the motor or engine. Excess heat ruins both electric motors and gasoline engines. This destructive heat is produced when a motor or engine is overloaded or its cooling system is clogged with debris. Motors and engines that are located low, near the ground, will get dirtier than those mounted higher.

The electric motors found on trimmers, brush cutters and blowers are equipped with a fan to circulate cool air around the motor. The motor may be equipped with a filter to prevent the entrance of dirt, grass and debris from passing around the motor. Usually the filter is an open cell pad that is easily accessible for cleaning or replacement. Clean the filter with mild soap and water only. Dry filter before reinstalling. Check condition of filter and discard if it is damaged or cannot be cleaned.

WARNING: Never operate electric equipment without filters in place. If motor overheats and flammable debris is ingested, a fire may result.

Cooling air for gasoline powered equipment must flow freely through the engine fan and across the cooling fins. Grass, leaves and dust can build up and block the flow of cool air causing the engine to overheat. The shrouds and baffles that cover the fan and form the cooling system air passages should be removed at least once a year so all debris can be cleaned out. More frequent cleaning may be necessary depending on usage. Trimmers with low-mounted engines should be cleaned more often. Clean any unit that has noticeable buildup. Use a brush, compressed air and a nonmetallic scraper to remove grass, dirt, leaves and any crusty deposits from fan and fins.

CAUTION: Cover openings to carburetor, exhaust, fuel tank vent and other engine openings when cleaning the cooling passages to prevent entrance of dirt and debris.

Excessive heat can ruin gasoline engines by breaking down the oil film that separates moving engine parts. Heat also damages seals and distorts components beyond design limits. Minor overheating may cause lowered engine performance; extreme overheating may result in seizure. Overheating is usually a result of inadequate cooling or overloading, and sometimes it is a combination of both. Proper maintenance and operating procedures will prevent most overheating occurrences.

CAUTION: Never attempt to cool an overheated engine or part by plunging it into water or by spraying on water. Rapid cooling may cause parts to break or become brittle. Uneven cooling may increase distortion and damage.

OVERLOADING

Overloading can be a problem for trimmers and brush cutters. Dirt or trash may wrap around the rotating parts and overload the drive system and engine. String trimmers with trimmer line too long for the cutting job will cause overloading. Dull cutting blades or attempting to cut beyond the equipment's capability will overload the engine and drive system.

Overloading the engine forces it to rotate at reduced speed. Engine output (and heat) is high, but reduced cooling air flow due to reduced cooling fan speed causes heat buildup and possible damage. An overloaded electric motor generally smells hot due to overheated wiring or smokes. Overloaded air-cooled engines may smell when overheated, but usually the only sign before seizure may be a drop in performance due to damaged parts. If the motor or engine is overheated, it should be inspected, as well as any nearby parts that may be damaged by heat, before equipment is operated again.

LUBRICATION

Lubrication of moving parts in motors and engines is necessary for their operation. Maintaining the presence of lubricating oil and grease at required points is important to obtain a long service life for all motors and engines. Most electric motors are equipped with no-maintenance bearings and bushings, which do not require lubrication. All gasoline engines use an oil system that provides lubricating oil to moving parts.

Two-stroke engines used on trimmers, brush cutters and blowers are lubricated by oil mixed with gasoline. The oil is specially formulated to mix with gasoline and lubricate internal engine parts when ingested with the fuel. Refer to service sections for the oil recommended by the manufacturer and the correct fuel:oil mixing ratio.

Do not allow dirt or debris to enter fuel or fuel tank when refueling engine. Dirt can also contaminate oil in a two-stroke engine when carried by air passing through the carburetor. A clean air filter prevents dirt from entering the engine. Service the air filter as needed and renew if it is damaged or cannot be cleaned.

STRING TRIMMER LINE

String trimmer cutting heads are constructed in a wide variety of designs, but all use a monofilament line for cutting.

The line is extended from many self-feeding heads by operating the unit while tapping the head against the ground. Centrifugal force draws the line out of the spool and a cutter blade on the protective shield cuts the line to the desired length. If the line is too short for centrifugal force to pull it out (usually less than 3 inches), the line must by pulled out manually. With engine stopped, or motor unplugged, depress center of hub while pulling out approximately 3-4 inches of line. Repeat as needed until sufficient line is extended. If line is not visible, spool may be empty or line may be broken or tangled inside hub. Disassembly is required to fix problem.

Cutting line is extended on some models by accelerating engine speed, slowing engine to idle, then accelerating engine to high speed. Proper line extension depends on size and weight of line, engine speed and tension of springs in cutting head. If line will not feed, stop engine and check the cutting head. If line is too short, centrifugal force will be insufficient to extend line and line must be extended manually. Remove cover, turn spool to extend line approximately 4 inches from eyelet and reassemble. If line is not visible, spool may be empty or line may be broken or tangled inside hub. Disassembly is required to fix problem.

CAUTION: The cutting head must be equipped with the correct string for proper operation. Refer to service section for recommended string dimensions.

Spools on most models can be refilled. Be sure to use the correct type and size of line as recommended by trimmer manufacturer. Some common line diameters are 0.051 inch (1.3 mm), 0.065 inch (1.6 mm), 0.080 inch (2.0 mm), 0.095 inch (2.4 mm) and 0.130 inch (3.3 mm). Cutting heads may contain a single cutting line or several lines. When renewing the spool, be sure the correct spool is reinstalled. When installing cutting line on spool, note arrow on spool that indicates direction to wind line around spool.

DRIVE SHAFT

Trimmers and brush cutters are equipped with a drive shaft that transmits power from the engine to the cutting head. Two types of drive shaft are used: flexible or solid. Flexible shafts are used on models with a curved housing while a solid shaft is used on models with a straight housing. Solid shafts do not generally require maintenance, but most flexible shafts must be lubricated periodically. Refer to trimmer service section for manufacturer's recommended service interval. If not indicated, service shaft after every 20 hours of operation.

To service a flexible drive shaft, remove and clean shaft. The shaft can be pulled from housing on most models after separating housing from cutter head or engine. Removal of the cutter head assembly from the drive shaft housing is generally easier. After cleaning shaft, apply lithium grease to shaft. Reverse ends of shaft during installation to relocate wear points and extend shaft life.

CAUTION: Be sure drive shaft and housing properly engage cutting head or engine during assembly. Misalignment can cause damage.

OTHER ADJUSTMENTS, SERVICES AND REPAIRS

ON-OFF IGNITION SWITCH

Electric Powered Units

Electric powered trimmers and blowers are equipped with a spring-loaded, trigger-type on-off switch. The trigger is usually located on the handle (Fig. 10) and spring-loaded as a safety feature so the motor stops when the trigger is released.

To renew the trigger switch, first disconnect the electrical lead to the unit. On most models, the switch is accessible by removing handle screws (Fig. 11). Note position of pieces and switch during disassembly (Fig. 12). Disconnect switch leads and remove switch.

Gasoline Powered Units

Gasoline powered units may be equipped with a simple spring-loaded ignition grounding switch (Fig. 13), an "on-off" toggle switch (Fig. 14) or a slider type switch (Fig. 15). The switch may be located on the engine cover/handle assembly, on a bracket attached to the engine or on the drive shaft housing tube.

Before renewing switch, check switch, wires and connections with an electrical tester. Be sure any ground wires are properly attached. Before disconnecting switch, check parts supplier to determine if switch is available individually or as part of a wired assembly.

On most models, it is necessary to remove cover or housing for access to switch. Note position of any wires during disassembly. When reinstalling cover or housing, be sure wires are not pinched, contacting exhaust system or will rub against moving components.

ENGINE CHOKE/PRIMER

Gasoline Powered Units

Gasoline powered units may be equipped with a choke or primer mechanism to enrich fuel starting mixture.

The choke may be a simple plunger that, when turned, closes off the carburetor opening (Fig. 16), or a more complex system using a choke plate activated by pulling a choke lever. The choke plate is usually connected to the choke lever by a wire control rod. Refer to the carburetor paragraphs in the appropriate engine service section of this manual for choke information.

Primer systems consist of a primer bulb (Fig. 18) located on the carburetor or, on engines with a full engine cover, it may be located at an external location and connected to the carburetor by a fuel tube. The primer bulb is compressed to provide a rich initial fuel charge for engine starting. Refer to the carburetor paragraphs in the appropriate engine service section of this manual for primer information.

ENGINE THROTTLE

Gasoline Powered Units

All gasoline powered units are equipped with a spring-loaded throttle trigger assembly. The throttle trigger is spring-loaded so the throttle will return to idle when released. The throttle trigger is usually connected to the carburetor throttle lever by either a solid control rod or by a wire cable. The trigger may be located on the engine cover, on a handle, on the drive shaft housing, or on blower tube.

The throttle cable on models so equipped should be lubricated after every 20 hours of operation. Apply SAE 30 oil to each end of inner wire. Throttle cable service and adjustment information is outlined in service sections in this manual.

ENGINE REMOVAL

Gasoline Powered Trimmers

The engine can be separated from the drive shaft housing tube of most models after loosening clamp bolt or bolts (Fig. 19). The drive shaft will separate from the drive shaft adapter or clutch adapter when the engine is removed. When reconnecting engine and drive shaft, be certain drive shaft engages adapter fully.

CAUTION: Be sure drive shaft and housing properly engage engine and drive shaft adapter during assembly. Misalignment can cause damage.

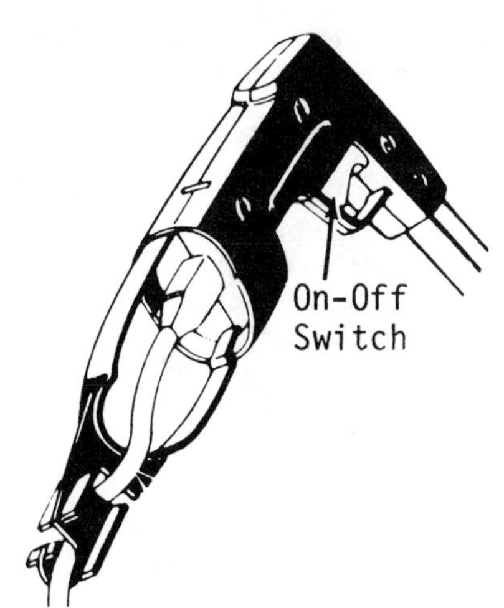

Fig. 10—View showing typical location for the spring loaded trigger type on-off switch used on electric trimmer models.

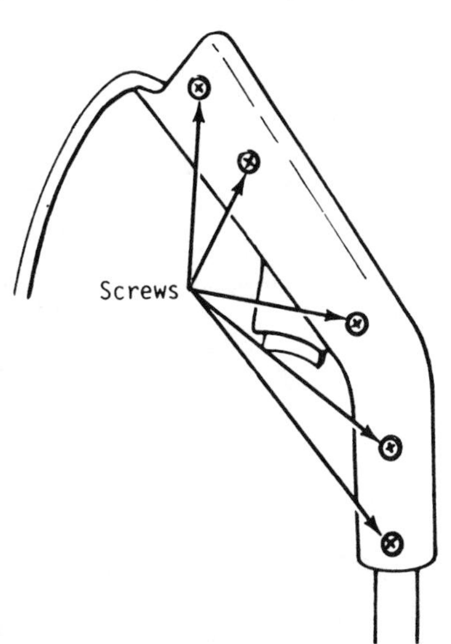

Fig. 11—Screws must be removed to separate handle for access to spring loaded trigger type switch used on many models.

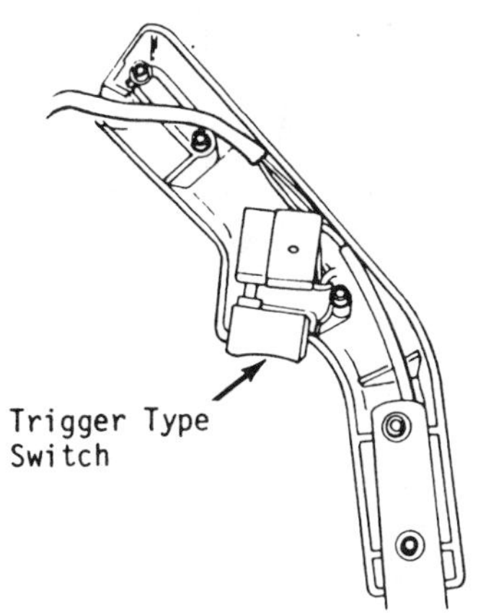

Fig. 12—Trigger assembly is trapped inside handle on many models.

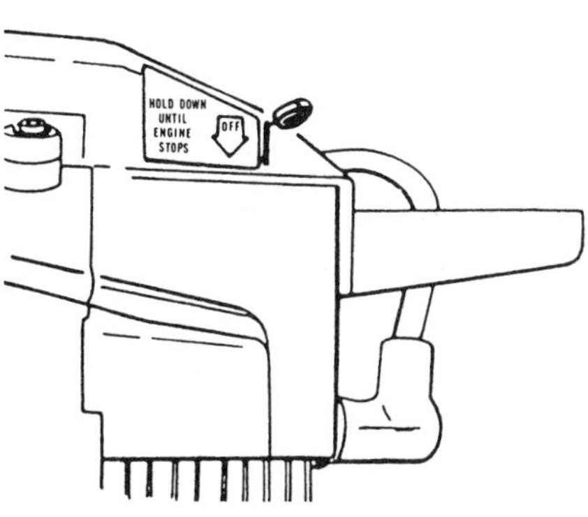

Fig. 13—A simple spring loaded grounding switch is used to stop engine on many models. Push spring down and hold switch lever until engine stops completely.

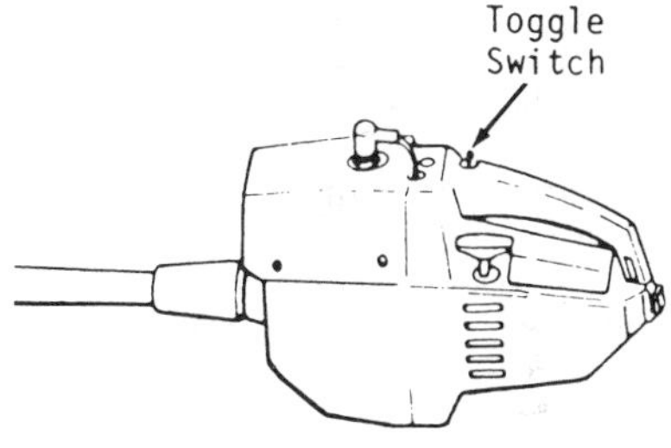

Fig. 14—A toggle switch is used for the ignition switch on many models.

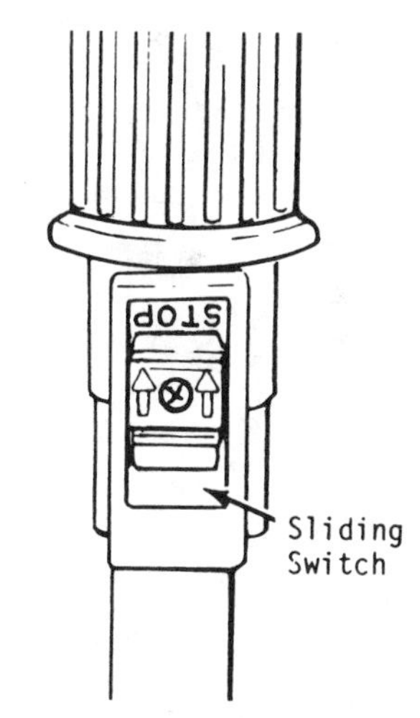

Fig. 15—Some models are equipped with a sliding type ignition switch.

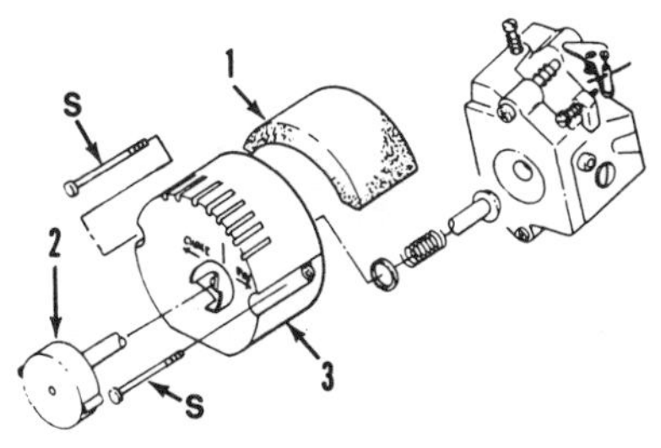

Fig. 16—Choke assembly on some models is a simple plunger (2) which rotates on a ramp and plugs carburetor opening.

Some models are equipped with a threaded collar that screws onto the engine adapter housing as shown in Fig. 20. Unscrew collar and separate engine from drive shaft housing tube. Drive shaft will separate from drive shaft adapter or clutch adapter when engine is removed. When reconnecting engine and drive shaft, be certain drive shaft engages adapter fully (see previous CAUTION).

On some models with a solid drive shaft, the clutch drum is threaded on the drive shaft. On these models, separate engine at adapter/clutch housing by removing screws securing housing to engine (Fig. 21).

Gasoline Powered Blowers

Removing the engine from a gasoline powered blower generally requires disassembly of surrounding shrouds and panels, which is apparent after inspecting the unit. In many cases, the engine can be separated from the blower assembly after detaching the blower impeller from the engine. Some means is necessary to secure the piston while unscrewing the impeller retaining nut. This may be accomplished using a special piston stop tool installed in spark plug hole. Some manufacturers recommend inserting a nylon or non-fraying rope through the spark plug hole, then rotating the piston against the rope.

DRIVE SHAFT ADAPTER/CLUTCH

Gasoline Powered Trimmers

Direct drive trimmer models (models without a clutch) are equipped with a drive shaft adapter that is threaded onto the crankshaft as shown in Fig. 22. The adapter may be an integral part of the flywheel nut. These models are equipped with a flexible drive shaft and the adapter is machined to engage the squared drive shaft end. When installing drive shaft, make certain squared end of drive shaft engages adapter fully to prevent drive shaft damage.

Models equipped with a clutch use an adapter that is attached to the clutch drum (Fig. 23). Models with a flexible drive shaft have an adapter that is machined to engage the squared end of the drive shaft. Models using a solid drive shaft may have an adapter machined to engage a splined drive shaft end, or the adapter may be threaded for use with a threaded drive shaft end (see Fig. 24).

When installing drive shaft on models equipped with a squared or splined end, be sure drive shaft end properly engages clutch adapter fully to prevent damage to drive shaft. On models with threads on the drive shaft end, apply locking compound to threads prior to connecting to clutch adapter.

BEARING HEAD/GEAR HEAD REMOVAL

All Trimmers

On most models equipped with a bearing head or gear head, the head may be removed by removing the clamp bolt or bolts and locating screw (Fig. 25). The drive shaft will separate from the drive shaft adapter when the shaft and adapter are disconnected. On models with the clutch mounted at the lower end of the

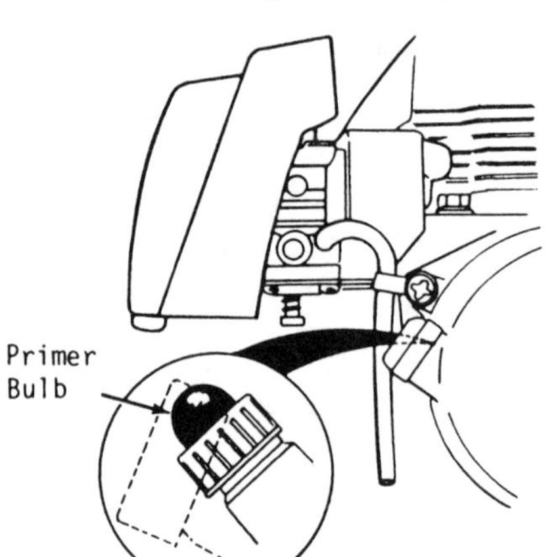

Fig. 18—Some models are equipped with a primer bulb which, when squeezed, injects a measured amount of fuel into carburetor.

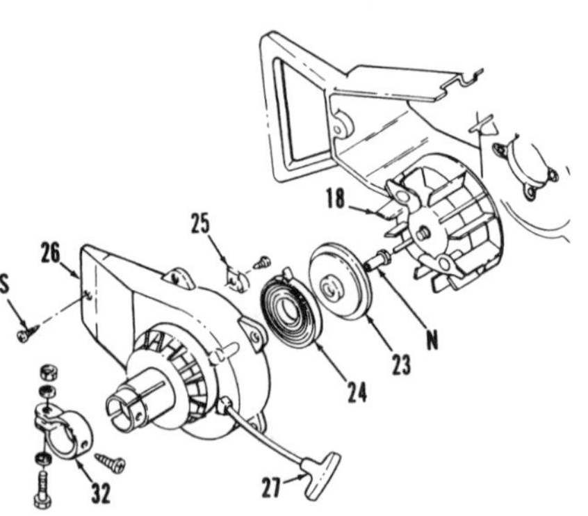

Fig. 19—A clamp (32) and bolt assembly secures engine to drive shaft housing tube on many models.

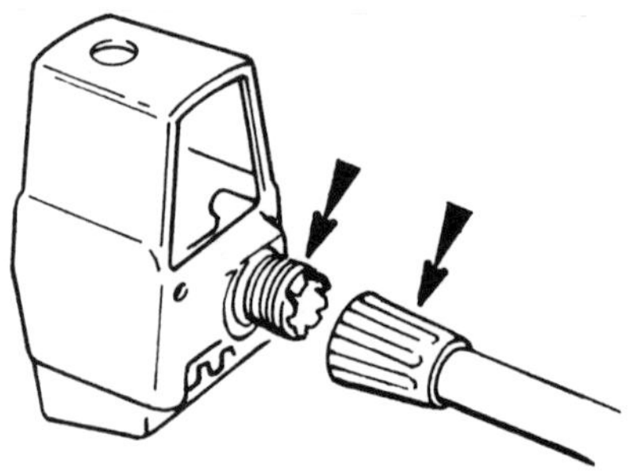

Fig. 20—Clutch housing or engine cover on some models are equipped with threads which engage a threaded collar on drive shaft housing tube to secure engine to drive shaft housing tube.

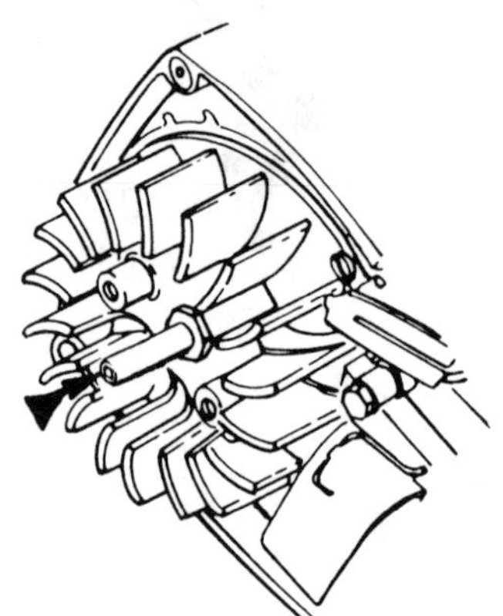

Fig. 22—Most direct drive models are equipped with a drive shaft adapter which also serves as the flywheel retaining nut.

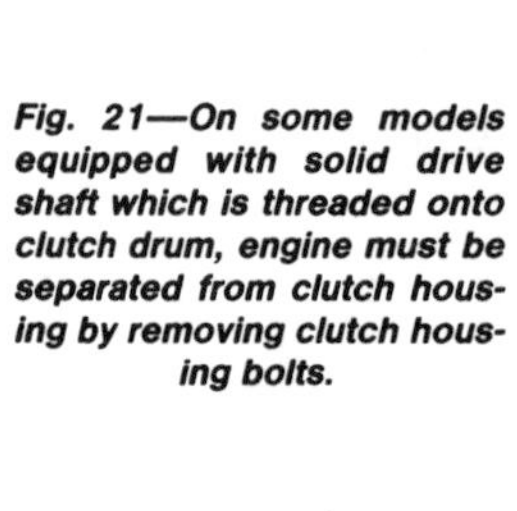

Fig. 21—On some models equipped with solid drive shaft which is threaded onto clutch drum, engine must be separated from clutch housing by removing clutch housing bolts.

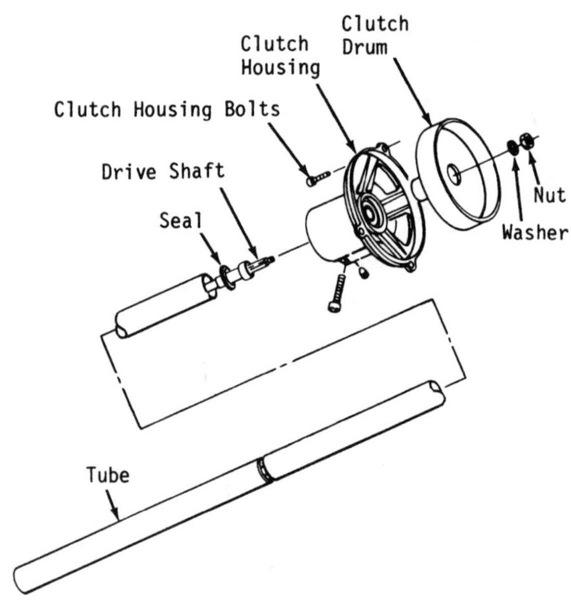

shaft, refer to appropriate service section for service information. On all models, refer to appropriate service section for service information on the bearing head or gear head.

DRIVE SHAFT HOUSING LINERS/BUSHINGS

All Trimmers

Models equipped with a flexible drive shaft in a curved drive shaft housing may be equipped with a drive shaft housing liner (2—Fig. 26). The liner may be renewed by separating the drive shaft housing tube from the bearing head and engine assemblies. Pull drive shaft (3) out of housing and liner. Mark location of liner (2) in housing (1) and pull liner out of housing. Install a new liner at the old liner location. Lubricate the drive shaft with lithium-base grease and install the shaft.

Models equipped with a solid drive shaft may have drive shaft support bushing (3—Fig. 25) located at intervals inside drive shaft housing (4). To renew bushings, separate the drive shaft housing tube from the trimmer head and engine assemblies. Mark locations of old bushings before removal. Install new bushings at locations of old bushings. A bushing installation tool is offered by some manufacturers and is indicated in trimmer service sections of this manual. Lubricate the drive shaft with lithium-base grease and install the shaft.

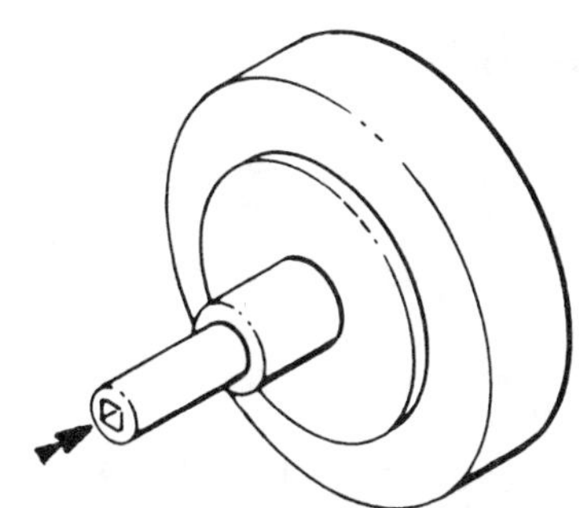

Fig. 23—Clutch drum on models equipped with a centrifugal clutch is equipped with a drive shaft adapter.

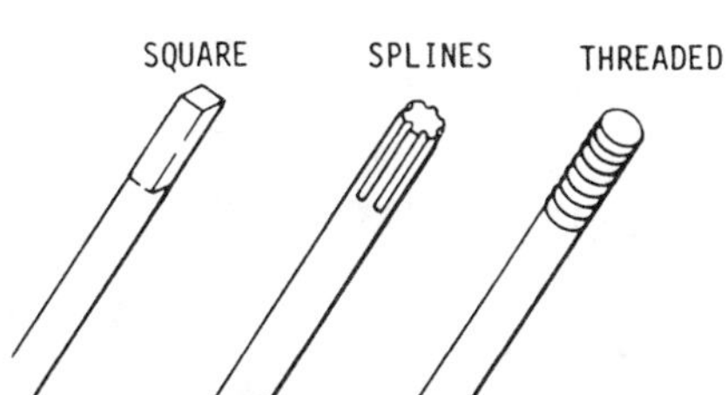

Fig. 24—Drive shaft ends may be square, equipped with splines or threaded.

GENERAL CARBURETOR SERVICE

TROUBLE-SHOOTING. Normally encountered difficulties resulting from carburetor malfunction, along with possible causes of difficulty, are as follows:

A. CARBURETOR FLOODS. Could be caused by:

- Dirt or foreign particles preventing inlet fuel needle from seating.
- Diaphragm lever spring not seated correctly on diaphragm lever.
- Improperly installed metering diaphragm. Also, when fuel tank is located above carburetor, flooding can be caused by leaking fuel pump diaphragm.

B. ENGINE RUNS LEAN. Could be caused by:

- Fuel tank vent plugged.
- Leak in fuel line or fittings between fuel tank and carburetor.
- Filter screen in carburetor or filter element in fuel pickup head plugged.
- Fuel orifice plugged.
- Hole in fuel metering diaphragm.
- Metering lever not properly set.
- Dirt in carburetor fuel channels or pulse channel to engine crankcase plugged.
- Leaky gaskets between carburetor and crankcase intake port. Also, check for leaking crankshaft seals, porous or cracked crankcase or other cause for air leak into crankcase. When fuel tank or fuel lever is below carburetor, lean operation can be caused by hole in fuel pump diaphragm or damaged valve flaps on pump diaphragm. On Walbro series SDC carburetor with diaphragm-type accelerating pump, a leak in accelerating pump diaphragm will cause lean operation.

C. ENGINE WILL NOT ACCELERATE SMOOTHLY. Could be caused by:

- Inoperative accelerating pump, on carburetors so equipped, due to plugged fuel channel, leaking diaphragm, stuck piston, etc.
- Idle or main fuel mixture too lean on models without accelerating pump.
- Incorrect setting of metering diaphragm lever.
- Diaphragm gasket leaking.
- Main fuel orifice plugged.

D. ENGINE WILL NOT IDLE. Could be caused by:

- Incorrect adjustment of idle fuel and/or idle speed stop screw.
- Idle discharge or air mixture ports clogged.
- Fuel channel clogged.
- Dirty or damaged main orifice check valve.
- Welch (expansion) plug covering idle ports not sealing properly allowing engine to run with idle fuel needle closed.
- Throttle shutter not properly aligned on throttle shaft causing fast idle.

E. ENGINE RUNS RICH. Could be caused by:

- Plug covering main nozzle orifice not sealing.
- When fuel level is above carburetor, leak in fuel pump diaphragm; worn or damaged adjustment needle and seat.

Refer to Fig. 28 for service hints on diaphragm-type carburetors and to following section for pressure testing procedure.

PRESSURE TESTING

DIAPHRAGM-TYPE CARBURETORS. With engine stopped and cool, first adjust carburetor low-speed and high-speed mixture screws to recommended initial settings. Remove fuel tank cap and withdraw fuel line out tank opening. If so equipped, detach

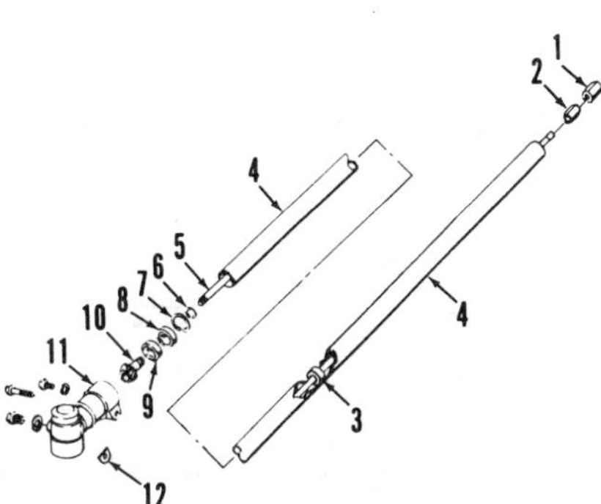

Fig. 25—Exploded view of a typical solid drive shaft and housing.

1. Adapter
2. Adapter
3. Bushing
4. Drive shaft housing
5. Drive shaft
6. Snap ring
7. Snap ring
8. Bearing
9. Bearing
10. Input shaft & gear
11. Gear head housing
12. Clamp shim

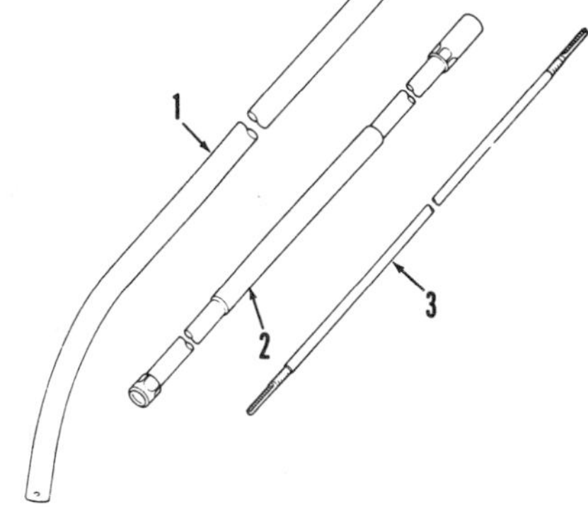

Fig. 26—Flexible drive shaft (3) on some models is supported in drive shaft housing tube (1) in a renewable liner (2).

strainer from end of fuel line and connect a suitable pressure tester to inlet end of fuel line as shown in Fig. 29. Pressurize system until 7 psi (48 kPa) is indicated on gage. Pressure reading must remain constant. If not, remove components as needed and connect pressure tester directly to carburetor inlet fitting as shown in Fig. 30. Pressurize system until 7 psi (48 kPa) is indicated on pressure gage. If pressure reading now remains constant, the fuel line is defective. If pressure reading decreases, the carburetor must be removed for further testing.

Connect pressure tester directly to carburetor inlet fitting and submerge carburetor assembly into a suitable container filled with a nonflammable solution or water as shown in Fig. 31. Pressurize system until 7 psi (48 kPa) is indicated on gage. Observe carburetor and note location of leaking air bubbles. If air bubbles escape from around jet needles or venturi, then inlet needle or metering mechanism is defective. If air bubbles escape at impulse opening, then pump diaphragm is defective. If air bubbles escape from around fuel pump cover, then cover gasket or pump diaphragm is defective.

To check inlet needle and metering mechanism, first rotate low- and high-speed mixture screws inward until seated. Pressurize system until 7 psi (48 kPa) is indicated on pressure gage. Use a suitable length and thickness of wire, and reach through vent hole in metering diaphragm cover. Slowly depress metering diaphragm. A slight drop in pressure reading should be noted as metering chamber becomes pressurized. If no drop in pressure reading is noted, then inlet needle is sticking. If pressure does not hold after a slight drop, then a defective metering mechanism or leaking high- or low-speed Welch plugs is indicated. To determine which component is leaking, submerge carburetor as previously outlined. Pressurize system until 7 psi (48 kPa) is indicated on pressure gage, then depress metering diaphragm as previously outlined. If bubbles escape around metering diaphragm cover, then metering diaphragm or gasket is defective. If bubbles escape from hole in metering diaphragm cover, then metering diaphragm is defective. If bubbles escape from within venturi, then determine which discharge port the air bubbles are escaping from to determine which Welch plug is leaking.

If low- or high-speed running problems are noted, the passage beneath the respective Welch plug may be restricted. To test idle circuit, adjust low-speed mixture screw to recommended initial setting and rotate high-speed mixture

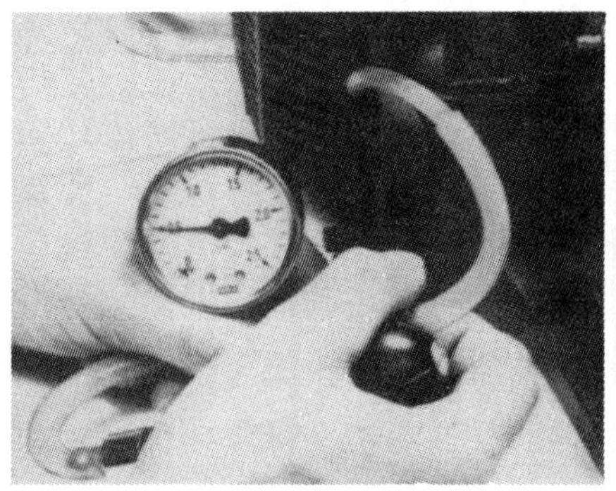

Fig. 29—View showing connection of pressure tester to fuel tank fuel line. Refer to text.

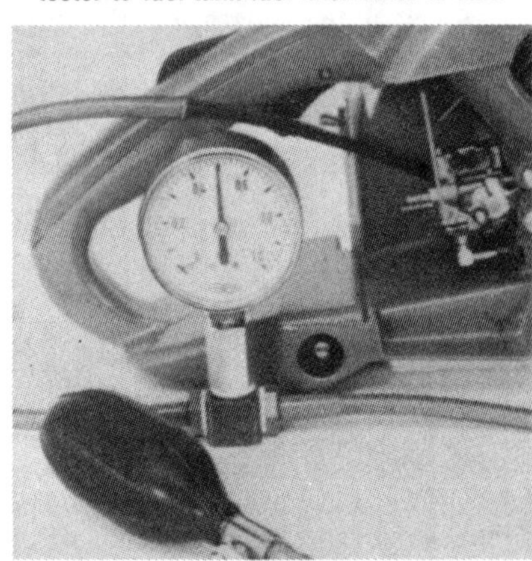

Fig. 30—View showing connection of pressure tester directly to carburetor inlet fitting. Refer to text.

THROTTLE SHUTTER COCKED CAUSING FAST IDLE
WELCH PLUG LOOSE CAUSING FLOODING
WELCH PLUG LOOSE CAUSING ENGINE TO RUN RICH WITH MAIN ADJ. CLOSED
FLANGE GASKET DEFECTIVE, ENGINE SPEEDS UP AND IDLE IS VERY LEAN AND ERRATIC
FILTER PLUG SCREW GASKET LEAKING CAUSING LEAN OPERATION
PLUGGED FILTER CAUSING LEAN OPERATION
IMPULSE CHANNEL PLUGGED CAUSING INOPERATIVE FUEL PUMP
DIRT UNDER INLET NEEDLE CAUSING FLOODING
DIRT IN IDLE SYSTEM CAUSING ERRATIC IDLE
LOW LEVER SETTING CAUSES LEAN OPERATION AND POOR ACCELERATION
DIRT IN REMOVABLE METERING JET CAUSING LEAN OPERATION & NO POWER
LEVER BINDING ON FULCRUM PIN CAUSES FLOODING OR LEAN OPERATION
HIGH LEVER SETTING CAUSED FLOODING OR RICH OPERATION
DIRT IN MAIN SYSTEM CAUSING LEAN OPERATION
BODY GASKETS DEFECTIVE CAUSING LEAN OPERATION
INLET CONNECTION GASKET NOT SEALING CAUSING LEAN OPERATION
BODY SCREWS LOOSE CAUSING LEAN OPERATION
HOLE IN METERING DIAPHRAGM CAUSING LEAN OPERATION
HOLE IN PUMP DIAPHRAGM CAUSING RICH OPERATION

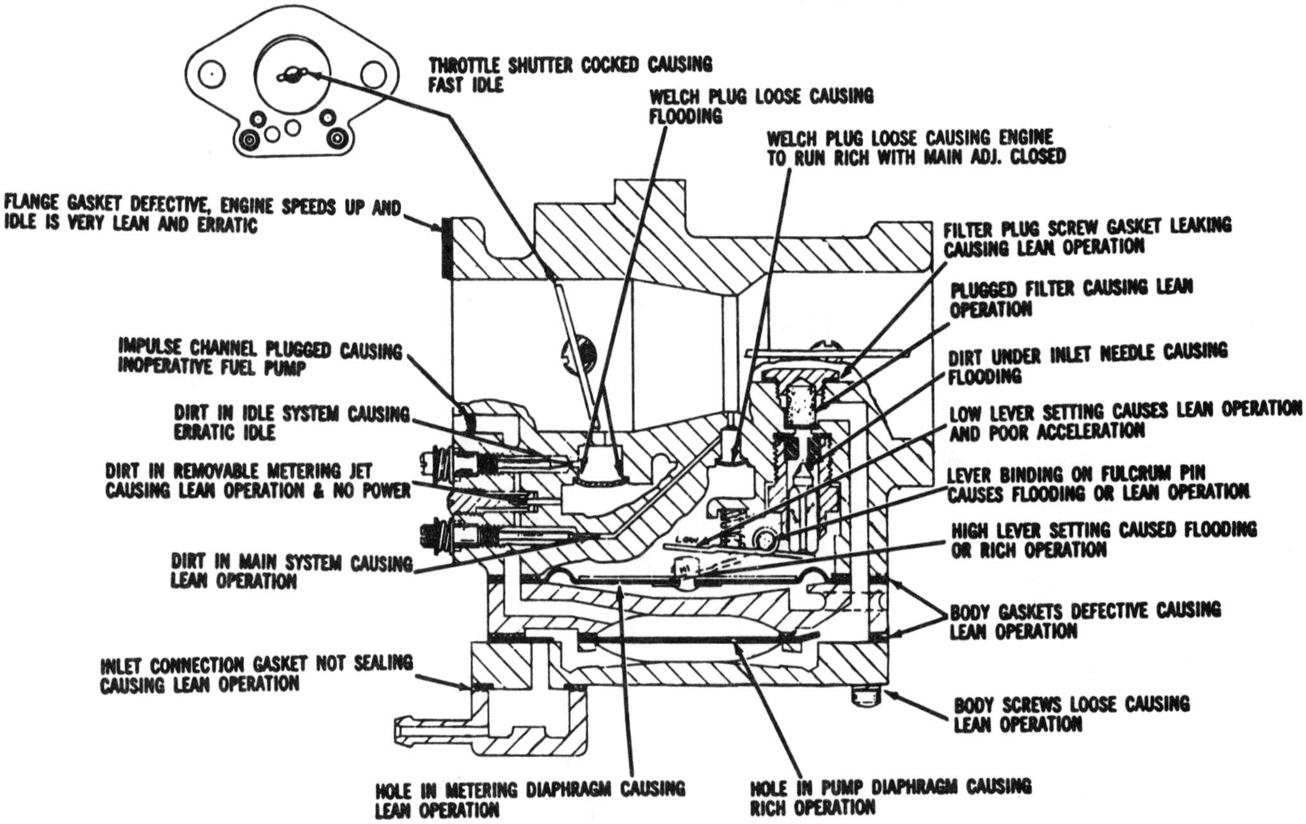

Fig. 28—Schematic cross-sectional view of a diaphragm-type carburetor illustrating possible causes of malfunction. Refer to appropriate engine repair section for adjustment information and for exploded and/or cross-sectional view of specific carburetor used.

screw inward until seated. Pressurize system until 7 psi (48 kPa) is indicated on pressure gage. Depress metering diaphragm as previously outlined. If pressure reading does not drop off or drops off very slowly, then a restriction is indicated. To test high-speed circuit, adjust high-speed mixture screw to recommended initial setting and rotate low-speed mixture screw inward until seated. Pressurize system and depress metering diaphragm as previously outlined and note reading on pressure gage. If pressure reading does not drop off or drops off very slowly, then a restriction is indicated.

Refer to specific carburetor service section in ENGINE SERVICE section and repair defect or renew defective component.

PRESSURE TEST CRANKCASE. Defective gaskets and oil seals or a crack in castings are the usual causes of crankcase leaks. A leak will allow supplementary air to enter the engine and thus upset the desired fuel:air mixture. An improperly sealed crankcase can cause:

A. Hard starting
B. Erratic running
C. Low power
D. Overheating

To test crankcase for leakage, remove muffler. Fabricate a seal using gasket paper or thin metal plate that will cover the exhaust port. Install the seal and muffler. Remove carburetor and fabricate an adapter plate with a fitting to which a rubber hose can be attached that will cover the intake port. Install adapter plate in place of carburetor. Connect a hand pump and pressure gage to adapter plate as shown in Fig. 32. Set piston at top dead center. Actuate hand pump to pump air into crankcase until gage indicates pressure of 7 psi (48 kPa). The pressure should remain constant for at least 10 seconds. If constant pressure cannot be maintained, use a soap and water solution to check crankcase seals, gaskets and castings for evidence of leakage.

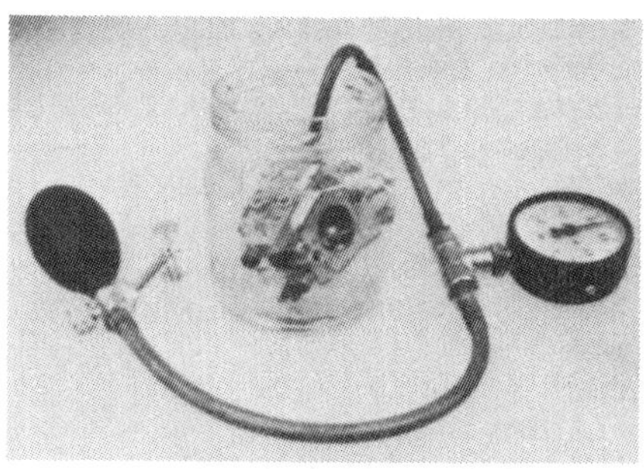

Fig. 31—Submerge carburetor into a suitable container filled with a nonflammable solution or water and pressure test as outlined in text.

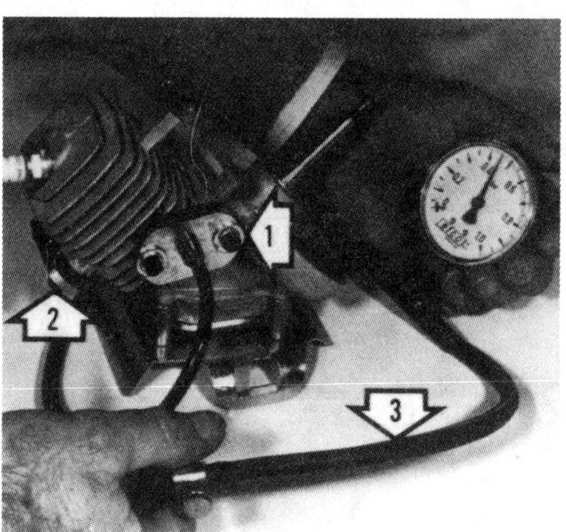

Fig. 32—Engine crankcase can be pressure tested for leaks by blocking off exhaust port and applying air pressure to intake port as shown. Refer to text.

SERVICE SHOP TOOL BUYER'S GUIDE

This listing of service shop tools is solely for the convenience of users of the manual and does not imply endorsement or approval by Intertec Publishing Corporation of the tools and equipment listed. The listing is in response to many requests for information on sources for purchasing special tools and equipment. Every attempt has been made to make the listing as complete as possible at time of publication and each entry is made from the latest material available.

Special engine service tools such as drivers, pullers, gages, etc., which are available from the engine manufacturer are not listed in this section of the manual. Where a special service tool is listed in the engine service section of this manual, the tool is available from the central parts or service distributors listed at the end of most engine service sections, or from the manufacturer.

NOTE TO MANUFACTURERS AND NATIONAL SALES DISTRIBUTORS OF ENGINE SERVICE TOOLS AND RELATED SERVICE EQUIPMENT. To obtain either a new listing for your products, or to change or add to an existing listing, write to Intertec Publishing Corporation, Book Division, P.O. Box 12901, Overland Park, KS 66282-2901.

Engine Service Tools

Ammco Tools, Inc.
Wacker Park
North Chicago, Illinois 60064
Valve spring compressor, torque wrenches, cylinder hones, ridge reamers, piston ring compressors, piston ring expanders.

Bloom, Inc.
Highway 939 West
Independence, Iowa 50644
Engine repair stand with crankshaft straightening attachment.

Brush Research Mfg. Co., Inc.
4642 East Floral Drive
Los Angeles, California 90022
Cylinder hones.

E-Z Lok
P.O. Box 2069
Gardena, California 90247
Thread repair insert kits.

Fairchild Fastener Group
3000 W. Lomita Blvd.
Torrance, California 90505
Thread repair insert kits (Keenserts) and installation tools.

Foley-Belsaw Company Outdoor Power Equipment Parts Div.
6301 Equitable Road
P.O. Box 419593
Kansas City, Missouri 64141
Crankshaft straightener and repair stand, valve refacer, valve seat grinder, parts washer, cylinder hone, ridge reamer, piston ring expander and compressor, flywheel puller, torque wrench.

Frederick Manufacturing Corp.
4840 E. 12th Street
Kansas City, Missouri 64127
Piston groove cleaner, compression tester, piston ring expander and compressor, valve spring compressor, valve seat grinder, valve refacer, cylinder hone, flywheel puller, flywheel wrench, flywheel holder, starter spring rewinder, condenser pliers.

Heli-Coil
Shelter Rock Lane
Danbury, Connecticut 06810
Thread repair kits, thread inserts, installation tools.

K-D Tools
3575 Hempland Road
Lancaster, Pennsylvania 17604
Thread repair kits, valve spring compressors, reamers, micrometers, dial indicators, calipers.

Keystone Reamer & Tool Co.
South Front Street
P.O. Box 308
Millersburg, Pennsylvania 17061
Valve seat cutter and pilots, reamers, screw extractors, taps and dies.

Ki-Sol Corporation
100 Larkin Williams Ind. Ct.
Fenton, Missouri 63026
Cylinder hone, ridge reamer, ring compressor, ring expander, ring groove cleaner, torque wrenches, valve spring compressor, valve refacing equipment.

K-Line Industries, Inc.
315 Garden Avenue
Holland, Michigan 49424
Cylinder hone, ridge reamer, ring compressor, valve guide tools, valve spring compressor, reamers.

K.O. Lee Company
200 South Harrison
P.O. Box 1416
Aberdeen, South Dakota 57402
Valve refacers, valve seat grinders, valve seat insert tools, valve guide tools.

Kwik-Way Mfg. Co.
500 57th Street
Marion, Iowa 52302
Cylinder boring equipment, valve facing equipment, valve seat grinding equipment.

Lisle Corporation
807 East Main
Clarinda, Iowa 51632
Cylinder hones, ridge reamers, ring compressors, valve spring compressors.

Microdot, Inc.
P.O. Box 3001
Fullerton, California 92634
Thread repair insert kits.

Mighty Midget Mfg. Co., Div. of Kansas City Screw Thread Co.
2908 E. Truman Road
Kansas City, Missouri 64127
Crankshaft straightener.

Neway Manufacturing, Inc.
1013 N. Shiawassee
Corunna, Michigan 48817
Valve seat cutters.

OTC
655 Eisenhower Drive
Owatonna, Minnesota 55060
Valve tools, spark plug tools, piston ring tools, cylinder hones.

Power Lawnmower Parts, Inc.
1920 Lyell Avenue
P.O. Box 60860
Rochester, New York 14606-0860
Flywheel pullers, starter wrench, flywheel holder, gasket cutter tool, gasket scraper tool, crankshaft cleaning tool, ridge reamer, valve spring compressor, valve seat cutters, thread repair kits, valve lifter, piston ring expander.

Precision Manufacturing & Sales Co., Inc.
2140 Range Road
Clearwater, Florida 34625
Cylinder boring equipment, measuring instruments, valve equipment, hones, hand tools, test equipment, threading tools, presses, parts washers, milling machines, lathes, drill presses, glass beading machines, dynos, safety equipment.

Sioux Tools, Inc.
2901 Floyd Blvd.
P.O. Box 507
Sioux City, Iowa 51102
Valve refacing and seat grinding equipment.

Sunnen Product Company
7910 Manchester Avenue
St. Louis, Missouri 63143
Cylinder hones, rod reconditioning, valve guide reconditioning.

Test Equipment and Gages

AW Dynamometer, Inc.
P.O. Box 428
Colfax, Illinois 61728
Engine test dynamometer.

B.C. Ames Company
131 Lexington
Waltham, Massachusetts 02254
Micrometers, dial gages, calipers.

Dixson, Inc.
287 27 Road
Grand Junction, Colorado 81503
Tachometer, compression gage, timing light.

Foley-Belsaw Company Outdoor Power Equipment Parts Div.
6301 Equitable Road
P.O. Box 419593
Kansas City, Missouri 64141
Cylinder gage, amp/volt testers, condenser and coil tester, magneto tester, ignition testers, tachometers, spark testers, compression gages, timing lights and gages, micrometers and calipers, carburetor testers, vacuum gages.

Frederick Manufacturing Corp.
4840 E. 12th Street
Kansas City, Missouri 64127
Ignition tester, tachometer, compression gage

Graham-Lee Electronics, Inc.
4220 Central Avenue N.E.
Minneapolis, Minnesota 55421
Coil and condenser tester.

K-D Tools
3575 Hempland Road
Lancaster, Pennsylvania 17604
Diode tester and installation tools, compression gage, timing light, timing gages.

Ki-Sol Corporation
100 Larkin Williams Ind. Ct.
Fenton, Missouri 63026
Micrometers, telescoping gages, compression gages, cylinder gages.

K-Line Industries, Inc.
315 Garden Avenue
Holland, Michigan 49424
Compression gage, leakdown tester, micrometers, dial gages.

Merc-O-Tronic Instruments Corporation
215 Branch Street
Almont, Michigan 48003
Ignition analyzers for conventional, solid-state and magneto systems, electric tachometers, electronic tachometer and dwell meter, power timing lights, ohmmeters, compression gages, mechanical timing devices.

OTC
655 Eisenhower Drive
Owatonna, Minnesota 55060
Feeler gages, hydraulic test gages.

Power Lawnmower Parts, Inc.
1920 Lyell Avenue
P.O. Box 60860
Rochester, New York 14606-0860
Compression gage, cylinder gage, magneto tester, compression gage, condenser and coil tester.

Prestolite Electronic Div.
An Allied Company
4 Seagate
Toledo, Ohio 43691
Magneto test plug.

Simpson Electric Company
853 Dundee Avenue
Elgin, Illinois 60120
Electrical and electronic test equipment.

L.S. Starrett Company
121 Crescent St.
Athol, Massachusetts 01331
Micrometers, dial gages, bore gages, feeler gages.

Stevens Instrument Company
P.O. Box 193
Waukegan, Illinois 60079
Ignition analyzers, timing lights, volt-ohm meter, tachometer, spark checkers, CD ignition testers.

Stewart-Warner Corporation
580 Slawin Ct.
Mt. Prospect, Illinois 60056
Compression gage, ignition tachometer, timing light, ignition analyzer.

Shop Tools and Equipment

AC Delco Division
General Motors Corp.
3031 W. Grand Blvd.
P.O. Box 33115
Detroit, Michigan 48232
Spark plug tools.

Black & Decker Mfg. Co.
626 Hanover Pike
Hampstead, Maryland 21074
Electric power tools.

Champion Pneumatic Machinery Co.
1301 N. Euclid Avenue
Princeton, Illinois 61356
Air compressors.

Champion Spark Plug Company
P.O. Box 910
Toledo, Ohio 43661
Spark plug cleaning and testing equipment, gap tools and wrenches.

Chicago Pneumatic Tool Co.
2200 Bleecker St.
Utica, New York 13501
Air impact wrenches, air hammers, air drills and grinders, nut runners, speed ratchets.

Cooper Tools
P.O. Box 728
Apex, North Carolina 27502
Chain type engine hoists and utility slings

E-Z Lok
P.O. Box 2069
Gardena, California 90247
Thread repair insert kits.

Fairchild Fastener Group
3000 W. Lomita Blvd.
Torrance, California 90505
Thread repair insert kits (Keenserts) and installation tools.

Foley-Belsaw Company
Outdoor Power Equipment Parts Div.
6301 Equitable Road
P.O. Box 419593
Kansas City, Missouri 64141
Torque wrenches, parts washers, micrometers and calipers.

Frederick Manufacturing Corp.
4840 E. 12th Street
Kansas City, Missouri 64127
Torque wrenches, gear pullers.

G&H Products, Inc.
P.O. Box 770
St. Paris, Ohio 43027
Equipment lifts.

General Scientific Equipment Co.
525 Spring Garden St.
Philadelphia, Pennsylvania 19122
Safety equipment.

Graymills Corporation
3705 N. Lincoln Avenue
Chicago, Illinois 60613
Parts washing equipment.

Heli-Coil
Shelter Rock Lane
Danbury, Connecticut 06810
Thread repair kits, thread inserts, installation tools.

Ingersoll-Rand
253 E. Washington Avenue
Washington, New Jersey 07882
Air and electric impact wrenches, electric drills and screwdrivers.

Jaw Manufacturing Co.
39 Mulberry St.
P.O. Box 213
Reading, Pennsylvania 19603
Files for repair or renewal of damaged threads, rethreader dies, flexible shaft drivers and extensions, screw extractors, impact drivers.

Jenny Division of Homestead Ind., Inc.
700 Second Avenue
Coraopolis, Pennsylvania 15108
Steam cleaning equipment, pressure washing equipment.

K-Line Industries, Inc.
315 Garden Avenue
Holland, Michigan 49424
Pullers, crack detectors, gloves, aprons, eyewear,

Keystone Reamer & Tool Co.
South Front Street
P.O. Box 308
Millersburg, Pennsylvania 17061
Adjustable reamers, twist drills, taps, dies.

Microdot, Inc.
P.O. Box 3001
Fullerton, California 92634
Thread repair insert kits.

OTC
655 Eisenhower Drive
Owatonna, Minnesota 55060
Bearing and gear pullers, hydraulic shop presses.

Power Lawnmower Parts, Inc.
1920 Lyell Avenue
P.O. Box 60860
Rochester, New York 14606-0860
Flywheel pullers, starter wrench,

Shure Manufacturing Corp.
1601 S. Hanley Road
St. Louis, Missour 63144
Steel shop benches, desks, engine overhaul stand.

Sioux Tools, Inc.
2901 Floyd Blvd.
P.O. Box 507
Sioux City, Iowa 51102
Air and electric impact tools, drills, grinders.

Sturtevant Richmont
3203 N. Wolf Rd.
Franklin Park, Illinois 60131
Torque wrenches, torque multipliers, torque analyzers.

Mechanic's Hand Tools

Channellock, Inc.
1306 South Main St.
P.O. Box 519
Meadville, Pennsylvania 16335

John H. Graham & Company
P.O. Box 739
Oradell, New Jersey 07649

Jaw Manufacturing Co.
39 Mulberry St.
P.O. Box 213
Reading, Pennsylvania 19603

K-D Tools
3575 Hempland Road
Lancaster, Pennsylvania 17604

K-Line Industries, Inc.
315 Garden Avenue
Holland, Michigan 49424

OTC
655 Eisenhower Drive
Owatonna, Minnesota 55060

Snap-On Tools
2801 80th Street
Kenosha, Wisconsin 53140

Triangle Corporation-Tool Division
P.O. Box 1807
Orangeburg, South Carolina 29115

Shop Supplies (Chemicals, Metallurgy Products, Seals, Sealers, Common Parts Items, etc.)

Clayton Manufacturing Co.
4213 N. Temple City Blvd.
El Monte, California 91731
Steam cleaning compounds and solvents.

E-Z Lok
P.O. Box 2069
Gardena, California 90247
Thread repair insert kits.

Eutectic+Castolin
40-40 172nd Street
Flushing, New York 11358
Specialized repair and maintenance welding alloys.

Fairchild Fastener Group
3000 W. Lomita Blvd.
Torrance, California 90505
Thread repair insert kits (Keenserts) and installation tools.

Foley-Belsaw Company Outdoor Power Equipment Parts Div.
6301 Equitable Road
P.O. Box 419593
Kansas City, Missouri 64141
Parts washers, cylinder head rethreaders, micrometers, calipers, gasket material, nylon rope, oil and grease products, bolt, nut, washer and spring assortments.

Frederick Manufacturing Corp.
4840 E. 12th Street
Kansas City, Missouri 64127
Thread repair kits.

Graymills Corporation
3705 N. Lincoln Avenue
Chicago, Illinois 60613
Parts cleaning fluids.

Heli-Coil
Shelter Rock Lane
Danbury, Connecticut 06810
Thread repair kits, thread inserts, installation tools.

K-Line Industries, Inc.
315 Garden Avenue
Holland, Michigan 49424
Machining lubricants, solvents, cleaning solutions.

Loctite Corporation
705 North Mountain Road
Newington, Connecticut 06111
Compounds for locking threads, retaining bearings and securing machine parts; sealants and adhesives.

Microdot, Inc.
P.O. Box 3001
Fullerton, California 92634
Thread repair insert kits.

Permatex Industrial
30 Tower Lane
Avon Park South
Avon, Connecticut 06001
Cleaning chemicals, gasket sealers, pipe sealants, adhesives, lubricants, thread locking and forming compounds.

Power Lawnmower Parts, Inc.
1920 Lyell Avenue
P.O. Box 60860
Rochester, New York 14606-0860
Grinding compound paste, gas tank sealer stick, shop aprons, eyewear.

Radiator Specialty Co.
1900 Wilkinson Blvd.
Charlotte, North Carolina 28208
Cleaning chemicals (Gunk) and solder seal.

ALPINA

GASOLINE POWERED TRIMMERS

Model	Engine Make	Engine Model	Displacement
160	Tanaka	...	22.6 cc (1.38 cu. in.)
180	Tanaka	...	31.0 cc (1.86 cu. in.)
200	Tanaka	...	37.4 cc (2.07 cu. in.)
VIP21	Own	21	20.5 cc (1.25 cu. in.)
VIP25, VIP25D	Own	25	24.8 cc (1.5 cu. in.)
VIP30	Own	30	27.4 cc (1.67 cu. in.)
VIP34, VIP34D & VIP34F	Own	34	32.5 cc (1.98 cu. in.)
VIP42, VIP42D & VIP42F	Own	42	41.1 cc (2.5 cu. in.)
VIP52, VIP52D & VIP52F	Own	52	52.3 cc (3.19 cu. in.)

"D" suffix indicates Duplex and "F" indicates Flex (backpack) model.

ENGINE INFORMATION

Tanaka (TAS) two-stroke air-cooled gasoline engines are used on models 160, 180 and 200. Other models are fitted with Alpina engines. Identify the engine by manufacturer and displacement and refer to the appropriate ALPINA or TANAKA Engine Service section of this manual.

FUEL MIXTURE

The manufacturer recommends mixing a quality 2-stroke engine oil with regular or unleaded gasoline at the ratio recommended by the oil manufacturer. If the oil manufacturer does not suggest a mixing ratio, use an oil designed for air cooled two-stroke engines mixed with gasoline at a ratio of 25:1.

STRING TRIMMER

Manual adjustment trimmer heads are available with either 2 lines or 4 lines. An automatic trimmer head with 2 lines is also available. Refer to Fig. AL1, Fig. AL2 or Fig. AL3.

The trimmer lines can be manually advanced with the engine stopped. Pull the cover and spool (3 and 4—Fig. AL1 or Fig. AL2) out and turn it until both lines are extended sufficiently, release the spool and allow the spring (2) to push the spool into the hub. If the spool is not completely seated, turn the spool until the pegs on the top of the spool engage the holes in the hub.

The trimmer lines of the automatic trimmer head should advance automatically when the engine speed is increased. If the lines do not advance, make sure that lines are not twisted or crossed.

On all models, all of the lines should extend from the hub the same amount. If a line does not extended, it may be broken inside the housing, making it necessary to disassemble the unit and feed the line through the eyelets (6—Fig. AL1, Fig. AL2 or Fig. AL3). If necessary to remove the spool, remove nut (1), then lift the spool(s) from the hub. Do not lose the spring (2—Fig.

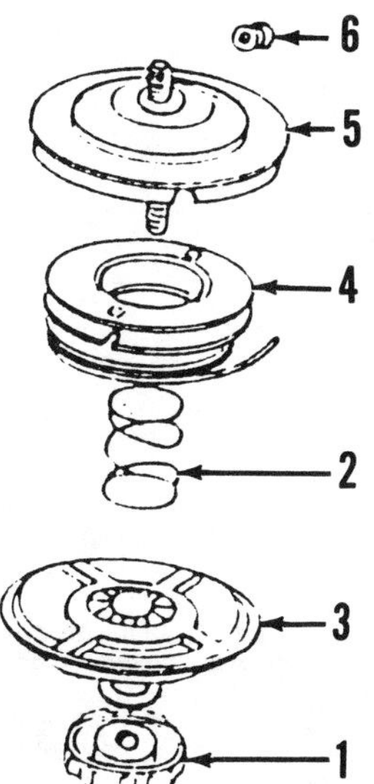

Fig. AL1—Exploded view of 2-line manual advance trimmer head used on some models.

1. Knob
2. Spring
3. Cover
4. Spool
5. Housing
6. Line guides (eyelets)

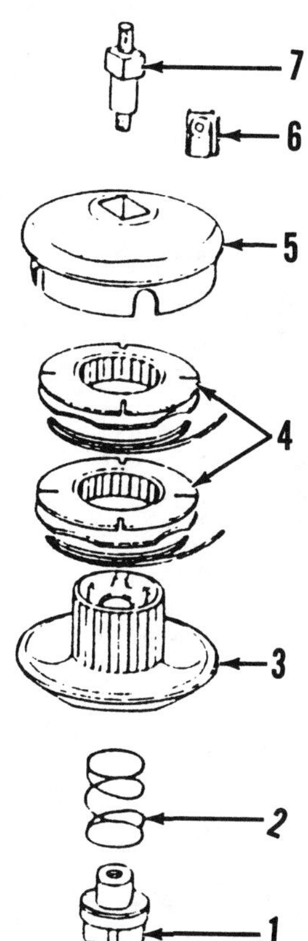

Fig. AL2—Exploded view of 4-line manual advance trimmer head used on some models.

1. Knob
2. Spring
3. Cover
4. Spools
5. Housing
6. Line guide (eyelets)
7. Adapter

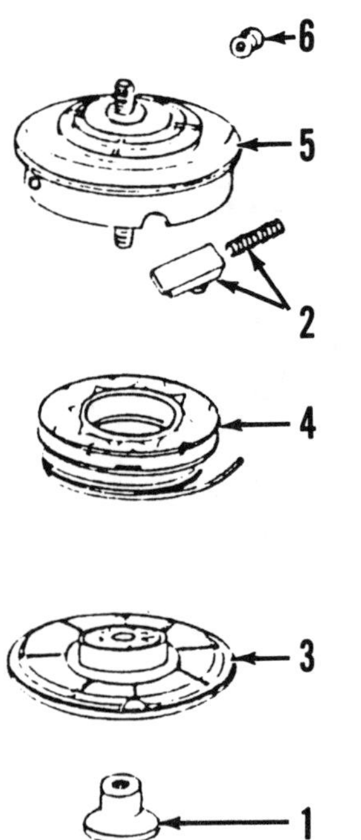

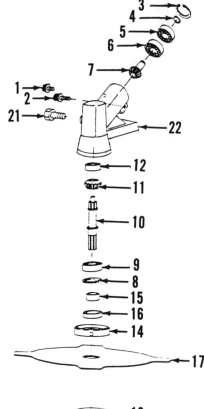

Fig. AL3—Exploded view of 2-line automatic advance trimmer head used on some models.

1. Knob
2. Ratchet
3. Cover
4. Spool
5. Housing
6. Line guides (eyelets)

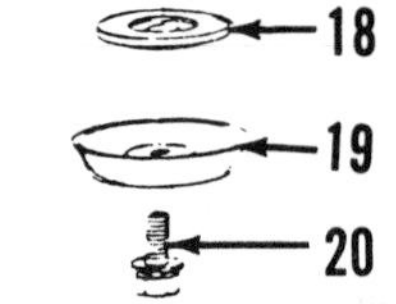

Fig. AL5—Exploded view of the gear head used on VIP 52 models.

1. Fitting screw
2. Clamp screws
3. Snap ring
4. Snap ring
5. Sealed bearing
6. Bearing
7. Drive gear
8. Snap ring
9. Bearing
10. Output shaft
11. Driven gear
12. Bearing
14. Cup washer
15. Seal spacer
16. Seal
17. Blade
18. Adapter plate
19. Cover
20. Screw
21. Fill plug
22. Gear housing

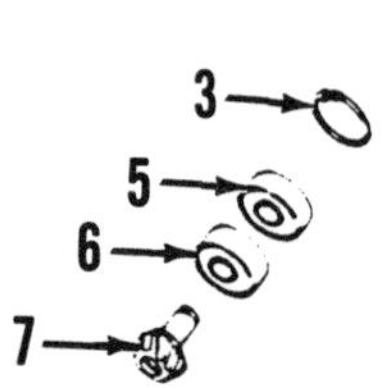

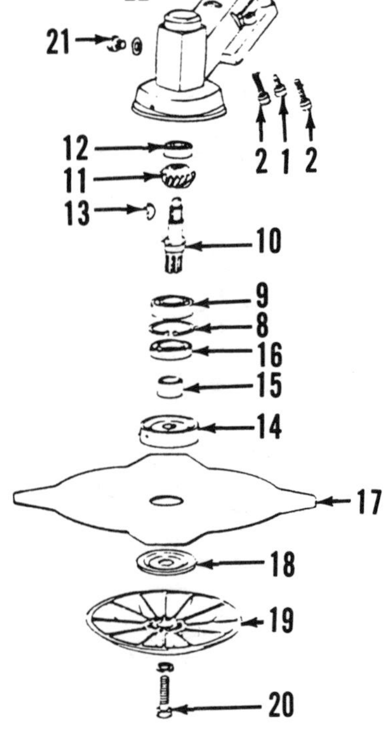

Fig. AL4—Exploded view of the gear head typical of the type used on most models.

1. Fitting screw
2. Clamp screws
3. Snap ring
5. Sealed bearing
6. Bearing
7. Drive gear
8. Snap ring
9. Bearing
10. Output shaft
11. Driven gear
12. Bearing
13. Woodruff key
14. Cup washer
15. Seal spacer
16. Seal
17. Blade
18. Adapter plate
19. Cover
20. Screw
21. Fill plug
22. Gear housing

AL1 or Fig. AL2) or the automatic advancing ratchet (2—Fig. AL3).

Clean and inspect all parts for damage. If new line is installed, it should be 0.095 in. (2.41 mm) diameter. Insert the lines through the attaching eye on the spool and pull the line through until it is the same length on both sides. Wrap both ends of the line on spool at the same time. Wind the line tightly and evenly from side to side and do not twist the lines. Install spool while directing the ends of both lines through the eyelets in the housing. Tighten the retaining nut (1—Fig. AL1, Fig. AL2 or Fig. AL3) securely.

BLADE

The weed and grass blade shown in Fig. AL4 or Fig. AL5 is available for installation on some models. The blades should be sharpened with a flat file at the same angle as original. Sharpen all of the blades evenly to maintain balance. Do not file into the radius at the root. Always make certain cup washer (14) is installed above the blade and adapter plate (18) is located below the blade. Be sure the cover (19) is in place and attaching screw (20) is tight.

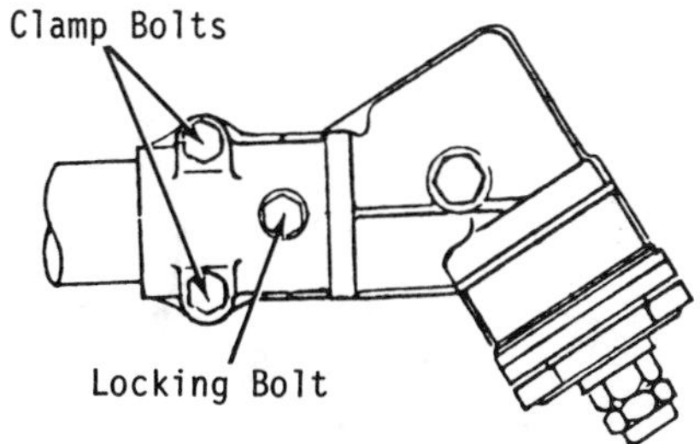

Fig. AL6—To separate the gear head from the drive shaft and housing, loosen or remove the clamp bolts and locking bolt.

GEAR HEAD

The gear head (Fig. AL4 or Fig. AL5) is located at the lower end of the drive shaft and housing. To remove the assembly, loosen or remove the locking bolt and clamp bolts (Fig. AL6), then pull the gear housing from the drive shaft housing. Remove the trimmer head or blade, then unbolt the protector shield. The seal (16—Fig. AL4 or Fig. AL5) can be pried from the housing.

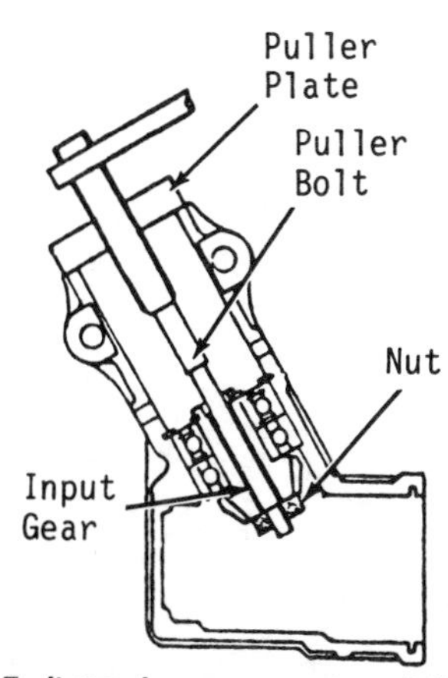

Fig. AL7—It may be necessary to pull the input shaft, gear and bearing assembly from the housing as shown.

To remove the gears and bearings, first remove snap ring (3). It may be possible to bump the open end of housing (22) to dislodge the bearings and gear (5, 6 and 7). If necessary, use a blind hole puller as shown in Fig. AL7 to pull the gear and bearings from the housing.

On some models it is necessary to remove snap ring (4—Fig. AL5) before the bearings (5 and 6) can be pressed from the gear. Remove spacer (15—Fig. AL4 or Fig. AL5) and seal (16), then remove snap ring (8). Pull the bearing and shaft (9 and 10) from the housing. A puller may be needed to remove the bearing (12) from its bore in housing.

Clean all parts and inspect for damage. Install new parts as necessary. Gears should be replaced as a set. Grease the lower seal (16) before pressing into the housing. Add multipurpose lithium grease to the housing until the cavity is approximately 2/3 full. Do not over-fill the housing with grease. Tighten fill plug (21) securely.

DRIVE SHAFT

All models are equipped with a solid high carbon steel drive shaft (1—Fig.

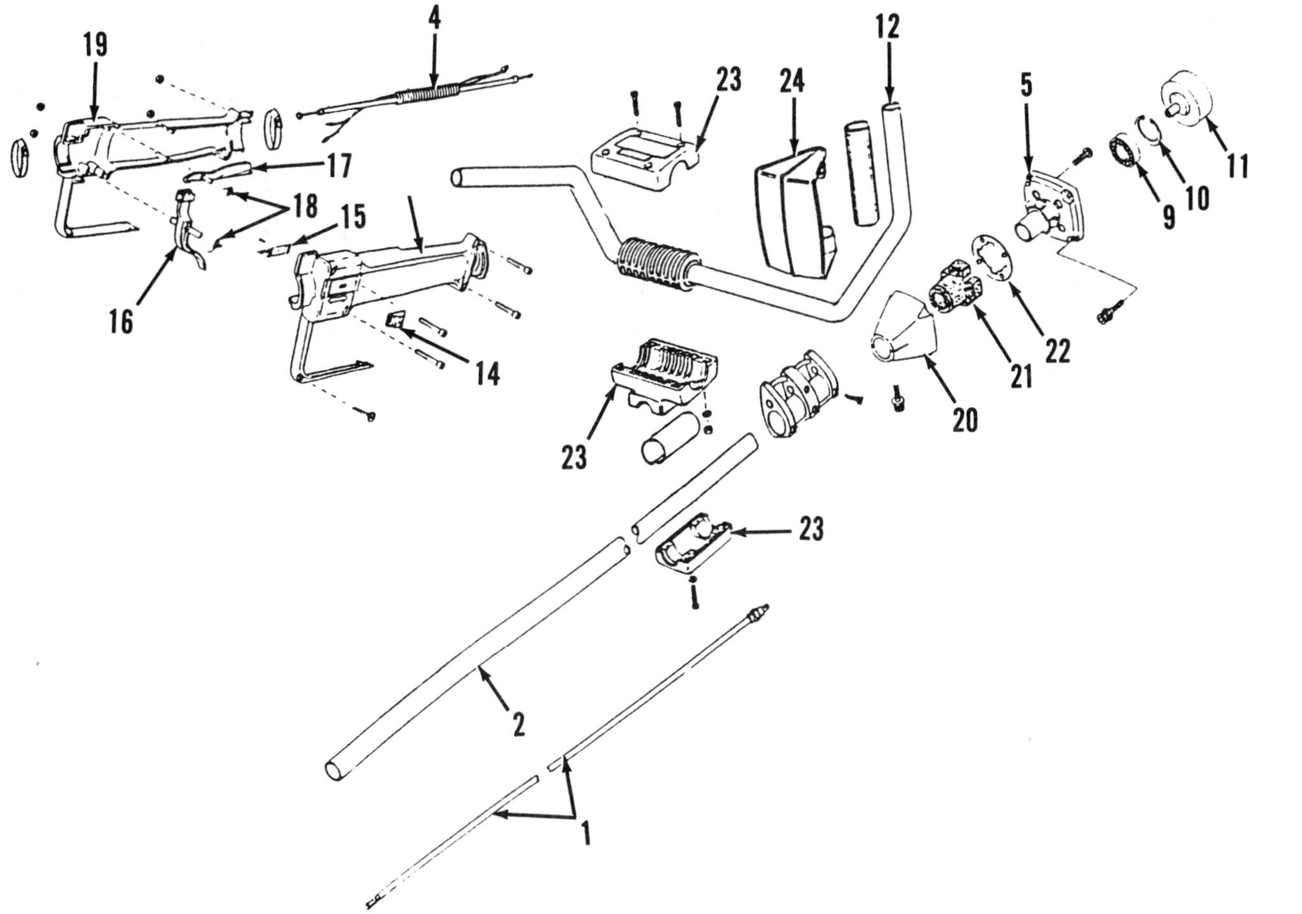

Fig. AL8—Exploded view of the drive shaft and engine controls typical of all except backpack models. Some models may be equipped with two bearings (9).

1. Drive shaft
2. Drive housing
4. Throttle cable & stop wires
5. Clutch housing
9. Bearing
10. Snap ring
11. Clutch drum
12. Handle bar
13. Grip half
14. Stop control
15. Stop switch
16. Throttle lever
17. Throttle interlock
18. Springs
19. Grip half
20. Clamp cover
21. Vibration isolator
22. Plate
23. Handle bar clamp
24. Hand protector

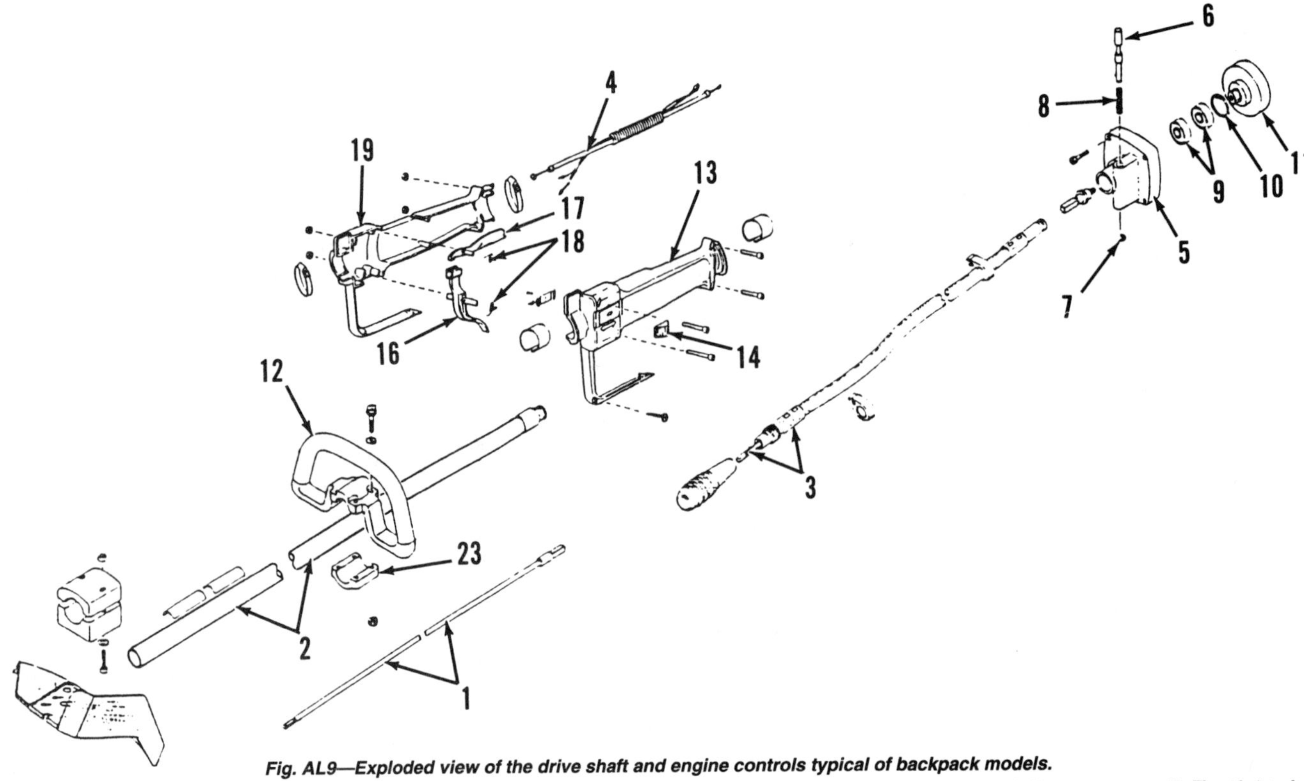

Fig. AL9—Exploded view of the drive shaft and engine controls typical of backpack models.

1. Drive shaft
2. Drive housing
3. Flexible shaft & housing
4. Throttle cable & stop wires
5. Clutch housing/shaft support
6. Release plunger
7. Retaining ring
8. Spring
9. Bearing
10. Snap ring
11. Clutch drum
12. Handle
13. Grip half
14. Stop control
15. Stop switch
16. Throttle lever
17. Throttle interlock
18. Springs
19. Grip half
23. Clamp

AL8 or Fig. AL9) that is supported in bushings located in the drive shaft housing (2). The shaft should be perfectly straight and drive surfaces at the ends should not be rounded. Any discoloration or wear on the steel drive shaft indicates bushing wear.

Flex (backpack) brush cutters are equipped with both a flexible shaft portion (3—Fig. AL9) and a solid high carbon steel drive shaft (1). The flexible shaft can be separated from the clutch housing (5) by pressing the lock plunger (6). Detach the engine stop switch wires and throttle control cable (4).

The bushings are not available for service and should not be removed. Lubricate the drive shaft with a good quality lithium based grease before installing it in the housing.

ENGINE CONTROLS

Engine throttle control is located within easy reach when the operator's hands are safely positioned on the grips. Refer to Fig. AL8 or Fig. AL9 for typical controls. The engine stop switch is also located in the grip housing. To replace control harness (4), separate handle grips (13 and 19) and disconnect control cable and wires from engine.

BLACK & DECKER

ELECTRIC STRING TRIMMERS

Model	Volts	Amps	Swath	Diameter	Cutting Line RPM
82205	120	1.4	9 in.	0.050 in.	10,500
82209	120	1.4	9 in.	0.050 in.	10,500
82210	120	1.5	10 in.	0.050 in.	9,500
82212	120	3.9	12 in.	0.065 in.	10,000
82214	120	4.3	14 in.	0.065 in.	8,500
82230	120	2.5	10 in.	0.050 in.	10,000
82232	120	3.2	12 in.	0.050 in.	9,500
82234	120	4.3	14 in.	0.050 in.	10,000

ELECTRICAL REQUIREMENTS

All models require electrical circuits with 120-volt alternating current. Extension cord length should not exceed 100 feet (30.5 m). Make certain all circuits and connections are properly grounded at all times.

STRING TRIMMER

Model 82205

Model 82205 is equipped with a manual advance line trimmer head designed to cut a 9 inch (229 mm) swath with 0.050 in. (1.3 mm) monofilament line. To extend line, disconnect power cord. Pull line up out of line slot (2-Fig. BD1) and pull line around spool in direction indicated by arrow and "UNWIND LINE" printed on spool. To renew line, push spool (8) in while turning in direction indicated by arrow and "REMOVE SPOOL" printed on spool. Remove spool, plastic line retainer (5) and any remaining old line. Insert one end of new line in hole in lower side of spool and wind new line onto spool in direction indicated by arrow on upper surface of spool. Insert line end through hole (4) in line retainer and install line retainer over spool. Install spool in housing and push spool in while turning spool to lock tabs (6) in housing (1).

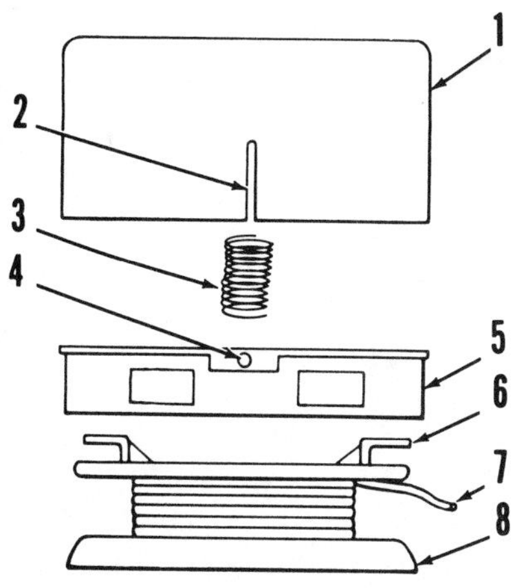

Fig. BD1—Exploded view of single strand manual trimmer head used on Model 82205.

1. Housing
2. Line slot
3. Spring
4. Line hole
5. Line retainer
6. Lock tabs
7. Line
8. Spool

Models 82209, 82210, 82212 And 82214

Models 82209, 82210, 82212 and 82214 are equipped with a single strand semi-automatic trimmer head shown in Fig. BD2. Models 82209 and 82210 are equipped with 0.050 inch (1.3 mm) line and Models 82212 and 82214 are equipped with 0.065 inch (1.6 mm) line. On all models, to extend line with trimmer motor off, push bump button (7) in while pulling on line end. Procedure may have to be repeated until desired line length has been obtained. To extend line with trimmer motor running, tap bump button (7) on the ground. Each time bump button is tapped on the ground a measured amount of new line will be advanced.

To renew line, disconnect power cord. Remove cover (8), button (7) and spool (6). Clean all parts thoroughly and remove any remaining old line from spool. Wind new line onto spool in direction indicated by arrow on spool. Insert line end through line guide opening in drum (1) and install spool, button and cover.

Models 82230, 82232 And 82234

Models 82230, 82232 and 82234 are equipped with a push button line feed system equipped with 0.050 inch (1.3 mm) line. Line is advanced by pushing button on secondary handle with trimmer motor running. Each time button is pushed, approximately 5/8 inch (16 mm) of line is advanced.

To renew line, disconnect power cord.

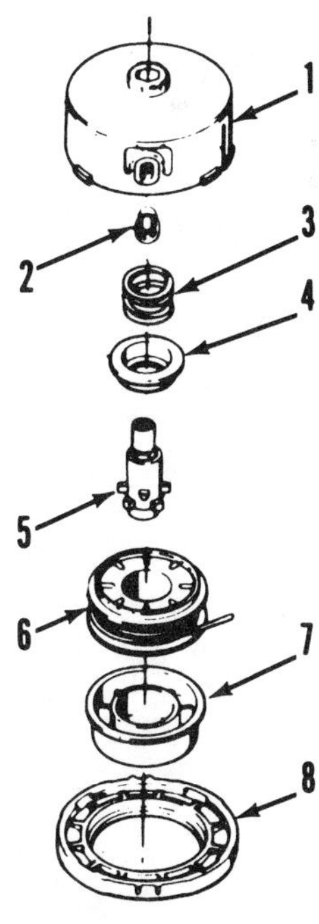

Fig. BD2—Exploded view of single strand semi-automatic head similar to the one used on Models 82209, 82210, 82212 and 82214.

1. Housing
2. Line guide
3. Spring
4. Spring adapter
5. Drive adapter
6. Spool
7. Bump button
8. Cover

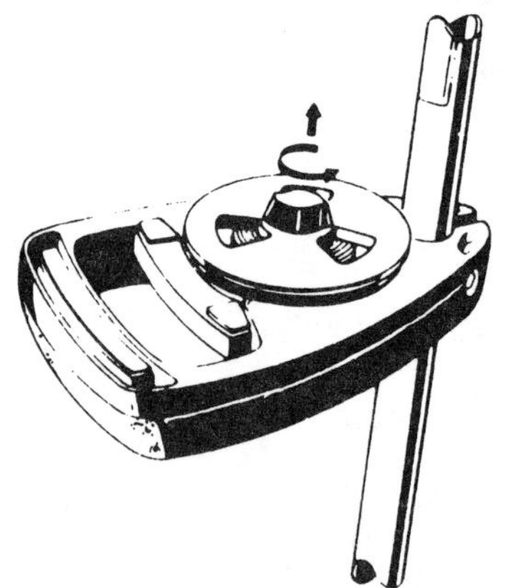

Fig. BD3—Turn spool nut in direction indicated to remove.

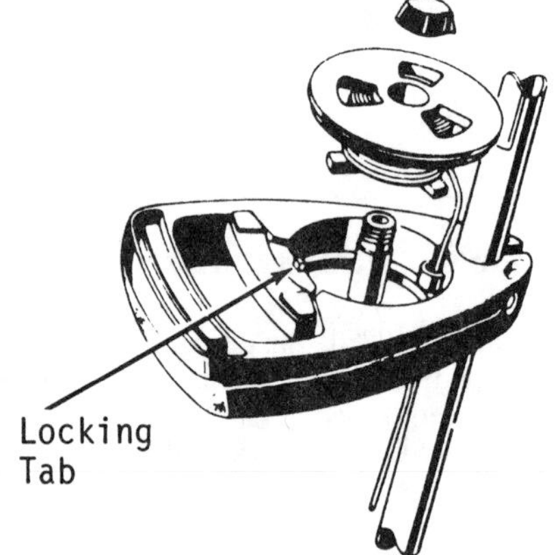

Fig. BD4—Insert line end through line hole as shown and install spool in bail.

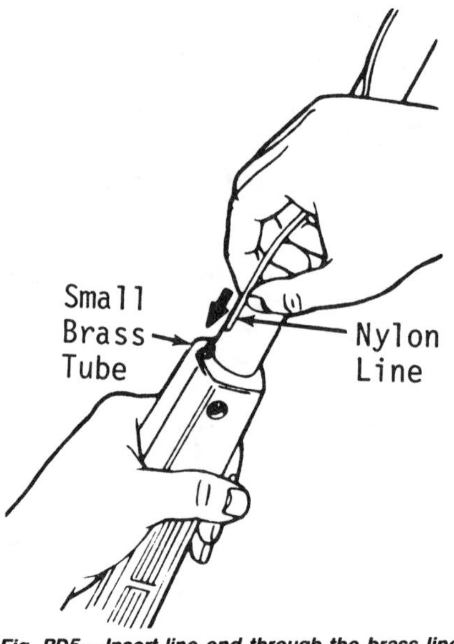

Fig. BD5—Insert line end through the brass line tube and work line down through tube until line is extending from line guide opening in trimmer head.

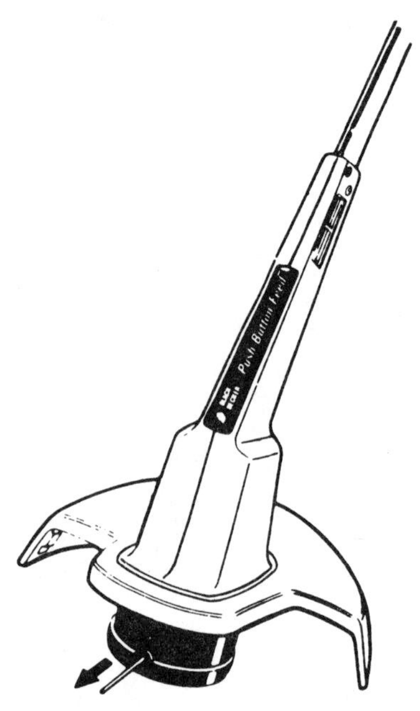

Fig. BD6—Line must extend from line guide opening in trimmer head after line installation.

Remove spool nut as shown in Fig. BD3. Lift spool out of handle assembly. Remove remaining old line and clean spool and bail assemblies. Wind new line onto spool leaving 3 feet (0.9 m) of line unwound from spool. Insert line end down through hole in bail handle assembly that is closest to handle tube (Fig. BD4). Install spool in bail assembly and install spool nut. Insert line end into line tube (Fig. BD5) and work entire length of free line through tube. At this point trimmer line should be extending from trimmer head line guide (Fig. BD6). If no line is at trimmer head, remove line spool and advance more free line before installing spool again.

BLACK & DECKER

GASOLINE POWERED STRING TRIMMER

Model	Engine Manufacturer	Engine Model	Displacement
8271-04	Kioritz	....	16.0 cc
8289-04	Kioritz	....	21.2 cc
82255	McCulloch	....	21.2 cc
82257	McCulloch	....	21.2 cc
82267	McCulloch	...	21.2 cc

ENGINE INFORMATION

All Models

Early models are equipped with Kioritz two-stroke air-cooled gasoline engines and later models are equipped with McCulloch two-stroke air-cooled gasoline engines. Identify engine model by engine manufacturer and engine displacement. Refer to KIORITZ ENGINE SERVICE or McCULLOCH ENGINE SERVICE section of this manual.

FUEL MIXTURE

All Models

Manufacturer recommends mixing regular grade gasoline (unleaded is an acceptable substitute) with a good quality two-stroke air-cooled engine oil at a 25:1 ratio. Do not use fuel containing alcohol.

STRING TRIMMER

Model 8271-04

Model 8271-04 is equipped with a single strand semi-automatic trimmer head shown in Fig. BD10. Line may be manually advanced with engine stopped by pushing in on housing (9) while pulling on line. Procedure may have to be repeated to obtain desired line length. To advance line with engine running, operate engine at full rpm and tap housing (9) on the ground. Each time housing is tapped on the ground, a measured amount of trimmer line will be advanced.

To renew trimmer line, remove cotter key (10) and twist housing (9) counterclockwise to remove housing. Remove foam pad (6) and any remaining line on spool (3). Clean spool and inside of housing. Cut off approximately 25 feet (7.6 m) of 0.080 inch (2 mm) monofilament line and tape one end of line to spool (Fig. BD12). Wind line on spool in direction indicated by arrow on spool (Fig. BD13). Install foam pad with line end protruding from between foam pad and spool as shown in Fig. BD13. Insert line end through line guide and install housing and spring assembly on spool.

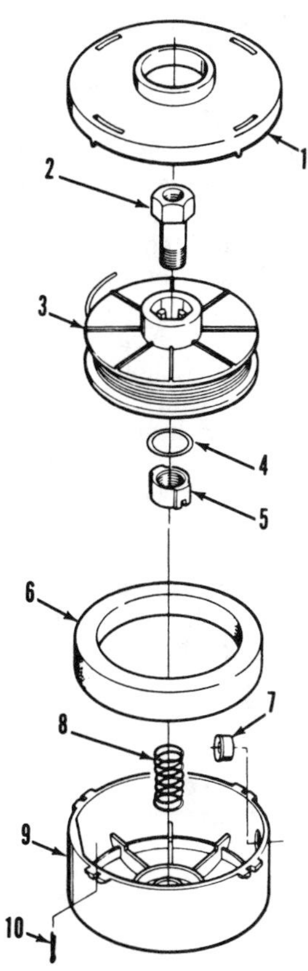

Fig. BD10—Exploded view of single strand semi-automatic trimmer head used on Model 8271-04.

1. Cover
2. Drive adapter
3. Spool
4. "O" ring
5. Drive adapter nut
6. Foam pad
7. Line guide
8. Spring
9. Housing
10. Cotter pin

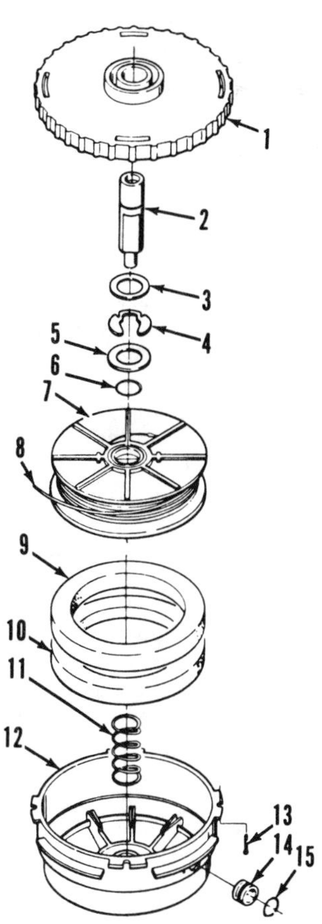

Fig. BD11—Exploded view of single strand semi-automatic trimmer head used on Models 8289-04, 82255, 82257 and 82267.

1. Cover
2. Drive adapter
3. Washer
4. Retainer
5. Washer
6. Retainer ring
7. Spool
8. Line
9. Foam pad
10. Foam pad
11. Spring
12. Housing
13. Cotter pin
14. Line guide
15. Retainer

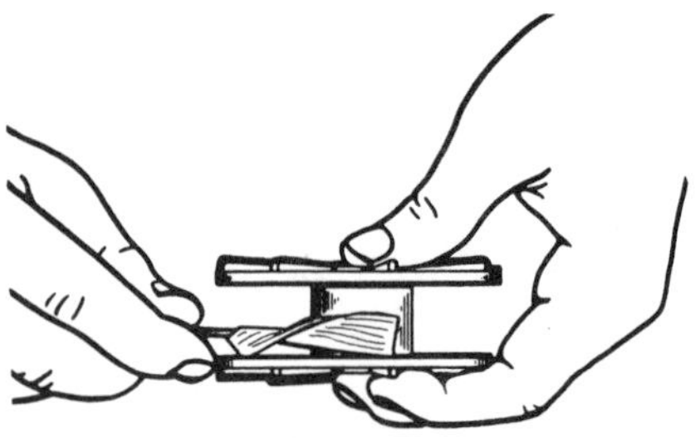

Fig. BD12—Tape one end of new line to center of spool as shown.

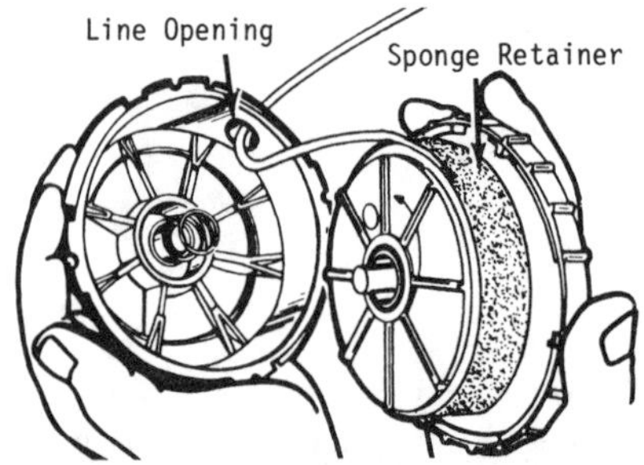

Fig. BD13—Install foam pad with line protruding between pad and spool as shown. Wind line in direction indicated by arrow on spool.

Push in on housing and twist housing to lock into position. Install cotter key through hole in housing and cover.

Model 8289-04, 82255, 82257 And 82267

A single strand semi-automatic trimmer head shown in Fig. BD11 may be used on these models. Line may be manually advanced with engine off by pushing in on housing (12) while pulling on line. Procedure may have to be repeated until desired line length is obtained. To advance line with engine running, operate trimmer engine at full rpm and tap housing (12) on the ground. Each time housing is tapped on the ground, a measured amount of trimmer line is advanced.

To renew trimmer line, remove cotter pin (13). Twist housing (12) counterclockwise and remove housing. Remove foam pads (9 and 10) and any remaining line from spool (7). Clean spool and

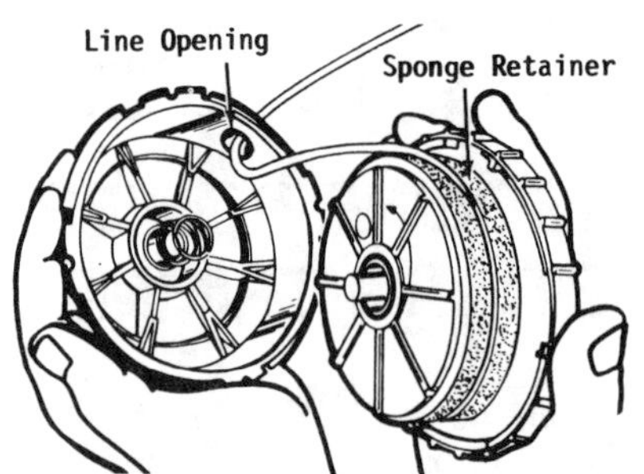

Fig. BD14—Install foam pads with line protruding from between pads. Wind line in direction indicated by arrow on spool.

inner area of housing. Cut off approximately 25 feet (7.6 mm) of 0.080 inch (2 mm) monofilament line and tape one end of line to spool (Fig. BD12). Wind line on spool in direction indicated by arrow on spool (Fig. BD14). Install foam pads (9 and 10—Fig. BD11) so line is protruding from center of foam pads (Fig. BD14). Insert end of line through line guide and install spool, housing and spring. Push in on housing and twist housing in clockwise direction to lock in position and install cotter pin (13—Fig. BD11).

DRIVE SHAFT

All Models

All models are equipped with a flexible drive shaft enclosed in the drive shaft housing tube. Drive shaft has squared ends which engage adapters at each end. Drive shaft should be removed for maintenance at 50 hour intervals of use. Remove screw (4—Fig. BD15) and bolt (3) at bearing head housing and separate bearing head from drive shaft housing. Pull flexible drive shaft from housing. Lubricate drive shaft with lithium base grease and reinstall in drive shaft housing with end which was previously at clutch end toward bearing head. Reversing drive shaft ends extends drive shaft life. Make certain ends of drive shaft are properly located into upper and lower square drive adapters when installing.

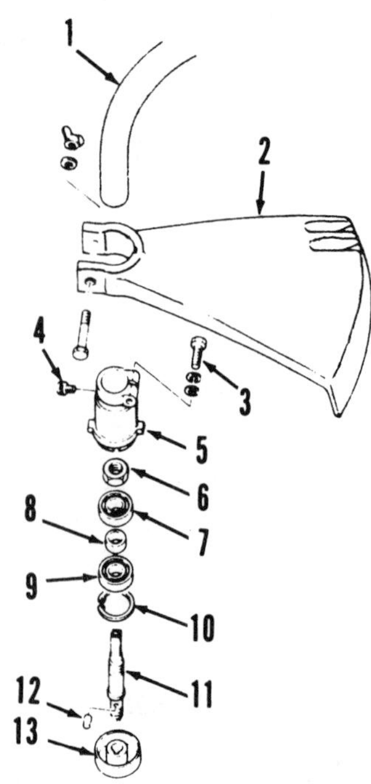

Fig. BD15—Exploded view of bearing head used on all models. Bearings (7 and 9) are sealed bearings and require no regular maintenance.

1. Drive shaft housing
2. Shield
3. Bolt
4. Screw
5. Housing
6. Nut
7. Bearing
8. Spacer
9. Bearing
10. Snap ring
11. Arbor (output) shaft
12. Pin
13. Cup washer

BEARING HEAD

All Models

All models are equipped with the bearing head shown in Fig. BD15. Bearing head is equipped with sealed bearings and requires no regular maintenance. To disassemble bearing head, remove trimmer head assembly and cup washer (13). Remove screw (4) and bolt (3) and separate bearing head from drive shaft housing tube. Remove snap ring (10) and use a suitable puller to remove arbor shaft (11) and bearing assembly. Remove nut (6) and press bearings (7 and 9) and spacer (8) from arbor shaft as reouired.

BUNTON

GASOLINE POWERED STRING TRIMMER

Model	Engine Manufacturer	Engine Model	Displacemen
LBF18K	Kawasaki	TD-18	18.4 cc
LBS24K	Kawasaki	TD-24	24.1 cc
LBS33K	Kawasaki	TD-33	33.3 cc

ENGINE INFORMATION

All Models

All models are equipped with a two-stroke air-cooled gasoline engine manufactured by Kawasaki. Refer to appropriate KAWASAKI ENGINE SERVICE section of this manual.

FUEL MIXTURE

All Models

Manufacturer recommends mixing a good quality two-stroke air-cooled engine oil with regular grade gasoline of at least 87 octane rating. Mix gasoline and oil at a 25:1 ratio. Unleaded regular gasoline is an acceptable substitute.

STRING TRIMMER

All Models

All models may be equipped with a dual strand manual trimmer head as shown in Figs. BT10 and BT11. To install trimmer head, refer to Fig. BT10 for assembly sequence for Model LBF18K and to Fig. BT11 for assembly sequence for Models LBS24K and LBS33K. Note that trimmer head retaining nut on all models has left-hand thread. On all models, line may be extended (with engine stopped) by loosening lock knob on underside of trimmer head and rotating spool in direction which will advance line. Tighten lock knob.

To renew line, remove lock knob and spool. Remove any remaining old line and install new line on spool. Wind line in direction indicated by arrow on spool Insert line ends through line guide openings in housing and install spool and lock knob.

BLADE

All Models

All models may be equipped with an eight blade weed and grass blade. Blade is installed on Model LBF18K as shown in Fig. BT12. Blade is installed on Models LBS24K and LBS33K as shown in Fig. BT13. Make certain adapter plate (7) is centered and seated squarely on blade during installation.

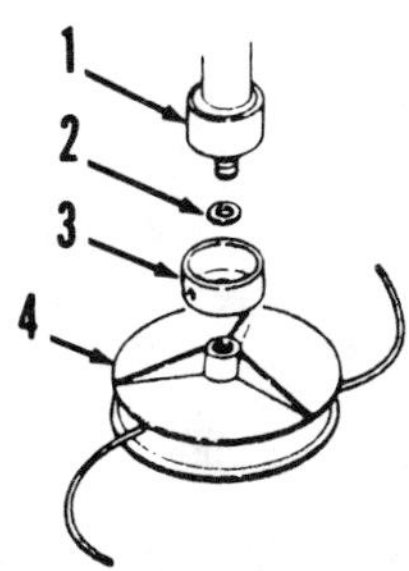

Fig. BT10—Trimmer head parts assembly sequence for trimmer head installation on Model LBF18K.

1. Drive shaft housing
2. Spacer
3. Cup washer
4. Trimmer head

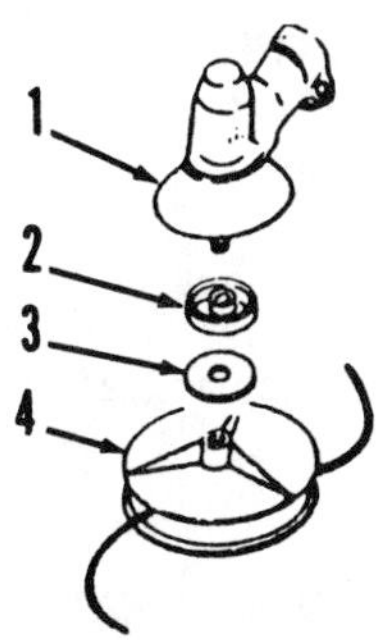

Fig. BT11—Trimmer head parts assembly sequence for trimmer head installation on Models LBS24K and LBS33K.

1. Gear head
2. Cup washer
3. Washer
4. Trimmer head

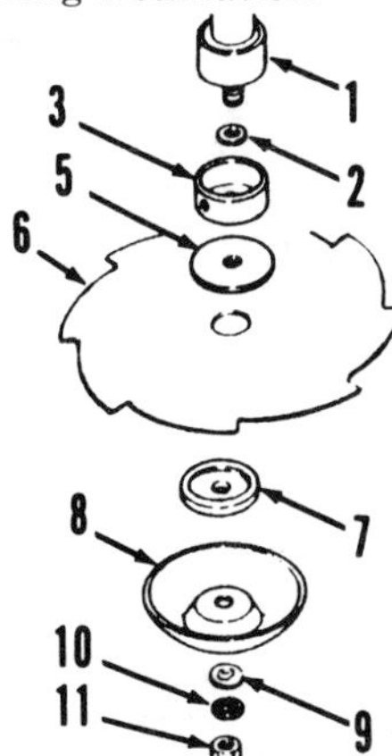

Fig. BT12—Parts assembly sequence for blade installation on Model LBF18K.

1. Drive shaft housing
2. Spacer
3. Cup washer
5. Washer
6. Blade
7. Adapter plate
8. Cover
9. Washer
10. Lock washer
11. Nut (LH)

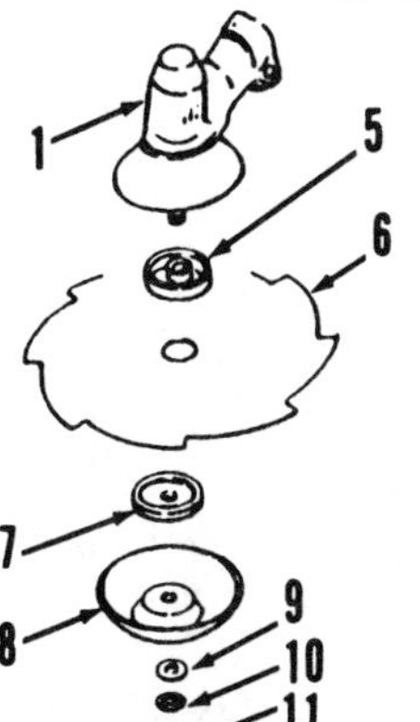

Fig. BT13—Parts assembly sequence for blade installation on Models LBS24K and LBS33K.

1. Gear head
5. Cup washer
6. Blade
7. Adapter plate
8. Cover
9. Washer
10. Lock washer
11. Nut (LH)

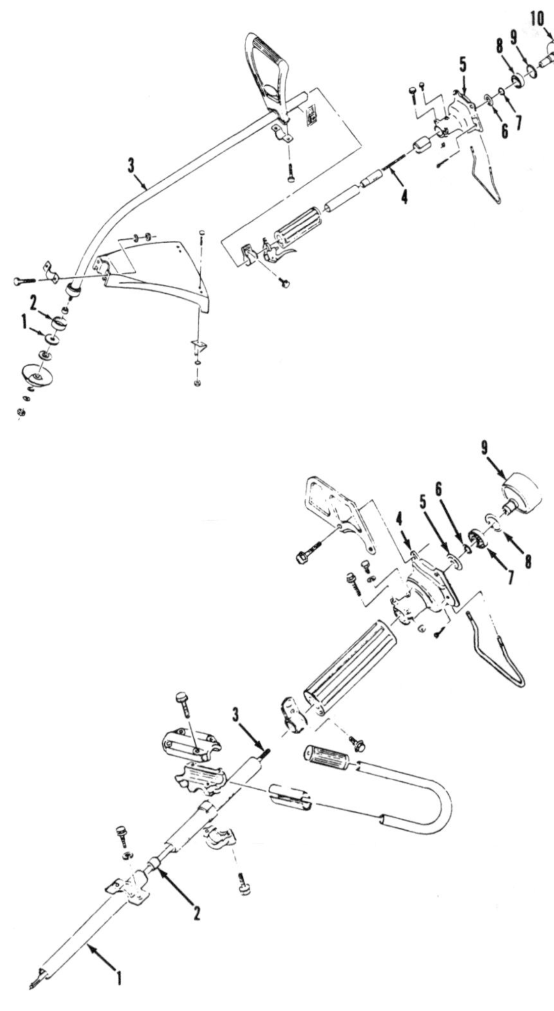

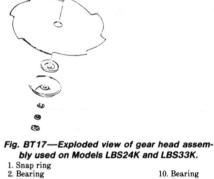

Fig. BT15—Exploded view of flexible drive shaft and housing on Model LBF18K.
1. Cup washer
2. Spacer
3. Drive shaft housing
4. Drive shaft
5. Clutch housing
6. Washer
7. Snap ring
8. Bearing
9. Snap ring
10. Clutch drum

Fig. BT16—Exploded view of drive shaft and housing used on Models LBS24K and LBS33K.
1. Drive shaft housing
2. Bushing
3. Drive shaft
4. Clutch housing
5. Washer
6. Snap ring
7. Bearing
8. Snap ring
9. Clutch drum

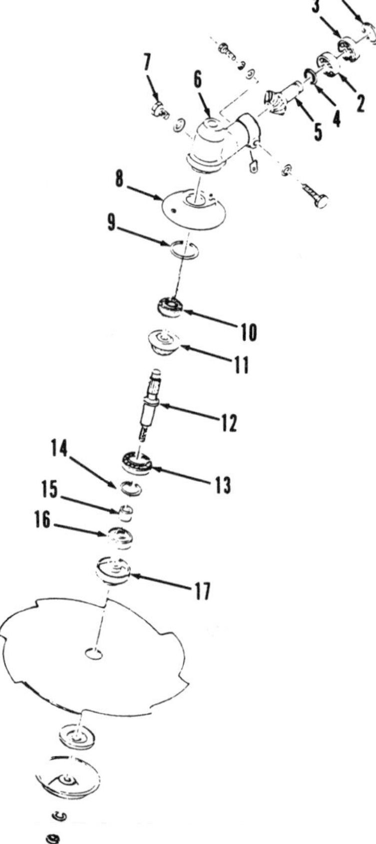

Fig. BT17—Exploded view of gear head assembly used on Models LBS24K and LBS33K.
1. Snap ring
2. Bearing
3. Bearing
4. Snap ring
5. Input shaft
6. Housing
7. Check plug
8. Anti-wrap cover
9. Snap ring
10. Bearing
11. Gear
12. Arbor shaft
13. Bearing
14. Snap ring
15. Spacer
16. Seal
17. Cup washer

DRIVE SHAFT

Model LBF18K

Models LBF18K is equipped with a flexible drive shaft (Fig. BT15) enclosed in the tube housing (3). Drive shaft has squared ends which engage clutch drum (10) adapter at engine end and head adapter at head end. Drive shaft should be removed for maintenance at 30 hour intervals. Remove and clean drive shaft after marking end positions. Inspect for damage. Coat with lithium base grease and make certain drive shaft is installed with ends in opposite locations. Alternating drive shaft squared ends between clutch and trimmer head ends will extend drive shaft life.

Models LBS24K And LBS33K

Models LBS24K and LBS33K are equipped with a solid drive shaft (3—Fig. BT16) supported in drive shaft housing (1) in bushings (2) and at gear head and clutch housing ends in sealed bearings. Drive shaft requires no regular maintenance however, if drive shaft is removed, lubricate drive shaft with lithium base grease before reinstallation. Drive shaft bushings (2) may be renewed. Mark locations of old bushings in drive shaft tube before removing. Install new bushings at old bushing locations in tube.

BEARING HEAD

Model LBF18K

Model LBF18K is equipped with a bearing head which is an integral part of drive shaft housing. If bearing head is worn or damaged, renew entire drive shaft housing.

GEAR HEAD

Models LBS24K And LBS33K

Models LBS24K and LBS33K are equipped with the gear head shown in Fig. BT17. At 30-hour intervals of use, remove trimmer head or blade assembly and install a grease fitting at check plug (7) opening. Pump lithium base grease into housing until new grease appears at seal (16) and spacer (15).

To disassemble gear head, remove trimmer head or blade assembly. Remove cup washer (17). Remove snap ring (1) and use a suitable puller to remove input shaft (5) and bearing assembly. Remove snap ring (4) and press bearings (2 and 3) from input shaft as required. Remove seal (16) and spacer (15). Remove snap ring (14) and use a suitable puller to remove arbor shaft (12) and bearing assembly as required. Press bearing (13) from arbor shaft. If bearing (10) stays in housing, heat housing to 140° F (60° C) and tap housing on wooden block to remove bearing.

JOHN DEERE

GASOLINE POWERED TRIMMERS

Model	Engine Manufacturer	Engine Model	Displacement
80G	Kioritz	...	21.2 cc (1.29 cu. in.)
82G & 83G	Poulan	...	26.2 cc (1.6 cu. in.)
85G	Tecumseh	AV520	85.0 cc (5.2 cu. in.)
90G	Kioritz	...	30.1 cc (1.84 cu. in.)
100G	Kioritz	...	16.0 cc (0.98 cu. in.)
110G	Deere	110	21.2 cc (1.29 cu. in.)
200G	Kioritz	...	21.2 cc (1.29 cu. in.)
210G	Deere	200	21.2 cc (1.29 cu. in.)
220G	Deere	220	21.2 cc (1.29 cu. in.)
240G	Deere	240	21.2 cc (1.29 cu. in.)
250G	Deere	250	21.2 cc (1.29 cu. in.)
260G	Deere	260	21.2 cc (1.29 cu. in.)
300G	Deere	300	24.4 cc (1.49 cu. in.)
350G	Deere	350	30.8 cc (1.88 cu. in.)
450G	Deere	450	40.2 cc (2.45 cu. in.)

ENGINE INFORMATION

Deere, Kioritz, Poulan and Tecumseh two stroke air-cooled gasoline engines are used. Identify the engine by manufacturer and displacement and refer to the appropriate DEERE, KIORITZ, POULAN or TECUMSEH Engine Service section of this manual.

FUEL MIXTURE

The manufacturer recommends mixing regular-grade gasoline, leaded or unleaded, with a high quality two-stroke engine oil. The use of gasohol or other alcohol blended fuels are not approved by manufacturer.

On Models 110G, 210G, 220G 240G, 250G, 260G 300G 350G and 450G, recommended fuel:oil ratio is 50:1 when using John Deere 2-Cycle Engine Oil. Fuel:oil ratio should be 32:1 when using any other two-stoke oil, regardless of recommended ratio on oil container.

On Models 90G, 100G and 200G, recommended fuel: oil ratio is 40:1 when using John Deere 2-Cycle Engine Oil. Fuel:oil ratio should be 32:1 when using any other two-stroke oil. On Model 85G, recommended fuel:oil ratio is 24:1. On Models 82G and 83G, recommended fuel:oil ratio is 32:1 when using John Deere 2-Cycle Engine Oil. Fuel:oil ratio should be 16:1 when using any other two-stroke oil. On Model 80G, recommended fuel:oil ratio is 32:1 when using John Deere 2-Cycle Engine Oil. Fuel:oil ratio should be 20:1 when using any other two-stroke oil.

STRING TRIMMER

Model 80G

Model 80G is equipped with the manual advance, single-strand trimmer head shown in Fig. JD10. To adjust line length, loosen knob (5) and pull out line.

To install new line, remove knob (5) and spool (4). Wind approximately 40 feet (12.2 m) of 0.080 inch (2 mm) diameter line in direction indicated by arrow on spool. Install spool in housing (2) with ribbed side visible and projections (P) positioned in line slots (L) of housing. Be sure line guides (3) are in place.

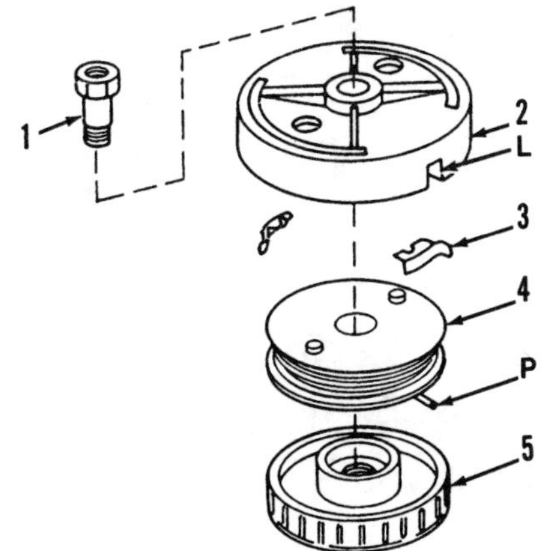

Fig. JD10—Exploded view of manual advance, single-strand trimmer head used on Model 80G.

1. Adapter
2. Housing
3. Line guide
4. Spool
5. Knob

Model 82G

Model 82G is equipped with a single-strand, semi-automatic head with 40 feet (12.2 m) of 0.080 inch (2 mm) diameter line. Early models are equipped with the head assembly shown in Fig. JD11. Later models are equipped with a similar head that is identified by grooves on top of drum (2); early models are smooth.

To adjust line length with engine stopped, depress button (8) and pull out line until it stops. Repeat procedure to extract more line. To extend line with engine running, operate trimmer at full throttle and tap button against ground.

To install new line, engine must be stopped. Depress latch (L—Fig. JD11) and rotate cover (9) counterclockwise to remove cover. Remove button (8) and spool (6). Inspect teeth on inner cam(5) and spool (6). Excessive wear indicates unnecessary pressure on button during operation. Remove any remaining old line and note direction of arrow on spool. Wind approximately 40 feet (12.2 m) of 0.080 inch (2 mm) diameter line in direction indicated by arrow on spool.

Install spool in drum (2) with arrow side visible. Install button (8) and cover (9). Rotate cover clockwise until it locks.

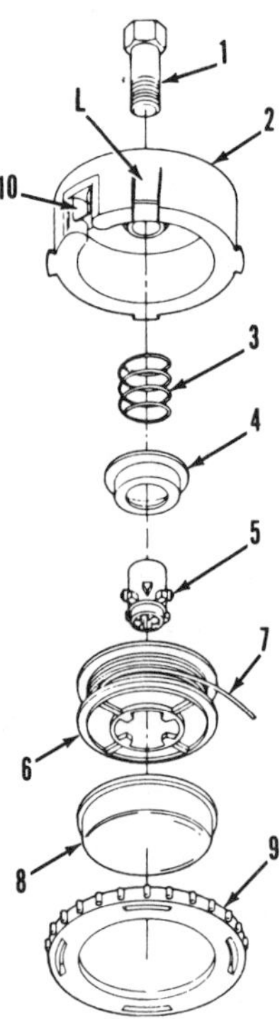

Fig. JD11—Exploded view of semi-automatic, single-strand trimmer head used on Model 82G.

1. Adapter
2. Drum
3. Spring
4. Spring adapter
5. Drive cam
6. Spool
7. Line
8. Button
9. Cover
10. Line guide

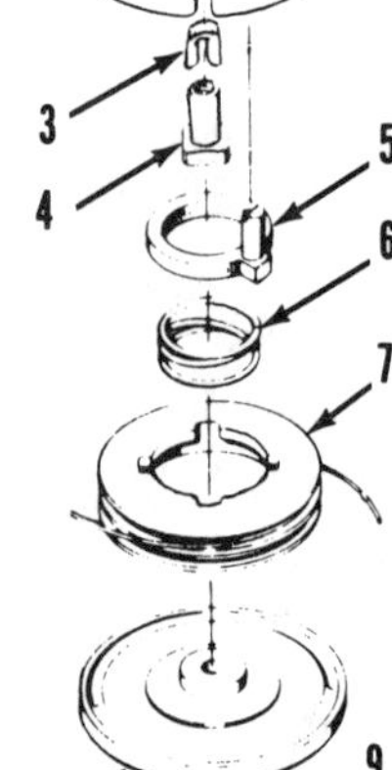

Fig. JD12—Exploded view of manual advance, dual-strand trimmer head used on Models 83G and 90G.

1. Release button
2. Housing
3. Line guide
4. Adapter
5. Lock ring
6. Spring
7. Spool
8. Cover
9. Screw

Models 83G and 90G

Models 83G and 90G trimmers are equipped with dual-strand, manual advance trimmer heads (Fig. JD12) that have double-grooved spools wound with approximately 50 feet (15.2 m) of 0.080 inch (2 mm) diameter line.

To adjust line length, depress release button (1) and pull out line from both line openings until line stops. Repeat procedure until at least 6 inches (15.2 cm) of line extends from both openings. Each line must be 6 inches (15.2 cm) long measured from line opening, if not cut line. Do not operate trimmer with line extended beyond recommended length.

To install new line, hold trimmer head and remove screw (9). Remove cover (8), spring (6) and spool (7). Each side of double spool will hold approximately 25 feet (7.6 m) of 0.080 inch (2 mm) line. Insert ends of new line in spool holes and wrap line around spool in direction indicated by arrow on spool. Make certain that line guides (3) are in position and place spool in housing (2). Install spool so side marked "THIS SIDE IN" is toward housing. Install spring and cover. Tighten cover screw (9) and cut line to proper length.

Model 85G

Model 85G is equipped with the manual advance, four-strand trimmer head shown in Fig. JD13. To extend line, depress top of each spool (3) and pull out line. Release spool being sure square portion of spool properly indexes with square hole in housing (1).

To install new line, remove Allen screw (7), cover (6), springs (5) and spools (3). Clean components. Each spool holds approximately 20 feet (6.1 m) of 0.080 inch (2 mm) diameter line. Wind line around spool in direction of arrow on spool. Note that there should be approximately the same amount of line on each spool so head is balanced.

Insert line ends through line guides and assemble components.

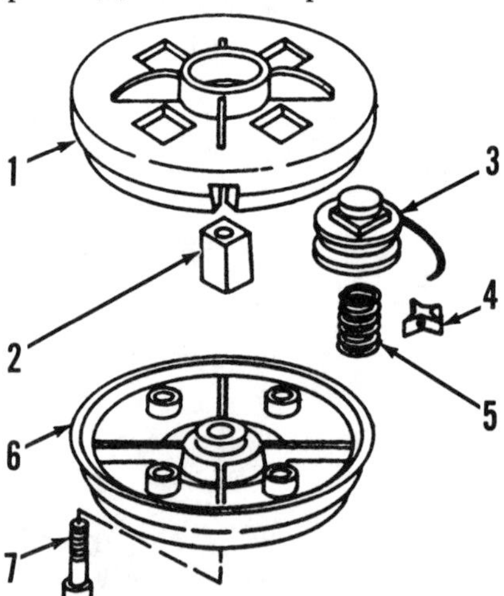

Fig. JD13—Exploded view of manual advance, four-strand trimmer head used on Model 85G.

1. Housing
2. Post
3. Spool
4. Retainer
5. Spring
6. Cover
7. Allen screw

Early 100G and Early 200G Models

Early 100G and early 200G models are equipped with a single-strand, semi-automatic trimmer head shown in Fig. JD14. The trimmer head will hold approximately 45 feet (13.7 m) of 0.080 inch (2 mm) diameter line. Line may be manually advanced with engine stopped by pushing in on housing (12) while pulling on line. Repeat procedure until desired line length is obtained. to advance line with engine running, operate trimmer engine at full rpm and tap housing (12) on ground. each time housing is tapped, measured amount of line is advanced.

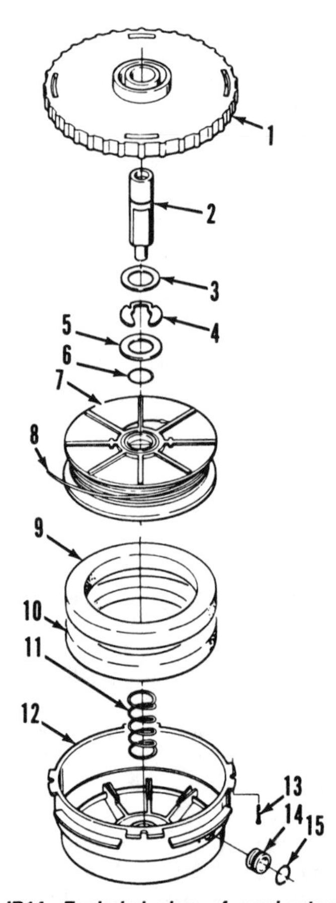

Fig. JD14—Exploded view of semi-automatic, single-strand trimmer head used on early 100G and early 200G models.

1. Cover
2. Adapter
3. Washer
4. Retainer
5. Washer
6. Retainer
7. Spool
8. Line
9. Foam pad
10. Foam pad
11. Spring
12. Housing
13. Cotter pin
14. Line guide
15. Retainer

To install new line, remove cotter pin (13). Twist housing (12) counterclockwise and remove housing. Remove foam pads (9 and 10) and any remaining line from spool (7). Clean spool and inner area of housing. Tape one end of new line to spool (Fig. JD15). Wind line on spool in direction indicated by arrow on spool (Fig. JD16). Install foam pads so line is protruding from center of pads as shown in Fig. JD16. Insert end of line through line guide and install spool, housing and spring. Push housing in and twist in clockwise direction to lock in position, then install cotter pin (13—Fig. JD14).

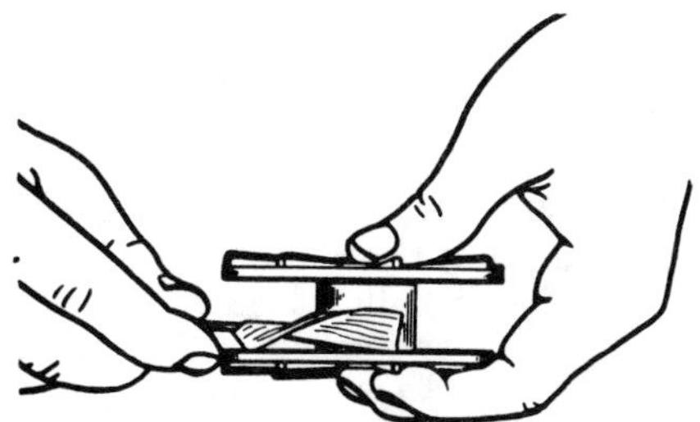

Fig. JD15—Tape end of new line to center of spool as shown.

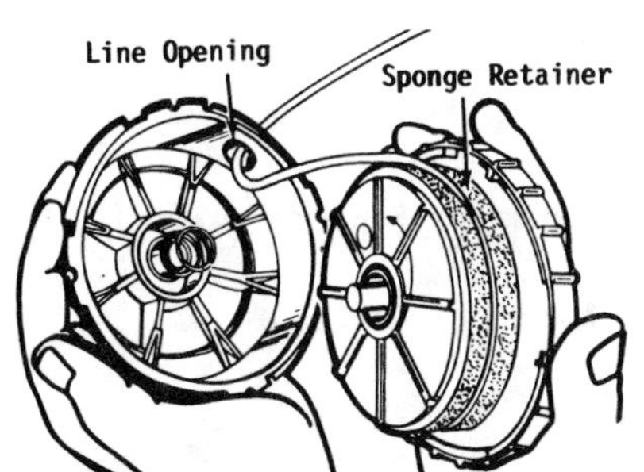

Fig. JD16—Install foam pads with line protruding from between pads. Wind line in direction indicated by arrow on spool.

Later 100G, 110G, Later 200G, 210G and 220G Models

These models are equipped with a dual-strand semi-automatic trimmer head. To manually advance line with engine stopped, push in button at bottom of head and pull on each line. To extend line with engine running, operate trimmer at full operating rpm and tap button on ground. Line will automatically advance a measured amount.

To install new line, press against tab marked "PUSH" and remove cover (8—Fig. JD17), button (7) and spool (6). Clean and inspect all parts. New line should be 0.080 inch (2 mm) diameter and 15 feet (4.6 m) long. Insert end of line through eye of spool as shown in Fig. JD18 so approximately 1 inch (25 mm) extends past eye. Wrap line on spool in clockwise direction as viewed from top side of spool (note arrow on spool). Install spool while directing line end through eye of drum (2—Fig. JD17). Install button and cover. Cover should snap into place after locking tabs of cover engage tabs on drum next to eye hole. Trim line so approximately 7 inches (18 cm) extend from drum.

If trimmer head retaining nut (4) must be unscrewed, prevent shaft rotation by inserting a pin through hole provided in bearing head to lock shaft.

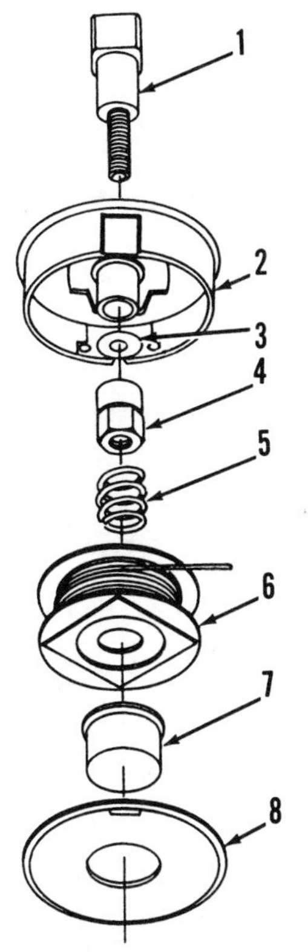

Fig. JD17—Exploded view of semi-automatic, dual-strand trimmer head used on later 100G, 110G, later 200G, 210G and 220G models.

1. Adapter
2. Housing
3. Line guide
4. Nut
5. Spring
6. Spool
7. Button
8. Cover

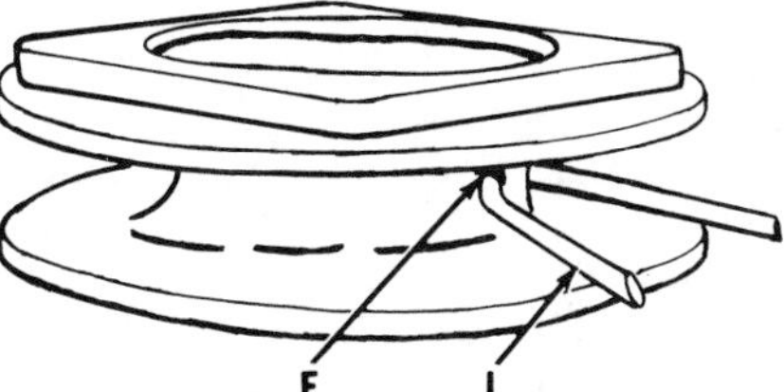

Fig. JD18—Insert end of line (L) through eye (E) of spool as shown so approximately 1 inch (25 mm) extends past eye.

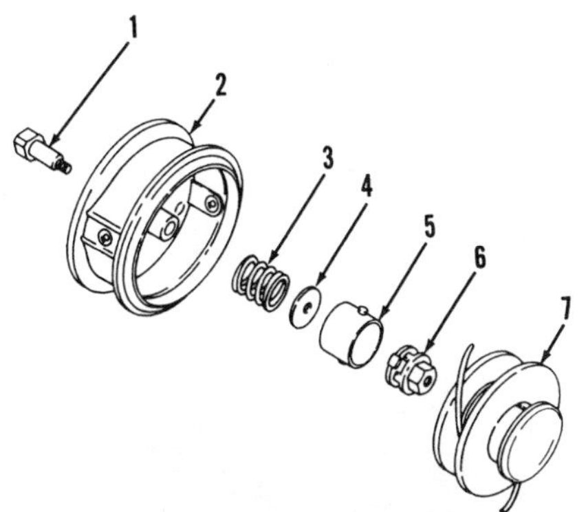

Fig. JD19—Exploded view of semi-automatic, dual-strand trimmer head used on 240G, later 250G, 260G, 300G, later 350G and later 450G models.

1. Adapter
2. Housing
3. Spring
4. Washer
5. Outer cam
6. Inner cam
7. Spool

Models 240G, Later 250G, 260G, 300G, 350G and 450G

These models are equipped with the dual-strand, semi-automatic trimmer head shown in Fig. JD19. To manually advance line with engine stopped, push in button at bottom of head and pull on each line. Procedure may have to be repeated to obtain desired line length. To extend line with engine running, operate trimmer at full operating rpm and tap button on ground. Line will automatically advance a given amount.

To install new line, hold drum firmly and turn spool in direction shown in Fig. JD20 to remove slack. Twist with a hard snap until plastic peg is between holes and separate spool from drum. Remove old line from spool. Spool will hold approximately 20 feet (6 m) of 0.095 inch (2.4 mm) diameter line. In-

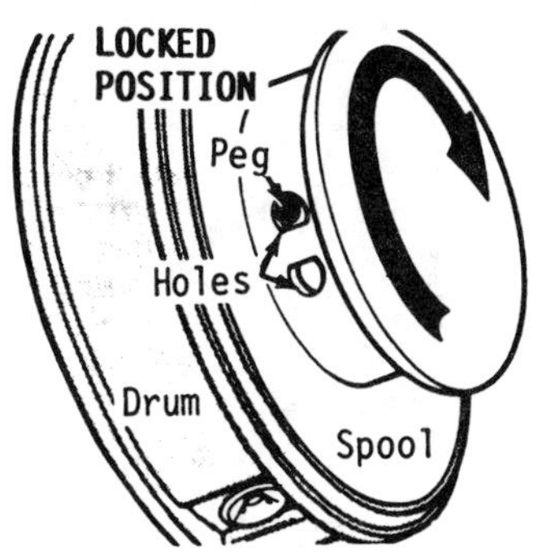

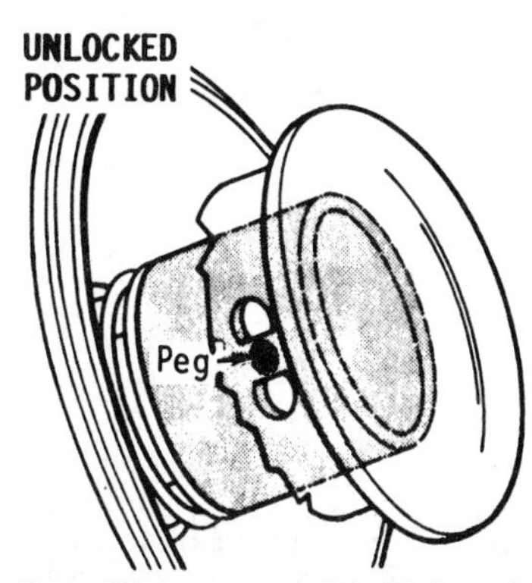

Fig. JD20—To remove spool, hold drum firmly and turn spool in direction shown to take up slack, then twist with a sudden snap until plastic peg is between holes as shown in lower view.

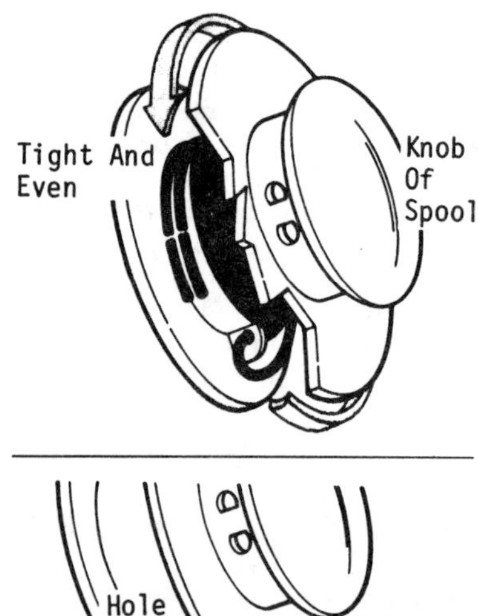

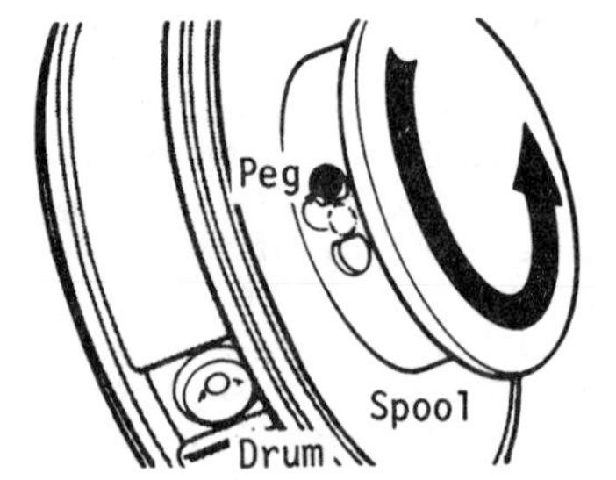

Fig. JD21—End of line must be inserted through hole on spool as shown in lower view. Wind line tightly in direction indicated by arrow on spool.

sert one end of new line through hole on spool (Fig. JD21) and pull line through until line is the same length on both sides of hole. Wind both ends of line at the same time in direction indicated by arrow on spool. Wind tightly and evenly from side-to-side and do not twist line. Insert ends of line through line guide openings, align pegs on drum with slots in spool and push spool into drum. Hold drum firmly, twist spool quickly in direction shown in Fig. JD22 so peg enters hole with a click and locks spool in position. Cut off lines to approximately 6 inches (15 cm).

If trimmer head inner drive cam (6—Fig. JD19) must be unscrewed, prevent shaft rotation by inserting a pin through hole located in bearing head. Cam has left-hand threads.

BLADE

Models 83G, 90G, 240G, 250G, 260G, 300G, 350G and 450G

Model 83G may be equipped with a four-tooth blade or a saw blade. Model 90G may be equipped with an eight-tooth blade. Models 240G, 250G, 260G, 300G, 350G and 450G may be equipped with an eight-tooth blade or a saw blade. When installing blade, make certain all adapter washers are centered and square with blade surface. Note that blade retaining nut has left-hand threads. Install blade so cutting surfaces will cut when blade rotates clockwise as viewed from ground side of blade.

Early 250G, Early 350G and Early 450G Models

Early Models 250G, 350G and 450G are equipped with the manual advance, dual-strand trimmer head shown in Fig. JD23. To pull out line, stop engine and loosen knob (6) approximately 1 1/2 turns clockwise (knob has left-hand threads). Line length should be approximately 5 inches (12.7 cm).

To install new line, remove screw (8) and washer (7). Unscrew knob (left hand threads) and remove cover (5), spring (4) and spool (3). New line should be 0.095 inch (2.4 mm) diameter. Each line is 12 feet (3.7 m) long. Insert line end through slot and into hole on opposite side of spool Line end should protrude 1/4 inch (6.4 mm). Without twisting lines, tightly wrap lines around spool in a counter-clockwise direction as viewed from slotted side of spool. Install spool with slotted side out while directing line ends through eyelets in drum. Install spring (4), cover (5), knob (6), washer (7) and screw (8). Be sure dogs (D—Fig. JD24) on spool properly engage slots (S) in cover. Cut line on each side so line length is 6 inches (15 cm).

DRIVE SHAFT HOUSING

All Models

REMOVE AND REINSTALL. The drive shaft housing may be separated from the engine clutch housing by unscrewing the housing clamp screws. If marks do not exist, place marks on clutch housing and drive shaft housing so the housings can be mated in their original positions.

Most models are equipped with a locating screw (S—Fig. JD25) that must be removed before separating lower end of drive shaft housing from gear head or bearing housing.

DRIVE SHAFT

Models 80G and 85G

Models 80G and 85G are equipped with flexible drive shafts that should be lubricated after every 10 hours of operation by injecting grease through the fitting on the shaft housing. Recommended lubricant is SAE high-temperature EP grease. Do not inject more than 1/2 teaspoon (2.5 mL) of

Fig. JD22—Hold drum firmly and twist suddenly to lock spool in position.

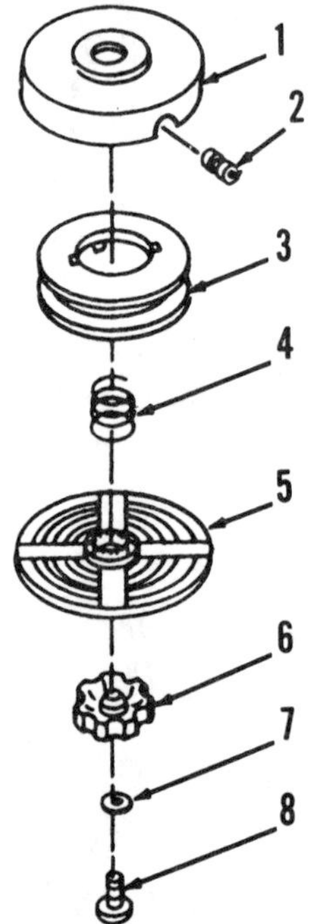

Fig. JD23—Exploded view of manual advance, dual-strand trimmer head used on early 250G, early 350G and early 450G models.

1. Housing
2. Eyelet
3. Spool
4. Spring
5. Cover
6. Knob
7. Washer
8. Screw

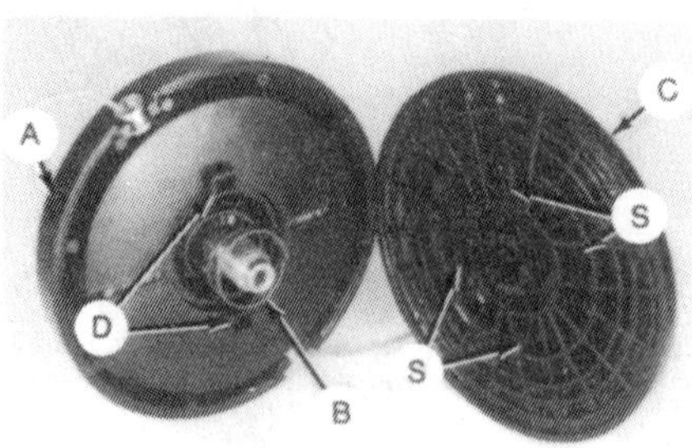

Fig. JD24—Dogs (D) on spool must engage slots (S) in cover (C).

Fig. JD25—Most models have a locating screw (S) that retains and positions the bearing housing or gear head on the drive shaft housing tube.

grease as over lubrication may force grease into clutch of trimmer head.

Models 82G, 100G and 200G

Models 82G, 100G and 200G are equipped with flexible drive shafts. Drive shafts should be removed from drive shaft housing, cleaned and installed with ends reversed after every 10 hours of operation.

To remove drive shaft, separate drive shaft housing from clutch housing. Mark drive shaft end and pull drive shaft from housing. Clean and lubricate drive shaft. Install with end that was at clutch end, now at trimmer head end. Reversing drive shaft ends extends drive shaft life.

Models 110G and 210G

Models 110G and 210G are equipped with flexible drive shafts that ride in renewable bushings. Drive shaft should be removed from drive shaft housing, cleaned and installed with ends reversed after every six months.

To remove drive shaft, separate drive shaft housing from bearing housing. Mark drive shaft end and pull drive shaft from housing. Clean and lubricate drive shaft. Install with end that was at clutch end, now at trimmer head end. Reversing drive shaft ends extends drive shaft life.

Models 240G and 260G

Models 240G and 260G are equipped with flexible drive shafts that ride in renewable bushings. Drive shaft should be removed from drive shaft housing, cleaned and lubricated annually.

To remove drive shaft, separate drive shaft housing from gear head.

Models 83G, 90G, 220G, 250G, 300G, 350G and 450G

These models are equipped with a solid shaft that rides in bushings in the drive shaft housing. Drive shaft requires no regular maintenance, However, if drive shaft is removed, it should be lubricated with lithium-base grease before installation. Manufacturer does not recommend renewal of bushings in drive shaft housing.

BEARING HEAD

Later Models 80G and 82G

Later Models 80G and 82G are equipped with the bearing head shown in Fig. JD26, which has sealed bearings and requires no maintenance.

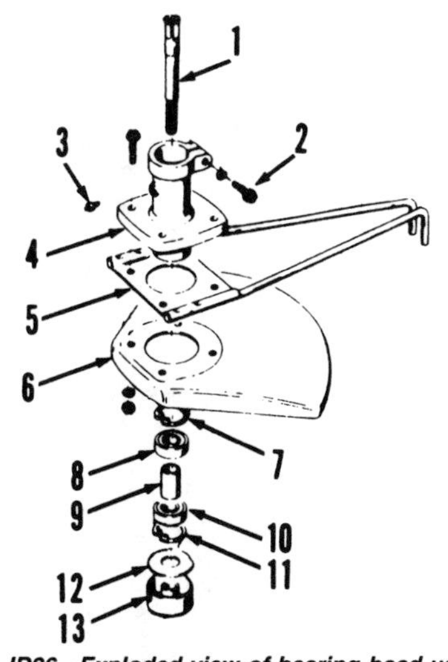

Fig. JD26—Exploded view of bearing head used on Models 80G and 82G.

1. Adapter
2. Clamp bolt
3. Locating screw
4. Housing
5. Bracket (if equipped)
6. Shield
7. Snap ring
8. Bearing
9. Spacer
10. Bearing
11. Snap ring
12. Washer
13. Drive disc

To disassemble bearing head, remove trimmer head. Remove clamp bolt (2) and locating screw (3). Separate bearing head assembly from drive shaft housing. Remove shield (6) and bracket (5), if so equipped. Remove cup washer (13) and washer (12). Carefully press drive shaft adapter (1) out of bearings. Remove snap rings (7 and 11), then press bearings (8 and 10) and spacer (9) out of housing.

Models 85G, 100G, 200G and 220G

Models 85G, 100G 200G and 220G are equipped with the bearing head shown in Fig. JD27, which has sealed bearings that do not require regular maintenance. To disassemble bearing head, remove screw (1) and clamp screw (2) and slide bearing head off drive shaft housing.

Remove adapter plate (10) and snap ring (8). Use a suitable puller or press and force shaft and bearing assembly out of housing (3). Unscrew nut (4) and remove bearings and spacer as required. Note that nut (4) has left-hand threads.

Models 110G and 210G

The bearing housings on Models 110G and 210G have no serviceable components and must be serviced as unit assemblies. No lubrication is required.

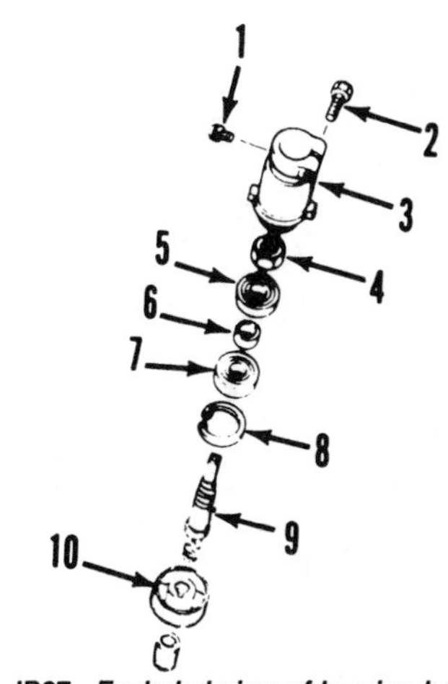

Fig. JD27—Exploded view of bearing head used on Models 100G, 200G and 220G. Model 85G is similar.

1. Locating screw
2. Clamp screw
3. Housing
4. Nug
5. Bearing
6. Spacer
7. Bearing
8. Snap ring
9. Shaft
10. Adapter plate & key

Model 83G

Lubricant level in gear housing should be checked after every 10 hours of operation. To check lubricant level, remove plug in side of gear housing. Gear housing should be two-thirds full of lubricant. Recommended lubricant is lithium-base grease.

The gear housing on Model 83G has no serviceable components and must be serviced as a unit assembly.

Model 90G

Lubricant level in gear housing should be checked after every 10 hours of operation. To check lubricant level, remove plug (20—Fig. JD28) in side of gear housing. Gear housing should be two-thirds full of lubricant. Recommended lubricant is lithium-base grease.

Before disassembly, note position of all spacers or shims so they can be reinstalled in their original position. Remove blade or trimmer head and separate gear head from drive shaft housing tube. Remove snap ring (19) and use a suitable puller to extract input shaft and bearing assembly from gear head. Remove plug (1) and snap ring (4). Remove seal (10) and snap ring (9). Press arbor (12) and bearing assembly out of gear head.

Inspect components and renew if excessively worn or damaged. Shims (15) may be installed to establish gear position and backlash. Gears should rotate smoothly without binding.

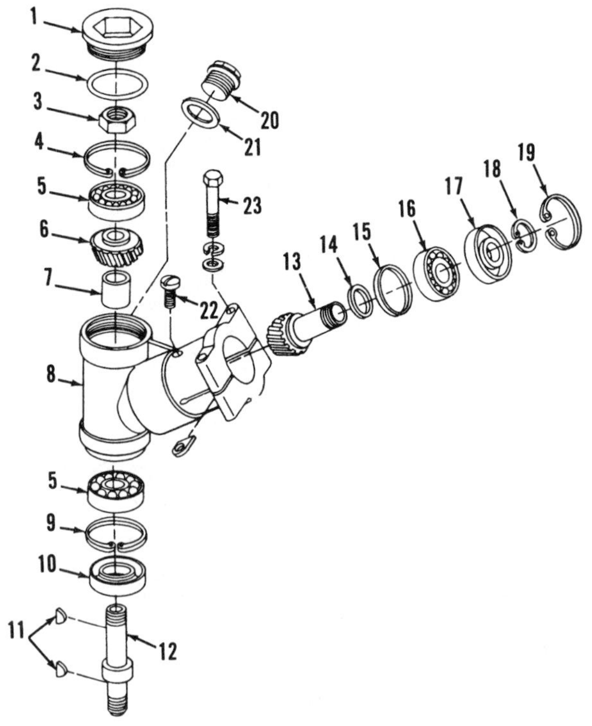

Fig. JD28—Exploded view of gear head used on Model 90G.

1. Plug
2. "O" ring
3. Nut
4. Snap ring
5. Bearing
6. Gear
7. Spacer
8. Housing
9. Snap ring
10. Seal
11. Keys
12. Arbor
13. Input gear
14. Washer
15. Shim
16. Bearnig
17. Bearing
18. Snap ring
19. Snap ring
20. Plug
21. Washer
22. Locating screw
23. Clamp bolt

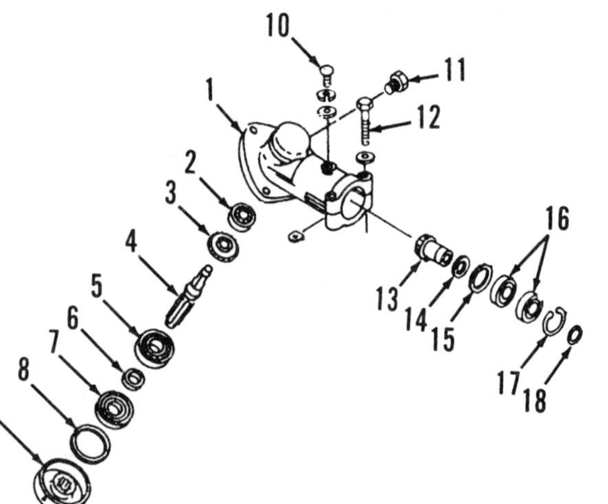

Fig. JD29—Exploded view of gear head used on Models 240G, later 250G and 260G.

1. Housing
2. Bearing
3. Gear
4. Arbor
5. Bearing
6. Washer
7. Seal
8. Snap ring
9. Adapter plate
10. Locating screw
11. Plug
12. Clamp bolt
13. Input gear
14. Washer
15. Shim
16. Bearings
17. Snap ring
18. Snap ring

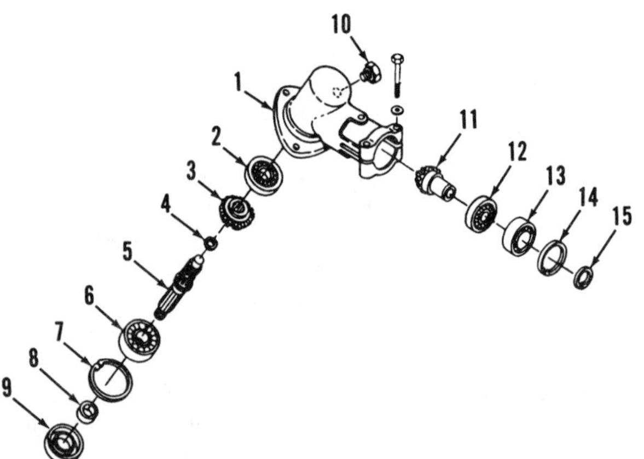

Fig. JD30—Exploded view of gear head used on early 250G and all 300G models.

1. Housing
2. Bearing
3. Gear
4. Snap ring
5. Arbor
6. Bearing
7. Snap ring
8. Washer
9. Seal
10. Plug
11. Input gear
12. Bearing
13. Bearing
14. Snap ring
15. Snap ring

Models 240G, Later 250G and 260G

Lubricant level in gear housing should be checked after every 10 hours of operation. To check lubricant level, remove plug (11—Fig. JD29) in side of gear housing. Gear housing should be nearly full of lubricant while leaving room for expansion. Recommended lubricant is lithium-base grease.

Before disassembly, note position of all spacers or shims so they can be reinstalled in their original position. Remove blade or trimmer head and separate gear head from drive shaft housing tube. Remove snap ring (17) and use a suitable puller to extract input shaft and bearing assembly from gear head. Remove adapter plate (9). Remove snap ring (8) and seal (7). Use a suitable puller to extract arbor (4), bearing (5) and gear (3) assembly. If bearing (2) is not free, heat housing and tap lightly to dislodge bearings. Inspect components and renew if excessively worn or damaged. Shims (15) may be installed to establish gear position and backlash. Gears should rotate smoothly without binding.

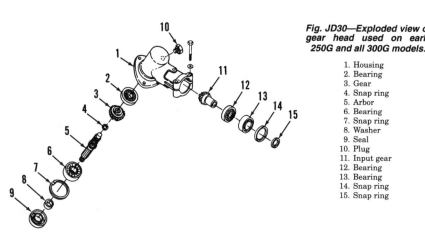

Early 250G and 300G

Lubricant level in gear housing should be checked after every 10 hours of operation. To check lubricant level, remove plug (10—Fig. JD30) in side of gear housing. Gear housing should be nearly full of lubricant while leaving room for expansion. Recommended lubricant is lithium-base grease.

To disassemble gear head, remove blade or trimmer head and separate gear head from drive shaft housing tube. Remove snap ring (14) and use a suitable puller to extract input shaft and bearing assembly from gear head. Remove adapter plate. Remove seal (9) and snap ring (7). Use a suitable puller to extract arbor (5), bearing (6) and gear(3) assembly. If bearing (2) is not free, heat housing and tap lightly to dislodge bearing. Inspect components and renew if excessively worn or damaged.

Model 350G

Lubricant level in gear housing should be checked after every 10 hours of operation. To check lubricant level, remove plug (11—Fig. JD31) in side of gear housing. Gear housing should be nearly full of lubricant while leaving room for expansion. Recommended lubricant is lithium-base grease.

Before disassembly, note position of all spacers or shims so they can be reinstalled in their original position. Remove blade or trimmer head and separate gear head from drive shaft housing tube. Remove snap ring (19) and use a suitable puller to extract input shaft and bearing assembly from gear head. Pull adapter plate (10) off shaft. Remove seal (9) and snap ring (8). Use a suitable puller to extract arbor (4), bearing (7) and gear (3) assembly. If bearing (2) is not free, heat housing and tap lightly to dislodge bearing.

Inspect components and renew if excessively worn or damaged. Shims (16) may be installed to establish gear position and backlash. Gears should rotate smoothly without binding.

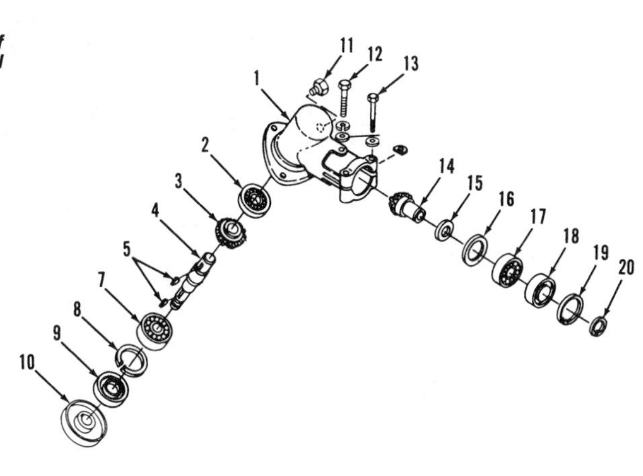

Fig. JD31—Exploded view of bearing head used on Model 350G.

1. Housing
2. Bearing
3. Gear
4. Arbor
5. Keys
7. Bearing
8. Snap ring
9. Seal
10. Adapter plate
11. Plug
12. Locating screw
13. Clamp bolt
14. Input gear
15. Washer
16. Shim
17. Bearing
18. Bearing
19. Snap ring
20. Snap ring

Model 450G

Lubricant level in gear housing should be checked after every 10 hours of operation. To check lubricant level, remove plug (11—Fig. JD32) in side of gear housing. Gear housing should be nearly full of lubricant while leaving room for expansion. Recommended lubricant is lithium-base grease.

Remove blade or trimmer head and separate gear head from drive shaft housing tube. Unscrew and separate input shaft housing (17) from gear housing (1). Detach snap ring (12) and force gear and bearing assembly out of housing by tapping on end of gear shaft. Detach snap ring (16) and separate bearings from shaft. To remove arbor shaft assembly, remove adapter plate from shaft and detach snap ring (9). Remove spacer (10) and use a suitable puller to remove shaft assembly. Disassemble shaft assembly as needed.

Inspect components for damage and excessive wear. Note during reassembly that sealed side of bearing (15) must be toward end of gear shaft.

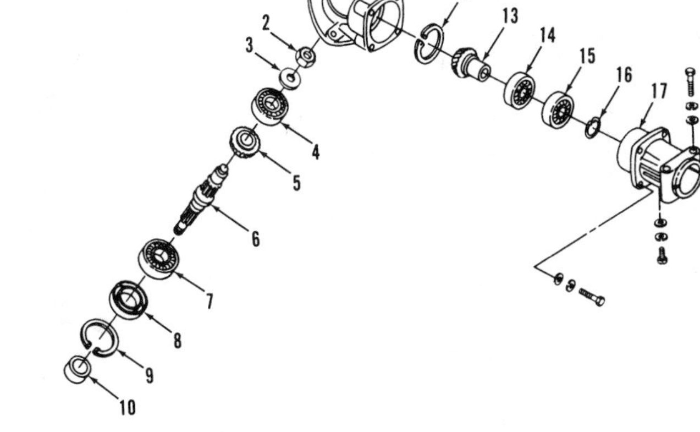

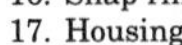

Fig. JD32—Exploded view of bearing head used on Model 450G.

1. Housing
2. Nut
3. Washer
4. Bearing
5. Gear
6. Arbor
7. Bearing
8. Seal
9. Snap ring
10. Spacer
11. Plug
12. Snap ring
13. Input gear
14. Bearing
15. Bearing
16. Snap ring
17. Housing

STARTER

Refer to the appropriate ENGINE SERVICE section for service to the starter assembly.

CLUTCH

Refer to the appropriate ENGINE SERVICE section for clutch removal and service procedures.

JOHN DEERE

GASOLINE POWERED TRIMMERS

Model	Engine Manufacturer	Engine Model	Displacement
21C	Own	....	21.2 cc (1.29 cu. in.)
21S	Own	....	21.2 cc (1.29 cu. in.)
25S	Own	....	24.4 cc (1.49 cu. in.)
30S	Own	....	30.5 cc (1.86 cu. in.)
38B	Own	....	37.4 cc (2.284 cu. in.)

ENGINE INFORMATION

Refer to the DEERE Engine Service section of this manual for service to the engines used on these models.

FUEL MIXTURE

The manufacturer recommends mixing John Deere 2-Cycle oil with regular or unleaded gasoline at a ratio of 50:1. When using regular BIA certified TC-W oil, mix at a ratio of 32:1.

Fuel tank capacity is 0.4 L (13.5 fl. oz.) for 21C and 21S models; 0.6 L (20.3 fl. oz.) for 25S model; 0.7 L (23.7 fl. oz.) for 30S model; 0.9 L (32.1 fl. oz.) for 38B model.

STRING TRIMMER

Models 21C

Refer to Fig. JD51 for the single line, semi-automatic string trimmer head typical of the type used. To manually advance the trimmer line with the engine stopped, push the button (7) at the bottom of the head and pull the line. To extend the line with the engine running, operate the trimmer at maximum speed and tap the button (7) on the ground. The line should extend a small amount automatically. If the line does not extend with the engine running, stop the engine and extend the line manually. If the line is broken inside the housing, it will be necessary to disassemble the unit and feed the line through the eyelet (3).

To disassemble, press the tab marked "PUSH," then twist the cover (8) to remove cover, button (7) and spool (6). Be careful not to lose the spring (5). Clean and inspect all parts for damage. A new eyelet (3) can be installed if worn. If new line is installed, it should be 0.080 in. (2.3 mm) diameter and should be 15 ft. (4.6 m) long. Insert the line through the eye of the spool as shown in Fig.

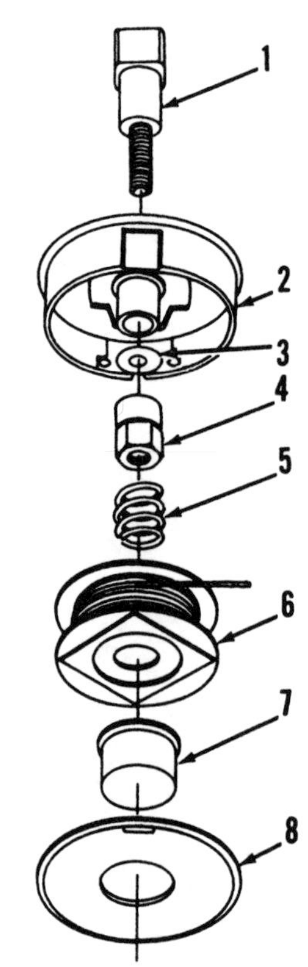

Fig. JD51—Exploded view of the single line string trimmer head used on 21C model.

1. Adapter
2. Housing
3. Eyelet (line guide)
4. Nut
5. Spring
6. Spool
7. Button
8. Cover

JD52. Wrap the line on spool in clockwise direction as viewed from the top of spool (note arrow on spool). Install spool while directing line through the eyelet (3—Fig. JD51) in the housing. Install the button and cover. The cover should snap in place when the locking tabs on cover and housing engage. Trim the line so the line extends approximately 7 in. (18 cm) from the drum.

If the trimmer head retaining nut (4) must be removed, lock the shaft to prevent it from rotating by inserting a pin

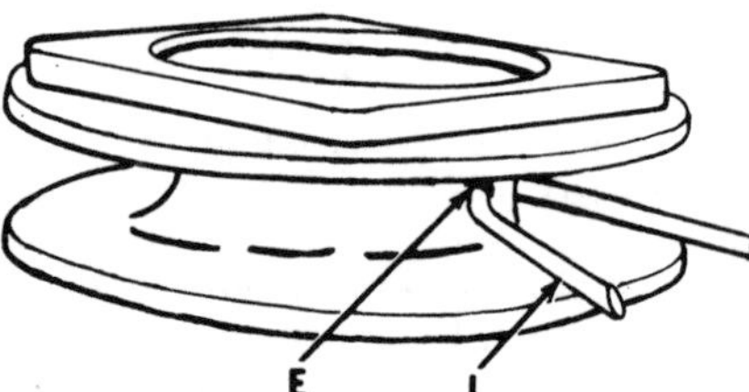

Fig. JD52—Insert the end of line (L) through the eye (E) of the spool as shown so approximately 1 inch (25 mm) extends past the eye.

through the hole in the bearing head. The nut has left hand thread.

Model 21S

Refer to Fig. JD53 for the dual line, semi-automatic string trimmer head typical of the type used. To manually advance the trimmer lines with the engine stopped, push the button (7) at the bottom of the head and pull both of the lines. To extend the lines with the engine running, operate the trimmer at maximum speed and tap the button (7) on the ground. Both lines should extend a small amount automatically. If the line does not extend with the engine running, stop the engine and extend the lines manually. If a line is broken inside the housing, it will be necessary to disassemble the unit and feed the line through the eyelet (3).

To disassemble, press the tab marked "PUSH," then twist the cover (8) to remove cover, button (7) and spool (6). Be careful not to lose the spring (5). Clean and inspect all parts for damage. New eyelets (3) can be installed if worn. If new line is installed, it should be 0.095 in. (2.41 mm) diameter. The spool will hold approximately 20 ft. (6 m) of line. Insert the line through the eye of the spool as shown in Fig. JD52 and pull the line through until it is the same length on both sides. Wrap both ends of the line on spool at the same time in clockwise direction as viewed from the top of spool (note arrow on spool). Wind the line tightly and evenly from side to

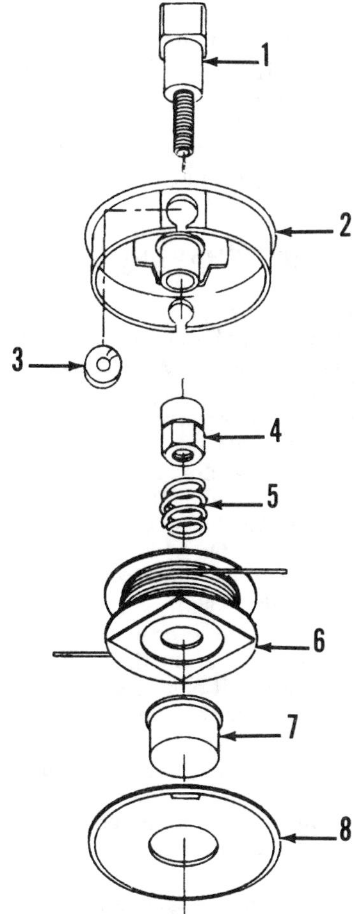

Fig. JD53—Exploded view of the dual line string trimmer head used on 21S model.

1. Adapter
2. Housing
3. Eyelets (line guide)
4. Nut
5. Spring
6. Spool
7. Button
8. Cover

side and do not twist the lines. Install spool while directing the ends of both lines through the eyelets (3) in the housing. Install the button and cover. The cover should snap in place when the locking tabs on cover and housing engage. Trim the line so the line extends approximately 6 in. (15 cm) from the drum.

If the trimmer head retaining nut (4) must be removed, lock the shaft to prevent it from rotating by inserting a pin through the hole in the bearing head. The nut has left hand thread.

Models 25S and 30S

Refer to Fig. JD54 for the dual line, semi-automatic string trimmer head typical of the type used. To manually advance the trimmer lines with the engine stopped, push the button at the bottom of the head and pull both of the lines. To extend the lines with the engine running, operate the trimmer at maximum speed and tap the button on the ground. Both lines should extend a small amount automatically. If the line does not extend with the engine running, stop the engine and extend the lines manually. If a line is broken inside the housing, it will be necessary to disassemble the unit and feed the line through the eyelet.

To remove and disassemble the string trimmer head, proceed as follows. Hold the drum firmly and turn spool in the direction shown in Fig. JD55 to remove slack. Twist with a hard snap until the plastic peg is between holes, then separate the spool from the drum.

Clean and inspect all parts for damage. If new line is installed, it should be 0.095 in. (2.41 mm) diameter. The spool will hold approximately 20 ft. (6 m) of line. Insert the line through the eye of the spool as shown in Fig. JD56 and pull the line through until it is the same length on both sides. Wrap both ends of the line on spool at the same time in clockwise direction as viewed from the top of spool. Wind the line tightly and evenly from side to side, but do not twist the lines. Install spool while directing the ends of both lines through the eyelets in the housing. Align the pegs on drum with slots in the spool and push the spool into drum. Hold the drum firmly, then twist spool quickly in the direction shown in Fig. JD57 so peg enters the hole with a click and locks the spool in position. Trim the line so the line extends approximately 6 in. (15 cm) from the drum.

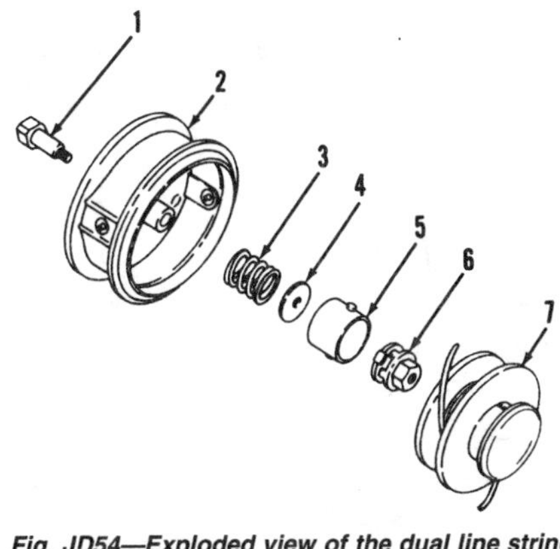

Fig. JD54—Exploded view of the dual line string trimmer head used on 25S and 30S model.

1. Adapter
2. Housing
3. Spring
4. Washer
5. Outer cam
6. Inner cam
7. Spool

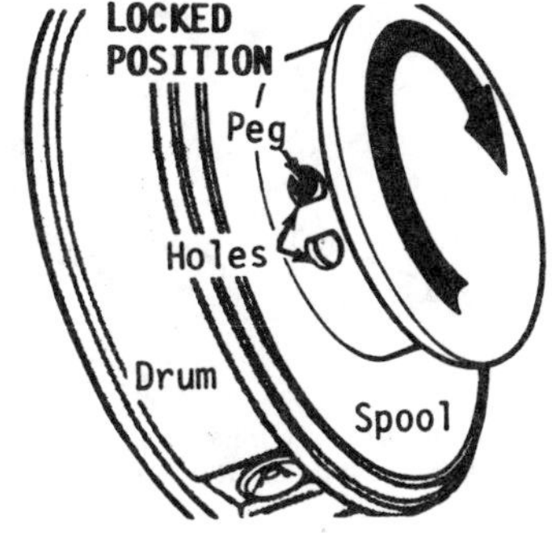

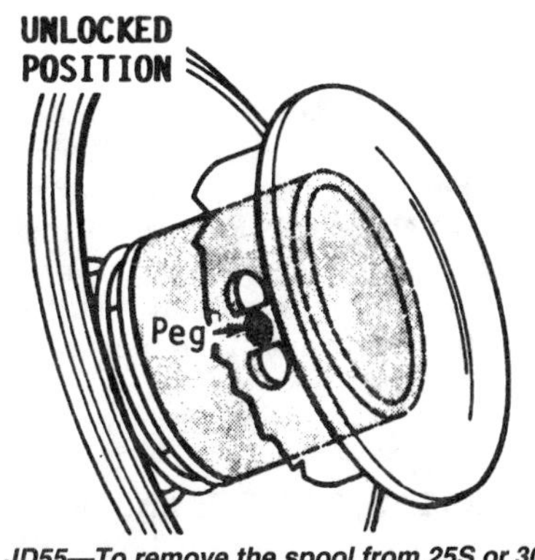

Fig. JD55—To remove the spool from 25S or 30S model, hold the drum firmly and turn the spool in the direction shown to take up slack, then twist with a sudden snap until the plastic peg is between the holes as shown in the lower view.

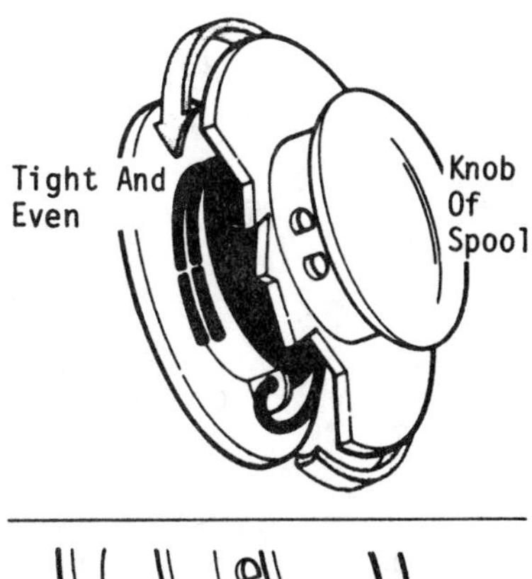

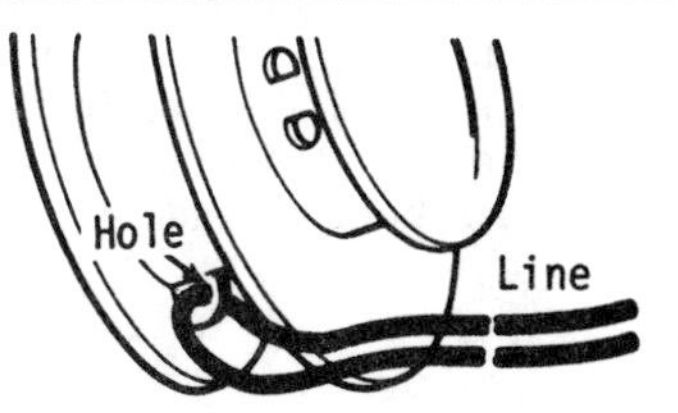

Fig. JD56—The end of the line must be inserted through the hole on spool as shown in the lower view. Wrap line tightly and evenly in the direction indicated by the arrow.

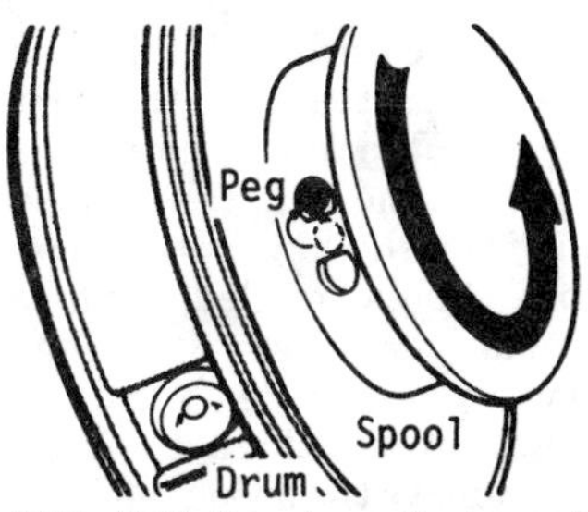

Fig. JD57—Hold the drum firmly and twist suddenly to lock the spool in position.

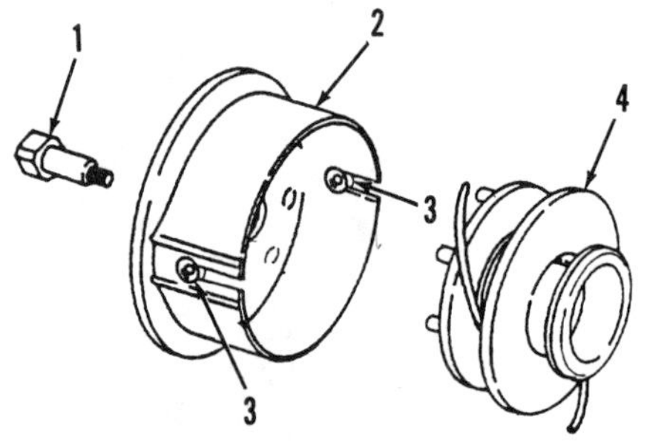

Fig. JD58—Exploded view of the dual line string trimmer head used on some 38B models.

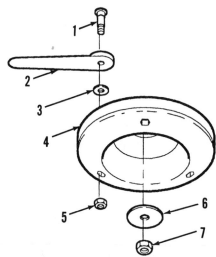

1. Adapter
2. Housing
3. Eyelets
4. Spool
5. Spring
6. Nut

If trimmer head drive cam (6—Fig. JD54) must be unscrewed, prevent shaft rotation by inserting a pin through hole located in bearing head. Cam has left hand threads.

Model 38B

Refer to Fig. JD58 for the dual line, string trimmer head typical of the type used. To manually advance the trimmer lines with the engine stopped, pull the spool out and turn it until both lines are extended sufficiently, release the spool and allow the spring (5) to push the spool into the hub. If the spool is not completely seated, turn the spool until the pegs on the top of the spool engage the holes in the hub. Both lines should extend from the hub the same amount. If a line is not extended, it may be broken inside the housing, making it necessary to disassemble the unit and feed the line through the eyelets. If necessary to remove the spool, remove nut (6) and spring (5), then lift the spool from the hub. If necessary to remove the adapter (1), hold the splined fitting plate and turn the adapter clockwise. The adapter has left hand thread.

Clean and inspect all parts for damage. If new line is installed, it should be 0.105 in. (2.7 mm) diameter. Insert the line through the eye of the spool as shown in Fig. JD56 and pull the line through until it is the same length on both sides. Wrap both ends of the line on spool at the same time in clockwise direction as viewed from the top of spool. Wind the line tightly and evenly from side to side, but do not twist the lines. Install spool while directing the ends of both lines through the eyelets in the housing. Install the spring (5—Fig. JD58) and nut (6). Tighten nut (6) securely. Trim the lines so each line extends approximately 6 in. (15 cm) from the drum.

TRI-CUT TRIMMER

All Models

The professional, tri-cut trimmer head shown in Fig. JD59 is available for all models. Each of the three cutter blades (2) can be replaced after removing the pivot screw (1). Be sure to install washers (3). Failure to install a washer or replacing the bolt or washer with a different part can result in the unit becoming out of balance.

Fig. JD59—Tri-cutter trimmer head is available for installation on 38B models.

1. Pivot bolt
2. Cutter blade
3. Washer
4. Hub
5. Nut
6. Washer
7. Nut

BLADE

Model 21S, 25S, 30S and 38B

An 8 in. diameter, 80 tooth saw blade or 8 tooth weed and grass blade is available for installation on 21S and 25S models. A 10 in. diameter, 80 tooth saw blade or 8 in. diameter, 8 tooth weed and grass blade is available for installation on 30S and 38B models.

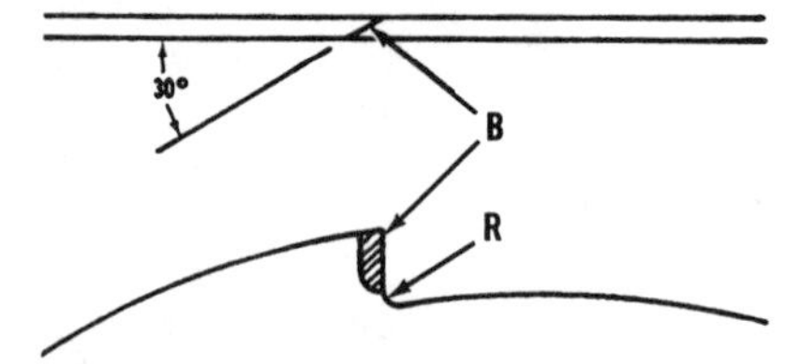

Fig. JD60—Steel blades can be installed on some models. The cutting face can be sharpened as shown.

The 8 tooth blades should be sharpened with a flat file as shown in Fig. JD60. Sharpen all of the blades evenly to maintain balance. Do not file into the radius at the root.

Sharpen the 80 tooth saw blades following the original sharpening angle and tooth set.

DRIVE SHAFT HOUSING

Before separating the drive shaft housing from the engine clutch housing, detach the throttle cable (10—Fig. JD61) and engine stop wires (8 and 9). Loosen the clamp screws (12), then pull the drive shaft housing (1) from the clamp (13) and clutch housing (16). On models with gear housing, remove the unit from the lower end of the drive shaft housing. On 21C models, remove the trimmer assembly from the lower end of the drive shaft and housing.

Inspect all parts for wear or damage. Check the ends of the drive shaft carefully for wear. If equipped with a solid drive shaft, make sure the shaft is straight. Lubricate the entire length of the drive shaft lightly with multipurpose grease. For most models, the bushings and drive shaft inner guide tube are available for service.

DRIVE SHAFT

Models 21C and 21S

These models are equipped with flexible drive shafts that should be removed, inspected and lubricated frequently. The 4-layer cable can be withdrawn from either end of drive shaft tube. If the drive shaft cannot be easily withdrawn or turned, it may be necessary to renew the housing as well as the drive shaft. Coat the shaft lightly with multipurpose grease, before installing.

Models 25S, 30S and 38B

These models are equipped with a solid drive shaft that rides in bushings located in the drive shaft housing. The drive shaft requires no regular maintenance; however, if the drive shaft is removed, it should be lightly coated with multipurpose grease before installing.

LOWER BEARING HOUSING

Model 21C

The lower bearing housing (2—Fig. JD62) can be removed after removing the trimmer head and loosening the clamp (3). Individual service parts are

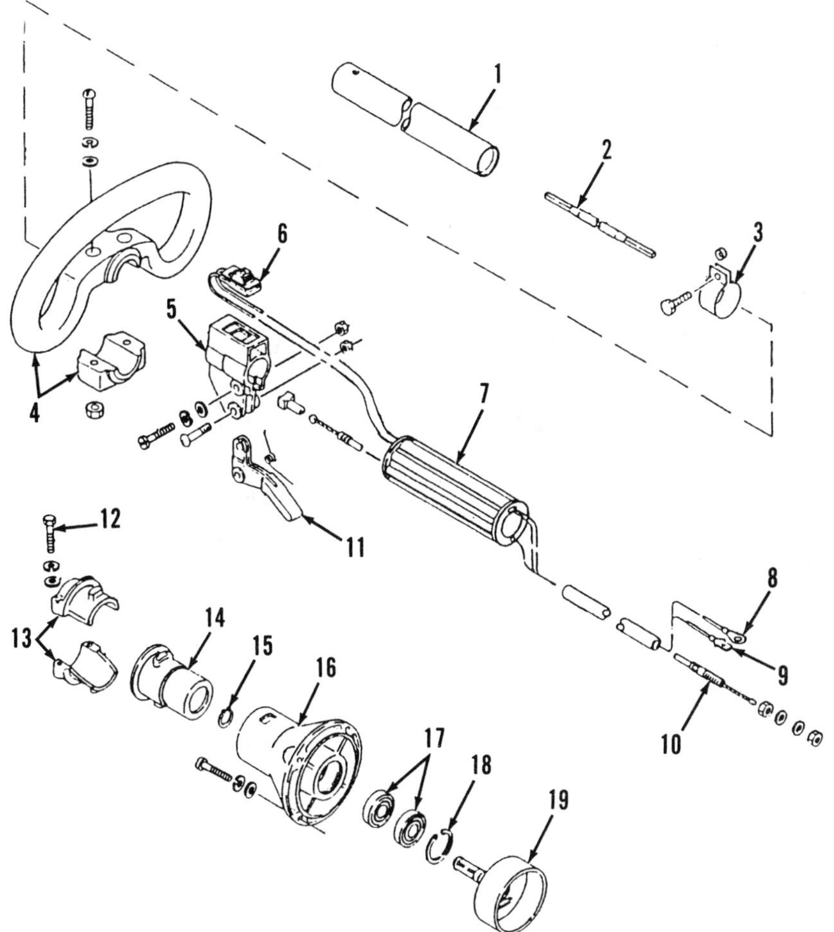

Fig. JD61—Typical drive shaft housing, clutch housing and clamp assembly.

1. Drive shaft housing
2. Drive shaft
3. Clamp
4. Handle
5. Bracket
6. On-off switch
7. Grip
8. Ground wire
9. Ignition module wire
10. Throttle cable
11. Throttle control
12. Screw
13. Holder
14. Cushion
15. Snap ring
16. Clutch housing
17. Bearings
18. Retaining ring
19. Clutch drum

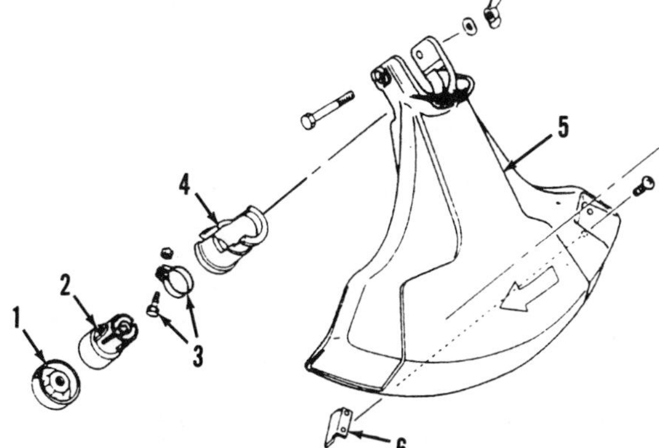

Fig. JD62—Individual service parts of the lower bearing head for 21C and 21S models are not available.

1. Lock plate
2. Lower bearing head
3. Clamp
4. Bracket
5. Protector shield

not available and the bearing head should not be disassembled.

GEAR HOUSING

Models 21S, 25S, 30S and 38B

The gear housing (Fig. JD63) is located at the lower end of the drive shaft and housing. To remove the assembly, loosen the fitting screw (1) and clamp bolts (2), then pull the gear housing from the drive shaft housing. Remove the trimmer head or blade, then unbolt the protector shield. The seal (16) can be pried from the housing.

To remove the gears and bearings, first remove snap ring (3). Use a 5/16 in. blind hole puller (part No. JTO 1720 and JTO 1724 or equivalent) to pull the gear and bearings (5, 6 and 7) from the housing.

NOTE: It may be possible to bump the open end of housing (14) to dislodge the bearings and gear (5, 6 and 7).

The bearings can be pressed from the gear after removing the snap ring (4). Remove snap ring (8), then pull the bearing and shaft (9 and 10) from the housing. A puller may be needed to remove the bearing (13) from its bore in housing.

Clean all parts and inspect for damage. Install new parts as necessary. Gears should be replaced as a set. Grease the lower seal (16) before pressing into the housing. Add multipurpose lithium-base grease to the housing until the cavity is approximately 2/3 full. Do not over fill the housing with grease. Tighten fill plug (21) securely.

RECOIL STARTER

Refer to Fig. JD64 for an exploded view of the starter. Unbolt and remove the starter from the engine. Remove the rope handle (3) and allow the rope to wind into the starter. Remove the center screw (7) and the pulley (10). The spring (11) may rewind uncontrollably causing injury. Wear appropriate safety eye wear and gloves before removing the recoil spring (11) from the housing (9).

Unscrew the lock nut and pawl plate (6) from the engine crankshaft. The lock nut may not be installed on some 21C and 21S models. The lock nut and pawl plate (6) have left-hand threads. Remove the clip from the front of the pawl to remove the pawl and spring (1 and 2). Install the pawl plate and tighten it to 8-10 N•m (70-90 in.-lb.) torque. Tighten the lock nut on 21C and 21S models so equipped to 16-20 N•m (140-175 in.-lb.) torque. Tighten the lock nut on 25S, 30S and 38B models to 16-17.5 N•m (140-155 in.-lb.) torque.

To assemble the starter, lubricate the center post and spring side of the housing with light grease. Attach the outer end of the spring to the clip in the housing, then wind the spring into the housing wrapping the spring in a counterclockwise direction until the spring is completely in the housing cavity. The inner end of the spring should contact the center post.

Attach the rope to the pulley (10), thread the rope through the housing and guide (4 and 9), then attach the

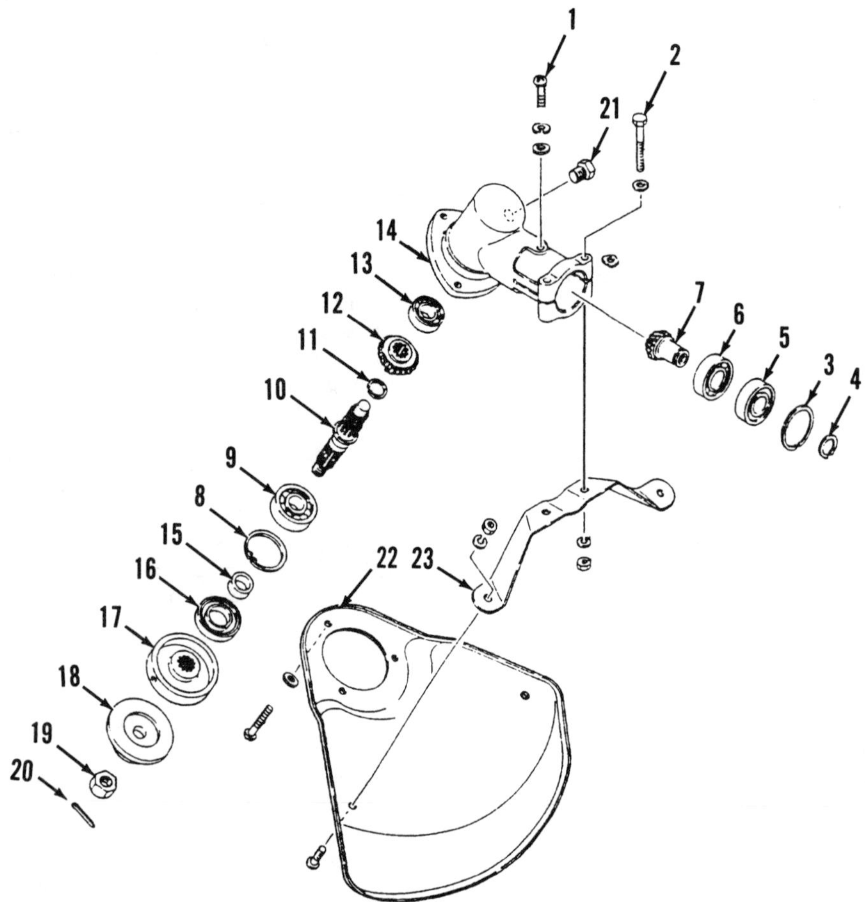

Fig. JD63—Exploded view of the gear housing typical of 21S, 25S, 30S and 38B models.

1. Fitting screw
2. Clamp screws
3. Snap ring
4. Snap ring
5. Bearing
6. Bearing
7. Gear
8. Snap ring
9. Bearing
10. Shaft
11. Snap ring
12. Gear
13. Bearing
14. Housing
15. Spacer
16. Seal
17. Lock plate
18. Drive plate
19. Nut
20. Cotter pin
21. Fill plug
22. Protector shield
23. Bracket

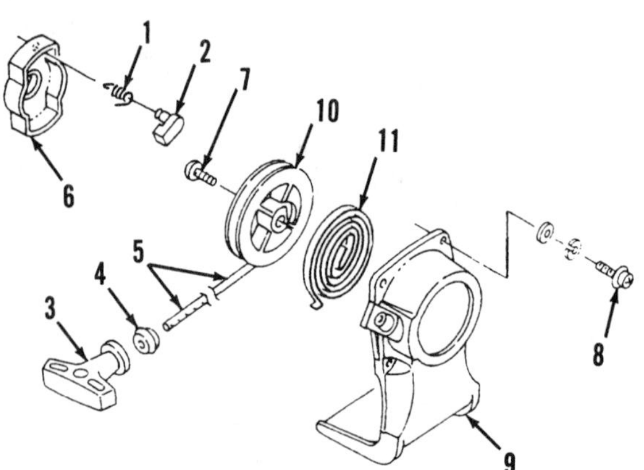

Fig. JD64—Exploded view of the recoil starter assembly typical of all models.

1. Pawl spring
2. Pawl
3. Handle
4. Guide
5. Rope
6. Pawl carrier
7. Screw
8. Screw
9. Housing
10. Pulley
11. Recoil spring

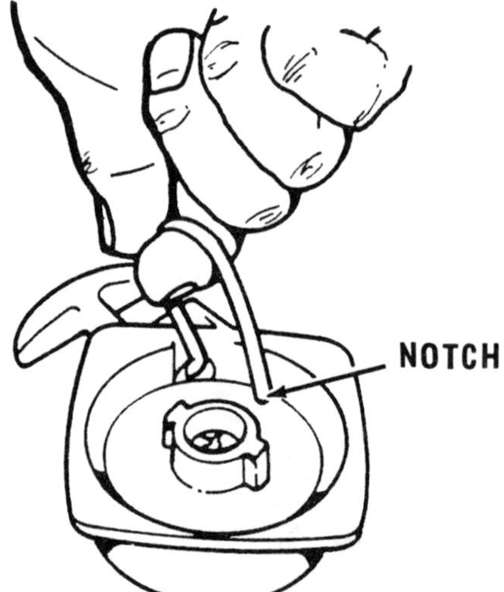

Fig. JD65—To set the preload of the starter recoil spring, pull a loop in the rope with the rope in the notch in the pulley, then wind the pulley as necessary. When the rope is released, it will pull out of the notch.

handle (3). Install the pulley over the center post of the housing while making sure the pulley engages the end of the rewind spring. Coat the threads of the retaining screw (7) with medium strength Loctite, then install and tighten the screw securely. Form a loop of rope in the pulley's notch as shown in Fig. JD65, hold the rope loop as shown and wind the pulley counterclockwise several turns. Pull the rope out with the handle and allow it to rewind. If the rope does not rewind properly, pull a loop in the rope as shown in Fig. JD65 and preload the spring another turn.

NOTE: If the rope is too long, it will bind before rewinding properly. Make sure the rope is not binding.

To make sure the spring is not tightened too much, pull the rope out completely, then turn the pulley an additional 1/2 turn. If the rope cannot be pulled out completely, the spring is bound and will break. Pull a loop in the rope as shown in Fig. JD65 and loosen the spring slightly as required. A proper setting will allow the rope to be fully extended and will also wind the rope onto the pulley fully.

ENGINE CONTROLS

Engine throttle control is located within easy reach of the operator's hands when safely positioned on the grips. Refer to Fig. JD66, Fig. JD67, Fig. JD68 and Fig. JD69. On some models, the engine stop switch is also located near the operator's grip.

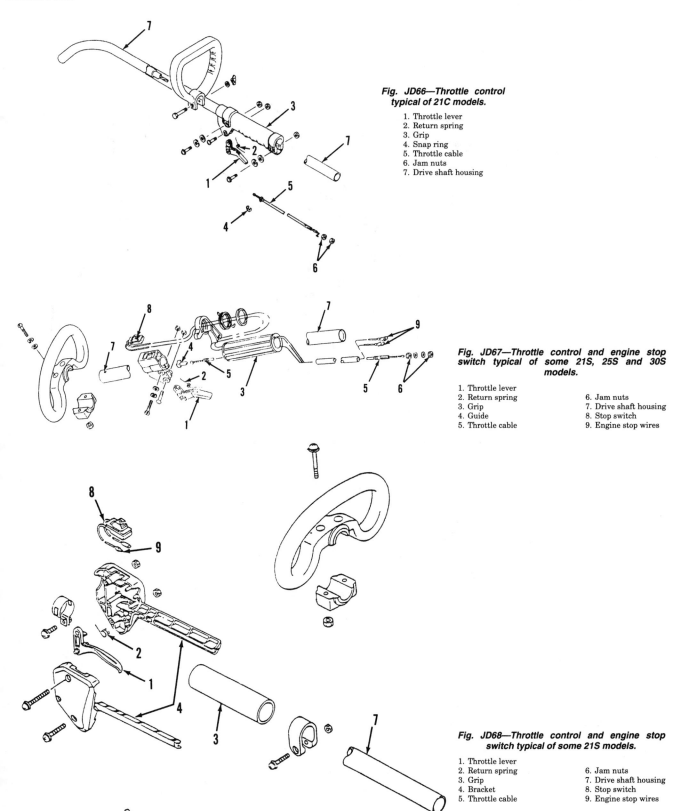

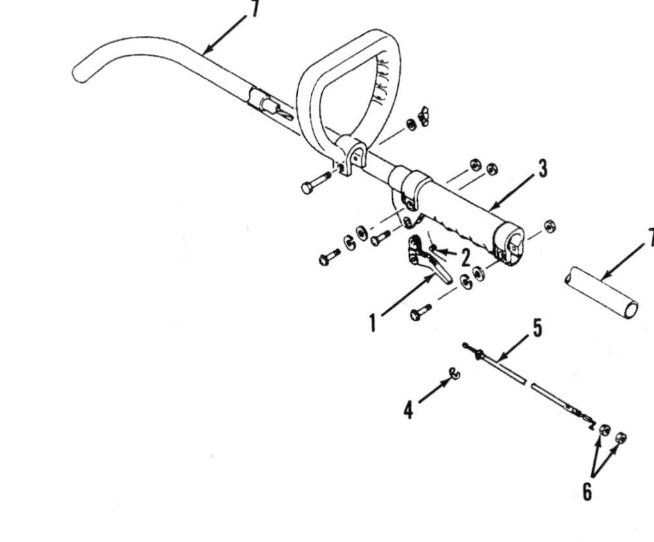

Fig. JD66—Throttle control typical of 21C models.

1. Throttle lever
2. Return spring
3. Grip
4. Snap ring
5. Throttle cable
6. Jam nuts
7. Drive shaft housing

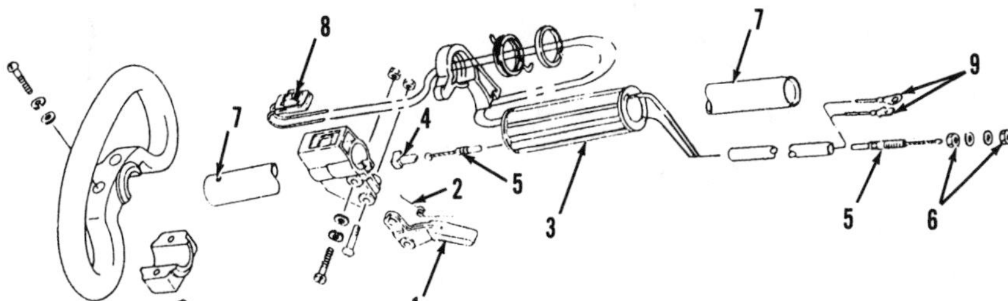

Fig. JD67—Throttle control and engine stop switch typical of some 21S, 25S and 30S models.

1. Throttle lever
2. Return spring
3. Grip
4. Guide
5. Throttle cable
6. Jam nuts
7. Drive shaft housing
8. Stop switch
9. Engine stop wires

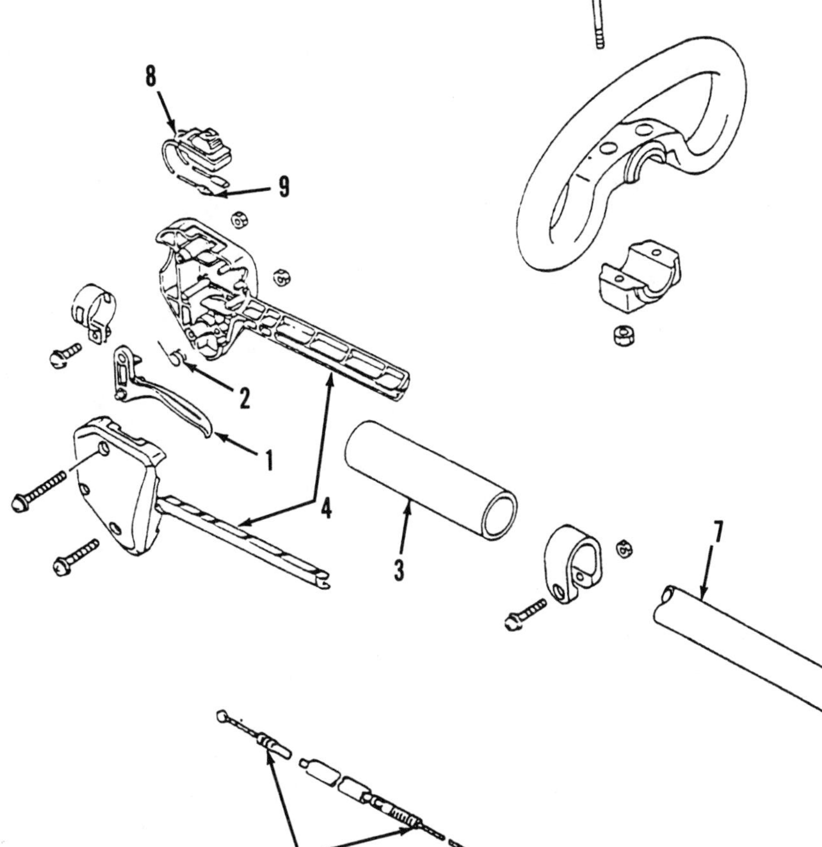

Fig. JD68—Throttle control and engine stop switch typical of some 21S models.

1. Throttle lever
2. Return spring
3. Grip
4. Bracket
5. Throttle cable
6. Jam nuts
7. Drive shaft housing
8. Stop switch
9. Engine stop wires

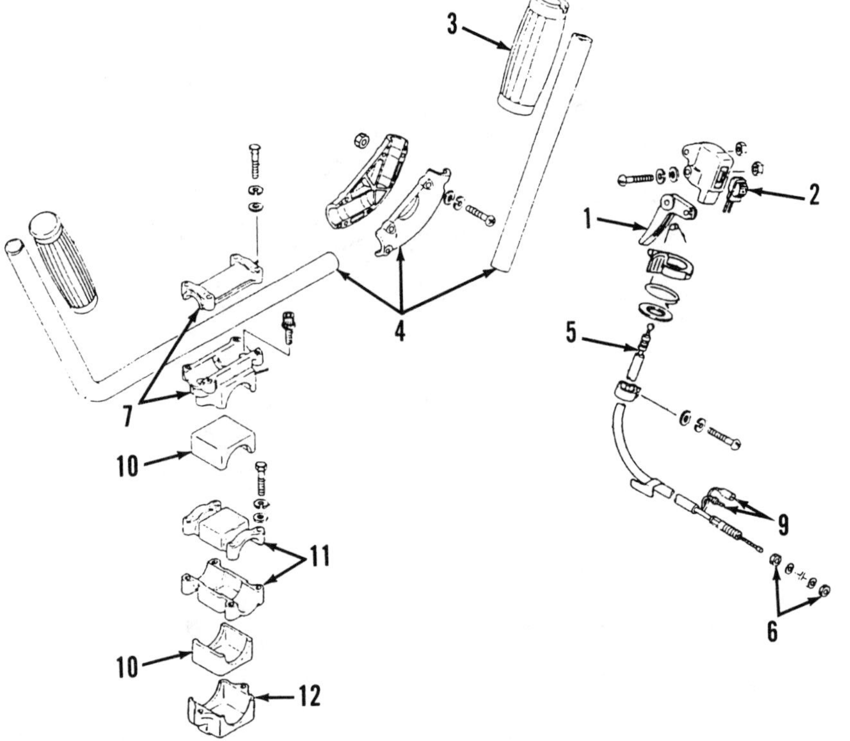

Fig. JD69—Throttle control and engine stop switch for 38B models. Some 21S, 25S and 30S models may be similarly equipped.

1. Throttle lever
2. Return spring
3. Grip
4. Handlebar
5. Throttle cable
6. Jam nuts
7. Handlebar upper clamp
8. Stop switch
9. Engine stop wires
10. Cushions
11. Drive shaft housing clamp
12. Handlebar lower clamp

JOHN DEERE

GASOLINE POWERED BLOWERS

Model	Engine Manufacturer	Engine Model	Displacement
2E	Kioritz	...	21.2 cc
3E	Kioritz	...	30.8 cc
4E	Kioritz	...	39.7 cc
5E	Kioritz	...	44.0 cc

FUEL MIXTURE

Manufacturer recommends mixing regular-grade gasoline, leaded or unleaded, with a high-quality, two-stroke engine oil with a BIA or NMMA certification for TC-W service. Recommended fuel:oil ratio is 50:1 when using John Deere 2-Cycle Engine Oil. Fuel:oil ratio should be 32:1 when using any other two-stroke oil, regardless of recommended ratio on oil container. Gasohol or other alcohol blended fuels are not approved by manufacturer.

ENGINE

Engine removal and installation procedures are outlined below. Refer to appropriate Deere engine service section for engine service procedures and specifications.

Model 2E

R&R ENGINE. To remove engine, drain fuel tank and remove tank. Remove recoil starter and ignition exciter coil. Use suitable puller to remove flywheel. Remove muffler guard and muffler. Unbolt and separate blower housing. Remove fan retaining nut and tap end of crankshaft with plastic mallet to loosen fan from crankshaft. Remove four engine mounting screws, separate engine from blower housing and disconnect throttle linkage. Remove carburetor, carburetor housing, ignition module, heat shield and cylinder cover. Unbolt and remove engine mounting bracket from engine.

To reinstall engine, reverse removal procedure. Tighten engine mounting bracket cap screws and engine to blower housing cap screws to 3.5-4.0 N·m (30-35 in.-lbs.).

Models 3E-5E

R&R ENGINE. To remove engine, remove recoil starter, engine cover, air cleaner, carburetor, air cleaner base, fuel tank, carburetor insulator, muffler and cylinder cover. Disconnect ignition switch wire. Remove backpack frame, handle, outer fan housing and blower fan. Unbolt and remove engine from fan housing.

To reinstall engine, reverse removal procedure. Tighten engine mounting cap screws to 3.5-4.0 N·m (30-35 in.-lbs.).

Model 4E

R&R ENGINE. To remove engine, drain fuel and remove fuel tank. Remove muffler, ignition coil and cylinder cover. Remove backpack frame, fan cover and fan. Remove engine mounting screws and separate engine from blower housing.

To reinstall engine, reverse removal procedure. Tighten engine mounting screws to 6.0-7.0 N·m (55-60 in.lbs.).

THROTTLE CABLE

Models 3E, 4E and 5E

The throttle cable should be adjusted so there is slight free play in throttle cable. To adjust, relocate nuts at carburetor end of throttle cable. Tighten nuts after adjustment.

FAN

Tighten fan nut or screws to 15-20 N·m (133-177 in.-lbs.) on Model 2E, 30 N·m (22 ft.-lbs.) on Models 3E and 5E and 3.5-4.0 N·m (31-35 in.-lbs.) on Model 4E. If equipped with a concave washer under retaining nut, install washer so concave side is next to fan.

DOLMAR

GASOLINE POWERED TRIMMERS

Model	Engine Manufacturer	Engine Model	Displacement
MS3300	Own	3300	33.0 cc (2.01 cu. in.)
MS4000	Own	4000	39.0 cc (2.44 cu. in.)
MS4500	Own	4500	45.0 cc (2.74 cu. in.)

ENGINE INFORMATION

All models are equipped with a Dolmar engine. Refer to the DOLMAR ENGINE SERVICE section of this manual.

FUEL MIXTURE

The manufacturer recommends mixing DOLMAR two-stroke oil (part No. 980 008 107) with regular grade gasoline at a ratio of 40:1. When using regular two-stroke engine oil, mix at a ratio of 25:1. Do not use fuel containing alcohol.

STRING TRIMMER

Refer to Fig. D1 for an exploded view of the dual line trimmer head used on some models. To advance the trimmer line, shut off the engine and wait until all head rotation has stopped. Loosen the knob (1) until the locating teeth between the spool (3) and body (6) are disengaged, then carefully pull each line to a length of about 4 in. (101 mm). The knob (1) and bolt (7) have left hand threads. After adjusting, make certain the locating grommets (5) engage the notches in the body and tighten knob (1) securely.

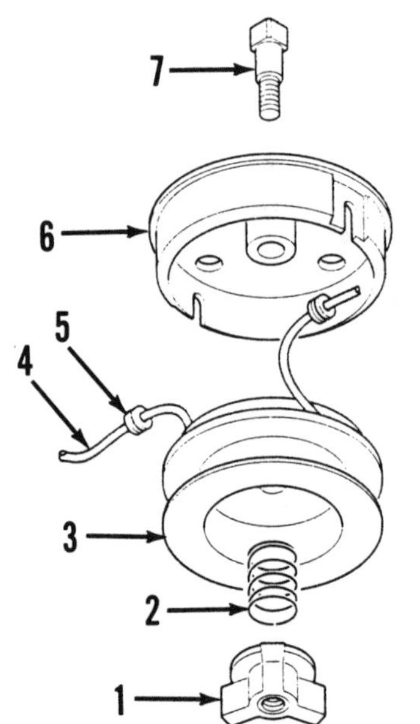

Fig. D1—Exploded view of the 2 strand trimmer head used on some models.

1. Nut
2. Spring
3. Spool
4. Trimmer line
5. Grommet
6. Body
7. Bolt

To renew trimmer line, remove knob (1), spring (2) and spool (3). Insert one end of line through hole in spool and pull line through hole until line is equal length on each side. Wind both ends of line in direction indicated by arrow on spool. Insert line ends through line guides (5), assemble spool, spring and knob to body (6). Trim string ends to a length of about 4 in. (101 mm).

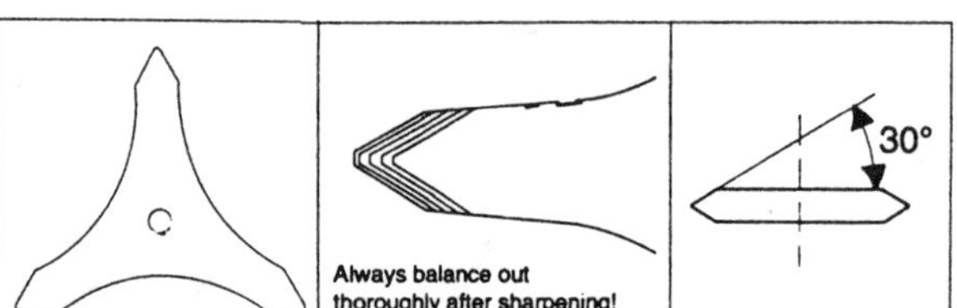

Fig. D2—Sharpen the 3 edged "brush" blade to the dimensions shown. Refer to text.

BLADE

The trimmer may be equipped with one of several different rigid cutting blades. Selection of the cutting blade will depend upon the trimming application.

Refer to Fig. D2 for sharpening blade with 3 cutting edges. The blades should be sharpened with a flat file to 30 degree angle as shown. Sharpen all blades the same to maintain balance.

Refer to Fig. D3 for sharpening blade with 4 cutting edges. Sharpen the edge of each blade with a flat file to maintain the 30 degree angle as shown. Sharpen all blades the same amount to maintain balance. Each blade edge should have the same length of sharpened edge as shown. Do not sharpen the last 10 mm of the blade near the root.

Fig. D3—Sharpen the 4 edged "star" blade to the dimensions shown. Refer to text.

Refer to Fig. D4 for sharpening blade with 8 cutting edges. Sharpen the blades with a flat file to maintain the 30 degree angle. Sharpen each of the 8 blades the same amount to maintain balance. The last 2 mm at the root of the blade should not be sharpened, but should maintain the original radius.

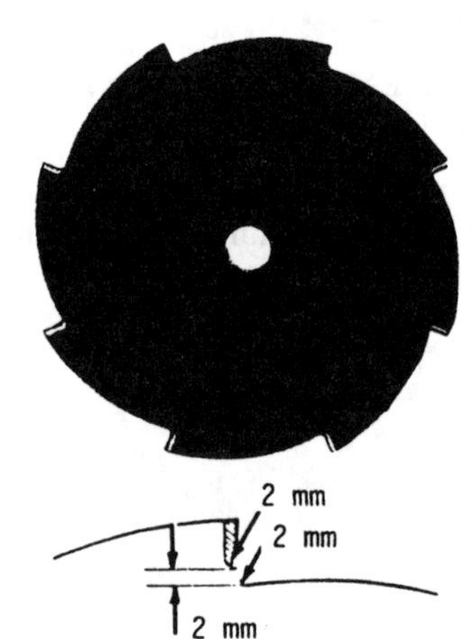

Fig. D4—Sharpen the 8 edged blade to the dimensions shown. Refer to text.

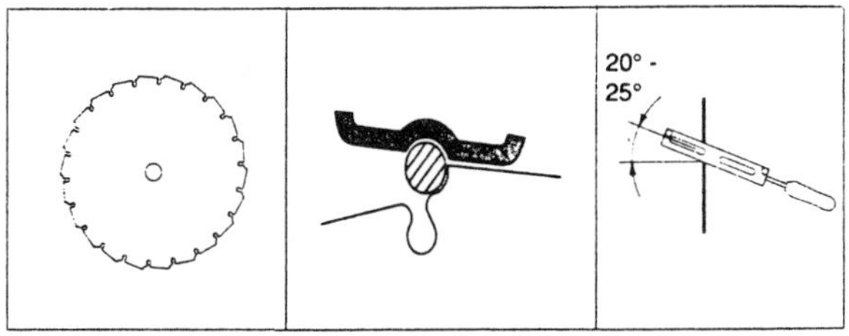

Fig. D5—Sharpen the "saw" blade to the dimensions shown. Refer to text.

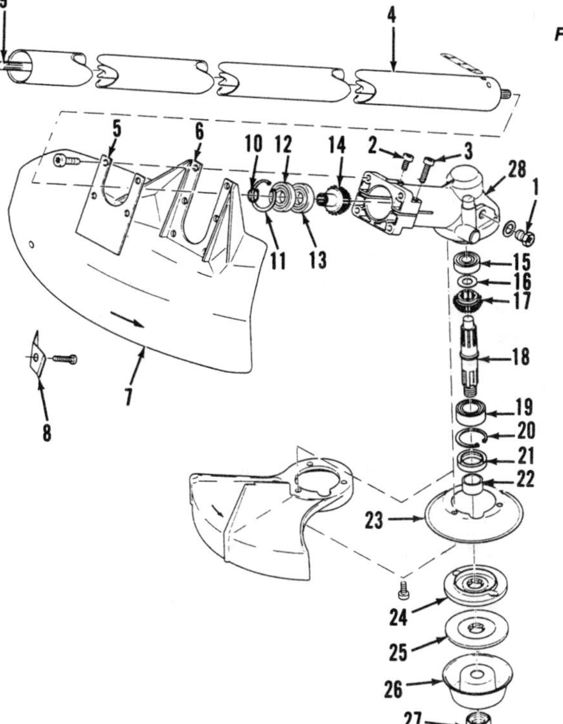

Fig. D6—Exploded view of the gear head.

1. Plug
2. Setting screw
3. Clamp screw
4. Drive shaft housing
5. Shim plate
6. Protection hood
7. Shield
8. Knife
9. Drive shaft
10. Snap ring
11. Snap ring
12. Seal
13. Bearing
14. Gear
15. Bearing
16. Shim
17. Gear
18. Shaft
19. Bearing
20. Snap ring
21. Seal
22. Spacer
23. Winding preventer
24. Drive plate
25. Pressure disc
26. Cup
27. Nut
28. Gear housing

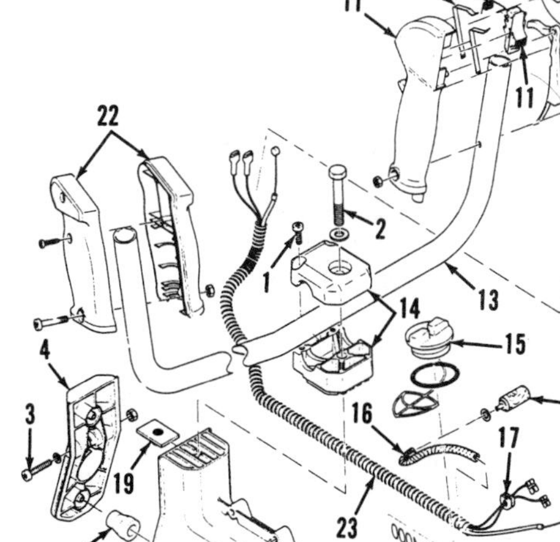

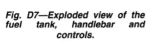

Fig. D7—Exploded view of the fuel tank, handlebar and controls.

1. Clamp screws
2. Attaching screw
3. Clamp screw
4. Clamp
5. Fuel filter
6. Fuel tank vent
7. Vibration isolators
8. Throttle trigger
9. Spring
10. Springs
11. On-off switch
12. Attaching screws
13. Handlebar
14. Clamp block
15. Tank cap
16. Fuel line
17. Grommet
18. Throttle cable retainer
19. Nut plate
20. Plate
21. Fuel ta

Refer to Fig. D5 for sharpening the saw blade. Use a 5.5 mm round file with a sharpening guide as shown. The face of the tooth should have 20-25 degree angle, depending upon the material cut. Make sure that all blade teeth are sharpened alike to maintain balance.

DRIVE SHAFT

The steel drive shaft (9—Fig. D6) is supported by bushings located in the drive shaft housing (4). The bushings are not renewable except by replacing the drive shaft housing. No regular maintenance is required.

GEAR HEAD

Refer to Fig. D6 for an exploded view of the gear head assembly used. Check lubrication of the gear head at least every 30 hours of operation. The gear head should be approximately 2/3 filled with a good quality lithium-base grease. Remove plug (1) to check and fill the gear head. Seals can be damaged by overfilling or using a grease gun to fill the gear head.

To remove the gear head, loosen the setting screw (2) and clamp screws (3), then pull the gear head assembly from the lower end of the drive shaft housing (4). It may be necessary to remove the protection hood from some models.

Tighten screws (2 and 3) securely. The steel shim (5) and protection hood (6) should be installed with the opening of the shim down when using a rigid cutting blade. The opening of the shim should be up when the 2-string trimmer head is used.

Internal parts for the gear head are not available and disassembly should be discouraged. Refer to Fig. D6 for an exploded view.

HANDLEBAR CONTROLS

The handle bar controls are usually contained in the grip located on the right-hand side. The grip can be removed after removing the two clamp screws and separating the halves of the grip. Refer to Fig. D7 for exploded view of the grip and controls. It will be necessary to remove the top cover before detaching the throttle cable from the carburetor or the shorting wires from the coil.

FUEL TANK

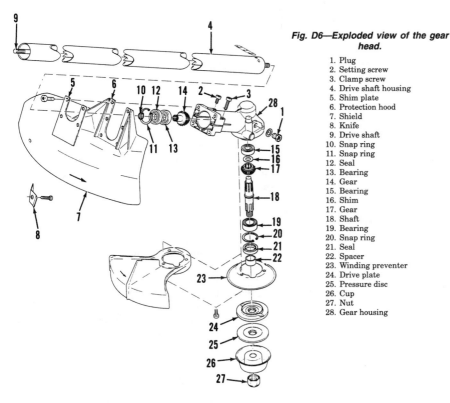

To remove the fuel tank, remove the 3 screws (1 and 2—Fig. D7) attaching the handle bar, then detach the handlebar assembly. Loosen clamp screw (3) and slide the clamping piece (4) down the drive shaft housing. Detach the fuel hose, throttle cable and shorting wires. Loosen the clamp attaching the drive shaft housing to the clutch housing, then slide the drive shaft housing away from the clutch housing. Slide the fuel tank from the drive shaft housing.

The fuel tank suction filter (5) can be removed and installed through the opening for the tank cap. The fuel tank vent assembly (6) can be withdrawn from the tank using needle nose pliers. New vibration isolators (7) should be installed if damaged. Assemble by reversing procedure.

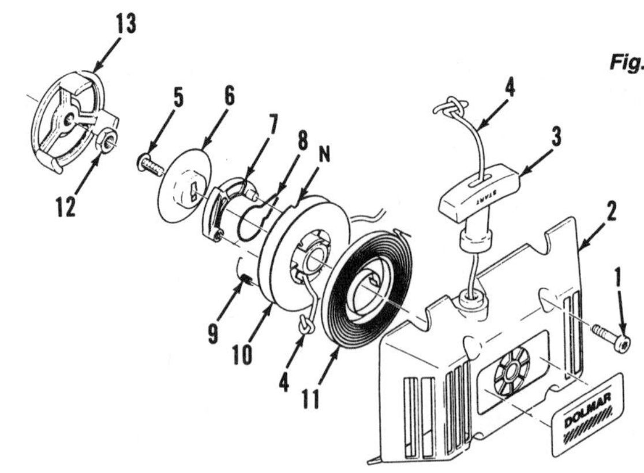

Fig. D9—Exploded view of the recoil starter assembly.

1. Screws
2. Cover
3. Handle
4. Rope (3 x 900 mm)
5. Screw
6. Cap
7. Starter pawl
8. Pawl spring
9. Brake spring
10. Pulley
11. Recoil spring
12. Nut
13. Starter cup

CLUTCH

To remove the clutch assembly, first separate the fuel tank from the engine. Remove the four screws attaching the clutch housing (1—Fig. D8) to the engine, then remove the clutch housing and clutch drum (2). The drum can be removed from the bearing after removing snap ring (3). Remove the two clutch pivot screws (4), then lift the clutch shoes (5) and spring (6) from the flywheel (7). Do not lose the two pivot bushings (8) or four washers (9) from the shoes and pivot screws.

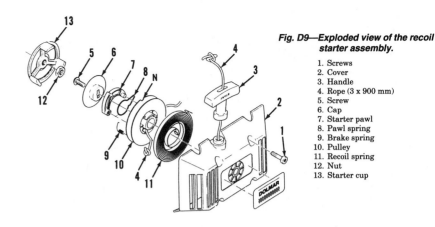

When assembling, make sure the shoes are positioned as shown in Fig. D8. Tighten screws (4) to 7-9 N•m torque. Tighten the screws attaching the housing (1) to 6-7 N•m torque. If a new engine housing has been installed, the screws should be tightened to 10-11 N•m. Inspect vibration isolators (10) and install new units if damaged.

REWIND STARTER

The rewind starter (Fig. D9) is attached to the rear of the engine with four screws (1). Release the spring tension before disassembling the starter. If the rope or rewind spring is broken, spring tension will already be released. The rope can be pulled out of the notch (N) in the pulley (10) and the pulley allowed to turn until the spring tension is released. Spring tension can also be released by removing the handle (3) and allowing the rope to be drawn into the pulley. Remove screw (5) and separate starter components using caution that recoil spring (11) does not uncoil uncontrollably.

The 3 mm diameter rope should be 900 mm long. Assemble the starter as shown in Fig. D9. Be sure that pawl spring (8) is positioned around leg of pawl (7). Preload the recoil spring enough to hold the handle against the housing when it is released.

The starter wheel (13) is attached to the crankshaft with nut (12). The crankshaft must be held from turning by using the piston stopper (part No. 944 601 030) or equivalent while removing or installing the nut.

Fig. D8—Exploded view of the clutch assembly. Bearing and housing (1) is only available as an assembly.

1. Clutch housing and bearing assembly
2. Clutch drum
3. Snap ring
4. Screw
5. Clutch shoe
6. Spring
7. Flywheel
8. Bushing
9. Washers
10. Vibration isolators
11. Clamp
12. Nut
13. Lock washer
14. Ignition coil

TIGHTENING TORQUE

Recommended tightening torques are as follows.

Carburetor
Attaching nuts. . . . . 4-5 N•m (35-45 in.-lb.)
Intermediate flange . . . . 5-6 N•m (45-55 in.-lb.)

Clutch housing
First assembly. . . . . 10-11 N•m (85-95 in.-lb.)
Second assembly . . . . 6-7 N•m (55-65 in.-lb.)

Clutch housing/
Drive shaft clamp . . . . 9-11 N•m (78-95 in.-lb.)

Clutch pivot screws . . . . 7-9 N•m (65-78 in.-lb.)

Crankcase/Engine housing

First assembly . . . . 10-11 N•m (85-95 in.-lb.)

Second assembly . . . . 6-7 N•m (55-65 in.-lb.)

Cylinder . . . . 10-11 N•m (85-95 in.-lb.)

Flywheel . . . . 19-21 N•m (165-185 in.-lb.)

Handle. . . . . 2 N•m (18 in.-lb.)

Ignition coil/module . . . . 7-9 N•m (65-78 in.-lb.)

Muffler

M5x55 . . . . 5-6 N•m (45-55 in.-lb.)

M5x16 . . . . 7-9 N•m (65-78 in.-lb.)

Spark plug . . . . 14-16 N•m (137-146 in.-lb.)

DOLMAR

GASOLINE POWERED TRIMMERS AND BRUSH CUTTERS

Models	Engine Make	Engine Model	Displacement
LT-16	Fuji	EC01	15.4 cc (0.94 cu. in.)
LT-250, BC-250, BC-330	Sachs	...	33.0 cc (2.01 cu. in.)
BC-400	Sachs	...	40.0 cc (2.44 cu. in.)

ENGINE INFORMATION

Fuji-Robin or Sachs-Dolmar two-stroke air-cooled gasoline engines are used. Identify the engine by manufacturer and model, then refer to the appropriate FUJI-ROBIN or SACHS-DOLMAR Engine Service section of this manual.

FUEL MIXTURE

These two-stroke engines are lubricated by mixing oil with the fuel. The manufacturer recommends mixing regular gasoline, leaded or unleaded, with a high-quality, two-stroke engine oil. The recommended mixing ratio is 24:1. Mix the gasoline and oil in a separate container; never in the fuel tank.

Fig. SD10—Exploded view of semi-automatic trimmer head used on Model LT-16.

1. Adapter
2. Hub
3. Line guide
4. Spring
5. Spring adapter
6. Drive post
7. Spool
8. Line
9. Button
10. Cover

STRING TRIMMER

Semi-Automatic. Refer to Fig. SD10 for an exploded view of the semi-automatic string trimmer head typical of the type used on some models. There may be either one or two lines, depending upon the model. To manually advance the trimmer line(s) with the engine stopped, push the button (9) at the bottom of the head and pull line(s). To extend the line(s) with the engine running, operate the trimmer at maximum speed and tap the button on the ground. Lines should extend a small amount automatically. If the line does not extend with the engine running, stop the engine and attempt to extend the line(s) manually. If a line is broken inside the housing, it will be necessary to disassemble the unit and feed the line through the eyelet.

To install new line, unsnap cover (10), then remove the cover, button (9) and spool (7). Clean all parts and remove any remaining line. The spool will hold approximately 25 ft. (7.6 m) of line. Attach the new line to the spool.

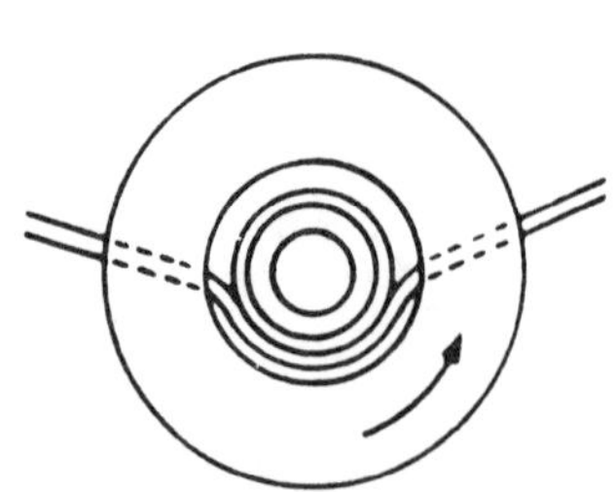

Fig. SD11—On models with two lines, the line should be inserted through the spool as shown and wrapped in the direction indicated by the arrow on the spool.

If equipped with two lines, insert the line through the eye of the spool as shown in Fig. SD11 and pull the line through until it is the same length on both sides. Wrap both ends of the line on spool at the same time in the direction indicated by the arrow on the spool. Do not twist the lines. Wind the line tightly and evenly from side to side.

On all models, wind the line tightly and evenly from side to side. Install spool while directing the end(s) through the line guide(s) (3). Install the spool (7), button (9) and cover (10).

Manual. Refer to Fig. SD12 for an exploded view of the dual line trimmer head used on some models. To advance the trimmer line, shut off the engine and wait until all head rotation has stopped. Loosen the knob (8) until the

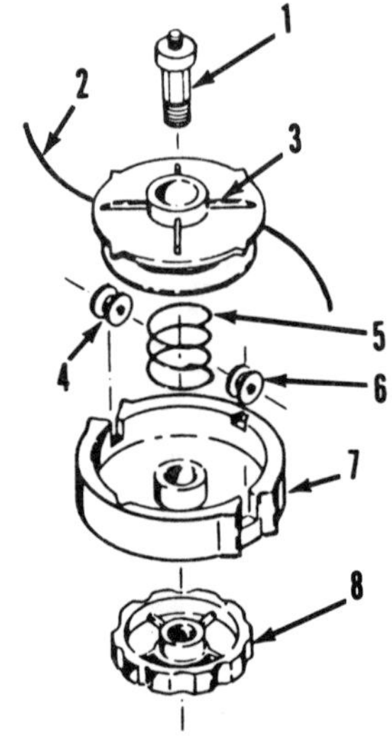

Fig. SD12—Exploded view of the manual trimmer head used on some models.

1. Adapter
2. Line
3. Spool
4. Line guide
5. Spring
6. Line guide
7. Body
8. Knob

locating teeth between the spool (3) and body (7) are disengaged, then carefully pull each line to a length of about 4 in. (101 mm). The knob (8) and bolt (1) have left hand threads. After adjusting, make certain the locating teeth on the spool are engaged and tighten knob (8) securely.

To install new line, remove knob (8), body (7), spring (5) and spool (3). Clean all parts and remove any remaining line. The spool will hold approximately 25 ft. (7.6 m) of line. Insert one end of the new line through the two holes in the spool (Fig. SD11), then pull the line until both ends are equal in length. Wind both ends of line in the same direction indicated by arrow on the spool. Wind the line tightly and evenly from side to side, but do not twist the lines. Install spool while directing the ends of both lines through the line guides (4 and 6—Fig. SD12). Install the spring (5), body (7) and knob (8). Tighten the knob securely.

BLADE

Some models may be equipped with a blade with four cutting edges (Fig. SD13), eight cutting edges (Fig. SD14 or Fig. SD15) or a multi-tooth saw blade (Fig. SD16). Certain models can be fitted with mulch cutting blade (Fig. SD17). Check with the manufacturer to be sure of correct application before installing a blade. The installation of any blade will increases the risk of injury and the unit can be quickly damaged if the unit is not designed for the blade.

Refer to Fig. SD18 for sharpening blade with 4 cutting edges. Sharpen the edge of each blade with a flat file to maintain the 30 degree angle as shown. Sharpen all blades the same amount to maintain balance. Each blade edge should have the same length and the same length of sharpened edge as shown. Do not sharpen the last 10 mm of the blade near the root.

The blade with 8 cutting edges shown in Fig. SD14 should be sharpened only for a length of 0.59-0.79 in. (15-20 mm). Sharpen the edge of each blade with a

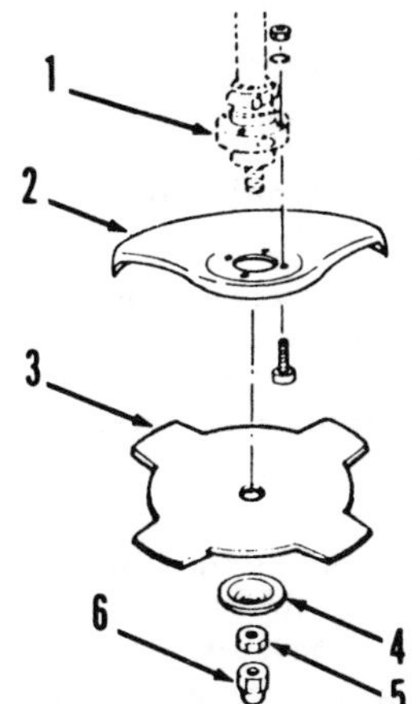

Fig. SD13—Exploded view of blade with four cutting edges and attaching parts typical of BC-250 and some other models.

1. Bearing head
2. Shield
3. Blade
4. Adapter
5. Nut
6. Jam nut

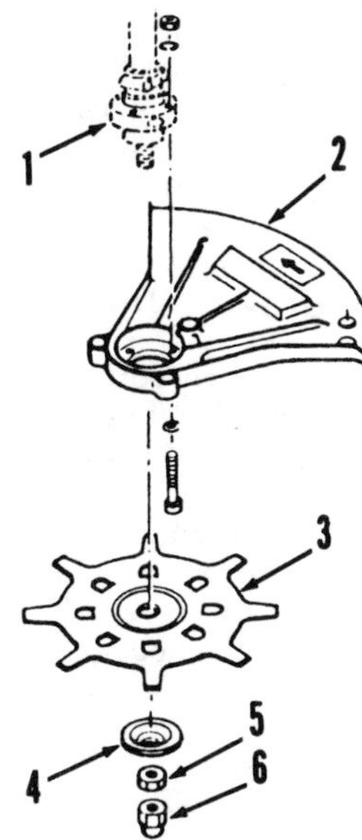

Fig. SD14—Exploded view of the blade with eight cutting edges used on some BC-250 models.

1. Bearing head
2. Shield
3. Blade
4. Adapter
5. Nut
6. Jam nut

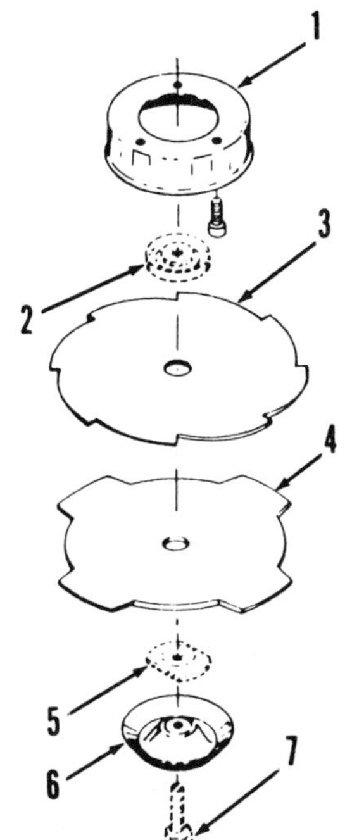

Fig. SD15—Exploded view of 4 tooth and 8 tooth blades used on some models.

1. Anti-wind plate
2. Adapter
3. Eight edge blade
4. Four edge blade
5. Adapter
6. Cap
7. Screw

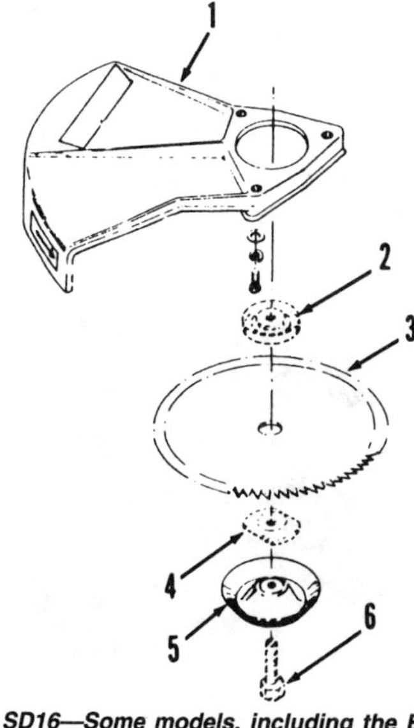

Fig. SD16—Some models, including the BC-330 and BC-400 shown, may be fitted with a multi tooth (saw) blade as shown.

1. Shield
2. Adapter
3. Blade
4. Adapter
5. Cap
6. Screw

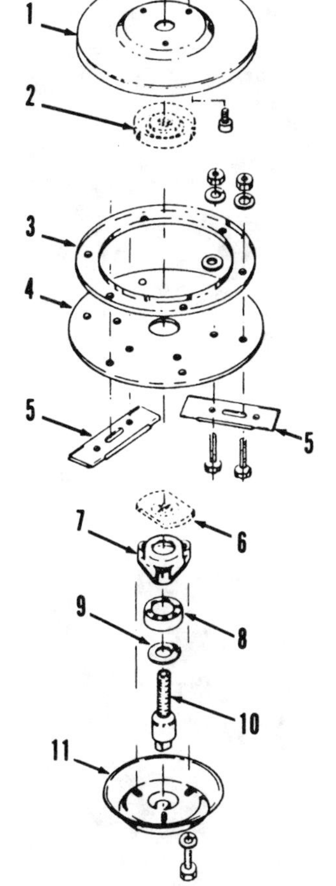

Fig. SD17—Exploded view of the mulch cutting blade available for BC-330 and BC-400 models.

1. Anti-wind plate
2. Adapter
3. Spacer
4. Blade plate
5. Blades
6. Adapter
7. Support bearing housing
8. Bearing
9. Washer
10. Arbor
11. Sliding cup

Illustrations courtesy Dolmar USA, Inc.

flat file to maintain the 30 degree angle as shown. Sharpen all blades the same amount to maintain balance. Each blade edge should have the same length and the same length of sharpened edge as shown. Do not sharpen the last 10 mm of the blade near the root. Use Fig. SD18 as a guide, except for sharpened length of the blades.

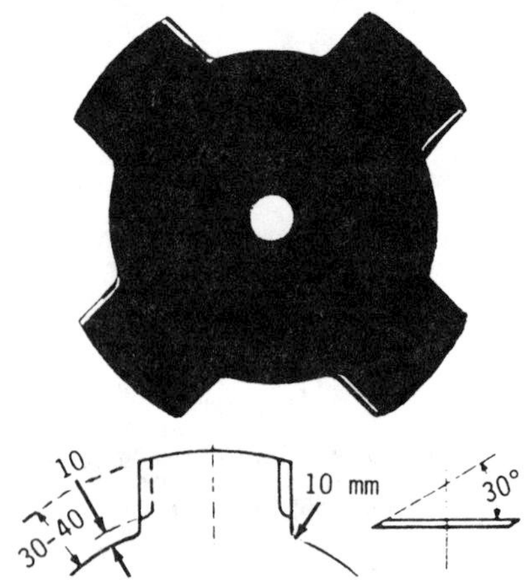

Fig. SD18—Sharpen the four cutting edge blade to the dimensions shown. Refer to text.

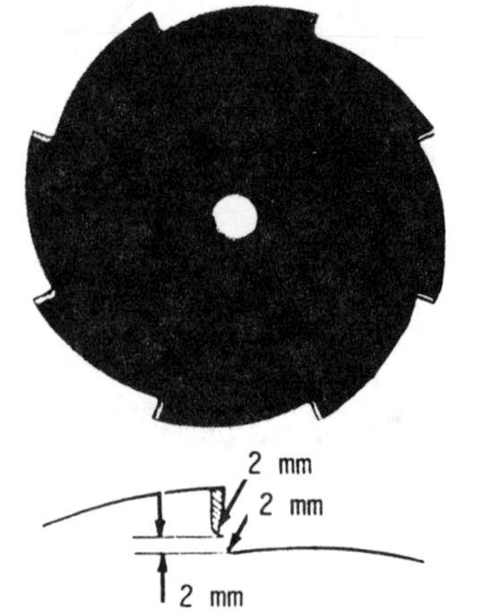

Fig. SD19—Sharpen the eight cutting edge blade to dimensions shown. Refer to text.

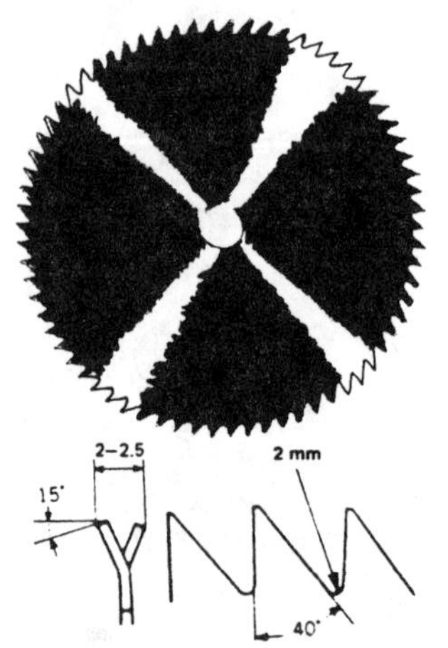

Fig. SD20—Set and sharpen saw blade teeth to dimensions shown. Refer to text.

Refer to Fig. SD19 for sharpening blade with 8 cutting edges shown in Fig. SD15. The blades with a flat file to maintain the 30 degree angle as shown. Sharpen each of the 8 blades the same amount to maintain balance. The last 2 mm at the root of the blade should not be sharpened, but should maintain the original radius.

To sharpen multi-tooth blades, follow the original sharpening angles and tooth set. Refer to Fig. SD20 for a blade available from the manufacturer. Be sure to maintain the 0.08-0.09 in. (2-2.5 mm) radius at the root of each tooth.

DRIVE SHAFT

Some models are equipped with a flexible drive shaft, while others use a solid steel shaft. The flexible shaft should be removed and lubricated lightly with a lithium based multipurpose grease after each 20 hours of operation. The drive shaft may be withdrawn from the housing after separating the engine from the drive shaft housing.

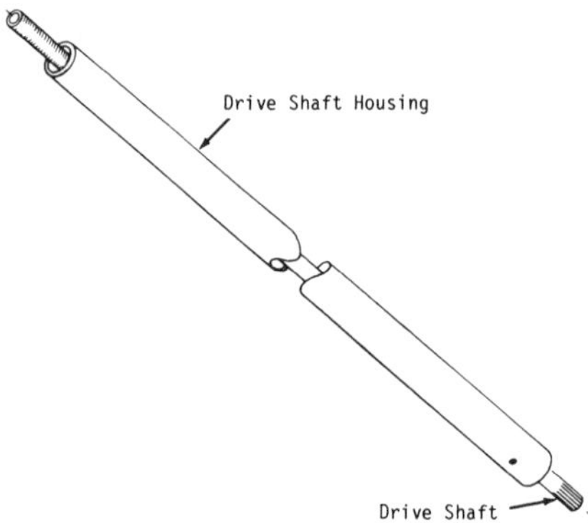

Fig. SD21—View of typical solid drive shaft.

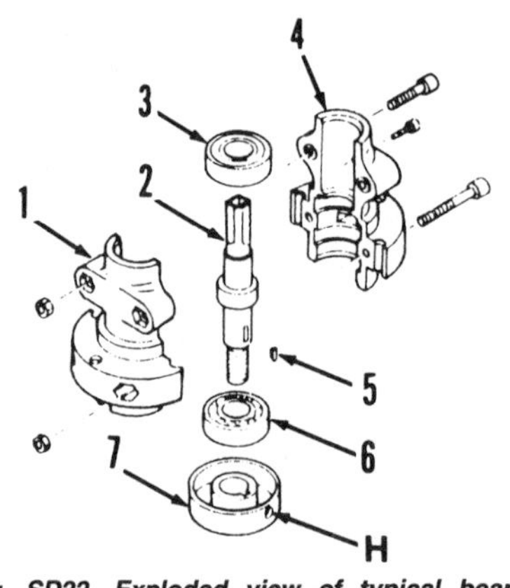

Fig. SD22—Exploded view of typical bearing head.

H. Hole
1. Housing
2. Arbor
3. Bearing
4. Housing
5. Key
6. Bearing
7. Cup washer

The solid steel drive shaft (Fig. SD21) requires no regular maintenance, but should be coated lightly with grease if it is removed for any reason.

Both types of drive shafts are supported by bushings located in the drive shaft housing. The bushings can not be serviced except by installing a new drive shaft housing and bushing assembly.

BEARING HEAD

Model LT-16

Model LT-16 bearing head is an integral part of the drive shaft housing. If the bearing head is damaged, the entire housing must be replaced.

Model LT-250

Refer to Fig. SD22 for an exploded view of the bearing head. Bearings (3 and 6) are sealed and require no regular maintenance. To disassemble the bearing head, remove bolts and separate the housing halves (1 and 4), then remove the arbor and bearings. Remove the cup washer (7) and Woodruff key (5) before pressing the bearings from the arbor.

The hole (H) in cup washer is to facilitate holding the arbor while tightening the trimmer head or blade retaining nut. Align the hole (H) with the hole in the housing and insert a 5/32 in. diameter Allen wrench or similar tool into the holes to prevent turning.

GEAR HEAD

Models BC-250, BC-330 And BC-400

Refer to Fig. SD23 or Fig. SD24. Remove plug (8) and check the level of grease in the unit after each 30 hours of operation or at least once each year. The housing should be 2/3 filled with lithium based multipurpose grease.

NOTE: Do not use a pressure grease gun to fill the housing. The high pressure can damage the housing or seals and may force bearing or seals from the housing.

To disassemble the gear head shown in Fig. SD23, first remove the trimmer or blade. Remove the clamp screws and locating screw, then separate the gear housing from the drive shaft housing. Remove the cup washer (13) and snap ring (12). Heat the gear head housing to approximately 212 degrees F (100 degrees C) and remove the output shaft

Illustrations courtesy Dolmar USA, Inc

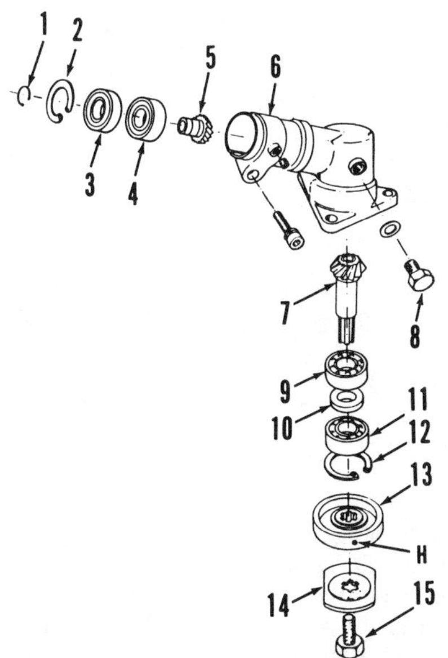

Fig. SD23—Exploded view of gear head typical of some models. Refer also to Fig. SD24 for another type used.

H. Hole
1. Snap ring
2. Snap ring
3. Bearing
4. Bearing
5. Input shaft & gear
6. Housing
7. Output shaft & gear
8. Plug
9. Bearing
10. Spacer
11. Sealed bearing
12. Snap ring
13. Cup washer
14. Adapter
15. Screw

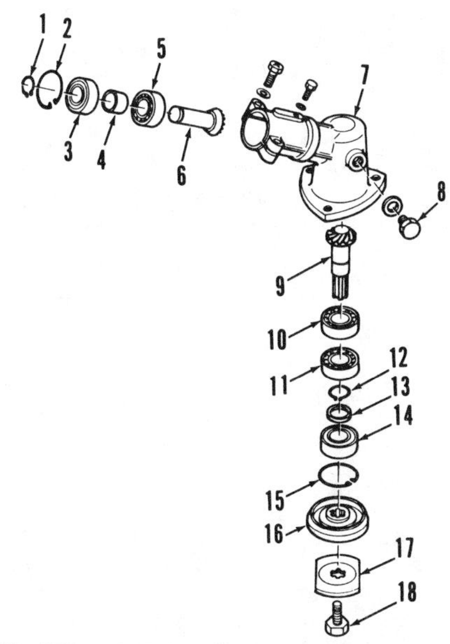

Fig. SD24—Exploded view of gear head typical of some models. Refer also to Fig. SD23 for another type used.

1. Snap ring
2. Snap ring
3. Bearing
4. Spacer
5. Bearing
6. Input shaft & gear
7. Housing
8. Plug
9. Output shaft & gear
10. Bearing
11. Bearing
12. Snap ring
13. Spacer
14. Seal
15. Snap ring
16. Cup washer
17. Adapter
18. Screw

and bearing assembly. Press bearing (11) from the output shaft (7). Remove spacer (10), then press bearing (9) from arbor shaft.

Remove snap ring (2). Insert a screwdriver or suitable wedge in the clamping split in housing to carefully expand the housing, then remove the input shaft and bearing assembly. Remove snap ring (1) and press bearings (3 and 4) from the input shaft. Install new parts as required. The housing should be 2/3 filled with lithium based multipurpose grease while assembling.

To disassemble the gear head shown in Fig. SD24, first remove the trimmer or blade. Remove the clamp screws and locating screw, then separate the gear housing from the drive shaft housing. Remove the cup washer (16) and snap ring (15). Heat the gear head housing to approximately 212 degrees F (100 degrees C) and remove the output shaft and bearing assembly. Remove spacer (13) and snap ring (12), then press bearings (10 and 11) from the output shaft (9).

Remove snap ring (2). Insert a screwdriver or suitable wedge in the clamping split in housing to carefully expand the housing, then remove the input shaft and bearing assembly. Remove snap ring (1) and press bearings (3 and 5) from the input shaft (6). Install new parts as required. The housing should be 2/3 filled with lithium based multipurpose grease while assembling.

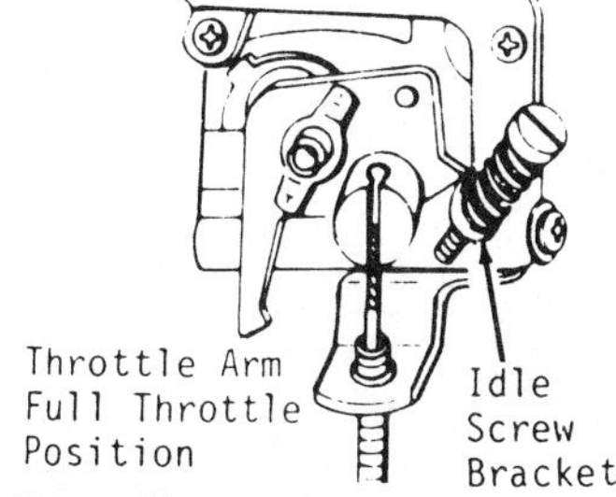

Fig. SD25—Adjust the threaded end of the throttle cable to limit cable end play. There must be some end play to be sure the throttle lever contacts the stop screw at idle.

THROTTLE TRIGGER AND CABLE

The throttle control trigger located on the drive shaft housing operates the carburetor throttle via a cable that operates inside a flexible housing. The cable should be lubricated with SAE 30 engine oil at least every 20 hours of operation. Adjust the engine idle speed to just slower than clutch engagement rpm, then check cable free play. Cable free play should be 0.08-0.10 in. (2-3 mm).

STARTER

Refer to the appropriate ENGINE SERVICE section for service to the starter assembly.

CLUTCH

Refer to the appropriate ENGINE SERVICE section for clutch removal and service procedures.

DOLMAR

GASOLINE POWERED BRUSHCUTTERS

Model	Engine Manufacturer	Engine Model	Displacement
BC-225-E	Fuji	....	22.5 cc
BC-377	Fuji	....	37.7 cc
BC-377-EES	Fuji	....	37.7 cc

ENGINE INFORMATION

Models BC-225-E, BC-377 and BC-377-EES brushcutters are equipped with Fuji two-stroke air-cooled gasoline engines. Identify engine by engine displacement or trimmer model number and refer to appropriate FUJI ENGINE SERVICE section of this manual.

FUEL MIXTURE

Manufacturer recommends mixing regular grade gasoline with an octane rating of at least 87, with a good quality two-stroke air-cooled engine oil at a ratio of 24:1. Do not use fuel containing alcohol.

BLADE

Model BC-225-E is equipped with a four cutting edge blade and Models BC-377 and BC-377-EES are equipped with a saw type blade (Fig. SD30). To remove blade from all models, align hole in cup washer with hole in gear head. Insert suitable tool (5—Fig. SD30) to prevent turning of arbor in gear head and remove jam nut (8) and nut (7). Remove adapter (6) and blade. When reassembling, tighten nut (7) to 130-215 in.-lbs. (15-24 N·m).

DRIVE SHAFT

All models are equipped with a solid steel drive shaft supported in sealed ball bearings and bushings in drive shaft housing tube (Figs. SD31 and SD32). Drive shaft requires no regular maintenance; however, if removed, lightly oil with SAE 30 oil before reinstalling drive shaft.

GEAR HEAD

Model BC-225-E

Refer to Fig. SD33 for an exploded view of the gear head used on Model BC-225-E. At 30-hour intervals of use,

Fig. SD30—Exploded view of saw blade available for Models BC-377 and BC-377-EES.

1. Gear head
2. Anti-wrap plate
3. Cup washer
4. Saw blade
5. Tool
6. Adapter
7. Nut
8. Jam nut

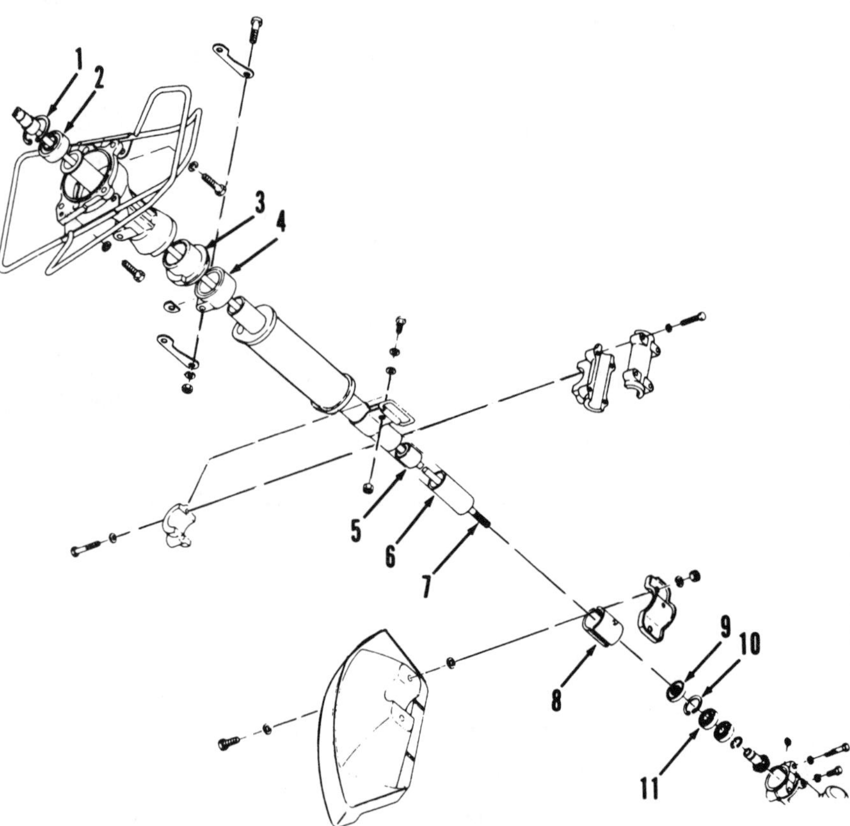

Fig. SD31—Exploded view of drive shaft and housing used on Model BC-225-E. Solid drive shaft is supported at each end in ball bearings and along drive shaft housing by bushings (5).

1. Snap ring
2. Bearing
3. Rubber vibration dampner
4. Locating collar
5. Bushing
6. Drive shaft housing
7. Drive shaft
8. Split spacer
9. Seal
10. Snap ring
11. Bearing

Illustrations courtesy Dolmar USA, Inc.

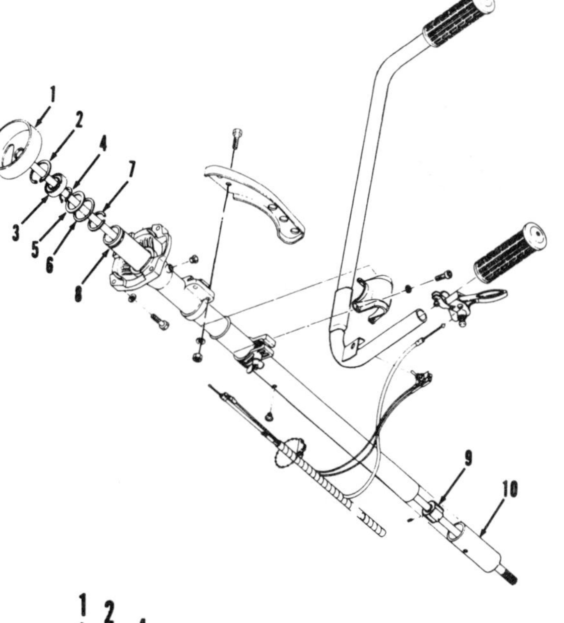

Fig. SD32—Exploded view of drive shaft and housing assembly used on Models BC-377 and BC-377-EES. Solid drive shaft is supported at each end by ball bearings and along drive shaft housing by bushings (9).

1. Drum & drive shaft assy.
2. Snap ring
3. Bearing
4. Snap ring
5. Spacer
6. Washer
7. Snap ring
8. Housing holder
9. Bushings
10. Housing

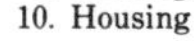

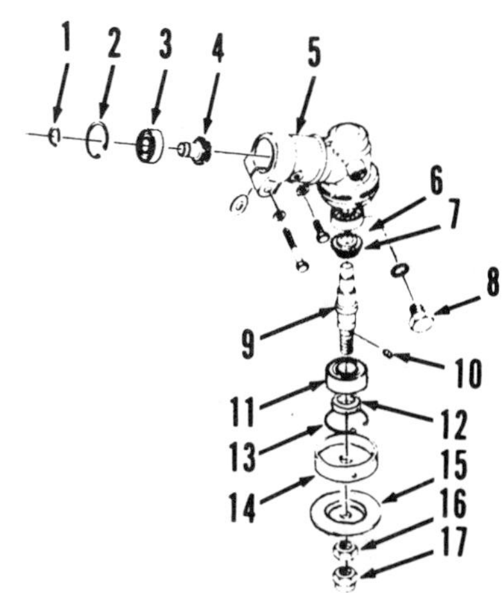

Fig. SD34—Exploded view of gear head used on Models BC-377 and BC-377-EES.

1. Snap ring
2. Snap ring
3. Bearing
4. Input shaft & gear
5. Housing
6. Bearing
7. Gear
8. Check plug
9. Arbor (output) shaft
10. Key
11. Bearing
12. Spacer
13. Snap ring
14. Cup washer
15. Adapter
16. Nut
17. Jam nut

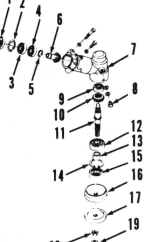

Fig. SD33—Exploded view of gear head assembly used on Models BC-225-E.

1. Seal
2. Snap ring
3. Bearing
4. Bearing
5. Snap ring
6. Input shaft
7. Housing
8. Check plug
9. Bearing
10. Gear
11. Arbor (output) shaft
12. Bearing
13. Spacer
14. Snap ring
15. Seal
16. Cup washer
17. Adapter
18. Nut
19. Jam nut

remove check plug (8) and pump a good-quality lithium-base grease into gear head housing until grease appears at lower seal (15).

To disassemble gear head, separate gear head from drive shaft housing. Remove blade. Remove seal (15) and snap ring (14). Use a suitable puller to remove arbor shaft (11) and bearing assembly. If bearing (9) stays in housing, heat housing to 140° F (60° C) and tap housing on wooden block to remove bearing. Remove seal (1) and snap ring (2). Insert screwdriver or suitable wedge into housing clamp split and carefully expand housing to remove input shaft (6) and bearing assembly. Remove snap ring (5) and press bearings (3 and 4) from input shaft.

Models BC-377 And BC-377-EES

Models BC-377 and BC-377-EES are equipped with gear housing shown in Fig. SD34. Remove check plug (8) at 30 hour intervals of use and make certain gear head housing is 2/3 full of a good quality lithium base grease. Do not use a pressure type grease gun to pump grease into housing as bearing seal damage will occur.

To disassemble gear head, separate gear head from drive shaft housing. Remove blade, adapters and spacer. Remove snap ring (13) and use a suitable puller to remove arbor (9) and bearing assembly. If bearing (6) stays in housing, heat housing to 140° F (60° C) and tap housing on wooden block to remove bearing. Remove snap ring (2). Insert screwdriver or suitable wedge into gear head housing clamp split and carefully expand housing to remove input shaft (4) and bearing assembly. Remove necessary snap rings to remove bearings and gears from shafts.

THROTTLE TRIGGER AND CABLE

Throttle trigger located on drive shaft housing tube controls engine rpm by a cable and housing assembly running from trigger to carburetor. Inner wire of throttle cable should be lubricated at each end with SAE 30 oil at 20 hour intervals of use. Adjusting nuts are installed on throttle cable housing at carburetor end to provide throttle cable adjustment. Cable should be adjusted so that carburetor throttle plate will be fully opened at high speed position of throttle trigger; however, throttle trigger should have 0.08-0.10 inch (2-3 mm) movement before beginning to operate throttle lever on carburetor.

DOLMAR

GASOLINE POWERED STRING TRIMMERS

Model	Engine Manufacturer	Engine Model	Displacement
LT-210	Fuji	...	21.2 cc
BC-210	Fuji	...	21.2 cc
BC-212	Fuji	...	21.2 cc

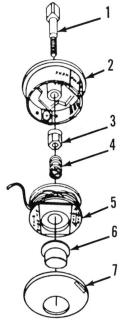

Fig. SD40—Exploded view of trimmer head used on Model LT-210.

1. Adapter
2. Drum
3. Nut (L.H.)
4. Spring
5. Spool
6. Button
7. Cover

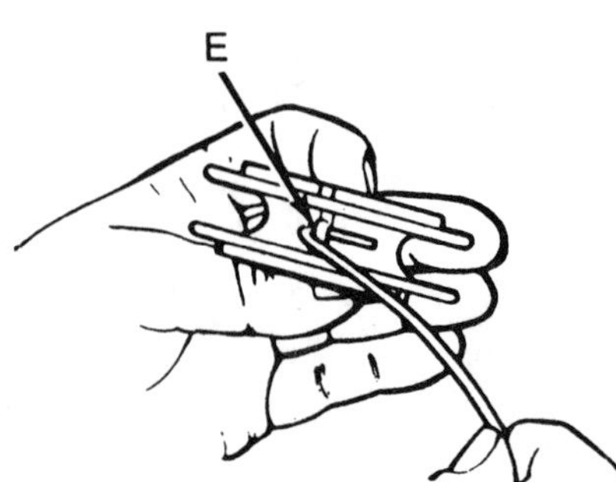

Fig. SD41—Insert trimmer line end through eye (E) on spool as shown so approximately 1 inch (25 mm) extends past eye.

ENGINE INFORMATION

The models in this section are equipped with a Fuji engine. Refer to Fuji engine service section for engine service information.

FUEL MIXTURE

Oil must be mixed with the fuel. Unleaded fuel may be used. Recommended fuel:oil ratio when using Sachs-Dolmar two-stroke oil is 40:1. When using other two-stroke oils, ratio should be 25:1.

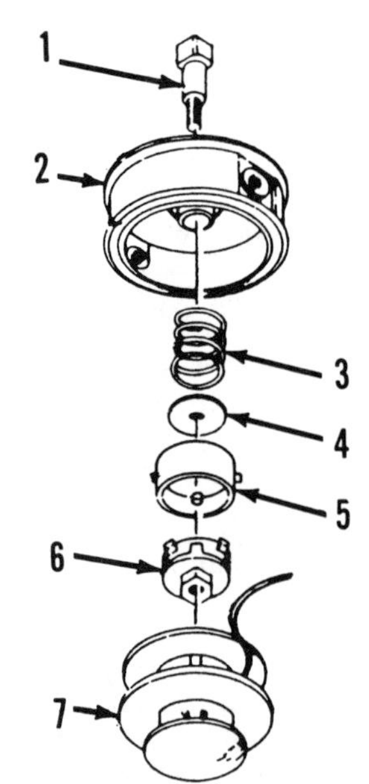

Fig. SD42—Exploded view of trimmer head used on Models BC-210 and BC-212. Unscrew cam (6) by turning clockwise.

1. Adapter
2. Drum
3. Spring
4. Washer
5. Outer drive cam
6. Inner drive cam
7. Spool

STRING TRIMMER

LT-210

Model LT-210 is equipped with a single-strand, semi-automatic trimmer head. To manually advance line with engine stopped, push in button at bottom of head and pull on line. To extend line with engine running, operate trimmer at full operating rpm and tap button on ground. Line will automatically advance a given amount.

To install new line, press against tab marked "PUSH" and remove cover (7—Fig. SD40), button (6) and spool (5). Clean and inspect all parts. New line should be 0.080-in. (2 mm) diameter and 12 feet (366 cm) long. Insert end of line through eye of spool as shown in Fig. SD41 so approximately 1 inch (25 mm) extends past eye. Wrap line on spool in clockwise direction as viewed from top side of spool (note arrow on spool). Install spool while directing line end through eye of drum (2—Fig. SD40). Install button and cover. Cover should snap into place after locking tabs of cover engage tabs on drum next to eye hole. Trim line so approximately 3 inches (75 mm) extend from drum.

If trimmer head retaining nut (3) must be unscrewed, prevent shaft rotation by inserting a pin through hole provided in bearing head to lock shaft.

Models BC-210 And BC-212

Models BC-210 and BC-212 are equipped with a dual-strand, semi-automatic trimmer head shown in Fig. SD42. To manually advance line with engine stopped, push in button at bottom of head and pull on each line. Procedure may have to be repeated to

Illustrations courtesy Dolmar USA, Inc.

obtain desired line length. To extend line with engine running, operate trimmer at full operating rpm and tap button on ground. Line will automatically advance a given amount.

To install new line, hold drum (2) firmly and turn spool (7) in direction shown in Fig. SD43 to remove slack. Twist with a hard snap until plastic peg is behind ridge and separate spool from drum. Remove old line from spool. Spool will hold approximately 20 feet (6 m) of 0.095 inch (2.4 mm) diameter line. Insert one end of new line through eye on spool (E—Fig. SD44) and pull line through until line is the same length on both sides of hole. Wind both ends of line at the same time in direction indicated by arrow on spool (Fig. SD44). Wind tightly and evenly from side-to-side and do not twist line. Position each line in notches (N—Fig. SD45) in spool and insert ends of line through line guide openings (O) in drum. Align pegs (P) on drum with slots in spool and push spool into drum. Hold drum firmly, twist spool quickly in direction shown in Fig. SD46 so peg enters hole with a click and locks spool in position. Cut off lines to approximately 4 inches (10 cm).

If trimmer head inner drive cam (6—Fig. SD42) must be unscrewed, prevent shaft rotation by inserting a pin through hole located in bearing head. Cam has left-hand threads.

BLADE

Models BC-210 and BC-212 may be equipped with an eight-edge cutting blade. Note that blade retaining nut has left-hand threads. When sharpening cutting edges, refer to Fig. SD47. Sharpened section must be kept 0.08 inch (2 mm) from the blade root. Root chamfer should have a 0.08 mm (2 mm) radius. Sharpen all teeth equally to maintain blade balance.

DRIVE SHAFT

Model LT-210

Model LT-210 is equipped with a flexible drive shaft. The drive shaft should be removed, cleaned and lubricated after every 20 hours of operation. Disconnect throttle cable and separate drive shaft housing (tube) from engine for access to shaft. Apply a high-quality lithium-base grease to drive shaft.

Models BC-210 And BC-212

Models BC-210 And BC-212 are equipped with a solid drive shaft supported in bushings. No maintenance is required. Drive shaft and tube are available separately.

BEARING HEAD

Model LT-210

The bearing head (2—Fig. SD48) may be separated from the drive tube (4) after loosening clamp bolt (6). Bearing head is available only as a unit assembly.

GEAR HEAD

Models BC-210 And BC-212

The amount of grease in the gear head should be checked after every 30 hours of operation. Remove screw (S—Fig. SD49) and fill unit with multipurpose grease as needed.

The gear head is available only as a unit assembly.

THROTTLE TRIGGER AND CABLE

The inner throttle cable (C—Fig. SD50) should be lubricated with engine oil after every 20 hours of operation.

Adjusting nuts (N) are located at carburetor end of throttle cable. Turn nuts as needed so carburetor throttle plate opens fully when throttle trigger is at full-speed position, and so there is 0.08-0.10 inch (2-3 mm) free play at throttle trigger when released.

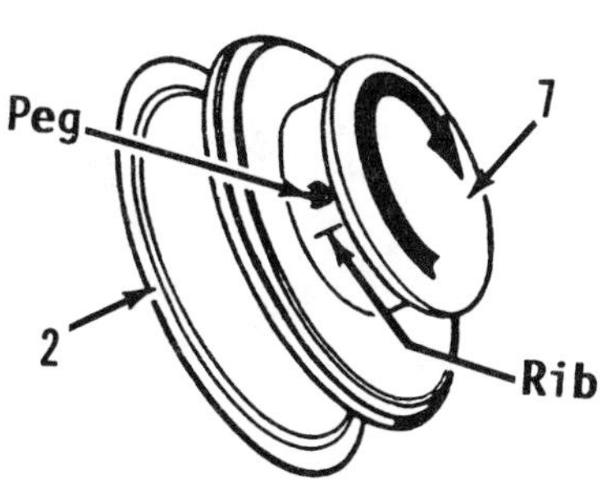

Fig. SD43—To remove spool (7), hold drum (2) firmly and turn spool in direction shown to take up slack, then twist with a sudden snap until plastic peg is behind rib.

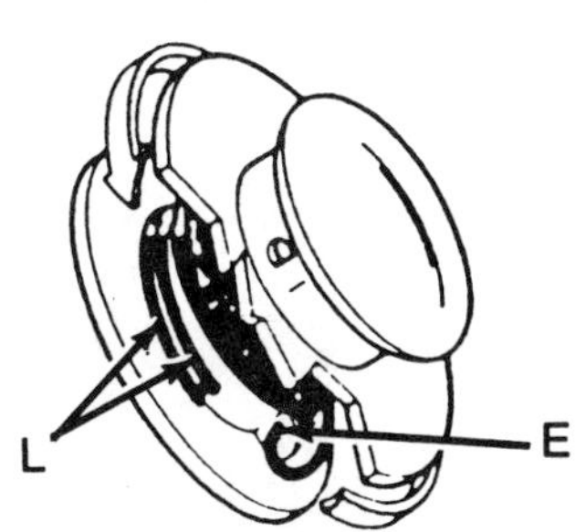

Fig. SD44—End of line on Models BC-210 and BC-212 must be inserted through eye on spool. Wind both strands of line at the same time in direction indicated on spool.

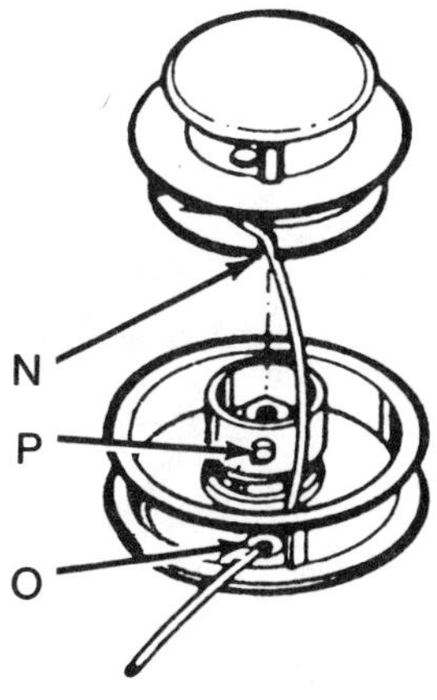

Fig. SD45—Position each line in notch (N) in spool and through opening (O) in drum. Align peg (P) with slot in spool and push spool into drum.

Fig. SD46—Hold drum firmly and twist quickly in direction indicated to lock spool in position.

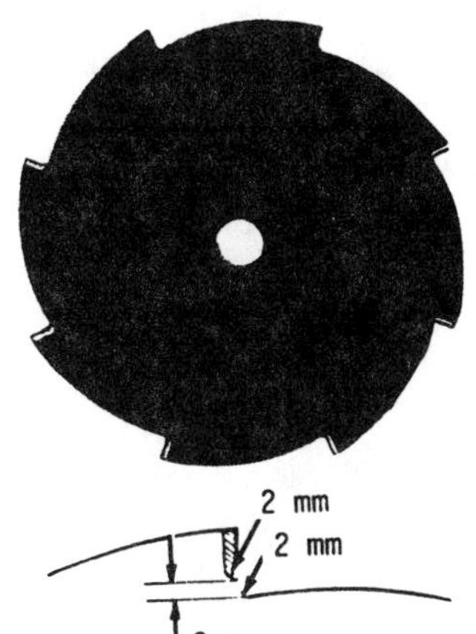

Fig. SD47—Sharpen blade edges to dimensions shown. Refer to text.

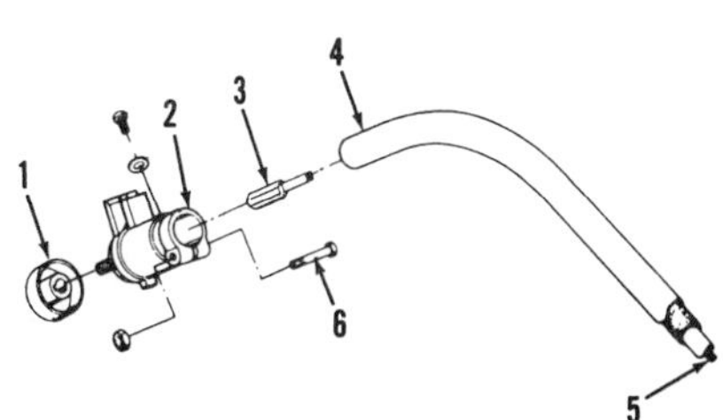

Fig. SD48—Trimmer bearing head (2), used on Model LT-210, is serviced as an assembly.

1. Mounting disc
2. Bearing head
3. Adapter
4. Drive shaft tube
5. Drive shaft
6. Clamp bolt

Illustrations courtesy Dolmar USA, Inc.

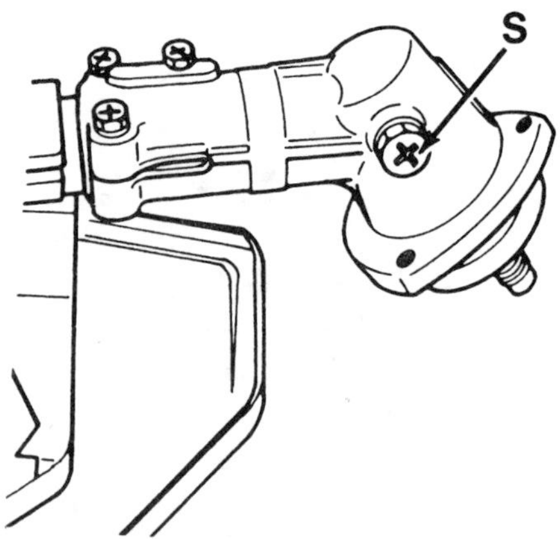

Fig. SD49—Fill gear head on Models BC-210 and BC-212 with grease through hole for screw (S).

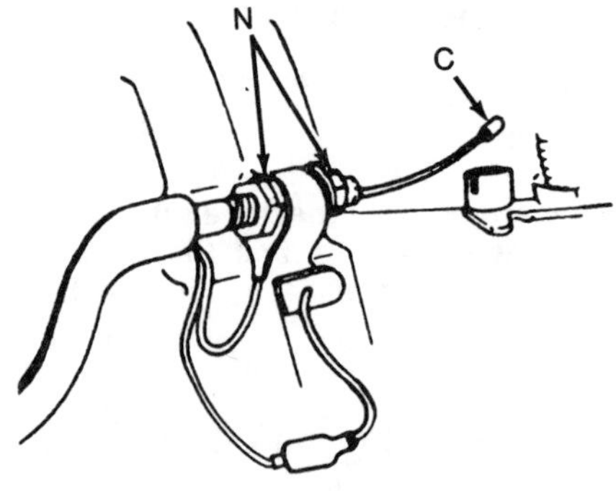

Fig. SD50—Throttle cable adjusting nuts (N) are located at carburetor end of cable (C).

ECHO

GASOLINE POWERED TRIMMERS

Model	Engine Make	Engine Displacement
GT-140, GT-140A, GT-140B	Echo	13.8 cc (0.842 cu. in.)
GT-160, GT-160A, GT-160AE	Echo	16.0 cc (0.976 cu. in.)
GT-200, GT-200A, GT-200B, GT-200BE, GT-200CE	Echo	21.2 cc (1.294 cu. in.)
SRM-140A, SRM-140D	Echo	13.8 cc (0.842 cu. in.)
SRM-200, SRM-200AE, SRM-200BE, SRM-200D, SRM-200DA, SRM-200DB, SRM-200E, SRM-201F, SRM-201FA, SRM-202D, SRM-202DA, SRM-202F, SRM-202FA, SRM-210AE, SRM-210E	Echo	21.2 cc (1.294 cu. in.)
SRM-300 & SRM-302ADX	Echo	30.1 cc (1.837 cu. in.)
SRM-300AE, SRM-300AE/1, SRM-300E, SRM-300E/1	Echo	30.8 cc (1.880 cu. in.)
SRM-400AE, SRM-400BE, SRM-402DE, SRM-400E	Echo	40.2 cc (2.452 cu. in.)

ENGINE INFORMATION

Echo two-stroke air-cooled gasoline engines are used on Echo trimmers and brush cutters. Identify the engine by displacement and refer to the ECHO Engine Service section of this manual.

FUEL MIXTURE

The manufacturer recommends mixing ECHO 2-Cycle oil with regular or unleaded gasoline at a ratio of 32:1. A good quality 2-stroke engine oil designed for air-cooled two-stroke engines can be used at a ratio of 25:1. The manufacturer discourages the use of gasoline containing alcohol.

CARBURETOR

Walbro WA diaphragm carburetors and Kehin float type carburetors have been used on these models. The manufacturer's name and model number is stamped on the carburetor. Refer to CARBURETOR section in the appropriate following Engine Service Section for tuning and service information. Refer to the table on the following page for original application and initial mixture settings.

STRING TRIMMER

Refer to Figs. E1 through E15 for an exploded view of string trimmer heads used. Not all heads will be covered in detail; however, the most widely used heads are covered. Service procedure for the remaining heads is similar.

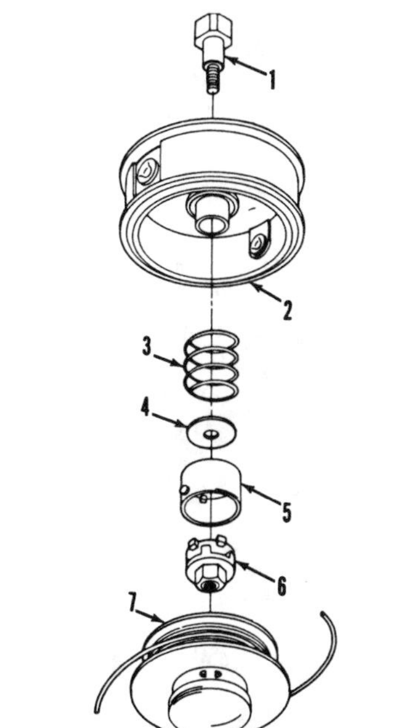

Fig. E1—Exploded view of dual strand semi-automatic trimmer head used on some SRM-200, SRM-201, SRM-202, SRM-300, SRM-302 and SRM-400 models.

1. Bolt
2. Drum
3. Spring
4. Washer
5. Outer drive
6. Inner cam
7. Spool

Semi-Automatic Dual Strand Trimmer Head

Refer to Fig. E1. To manually advance the trimmer line with the engine stopped, push the button in the center of spool (7) at the bottom of the head and pull the line. To extend the line with the engine running, operate the trimmer at maximum speed and tap the button on the ground. The line should extend a small amount automatically. If the line does not extend with the engine running, stop the engine and extend the line manually. If the line is broken inside the housing, it will be necessary to disassemble the unit and feed the line through the drum eyelet.

To remove and disassemble the string trimmer head, proceed as follows. Hold the drum firmly and turn spool in the direction shown in Fig. E2 to remove slack. Twist with a hard snap until the plastic peg is between holes, then separate the spool from the drum.

Clean and inspect all parts for damage. If new line is installed, it should be 0.095 in. (2.41 mm) diameter. The spool will hold approximately 20 ft. (6 m) of

Illustrations courtesy Echo Inc.

	Carburetor Model	Low-speed Needle	High-speed Needle
GT-140	Walbro WA-46	1 1/4	1 1/4
	Walbro WA-80	1 1/4	1 1/4
GT-140A	Walbro WA-80	1 1/4	1 1/4
GT-140B	Walbro WA-80	1 1/4	1 1/4
GT-160	Walbro WA-123	1 1/4	1 3/8
GT-160A	Walbro WA-138A	1 1/8	1
GT-160AE	Walbro WA-138A	1 1/8	1
GT-200	Walbro WA-59	1	1
	Walbro WA-59R	1	1
GT-200A	Walbro WA-81	1 1/4	1 3/8
GT-200B	Walbro WA-143	7/8	1 3/8
GT-200BE	Walbro WA-143	7/8	1 3/8
GT-200CE	Walbro WA-143	7/8	1 3/8
SRM-140A	...	...	...
SRM-140D	Walbro WA-46	1 1/4	1 1/4
	Walbro WA-80	1 1/4	1 1/4
SRM-140DA	Walbro WA-46	1 1/4	1 1/4
	Walbro WA-80	1 1/4	1 1/4
SRM-200	Walbro WA-81	1 1/4	1 3/8
SRM-200AE	Walbro WA-81	1 1/4	1 3/8
SRM-200BE	Walbro WA-143	7/8	1 3/8
SRM-200CE	Walbro WA-143	7/8	1 3/8
SRM-200D	Walbro WA-21	1	1
SRM-200DA	Walbro WA-59	1 1/4	1 1/8
	Walbro WA-59R	1 1/4	1 1/8
SRM-200DB	Walbro WA-59	1 1/4	1 1/8
	Walbro WA-59R	1 1/4	1 1/8
SRM-200E	...	...	...
SRM-201F	...	...	...
SRM-201FA	...	...	...
SRM-202D	...	...	...
SRM-202DA	Walbro WA-21	1	1
SRM-202F			
SRM-202FA	M-11 Kehin	...	...
SRM-210AE	Walbro WA-143	7/8	1 3/8
SRM-210E	Walbro WA-81	1 1/4	1 3/8
SRM-300	Walbro WA-87	1 1/8	1 1/4
SRM-302ADX	Walbro WA-7A	1	1
	Walbro WA-7B	1	1
SRM-300AE	Walbro WA-141	1	1 1/8
SRM-300AE/1	Walbro WA-141	1	1 1/8
SRM-300E	Walbro WA-87	1 1/8	1 1/4
SRM-300E/1	Walbro WA-87	1 1/8	1 1/4
SRM-400AE	Walbro WA-142	1 1/8	1 1/8
SRM-400BE	Walbro WA-142	1 1/8	1 1/8
SRM-400E	Walbro WA-106	1 1/4	1 3/8
SRM-402DE	...	...	...

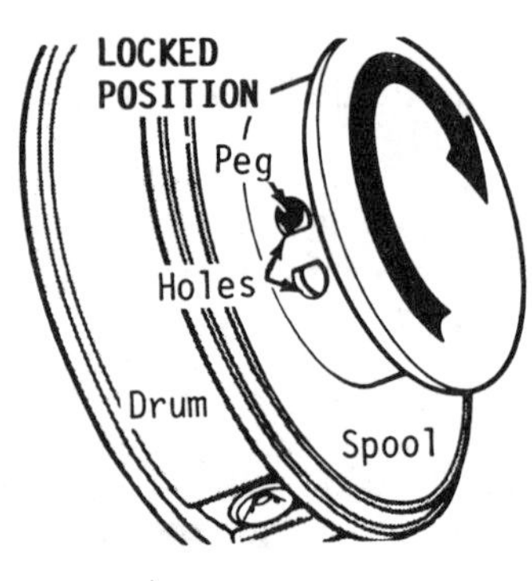

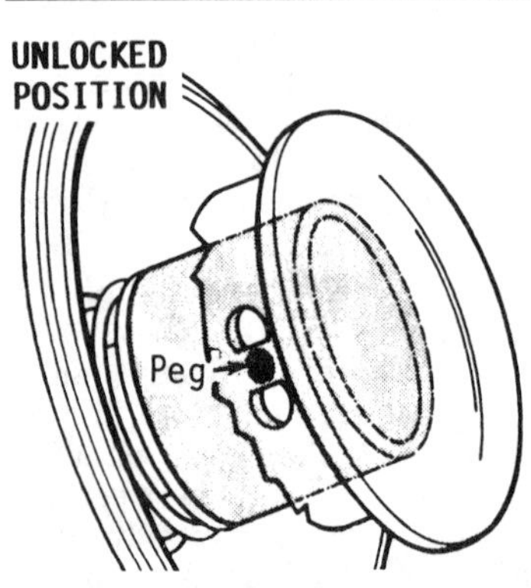

Fig. E2—To remove spool, hold drum firmly and turn spool in direction shown to take up slack, then twist with a sudden snap until plastic peg is between holes as shown in lower view.

line. Insert the line through the hole of the spool as shown in Fig. E3 and pull the line through until it is the same length on both sides. Wrap both ends of the line on spool at the same time in the direction indicated by an arrow marked "cc" on the edge of the spool. Wind the line tightly and evenly from side to side and do not twist the lines. Install spool while directing the ends of both lines through the eyelets in the housing. Align the pegs on drum with slots in the spool and push the spool into drum. Hold the drum firmly, then twist spool quickly in the direction shown in Fig. E4 so peg enters the hole with a click and locks the spool in position. Trim the lines to the desired length before starting the engine.

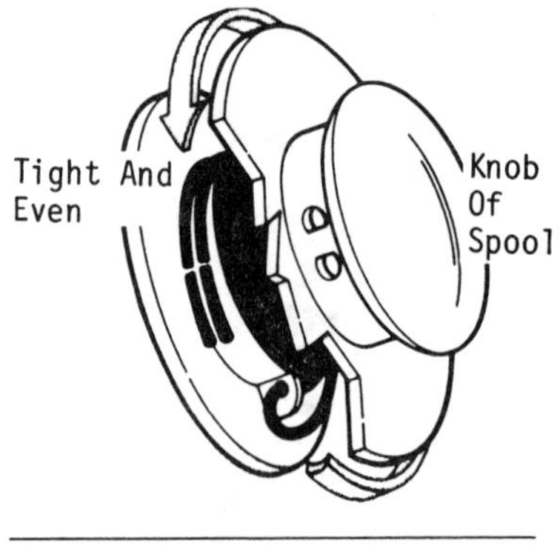

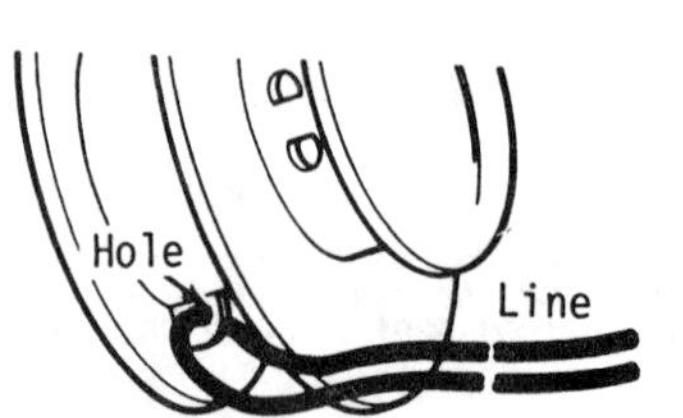

Fig. E3—End of line must be inserted through hole on spool as shown in lower view. Wind line tightly in direction indicated by arrow on spool.

Manual Advance Dual Strand Trimmer Head

Refer to Fig. E5. To manually advance the trimmer line, stop the engine and wait for the trimmer head to stop rotating. Loosen lock knob (6) approximately one turn. Pull lines from each

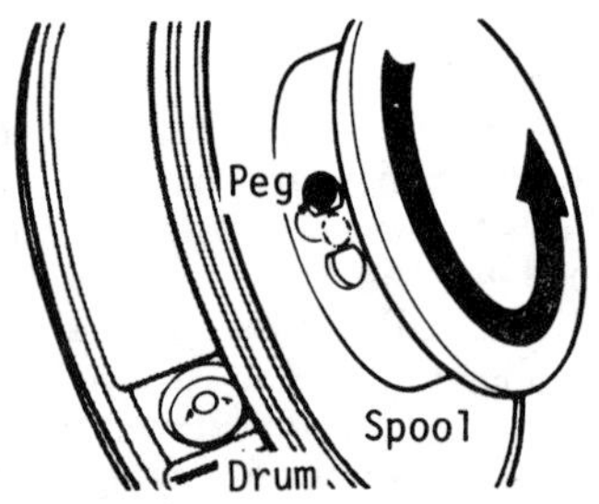

Fig. E4—Hold drum firmly and twist suddenly to lock spool in position.

Illustrations courtesy Echo Inc.

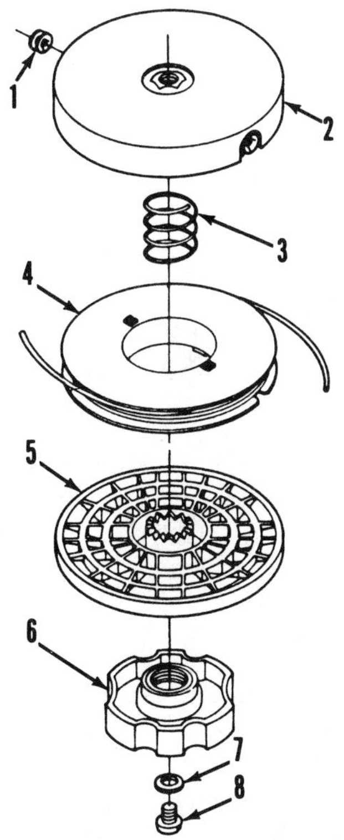

Fig. E5—Exploded view of manual trimmer head used on some SRM-200, SRM-201, SRM-202, SRM-300, SRM-302 and SRM-400 models. This head is no longer available.

1. Line guide
2. Hub
3. Spring
4. Spool
5. Cover
6. Knob
7. Washer
8. Screw

side until both are the desired distance from the drum, then tighten knob (6).

To remove the spool for installing new line or other service, remove the slotted screw (8) and washer (7). Unscrew knob (6), then remove cover (5), spool (4) and spring (3). Clean and inspect all parts for damage.

To install new line, cut two 12 ft. (3.65 m) lengths of 0.095 in. (2.41 mm) diameter line. Insert one end of each line into the locating hole at the bottom of the spool. The ends of lines should extend approximately 1/4 in. (6.4 mm) through the locating holes. Wrap ends of both lines on spool at the same time in counterclockwise direction as viewed from the bottom of spool. Wind the line tightly and evenly from side to side and do not twist the lines. Insert the ends of both lines through the line guides (1) in the housing while installing the spool. Install the spring (3), cover (5), knob (6), washer (7) and screw (8). Make sure screw (8) is tight, loosen knob (6), extend the lines if necessary, then tighten knob (6). Trim the lines to the desired length before starting the engine.

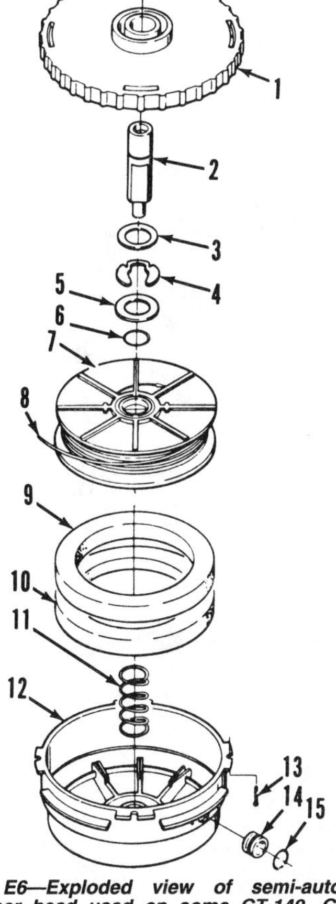

Fig. E6—Exploded view of semi-automatic trimmer head used on some GT-140, GT-160, GT-200 and GT-210 models.

1. Plate
2. Adapter
3. Washer
4. Retainer ring
5. Washer
6. Retainer ring
7. Spool
8. Line
9. Foam pad
10. Foam pad
11. Spring
12. Housing
13. Cotter pin
14. Line guide
15. Retainer

Semi-Automatic Single Strand Trimmer Head

Refer to Fig. E6. Line may be manually advanced with the engine stopped by pressing the housing (12) while pulling line from the spool. To extend the line with the engine running, operate the trimmer at maximum speed and "bump" housing (12) on the ground. The line should extend a small amount automatically. If the line does not extend with the engine running, stop the engine and attempt to extend the line manually. If the line is broken inside the housing, it will be necessary to disassemble the unit and feed the line through the line guide (14).

To install new line, first remove cotter pin (13). Rotate housing (12) counterclockwise, then remove the housing and spool (7). Remove foam pads (9 and 10) and any remaining line. Clean the spool and housing. Inspect the indexing teeth on the spool and in housing for damage. The spool will hold approximately 25 ft. (7.6 m) of 0.080 in. (2 mm) diameter line. Tape one end of new line to the spool as shown in Fig. E7. Wind the line on spool in the direction indicated by arrow on spool as shown in Fig. E8. Install both foam pads (9 and 10—Fig. E6) and install the spool assembly. Insert the end of line through the line guide as shown in Fig. E8, while installing the housing. Push the housing in and rotate it clockwise to lock it in position, then install cotter pin (13—Fig. E6). Trim the line to the desired length before starting the engine.

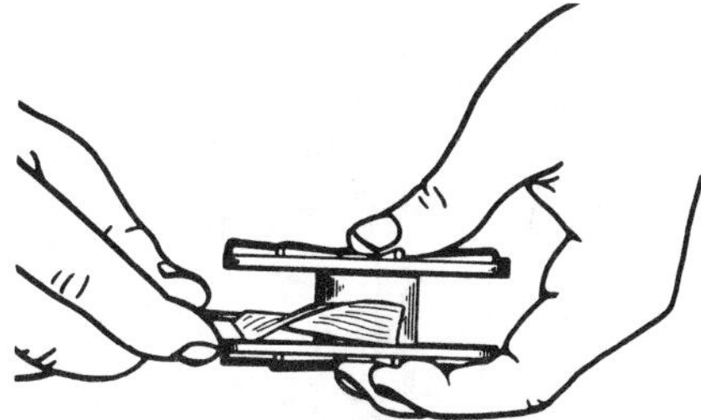

Fig. E7—Tape one end of line to center of spool.

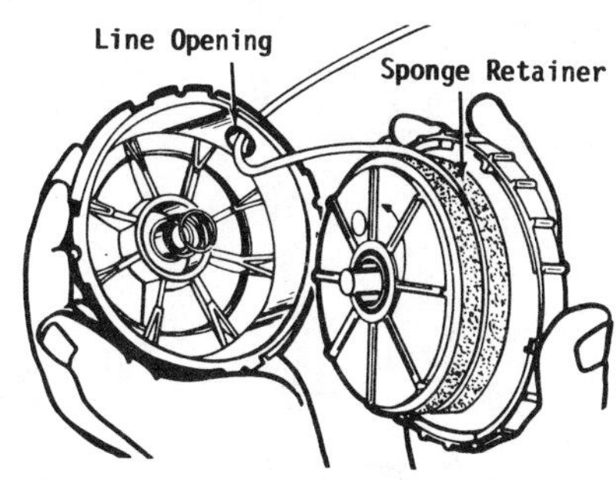

Fig. E8—Foam pads are installed on spool with trimmer line between them.

Semi-Automatic Single and Dual Strand Trimmer Heads

Some GT and SRM models may be equipped with a semi-automatic trimmer head as shown in Fig. E9, Fig. E10 or Fig. E11. Line may be manually advanced with engine stopped by depressing the "bump" button or spool and pulling line out as required.

To renew line, remove line spool and remove any remaining old line. Install new line of same diameter, winding line on spool in direction indicated by arrow on spool. On dual strand heads, wind both ends of line at the same time in the same direction. Wind tightly and evenly from side to side and do not twist line. Insert end of line through drum eyelet leaving approximately 6 inches (152 mm) of line extending from spool.

Illustrations courtesy Echo Inc.

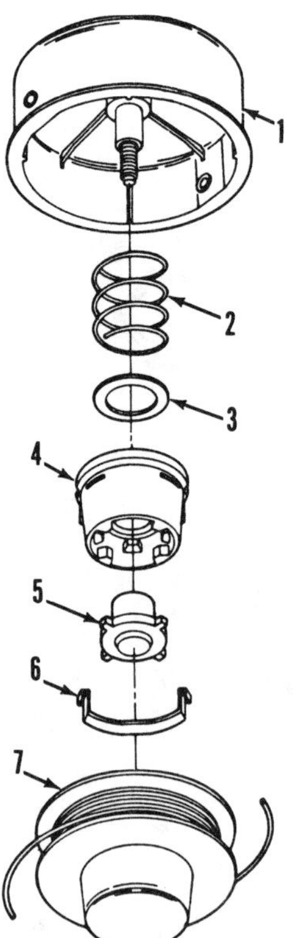

Fig. E9—Exploded view of semi-automatic trimmer head used on some SRM-140D and SRM-140DA models.

1. Hub
2. Spring
3. Washer
4. Outer drive
5. Inner cam
6. Clip
7. Spool

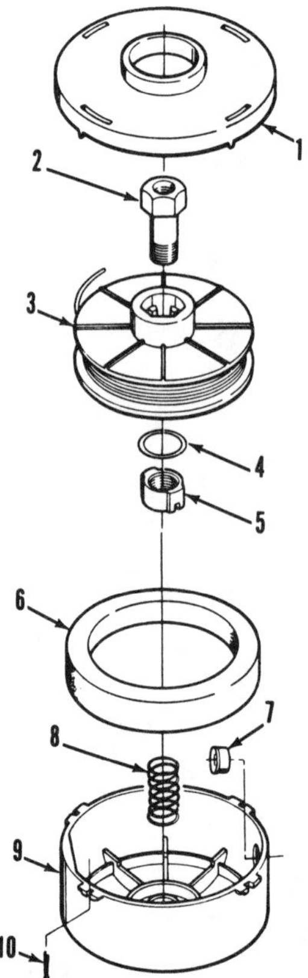

Fig. E10—Exploded view of semi-automatic trimmer head used on some GT-140B, GT-160, GT160-A, GT-200A, GT-200B and SRM-210E models. This head is no longer available.

1. Plate
2. Drive adapter
3. Spool
4. "O" ring
5. Drive adapter nut
6. Foam pad
7. Line guide
8. Spring
9. Hub
10. Cotter pin

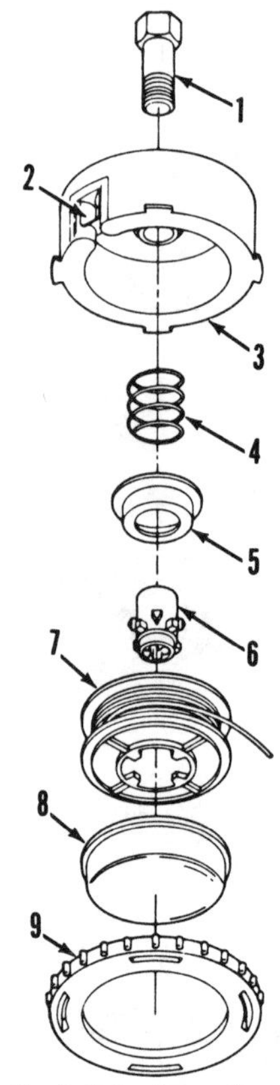

Fig. E11—Exploded view of semi-automatic trimmer head used on GT-200 model. This head is no longer available.

1. Bolt
2. Line guide
3. Drum
4. Spring
5. Spring adapter
6. Inner cam
7. Spool
8. Button
9. Cover

Manual Single and Dual Strand Trimmer Heads

Some GT and SRM models may be equipped with manual advance trimmer head as shown in Fig. E12, Fig. E13, E14 or Fig. E15. To extend line, stop engine and loosen spool lock knob or nut. Pull out the line to desired length.

To renew line, remove line spool and remove any remaining old line. Install new line of same diameter, winding line on spool in direction indicated by arrow on spool. On dual strand head, wind both ends of line at the same time in the same direction. Wind tightly and evenly from side to side and do not twist line. Insert end of line through drum eyelet leaving approximately 6 inches (152 mm) of line extending from spool.

Maxicut Trimmer Head

The "Maxicut" trimmer head (Fig. E16) is equipped with three plastic blades (2) attached to a plastic mounting disc (3) and is available as an aftermarket item. Note that nut (6) may have either left- or right-hand threads depending upon the model being serviced.

BLADE

An eight tooth weed and grass blade (A—Fig. E17) and an eighty tooth saw blade are available for some models. To install either blade, rotate the drive shaft until the holes in upper adapter plate and the gear or bearing head are aligned. Insert a locking rod (Fig. E18) into holes. Install blade making certain that it is centered correctly on the adapter plate. Install lower adapter plate and locking nut. Install cotter pin.

To sharpen the eight tooth weed and grass blade, round the tooth bottom 1-2 mm (0.4-0.8 in.) as shown in Fig. E19 to prevent blade cracking. Length of cutting edge must be about 10 mm (0.4 in.) from the base of the tooth, but the rounded 2 mm part is not to be sharpened. Sharpen each blade equally to retain balance.

To sharpen the eighty tooth saw blade, setting can be done by using a

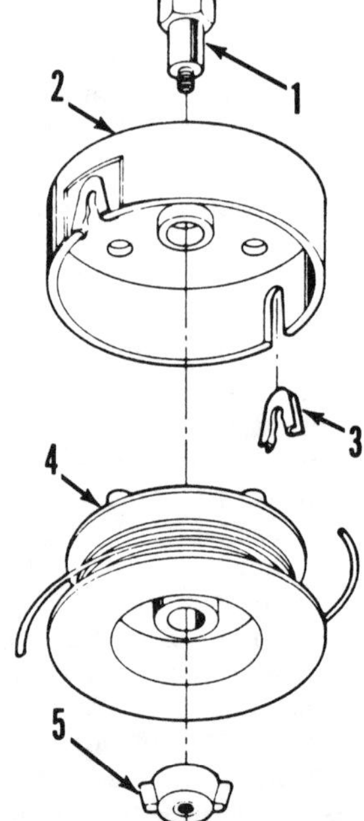

Fig. E12—Exploded view of manual trimmer head used on some GTL-140 and SRM-140 models. This head has also been used on light duty SRM-200, SRM-201 and SRM-202 models. Bolt (1) may be right or left hand thread according to model.

1. Bolt
2. Drum
3. Line guide
4. Spool
5. Wing nut

Illustrations courtesy Echo Inc.

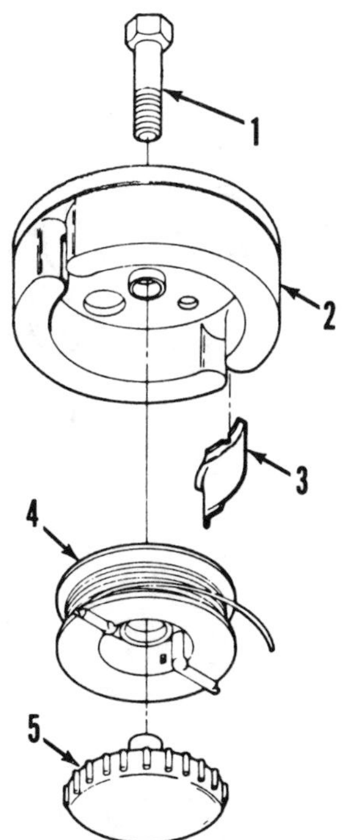

Fig. E13—Exploded view of manual trimmer head used on some GT-140B, GT-160, GT-160AE, GT-200A, GT-200B, GT-200CE, SRM-210E and SRM-210AE models.

1. Bolt
2. Drum
3. Line guide
4. Spool
5. Ball lock

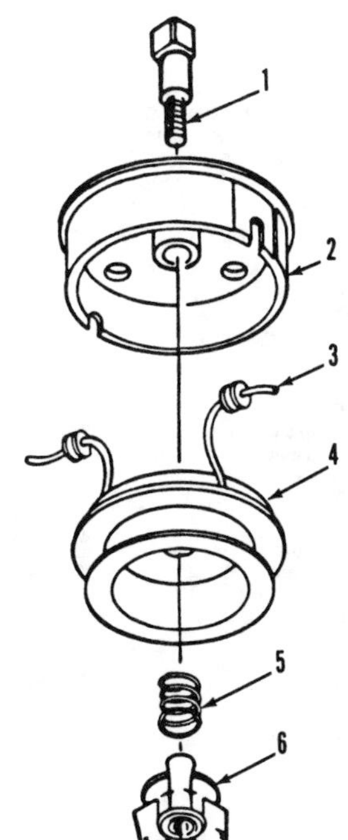

Fig. E15—Exploded view of heavy duty manual trimmer head used on some SRM-200, SRM-201, SRM-202, SRM-250 SRM-300, SRM-302 and SRM-400 models.

1. Bolt
2. Housing
3. Line guide
4. Spool
5. Spring
6. Knob

Fig. E17—Weed and grass blade (A) and brush blade (B) are available for some models.

Fig. E18—Make certain blade is centered on adapter plate (fixing plate) during installation.

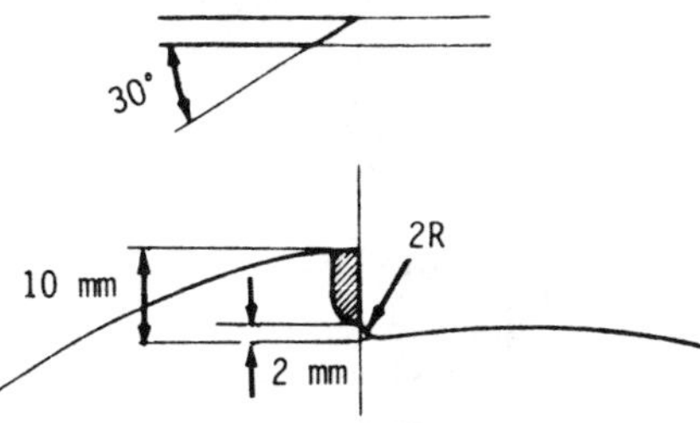

Fig. E19—The eight tooth weed and grass blade may be sharpened as shown.

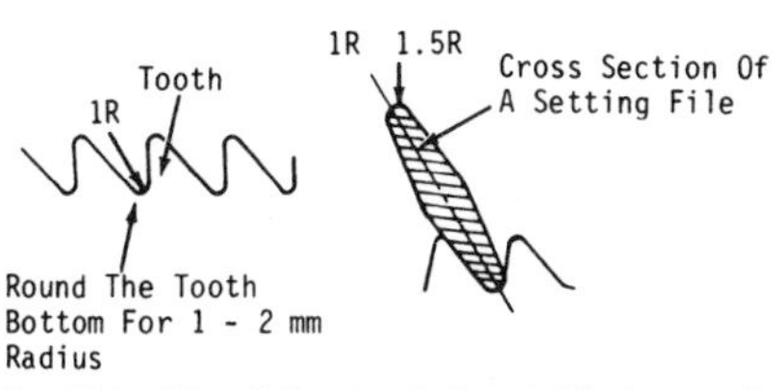

Fig. E20—The eighty tooth brush blade may be sharpened as shown.

Fig. E14—Exploded view of manual trimmer head used on some GT-140, GT-140A and GT-200 models. Nut (3) is right hand thread for GT-140A and GT-200 models but is left hand thread for GT-140 model.

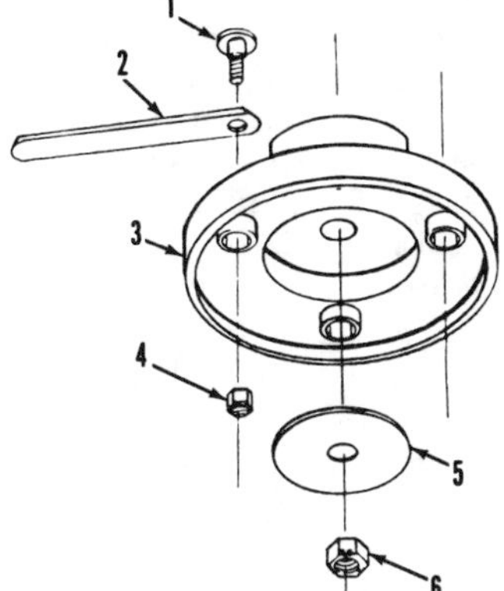

Fig. E16—Exploded view of "Maxicut" head which is available for all GT and SRM trimmers. Nut (6) may have left or right hand threads depending upon model.

1. Bolt
2. Blade
3. Body
4. Nut
5. Washer
6. Nut

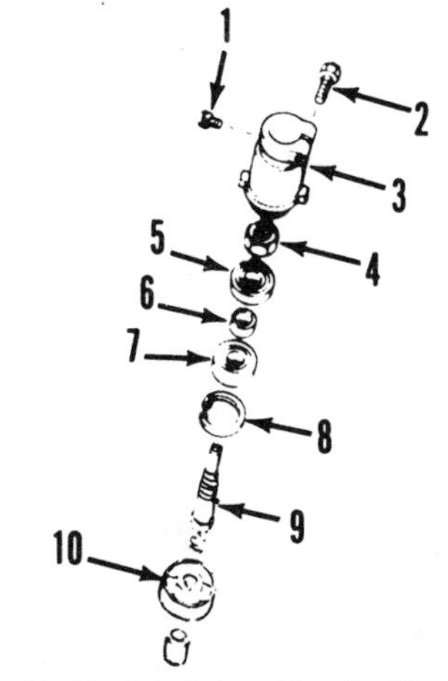

Fig. E21—Exploded view of bearing head used on some models.

1. Screw
2. Clamp screw
3. Housing
4. Nut
5. Bearing
6. Spacer
7. Bearing
8. Snap ring
9. Shaft
10. Adapter plate & key

circular saw setter. Sharpen blade as shown in Fig. E20.

BEARING HEAD

All Models So Equipped

Bearing heads (Fig. E21 or E22) are equipped with sealed bearings and require no periodic maintenance. To disassemble either bearing head, remove screw (1) and clamp screw (2). Remove adapter plate (10) and snap ring (8). Use suitable puller to remove bearing and arbor assemblies. Remove nut (4) and remove bearings and spacer as required.

GEAR HEAD

All Models So Equipped

Gear heads (Figs. E23, E24, E25 and E26 should have gear lubricant checked at 50 hour intervals. To check, remove check plug (15). Gear head housing should be 2/3 full of lithium base grease.

To disassemble gear heads shown in Figs. E23 and E24, remove trimmer head or blade assembly. Remove screw (14) and clamp bolt (16). Pry seal (5) from housing (13) and remove snap ring (7). Remove bushing (6) as equipped. Remove snap ring (20). Use suitable puller to remove input shaft and gear (17). Use suitable puller to remove arbor shaft (9).

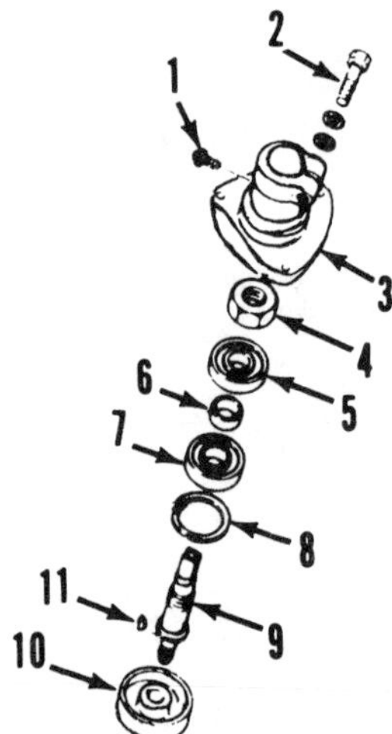

Fig. E22—Exploded view of bearing head used on some models.

1. Screw
2. Clamp screw
3. Housing
4. Nut
5. Bearing
6. Spacer
7. Bearing
8. Snap ring
9. Shaft
10. Adapter
11. Key

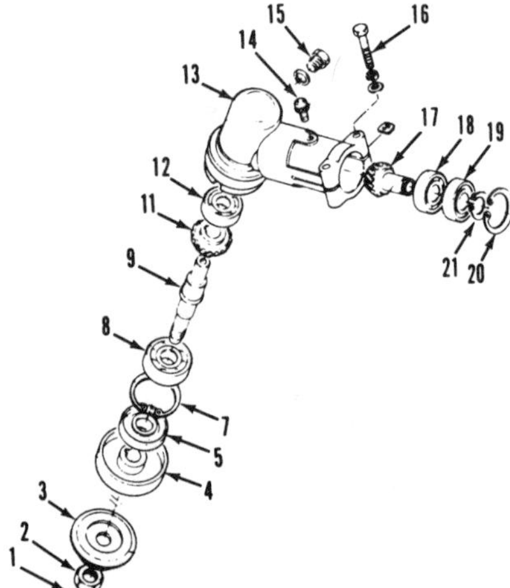

Fig. E23—Exploded view of gear head used on many models. Note arbor shaft (9) is cut for keys. Refer also to Fig. E25.

1. Cotter pin
2. Nut
3. Adapter plate
4. Adapter plate
5. Seal
7. Snap ring
8. Bearing
9. Arbor shaft
11. Gear
12. Bearing
13. Housing
14. Screw
15. Level check plug
16. Clamp bolt
17. Gear
18. Bearing
19. Bearing
20. Snap ring
21. Snap ring

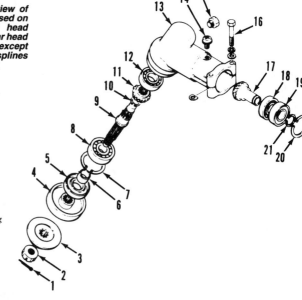

Fig. E24—Exploded view of gear head assembly used on many models. Gear head shown is similar to gear head shown in Fig. E24 except arbor shaft has splines instead of keys.

1. Cotter pin
2. Nut
3. Adapter plate
4. Adapter plate
5. Seal
6. Bushing
7. Snap ring
8. Bearing
9. Arbor shaft
10. Snap ring
11. Gear
12. Bearing
13. Housing
14. Screw
15. Level check plug
16. Clamp bolt
17. Gear
18. Bearing
19. Bearing
20. Snap ring
21. Snap ring

Remove required snap rings and remove bearings and gears.

Gear heads shown in Figs. E25 and E26 are similarly constructed. Spacers (17 and 18—Fig. E26) may also be used in gear head shown in Fig. E25. Remove trimmer head or blade assembly. Remove screw (13—Fig. E25 or E26) and clamp bolt (14). Separate gear head from drive shaft housing tube. Remove seal (6), snap ring (5) and bushing (7). On gear head shown in Fig. E25, seal (6) must be removed to gain access to snap ring (5). Remove snap ring (21—Fig. E25 or E26).

Use suitable pullers to remove input shaft and arbor shaft assemblies. Remove required snap rings and remove bearings, gears and spacers.

To disassemble gear head shown in Fig. E27, separate gear head from drive shaft housing tube. Remove cotter pin (1), nut (2), adapter plate (3), blade and adapter plate (4). Remove snap ring (25) and use suitable puller to remove input shaft (20) and bearings assembly. Remove plug (16). Remove seal (7) and snap ring (8). Remove snap ring (14). Press arbor and bearing assembly from housing (19).

DRIVE SHAFT

All Models With Flexible Drive Shaft

Flexible drive shaft should be removed, cleaned and lubricated with lithium base grease at 18 hour intervals of use.

To remove, separate drive shaft housing tube from engine assembly. Mark position of flexible drive shaft ends and remove drive shaft from housing. Reverse ends of drive shaft then reinstall shaft in housing. Reversing drive shaft each time it is serviced will greatly extend drive shaft life.

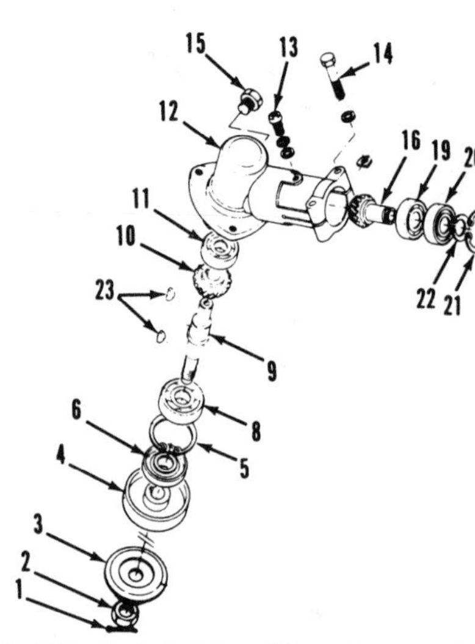

Fig. E25—Exploded view of flange type gear head with arbor shaft cut for keys (23). Refer to Fig. E26 for identification of parts.

All Models With Solid Drive Shaft

A solid steel drive shaft is used on heavy duty models which may be equipped with grass and weed or saw blade. Drive shaft runs through housing and is supported in bushing in drive shaft housing tube (Fig. E28). No regular maintenance is required; however if drive shaft is removed, lubricate with lithium base grease before reinstalling.

Illustrations courtesy Echo Inc.

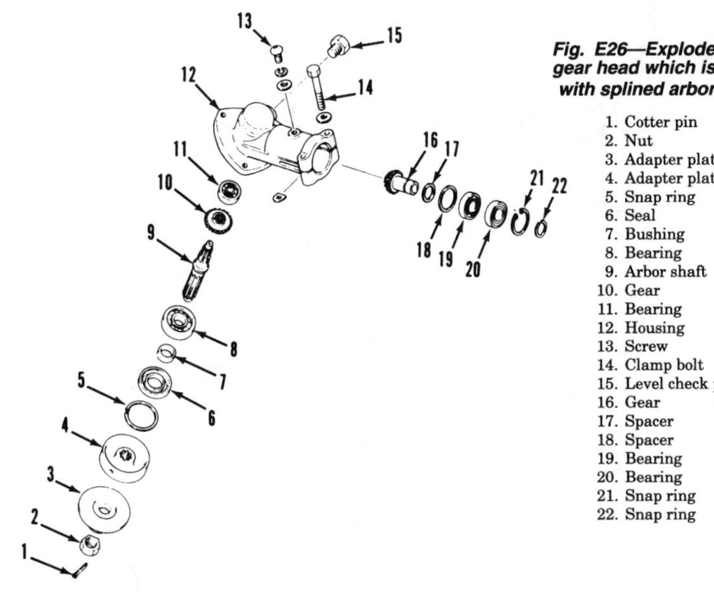

Fig. E26—Exploded view of gear head which is equipped with splined arbor shaft (9).

1. Cotter pin
2. Nut
3. Adapter plate
4. Adapter plate
5. Snap ring
6. Seal
7. Bushing
8. Bearing
9. Arbor shaft
10. Gear
11. Bearing
12. Housing
13. Screw
14. Clamp bolt
15. Level check plug
16. Gear
17. Spacer
18. Spacer
19. Bearing
20. Bearing
21. Snap ring
22. Snap ring

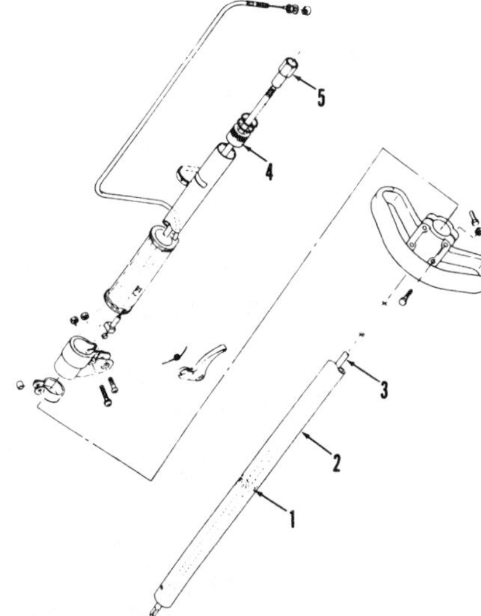

Fig. E28—Exploded view of housing and solid drive shaft.

1. Internal drive shaft bearing
2. Drive shaft housing
3. Solid steel drive shaft
4. Drive shaft bearing
5. Drive shaft adapter

Fig. E27—Exploded view of gear head used on SRM-302ADX models.

1. Cotter pin
2. Nut
3. Adapter plate
4. Adapter plate
5. Arbor shaft
6. Keys
7. Seal
8. Snap ring
9. Bearing
10. Spacer
11. Gear
12. Snap ring
13. Bearing
14. Snap ring
15. Level check plug
16. Plug
17. Nut
18. Clamp bolt
19. Housing
20. Gear
21. Spacer
22. Bearing
23. Bearing
24. Snap ring
25. Snap ring

STARTER

Refer to the appropriate ENGINE SERVICE section for service to the starter assembly.

CLUTCH

Refer to the appropriate ENGINE SERVICE section for clutch removal and service procedures.

ECHO

GASOLINE POWERED TRIMMERS

Model	Engine Make	Displacement
GT-1000, GT1100, GT-2000, GT-2101, GT-2102, GT-2103,	Echo	16.0 cc (0.976 cu. in.)
GT-2200	Echo	21.2 cc (1.294 cu. in.)
GT-2400	Echo	23.6 cc (1.440 cu. in.)
PE-2000 Edger, PE-2201	Echo	21.2 cc (1.294 cu. in.)
PE-2400 Edger	Echo	23.6 cc (1.440 cu. in.)
SRM-1500, SRM-1501, SRM-2000, SRM-2100, SRM-2110, SRM-2200, SRM-2201, SRM-2300, SRM-2301, SRM-2310	Echo	21.2 cc (1.294 cu. in.)
SRM-2400, SRM-2410	Echo	23.6 cc (1.440 cu. in.)
SRM-2500, SRM-2501, SRM-2501S, SRM-2503, SRM-2510	Echo	24.4 cc (1.489 cu. in.)
SRM-3000, SRM-3001	Echo	30.8 cc (1.88 cu. in.)
SRM-3100, SRM-3100S, SRM-3110	Echo	30.5 cc (1.861 cu. in.)
SRM-3400	Echo	34.0 cc (2.08 cu. in.)
SRM-3800	Echo	37.4 cc (2.284 cu. in.)
SRM-4600	Echo	45.7 cc (2.790 cu. in.)

ENGINE INFORMATION

Echo two-stroke air-cooled gasoline engines are used. Identify the engine by displacement and refer to the ECHO Engine Service section of this manual.

FUEL MIXTURE

The manufacturer recommends mixing ECHO 2-Cycle oil with regular or unleaded gasoline at a ratio of 32:1. A good-quality 2-stroke engine oil designed for air-cooled two-stroke engines can be used a ratio of 25:1. The manufacturer discourages the use of gasoline containing alcohol.

CARBURETOR

Walbro WA, Walbro WY, Walbro WYL and Zama C1U diaphragm carburetors have been used on these models. The manufacturer's name and model number is stamped on the carburetor. Refer to CARBURETOR section in the appropriate following Engine Service Section for tuning and service information. Refer to the table on the following page for original application and initial mixture settings.

Initial setting of the idle-speed mixture needle of models indicated by * is set by counting the turns IN (clockwise) after threads of the needle just engage carburetor body. Initial setting for other models is set by counting the turns **OUT** from lightly seated position.

STRING TRIMMER

Semi-Automatic Dual Strand Trimmer Head

Refer to Fig. E51. To manually advance the trimmer line with the engine stopped, push the button in the center of spool (7) at the bottom of the head and pull the line. To extend the line with the engine running, operate the trimmer at maximum speed and tap the button on the ground. The line should extend a small amount automatically. If the line does not extend with the engine running, stop the engine and extend the line manually. If the line is broken inside the housing, it will be necessary to disassemble the

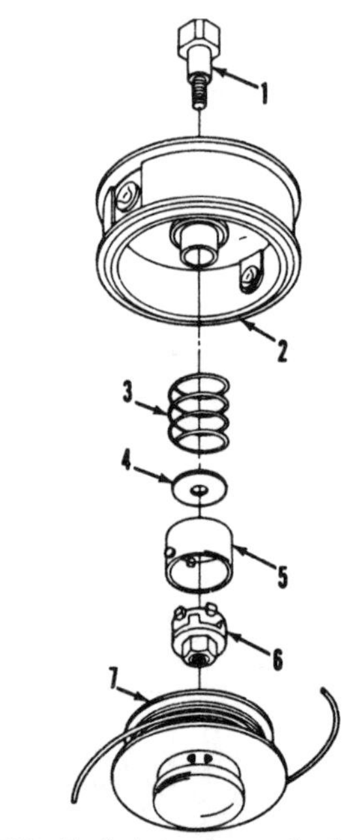

Fig. E51—Exploded view of dual strand semi-automatic head typical of type used on some models.

1. Bolt
2. Drum
3. Spring
4. Washer
5. Outer drive
6. Inner cam
7. Spool

Illustrations courtesy Echo Inc.

	Carburetor Model	Low-speed Needle	High-speed Needle
GT-1000	Walbro WA-168	1 1/4	1
GT-1100	Walbro WYL-1	12*	...
	Walbro WYL-6	12*	...
	Walbro WYL-10	12*	...
	Zama C1U-K29	1	1
GT-1100B	Zama C1U-K16	1	1
GT-2000	...	...	...
GT-2100	Zama C1U-K4	1	1
GT-2101	Walbro WYL-1	12*	...
GT-2102	Walbro WYL-1	12*	...
	Walbro WYL-6	12*	...
GT-2103	Zama C1U-K12	1 1/8	1
	Zama C1U-K16	1	1
GT-2200	Walbro WY-18	7*	...
GT-2400	Zama C1U-K23	1 1/4	1
PE-2000 Edger	...	...	...
PE-2201	Walbro WY-18	7*	...
PE-2400 Edger	Zama C1U-K23	1 1/4	1
SRM-1500	Zama C1U-K9	1 1/8	1 1/8
SRM-1501	Zama C1U-K9	1 1/8	1 1/8
	Zama C1U-K16	1	1
SRM-2000	Walbro WY-18	7*	...
SRM-2100	...	...	...
SRM-2110	...	...	...
SRM-2200	Walbro WY-18	7*	...
SRM-2201	Walbro WY-18	7*	...
SRM-2300	Zama C1U-K9	1 1/8	1 1/8
SRM-2301	Zama C1U-K12	1 1/8	1
SRM-2310	Zama C1U-K12	1 1/8	1

Carburetor	Low-speed Model	High-speed Needle	Needle
SRM-2400	Zama C1U-K23	1 1/4	1
SRM-2410	Zama C1U-K31	7/8	1 1/4
SRM-2500	Walbro WY-21	7*	...
SRM-2501	Walbro WY-21	7*	...
	Zama C1U-K20	1 1/8	1
	Zama C1U-K20A	1 1/8	1/2
SRM-2502	Walbro WY-21	7*	...
SRM-2503			
SRM-2510	Zama C1U-K20	1 1/8	1
	Zama C1U-K20A	1 1/8	1/2
SRM-2600	...	1 2/4	1
SRM-3000	Walbro WY-21	7*	...
	Zama C1U-K21	1	1
SRM-3001	Walbro WY-21	7*	...
SRM-3010	Walbro WY21	7*	...
SRM-3100	Walbro WT-333	Limiter caps	
SRM-3100S	Walbro WT-334	1	1 1/2
SRM-3110	Walbro WY-21	7*	...
	...	1	1 2/2
SRM-3150		1 1/4	1 1/8
SRM-3400 & SRM-3410	Walbro WT-333	Limiter caps	
SRM-3600	Walbro WT-334	1	1 1/2
SRM-3800	Walbro WT-74	1	N/A
	Walbro WT-74A	1	N/A
SRM-4600	Walbro WT-77	1	1
	Walbro WT-120A	1 1/4	1 1/4
	Walbro WT-120B	1 1/8	1 1/4

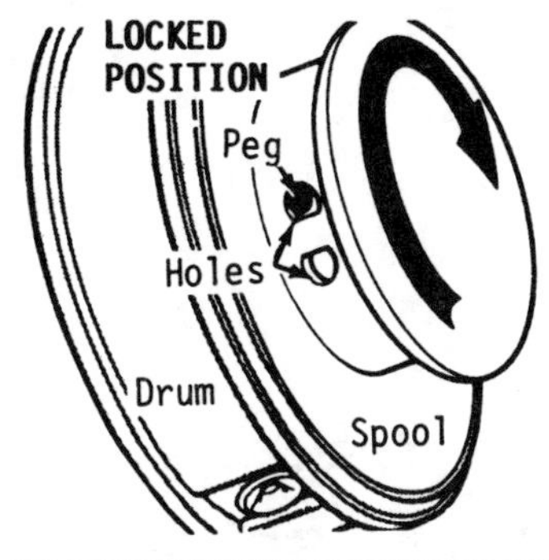

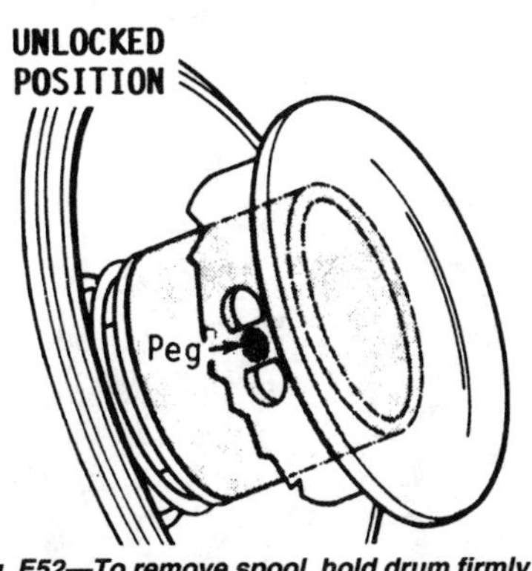

Fig. E52—To remove spool, hold drum firmly and turn spool in direction shown to take up slack, then twist with a sudden snap until plastic peg is between holes as shown in lower view.

unit and feed the line through the drum eyelet (2).

To remove and disassemble the string trimmer head, proceed as follows. Hold the drum firmly and turn spool in the direction shown in Fig. E52 to remove slack. Twist with a hard snap until the plastic peg is between holes, then separate the spool from the drum.

Clean and inspect all parts for damage. If new line is installed, it should be 0.095 in. (2.41 mm) diameter. The spool will hold approximately 20 ft. (6 m) of line. Insert the line through the hole of the spool as shown in Fig. E53 and pull the line through until it is the same length on both sides. Wrap both ends of the line on spool at the same time in the direction indicated by an arrow marked "cc" on the edge of the spool. Wind the line tightly and evenly from side to side and do not twist the lines. Install spool while directing the ends of both lines through the eyelets in the housing. Align the pegs on drum with slots in the spool and push the spool into drum. Hold the drum firmly, then twist spool quickly in the direction shown in Fig. E54 so peg enters the hole with a click and locks the spool in position. Trim the lines to the desired length before starting the engine.

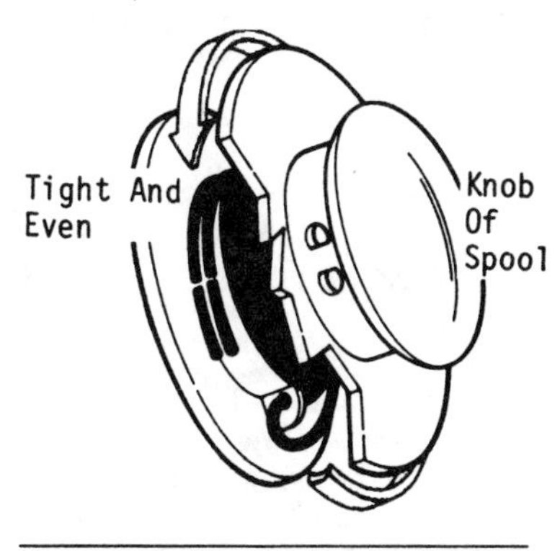

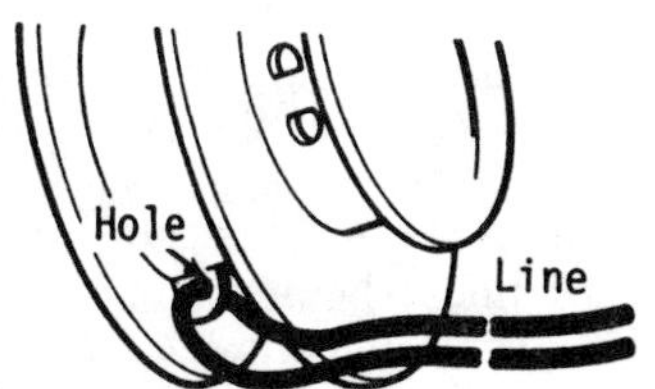

Fig. E53—End of line must be inserted through hole on spool as shown in lower view. Wind the line tightly in direction indicated by arrow on spool.

Illustrations courtesy Echo Inc.

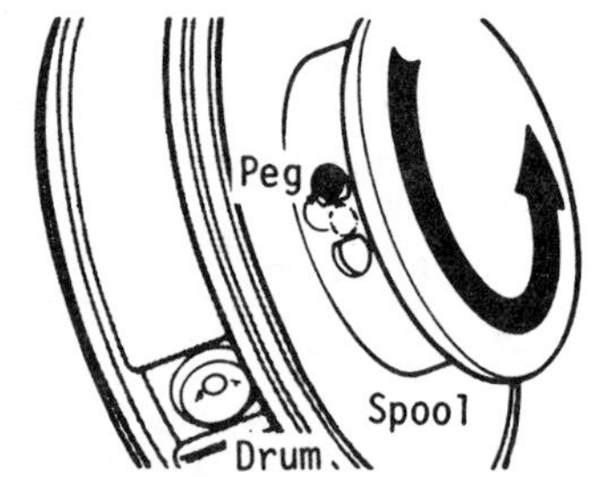

Fig. E54—Hold drum firmly and twist suddenly to lock spool in position.

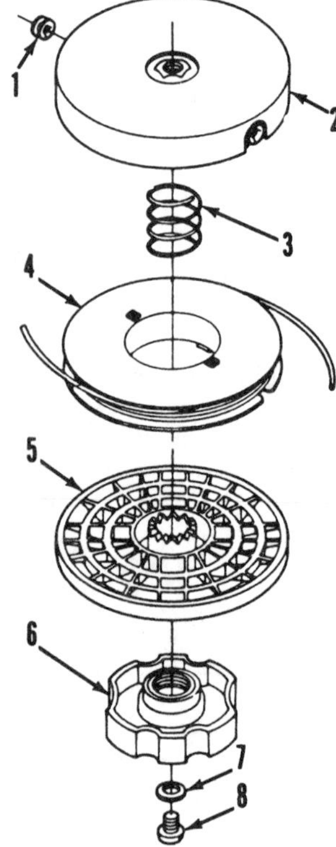
Fig. E55—Exploded view of manual trimmer head used on some models.

1. Line guide
2. Hub
3. Spring
4. Spool
5. Cover
6. Knob
7. Washer
8. Screw

Manual Advance Dual Strand Trimmer Head

Refer to Fig. E55. To manually advance the trimmer line, stop the engine and wait for the trimmer head to stop rotating. Loosen lock knob (6) approximately one turn. Pull lines from each side until both are the desired distance from the drum, then tighten knob (6). If the spool is not completely seated, turn the spool until the pegs on the top of the spool engage the holes in the hub.

Both lines should extend from the hub the same amount. If a line is not extended, it may be broken inside the housing, making it necessary to disassemble the unit and feed the line through the eyelets.

To remove the spool for installing new line or other service, remove the slotted screw (8) and washer (7). Unscrew knob (6), then remove cover (5), spool (4) and spring (3). Clean and inspect all parts for damage.

If new line is installed, it should be the same diameter as originally installed. Insert one end of each line into the locating hole at the bottom of the spool. The ends of lines should extend approximately 1/4 in. (6.4 mm) through the locating holes. Wrap ends of both lines on spool at the same time in counterclockwise direction as viewed from the bottom of spool. Wind the line tightly and evenly from side to side and do not twist the lines. Insert the ends of both lines through the line guides (1) in the housing while installing the spool. Install the spring (3), cover (5), knob (6), washer (7) and screw (8). Make sure screw (8) is tight, loosen knob (6), extend the lines if necessary, then tighten knob (6). Trim the lines to the desired length before starting the engine.

Semi-Automatic Single Strand Trimmer Head

Refer to Fig. E56. Line may be manually advanced with the engine stopped by pressing the housing (12) while pulling line from the spool. To extend the line with the engine running, operate the trimmer at maximum speed and "bump" housing (12) on the ground. The line should extend a small amount automatically. If the line does not extend with the engine running, stop the engine and attempt to extend the line manually. If the line is broken inside the housing, it will be necessary to disassemble the unit and feed the line through the line guide (14).

To install new line, first remove cotter pin (13). Rotate housing (12) counterclockwise, then remove the housing and spool (7). Remove foam pads (9 and 10) and any remaining line. Clean the spool and housing. Inspect the indexing teeth on the spool and in housing for damage. The spool will hold approximately 25 ft. (7.6 m) of 0.080 in. (2 mm) diameter line.

Tape one end of new line to the spool as shown in Fig. E57. Wind the line on spool in the direction indicated by arrow on spool as shown in Fig. E58. Install both foam pads (9 and 10—Fig. E56) and install the spool assembly. Insert the end of line through the line guide as shown in Fig. E58, while installing the housing. Push the housing in and rotate it clockwise to lock it in position, then install cotter pin

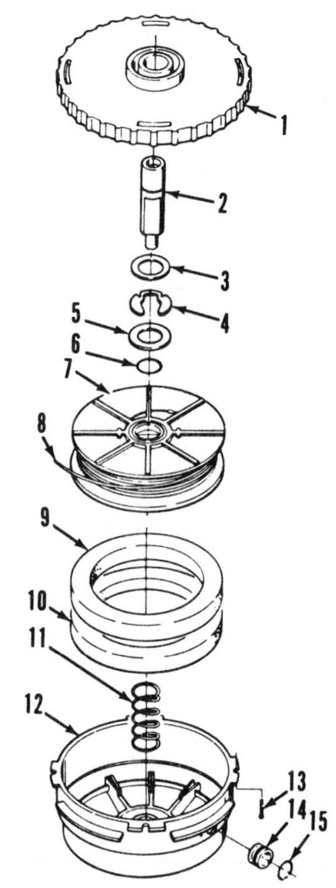
Fig. E56—Exploded view of semi-automatic trimmer head used on some models.

1. Plate
2. Adapter
3. Washer
4. Retainer ring
5. Washer
6. Retainer ring
7. Spool
8. Line
9. Foam pad
10. Foam pad
11. Spring
12. Housing
13. Cotter pin
14. Line guide
15. Retainer

Fig. E57—Tape one end of line to center of the spool.

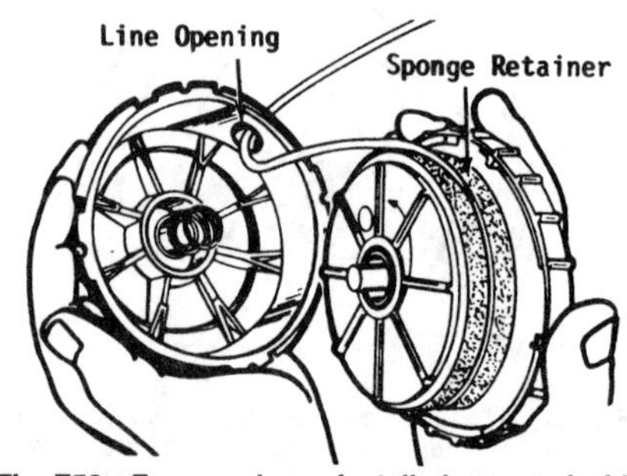

Fig. E58—Foam pads are installed on spool with trimmer line between pads.

Illustrations courtesy Echo Inc.

(13—Fig. E56). Trim the line to the desired length before starting the engine.

BLADE

A variety of hard cutting blades are available for installation on most models. All of the available hard blades can be dangerous and should be selected and used with great care. Blades of different diameters should be matched to the specific model of the powerhead. A blade too small or too large will reduce the effectiveness of operation and may increase the chance for damage or injury. Sharpen each tooth following the original sharpening angle and tooth set. Sharpen all teeth evenly to maintain balance and do not file into the radius at the root.

To remove or install blade, insert a tool into hole in upper adapter and gear head to prevent the drive shaft from turning. Remove bolt, lower adapter and blade.

BEARING HEAD

The bearing head (Fig. E59) is equipped with sealed bearings and requires no periodic maintenance. Some parts may not be available. To disassemble the bearing head, remove screw (1) and clamp screw (2). Remove adapter plate (10) and snap ring (8). Use a suitable puller to remove the bearing and arbor assemblies. Remove nut (4), then remove bearings and spacer as necessary.

GEAR HEAD

The gear housing (Fig. E60 or Fig. E61) is located at the lower end of the drive shaft and housing. To remove the assembly, loosen the fitting screw (13) and clamp bolts (14), then pull the gear housing from the drive shaft housing. Remove the trimmer head or blade, then unbolt the protector shield. On some models it is necessary to remove snap ring (5—Fig. E61) before prying seal (6) from the housing.

To remove the gears and bearings, first remove snap ring (21—Fig. E60 or Fig. E61). Use a blind hole puller to pull the gear and bearings (16, 19 and 20) from the housing.

NOTE: It may be possible to bump the open end of housing (12) to dislodge the bearings and gear (16, 19 and 20).

The bearings can be pressed from the gear after removing the snap ring (22). Remove snap ring (5), then pull the bearing and shaft (8 and 9) from the housing. A puller may be needed to remove the bearing (11) from its bore in housing.

Clean all parts and inspect for damage. Install new parts as necessary. Gears should replaced as a set. Grease the lower seal (6) before pressing into the housing. Add multipurpose lithium-base grease to the housing until the cavity is approximately 2/3 full. Do not over fill the housing with grease. Tighten fill plug (15) securely.

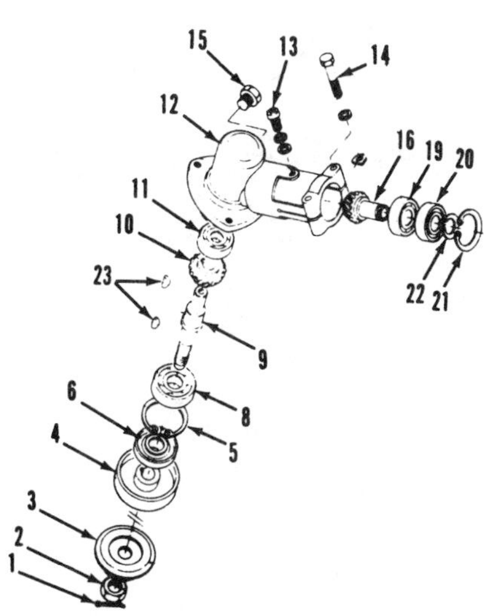

Fig. E60—Exploded view typical of the gear head used on some models. The Arbor shaft (9) is fitted with drive keys (23) Refer also to Fig. E61.

1. Cotter pin
2. Nut
3. Adapter plate
4. Drive plate
5. Snap ring
6. Seal
8. Bearing
9. Arbor shaft
10. Gear
11. Bearing
12. Housing
13. Fitting screw
14. Clamp bolt
15. Lubrication check plug
16. Gear
19. Bearing
20. Bearing
21. Snap ring
22. Snap ring
23. Woodruff keys

DRIVE SHAFT

The flexible drive shaft should be removed, inspected and lubricated frequently. The 4-layer cable can be withdrawn from either end. If the drive shaft cannot be easily withdrawn or turned, it may be necessary to install the housing as well as the drive shaft. Coat the shaft lightly with multipurpose lithium-base grease, before installing. Reverse ends of the drive shaft, before installing. Reversing the drive shaft frequently will extend the life of the shaft.

STARTER

Refer to the appropriate ENGINE SERVICE section for service to the starter assembly.

CLUTCH

Refer to the appropriate ENGINE SERVICE section for clutch removal and service procedures.

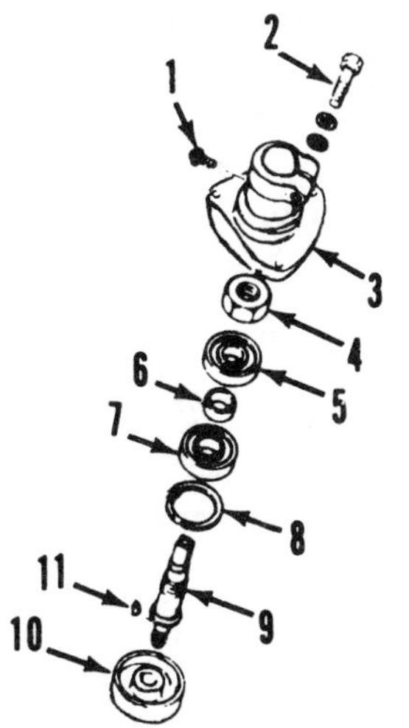

Fig. E59—Exploded view of bearing head typical of the type used on some models.

1. Screw
2. Clamp screw
3. Housing
4. Nut
5. Bearing
6. Spacer
7. Bearing
8. Snap ring
9. Shaft
10. Adapter
11. Key

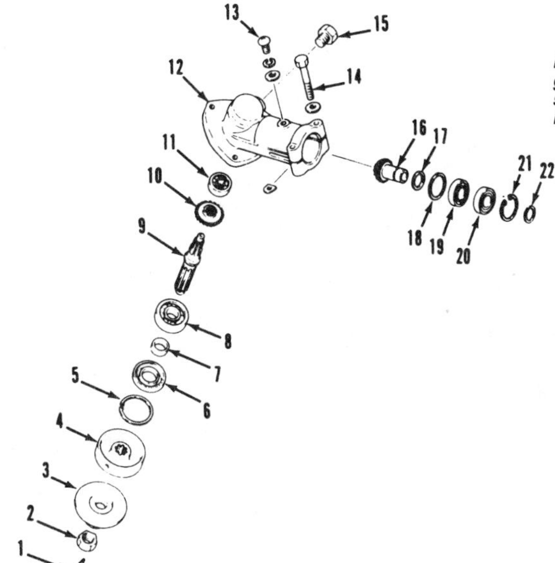

Fig. E61—Exploded view of the gear head assembly used on some models. The arbor shaft (9) is splined to gear (11) and drive plates (3 and 4).

1. Cotter pin
2. Nut
3. Adapter plate
4. Drive plate
5. Snap ring
6. Seal
7. Spacer
8. Bearing
9. Arbor shaft
10. Gear
11. Bearing
12. Housing
13. Fitting screw
14. Clamp bolt
15. Lubrication check plug
16. Gear
17. Spacer
18. Spacer
19. Bearing
20. Bearing
21. Snap ring
22. Snap ring

Illustrations courtesy Echo Inc.

ECHO

GASOLINE POWERED HEDGE CLIPPERS AND POWER BLOWERS

Model	Engine Manufacturer	Engine Displacement
HC-140	Echo/Kioritz	13.8 cc (0.842 cu. in.)
HC-160	Echo/Kioritz	16.0 cc (0.976 cu. in.)
HC-200, HC-210E	Echo/Kioritz	21.2 cc (1.294 cu. in.)
HC-1000, HC-1001	Echo/Kioritz	21.2 cc (1.294 cu. in.)
HC-1500, HC-1600	Echo/Kioritz	21.2 cc (1.294 cu. in.)
HC-2000, HC-2100, HC-2400, HC-2401	Echo/Kioritz	23.6 cc (1.440 cu. in.)
PB-200, PB-202, PB-210E	Echo/Kioritz	21.2 cc (1.294 cu. in.)
PB-300E	Echo/Kioritz	30.8 cc (1.88 cu. in.)
PB-1000 & PB-1010	Echo/Kioritz	21.2 cc (1.294 cu. in.)

ENGINE INFORMATION

Echo or Kioritz two-stroke air-cooled gasoline engines are used. Identify the engine by displacement and refer to the ECHO or KIORITZ Engine Service section of this manual. Some differences may be noted between the engines used on this equipment and the engines described in the service section.

FUEL MIXTURE

The manufacturer recommends mixing ECHO 2-Cycle oil with regular or unleaded gasoline at a ratio of 32:1. A good quality 2-stroke engine oil designed for air-cooled two-stroke engines can be used a ratio of 25:1. The manufacturer discourages the use of gasoline containing alcohol.

CARBURETOR

Walbro WA, Walbro WT, Walbro WY, Walbro WYL and Zama C1U diaphragm carburetors or Kehin float type carburetors have been used on these models. The manufacturer's name and model number is stamped on the carburetor. Refer to CARBURETOR section in the appropriate following Engine Service Section for tuning and service information. Refer to the table on the following page for original application and initial mixture settings.

Initial setting of the idle-speed mixture needle of models idicated by * is set by counting the turns IN (clockwise) after threads of the needle just engage carburetor body. Initial setting for other models is set by counting the turns OUT from lightly seated position.

HEDGE CLIPPER

Drive for the clippers consists of eccentrics that cause the two blades to reciprocate in opposite directions.

Refer to Fig. E75 for an exploded view of a typical HC model hedge clipper. The engine crankshaft is perpendicular to the cutting blades. The pinion of the clutch drum (15) drives the gear and eccentric (5). Connecting rods (4) transfer the movement of the eccentric to the cutters (8 and 9). The gear case should be 2/3 full of multipurpose lithium base grease.

Refer to Fig. E76 for an exploded view of a typical shaft drive hedge clipper. The cutter is driven by an engine with the crankshaft parallel to the cutting blades. Bevel pinion (21), connected to the engine drive shaft, drives gear (14) that is attached to the drive pinion (12). Pinion (12) drives gears and eccentrics (3 and 7). The eccentric operates within the cam at the end of each cutting blade (4 and 6) to move the cutter. When assembling, gears (3 and 7) must be installed so the blades move in opposite directions. When the top blade is fully extended, the lower blade must be back as far as possible. The gear case should be 2/3 full of multipurpose lithium base grease.

POWER BLOWER

The blower fan (4—Fig. E77) is attached directly to the engine crankshaft. Disassembly procedure will depend upon the model and the service required. The fan can be removed after removing the fan case (6) and nut (1). The engine can be unbolted and removed from the housing (7) after removing the cover (16).

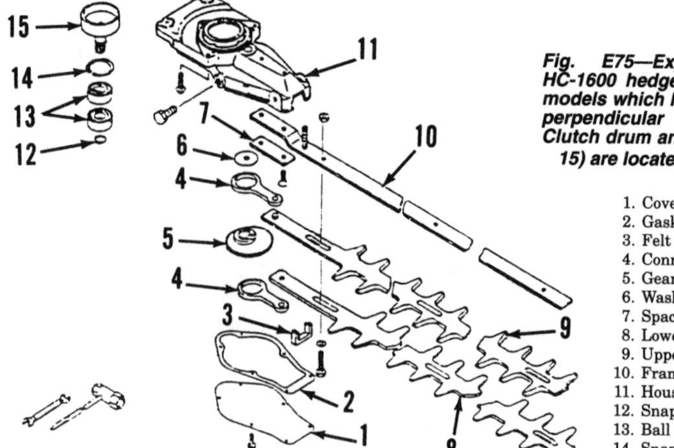

Fig. E75—Exploded view of HC-1600 hedge clipper typical of models which have the crankshaft perpendicular to the cutters. Clutch drum and bearings (13 and 15) are located in housing (11).

1. Cover
2. Gasket
3. Felt
4. Connecting rods
5. Gear and eccentric
6. Washer
7. Spacer
8. Lower cutter
9. Upper cutter
10. Frame bar
11. Housing
12. Snap ring
13. Ball bearings
14. Snap ring
15. Drum and pinion

Illustrations courtesy Echo Inc.

	Carburetor Model	Low-speed Needle	High-speed Needle
HC-140	Walbro WA-89	1 1/8	1 1/4
HC-160	Walbro WA-89	1 1/8	1 1/4
HC-160A	Walbro WA-89	1 1/8	1 1/4
HC-200	Walbro WA-91	1 1/8	N/A
	Walbro WA-91A	1 1/8	N/A
	Walbro WA-91B	1 1/8	1 1/4
HC-210E	Walbro WA-148	1	1
	Walbro WA-148A	1	1
HC-1000	Zama C1U-K7	1	1
HC-1001	Walbro WYL-3	12*	...
	Walbro WYL-7	12*	...
	Walbro WYL-11	12*	...
HC-1500	Zama C1U-K17	1 1/4	1
HC-1600	Walbro WT-168	1 1/8	1/2
	Walbro WT-168A	1 1/4	1/2
	Zama C1U-K18	1	½
HC-2000	Zama C1U-K18	1	1/2

	Carburetor Model	Low-speed Needle	High-speed Needle
HC-2100 & HC-2300	Zama C1U-K13	1	1
	Zama C1U-K18	1	1/2
	Walbro WT-168	1 1/8	1/2
	Walbro WT-168A	1 1/4	1/2
HC-2400	Zama C1U-K31	1 1/4	7/8-1
HC-2410	Zama C1U-K31	1 1/4	7/8-1
PB-200	Walbro WA-66	1	1
PB-202	Kehin float	...	...
PB-210E	Walbro WA-157	1 1/4	1 1/4
PB-300E	Walbro WA-162	1 1/4	1 1/4
PB-1000	Zama C1U-K11	1 1/8	1 1/8
	Zama C1U-K14	1 1/8	1 1/8
	Zama C1U-K26	1 1/8	1
PB-1010	Zama C1U-K11	1 1/8	1 1/8
	Zama C1U-K14	1 1/8	1 1/8
	Zama C1U-K26	1 1/8	1

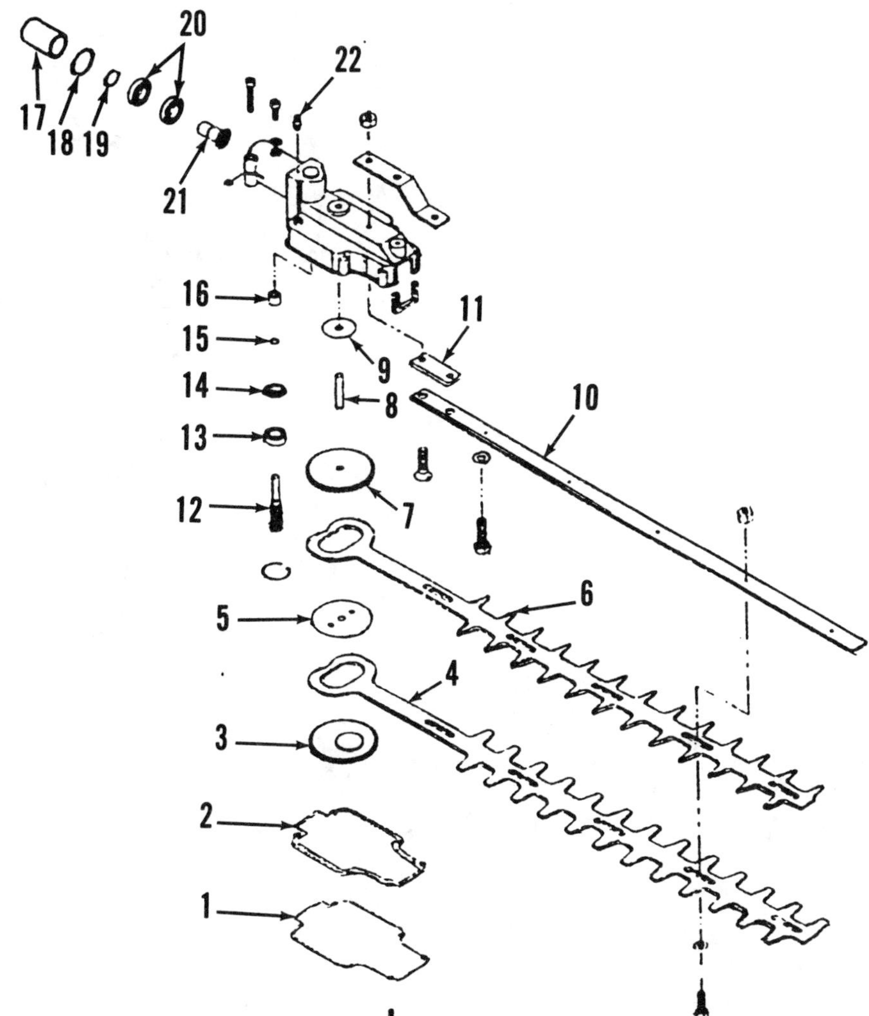

Fig. E76—Exploded view of SHC-1700 hedge clipper typical of models which have the engine crankshaft parallel to the cutters. The engine drives pinion gear (21).

1. Cover
2. Gasket
3. Lower gear and eccentric
4. Cutter and cam
5. Washer
6. Cutter and cam
7. Upper gear and eccentric
8. Gear shaft
9. Washer
10. Frame bar
11. Spacer
12. Spur pinion
13. Ball bearing
14. Bevel pinion
15. Snap ring
16. Needle bearing
17. Adapter collar
18. Snap ring
19. Snap ring
20. Ball bearings
21. Bevel drive gear
22. Grease fitting

ENGINE CONTROLS

The throttle control and the engine stop switch are located in or near the handle. Refer to Fig. E77, Fig. E78 or Fig. E79 for views of controls typical of most models.

RECOIL STARTER

Refer to Fig. E77 or Fig. E80 for an exploded view of typical recoil starters. Unbolt and remove the starter from the engine. Remove the rope handle and allow the rope to wind into the starter. Remove the center screw (29—Fig. E77 or 7—Fig. E80) and the pulley. The spring (33—Fig. E77 or 11—Fig. E80) may rewind uncontrollably causing injury. Wear appropriate safety eye wear and gloves before removing the recoil spring from the housing.

To remove the pawl plate (6—Fig. E80) from models so equipped, unscrew the lock nut and the pawl plate from the engine crankshaft. Remove the clip (12) from the front of the pawl to remove the pawl and spring (1 and 2). Install the pawl plate and tighten it to 8-10 N•m (70-90 in.-lb.) torque. Tighten the lock nut to 16-17.5 N•m (140-155 in.-lb.) torque.

On some models, the starter pawl (24—Fig. E77) is located on the flywheel. The spring (23) should cause the pawl to engage the starter pulley until the engine starts.

To assemble the starter, lubricate the center post and spring side of the housing with light grease. Attach the outer end of the spring to the clip in the housing, then wind the spring into the housing. Wind the spring in the correct direction, depending upon engine rotation, until the spring is completely in the housing cavity. The inner end of the

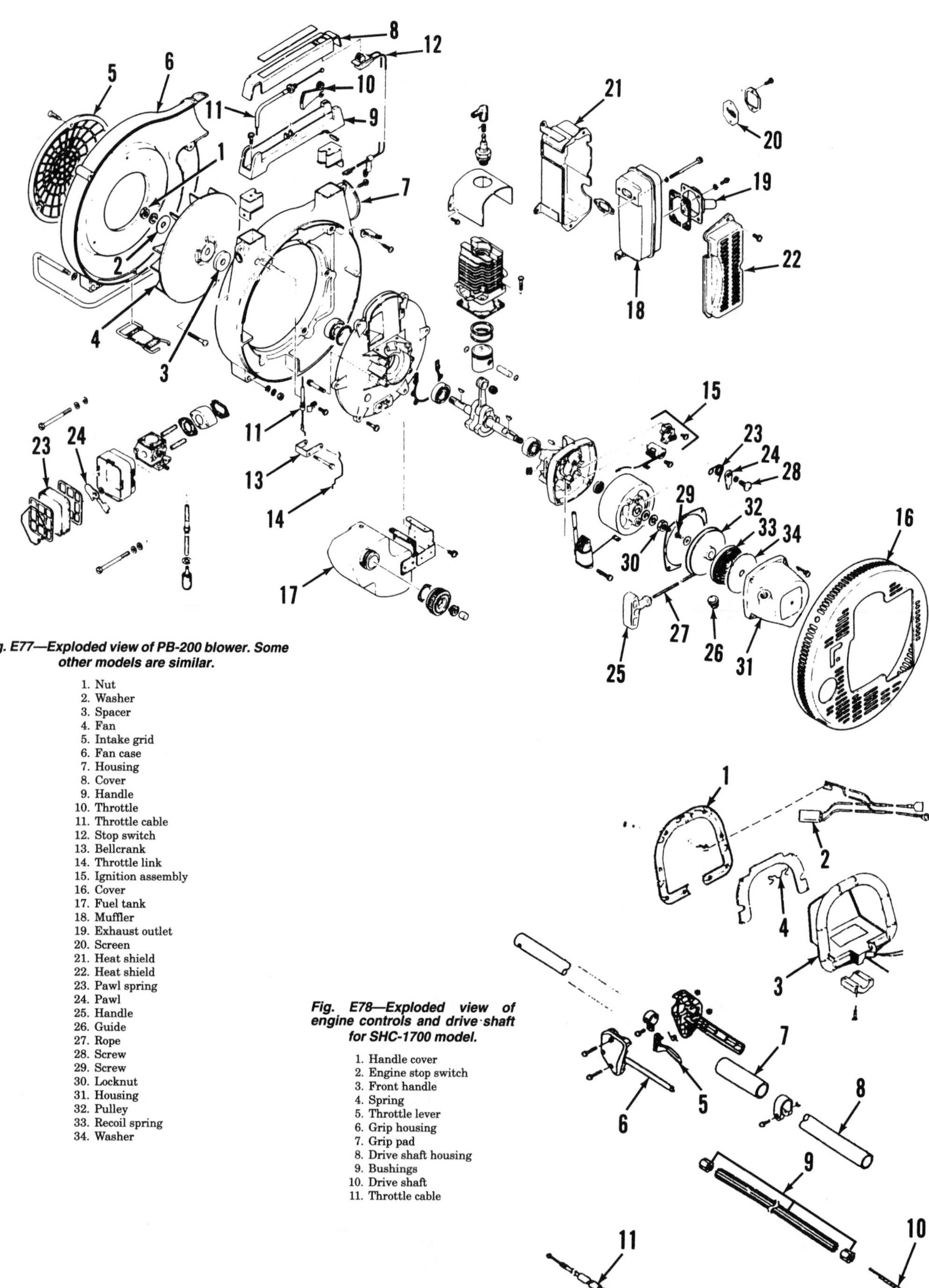

Fig. E77—Exploded view of PB-200 blower. Some other models are similar.

1. Nut
2. Washer
3. Spacer
4. Fan
5. Intake grid
6. Fan case
7. Housing
8. Cover
9. Handle
10. Throttle
11. Throttle cable
12. Stop switch
13. Bellcrank
14. Throttle link
15. Ignition assembly
16. Cover
17. Fuel tank
18. Muffler
19. Exhaust outlet
20. Screen
21. Heat shield
22. Heat shield
23. Pawl spring
24. Pawl
25. Handle
26. Guide
27. Rope
28. Screw
29. Screw
30. Locknut
31. Housing
32. Pulley
33. Recoil spring
34. Washer

Fig. E78—Exploded view of engine controls and drive shaft for SHC-1700 model.

1. Handle cover
2. Engine stop switch
3. Front handle
4. Spring
5. Throttle lever
6. Grip housing
7. Grip pad
8. Drive shaft housing
9. Bushings
10. Drive shaft
11. Throttle cable

Illustrations courtesy Echo Inc.

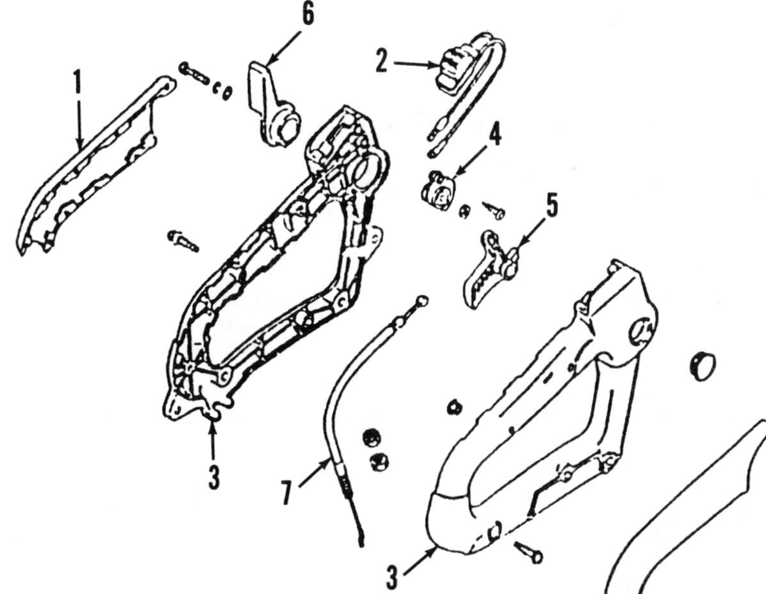

Fig. E79—Exploded view of the handle and engine controls for PB-2400 model.

1. Handle grip
2. Engine stop switch
3. Handle
4. Throttle bracket
5. Throttle lever
6. Throttle lever
7. Throttle cable

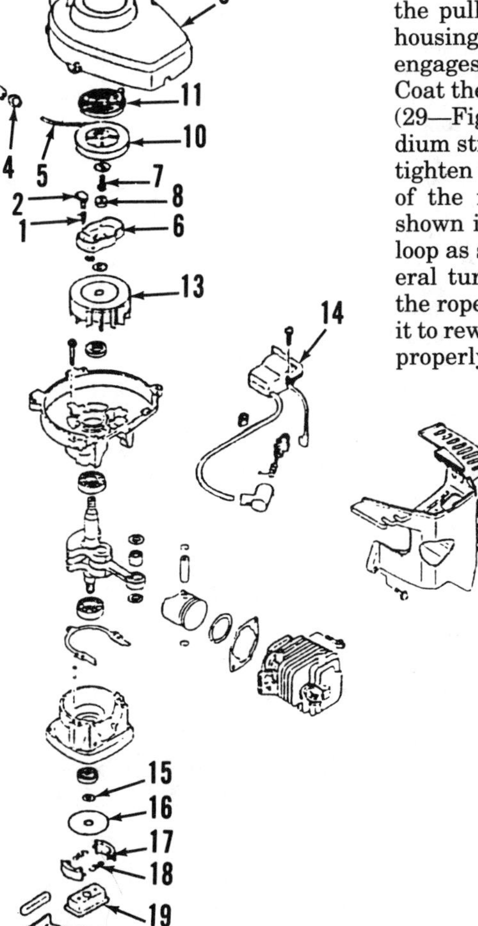

Fig. E80—Exploded view of the recoil starter and engine assembly used on HC-1600 models.

1. Pawl spring
2. Pawl
3. Handle
4. Guide
5. Rope
6. Pawl carrier
7. Screw
8. Locknut
9. Housing
10. Pulley
11. Recoil spring
12. Snap ring
13. Flywheel
14. Ignition coil
15. Spacer
16. Washer
17. Clutch shoe
18. Spring
19. Clutch hub

spring should nearly contact the center post.

Attach the rope to the pulley (32—Fig. E77 or 10—Fig. E80), thread the rope through the housing and guide, then attach the handle. Install the pulley over the center post of the housing while making sure the pulley engages the end of the rewind spring. Coat the threads of the retaining screw (29—Fig. E77 or 7—Fig. E80) with medium strength Loctite, then install and tighten the screw securely. Form a loop of the rope at the pulley's notch as shown in Fig. E81, then hold the rope loop as shown and wind the pulley several turns to preload the spring. Pull the rope out with the handle and allow it to rewind. If the rope does not rewind properly, pull a loop in the rope as shown in Fig. E81 and preload the spring another turn.

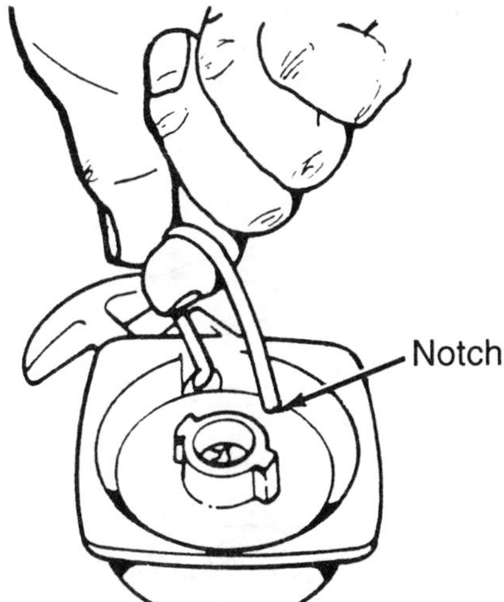

Fig. E81—To set the preload of the starter recoil spring, pull a loop in the rope with the rope in the notch in the pulley, then wind the pulley as necessary. When the rope is released, it will pull out of the notch.

NOTE: If the rope is too long, it will bind before rewinding properly. Make sure the rope is not binding.

To make sure the spring is not tightened too much, pull the rope out completely, then turn the pulley an additional 1/2 turn. If the rope cannot be pulled out completely, the spring is bound and will break. Pull a loop in the rope as shown in Fig. E81 and loosen the spring slightly as required. A proper setting will allow the rope to be fully extended and will also wind the rope onto the pulley fully.

ELLIOT

GASOLINE POWERED STRING TRIMMERS

Model	Engine Manufacturer	Engine Model	Displacement
Tiger 4100	Kioritz	.....	16.0 cc
Tiger 4200	Kioritz	.....	21.2 cc

ENGINE INFORMATION

All Models

All Elliot trimmer models listed are equipped with Kioritz two-stroke air-cooled gasoline engines. Identify engine model by trimmer model or engine displacement. Refer to KIORITZ ENGINE SERVICE section of this manual.

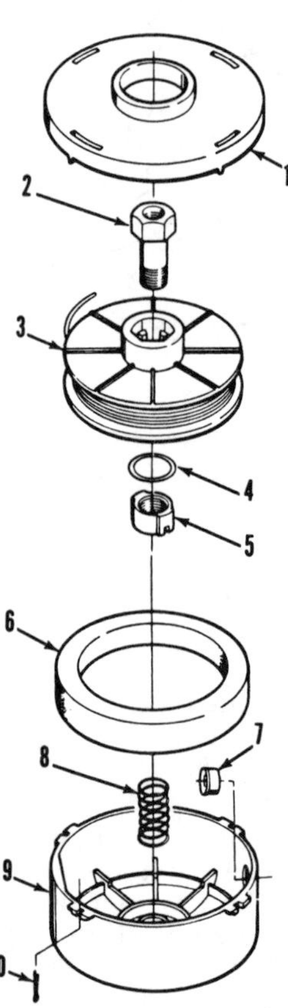

Fig. EL10—Exploded view of single strand semi-automatic trimmer head used on Tiger 4100 model.

1. Cover
2. Drive adapter
3. Spool
4. "O" ring
5. Drive adapter nut
6. Foam pad
7. Line guide
8. Spring
9. Housing
10. Cotter pin

FUEL MIXTURE

All Models

Manufacturer recommends mixing regular grade gasoline (unleaded is an acceptable substitute) with a good quality two-stroke air-cooled engine oil at a 25:1 ratio. Do not use fuel containing alcohol.

STRING TRIMMER

Tiger 4100 Model

Tiger 4100 model is equipped with a single strand semi-automatic trimmer head shown in Fig. EL10. Line may be manually advanced with engine stopped by pushing in on housing (9) while pulling on line. Procedure may have to be repeated to obtain desired line length. To advance line with engine running, operate engine at full rpm and tap housing (9) on the ground. Each time housing is tapped on the ground, a measured amount of trimmer line will be advanced.

To renew trimmer line, remove cotter key (10) and twist housing (9) counterclockwise to remove housing. Remove foam pad (6) and any remaining line on spool (3). Clean spool and inside of housing. Cut off approximately 25 feet (7.6 m) of 0.080 inch (2 mm) monofilament line and tape one end of line to spool (Fig. EL12). Wind line on spool in direction indicated by arrow on spool (Fig. EL13). Install foam pad with line end protruding from between foam pad and spool as shown in Fig. EL13. Insert line end through line guide and install housing and spring assembly on spool. Push in on housing and twist housing in a clockwise direction to lock into position. Install cotter key through hole in housing and cover.

Tiger 4200 Model

Tiger 4200 model is equipped with a single strand semi-automatic trimmer head shown in Fig. EL11. Line may be manually advanced with engine stopped by pushing in on housing (12) while pulling on line. Procedure may have to be repeated until desired line length is obtained. To advance line with engine running, operate trimmer engine at full rpm and tap housing (12) on the ground. Each time housing is tapped on the ground, a measured amount of trimmer line is advanced.

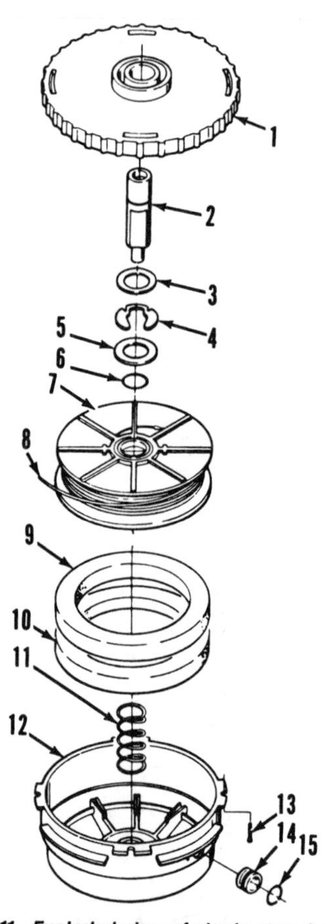

Fig. EL11—Exploded view of single strand semi-automatic trimmer head used on Tiger 4200 model.

1. Cover
2. Drive adapter
3. Washer
4. Retainer
5. Washer
6. Retainer ring
7. Spool
8. Line
9. Foam pad
10. Foam pad
11. Spring
12. Housing
13. Cotter pin
14. Line guide
15. Retainer

To renew trimmer line, remove cotter pin (13). Twist housing (12) counterclockwise and remove housing. Remove foam pads (9 and 10) and any remaining line from spool (7). Clean spool and inner area of housing. Cut off approximately 25 feet (7.6 m) of 0.080 inch (2 mm) monofilament line and tape one end of line to spool (Fig. EL12). Wind line on spool in direction indicated by arrow on spool (Fig. EL14). Install foam pads (9 and 10—Fig. EL11) so line is protruding from center of foam pads (Fig. EL 14). Insert end of line through line guide and install spool, housing and spring. Push in on housing and twist housing in a clockwise direction to lock in position and install cotter pin (13—Fig. EL11).

DRIVE SHAFT

All Models

All models are equipped with a flexible drive shaft enclosed in the drive shaft housing tube. Drive shaft has squared ends which engage adapters at each end. Drive shaft should be removed for maintenance at 50 hour intervals of use. Remove screw (4—Fig. EL15) and bolt (3) at bearing head housing and separate bearing head from drive shaft housing. Pull flexible drive shaft from housing.

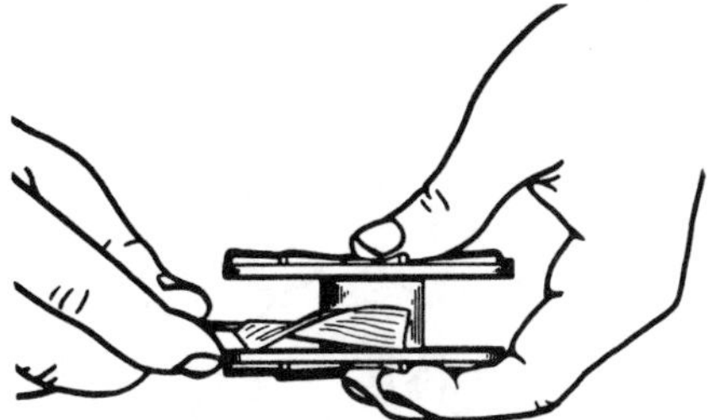

Fig. EL12—Tape one end of new line to center of spool as shown.

Lubricate drive shaft with lithium base grease and reinstall in housing with end that was previously at clutch end, at bearing head end. Reversing drive shaft ends extends drive shaft life. Make certain ends of drive shaft properly engage upper and lower square drive adapters when installing.

BEARING HEAD

All Models

All models are equipped with the bearing head shown in Fig. EL15. Bearing head is equipped with sealed bearings and requires no regular maintenance. To disassemble bearing head, remove trimmer head assembly and cup washer (13). Remove screw (4) and bolt (3) and separate bearing head from drive shaft housing tube. Remove trimmer head assembly and cup washer (13). Remove snap ring (10) and use a suitable puller to remove arbor shaft (11) and bearing assembly. Remove nut (6) and press bearings (7 and 9) and spacer (8) from arbor shaft as required.

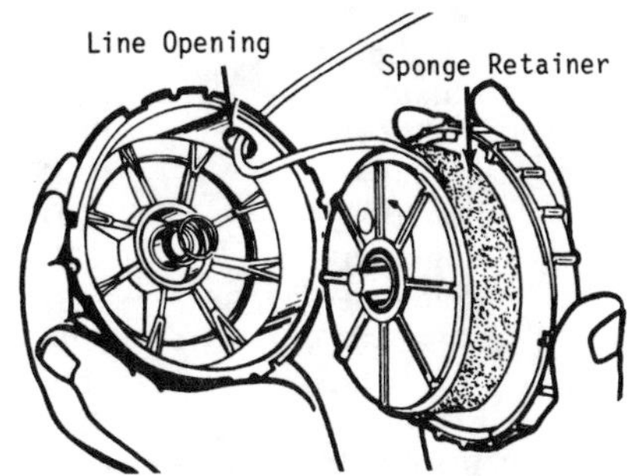

Fig. EL13—Install foam pad with line protruding between pad and spool as shown. Wind line in direction indicated by arrow on spool.

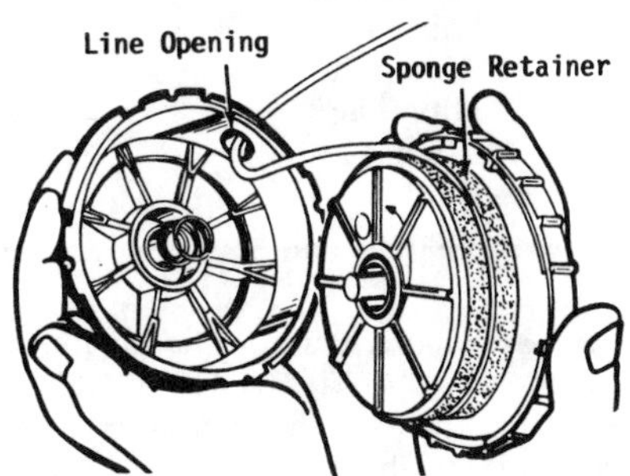

Fig. EL14—Install foam pads with line protruding from between pads. Wind line in direction indicated by arrow on spool.

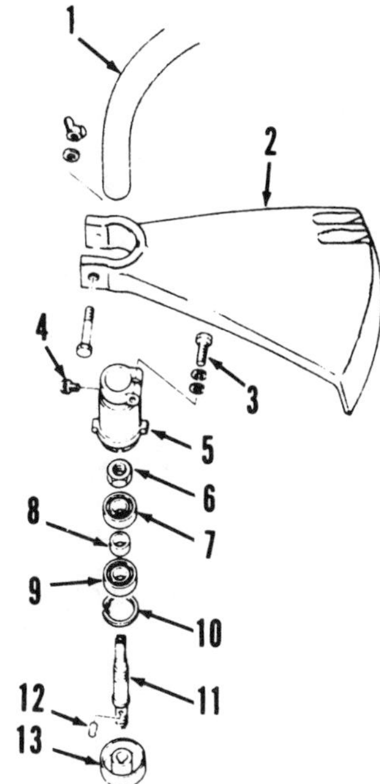

Fig. EL15—Exploded view of bearing head used on all models. Bearings (7 and 9) are sealed bearings and require no regular maintenance.

1. Drive shaft housing
2. Shield
3. Bolt
4. Screw
5. Housing
6. Nut
7. Bearing
8. Spacer
9. Bearing
10. Snap ring
11. Arbor (output) shaft
12. Pin
13. Cup washer

GREEN MACHINE

GASOLINE POWERED STRING TRIMMERS

Model	Engine Manufacturer	Engine Model	Displacement
1600	PPP	99D	31.0 cc
1730	Komatsu	G2E	25.4 cc
1800	PPP	99D	31.0 cc
1930	McCulloch	...	21.2 cc
1940	McCulloch	...	21.2 cc
2130	McCulloch	...	21.2 cc
2200	Komatsu	G2E	25.4 cc
2230	PPP	99E	31.0 cc
2340	Komatsu	G2E	25.4 cc
2500LP	Komatsu	G2D	22.5 cc
2510LP	Komatsu	G2D	22.5 cc
2540LP	Komatsu	G2D	22.5 cc
2800	Mitsubishi	T140	24.1 cc
2840	Mitsubishi	T140	24.1 cc
3000LP	Komatsu	G2K	25.4 cc
3000M	Mitsubishi	T140	24.1 cc
3000SS	Shindaiwa	...	24.1 cc
3010M	Mitsubishi	T140	24.1 cc
3040M	Mitsubishi	T140	24.1 cc
3540	Shindaiwa	...	24.1 cc
4000LP	Komatsu	G4K	41.5 cc
4000M	Mitsubishi	T200	40.6 cc
4500LP	Komatsu	G4K	41.5 cc

ENGINE INFORMATION

The models in this section are equipped with Komatsu, McCulloch, Mitsubishi, Piston Powered Products (PPP) or Shindaiwa engines. Refer to appropriate engine service section for engine service information.

FUEL MIXTURE

Manufacturer recommends mixing regular-grade gasoline, leaded or unleaded, with HMC One-Mix two-stroke engine oil mixed as indicated on container. Fuel:oil ratio should be 25:1 (5.12 ounces of oil to one U.S. gallon of gasoline) when using any other two-stroke oil, regardless of recommended ratio on oil container. Gasohol or other alcohol blended fuels are not approved by manufacturer.

STRING TRIMMER

All Models except 2200 and 3000SS

All models except 2200 and 3000SS may be equipped with the dual strand, semi-automatic trimmer head (Tap-For-Cord) shown in Figs. GM10 or GM11. To extend line with trimmer engine stopped, push in on spool button and pull line ends out to desired length. To extend line with trimmer engine running, run engine at full rpm and tap spool button against the ground. Each time button is tapped a measured amount of line is advanced.

To renew trimmer line, refer to Fig. GM10. Push in on the two lock tabs on cap (10) and remove cap and spool. Remove any remaining line on spool. Clean spool, cap and inner cavity of housing. Refer to following table for line length and diameter:

	Line Length	Line Diameter
1600, 1730, 1800, 1930, 1940, 2130, 2230	15 ft. (4.6 m)	0.080 in. (2 mm)
2340, 2500LP, 2510LP,2540LP, 2800, 2840, 3540	30 ft. (9.2 m)	0.080 in. (2 mm)

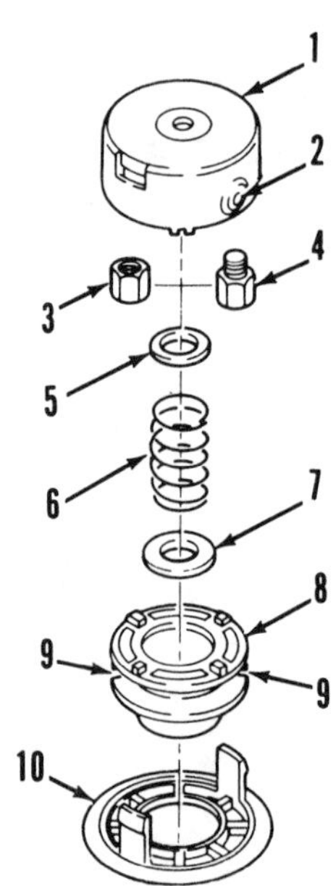

Fig. GM10—Exploded view of dual strand, semi-automatic (Tap-For-Cord) trimmer head used on most models except 2200 and 3000SS. Refer also to Fig. GM11. Note that only one adapter (3 or 4) is used according to model.

1. Housing
2. Line guides
3. Adapter
4. Adapter
5. Washer
6. Spring
7. Washer
8. Spool
9. Line notch
10. Cap

3000LP, 3000M, 3010M, 3040M	50 ft. (15.2 m)	0.095 in. (2.4 mm)
4000LP, 4000M, 4500LP....	40 ft. (12.2 m)	0.105 in. (2.6 mm)

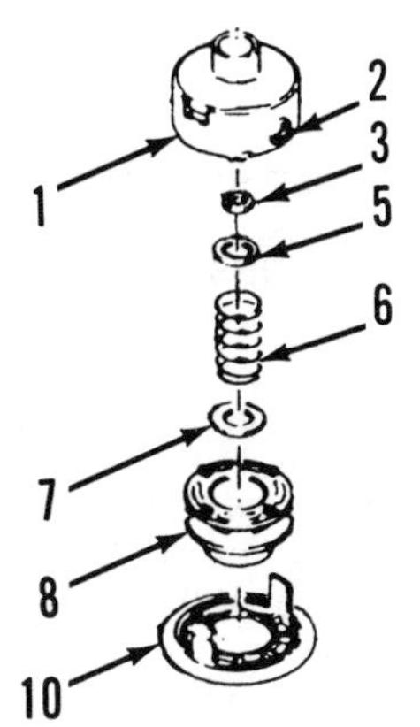

Fig. GM11—Exploded view of trimmer head used on some models that is similar to head shown in Fig. GM10. Note difference in housing and lack of adapter (3 or 4—Fig. GM10).

1. Housing
2. Line guides
3. Pal nut
5. Washer
6. Spring
7. Washer
8. Spool
10. Cap

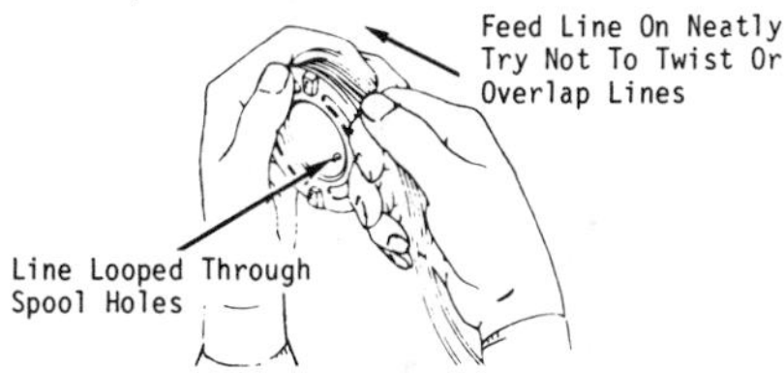

Fig. GM12—Rotate spool to wind line in direction indicated by arrow on spool.

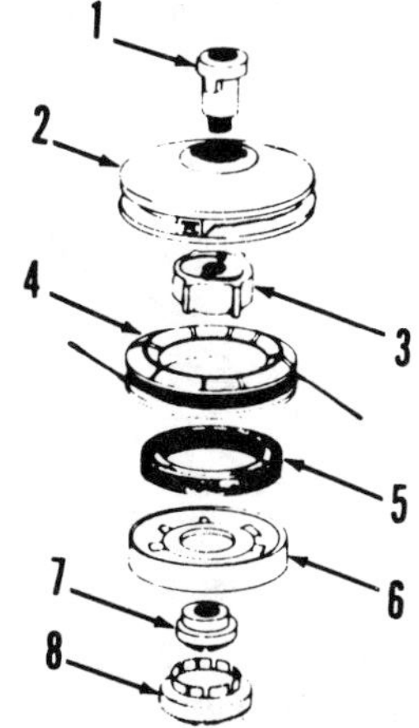

Fig. GM13—Exploded view of dual strand, semi-automatic trimmer head used on Model 2200.

1. Adapter
2. Upper housing
3. Cam
4. Spool
5. Foam pad
6. Lower housing
7. Screw (L.H.)
8. Button

Loop one end of new line through the two holes in spool (Fig. GM12) and rotate spool so line is wound tightly and neatly in direction indicated by arrow on spool. Slip lines into notches in spool (8—Fig. GM10 or GM11), insert line ends through line guides (2) and install spool in housing. Align locking tabs of trimmer head cap (10) with notches in housing (1) and snap cap onto housing. Advance line manually to make certain line is free.

Model 2200

Model 2200 is equipped with a dual strand, semi-automatic trimmer head shown in Fig. GM13. To extend line with trimmer engine stopped, pull on lines while pushing in on button (8). To extend line with engine running, operate trimmer engine at full rpm and tap button on the ground. Each time button is tapped a measured amount of new line will be advanced.

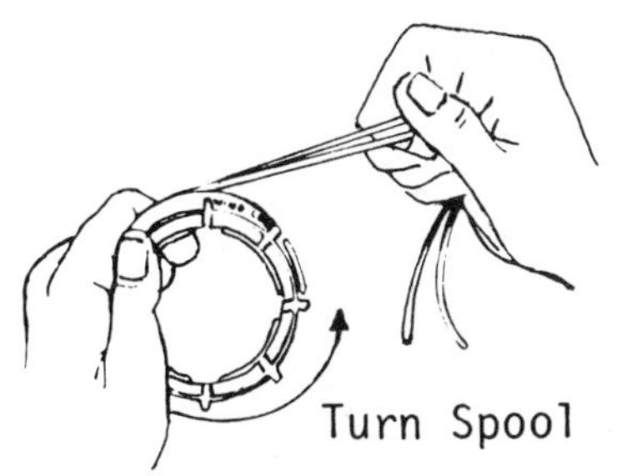

Fig. GM14—Rotate spool to wind line in direction indicated by arrow on spool.

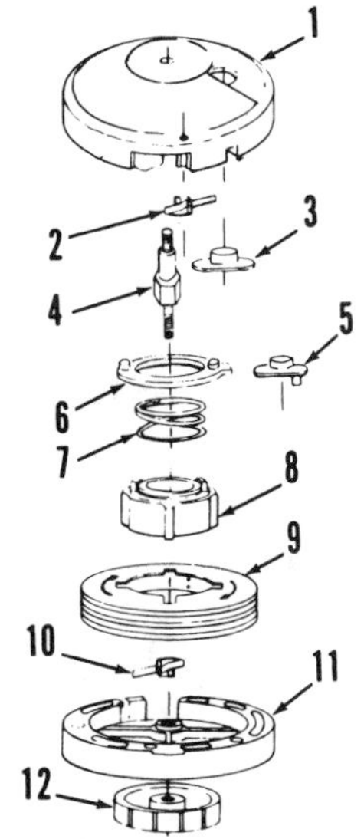

Fig. GM15—Exploded view of trimmer head used on Model 3000SS. Trimmer head may be manual line feed or semi-automatic line feed according to parts installed. Note parts designated (TFC) are for semi-automatic line feed heads and parts designated (M) are for manual line feed heads.

1. Upper housing
2. Line saver
3. Button (M)
4. Arbor
5. Button (TFC)
6. Lock ring (M)
7. Spring
8. Cam
9. Spool
10. Line saver
11. Lower housing
12. Lock knob

To renew line, unsnap button (8) from screw (7). Note that screw has left-hand threads. Remove screw (7), cover (6) and spool (4). Remove any remaining line from spool. Clean spool, cover and housing (2). Cut two 10-ft. (3.9 m) lengths of 0.080-in. (2 mm) diameter monofilament line. Insert one end of each line into each of the two holes in spool. Rotate spool to wind line evenly in direction indicated by arrow on spool (Fig. GM14). Install foam pad (5—Fig. GM13). Insert line ends through line guides and reinstall spool into housing. Spool is installed so side of spool with arrow will be towards the ground. Install cover, screw and snap button onto screw.

Model 3000SS

Model 3000SS may be equipped with trimmer head shown in Fig. GM15. Trimmer head may be a manual line feed or a semi-automatic (Tap-For-Cord) line feed according to model.

To extend line on manual models, stop trimmer engine. Loosen lock knob (12) and pull line ends out of housing until desired line length is obtained.

To extend line on semi-automatic trimmer head with engine stopped, push in on lock knob (12) while pulling lines from housing. Procedure may have to be repeated until desired line length has been obtained. To extend line with engine running, operate trimmer engine at full rpm and tap lock knob on the ground. Each time lock knob is tapped on the ground a measured amount of new line will be advanced.

To renew line on either model, remove lock knob (12—Fig. GM15) (note that lock knob has left-hand threads), cover (11) and spool (9). Remove any remaining line from spool. Clean spool, cover and inner cavity of housing (1). Cut two 20-ft. (6.1 m) lengths of 0.095-in. (2.4 mm) diameter monofilament line. Insert one end of each line into each of the two holes in inside wall of spool. Rotate spool to wind lines in direction indicated by arrow on spool (Fig. GM16). Insert line ends through line guides and install spool into upper housing with notched

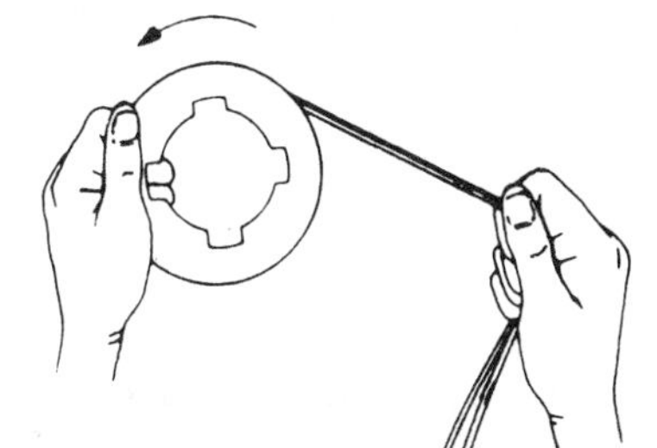

Fig. GM16—Rotate spool to wind line in direction indicated by arrow on spool.

side towards housing. Install cover and lock knob.

BLADE

All Models So Equipped

Some models may be equipped with one of the blades shown in Fig. GM17. To install blade, assemble parts in sequence shown in Fig. GM18. Note that screw (7) has left-hand threads. Make certain splines in cup washers (2 and 4) are aligned with splines on arbor and cup washer (4) is seated squarely.

DRIVE SHAFT

Curved Shaft Models

Models with a curved drive shaft housing tube are equipped with a flexible drive shaft. The drive shaft should be removed, cleaned and lubricated with lithium-base grease after every 10 hours of operation. Mark ends of drive shaft during removal so drive shaft can be reinstalled with ends in original position. The drive shaft cable may be wound for rotation in one direction only.

Straight Shaft Models

Models with a straight drive shaft housing tube may be equipped with a wire-wound shaft or a solid shaft. Periodic maintenance is not required. If shaft is removed, lubricate with lithium-based grease before installation.

On some models the bushings (5—Fig. GM20) in the drive shaft housing (6) are renewable. A bushing removal and installation tool is available that is marked for correct locations of bushings. If tool is not available, mark locations of old bushings before removal so new bushings can be installed in correct location.

BEARING HEAD

Models 1600, 1730 and 1930

Models 1600, 1730 and 1930 are equipped with the bearing head shown in Fig. GM21. Bearing head requires no regular maintenance. A bearing kit (part 160305) is available for bearing head repair.

BEARING HEAD/LOWER CLUTCH

Model 1800

Model 1800 is equipped with a bearing head incorporated in the lower clutch unit (Fig. GM22). Bearing head is equipped with sealed bearings and requires no regular maintenance.

To renew bearings or remove clutch assembly, remove trimmer head and cup washer (15). Remove the three bolts retaining bearing plate (11) to housing (4). Separate housing from bearing plate. Remove clutch shoe assembly (6) as required. Remove clutch drum (7) and shield (5). Press arbor shaft (8) from bearings. Remove snap rings (9 and 14). Remove bearings (10 and 13) and spacer (12).

GEAR HEAD

Split Gear Housing

Some models are equipped with a gear head that has a split housing (2 and 18—Fig. GM23). Lubricate gear head after every 10 hours of operation. To lubricate gear head, remove trimmer head or blade assembly. Pump a lithium-based grease through fitting on side of head until old grease is forced out. Failure to remove trimmer head or blade prior to lubrication will result in bearing/gear housing damage.

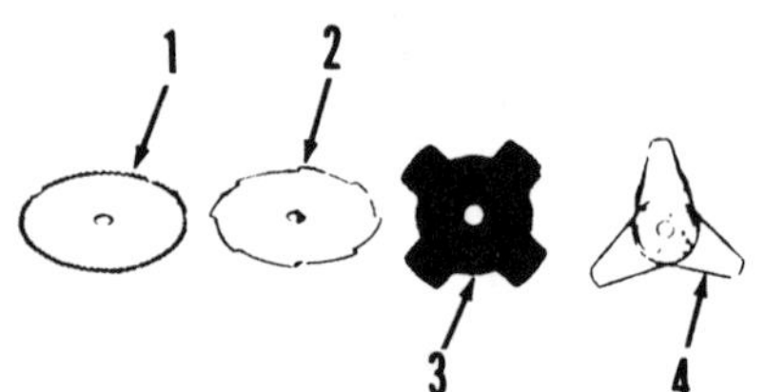

Fig. GM17—A variety of blades are offered for some models.

1. Saw blade
2. Eight-edge blade
3. Four-edge blade
4. Three-edge blade

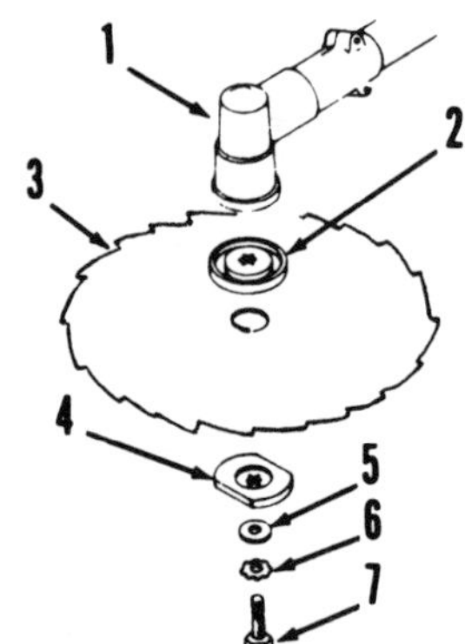

Fig. GM18—Exploded view of blade and attaching parts. Refer to text.

1. Gear head
2. Upper cup washer
3. Blade
4. Lower cup washer
5. Flat washer
6. Lockwasher
7. Screw (L.H.)

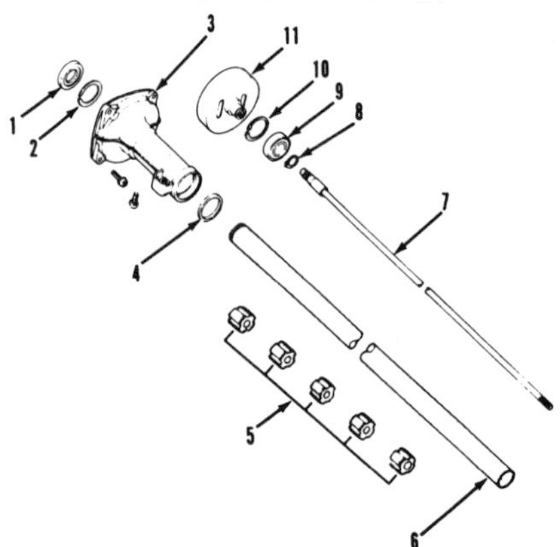

Fig. GM20—Exploded view of drive shaft with renewable bushings.

1. Seal
2. Snap ring
3. Housing
4. Seal
5. Bushings
6. Drive shaft housing
7. Drive shaft
8. Snap ring
9. Bearing
10. Snap ring
11. Clutch drum

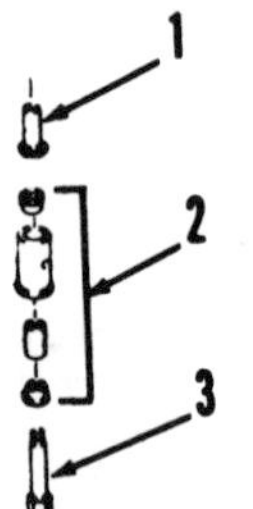

Fig. GM21—Exploded view of lower bearing (bushing) head used on Models 1600, 1730 and 1930.

1. Arbor
2. Bushing kit
3. Arbor

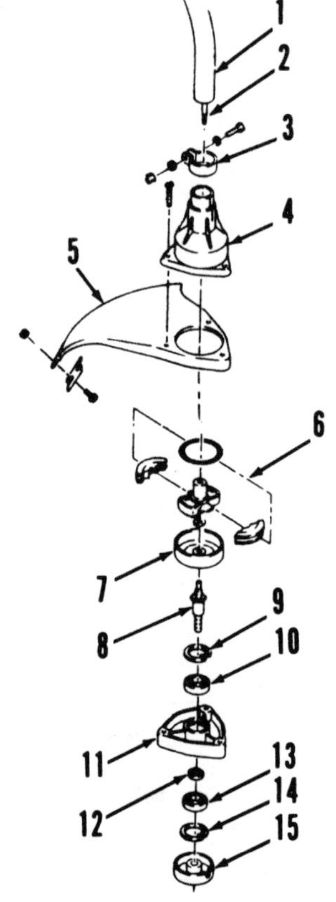

Fig. GM22—Exploded view of lower clutch and bearing head unit used on Model 1800.

1. Drive shaft housing
2. Drive shaft
3. Clamp
4. Housing
5. Shield
6. Clutch assy.
7. Clutch drum
8. Arbor
9. Snap ring
10. Bearing
11. Bearing plate
12. Spacer
13. Bearing
14. Snap ring
15. Upper cup washer

To disassemble gear head, remove trimmer head or blade assembly and separate gear head from drive shaft housing. Remove all bolts (19) and separate gear housing halves (2 and 18). Remove shaft, bearing and gear assemblies. Press bearings and gears from input shaft (14) and arbor (5). Lubricate parts during reassembly and pack housing with lithium-base grease prior to reassembly.

Fig. GM23—Exploded view of a typical gear housing with a split housing.

1. Check plug
2. Housing
3. Bearing
4. Gear
5. Arbor
6. Bearing
7. Seal
8. Spacer
9. Upper cup washer
10. Lower cup washer
11. Flat washer
12. Lockwasher
13. Screw (L.H.)
14. Input shaft
15. Bearing
16. Bearing
17. Snap ring
18. Housing
19. Bolts

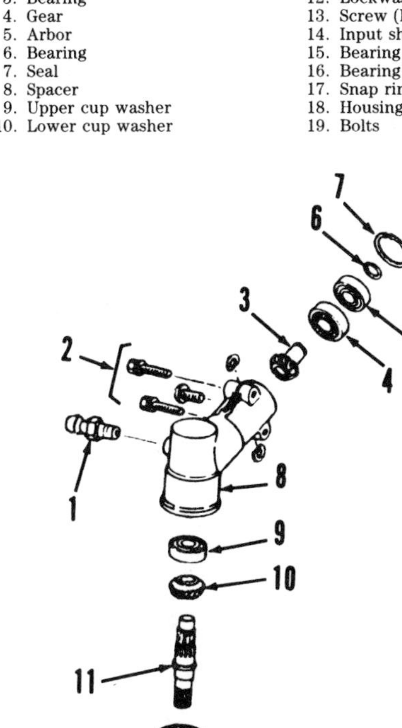

Fig. GM24—Exploded view of typical gear housing with a one-piece housing.

1. Grease fitting
2. Bolts
3. Input shaft
4. Bearing
5. Bearing
6. Snap ring
7. Snap ring
8. Housing
9. Bearing
10. Gear
11. Arbor
12. Bearing
13. Seal
14. Snap ring
15. Spacer
16. Upper cup washer
17. Lower cup washer
18. Flat washer
19. Lockwasher
20. Bolt (L.H.)

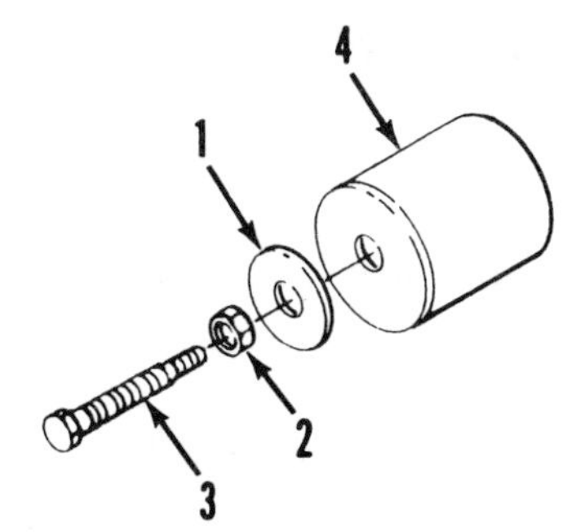

Fig. GM25—Shaft puller is used to pull arbor and input shaft.

1. Washer
2. Nut
3. Bolt
4. Puller body

Fig. GM26—Loosen set screw (S) and move throttle cable to obtain throttle trigger free play of approximately 0.040 inch (1 mm).

Fig. GM27—Loosen jam nut (3) and rotate adjuster nut (4) to obtain throttle trigger free play of approximately 0.040 inch (1 mm). Inner cable (1) slides in outer cable (2).

1. Inner throttle cable
2. Throttle cable housing
3. Jam nut
4. Adjustment nut

One-Piece Gear Housing

Some models are equipped with the one-piece gear housing shown in Fig. GM24. Lubricate gear head after every 30 hours of operation. To lubricate gear head, remove trimmer head or blade assembly. Pump lithium-base grease into grease fitting (1) until grease appears at seal (13) and pushes spacer (15) out. Make certain spacer (15) is pushed back into position and reinstall trimmer head or blade assembly. Failure to remove trimmer head or blade assembly prior to lubrication may result in bearing or housing damage.

To disassemble gear head, remove trimmer head or blade assembly. Separate gear head from drive shaft housing. Remove snap ring (7). Insert a screwdriver or suitable wedge into gear head housing split and carefully expand housing. Remove input shaft (3) and bearings as an assembly. Remove snap ring (6) and press bearings (4 and 5) from input shaft. Remove spacer (15) and snap ring (14). Use a suitable puller (Fig. GM25) to remove arbor (11—Fig. GM24) and bearing assembly. If bearing (9) stays in housing (8), heat housing to 140° F (60° C) and tap housing on a wooden block to remove bearing (9). Press bearing (12) and gear (10) from arbor. Lubricate all parts during reassembly. Pack housing with lithium-base grease prior to installing shaft and bearing assemblies.

THROTTLE TRIGGER AND CABLE

The inner throttle cable should be lubricated with engine oil after every 20 hours of operation.

The throttle cable should be adjusted so there is approximately 0.040-in. (1 mm) throttle trigger free play. To adjust free play, refer to Figs. GM26, GM27 or GM28, depending on type of carburetor, and reposition adjuster as needed.

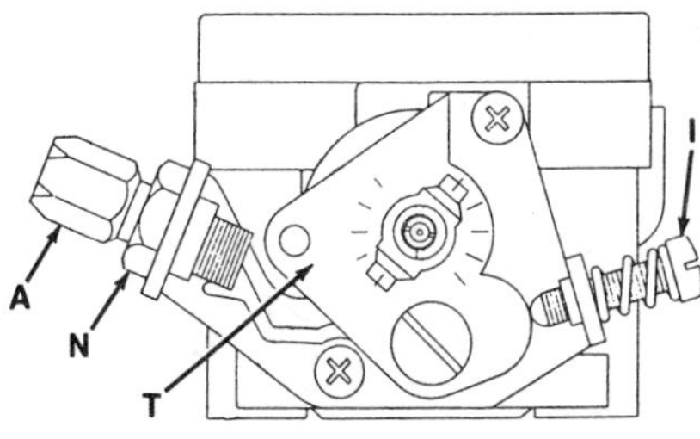

Fig. GM28—Loosen jam nut (N) and rotate adjuster nut (A) to obtain throttle trigger free play of approximately 0.040 inch (1 mm).

A. Cable adjuster nut
I. Idle speed adjustment screw
N. Jam nut
T. Throttle lever

GREEN MACHINE

GASOLINE POWERED BLOWERS

Model	Engine Manufacturer	Engine Model	Displacement
2600	Komatsu	G2D	22.5 cc
4600LP	Komatsu	...	41.5 cc

ENGINE INFORMATION

The models in this section are equipped with a Komatsu engine. Refer to Komatsu engine service section for engine service information.

FUEL MIXTURE

Manufacturer recommends mixing regular grade gasoline, leaded or unleaded, with HMC One-Mix two-stroke engine oil mixed as indicated on container. Fuel:oil ratio should be 25:1 (5.12 ounces oil mixed with one U.S. gallon of gasoline) when using any other two-stroke oil, regardless of recommended ratio on oil container. Gasohol or other alcohol blended fuels are not approved.

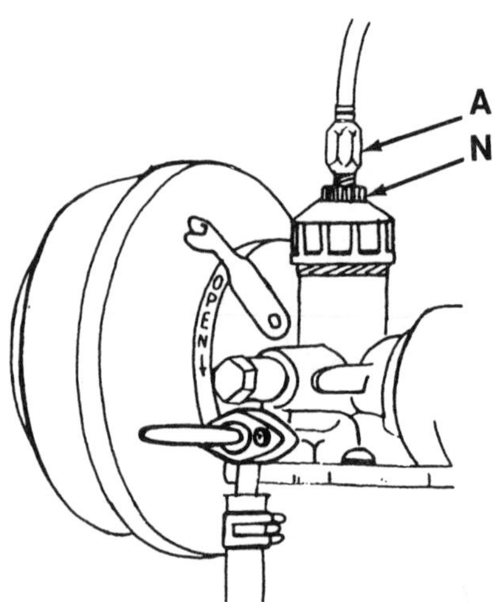

Fig. GM51—Loosen nut (N) and rotate adjuster (A) to adjust idle speed on Model 2600.

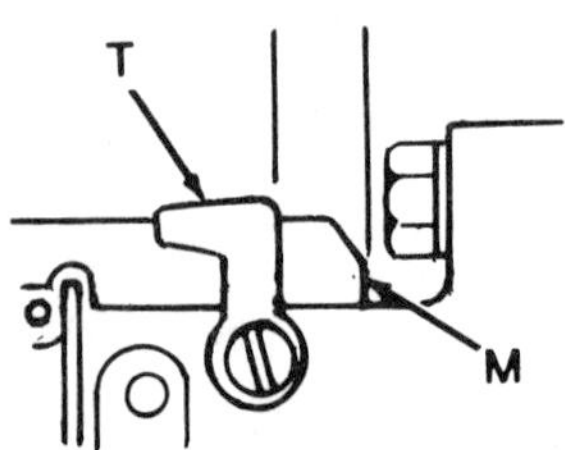

Fig. GM52—At wide-open throttle the carburetor throttle stop arm (T) should be parallel with carburetor mounting face (M).

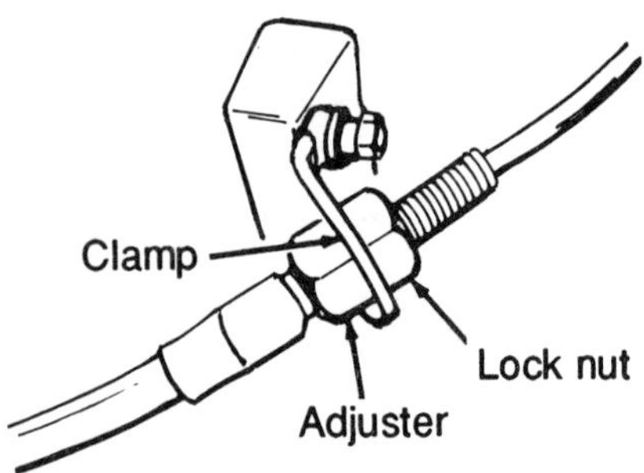

Fig. GM53—Turn cable adjusting nuts so carburetor throttle stop arm (T—Fig. GM52) is parallel with carburetor mounting face (M).

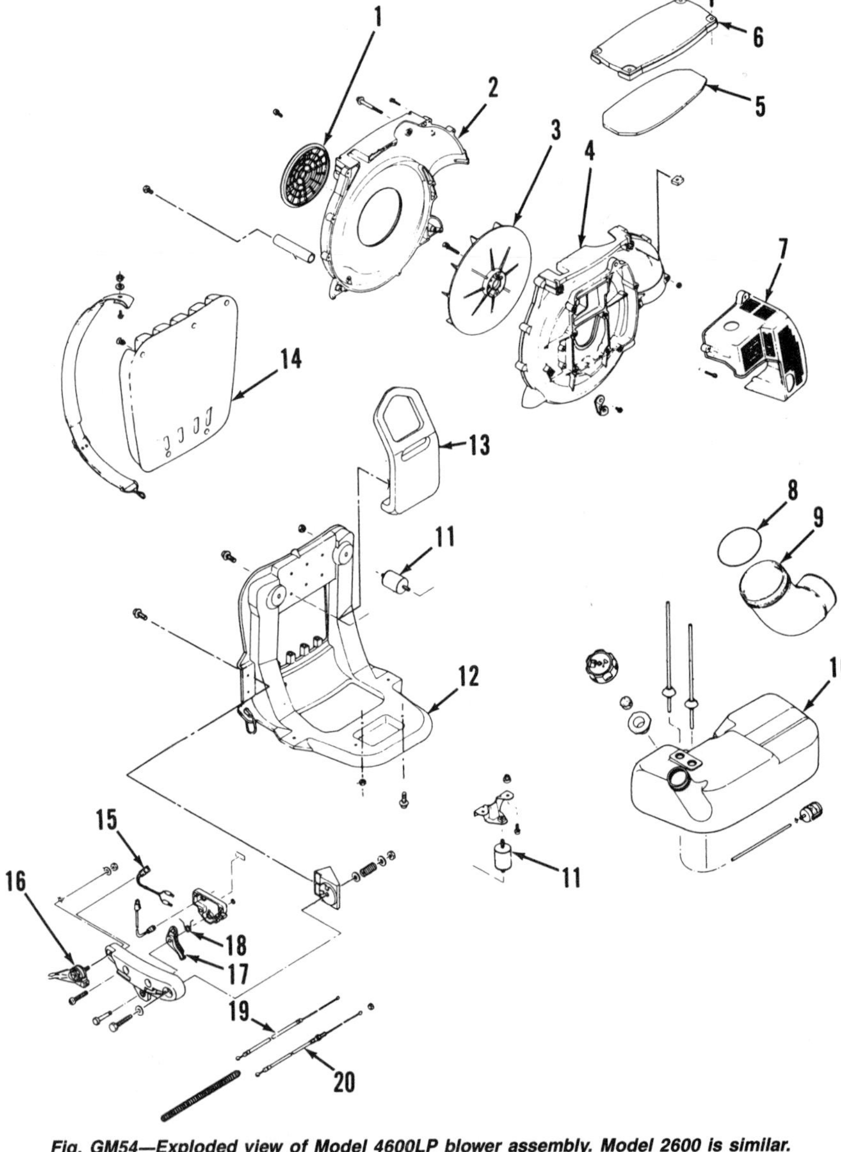

Fig. GM54—Exploded view of Model 4600LP blower assembly. Model 2600 is similar.

1. Intake guard	6. Cover	11. Rubber mounts	16. Throttle lever
2. Blower housing half	7. Engine cover	12. Backpack frame	17. Lever
3. Blower fan	8. "O" ring	13. Hanger bracket	18. Spring
4. Blower housing half	9. Elbow	14. Backpad	19. Choke cable
5. Gasket	10. Fuel tank	15. Stop switch	20. Throttle cable

THROTTLE CABLE

Model 2600

There is no free play in the throttle cable. Idle speed is adjusted by loosening lock ring (N—Fig. GM51) and rotating adjuster (A). Turn adjuster counterclockwise to increase idle speed. Recommended idle speed is 2800-3100 rpm.

Model 4600LP

The throttle cable should be adjusted so the throttle trigger and carburetor throttle plate are synchronized. With throttle trigger in wide-open position, the throttle stop arm (T—Fig. GM52) should be parallel with the carburetor mounting face (M). To adjust, relocate nuts (Fig. GM53) at throttle cable end. Tighten nuts after adjustment.

BLOWER FAN

To remove engine from blower housing, remove fuel tank (10—Fig. GM54) and engine cover (7). Remove screw retaining crankcase to backpack frame (12). Remove backpad (14) and pry off intake guard (1). Remove screws attaching blower fan (3) to flywheel. Remove four engine mounting screws and remove engine from blower housing.

To remove blower fan (3), remove cover (6) from blower housing. Remove screws holding blower housing halves (2 and 4) together. Separate blower housing and remove fan.

GREEN MACHINE BY JOHN DEERE

GASOLINE POWERED TRIMMERS

Model	Engine Make	Engine Displacement
1930 & 1940 (Late)	Homelite	30.0 cc (1.83 cu. in.)
2600	Mitsubishi	22.6 cc (1.38 cu. in.)
2800 & 2840	Mitsubishi	26.1 cc (1.59 cu. in.)
3000b (brush cutter) & 3000j (J handle)	Mitsubishi	26.1 cc (1.59 cu. in.)
4000b (brush cutter) & 4000j (J handle)	Mitsubishi	40.6 cc (2.48 cu. in.)

ENGINE INFORMATION

Refer to the appropriate HOMELITE or MITSUBISHI Engine Service section of this manual for service to the engines used on these models.

FUEL MIXTURE

The manufacturer recommends mixing Green Machine Premium Extract Mix or Green Machine 32:1 oil with regular or unleaded gasoline at the ratio indicated on the container. If this oil is not available, use a good quality oil designed for use in air-cooled, 2-stroke engines. Do not use oil designed for outboard motors or automotive oil.

STRING TRIMMER

Refer to Fig. JDG1 for the dual line, semi-automatic string trimmer head typical of the type available for all models. To manually advance the trimmer lines with the engine stopped, push the button at the bottom of the spool (8) and pull both of the lines. To extend the lines with the engine running, operate the trimmer at maximum speed and tap the spool button on the ground. Both lines should extend a small amount automatically. If the line does not extend with the engine running, stop the engine and extend the lines manually. If a line is broken inside the housing, it will be necessary to disassemble the unit and feed the line through the housing eyelet (2).

To disassemble, press the two lock tabs, then remove the cap (10) and spool (8). Be careful not to lose the spring (6) or washers (5 and 7). Clean and inspect all parts for damage. A new eyelet (2) can be installed if worn.

If new line is installed, make sure it is the proper diameter. The spool will hold approximately 15 ft. (4.6 m) of 0.080 in. (2 mm) diameter of line for 1930 and 1940 models; approximately 30 ft. (9.1 m) of 0.080 in. (2 mm) diameter line for 2600, 2800 and 2840 models; approximately 50 ft. (15.2 m) of 0.95 in. (2.4 mm) diameter line for 3000b, 3000j, 4000b and 4000j models. Loop the line through the holes in the center of the spool, then pull the line through the holes until it is the same length on both sides. Wrap both ends of the line on spool at the same time in counterclockwise direction as viewed from the top of spool (note arrow on spool). Wind the line tightly and evenly from side to side and do not twist the lines. Install spool while directing the ends of both lines through the eyelets (2) in the housing. Install the cap, making sure the tabs snap in place. Trim the line so the ends extend to the cutoff blade in the protective cover.

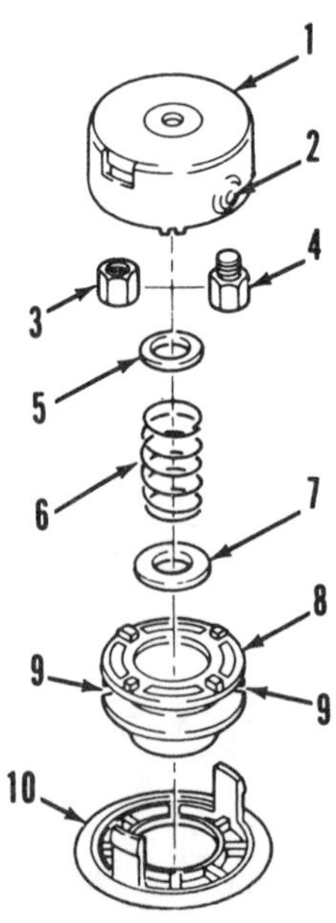

Fig. JDG1—Exploded view of dual strand trimmer head typical of the type available on all models. Note that only one adapter (3 or 4) is used according to the application.

1. Housing
2. Eyelet
3. Adapter
4. Adapter
5. Washer
6. Spring
7. Washer
8. Spool
9. Line
10. Cap

If the trimmer head must be removed, hold the shaft to prevent it from rotating, then turn the trimmer head clockwise (viewed from the bottom). The cutter adapter has left-hand threads.

BLADE

An 8 in. diameter, saw blade or 8 tooth brush blade is available for installation on some models. The 8 tooth blades should be sharpened with a flat file as shown in Fig. JDG2. Sharpen all of the blades evenly to maintain balance. Do not file into the radius (R) at the root.

The brush cutter blade available for some models can be sharpened using a

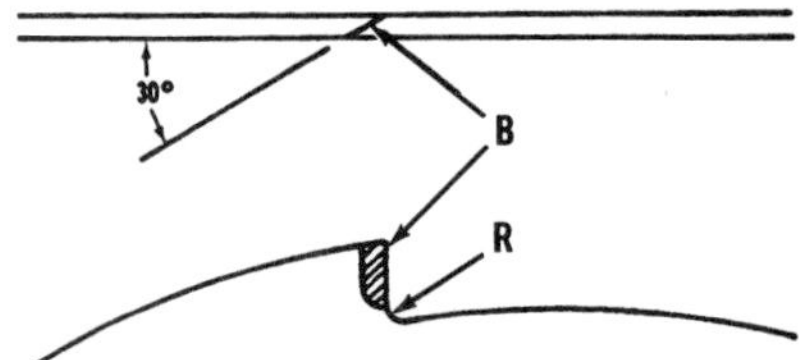

Fig. JDG2—Steel blades with 8 teeth can be installed on some models. The cutting face can be sharpened as shown.

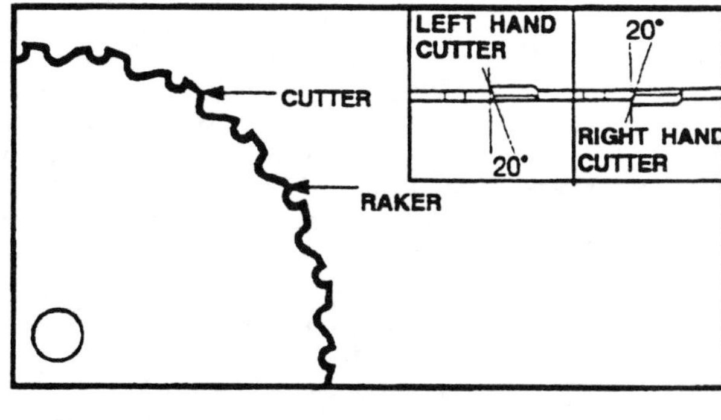

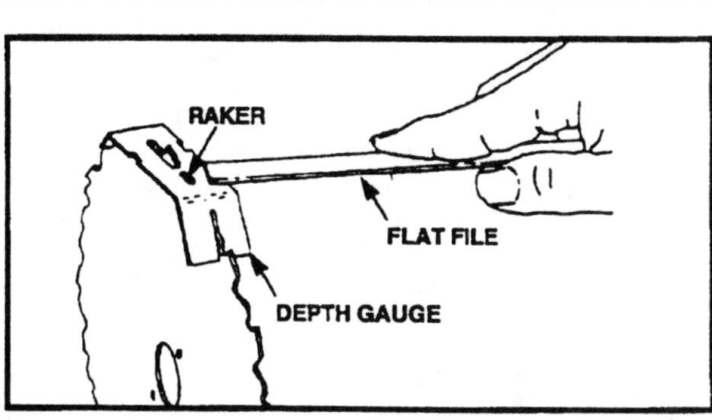

Fig. JDG3—Steel brush cutter blades used on some models should be sharpened as described in the text.

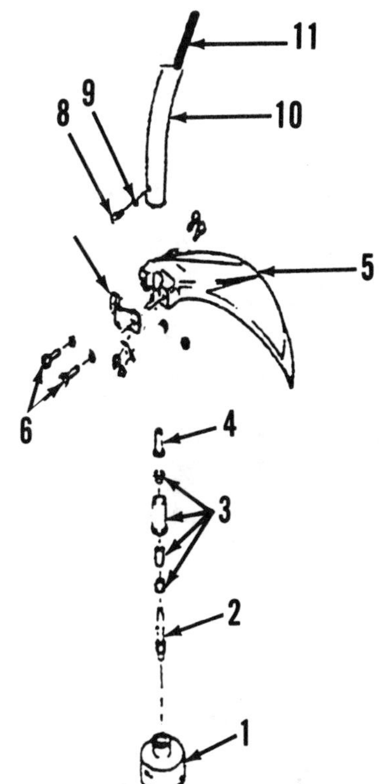

Fig. JDG5—On models without gearcase, the lower end of the drive shaft tube is equipped with bearing assembly (3).

1. Trimmer head
2. Arbor
3. Bearing assembly
4. Arbor adapter
5. Proctor shield
6. Clamp bolts
7. Clamp
8. Fitting screw
9. Washer
10. Drive shaft housing
11. Drive shaft

7/32 in. diameter round file (part No. A-92615 or equivalent) as shown in Fig. JDG3. The face of the cutters should be sharpened to the 20 degree angle as shown. A depth gauge (part No. D-92609) should be used to check the height of the rakers after sharpening the blades. If necessary, use a 6 in. flat file to reduce the height of the rakers.

If other blades are used, sharpen the blades following the original sharpening angle and tooth set.

DRIVE SHAFT AND HOUSING

The drive shaft and housing of some models is provided with a coupler (Fig. JDG4) that permits a variety of devices (such as a cultivator, snow thrower, blower and edger as well as the trimmer or brush cutter) to be driven by the power head. On these models, first separate the drive shaft from the attachment at the coupling. Additional service procedure will depend upon whether the upper or lower shaft/housing tube is being serviced, but will generally follow the procedure described for units with one drive shaft and housing.

Before separating the drive shaft housing from the clutch housing and engine, detach the throttle cable and engine stop wires. Loosen the screw(s) that clamps the drive shaft housing in the clutch housing, then pull the drive shaft housing from the clutch housing. If so equipped, remove the gearcase from the lower end of the drive shaft housing. On model without gearcase, remove the trimmer assembly from the lower end of the drive shaft housing.

Inspect the ends of the drive shaft (10—Fig. JDG4 or 11—Fig. JDG5) carefully for wear. The flexible cable does not require regular maintenance, unless it is removed. If the drive shaft cannot be easily withdrawn or turned, it may be necessary to install the housing as well as the drive shaft.

If the drive shaft cable is removed, it should be cleaned, inspected and lubricated. If damaged, a new cable should be installed. Lubricate the entire length of the drive shaft with No. 2 multipurpose grease (part No. 18453 or equivalent).

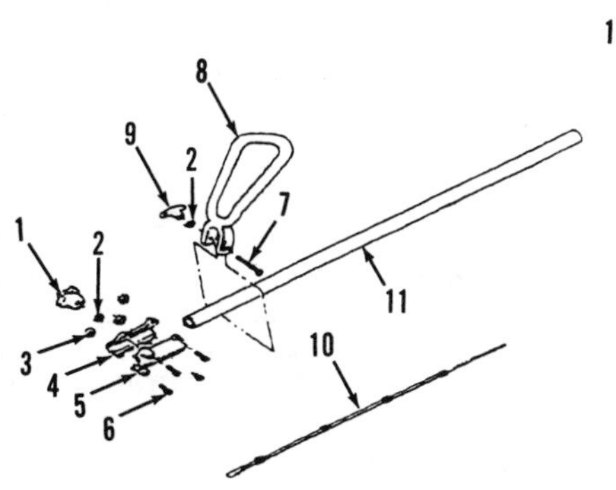

Fig. JDG4—View of the drive shaft and housing for models with coupling (4 and 5) for attaching the drive shaft to various equipment.

1. Knob
2. Washers
3. Nuts
4. Coupler half
5. Coupler half
6. Bolt
7. Bolt
8. Handle
9. Knob
10. Drive shaft
11. Housing
13. Grip

Service bushings for the drive shaft housing may be available for some models. A renewable bearing assembly (3—Fig. JDG5) is located at the lower end of the drive shaft housing of models not equipped with a gearcase. Install new arbor post (2), Bearing assembly (3) and arbor adapter (4) if worn excessively.

GEARCASE

On some models, a gearcase (Fig. JDG6) is located at the lower end of the drive shaft and housing. To remove the assembly, loosen the fitting screw (4) and clamp bolts (1), then pull the gear housing from the drive shaft housing. The gearcase and related components can be removed, cleaned and inspected after removing the screws attaching the halves of the case (2 and 3) together.

The case should be partially filled with No. 2 multipurpose grease (part No. 18453 or equivalent) when assembling. The manufacturer suggests the following maintenance after each 10 hours of operation. Remove the trimmer head or blade and holders (9 and

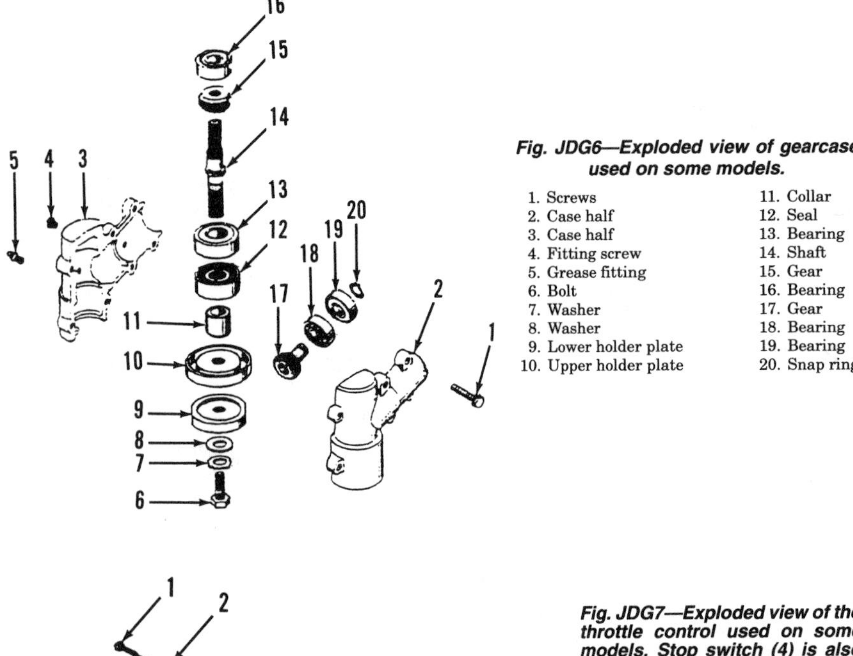

Fig. JDG6—Exploded view of gearcase used on some models.

1. Screws
2. Case half
3. Case half
4. Fitting screw
5. Grease fitting
6. Bolt
7. Washer
8. Washer
9. Lower holder plate
10. Upper holder plate
11. Collar
12. Seal
13. Bearing
14. Shaft
15. Gear
16. Bearing
17. Gear
18. Bearing
19. Bearing
20. Snap ring

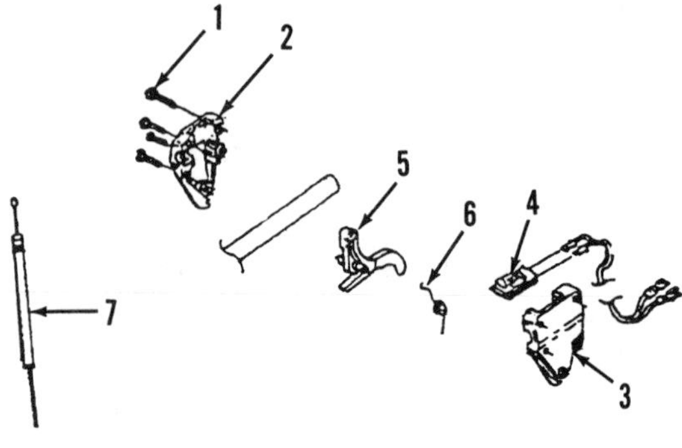

Fig. JDG7—Exploded view of the throttle control used on some models. Stop switch (4) is also located in the housing. See also Fig. JDG8.

1. Screws
2. Housing half
3. Housing half
4. Engine stop switch
5. Throttle lever
6. Return spring
7. Throttle cable

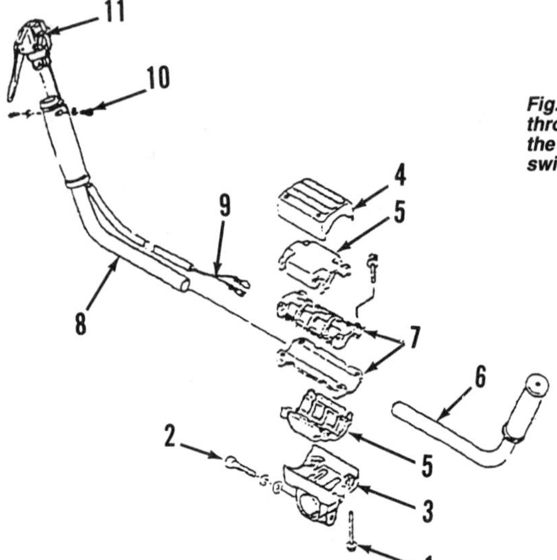

Fig. JDG8—Exploded view of the throttle control used on models with the wide handle assembly. The stop switch is also located at the grip. See Fig. JDG7 for other models.

1. Screws
2. Clamp screw
3. Clamping bracket
4. Upper clamp
5. Isolating rubber
6. Left bar
7. Bar clamp
8. Right bar
9. Engine stop wires
10. Fitting screws
11. Throttle & stop switch assy.

10), then insert grease through fitting (5) until it comes from around the collar (11) and shaft (14).

ENGINE CONTROLS

Engine throttle control is located within easy reach when the operator's hands are safely positioned on the grips. Refer to Fig. JDG7 or Fig. JDG8. On some models, the engine stop switch is also located near the operator's grip.

RECOIL STARTER

Models 1930, 1940, 2600, 2800, 2840, 3000b and 3000j

Refer to Fig. JDG9 for an exploded view of the starter. Unbolt and remove the starter from the engine. Remove the rope handle (3) and allow the rope to wind into the starter. Remove the center screw (7) and the pulley (10). The spring (11) may rewind uncontrollably causing injury. Wear appropriate safety eye wear and gloves before removing the recoil spring (11) from the housing (9).

Unscrew the lock nut and pawl plate (6) from the engine crankshaft. The lock nut may not be installed on all models. The lock nut and pawl plate (6) have left-hand threads. Remove the clip from the front of the pawl to remove the pawl and spring (1 and 2). Install the pawl plate and tighten it to 8-10 N•m (70-90 in.-lb.) torque. Tighten the lock nut on 1930 and 1940 models so equipped to 16-20 N•m (140-175 in.-lb.) torque. Tighten the lock nut on 2600, 2800 and 3000 models to 16-17.5 N•m (140-155 in.-lb.) torque.

To assemble the starter, lubricate the center post and spring side of the housing with light grease. Attach the outer end of the spring to the clip in the housing, then wind the spring into the housing wrapping the spring in a counterclockwise direction until the spring is completely in the housing cavity. The inner end of the spring should contact the center post.

Attach the rope to the pulley (10), thread the rope through the housing and guide (4 and 9), then attach the handle (3). Install the pulley over the center post of the housing while making sure the pulley engages the end of the rewind spring. Coat the threads of the retaining screw (7) with medium strength Loctite, then install and tighten the screw securely. A loop of the rope should be in the pulley's notch as shown in Fig. JDG10. Hold the rope loop as shown in Fig. JDG10 and wind the pulley counterclockwise several turns. Pull the rope out with the handle and allow it to rewind. If the rope does not rewind properly, pull a loop in the rope as shown in Fig. JDG10 and preload the spring another turn.

NOTE: If the rope is too long, it will bind before rewinding properly. Make sure the rope is not binding.

To make sure the spring is not tightened too much, pull the rope out completely, then turn the pulley an additional 1/2 turn. If the rope cannot be pulled out completely, the spring is bound and will break. Pull a loop in the rope as shown in Fig. JDG10 and loosen the spring slightly as required. A proper setting will allow the rope to be

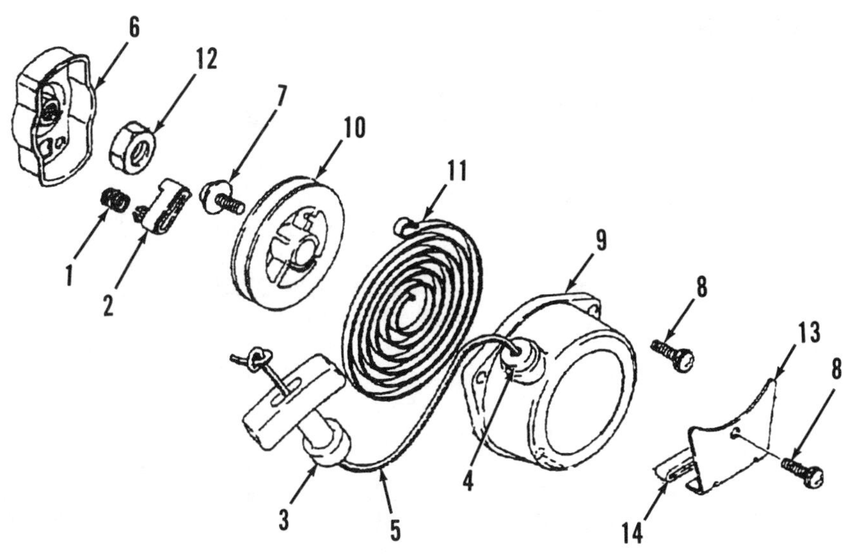

Fig. JDG9—Exploded view of the recoil starter assembly typical of most models except 4000 series.

1. Pawl spring
2. Pawl
3. Handle
4. Guide
5. Rope
6. Pawl carrier
7. Screw
8. Screw
9. Housing
10. Pulley
11. Recoil spring
12. Lock nut
13. Bracket
14. Pad

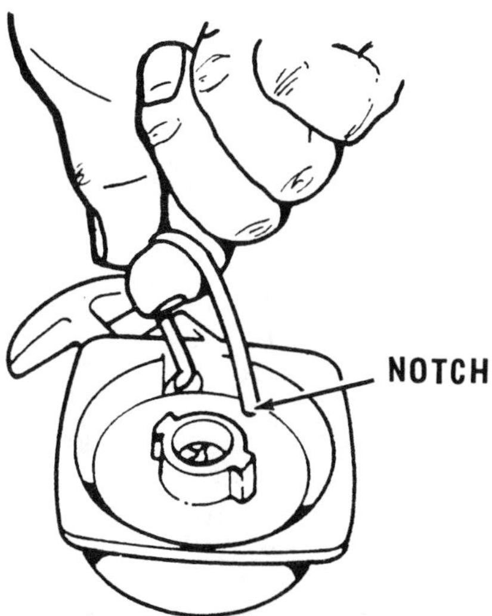

Fig. JDG10—To set the preload of the starter recoil spring, pull a loop in the rope with the rope in the notch in the pulley, then wind the pulley as necessary. When the rope is released, it will pull out of the notch.

fully extended and will also wind the rope onto the pulley fully.

Models 4000b and 4000j

The rewind starter (Fig. JDG11) is attached to the rear of the engine with 4 screws (1). Release the spring tension before disassembling the starter. If the rope or rewind spring is broken, spring tension will already be released. The rope can be pulled out of the notch in the pulley (10) and the pulley allowed to turn until the spring tension is released. Spring tension can also be released by removing the handle (3) and allowing the rope to be drawn into the pulley.

Assemble the starter as shown in Fig. JDG11. Preload the recoil spring enough to hold the handle against the housing when it is released.

The starter wheel (12) is attached to the crankshaft with nut. The crankshaft must be held from turning by using the piston stopper while removing or installing the nut.

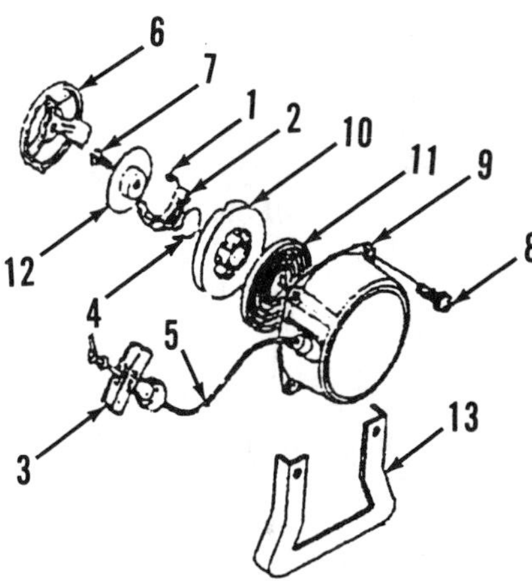

Fig. JDG11—Exploded view of recoil starter used on 4000 series.

1. Screws
2. Cover
3. Handle
4. Rope
5. Screw
6. Cap
7. Shoe
8. Friction spring
9. Spring
10. Pulley
11. Recoil spring
12. Starter cup
13. Stand

HOFFCO

GASOLINE POWERED TRIMMERS

Model	Engine Make	Engine Model	Displacement
Critter	McCulloch	SI-410	21.2 cc (1.29 cu. in.)
GT14	Echo	F2/2	13.8 cc (0.842 cu. in.)
GT14B	Echo	G1AH	13.8 cc (0.842 cu. in.)
GT160B, GT160T, GT160TL	Fuji	EC01-R	15.4 cc (0.94 cu. in.)
GT21, GT210, GT211, GT211A	McCulloch	SI-410	21.2 cc (1.29 cu. in.)
GT215	Echo	...	21.2 cc (1.29 cu. in.)
GT225 & GT225SPL	Fuji	EC02-R	22.5 cc (1.37 cu. in.)
GT256SPL	Fuji	EC02-F	25.6 cc (1.56 cu. in.)
GT320	Tecumseh	TC200	32.8 cc (2.0 cu. in.)
Hoffie 22	Fuji	EC02-R	22.5 cc (1.37 cu. in.)
JP215	Echo	...	21.2 cc (1.29 cu. in.)
JP220F	Fuji	EC022GA	21.7 cc (1.32 cu. in.)
JP225	Fuji	EC02-R	22.5 cc (1.37 cu. in.)
JP260, JP260A, JP260C	McCulloch	SI-410	21.2 cc (1.29 cu. in.)
JP270	Echo	...	21.2 cc (1.29 cu. in.)
JP300, JP300A, JP300B	Fuji	EC02-F	25.6 cc (1.56 cu. in.)
JP300C	McCulloch	...	25.0 cc (1.52 cu. in.)
JP300F	Fuji	EC02-F	25.6 cc (1.56 cu. in.)
JP320	Fuji	EC02-R	22.5 cc (1.37 cu. in.)
JP390, JP390A, JP390C, JP390XL	Fuji	EC03-F	30.5 cc (1.86 cu. in.)
JP420, JP420D, JP420GT	Tecumseh	TC200	32.8 cc (2.0 cu. in.)
JP660	Fuji	EC02-R	22.5 cc (1.37 cu. in.)
Lil Whizz 1600	Fuji	EC01-R	15.4 cc (0.94 cu. in.)
Lil Whizz 600	Echo	G1AH	13.8 cc (0.842 cu. in.)
P10A, P250 & P85	Tecumseh	AV520-670	85.0 cc (5.2 cu. in.)
PC225, PC380	Fuji	EC02-R	22.5 cc (1.37 cu. in.)
WT14H	Echo	G1AH	13.8 cc (0.842 cu. in.)
WT160, WT160H, WT160HT, WT230HT	Fuji	EC02-R	22.5 cc (1.37 cu. in.)
WT250C	McCulloch	...	25.0 cc (1.52 cu. in.)
WT250HT, WT250HT-A	Fuji	EC02-F	25.6 cc (1.56 cu. in.)
WT320H, WT320T	Tecumseh	TC200	32.8 cc (2.0 cu. in.)
WW850, WW88	Tecumseh	AV520-670	85.0 cc (5.2 cu. in.)

ENGINE INFORMATION

Echo, Fuji-Robin, McCulloch and Tecumseh two-stroke air-cooled gasoline engines are used. Identify the engine by displacement and model if available, then refer to the appropriate ECHO, FUJI-ROBIN, McCULLOCH or TECUMSEH Engine Service section of this manual.

FUEL MIXTURE

Hoffco recommends a fuel:oil mixture ratio of 24:1. Mix regular grade gasoline with a high quality oil designed for two-stroke, air-cooled engines. Gasohol or other alcohol blended fuels are not approved by manufacturer.

STRING TRIMMER

Single Strand Trimmer Head

EARLY MODELS. Refer to Fig. HF10 for an exploded view of the semi-automatic, single strand trimmer head used on early models. To manually advance line with engine stopped, push hub assembly towards drive tube while

Illustrations courtesy Hoffco Inc.

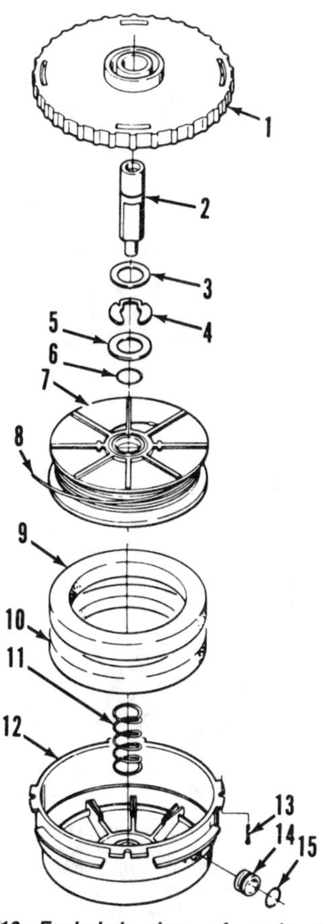

Fig. HF10—Exploded view of early type semi-automatic, single strand trimmer head.

1. Plate
2. Adapter
3. Washer
4. Retainer ring
5. Washer
6. Retainer ring
7. Spool
8. Line
9. Foam pad
10. Foam pad
11. Spring
12. Hub
13. Cotter pin
14. Line guide
15. Retainer

Fig. HF11—Tape line to spool center when installing new line.

pulling out line. Procedure may require repeating to provide adequate line length. To advance line with engine running, tap hub assembly on the ground with engine running at full throttle. Line will automatically advance a measured amount.

To disassemble trimmer head, remove cotter pin (13—Fig. HF10) and twist hub (12) counterclockwise. Remove hub and spool (7). Remove foam pads (9 and 10) and remaining old line. Clean parts.

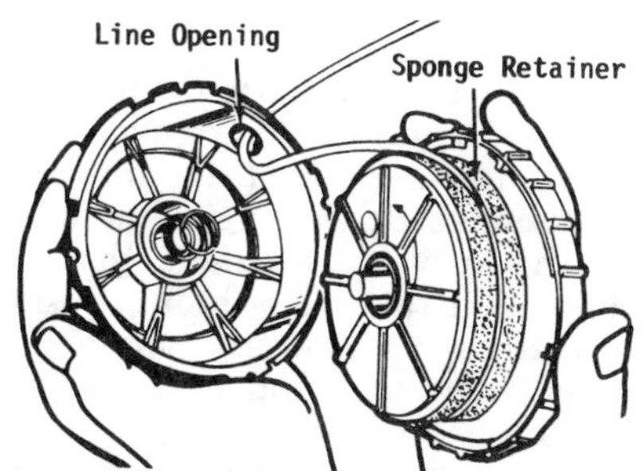

Fig. HF12—After line is wound on spool, install foam pads with line protruding as shown.

New line length should be 25 ft. (7.6 m) long with diameter of 0.080 in. (2 mm). Tape one end to center of spool (Fig. HF11) and carefully wind line in direction indicated by arrow on spool (Fig. HF12). Leave a short length of line extending from spool and install foam pads (9 and 10—Fig. HF10) so line is between pads after installation (Fig. HF12). One side of spool is marked "motor" and the other side is marked "top." The side marked "motor" is installed towards hub (12). Slip extended line end through line guide (14) in hub (12) and install spool in hub. Install hub and spool assembly on cover (1). Push in on hub against spring tension and rotate in a clockwise direction to engage lock tabs. Install cotter pin (13).

LATER TYPE Fig. HF13. The single strand semi-automatic trimmer head shown in Fig. HF13 is used on some models including Critter and GT211. The line can be extended manually as follows. Make sure the engine is stopped, push the button (7) and pull the line. The procedure may have to be repeated several times to obtain the desired length. To extend the line with the engine running, operate the engine at maximum speed and tap the button (7) on the ground. The line should advance each time the button is tapped.

To install new line, the unit must be disassembled. Push in on the tabs retaining cover (5) to the drum (1) and remove the cover. Remove spool (4) and be careful not to lose the spring (3) or other parts. Clean all parts and remove any old line remaining on the spool. Insert the end of 0.080 in. (2 mm) line through the hole in the spool and wind the line onto the spool in the direction indicated by the arrow on spool. Do not install so much line on the spool that it causes it to bind. Install the button (7) and spool (5) while inserting the free end of line (6) through the line guide opening in the drum (1). Install cover (5) making sure tabs are properly engaged.

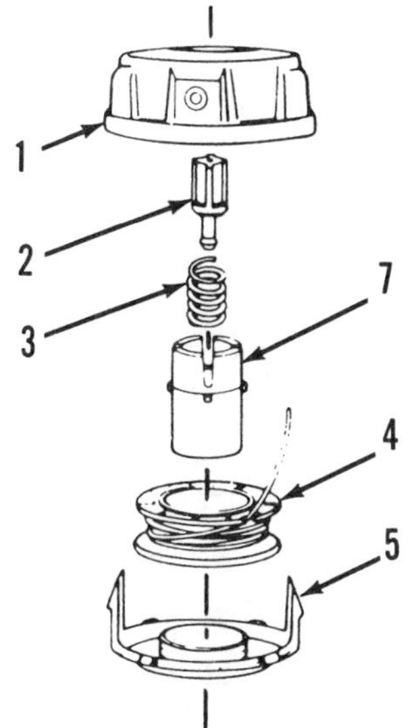

Fig. HF13—Exploded view of single strand semi-automatic trimmer head used on some models.

1. Drum
2. Adapter
3. Spring
4. Spool
5. Cover
7. Button

LATER TYPE (Fig. HF14). The single strand semi-automatic trimmer head shown in Fig. HF14 is installed on some models. To extended the line manually, first make sure the engine is stopped. Push the button (7) and pull

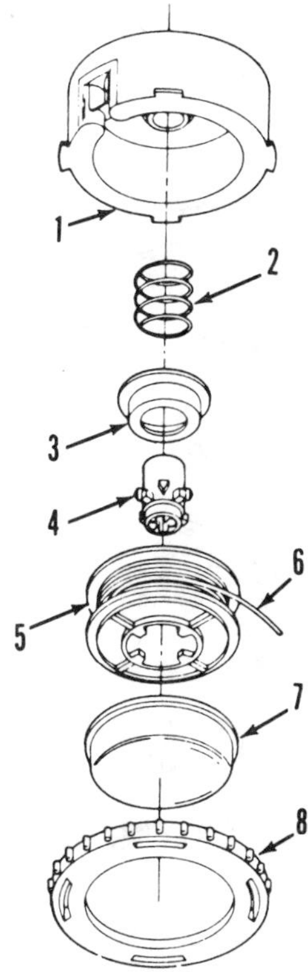

Fig. HF14—Exploded view of late style semi-automatic, single line trimmer head used on some models.

1. Drum
2. Spring
3. Spring adapter
4. Inner cam
5. Spool
6. Line
7. Button
8. Cover

Illustrations courtesy Hoffco Inc.

the line. The procedure may have to be repeated several times to obtain the desired length. To extend the line with the engine running, operate the engine at maximum speed and tap the button (7) on the ground. The line should advance each time the button is tapped.

To install new line, the unit must be disassembled. Remove cover (8) and lift the button (7) and spool (5) from the drum (1). Be careful not to lose any parts. Clean all parts and remove any old line remaining on the spool. Insert the end of 0.080 in. (2 mm) line through the hole in the spool and wind the line onto the spool in the direction indicated by the arrow on spool. Do not install so much line on the spool that it causes it to bind. Install the spool while inserting the free end of the line through the line guide opening in the drum (1). Install button (7) and cover (5).

LATER TYPE (Fig. HF15). The single strand semi-automatic trimmer head shown in Fig. HF15 is installed on some models including WT250F, GT211A and GT21. To manually advance the trimmer line with the engine stopped, push the button (7) at the bottom of the head and pull the line. To extend the line with the engine running, operate the trimmer at maximum speed and tap the button (7) on the ground. The line should extend a small amount automatically. If the line does not extend with the engine running, stop the engine and extend the line manually. If the line is broken inside the housing, it will be necessary to disassemble the unit and feed the line through the eyelet (3).

To disassemble, press the tab marked "PUSH," then twist the cover (8) to remove cover, button (7) and spool (6). Be careful not to lose the spring (5). Clean and inspect all parts for damage. A new eyelet (3) can be installed if worn. If new line is installed, it should be 0.080 in. (2 mm) diameter and should be approximately 15 ft. (4.6 m) long. Insert the line through the eye of the spool, then wrap the line on spool in direction indicated by the arrow on spool. Install spool while directing line through the eyelet (3) in the housing. Install the button and cover. The cover should snap in place when the locking tabs on cover and housing engage. Trim the line so the line extends approximately 3 in. (75 mm) from the drum.

If the trimmer head retaining nut (4) must be removed, lock the shaft to prevent it from rotating by inserting a pin through the hole in the bearing head.

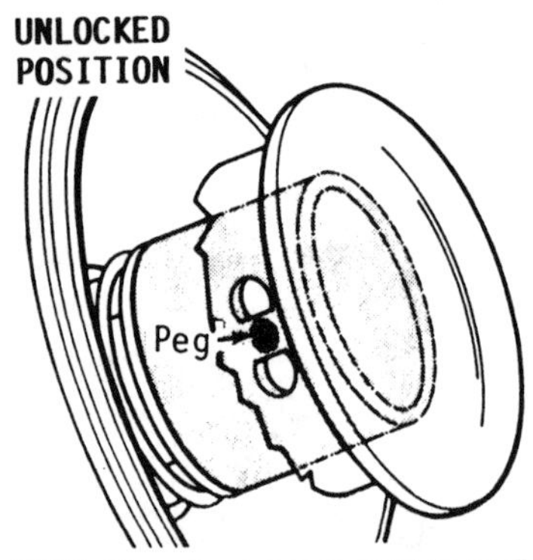

Fig. HF17—To remove spool, hold drum firmly and turn spool in direction shown to take up slack, then twist it with a sudden snap until the plastic peg is between the holes as shown in the lower view.

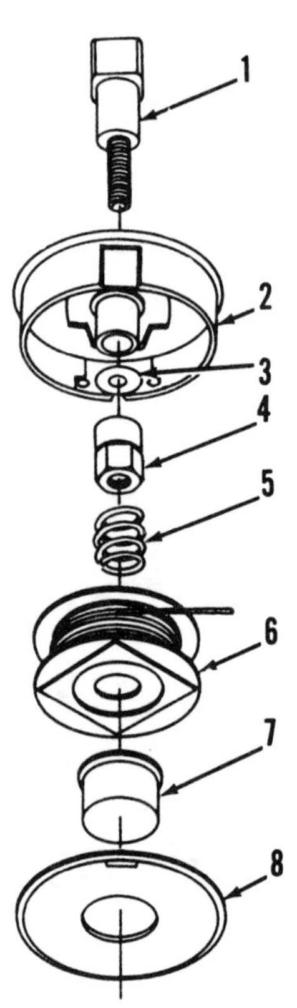

Fig. HF15—Exploded view of the single line string trimmer head used on some late models including WT250F, GT211A and GT21.

1. Adapter
2. Housing
3. Eyelet (line guide)
4. Nut
5. Spring
6. Spool
7. Button
8. Cover

Dual Strand Trimmer Head

Refer to Fig. HF16 for an exploded view of the dual line, semi-automatic string trimmer head typical of the type used. To manually advance the trimmer lines with the engine stopped, push the button at the bottom of the head and pull both of the lines. To extend the lines with the engine running, operate the trimmer at maximum speed and tap the button on the ground. Both lines should extend a small amount automatically. If the line does not extend with the engine running, stop the engine and extend the lines manually. If a line is broken inside the housing, it will be necessary to disassemble the unit and feed the line through the eyelet.

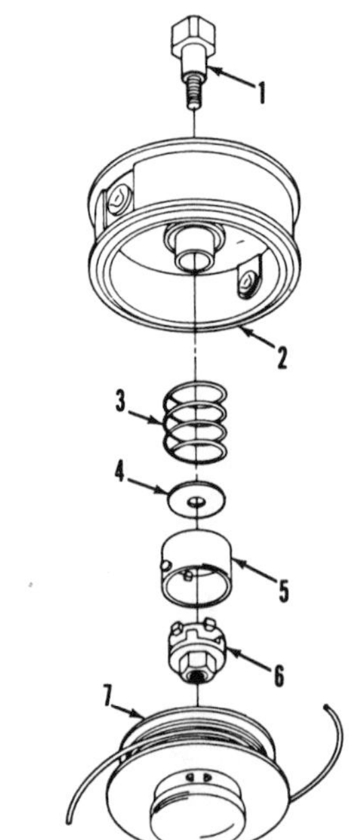

Fig. HF16—Exploded view of semi-automatic dual line trimmer head.

1. Adapter
2. Drum
3. Spring
4. Washer
5. Outer cam
6. Inner cam
7. Spool

To remove and disassemble the string trimmer head, proceed as follows. Hold the drum firmly and turn spool in the direction shown in Fig. HF17 to remove slack. Twist with a hard snap until the plastic peg is between holes, then separate the spool from the drum.

Clean and inspect all parts for damage. If new line is installed, it should be 0.095 in. (2.41 mm) diameter. The spool will hold approximately 20 ft. (6 m) of line. Insert the line through the eye of the spool as shown in Fig. HF18 and pull the line through until it is the same length on both sides. Wrap both ends of

Illustrations courtesy Hoffco Inc.

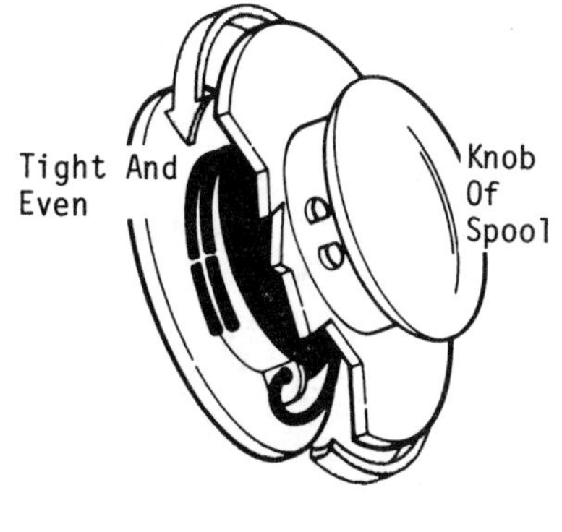

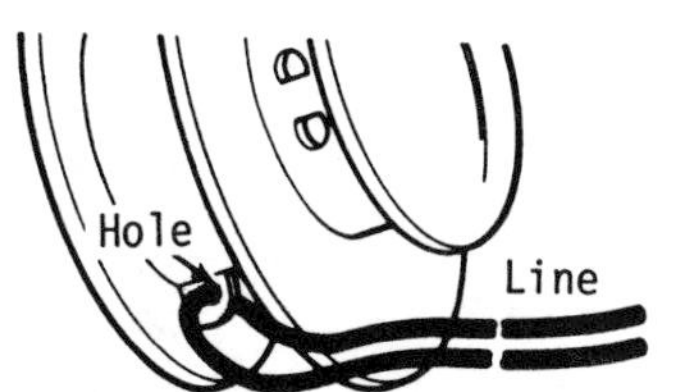

Fig. HF18—Line should be inserted through hole in spool as shown in lower view. Wind the line tightly in direction indicated on spool.

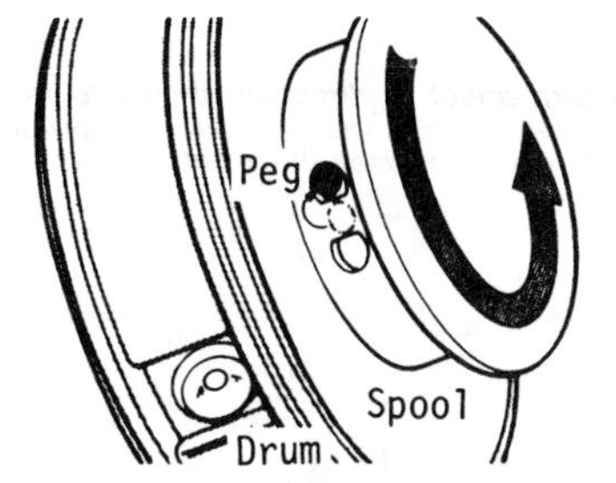

Fig. HF19—Hold drum firmly, then twist suddenly to lock spool in position.

the line on spool at the same time in the direction indicated by the arrow on the spool. Wind the line tightly and evenly from side to side, but do not twist the lines. Install spool while directing the ends of both lines through the eyelets in the housing. Align the pegs on drum with slots in the spool and push the spool into drum. Hold the drum firmly, then twist spool quickly in the direction shown in Fig. HF19 so peg enters the hole with a click and locks the spool in position. Trim the line so the line extends approximately 6 in. (15 cm) from the drum.

Triple Strand Trimmer Head

Refer to Fig. HF20 for an exploded view of the triple strand trimmer head used on some models.

To install new trimmer line, align hole in cup washer with hole in bearing head or gear housing. Insert a 5/32 in. Allen wrench or similar tool into holes in cup washer and head to prevent drive shaft from turning. Turn tri-line head counterclockwise to remove the head. Unscrew bolt (6) and cover (5). Clean inside of rotary head. Wind new line on spools as shown in Fig. HF21. Place spools (3—Fig. HF20) back in upper body (1), install springs (4) and cover (5).

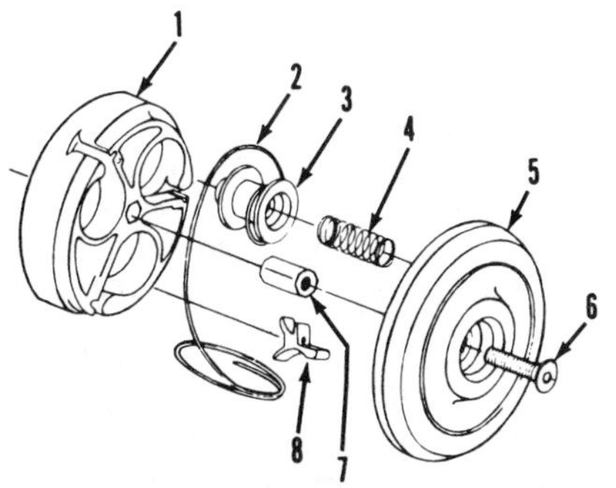

Fig. HF20—Exploded view of "Tri-Line" trimmer head used on some models.

1. Body
2. Line
3. Spool (3)
4. Spring
5. Cover
6. Screw
7. Retainer
8. Line retainer

Fig. HF21—Line is wound on "Tri-Line" spools and routed as shown.

BLADES

Some models may be equipped with "TRI-KUT" or brush blades (Fig. HF22) for cutting heavier weeds, grasses or brush. All of the available hard blades can be dangerous and should be selected and used with great care. Blades should be matched to the specific model of the powerhead. Check the manufacturer's recommended application for your specific model. A blade too small or too large will reduce the effectiveness of operation and may be dangerous to operate.

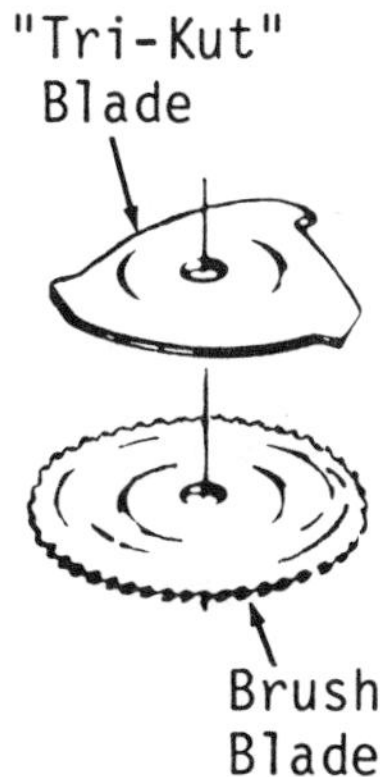

Fig. HF22—A "TRI-CUT" weed and grass blade and a brush blade are available for some models.

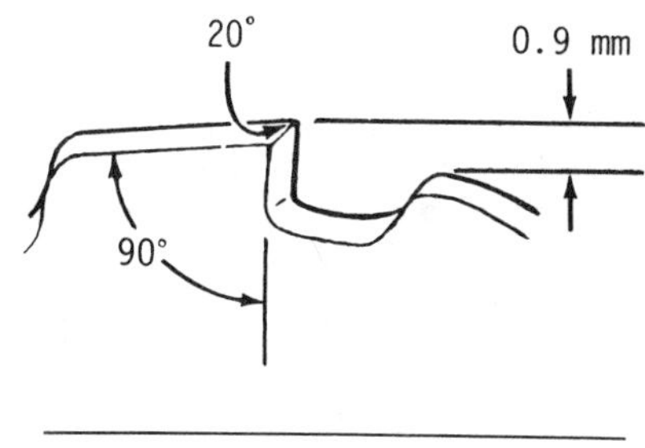

Fig. HF23—Sharpen brush blade to dimensions shown. Refer to text.

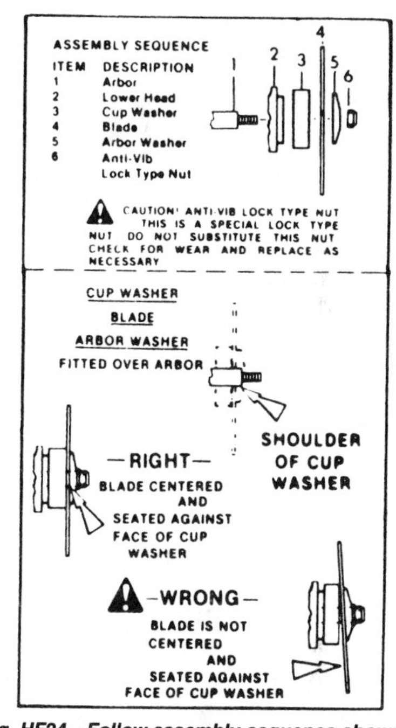

Fig. HF24—Follow assembly sequence shown to install blade.

To sharpen brush blade, refer to Fig. HF23. Sharpen each tooth of brush blade following the original sharpening angle and tooth set. Sharpen all teeth evenly to maintain balance and do not file into the radius at the root. If a blade has hit a stone or other solid object, the entire damaged section must be filed away and all of the blades must be filed the same to maintain proper balance. File templates are available from the manufacturer for sharpening some brush blades.

To install "TRI-KUT" or brush blade, note that rotation is clockwise as viewed from engine end looking down the shaft. Make certain blade is centered on arbor and seated against the face of cup washer (3—Fig. HF24). Assemble the blade, arbor washer and anti-vibration lock nut in sequence shown in Fig. HF24. Insert a screwdriver tip into the aligned notches of the lower head casting and cup washer, and hold them together. make certain that cup washer remains in place flush against the lower head casting. This will allow nut, washer and blade to be tightened into position.

DRIVE SHAFT

All models are equipped with a flexible drive shaft (2—Fig. HF25). Some models are equipped with a grease fitting at upper end of drive shaft housing. Drive shaft should be removed, cleaned and inspected after every 20 hours of operation.

To remove drive shaft, disconnect throttle cable and stop switch wires (Fig. HF26). Remove clamp bolt from clutch housing, then separate engine and clutch assembly from drive shaft tube. Mark drive shaft end locations, then withdraw drive shaft from tube.

Clean and inspect drive shaft. Drive shaft is available as a unit assembly with drive shaft housing tube. Lubricate drive shaft with a high quality, high-temperature wheel bearing grease. Exchange drive shaft ends before installation to extend drive shaft life. Be sure drive shaft properly engages clutch and trimmer head. Refer to Fig. HF26 for illustration showing installation of throttle cable and engine kill wires typical of most models.

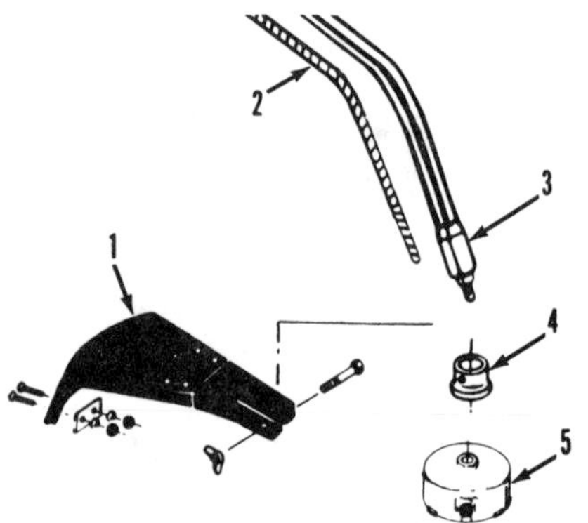

Fig. HF25—Exploded view of drive shaft housing and trimmer head.

1. Shield
2. Flexible drive shaft
3. Housing
4. Adapter
5. Trimmer head

BEARING HEAD

Integrated Drive Shaft Housing/Bearing Head. Light-duty models are equipped with an integrated drive shaft housing/bearing head assembly (Fig. HF25). Bearings consist of two powdered-metal bushings at upper end of housing and two prelubricated, precision ball bearings located between double seals. If bearing failure occurs, entire housing assembly must be renewed.

Kick-Stand Type Bearing Head. Refer to Fig. HF27 for an exploded view of kick-stand type bearing head. To service, remove clamping screw (3) and set screw (7). Slip head off drive shaft tube. Remove trimmer head or blade assembly. Remove snap ring (11). Secure head assembly in a vise. Place a 1-3/8 inch diameter wooden dowel with a 3/4 inch hole drilled through the center over the arbor, against the square coupling end. Tap wooden dowel with a mallet. Bearings and arbor assembly will slip from lower head. Disassemble bearings, coupling and arbor assembly as necessary.

To reassemble, place coupling (4) and washer (5) on arbor (12). Press one bearing onto arbor. Install assembly into housing. Install spacer (9) and press remaining bearing onto arbor and into housing. Install snap ring.

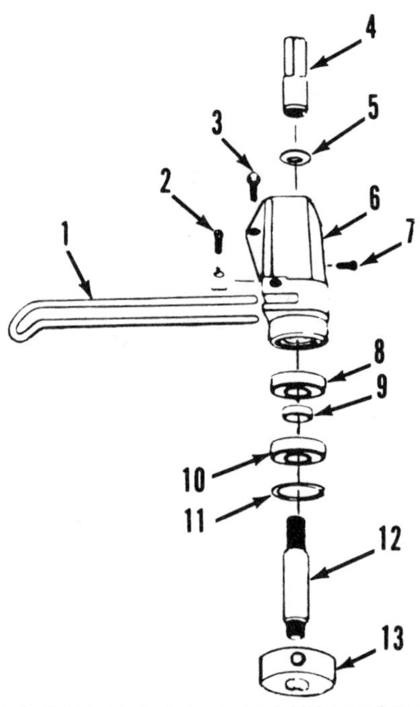

Fig. HF27—Exploded view of kick-stand type bearing head.

1. Kick stand
2. Screw
3. Screw
4. Adapter
5. Washer
6. Housing
7. Screw
8. Bearing
9. Spacer
10. Bearing
11. Snap ring
12. Arbor
13. Cup washer

Flange Type Bearing Head. Refer to Fig. HF28 for an exploded view of flange type bearing head used on some models. To service, remove shield (5). Remove clamp and screw securing head to drive shaft tube. Separate head from drive shaft housing tube. Remove trimmer head and cup washer (6). Remove snap ring (4) and press bearing and arbor assembly (3) from housing (1). Remove washer (2). Arbor and bearings (3) are renewed as an assembly.

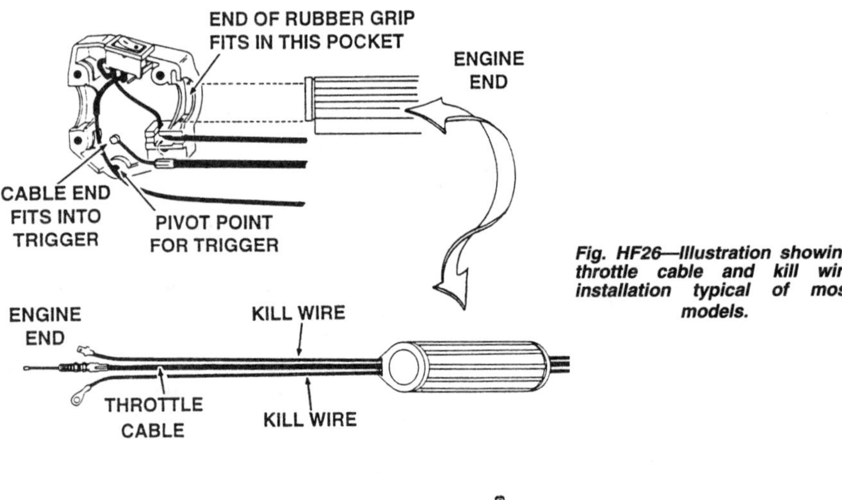

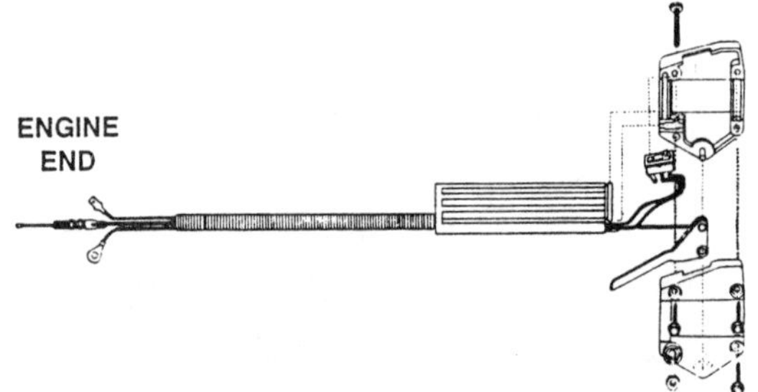

Fig. HF26—Illustration showing throttle cable and kill wire installation typical of most models.

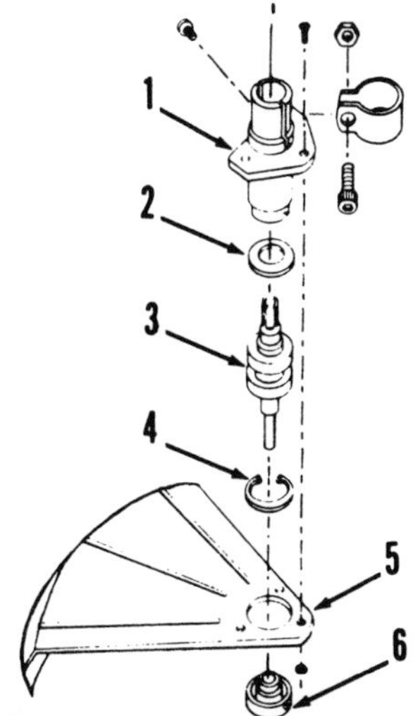

Fig. HF28—Exploded view of flange type bearing head used on some models.

1. Housing
2. Washer
3. Arbor & bearing assy.
4. Snap ring
5. Shield
6. Cup washer

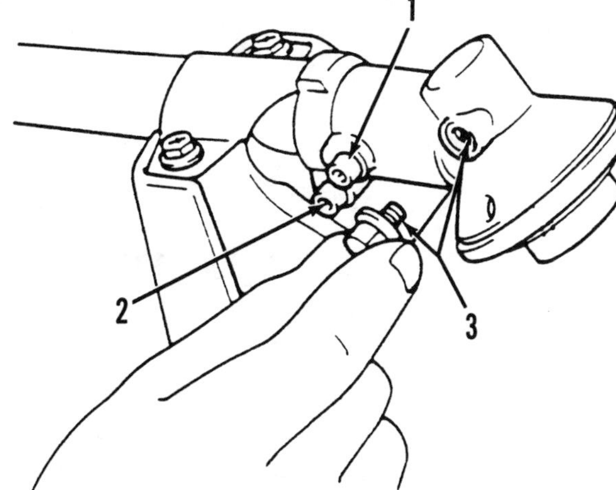

Fig. HF29—Some models are equipped with a gear head which has a one piece housing. Service parts are not available for this gear head.

1. Locating screw
2. Clamp screw
3. Filler plug

GEAR HEAD ASSEMBLY

A gear head is located at the lower end of the drive shaft and housing of some models. To remove the assembly, loosen the fitting screw and clamp bolts, then pull the gear head from the drive shaft housing. Check for parts availability before attempting repairs.

The gear head housing of some models has one piece housing while for other models the housing is made in two pieces.

Parts for the one piece gear housing are not available and service is limited to inspection, adding lubricant and installing a new unit. To check the lubricant in the gear head, remove plug from filler opening (3—Fig. HF29). Add multipurpose grease to the housing until the cavity is approximately 2/3 full. Do not over fill the housing with grease and tighten fill plug securely.

Refer to Fig. HF30 for an exploded view of the unit which has two piece housing. The gear head is equipped with sealed bearings, and periodic maintenance is not required. The halves of the housing can be separated after removing the unit from the drive shaft housing. Remove the trimmer head or blade before removing the screws that attach the halves together.

STARTER

Refer to the appropriate ENGINE SERVICE section for service to the starter assembly.

CLUTCH

Refer to the appropriate ENGINE SERVICE section for clutch removal and service procedures.

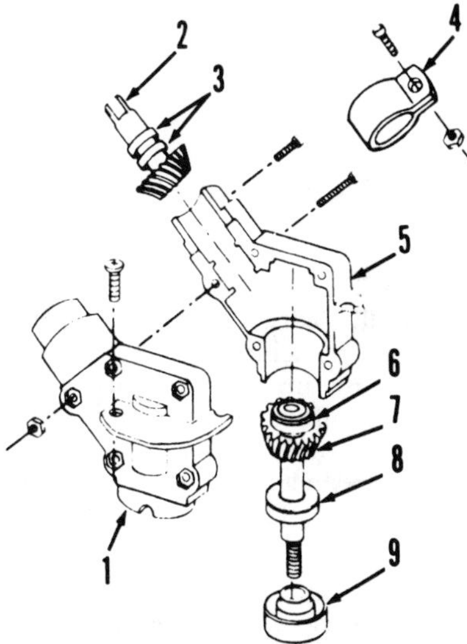

Fig. HF30—Exploded view of gear head typical of models with two piece housing.

1. Housing half
2. Input gear
3. Bearings
4. Clamp
5. Housing half
6. Bearing
7. Output gear & arbor
8. Bearing
9. Cup washer

HOMELITE

ELECTRIC STRING TRIMMERS

Model	Volts	Amps	Cutting Swath	Line Diameter
ST-20	120	2.2	10 in.	0.065 in.
ST-40	120	3.3	14 in.	0.065 in.
ST-60	120	4.0	16 in.	0.065 in.

ELECTRICAL REQUIREMENTS

Model ST-20, ST-40 and ST-60 string trimmers are designed to be used on electrical circuits with 120-volt alternating current. All models are double-insulated and do not require a ground wire. A two-wire extension cord is recommended and wire gage should be matched to cord length to prevent power loss. Use no more than 100 feet (30.5 m) of #18 wire or no more than 150 feet (45.7 m) of #16 wire.

All models are equipped with an automatic string advance system. The string trimmer will automatically feed out string by cycling the trimmer motor from on to off. The string spool must stop completely to advance the string, and if sufficiently short, it may be necessary to cycle the trimmer on and off several times. Operation is similar to that described in OPERATING SAFETY section in this manual.

If string will not advance on ST-40 or ST-60 models, it may be necessary to remove the high speed slider spring (the larger of the two springs) and compress the spring several times. This will reduce spring tension and allow the high speed slider to cock at a lower rpm. If a new high speed slider spring is being installed, it should also be compressed a couple of times before installation.

NOTE
All wiring must be routed exactly as shown in wiring diagram.

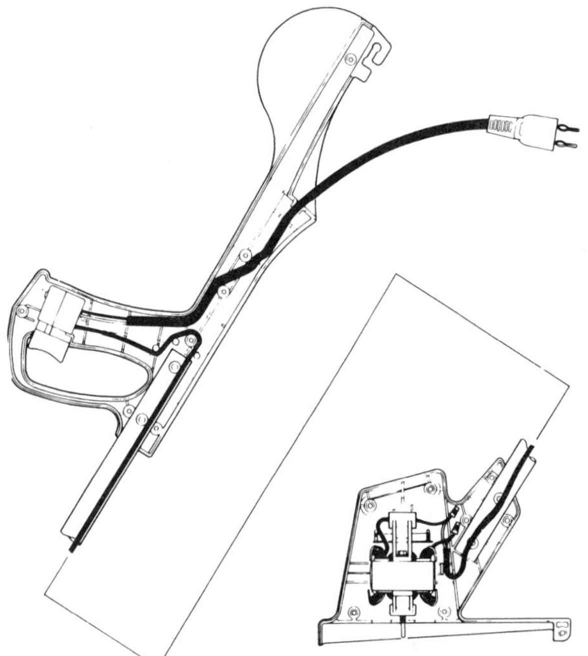

Fig. HL27-1—Wiring diagram showing correct routing of wire on Model ST-20.

NOTE
All wiring must be routed exactly as shown in wiring diagram.
CAUTION
Make sure that the wire terminals do not touch after assembly of the motor housing

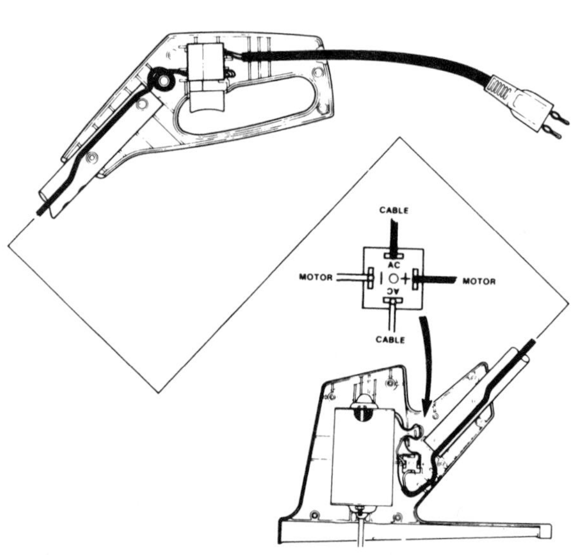

Fig. HL27-2—Wiring diagram showing correct routing of wire on Models ST-40 and ST-60.

HOMELITE

ELECTRIC STRING TRIMMERS

Model	Volts	Amps	Cutting Swath	Line Diameter
ST-10, ST-10A	120	2.0	10 in.	0.065 in.
ST-30, ST-30C	120	3.3	12 in.	0.065 in.
ST-70	120	5.0	16 in.	0.065 in.

ELECTRICAL REQUIREMENTS

Models ST-10, ST-10A, ST-30, ST-30C and ST-70 string trimmers are designed to be used on electrical circuits with 120-volt alternating current. All models are double-insulated and do not require a ground wire. A two-wire extension cord is recommended and wire gage should be matched to cord length to prevent power loss. Use no more than 100 feet (30.5 m) of #16 wire or no more than 150 feet (45.7 m) of #14 wire.

STRING TRIMMER

Model ST-10

Model ST-10 is equipped with a single strand, manual advance trimmer head. To extend line, pull string down and around head until string extends from next slot in head.

To install new string, unscrew spool retaining nut and remove spool. New string length should be 15 feet (4.6 m). Attach string to hole in spool and wind string around spool in direction of arrow on spool. Reassemble trimmer head.

Models ST-10A, ST-30 And ST-30C

Models ST-10A, ST-30 and ST-30C are equipped with a single strand, automatic advance trimmer head. The string is advanced by a slider and spring mechanism when the trimmer motor is accelerated or decelerated.

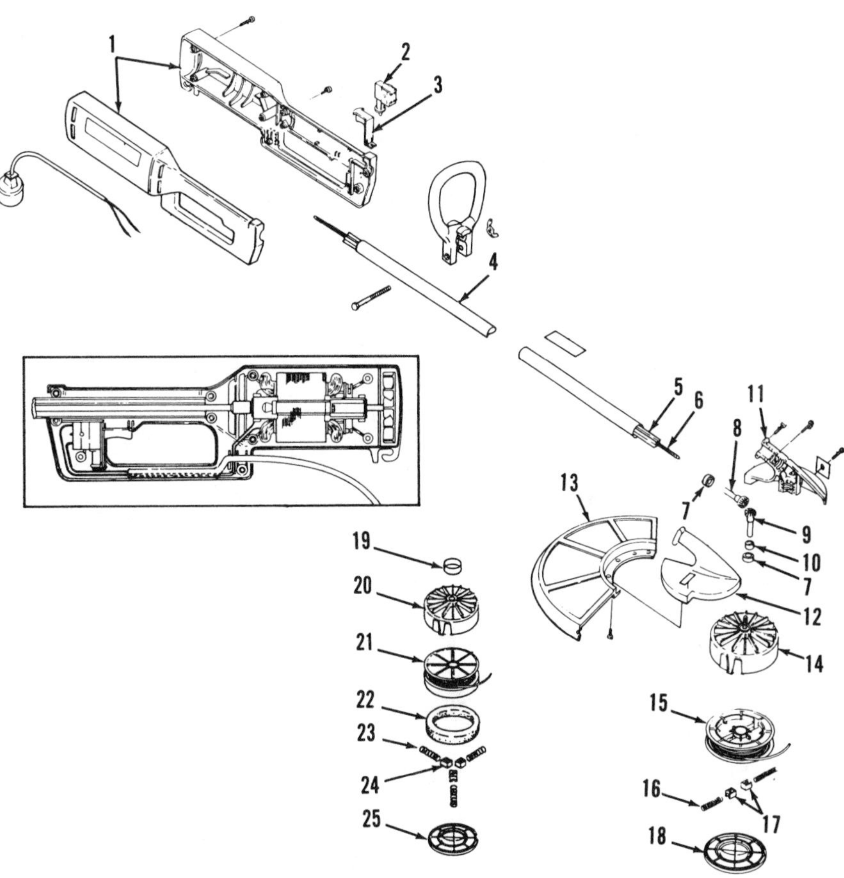

Fig. HL28-1—Exploded view of trimmer. Trimmer head components (19 through 25) are used on later ST-70 models.

1. Motor housing
2. Switch
3. Trigger
4. Drive shaft housing
5. Liner
6. Drive shaft
7. Bearing
8. Gears
9. Gears
10. Spacer
11. Gear head housing
12. Deflector
13. Gear head housing
14. Housing
15. Spool
16. Spring
17. Slider
18. Cover
19. Cupped washer
20. Housing
21. Spool
22. Foam ring
23. Spring
24. Slider
25. Cover

To install new string, twist and detach cover (18—Fig. HL28-1) and remove spool. New line length is 26 feet (7.9 m). Insert new line through hole in spool and tie end around post as shown in Fig. HL28-2. Wrap line around spool in direction indicated on spool. Install spool with 3 inches (7.6 cm) of line extended past eyelet and install cover.

Model ST-70

Model ST-70 may be equipped with an automatic advance trimmer head with single or dual strings. The string is advanced by a slider and spring mechanism when the trimmer motor is accelerated or decelerated. Refer to previous section covering ST-30 models for string installation on single string head.

To install string on dual strand trimmer head, twist and detach cover (25—Fig. HL28-1). New line length should be 30 feet (9.1 m). Insert string through holes in the spool (Fig. HL28-3) and center the spool between the string ends. Pull loop tight and wind both lengths of string around the spool in direction indicated on spool. Position foam ring (22—Fig. HL28-1) around spool so string ends extend from top and bottom of foam ring. Place string ends in slots on spool as shown in Fig. HL28-3 (one string end will bend over outside of foam ring). Pass string ends through housing eyelets and reassemble trimmer head.

Fig. HL28-2—When installing new line, attach string end to post. If line is proper diameter, the line will fit snugly in gage slot.

DRIVE SHAFT

The drive shaft does not require periodic maintenance. Lubricate drive shaft with molybdenum disulfide grease if removed. The drive shaft liner (5—Fig. HL28-1) is available separately.

GEAR HEAD

Models ST-30, ST-30C And ST-70

Models ST-30, ST-30C and ST-70 are equipped with a gear head. Periodic maintenance is not required. Individual gears and bearings are available. Gears should be lubricated with molybdenum disulfide grease if unit is disassembled.

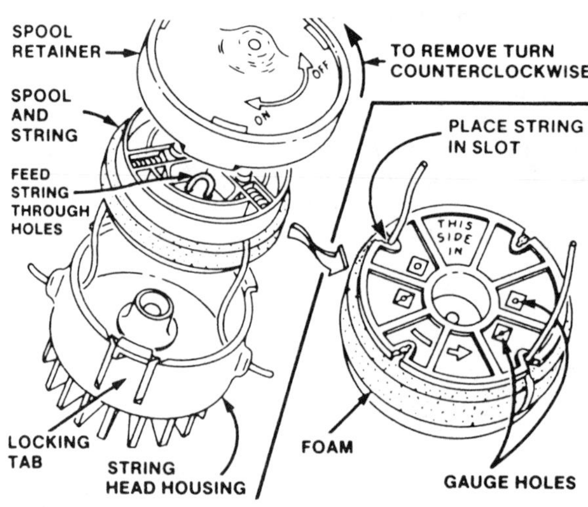

Fig. HL28-3—View of properly assembled trimmer head on Model ST-70 with dual strings. Note gage holes in spool to determine if line is proper diameter. Line will pass through one hole but not "no go" hole.

HOMELITE

GASOLINE POWERED STRING TRIMMERS

Models	Make	Engine Displacement
ST-80, ST100, ST-120, ST-160, ST-160A, ST-165 & ST-180	Homelite	26.2 cc (1.6 cu. in.)
ST-200 & ST-210	Homelite	31.2 cc (1.9 cu. in.)
ST-260	Homelite	26.2 cc (1.6 cu. in.)
ST-310	Homelite	31.2 cc (1.9 cu. in.)

ENGINE IDENTIFICATION

All models are equipped with a Homelite engine. Refer to the HOMELITE Engine Service section of this manual for service to the engine used.

FUEL MIXTURE

The manufacturer recommends mixing Homelite 2-Cycle oil with regular or unleaded gasoline at the ratio indicated on the package. When using regular BIA certified TC-W oil, mix at a ratio of 32:1.

An antioxidant fuel stabilizer (such as Sta-Bil) should be added to the fuel if Homelite oil is not used. Homelite oil contains an antioxidant fuel stabilizer.

STRING TRIMMER

All Models Except ST-160A, ST-165, ST-260 And ST-310

These models are equipped with an automatic string advance system (Model ST-210 is a brushcutter in a standard configuration but may be optionally equipped as a string trimmer). The string trimmer will automatically feed out string by cycling the engine throttle from full speed to idle speed. String head (17—Fig. HL29-1, Fig. HL29-3 and Fig. HL29-4) encases two slider and spring pairs for high speed and low speed engagements of string spool (18). Heavy spring (13) is used with high speed slider (14) and light spring (16) is used with low speed slider (15). Note position of lugs in Fig. HL29-2 to identify sliders. When string length is at desired cutting length engine speed is approximately 6500 rpm and high speed slider lug drives the string spool. As the string is shortened, engine speed will increase so that centrifugal force disengages the high speed slider lug from the string spool lug. The low speed slider lug picks up a string spool lug which allows the high speed slider to cock behind a string spool lug.

When the engine is slowed to idle speed, the low speed slider will disengage and the high speed slider will engage the next string spool lug thereby allowing the string spool to rotate 1/6 turn and feed out string. The amount of string advanced automatically is determined by the amount of string on the spool. Approximately 2 1/4 inches (57 mm) of string will be advanced from a

Fig. HL29-1—Exploded view of lower head on Model ST-200. Components (11 through 21) are used on Models ST-80, ST-100 and ST-120.

1. Spindle
2. Needle bearing
3. Housing
4. Washer
5. Socket head screw
6. Ball bearing
7. Screw
8. Snap ring
9. Spacer
10. Grass shield
11. Connector
12. "O" ring
13. Heavy spring
14. High speed slider
15. Low speed slider
16. Light spring
17. String head
18. String spool
19. String
20. Weldnot tube
21. Retainer

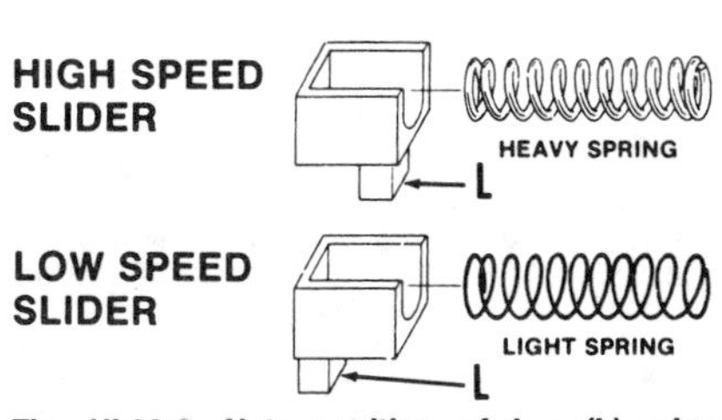

Fig. HL29-2—Note position of lug (L) when identifying high and low speed sliders. Be sure correct spring is installed in slider.

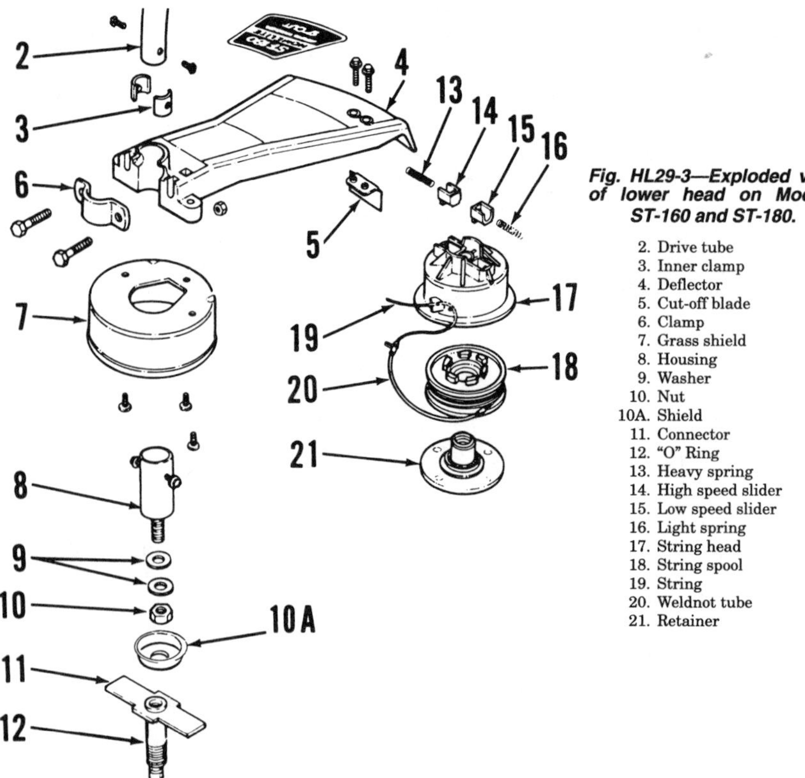

Fig. HL29-3—Exploded view of lower head on Models ST-160 and ST-180.

2. Drive tube
3. Inner clamp
4. Deflector
5. Cut-off blade
6. Clamp
7. Grass shield
8. Housing
9. Washer
10. Nut
10A. Shield
11. Connector
12. "O" Ring
13. Heavy spring
14. High speed slider
15. Low speed slider
16. Light spring
17. String head
18. String spool
19. String
20. Weldnot tube
21. Retainer

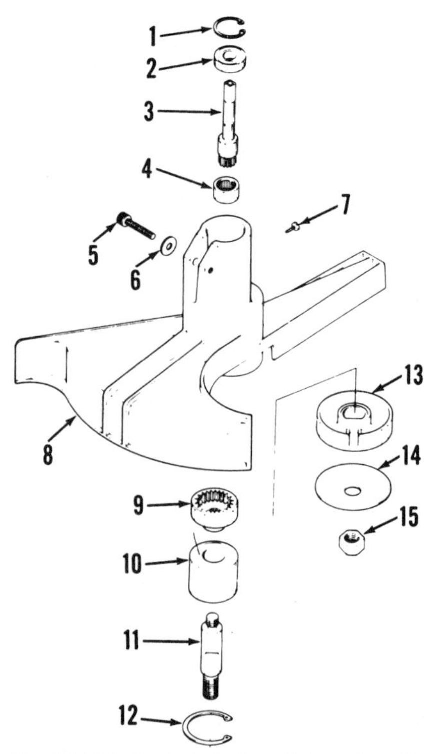

Fig. HL29-5—Exploded view of brusch cutter head which is standard on Model ST-210 and optional on Model ST-200.

1. Snap ring
2. Ball bearing
3. Pinion shaft
4. Needle bearing
5. Clamp screw
6. Washer
7. Socket head screw
8. Head
9. Ring gear
10. Ball bearing
11. Spindle
12. Snap ring
13. Cup washer
14. Shield
15. Nut

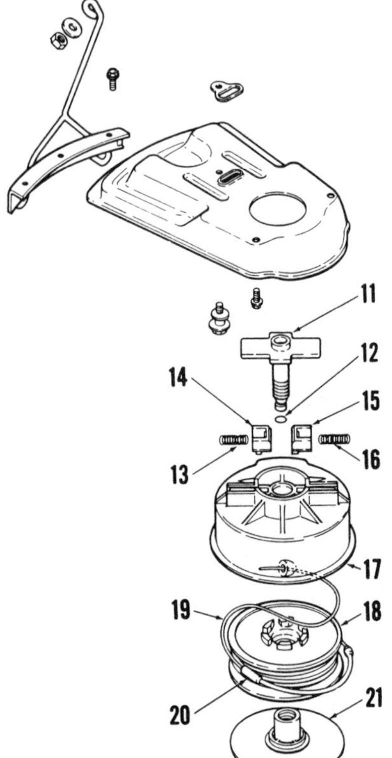

Fig. HL29-4—Exploded view of lower head on Model ST-80. Models ST-100 and ST-120 are similar.

11. Connector
12. "O" ring
13. Heavy spring
14. High speed slider
15. Light spring
17. String head
18. String spool
19. String
20. Weldnot tube
21. Retainer

full spool, and about 3/4 inch (19 mm) from a nearly empty spool.

If automatic string advance malfunctions, be sure proper string is used, string advance components move freely and engine is properly tuned and will run at full speed of at least 7500 rpm. Engine must idle below 4200 rpm (refer to engine service section for carburetor adjustment).

Insufficient string length (less than 2 inches) will not allow automatic string advance. If string is less than 2 inches, remove string head and manually extract sting until string length is 5 inches. Install Weldnot tube so large end is towards outer string end.

Spool retainer (21—Figs. HL29-1, HL29-3 and HL29-4) has left-hand threads and must be turned clockwise for removal. Connector (11) has left-hand threads.

Models ST-200 and ST-210, remove snap ring (8—Fig. HL29-1) and press bearings out of housing. When installing bearings, install needle bearing (2) with lettered end up and ball bearing (6) with sealed end out. Install snap ring (8) with square edge to outside.

Be sure connector (11—Figs. HL29-1, HL29-3 and HL29-4) is fully seated in recess of string head (17) to prevent slider ejection. Apply a light coat of multipurpose grease to bore of spool before installation.

Models ST-160A, ST-165, ST-260 And ST-310

Refer to Fig. HL29-6 for an exploded view of the string trimmer head assembly. To remove string trimmer spool (13), unscrew retainer (14)—retainer has left-hand threads. When installing string, insert string end through holes in spool as shown in Fig. HL29-7. Wrap string around spool in direction of arrow on spool. Do not wrap more than 25 feet (7.6 m) of string onto spool. Position string between lugs on spool before passing string through outlet of string head. To check string advance operation, alternately press down and release retainer (14) while pulling on string.

To separate lower drive shaft assembly (8) from string head (10), retaining ring (11) must be cut and removed. To gain access to the retaining ring press drive shaft assembly down into string head approximately 1/4 inch (6.4 mm). Cut retaining ring, then remove and discard ring.

NOTE: DO NOT attempt to reuse retaining ring.

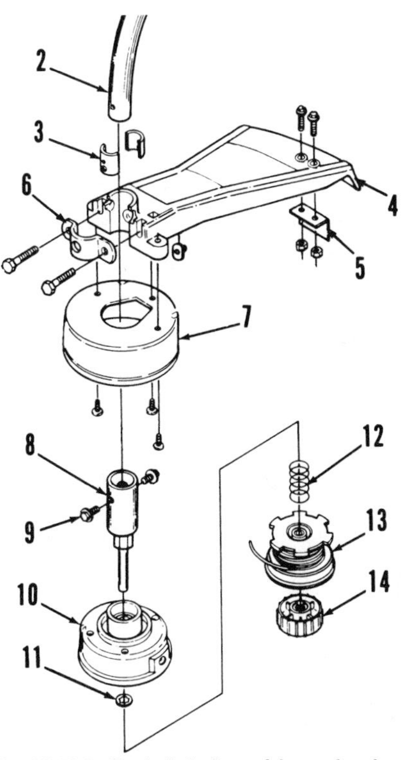

Fig. HL29-6—Exploded view of lower head on Models ST-160A, ST-165 and ST-310.

2. Drive tube
3. Inner clamp
4. Deflector
5. Cut-off blade
6. Clamp
7. Grass shield
8. Lower drive shaft assy.
9. Screw
10. String head
11. Retaining ring
12. Spring
13. String spool
14. Retainer

Separate drive shaft assembly from string head. When installing drive shaft assembly and string head, install retaining ring so inner points are towards end of drive shaft.

BRUSH CUTTER

A brush cutter head is standard on Model ST-210 and optional on Model ST-200. Refer to Fig. HL29-5 for an exploded view. Blade retaining nut (15) has left-hand threads and must be turned clockwise for removal. Head (8) is aligned with drive tube by screw (7) which aligns holes in head and drive tube.

Loosen clamp screw (5) to remove head from drive tube. When assembling head, install bearing (2) with sealed side up.

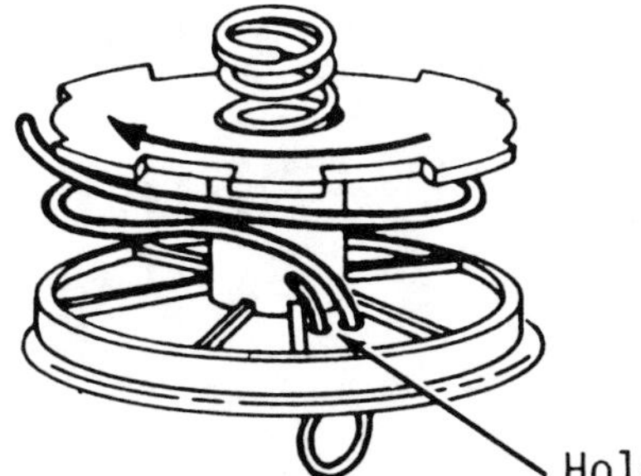

Fig. HL29-7—Insert string end through holes in spool as shown on Models ST-160A, ST-165, ST-260 and ST-310.

Note that the brushcutter kit for early Model ST-200 uses ball bearing (2) and needle bearing (4) to support pinion shaft (3). Two ball bearings (2) are used to support the pinion shaft on later models.

DRIVE SHAFT

Models ST-160 and ST-180 are equipped with a flexible drive shaft which should be inspected and greased annually. Detach drive tube from engine housing and pull drive shaft from drive tube.

Clean drive shaft. Swap drive shaft end-to-end before inserting in drive tube to prolong shaft service life. While inserting drive shaft into drive tube, apply molybdenum disulfide grease to shaft; do not apply excess grease. Reconnect drive tube to engine housing while being sure drive shaft is properly connected.

Models ST-200 and ST-210 are equipped with a flexible drive shaft between the engine and drive head. The flexible drive shaft should be removed, inspected and lubricated after every 25 hours of operation. To remove drive shaft, remove screw (7—Fig. HL29-1 or HL29-5) and loosen clamp screw (5). Slide head off drive tube and pull flexible shaft from tube.

Clean and inspect shaft, then lubricate shaft with lithium grease. Insert shaft into drive tube (shaft ends are identical and shaft ends may be reversed to extend shaft life). Install head while turning head to engage shaft ends in engine and head. Align holes in front side of head and drive tube and install screw (7). Tighten clamp screw (5) so head will not turn.

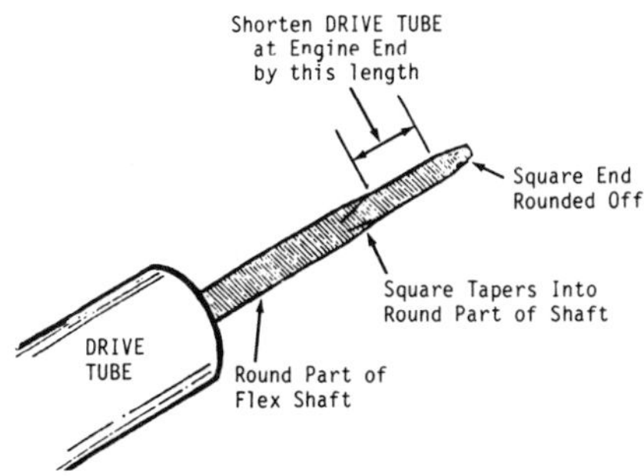

Fig. HL29-8—Shorten drive shaft as shown to prevent rounding off cable end.

For early Models ST-200 and ST-210, bushing kit number A-96064 is available to install a bushing in the lower end of the drive tube. There must be at least 1 1/4 inches from bottom of drive tube to bottom of flex shaft. New drive tubes are equipped with bushings.

Early production ST-200 and ST-210 models were produced with a drive shaft housing having a bump on the end which was designed to index with a notch in the engine housing. Service parts will supply a drive shaft housing, part number A-96205-1, without a bump which is designed to fit all early and late models.

Some ST-160 and ST-180 models may have a drive shaft housing that is too long to allow full engagement of the flexible drive shaft. When a failure occurs, the drive shaft will be rounded off at the end as shown in Fig. HL29-8. Measure the length of the square tapers on the drive shaft and shorten the drive shaft housing at the engine end the same amount.

STARTER

Refer to the appropriate ENGINE SERVICE section for service to the starter assembly.

CLUTCH

Refer to the appropriate ENGINE SERVICE section for clutch removal and service procedures.

HOMELITE

GASOLINE POWERED TRIMMERS

Models	Make	Engine Displacement
BP-250, HB-100, HB-180, HLT-15, ST-145, ST-155, ST-175, ST-185, ST-285, ST-385, ST-485, SX-135, 625, 725, 825*	Homelite	25.0 cc (1.53 cu. in.)
HLT-16, HLT-17, HBC-18, HLT-18, HBC-30, 630, 730, 830*	Homelite	30.0 cc (1.83 cu. in.)
PSE-3000, PLT-3200, PLT-3400, PBC-3400, PBC-3600	Homelite	30.0 cc (1.83 cu. in.)
HBC-38, HBC-40, PBC-3800, PBC-4000	Homelite	40.0 cc (2.46 cu. in.)

* Refer to Fig. HL1 for explanation of model code prefix and suffix.

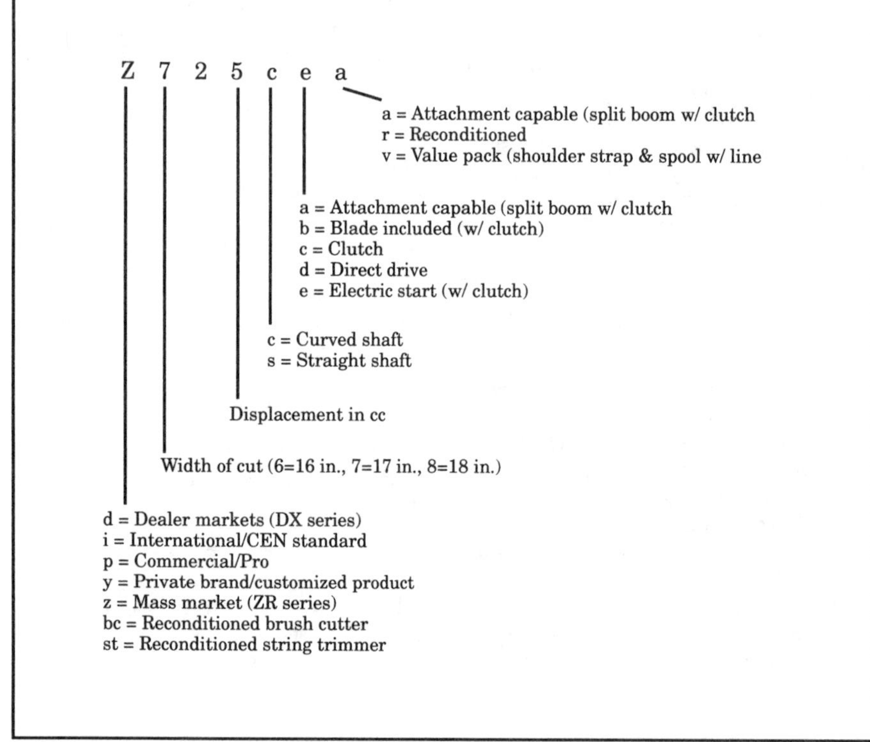

ENGINE IDENTIFICATION

All models are equipped with a Homelite engine. Refer to the HOMELITE Engine Service section of this manual for service to the engine used.

FUEL MIXTURE

The manufacturer recommends mixing Homelite 2-Cycle oil with regular or unleaded gasoline at the ratio indicated on the package. When using regular BIA certified TC-W oil, mix at a ratio of 32:1.

STRING TRIMMER

All models can be fitted with an adjustable string trimmer head. Different styles have been used including both semi-automatic and manual adjustment types. Refer to the appropriate following paragraphs for service.

E-Z Line Advance. This semi-automatic, single or dual line advance shown in Fig. HL2 is used on some models. To extend the lines with the engine running, operate the trimmer at maximum speed and tap the spool retainer (1—Fig. HL2) on the ground. The line(s) should extend a small amount automatically. If the line does not extend with the engine running, stop the engine and extend the lines manually. If a line is broken inside the housing, it will be necessary to disassemble the unit and feed the line through the eyelet. To manually advance the trimmer lines with the engine stopped, push the retainer (1—Fig. HL2) at the bottom of the head and pull the line (both lines if so equipped).

To replace or rewind the spool, remove the spool retainer (1) by turning counterclockwise. Lift the spool (2) and the spring (3) from the spool housing (4). Inspect the spool lugs and shaft bore for wear or excessive damage. Replace if necessary. Replacement spools are available prewound with the proper size and length of line.

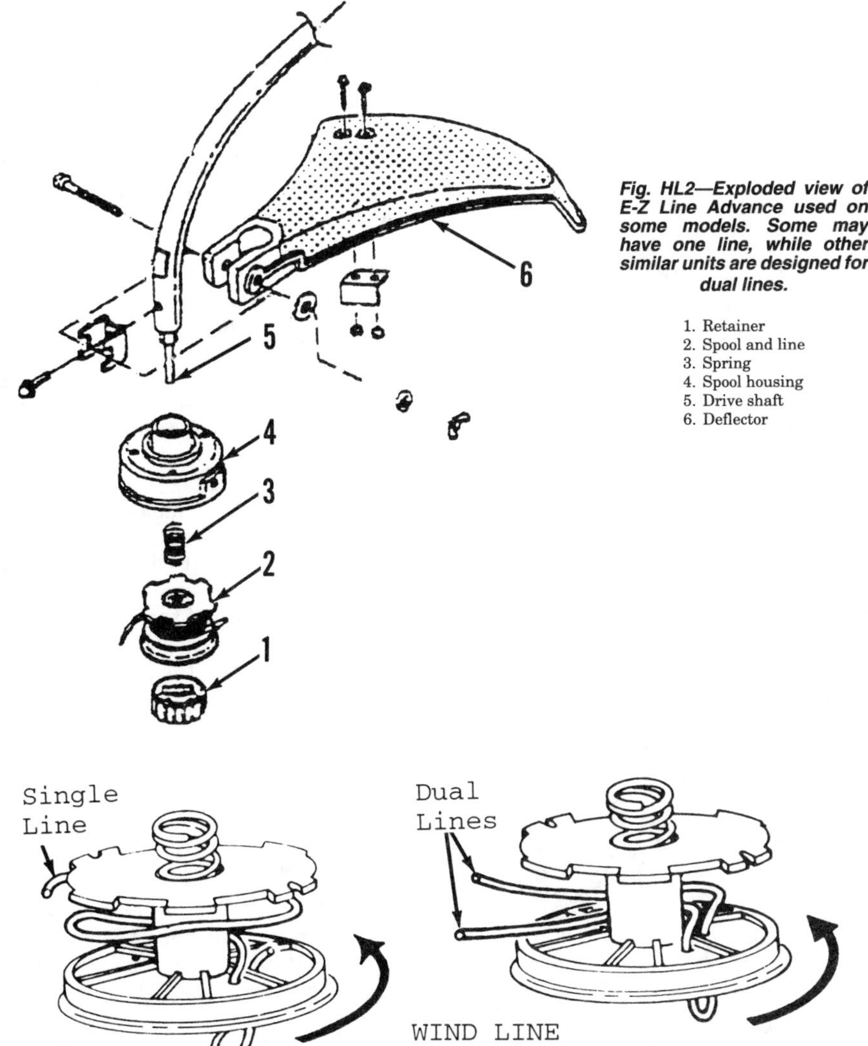

Fig. HL2—Exploded view of E-Z Line Advance used on some models. Some may have one line, while other similar units are designed for dual lines.

1. Retainer
2. Spool and line
3. Spring
4. Spool housing
5. Drive shaft
6. Deflector

Fig. HL3—On spool for E-Z Line Advance trimmer, wind the line in the direction shown. The left view shows proper attachment of line to the spool for single line models; drawing on the right shows correct attachment for dual line models.

To wind line on the spool for a single line system, insert one end of a 25 ft. (7.6 m) length of premium quality 0.080-in. (2 mm) diameter line through one of the two holes in the outer spool flange, then back through the other hole forming a small loop. Pull the loop tight. See left side of Fig. HL3. Wind the line clockwise (when viewed from the bottom of the spool flange). Wind the line onto the spool evenly as shown in Fig. HL4.

To wind line on the spool for a dual line system, first determine the proper size of line to install. HLT-15, ST-145, ST-155, ST-175, ST-185, ST-285, SX-135, 625, 725 and 825 models are originally equipped with 0.080 in. (2 mm) diameter line. ST-385 and ST-485 models are originally equipped with 0.105 in. line. HLT-16, HLT-17, HBC-18, HBC-30, 630, 730 and 830 models are originally equipped with 0.095 in. (2.41 mm) diameter line. The proper length of the line will vary, but will usually be about 25 ft. (7.6 m). Insert one end of the line through one of the two holes in the outer spool flange, then back through the other hole. Center the spool on the line, then pull both ends of the line until the small loop is tight. See right side of Fig. HL3. Wind both lines clockwise (when viewed from the bottom of the spool flange), being careful not to twist the lines. Wind the line onto the spool evenly as shown in Fig. HL4.

Install the spring (3—Fig. HL2), spool (2) and line into the spool housing while directing the ends of line(s) through the eyelets in the string head as shown in Fig. HL5. Push the spool into the string head and install the retainer (1—Fig. HL2).

To check operation, pull the line(s) while pressing down on the retainer.

Semi-Automatic Advance. Refer to Fig. HL6 for the dual line, semi-automatic string trimmer head typical of the type used on some models. To manually advance the trimmer lines with the engine stopped, push the button at the bottom of the head and pull both of the lines. To extend the lines with the engine running, operate the trimmer at maximum speed and tap the button on the ground. Both lines should extend a small amount automatically. If the line does not extend with the engine running, stop the engine and extend the lines manually. If a line is broken inside the housing, it will be necessary to disassemble the unit and feed the line through the eyelet.

To remove and disassemble the string trimmer head, proceed as follows. Hold the drum firmly and turn spool in the direction shown in Fig. HL7

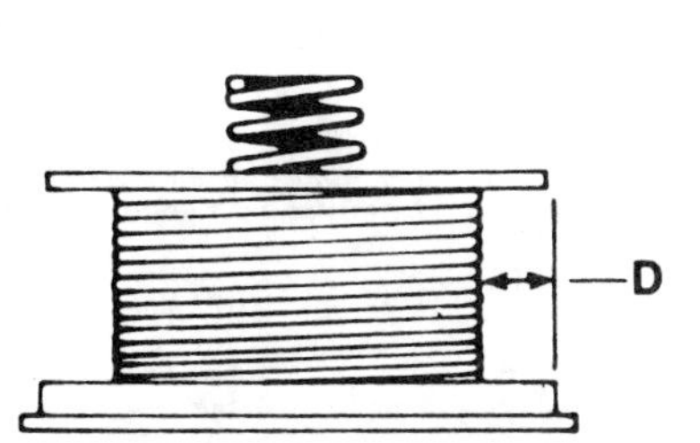

Fig. HL4—Wind line evenly around the spool until it is about 1/4 in. (6.4 mm) from the top (d).

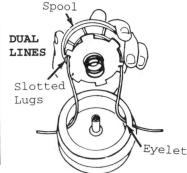

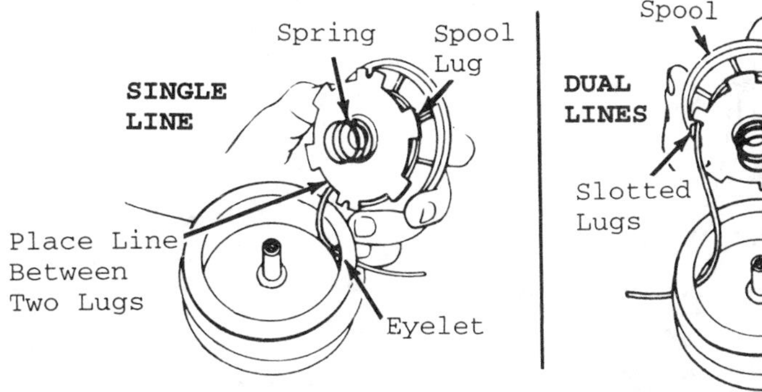

Fig. HL5—Install the spool in models with E-Z Line Advance trimmer head as shown. On single line models, position the line between lugs as shown at the left. On models with dual lines, the lines should be located in the slotted lugs as shown at the right.

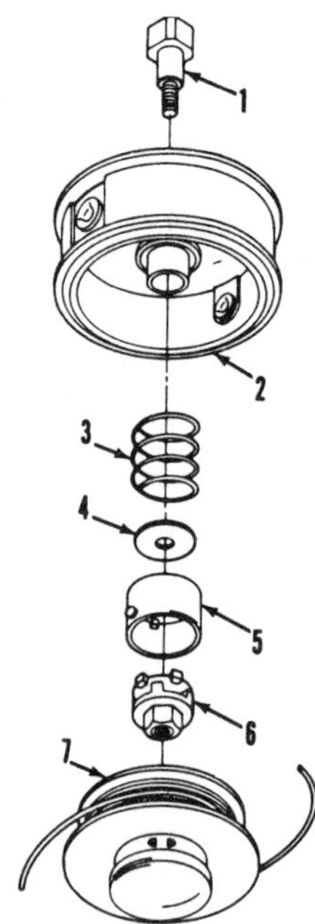

Fig. HL6—Exploded view of the dual line semi-automatic trimmer head used on some models.

1. Adapter
2. Housing
3. Spring
4. Washer
5. Outer cam
6. Inner cam
7. Spool

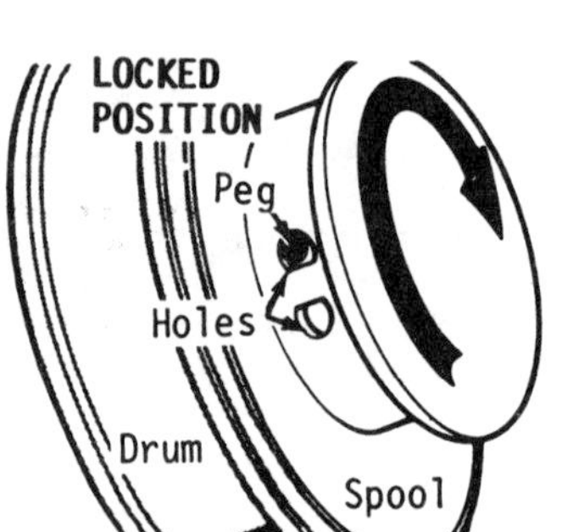

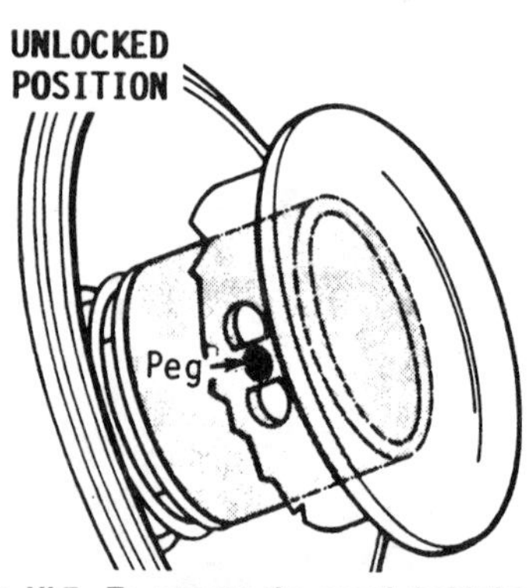

Fig. HL7—To remove the spool, hold the drum firmly and turn the spool in the direction shown to take up slack, then twist with a sudden snap until the plastic peg is between the holes as shown in the lower view.

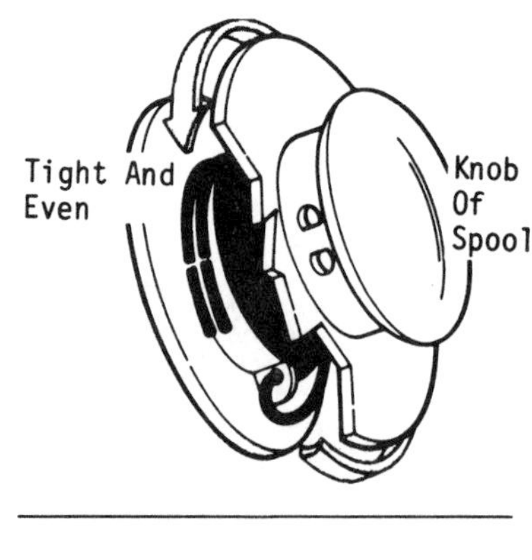

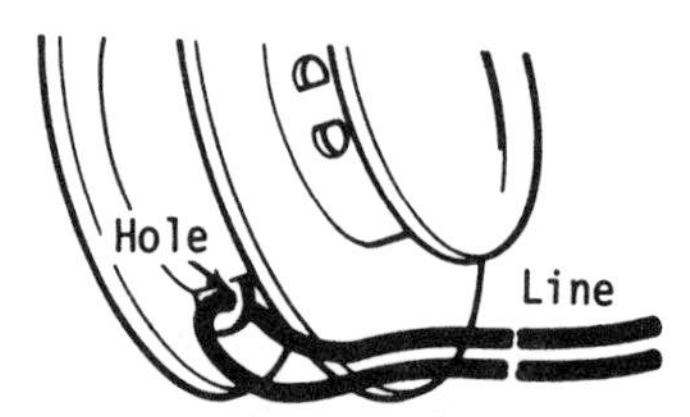

Fig. HL8—The end of the line must be inserted through the hole on spool as shown in the lower view. Wrap line tightly and evenly in the direction indicated by the arrow.

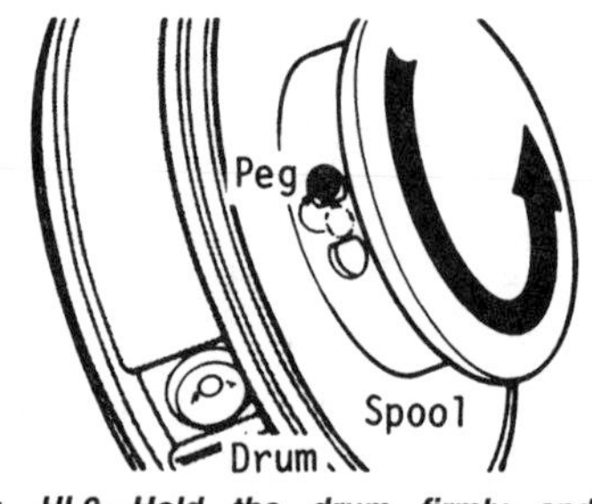

Fig. HL9—Hold the drum firmly and twist suddenly to lock the spool in position.

to remove slack. Twist with a hard snap until the plastic peg is between holes, then separate the spool from the drum.

Clean and inspect all parts for damage. If new line is installed, it should be 0.095 in. (2.41 mm) diameter. The spool will hold approximately 20 ft. (6 m) of line. Insert the line through the eye of the spool as shown in Fig. HL8 and pull the line through until it is the same length on both sides. Wrap both ends of the line on spool at the same time in clockwise direction as viewed from the top of spool. Wind the line tightly and evenly from side to side and do not twist the lines. Install spool while directing the ends of both lines through the eyelets in the housing. Align the pegs on drum with slots in the spool and push the spool into drum. Hold the drum firmly, then twist spool quickly in the direction shown in Fig. HL9 so peg enters the hole with a click and locks the spool in position. Trim the line so the line extends approximately 6 in. (15 cm) from the drum.

Manual Advance. Some models may be equipped with a manual advance trimmer head shown in Fig. HL10. To advance the trimmer lines with the engine stopped, pull the spool out and turn it until both lines are extended sufficiently, release the spool and allow the spring (5) to push the spool into the hub. If the spool is not completely seated, turn the spool until the pegs on the top of the spool engage the holes in the hub. Both lines should extend from the hub the same amount. If a line is not extended, it may be broken inside the housing, making it necessary to disassemble the unit and feed the line through the eyelets. If necessary to remove the spool, remove nut (6) and spring (5), then lift the spool from the hub. If necessary to remove the adapter (1), hold the splined fitting plate and turn the adapter clockwise. The adapter has left hand thread.

Clean and inspect all parts for damage. If new line is installed, it should be 0.105 in. (2.7 mm) diameter. Insert the line through the eye of the spool as shown in Fig. HL8 and pull the line through until it is the same length on both sides. Wrap both ends of the line on spool at the same time in clockwise direction as viewed from the top of spool. Wind the line tightly and evenly from side to side and do not twist the lines. Install spool while directing the ends of both lines through the eyelets in the housing. Install the spring (5—Fig. HL10) and nut (6). Tighten nut (6) securely.

BLADE

Saw, XRT, Machete, tri-arc blade, and 8 tooth blades are available for in-

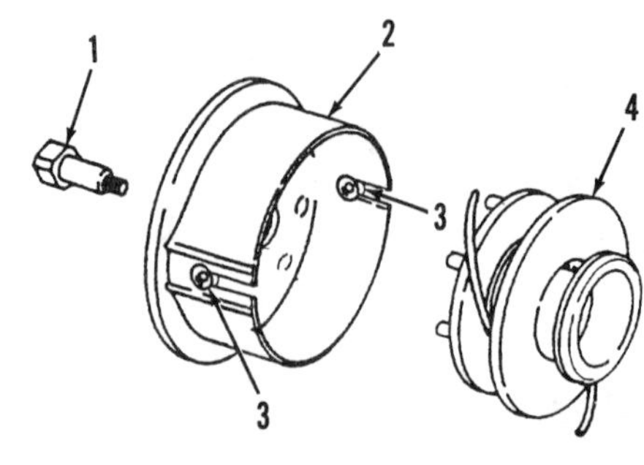

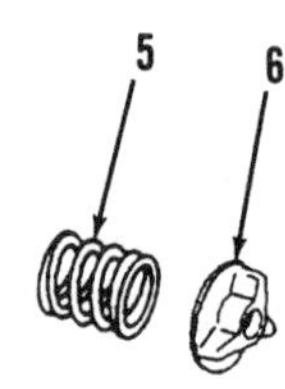

Fig. HL10—Exploded view of the dual line string trimmer head used on some models.

1. Adapter
2. Housing
3. Eyelets
4. Spool
5. Spring
6. Nut

stallation on some models. All of the available hard blades can be dangerous and should be selected and used with great care. Blades of different diameters should be matched to the specific model of the powerhead. Check the manufacturer's recommended application for your specific model. A blade too small or too large will reduce the effectiveness of operation and may be dangerous to operate. Sharpen each tooth following the original sharpening angle and tooth set. Sharpen all teeth evenly to maintain balance and do not file into the radius at the root.

DRIVE SHAFT AND HOUSING

The drive shaft and housing of some models is provided with a coupler (Fig. HL11) that permits a variety of devices (such as a cultivator, snow thrower, blower and edger as well as the trimmer or brush cutter) to be driven by the power head. On these models, first separate the drive shaft from the attachment at the coupling. Additional service procedure will depend upon whether the upper or lower shaft/housing tube is being serviced, but will generally follow the procedure described for units with one drive shaft and housing.

Before separating the drive shaft housing from the clutch housing and engine, detach the throttle cable and engine stop wires. Loosen the screw(s) that clamps the drive shaft housing in the clutch housing, then pull the drive shaft housing from the clutch housing. If so equipped, remove the gear head from the lower end of the drive shaft housing. On model without gear head, remove the trimmer assembly from the lower end of the drive shaft housing.

Inspect the ends of the drive shaft (21—Fig. HL12 or 21—Fig. HL13) care-

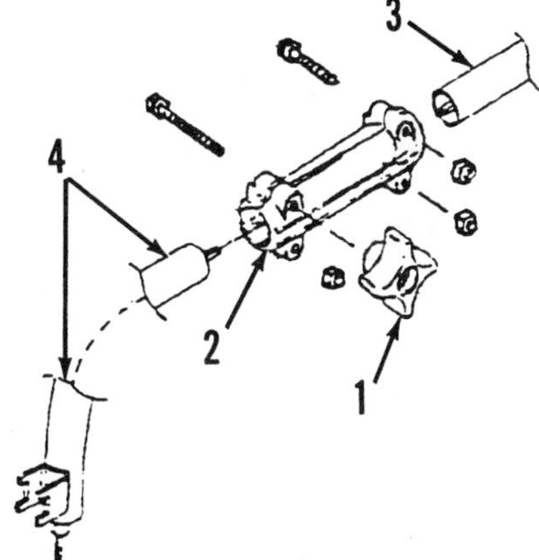

Fig. HL11—View of the coupler (2) used on some models to attach the drive shaft (3) from the power head to the drive shaft (4) of various equipment.

1. Knob
2. Coupler
3. Upper drive shaft
4. Lower drive shaft

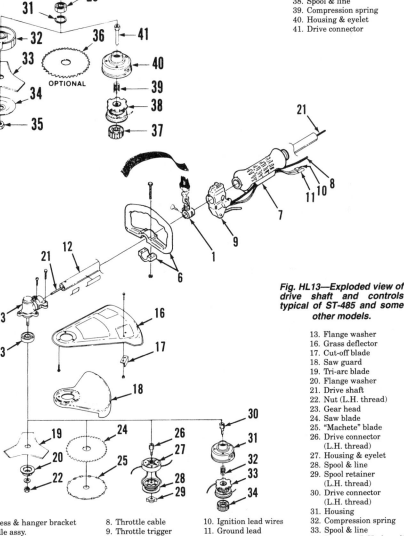

Fig. HL12—Exploded view of the drive shaft and controls typical of HBC-18, ST-185 and some other models.

1. Harness
2. Nut
3. Switch plate
4. Grounding washer
5. Stop switch
7. Grip half
8. Throttle cable
9. Throttle trigger
10. Stop switch lead wires
12. Drive shaft housing
14. Spindle shaft (adapter)
15. Grip half
16. Grass protector
17. Cut-off blade
18. Handle bar clamp
19. Hanger bracket
21. Flexible shaft
22. Handle bar
24. Lower bearing housing
28. Thrust washer
29. Ball bearing
30. Spacer
31. Snap ring
32. Flange washer
33. Tri-arc blade
34. Cupped washer
35. Locknut
36. Saw blade
37. Spool retainer
38. Spool & line
39. Compression spring
40. Housing & eyelet
41. Drive connector

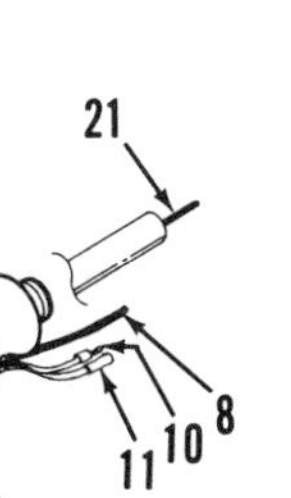

Fig. HL13—Exploded view of drive shaft and controls typical of ST-485 and some other models.

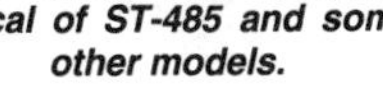

1. Harness & hanger bracket
6. Handle assy.
7. Grip
8. Throttle cable
9. Throttle trigger & ignition switch
10. Ignition lead wires
11. Ground lead
12. Drive shaft housing
13. Flange washer
16. Grass deflector
17. Cut-off blade
18. Saw guard
19. Tri-arc blade
20. Flange washer
21. Drive shaft
22. Nut (L.H. thread)
23. Gear head
24. Saw blade
25. "Machete" blade
26. Drive connector (L.H. thread)
27. Housing & eyelet
28. Spool & line
29. Spool retainer (L.H. thread)
30. Drive connector (L.H. thread)
31. Housing
32. Compression spring
33. Spool & line
34. Retainer (L.H. thread)

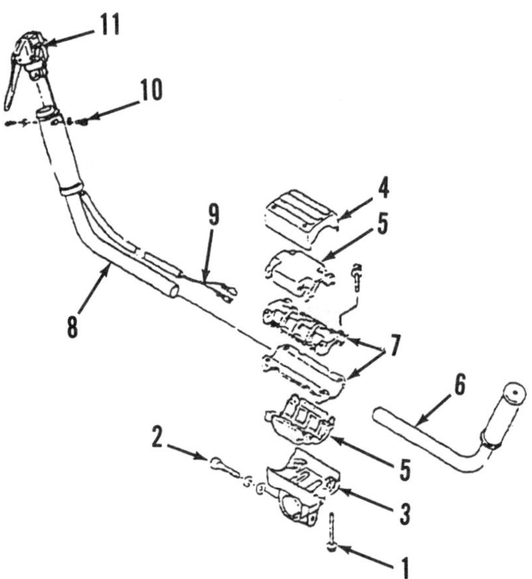

Fig. HL14—Exploded view of the throttle control typical of some models with the wide handle assembly. The stop switch is also located at the grip.

1. Screws
2. Clamp screw
3. Clamping bracket
4. Upper clamp
5.I solating rubber
6. Left bar
7. Bar clamp
8. Right bar
9. Engine stop wires
10. Fitting screws
11. Throttle and stop switch assembly

fully for wear. The flexible cable or solid drive shaft does not require regular maintenance unless it is removed. If the drive shaft cannot be easily withdrawn or turned, it may be necessary to install the housing as well as the drive shaft.

If the drive shaft cable is removed, it should be cleaned, inspected and lubricated. If damaged, a new cable should be installed. Lubricate the entire length of the drive shaft with No. 2 multipurpose grease (part No. 18453 or equivalent). Service bushings for the drive shaft housing may be available for some models. Renewable bearings (29—Fig. HL12) may be located in the bearing head at the lower end of the drive shaft housing of some models.

GEAR HEAD

A gear head (23—Fig. HL13) is located at the lower end of the drive shaft and housing of some models. To remove the assembly, loosen the fitting screw and clamp bolts, then pull the gear head from the drive shaft housing. The gear head is lubricated by the manufacturer and should need no further maintenance.

ENGINE CONTROLS

Engine throttle control is located within easy reach of the operator's hands when safely positioned on the grips. Refer to Fig. HL12, Fig. HL13, Fig. HL14 or Fig. HL15. On some models, the engine stop switch is also located near the operator's grip.

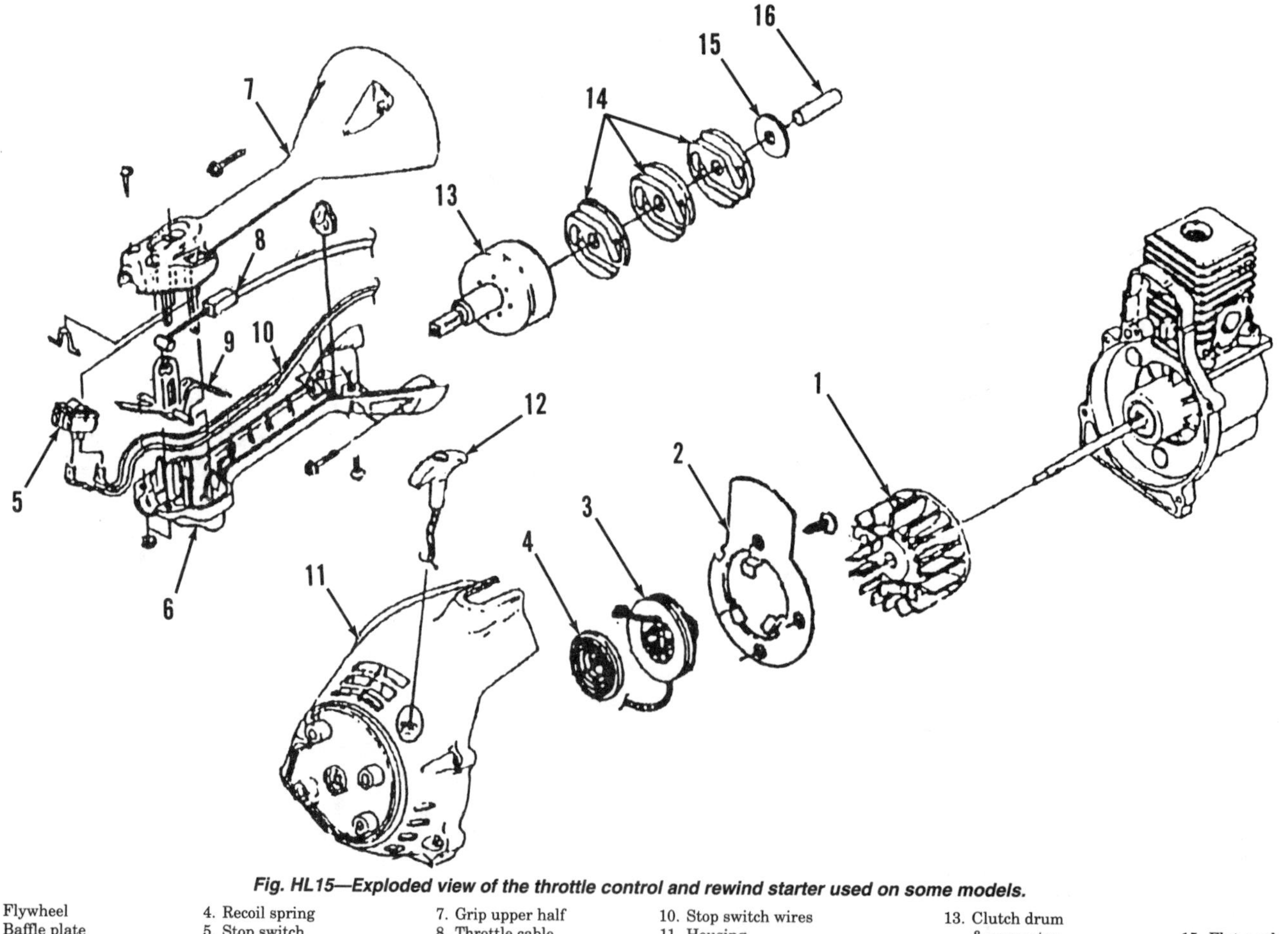

Fig. HL15—Exploded view of the throttle control and rewind starter used on some models.

1. Flywheel
2. Baffle plate
3. Starter pulley
4. Recoil spring
5. Stop switch
6. Grip lower half
7. Grip upper half
8. Throttle cable
9. Throttle trigger
10. Stop switch wires
11. Housing
12. Starter handle
13. Clutch drum & connector
14. Clutch
15. Flat washer
16. Spacer

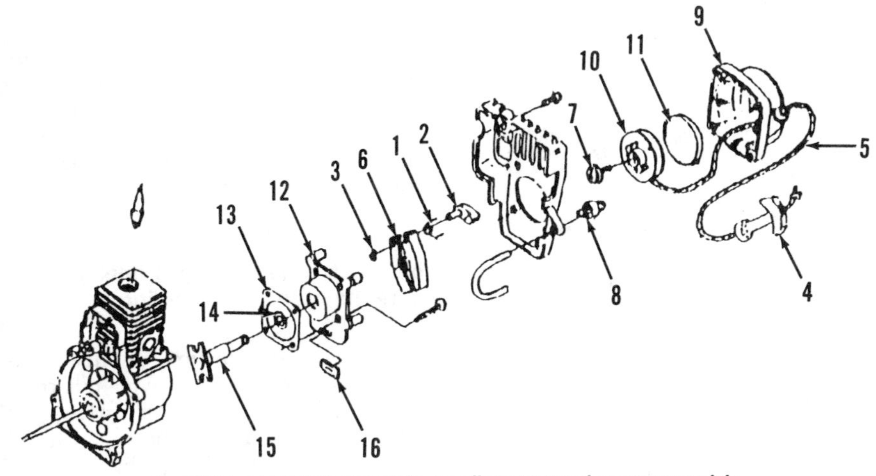

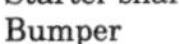

Fig. HL16—Exploded view of the recoil starter used on some models.

1. Pawl spring
2. Pawl
3. Clip
4. Handle
5. Rope
6. Pawl carrier
7. Screw
8. Air purge bulb
9. Housing
10. Pulley
11. Recoil spring
12. Crankcase cover
13. Gasket
14. Spacer
15. Starter shaft
16. Bumper

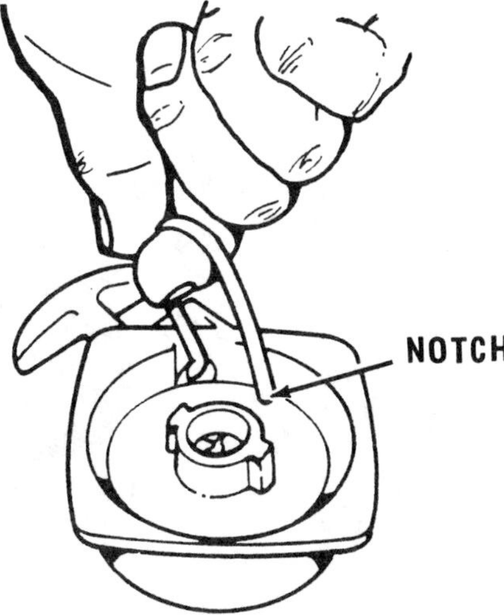

Fig. HL17—To set the preload of the starter recoil spring, pull a loop in the rope with the rope in the notch in the pulley, then wind the pulley as necessary. When the rope is released, it will pull out of the notch.

RECOIL STARTER

The recoil starter is located in the engine housing at the front of the power head of 25 cc engine and many 30 cc engine models. Refer to Fig. HL15 for an exploded view of a typical application. On some 30 cc and 40 cc models, the recoil starter is mounted at the rear (Fig. HL16). On these models, the starter can be removed and service can be accomplished without disassembling the power head.

Front Mounted Starter. To service front mounted starter (Fig. HL15), detach stop switch wires (5) and throttle cable (8). Remove handle grips (7 and 10) and clutch assembly (13-16). Unbolt and remove starter housing (11). If rope is not broken, remove rope handle and allow rope to wind into the starter housing. Wear appropriate safety eye wear and gloves before disengaging pulley (3) from starter housing as rewind spring may uncoil uncontrolled. Remove screws attaching pulley retainer (2) to starter housing and remove pulley (3) and rope.

Lubricate starter center post and rewind spring (4) lightly with grease before assembling. Starter rope should be wound on pulley in clodkwise direction as viewed from flywheel side of pulley. Insert outer end of rope through opening in starter housing and attach rope handle. To preload rewind spring, pull a loop in the rope at the notch in starter pulley. Turn starter pulley clockwise several turns while holding the rope in the notch in pulley. Release the rope from the pulley notch and let the spring unwind slowly while winding the rope on the pulley. The spring should be preloaded enough to rewind the rope completely and should hold the starter handle against the guide, but the spring must not bind before the rope is fully extended. When the rope is fully extended, it should be possible to turn the pulley at least ¼ turn before the spring binds.

30 cc Engine Models. Refer to Fig. HL16 for an exploded view of this rear mounted unit. Unbolt and remove the starter from the engine. Remove the rope handle (4) and allow the rope to wind into the starter. Remove the center screw (7) and the pulley (10). The spring (11) may rewind uncontrollably causing injury. Wear appropriate safety eye wear and gloves before removing the recoil spring (11) from the housing (9).

Unscrew the lock nut and pawl plate (6) from the engine crankshaft. Remove the clip (3) from the front of the pawl to remove the pawl and spring (1 and 2). Install the pawl plate and tighten it to 8-10 N•m (70-90 in.-lb.) torque. Tighten the lock nut on models so equipped to 16-17.5 N•m (140-155 in.-lb.) torque.

To assemble the starter, lubricate the center post and spring side of the housing lighly with grease before assembling. Attach the outer end of the spring to the clip in the housing, then wind the spring into the housing wrapping the spring in a counterclockwise direction until the spring is completely in the housing cavity. The inner end of the spring should contact the center post.

Attach the rope to the pulley (10), thread the rope through the housing (9), then attach the handle (4). Install the pulley over the center post of the housing while making sure the pulley engages the end of the rewind spring. Coat the threads of the retaining screw (7) with medium strength Loctite, then install and tighten the screw securely. A loop of the rope should be in the pulley's notch as shown in Fig. HL17. Hold the rope loop as shown and wind the pulley counterclockwise several turns. Pull the rope out with the handle and allow it to rewind. If the rope does not rewind properly, pull a loop in the rope as shown in Fig. HL17 and preload the spring another turn.

NOTE: If the rope is too long, it will bind before rewinding properly. Make sure the rope is not binding.

To make sure the spring is not tightened too much, pull the rope out completely, then turn the pulley an additional 1/2 turn. If the rope cannot be pulled out completely, the spring is bound and will break. Pull a loop in the rope as shown in Fig. HL17 and loosen the spring slightly as required. A proper setting will allow the rope to be fully extended and will also wind the rope onto the pulley fully.

40 cc Engine Models. Refer to Fig. HL18 for an exploded view of this rear mounted starter. Unbolt and remove the starter housing (7) from the engine. Release the spring tension before disassembling the starter. If the rope or rewind spring is broken, spring tension will already be released. The rope can be pulled out of the notch in the pulley (5) and the pulley allowed to turn until the spring tension is released. Spring tension can also be released by removing the handle (8) and allowing the rope to be drawn into the pulley.

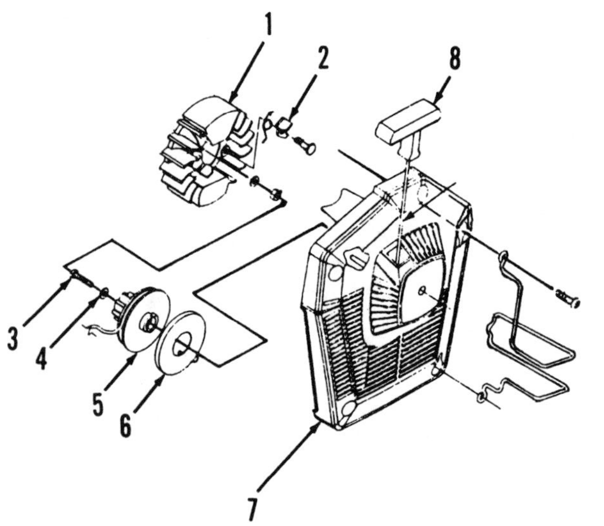

Fig. HL18—Exploded view of rewind starter used on some models.

1. Flywheel
2. Pawl assy.
3. Screw
4. Washer
5. Pulley
6. Rewind spring
7. Housing
8. Rope handle

Remove the center screw (3) and the pulley (5) being careful not to dislodge the recoil spring (6). The spring (6) may rewind uncontrollably causing injury. Wear appropriate safety eye wear and gloves before removing the recoil spring (6) from the housing.

To assemble the starter, lubricate the center post and spring side of the housing with light grease. Attach the outer end of the spring to the clip in the housing, then wind the spring into the housing. Wrap the spring in a counterclockwise direction until the spring is completely in the housing cavity. The inner end of the spring should contact the center post.

Attach the rope to the pulley (5), thread the rope through the housing (7), then attach the handle (8). Install the pulley over the center post of the housing while making sure the pulley engages the end of the rewind spring. Coat the threads of the retaining screw (3) with medium strength Loctite, then install and tighten the screw securely. A loop of the rope should be in the pulley's notch as shown in Fig. HL17. Hold the rope loop and wind the pulley counterclockwise several turns. Pull the rope out with the handle and allow it to rewind. If the rope does not rewind properly, pull a loop in the rope as shown in Fig. HL17 and preload the spring another turn.

NOTE: If the rope is too long, it will bind before rewinding properly. Make sure the rope is not binding.

To make sure the spring is not tightened too much, pull the rope out completely, then turn the pulley an additional 1/2 turn. If the rope cannot be pulled out completely, the spring is bound and will break. Pull a loop in the rope as shown in Fig. HL17 and loosen the spring slightly as required. A proper setting will allow the rope to be fully extended and will also wind the rope onto the pulley fully.

ELECTRIC STARTER

An electric starter motor is incorporated in the housing (11—Fig. HL19) of some models. The starter is energized by the battery pack (18) when the starter switch (12) is pressed. When troubleshooting, attempt to start the unit and carefully observe what happens as well as what does not happen. If the starter turns freely, without turn-

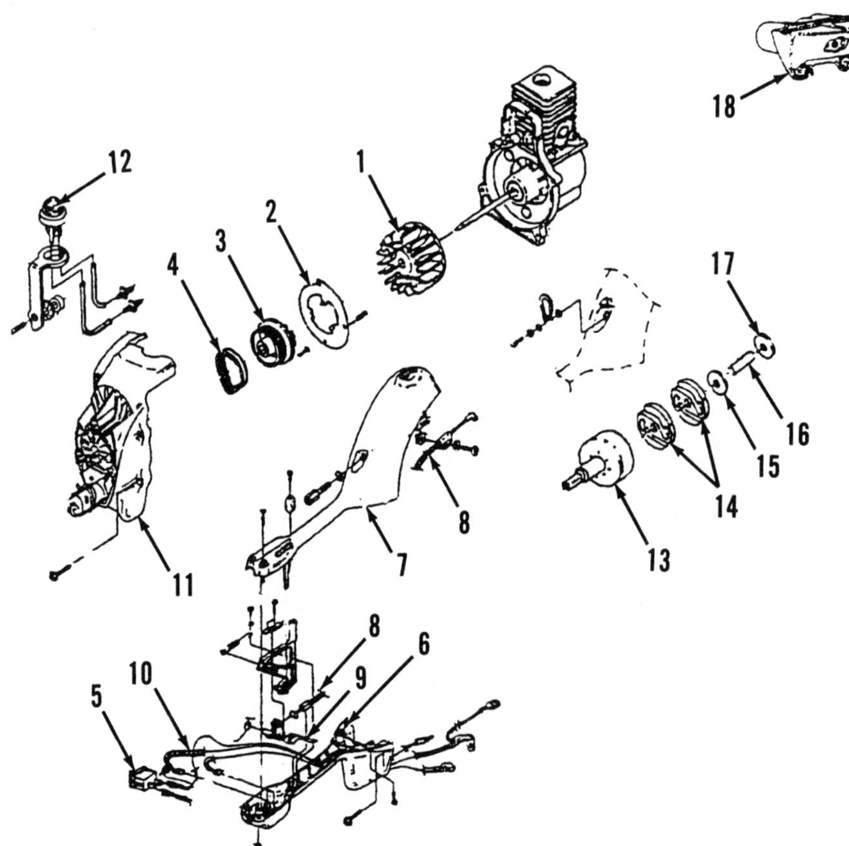

Fig. HL19—Exploded view of the electric starter and associated parts used on some models. The starter motor is located in housing (11).

1. Flywheel
2. Baffle plate
3. Starter pulley
4. Starter belt
5. Stop switch
6. Grip lower half
7. Grip upper half
8. Throttle cable
9. Throttle trigger
10. Stop switch wires
11. Housing & starter motor
12. Starter button (switch)
13. Clutch drum & connector
14. Clutch
15. Flat washer
16. Spacer
17. Washer
18. Battery pack
19. Battery charger

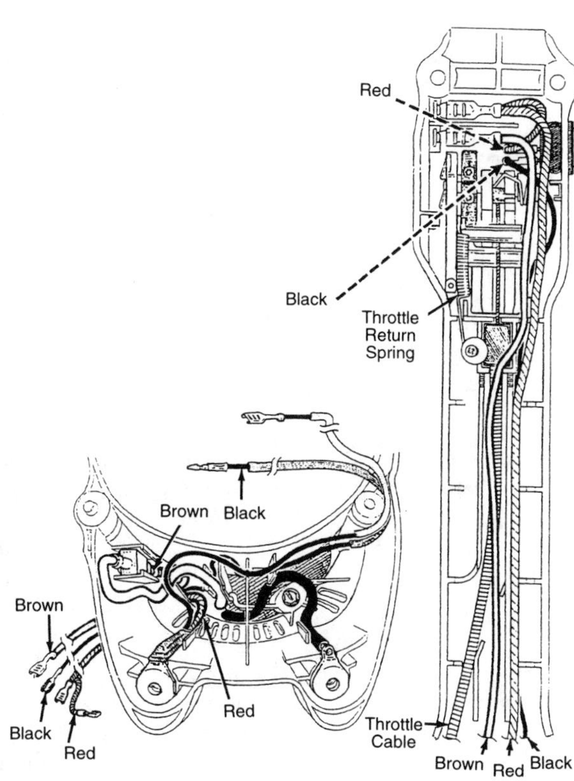

Fig. HL20—Drawings of the grip of models with electric starter showing location of wires and other components.

ing the engine, check the belt and pulley (3 and 4). If the starter tries but does not turn the engine, check the condition of the battery. Damage to the engine may also prevent turning the engine or slow the speed causing difficult starting. Refer to Fig. HL20 for location of the wires, throttle cable and other components in the lower grip.

CLUTCH

Refer to the appropriate ENGINE SERVICE section for clutch removal and service procedures.

HOMELITE

BRUSHCUTTER

Model	Engine Make	Displ.
ST-400	Homelite	54 cc

ENGINE INFORMATION

Model ST-400 brushcutter is powered by a Homelite engine. Refer to appropriate HOMELITE ENGINE SERVICE section of this manual.

SAW BLADE

The saw blade may be removed after unscrewing retaining nut. Prevent shaft rotation by inserting a suitable pin through the grass shield. Note when installing a toothed saw blade that shaft rotation is clockwise as viewed from underside.

DRIVE SHAFT

The flexible drive shaft should be removed, inspected and lubricated after every 25 hours of operation. To remove drive shaft, loosen clamp screw and remove screw in front side of lower head (26—Fig. HL32-1). Slide head off drive tube (23) and pull flexible shaft (15) from tube. Clean and inspect shaft, then lubricate shaft with Homelite Multi-Purpose Grease 17237 or a suitable lithium grease. Insert shaft into drive tube (shaft ends are identical and shaft ends may be reversed to extend shaft life). With 3-5 inches (7.6-12.7 cm) of shaft extending from drive tube engage shaft in lower head. Then while turning lower head so upper end of shaft engages clutch drum, install lower head on drive tube. Align holes in front side of lower head and drive tube and install screw. Tighten clamp screw so lower head will not turn.

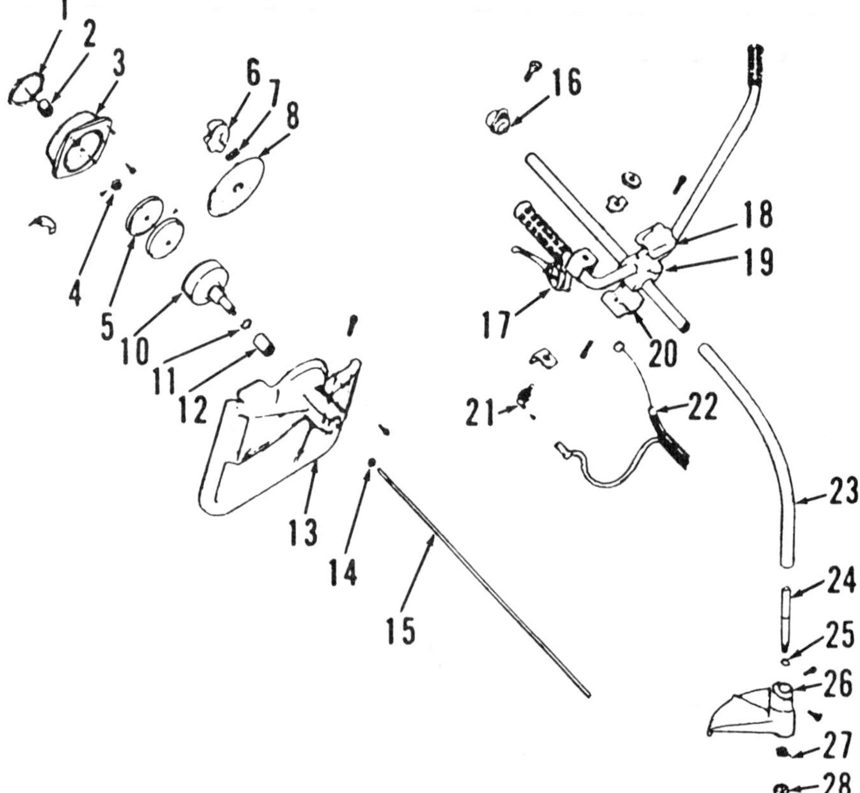

Fig. HL32-1—Exploded view of ST-400 brushcutter.

1. Gasket
2. Bearing
3. Drivecase
4. Seal
5. Cover
6. Clutch shoe
7. Spring
8. Clutch hub
10. Clutch drum
11. Snap ring
12. Bearing
13. Upper head
14. Snap ring
15. Drive shaft
16. Hanger
17. Throttle lever
18. Clamp
19. Block
20. Clamp
21. Ignition switch
22. Throttle cable
23. Drive tube
24. Spindle
25. Snap ring
26. Lower head
27. Bearing
28. Snap ring

HOMELITE

GASOLINE POWERED TRIMMER/BRUSHCUTTER

Models	Engine Make	Engine Model	Displacement
HK-18	Homelite	...	18.4 cc (1.12 cu. in.)
HK-24	Homelite	...	24.1 cc (1.47 cu. in.)
HK-33	Homelite	...	33.3 cc (2.03 cu. in.)

ENGINE IDENTIFICATION

All models are equipped with a Homelite engine. Refer to the HOMELITE Engine Service section of this manual for service to the engine used.

FUEL MIXTURE

The manufacturer recommends mixing Homelite 2-Cycle oil with regular or unleaded gasoline at the ratio indicated on the package. When using regular BIA certified TC-W oil, mix at a ratio of 32:1.

An antioxidant fuel stabilizer (such as Sta-Bil) should be added to the fuel if Homelite oil is not used. Homelite oil contains an antioxidant fuel stabilizer.

STRING TRIMMER

Model HK-18 is equipped with a string trimmer head while Models HK-24 and HK-33 may be equipped with a string trimmer head or brush cutting blade (Fig. HL33-1 or Fig. HL33-2).

The string trimmer head may be removed after unscrewing retaining nut, then pulling out spool so lugs disengage while rotating spool. Trimmer line will be expelled from outlet holes if spool is rotated in proper direction. Push spool back into head while engaging lugs in holes of head. Reinstall retainer nut.

To install line on an empty spool, a length of line 15 feet (4.5 m) long should be inserted through the holes in the spool as shown in Fig. HL33-3. The spool should be centered between both ends of the line. Wrap both ends of line around spool in the same direction. Install the spool in the head while inserting string ends through the outlet holes in the head. Do not trap string between

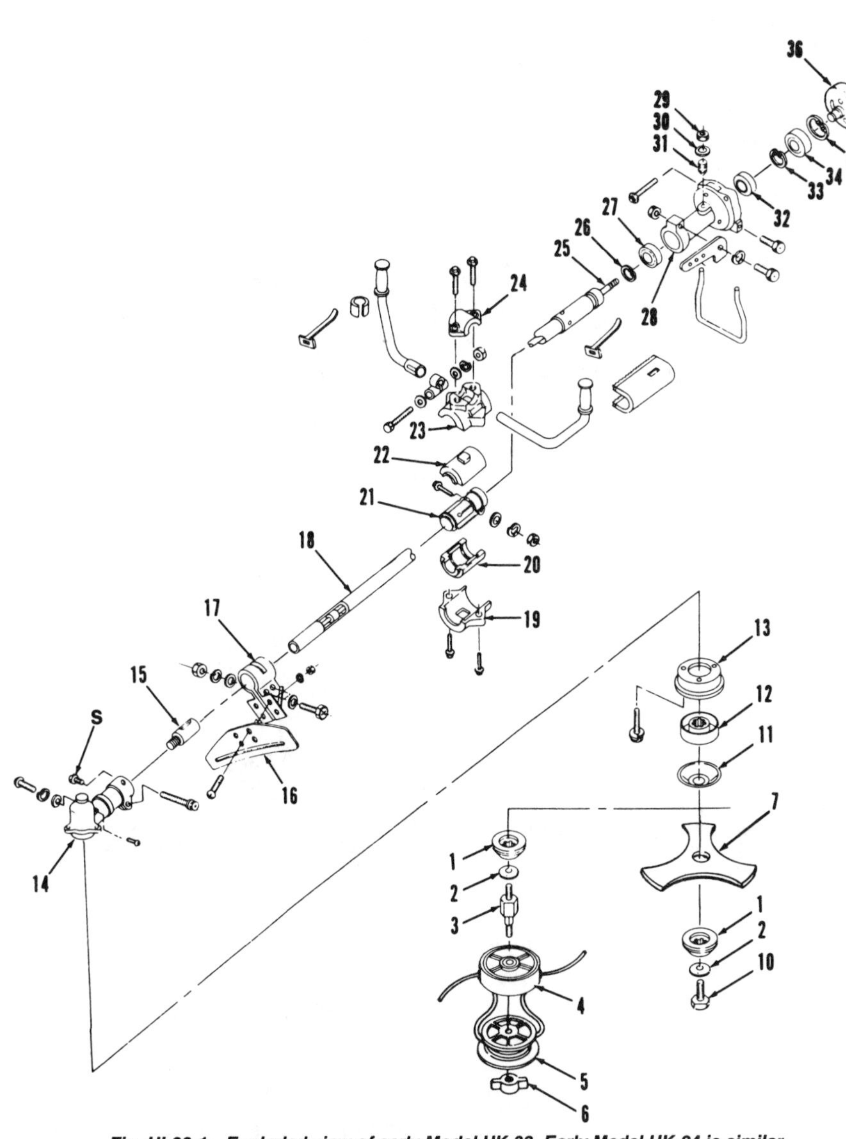

Fig. HL33-1—Exploded view of early Model HK-33. Early Model HK-24 is similar.

1. Lower flange
2. Wave washer
3. Shaft bolt
4. Head
5. Spool
6. Nut (L.H.)
7. Blade
10. Screw (L.H.)
11. Cup
12. Upper flange
13. Cover
14. Gear head
15. Connector
16. Guard blade
17. Bracket
18. Drive
19. Bracket
20. Isolator
21. Handle hoop
22. Isolator
23. Bracket
24. Bracket
25. Drive shaft
26. Snap ring
27. Collar
28. Clutch housing
29. Locknut
30. Washer
31. Screw
32. Collar
33. Snap ring
34. Bearing
35. Snap ring
36. Clutch drum

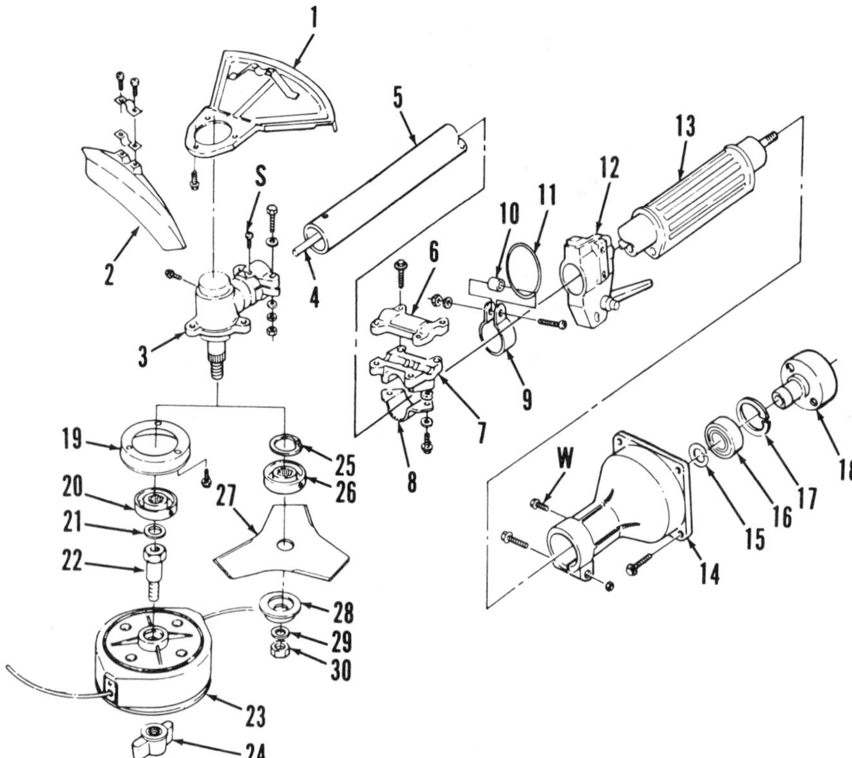

Fig. HL33-2—Exploded view of later Model HK-24 and HK-33. Model HK-18 is similar. Washer (21) is not used on Model HK-18.

1. Shield
2. Shield
3. Gear head
4. Drive shaft
5. Drive shaft housing
6. Bracket
7. Bracket
8. Bracket
9. Hanger
10. Spacer
11. Ring
12. Throttle assy.
13. Grip
14. Clutch housing
15. Snap ring
16. Bearing
17. Snap ring
18. Clutch drum
19. Cover
20. Upper flange
21. Special washer
22. Shaft bolt
23. Trimmer assy.
24. Nut (L.H.)
25. Snap ring
26. Upper flange
27. Blade
28. Lower flange
29. Special washer
30. Nut (L.H.)

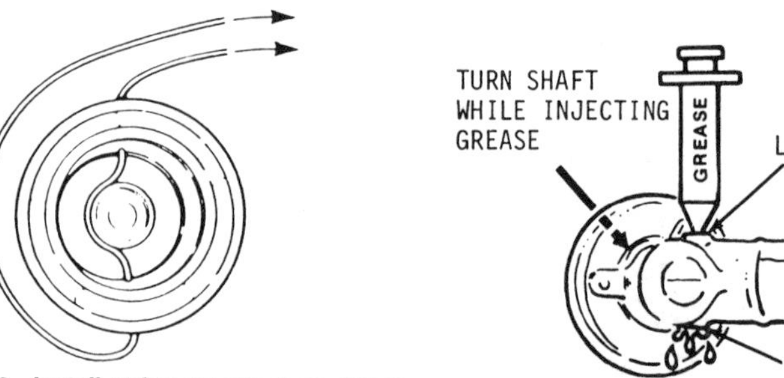

Fig. HL33-30—Install string on spool as shown and as outlined in text. Ends may be wrapped around spool in either direction as long as both ends are in the same direction.

Fig. HL33-4—Lubricate gear head by injecting grease into gear head as shown.

underside of spool and head. Complete assembly of trimmer head.

SAW BLADE

The saw blade may be removed after unscrewing retaining screw or nut. Note that screw or nut has left-hand threads. Prevent blade rotation by inserting shaft holder tool into lower flange (1—Fig. HL33-1 or 28—Fig. HL33-2). Install saw blade so blade cuts when turning clockwise as viewed from underside.

GEAR HEAD

Gear head (14—Fig. HL33—1 or 3—Fig. HL33-2) is lubricated using multipurpose grease. The gear head should be lubricated after every 50 hours of operation.

To lubricate gear head, remove large slotted screw and small Phillips head screw on sides of gear head. While rotating gear head shaft, inject grease into large screw hole as shown in Fig. HL33-4 until grease is expelled from small screw hole. Reinstall screws and clean off excess grease.

To remove shaft bolt (3—Fig. HL33-1) on early models, secure lower flange (1) using shaft holder tool and turn bolt clockwise (L.H. threads). To remove shaft bolt (22—Fig. HL33-2) on later models, prevent shaft rotation by inserting a 3/16 inch (4 mm) rod through cover (19) and into upper flange (20). Turn shaft bolt clockwise (L.H. threads) to remove.

To remove gear head, back out alignment screw (S—Fig. HL33-1 or Fig. HL33-2) approximately 1/8 inch (3.2 mm). Loosen clamp screw(s) and separate gear head from drive shaft housing. On early models, use a suitable tool to engage shaft connector (15—Fig. HL33-1) and unscrew connector from gear head shaft.

The gear head on all models must be serviced as a unit assembly. Individual components are not available.

DRIVE SHAFT

The drive shaft does not normally require lubrication. If a new drive shaft is installed or the old drive shaft is removed, the drive shaft should be lubricated. Apply Homelite Multipurpose Grease 17237 or a suitable lithium base grease to the drive shaft. Do not apply an excessive amount of grease.

To remove drive shaft assembly, refer to preceding section and remove gear head. On Model HK-18, detach throttle cable bracket from engine fan housing, disconnect throttle cable and disconnect stop switch wire at connector adjacent to throttle cable bracket. On Model HK-24 and HK-33, loosen throttle cable guide-nut (Fig. HL33-5), unscrew carburetor cap and lift out throttle valve assembly (cover carburetor opening and be careful not to damage throttle valve components).Remove four screws securing clutch housing (28—Fig. HL33-1 or 14—Fig. HL33-2) to engine and detach clutch housing with drive shaft housing.

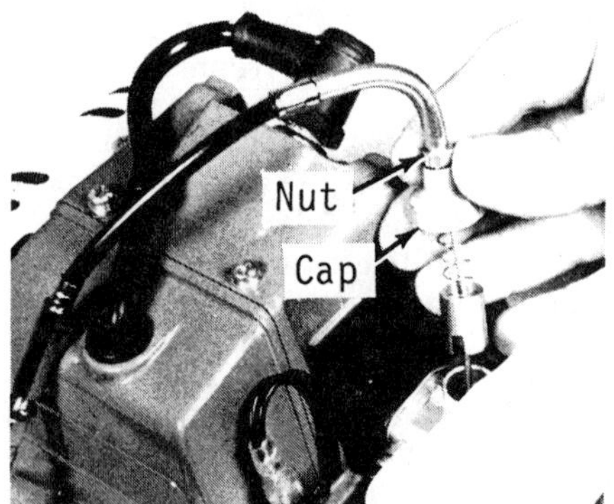

Fig. HL33-5—Loosen nut and cap and withdraw throttle valve assembly from carburetor on Models HK-24 and HK-33.

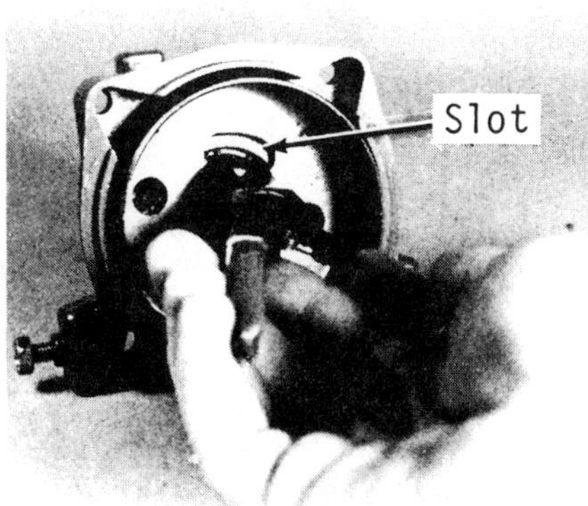

Fig. HL33-6—Snap ring is accessible through slot in clutch drum.

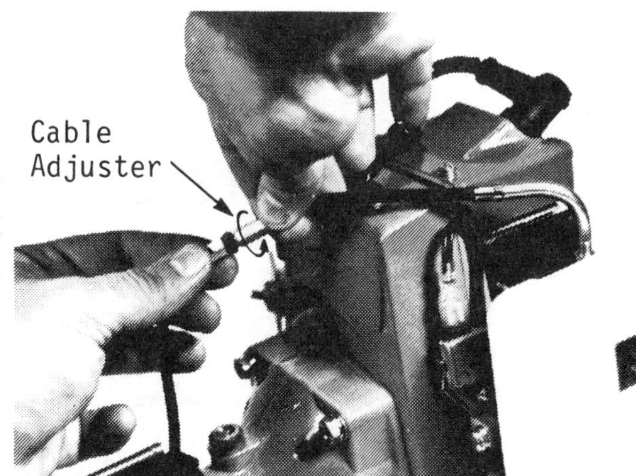

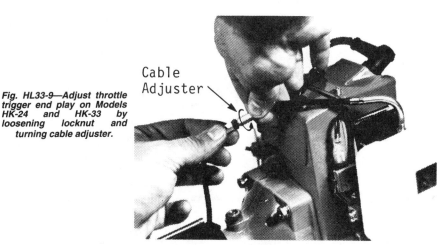

Fig. HL33-9—Adjust throttle trigger end play on Models HK-24 and HK-33 by loosening locknut and turning cable adjuster.

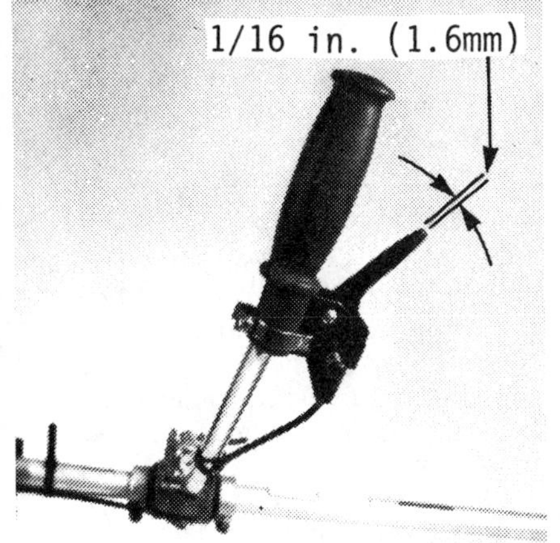

Fig. HL33-7—Throttle trigger end play should be 1/16 inch (1.6 mm) measured at end of lever.

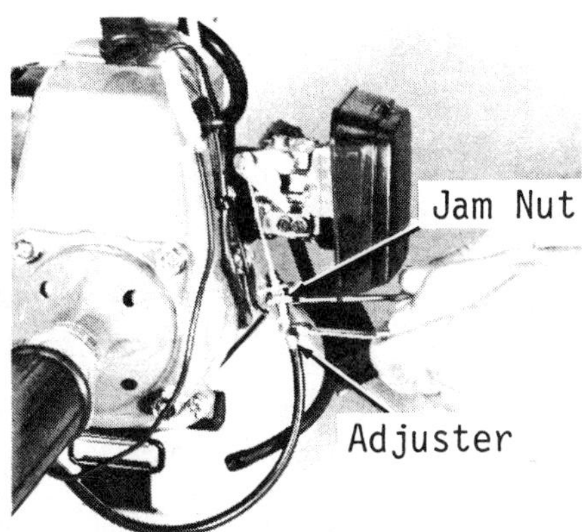

Fig. HL33-8—Adjust throttle trigger end play on Model HK-18 by loosening locknut and turning cable adjuster.

On early Model HK-33, loosen locknuts (29—Fig. HL33-1) and back out locating screws (31). On later models, back out housing alignment screw (W—Fig. HL33-2). On all models, loosen clamp screw and withdraw drive shaft housing from clutch housing. Drive shaft will remain attached to clutch.

To detach the drive shaft from the clutch drum, proceed as follows: On early models, insert a suitable rod through the clutch housing and the holes in the clutch drum so the drum cannot rotate.

Grasp the opposite end of the drive shaft with a wrench and unscrew the drive shaft from the clutch drum. On later models, grasp the drive shaft in a soft-jawed vise then use a suitable tool inserted in the two-holes in the clutch drum and unscrew the drum off the drive shaft.

Reassemble by reversing the disassembly procedure. Be sure throttle valve assembly is properly installed on Model HK-18.

CLUTCH

The clutch assembly is accessible after removing the clutch housing as outlined in the preceding DRIVE SHAFT section. Inspect components and renew any which are damaged or excessively worn.

To remove the clutch drum on early Model HK-33, remove the drive shaft as previously outlined. Working through the elongated slot in the clutch drum, detach snap ring (35—Fig. HL33-1) as shown in Fig. HL33-6. Using Homelite tool 94455 or a suitable equivalent, press clutch drum and bearing (34—Fig. HL33-1) out of clutch housing. Remove snap ring (33) and press clutch drum out of bearing. If necessary, remove rear collar (32), snap ring (26) and front collar (27).

To remove the clutch drum on Models HK-18, HK-24 and later Model HK-33, remove snap ring (33—Fig. HL33-1 or 16—Fig. HL33-2). Press clutch drum out of bearing. Remove snap ring (35-Fig. HL33-1 or 17—Fig. HL33-2). Using Homelite tool 94455 or a suitable equivalent, press bearing out of clutch housing.

Reassemble by reversing disassembly procedure.

THROTTLE TRIGGER

Throttle trigger end play must be properly adjusted to obtain desired engine operation and to allow clutch to disengage. Throttle trigger end play should be 1/16 inch (1.6 mm) measured at end of trigger lever. See Fig. HL33-7.

Loosen locknut and rotate cable adjuster shown in Fig. HL33-8 or HL33-9 to adjust end play. Tighten locknut against adjuster after performing adjustment.

NOTE: Insufficient throttle trigger end play may not allow engine to reach idle speed and clutch may not disengage.

STARTER

Refer to the ENGINE SERVICE section for service to the recoil starter assembly.

HOMELITE

TRIMMERS/BRUSHCUTTERS

Model	Cutting Swath	Line Diameter	Engine Make	Displacement
HBC-38	18 in.	0.105 in.	Homelite	40 cc
HBC-40	20 in.	0.105 in.	Homelite	40 cc

ENGINE INFORMATION

All models are equipped with a Homelite engine. Refer to appropriate Homelite engine section for service information.

STRING TRIMMER

The brushcutter may be equipped with a dual string, manual advance string trimmer head. Advancing the trimmer line is accomplished by loosening retainer nut (12—Fig. HL34-1) by turning clockwise (L.H. thread). Loosen retainer enough so line can be pulled out about $^1/_4$ inch (6.4 mm) from string head. Pull down on spool (10) and rotate to advance line. Each line should measure approximately $6^3/_4$ inches (17 cm) on Model HBC-38 or $7^3/_4$ inches (19.7 cm) on Model HBC-40.

After advancing the line, rotate spool slightly in either direction to line up locating lugs on spool with locating holes in string head. Tighten retainer by turning counterclockwise (L.H. thread).

To replace or rewind the spool, remove retainer (12) by turning clockwise (L.H. thread). Pull spool from string head. To rewind new line on spool, insert one end of an 18-ft. (5.5 m) length of premium quality 0.105-in. (2.7 mm) diameter monofilament line through hole in the spool (Fig. HL34-2). Center the spool in the 18-ft. (5.5 m) length of line. Pull loop tight and wind both lengths of line around the spool in clockwise direction as viewed from top of spool, taking care not to twist the line.

Install spool and line into string head. Feed $6^1/_2$ inches (16.5 cm) of line through each eyelet. Tilt spool and place into string head taking care that the line does not slip under the spool flange. Rotate spool slightly in either direction to engage locating lugs on spool with locating holes in string head. Install retainer by turning counterclockwise (L.H. thread).

BLADE

The brushcutter may be equipped with either a Tri-Arc or "machete" blade. Refer to Fig. HL34-1 for configuration of blade components. Note that nut (7) has left-hand threads.

DRIVE SHAFT

Models HBC-38 and HBC-40 are equipped with a solid drive shaft (2—Fig. HL34-1) that does not require periodic maintenance. Lubricate shaft if removed.

GEAR HEAD

The gear head (3—Fig. HL34-1) should be lubricated after every 100 hours of operation. Recommended lubricant is Homelite All-Temp Multi-Purpose Grease or equivalent. Remove plug (P) in side of gear head and inject grease into gear head.

To remove gear head, loosen the two clamp screws and locating screw. Slide gear head from drive shaft housing. Gear head must be serviced as a unit assembly; individual components are not available.

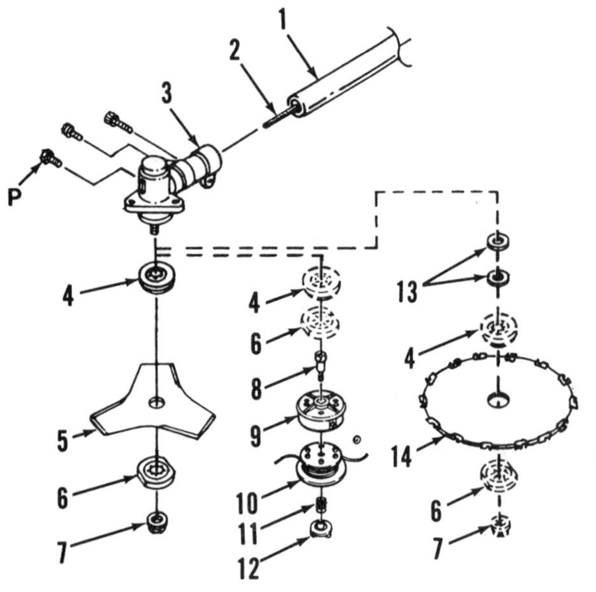

Fig. HL34-1—Exploded view of trimmer and brushcutter components.

1. Drive shaft housing
2. Drive shaft
3. Gear head
4. Washer
5. Tri-Arc blade
6. Washer
7. Nut (L.H. threads)
8. Drive connector
9. Housing & eyelet
10. Spool
11. Spring
12. Retainer nut (L.H. threads)
13. Washers
14. "Machete" blade

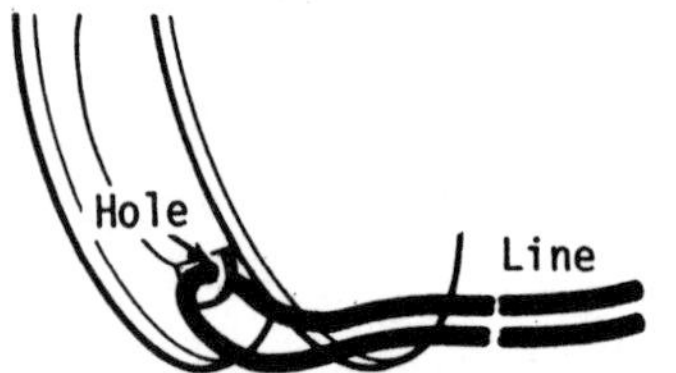

Fig. HL34-2—End of trimmer line must be routed through hole on spool.

HOMELITE

GASOLINE POWERED BLOWERS

Model	Engine Manufacturer	Engine Model	Displacement
BP-250	Homelite	...	1.53 cu. in.
HB-100	Homelite	...	1.53 cu. in.
HB-180	Homelite	...	1.53 cu. in.
HB-280	Homelite	...	1.6 cu. in.
HB-380	Homelite	...	1.6 cu. in.
HB-480	Homelite	...	1.9 cu. in.
HB-680	Homelite	...	1.9 cu. in.

ENGINE INFORMATION

The models included in this section are powered by a Homelite engine. Refer to appropriate Homelite engine service section for service procedures and specifications.

R&R ENGINE

All Models

To remove engine, first unbolt and remove back rest pad and back rest on models so equipped. On all models, remove engine cover (1—Fig. HL37-1). Remove screws holding blower volute halves (4 and 7) together and separate volute halves. Disconnect throttle cable and ignition wires from engine. Remove blower fan (6) from flywheel (5). Unbolt and remove engine from blower volute half (4).

REWIND STARTER

Models BP-250, HB-100 And HB-180

The rewind starter is located in the blower volute half adjacent to the engine. The engine must be removed to service the starter.

To disassemble starter, remove rope handle (4—Fig. HL37-2) and allow rope to wind into starter. Remove pulley retainer (7) and remove starter components as needed. Wear appropriate safety eyewear and gloves when working with or around rewind spring (5) as spring may uncoil uncontrolled.

Before assembling starter, lubricate center post of housing and side of spring with light grease. Install rewind spring (4) in a clockwise direction from outer end. Rope length should be 46 inches (117 cm). Assemble starter while passing rope through housing rope outlet and attach rope handle to rope. To place tension on starter rope, rotate pulley clockwise so notch in pulley is aligned with rope outlet, then hold pulley to prevent pulley rotation. Pull rope back into housing while positioning rope in pulley notch. Turn rope pulley clockwise until spring is tight. Allow pulley to turn counterclockwise until notch aligns with rope outlet. Disengage rope from notch then release pulley and allow rope to wind on pulley. Check starter operation. Rope handle should be held against housing by spring tension, but it must be possible to rotate pulley at least $^1/_4$ turn clockwise when rope is pulled out fully.

Models HB-280, HB-380, HB-480 And HB-680

The backrest pad and backrest must be removed on Models HB-480 and HB-

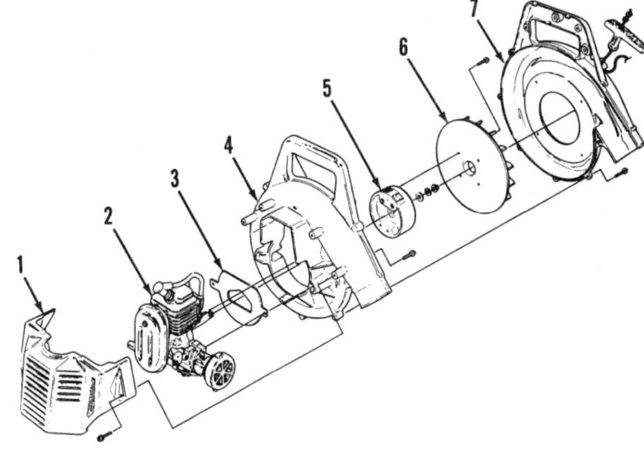

Fig. HL37-1—Exploded view of Model HB280 blower assembly. Other models are similar.

1. Cover
2. Engine
3. Backplate
4. Blower volute
5. Flywheel
6. Blower fan
7. Blower volute

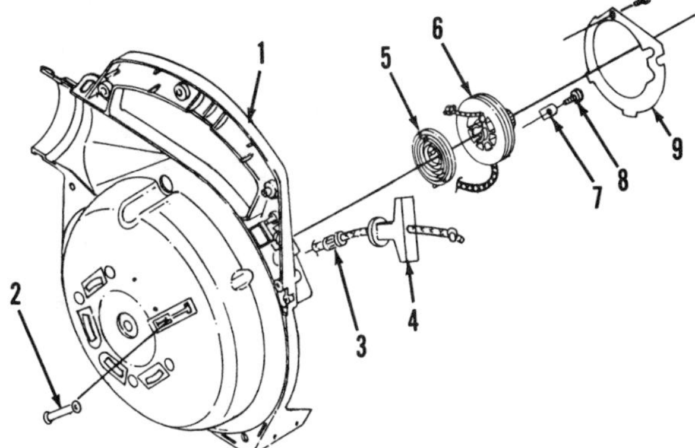

Fig. HL37-2—Exploded view of rewind starter used on Models BP-250, HB-100 And HB-180.

1. Volute half
2. Rope guide
3. Rope guide
4. Rope handle
5. Rewind spring
6. Pulley
7. Retainer
8. Screw
9. Plate

680 for access to starter. On all models, unscrew mounting screws and remove starter. remove rope handle and allow rope to wind into starer. Unscrew retaining screw (3—Fig. HL37-3) and remove ratchet (5) and pulley while being careful not to dislodge rewind spring in housing. Wear appropriate safety eyewear and gloves when working with or around rewind spring as spring may uncoil uncontrolled.

When assembling starter, wind rope around rope pulley in a clockwise direction as viewed with pulley in housing. To place tension on rewind spring, pass rope through rope outlet in housing and install rope handle. Pull rope out and hold rope pulley so notch in pulley is adjacent to rope outlet. Pull rope back through outlet between notch in pulley and housing. Turn rope pulley clockwise to place tension on spring. Release pulley and check starter action. Do not place more tension on rewind spring than is necessary to draw rope handle up against housing. Install ratchet (5) with hooked end of ratchet lever wire (6) up and between posts of starter housing. Install screw (3) and washer (4) then install starter housing.

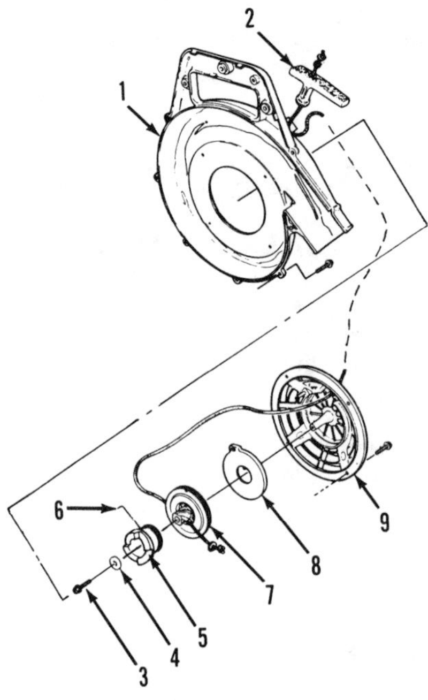

Fig. HL37-3—Exploded view of rewind starter used on Models HB-280, HB-380, HB-480 and HB-680.

1. Volute half
2. Rope handle
3. Screw
4. Washer
5. Ratchet
6. Ratchet lever wire
7. Pulley
8. Rewind spring
9. Starter housing

HUSQVARNA

GASOLINE POWERED STRING TRIMMERS

Model	Engine Manufacturer	Engine Model	Displacement
18RL	Husqvarna	18	18.5 cc
22LD	Husqvarna	22	21.2 cc
22R, 22RL	Husqvarna	22	21.2 cc
25BL, 25BT	Husqvarna	25	24.1 cc
25R, 25RD, 25RL	Husqvarna	25	24.1 cc
26LC	Husqvarna	26	26 cc
26RLC	Husqvarna	26	26 cc
32LC	Husqvarna	32	32 cc
32R, 32RL, 32RLC	Husqvarna	32	32 cc
36R	Husqvarna	36	36 cc
39R	Husqvarna	39	40 cc
125L, 125LD	Husqvarna	125	25.4 cc
125R, 125RD	Husqvarna	125	25.4 cc
132L, 132LD	Husqvarna	132	31.8 cc
132R, 132RD	Husqvarna	132	31.8 cc
140R	Husqvarna	140	40 cc
165R, 165RX	Husqvarna	165	65 cc
240R	Husqvarna	240	40 cc
244R, 244RX	Husqvarna	244	44 cc
245R, 245RX	Husqvarna	245	44 cc
250RX	Husqvarna	250	49 cc

ENGINE INFORMATION

The models in this section are equipped with a Husqvarna engine. Refer to appropriate engine service section for engine service information.

FUEL MIXTURE

Manufacturer recommends mixing regular unleaded grade gasoline with a high-quality, two-stroke engine oil designed for air-cooled engines. Recommended oil is Husqvarna oil mixed at fuel:oil ratio indicated on oil container. Fuel:oil ratio should be 16:1 when using any other two-stroke oil.

STRING TRIMMER

The unit may be equipped with a manual advance or semi-automatic advance string trimmer head. The trimmer head may be equipped with right- or left-hand threads. Observe arrow on trimmer head when removing head.

Refer to Fig. HQ10 for an exploded view of a typical manual advance trimmer head. Refer to Fig. HQ11 for an exploded view of one version of the semi-automatic trimmer head used on some models. When installing string on this type, route string around pin (P—Fig. HQ12), otherwise string will feed continuously. On some semi-automatic trimmer heads, new string can be fed into head as shown in Fig. HQ13 and wound on spool by turning lower plate.

BLADE

Some models may be equipped with a blade, which may be a three- or four-edge blade, or a saw blade. To remove blade, carefully rotate blade until hole in upper driving disc is aligned with hole in gear housing as shown in Fig. HQ14. Insert a 4.5 mm (0.16 in.) round rod into holes to prevent blade rotation. Blade retaining nut has left-hand threads. Remove nut and blade assembly. When installing blade, tighten nut to 35-50 N·m (26-30 ft.-lbs.).

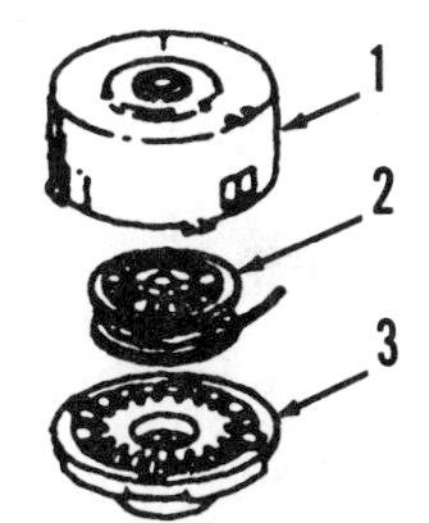

Fig. HQ10—Exploded view of manual trimmer head used on some models.
1. Housing
2. Spool
3. Cover

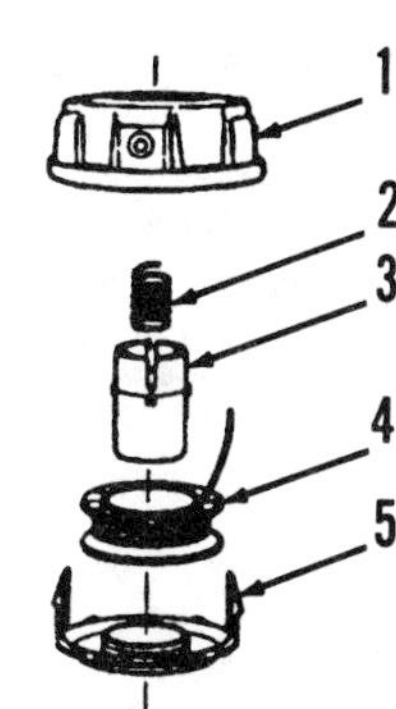

Fig. HQ11—Exploded view of semi-automatic trimmer head used on some models.
1. Housing
2. Spring
3. Button
4. Spool
5. Cover

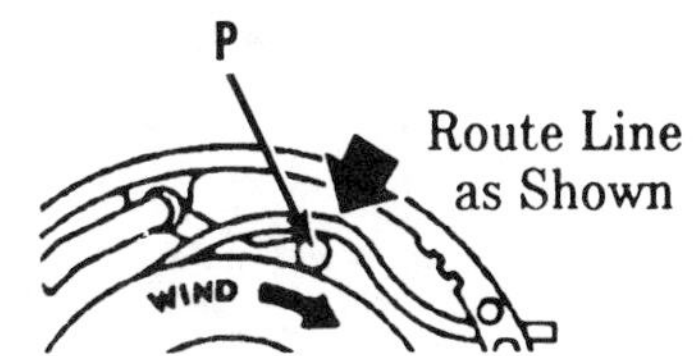

Fig. HQ12—On models so equipped, route string around pin (P) as shown.

To sharpen saw blade, use a 5.5 mm (7.32 in.) round file in file holder 501 58 02-01 and follow sharpening procedure depicted in Figs. HQ15 through HQ21. Three-edge and four-edge blades may be sharpened using a single-cut flat file.

DRIVE SHAFT

The flexible drive shaft on models with a curved drive shaft tube should be removed and lubricated after every 10 hours of operation. Recommended lubricant is Husqvarna lubricant 530-030102 or equivalent.

The drive shaft on models with a straight drive shaft tube does not require periodic lubrication. If removed, lubricate drive shaft with Husqvarna lubricant 530-030102 or equivalent before reinstalling drive shaft.

GEAR HEAD

Series 22, 25, 125 And 132

These models are equipped with the gear head shown in Fig. HQ22. Gear

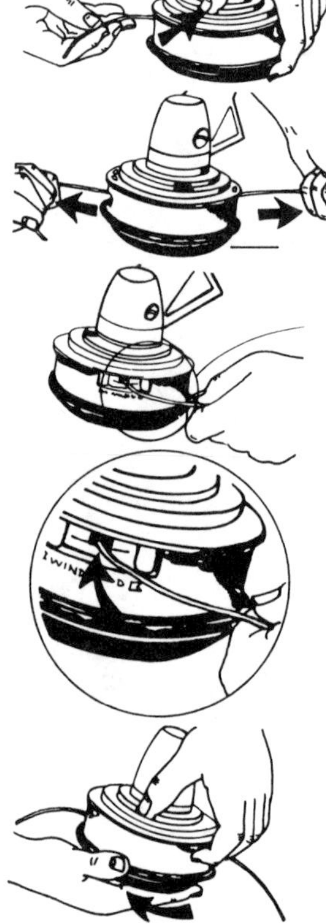

Fig. HQ13—To extend line on trimmer head shown, follow procedure in top two views. To install line, insert line then turn lower plate as shown in bottom three views.

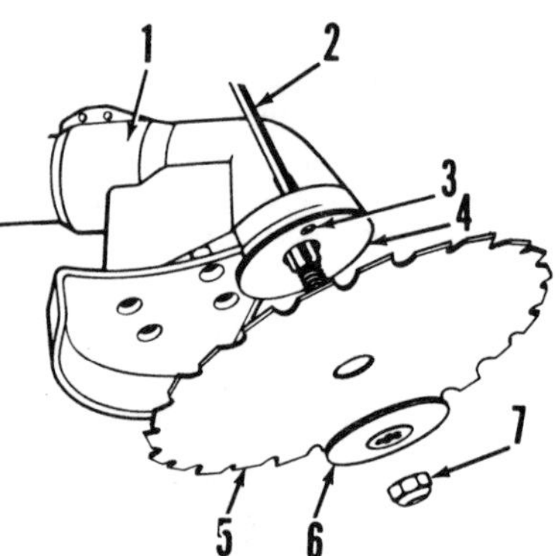

Fig. HQ14—View showing location of blade assembly components on some models.

1. Gear head
2. Tool
3. Hole
4. Drive disc
5. Blade
6. Washer
7. Nut (L.H.)

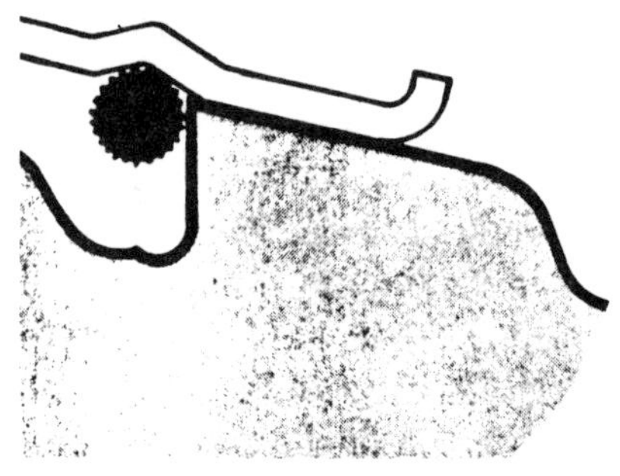

Fig. HQ15—Sharpen front edge of tooth only. Make certain file holder is held firmly against edge of tooth.

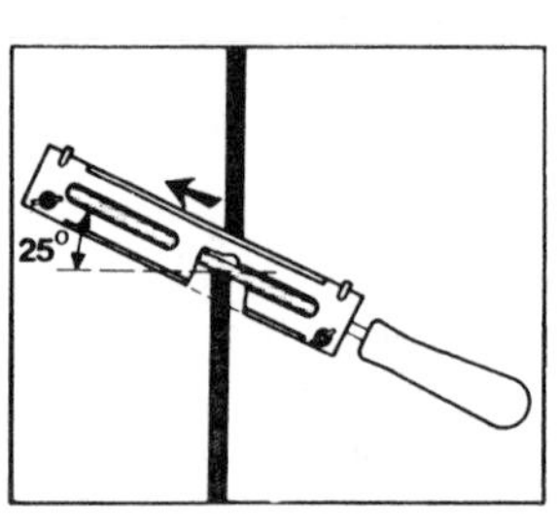

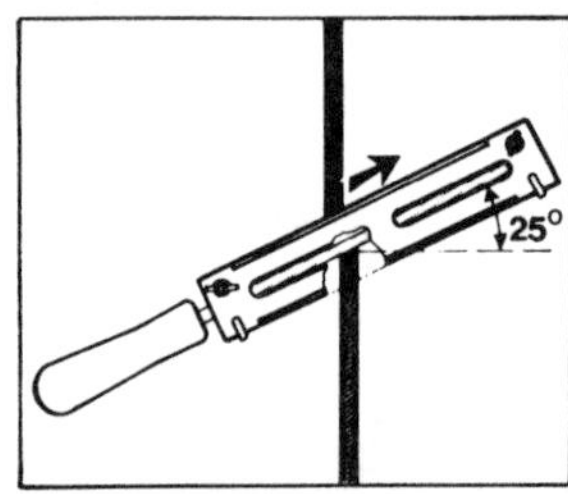

Fig. HQ16—Alternate filing one tooth to the right and the next tooth to the left. File at a 25-degree angle.

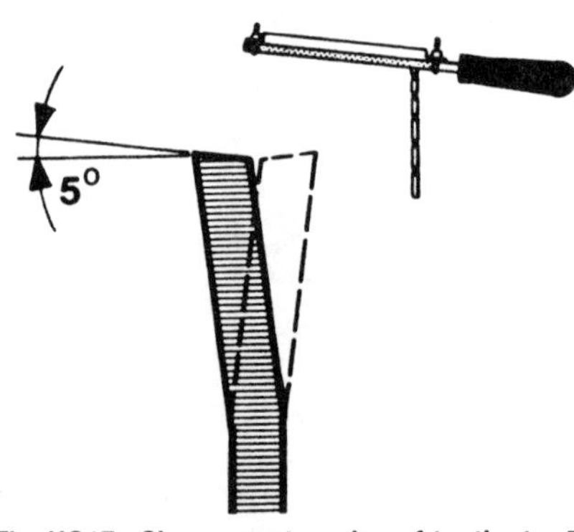

Fig. HQ17—Sharpen outer edge of tooth at a 5-degree angle.

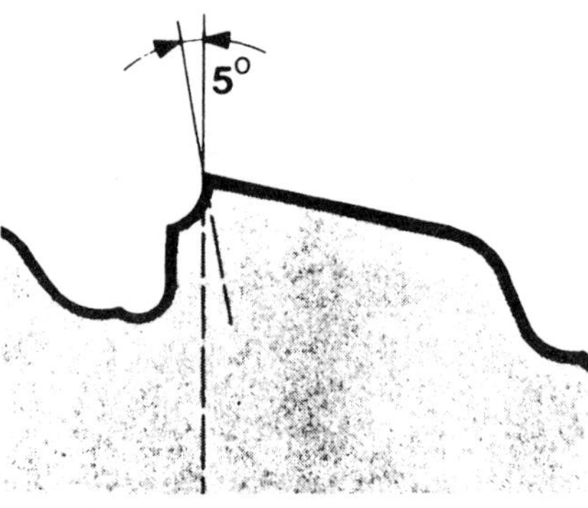

Fig. HQ18—Tooth front edge angle should be 5-degree. Hard wood and large trees may require a smaller angle.

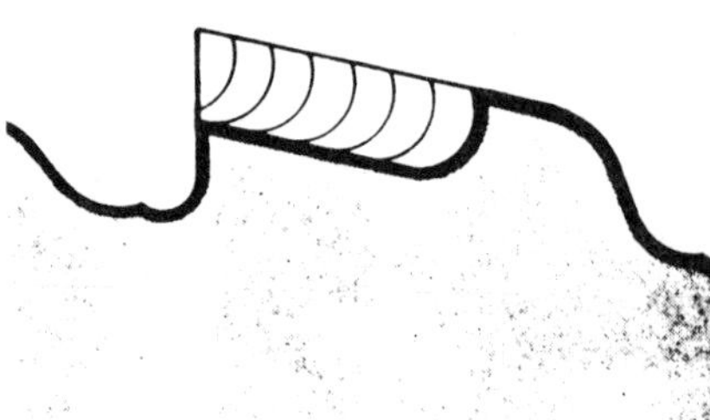

Fig. HQ19—Reduce tooth height evenly during repeated sharpening.

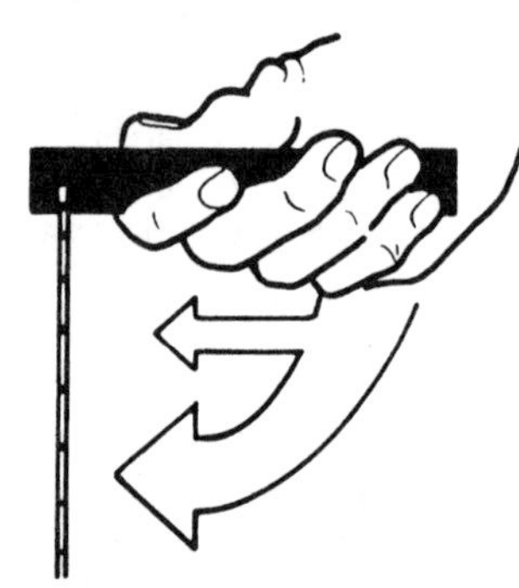

Fig. HQ20—Use set gage (501 31 77-01) to adjust tooth set when teeth have been filed down approximately 50 percent.

Fig. HQ21—Tooth set should provide 1 mm (0.04 in.) distance between tooth tips.

Illustrations courtesy Husqvarna Forest & Garden

head lubricant level should be checked after every 50 hours of operation. Remove plug (9) to check lubricant level and inject grease. Gear head should be ³/₄ full. Recommended lubricant is a lithium-base grease.

To disassemble gear head, remove trimmer head or blade assembly. Detach gear head from drive shaft housing tube. Remove snap ring (14) and pull arbor shaft (12) from gear head (8). Remove snap ring (1) and pull input shaft (7) and bearings from gear head. If necessary, heat housing to ease removal of bearings.

To reassemble, reverse disassembly procedure.

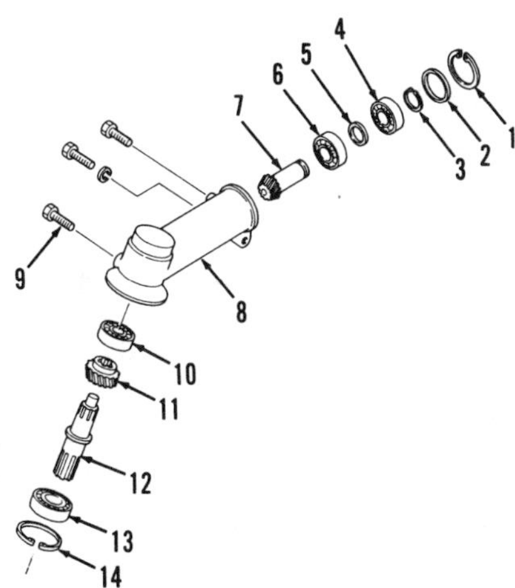

Fig. HQ22—Exploded view of gear head used on Series 22, 25, 125 and 132 models. Spacers (2 and 5) are not used on later models.

1. Snap ring
2. Spacer
3. Snap ring
4. Bearing
5. Spacer
6. Bearing
7. Input shaft
8. Housing
9. Plug
10. Bearing
11. Gear
12. Arbor
13. Bearing
14. Snap ring

Models 36R, 140R, 244R And 244RX

Models 36R, 140R, 244R and 244RX are equipped with the gear head shown in Fig. HQ23. Gear head lubricant level should be checked after every 50 hours of operation. Remove plug (11) to check lubricant level and inject grease. Gear head should be ³/₄ full. Recommended lubricant is a lithium-base grease.

To disassemble gear head, remove trimmer head or blade assembly. Remove four screws (3) retaining cover (5) and use puller 502 50 09-11 to separate cover from housing. Separate gear head from drive shaft housing tube. Remove sleeve (19) using remover 502 51 11-01. Heat housing to 140° F (60° C) and remove input shaft (16) and bearing assembly, and arbor (9) and bearing assembly. If bearing (10) remains in housing, tap housing against a wooden block while housing is still hot to remove bearing. Remove snap ring (21) and press bearings (17 and 18) from input shaft as required. Remove bearing (7) and spacer (8) if required.

To reassemble, reverse disassembly procedure.

Model 165R

Model 165 is equipped with the gear head shown in Fig. HQ24. Gear head lubricant level should be checked after every 50 hours of operation. Remove plug (9) to check lubricant level and inject grease. Gear head should be ³/₄ full. Recommended lubricant is a lithium-base grease.

To disassemble gear head, remove trimmer head or blade assembly. Remove five screws (4) from the blade guard and remove guard. Separate gear head from drive shaft housing tube. Heat housing to 140° F (60° C) and use puller 502 50 65-01 to remove arbor (7) and bearing assembly. Remove locking screw (16) and use puller 502 50 63-01 to remove input shaft (13) and bearing assembly. Press bearings and spacer (12) from input shaft if required.

To reassemble, reverse disassembly procedure.

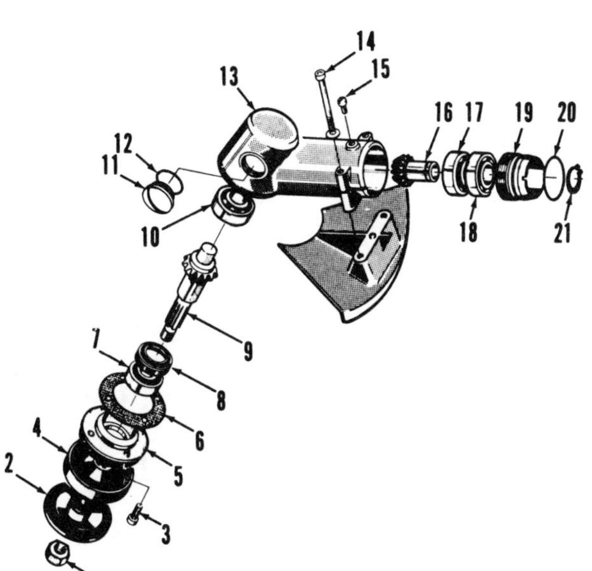

Fig. HQ23—Exploded view of gear head used on Models 36R, 140R, 244R and 244RX.

1. Nut (L.H.)
2. Adapter washer
3. Screw
4. Drive disc
5. Cover
6. Gasket
7. Bearing
8. Spacer
9. Arbor
10. Bearing
11. Plug
12. "O" ring
13. Housing
14. Clamp bolt
15. Locating screw
16. Input shaft
17. Bearing
18. Bearing
19. Sleeve
20. "O" ring
21. Snap ring

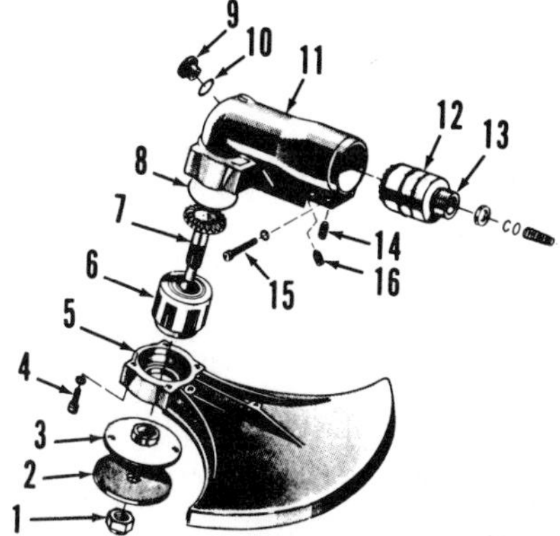

Fig. HQ24—Exploded view of gear head used on Model 165R.

1. Nut (L.H.)
2. Adapter washer
3. Drive disc
4. Screw
5. Shield & cover assy.
6. Bearing
7. Arbor
8. "O" ring
9. Plug
10. "O" ring
11. Housing
12. Bearing & spacer assy.
13. Input shaft
14. Locating screw
15. Clamp bolt
16. Locking screw

Illustrations courtesy Husqvarna Forest & Garden

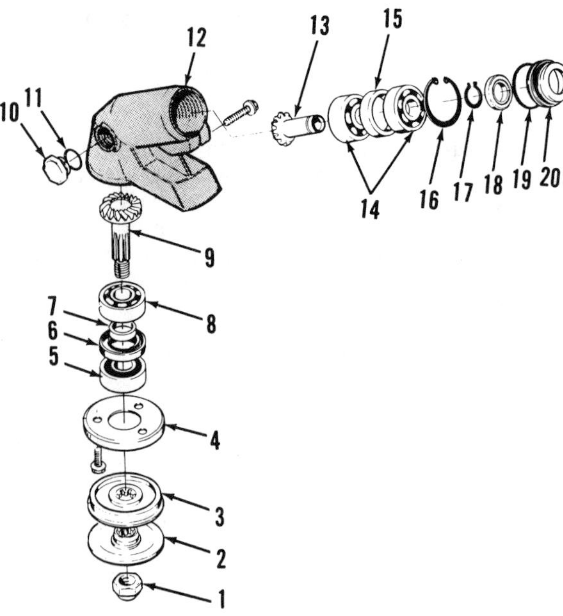

Fig. HQ25—Exploded view of gear head used on Models 240R, 245R and 245RX. Model 165RX is similar but snap ring (16) is not used.

1. Nut (L.H.)
2. Adapter washer
3. Drive disc
4. Cover
5. Bearing
6. Seal
7. Spacer
8. Bearing
9. Arbor
10. Plug
11. "O" ring
12. Housing
13. Input shaft
14. Bearing
15. Spacer
16. Snap ring
17. Snap ring
18. Seal
19. "O" ring
20. Sleeve

Models 165RX, 240R, 245R And 245RX

Models 165RX, 240R, 245R and 245RX are equipped with the gear head shown in Fig. HQ25. Gear head lubricant level should be checked after every 50 hours of operation. Remove plug (10) to check lubricant level and inject grease. Gear head should be $^{3}/_{4}$ full. Recommended lubricant is a lithium-base grease.

To disassemble gear head, remove trimmer head or blade assembly. Separate gear head from drive shaft housing tube. Unscrew and remove cover (4). Remove sleeve (20) and detach snap ring (16). Remove components as needed. Heat housing to ease removal of bearings.

To reassemble, reverse disassembly procedure.

IDC

GASOLINE POWERED STRING TRIMMERS

Model	Engine Manufacturer	Engine Model	Displacement
364	IDC	...	31.0 cc
500	IDC	...	28.5 cc
520	IDC	...	28.5 cc
540	IDC	...	31.0 cc
580	IDC	...	31.0 cc

ENGINE INFORMATION

The models in this section are equipped with an Inertia Dynamics Corporation (IDC) engine. Refer to IDC engine service section for engine service information.

FUEL MIXTURE

Manufacturer recommends mixing regular grade gasoline, leaded or unleaded, with a high-quality, two-stroke engine oil. Recommended fuel:oil ratio is 32:1 when using IDC Two-Cycle Engine Oil. When using any other two-stroke oil, mix 6 ounces (0.177 mL) of oil with 1 gallon (3.8 L) of gasoline, regardless of recommended ratio on oil container. The use of gasohol or other alcohol blended fuels are not approved by manufacturer.

STRING TRIMMER

Model 364

Model 364 is equipped with a single line, semi-automatic trimmer head (Fig. ID10). To extend line with engine stopped, push in on bump button (20) and pull on line until desired length is obtained. To extend line with engine running, operate trimmer engine at full rpm and tap bump button (20) on the ground. Line will automatically advance a measured amount.

To renew trimmer line, hold drum (15) and unscrew bump button (20). Remove spool (19). Clean inner surface of drum and spool. Check indexing teeth on spool and drum for wear. Insert one end of a 25-ft. (7.6 m) length of 0.080-in. (2 mm) diameter monofilament line into one of the holes in spool from the inside out, and back through the second hole to the inside. Wind line in direction indicated by arrow on spool until all but about 3 inches (76.2 mm) of line is wrapped, then clip line temporarily in one of the line lock slots (LS) on spool.

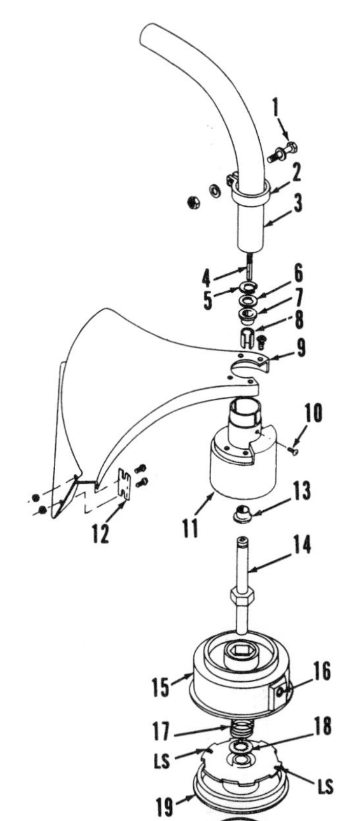

Fig. ID10—Exploded view of single strand, semi-automatic trimmer head used on Model 364.

1. Bolt
2. Clamp
3. Drive shaft housing
4. Drive shaft
5. Retaining ring
6. Washer
7. Bushing
8. Bushing
9. Shield
10. Locating screw
11. Bushing housing
12. Line length trimmer
13. Bushing
14. Shaft
15. Drum
16. Line guide
17. Spring
18. Retainer
19. Spool
20. Bump button

LS. Line slot

Insert line end through line guide (16) in drum and install spool and bump button. Pull line to release from line lock slot on spool after assembly is complete.

Models 500, 520, 540 And 580

These models are equipped with a dual strand, semi-automatic trimmer head (Fig. ID11). To extend line with engine off, push bump button (8) in and pull lines out. Procedure may have to be repeated until desired line length has been obtained. To extend line with engine running, operate trimmer engine at full operating rpm and tap bump button

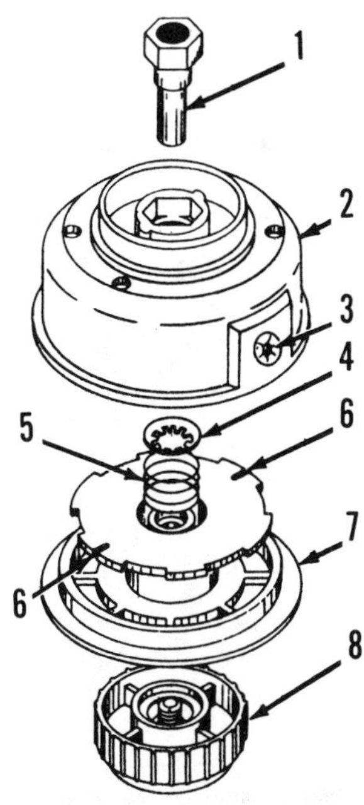

Fig. ID11—Exploded view of dual strand, semi-automatic trimmer head used on Models 500, 520 and 540. Model 580 is similar.

1. Adapter
2. Drum
3. Line guide
4. Retainer
5. Spring
6. Line slot
7. Spool
8. Bump button

on the ground. Each time bump button is tapped on the ground, approximately 1 inch (25 mm) of new line will be advanced.

To renew line, hold drum (2) and unscrew bump button (8). Note that screw in bump button on Model 580 has left-hand threads. Remove spool (7) and remove any remaining old line. Clean spool and inner surface of drum. Check indexing teeth in drum and on spool. On Models 500, 520 and 540, loop a 25-ft. (7.6 cm) length of 0.080-in. (2 mm) diameter monofilament line into two equal lengths. On Model 580, loop a 50-ft. (15.2 m) length of 0.095-in. (2.4 mm) diameter line into two equal lengths. Insert the two line ends into the two holes in spool from the bottom and pull line out until end of loop is against spool. Wind both strands of line around spool in direction indicated by arrow on spool. Wind in tight even layers. Clip lines into line slots (6) in spool. Insert line ends through line guides (3) in drum and install spool and bump button. Bump button screw on Model 580 has left-hand threads. Pull line ends to free from line slots.

On Model 580, note that trimmer housing (2) has left-hand threads.

BLADE

Models 540 And 580

Models 540 and 580 may be equipped with a four-edge cutting blade (9—Figs. ID12 and ID13). To install blade, refer to Figs. ID12 or ID13 for assembly sequence. Note that nut (11) on Model 580 has left-hand threads. Tighten nut (11) to 225-250 in.-lbs. (26-28 N·m).

DRIVE SHAFT

All Models Except 580

All models except Model 580 are equipped with a flexible drive shaft enclosed in the drive shaft housing. The drive shaft has squared ends that engage adapters at each end. The drive shaft should be removed for maintenance after every 10 hours of operation.

To remove drive shaft, loosen clamp (2—Fig. ID10 or 6—Fig. ID12) and remove set screw attaching drive shaft tube to trimmer bearing housing. Remove and clean drive shaft, then inspect shaft for damage. Coat with a high-quality, high-temperature wheel bearing grease and install drive shaft. Make certain ends of shaft are properly located in upper and lower drive adapters.

Model 580

Model 580 is equipped with a solid steel drive shaft (2—Fig. ID13) that rides in bushings in the drive shaft housing (1). The drive shaft requires no maintenance. If shaft is removed, it should be lubricated with high-temperature wheel bearing grease before installation.

BEARING HOUSING

Models 364, 500, And 520

Refer to Fig. ID10 for an exploded view of the bearing housing used on Models 364, 500, and 520. Bushings are available only with housing (11), not separately.

Model 540

The bearing head (7—Fig. ID12) on Model 540 is equipped with a sealed bearing and must be serviced as a unit assembly.

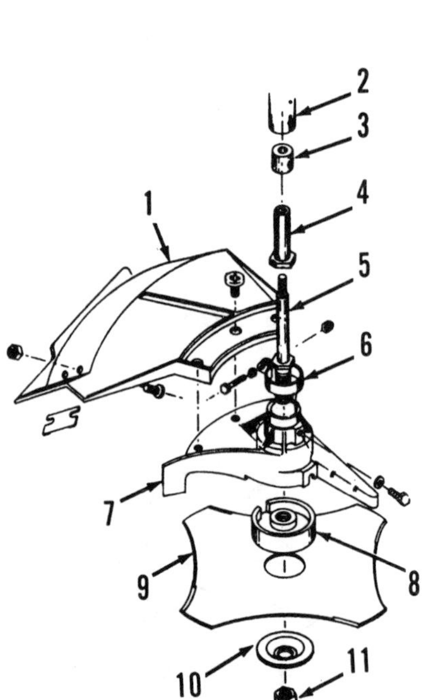

Fig. ID12—Exploded view of weed, grass and light brush blade assembly used on Model 540.

1. Shield
2. Drive shaft housing
3. Retainer & bushing
4. Drive shaft adapter
5. Head drive shaft
6. Clamp assy.
7. Bearing housing assy.
8. Blade adapter
9. Blade
10. Lower blade adapter
11. Nut

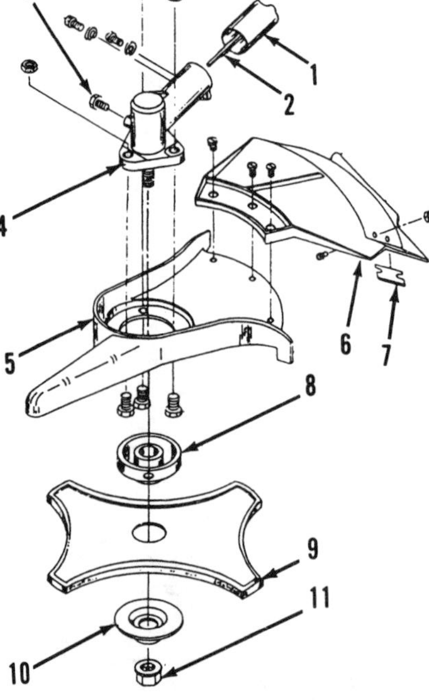

Fig. ID13—Exploded view of weed, grass and light brush blade assembly used on Model 580. Nut (11) has left-hand threads.

1. Drive shaft housing
2. Drive shaft
3. Lubricant check plug
4. Gear head
5. Guard mount
6. Guard
7. Line length trimmer blade
8. Blade adapter
9. Blade
10. Retaining washer
11. Nut

GEAR HEAD

Model 580

Model 580 is equipped with a gear head assembly (4—Fig. ID13). Plug (3) in side of gear head should be removed and lubricant level checked after every 50 hours of operation. Housing should be $^2/_3$ full of lithium-base grease. Service parts are not available. Gear head must be renewed as a complete unit.

THROTTLE TRIGGER AND CABLE

All Models

The throttle trigger assembly is attached to the drive shaft housing (Fig. ID14) on all models. The throttle cable inner wire (2) should be lubricated after every 20 hours of operation. Apply SAE 30 oil to each end of wire. The throttle cable should be adjusted to provide 0.02-0.04-in. (0.5-1.0 mm) throttle trigger movement before the carburetor throttle lever begins to move. Adjust by

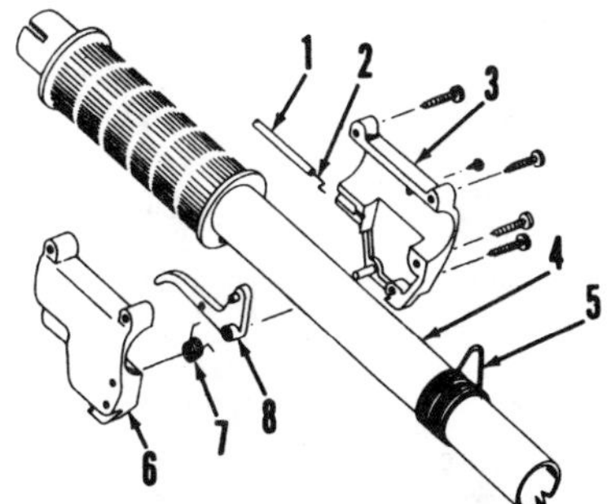

Fig. ID14—Exploded view of throttle trigger and cable assembly used on all models.

1. Throttle cable housing
2. Inner throttle cable
3. Throttle trigger housing
4. Drive shaft housing
5. Strap bracket
6. Throttle trigger housing
7. Spring
8. Throttle trigger

loosening set screw (S—Fig. ID15) and moving cable housing and inner wire to provide specified free play. Tighten set screw (S).

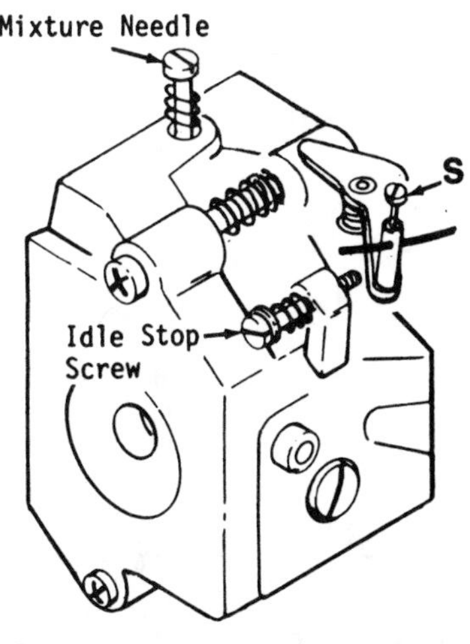

Fig. ID15—Loosen screw (S) and move throttle cable and housing to provide correct throttle trigger free play. Refer to text.

IDC

GASOLINE POWERED BLOWERS

Model	Engine Manufacturer	Engine Model	Displacement
200	IDC	...	31.0 cc
300BV	IDC	...	31.0 cc

ENGINE INFORMATION

The models in this section are equipped with an Inertia Dynamics Corporation (IDC) engine. Refer to IDC engine service section for engine service information.

FUEL MIXTURE

Manufacturer recommends mixing regular grade gasoline, leaded or unleaded, with a high-quality, two-stroke engine oil. Recommended fuel:oil ratio is 32:1 when using IDC Two-Cycle Engine Oil. When using any other two-stroke oil, mix 6 ounces (0.177 mL) of oil with 1 gallon (3.8 L) of gasoline, regardless of recommended ratio on oil container. Gasohol or other alcohol blended fuels are not approved by manufacturer.

BLOWER ASSEMBLY

Model 200

Refer to Fig. ID75 for exploded view of blower assembly. To remove blower impeller (4), remove mounting screws from starter housing (1) and blower housing (3). Separate blower housing halves (3 and 6). Remove mounting screws from blower impeller (4) and separate impeller from flywheel.

To separate engine from blower housing, remove impeller as outlined above. Remove engine cover (10). Disconnect fuel line, throttle cable and ignition wires from engine. Remove engine mounting screws and withdraw engine from blower housing half (6).

Model 300BV

Refer to Fig. ID76 for exploded view of blower assembly. To remove blower impeller (8), remove blower tube (12). Remove screws attaching blower lower housing (10) to upper housing (7) and separate housing. Remove impeller mounting screw and separate impeller (8) from flywheel.

To separate engine from blower housing, remove impeller as outlined above. Remove screws securing engine covers (1 and 4). Separate covers and disconnect throttle cable, fuel line and ignition wires from engine. Remove engine mounting screws and withdraw engine from blower upper housing (7).

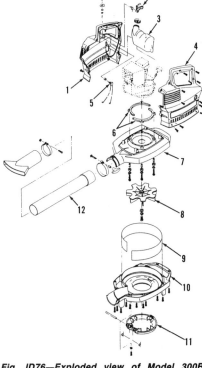

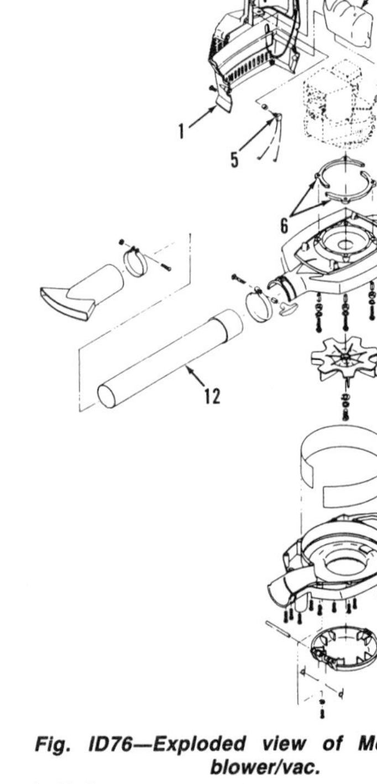

Fig. ID76—Exploded view of Model 300BV blower/vac.

1. Engine cover
2. Throttle trigger
3. Fuel tank
4. Engine cover
5. Stop switch
6. Gasket
7. Blower upper housing
8. Impeller
9. Shield
10. Blower lower housing
11. Intake cover
12. Blower tube

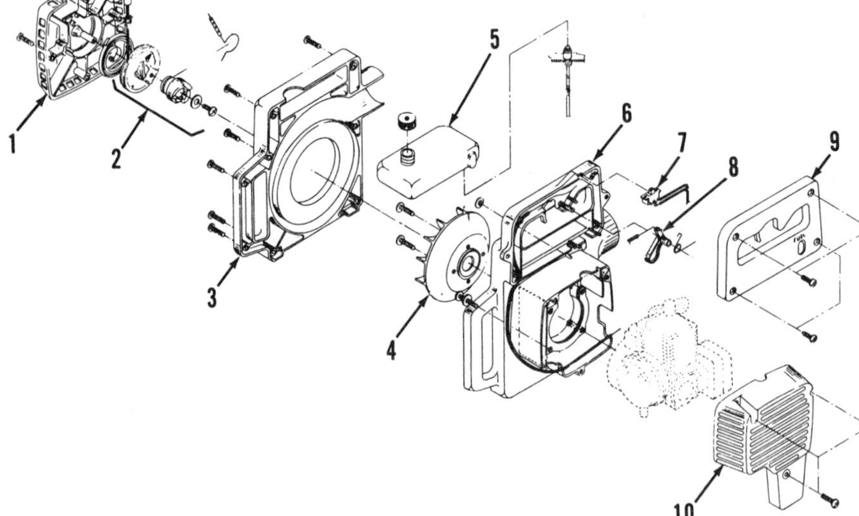

Fig. ID75—Exploded view of Model 200 blower.

1. Starter housing
2. Recoil starter assy.
3. Blower housing half
4. Impeller
5. Fuel tank
6. Blower housing half
7. Stop switch
8. Throttle trigger
9. Handle
10. Engine cover

Illustrations courtesy Ryobi Outdoor Products

JONSERED

GASOLINE POWERED STRING TRIMMERS

Model	Engine Manufacturer	Engine Model	Displacement
J200B	EFCO	200	22.5 cc
J200L	EFCO	200	22.5 cc
J220B	EFCO	220	22.5 cc
J220L	EFCO	220	22.5 cc
J260B	EFCO	260	25.4 cc
J260L	EFCO	260	25.4 cc
J300B	EFCO	300	30.5 cc
J320B	EFCO	300	30.5 cc
J400B	EFCO	400	37.7 cc
J420B	EFCO	400	37.7 cc
J450B	EFCO	450	37.7 cc
J460B	EFCO	450	37.7 cc

ENGINE INFORMATION

The models in this section are equipped with an EFCO engine. Refer to EFCO engine service section for engine service information.

FUEL MIXTURE

Manufacturer recommends mixing regular grade gasoline, preferably leaded, with a high-quality, two-stroke engine oil. Recommended fuel:oil ratio is 40:1.

STRING TRIMMER

All models are equipped with a manual advance, dual strand trimmer head. To pull out line, stop engine and push up against spool (against spring pressure). While pushing spool up, turn spool counterclockwise (as viewed from bottom) to eject new line. Release spool.

To install new line, unscrew retaining screw (5—Fig. J11)—screw has left-hand threads. Remove housing (4), spool (3) and spring (2). Remove old string and clean components. Specified string diameter on Models J300B, J320B, J400B, J420B, J450B and J460B is 0.095 inch (2.4 mm). Specified string diameter for all other models is 0.080 inch (2.0 mm). Spool capacity is 36 feet (11 m) for Models J300B, J320B, J400B, J420B, J450B and J460B and 42 feet (13 m) for all other models. Insert line (6) through holes in spool as shown in Fig. J11 and pull line through holes until ends are even. Wrap line around spool in direction indicated by arrows on spool. Do not twist lines. Reassemble trimmer head. Tighten retaining screw (5—Fig. J11) to 25 N·m (18 ft.-lbs.).

BLADE

All straight-shaft models may be equipped with a blade. Refer to Figs. J13, J14 or J15 for configuration of blade assembly. Blade retaining screw has left-hand threads. Note that direction of blade rotation is usually indicated by an arrow on the gear head. Tighten retaining screw to 25 N·m (18 ft.-lbs.).

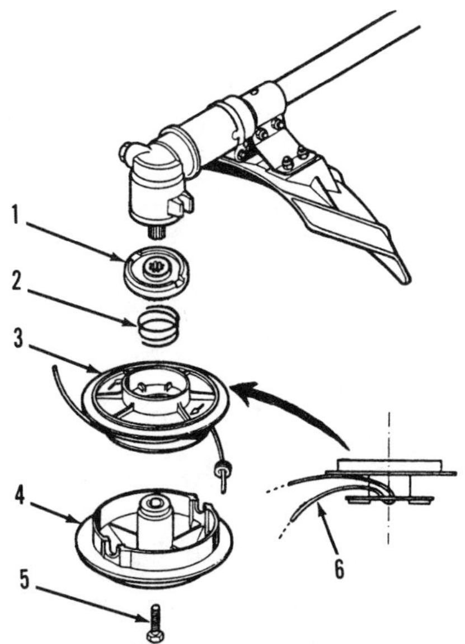

Fig. J11—Exploded view of dual strand, manual advance trimmer used on Models J200B, J200L, J220B, J220L, J260B and J260L. All other models are similar. Insert new trimmer line (6) through spool holes as shown.

1. Flange
2. Spring
3. Spool
4. Cup washer
5. Lockwasher
6. Screw (L.H.)

DRIVE SHAFT

Models J200B and J200L

Models J200B and J200L are equipped with a flexible drive shaft. Periodically remove drive shaft and lubricate with a lithium-base grease. To remove drive shaft, remove bearing head and extract drive shaft. When installing drive shaft, be sure drive shaft end is properly seated at drive end.

All Other Models

All models except Models J200B and J200L are equipped with a solid drive

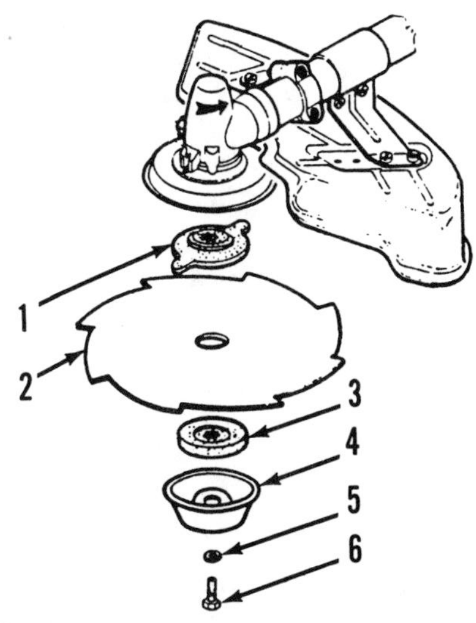

Fig. J13—Blade assembly used on some models.

1. Flange
2. Blade
3. Washer
4. Housing
5. Screw (L.H.)
6. Trimmer line

shaft that does not require periodic lubrication. If drive shaft is removed, apply a lithium-base grease to drive shaft. The drive shaft rides in bushings that are renewable. If bushings are to be renewed, mark position of old bushings before removal so new bushings can be installed in original positions.

BEARING HEAD

Models J200B and J200L

The bearing head does not require periodic lubrication.

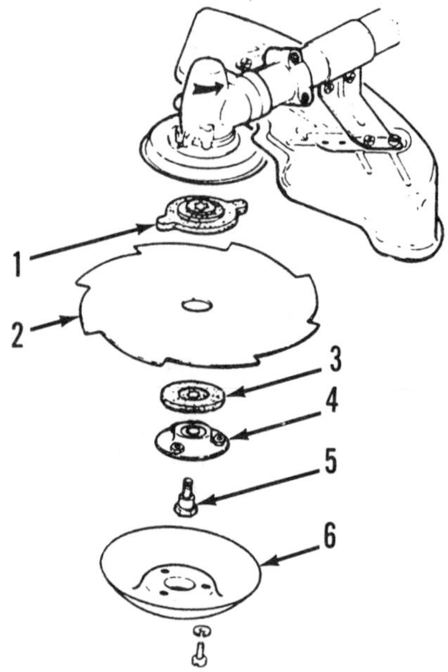

Fig. J14—Blade assembly used on some models.

1. Flange
2. Blade
3. Washer
4. Shield flange
5. Screw (L.H.)
6. Shield

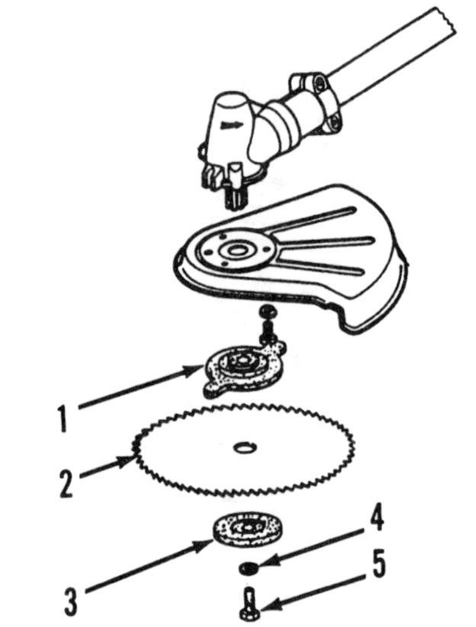

Fig. J15—Blade assembly used on some models.

1. Flange
2. Blade
3. Washer
4. Lockwasher
5. Screw (L.H.)

To disassemble bearing head, remove trimmer assembly (trimmer head retaining screw has left-hand threads). Separate bearing head from drive shaft tube. Detach snap ring (5—Fig. J16). Use a suitable puller and extract arbor (3) with bearings (4) from housing (1). Press or pull bearings off arbor. Reassemble by reversing disassembly procedure.

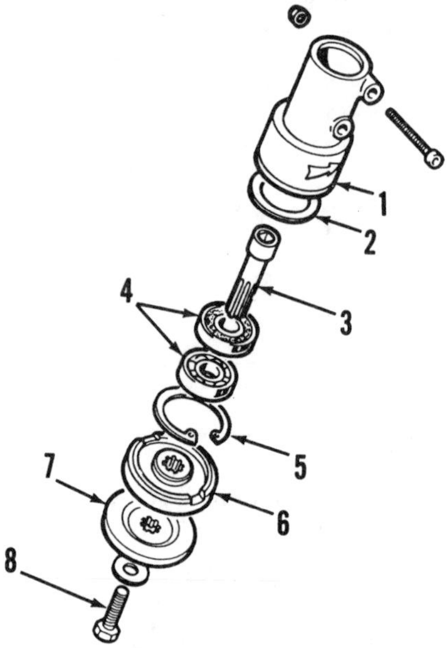

Fig. J16—Exploded view of bearing head used on Models J200B and J200L.

1. Housing
2. Washer
3. Arbor
4. Bearings
5. Snap ring
6. Flange
7. Flange
8. Screw (L.H.)

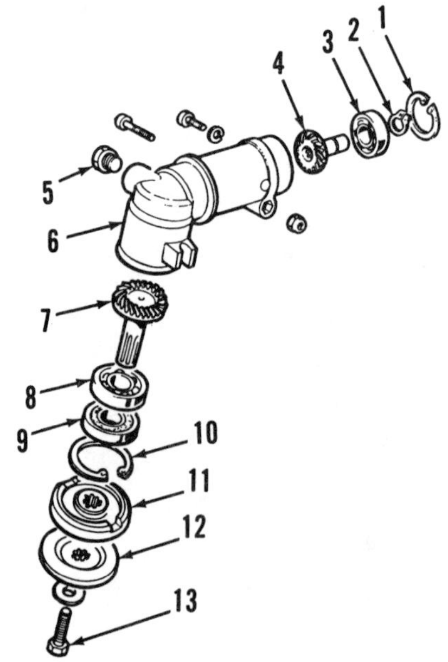

Fig. J17—Exploded view of gear head used on Models J220B, J220L, J260B and J260L.

1. Snap ring
2. Snap ring
3. Bearing
4. Input gear
5. Plug
6. Housing
7. Output gear
8. Bearing
9. Bearing
10. Snap ring
11. Flange
12. Flange
13. Screw (L.H.)

GEAR HEAD

Models J220B, J220L, J260B and J260L

Models J220B, J220L, J260B and J260L are equipped with the gear head shown in Fig. J17. Lubricant level should be checked after every 80 hours of operation. Remove fill plug (5) in side of housing and add lubricant so housing is ½ full. Maximum amount that should be added if housing is dry is 9 mL (0.3 oz.). Recommended lubricant is molybdenum disulfide grease.

To disassemble gear head, remove trimmer or blade assembly (retaining screw has left-hand threads). Separate gear head from drive shaft tube. Remove flange (11) and detach snap ring (10). Use a suitable puller and extract gear (7) and bearings. Press or pull bearings off gear shaft. Detach snap ring (1). Reach through output opening of housing and drive out input shaft (4) and bearing (3). Remove snap ring (2) and separate bearing from shaft.

Reassemble by reversing disassembly procedure. Note that lower bearing (9) is a sealed bearing.

Models J300B, J320B, J400B, J420B, J450B and J460B

Models J300B, J320B, J400B, J420B, J450B and J460B are equipped with the bearing head shown in Fig. J18. Lubricant level should be checked after eve-

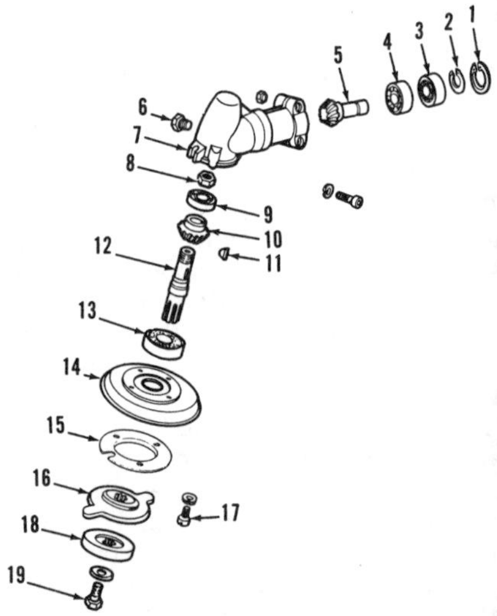

Fig. J18—Exploded view of gear head used on Models J300B, J320B, J400B, J420B, J450B and J460B.

1. Snap ring
2. Snap ring
3. Bearing
4. Bearing
5. Input gear
6. Plug
7. Housing
8. Nut
9. Bearing
10. Output gear
11. Key
12. Arbor
13. Bearing
14. Shield
15. Retainer
16. Flange
17. Screw
18. Flange
19. Screw (L.H.)

Illustrations courtesy Jonsered Power Products

ry 80 hours of operation. Remove fill plug (6) in side of housing and add lubricant so housing is ½ full. Maximum amount that should be added if housing is dry is 11 mL (0.37 oz.). Recommended lubricant is molybdenum disulfide grease.

To disassemble gear head, remove blade or trimmer head. Detach gear head from drive shaft tube. Remove snap ring (1—Fig. J18) and using a suitable puller, extract pinion gear (5) and bearings as an assembly from housing. Detach snap ring (2) and press or pull bearings (3 and 4) off pinion gear (5). Remove flange (16), retainer (15) and shield (14). Using a suitable puller, extract arbor (12) assembly. Pull bearing (13) off of arbor (12). Unscrew nut (8) and remove gear (10) and bearing (9) from arbor.

Clean and inspect components. Reassemble by reversing disassembly procedure. Tighten pinion gear retaining nut (8) to 30 N·m (22 ft.-lbs.). Align slot in retainer (15) with hole (H—Fig. J19) in shield (14). Before tightening screws (17), position flange (16—Fig. J18) on arbor shaft to center the retainer (15). Then, remove flange and tighten screws (17).

Fig. J19—Align slot on retainer (15) with hole (H) in shield (14). Center retainer before tightening screws (17). Refer to text.

THROTTLE FREE PLAY

To adjust throttle free play, loosen locknut (N—Fig. J20) and turn adjuster (A) so cable free play at carburetor is 1 mm (0.04 in.). Tighten locknut. The carburetor throttle plate should be fully open when throttle trigger is in full throttle position.

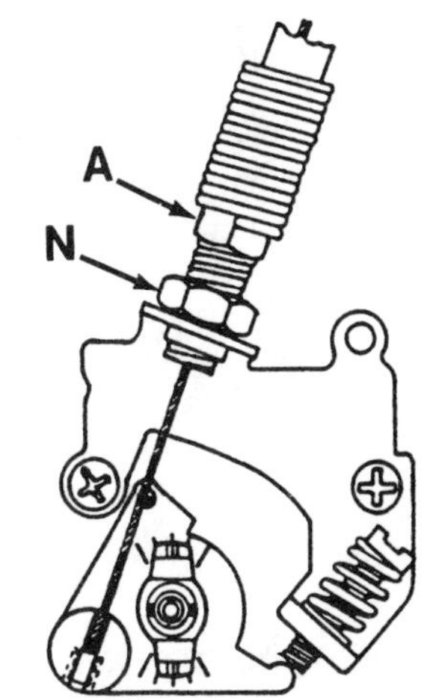

Fig. J20—Adjust throttle free play by loosening nut (N) and turning adjuster (A).

JONSERED

GASOLINE POWERED TRIMMERS

Model	Engine Make	Engine Model	Engine Displacement
JBP40	Own	BP40	36.3 cc (2.2 cu. in.)
JGR26C, JGR26D, JGR26L	Own	GR26	25.4 cc (1.55 cu. in.)
JGR32C, JGR32D, JGR32L	Own	GR32	30.8 cc (1.88 cu. in.)
JGR36C, JGR36D	Own	GR36	36.3 cc (2.2 cu. in.)
JGR41	Own	GR41	40.2 cc (2.5 cu. in.)
JGR50	Own	GR50	48.7 cc (2.97 cu. in.)
JGT21L, JGT22L, JGT24L	ElectroLux	...	21.2 cc (1.29 cu. in.)
RS44	Own	RS44	44.3 cc (2.7 cu. in.)
RS51 Pro	Own	RS51	50.8 cc (3.1 cu. in.)

ENGINE INFORMATION

The models in this section are equipped with ElectroLux or Jonsered engines. Refer to the appropriate engine service section for servicing the engine.

FUEL MIXTURE

The manufacturer recommends mixing a quality 2-stroke engine oil with regular or unleaded gasoline at the ratio recommended by the oil manufacturer. If the oil manufacturer does not suggest a mixing ratio, use an oil designed for air cooled two-stroke engines mixed with gasoline at a ratio of 40:1.

STRING TRIMMER

The semi-automatic single strand trimmer (Fig. J30) is used on some models including JGT21L and JGT22L. The line can be extended manually as follows. Make sure the engine is stopped, push the button (7) and pull the line. The procedure may have to be repeated several times to obtain the desired length. To extend the line with the engine running, operate the engine at maximum speed and tap the button (7) on the ground. The line should advance each time the button is tapped. To install new line, the unit must be disassembled. Push in on the tabs retaining cover (5) to the drum (1) and remove the cover. Remove spool (4) and be careful not to lose the spring (3) or other parts. Clean all parts and remove any old line remaining on the spool. Insert the end of 0.080 in. (2 mm) line through the hole in the spool and wind the line onto the spool in the direction indicated by the arrow on spool. Do not install so much line on the spool that it causes it to bind. Install the button (7) and spool (5) while inserting the free end of line (6) through the line guide opening in the drum (1). Install cover (5) making sure tabs are properly engaged.

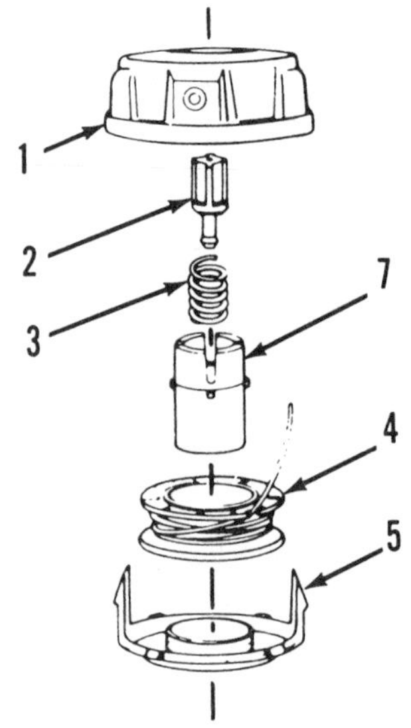

Fig. J30—Exploded view of the single strand trimmer used on JGT21L and JGT22L models.

1. Drum
2. Adapter
3. Spring
4. Spool
5. Cover
7. Button

The semi-automatic single strand trimmer (Fig. J31) is used on some models including JGT24L. To extend the line manually, first make sure the engine is stopped. Push the button (7) and pull the line. The procedure may have to be repeated several times to obtain the desired length. To extend the line with the engine running, operate the engine at maximum speed and tap the button (7) on the ground. The line should advance each time the button is tapped. To install new line, the unit must be disassembled. Remove cover

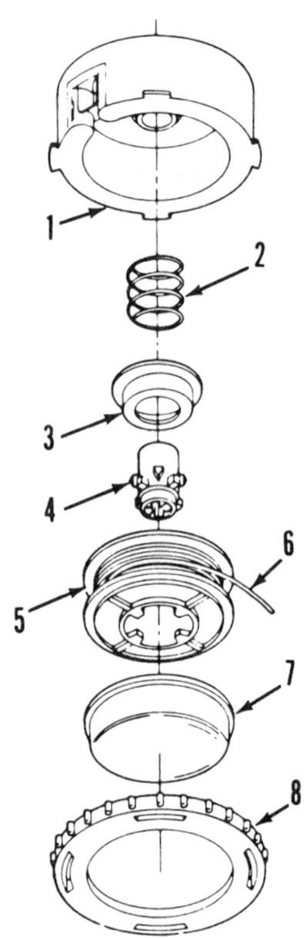

Fig. J31—Exploded view of the single strand trimmer used on JGT24L models.

1. Adapter
2. Drum
3. Spring
4. Washer
5. Outer cam
6. Inner cam
7. Spool

(8) and lift the button (7) and spool (5) from the drum (1). Be careful not to lose any parts. Clean all parts and remove any old line remaining on the spool. Insert the end of 0.080 in. (2 mm) line through the hole in the spool and wind the line onto the spool in the direction indicated by the arrow on spool. Do not install so much line on the spool that it causes it to bind. Install the spool while inserting the free end of the line through the line guide opening in the drum (1). Install button (7) and cover (5).

BLADE

Models JBP, JGR and RS models can be fitted with brush blades for cutting heavier weeds, grasses or brush. All of the available hard blades can be dangerous and should be selected and used with great care. Different types of blades may be used, but should be matched to the job and to each model. Check the manufacturer's recommended application for your specific model. The wrong blade will reduce the effectiveness of operation and may be dangerous to operate. Refer to Fig. J32 for typical installation.

Sharpen each tooth following the original sharpening angle and tooth set. Sharpen all teeth evenly to maintain balance and do not file into the radius at the root. If a blade has hit a stone or other solid object, the entire damaged section must be filed away and all of the blades must be filed the same to maintain proper balance.

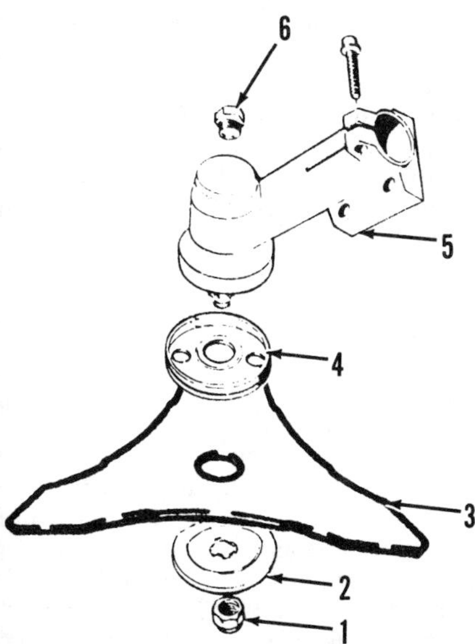

Fig. J32—Brush cutting blades may have 3, 4, 8 or more cutting edges and should be matched to the job and the specific model.

1. Nut
2. Lower plate
3. Blade
4. Cup
5. Gear housing
6. Filler plug

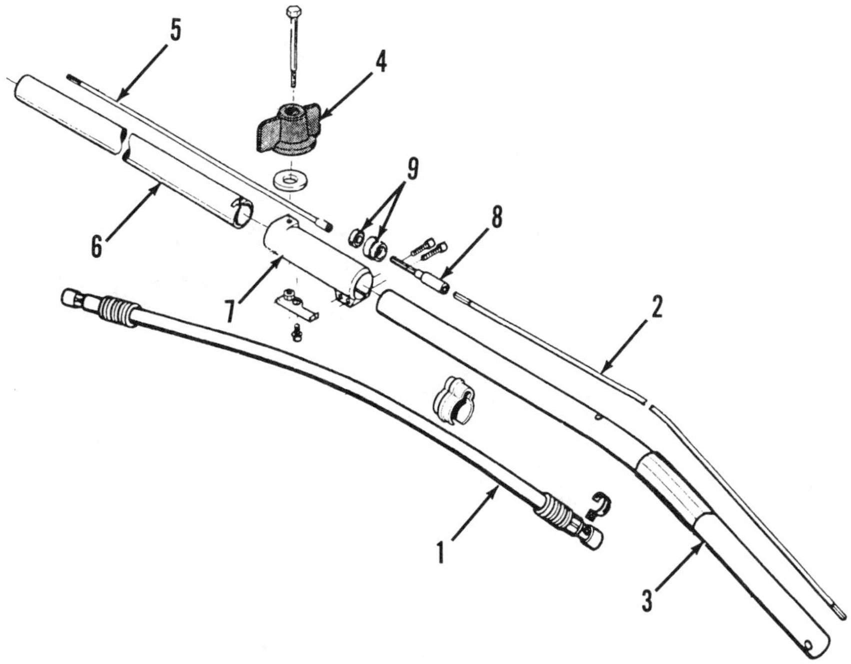

Fig. J33—Back pack BP40 models are equipped with both rigid and flexible drive shafts and drive shaft housings.

1. Flexible housing & shaft
2. Flexible drive shaft
3. Lower housing
4. Knob
5. Drive shaft
6. Housing
7. Clamp
8. Adapter
9. Bearing & seal

DRIVE SHAFT

Models JGT21L and JGT22L are equipped with a flexible drive shaft that operates inside a curved housing. The drive shaft should be removed periodically and lubricated with lithium based multipurpose grease. To remove the drive shaft, separate the clutch and power head assembly from the upper end of the drive shaft housing, then extract the drive shaft. If the drive shaft can not be withdrawn easily, it may be necessary to install a new housing and bearing assembly as well as the drive shaft. When installing, be sure that both ends of drive shaft are properly seated.

On JGR and RS models, the upper end of drive shaft is threaded into the clutch drum. To remove the drive shaft, separate the clutch housing from the engine and the upper end of the drive shaft housing from the clutch housing. Clamp the drive shaft in a vise, then unscrew the clutch drum from the drive shaft. It will be necessary to remove the vibration isolating covers and engine controls from most models. Some models have a two piece drive shaft housing which must be separated before removing the upper drive shaft. The lower drive shaft of models with two piece housing can be withdrawn after removing the gear head assembly. Regular maintenance is not required, but if removed, the drive shaft should be lubricated with lithium based multipurpose grease. When installing, be sure that both ends of drive shaft are properly seated.

Model BP40 is equipped with both rigid and flexible drive shaft housings as shown in Fig. J33. Service and lubrication of the drive shaft (5) located in the rigid housing is similar to other models. The flexible housing (1) and the flexible drive shaft (2) located inside the housing are available only as an assembly.

BEARING HEAD

The bearing head located at the lower end of models with a curved drive shaft housing is integral with the drive shaft housing. Service is limited to installing a new drive shaft housing and bearing head.

GEAR HEAD

A gear head is located at the lower end of the drive shaft and housing of some models. To check the lubricant in the gear head, remove plug from filler opening (6—Fig. J32). Add multipurpose lithium base grease to the housing until the cavity is approximately 2/3 full. Do not over fill the housing with grease. Tighten fill plug securely.

To remove the assembly, loosen the fitting screw and clamp bolts, then pull the gear head from the drive shaft

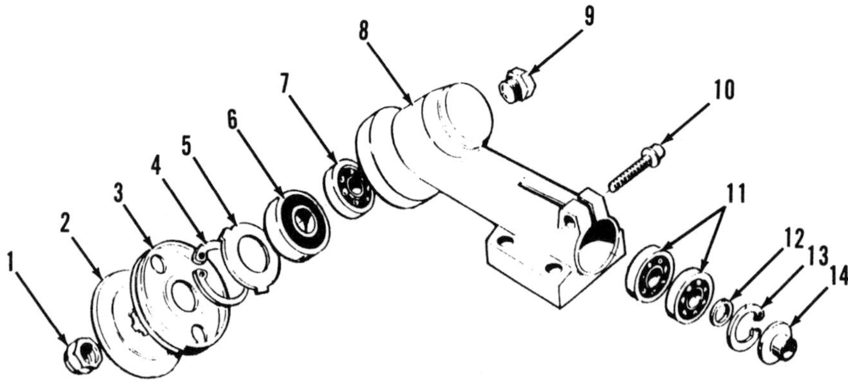

Fig. J34—Exploded view of the gear head typical of JGR26, JGR32, JGR36, JBP40 and some other models.

1. Nut
2. Lower plate
3. Cup
4. Snap ring
5. Retainer
6. Sealed bearing
7. Bearing
8. Housing
9. Filler plug
10. Clamp screw
11. Bearings
12. Spacer
13. Snap ring
14. Protector

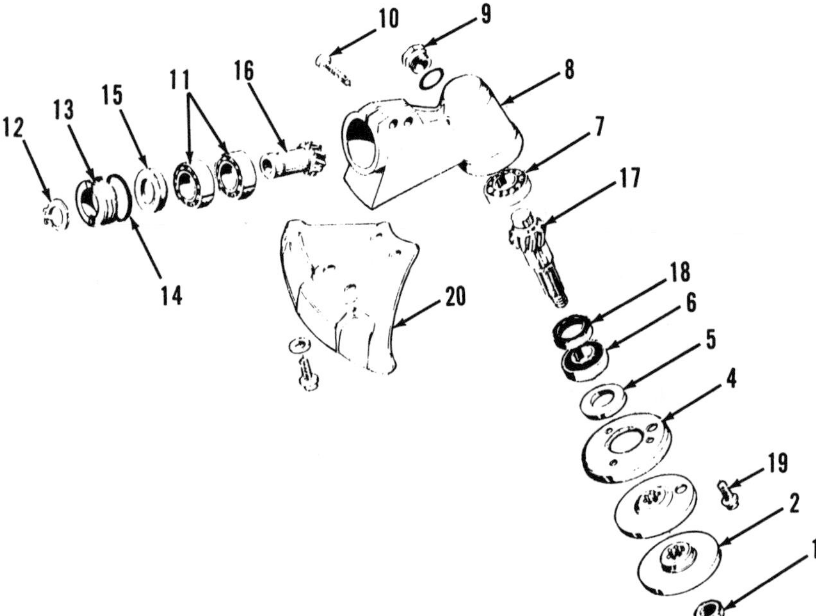

Fig. J35—Exploded view of the gear head for RS51 model. The gear head of JGR41, JGR50 and RS44 models is similar.

1. Nut
2. Lower plate
3. Cup
6. Bearing
7. Bearing
8. Housing
9. Filler plug
10. Clamp screw
11. Bearings
12. Snap ring
13. Seal retainer
14. "O" ring
15. Seal
16. Input gear
17. Output gear & shaft
18. Spacer
19. Screw
20. Shield

housing. Check for parts availability before attempting repairs. Parts for the one piece gear housing may not be available.

Before servicing the removed unit, remove the trimmer head or blade, then unbolt the protector shield. On JGT24L model, the lower seal can be pried from the housing.

To remove the gears and bearings from the gear head shown in Fig. J34, remove snap rings (4 and 13). Use suitable pullers to pull the gears and bearings from the housing.

To remove the gears and bearings from the gear head shown in Fig. J35, use special tool (part No. 502 51 11-01 or equivalent) to unscrew seal retainer (13) from the housing. Use a suitable puller to remove gear (16) and bearings as an assembly from the housing. Remove screws (19), then use a suitable puller to remove the seal housing (4). Pull the shaft and gear (17) from the housing.

NOTE: It may be possible to bump the open end of housing (8) to dislodge the bearings and gears.

On all models, the bearings can be pressed from the gears if replacement is required. Clean all parts and inspect for damage. Install new parts as necessary. Gears and shafts may only be available as an assembly with the housing. Grease bearings that are not sealed before pressing into the housing. Coat threads of screws with Loctite before tightening. Screws (19—Fig. J35) should be tightened to 9 Nm (80 in.-lb.) torque. Add Jonsered special grease (part No. 504 98 00-20) or equivalent to the housing until the cavity is approximately 3/4 full. Do not over fill the housing with grease and tighten fill plug (9—Fig. J34 or Fig. J35) securely.

ENGINE CONTROLS

Engine throttle control is located within easy reach of the operator's hands when safely positioned on the grips. Refer to Fig. J36, Fig. J37 or Fig. J38. On some models, the engine stop switch is also located near the operator's grip.

RECOIL STARTER

If the recoil starter is located in the fan housing at the output shaft end of the engine, refer to Fig. J39 (GT21L) or Fig. J40 (JGT22L and JGT24L). Refer to Fig. J41 or Fig. J42 for other models that have the recoil starter opposite the output (drive shaft) end of the engine.

To remove the recoil starter from direct drive JGT21L models, first loosen the clamp screws (1—Fig. J39) and withdraw the drive shaft housing. Unbolt and remove the fan and starter housing (2).

To remove the recoil starter from JGT22L or JGT24L models, first disassemble the throttle lever and grip assembly (Fig. J36). Unbolt the clutch housing (1—Fig. J40) from the fan housing (2) and separate the housings. Remove nut and clutch assembly (9-12), then unbolt and remove the fan and starter housing (2).

To remove the starter assembly from other models, unbolt the housing (1—Fig. J41 or Fig. J42) and remove the starter assembly from the engine.

To disassemble starter, remove rope handle and allow pulley to unwind slowly to release spring tension. On Models 21/22/24, remove pulley lock plates (5—Fig. J39 or Fig. J40) and lift starter pulley (4) from starter housing. On all other models, remove screw (3—Fig. J41 or Fig. J42) from center of pulley (4) and lift starter pulley from starter housing. Remove rope from pulley if renewal is necessary. Use caution

Illustrations courtesy Jonsered Power Product

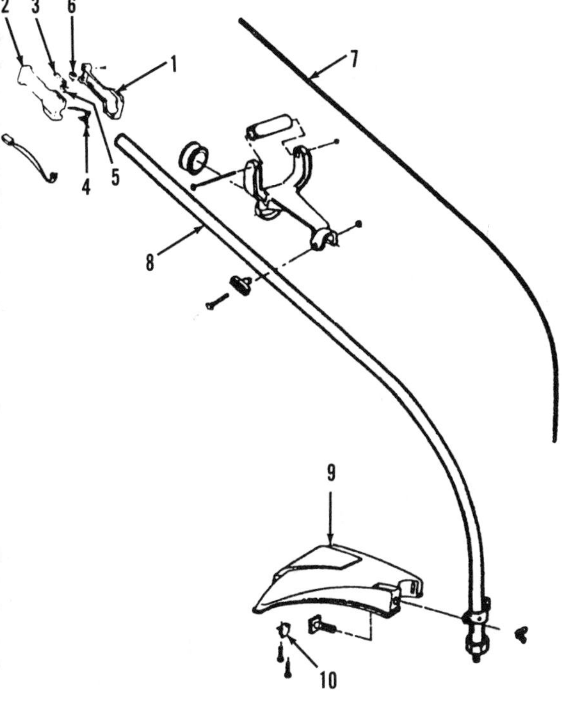

Fig. J36—View of engine controls and drive shaft typical of JGT22L. Models JGT21L and JGT24L are similar.

1. Grip half
2. Grip half
3. Interlock
4. Throttle lever
5. Spring
6. Stop switch
7. Drive shaft
8. Drive shaft housing
9. Shield
10. Line cutter

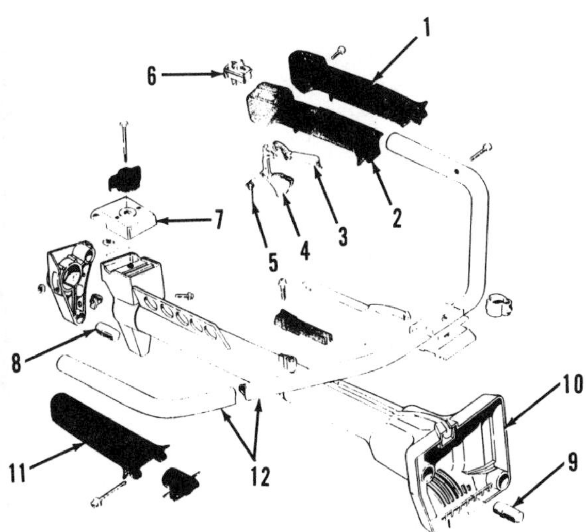

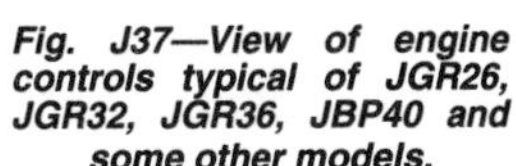

Fig. J37—View of engine controls typical of JGR26, JGR32, JGR36, JBP40 and some other models.

1. Grip half
2. Grip half
3. Interlock
4. Throttle lever
5. Spring
6. Stop switch
7. Clamp
8. Vibration isolators
9. Vibration isolators
10. Housing
11. Grip
12. Handlebar

when servicing rewind spring as it may uncoil uncontrolled. Wear suitable eye protection and gloves when removing and installing the spring.

When reassembling, lubricate center post of housing and spring side of pulley with light grease. On models equipped with spring cassette (Fig. J41), install new spring and cassette in starter housing and secure with retaining screw. On models without cassette (Fig. J42), push the spring into position in the starter housing while letting the locking shackle slide over the spring. Install spring cover (5) and secure with screws. On Models 21/22/24 with a loose cassette, install cassette and spring into starter housing with spring facing downward. Be sure that the spring outer hook engages notch in starter housing.

Wind rope approximately 4 turns clockwise around the pulley. For Models 26/32/36/40/51, rope should be wound in counterclockwise direction. Pass rope through housing eyelet and attach handle. Rotate starter pulley to preload the rewind spring so that rope handle is held snugly against starter housing. Pull out starter rope fully; it should be possible to rotate pulley at least another half turn.

CLUTCH

The clutch used on JGT22L and JGT24L is shown in Fig. J40. To remove the clutch, first disassemble the throttle lever and grip assembly (Fig. J36). Unbolt the clutch housing (1—Fig. J40) from the fan housing (2) and separate the housings. The clutch drum is contained in the clutch housing and the

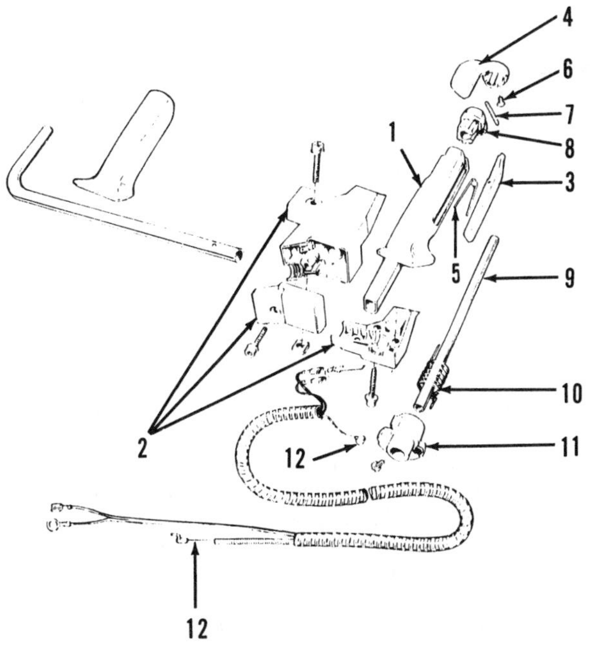

Fig. J38—View of engine controls for RS51 models.

1. Grip
2. Grip half
3. Interlock
4. Throttle lever
5. Spring
6. Screw
7. Pin
8. Adapter
9. Throttle shaft
10. Return spring
11. Lever
12. Throttle cable

Illustrations courtesy Jonsered Power Product

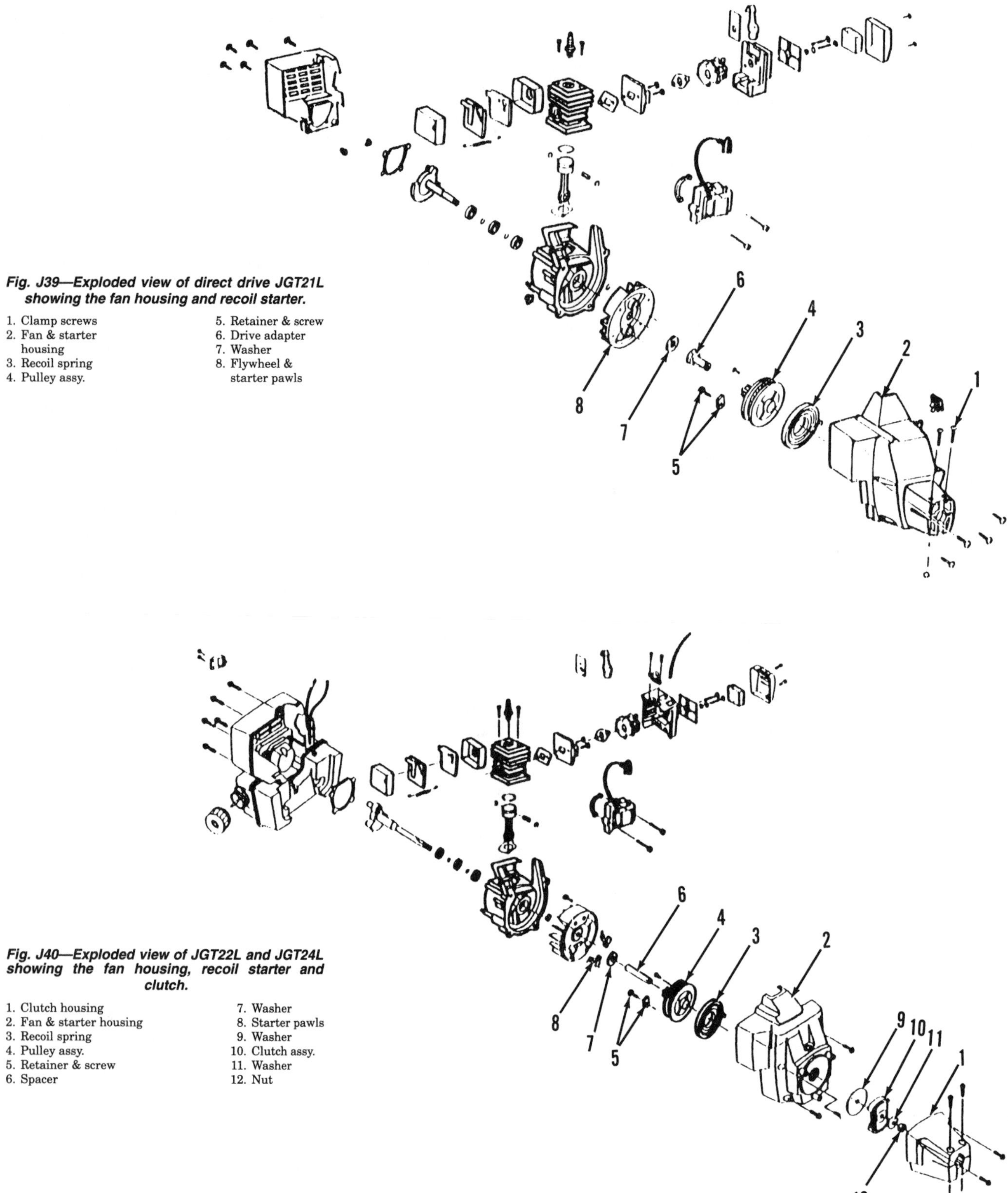

Fig. J39—Exploded view of direct drive JGT21L showing the fan housing and recoil starter.

1. Clamp screws
2. Fan & starter housing
3. Recoil spring
4. Pulley assy.
5. Retainer & screw
6. Drive adapter
7. Washer
8. Flywheel & starter pawls

Fig. J40—Exploded view of JGT22L and JGT24L showing the fan housing, recoil starter and clutch.

1. Clutch housing
2. Fan & starter housing
3. Recoil spring
4. Pulley assy.
5. Retainer & screw
6. Spacer
7. Washer
8. Starter pawls
9. Washer
10. Clutch assy.
11. Washer
12. Nut

drum, ball bearing and housing must be replaced as an assembly. Remove nut and clutch assembly (9-12) from the end of the crankshaft. The outside lip of the shoes should be at least 1 mm thick. Both shoes must be replaced as a set. Be sure to install large washer (9). The side of the clutch hub marked "OFF" and "HOLD TO TURN NUT" should be toward the outside before installing smaller washer (11) and nut (12).

The two shoe clutch used on JGR26, JGR32 and JBP40 can be removed after detaching the upper drive shaft. The drive shaft (1—Fig. J43) of JGR26 and JGR32 models is threaded into the clutch drum(4). On JBP40 model, drive adapter (1—Fig. J44) is threaded into the clutch drum. The clutch drum (4—Fig. J43 or Fig. J44), bearing and housing (3) are available as an assem-

Illustrations courtesy Jonsered Power Product

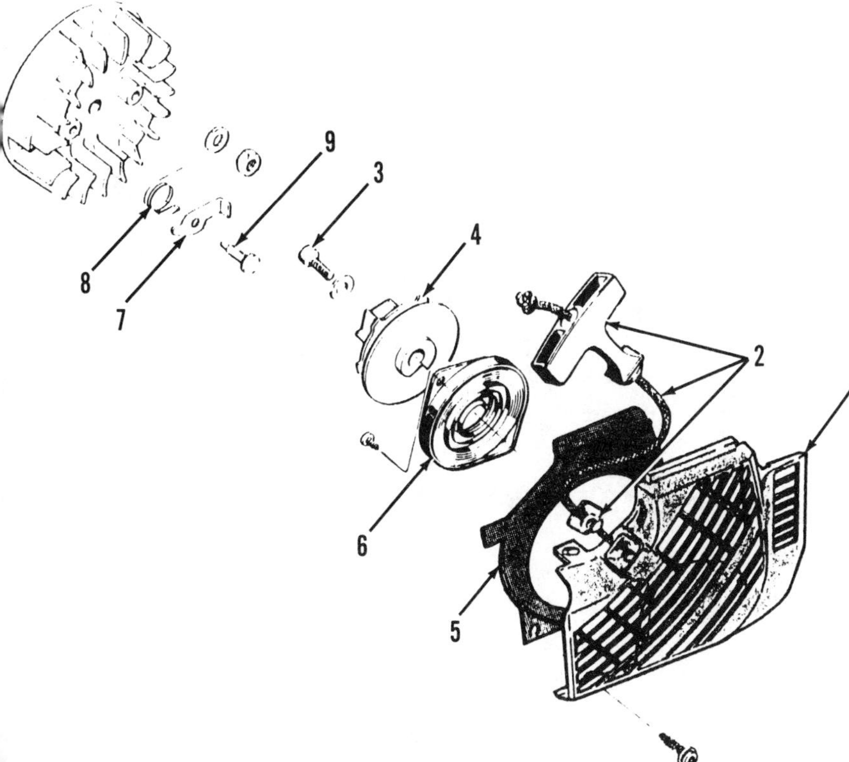

Fig. J41—Exploded view of starter typical of JBP40, JGR26, JGR32, JGR36, JGR41, JGR50 and RS44 models.

1. Starter housing
2. Handle, rope & guide
3. Screw
4. Pulley
5. Plate
6. Spring & case
7. Pawl
8. Spring
9. Pivot screw

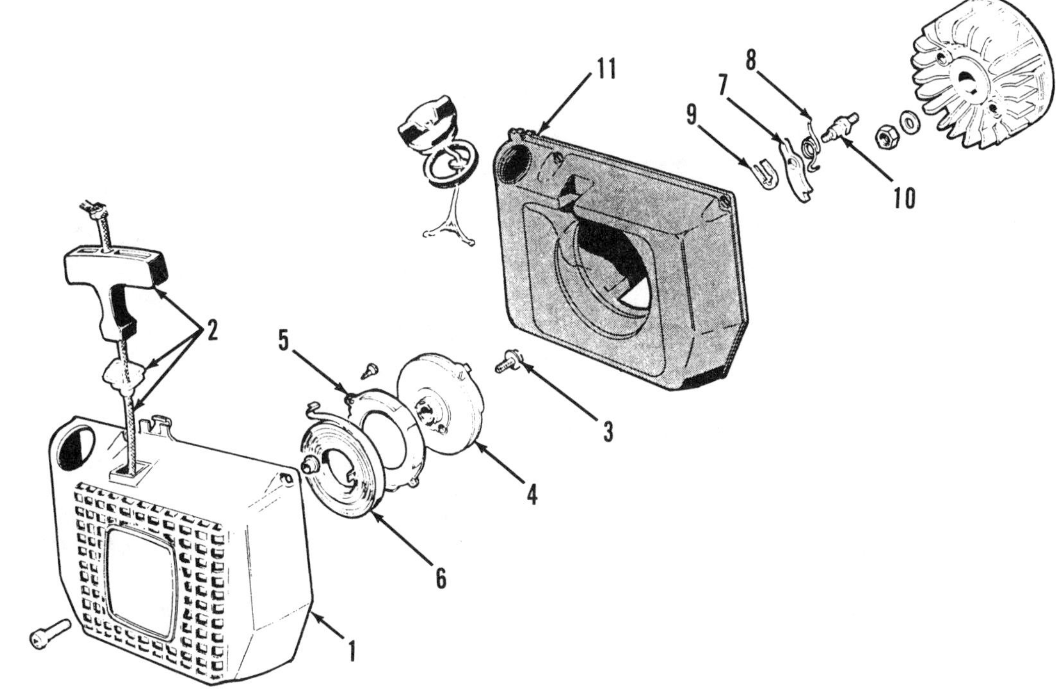

Fig. J42—Exploded view of starter for RS51 models.

1. Starter housing
2. Handle, rope & guide
3. Screw
4. Pulley
5. Spring housing
6. Spring
7. Pawl
8. Spring
9. Retainer clip
10. Pivot stud
11. Fuel tank

Illustrations courtesy Jonsered Power Product

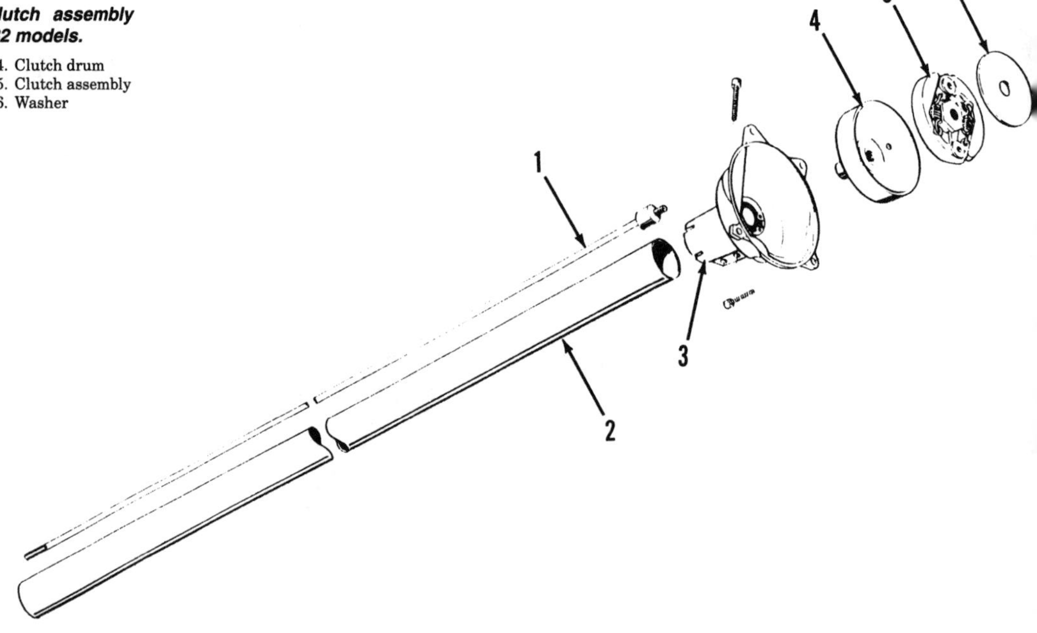

Fig. J43—Exploded view of clutch assembly typical of JGR26 and JGR32 models.

1. Drive shaft
2. Drive shaft housing
3. Clutch housing
4. Clutch drum
5. Clutch assembly
6. Washer

bly. If disassembled, the shoes can be aligned so hub can be installed by clamping the shoes and springs in a vise. Tighten the vise until the shoes are aligned and hub can be inserted into shoes easily. Be sure to install the large washer (6) on the crankshaft before installing the clutch assembly.

The three shoe clutch used on JGR36 can be removed after loosening the plastic covers of the drive shaft housing and sliding the covers forward (down) far enough to remove the screws attaching the clutch housing (3—Fig. J45). It may be necessary to disassemble the throttle grip to detach the throttle cable and engine stop switch wires. Install a piston stop (part No. 504 91 06-05 or

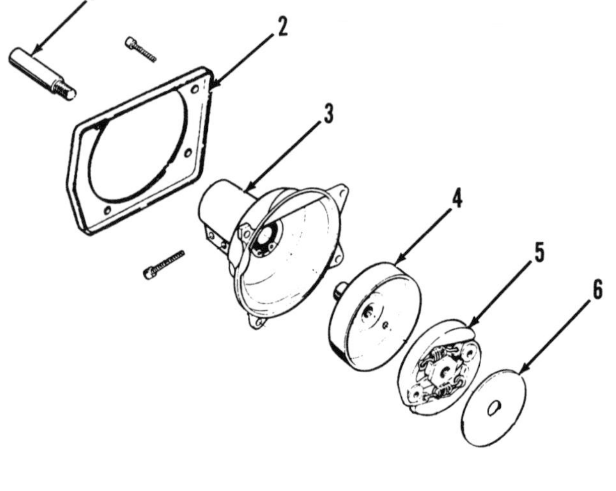

Fig. J44—Exploded view of clutch assembly for BP40 model.

1. Drive adapter
2. Plate
3. Clutch housing
4. Clutch drum
5. Clutch assembly
6. Washer

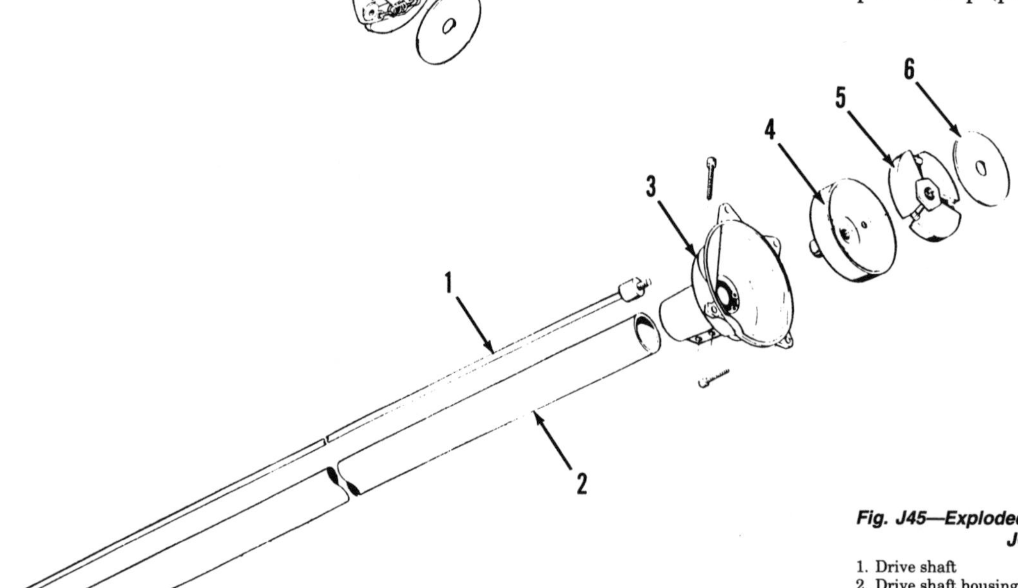

Fig. J45—Exploded view of clutch assembly for JGR36 model.

1. Drive shaft
2. Drive shaft housing
3. Clutch housing
4. Clutch drum
5. Clutch assembly
6. Washer

Illustrations courtesy Jonsered Power Product

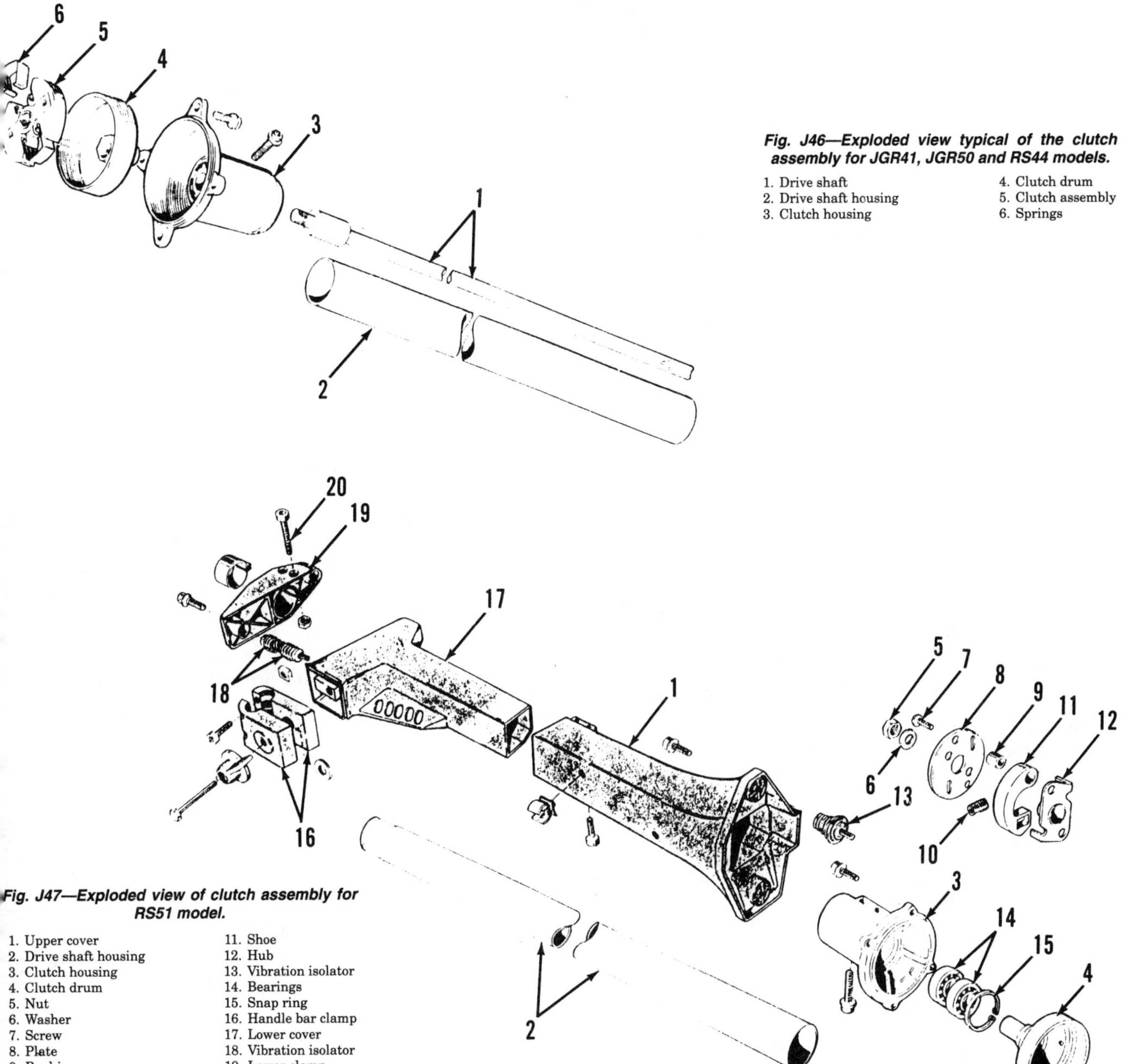

Fig. J46—Exploded view typical of the clutch assembly for JGR41, JGR50 and RS44 models.

1. Drive shaft
2. Drive shaft housing
3. Clutch housing
4. Clutch drum
5. Clutch assembly
6. Springs

Fig. J47—Exploded view of clutch assembly for RS51 model.

1. Upper cover
2. Drive shaft housing
3. Clutch housing
4. Clutch drum
5. Nut
6. Washer
7. Screw
8. Plate
9. Bushing
10. Spring
11. Shoe
12. Hub
13. Vibration isolator
14. Bearings
15. Snap ring
16. Handle bar clamp
17. Lower cover
18. Vibration isolator
19. Lower clamp
20. Clamp screw

equivalent) in the spark plug hole to stop the crankshaft from turning, then unscrew the clutch using a 6-point socket. The outside lip of the shoes should be at least 1 mm thick. All three shoes must be replaced as a set. If disassembled, the connection point of the spring ends should be located in the center on one of the clutch shoes.

The two shoe clutch used on JGR41, JGR50 and RS44 models can be removed after loosening the plastic covers of the drive shaft housing and sliding the covers forward (down) far enough to remove the screws attaching the clutch housing (3—Fig. J46). Install a piston stop (part No. 504 91 06-05 or equivalent) in the spark plug hole to stop the crankshaft from turning, then use a hammer and punch to unscrew the clutch hub from the crankshaft. If necessary, snap ring pliers can be used to expand the springs (6) for removal or installation. The pins must be driven from the clutch shoes before the shoes can be removed from the hub. Make sure the pins are properly in place and that springs correctly engage the shoes when assembling.

The two shoe clutch used on RS51 model can be removed after loosening the plastic covers (1, 17 and 19—Fig. J47) and sliding the covers forward (down) the drive shaft housing (2) far enough to remove the screws attaching the clutch housing (3). Install a piston stop (part No. 504 91 06-05 or equivalent) in the spark plug hole to stop the crankshaft from turning, then remove nut (5), washer (6). Use a special knocking tool (part No. 505 26 79-12 or equivalent) to dislodge the clutch assembly from the engine crankshaft. The outside lip of the shoes should be at least 1 mm thick. If the shoes or any other part is damaged, the clutch should be replaced as an assembly. The clutch drum is provided with two holes which will engage the two pins of special tool (502 52 16-01) when removing the drum from the drive shaft.

KAAZ

GASOLINE POWERED BRUSH CUTTERS

Model	Engine Manufacturer	Engine Model	Displacement
V20	Mitsubishi	T110PD	21.2 cc
V20	Kawasaki	TD18	18.4 cc
V25	Mitsubishi	T140PD	24.1 cc
V25	Kawasaki	TD24	24.1 cc
V35	Mitsubishi	T180PD	32.5 cc
V35	Kawasaki	TD33	33.3 cc
V40	Mitsubishi	T200PD	40.6 cc

ENGINE INFORMATION

All Models

Kaaz brush cutters are available in each model with Kawasaki or Mitsubishi two-stroke air-cooled gasoline engines. Engines may be identified by engine model number and engine displacement. Refer to KAWASAKI ENGINE SERVICE or MITSUBISHI ENGINE SERVICE sections of this manual.

FUEL MIXTURE

All Models

Manufacturer recommends mixing regular grade gasoline (unleaded is an acceptable substitute) with a good quality two-stroke air-cooled engine oil at a 25:1 ratio. Do not use fuel containing alcohol.

BLADE

All Models

All models may be equipped with a four cutting edge brush blade, an eight cutting edge blade or a sixty tooth saw blade. Make certain upper cup washer and lower adapter washer are centered and squarely seated on blade.

DRIVE SHAFT

All Models

All models are equipped with a solid steel drive shaft supported in bushings located in drive shaft housing tube. Drive shaft requires no regular maintenance; however, if drive shaft has been removed, lubricate drive shaft with lithium base grease before reinstallation. Bushings (2-Fig. KZ10) in drive shaft housing tube (1) may be renewed. Mark locations of old bushings in drive shaft housing before removing bushings. Install new bushings at old bushing locations.

GEAR HEAD

All Models

Refer to Fig. KZ11 for an exploded view of the gear head used on all models. Gear head lubricant level should be checked at 30 hour intervals of use. To check, remove check plug (8). Gear head housing should be 2/3 full of lithium base grease.

To disassemble gear head, remove blade assembly. Remove clamp bolts (10) and locating screw (9) and separate gear head from drive shaft housing. Remove snap ring (16) and use a suitable puller to remove input shaft (12) and bearing assembly. Remove snap ring (1) and use a suitable puller to remove arbor shaft (4) and bearing assembly. If bearing (6) stays in housing (7), heat housing to 140° F (60° C) and tap housing on wooden block to remove bearing. Note spacers (11) are installed at gear head housing clamp split to prevent housing damage from overtightening clamp bolts.

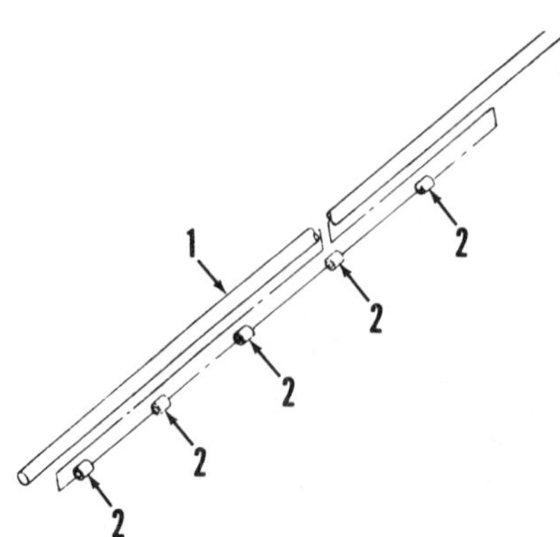

Fig. KZ10—Exploded view of drive shaft housing (1) and bushings (2) used on most models.

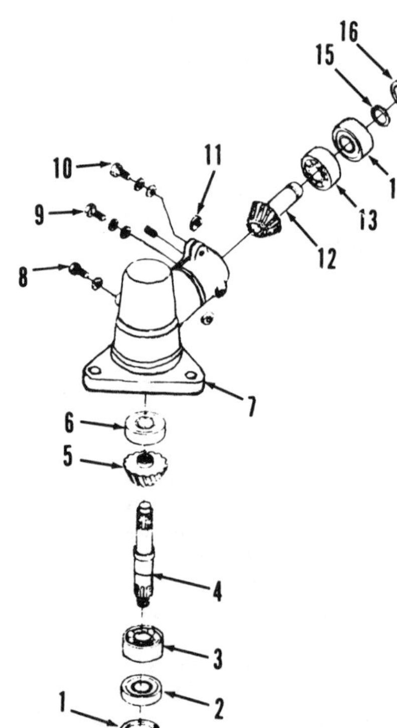

Fig. KZ11—Exploded view of gear head assembly used on all models.

1. Snap ring
2. Seal
3. Bearing
4. Arbor shaft
5. Gear
6. Bearing
7. Housing
8. Check plug
9. Locating plug
10. Clamp bolts
11. Shim (spacer)
12. Input shaft
13. Bearing
14. Bearing
15. Snap ring
16. Snap ring

LAWN BOY

GASOLINE POWERED STRING TRIMMER

Model	Engine Manufacturer	Engine Model	Displacement
SSI	PPP	....	31.0 cc
SSII	PPP	....	31.0 cc
1100	PPP	....	31.0 cc
1150	PPP	....	31.0 cc
1400	PPP	....	31.0 cc
1480	PPP	....	31.0 cc

ENGINE INFORMATION

All Models

All models are equipped with a two-stroke engine manufactured by Piston Powered Products. Refer to PISTON POWERED PRODUCTS ENGINE SERVICE section of this manual. Trimmer model number decal is located on engine cover.

FUEL MIXTURE

All Models

Manufacturer recommends mixing 8 ounces (236.6 mL) of Lawn Boy 2 cycle oil with 2 gallons (7.5 L) of regular grade gasoline of at least 87 octane rating. Unleaded regular gasoline is an acceptable substitute.

STRING TRIMMER

Trimmer may be equipped with a single strand semi-automatic trimmer head or a dual strand semi-automatic trimmer head. Refer to appropriate paragraph for model being serviced.

Single Strand Trimmer Head

To extend line on single strand trimmer head (Fig. LB10) with engine off, push in on bump button (20) and pull on line until desired length is obtained. To extend line with engine running, operate trimmer engine at full rpm and bump the button (20) on the ground. Line will automatically advance a measured amount.

To renew trimmer line, hold drum (15) and unscrew bump button (20). Remove spool (19). Clean inner surface of drum and spool. Check indexing teeth on spool and drum for wear. Insert one end of a 25 foot (7.6 m) length of 0.080 inch (2 mm) monofilament line into one of the holes in spool from the inside out, and back through the second hole to the inside. Wind line in direction indicated by arrow on spool until all but about 3 inches (76.2 mm) of line is wrapped on spool, then clip line temporarily into one of the line lock slots (LS) on spool. Insert line end through line guide in drum and install spool and bump button. Pull line to release from line lock slot on spool after assembly is complete.

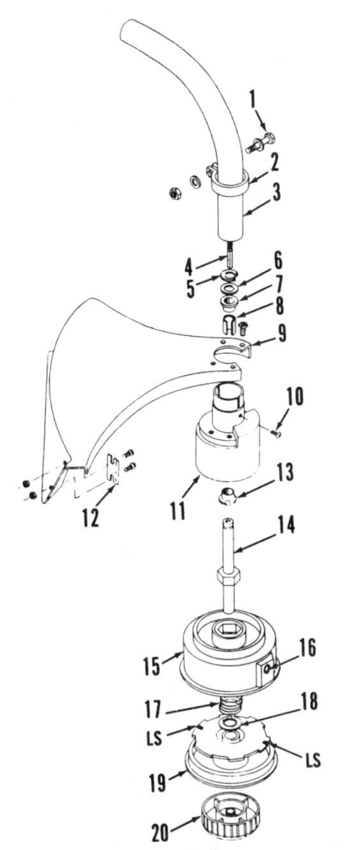

Fig. LB10—Exploded view of single strand semi-automatic trimmer head used on some models.

1. Bolt
2. Clamp
3. Drive shaft housing
4. Drive shaft
5. Retainer
6. Washer
7. Bushing
8. Bushing
9. Shield
10. Locating screw
11. Bushing housing
12. Line cutter
13. Bushing
14. Drive shaft adapter
15. Housing
16. Line guide
17. Spring
18. Retainer
19. Spool
20. Lock knob & bump button

LS. Line slot

Dual Strand Trimmer Head

To extend line on the dual strand semi-automatic trimmer head (Fig. LB11) with engine off, push in on bump button (8) while pulling lines out. Procedure may have to be repeated until desired line length has been obtained. To extend line with engine running, operate trimmer engine at full operating rpm and bump the button (8) on the ground. Each time bump button is tapped on the ground, approximately 1 inch (25 mm) of new line will be advanced.

To renew line, hold drum (2) and unscrew bump button (8). Remove spool (7) and remove any remaining old line. Clean spool and inner surface of drum. Check indexing teeth in drum and on spool. Loop a 25 foot (7.6 m) length of 0.080 inch (2 mm) monofilament line into two equal lengths. Insert the two line ends into the two holes in spool from the bottom and pull line out until loop is against spool. Wind both strands of line around spool at the same time and in the direction indicated by arrow on spool. Wind in tight even layers until almost all line is wrapped around spool, then temporarily clip each line into one of the two line slots (6). Insert line ends through line guides (3) in housing (2), install spool and tighten lock knob and bump button (8). Pull line ends to free from line slots after assembly is complete.

BLADE

Model 1480

Model 1480 may be equipped with the optional four-point brush blade (Fig. LB13). To install blade, refer to Fig. LB13 for assembly sequence. Tighten nut (11) to 225-250 in.-lbs. (26-28 N·m).

DRIVE SHAFT

Models SSI, SSII, 1100, 1150 And 1400

Models SSI, SSII, 1100, 1150 and 1400 are equipped with a flexible drive shaft enclosed in the drive shaft housing tube. Models 1100 and 1150 are direct drive models with no clutch. All other models are equipped with a centrifugal clutch. Drive shaft has squared ends which engage clutch adapter at engine end and head adapter at trimmer head end. Drive shaft should be removed for maintenance at 10 hour intervals of continuous use. Remove drive shaft, mark end positions, then clean shaft and inspect for damage. Lubricate drive shaft with a good quality high temperature wheel bearing grease and make certain shaft is installed with ends in opposite locations. Alternating drive shaft squared ends between clutch and trimmer head ends will extend life of the shaft.

Model 1480

Model 1480 is equipped with a solid steel drive shaft mounted in bushings in the drive shaft housing. Drive shaft requires no regular maintenance; however, if drive shaft has been removed, lubricate with lithium base grease before reinstallation.

LOWER DRIVE SHAFT BUSHINGS

Models SSI, 1100, 1150 And 1400

Models SSI, 1100, 1150 and 1400 are equipped with drive shaft support bushings located in bushing head as shown in Fig. LB14. Bushing head requires no regular maintenance. A bushing kit (2) is available for service.

BEARING HEAD/LOWER CLUTCH

Model SSII

Model SSII is equipped with a bearing head incorporated in the lower clutch unit (Fig. LB15). Bearing head is equipped with sealed bearings and requires no regular maintenance.

To renew bearings or remove clutch assembly, remove trimmer head and cup washer (15). Remove the three bolts retaining bearing plate (11) to housing (4). Separate housing from bearing plate. Remove clutch shoe assembly (6) as required. Remove clutch drum (7) and shield (5). Press arbor shaft (8) from bearings. Remove snap rings (9 and 14). Remove bearings (10 and 13) and spacer (12).

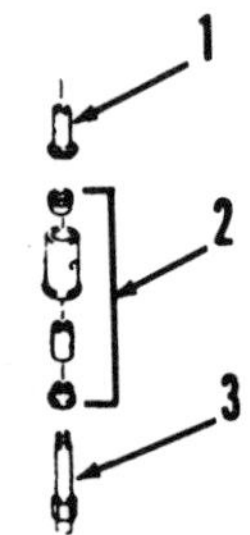

Fig. LB14—Exploded view of lower drive shaft support bushing assembly.

1. Adapter
2. Bushing kit
3. Drive shaft (head)

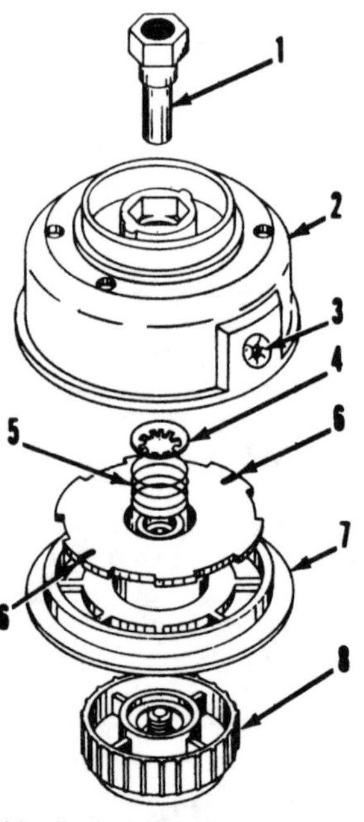

Fig. LB11—Exploded view of dual strand semi-automatic trimmer head used on most models.

1. Drive shaft adapter
2. Housing
3. Line guide
4. Retainer
5. Spring
6. Line slot
7. Spool
8. Lock knob & bump button

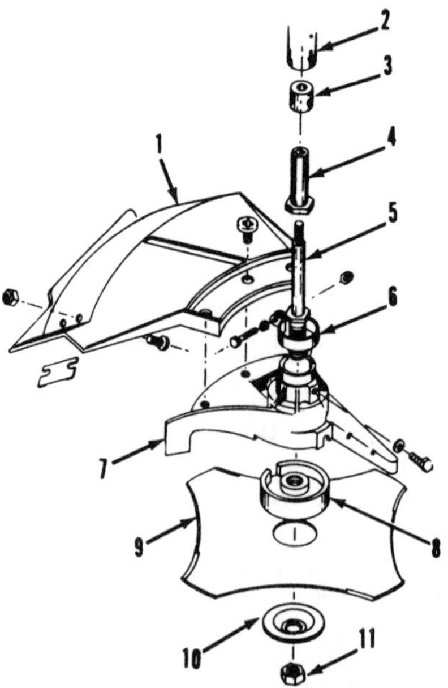

Fig. LB13—Exploded view of blade assembly.

1. Shield
2. Drive shaft housing
3. Sleeve
4. Drive shaft adapter
5. Drive shaft (head)
6. Clamp
7. Bearing housing
8. Cup washer
9. Blade
10. Adapter plate
11. Nut

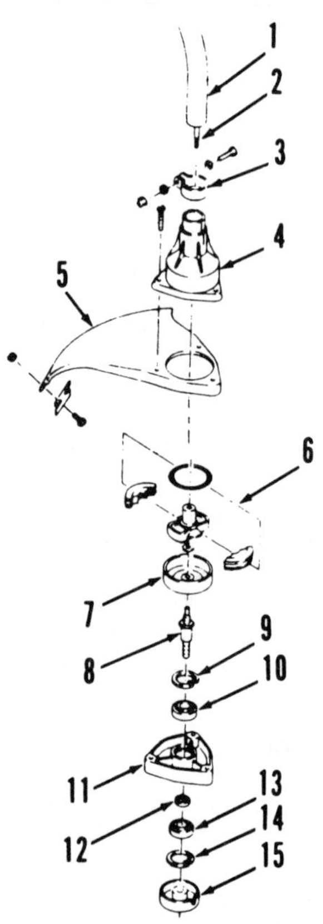

Fig. LB15—Exploded view of lower clutch and bearing head assembly used on Model SSII.

1. Drive shaft housing
2. Drive shaft
3. Clamp
4. Housing
5. Shield
6. Clutch assy.
7. Clutch drum
8. Shaft
9. Snap ring
10. Bearing
11. Bearing plate
12. Spacer
13. Bearing
14. Snap ring
15. Cup washer

GEAR HEAD

Model 1480

Model 1480 is equipped with a gear head assembly. Check plug in gear head should be removed and lubricant level checked at 50 hour intervals of use. Gear head housing should be 2/3 full of lithium base grease. Service parts are not available from Lawn Boy. Gear head must be renewed as a complete unit.

ENGINE COVER

Models SSI And SSII

Models SSI and SSII are equipped with a full engine cover (Fig. LB17). To remove cover, remove all Phillips screws around outer cover. Remove head adjustment screw (12). Remove the side of housing (7) opposite fuel tank filler cap (11). Covers are mounted in rubber grommets (1) also and may be slightly difficult to remove. Note locations of starter rope guide (2), throttle trigger (5), spring (6), switch (3) and fuel tank mounting before removing cover side (10). Fuel tank cap (11) must be removed to separate cover from fuel tank.

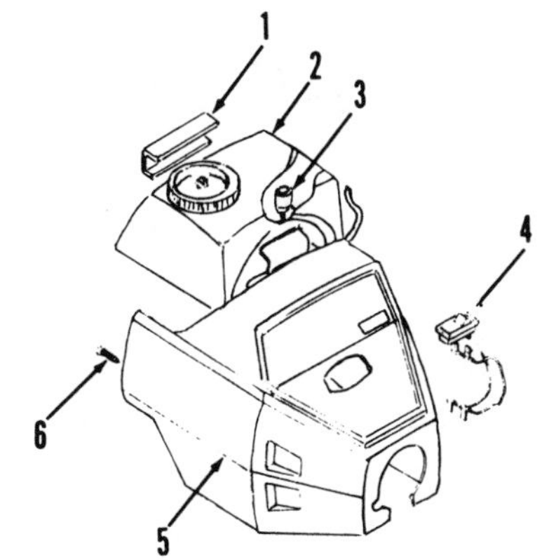

Fig. LB18—Exploded view of partial engine cover used on Models 1150, 1400 and 1480.

1. Fuel tank mount
2. Fuel tank
3. Fuel line assy.
4. Switch
5. Engine cover
6. Screw

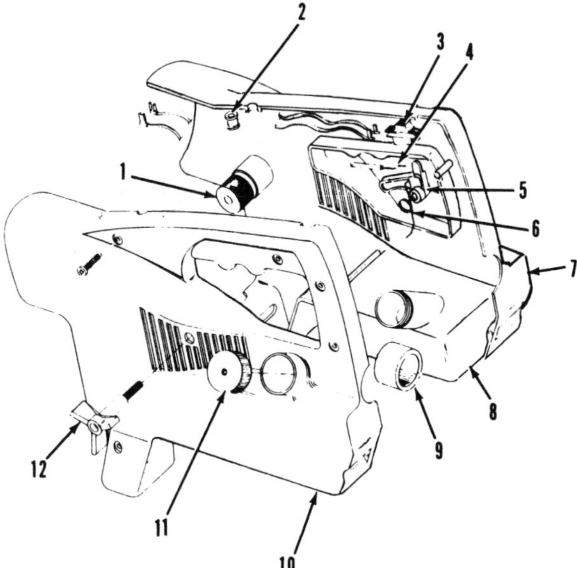

Fig. LB17—Exploded view of engine cover assembly used on SSI and SSII models.

1. Rubber grommet
2. Rope guide
3. Switch
4. Throttle cable
5. Throttle trigger
6. Throttle spring
7. Cover half
8. Fuel tank
9. Rubber sleeve
10. Cover half
11. Fuel tank cap
12. Tube clamp screw

Models 1150, 1400 And 1480

Models 1150, 1400, and 1480 are equipped with a partial engine cover (Fig. LB18). To remove cover, disconnect spark plug lead and remove screw retaining cover extension stand (8— Fig. LB19). Remove cover extension stand. Disconnect the two wire leads at the ignition module. Remove the two inner engine cover retaining screws located just under fuel tank at each side (6— Fig. LB18). A long screwdriver is required to reach inner screws. Slide cover forward on tube as starter handle is worked through opening in engine cover.

Before reinstalling engine cover make certain the two ignition module wire leads are secured in retainer slot.

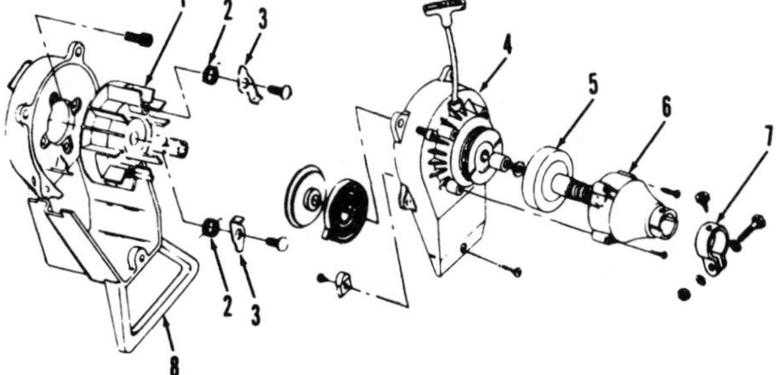

Fig. LB19—Exploded view of engine inner cover assembly.

1. Flywheel
2. Spring
3. Pawl
4. Recoil housing
5. Clutch drum
6. Clutch cover
7. Clamp
8. Stand

MAKITA

GASOLINE POWERED TRIMMERS

Models	Engine Make	Engine Model	Displacement
RBC220, RBC221	Makita	...	21.7 cc
RBC230	Makita	...	22.2 cc
RBC250, RBC251	Makita	...	24.5 cc
RBC260, RBC261	Makita	...	25.4 cc
RBC310, RBC311	Makita	...	30.5 cc
RST250	Makita	...	24.5 cc

ENGINE INFORMATION

The models in this section are equipped with Makita two-stroke engines. Refer to the appropriate ENGINE SERVICE section of this manual for service to the engines used on these models.

FUEL MIXTURE

These two-stroke engines are lubricated by mixing oil with the fuel. The manufacturer recommends mixing regular gasoline, leaded or unleaded, with a high-quality, two-stroke engine oil. The recommended mixing ratio is 50:1 when using Makita Genuine 2 Cycle Engine Oil. If other 2-Stroke oil is used, mix at a ratio of 25:1. Mix the gasoline and oil in a separate container; never in the fuel tank. The use of oxygenated (alcohol blended) gasoline is discouraged

STRING TRIMMER

The string trimmer head should adjust the line length automatically during normal operation by increasing the speed of the engine. If the length of the two cutting lines do not adjust, stop the engine and use pliers to pull the lines 40-80 mm (1 9/16-3 1/8 in.) from the head. If either line is broken off inside the housing or if the lines are twisted inside the housing, the trimmer head should be disassembled and the problem corrected.

To disassemble the type shown in Fig. MK1, press the tabs (A) and remove the cover as shown. Lift the spool from the housing. Remove the remaining line. Clean the drum and spool, then inspect all parts for damage. Make sure new line is the proper diameter. Insert the line through the spool until one end is approximately 80 mm (3 1/8 in.) longer than the other. Wrap the line on spool in the direction opposite that of normal trimmer head rotation as indicated by the arrow on the spool (Fig. MK2). Wind both lines at the same time, tightly and evenly from side to side. Be careful not to twist the lines.

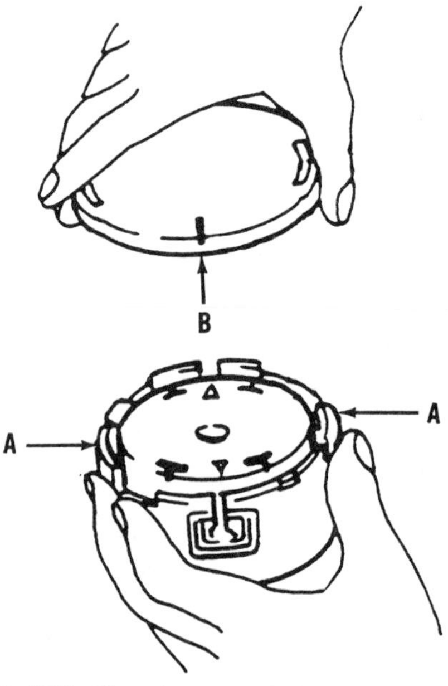

Fig. MK1—View of one type of trimmer head used on RBC220, RBC221, RBC250, RST250 and RBC251 models. To disassemble, depress tabs (A) and remove cover. Install cover so slot (B) in cover aligns with line guides.

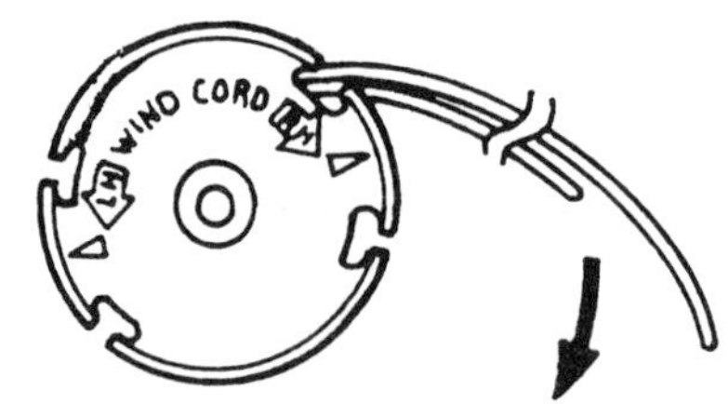

Fig. MK2—Wrap both ends of line on spool at the same time in direction of arrow.

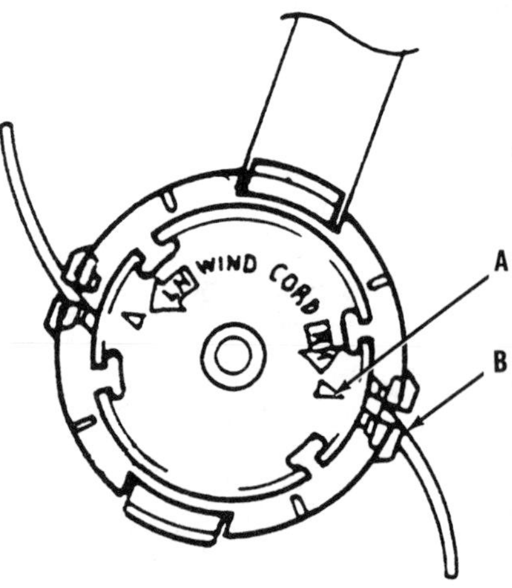

Fig. MK3—When assembling, align the arrows (A) on the spool with the line guides (B) in the housing.

Install the spool while directing the ends of the lines through the line guides in the drum. Align the arrows on the spool with the line guides as shown in Fig. MK3. The lines should protrude 40-80 mm (1 9/16-3 1/8 in.) from the head. Install the cover with the marks (B—Fig. MK1) on the cover aligned with the line guides.

To disassemble the type shown in Fig. MK4, remove the knob (1), then lift the cover (2) and spool (3) from the housing (4). Remove any remaining line from the spool. Clean the drum and spool, then inspect all parts for damage. Make sure new line is the proper diameter. Insert the line through the spool until one end is approximately 120 mm (4 3/4 in.) longer than the other. Wrap the line on spool in the direction of the "WIND CORD LH" indicated by the arrow on the spool (Fig, MK5). Wind both lines at the same time, tightly and evenly from side to side. Be careful not to twist the lines. When spool is filled, the ends of the line

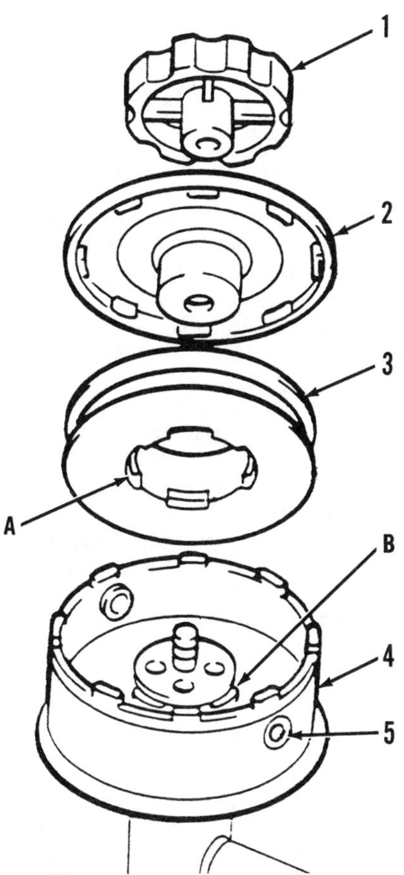

Fig. MK4—View of one type of trimmer head used on RBC230, RBC260, RBC261, RBC310 and RBC311 models.

A. Notch
B. Projection
1. Knob
2. Cover
3. Spool
4. Housing
5. Line guide

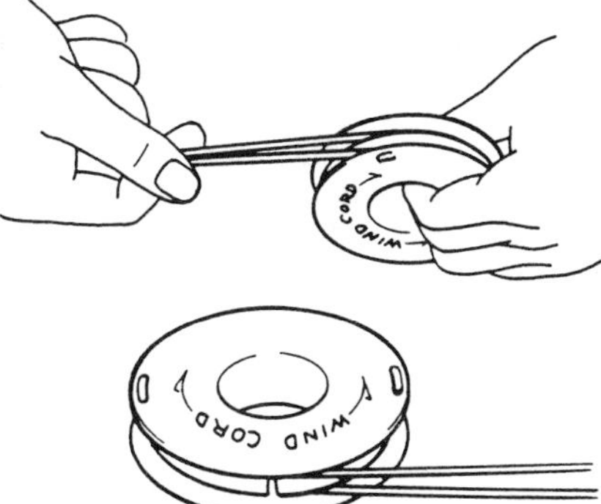

Fig. MK5—Wind both ends of line on spool at the same time in direction of arrow. Refer to text.

can be looped through the two holes provided in the spool to prevent the lines from loosening on the spool. Direct the ends of both lines through the line guides (C—Fig. MK6) in the drum until the lines protrude 120 mm (4 3/4 in.) from the head. Install the spool engaging the notches (A—Fig. MK6) in the center of the spool with the projections (B) inside the housing. Install the

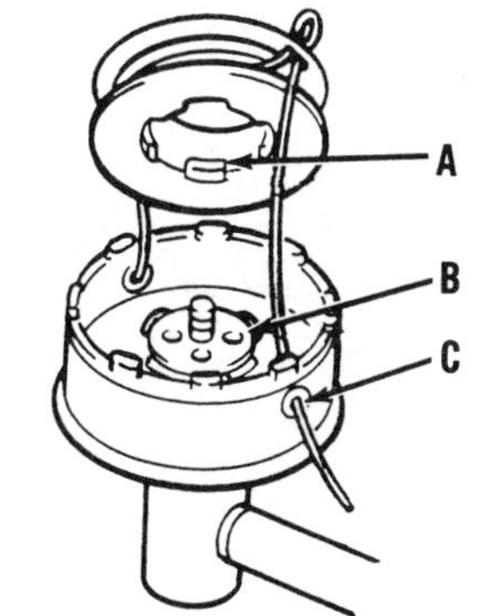
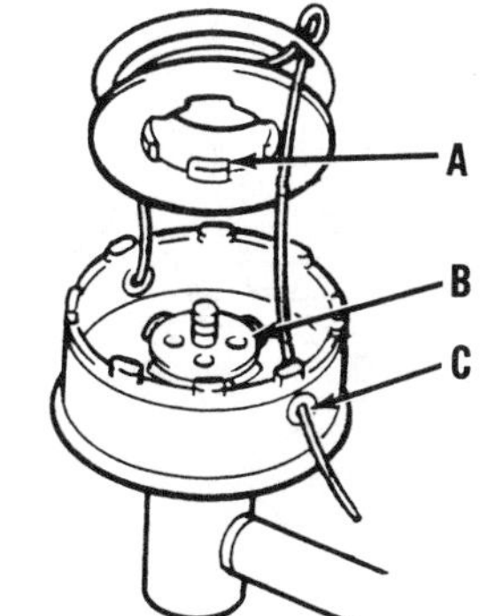

Fig. MK6—Install spool engaging notches (A) with projections (B) inside the housing.

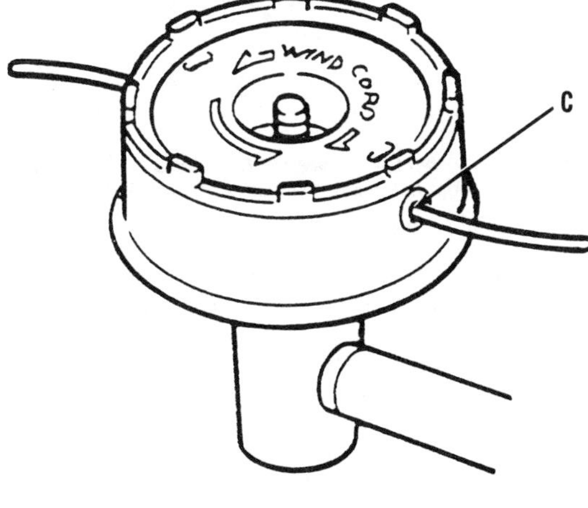

Fig. MK7—Small holes (H) on cover should be aligned with line guides (C).

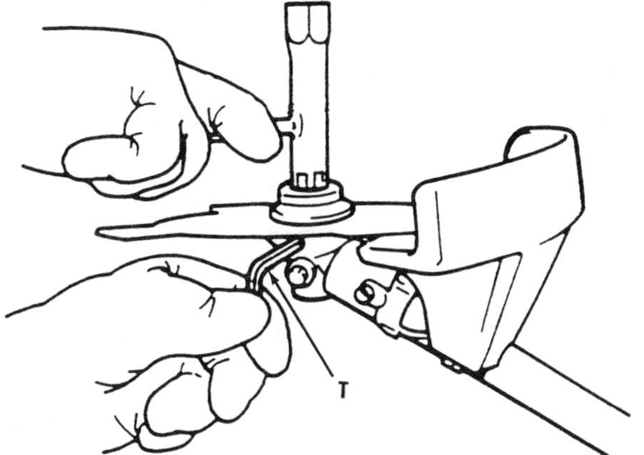

Fig. MK8—Use the locking tool (T) to hold the shaft while loosening the blade attaching nut or trimmer head.

cover with the small holes (H—Fig. MK7) on the cover aligned with the line guides (C) and tighten the retaining knob.

On both models, test operation after assembling.

BLADE

A four-edge cutting blade is available for use on some models. The locking tool (T—Fig. MK8) should be inserted into the slot in the casting and into the blade adapter before loosening or tightening the blade retaining nut. When sharpening, follow the original sharpening angle (A—Fig. MK9). Make sure the inner edge of the sharpened area (C) is rounded to prevent breakage. Install the blade and tighten the blade attaching nut securely.

DRIVE SHAFT

The drive shaft is enclosed in the drive shaft housing (tube) and requires no regular maintenance. It may be necessary to separate the drive shaft hous-

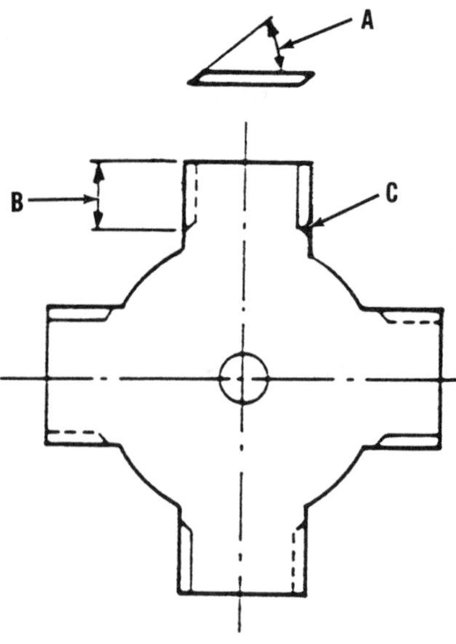

Fig. MK9—Follow the original 30 degree angle (A) when sharpening. Sharpen only the original length (B) and make sure to radius the inner surface (C).

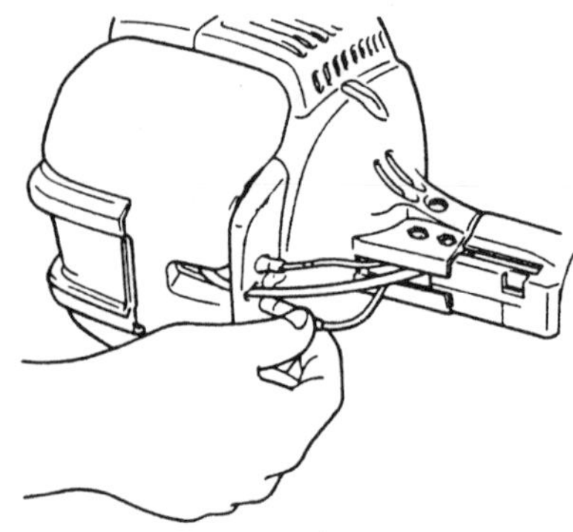

Fig. MK10—Wires to the engine stop switch must be detached before separating the drive shaft housing from the engine assembly.

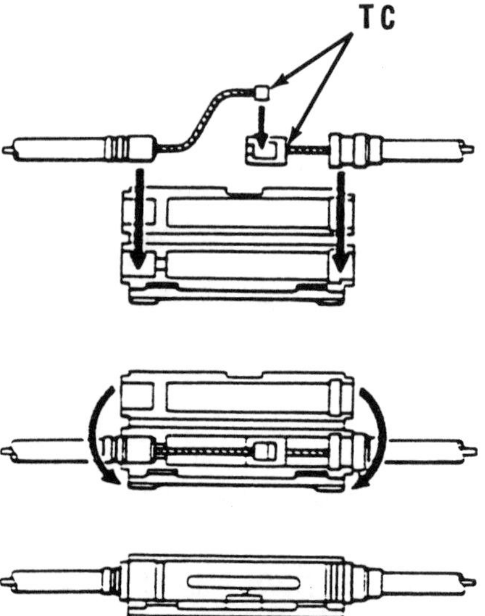

Fig. MK11—On some models, the throttle control cable (TC) is equipped with a connector that can be separated when removing the engine drive shaft housing.

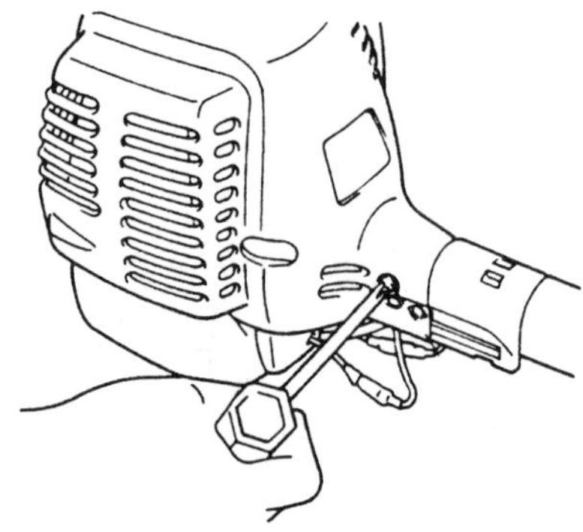

Fig. MK12—The drive shaft housing is located in the engine housing by screw shown.

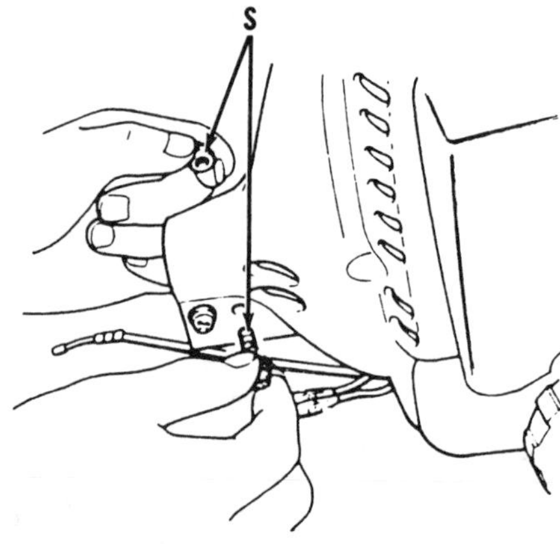

Fig. MK13—Drive shaft housing is clamped in the engine housing by clamp screws (S) as shown.

ing from the engine assembly and to remove the drive shaft from the housing for other service. Remove, inspect and lubricate the drive shaft as follows if damage is suspected or for other service.

If the engine stop switch is located on the grip, find the connector for the wires and separate the wires (Fig. MK10). Detach the throttle cable from the control handle or the carburetor if equipped with a one-piece throttle ca-

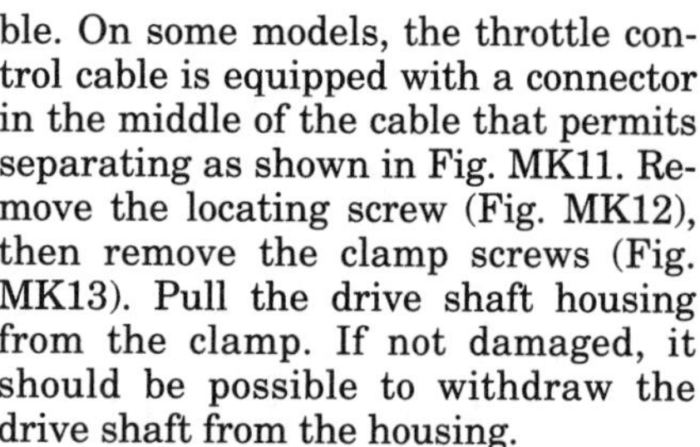

ble. On some models, the throttle control cable is equipped with a connector in the middle of the cable that permits separating as shown in Fig. MK11. Remove the locating screw (Fig. MK12), then remove the clamp screws (Fig. MK13). Pull the drive shaft housing from the clamp. If not damaged, it should be possible to withdraw the drive shaft from the housing.

When assembling, insert the drive shaft and housing 60 mm (2 3/8 in.) into the engine clamp. If it cannot be inserted completely, separate the two assemblies, turn the drive shaft slightly to align the end of the drive shaft with the engine coupling. Align the hole in the drive shaft housing with the locating screw (Fig. MK12), then install the screw. Install and tighten clamp screws (Fig. MK13) after installing the locating screw. Attach the throttle cable and stop switch wires. Make sure the cable and wires are correctly routed and out of the way.

GEAR HEAD

A gear housing is located at the lower end of the drive shaft and housing of some models. To remove the assembly, first remove the trimmer head or blade, then unbolt the protector shield. Loosen the fitting screw (1—Fig. MK14) and clamp bolt(s) (2), then pull the gear housing from the drive shaft housing.

Parts for the gear housing are not available and service is limited to inspection, adding lubricant and installing a new unit.

To check the lubricant in the gear head, remove plug from filler opening (3—Fig. MK14). Add multipurpose lithium grease to the housing until the cavity is approximately 2/3 full. Do not over fill the housing with grease. Tighten fill plug securely.

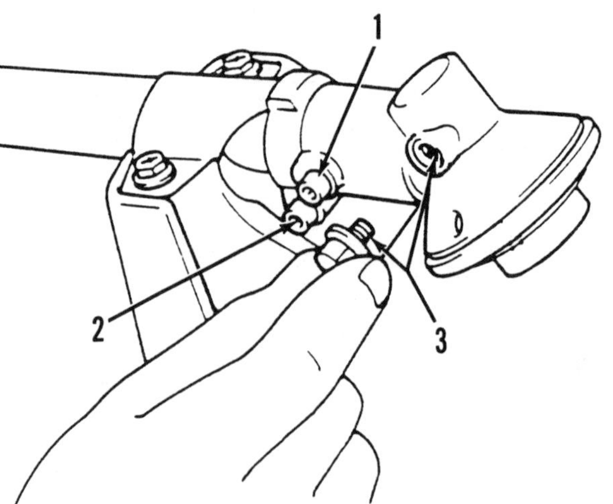

Fig. MK14—On some models gear head is attached to drive shaft by locating screw (1) and clamp screw (2). Gear head is lubricated through filler opening (3).

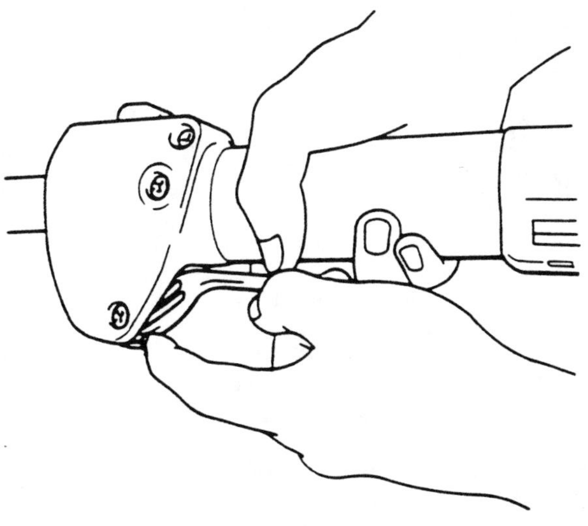

Fig. MK15—View of throttle located on the drive shaft housing. On the unit shown, the engine stop switch is located at the top of the grip.

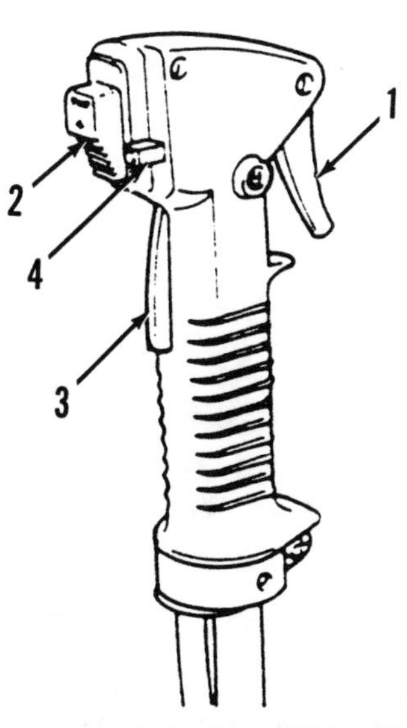

Fig. MK16—On models with handle bar, the grip is fitted with throttle and engine stop switch as shown. The unit shown also has interlock (3).

1. Throttle trigger
2. Stop switch
3. Throttle interlock
4. Lock button

ENGINE CONTROLS

Engine throttle control is located within easy reach of the operator's hands when safely positioned on the grips. Refer to Fig. MK15 and Fig. MK16. On most models, the engine stop switch is also located near the operator's grip.

MARUYAMA

GASOLINE POWERED STRING TRIMMERS

Model	Engine Manufacturer	Engine Model	Displacement
BC184	Kawasaki	KE18	18.4 cc
BC184C	Kawasaki	KE18	18.4 cc

ENGINE INFORMATION

All Models

Maruyama line trimmers and brush cutters are equipped with Kawasaki two-stroke air-cooled gasoline engines. Engines may be identified by manufacturer, engine model number and engine displacement. Refer to KAWASAKI ENGINE SERVICE section of this manual.

FUEL MIXTURE

All Models

Manufacturer recommends mixing regular grade gasoline (unleaded is an acceptable substitute) with a good quality two-stroke air-cooled engine oil at a 25:1 ratio. Do not use fuel containing alcohol.

STRING TRIMMER

All Models

Refer to Fig. MA10 for an exploded view of the dual strand manual trimmer head used on most models. To extend line, stop trimmer engine and wait until all head rotation has stopped. Loosen lock knob (6) (left-hand thread) until line ends may be pulled from housing. Pull lines until desired length has been obtained. Correct line length is 3.4-4.7 inches (10-12 cm).

To renew line, remove lock knob (6) and housing (5). Remove any remaining line on spool (2) and clean spool and housing. Install new line on spool. Wind line in direction indicated by arrow on spool. Diameter when new line is wound on spool must not exceed spool flange diameter. Insert line ends through line guides (4) then reinstall housing and lock knob.

BLADE

Model BC184

Model BC184 may be equipped with a 9 inch blade. Blade may be a four cutting edge blade, an eight cutting edge blade or a saw blade. To remove blade, rotate anti-wrap guard (1-Fig. MA11) until hole (H) in guard is aligned with hole (H) in cup washer (2). Insert a round tool into aligned holes to prevent blade rotation. Remove bolt (7) (left-hand thread), washer (6), cover (5) and adapter (4). Remove blade (3). When installing blade, tighten bolt (7) to 250 in.-lbs. (28 N·m).

DRIVE SHAFT

Model BC184

Model BC184 is equipped with a solid steel drive shaft supported in drive shaft housing tube. Drive shaft requires no regular maintenance; however, if drive shaft has been removed, lubricate drive shaft with lithium base grease before reinstallation.

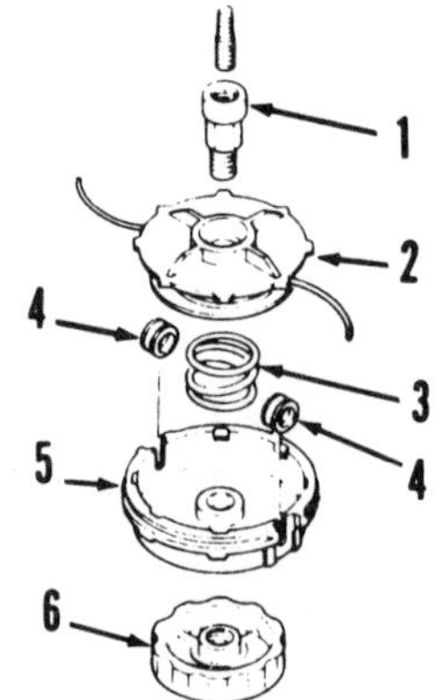

Fig. MA10—Exploded view of the dual strand manual trimmer head standard on most models.

1. Drive shaft adapter
2. Spool
3. Spring
4. Line guides
5. Housing
6. Lock knob

Model BC184C

Model BC184C is equipped with a flexible drive shaft enclosed in the drive shaft housing tube. Drive shaft has squared ends which engage adapters at each end. Drive shaft should be removed for maintenance at 20 hour intervals of use. To remove, separate drive shaft housing from engine. Mark locations of drive shaft ends and pull drive shaft out of housing. Clean drive shaft and lubricate with lithium base grease. Reinstall drive shaft in housing. Make certain drive shaft ends are installed at original location.

BEARING HEAD

Model BC184C

Model BC184C is equipped with sealed bearing housing (3-Fig. MA12). No regular maintenance is required and no service parts are available.

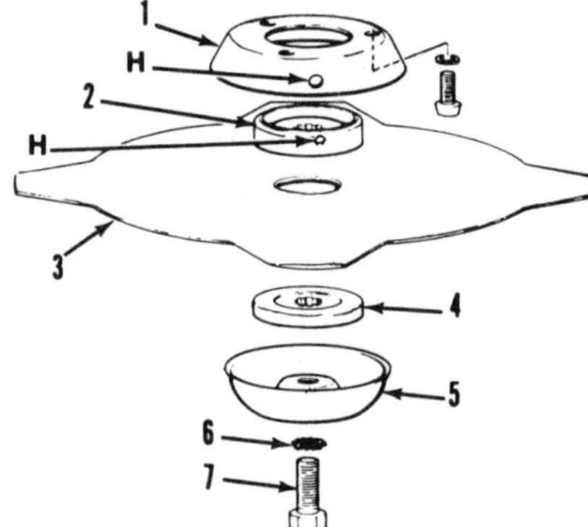

Fig. MA11—Exploded view of blade assembly on Model BC184.

1. Anti-wrap guard
2. Cup washer
3. Blade
4. Adapter plate
5. Cover
6. Washer
7. Bolt (LH)

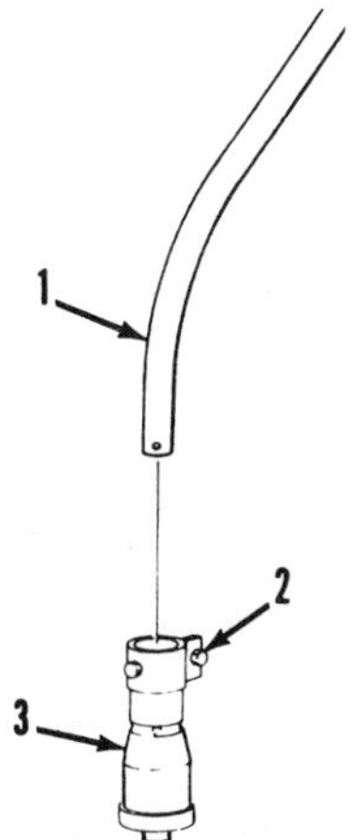

Fig. MA12—Bearing head assembly (3) is attached to drive shaft housing tube (1) by clamp (2). No service parts are available for bearing head.

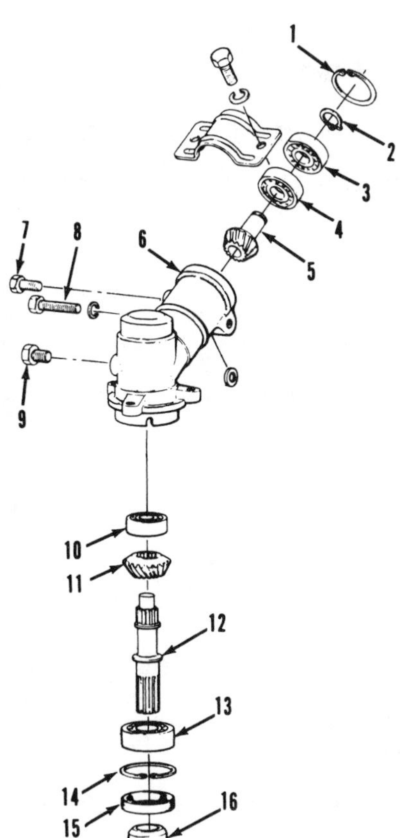

Fig. MA13—Exploded view of gear head used on Model BC184.

1. Snap ring
2. Snap ring
3. Bearing
4. Bearing
5. Input shaft
6. Housing
7. Locating screw
8. Clamp bolt
9. Check plug
10. Bearing
11. Gear
12. Arbor (output) shaft
13. Bearing
14. Snap ring
15. Seal
16. Spacer

GEAR HEAD

Model BC184

Model BC184 is equipped with the gear head shown in Fig. MA13. Gear head lubricant level should be checked at 50 hour intervals of use by removing check plug (9). Gear head housing should be 2/3 full of lithium base grease. Do not use a pressure grease gun to install grease as bearing seal and housing damage will occur.

To disassemble gear head, remove trimmer head or blade assembly. Remove locating screw (7) and clamp bolt (8) then separate gear head from drive shaft housing. Remove snap ring (1). Insert a screwdriver into clamp split in gear head housing and carefully expand housing. Remove input shaft (5) and bearing assembly. Remove snap ring (2) and press bearings (3 and 4) as required. Remove spacer (16) and seal (15). Remove snap ring (14) and use a suitable puller to remove arbor shaft (12) and bearing assembly. If bearing (10) stays in housing, heat housing to 140° F (60° C) and tap housing on wooden block to remove bearing. Remove gear (11) from arbor shaft. Press bearing (13) from arbor shaft as required.

McCULLOCH

GASOLINE POWERED STRING TRIMMERS

Model	Engine Manufacturer	Engine Model	Displacement
MAC 60, 70	Kioritz	...	13.8 cc
MAC 80, 95	Kioritz	...	21.2 cc
MAC 60A, 80A, 85A	McCulloch	...	21.2 cc
MAC 90A, 95A, 100A, 100A-HD	McCulloch	...	21.2 cc
PRO SCAPER I, II, II-HD	McCulloch	...	21.2 cc
SUPER MAC 90A, 95A	McCulloch	...	21.2 cc
SUPER EAGER BEAVER IV	McCulloch	...	21.2 cc

ENGINE INFORMATION

All Models

Early model trimmers and brush cutters are equipped with engines manufactured by Kioritz. Late model trimmers and brush cutters are equipped with engines manufactured by McCulloch. Service procedure and specifications are similar. Identify engine by manufacturer and engine displacement. Refer to appropriate McCULLOCH ENGINE SERVICE or KIORITZ ENGINE SERVICE section of this manual.

FUEL MIXTURE

All Models

Manufacturer recommends mixing regular or unleaded gasoline with a high-quality, two-stroke engine oil designed for air-cooled engines. Recommended fuel:oil ratio is 40:1 when using McCulloch Custom Lubricant. Fuel:oil ratio should be 20:1 when using any other two-stroke oil, regardless of recommended ratio on oil container. Manufacturer recommends addition of Sta-Bil to fuel to prevent fuel degradation. Manufacturer does not recommend using fuel blended with any type of alcohol (gasohol).

STRING TRIMMER

All Models

Trimmer may be equipped with a single strand semi-automatic trimmer head or dual strand trimmer head. Two basic single strand trimmer heads have been used. An early model head (Fig. MC10) and a late model head (Fig. MC14). The dual strand semi-automatic trimmer head is shown in Fig. MC16.

Early Style Single Strand Trimmer Head

Early style single strand semi-automatic trimmer head is shown in Fig. MC10. Line may be manually advanced with engine stopped by pushing in on housing (9) while pulling on line. Procedure may have to be repeated to obtain desired line length. To advance line with engine running, operate engine at full rpm and tap housing (9) on the ground. Each time housing is tapped on the ground, a measured amount of trimmer line will be advanced.

To renew trimmer line, remove cotter pin (10) and twist housing (9) counterclockwise to remove housing. Remove foam pad (6) and any remaining line on spool (3). Clean spool and inside of housing. Cut off approximately 25 feet (7.6 m) of 0.080 inch (2 mm) monofilament line and tape one end of line to spool (Fig. MC11). Wind line on spool in direction indicated by arrow on spool (Fig. MC12). Install foam pad with line end protruding from between foam pad and spool as shown in Fig. MC12. Insert end of line through line guide and install spool, housing and spring. Push housing in and twist in clockwise direction to lock in position, then install cotter pin (10—Fig. MC10).

Late Style Single Strand Trimmer Head

Late style single strand semi-automatic trimmer head is shown in Fig. MC14. Line may be manually advanced with engine stopped by pushing in on housing (12) while pulling on line. Procedure may have to be repeated until desired line length is obtained. To advance line with engine running, operate

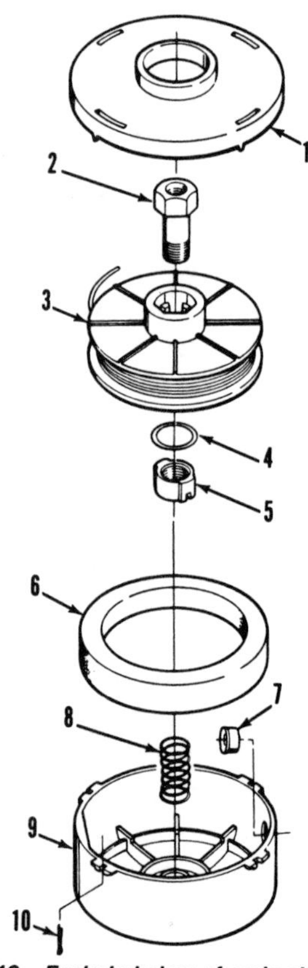

Fig. MC10—Exploded view of early style single strand semi-automatic trimmer head used on some models.

1. Cover
2. Drive shaft adapter
3. Spool
4. "O" ring
5. Drive adapter nut
6. Foam pad
7. Line guide
8. Spring
9. Housing
10. Cotter pin

Illustrations courtesy McCulloch Corp.

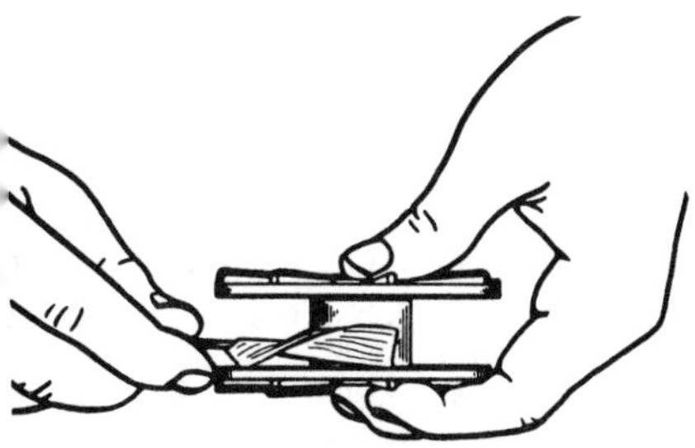

Fig. MC11—Tape end of new line to center of spool as shown.

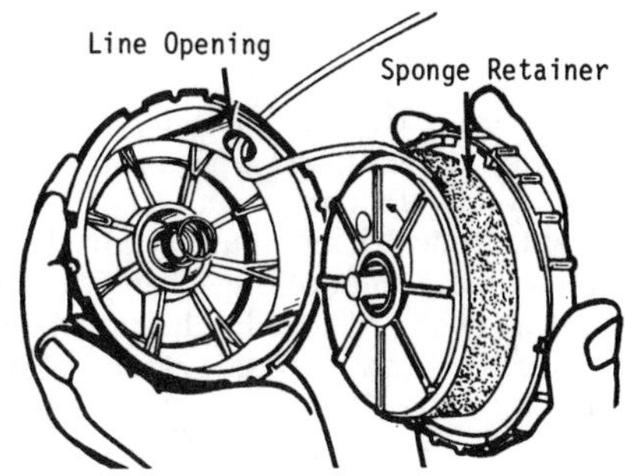

Fig. MC12—Install foam pad with line protruding from between pad and spool. Wind line in direction indicated on spool.

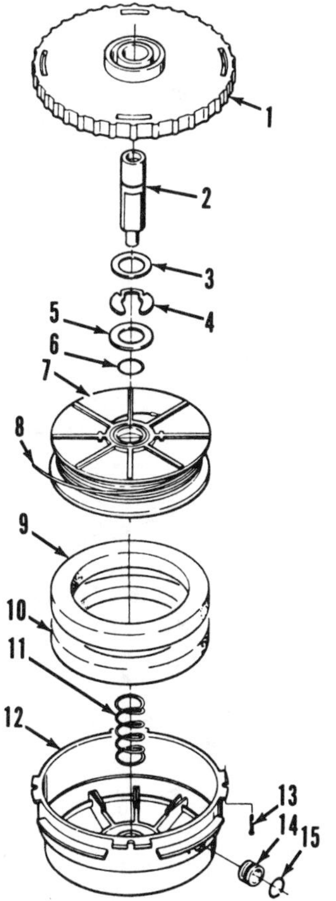

Fig. MC14—Exploded view of the single strand semi-automatic trimmer head used on some late models.

1. Cover
2. Drive shaft adapter
3. Washer
4. Retainer
5. Washer
6. Retainer
7. Spool
8. Line
9. Foam pad
10. Foam pad
11. Spring
12. Housing
13. Cotter pin
14. Line guide
15. Retainer

trimmer engine at full rpm and tap housing (12) on the ground. Each time housing is tapped on the ground, a measured amount of trimmer line is advanced.

To renew trimmer line, remove cotter pin (13). Twist housing (12) counterclockwise and remove housing. Remove foam pads (9 and 10) and any remaining line from spool (7). Clean spool and inner area of housing. Cut off approximately 25 feet (7.6 m) of 0.080 inch (2 mm) diameter monofilament line and tape one end of line to spool (Fig. MC11). Wind line on spool in direction indicated by arrow on spool (Fig. MC15). Install foam pads so line is protruding from center of pads (Fig. MC15). Insert end of line through line guide and install spool, housing and spring. Push housing and twist in clockwise direction to lock in position, then install cotter pin (13—Fig. MC14).

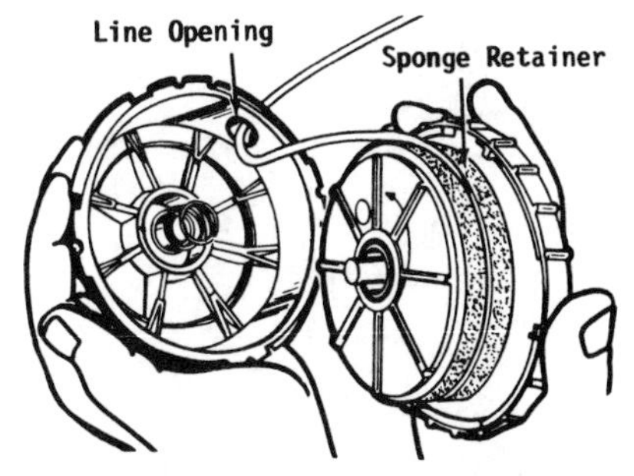

Fig. MC15—Install foam pads with line protruding from between pads. Wind line in direction indicated by arrow on spool.

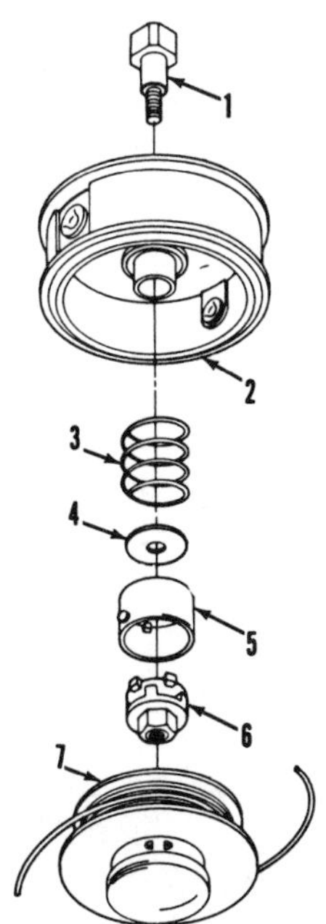

Fig. MC16—Exploded view of the dual strand semi-automatic trimmer head used on some models.

1. Drive shaft adapter
2. Housing
3. Spring
4. Washer
5. Outer cam
6. Inner cam
7. Spool & button

Dual Strand Trimmer Head

Heavy duty dual strand trimmer head is shown in Fig. MC16. To manually advance line with engine stopped, push in on button (7) and pull on each line. Procedure may have to be repeated to obtain desired line length. To extend line with engine running, operate trimmer at full operating rpm and tap button (7) on the ground. Line will automatically advance a measured amount.

To renew trimmer line, hold drum firmly and turn spool in direction shown in Fig. MC17 to remove slack. Twist with a hard snap until plastic peg is between holes. Pull spool out of drum. Remove old line from spool. Spool will hold approximately 20 feet (6 m) of monofilament line. Insert one end of new line through hole on spool (Fig. MC18) and pull line through until line is the same length on both sides of hole. Wind both ends of line at the same time in direction indicated by arrow on spool. Wind line tightly and evenly from side to side and do not twist line.

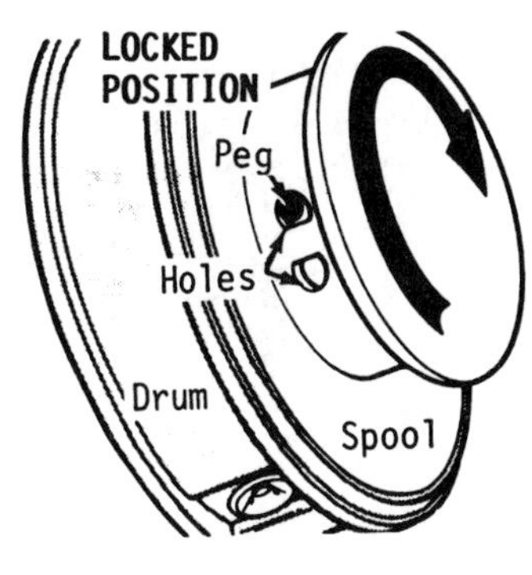

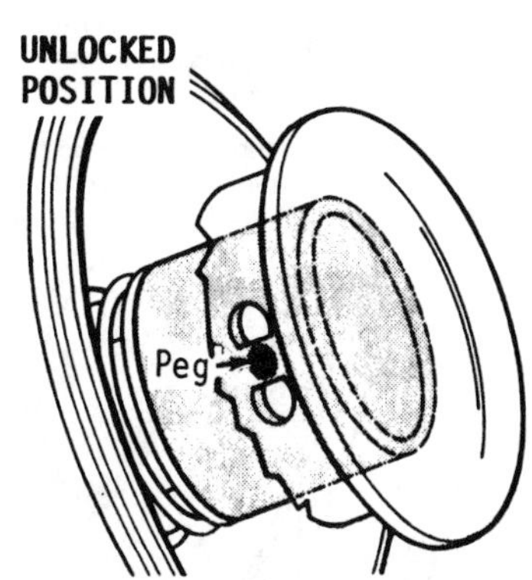

Fig. MC17—To remove spool, hold drum firmly and turn spool in direction shown to take up slack, then twist with a sudden snap until plastic peg is between holes as shown in lower view.

Insert ends of line through line guide openings, align pegs on drum with slots in spool and push spool into drum. Hold drum firmly, twist spool suddenly in direction shown in Fig. MC19 until peg enters hole with a click and locks spool in position. Trim extending lines to desired length.

BLADE

All Models So Equipped

Some models may be equipped with a four cutting edge blade (Fig. MC20) or a saw blade (Fig. MC21). To remove blade, rotate cup washer (2—Figs. MC20 or MC21) and align hole in cup washer with hole in gear head housing. Insert a suitable tool into hole to prevent drive shaft from turning. Remove cotter pin (6—Figs. MC20 or MC21). Nut (5—Figs. MC20 or MC21) has left-hand threads. Remove nut (5), adapter and blade. Tighten nut (5) to 260 in.-lbs. (30 N·m) and install a new cotter pin.

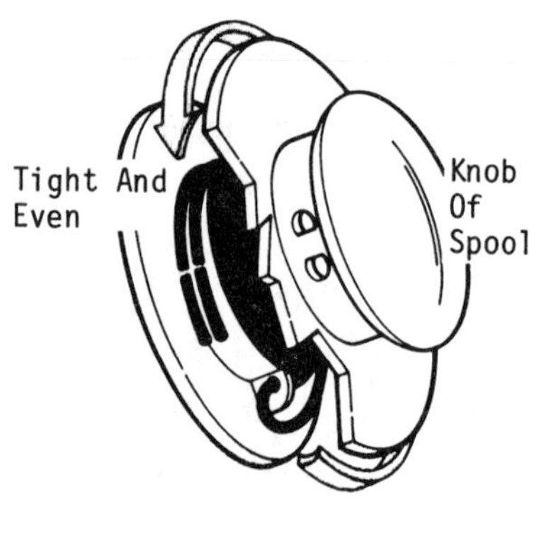

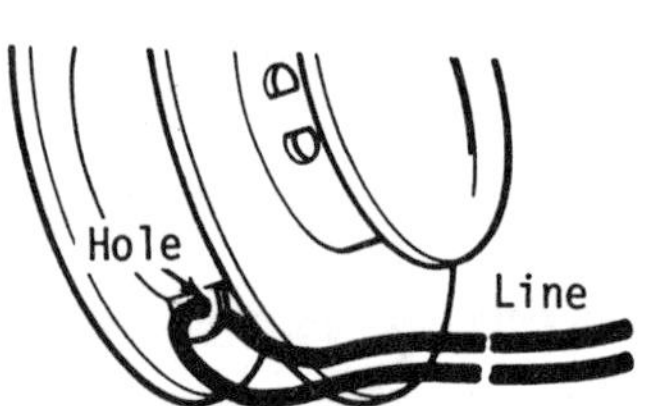

Fig. MC18—End of line must be inserted through hole on spool as shown in lower view. Wind line tightly in direction indicated by arrow on spool.

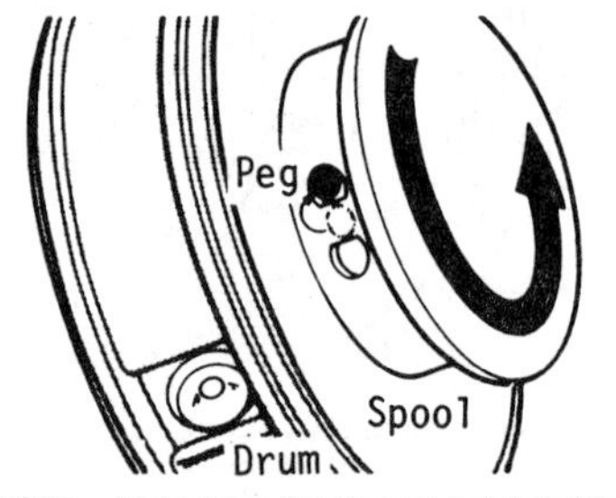

Fig. MC19—Hold drum firmly and twist suddenly to lock spool in position.

DRIVE SHAFT

Models With Curved Drive Shaft Housing

All models with a curved drive shaft housing are equipped with a flexible drive shaft enclosed in the drive shaft housing tube. Drive shaft has squared ends which engage adapters at each end. Drive shaft should be removed for maintenance at 20 hour intervals of use. To remove, separate drive shaft housing from engine. Mark locations of drive shaft ends and pull drive shaft out of housing. Clean drive shaft and lubricate with lithium base grease. Reinstall drive shaft in housing with the drive shaft end previously at engine now at trimmer head end. Reversing drive shaft in this manner will extend drive shaft life.

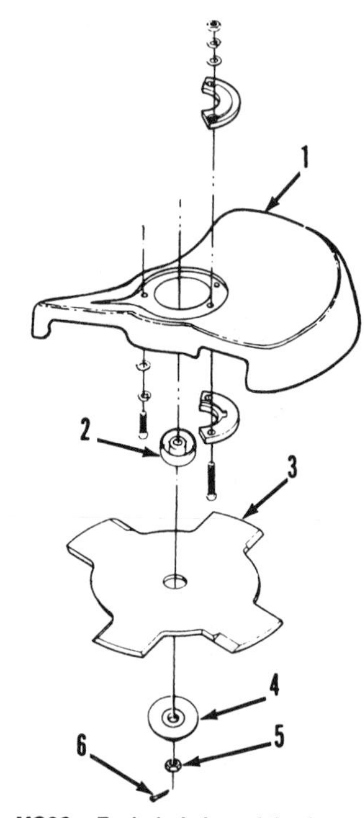

Fig. MC20—Exploded view of the four edge cutting blade used on some models.

1. Shield
2. Cup washer
3. Blade
4. Adapter washer
5. Nut
6. Cotter pin

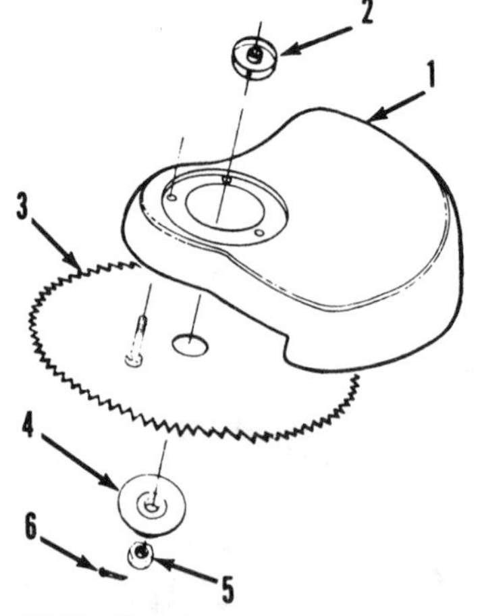

Fig. MC21—Exploded view of saw blade used on some models.

1. Shield
2. Cup washer
3. Saw blade
4. Adapter washer
5. Nut
6. Cotter pin

Models With Straight Drive Shaft Housing

Models with straight drive shaft housings are equipped with a solid steel drive shaft supported in drive shaft housing tube. Drive shaft requires no regular maintenance; however, if drive shaft has been removed, lubricate drive shaft with lithium base grease before reinstallation.

BEARING HEAD

All Models So Equipped

Refer to Fig. MC24 and MC25 for an exploded view of the two different bearing heads used on some models. Bearing heads are equipped with sealed bearings and require no regular maintenance.

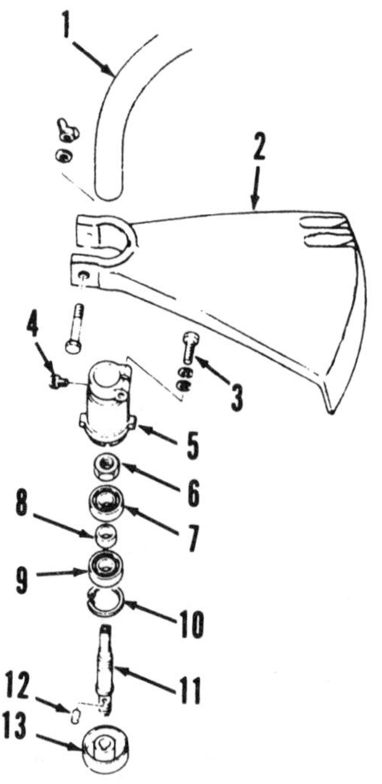

Fig. MC24—Exploded view of bearing head used on some models.

1. Drive shaft housing
2. Shield
3. Clamp bolt
4. Locating screw
5. Housing
6. Nut
7. Bearing
8. Spacer
9. Bearing
10. Snap ring
11. Arbor (output) shaft
12. Pin
13. Cup washer

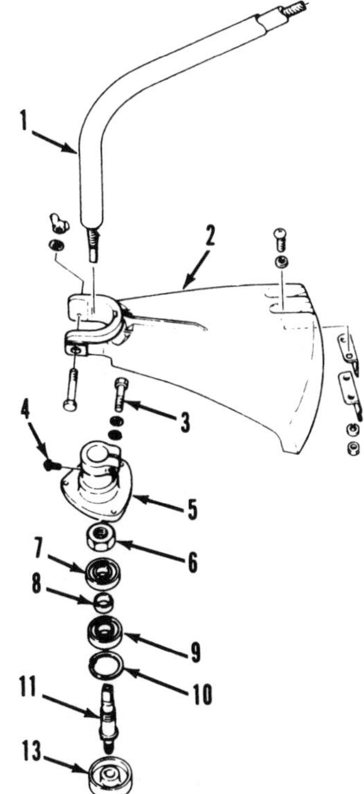

Fig. MC25—Exploded view of bearing head assembly used on some models.

1. Drive shaft housing
2. Shield
3. Clamp bolt
4. Locating screw
5. Housing
6. Nut
7. Bearing
8. Spacer
9. Bearing
10. Snap ring
11. Arbor (output) shaft
13. Cup washer

To disassemble either bearing head, remove clamp bolt (3—Figs. MC24 or MC25) and locating screw (4). Separate bearing head from drive shaft housing. Remove trimmer head or blade assembly and cup washer (13). Remove snap ring (10) and use a suitable puller to remove arbor shaft and bearing assembly. Remove nut (6) and press bearings from arbor shaft as required.

GEAR HEAD

All Models So Equipped

Refer to Fig. MC26 for an exploded view of the gear head used on heavy duty string trimmers and brush cutters. Check plug (15) should be removed and gear head housing lubricant level checked at 30 hour intervals of use. Gear head should be 2/3 full of lithium base grease. Do not use a pressure grease gun to install grease as bearing seal and housing damage will occur.

To disassemble gear head, remove trimmer head or blade assembly. Remove clamp bolts (14) and locating screw (13) and separate gear head from drive shaft housing tube. Remove snap ring (21). Insert screwdriver or other suitable wedge into clamp splits in housing and carefully expand housing. Remove input shaft (16) and bearing assembly. Remove snap ring (22) and press bearings from input shaft as required. Remove snap ring (5) and seal (6). Use a suitable puller to remove arbor shaft and bearing assembly. If bearing (11) stays in housing, heat housing to 140° F (60° C) and tap housing on wooden block to remove bearing. Press bearings and gear from arbor shaft as required.

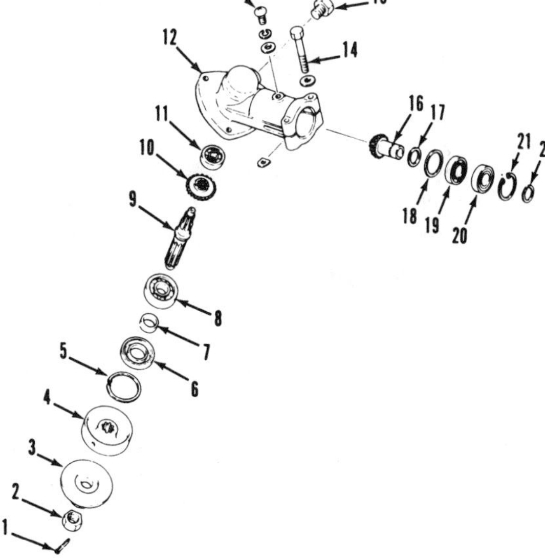

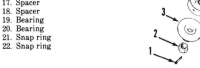

Fig. MC26—Exploded view of gear head used on heavy duty trimmers and brush cutters.

1. Cotter pin
2. Nut
3. Adapter plate
4. Cup washer
5. Snap ring
6. Seal
7. Spacer
8. Bearing
9. Arbor shaft
10. Gear
11. Bearing
12. Housing
13. Locating screw
14. Clamp bolt
15. Check plug
16. Input shaft
17. Spacer
18. Spacer
19. Bearing
20. Bearing
21. Snap ring
22. Snap ring

Illustrations courtesy McCulloch Corp.

McCULLOCH

GASOLINE POWERED STRING TRIMMERS

Model	Engine Manufacturer	Engine Model	Displacement
EAGER BEAVER I-SX, II-SX	McCulloch	...	21.2 cc
EAGER BEAVER III-SL, III-SX, IV-SL	McCulloch	...	21.2 cc
EAGER BEAVER SUPER, SUPER-SL	McCulloch	...	21.2 cc
MAC 60-SX, 65, 65-SL	McCulloch	...	21.2 cc
MAC 80-SX, 85-SL, 85-SX, 99-SL	McCulloch	...	21.2 cc
PRO SCAPER I-SX	McCulloch	...	21.2 cc
PRO SCAPER III, IV	McCulloch	...	30.0 cc
PRO SCAPER V	McCulloch	...	38.0 cc
ROADRUNNER	McCulloch	...	21.2 cc
SUPER EAGER BEAVER I-SX SPECIAL	McCulloch	...	21.2 cc

ENGINE INFORMATION

The models included in this section are powered by a McCulloch engine. Refer to appropriate McCulloch engine service section for service procedures and specifications.

FUEL MIXTURE

Manufacturer recommends mixing regular or unleaded grade gasoline with a high-quality two-stroke engine oil designed for air-cooled engines. Recommended fuel:oil ratio is 40:1 when using McCulloch Custom Lubricant. Fuel:oil ratio should be 20:1 when using any other two-stroke oil, regardless of recommended ratio on oil container. Manufacturer recommends addition of Sta-Bil to fuel to prevent fuel degradation. Manufacturer does not recommend using fuel blended with any type of alcohol (gasohol).

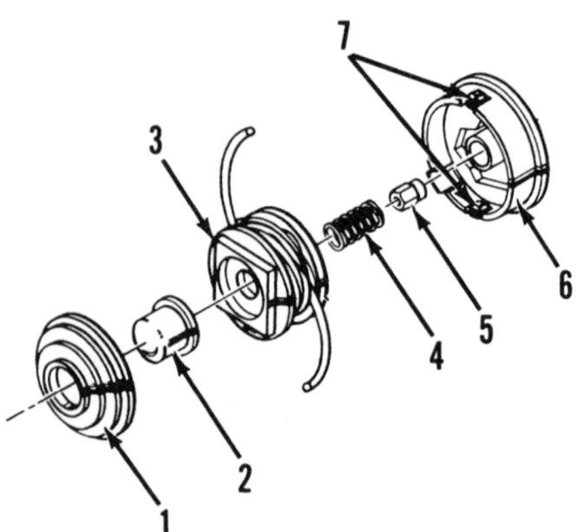

Fig. MC30—Exploded view of string trimmer head used on EAGER BEAVER III-SL, III-SX, IV-SL; MAC 85-SL, 85-SX, 99-SL; PRO SCAPER I-SX.

1. Cover
2. Button
3. Spool
4. Spring
5. Nut
6. Drum
7. Eyelets

STRING TRIMMER

Models EAGER BEAVER III-SL, III-SX, IV-SL; MAC 85-SL, 85-SX, 99-SL; PRO SCAPER I-SX

These models are equipped with the semi-automatic string trimmer head shown in Fig. MC30. Models EAGER BEAVER III-SX, MAC 85-SX and PRO SCAPER I-SX are equipped with a single strand head; other models are equipped with a dual strand head.

To advance line with engine stopped, push in on button (2—Fig. MC30) and pull on line. Procedure may have to be repeated to obtain desired line length. To extend line with engine running, operate trimmer at full operating rpm and tap button (2) on ground. Line will automatically advance a measured amount.

To install new line on single strand head, press against tab marked "PUSH" and remove cover (1—Fig. MC30), button (2) and spool (3). Clean and inspect all parts. New line should be 0.095 inch (2.4 mm) diameter and 12 feet (3.7 m) long. Insert end of line through eye of spool as shown in Fig. MC31 so approximately 1 inch (25 mm) extends past eye. Wrap line on spool in direction indicated by arrow on spool. Install spool while directing line end through eye of drum (6—Fig. MC30). Install button and cover. Cover should snap into place after locking tabs of cover engage tabs on drum next to eye hole. Trim line so approximately 3 inches (75 mm) of line extends from drum.

To install new line on dual strand head, press against tab marked "PUSH" and remove cover (1—Fig. MC30), button (2) and spool (3). Clean and inspect all parts. New line should be 0.095 inch (2.4 mm) diameter and 15 feet (4.6 m) long. Insert line through eye in spool and pull line through eye until ends of line are even. Wrap line on spool in direction indicated by arrow on spool as shown in Fig. MC31A. Install spool while directing line end through each eye (7—Fig. MC30) of drum. Install button and cov-

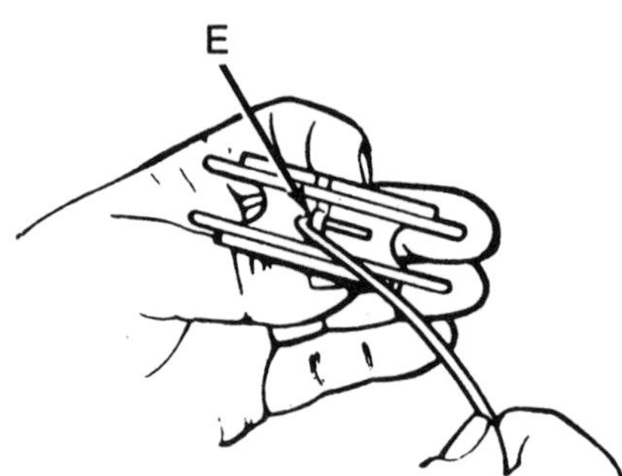

Fig. MC31—Insert trimmer line end through eye (E) on spool as shown so approximately 1 inch (25 mm) extends past eye.

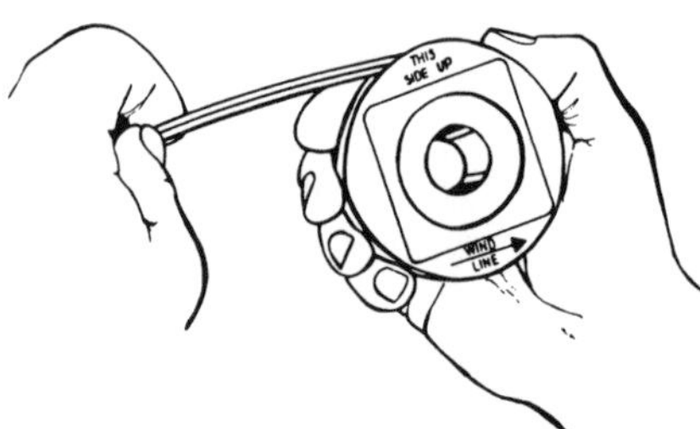

Fig. MC31A—Wind line onto trimmer spool in direction indicated by arrow on spool. Dual line spool is shown; single line spool is similar.

Illustrations courtesy McCulloch Corp.

er. Cover should snap into place after locking tabs of cover engage tabs on drum next to eye hole. Trim line so approximately 4 inches (102 mm) of line extends from drum.

If trimmer head retaining nut (5—Fig. MC30) must be unscrewed, prevent shaft rotation by inserting a pin through hole provided in bearing head to lock shaft.

Models EAGER BEAVER SUPER, SUPER SL; MAC 65, 65-SL; ROAD RUNNER

These models are equipped with the semi-automatic string trimmer head shown in Fig. MC32. Models EAGER BEAVER SUPER, MAC 65 and early ROAD RUNNER are equipped with a single strand head; Models EAGER BEAVER SUPER SL, MAC 65-SL and later ROAD RUNNER are equipped with a dual strand head.

To advance line with engine stopped, push in on button (B—Fig. MC32) and pull on line. Procedure may have to be repeated to obtain desired line length. To extend line with engine running, operate trimmer at full operating rpm and tap button on ground. Line will automatically advance a measured amount.

To install new line on Models EAGER BEAVER SUPER, MAC 65 and early ROAD RUNNER, press against tab marked "PUSH" and twist cover (8—Fig. MC32) counterclockwise. Remove cover and spool (7) assembly. Clean and inspect all parts. New line should be 0.095 inch (2.4 mm) diameter and 12 feet (3.7 m) long. Insert end of line through eye of spool as shown in Fig. MC33 so approximately $^{3}/_{4}$ inch (19 mm) extends past eye. Wrap line on spool in clockwise direction (note arrow on spool). Install spool while directing line end through eye (2—Fig. MC32) of drum (3). Install cover (8) so lug aligns with tab of drum and twist clockwise so cover snaps into place. Trim line so approximately 3 inches (75 mm) extend from drum.

To install new line on Models EAGER BEAVER SUPER SL, MAC 65-SL and later ROAD RUNNER, press against tab marked "PUSH" and twist cover (8—Fig. MC32) counterclockwise. Remove cover and spool (7) assembly. Clean and inspect all parts. New line should be 0.095 inch (2.4 mm) diameter and 12 feet (3.7 m) long. Insert line through eye and pull line through eye until ends of line are even. Wrap line on spool in clockwise direction (note arrow on spool). Install spool while directing line ends through eyes (2—Fig. MC32) of drum. Install cover by twisting clockwise so cover snaps into place. Trim line so approximately 3 inches (75 mm) extend from drum.

Models EAGER BEAVER I-SX, II-SX; MAC 60-SX, 80-SX; SUPER EAGER BEAVER I-SX SPECIAL

These models are equipped with the semi-automatic single strand string trimmer head shown in Fig. MC34.

To advance line with engine stopped, push in on button and pull on line. Procedure may have to be repeated to obtain desired line length. To extend line with engine running, operate trimmer at full operating rpm and tap button on ground. Line will automatically advance a measured amount.

To install new line, remove screw (1—Fig. MC34) and separate trimmer spool assembly (2) from head. Clean and inspect all parts. New line on EAGER BEAVER I-SX, MAC 60-SX and SUPER EAGER BEAVER I-SX SPECIAL should be 0.080 inch (2 mm) diameter and 17 feet (5.2 m) long. New line on EAGER BEAVER II-SX and MAC 80-SX should be 0.095 inch (2.4 mm) diameter and 14 feet (4.3 m) long. Using a 2 inch (50 mm) piece of tape, wrap tape around 1 inch (25 mm) of line end and attach remainder of tape to spool as shown in Fig. MC35. Wind line around spool in direction indicated by arrow on spool. Install spool while directing line end through eye of drum (6—Fig. MC34). Install retaining screw (1). Trim line so approximately 3 inches (75 mm) extend from drum.

Models PRO SCAPER III, IV, V

Models PRO SCAPER III, PRO SCAPER IV and PRO SCAPER V are equipped with the manual advance, dual strand string trimmer head shown in Fig. MC36. To extend line, loosen lock knob (8) approximately two turns by turning knob clockwise (note that knob has left-hand threads). Pull out 6 inches (152 mm) of line from each side.

To install new line, remove screw (9) and washer. Unscrew lock knob (8) by turning clockwise (note that knob has left-hand threads). Remove cover (6), spring (5) and spool (4); do not lose eyelets (3). New line should be 0.095 inch (2.4 mm) diameter and $17^{1}/_{2}$ feet (5.3 m) long. Loop the line through two holes in spool and pull both ends so each strand is equal length. Then, wrap both strands at the same time onto spool in clockwise direction as viewed from unnotched side of spool shown in Fig. MC37. Place eyelets (3—Fig. MC36) on line ends and install spool (4) into drum (2) with notched side out. Snap eyelets into drum. Install spring (5), cover (6), knob

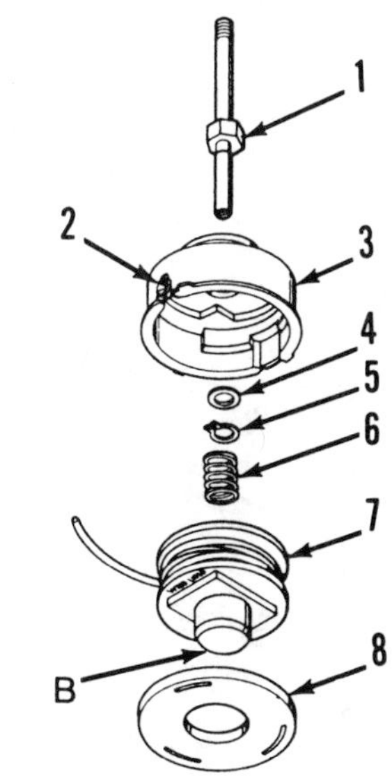

Fig. MC32—Exploded view of string trimmer head used on EAGER BEAVER SUPER, SUPER SL; MAC 65, 65-SL; ROAD RUNNER.

1. Arbor
2. Eyelet
3. Drum
4. Washer
5. Snap ring
6. Spring
7. Spool
8. Cover

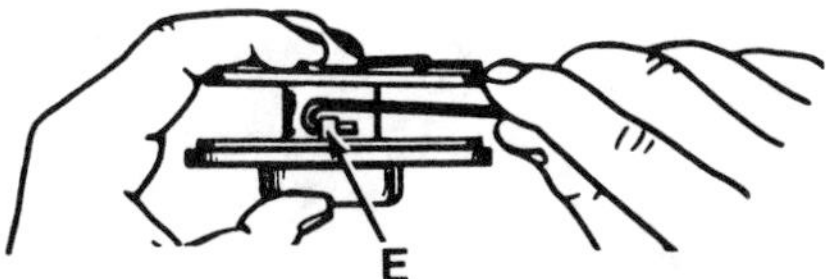

Fig. MC33—Insert trimmer line end through eye (E) on spool as shown so approximately $^{3}/_{4}$ inch (19 mm) extends past eye.

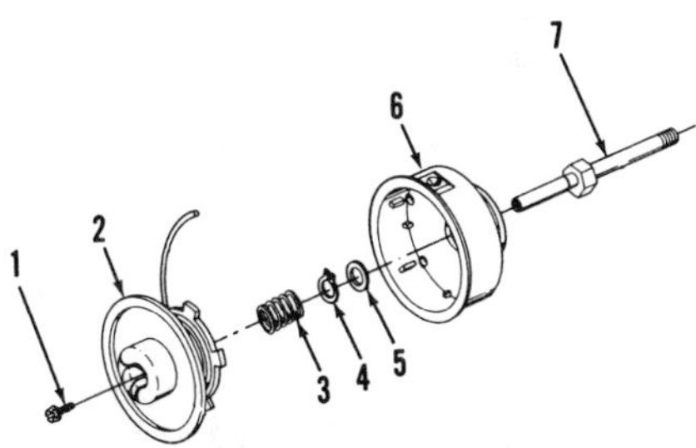

Fig. MC34—Exploded view of string head used on EAGER BEAVER I-SX, II-SX; MAC 60-SX, 80-SX; SUPER EAGER BEAVER I-SX SPECIAL.

1. Screw
2. Spool
3. Spring
4. Snap ring
5. Washer
6. Drum
7. Arbor

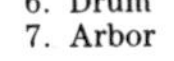

Fig. MC35—Using a 2-in. (50 mm) piece of tape (T), wrap tape around 1 inch (25 mm) of line end and attach remainder of tape to spool.

(8), washer and screw (9). Trim line on each side so line length is 6 inches (152 mm).

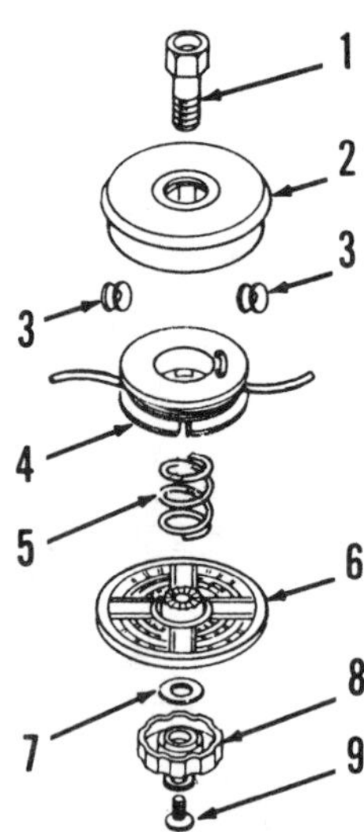

Fig. MC36—Exploded view of string head used on PRO SCAPER III, IV, V.

1. Adapter
2. Drum
3. Eyelets
4. Spool
5. Spring
6. Cover
7. Washer
8. Knob
9. Screw

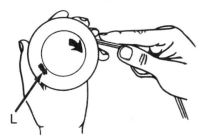

Fig. MC37—Pull line (L) through holes in spool so each line is of equal length, then wrap both strands of line around spool as shown.

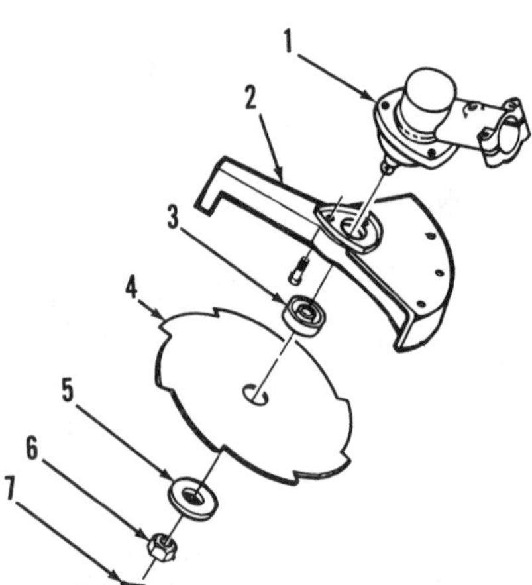

Fig. MC38—Exploded view of typical blade installation on EAGER BEAVER III-SL, III-SX, IV-SL; MAC 85-SL, 85-SX, 99-SL. Nut (6) has left-hand threads on EAGER BEAVER III-SX, EAGER BEAVER IV-SL, MAC 85-SX and MAC 99-SL.

1. Gear head
2. Shield
3. Cup washer
4. Blade
5. Washer
6. Nut
7. Cotter pin

BLADE

Models EAGER BEAVER III-SL, III-SX, IV-SL; MAC 85-SL, 85-SX, 99-SL; PRO SCAPER IV, V

These models may be equipped with a blade. Refer to Figs. MC38 or MC39. To remove blade (4), rotate cup (3) so hole in cup aligns with hole in head (1). Insert a suitable pin through holes and unscrew blade retaining nut or screw. Note that nut or screw on Models EAGER BEAVER III-SX, EAGER BEAVER IV-SL, MAC 85-SX, MAC 99-SL, PRO SCAPER IV and PRO SCAPER V has left-hand threads. Blade nut on Models MAC 85-SL and EAGER BEAVER III-SL has right-hand threads.

Install blade on Models EAGER BEAVER III-SX, EAGER BEAVER IV-SL, MAC 85-SX, MAC 99-SL, PRO SCAPER IV and PRO SCAPER V so teeth point in clockwise direction as viewed from ground side of blade. Install blade on Models MAC 85-SL and EAGER BEAVER III-SL so teeth point in counterclockwise direction as viewed from ground side of blade. On models shown in Fig. MC39, install washer (5) with concave side against blade. Tighten blade nut or screw to 176-265 in.-lbs. (20-30 N·m).

DRIVE SHAFT

All Models

The drive shaft should be removed, cleaned and lubricated after every 50 hours of operation. Separate drive shaft housing (tube) from engine for access to shaft. Apply a high-quality, lithium-base grease to drive shaft.

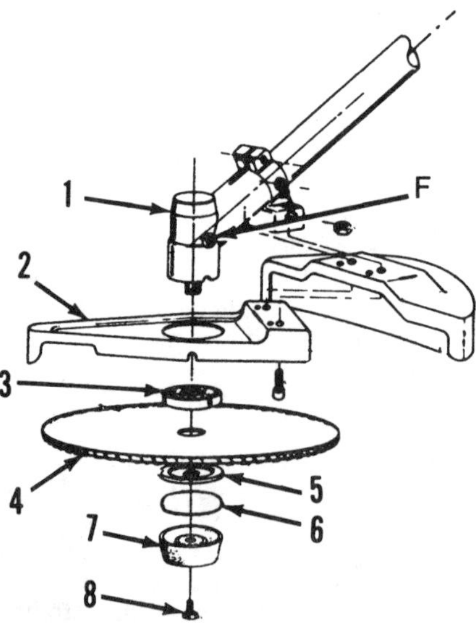

Fig. MC39—Exploded view of blade installation on PRO SCAPER IV and PRO SCAPER V. Install step washer (5) with concave side towards blade. Screw (8) has left-hand threads. Gear head is lubricated by injecting grease through fitting (F).

1. Gear head
2. Shield
3. Collar
4. Blade
5. Step washer
6. Washer
7. Scuff plate
8. Screw (L.H.)

BEARING HEAD

All Models So Equipped

The bearing head is sealed and does not require maintenance.

Bearing head must be serviced as a unit assembly; no components are available.

GEAR HEAD

All Models So Equipped

The gear head on Models PRO SCAPER III, PRO SCAPER IV and PRO SCAPER V should be lubricated after every 50 hours of operation by injecting a high-quality lithium-base grease through grease fitting (F—Fig. MC39) located on side of gear head.

On other models with a gear head, periodically check grease level by removing screw (S—Fig. MC40). Gear head should be $^2/_3$ full of lithium-base grease. Rotate shaft to be sure grease is distributed throughout. Do not install grease with a pressure grease gun.

Gear head must be serviced as a unit assembly; no components are available.

THROTTLE TRIGGER AND CABLE

Adjusting nuts are located at carburetor end of throttle cable. Turn nuts as needed so carburetor throttle plate opens fully when throttle trigger is at full-speed position, and so there is slight free play at throttle trigger when released.

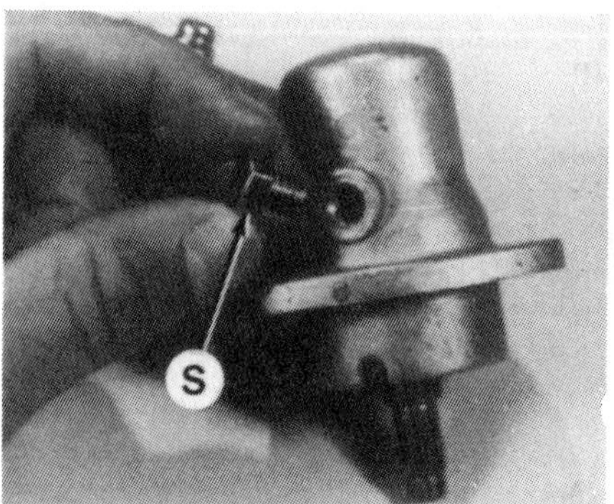

Fig. MC40—Periodically check gear head lubricant level by removing screw (S). Gear head should be $^2/_3$ full of lithium-base grease.

Illustrations courtesy McCulloch Corp.

McCULLOCH

GASOLINE POWERED TRIMMERS

Models	Engine Make	Engine Displacement
Titan 2000, 2030, 2100, 2200	McCulloch	21.2 cc (1.29 cu. in.)
Titan 2250	McCulloch	25.0 cc (1.52 cu. in.)
Titan 2300, 2310, 2360	McCulloch	21.2 cc (1.29 cu. in.)
Titan 2500AV, 2560AV, 2565AV	McCulloch	25.0 cc (1.52 cu. in.)
Titan 3000AV	McCulloch	30 cc (1.83 cu. in.)
Titan 3900AV	McCulloch	38 cc (2.32 cu. in.)

ENGINE INFORMATION

The models included in this section are powered by a McCulloch engine. Refer to appropriate McCulloch engine service section for service procedures and specifications.

FUEL MIXTURE

Manufacturer recommends mixing regular or unleaded gasoline with a high-quality two-stroke engine oil designed for air-cooled engines. Recommended fuel:oil ratio is 40:1 when using McCulloch Custom Lubricant. Fuel:oil ratio should be 20:1 when using any other two-stroke oil, regardless of recommended ratio on oil container.

Manufacturer recommends addition of Sta-Bil or other equivalent fuel conditioner to the fuel to prevent fuel degradation. Manufacturer does not recommend using fuel blended with any type of alcohol (gasohol).

STRING TRIMMER

All models are equipped with the dual strand, semi-automatic string trimmer head shown in Fig. MC50.

To manually advance trimmer line with engine stopped, push in on button (2—Fig. MC50) and pull line out to desired length. To extend line with engine running, operate trimmer at full operating rpm and tap button (2) on ground. Line will automatically advance a measured amount. Repeat procedure if necessary until line is at desired length.

To install new line, press against tab marked "PUSH" and remove cover (1—Fig. MC50), button (2) and spool (3). Remove any old line remaining on spool. New line should be 0.095 in. (2.4 mm) diameter for all models. Maximum line length is 20 ft. (6 m) for Models 2000, 2030, 2100, 2200 and 2250. Maximum line length for all other models is 30 ft. (9 m).

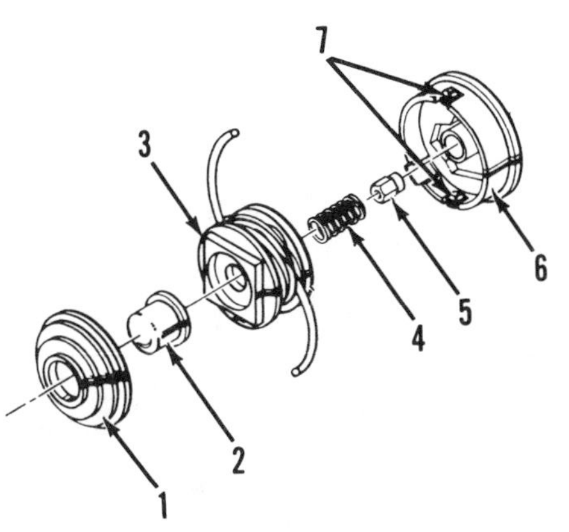

Fig. MC50—Exploded view of dual strand, semi-automatic string trimmer head used on all models.

1. Cover
2. Button
3. Spool
4. Spring
5. Nut
6. Drum
7. Eyelets

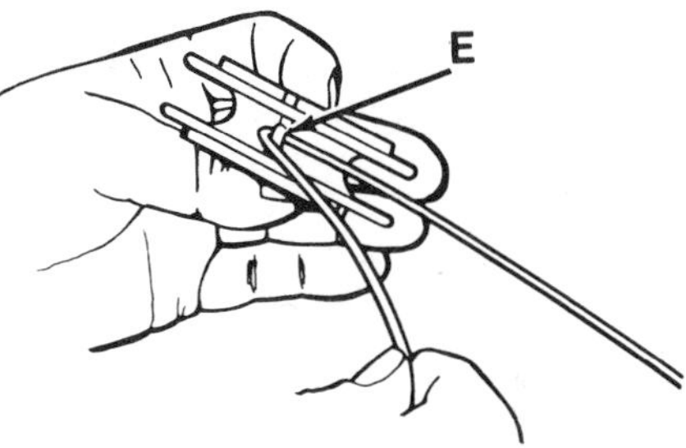

Fig. MC51—Thread new line through spool eye (E) so both ends are equal length.

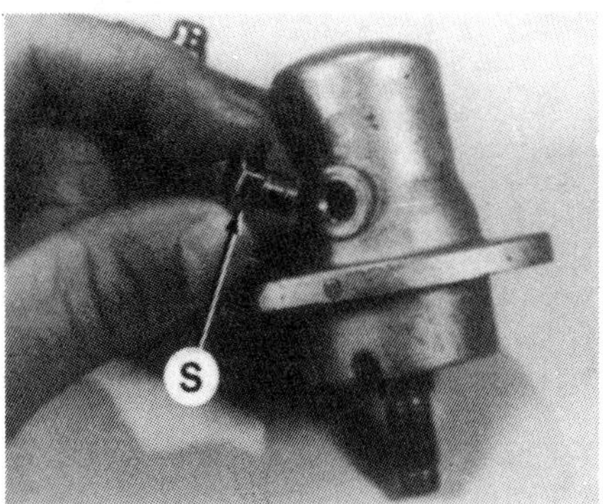

Fig. MC52—Periodically check gear head lubricant level by removing screw (S). Gear head should be 2/3 full of multipurpose grease.

Insert line through eye of spool (Fig. MC51) and pull line through eye until ends of line are even. Wrap both strands of line at the same time on spool in direction indicated by arrow on spool. Do not allow lines to cross over each other.

Install spool while directing line ends through eyes (7—Fig. MC50) of drum (6). Install button (2) and cover (1). Cover should snap into place after locking tabs of cover engage tabs on drum. Trim line so each end extends approximately 4 in. (100 mm) from drum.

If trimmer head retaining nut (5—Fig. MC50) must be removed, prevent shaft rotation by inserting a pin through hole provided in bearing head to lock shaft. Note that nut on some models has left-hand threads and nut or trimmer head must be rotated clockwise for removal.

BEARING HEAD

Curved Shaft Models

The spindle bearing head is sealed and does not require maintenance.

Bearing head must be serviced as a unit assembly; no components are available for service.

GEAR HEAD

Straight Shaft Models

Periodically remove screw (S—Fig. MC52) and check grease level. Gear

Illustrations courtesy McCulloch Corp.

head should be 2/3 full of multipurpose grease.

Gear head must be serviced as a unit assembly; no components are available for service.

THROTTLE TRIGGER AND CABLE

Adjusting nuts are located at carburetor end of throttle cable. Turn nuts as needed so carburetor throttle plate opens fully when throttle trigger is at full-sped position. There should be slight free play at throttle trigger when release.

Illustrations courtesy McCulloch Corp.

McCULLOCH

GASOLINE POWERED BLOWERS

Engine Model	Engine Manufacturer	Model	Displacement
EAGER BEAVER	McCulloch	...	21.2 cc
EAGER BEAVER III, IV	McCulloch	...	21.2 cc
PRO STREAM	McCulloch	...	21.2 cc
SUPER AIR STREAM III, IV, V	McCulloch	...	21.2 cc

ENGINE INFORMATION

The models included in this section are powered by a McCulloch engine. Refer to appropriate McCulloch engine service section for service procedures and specifications.

FUEL MIXTURE

Manufacturer recommends mixing regular or unleaded gasoline with a high-quality, two-stroke engine oil designed for air-cooled engines. Recommended fuel:oil ratio is 40:1 when using McCulloch Custom Lubricant. Fuel:oil ratio should be 20:1 when using any other two-stroke oil, regardless of recommended ratio on oil container. Manufacturer recommends addition of Sta-Bil to fuel to prevent fuel degradation. The use of any fuel blended with any type of alcohol (gasohol) is not recommended by the manufacturer.

ENGINE AIR FILTER

Engine air filter element should be removed, inspected and cleaned (if necessary) after each use of blower. Tap the filter element to remove loose dirt. Filter may be washed in warm, soapy water. Rinse in clean water and allow to dry completely before installing.

If filter is damaged, install a new filter. Engine will be damaged if operated with a faulty filter. Do not operate engine without the air filter.

MUFFLER

Muffler and exhaust ports should be inspected periodically for carbon buildup. Rotate crankshaft until piston skirt covers the exhaust ports, then use a wooden scraper to clean carbon from ports. Use scraper or wire brush to clean carbon from muffler and spark arrestor screen as necessary.

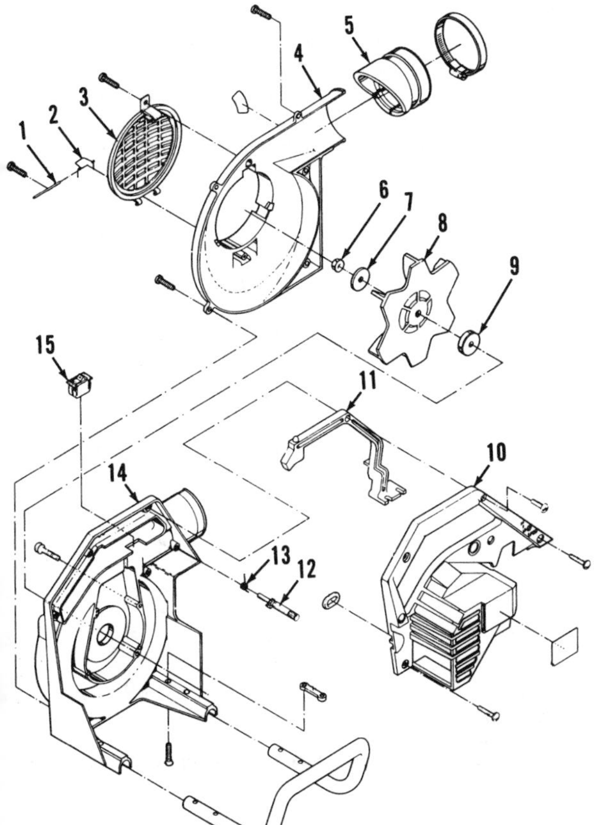

Fig. MCB1—Exploded view of typical blower/vac assembly.

1. Pin
2. Spring
3. Inlet cover
4. Impeller housing, outer
5. Adapter tube
6. Nut
7. Washer
8. Impeller
9. Drive disc
10. Engine shroud
11. Throttle trigger
12. Throttle lock
13. Spring
14. Impeller housing, inner
15. Ignition switch

BLOWER ASSEMBLY

To disassemble blower, remove blower tube and adapter (5—Fig. MCB1) from impeller housing. Remove screws holding impeller housing halves (4 and 10) together. Remove spark plug and insert end of a rope into cylinder to lock the piston and crankshaft. Remove blower impeller retaining nut (6) and remove impeller (8) from engine crankshaft.

To reassemble, reverse disassembly procedure. Tighten impeller nut (6) to 90-100 in.-lbs. (10.2-11.3 N·m). Tighten impeller housing screws to 20-25 in.-lbs. (2.3-2.8 N·m).

Illustrations courtesy McCulloch Corp.

OLYMPYK

GASOLINE POWERED STRING TRIMMERS

Model	Engine Manufacturer	Engine Model	Displacement
OL200B	EFCO	200	22.5 cc
OL200L	EFCO	200	22.5 cc
OL220B	EFCO	220	22.5 cc
OL220L	EFCO	220	22.5 cc
OL260B	EFCO	260	25.4 cc
OL260L	EFCO	260	25.4 cc
OL300B	EFCO	300	30.5 cc
OL320B	EFCO	300	30.5 cc
OL400B	EFCO	400	37.7 cc
OL420B	EFCO	400	37.7 cc
OL450B	EFCO	450	37.7 cc
OL460B	EFCO	450	37.7 cc

ENGINE INFORMATION

The models in this section are equipped with an EFCO engine. Refer to EFCO engine service section for engine service information.

FUEL MIXTURE

Manufacturer recommends mixing regular grade gasoline, preferably leaded, with a high-quality, two-stroke engine oil. Recommended fuel:oil ratio is 40:1

STRING TRIMMER

All models are equipped with a manual advance, dual strand trimmer head. To pull out line, stop engine and push up against spool (against spring pressure). While pushing spool up, turn spool counterclockwise (as viewed from bottom) to eject new line. Release spool.

To install new line, unscrew retaining screw (5—Fig. OL11). Screw has left-hand threads. Remove housing (4), spool (3) and spring (2). Remove old string and clean components. Specified string diameter on Models OL300B, OL320B, OL400B, OL420B, OL450B and OL460B is 0.095 inch (2.4 mm). Specified string diameter for all other models is 0.080 inch (2.0 mm). Spool capacity is 36 feet (11 m) for Models OL300B, OL320B, OL400B, OL420B, OL450B and OL460B and 42 feet (13 m) for all other models. Insert line (6) through holes in spool as shown in Fig. OL11 and pull line through holes until ends are even. Wrap line around spool in direction indicated by arrows on spool. Do not twist lines. Reassemble trimmer head. Tighten retaining screw (5—Fig. OL11) to 25 N·m (18 ft.-lbs.).

BLADE

All straight-shaft models may be equipped with a blade. Refer to Figs. OL13, OL14 or OL15 for configuration of blade assembly. Blade retaining screw has left-hand threads. Note that direction of blade rotation is usually indicated by an arrow on the gear head. Tighten retaining screw to 25 N·m (18 ft.-lbs.).

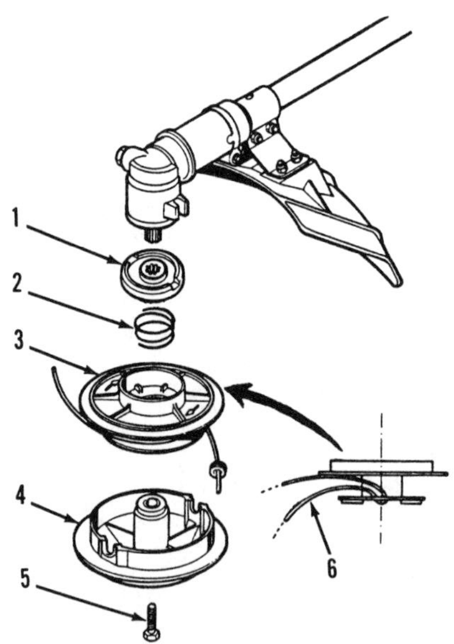

Fig. OL11—Exploded view of dual strand, manual advance trimmer used on Models OL200B, OL200L, OL220B, OL220L, OL260B and OL260L. All other models are similar. Insert trimmer line through spool holes as shown.

1. Flange
2. Spring
3. Spool
4. Housing
5. Screw (L.H.)
6. Line

DRIVE SHAFT

Models OL200B And OL200L

Models OL200B and OL200L are equipped with a flexible drive shaft. Periodically remove drive shaft and lubricate with a lithium-base grease. To remove drive shaft, remove bearing head and extract drive shaft. When installing drive shaft, be sure drive shaft end is properly seated at drive end.

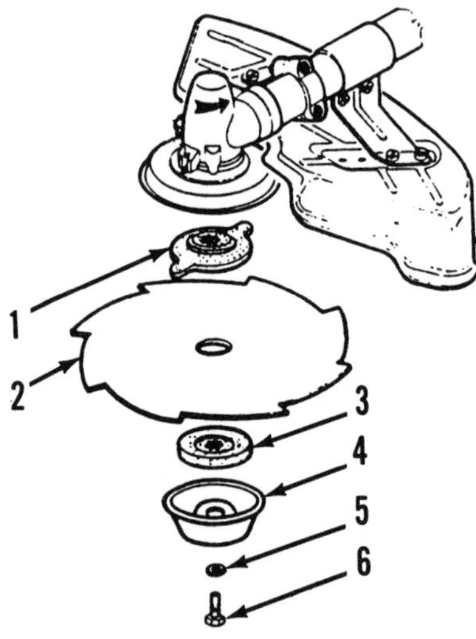

Fig. OL13—Blade assembly used on some models.

1. Flange
2. Blade
3. Washer
4. Cup washer
5. Lockwasher
6. Screw (L.H.)

Illustrations courtesy Olympyk/Oleo-Mac

All Other Models

All models except Models OL200B and OL200L are equipped with a solid drive shaft that does not require periodic lubrication. If drive shaft is removed, apply a lithium-base grease to drive shaft. The drive shaft rides in bushings that are renewable. If bushings are to be renewed, mark position of old bushings before removal so new bushings can be installed in original positions.

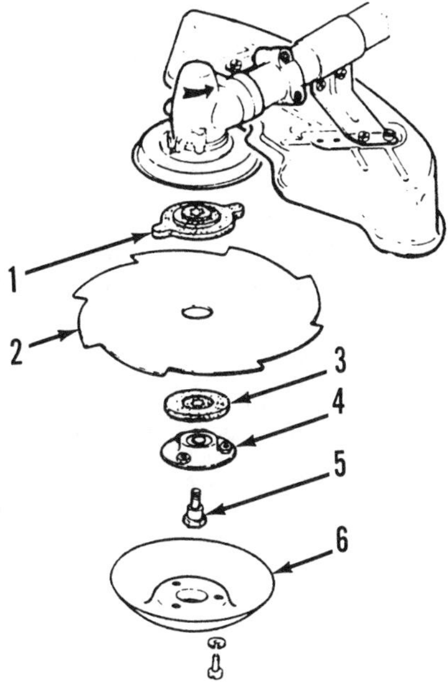

Fig. OL14—Blade assembly used on some models.

1. Flange
2. Blade
3. Washer
4. Shield flange
5. Screw (L.H.)
6. Shield

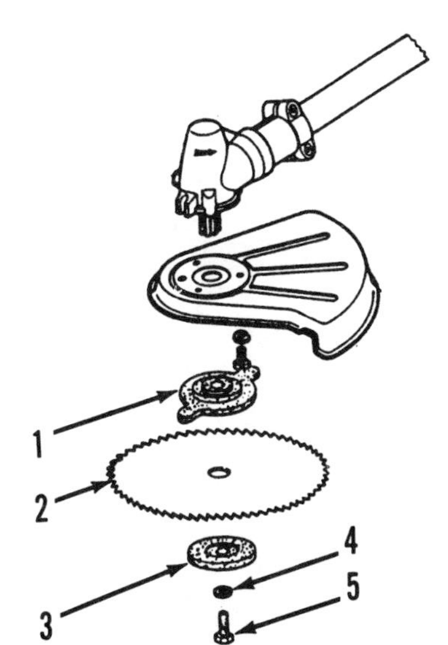

Fig. OL15—Blade assembly used on some models.

1. Flange
2. Blade
3. Washer
4. Lockwasher
5. Screw (L.H.)

BEARING HEAD

Models OL200B And OL200L

The bearing head does not require periodic lubrication.

To disassemble bearing head, remove trimmer assembly (trimmer head retaining screw has left-hand threads). Separate bearing head from drive shaft tube. Detach snap ring (5—Fig. OL16). Use a suitable puller and extract arbor (3) with bearings (4) from housing (1). Press or pull bearings off arbor. Reassemble by reversing disassembly procedure.

GEAR HEAD

Models OL220B, OL220L, OL260B And OL260L

Models OL220B, OL220L, OL260B and OL260L are equipped with the gear head shown in Fig. OL17. Lubricant level should be checked after every 80 hours of operation. Remove fill plug (5) in side of housing and add lubricant so housing is 1/2 full. Maximum amount that should be added if housing is dry is 9 mL (0.3 oz.). Recommended lubricant is molybdenum disulfide grease.

To disassemble gear head, remove trimmer or blade assembly (retaining screw has left-hand threads). Separate gear head from drive shaft tube. Remove flange (11) and detach snap ring (10). Use a suitable puller and extract gear (7) and bearings as an assembly. Press or pull bearings (8 and 9) off gear shaft. Detach snap ring (1). Reach through output opening of housing and drive out input shaft (4) and bearing (3). Remove snap ring (2) and separate bearing from shaft.

Reassemble by reversing disassembly procedure. Note that lower bearing (9) is a sealed bearing.

Models OL300B, OL320B, OL400B, OL420B, OL450B And OL460B

Models OL300B, OL320B, OL400B, OL420B, OL450B and OL460B are equipped with the gear head shown in Fig. OL18. Lubricant level should be checked after every 80 hours of operation. Remove fill plug (6) in side of housing and add lubricant so housing is 1/2 full. Maximum amount that should be added if housing is dry is 11 mL (0.37 oz.). Recommended lubricant is molybdenum disulfide grease.

To disassemble gear head, remove blade or trimmer head. Detach gear head from drive shaft tube. Remove snap ring (1—Fig. OL18) and, using a suitable puller, extract pinion gear (5) and bearings as an assembly from housing. Detach snap ring (2) and press or pull bearings (3 and 4) off pinion gear (5). Remove flange (16), retainer (15) and shield (14). Using a suitable puller, extract arbor (12) assembly. Pull bearing (13) off arbor (12). Unscrew nut (8) and

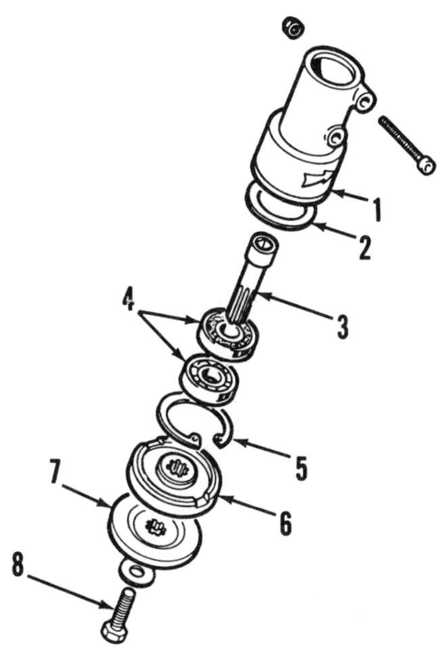

Fig. OL16—Exploded view of bearing head used on Models OL200B and OL200L.

1. Housing
2. Washer
3. Arbor
4. Bearings
5. Snap ring
6. Flange
7. Flange
8. Screw (L.H.)

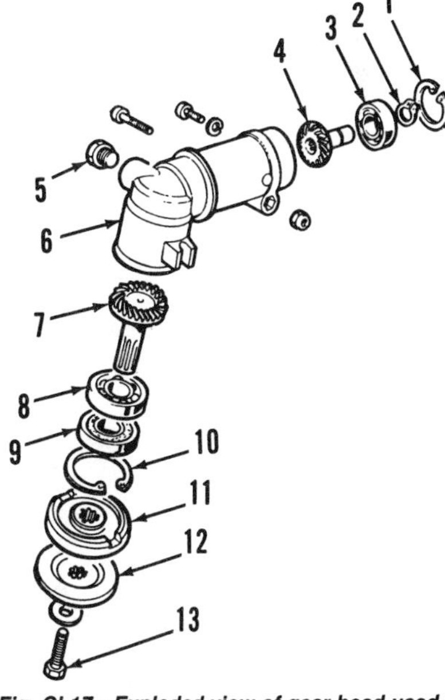

Fig. OL17—Exploded view of gear head used on Models OL220B, OL220L, OL260B and OL260L.

1. Snap ring
2. Snap ring
3. Bearing
4. Input gear
5. Plug
6. Housing
7. Output gear
8. Bearing
9. Bearing
10. Snap ring
11. Flange
12. Flange
13. Screw (L.H.)

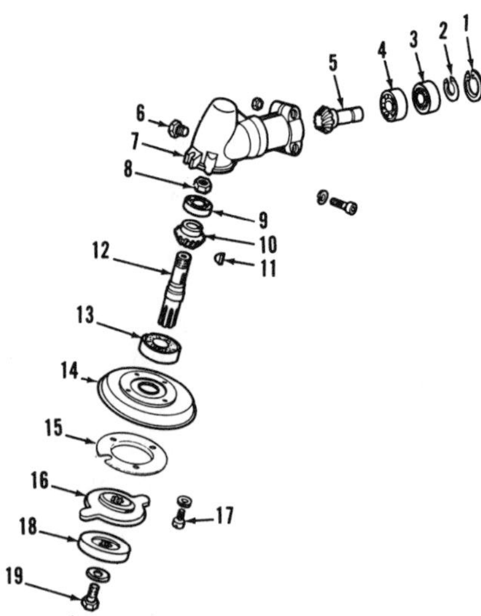

Fig. OL18—Exploded view of gear head used on Models OL300B, OL320B, OL400B, OL420B, OL450B and OL460B.

1. Snap ring
2. Snap ring
3. Bearing
4. Bearing
5. Input gear
6. Plug
7. Housing
8. Nut
9. Bearing
10. Output gear
11. Key
12. Arbor
13. Bearing
14. Shield
15. Retainer
16. Flange
17. Screw
18. Flange
19. Screw

remove gear (10) and bearing (9) from arbor.

Clean and inspect components. Reassemble by reversing disassembly procedure. Tighten nut (8) to 30 N·m (22 ft.-lbs.). Align slot in retainer (15) with hole (H—Fig. OL19) in shield (14). Before tightening screws (17), position flange (16—Fig. OL18) on arbor shaft to center the retainer (15). Then, remove flange and tighten screws (17).

Fig. OL19—Align slot on retainer (15) with hole (H) in shield (14). Center retainer before tightening screws (17).

THROTTLE FREE PLAY

To adjust throttle free play, loosen locknut (N—Fig. OL20) and turn adjuster (A) so cable free play at carburetor is 1 mm (0.04 in.). Tighten locknut. The carburetor throttle plate should be fully open when throttle trigger is in full throttle position.

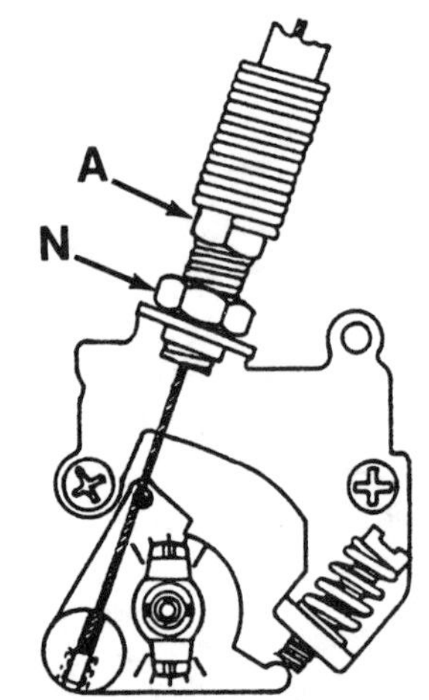

Fig. OL20—Adjust throttle free play by loosening nut (N) and turning adjuster (A).

Illustrations courtesy Olympyk/Oleo-Mac

PIONEER/PARTNER

GASOLINE POWERED STRING TRIMMERS

Model	Engine Manufacturer	Engine Model	Displacement
B180	Kawasaki	KE18	18.4 cc
B250	Kawasaki	KE24	24.1 cc
B370	Husqvarna	....	44.0 cc
B440	Husqvarna	....	44.0 cc

ENGINE INFORMATION

All Models

Pioneer/Partner line trimmers and brush cutters are equipped with a Kawasaki or Husqvarna two-stroke air-cooled gasoline engines. Engines may be identified by engine manufacturer, trimmer model number or engine displacement. Refer to KAWASAKI ENGINE SERVICE or HUSQVARNA ENGINE SERVICE sections of this manual.

FUEL MIXTURE

All Models

Manufacturer recommends mixing regular grade gasoline (unleaded is an acceptable substitute) with a good quality two-stroke air cooled engine oil at a 25:1 ratio. Do not use fuel containing alcohol.

STRING TRIMMER

Models B180 And B250

Refer to Fig. PR10 for an exploded view of the dual strand manual trimmer head used on Models B180 and B250. To extend line, stop trimmer engine and wait until all head rotation has stopped. Loosen lock knob (6) (left-hand thread) until line ends may be pulled from housing. Pull lines until desired length has been obtained. Correct line length is 3.4-4.7 inches (10-12 cm).

To renew line, remove lock knob (6) and housing (5). Remove any remaining line on spool (2) and clean spool and housing. Install new line on spool. Wind line in direction indicated by arrow on spool. Diameter when new line is wound on spool must not exceed spool flange diameter. Insert line ends through line guides (4) then reinstall housing and lock knob.

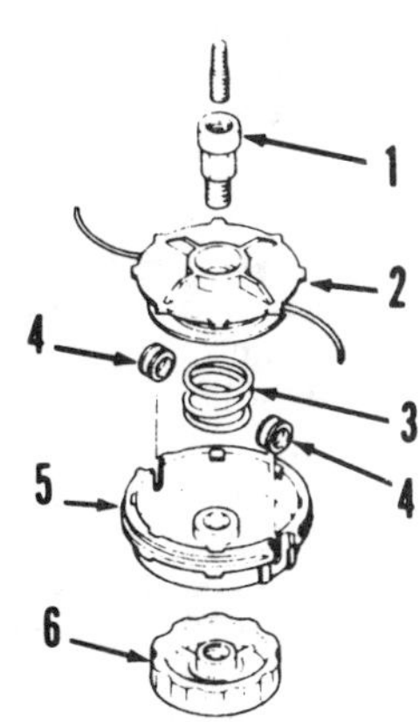

Fig. PR10—Exploded view of dual strand manual trimmer head used on Models B180 and B250.
1. Drive shaft adapter
2. Spool
3. Spring
4. Line guides
5. Lower housing
6. Lock knob

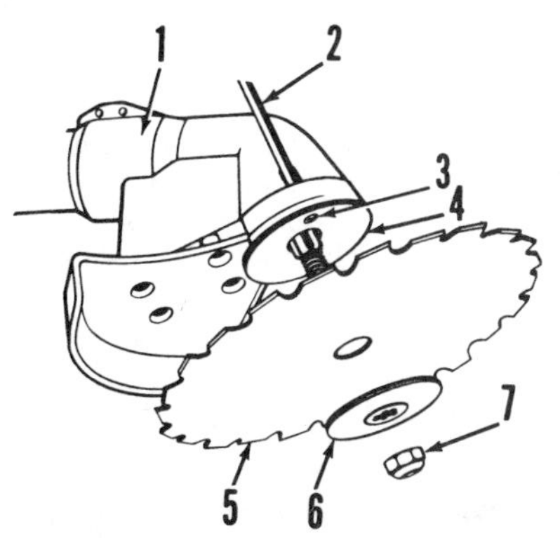

Fig. PR11—View showing parts assembly sequence to install blade on Models B370 and B440.
1. Gear head
2. Locking tool
3. Hole
4. Drive disc
5. Blade
6. Adapter washer
7. Nut (LH)

Models B370 And B440

Models B370 and B440 may be equipped with a trimmer head as an option. To install trimmer head, insert a locking rod (2—Fig. PR 11) in hole in gear head and hole in drive disc (4). Some models have a slot at front of gear head housing instead of hole. Remove left-hand threaded nut (7), adapter washer (6) and blade (5). Some models may have a cover between nut (7) and adapter washer (6). Install trimmer head as shown in Fig. PR12. Tighten trimmer head to 20 N·m (15 ft.-lbs.).

To renew line in trimmer head, align hole in trimmer housing and line guide opening and feed new line onto spool while winding lower plate (Fig. PR13).

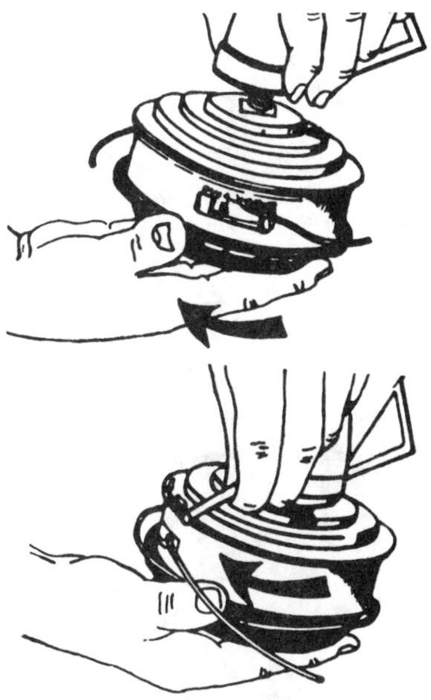

Fig. PR12—Trimmer head available for Models B370 and B440 has left-hand threads. Tighten trimmer head to 20 N·m (15 ft.-lbs.).

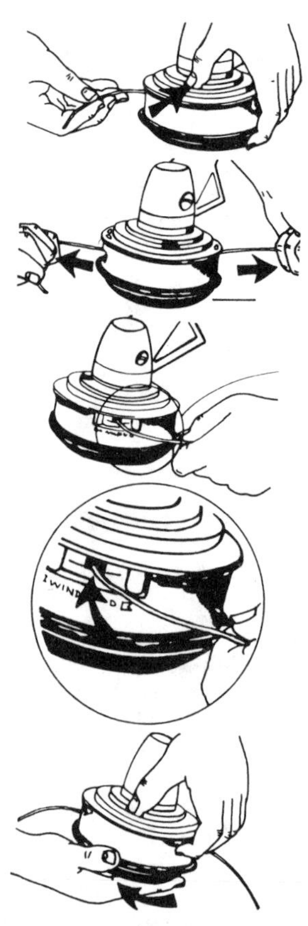

Fig. PR13—To renew line on Models B370 and B440 trimmer head, refer to text and follow sequence in illustration.

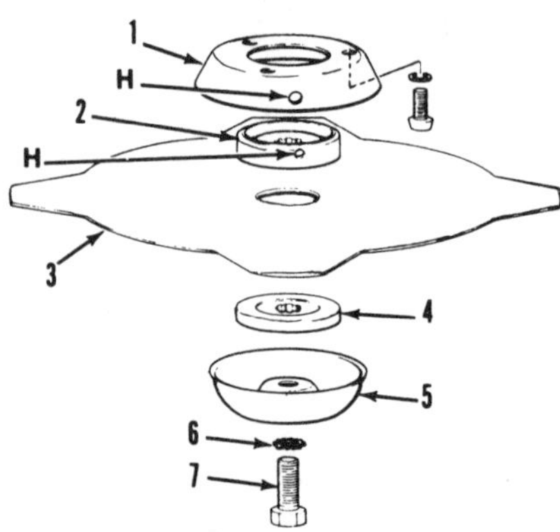

Fig. PR14—View showing parts assembly sequence to install blade on Model B250.

1. Anti-wrap guard
2. Cup washer
3. Blade
4. Adapter plate
5. Cover
6. Washer
7. Bolt (LH)

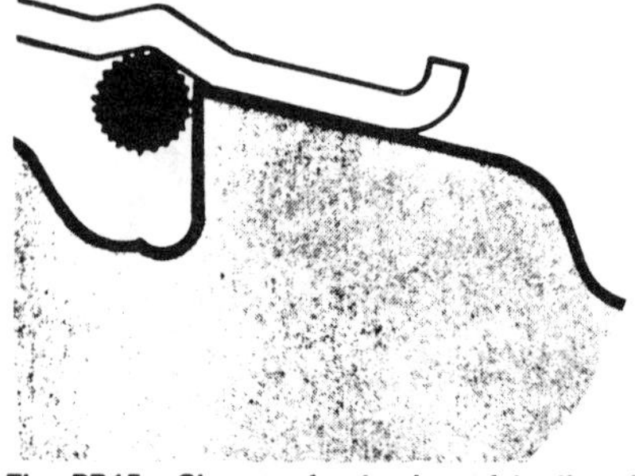

Fig. PR15—Sharpen front edge of tooth only. Make certain file holder is held firmly against the edge of tooth.

BLADE

Model B250

Model B250 may be equipped with a four cutting edge blade (Fig. PR14). To remove blade, rotate anti-wrap guard (1) until hole (H) in guard is aligned with hole (H) in cup washer (2). Insert a round tool into aligned holes to prevent blade rotation. Remove bolt (7) (left-hand thread), washer (6), cover (5) and adapter (4). Remove blade (3). When installing blade, tighten bolt (7) to 28 N·m (250 in.-lbs.).

Models B370 And B440

Models B370 and B440 may be equipped with a saw blade, a four cutting edge blade or a three cutting edge blade. To remove blade, carefully rotate blade until hole in upper driving disc is aligned with hole or slot in gear head housing. Insert a 4.5 mm (0.16 in.) round rod into holes to prevent blade rotation. Note nut retaining blade has left-hand threads and remove nut, cover, drive disc and blade. When installing blade, tighten left-hand thread nut to 35-50 N·m (26-30 ft.-lbs.).

To sharpen saw blade, use a 5.5 mm (7.32 in.) round file in file holder (part number 501 58 02-01). File front edge of tooth only with file holder firmly against the rear edge of tooth (Fig. PR15). Alternate filing one tooth to the right and the next tooth to the left at a 25° angle (Fig. PR16). Sharpen outer edge of tooth at a 5° angle (Fig. PR17). Use tooth set gage (part number 501 31 77-01) to adjust tooth set when teeth have been filed down 50 percent (Fig. PR18). Correct tooth set should provide 1 mm (0.04 in.) distance between tooth tips (Fig. PR19).

DRIVE SHAFT

Model B180

Model B180 is equipped with a flexible drive shaft enclosed in the drive shaft housing tube. Drive shaft has squared ends which engage adapters at each end. Drive shaft should be removed for maintenance at 20 hour intervals of use. To remove, separate drive shaft housing from engine. Clean drive shaft and lubricate with lithium base grease. Reinstall drive shaft in housing.

Models B250, B370 And B440

Models B250, B370 and B440 are equipped with a solid steel drive shaft supported in drive shaft housing tube. Drive shaft requires no regular maintenance; however, if drive shaft has been removed, lubricate drive shaft with lithium base grease before reinstallation.

BEARING HEAD

Model B180

Model B180 is equipped with sealed bearing housing (3—Fig. PR20). No regular maintenance is required and no service parts are available.

GEAR HEAD

Model B250

Model B250 is equipped with the gear head shown in Fig. PR21. Gear head lubricant level should be checked at 50 hour intervals of use by removing check plug (9). Gear head housing should be 2/3 full of lithium base grease. Do not use a pressure grease gun to install grease as bearing seal and housing damage will occur.

To disassemble gear head, remove trimmer head or blade assembly. Remove locating screw (7) and clamp bolt (8) then separate gear head from drive shaft housing. Remove spacer (16) and seal (15). Remove snap ring (14) and use a suitable puller to remove arbor shaft (12) and bearing assembly. If bearing (10) stays in housing, heat housing to 140° F (60° C) and tap housing on wooden block to remove bearing. Remove gear (11) from arbor shaft. Press bearing (13) from arbor shaft as required. Remove snap ring (1). Insert a screwdriver into clamp split in gear head housing and carefully expand housing. Remove input shaft (5) and bearing

Fig. PR16—Alternate filing one tooth to the right and the next tooth to the left. File at a 25° angle.

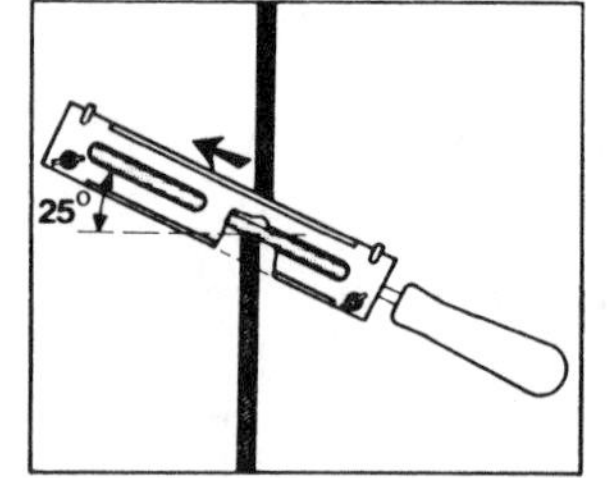

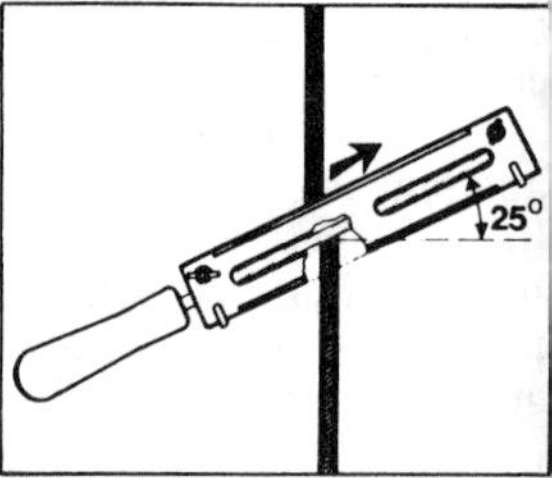

assembly. Remove snap ring (2) and press bearings (3 and 4) as required.

Models B370 And B440

Models B370 and B440 are equipped with gear head shown in Fig. PR22. Gear head lubricant level should be checked at 50 hour intervals of use. To check, remove check plug (11). Gear head housing should be kept 3/4 full of lithium base grease.

To disassemble gear head, remove trimmer head or blade assembly. Remove the four screws (3) retaining cover (5) to housing and use puller (part number 502 50 09-01) to remove cover. Remove clamp bolts (14) and locating screw (15). Separate gear head assembly from drive shaft housing tube. Remove sleeve (19) using remover (part number 502 51 09-01). Heat housing (13) to 140° F (60° C) and remove input shaft (16) and bearing assembly and arbor shaft (9) and bearing assembly. If bearing (10) remains in housing, tap housing against a wooden block while housing is still hot to remove bearing. Remove snap ring (21) and press bearings (17 and 18) from input shaft as required. Remove bearing (7) and spacer (8) as required.

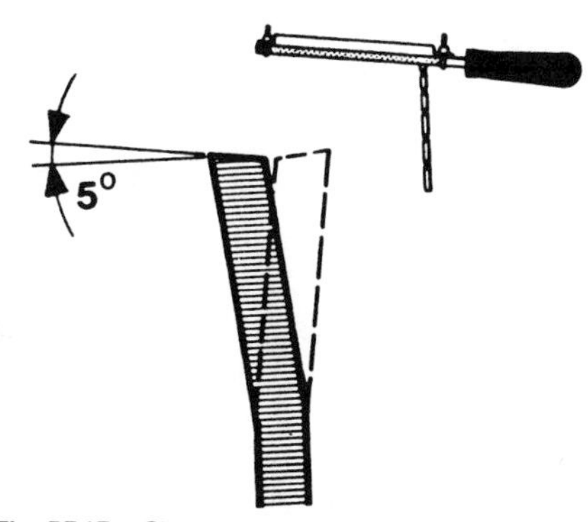

Fig. PR17—Sharpen outer edge of tooth at a 5° angle.

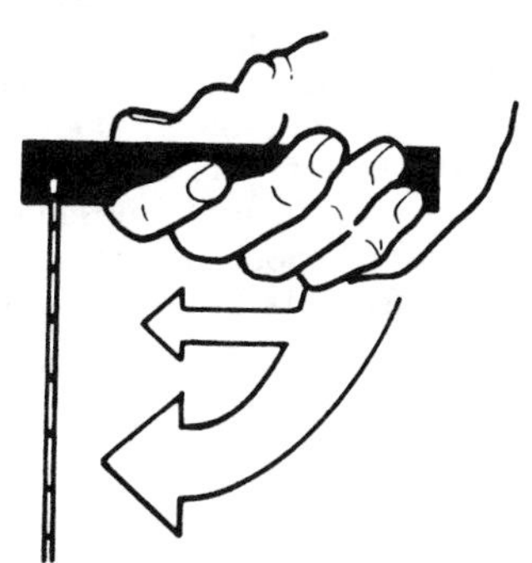

Fig. PR18—Use set gage (part number 501 31 77-01) to adjust tooth set when teeth have been filed down approximately 50 percent.

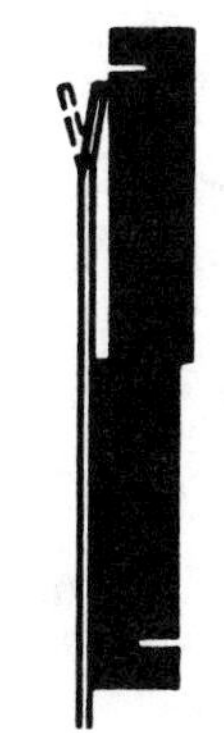

Fig. PR19—Tooth set should provide 1 mm (0.04 in.) distance between tooth tips.

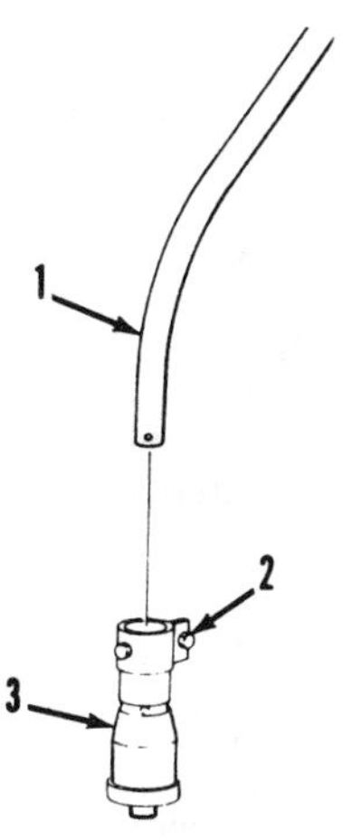

Fig. PR20—View of bearing head assembly used on Model B180.

1. Drive shaft housing
2. Clamp bolt
3. Bearing head

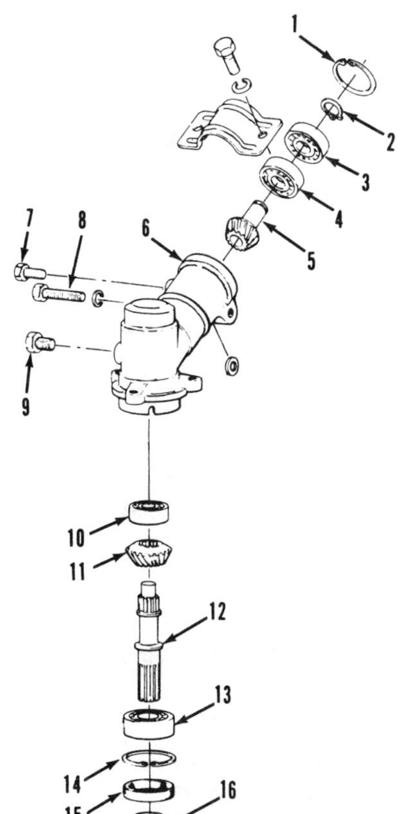

Fig. PR21—Exploded view of gear head used on Model B250.

1. Snap ring
2. Snap ring
3. Bearing
4. Bearing
5. Input gear
6. Housing
7. Bolt
8. Clamp bolt
9. Check plug
10. Bearing
11. Gear
12. Arbor shaft
13. Bearing
14. Snap ring
15. Seal
16. Spacer

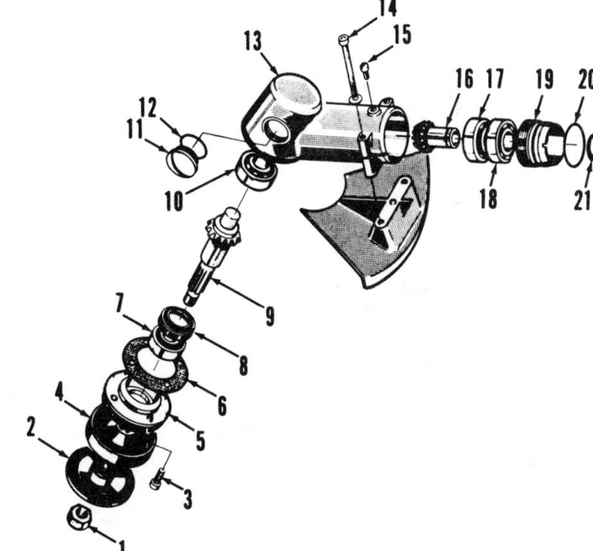

Fig. PR22—Exploded view of gear head used on Models B370 and B440.

1. Nut (LH)
2. Adapter plate
3. Screw
4. Drive disc
5. Cover
6. Gasket
7. Bearing
8. Spacer
9. Arbor shaft
10. Bearing
11. Check plug
12. Sealing ring
13. Housing
14. Clamp bolts
15. Locating screw
16. Input gear
17. Bearing
18. Bearing
19. Sleeve
20. "O" ring
21. Snap ring

POULAN

GASOLINE POWERED STRING TRIMMERS

Model	Engine Manufacturer	Engine Model	Displacement
111	Poulan	...	22 cc
114	Poulan	...	30 cc
117	Poulan	...	30 cc
175	Poulan	...	30 cc
185	Poulan	...	30 cc
195	Poulan	...	30 cc
2600	Poulan	...	26.2 cc
2610	Poulan	...	26.2 cc
2620	Poulan	...	26.2 cc

ENGINE INFORMATION

The models in this section are equipped with a Poulan engine. Refer to appropriate engine service section for engine service information.

FUEL MIXTURE

Manufacturer recommends mixing regular grade gasoline with Poulan/Weed Eater two-stroke engine oil mixed as indicated on container. Gasohol or other alcohol blended fuels are not approved by manufacturer.

STRING TRIMMER

Models 2600 And 2610

Models 2600 and 2610 are equipped with the single strand, semi-automatic trimmer head shown in Figs. PN10 or PN11. Early type trimmer head (Fig. PN10) is identified by the adapter (1) that drives the trimmer head. Service procedure for both heads is similar.

To extend line with trimmer engine stopped, push in on button (7) while pulling on line end. Repeat procedure as needed to obtain desired line length. To extend line with trimmer engine running and head rotating, tap button (7) on ground. Each time button is tapped on ground a measured amount of line is advanced.

To install new line, remove cover (8), button (7) and spool (6). Clean all parts thoroughly and remove any remaining old line from spool. Wind approximately 30 feet (9 m) of 0.080 inch (2 mm) diameter monofilament line on spool in direction indicated by arrow on spool. Insert line end through line guide opening in housing (2) and install spool, button and cover.

Model 2620

Model 2620 is equipped with the dual strand, manual trimmer head shown in Fig. PN12. To extend line, stop trimmer engine and push in on plate (8) while pulling each line out of housing (2).

To install new trimmer line, remove screw (9), plate (8), spring (6) and spool (7). Remove any remaining line from each side of spool. Clean spool, housing and plate. Insert ends of two new 0.095 inch (2.4 mm) diameter lines in holes located within spool and wind lines in direction indicated by arrow on spool.

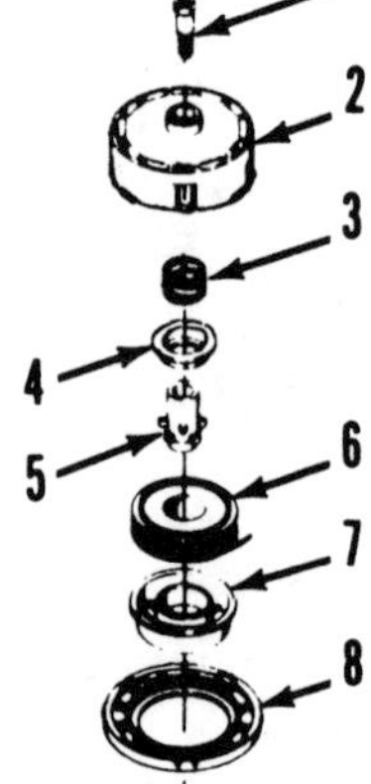

Fig. PN10—Exploded view of early-style, single strand, semi-automatic trimmer head used on early Models 2600 and 2610.

1. Drive shaft adapter
2. Housing
3. Spring
4. Spring adapter
5. Drive cam
6. Spool
7. Button
8. Cover

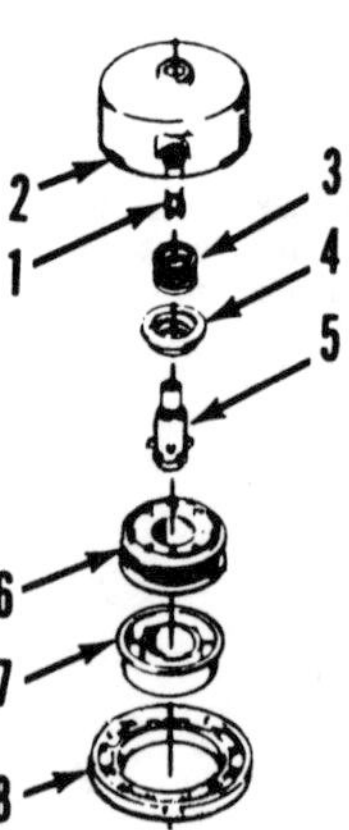

Fig. PN11—Exploded view of later-style, single strand, semi-automatic trimmer head used on Models 2600 and 2610.

1. Line guide
2. Housing
3. Spring
4. Spring adapter
5. Drive cam
6. Spool
7. Button
8. Cover

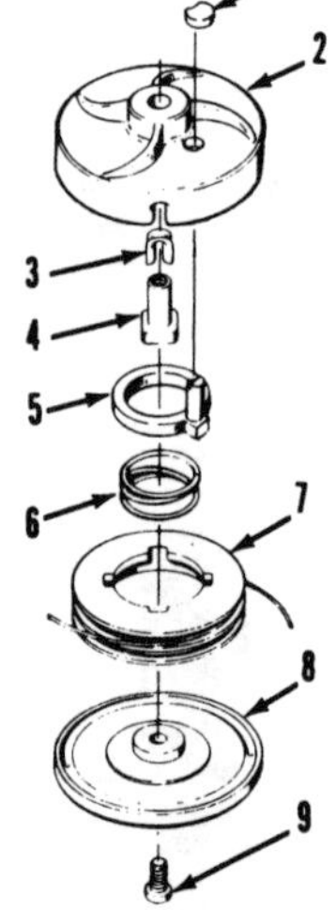

Fig. PN12—Exploded view of dual strand, manual trimmer head used on Model 2620.

1. Lock ring cap
2. Housing
3. Line guide
4. Drive shaft adapter
5. Lock ring
6. Spring
7. Spool
8. Cover
9. Screw

Illustrations courtesy Poulan/Weed Eater

Total amount of installed line should not exceed spool diameter. Make certain line savers (3) are in position and install spool in housing with the "THIS SIDE IN" instructions on spool toward inside

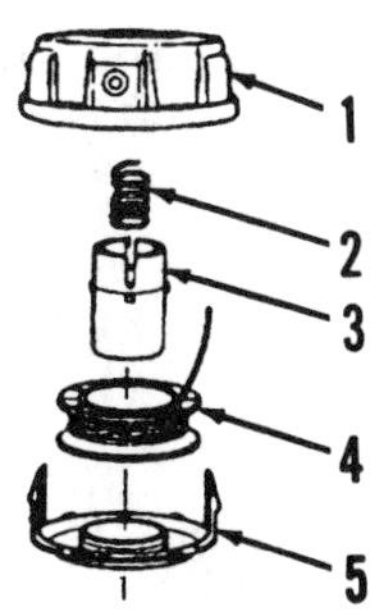

Fig. PN13—Exploded view of single strand, semi-automatic trimmer head used on some Models 111, 114 and 117.

1. Housing
2. Spring
3. Button
4. Spool
5. Cover

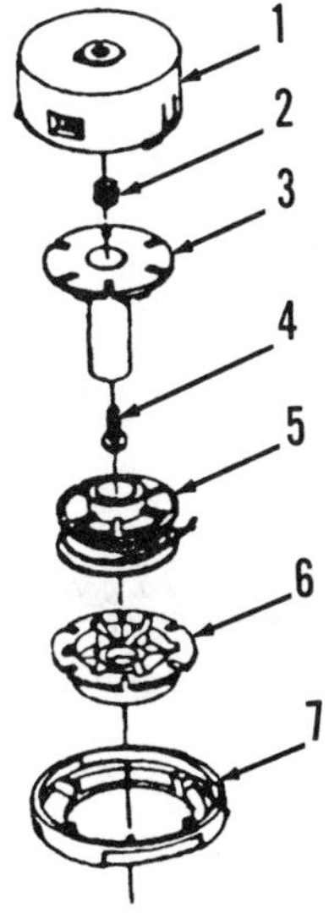

Fig. PN14—Exploded view of single strand, semi-automatic trimmer head used on some Models 111, 114, 117, 175, 185 and 195.

1. Housing
2. Spring
3. Spool post
4. Screw
5. Spool
6. Button
7. Cover

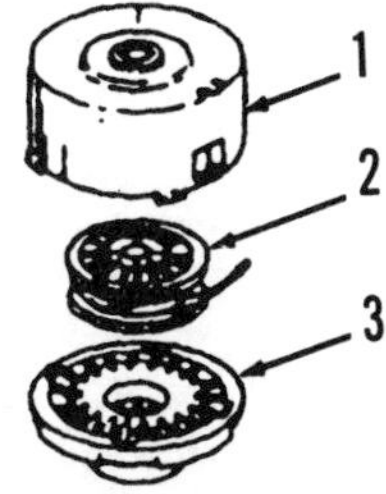

Fig. PN15—Exploded view of single strand, semi-automatic trimmer head used on some Models 111, 114, 117, 175 and 195.

1. Housing
2. Spool
3. Cover & button assy.

of trimmer head. Install spring (6), cover (8) and screw (9).

Models 111, 114 And 117

Models 111, 114 and 117 may be equipped with the single strand, semi-automatic trimmer head shown in Fig. PN13.

To extend line with trimmer engine stopped, push in on button (3) while pulling on line end. Repeat procedure as needed to obtain desired line length. To extend line with trimmer engine running and head rotating, tap button (3) on ground. Each time button is tapped on ground a measured amount of line is advanced.

To install new line, disengage tabs on cover (5) from housing (1). Remove old line and clean parts. Recommended line diameter is 0.080 inch (2 mm). Wind line around spool in direction indicated by arrow on spool.

Models 111, 114, 117, 175, 185 And 195

Models 111, 114, 117, 175, 185 and 195 may be equipped with the single strand, semi-automatic trimmer head shown in Fig. PN14.

To extend line with trimmer engine stopped, push in on button (6) while pulling on line end. Repeat procedure as needed to obtain desired line length. To extend line with trimmer engine running and head rotating, tap button (6) on ground. Each time button is tapped on ground a measured amount of line is advanced.

To install new line, remove cover (7), button (6) and spool (5). Clean all parts thoroughly and remove any remaining old line from spool. Wind 0.080 inch (2 mm) diameter monofilament line on spool in direction indicated by arrow on spool. Insert line end through line guide opening in housing (1) and install spool, button and cover.

Models 111, 114, 117, 175 And 195

Models 111, 114, 117, 175 and 195 may be equipped with the single strand, semi-automatic trimmer head shown in Fig. PN15.

To extend line with trimmer engine stopped, push in on button while pulling on line end. Repeat procedure as needed to obtain desired line length. To extend line with trimmer engine running and head rotating, tap button on ground. Each time button is tapped on ground a measured amount of line is advanced.

To install new line, detach cover (3) from housing (1). Remove old line and clean parts. Recommended line diameter is 0.080 inch (2 mm). Wind line around spool in direction indicated by arrow on spool.

BLADE

Some models may be equipped with a blade. When installing blade, be sure all adapter plates are centered and seated squarely against blade. Blade nut has left-hand threads.

DRIVE SHAFT

Curved Shaft Models

Models with a curved drive shaft housing are equipped with a flexible drive shaft. The drive shaft should be removed, cleaned and lubricated after every 20 hours of operation. Detach head assembly from drive shaft housing and remove shaft. Apply lithium-based grease to shaft.

Straight Shaft Models

Periodic maintenance is not required for the drive shaft on models with a straight drive shaft housing. If removed, apply lithium-based grease to shaft.

BEARING HEAD

Models 111, 114 And 117

These models are equipped with a bearing head that is an integral part of the drive shaft housing tube. Regular maintenance is not required. Service parts are not available.

Early Models 2600 And 2610

Early Models 2600 And 2610 are equipped with the bearing head shown in Fig. PN16. To disassemble bearing head, remove trimmer head assembly. Remove locating screw (2) and slip bearing head off drive shaft housing tube. Remove dust cover (6), spacer (5) and arbor shaft (4). Lubricate arbor with lithium-base grease before installation.

Late Models 2600 And 2610

Late Models 2600 And 2610 are equipped with the bearing head shown in Fig. PN17. The bearing head is equipped with sealed bearings; regular maintenance is not required.

To disassemble bearing head, remove trimmer head or blade assembly. Remove clamp bolt (2) and locating screw (3). Separate bearing head assembly from drive shaft housing. Remove shield (6) and bracket (5), if so equipped. Re-

Illustrations courtesy Poulan/Weed Eater

move cup washer (13) and washer (12). Carefully press drive shaft adapter (1) out of bearings. Remove snap rings (7 and 11). Press bearings (8 and 10) and spacer (9) out of housing.

GEAR HEAD

Models 175, 185, 195 And 2620

The gear head should be lubricated after every 10 hours of operation by injecting lithium-based grease through screw hole in side of gear head. Fill housing so it is approximately two-thirds full of grease.

The gear head on Models 175, 185 and 195 must be serviced as a unit assembly; individual components are not available.

Model 2620 is equipped with the gear head shown in Fig. PN18. To disassemble gear, remove trimmer head or blade assembly. Remove clamp bolt and head locating screw and separate gear head from drive shaft housing tube. Remove cup washer (17) and spacer (14). Remove snap ring (2) and use a suitable puller to remove input shaft (5) and bearing assembly. Remove snap ring (1) and press bearings (3 and 4) from input shaft as required. Remove seal (16) and snap ring (15). Use a suitable puller to remove arbor (12) and bearing assembly. Press bearing (13) and gear (11) from shaft as required. If bearing (10) remains in housing (6), heat housing to 140° F (60° C) and tap housing on wooden block to remove bearing.

ENGINE COVER

All Models So Equipped

Some models are equipped with the full engine cover shown in Fig. PN19. Note that two styles (9 or 10) have been used. Style (9) is secured to drive shaft housing by a clamp bolt (8). Style (10) has a threaded collar on drive shaft tube that connects to threads on housing. To remove engine cover, separate engine assembly from drive shaft housing. Remove the four 10-24 screws and separate housings (5) and (9 or 10) slightly. Disconnect ignition wire from module and separate fuel line so junction fitting stays with crankcase side of fuel line. Separate housings completely. Remove the three 8-24 screws from inner side of housing (5) and remove the air baffle. Remove the five 10-24 screws located under air baffle and separate housing (4) from housing (5). Remove fuel tank cap and remove fuel tank. Remove the four screws securing carburetor cover plate and remove carburetor cover. Disconnect spark plug, remove the four 10-24 screws at drive shaft housing side of cover (9 or 10), then remove cover.

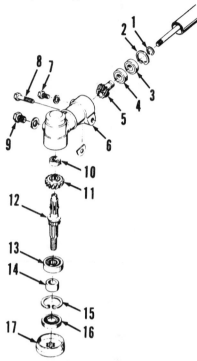

Fig. PN18—Exploded view of gear head used on Model 2620.

1. Snap ring
2. Snap ring
3. Bearing
4. Bearing
5. Input shaft
6. Housing
7. Clamp bolt
8. Bolt
9. Check plug
10. Bearing
11. Gear
12. Arbor shaft
13. Bearing
14. Spacer
15. Snap ring
16. Seal
17. Cup washer

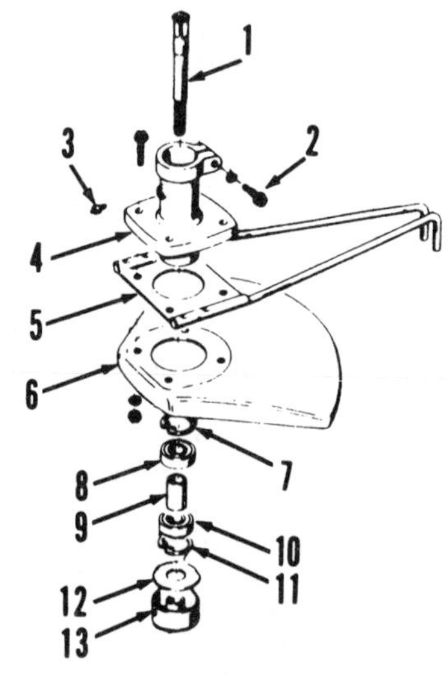

Fig. PN17—Exploded view of bearing head used on late Models 2600 and 2610.

1. Drive shaft adapter
2. Clamp bolt
3. Locating screw
4. Housing
5. Bracket (if equipped)
6. Shield
7. Snap ring
8. Bearing
9. Spacer
10. Bearing
11. Snap ring
12. Washer
13. Drive disc

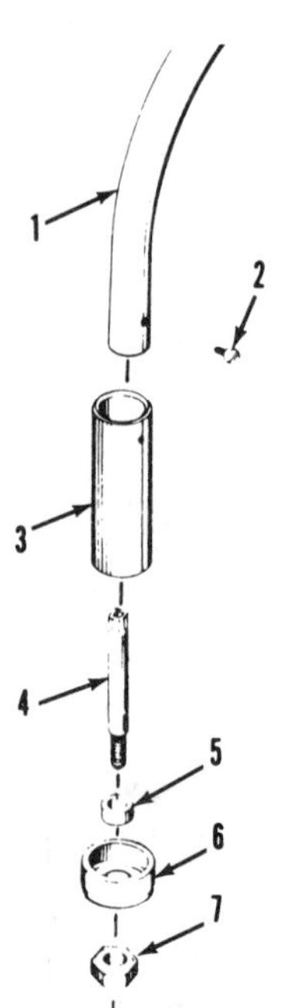

Fig. PN16—Exploded view of drive shaft and bearing head used on early Models 2600 and 2610.

1. Drive shaft housing
2. Locating screw
3. Bearing housing
4. Arbor
5. Spacer
6. Dust cover
7. Nut

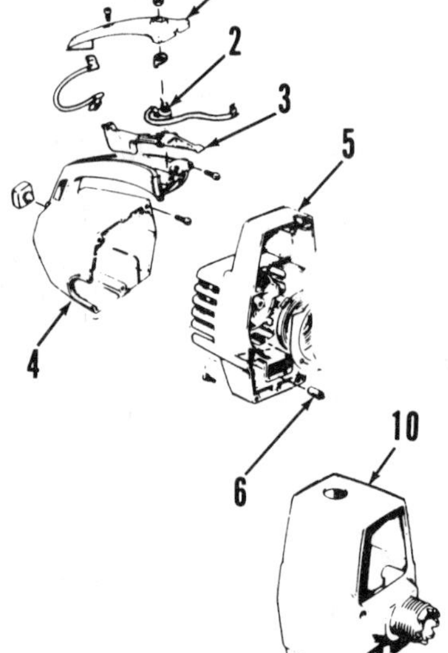

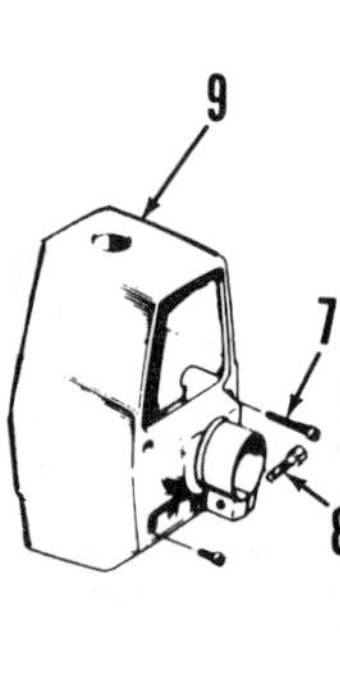

Fig. PN19—Exploded view of engine cover assembly used on some models.

1. Throttle housing cover
2. Ignition switch
3. Throttle trigger
4. Handle
5. Fan housing
6. Spacer
7. Screw
8. Clamp bolt
9. Cover (clamp style)
10. Cover (threaded style)

POULAN

GASOLINE POWERED BLOWERS

Model	Engine Manufacturer	Engine Model	Displacement
420	Poulan	...	26.2 cc
422	Poulan	...	22 cc
432	Poulan	...	30 cc

ENGINE INFORMATION

The models in this section are equipped with a Poulan engine. Refer to appropriate engine service section for engine service information.

FUEL MIXTURE

Manufacturer recommends mixing regular grade gasoline with Poulan/Weed Eater two-stroke engine oil mixed as indicated on container. Gasohol or other alcohol blended fuels are not approved by manufacturer.

FAN

To remove blower fan (11—Fig. PN40) on Model 420, remove tube clamp (9) from blower housing. Remove blower housing screws and separate blower housing halves (6 and 13). Remove fan mounting nut (12) and withdraw fan from drive shaft (4). When installing fan, tighten fan retaining nut to 19-20 N·m (14-15 ft.-lbs.).

To remove blower fan (3—Fig. PN41) on Model 422, remove screws from blower housing and separate outer

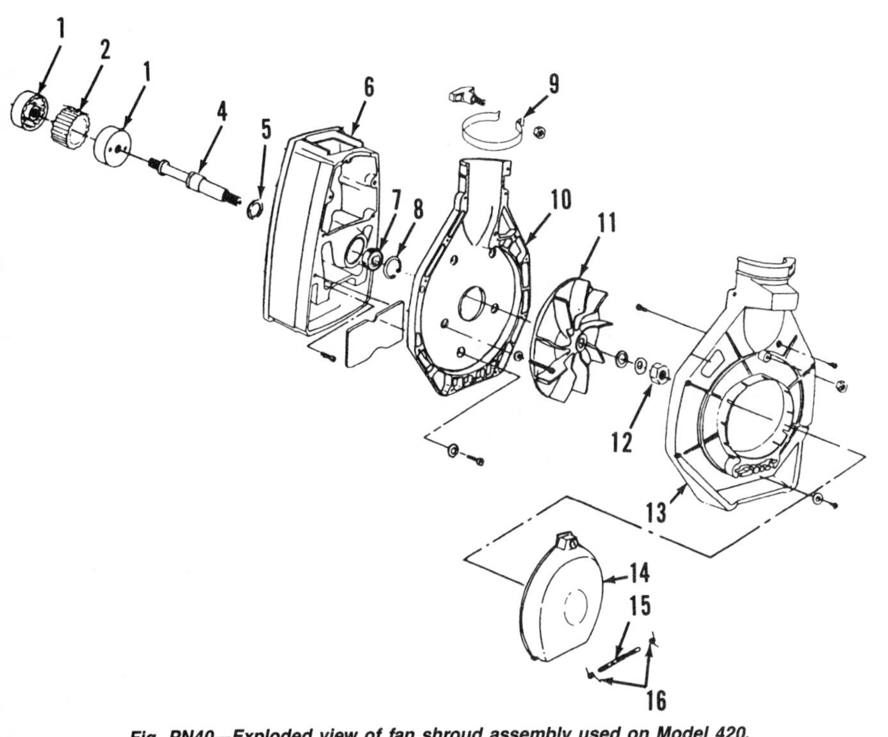

Fig. PN40—Exploded view of fan shroud assembly used on Model 420.

1. Shaft coupling
2. Coupling hub
4. Fan shaft
5. Washer
6. Shroud
7. Bearing
8. Snap ring
9. Clamp
10. Blower housing
11. Fan
12. Nut
13. Blower housing
14. Inlet door
15. Pivot pin
16. Springs

blower housing (4) and recoil starter assembly from inner blower housing (2). Remove screws mounting fan (3) to flywheel (1) and remove fan.

To remove blower fan (7—Fig. PN42) on Model 432, remove retaining screws from blower housing and separate blower housing halves (5 and 12). Remove fan retaining nut (11) and withdraw fan from end of crankshaft.

SHROUD BEARING

The fan shaft (4—Fig. PN40) on Model 420 is supported by a bearing (7) in the fan shroud (6). To remove bearing and drive shaft, first remove blower housing (10 and 13) and fan (11). Unbolt and remove fan shroud from engine. Detach snap ring (8), then heat shroud to 300° F (149° C) and remove bearing and shaft.

The fan end of crankshaft on Model 432 is supported by bearing (3—Fig. PN42) in starter housing (1). To remove bearing, first separate blower housing (5 and 12), fan (7) and starter housing (1) from engine. Press bearing out of starter housing.

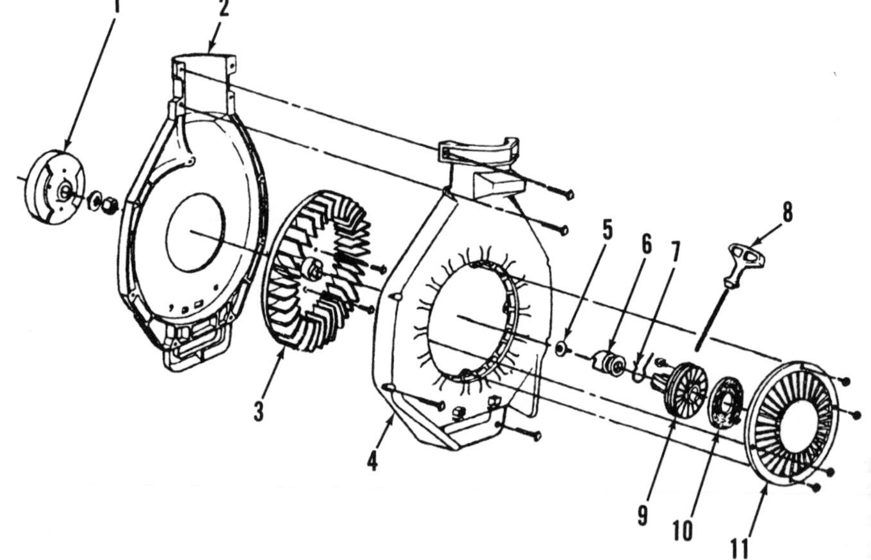

Fig. PN41—Exploded view of fan shroud assembly used on Model 422.

1. Flywheel
2. Blower housing
3. Fan
4. Blower housing
5. Screw
6. Starter pinion
7. Spring
8. Rope handle
9. Starter pulley
10. Recoil spring
11. Pulley housing

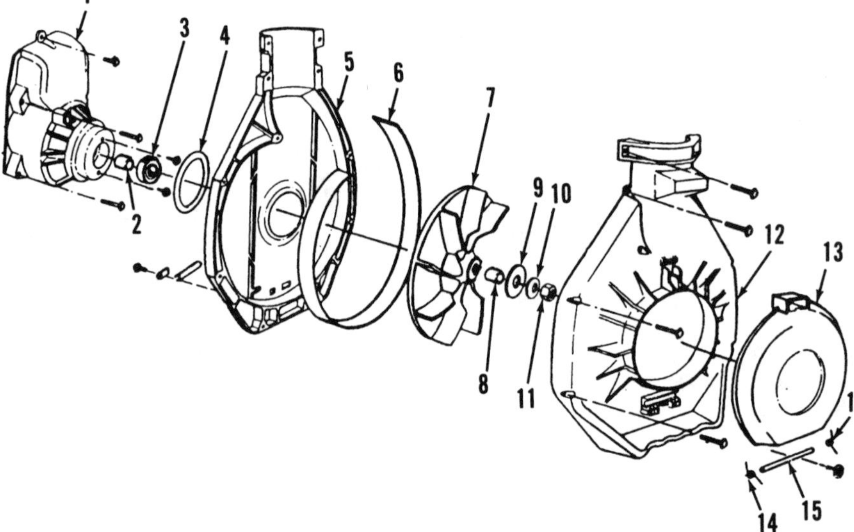

Fig. PN42—Exploded view of fan shroud assembly used on Model 432.

1. Starter housing
2. Spacer
3. Bearing
4. "O" ring
5. Housing
6. Band
7. Fan
8. Spacer
9. Washer
10. Washer
11. Nut
12. Housing
13. Inlet door
14. Springs
15. Pivot pin

Illustrations courtesy Poulan/Weed Eater

REDMAX

GASOLINE POWERED TRIMMERS

Model	Engine Make	Engine Model	Displacement
BC220DL & BC2000DL	Komatsu/Zenoah	G2D	22.5 cc (1.37 cu. in.)
BT2000, BC2001DL, BC2300DL	Komatsu/Zenoah	G23L	22.5 cc (1.37 cu. in.)
BC260DL	Komatsu/Zenoah	G2K	25.4 cc (1.55 cu. in.)
BC2600DL	Komatsu/Zenoah	G26L	25.4 cc (1.55 cu. in.)
BC340DL & BC342DL	Komatsu/Zenoah	G3K	33.6 cc (2.05 cu. in)
BC430DWM, BC440DWM, BC442DWM	Komatsu/Zenoah	G4K	41.5 cc (2.53 cu. in.)
BT17	Komatsu/Zenoah	G1E	17.2 cc (1.05 cu. in.)
BT220	Komatsu/Zenoah	G2KC	22.5 cc (1.37 cu. in.)
SGC220DL	Komatsu/Zenoah	G2KC	22.5 cc (1.37 cu. in.)

ENGINE INFORMATION

Komatsu/Zenoah two stroke air-cooled gasoline engines are used. Identify the engine by displacement and model if available, then refer to the appropriate KOMATSU/ZENOAH Engine Service section of this manual.

FUEL MIXTURE

Manufacturer recommends mixing regular or unleaded grade gasoline with a high-quality two-stroke engine oil designed for air-cooled engines.

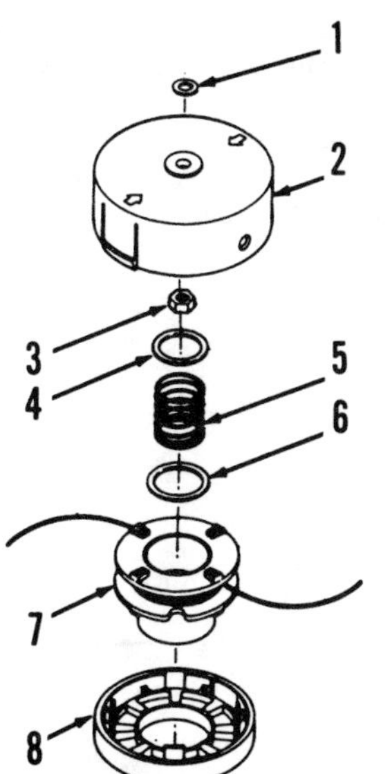

Fig. RM11—Exploded view of trimmer head used on BT and some BC models. Nut (3) may not be used with some applications.

1. Washer
2. Drum
3. Nut
4. Washer
5. Spring
6. Washer
7. Spool
8. Cover

Recommended fuel: oil ratio is 32:1 when using RedMax oil or any other high-quality two-stroke oil. Manufactgurer does not recommend using gasolhol or other fuels that include alcohol.

STRING TRIMMER

Different style trimmer heads have been used. Identify the type by referring to the illustrations.

Fig. RM11. The dual cutter lines of the semi-automatic trimmer head shown in Fig. RM11 can be extended with the engine stopped or with the engine running. To manually advance the trimmer lines with the engine stopped, push the spool button at the bottom of the head and pull both of the lines. To extend the lines with the engine running, operate the trimmer at maximum speed and tap the button on the ground. Both lines should extend a small amount automatically. If the line does not extend with the engine running, stop the engine and extend the lines manually. If a line is broken inside the drum, it will be necessary to disassemble the unit and feed the line through the eyelet in the drum (2).

To install new line, press the tabs on cover (8) and remove the cover, spool (7), washers (4 and 6) and spring (5). Clean and inspect all parts for damage. If new line is installed, be sure the new line is the correct diameter. Some models use 0.080 in. (2 mm) diameter line while other models use 0.095 in. (2.4 mm) diameter. Depending upon the model and the diameter of line, the spool will hold either 15 ft. (4.6 m) or 20 ft. (6 m) of line. Insert the line through the eye of the spool as shown in Fig. RM12 and pull the line through until it

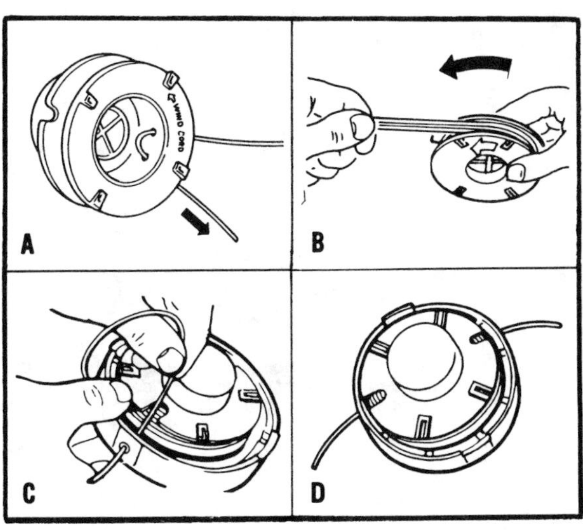

Fig. RM12—Insert end of trimmer line through hole in spool and pull line through until ends are the same length. Refer to text.

Illustrations courtesy Redmax

is the same length on both sides. Wrap both ends of the line on spool at the same time in the direction indicated by the arrow on the spool. Wind the line tightly and evenly from side to side, but do not twist the lines. Install washers (4 and 6—Fig. RM11), spring (5) and spool (7) while directing the ends of both lines through the eyelets in the housing (C—Fig. RM12). Install the cover making sure the locking tabs of the drum (2) properly engage the slits in the cover (8). Trim the line so each extends approximately 6 in. (15 cm) from the drum.

If the trimmer head retaining nut (3) and drum (2) must be removed, hold the drum while removing nut.

Fig. RM13. The dual cutter lines of the semi-automatic trimmer head shown in Fig. RM13 can be extended with the engine stopped or with the engine running. To extend the line with the engine running, allow the engine to run at idle speed, accelerate the engine to full speed very quickly, then return the speed to idle. Lines should extend when the engine speed is increased rapidly. If necessary, repeat the procedure. If the line does not extend with the engine running, stop the engine and extend the lines manually. To manually extend the lines with the engine stopped, loosen knob (10), then pull both lines the desired length from the drum. If a line is broken inside the drum (2), it will be necessary to disassemble the unit and feed the line through the eyelet (3) in the drum.

To install new line, remove knob (10), then remove cover (9) and spool (8). Clean and inspect all parts for damage. If new line is installed, be sure the new line is the correct diameter and length. Insert the line through the eye of the spool and pull the line through until it is the same length on both sides. Wrap both ends of the line on spool at the same time in the direction indicated by the arrow on the spool. Wind the line tightly and evenly from side to side, but do not twist the lines. Install the spool while guiding the ends of the line through eyelets (3).

Fig. RM13—Exploded view of trimmer head used on most BC models.

1. Adapter
2. Drum
3. Eyelet
4. Slider
5. Spring
6. Cam disc
7. Retainer
8. Spool
9. Cover
10. Knob

BRUSH CUTTING BLADE

Some trimmer (BT) models may be fitted with an eight-tooth blade (Fig. RM14). Some brush cutter (BC) models may be fitted with a trimmer head, four-tooth blade or eight-tooth head (Fig. RM15). A finer (saw) tooth blade may also be installed on some models.

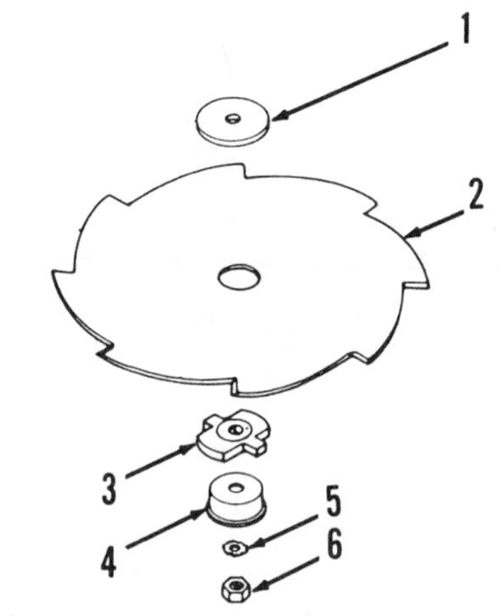

Fig. RM14—Certain BT models may be fitted with the eight-tooth blade shown.

1. Washer
2. Blade
3. Flange
4. Cup
5. Washer
6. Nut

Fig. RM15—BC Models may be equipped with the eight-tooth blade (1). Certain models may also be fitted with a four-tooth blade (2) or a fine-tooth saw type blade.

1. Blade
2. Blade
3. Washer
4. Cup
5. Washer
6. Lockwasher
7. Screw (L. H.)

Before removing a trimmer and installing any of these blades, check with a dealer to be sure the application is acceptable to the manufacturer. Damage or injury can occur as a result of improper installation. When sharpening follow the original sharpening angle.

When installing, make sure the concave side of flange (3—Fig. RM14) or washer (3—Fig. RM15) is against the blade. Install the blade so teeth are facing the direction of rotation. BT models without gear head rotate clockwise as viewed by the operator; BC models are equipped with gear head and rotate counterclockwise. Tighten the blade retaining nut to 14.7-19.7 Nm (130-174 in.-lb.) torque.

RECIPROCATOR BLADES

The reciprocating blades of SGC models cut by shearing material trapped between the blades. Refer to the RECIPROCATOR GEAR HEAD paragraphs for servicing the mechanism that moves the blades.

Blades can be sharpened to restore cutting efficiency without removing the blades. To sharpen the blades, insert a hex wrench in the screw located on top the gear head as shown in Fig. RM16. Turn the hex wrench to move the blades until they are offset 3.1 mm (1/8 in.) as shown. Grind the cutting surfaces lightly to the shape and angle shown in Fig. RM17. After sharpening one side of each blade, use the hex wrench (Fig. RM16) to reposition the blades the other sides can be sharpened.

NOTE: When sharpening, grind the surfaces quickly to avoid overheating the blade. Heat can disturb the temper of the metal and cause the blades to dull more quickly. Corners (T—Fig. RM17) of the blade should be sharp.

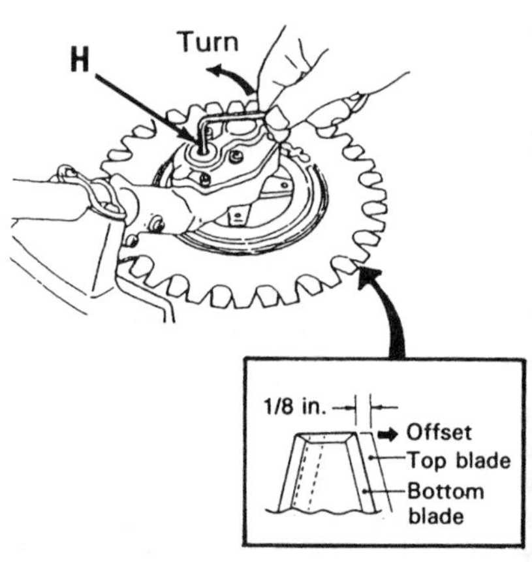

Fig. RM16—The blades of Reciprocator (SGC models) can be rotated with the engine stopped using a hex wrench in screw (H) located in the top of gear head. To sharpen blades, turn the hex screw to the position shown in the inset.

Illustrations courtesy Redmax

not rounded. The desired angle for all cutting angles is 55 degrees.

Install new blades when the width (W) at the tip is less than 8 mm (5/16 in.), if thickness is less than 6.65 mm (0.262 in.) or if the blades are severely damaged. To remove the blades, remove the attaching screws shown in Fig. RM18. When new, the blades are identical. Tighten the blade fitting screws to 11.8-14.7 N•m (104-130 in.-lb.) and the screws attaching the stabilizer (7) to 2.0-2.9 N•m (18-26 in.-lb.) torque.

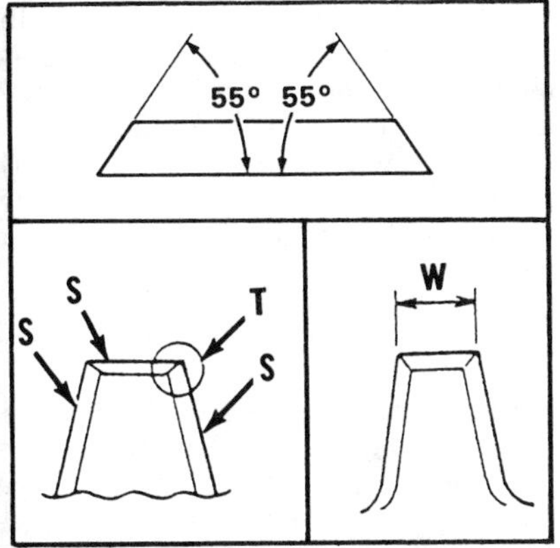

Fig. RM17—The desired angle for the cutting edge for SGC models is 55 degrees. Sharpen all three surfaces (S), making sure the corners (T) are sharp, not rounded. Install new blade when tip width (W) is less than 8 mm (5/16 in.).

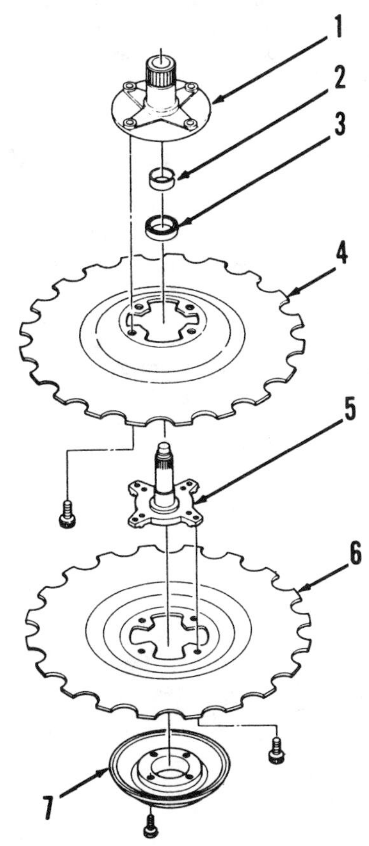

Fig. RM18—Exploded view of the blade assembly of SGC models.

1. Outer shaft
2. Bushing
3. Seal
4. Blade
5. Inner shaft
6. Blade
7. Stabilizer

MOWER

Some models may be equipped with the mower assembly shown in Fig. RM19. New blades (5) can be installed, but should be installed in sets. The assembly may become dangerously out of balance if only one or two blades are renewed.

DRIVE SHAFT

BT Models. These models have a flexible drive shaft cable that runs inside the curved housing. Periodic drive shaft maintenance is not required, but if removed, the drive shaft should be cleaned, inspected and lubricated with lithium base grease before installing. The drive shaft housing is lined, but liner is not available separately for service.

To remove the drive shaft, first separate the engine from the drive shaft housing as follows. Detach the engine stop switch wire and the throttle cable. If so equipped, loosen clamp (C—Fig. RM20), then separate the drive shaft housing (H) from the engine assembly. To separate the engine from the drive shaft of models shown in Fig. RM21, remove the two retaining screws (S) and pull the handle (H) and drive shaft housing from the engine assembly. It should be possible to easily withdraw the drive shaft (D—Fig. RM20 or Fig. RM21) from the housing. If the drive shaft is stuck and cannot be withdrawn, the housing and shaft should both be replaced. When installing, the end of the drive shaft should protrude 18 mm (0.7 in.) as shown at P—Fig. RM22. Be sure the drive shaft fully engages the clutch when attaching the drive shaft housing to the engine assembly.

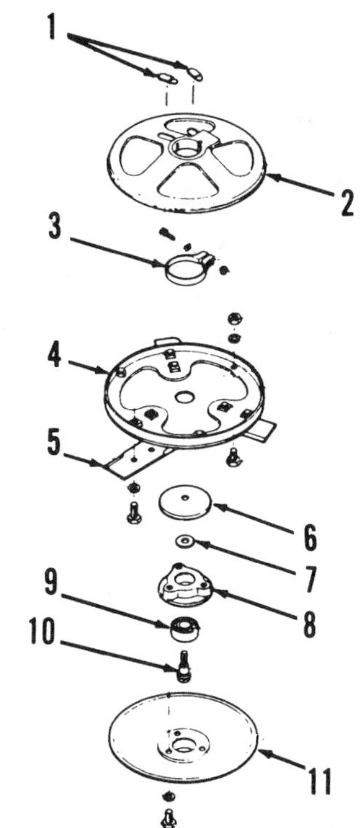

Fig. RM19—Exploded view of the mower unit that may be fitted to some BC models.

1. Plugs
2. Cover
3. Clamp
4. Ring
5. Blade
6. Cover
7. Spacer
8. Bearing holder
9. Bearing
10. Stabilizer

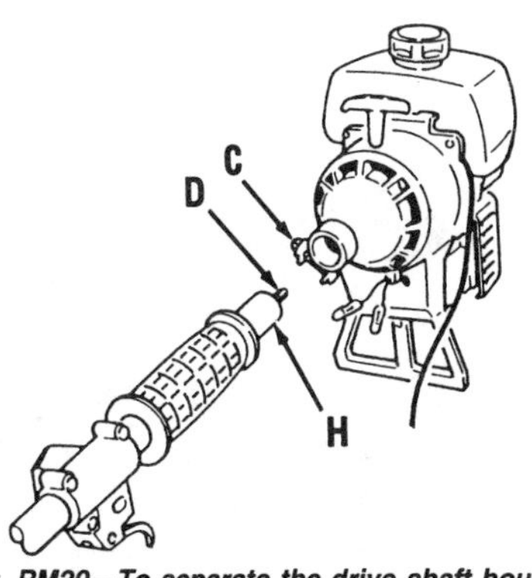

Fig. RM20—To separate the drive shaft housing from the engine assembly of some models, loosen clamp (C), then pull the drive shaft housing (H) from the clamp housing.

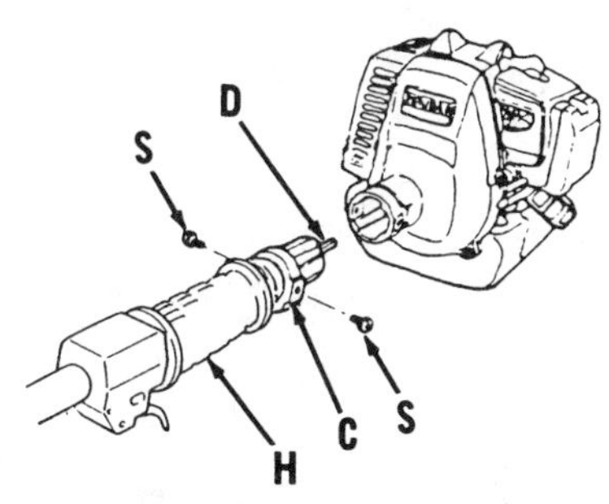

Fig. RM21—The two retaining screws (S) must be removed from collar (C) before separating the drive shaft housing (H) from the engine assembly of some models.

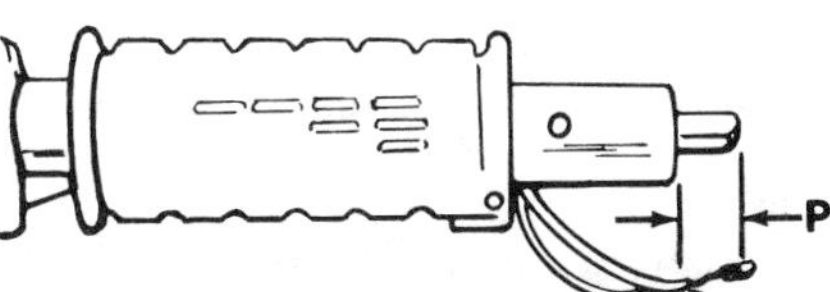

Fig. RM22—The drive shaft should extend (P) about 18 mm (0.7 in.) from the end of the drive shaft housing.

BC Models. These models are equipped with a straight, solid drive

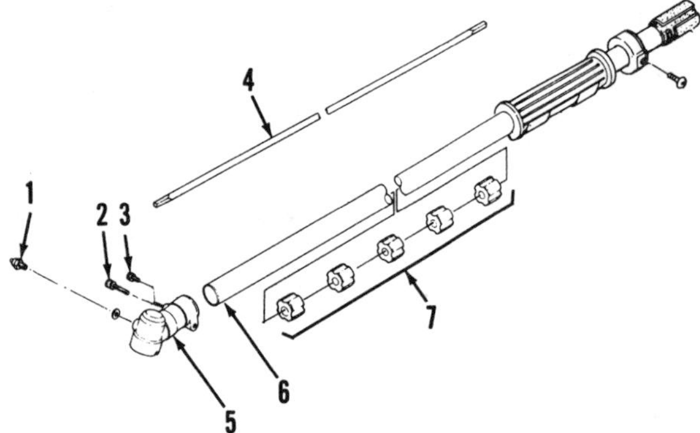

Fig. RM23—Exploded view of the solid drive shaft and housing used on some models.

1. Grease fitting
2. Clamp screw
3. Locating screw
4. Drive shaft
5. Gear head
6. Housing
7. Bushings

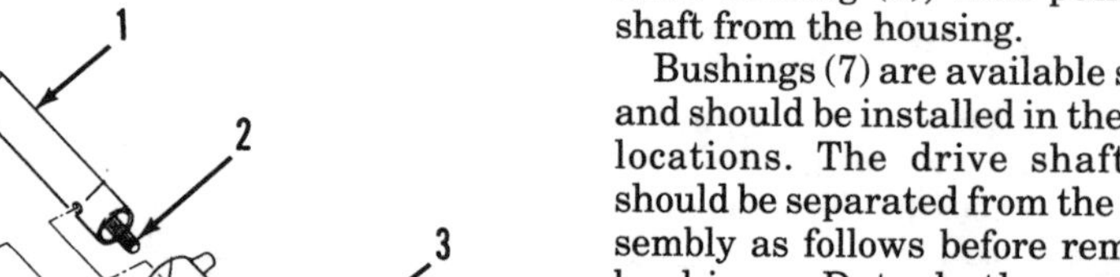

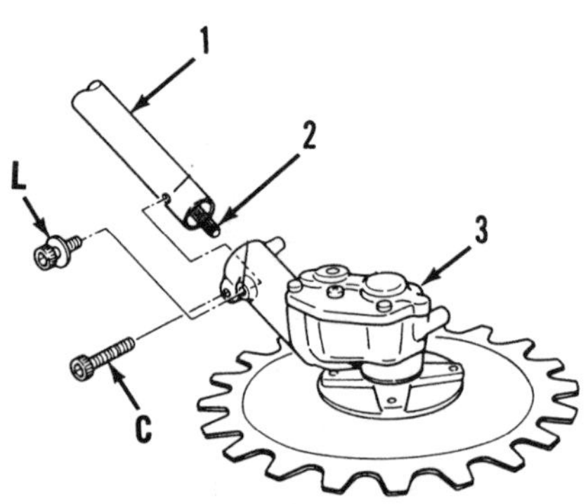

Fig. RM24—To remove the drive shaft from Reciprocator (SGC models), remove the locating screw (L) and clamp screw (C).

1. Drive shaft housing
2. Drive shaft
3. Reciprocator gear head

shaft that rides in bushings within the drive shaft housing. Periodic drive shaft maintenance is not required, but if removed, the drive shaft should be cleaned, inspected and lubricated with lithium base grease before installing.

To remove the drive shaft, first remove the gear head from the lower end of the drive shaft housing as follows. Remove the locating screw (3—Fig. RM23) and clamp screw (2). Pull the gear head (5) from the end of the drive shaft housing (6), then pull the drive shaft from the housing.

Bushings (7) are available separately and should be installed in their original locations. The drive shaft housing should be separated from the engine assembly as follows before removing the bushings. Detach the engine stop switch wire and the throttle cable. Remove the two retaining screws (S—Fig. RM21) and pull the handle (H) and drive shaft housing from the engine assembly.

When assembling, tighten the gear head locating screw (3—Fig. RM23) to 2.0-2.9 N•m (18-26 in.-lb.) and the clamp screw (2) to 5.0-8.8 N•m (44-78 in.-lb.) torque.

SGC Model. The straight, solid drive shaft rides in bushings within the drive shaft housing. Periodic drive shaft maintenance is not required, but if removed, the drive shaft should be cleaned, inspected and lubricated with lithium base grease before installing.

To remove the drive shaft, first remove the gear head from the lower end of the drive shaft housing as follows. Remove the locating screw (L—Fig. RM24) and clamp screw (C). Pull the reciprocator gear head (3) from the end of the drive shaft housing (1), then pull the drive shaft from the housing. It may be necessary to heat the clamp area if the drive shaft housing is stuck in the gear head.

Bushings (3—Fig. RM25) are available separately. Mark the original position of each bushing before removing then install new bushings in the same location as the original. Separate the drive shaft housing from the engine and gear reduction assembly as follows before removing the bushings. Remove interfering covers, then detach the engine stop switch wire and the throttle cable. Remove the two locating screws (5) and pull the housing (1) from the gear reduction case (6).

BEARING HEAD

The bearing head of BT models is shown in Fig. RM26. Periodic maintenance is not required. To disassemble remove the trimmer head of blade. Insert a suitable tool in the hole in bearing head to prevent shaft rotation. If so equipped, unscrew nut (8). Remove cover (7) and snap ring (4). Attach puller (part No. 3238-99100 or equivalent) to arbor (2) and pull arbor and bearing assembly (3) from the housing (1). Clean and inspect components, then install new parts as necessary. Reverse disassembly procedure to assemble unit.

BRUSH CUTTER GEAR HEAD

BC Models. The gear head should be lubricated after each 30 hours of operation. Remove trimmer or blade and use a hand operated grease gun to inject lithium base grease into the grease fitting (F—Fig. RM27). Old grease should be expelled from around the arbor (9—Fig. RM28) and damage could result if the trimmer head or blade is not removed before filling.

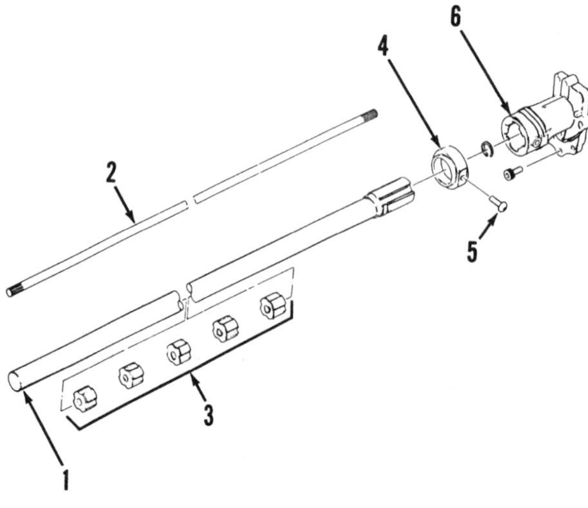

Fig. RM25—Exploded view of the solid drive shaft used on Reciprocator (SGC models). Loosen locator screws (5) to separate the drive shaft housing (1) from the gear reduction case (6).

1. Drive shaft housing
2. Drive shaft
3. Bushings
4. Collar
5. Locating screw (2 used)
6. Gear reduction case

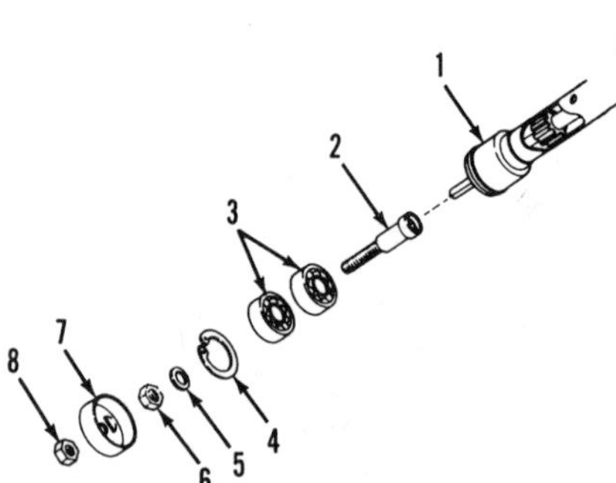

Fig. RM26—Exploded view of the bearing head typical of BT models.

1. Drive shaft housing
2. Arbor
3. Bearings
4. Snap ring
5. Washer
6. Nut
7. Cover
8. Nut

Illustrations courtesy Redmax

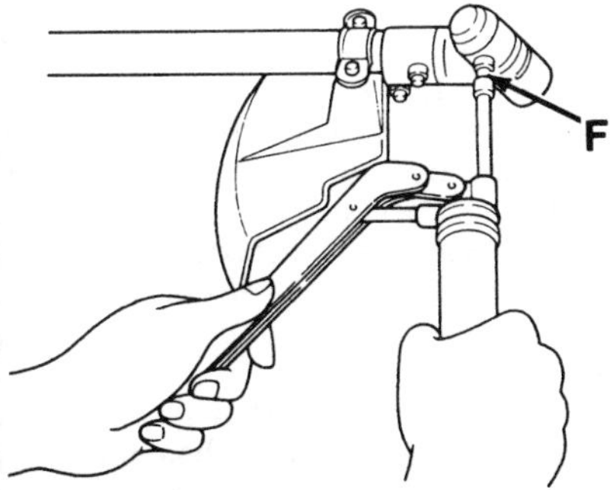

Fig. RM27—The gear housing should be 2/3 filled with lithium based multipurpose grease. Refer to text.

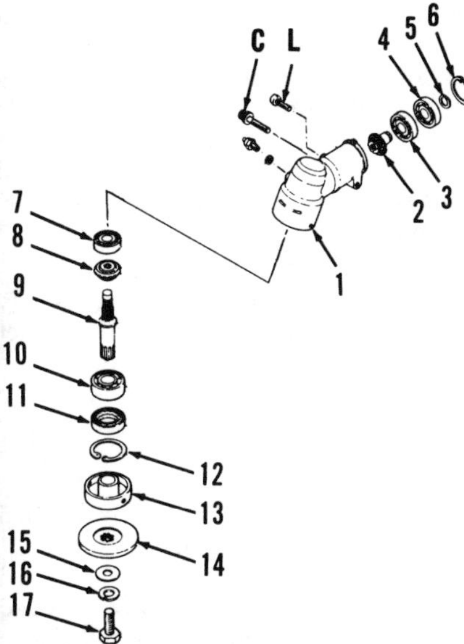

Fig. RM28—Exploded view typical of the gear head used on BC models. Snap ring (12) may be located on either side of seal (11), depending upon application.

1. Housing
2. Pinion gear
3. Bearing
4. Bearing
5. Snap ring
6. Snap ring
7. Bearing
8. Gear
9. Arbor
10. Bearing
11. Seal
12. Snap ring
13. Cover
14. Washer
15. Washer
16. Lockwasher
17. Screw (L. H.)

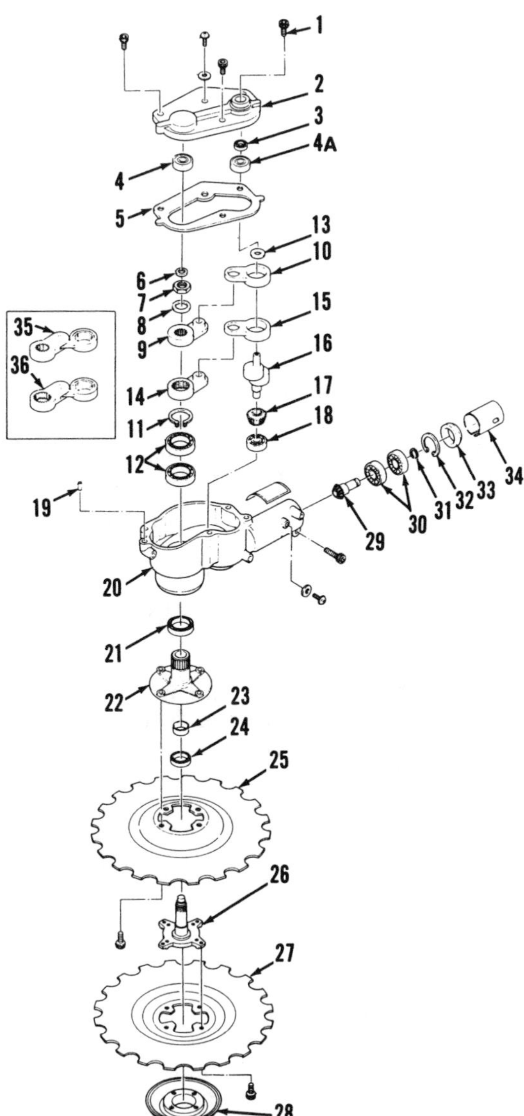

Fig. RM29—Exploded view of the Reciprocator gear head used on SGC models. Links (35 and 36) are typical of the type used in early production models.

1. Hex screw
2. Cover
3. Seal
4. Bearing
4A. Bearing
5. Gasket
6. Spacer
7. Nut
8. Shim
9. Splined link end
10. Link end
11. Snap ring
12. Bearings
13. Washer
14. Splined link end
15. Link end
16. Crankshaft
17. Bevel gear
18. Bearing
19. Dowel pin
20. Housing
21. Seal
22. Outer shaft
23. Bushing
24. Seal
25. Upper blade
26. Inner shaft
27. Lower blade
28. Stabilizer
29. Pinion gear
30. Bearings
31. Snap ring
32. Snap ring
33. Packing
34. Sleeve
35. Link assy.
36. Link assy.

To disassemble the gear head, first insert a suitable tool in cover (13—Fig. RM28)) to hold the shaft, then remove the trimmer or blade. Remove the locating screw (L) and clamp screw (C), then pull the gear head from the end of the drive shaft housing. Remove snap ring (6), then use a suitable puller to pull the pinion (2) and bearings (3 and 4) from the housing. It may be necessary to heat the housing and spread the clamping gap to facilitate removal.

CAUTION: Excessive force while spreading the clamp or excessive heat can damage the housing. Use caution when using either method.

Remove snap ring (5—Fig. RM28) and press bearings from pinion if renewal is required. Snap ring (12) may be either above or below seal (11) depending upon the model. Remove seal (11) and snap ring (12), then withdraw arbor (9), gear (8) and bearings (7 and 10). If stuck in housing, bearing (7) can usually be dislodged by heating the housing and bumping the housing against a wood block.

Inspect and clean components. Reassemble by reversing disassembly procedure. Tighten the locating screw (L) to 2.0-2.9 N·m (18-26 in.-lb.) and clamp screw (C) to 5.0-5.8 N·m (44-78 in.-lb.) torque.

RECIPROCATOR GEAR HEAD

SGC Models are equipped with two blades that reciprocate back and forth to shear material trapped between the blades. The mechanism shown in Fig. RM29 transmits the rotating motion of the drive shaft to the oscillating motion of the blades.

LUBRICATION. The gear head should be lubricated after every 50 hours of use or at least once each year. Remove screw (S—Fig. RM30) and

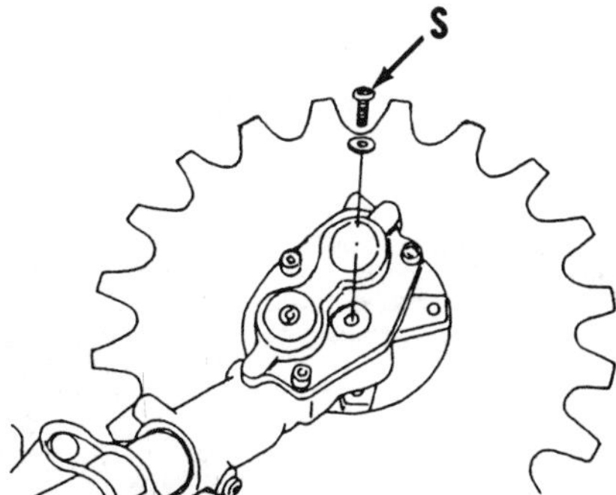

Fig. RM30—Grease can be injected into the gear head of Reciprocator models through hole for plug (S).

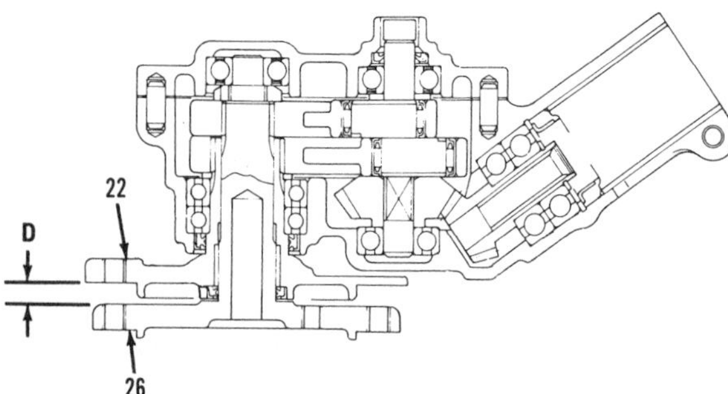

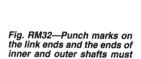

Fig. RM31—Refer to text for measuring and setting blade base gap (D) between shaft flanges (22 and 26).

check the level of grease inside the housing. The housing should contain 40 grams (1.4 oz.) of multipurpose lithium base grease. With this amount, the housing will be approximately 2/3 filled. Grease can be added through opening for screw (S) if necessary, but do not overfill.

BLADE BASE GAP. To cut properly, the proper distance between the blades must be maintained. Blade position is determined by distance (D—Fig. RM31) between flanges of the blade drive shafts.

To measure the gap, first remove the stabilizer (28—Fig. RM29), then unbolt and remove both blades (25 and 27). Measure the distance (D—Fig. RM31) and compare the measured distance with the desired clearance of 11.8-12.0 mm (0.465-0.472 in.). If distance is incorrect, check at several locations to determine if the flange is bent and check to be sure the shafts are tight in the bearings. The distance should not change during normal operation unless parts are worn or damaged. Gap is changed by varying the thickness of shim (8—Fig. RM29). Refer to the OVERHAUL paragraph for replacing damaged parts or for changing the thickness of shim.

OVERHAUL. Before removing, lock the blades from turning using a soft wood block and loosen hex screw (1—Fig. RM29). It may be necessary to use heat to soften Loctite applied to the threads when assembling. Unbolt and remove the blades (25 and 27). Measure and record distance (D—Fig. RM31) as described in the BLADE BASE GAP paragraph. Remove locating screw (L—Fig. RM24) and clamp screw (C), then pull the gear head from the end of the drive shaft housing.

NOTE: It may be necessary to spread the slot and heat the clamp area if the drive shaft housing is stuck in the gear head.

Remove screws attaching top cover (2), then remove the cover, being careful not to lose spacers (6 and 13). The spacers may stick to bearings (4 and 4A) that may remain in the cover. Use a suitable puller to remove bearing (4) if it remains on the shaft. Remove nut (7).

If this procedure is being followed to adjust the blade base gap, remove or add shims (8) as required to set distance (D—Fig. RM31) to the dimension listed in the BLADE BASE GAP paragraph. Shims are available in thickness of 0.1, 0.2 and 0.3 mm. Tighten the inner shaft nut (7—Fig. RM29) to 29.4-39.2 N•m (22-29 in.-lb.) and the cover screws to 4.9-6.8 N•m (44-71 in.-lb.) torque. If loosened, apply thread lock to the hex screw (1).

Remove shim (8), then tap the inner shaft (26) down to withdraw it from the gearcase. Remove links, crankshaft (16) and bevel gear (17). Remove snap ring (11), then tap outer shaft down to remove it. Remove bearings (12) and oil seal (21). It may be necessary to heat the housing and use a suitable puller to remove bearings from bores. Use a hook shaped tool to pull sleeve (34) and packing (33) from the housing. Remove snap ring (32) and pull pinion gear (29) and bearings (30) from the housing. Remove snap ring (31) and press bearings from the shaft. Pull bearing (18) from housing bore.

Inspect components for wear and damage. Note that two types of links have been used. Early links are equipped with roller bearings and link ends are inseparable. The roller bearing for early link is not available separately. Later links (9, 10, 14 and 15) do not have bearing in crankshaft end, but can be separated. The crankshafts used with early and later links are not interchangeable.

Reverse disassembly procedure to assemble, noting the following. Apply grease to links, bearings and contact surfaces of the crankshaft (16). Punch marks on the links must be visible and must align with similar punch marks on ends of shafts (22 and 26) as shown in Fig. RM32. Install seal (3—Fig. RM29) with **open** side and lip toward top (outside) of cover. Install seals (21 and 24) with open side and lip toward inside. Install packing (33) so tapered side is toward sleeve (34). Install sleeve (34) so hole in side aligns with the locating screw hole in housing.

Before installing the top cover (2), measure distance (D—Fig. RM31) as described in BLADE BASE GAP paragraph. If necessary, remove nut (7—Fig. RM29) and change the thickness of shims (8). Tighten inner shaft nut (7) to 29.4-39.2 N•m (22-29 ft.-lb.) and cover screws to 4.9-6.8 N•m (44-61 in.-lb.) torque. Apply Loctite to threads of hex screw (1) before installing.

After the unit is filled with grease and assembled, turn the shafts with hex screw (H—Fig. RM16) and check for smooth operation. If screw/shafts are difficult to turn, tap the housing to seat the gears and bearings, then recheck. If it is still binding, remove the cover and disassemble as necessary to find and correct the problem.

Fig. RM32—Punch marks on the link ends and the ends of inner and outer shafts must be aligned as shown.

GEAR REDUCTION

SGC Reciprocator models are equipped with a gear reduction unit (Fig. RM33) that is attached to the front of the engine. The clutch drum (26) transmits power to the gear unit from the engine. The bore of the output

Illustrations courtesy Redmax

Fig. RM33—Exploded view of the gear reduction unit used on SGC Reciprocator models. Idler gear (15) is the type used on early production units.

1. Drive shaft housing
2. Collar
3. Snap ring
4. Locating screws (2 used)
5. Front case
6. Dowel pin
7. Thrust washer
8. Shaft
9. Idler gear
11. Sealed bearing
12. Bearing
13. Outer gear
14. Bushing
15. Idler gear
16. Bushing
17. Cover
18. Gasket
20. Snap ring
21. Input gear
22. Snap ring
23. Bearing
24. Sealed bearing
25. Rear case
26. Clutch drum

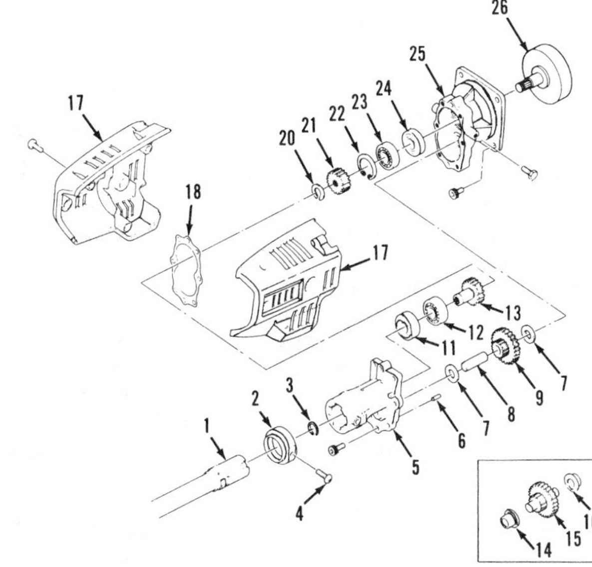

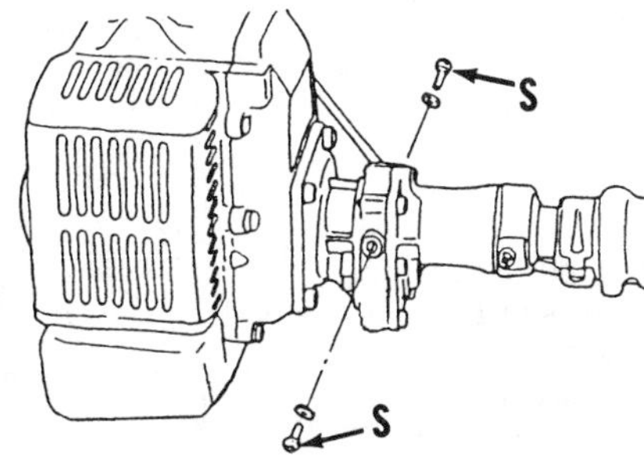

Fig. RM34—The reduction case is lubricated by removing screws (S) and injecting lithium based multipurpose grease into one side until grease is expelled from the other side.

gear (13) accepts the upper end of the drive shaft.

LUBRICATION. After every 50 hours of operation, check and fill the gear reduction unit with grease if necessary. Remove the cover (17—Fig. RM33) and screws (S—Fig. RM34) from both sides of the housing. Inject multipurpose lithium based grease in one side until grease is expelled from the hole on the other side.

OVERHAUL. Remove the covers (17—Fig. RM33), then detach the throttle cable and engine stop switch wires. Loosen both locating screws (4) and collar (2). Separate the drive shaft housing (1) from the front case (5) of the gear reduction housing. If the drive shaft is stuck in the case, it may be necessary to heat the case. Remove the four screws attaching the rear case (25) to the engine. Remove the attaching screws and separate the front case (5) from the rear case (25). Remove snap ring (3) and press the output gear (13) from the bearings (11 and 12) if the gear or bearings require replacement. Remove snap ring (20) and gear (21), then press the clutch drum (26) from bearings (23 and 24). If bearings (23 and 24) require replacement, remove snap ring (22) and press bearings from the housing.

Two different idler gear assemblies have been used. Components (14, 15 and 16) were used on early models; idler gear components (7, 8 and 9) are typical of later models. Cases (5 and 25) are machined to accept only one type of idler assembly and components cannot be interchanged.

Reverse disassembly procedure to assemble the gear reduction unit. Note that outer bearings (11 and 24) are sealed. On early type idler assembly, fill bushings (14 and 16) and the cavities in the cases with multipurpose lithium based grease before installing the idler gear. Tighten the screws attaching the front case (5) in a crossing pattern to 6.9 N•m (61 in.-lb.) torque. Attach the gear reduction unit to the engine and install the drive shaft and housing. After the unit is installed, remove both screws (S—Fig. RM34) and inject grease into one side until grease is expelled from the other side.

THROTTLE FREE PLAY

Throttle cable may have adjuster installed as shown in Fig. RM35, Fig. RM36 or Fig. RM37. Refer to the appropriate following paragraph for adjustment procedure.

On some models it is necessary to remove the air cleaner or cover for access to the carburetor. On some models it is necessary to pull the protective sleeve (S—Fig. RM36) back. On all models, loosen locknut (N—Fig. RM35, Fig. RM36 or Fig. RM37) and turn adjuster (A) so cable free play (P) at carburetor is 1-2 mm (0.04-0.08 in.). Tighten the locknut when free play is correct.

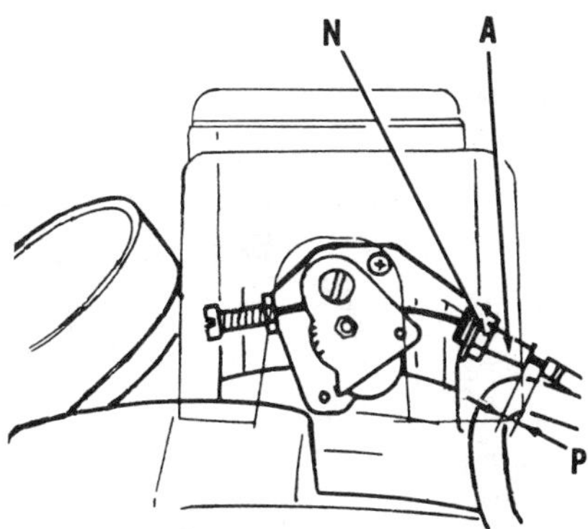

Fig. RM35—One type of throttle cable adjustment used on some BC220, BC260, BT220 and SGC220 models.

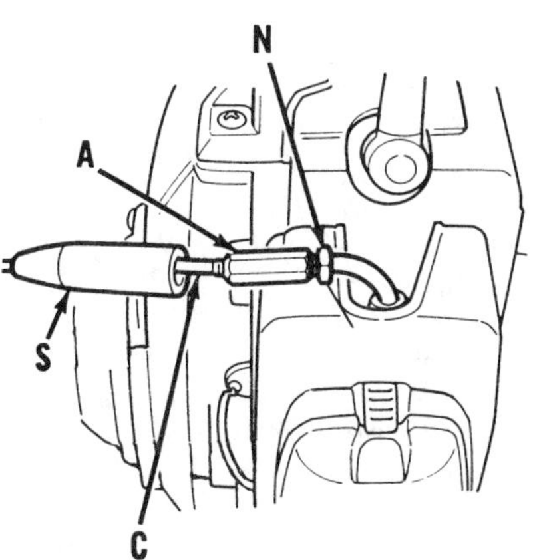

Fig. RM36—One type of throttle cable adjustment used on some BC340 models.

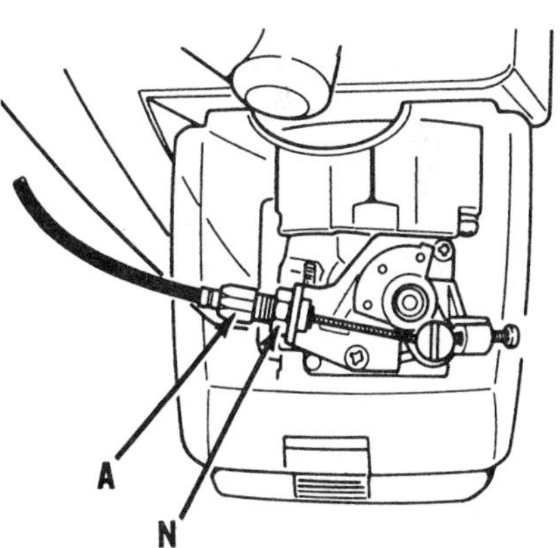

Fig. RM37—One type of throttle cable adjustment used on some BC440 models.

REWIND STARTER

Refer to Fig. RM38 for exploded views of rewind starters used. To disassemble the starter, unbolt and remove the housing (1) from the engine. Remove handle from the rope and allow the rope to wind into the starter. Re-

Illustrations courtesy Redmax

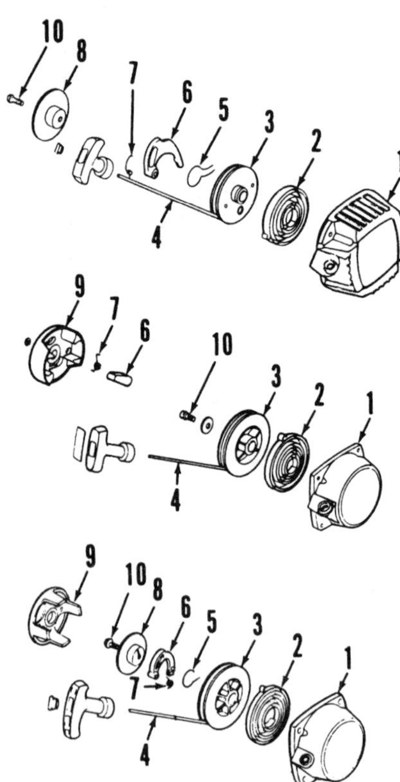

Fig. RM38—Exploded view of the rewind starter assemblies typical of those used.

1. Housing
2. Rewind spring
3. Pulley
4. Rope
5. Friction spring
6. Ratchet
7. Spring
8. Friction plate
9. Starter plate
10. Screw

move center screw (10) and remove the rope pulley (3). Wear appropriate eyewear and gloves to protect against injury when removing the spring (2). The spring may unwind from the housing uncontrollably. If necessary to remove the pulley plate (9), use a suitable puller.

The rope must be the correct diameter and length for the starter to operate properly. If the rope is too large in diameter or too long, the rope may bind when trying to wind onto the pulley. When installing new rope, measure the length and diameter of the old rope, then install new rope that matches the original. Refer to the following for some starter rope applications.

Model	Diameter mm (in.)	Length mm (in.)
BC220 & BT220	3 (0.118)	880 (34.6)
BC260DL, BC340DL & BC342DL	3.5 (0.138)	1000 (39)
BC430DWM, BC440DWM	3.5 (0.138)	1000 (39)
BC442DWM	4.0 (0.15)	1065 (42)
HT230	3.5 (0.138)	830 (32.7)

To assemble the starter, apply a small amount of light grease to the starter housing post, spring and the back of the pulley. Install the rewind spring so it is wound counterclockwise from the outer end. Attach the rope to the pulley (3), making sure the knot is fully nested in the pocket. Pull the rope tight and wind the rope counterclockwise as viewed from the pawl (engine) side. Install the pulley/rope and rotate slightly until the spring hooks into the pulley and the pulley drops into the housing. Guide the end of the rope through the housing and attach the handle.

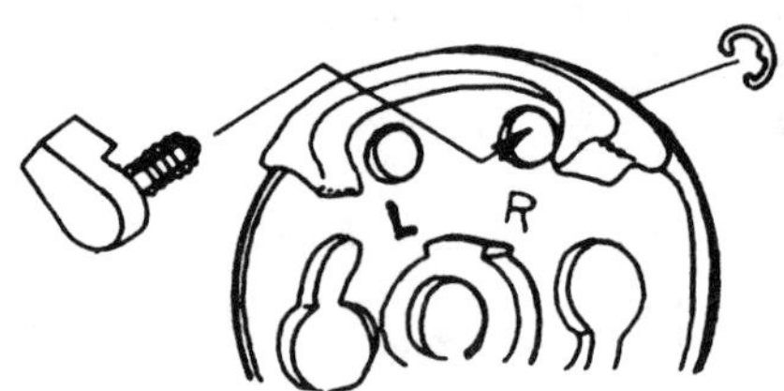

Fig. RM39—Starter ratchet must be installed in pulley hole marked "R".

When assembling or if the starter rope does not fully rewind, preload the recoil spring as follows. Hold the pulley to keep it from turning, then pull a small loop in the rope between the pulley and the inside of the housing (1). Hold the rope and wind the pulley to preload the pulley, allow the pulley to rewind the rope, then check operation. The spring should wind the rope around the pulley fully, but the spring must not bind when the rope is fully extended. It should be possible to rotate the pulley at least 1/4 turn when the rope is pulled out completely. Complete the assembly by reversing the disassembly procedure when the spring preload is correctly set.

On models with starter ratchet (6), the ratchet should be installed in the hole marked "R" as shown in Fig. RM39. The spring (7—Fig. RM38) should hold the ratchet out lightly.

Illustrations courtesy Redmax

REDMAX

GASOLINE POWERED BLOWERS

Model	Engine Manufacturer	Engine Model	Displacement
EB430, EBA430	Komatsu	...	41.5 cc
EB440, EBA440	Komatsu	...	41.5 cc
HB260	Komatsu	...	25.4 cc

ENGINE INFORMATION

The models included in this section are powered by a Komatsu engine. Refer to appropriate Komatsu engine service section for service procedures and specifications.

FUEL MIXTURE

Manufacturer recommends mixing regular or unleaded gasoline with a high-quality, two-stroke engine oil designed for air-cooled engines. Recommended fuel:oil ratio is 32:1 when using RedMax oil or any other high-quality two-stroke oil. Manufacturer does not recommend using gasohol or other fuels that include alcohol.

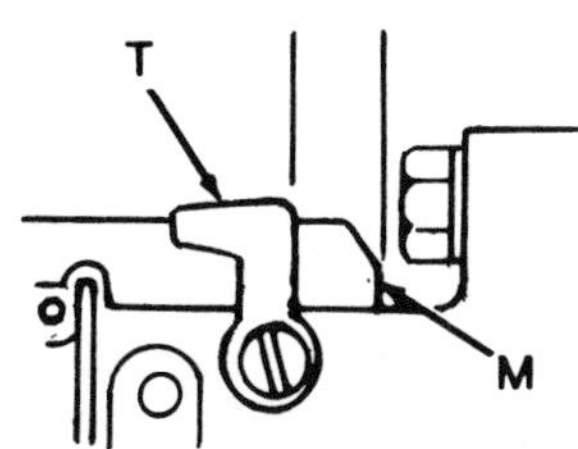

Fig. RM101—At wide-open throttle, the carburetor throttle stop arm (T) should be parallel with carburetor mounting face (M).

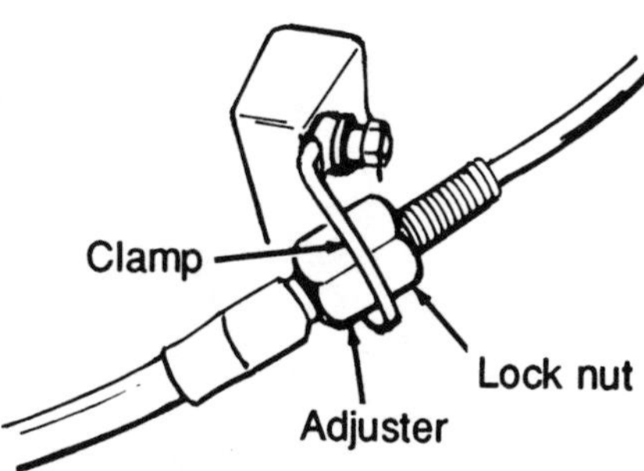

Fig. RM102—Turn cable adjusting nuts so carburetor throttle stop arm (T—Fig. RM101) is parallel with carburetor mounting face (M).

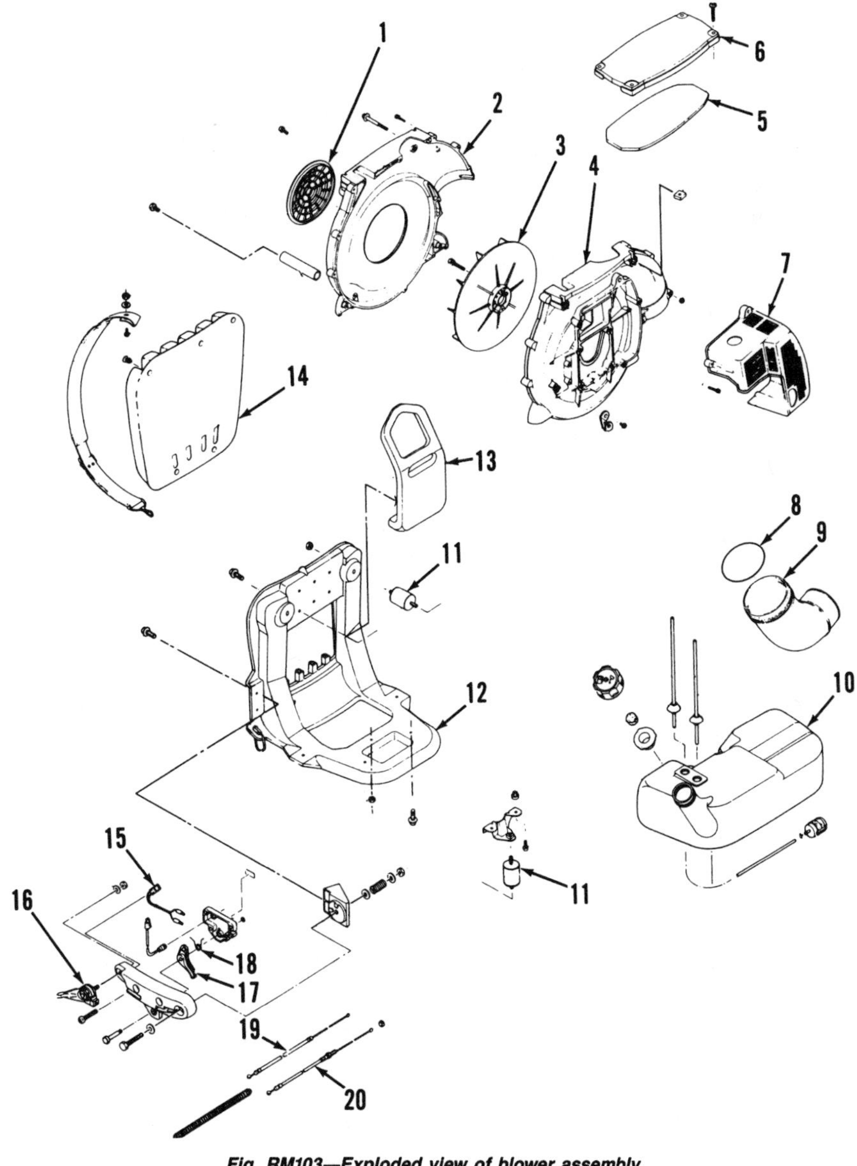

Fig. RM103—Exploded view of blower assembly.

1. Intake guard
2. Blower housing half
3. Blower fan
4. Blower housing half
5. Gasket
6. Cover
7. Engine cover
8. "O" ring
9. Elbow
10. Fuel tank
11. Rubber mounts
12. Backpack frame
13. Hanger bracket
14. Backpad
15. Stop switch
16. Throttle lever
17. Lever
18. Spring
19. Choke cable
20. Throttle cable

THROTTLE CABLE

Models EB430, EB440, EBA430 And EBA440

The throttle cable should be adjusted so the throttle trigger and carburetor throttle plate are synchronized. With throttle trigger in wide-open position, the throttle stop arm (T—Fig. RM101) should be parallel with the carburetor mounting face (M). To adjust, loosen locknut (RM102) at throttle cable end and reposition adjusting nut as necessary. Tighten nuts after adjustment.

Blower Fan

To remove engine from blower housing, remove fuel tank (10—Fig. RM103) and engine cover (7). Remove screw retaining crankcase to backpack frame (12). Remove backpad (14) and pry off intake guard (1). Remove screws attaching blower fan (3) to flywheel. Remove four engine mounting screws and remove engine from blower housing.

To remove blower fan (3), remove cover (6) from blower housing. Remove screws holding blower housing halves (2 and 4) together. Separate blower housing and remove fan.

Illustrations courtesy Redmax

ROBIN

GASOLINE POWERED STRING TRIMMERS

Model	Engine Manufacturer	Engine Model	Displacement
NB02, NB02-3A, NB02-3B, NB02T*	Fuji	EC02	22.2 cc
NB04	Fuji	EC04	37.7 cc
NB16, NB16F, NB16S, NB16T†	Fuji	EC01	15.4 cc
NB23, NB23F, NB23S, NB23T‡	Fuji	EC02	22.2 cc
NB26	Fuji	EC02	25.6 cc
NB30	Fuji	EC03	30.5 cc
NB50L	Fuji	EC05	51.7 cc
NB211, NB211C, NB211T§	Fuji	EC02	20.3 cc
NB231	Fuji	EC02	22.2 cc
NB351	Fuji	EC03	34.4 cc
NB411	Fuji	EC04	40.2 cc
NBF171	Fuji	EC01	15.4 cc
PT	Fuji	EC01	15.4 cc

*May be designated Series NB02 in text.
†May be designated Series NB16 in text.
‡May be designated Series NB23 in text.
§May be designated Series NB211 in text.

ENGINE INFORMATION

All models are equipped with Fuji two-stroke, air-cooled gasoline engines. Refer to Fuji engine section in this manual for engine service information.

FUEL MIXTURE

Manufacturer recommends mixing regular grade gasoline (unleaded gasoline is acceptable) and a high-quality oil designed for use in a two-stroke, air-cooled engine. Recommended fuel:oil ratio is 24:1. Do not use gasoline containing alcohol.

STRING TRIMMER

Models NB231, NBF171 And Series NB02, NB16, NB23, And NB211 With Semi-Automatic Head

These models may be equipped with the dual strand, semi-automatic trimmer head shown in Fig. RB10. To extend line with trimmer engine stopped, push in on spool button (7) while pulling on each line. Procedure may have to be repeated until desired line length is obtained. To extend line with trimmer engine running, operate trimmer at full rpm and tap button on the ground. Each time button is tapped on the ground, a measured amount of line will be advanced.

To install new trimmer line, hold drum firmly and turn spool in direction shown in Fig. RB11 to remove slack. Twist with a hard snap until plastic peg is between holes. Pull spool out of drum. Remove old line from spool. Spool will hold approximately 20 feet (6 m) of monofilament line. Insert one end of new line through hole on spool (Fig. RB12) and pull line through until line is the same length on both sides of hole. Wind both ends of line at the same time in direction indicated by arrow on spool. Wind tightly and evenly from side to side and do not twist line. Insert ends of line through line guide openings, align pegs on drum with slots in spool and push spool into drum. Hold drum firmly, twist spool suddenly in direction shown in Fig. RB13 until peg enters hole with a click and locks spool in position.

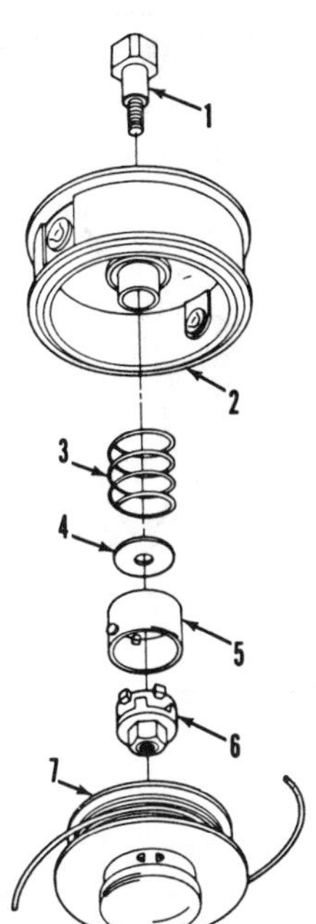

Fig. RB10—Exploded view of the dual strand, semi-automatic trimmer head used on Models NB231, NBF171 and Series NB02, NB16, NB23 and NB211.

1. Drive shaft adapter
2. Housing
3. Spring
4. Washer
5. Outer cam
6. Inner cam
7. Spool

Illustrations courtesy Robin

Models NB231, NBF171 And Series NB02, NB16, NB23, And NB211 With Low Profile Manual Head

These models may be equipped with the Low Profile manual trimmer head

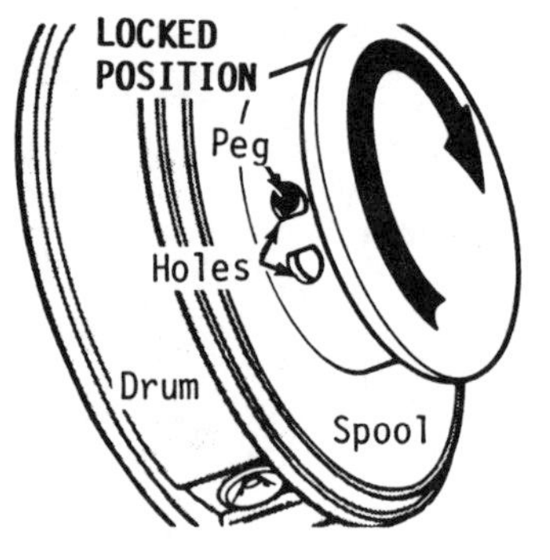

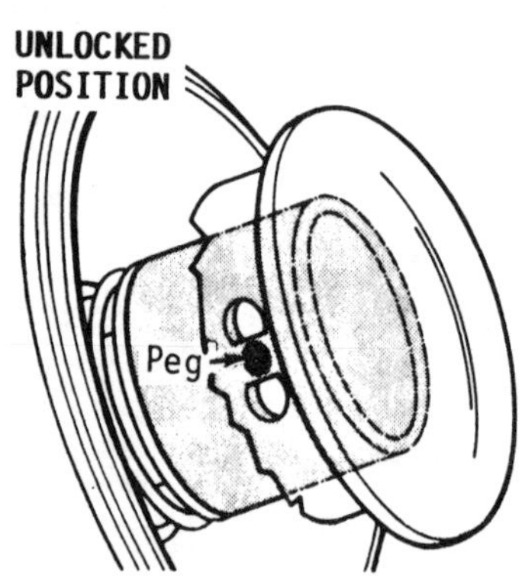

Fig. RB11—To remove spool, hold drum firmly and turn spool in direction shown to take up slack, then twist with a sudden snap until plastic peg is between holes as shown in lower view.

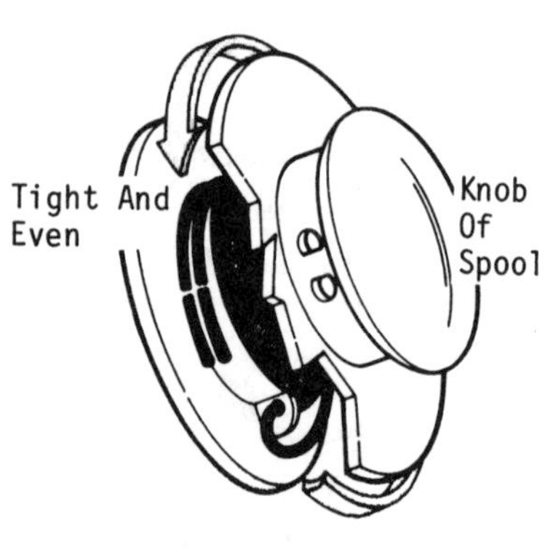

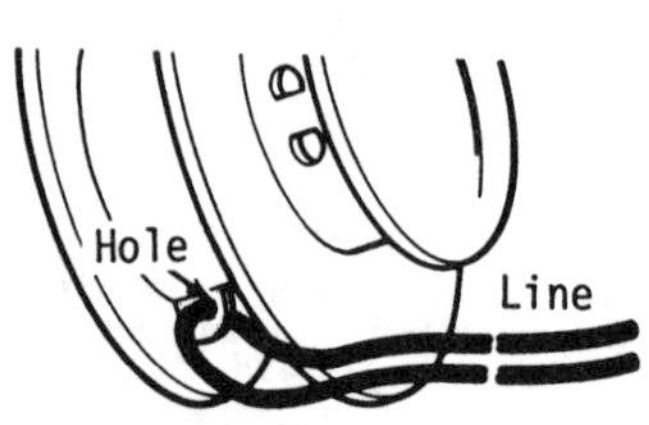

Fig. RB12—End of line must be inserted through hole on spool as shown in lower view. Wind line tightly in direction indicated by arrow on spool.

shown in Fig. RB14. To extend line, stop trimmer engine and wait until head rotation has stopped. Loosen knob (6) until spool (4) may be turned to advance line. Tighten knob when desired line length has been obtained.

To install new line, remove lock knob (6), spring (5) and spool (4). Remove any remaining old line. Wind new line in direction indicated by arrow on spool. Do not exceed spool diameter with line. Insert line ends through line guides (3) of housing (2) and install spool, spring and lock knob.

Models NB04, NB30 And NB50L

Models NB04, NB30 and NB50L may be equipped with the four strand, manual head shown in Fig. RB15. To extend line, loosen lock knob (8) and pull each of the four lines out until desired line length is obtained. Tighten lock knob (8).

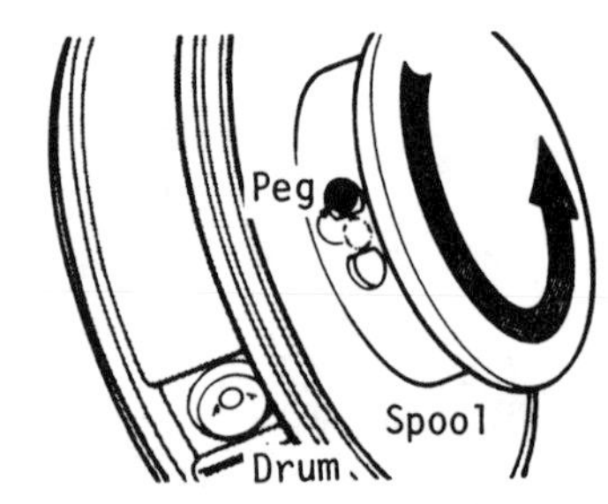

Fig. RB13—Hold drum firmly and twist suddenly to lock spool in position.

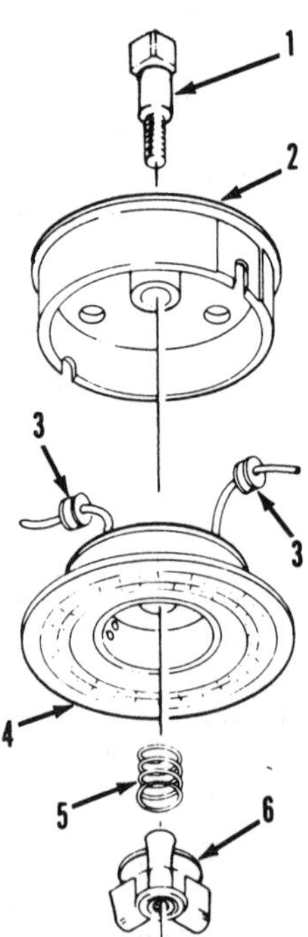

Fig. RB14—Exploded view of low profile manual trimmer head used on Models NB231, NBF171 and Series NB02, NB16, NB23 and NB211.

1. Drive shaft adapter
2. Housing
3. Line guides
4. Spool
5. Spring
6. Lock knob

To install new line, remove lock knob (8), cover (7), spools (5 and 3) and spring (4). Remove any remaining old line. Wind new line on spools in direction indicated by arrow on spool. Do not wrap line to greater diameter than diameter of spool. Insert line ends through line guides (6), then install spools, spring cover (7) and lock knob (8).

Models NB04, NB30 And NB50L

Models NB04, NB30 and NB50L may be equipped with a manual trimmer head (Fig. RB16) that is similar to Low Profile head (Fig. RB14). Refer to preceding paragraph for service information.

BLADE

Some models may be equipped with a blade. Refer to Fig. RB17 for a typical arrangement of parts. Note that some models use a lockwasher (7) and nut (8), while other models use two nuts.

To sharpen the four-cutting-edge blade, refer to Fig. RB18. Blade edge should have a length of 1.18-1.58 inch (30-40 mm). Do not grind the chamfered section of the blade root. Make certain the root of cutting blade remains chamfered to prevent breakage. Sharpen all teeth equally to maintain blade balance.

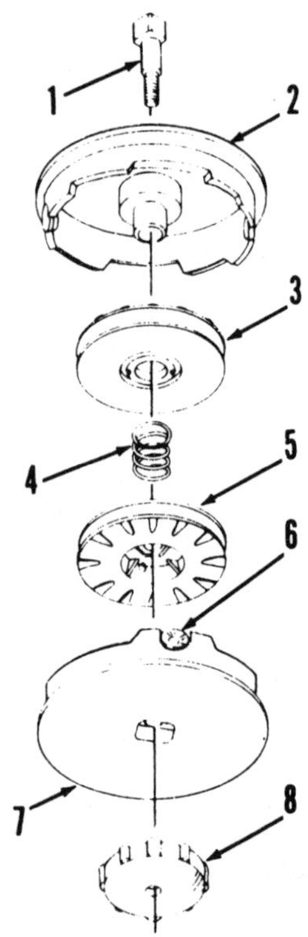

Fig. RB15—Exploded view of the four strand, manual trimmer head used on Models NB04, NB30 and NB50L.

1. Drive shaft adapter
2. Upper housing
3. Spool
4. Spring
5. Spool
6. Line guides
7. Lower housing
8. Lock knob

To sharpen the eight cutting edge blade, refer to Fig. RB19. Sharpened section must not be closer than 0.08 inch (2 mm) to the root. Root chamfer should have a 0.08 inch (2 mm) radius. Sharpen all teeth equally to maintain blade balance.

To sharpen the saw blade, refer to Fig. RB20. Maintain a 0.04-0.08 inch (1-2 mm) radius at the tooth root. Maintain a 0.08-0.09 inch (2-2.5 mm) tooth set. Sharpen all teeth equally to maintain blade balance.

DRIVE SHAFT

Series NB16 And NB23

Series NB16 and NB23 are equipped with a flexible drive shaft supported in a drive shaft housing tube (Fig. RB21). The drive shaft should be removed, cleaned and lubricated with lithium-base grease after every 30 hours of operation.

Model NB26 And Series NB02

These trimmers are equipped with a solid steel drive shaft (14—Fig. RB22) supported in renewable bushings (13) located in the drive shaft housing tube (12). Drive shaft requires no maintenance; however, if removed, the drive shaft should be lubricated with lithium-base grease before reinstalling. Drive shaft bushings (13) may be renewed. Mark locations of old bushings in drive shaft housing before removing so new bushings can be installed at the same locations.

Models NB04, NB30, NB351 And NB411

Models NB04, NB30, NB351 and NB411 are equipped with a solid steel drive shaft supported in renewable bushings located in drive shaft housing tube (Fig. RB23 or RB24). Drive shaft requires no maintenance; however, if removed, the drive shaft should be lubricated with lithium-base grease before reinstalling. Drive shaft bushings may be renewed. Mark locations of old bushings in drive shaft housing before removing so new bushings can be installed at the same locations. On some models, bushings may be held in position by pins through drive shaft housing and bushing.

Model NB231 And Series NB211

Model NB231 and Series NB211 trimmers are equipped with a solid steel drive shaft (8—Fig. RB25) supported in renewable bushings (7) located in drive shaft housing tube (6). Drive shaft requires no maintenance; however, if removed, the drive shaft should be lubricated with lithium-base grease before reinstalling. Drive shaft bushings (7) may be renewed. Mark locations of old bushings in drive shaft housing before removing so new bushings can be installed at the same locations.

BEARING HEAD

Model PT

The drive shaft rides in a bushing at drive end of drive shaft housing. Parts are not available and service is not possible.

Model NBF and Series NB16 And NB23

Series NB16 and NB23 trimmers are equipped with sealed bearings in the

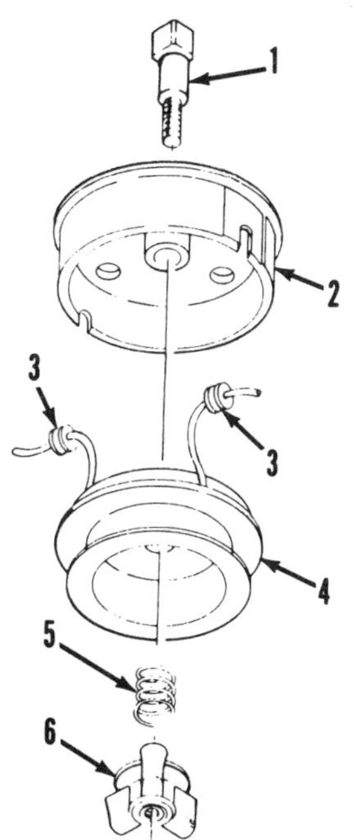

Fig. RB16—Exploded view of the dual strand, manual trimmer head used on NB04, NB30 and NB50L.

1. Drive shaft adapter
2. Housing
3. Line guides
4. Spool
5. Spring
6. Lock knob

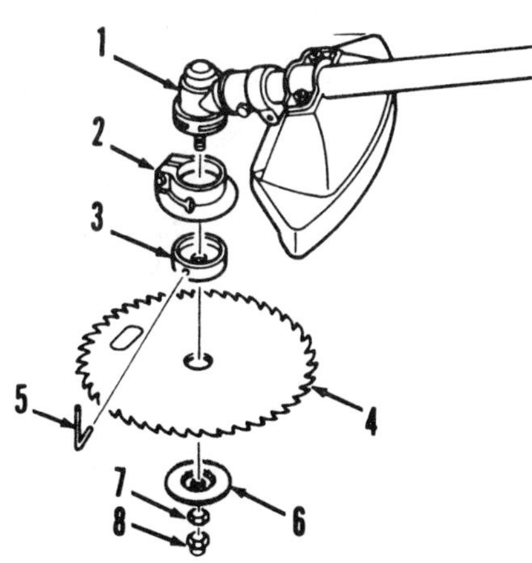

Fig. RB17—Exploded view of typical blade assembly.

1. Gear head
2. Grass guard
3. Cup washer
4. Blade
5. Tool
6. Adapter plate
7. Washer
8. Nut

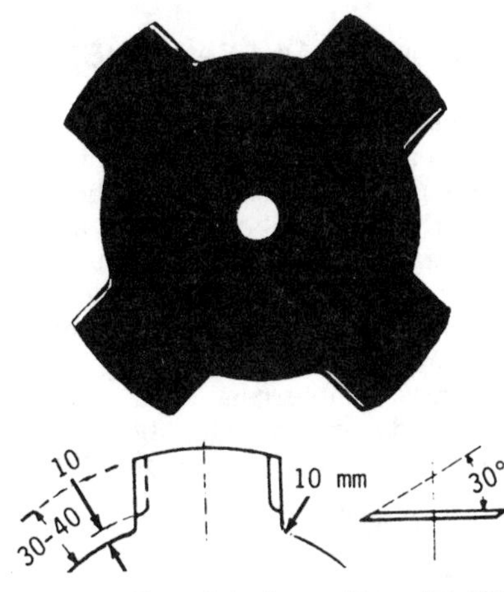

Fig. RB18—View of the four-cutting-edge blade available for some models. Sharpen to dimensions shown and outlined in text.

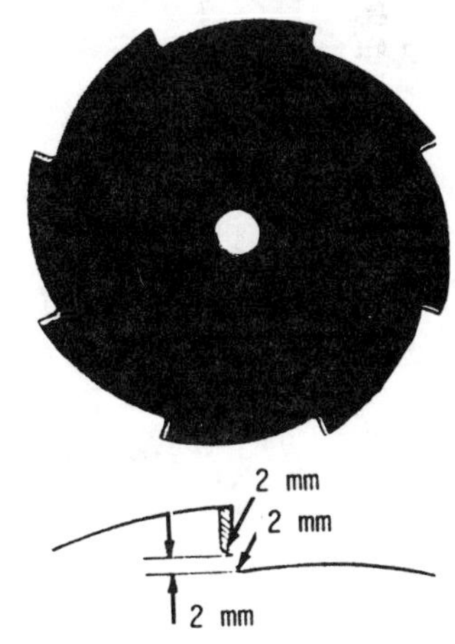

Fig. RB19—View of the eight-cutting-edge blade available for some models. Sharpen to dimensions shown and outlined in text.

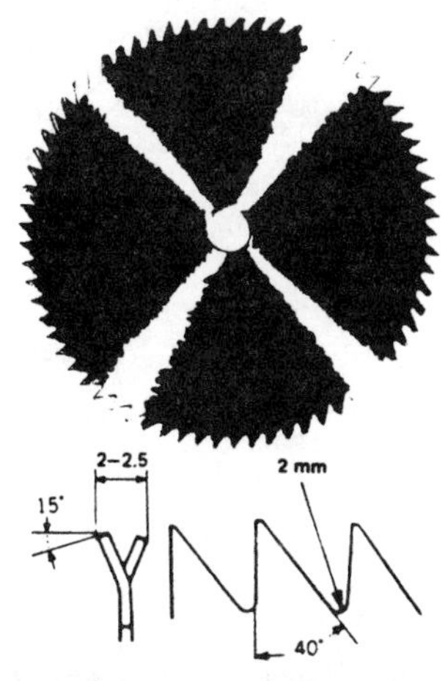

Fig. RB20—View of saw blade available for some models. Sharpen to dimensions shown and outlined in text.

bearing head (Fig. RB26). Bearing head requires no maintenance. To renew bearings (3 and 4), remove trimmer head or blade assembly and separate bearing head from drive shaft housing tube. Remove snap ring (5) and use a suitable puller to remove arbor (2) and bearing assembly. Press bearings from arbor.

Model NB26 And Series NB02

These models are equipped with the gear head shown in Fig. RB27. Remove check plug (8) after every 30 hours of operation and make certain that gear head housing is 2/3 full of lithium-base grease. Do not force grease into housing with a pressure-type gun as seal may be damaged.

To disassemble gear head, separate gear head from drive shaft housing. Remove blade, adapters (16 and 17) and spacer (13). Pry out seal (1) and remove snap ring (2). Insert a screwdriver or other suitable wedge into gear head housing clamp splits and carefully expand housing. Remove input shaft (6) and bearings as an assembly. Remove snap ring (5) and press bearings (3 and 4) off input shaft. Remove snap ring (14) and use a suitable puller to remove arbor (11) and bearing assembly. If bearing (9) stays in housing, heat housing to 140° F (60° C) and tap housing on a wood block to dislodge bearing.

Models NB04, NB30, NB50L, NB351 And NB411

Models NB04, NB30, NB50L, NB351 and NB411 are equipped with the gear head shown in Fig. RB28. Remove check plug (8) after every 30 hours of operation and make certain that gear head housing is 2/3 full of lithium-base grease. Do not force grease into housing with a pressure-type gun as seal may be damaged.

To disassemble gear head, separate gear head from drive shaft housing. Remove trimmer head or blade assembly. Remove snap ring (2). Insert a screwdriver or other suitable wedge into gear head housing clamp split and carefully expand housing. Remove input shaft (4) and bearing assembly. Remove snap ring (1) and press bearing (3) from input shaft. Remove snap ring (13) and use a suitable puller to remove arbor shaft (9) and bearing assembly. If bearing (6) stays in housing, heat housing to 140° F (60° C) and tap housing on a wood block to dislodge bearing. Remove bearing (11) and gear (7) from arbor.

Model NB231 And Series NB211

These models are equipped with the gear head shown in Fig. RB29. Remove check plug (6) after every 30 hours of operation and make certain that gear head housing is 2/3 full of lithium-base grease. Do not force grease into housing with a pressure-type gun as seal may be damaged.

To disassemble gear head, separate gear head from drive shaft housing. Remove trimmer head or blade assembly. Remove snap ring (1). Extract input shaft (4) and bearing assembly. Remove snap ring (2) and press bearing (3) off input shaft. Detach snap ring (10) and pry out seal (11). Remove arbor (8) and bearing assembly. Remove bearing (9) from shaft.

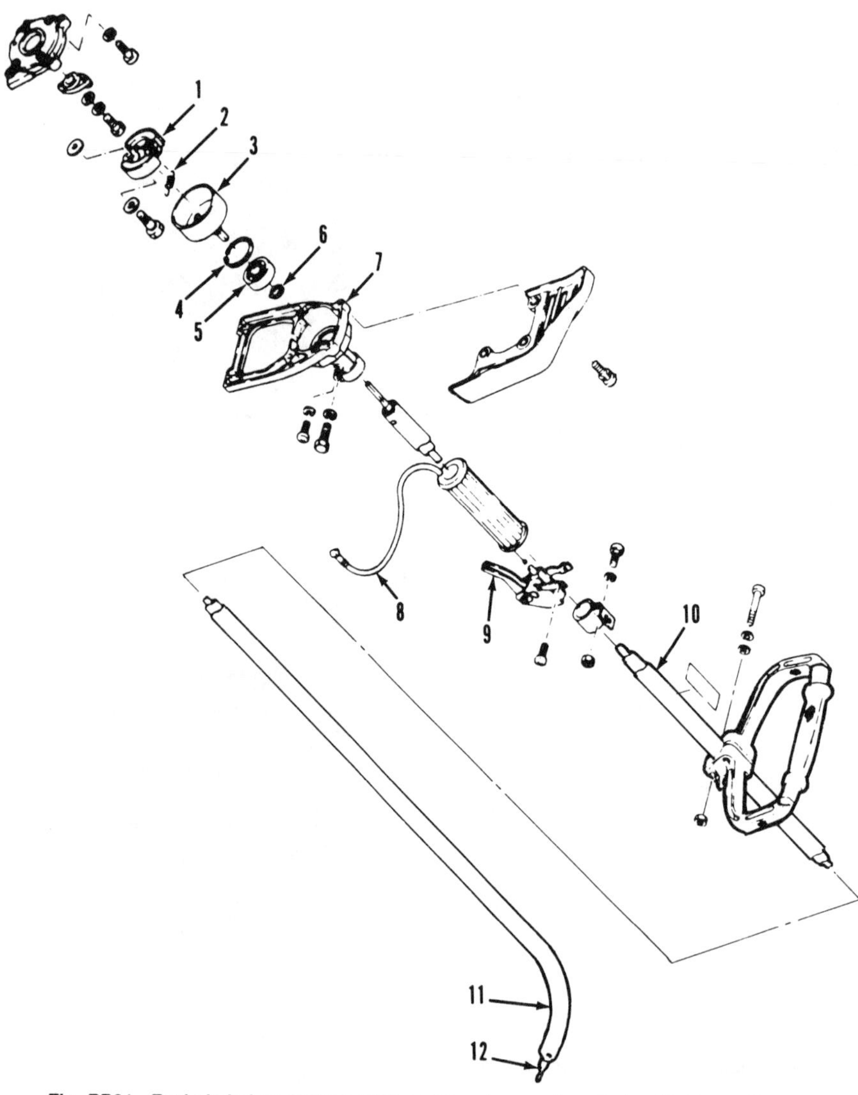

Fig. RB21—Exploded view of drive shaft and housing used on Series NB16 and NB23.

1. Clutch assy.
2. Clutch spring
3. Clutch drum
4. Snap ring
5. Bearing
6. Snap ring
7. Housing
8. Throttle cable
9. Throttle trigger
10. Drive shaft housing
11. Drive shaft housing
12. Drive shaft

Illustrations courtesy Robin

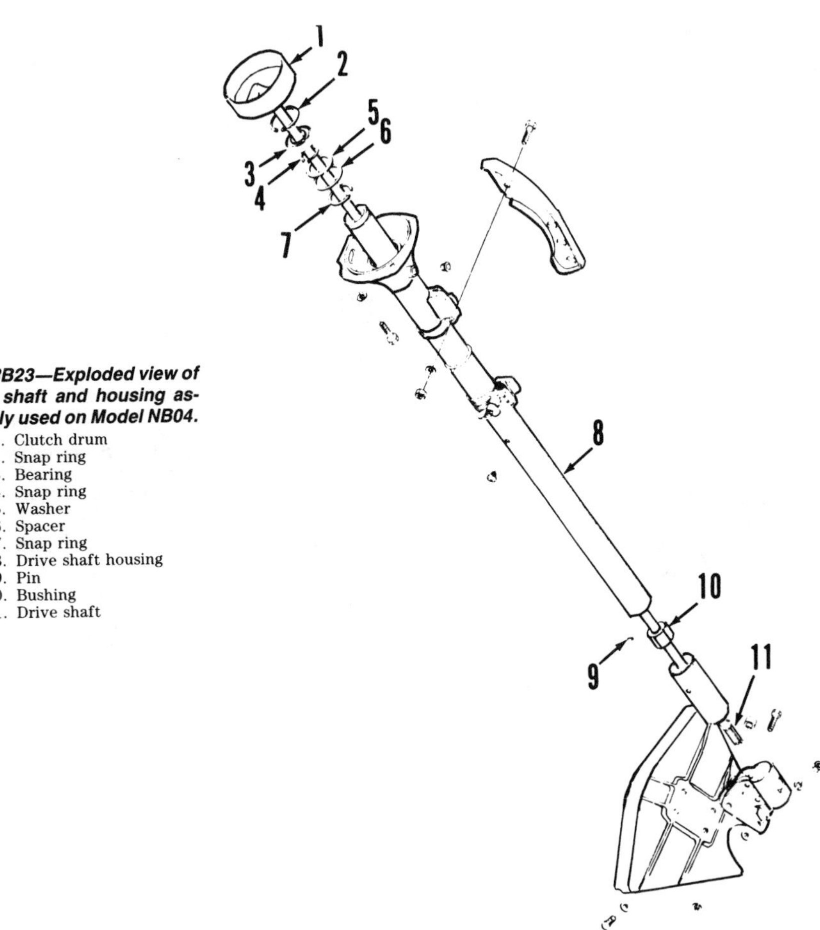

Fig. RB23—Exploded view of drive shaft and housing assembly used on Model NB04.

1. Clutch drum
2. Snap ring
3. Bearing
4. Snap ring
5. Washer
6. Spacer
7. Snap ring
8. Drive shaft housing
9. Pin
10. Bushing
11. Drive shaft

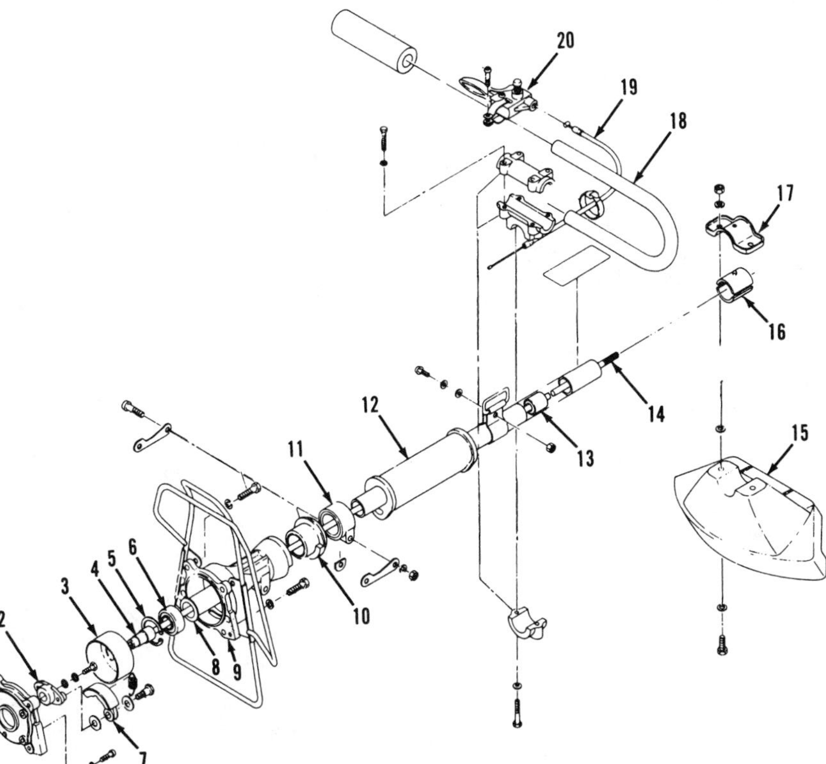

Fig. RB22—Exploded view of drive shaft and housing used on Series NB02. Model NB26 is similar.

1. Locating plate
2. Clutch hub
3. Clutch drum
4. Adapter
5. Snap ring
6. Bearing
7. Clutch shoe
8. Drive tube
9. Drive housing
10. Insulator
11. Clamp
12. Hand grip
13. Bushing
14. Drive shaft
15. Safety cover
16. Spacer
17. Clamp
18. Handle
19. Throttle cable
20. Throttle trigger

Illustrations courtesy Robin

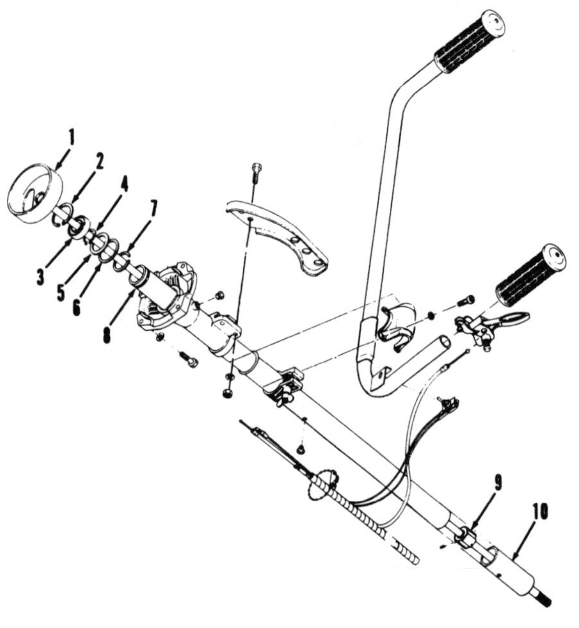

Fig. RB24—Exploded view of drive shaft and housing assembly used on Model NB30. Models NB351 and NB411 are similar.

1. Clutch drum
2. Snap ring
3. Bearing
4. Snap ring
5. Washer
6. Spacer
7. Snap ring
8. Drive shaft housing
9. Bushing
10. Drive shaft housing

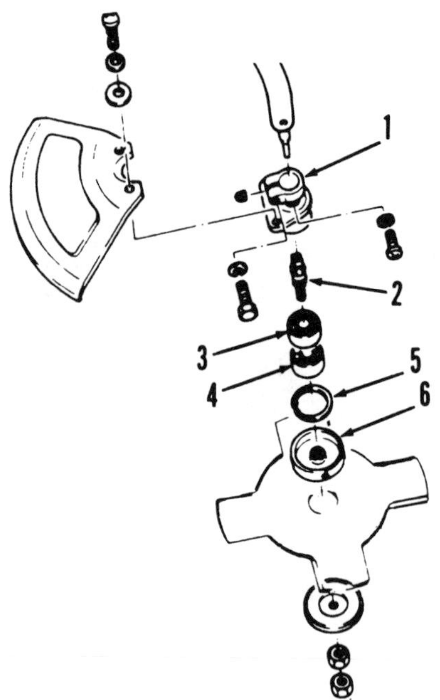

Fig. RB26—Exploded view of bearing head assembly used on Model NBF171 and Series NB16 and NB23.

1. Housing
2. Arbor
3. Bearing
4. Bearing
5. Snap ring
6. Cup washer

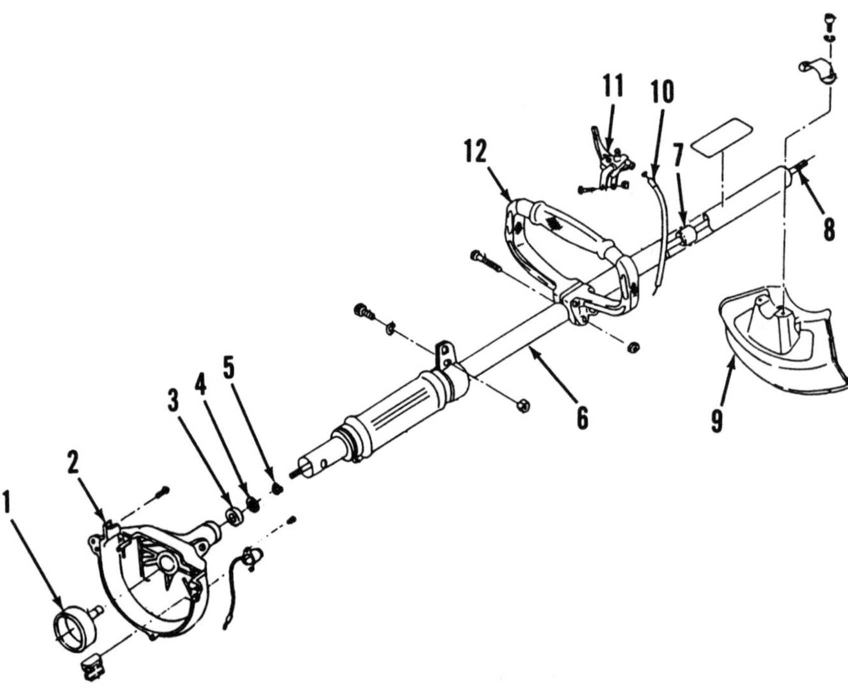

Fig. RB25—Exploded view of drive shaft and housing assembly used on Series NB211 and Model NB231.

1. Clutch drum
2. Clutch housing
3. Bearing
4. Snap ring
5. Snap ring
6. Drive shaft housing
7. Bushing
8. Drive shaft
9. Safety shield
10. Throttle cable
11. Throttle trigger
12. Handle

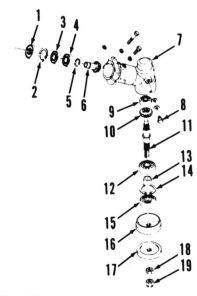

Fig. RB27—Exploded view of gear head used on Model NB26 and Series NB02.

1. Seal
2. Snap ring
3. Bearing
4. Bearing
5. Snap ring
6. Input shaft
7. Housing
8. Check plug
9. Bearing
10. Gear
11. Arbor
12. Bearing
13. Spacer
14. Snap ring
15. Seal
16. Cup washer
17. Adapter plate
18. Nut
19. Jam nut

Illustrations courtesy Robin

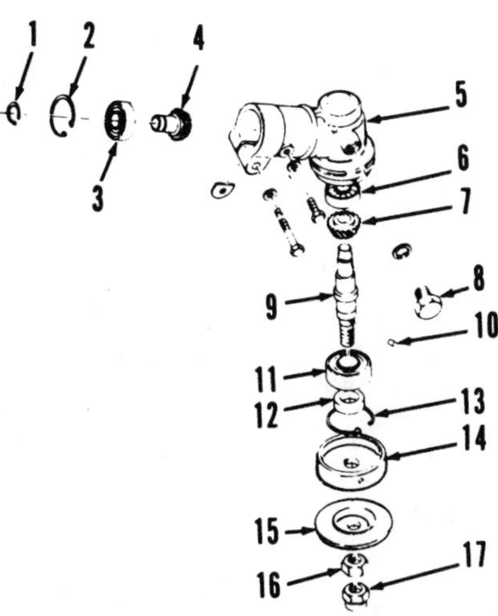

Fig. RB28—Exploded view of gear head used on Models NB04, NB30, NB50L, NB351 and NB411.

1. Snap ring
2. Snap ring
3. Bearing
4. Input shaft
5. Housing
6. Bearing
7. Gear
8. Check plug
9. Arbor
10. Pin
11. Bearing
12. Spacer
13. Snap ring
14. Cup washer
15. Adapter plate
16. Nut
17. Jam nut

Fig. RB29—Exploded view of gear head used on Model NB231 and Series NB211.

1. Snap ring
2. Snap ring
3. Bearing
4. Input shaft
5. Gear head
6. Check plug
7. Safety guard
8. Arbor & gear
9. Bearing
10. Snap ring
11. Seal
12. Cup washer
13. Adapter plate
14. Lockwasher
15. Nut

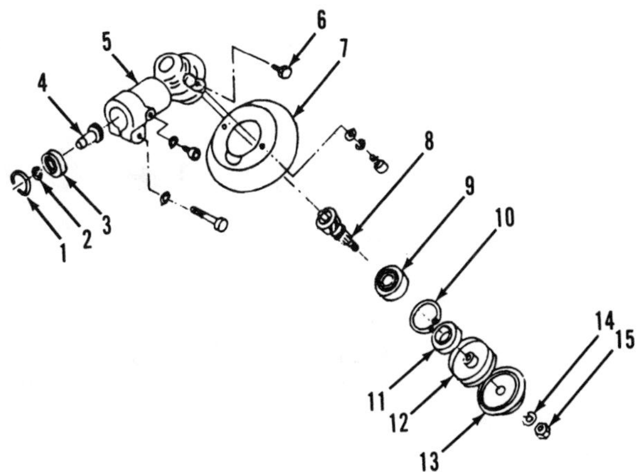

Illustrations courtesy Robin

ROBIN

GASOLINE POWERED BLOWERS

Model	Engine Manufacturer	Engine Model	Displacement
FL21	Fuji	EC02	20.3 cc
FL40, FL40A	Fuji	EC04	37.7 cc
FL411	Fuji	EC04	37.7 cc
NF40	Fuji	EC04	37.7 cc

ENGINE INFORMATION

The models included in this section are powered by a Fuji engine. Refer to appropriate Fuji engine service section for service procedures and specifications.

FUEL MIXTURE

Manufacturer recommends mixing regular grade gasoline (unleaded gasoline is acceptable) and a good quality oil designed for use in a two-stroke, air-cooled engine. Recommended fuel:oil ratio is 24:1. Do not use gasoline containing alcohol.

IMPELLER

The blower impeller (5—Fig. RB51) is attached to the flywheel. The impeller and flywheel on some models are marked to insure proper balance. To remove impeller, first separate engine and blower housing from back pack frame (13) if so equipped. Remove blower tube elbow (16). Remove screws securing blower case halves (3 and 7) and separate case halves. Remove impeller mounting screws or nut and withdraw impeller (5) from flywheel.

When installing impeller, align marks (if used) on impeller and flywheel as shown in Fig. RB52. Tighten fan nut or screws to following torque:

FL21 . . . . 3.9-4.9 N·m (35-43 in.-lbs.)
FL40, FL40A & NF40 . . . 27.4-37.2 N·m (20-27 ft.-lbs.)
FL411 . . . . 8.8-9.8 N·m (78-87 in.-lbs.)

ENGINE

To remove engine from blower, first remove impeller as outlined above. Remove engine cover. Disconnect throttle cable, fuel line and stop switch wire from engine. Remove engine mounting screws and separate engine from blower case.

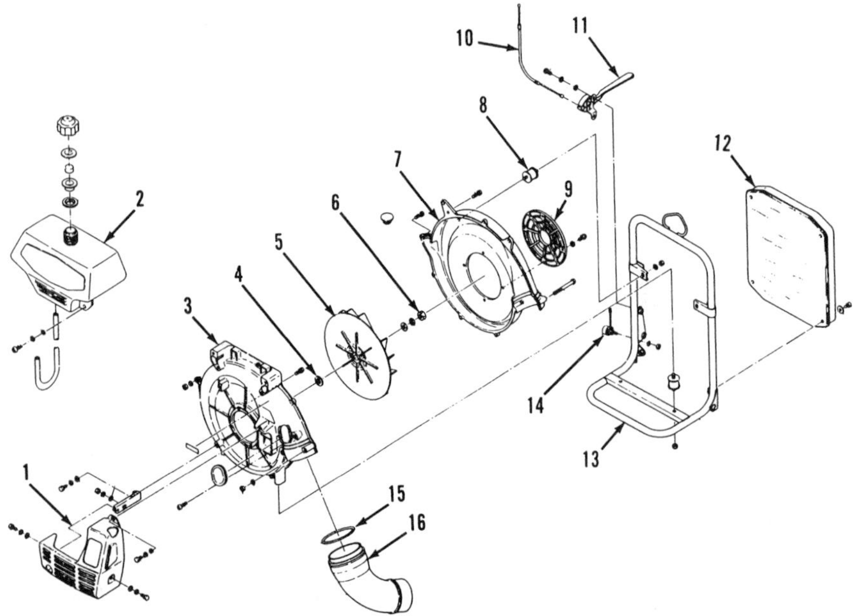

Fig. RB51—Exploded view of blower unit typical of all models.

1. Engine cover
2. Fuel tank
3. Blower case (rear)
4. Spacer
5. Impeller
6. Nut
7. Blower case (front)
8. Vibration insulator
9. Cover
10. Throttle cable
11. Throttle trigger
12. Shoulder pad
13. Back-pack frame
14. Stop switch
15. "O" ring
16. Blower pipe

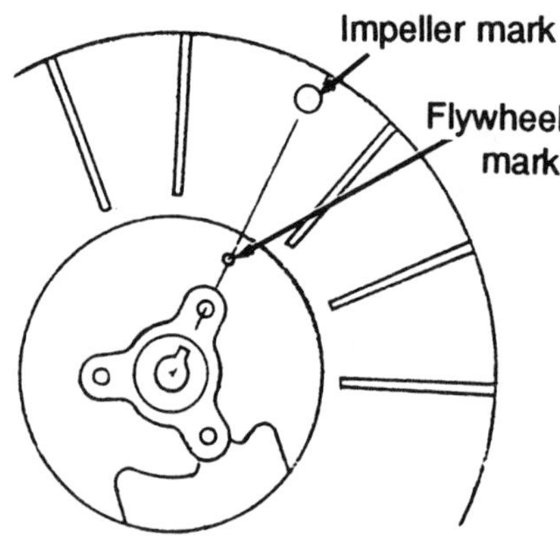

Fig. RB52—Align marks (if used) on fan and flywheel during assembly.

Illustrations courtesy Robin

RYAN

GASOLINE POWERED STRING TRIMMERS

Model	Engine Manufacturer	Engine Model	Displacement
261	PPP	99E	31.0 cc
264	IDC	...	31.0 cc
265	PPP	99E	31.0 cc
275	PPP	99E	31.0 cc
284	IDC	...	31.0 cc
285	PPP	99E	31.0 cc

ENGINE INFORMATION

The models in this section are equipped with an Inertia Dynamics Corporation (IDC) or Piston Powered Products (PPP) engine. Refer to appropriate engine service section for engine service information.

FUEL MIXTURE

Manufacturer recommends mixing regular gasoline, leaded or unleaded, with a high-quality two-stroke engine oil. Recommended fuel:oil ratio is 32:1 when using IDC Two-Cycle Engine Oil. When using any other two-stroke oil, mix 6 oz. (0.177 mL) of oil with 1 gal. (3.8 L) of gasoline, regardless of recommended ratio on oil container. Gasohol or other alcohol blended fuels are not approved by manufacturer.

STRING TRIMMER

Models 261, 264, 265 And 275

These models are equipped with a single line, semi-automatic trimmer head (Fig. RN10). To extend line with engine stopped, push in on bump button (20) and pull on line until desired length is obtained. To extend line with engine running, operate trimmer engine at full rpm and tap bump button (20) on the ground. Line will automatically advance a measured amount.

To renew trimmer line, hold drum (15) and unscrew bump button (20). Remove spool (19). Clean inner surface of drum and spool. Check indexing teeth on spool and drum for wear. Insert one end of a 25-ft. (7.6 m) length of 0.080 in. (2 mm) diameter monofilament line into one of the holes in spool from the inside out, then back through the second hole to the inside. Wind line in direction indicated by arrow on spool until all but about 3 inches (76.2 mm) of line is wrapped, then clip line temporarily in one of the line lock slots (LS) on spool. Insert line end through line guide (16) in drum and install spool and bump button. Pull line to release from line lock slot on spool after assembly is complete.

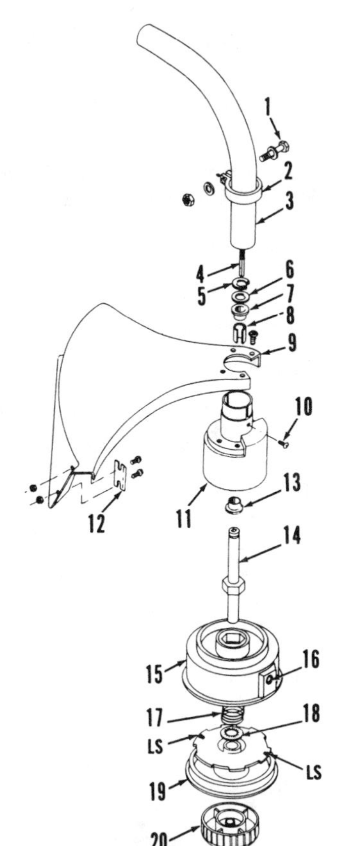

Fig. RN10—Exploded view of single strand, semi-automatic trimmer head used on Models 261, 264, 265 and 275.

1. Bolt
2. Clamp
3. Drive shaft housing
4. Drive shaft
5. Retaining ring
6. Washer
7. Bushing
8. Bushing
9. Shield
10. Locating screw
11. Bushing housing
12. Line length trimmer
13. Bushing
14. Shaft
15. Drum
16. Line guide
17. Spring
18. Retainer
19. Spool
20. Bump button

LS. Line slot

Models 274, 284 And 285

These models are equipped with a dual strand, semi-automatic trimmer head (Fig. RN11). To extend line with engine off, push bump button (8) in and pull lines out. Procedure may have to be repeated until desired line length has been obtained. To extend line with engine running, operate trimmer engine at full operating rpm and tap bump button on the ground. Each time bump button

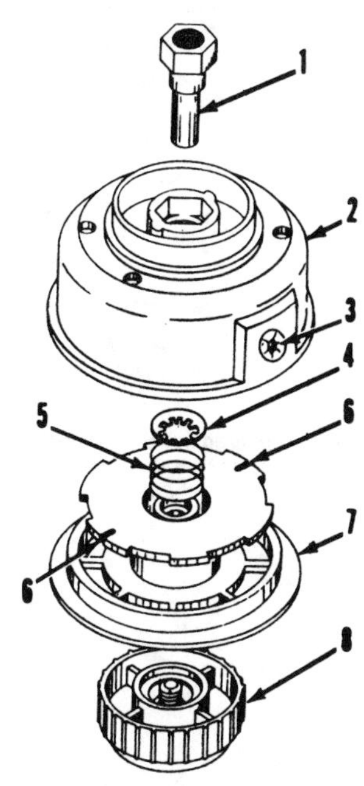

Fig. RN11—Exploded view of dual strand, semi-automatic trimmer head used on Models 284 and 285.

1. Adapter
2. Drum
3. Line guide
4. Retainer
5. Spring
6. Line shot
7. Spool
8. Bump button

Illustrations courtesy Ryobi Outdoor Products

is tapped on the ground, approximately 1 inch (25 mm) of new line will be advanced.

To renew line, hold drum (2) and unscrew bump button (8). Remove spool (7) and remove any remaining old line. Clean spool and inner surface of drum. Check indexing teeth in drum and on spool. Loop a 25-ft. (7.6 m) length of 0.080 in. (2 mm) diameter monofilament line into two equal lengths. Insert the two line ends into the two holes in spool from the bottom and pull line out until loop is against spool. Wind both strands of line around spool in direction indicated by arrow on spool. Wind in tight even layers. Clip lines into line slots (6). Insert line ends through line guides (3) in drum and install spool and bump button. Pull line ends to free from line slots.

BLADE

Models 284 And 285

Models 284 and 285 may be equipped with a four-edge cutting blade (Fig. RN12). To install blade, refer to Fig. RN12 for assembly sequence. Tighten nut (11) to 225-250 in.-lbs. (26-28 N·m).

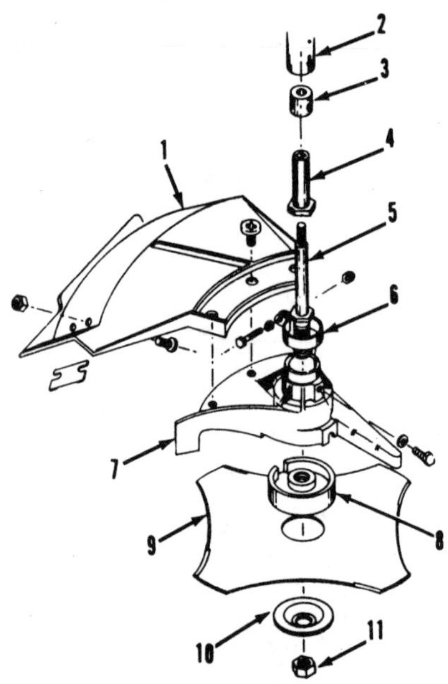

Fig. RN12—Exploded view of weed, grass and light brush blade assembly used on Models 284 and 285.

1. Shield
2. Drive shaft housing
3. Retainer & bushing
4. Drive shaft adapter
5. Head drive shaft
6. Clamp assy.
7. Bearing housing assy.
8. Blade adapter
9. Blade
10. Lower blade adapter
11. Nut

DRIVE SHAFT

All Models

All models are equipped with a flexible drive shaft enclosed in the drive shaft housing. The drive shaft has squared ends that engage adapters at each end. The drive shaft should be removed for maintenance after every 10 hours of operation. Remove and clean drive shaft, then inspect shaft for damage. Coat with a high-quality, high-temperature wheel bearing grease and install drive shaft. Make certain ends of shaft are properly located in upper and lower drive adapters.

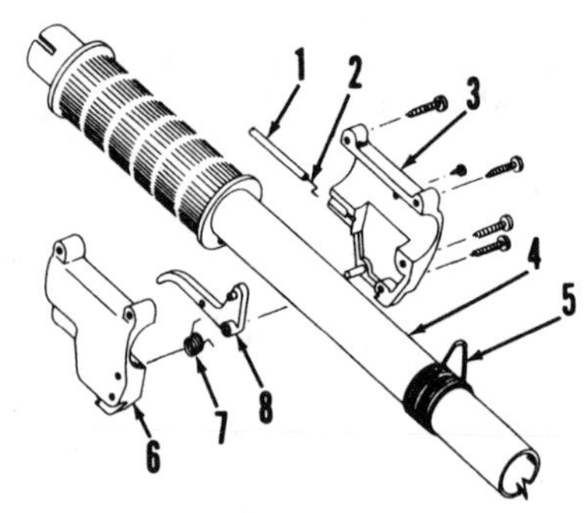

Fig. RN13—Exploded view of throttle trigger and cable assembly used on all models.

1. Throttle cable housing
2. Inner throttle cable
3. Throttle trigger housing
4. Drive shaft housing
5. Strap bracket
6. Throttle trigger housing
7. Spring
8. Throttle trigger

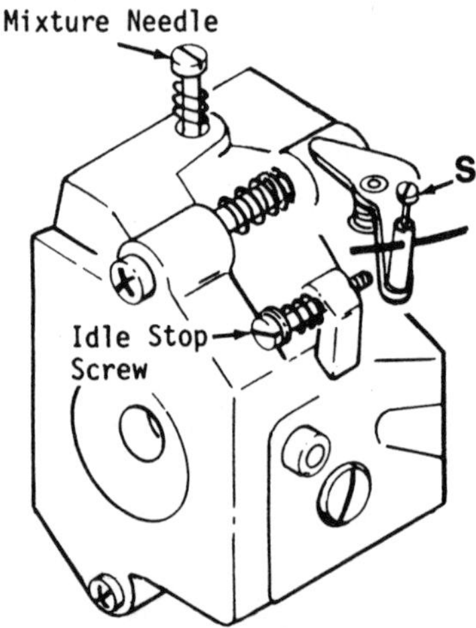

Fig. RN14—Loosen screw (S) and move throttle cable and housing to provide correct throttle trigger free play. Refer to text.

BEARING HOUSING

Models 261, 264, 265 And 275

Refer to Fig. RN10 for an exploded view of the bearing housing used on Models 261, 264, 265 and 275. Bushings are not available separately, only with housing (11).

Models 284 And 285

The bearing housing (7—Fig. RN12) on Models 284 and 285 is equipped with a sealed bearing and must be serviced as a unit assembly.

THROTTLE TRIGGER AND CABLE

All Models

The throttle trigger assembly is attached to the drive shaft housing (Fig. RN13) on all models. The throttle cable inner wire (2) should be lubricated after every 20 hours of operation. Apply SAE 30 oil to each end of wire. The throttle cable should be adjusted to provide 0.02-0.04 inch (0.5-1.0 mm) throttle trigger movement before the carburetor throttle lever begins to move. Adjust by loosening set screw (S—Fig. RN14) and moving cable housing and inner wire to provide specified free play. Tighten set screw (S)

RYAN

GASOLINE POWERED BLOWERS

Model	Engine Manufacturer	Engine Model	Displacement
200	IDC	...	31.0 cc
300BV	IDC	...	31.0 cc

ENGINE INFORMATION

The models in this section are equipped with an Inertia Dynamics Corporation (IDC) engine. Refer to IDC engine service section for engine service information.

FUEL MIXTURE

Manufacturer recommends mixing regular gasoline, leaded or unleaded, with a high-quality, two-stroke engine oil. Recommended fuel:oil ratio is 32:1 when using IDC Two-Cycle Engine Oil. When using any other two-stroke oil, mix 6 oz. (0.177 mL) of oil with 1 gal. (3.8 L) of gasoline, regardless of recommended ratio on oil container. Gasohol or other alcohol blended fuels are not approved by manufacturer.

BLOWER ASSEMBLY

Model 200

Refer to Fig. RN50 for exploded view of blower assembly. To remove blower impeller (4), remove mounting screws from starter housing (1) and blower housing (3). Separate blower housing halves (3 and 6). Remove mounting screws from blower impeller (4) and separate impeller from flywheel.

To separate engine from blower housing, remove impeller as outlined above. Remove engine cover (10). Disconnect fuel line, throttle cable and ignition wires from engine. Remove engine mounting screws and withdraw engine from blower housing half (6).

Model 300BV

Refer to Fig. RN51 for exploded view of blower assembly. To remove blower impeller (8), remove blower tube (12). Remove screws attaching blower lower housing (10) to upper housing (7) and separate housing. Remove impeller mounting screw and separate impeller (8) from flywheel.

To separate engine from blower housing, remove impeller as outlined above. Remove screws securing engine covers (1 and 4). Separate covers and disconnect throttle cable, fuel line and ignition wires from engine. Remove engine mounting screws and withdraw engine from blower upper housing (7).

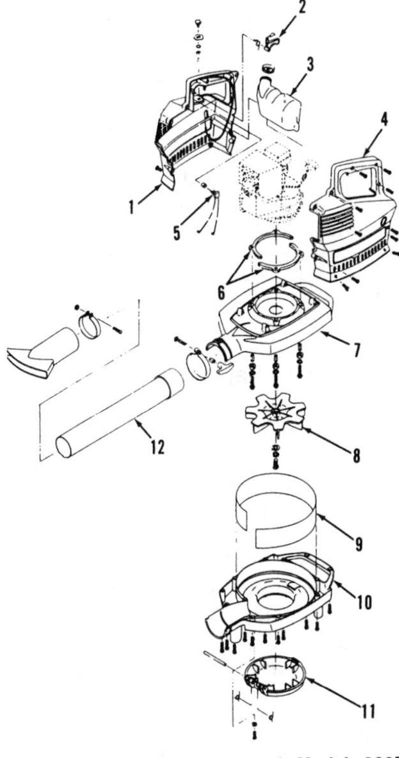

Fig. RN51—Exploded view of Model 300BV blower/vac.

1. Engine cover
2. Throttle trigger
3. Fuel tank
4. Engine cover
5. Stop switch
6. Gasket
7. Blower upper housing
8. Impeller
9. Shield
10. Blower lower housing
11. Intake cover
12. Blower tube

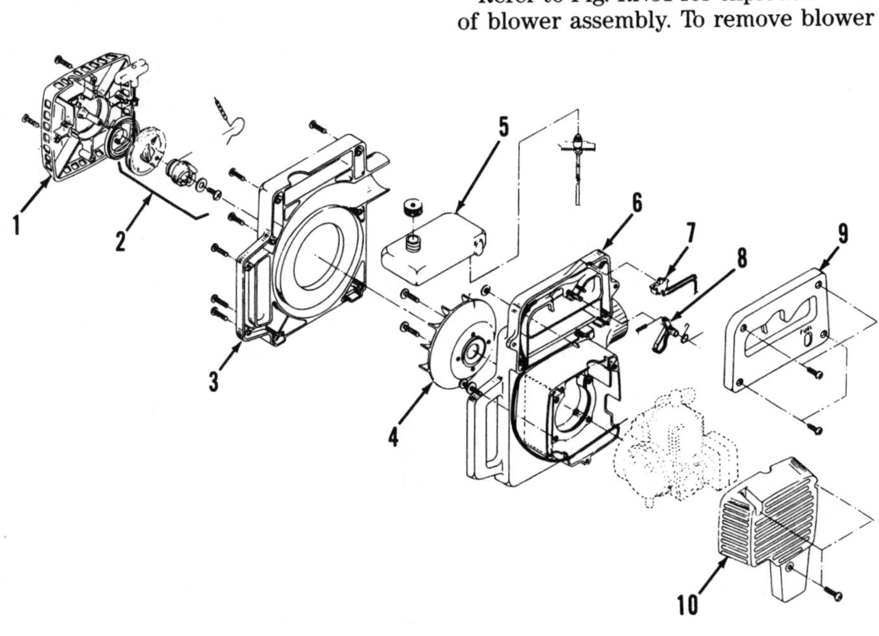

Fig. RN50—Exploded view of Model 200 blower.

1. Starter housing
2. Recoil starter assy.
3. Blower housing half
4. Impeller
5. Fuel tank
6. Blower housing half
7. Stop switch
8. Throttle trigger
9. Handle
10. Engine cover

Illustrations courtesy Roybi Outdoor Products

RYOBI

GASOLINE POWERED TRIMMERS

Models	Engine Make	Engine Model	Displacement
700r, 705r, 710r, 720r, 725r, 740r, 750r	IDC	A31	31.0 cc
760r, 765r, 767r, 770r, 775r, 780r, 790r	IDC	A31	31.0 cc
865r & 885r	IDC	A28	28.5 cc
920r, 960r, 970r, 975r, 990r 4 cycle	IDC	AC-1	26.2 cc

ENGINE INFORMATION

The models in this section are equipped with an IDC engine. Four-stroke (cycle) engines are used on all 920r, 960r, 970r, 975r and 990r models. Other 700 and 800 series models are equipped with two-stroke engines. Refer to the appropriate IDC Engine Service section of this manual for service to the engines used on these models.

FUEL AND LUBRICATION

The two-stroke engine used on 700 and 800 series is lubricated by mixing oil with the fuel, but the four-stroke engine used in 900 series should **not** have oil mixed with the fuel. Refer to the appropriate following paragraphs, depending upon the engine used.

700 and 800 Series Two-Stroke Engines

These two-stroke engines are lubricated by mixing oil with the fuel. The manufacturer recommends mixing regular gasoline, leaded or unleaded, with a high-quality, two-stroke engine oil. The recommended mixing ratio is 32:1 when using IDC or RYOBI Two-Cycle Engine Oil. Mix the gasoline and oil in a separate container; never in the fuel tank. The use of oxygenated (alcohol blended) gasoline is discouraged, but if used observe the following procedures.

1. Use fresh fuel and mix the proper oil in the correct proportions.
2. Use an additive such as Gold Eagle brand Alcohol Protector (or equivalent) to inhibit corrosion and reduce the tendency of the oil and fuel to separate. Follow the mixing ratio suggested by the additive manufacturer and always mix additives in a separate container; not in the fuel tank.
3. Agitate the fuel mix frequently, especially before refueling.
4. Drain the fuel tank and run the engine until it stops before storing the unit for even a short time.

900 Series Four-Stroke Engines

The engine on these four-stroke models is lubricated by oil contained in the engine crankcase. The crankcase contains only 3.4 fl. oz (100 ml) of oil, so it is important to check the oil frequently (at least before each use) and maintain the oil at the proper level. A dipstick is attached to the fill plug. To check the oil level, make sure the engine has cooled and the oil has had time to return to the crankcase. Position the unit with engine level and the drive shaft straight. Remove the fill plug, wipe the plug dry with a clean cloth, then reinstall and tighten the plug. Remove the plug and observe the level of the oil on the dipstick. Oil level should be maintained at the top of the dipstick. The engine crankcase should be drained and filled with new oil after the first 10 hours of operation and after each 25 hours of operation thereafter. The oil should also be changed before storing the unit for an extended time.

Change the engine oil as follows. Be sure to catch and discard the oil in a safe and approved method. Start the engine and allow it to run until it reaches normal operating temperature. Stop the engine, remove the oil fill plug, then tip the unit and pour all of the oil from the opening. Be sure to allow all of the oil to drain and be removed. Refill the crankcase with 3.4 fl. oz. (100 ml) of RYOBI Four-Cycle Engine Oil or a good quality SAE 30 oil designated API service class SG, SF or SH. Be sure the O-ring is installed on the fill plug and tighten the plug securely.

The fuel tank should be filled with fresh regular or unleaded gasoline only. Do not mix oil with the fuel. The use of oxygenated (alcohol blended) gasoline is discouraged, but if used it should as fresh as possible. Never use oxygenated fuel that has been stored 60 days or longer. Drain the fuel tank and run the engine until it stops before storing the unit. The manufacturer also recommends mixing 0.8 fl. oz. (23 ml) of STA-BIL or an equivalent fuel additive with each gallon of oxygenated gasoline. Always mix additives with the gasoline in a separate container; never in the fuel tank.

STRING TRIMMER

Models 700r, 705r and 710r

The single line, semi-automatic trimmer head (Fig. RY10) is used on some models. To extend the line with the engine stopped, push the bump button (20) and pull the line until it is the desired length. To extend the line with the engine running, operate the trimmer at full rpm and tap the bump button (20) on the ground. Line should extend slightly.

To install new trimmer line, hold the drum (15) and unscrew the bump button (20). Remove the spool and clean the drum and spool. Check the indexing teeth on the spool and drum for wear or other damage. The 0.080 in. (2 mm) diameter trimmer line should be approxi-

Illustrations courtesy Ryobi Outdoor Products

nately 25 ft. (7.6 m) long. Insert one end of the new line into one of the holes in the spool from the inside out, then back through the second hole to the inside. Wind the line in the direction indicated by the arrow on the spool until all but about 3 inches (76.2 mm) of line is wrapped. Clip the line temporarily in one of the line lock slots (LS) on spool. Insert the end of the line through the line guide (16) in drum and install the spool and bump button. After assembly is complete, pull the line to release it from the line lock slot on the spool.

If the trimmer head must be removed, hold the shaft to prevent it from rotating, then turn the trimmer head clockwise (viewed from the bottom). The cutter adapter has left-hand threads.

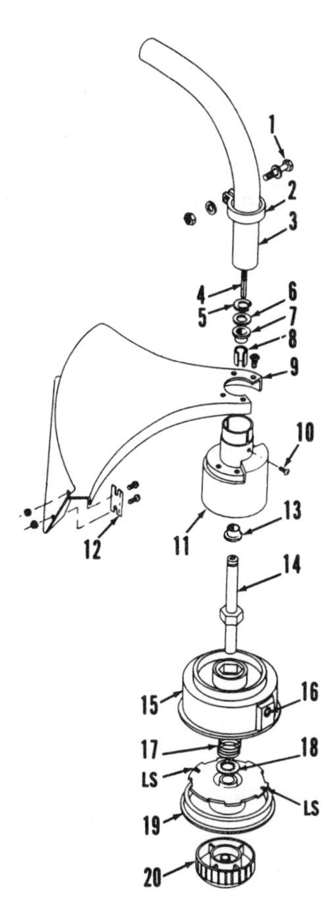

Fig. RY10—Exploded view of the single line, semi-automatic trimmer typical of the type used on 700r and other models.

LS. Line slot
1. Bolt
2. Clamp
3. Drive shaft housing
4. Drive shaft
5. Retaining ring
6. Washer
7. Bushing
8. Bushing
9. Protective shield
10. Locating screw
11. Bushing housing
12. Line length cutter blade
13. Bushing
14. Shaft
15. Drum
16. Line guide
17. Spring
18. Retainer
19. Spool
20. Bump button

Models 760r, 765r, 767r, 770r, 775r, 960r, 970r and 975r

Refer to Fig. RY11 for the trimmer head typical of that used on some models. To extend the line with the engine stopped, push the bump button (11) and pull the line until it is the desired length. To extend the line with the engine running, operate the trimmer at full rpm and tap the bump button (11) on the ground. Line should extend slightly.

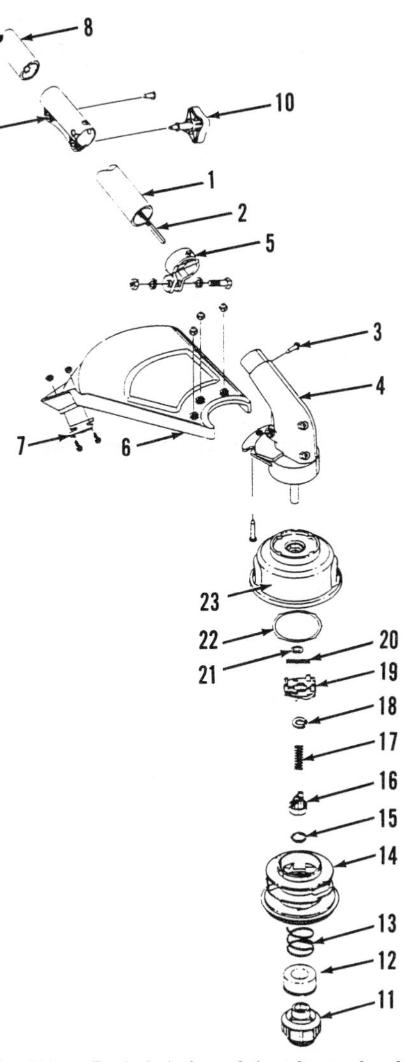

Fig. RY11—Exploded view of the trimmer head, drive shaft and drive used on 975r and other models. The drive shaft shown separates in the middle. The two piece drive shaft is also used on some models with different type of drive.

1. Lower drive shaft housing
2. Lower drive shaft
3. Locating screw
4. Gear head
5. Clamp
6. Protective shield
7. Line length cutter blade
8. Upper drive shaft
9. Coupler clamp
10. Knob
11. Bump knob
12. Foam seal
13. Spring
14. Spool
15. C-clip
16. Plunger
17. Spring
18. E-clip
19. Slider
20. Spring
21. Retainer
22. Thrust washer
23. Drum assy.

To install new trimmer line, hold the drum (23) and unscrew the bump button (11). Remove the spool, being careful not to lose the springs or other parts. Clean the drum and spool, then inspect all parts for damage. If new line is installed, make sure it is the proper diameter. Approximately 12 ft. (3.6 m) of line will be required to fill the spool. Insert the end of the line into the spool and wrap the line on spool in the direction indicated by the arrow on the spool. Wind the line tightly and evenly from side to side and do not twist the lines. Assemble parts (15-22) and install the spool while directing the ends of the line through the line guide in the drum. Install the spring (13), filter (12) and bump button (11). After assembly is complete, trim the line so the end extends to the cutoff blade (7) in the protective cover.

Other Models

Refer to Fig. RY12 for the dual line, semi-automatic trimmer head used on some models. To manually advance the trimmer lines with the engine stopped, push the button at the bottom of the spool (8) and pull both of the lines. To extend the lines with the engine running, operate the trimmer at maximum speed and tap the spool button on the ground. Both lines should extend a small amount automatically. If the line does not extend with the engine run-

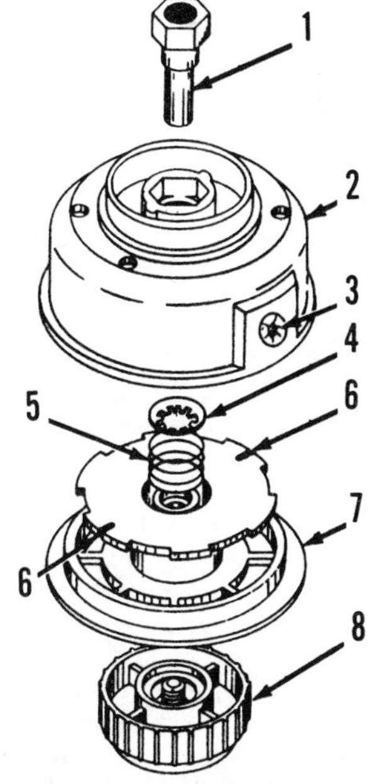

Fig. RY12—Exploded view of the dual line, semi-automatic trimmer head typical of the type used on most models.

1. Adapter
2. Drum
3. Line guide
4. Retainer
5. Spring
6. Line slot
7. Spool
8. Bump button

ning, stop the engine and extend the lines manually. If a line is broken inside the housing, it will be necessary to disassemble the unit and feed the line through the eyelet.

To disassemble, hold the drum (2) and unscrew the bump button (8). Notice that the screw on some models has left hand thread. Remove the spool (7), then remove any old line that remains on the spool. Be careful not to lose the spring (5) or retainer (4). Clean and inspect all parts for damage. Check the indexing teeth in the drum (2) and on spool. A new line guide (3) can be installed if worn.

If new line is installed, make sure it is the proper diameter. On some models, the spool will hold a loop of line 0.080 in. (2 mm) diameter approximately 25 ft. (7.6 m) long. On other models, the spool will hold a loop of 0.095 in. (2.4 m) diameter line approximately 50 ft. (15.2 m) long. Insert the two ends into the two holes in the spool from the bottom and pull the line out until the loop is against the spool and the two lengths of line are the same length. Wrap both ends of the line on spool at the same time in the direction indicated by the arrow on the spool. Wind the line tightly and evenly from side to side and do not twist the lines. Clip the lines into the lines slots (6). Install spool while directing the ends of both lines through the line guides (2) in the drum and install the spool and bump button. After assembly is complete, pull the lines to release them from the line lock slots on the spool. Trim the lines so the ends extend to the cutoff blade in the protective cover.

If the trimmer head must be removed, hold the shaft to prevent it from rotating, then turn the trimmer head clockwise (viewed from the bottom). The cutter adapter has left-hand threads.

BLADE

A four-edge cutting blade (9—Fig. RY13 or Fig. RY14) is available for use on some models. The locking tool should be inserted into the slot in the casting (7—Fig. RY13 or 5—Fig. RY14) and into the blade adapter (8) before loosening or tightening the nut (11). The attaching nut (11) has left-hand threads. When sharpening, follow the original sharpening angle. Tighten the blade attaching nut to 225-250 in.-lb. (25.3-28.1 N•m) torque. If a torque wrench is not available, tighten the nut by hand until the blade adapter, blade and retaining washer are held firmly together, then turn the nut an additional 1/2-3/4 turn. Check that the edge of the blade is aligned with the mark cast into the casting (7—Fig. RY13 or 5—Fig. RY14).

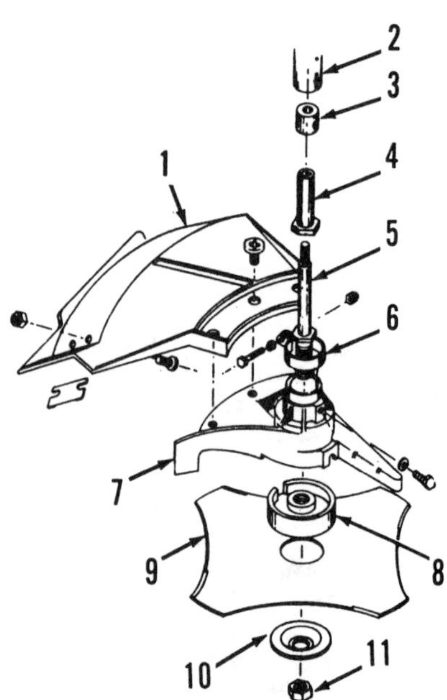

Fig. RY13—Exploded view of the drive and light brush blade typical of 740r and some other models.

1. Protective shield
2. Drive shaft housing
3. Retainer & bushing
4. Drive shaft adapter
5. Head drive shaft
6. Clamp assy.
7. Bearing housing assy.
8. Blade adapter
9. Blade
10. Lower blade adapter
11. Nut

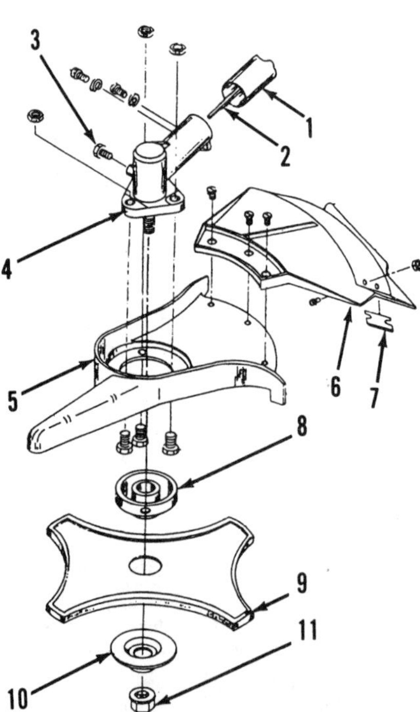

Fig. RY14—Exploded view of the drive and light brush blade assembly typical of the type used on some models.

1. Drive shaft housing
2. Drive shaft
3. Lubrication check plug
4. Gear head
5. Guard mount
6. Protective shield
7. Line length cutter blade
8. Blade adapter
9. Blade
10. Retaining washer
11. Nut

DRIVE SHAFT

A flexible drive shaft(s) is used on most models; however, a solid shaft is used on 780r models. The shaft housing between the engine and the attachment of some models is equipped with a coupling (9 and 10—Fig. RY11) that allows separation so that other tools can be attached to the power head. The two piece drive shaft can be separated after loosening the clamp screw, then pressing the release button. Make sure the drive shaft halves are fully engaged and the release button engages one of the holes in the coupling. Holes on some models are located every 90 degrees so the various attachments can be properly aligned. Tighten the coupling screws before operating the equipment.

The drive shaft is enclosed in the drive shaft housing and the ends of the shaft(s) are square to engage adapters. Flexible drive shaft(s) should be removed after each 10 hours of operation, inspected and lubricated.

To remove the drive shaft, loosen the clamp (2—Fig. RY10, 5—Fig. RY11 or 6—Fig. RY13) and remove the set screw attaching the drive shaft tube to the trimmer housing. Remove and clean the drive shaft, then inspect the shaft for damage. Coat the shaft with a high-quality, multipurpose lithium grease. Make sure the ends of the shaft are properly located in the drive adapters when assembling.

BEARING HOUSING

Models 700r, 705r, 710r, 720r and 725r

Refer to Fig. RY10 for an exploded view of the bearing housing typical of the type used on some models. Bushings are not available separately. Wear or damage is corrected by installing a new bearing housing assembly (11).

Models 740r, 750 and 920r

The bearing head (7—Fig. RY13) is equipped with a sealed bearing. If damaged, install a new bearing and housing assembly.

GEAR HEAD

Models 760r, 765r, 767r, 770r, 775r, 960r, 970r and 975r

These models are equipped with a split gear head typical of that shown in Fig. RY11. Individual parts of the gear head are not available and a new assembly should be installed if damaged.

Illustrations courtesy Ryobi Outdoor Products

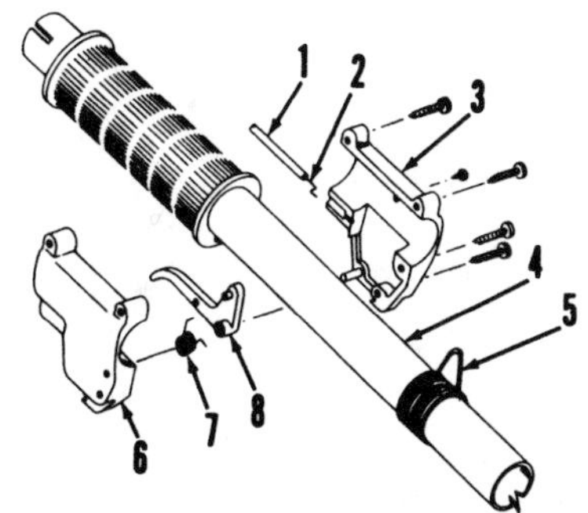

Fig. RY15—Exploded view of the throttle trigger assembly typical of the type used on some models.

1. Throttle cable housing
2. Inner throttle cable
3. Throttle trigger housing
4. Drive shaft housing
5. Shoulder strap attachment
6. Throttle trigger housing
7. Spring
8. Throttle trigger

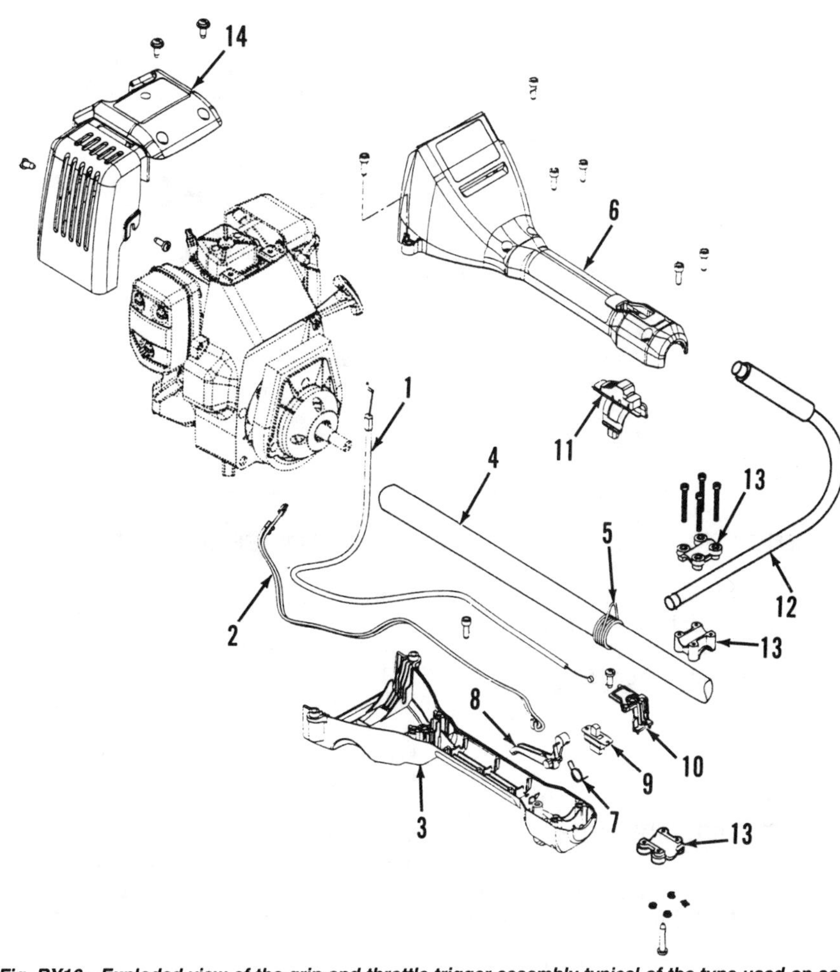

Fig. RY16—Exploded view of the grip and throttle trigger assembly typical of the type used on some models.

1. Throttle cable
2. Engine stop wires
3. Grip lower housing
4. Drive shaft housing
5. Shoulder strap attachment
6. Grip upper housing
7. Throttle return spring
8. Throttle trigger
9. Engine stop switch
10. Trigger & switch retainer
11. Engine stop switch slider
12. J handle
13. Clamp assembly

Models 780r, 790r, 865r, 885r and 990r

These models are equipped with a gear head typical of the type shown in Fig. RY14. Individual parts are not available and a new assembly should be installed if damaged. Plug (3) located in the side of the gear head should be removed and the lubricant level checked after each 50 hours of operation. Lubricant level should be maintained at the lower edge of the hole for plug (3). If necessary, add multipurpose lithium grease and install the plug.

ENGINE CONTROLS

Engine throttle control is located within easy reach when the operator's hands are safely positioned on the grips. Refer to Fig. RY15 or Fig. RY16.

STARTER

Refer to the appropriate ENGINE SERVICE section for service to the starter assembly.

CLUTCH

Refer to the appropriate ENGINE SERVICE section for clutch removal and service procedures.

RYOBI

GASOLINE POWERED BLOWERS

Model	Engine Manufacturer	Engine Model	Displacement
210r	IDC	...	31.0 cc
310BVR	IDC	...	31.0 cc

ENGINE INFORMATION

The models in this section are equipped with an Inertia Dynamics Corporation (IDC) engine. Refer to IDC engine service section for engine service information.

FUEL MIXTURE

Manufacturer recommends mixing regular grade gasoline, leaded or unleaded, with a high-quality, two-stroke engine oil. Recommended fuel:oil ratio is 32:1 when using IDC Two-Cycle Engine Oil. When using any other two-stroke oil, mix 6 oz. (0.177 mL) of oil with 1 gal. (3.8 L) of gasoline, regardless of recommended ratio on oil container. Gasohol or other alcohol blended fuels are not approved by manufacturer.

BLOWER ASSEMBLY

Model 210r

Refer to Fig. RY50 for exploded view of blower assembly. To remove blower impeller (4), remove mounting screws from starter housing (1) and blower housing (3). Separate blower housing halves (3 and 6). Remove mounting screws from blower impeller (4) and separate impeller from flywheel.

To separate engine from blower housing, remove impeller as outlined above. Remove engine cover (10). Disconnect fuel line, throttle cable and ignition wires from engine. Remove engine mounting screws and withdraw engine from blower housing half (6).

Model 310BVR

Refer to Fig. RY51 for exploded view of blower assembly. To remove blower impeller (8), remove blower tube (12). Remove screws attaching blower lower housing (10) to upper housing (7) and separate housing. Remove impeller mounting screws and separate impeller (8) from flywheel.

To separate engine from blower housing, remove impeller as outlined above. Remove screws securing engine covers (1 and 4). Separate covers and disconnect throttle cable, fuel line and ignition wires from engine. Remove engine mounting screws and withdraw engine from blower upper housing (7).

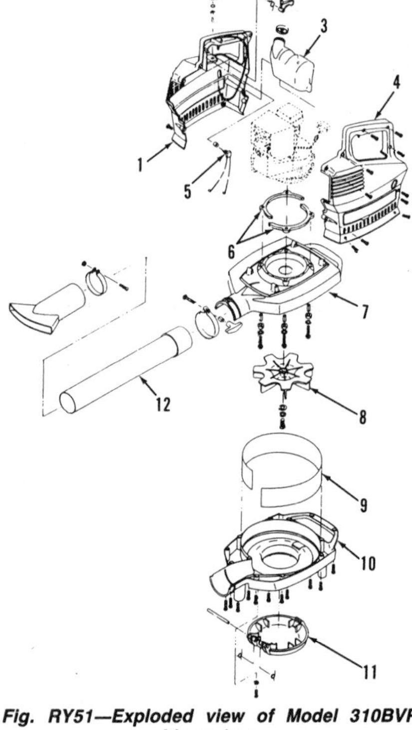

Fig. RY51—Exploded view of Model 310BVR blower/vac.

1. Engine cover
2. Throttle trigger
3. Fuel tank
4. Engine cover
5. Stop switch
6. Gasket
7. Blower upper housing
8. Impeller
9. Shield
10. Blower lower housing
11. Intake cover
12. Blower tube

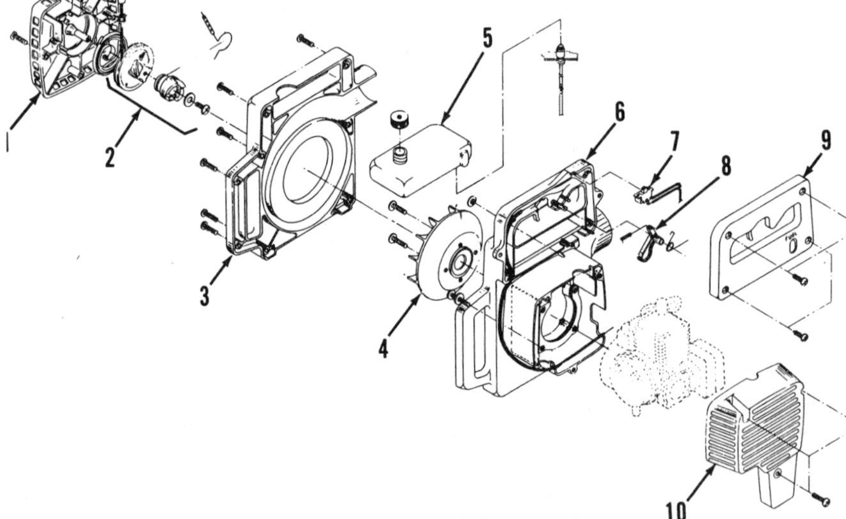

Fig. RY50—Exploded view of Model 210r blower.

1. Starter housing
2. Recoil starter assy.
3. Blower housing half
4. Impeller
5. Fuel tank
6. Blower housing half
7. Stop switch
8. Throttle trigger
9. Handle
10. Engine cover

Illustrations courtesy Ryobi Outdoor Products

SEARS
GASOLINE POWERED STRING TRIMMERS

Model	Engine Manufacturer	Engine Model	Displacement
28151	Kioritz	....	21.2 cc
281510	Kioritz	....	21.2 cc
281511	Kioritz	....	21.2 cc
281512	Kioritz	....	21.2 cc
28161	Kioritz	....	30.1 cc
281610	Kioritz	....	30.1 cc
281611	Kioritz	....	30.1 cc
28171	Kioritz	....	13.8 cc
281711	Kioritz	....	13.8 cc
79545	Fuji	....	37.7 cc
79555	Poulan	....	26.2 cc
79556	Fuji	....	28.0 cc
79558	Poulan	....	26.2 cc
79559	Fuji	....	28.0 cc
79623	Fuji	....	37.7 cc
79812	Poulan	....	26.2 cc
79813	Poulan	....	26.2 cc
79814	Fuji	....	28.0 cc
79821	Fuji	....	28.0 cc
79822	Fuji	....	28.0 cc

ENGINE INFORMATION

All Models

Sears and Sears "Brushwacker" line trimmers and brush cutters are equipped with Kioritz, Fuji or Poulan two-stroke air-cooled gasoline engines. Identify engine manufacturer by trimmer model number or engine displacement and refer to appropriate POULAN, KIORITZ or FUJI ENGINE SERVICE section in this manual.

FUEL MIXTURE

All Models

Manufacturer recommends mixing regular grade gasoline (unleaded is an acceptable substitute) with a good quality two-stroke air-cooled engine oil at a 25:1 ratio. Do not use fuel containing alcohol.

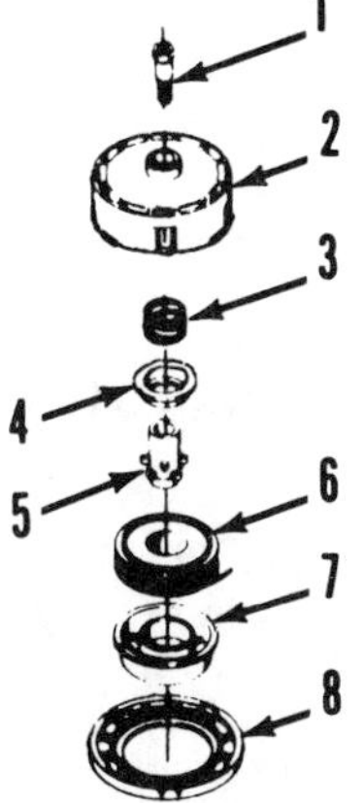

Fig. SR10—Exploded view of old style single strand semi-automatic trimmer head used on some early models.

1. Drive shaft adapter
2. Housing
3. Spring
4. Spring adapter
5. Drive cam
6. Spool
7. Button
8. Cover

STRING TRIMMER

All Models

Single Strand Semi-Automatic Head. All models may be equipped with a single strand semi-automatic line trimmer head shown in Figs. SR10 and SR11. Fig. SR10 shows an exploded view of early style trimmer head which may be identified by the rough portion of upper housing (2). Fig. SR11 shows an exploded view of late style trimmer head which may be identified by the smooth portion of upper housing (2). Service procedure for both heads is similar.

To extend line with trimmer engine stopped, push in on button (7) while pulling on line end. Procedure may have to be repeated to obtain desired line length. To extend line with trimmer engine running, operate trimmer engine at full rpm and tap button (7) on the ground. Each time button (7) is tapped on the ground a measured amount of new line will be advanced.

To renew line, remove cover (8), button (7) and spool (6). Clean all parts thoroughly and remove any remaining old line from spool. Wind approximately 30 feet (9 m) of 0.080 inch (2 mm) monofilament line on spool in

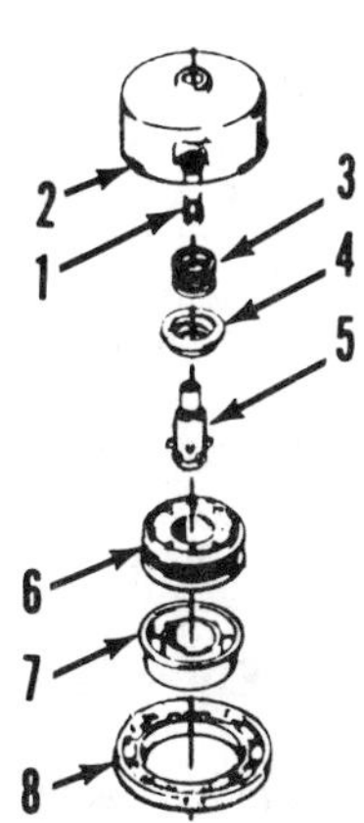

Fig. SR11—Exploded view of late style single strand semi-automatic trimmer head used on some models.

1. Line guide
2. Housing
3. Spring
4. Spring adapter
5. Drive cam
6. Spool
7. Button
8. Cover

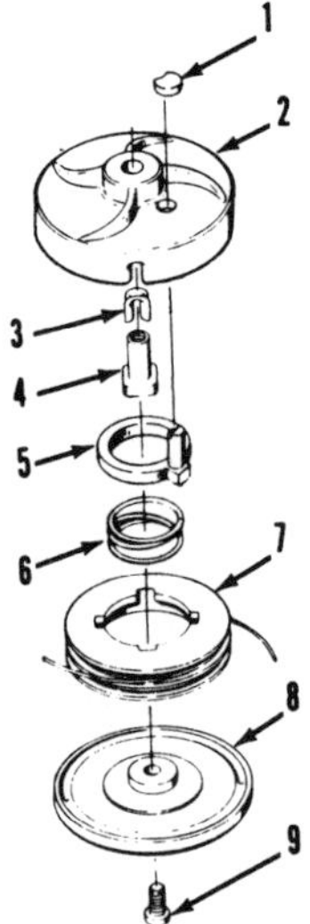

Fig. SR12—Exploded view of dual strand manual trimmer head used on some models.

1. Lock ring cap
2. Housing
3. Line guide
4. Drive shaft adapter
5. Lock ring
6. Spring
7. Spool
8. Cover
9. Screw

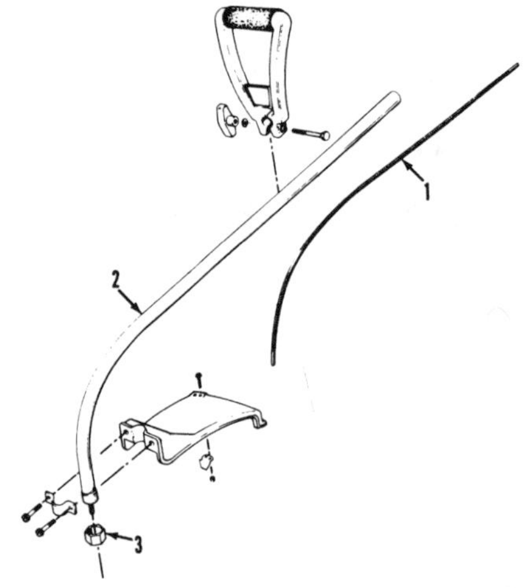

Fig. SR13—Exploded view of typical flexible drive shaft (1), drive shaft housing tube (2) and dust cover (3) used on some models. Note this style drive shaft and housing are also used with heavy duty bearing head models.

Fig. SR14—Exploded view of bearing head used on Models 281512, 28171 and 281711.

1. Locating screw
2. Clamp bolt
3. Bearing housing
4. Nut
5. Bearing
6. Spacer
7. Bearing
8. Snap ring
9. Arbor shaft
10. Cup washer
11. Pin

direction indicated by arrow on spool. Insert line end through line guide opening in housing (2) and install spool, button and cover.

Dual Strand Manual Head. Some models may be equipped with a dual strand manual trimmer head shown in Fig. SR12. To extend line, stop trimmer engine and wait until all trimmer head rotation has stopped. Push in on plate (8) while pulling each line out of housing (2).

To renew trimmer line, remove screw (9), plate (8), spring (6) and spool (7). Remove any remaining line from each side of spool. Clean spool, housing and plate. Insert ends of two new 0.095 inch (2.4 mm) lines in holes located within spool and wind lines in direction indicated by arrow on spool. Diameter of line wound on spool should not exceed diameter of spool sides. Make certain line savers (3) are in position and install spool in housing with the "THIS SIDE IN" instructions on spool toward inside of trimmer head. Install spring (6), cover (8) and screw (9).

BLADE

All Models So Equipped

Some models may be equipped with a four cutting edge grass and weed blade or a saw blade. When installing blade, make certain all adapter plates are centered and seated squarely against blade and tighten nut (left-hand thread) securely.

DRIVE SHAFT

Flexible Drive Shaft Models

Most models equipped with a flexible drive shaft (1—Fig. SR13) have a curved drive shaft housing tube (2). Drive shaft has squared ends which engage adapters at each end. Drive shaft should be removed for maintenance at 20 hour intervals of use. To remove, separate drive shaft housing from engine. Mark locations of drive shaft ends and pull drive shaft out of housing. Clean drive shaft and lubricate with lithium base grease. Reinstall drive shaft in housing making certain ends are not reversed.

Solid Drive Shaft

Models equipped with a solid steel drive shaft have a straight drive shaft housing tube. Drive shaft requires no regular maintenance; however, if drive shaft has been removed, lubricate drive shaft with lithium base grease before reinstallation.

BEARING HEAD

Models 79812 And 79813

Models 79812 and 79813 are equipped with a bearing head which is an integral part of drive shaft housing (Fig. SR13). Bearing head requires no regular maintenance and service parts are not available.

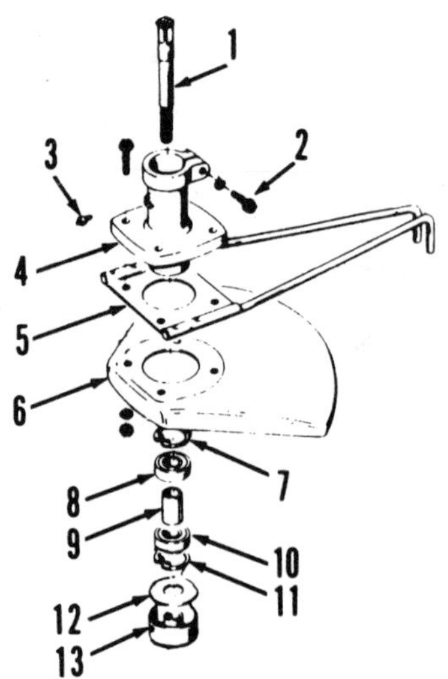

Fig. SR15—Exploded view of bearing head used on Models 79814 and 79821.

1. Drive shaft adapter
2. Clamp bolt
3. Locating screw
4. Housing
5. Bracket (as equipped)
6. Shield
7. Snap ring
8. Bearing
9. Spacer
10. Bearing
11. Snap ring
12. Washer
13. Drive disc

Models 281512, 28171 And 281711

Models 281512, 28171 and 281711 are equipped with the bearing head shown in Fig. SR14. Bearing head is equipped with sealed bearings and requires no regular maintenance.

To disassemble bearing head, remove trimmer head assembly and cup washer (10). Remove clamp bolt (2) and locating screw (1). Separate bearing head from drive shaft housing tube. Remove snap ring (8) and use a suitable puller to remove arbor shaft (9) and bearing assembly. Remove nut (4), bearing (5), spacer (6) and bearing (7) as required.

Models 79814 And 79821

Models 79814 and 79821 are equipped with the bearing head shown in Fig. SR15. Bearing head is equipped with sealed bearings and requires no regular maintenance.

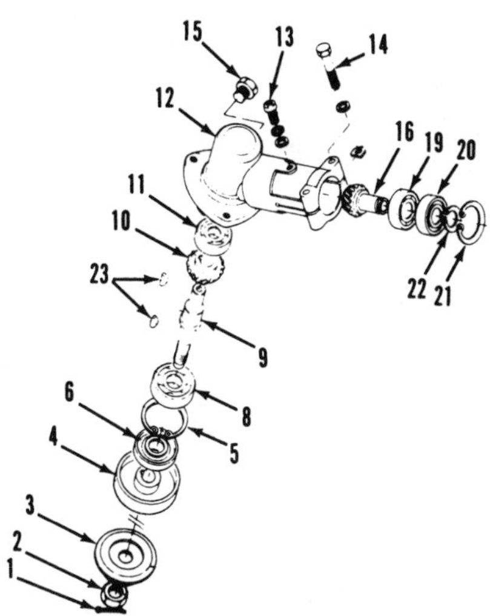

Fig. SR16—Exploded view of gear head used on Models 28151, 281510 and 281511.

1. Cotter pin
2. Nut
3. Adapter plate
4. Adapter plate
5. Snap ring
6. Seal
8. Bearing
9. Arbor shaft
10. Gear
11. Bearing
12. Housing
13. Screw
14. Clamp bolt
15. Level check plug
16. Gear
19. Bearing
20. Bearing
21. Snap ring
22. Snap ring
23. Keys

Fig. SR17—Exploded view of gear head used on Models 28161, 281610 and 281611.

1. Cotter pin
2. Nut
3. Adapter plate
4. Adapter plate
5. Arbor shaft
6. Keys
7. Seal
8. Snap ring
9. Bearing
10. Spacer
11. Gear
12. Snap ring
13. Bearing
14. Snap ring
15. Level check plug
16. Plug
17. Nut
18. Clamp bolt
19. Housing
20. Gear
21. Spacer
22. Bearing
23. Bearing
24. Snap ring
25. Snap ring

To disassemble bearing head, remove trimmer head or blade assembly. Remove clamp bolt (2) and locating screw (3). Separate bearing head assembly from drive shaft housing. Remove shield (6) and bracket (5) (as equipped). Remove cup washer (13) and washer (12). Carefully press drive shaft adapter (1) out of bearings. Remove snap rings (7 and 11). Press bearings (8 and 10) and spacer (9) out of housing.

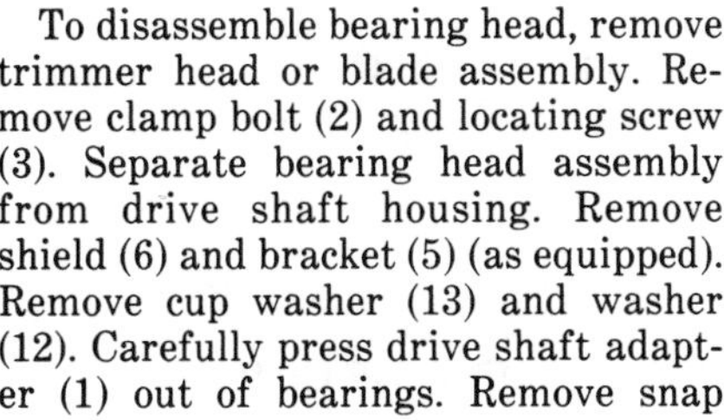

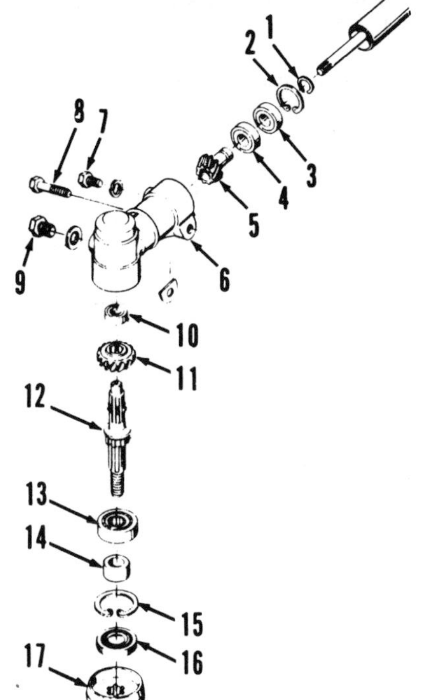

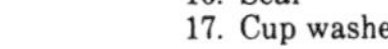

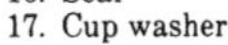

Fig. SR18—Exploded view of gear head used on Model 79822.

1. Snap ring
2. Snap ring
3. Bearing
4. Bearing
5. Input shaft
6. Housing
7. Clamp bolt
8. Bolt
9. Check plug
10. Bearing
11. Gear
12. Arbor shaft
13. Bearing
14. Spacer
15. Snap ring
16. Seal
17. Cup washer

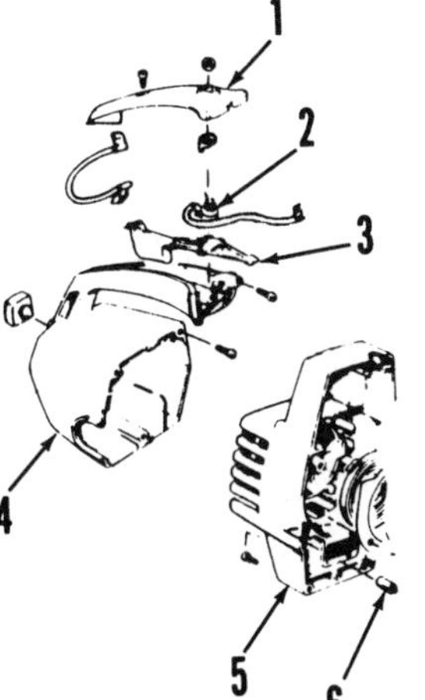

GEAR HEAD

Models 28151, 281510 And 281511

Models 28151, 281510 and 281511 are equipped with the gear head shown in Fig. SR16. Remove check plug (15) and check lubricant level at 50 hour intervals of use. Gear head housing should be kept 2/3 full of lithium base grease.

To disassemble gear head, remove trimmer head or blade assembly. Separate gear head from drive shaft housing tube. Remove snap ring (21) and use suitable puller to remove input shaft (16) and bearing assembly. Remove snap ring (22) and press bearings (19 and 20) from input shaft as required. Remove seal (6) and snap ring (5). Use suitable puller to remove arbor shaft (9) and bearing assembly. Press bearings from arbor shaft as required. Remove gear (10). If bearing (11) stays in housing (12), heat housing to 140° F (60° C) and tap housing on wooden block to remove bearing.

Models 28161, 281610 And 281611

Models 28161, 281610 and 281611 are equipped with the gear head shown in Fig. SR17. Remove check plug (15) and check lubricant level at 50 hour intervals of use. Gear head housing should be kept 2/3 full of lithium base grease.

To disassemble gear head, remove trimmer head or blade assembly. Separate gear head from drive shaft housing tube. Remove snap ring (25) and use suitable puller to remove input shaft and bearing assembly (20). Remove plug (16). Remove seal (7) and snap ring (8). Remove snap ring (14). Press arbor (5) and bearing assembly from housing (19).

Model 79822

Model 79822 is equipped with the gear head shown in Fig. SR18. Check plug (9) should be removed and gear

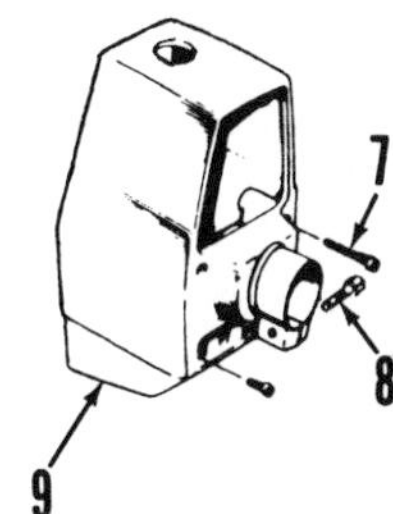

Fig. SR19—Exploded view of engine cover used on some models.

1. Throttle housing cover
2. Ignition switch
3. Throttle trigger
4. Handle
5. Fan housing
6. Spacer
7. Screw
8. Clamp bolt
9. Cover

head lubricant checked at 10 hour intervals of use. Gear head housing should be kept 2/3 full of lithium base grease.

To disassemble gear head, remove trimmer head or blade assembly. Remove clamp bolt and head locating screw and separate gear head from drive shaft housing. Remove cup washer (17) and spacer (14). Remove snap ring (2) and use a suitable puller to remove input shaft (5) and bearing assembly. Remove snap ring (1) and press bearings (3 and 4) from input shaft as required. Remove seal (16) and snap ring (15). Use suitable puller to remove arbor shaft (12) and bearing assembly. Press bearing (13) and gear (11) from shaft as required. If bearing (10) remains in housing (6), heat housing to 140° F (60° C) and tap housing on wooden block to remove bearing.

ENGINE COVER

Models 79812, 79813, 79814, 79821 And 79822

Models 79812, 79813, 79814, 79821 and 79822 are equipped with a full engine cover (Fig. SR19). To remove engine cover, remove clamp bolt (8) and separate engine assembly from drive shaft housing. Remove the four 10-24 screw and separate housings (5) and (9 slightly. Disconnect ignition wire fron module and separate fuel line so junction fitting stays with crankcase side o fuel line. Separate housings completely Remove the three 8-24 inch screws fron inner side of housing (5) and remove the air baffle. Remove the five 10-2 screws located under air baffle and separate housing (4) from housing (5) Remove fuel tank cap and remove fue tank. Remove the four screws securing carburetor cover plate and remove carburetor cover. Disconnect spark plug and remove the four 10-24 screws a drive shaft housing side of cover (9) and remove cover (9).

SHINDAIWA

GASOLINE POWERED TRIMMERS

Models	Engine Make	Engine Model	Displacement
F-18 & T-18	Own	S18	18.4 cc (1.1 cu. in.)
F-20	Own	S20	19.8 cc (1.21 cu. in.)
T-20 & F-21	Own	S21	21.1 cc (1.29 cu. in.)
C-230, F-230, T-230, LE-230 Edger	Own	S230	22.5 cc (1.37 cu. in.)
C-250, T-250, LE-250 Edger	Own	S250	24.1 cc (1.47 cu. in.)
C-25 & T-25	Own	S25	24.1 cc (1.47 cu. in.)
C-27 & T-27	Own	S27	27.2 cc (1.7 cu. in.)
BP-35 & C-35	Own	S35	33.6 cc (2.05 cu. in.)
B-40	Own	S40	39.4 cc (2.40 cu. in.)
B-45	Own	S45	41.5 cc (2.6 cu. in.)
RC-45 Clearing Saw	Own	S45	41.5 cc (2.6 cu. in.)

B = Brush cutter (handlebar handles)
BP = Backpack brush cutter
C = Brush cutter (handlebar handles)
F = Curved shaft models
LE = Lawn edger
RC = Clearing saw
T = Straight shaft models

ENGINE INFORMATION

All models are equipped with a Shindaiwa engine. The model number and serial number are located on a plate attached to the side of the engine. Refer to the SHINDAIWA ENGINE SERVICE section of this manual for service to the engine used.

FUEL MIXTURE

These two-stroke engines are lubricated by mixing oil with the fuel. The manufacturer recommends mixing regular gasoline, leaded or unleaded, with Shindaiwa Premium 2-Cycle engine oil or another high-quality, two-stroke engine oil. The recommended mixing ratio is 40:1. Mix the gasoline and oil in a separate container; never in the fuel tank. The use of oxygenated (alcohol blended) gasoline is discouraged, but if used observe the following procedures.

1. Use fresh fuel and mix the proper oil in the correct proportions.
2. Choose an ether-based oxygenate over one containing alcohol. Never use fuel containing more than 10% alcohol by volume.
3. Reduce the risk of seizure by enriching the fuel mixture slightly. Refer to the carburetor section of the engine service section.
4. Use a fuel stabilizer such as Sta-Bil. Follow the mixing ratio suggested by the additive manufacturer and always mix additives in a separate container; not in the fuel tank.
5. Agitate the fuel mix frequently, especially before refueling.
6. Never store the unit, even for a short time, with fuel in the tank. Drain the fuel tank and run the engine until it stops before storing.

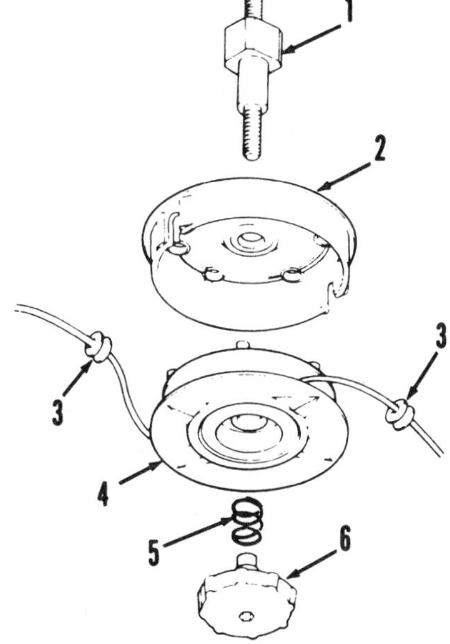

Fig. SH9—Exploded view of the manually adjusted trimmer head used on some models.

1. Adapter
2. Drum
3. Line guides
4. Spool
5. Spring
6. Knob

STRING TRIMMER

Refer to Fig. SH9 and Fig. SH10 for an exploded view of two of the trimmer heads used. To remove the head from the drive shaft tube (housing), insert a tool into the cup washer and bearing head (Fig. SH11) to lock the head in position. Turn the head counterclockwise to remove.

The trimmer shown in Fig. SH9 is manually adjusted only. To advance the trimmer lines, first stop the engine. Pull the spool (4) out and turn it until both lines are extended sufficiently, then release the spool and allow the spring (5) to push the spool into the

Fig. SH10—Exploded view of the semi-automatic string trimmer head typical of the type used on some models.

1. Adapter
2. Housing
3. Spring
4. Washer
5. Outer cam
6. Inner cam
7. Spool

Illustrations courtesy Shindaiwa Inc.

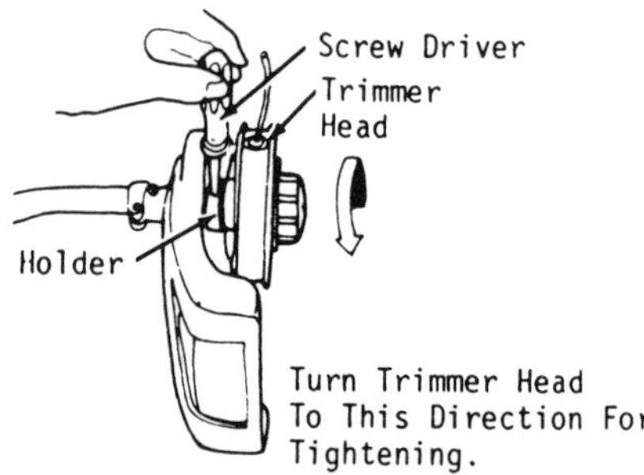

Fig. SH11—Us a 5/32 inch Allen wrench or similar tool inserted into the hole in cup casher and the drive shaft housing to prevent the drive shaft from turning when removing the trimmer head.

hub. If the spool is not completely seated, turn the spool until the pegs on the top of the spool engage the holes in the hub. Both lines should extend from the hub the same amount. If a line is not extended, it may be broken inside the housing, making it necessary to disassemble the unit and feed the line through the eyelets.

If necessary to remove the spool, remove nut (6) and spring (5), then lift the spool from the hub. To install new 0.095 in. (2.4 mm) diameter line, insert the line through the eye of the spool and pull the line through until it is the same length on both sides. Wrap both ends of the line on the spool at the same time. Wind the line tightly and evenly from side to side and do not twist the lines. Insert the ends of line through line guides (3) and install the spool in drum (2) making sure the guides are properly fitted in the drum. Install spring (5) and tighten knob (6).

The dual line semi-automatic string trimmer head shown in Fig. SH10 is typical of one of the types used. To manually advance the trimmer lines with the engine stopped, push the button at the bottom of the head and pull both of the lines. To extend the lines with the engine running, operate the trimmer at maximum speed and tap the button on the ground. Both lines should extend a small amount automatically. If the line does not extend with the engine running, stop the engine and extend the lines manually. If a line is broken inside the housing, it will be necessary to disassemble the unit and feed the line through the eyelet.

To remove and disassemble the string trimmer head, proceed as follows. Hold the drum firmly and turn spool in the direction shown in Fig. SH12 to remove slack. Twist with a hard snap until the plastic peg is between holes, then separate the spool from the drum.

Clean and inspect all parts for damage. Insert the line through the eye of the spool as shown in Fig. SH13 and pull the line through until it is the same length on both sides. Wrap both ends of the line on spool at the same time in clockwise direction as viewed from the top of spool. Wind the line tightly and evenly from side to side and do not twist the lines. Install spool while directing the ends of both lines through the eyelets in the housing. Align the pegs on drum with slots in the spool and push the spool into drum. Hold the drum firmly, then twist spool quickly in the direction shown in Fig. SH14 so peg enters the hole with a click and locks the spool in position. Trim the line so the line extends approximately 6 in. (15 cm) from the drum.

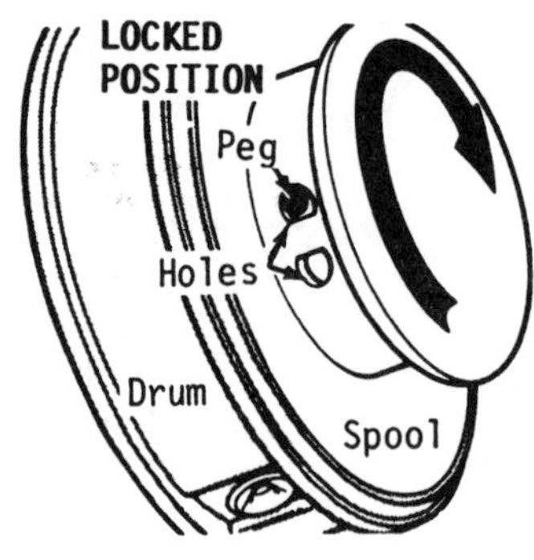

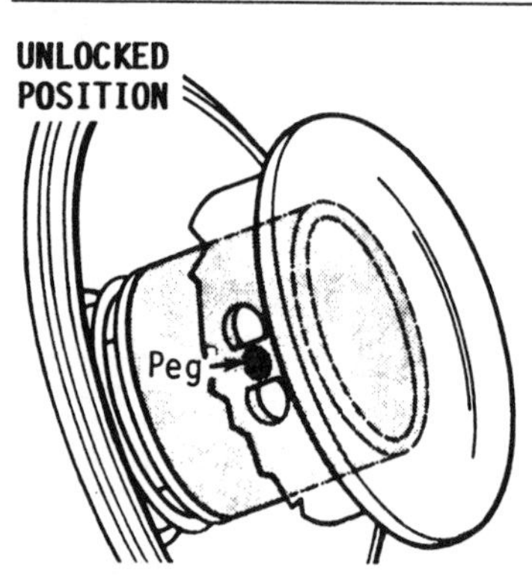

Fig. SH12—To remove the spool from trimmer head shown in Fig. SH10, hold the drum firmly and turn the spool in the direction shown to take up slack, then twist with a sudden snap until the plastic peg is between the holes as shown in the lower view.

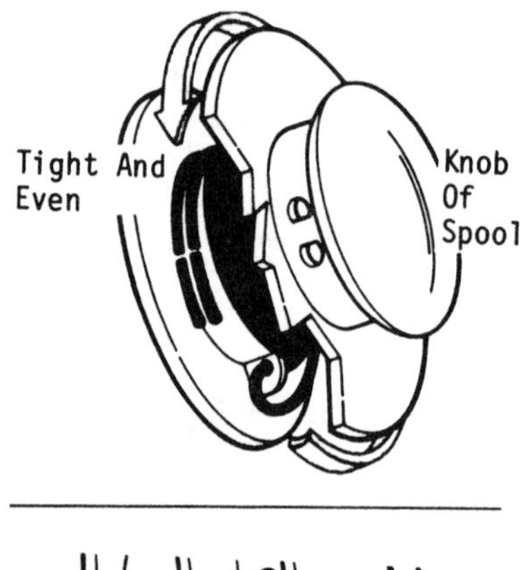

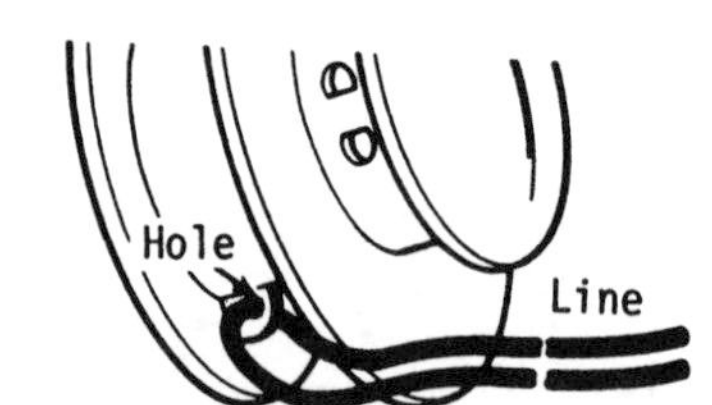

Fig. SH13—The end of the line must be inserted through the hole on spool as shown in the lower view. Wrap line tightly and evenly in the direction indicated by the arrow.

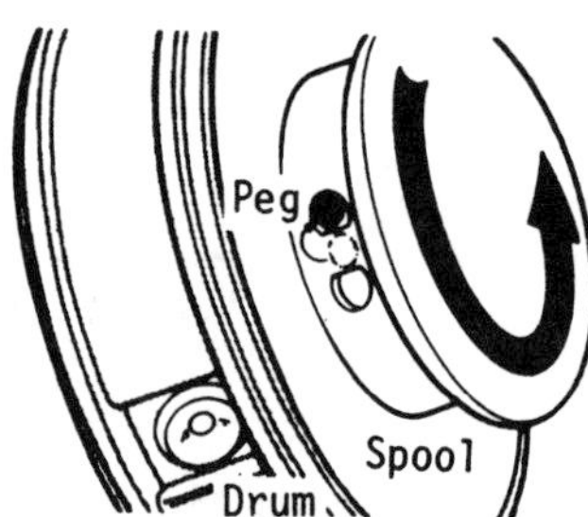

Fig. SH14—Hold the drum firmly and twist suddenly to lock the spool in position.

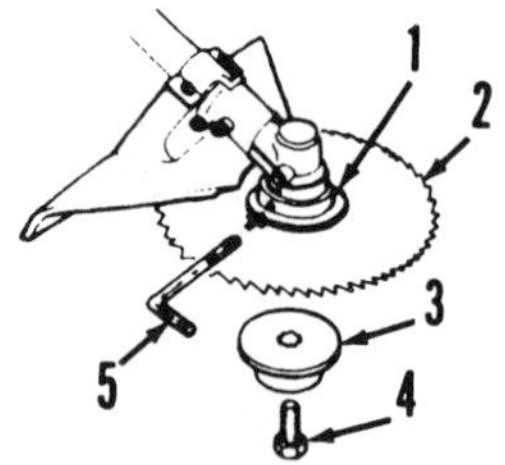

Fig. SH15—Use 5/32 in. Allen wrench or similar tool to lock the drive shaft when removing or installing a brush blade.

BLADE

A variety of hard cutting blades are available for installation on most models. All of the available hard blades can be dangerous and should be selected and used with great care. Blades of different diameters should be matched to the specific model of the powerhead. A blade too small or too large will reduce the effectiveness of operation and may increase the chance for damage or injury. Sharpen each tooth following the original sharpening angle and tooth set. Sharpen all teeth evenly to maintain balance and do not file into the radius at the root.

To remove or install blade, insert tool (5—Fig. SH15) into hole in upper adapter (1) and gear head to prevent the drive shaft from turning. Remove bolt (4), lower adapter (3) and blade (2).

DRIVE SHAFT AND HOUSING

F and BP Models

All F models are equipped with a 6 mm flexible steel drive shaft contained in a curved housing. An 8 mm diameter

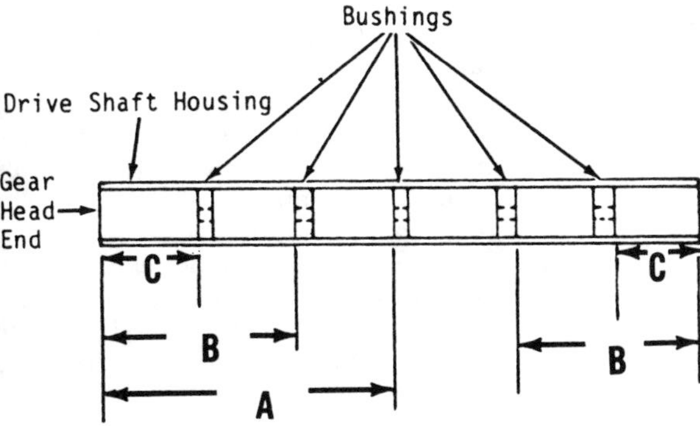

Fig. SH16—Refer to the text for proper installation of the bushings.

flexible steel drive shaft is used on BP models. The drive shaft should be removed, cleaned and lubricated at 20 hour intervals of use. Use Shindaiwa Premium Gearcase Lube or a good quality No. 2 multipurpose lithium grease.

B, BP, C, RC and T Models

These models are equipped with a solid high carbon steel drive shaft that is splined on both ends. The straight drive shaft is supported in bushings located in the drive shaft housing. The shaft should be perfectly straight and all splined surfaces should be sharp, not rounded. Any discoloration or wear on the steel drive shaft indicates bushing wear.

Model BP Backpack brush cutters are equipped with both a flexible shaft portion and a solid high carbon steel drive shaft. To separate the flexible shaft from the straight shaft, detach the engine stop switch wires and remove the index screw from the rear handle grip near the end of the straight shaft. The two parts should pull apart easily.

The bushings can be removed and installed with Shindaiwa driver (part No. 22000-96101). All of the bushings can be driven from the housing at the same time using the driver to drive all of the bearings to one end, then out of the tube (housing). A lightweight oil such as WD-40 can be used to facilitate movement of the bushings. Inspect the housing tube carefully and install if any distortion or cracks are found or if the housing is bent. The bushings should be installed at approximately equal distance apart in the housing as shown in Fig. SH16. Install the bushings to the following depths.

All T models
Distance A—Fig. SH16 .... 740 mm (29.1 in.)
Distance B—Fig. SH16 .... 490 mm (19.1 in.)
Distance C—Fig. SH16 .... 240 mm (9.45 in.)

C-20, C-25, C-27, C-230, C-250
Distance A—Fig. SH16 .... 740 mm (29.1 in.)
Distance B—Fig. SH16 .... 490 mm (19.1 in.)
Distance C—Fig. SH16 .... 240 mm (9.45 in.)

C-35, B-40, B-45, RC-45 models
Distance A—Fig. SH16 .... 690 mm (27.3 in.)
Distance B—Fig. SH16 .... 456 mm (17.9 in.)
Distance C—Fig. SH16 .... 223 mm (8.78 in.)

BP-35 models
Four bushings each 280 mm (11.02 in.) apart.

Install bushings to the specific distances from the ends of the housing. Begin by installing the center bushing, then installing the next bushing toward the ends. Installation is easier if the driver (Shindaiwa part No. 22000-96101) is marked and used to drive the bushings in to the correct distance. A lightweight oil such as WD-40 can be used to facilitate movement of the bushings. Lubricate the drive shaft with a good quality lithium based grease before installing it in the housing. If the drive shaft has a smaller section near one end, that end should be installed closest to the engine.

BEARING HEAD

All F Models

These models are equipped with a flange type bearing head equipped with sealed bearings. The bearing head requires no maintenance except external cleaning.

To disassemble the bearing head, refer to Fig. SH17. Remove the trimmer head by inserting a tool into the cup washer and bearing head as shown in Fig. SH11, then turning the head counterclockwise. Remove the locating screw (1—Fig. SH17) and clamp bolt (2). Pull the bearing head from the drive shaft housing. Remove the snap ring (8), then use a suitable puller to remove the arbor (4) and bearing assembly from the housing. If necessary, the bearings can be pressed from the arbor shaft.

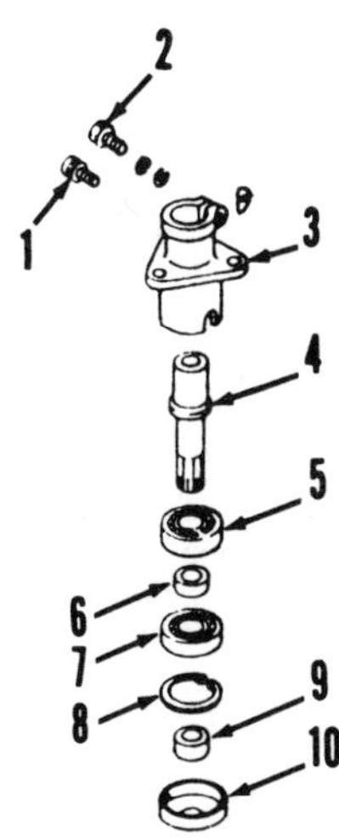

Fig. SH17—Exploded view of the bearing head used on models with curved shaft.

1. Locating screw
2. Clamp bolt
3. Housing
4. Arbor
5. Bearing
6. Spacer
7. Bearing
8. Snap ring
9. Spacer
10. Adapter plate

GEAR HEAD

Refer to Fig. SH18 for a cut-away view typical of the gear head used on all models. The gear head should be lubricated at 50 hour intervals as follows. Remove the trimmer head or blade assembly. Remove the shaft collar from around the output shaft. Remove the grease plug from the side of the housing and pump grease into the gear head until clean, but used grease comes from around the seal and output shaft. See Fig. SH19.

To disassemble the gear head, remove the trimmer head or blade assembly from the unit. Remove the locking bolt and loosen the clamp bolts (Fig.

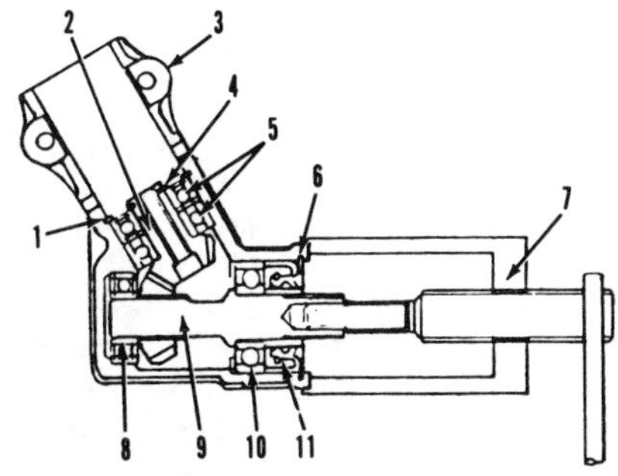

Fig. SH18—Cross section of the gear head used on models so equipped.

1. Snap ring
2. Input shaft & gear
3. Housing
4. Snap ring
5. Bearings
6. Snap ring
7. Puller
8. Bearing
9. Arbor shaft & gear
10. Bearing
11. Seal

Illustrations courtesy Shindaiwa Inc.

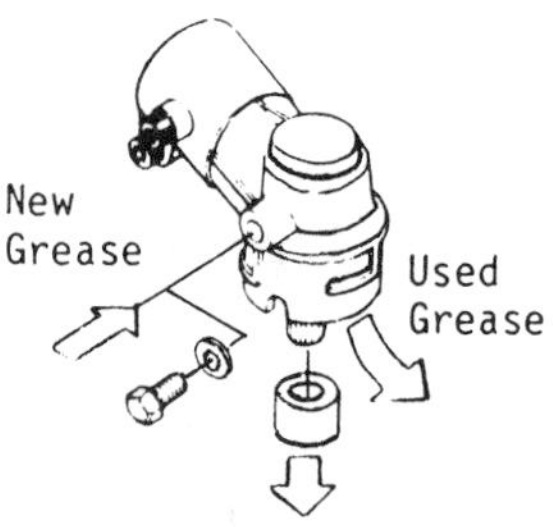

Fig. SH19—Pump grease into the gear head through the opening for the filler plug until grease comes from around the output shaft and seal. If the seal collar is not removed, the seal may be damaged.

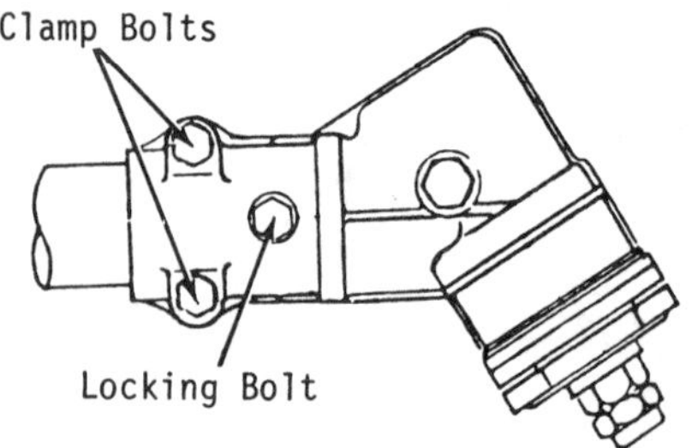

Fig. SH20—To remove the gear head from the drive shaft housing, remove the locking bolt and loosen or remove the clamp bolts.

SH20), then pull the unit from the end of the drive shaft housing.

NOTE: On some models, the lower (output shaft) seal must be removed before the snap ring (6—Fig. SH18). If the snap ring is located outside the seal, the seal can be pulled from the housing at the same time as the shaft and bearings.

On models except T-250 and C-250, remove the snap ring (6—Fig. SH18), then attach a suitable puller (7) as illustrated. Use the puller to withdraw the shaft (9), and bearing (10) from the housing. The bearing (8) can be removed after the input shaft and gear are removed as follows. Remove snap ring (1) and use a suitable puller as shown in Fig. SH21 to pull the input shaft from the housing. The puller bolt must pass through the input shaft and a nut is then installed at the bottom. Bearings (5—Fig. SH18) can be pressed from the shaft is necessary. Heat the housing to 212 degrees F (100 degrees C) and tap the housing on a flat wood surface to remove the inner bearing (8).

On T-250 and C-250 models, remove the snap ring (1—Fig. SH18). Heat the housing to approximately 212 degrees F (100 degrees C) and tap the housing on a flat wood surface to remove the input bearings (5), shaft and gear (2). It may be necessary to insert a screwdriver in the clamping slot to assist removal. Remove the seal (11) from the

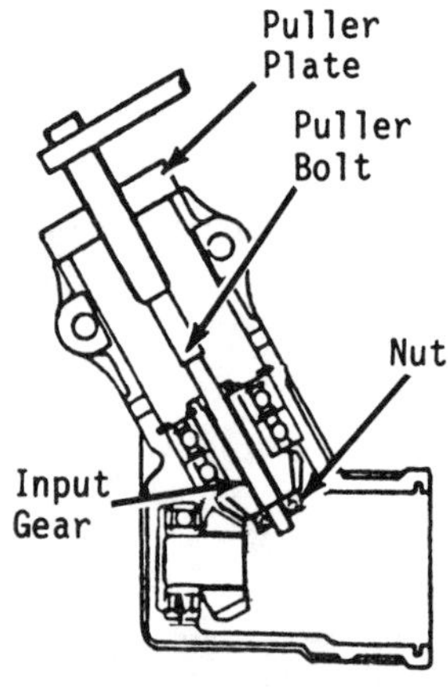

Fig. SH21—On some models, a puller can be used to remove the input shaft and gear assembly.

output end of the housing, then remove the snap ring (6) that is located between the bearing and seal of these models. A puller (7) can be attached to pull the shaft, gear and bearing (10) from the housing. If the inner bearing (8) is not removed with the shaft, it may be necessary to heat the housing. Bearings (5) can be pressed from the input shaft if necessary after removing the snap ring (4).

On all models, use a bearing driver of the proper size to install the inner bearing (8). Install the output shaft (9), gear and bearing (10). using a driver that contacts only the outer race of the bearing (10). Depending upon construction type, install the snap ring (6), then seal (11) or the seal (11) followed by the snap ring (6).

NOTE: Snap rings are manufactured with a sharp side and a rounded side. Install snap rings with the rounded edge toward the bearing race or seal. The sharp edge should engage the housing or shaft.

Install the input gear and shaft (2), bearings (5) and snap ring (4) as an assembly. Install the retaining snap ring (1) when properly seated. Check to make sure the assembly is free to turn. If binding is noticed, bump the housing near the clamping surface of the housing to move the input shaft assembly against the snap ring (1). Remove the grease plug from the side of the housing and pump grease into the gear head until grease comes from around the seal and output shaft. See Fig. SH19. Install grease plug, seal collar and gear head assembly.

RECOIL STARTER

Different types of recoil starters have been used (Fig. SH22, Fig. SH23, Fig. SH24 and Fig. SH25). The recoil starter is attached to the rear of the engine and can be removed without disassembling the power head. Refer to the following for service to the recoil starter.

Refer to Fig. SH22 for the starter used on C-27, T-27, RC-45, C-250 and T-250 and Fig. SH23 for C-20, T-20, F-21 models. Remove handle (1) and allow the rope to wind into the starter. Remove the center screw (2) and the pulley (3). The spring (4) may rewind uncontrollably causing injury. Wear appropriate safety eye wear and gloves before removing the recoil spring (4) from the housing (5). Unscrew the lock nut (6) and pawl plate (7) from the engine crankshaft. Remove the clip (8) from the front of the pawl to remove the pawl and spring (9 and 10).

Some starters may turn in opposite directions as shown in Fig. SH23. The pawl (9) is located at the opposite side of the plate (7), the rope is wrapped the other direction and spring (4) is installed so it will recoil the correct direction. Make sure the starter is assembled correctly.

Install the pawl plate (7) and tighten securely, then install and tighten the lock nut (6). Lubricate the center post and spring side of the housing with light grease. Attach the outer end of the spring to the clip in the housing, then

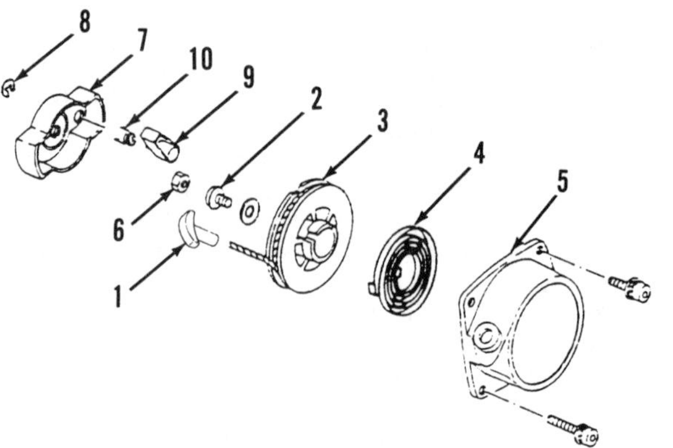

Fig. SH22—Exploded view of the starter typical of the type used on C-27, T-27, RC-45, C-250 and T-250 models.

1. Handle
2. Screw
3. Pulley and rope
4. Recoil spring
5. Housing
6. Nut
7. Pawl retainer
8. "E" ring
9. Pawl
10. Spring

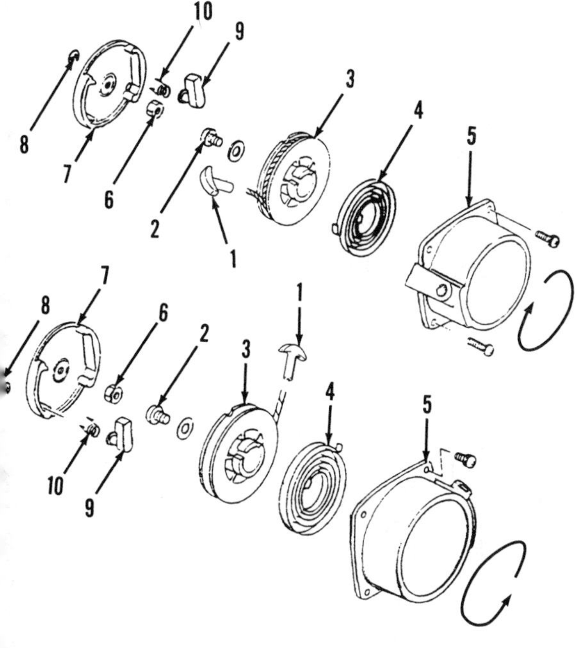

Fig. SH23—Exploded view of starters typical of the types used on some models. The upper view is for C-20, T-20 and F-21. The lower view is assembled to turn the opposite direction for use on F-20 models.

1. Handle
2. Screw
3. Pulley and rope
4. Recoil spring
5. Housing
6. Nut
7. Pawl retainer
8. "E" ring
9. Pawl
10. Spring

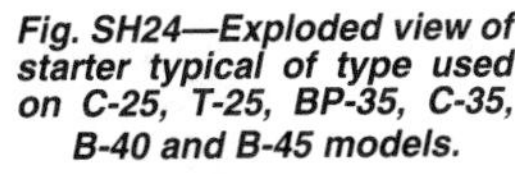

Fig. SH24—Exploded view of starter typical of type used on C-25, T-25, BP-35, C-35, B-40 and B-45 models.

1. Handle
2. Screw
3. Friction plate
4. Ratchet
5. Friction spring
6. Spring
7. Pulley and rope
8. Recoil spring
9. Housing
10. Nut
11. Plate

Fig. SH25—Exploded view of starter typical of type used on F-18, T-18, C-230 and T-230 models.

1. Handle
2. Screw
3. Washer
4. Plate
5. Wave washer
6. Ratchet
7. Pulley and rope
8. Recoil spring
9. Housing
10. Nut
11. Plate

wind the spring into the housing. The inner end of the spring should contact the center post.

Refer to Fig. SH24 for the starter used on C-25, T-25, BP-35, C-35, B-40 and B-45 models. Remove handle (1) and allow the rope to wind into the starter. Remove the center screw (2) and friction plate (3). Remove the ratchet (4), friction spring (5) and spring (6), then remove the pulley (7). The recoil spring (8) may rewind uncontrollably causing injury. Wear appropriate safety eye wear and gloves before removing the recoil spring (8). If necessary, unscrew the lock nut (10) and remove plate (11) from the engine crankshaft. On some models, the recoil spring (8) is contained in a cassette.

Refer to Fig. SH25 while disassembling and assembling the starter used on F-18, T-18, C-230 and T-230 models.

It is important to use the correct diameter and length of rope as follows.

Model	Diameter	Length
F-18, T-18, C-230, F-230, T-230, LE-230	0.130 in. (3 mm)	29.875 in. (75.9 cm)
C-20, F-20, T-20, LT-20, F-21	0.130 in. (3 mm)	33.25 in. (84.5 cm)
C-25, T-25, C-35	0.140 in. (3.5 mm)	31.75 in. (80.6 cm)
C-27, T-27, C-250, LE-250, T-250	0.140 in. (3.5 mm)	32.5 in. (82.6 cm)
BP-35, B-40, B-45, RC-45	0.170 in. (4 mm)	31.875 in. (81 cm)

On all models, attach the rope to the pulley, then wrap the rope onto the pulley leaving about 6-8 in. of rope hanging free. Install the pulley over the center post of the housing while making sure the pulley engages the end of the rewind spring. Preload the rewind spring by turning the pulley 2-3 turns, then thread the rope through the housing and attach handle. Coat the threads of the retaining screw with medium strength Loctite, then install and tighten the screw securely. Pull the handle, then allow the rope to rewind. If the rope does not rewind properly, preload the spring another turn.

NOTE: If the rope is too long or too large in diameter, it will bind before rewinding properly. Make sure the rope is not binding.

To make sure the spring is not tightened too much, pull the rope out completely, then turn the pulley an additional 1/2-3/4 turn. If the rope cannot be pulled out completely, the spring is bound and will break. Loosen the spring slightly if required. A proper setting will allow the rope to be fully extended and will also wind the rope onto the pulley fully.

CLUTCH

Refer to the appropriate ENGINE SERVICE section for clutch removal and service procedures.

Illustrations courtesy Shindaiwa Inc.

SMC

GASOLINE POWERED STRING TRIMMERS

Model	Engine Manufacturer	Engine Model	Displacement
GT-140	Kioritz	....	13.8 cc
GT-200	Kioritz	....	21.2 cc

ENGINE INFORMATION

All Models

All models are equipped with Kioritz two-stroke air-cooled engines. Identify engine model by trimmer model or engine displacement. Refer to KIORITZ ENGINE SERVICE section of this manual.

FUEL MIXTURE

All Models

Manufacturer recommends mixing regular grade gasoline (unleaded is an acceptable substitute) with a good quality two-stroke air-cooled engine oil at a 25:1 ratio. Do not use fuel containing alcohol.

STRING TRIMMER

Model GT-140

Model GT-140 is equipped with a single strand semi-automatic trimmer head shown in Fig. SC10. Line may be manually advanced with engine stopped by pushing in on housing (9) while pulling on line. Procedure may have to be repeated to obtain desired line length. To advance line with engine running, operate engine at full rpm and tap housing (9) on the ground. Each time housing is tapped on the ground, a measured amount of trimmer line will be advanced.

To renew trimmer line, remove cotter key (10) and twist housing (9) counterclockwise to remove housing. Remove foam pad (6) and any remaining line on spool (3). Clean spool and inside of housing. Cut off approximately 25 feet (7.6 m) of 0.080 inch (2 mm) monofilament line and tape one end of line to spool (Fig. SC12). Wind line on spool in direction indicated by arrow on spool (Fig. SC13). Install foam pad with line end protruding from between foam pad and spool as shown in Fig. SC13. Insert line end through line guide and install housing and spring assembly on spool. Push in on housing and twist housing to lock into position. Install cotter key through hole in housing and cover.

Model GT-200

Model GT-200 is equipped with a single strand semi-automatic trimmer head shown in Fig. SC11. Line may be manually advanced with engine stopped by pushing in on housing (12) while pulling on line. Procedure may have to be repeated until desired line length is obtained. To advance line with engine running, operate trimmer engine at full rpm and tap housing (12) on the ground. Each time housing is tapped on the ground, a measured amount of trimmer line is advanced.

To renew trimmer line, remove cotter pin (13). Twist housing (12) counterclockwise and remove housing. Remove

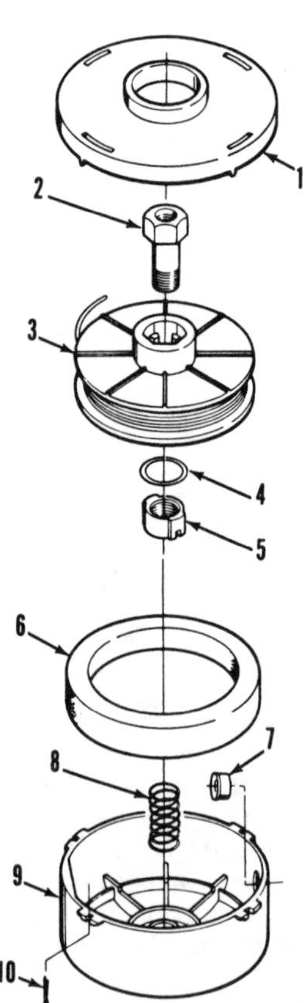

Fig. SC10—Exploded view of single strand semi-automatic trimmer head used on Model GT-140.

1. Cover
2. Drive adapter
3. Spool
4. "O" ring
5. Drive adapter nut
6. Foam pad
7. Line guide
8. Spring
9. Housing
10. Cotter pin

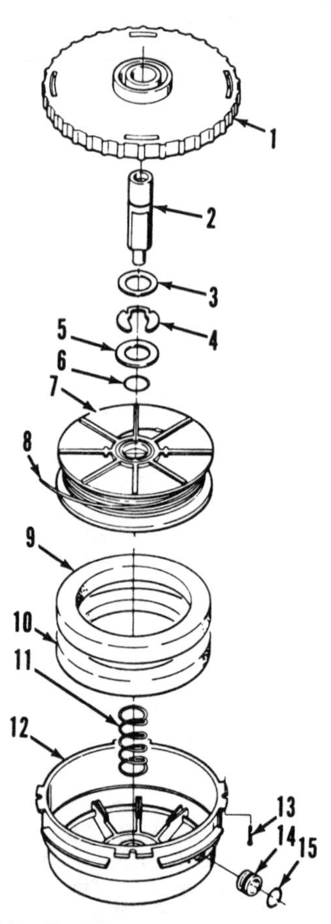

Fig. SC11—Exploded view of single strand semi-automatic trimmer head used on Model GT-200.

1. Cover
2. Drive adapter
3. Washer
4. Retainer
5. Washer
6. Retainer ring
7. Spool
8. Line
9. Foam pad
10. Foam pad
11. Spring
12. Housing
13. Cotter pin
14. Line guide
15. Retainer

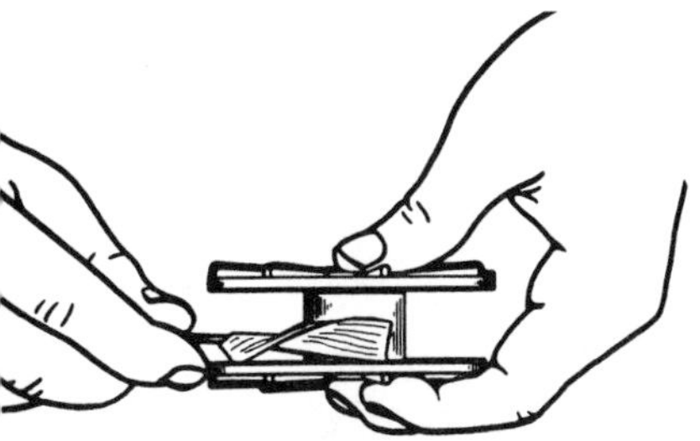

Fig. SC12—Tape one end of new line to center of spool as shown.

foam pads (9 and 10) and any remaining line from spool (7). Clean spool and inner area of housing. Cut off approximately 25 feet (7.6 mm) of 0.080 inch (2 mm) monofilament line and tape one end of line to spool (Fig. SC12). Wind line on spool in direction indicated by arrow on spool (Fig. SC14). Install foam pads (9 and 10—Fig. SC11) so line is protruding from center of foam pads (Fig. SC14). Insert end of line through line guide and install spool, housing and spring. Push in on housing and twist housing to lock in position and install cotter pin (13—Fig. SC11).

DRIVE SHAFT

All Models

All models are equipped with a flexible drive shaft enclosed in the drive shaft housing tube. Drive shaft has squared ends which engage adapters at each end. Drive shaft should be removed for maintenance at 50-hour intervals of use. Remove screw (4—Fig. SC15) and bolt (3) at bearing head housing and separate bearing head from drive shaft housing. Pull flexible drive shaft from housing. Lubricate drive shaft with lithium base grease and reinstall in drive shaft housing with end which was previously at clutch end bearing head end. Reversing drive shaft ends extends drive shaft life. Make certain ends of drive shaft are properly located into upper and lower square drive adapters when installing.

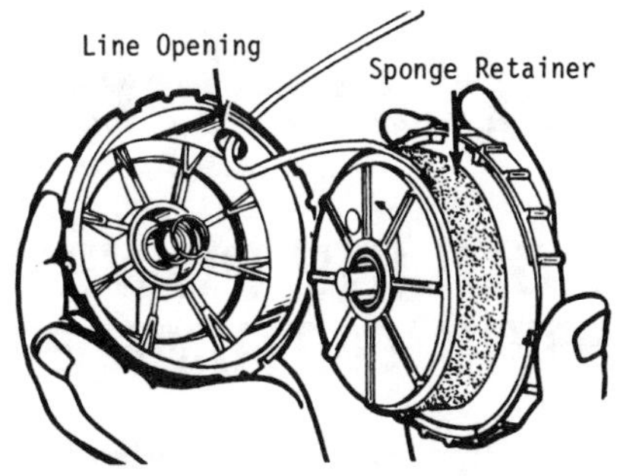

Fig. SC-13—Install foam pad with line protruding between pad and spool as shown. Wind line in direction indicated by arrow on spool.

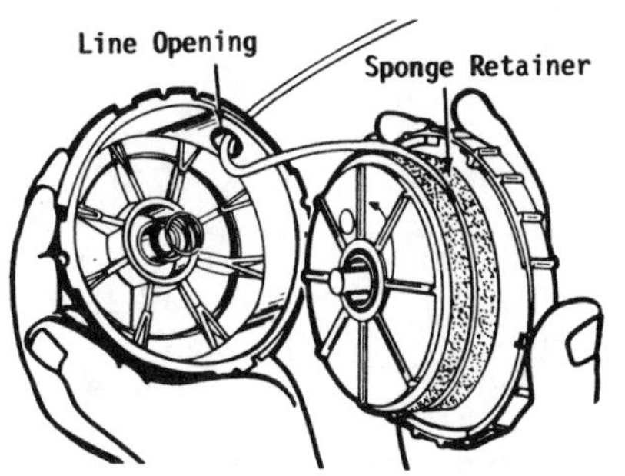

Fig. SC-14—Install foam pads with line protruding from between pads. Wind line in direction indicated by arrow on spool.

BEARING HEAD

All Models

All models are equipped with the bearing head shown in Fig. SC15. Bearing head is equipped with sealed bearings and requires no regular maintenance. To disassemble bearing head, remove screw (4) and bolt (3) and separate bearing head from drive shaft housing tube. Remove trimmer head assembly and cup washer (13). Remove snap ring (10) and use a suitable puller to remove arbor shaft (11) and bearing assembly. Remove nut (6) and press bearings (7 and 9) and spacer (8) from arbor shaft as required.

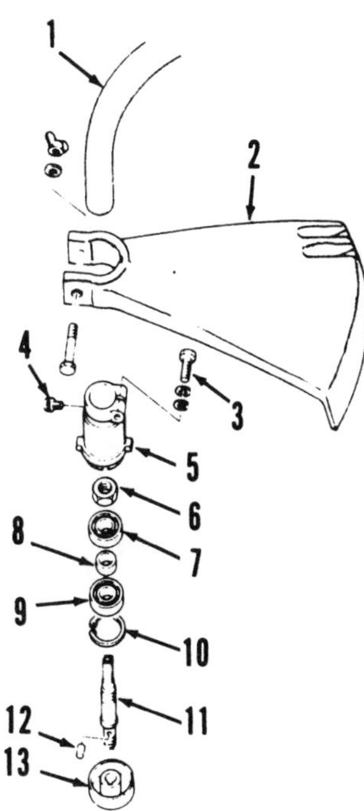

Fig. SC15—Exploded view of bearing head used on all models. Bearings (7 and 9) are sealed bearings and require no regular maintenance.

1. Drive shaft housing
2. Shield
3. Bolt
4. Screw
5. Housing
6. Nut
7. Bearing
8. Spacer
9. Bearing
10. Snap ring
11. Arbor (output) shaft
12. Pin
13. Cup washer

SNAPPER

GASOLINE POWERED STRING TRIMMERS

Model	Engine Manufacturer	Engine Model	Displacement
210SS	Mitsubishi	T110	21.2 cc
211SST	Mitsubishi	T110	21.2 cc
212CST	McCulloch	...	21.2 cc
213CST	McCulloch	...	21.2 cc
214DCST	McCulloch	...	21.2 cc
215SST	McCulloch	...	21.2 cc
240SS	Mitsubishi	T140	24.1 cc
240SST	Mitsubishi	T140	24.1 cc
311	PPP	99E	31.0 cc
410	Mitsubishi	T200-PD	40.6 cc
2111SST	Mitsubishi	TMX-21	21.2 cc
2401SST	Mitsubishi	TM-24	24.1 cc
4111SST	Mitsubishi	T200	40.6 cc
P212CST	McCulloch	...	21.2 cc

ENGINE INFORMATION

The models in this section are equipped with a McCulloch, Mitsubishi or Piston Powered Products (PPP) engine. Refer to appropriate engine service section for engine service information.

FUEL MIXTURE

Manufacturer recommends mixing leaded or unleaded gasoline with a high-quality two-stroke engine oil designed for air-cooled engines. Recommended fuel:oil ratio is 32:1 when using Snapper two-stroke oil. Use of 50:1 oils is not recommended. Manufacturer recommends addition of a fuel stabilizer, such as Sta-Bil, to fuel to prevent fuel degradation.

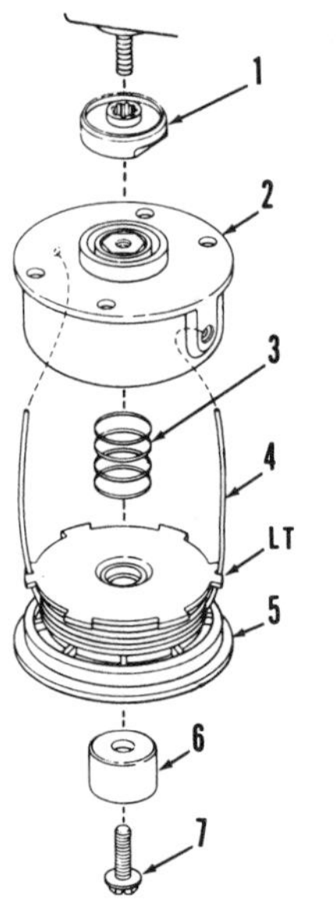

Fig. SP10—Exploded view of semi-automatic trimmer head used on Models 210SS, 211SST and 311, and as an option on some other models.

1. Washer
2. Hub
3. Spring
4. Line
5. Spool
6. Button
7. Screw
LT. Lock tab (line)

STRING TRIMMER

Models 210SS, 211SST And 311

Models 210SS, 211SST and 311 are equipped with a dual strand, semi-automatic trimmer head (Fig. SP10). To extend line with engine stopped, push up on bump button (6) and pull out each line. Repeat procedure if needed to reach desired length.

To extend line with engine running, operate trimmer at full rpm and tap button (6) on the ground. Each time button is tapped a measured amount of line is automatically advanced.

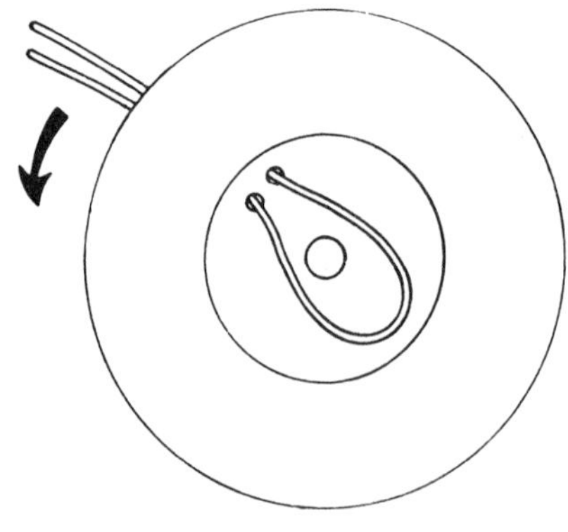

Fig. SP11—Insert line ends through holes in spool and pull line out in two equal lengths. Wind line in direction indicated by arrow on spool.

To install new trimmer line, hold hub (2) and push spool (5) upward against hub. Twist spool to the left until tabs lock the spool to the hub. Tabs can be viewed through the four noles in the hub. Remove screw (7) and bump button (6). Twist spool to the right to unlock tabs and pull spool downward to remove. Loop 40 feet (12 m) of 0.095-in. (2.4 mm) diameter monofilament line into two equal lengths. Insert line ends through the two holes in spool as shown in Fig. SP11. Wind both lines in direction indicated by arrow on spool. Snap lines into lock tabs (LT—Fig. SP10) of spool and insert line ends through the line guide holes in hub. Install spool and bump button. Install screw. Pull lines to free them from lock tabs.

Models 240SS, 240SST And 410

Models 240SS, 240SST and 410 are equipped with a heavy-duty manual, dual strand trimmer head (Fig. SP12). To extend line, stop trimmer engine. Loosen knob (9) and pull each line until desired length is obtained. Tighten knob.

To install new line, cut 15 feet (4.6 m) of 0.095-in. (2.4 mm) diameter monofilament line. Remove lock knob (9) and remove lower housing (8) and spool (5). Remove any remaining old line. Clean all parts of trimmer head with a wet, soapy cloth. Pull line guides (3) down (do not remove) and clean outside surfaces. Apply a few drops of oil into cavities after cleaning. Loop new line into two equal lengths and insert line ends through holes at center of spool. Pull line ends out until stopped by spool. Wind both lines in direction indicated by arrow on spool. Insert line ends in line guides and reinstall spool, lower housing and lock knob.

Models 212CST, 213CST, 214DCST, 215SST, 2111SST And P212CST

Models 212CST, 213CST, 214DCST, 215SST, 2111SST and P212CST are equipped with the dual strand, semi-automatic trimmer head shown in Fig. SP13. To extend line with engine stopped, push up on bump button (9) and pull out each line. Repeat procedure if needed to reach desired length.

To extend line with engine running, operate trimmer at full rpm and tap button (9) on the ground. Each time button is tapped a measured amount of line is automatically advanced.

To install new line, unscrew cover (7) by rotating clockwise (L.H. threads). Remove spool and remaining old line. Clean parts. Loop 20 feet (6 m) of 0.080-in. (2 mm) diameter monofilament line into two equal lengths. Insert loop in slot (S—Fig. SP14) on spool and wind both lines in clockwise direction as viewed from ground side of spool. Leave 6 inches (152 mm) extending at each end. While positioning string ends in line guides, reassemble trimmer head.

Models 2401SST And 4111SST

Models 2401SST and 4111SST are equipped with a multiple strand, fixed trimmer head. Trimmer string is routed between two flanges. To install new string, insert new string in passages between flanges.

BLADE

Some models may be equipped with the blades shown in Fig. SP15. Install blade as shown in Fig. SP16.

To sharpen saw blade, refer to Fig. SP17. Check blade for nicks and cracks and discard blade if damaged. Sharpen blade cutting edges as shown in Fig. SP17. Maintain radius at base of tooth to prevent blade cracking. Note also that idle speed of engine must be lowered when blade is installed.

DRIVE SHAFT

Models 212CST, 213CST, 214DCST, 311 And P212CST

Models 212CST, 213CST, 214DCST, 311 and P212CST are equipped with a flexible drive shaft. The drive shaft should be removed, cleaned and lubricated with lithium-base grease after every 20 hours of operation. Mark shaft ends before removal, then reverse ends during installation to extend life of drive shaft. Be sure drive shaft is properly seated at engine end.

All Other Models

These models are equipped with a straight, steel drive shaft. Bushings on Model 215SST are not renewable. Bushings on all other models are renewable. Periodic maintenance is not required. If

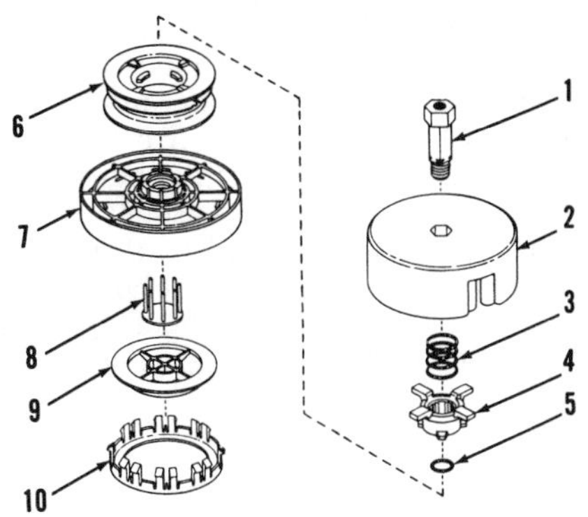

Fig. SP13—Exploded view of dual strand, semi-automatic trimmer head used on Models 212CST, 213CST, 214DCST, 215SST, 2111SST and P212CST.

1. Adapter
2. Housing
3. Spring
4. Indexer
5. Retainer
6. Spool
7. Cover
8. Actuator
9. Button
10. Retainer

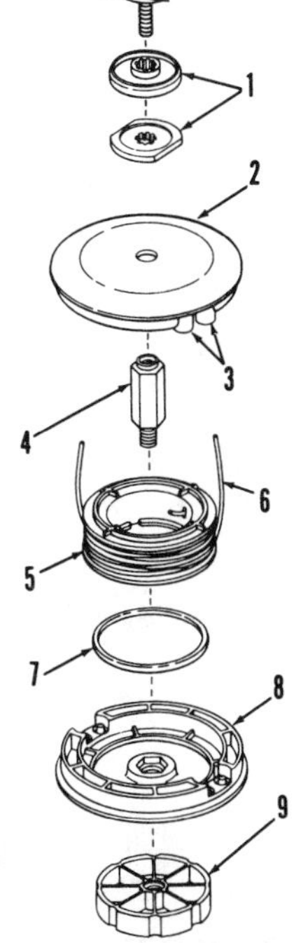

Fig. SP12—Exploded view of manual advance, dual strand trimmer head used on Models 240SS, 240SST and 410, and as an option on some other models.

1. Washers
2. Upper housing
3. Line guides
4. Adapter
5. Spool
6. Line
7. "O" ring
8. Lower housing
9. Lock knob

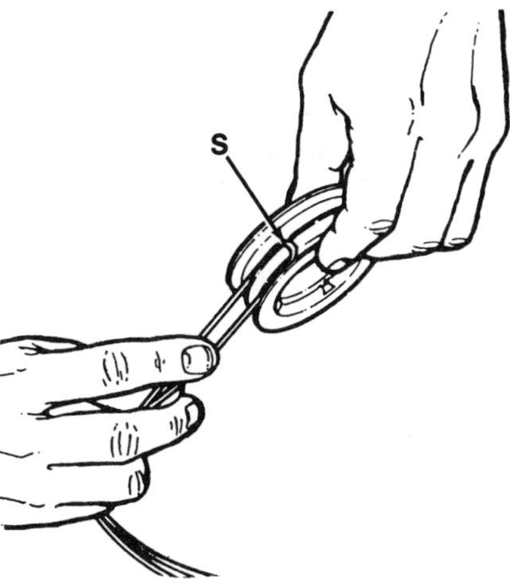

Fig. SP14—When installing new line, insert looped end of line into slot (S) in spool.

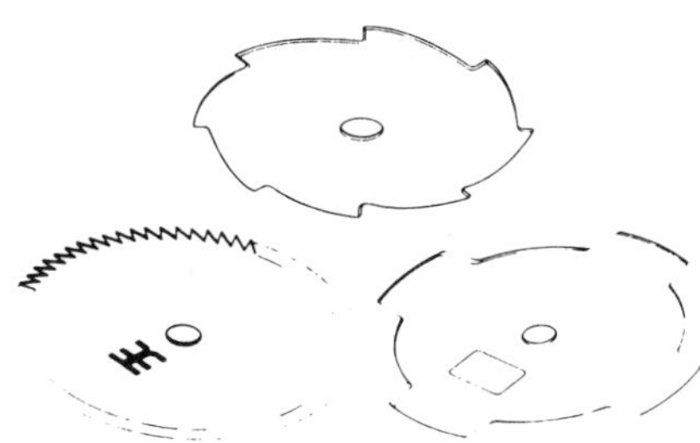

Fig. SP15—Some models may be equipped with a four-edge cutting blade, eight-edge cutting blade or saw blade.

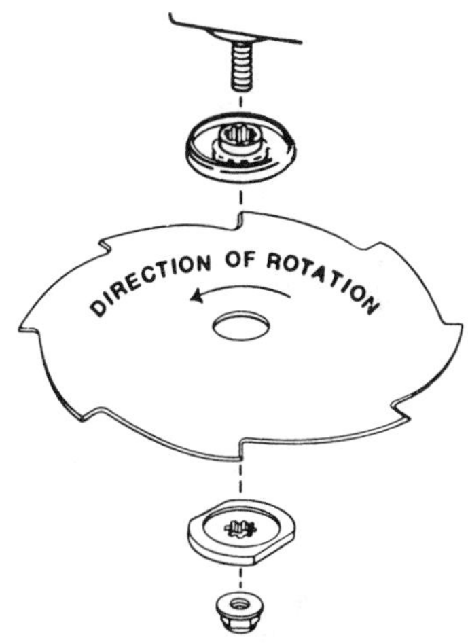

Fig. SP16—Install blade with cutting edges located as shown.

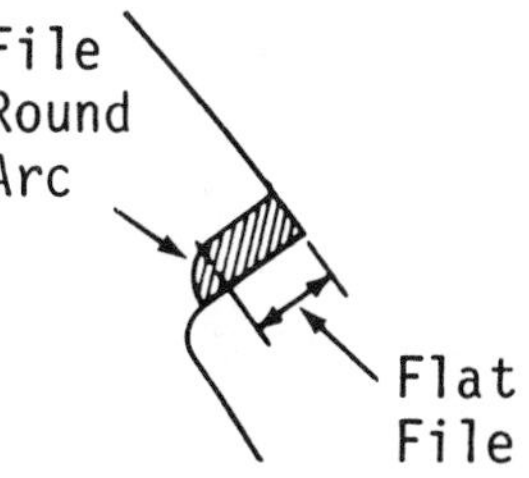

Fig. SP17—To prevent blade cracking, the blade teeth must be sharpened as shown so the arc in the cutting edge is maintained.

drive shaft is removed, lubricate shaft with lithium-base grease before installation.

To renew bushings, except on Model 215SST, mark location of old bushings so new bushings can be installed in original position. Use a suitable puller or driver to dislodge bushings.

BEARING HEAD

Models 212CST, 213CST, 214DCST, 311 And P212CST

The bearing head on Models 212CST, 213CST, 214DCST, 311 and P212CST has sealed bearings so periodic maintenance is not required. Bearing and arbor assembly (2—Fig. SP18) on Model 214DCST is available separately from housing. The bearing head on all other models so equipped is available only as a unit assembly.

GEAR HEAD

All Models So Equipped

The gear head, on models so equipped, should be lubricated after every 50 hours of operation. Remove trimmer head or blade assembly and inject lithium-base grease through grease fitting in side of housing (see Fig. SP19) until grease appears at lower seal. Failure to remove trimmer head or blade assembly before injecting grease may damage bearing, seal or housing.

To disassemble gear, remove trimmer head or blade, adapters and spacer. Separate gear head from drive shaft housing. Remove snap ring (1—Fig. SP20). Insert a screwdriver or suitable wedge into gear head housing clamp split and carefully expand housing to remove input shaft (7) and bearing assembly. Remove snap ring (2) and press bearings (3 and 4) from input shaft. Remove seal (16) and detach snap ring (15), then use a suitable puller to remove arbor (13) and bearing (14) as an assembly. If bearing (11) remains in housing, heat housing to 140° F (60° C) and tap housing on a wood block to dislodge bearing.

THROTTLE TRIGGER AND CABLE

The inner throttle cable should be lubricated with engine oil after every 20 hours of operation.

The throttle cable should be adjusted so there is approximately 0.04 inch (1 mm) throttle trigger free play. To adjust free play, refer to Figs. SP21, SP22 or SP23, depending on type of carburetor, and reposition adjuster or cable as needed.

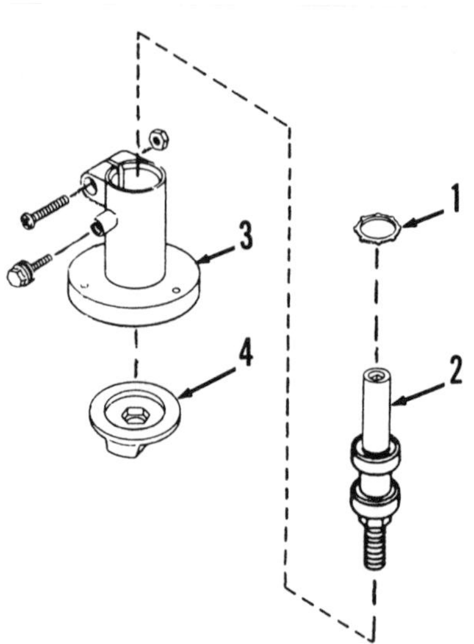

Fig. SP18—Exploded view of bearing head used on Model 214DCST.

1. Retainer
2. Arbor & bearing assy.
3. Housing
4. Washer

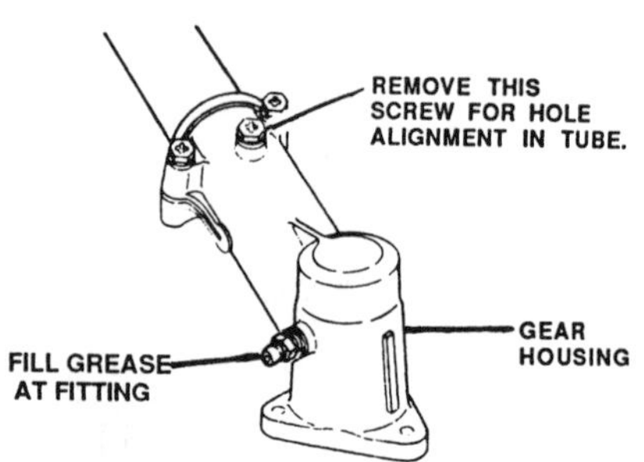

Fig. SP19—To lubricate gear head, inject grease through grease fitting until grease appears at lower seal.

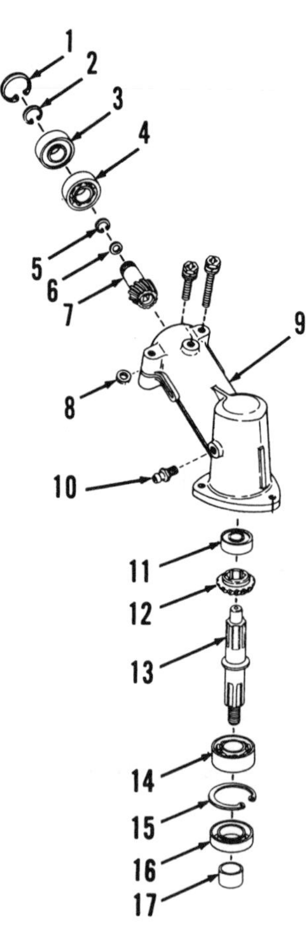

Fig. SP20—Exploded view of gear head used on models with straight drive shaft tube.

1. Snap ring
2. Snap ring
3. Bearing
4. Bearing
5. Snap ring
6. Washer
7. Input shaft
8. Spacer
9. Housing
10. Grease fitting
11. Bearing
12. Gear
13. Arbor
14. Bearing
15. Snap ring
16. Seal
17. Spacer

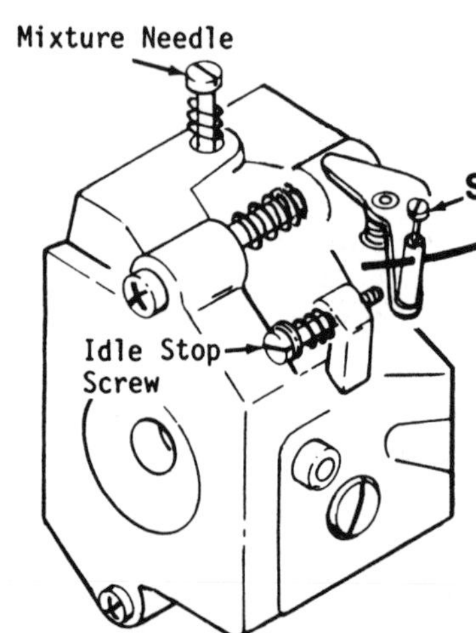

Fig. SP21—Loosen set screw (S) and move throttle cable to obtain throttle trigger free play of approximately 0.4 inch (1 mm).

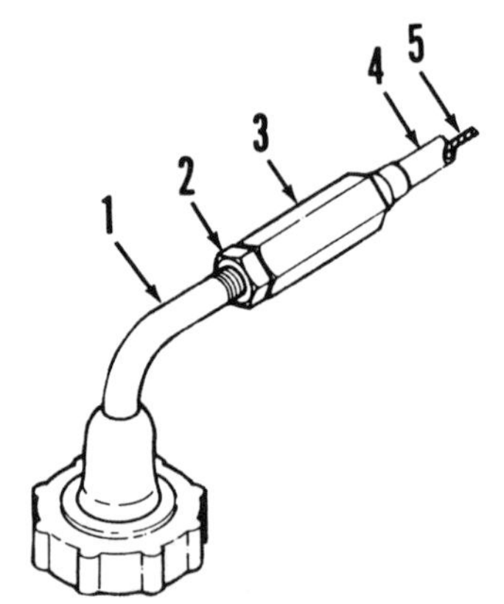

Fig. SP22—Loosen jam nut (2) and rotate adjuster nut (3) to obtain throttle trigger free play of approximately 0.4 inch (1 mm).

1. Cable housing
2. Jam nut
3. Adjuster nut
4. Housing
5. Inner cable

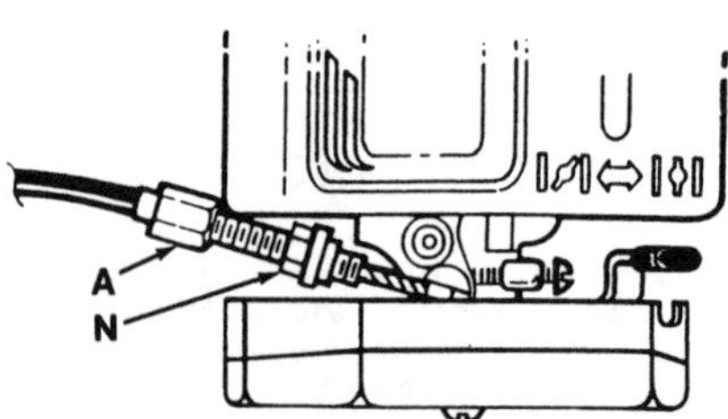

Fig. SP23—Loosen jam nut (N) and rotate adjuster nut (A) to obtain throttle trigger free play of approximately 0.4 inch (1 mm).

SOLO

GASOLINE POWERED TRIMMERS

Model	Engine Make	Displacement
120, 124 & 126	Solo	25 cc
134	Solo	34 cc
140	Solo	40 cc
S100 & S200	Kawasaki	18.4 cc
S300	Kawasaki	24.1 cc
S400	Kawasaki	40.2 cc

ENGINE INFORMATION

Solo or Kawasaki two-stroke air-cooled gasoline engines are used. Service information for Solo engines was not available at the time of printing this manual. For Kawasaki engines, refer to the KAWASAKI Engine Service section of this manual.

FUEL MIXTURE

Manufacturer recommends mixing gasoline with Solo Superior or Castrol Super TT two-stroke, air-cooled engine oil at a ratio of 40 parts fuel and one part oil (40:1). If a two-stroke, air-cooled engine oil other than Solo Superior or Castrol Super TT is used, manufacturer recommends mixing fuel and oil at a ratio of 25:1.

STRING TRIMMER

Manual Advance Trimmer

Refer to Fig. SO1 for an exploded view of manual advance, dual line trimmer head used on some models.. To advance trimmer line, shut off engine. Loosen knob (6) until spool housing (5) can be turned. Pull out line ends so they are approximately 10 cm (4 in.) long. Make certain that spool locating teeth engage notches in housing (5), then tighten knob (6).

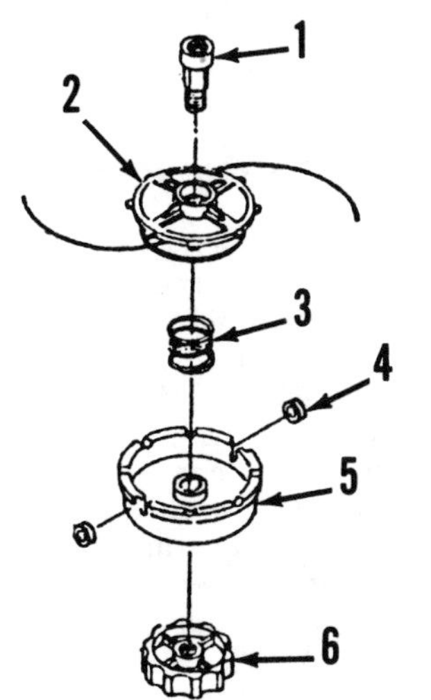

Fig. SO1—Fig. Exploded view of manual dual strand trimmer head used on some models.

1. Shaft bolt
2. Spool
3. Spring
4. Line guide
5. Hub
6. Knob

To install new line, remove knob (6). Note that knob may have LH or RH threads. Separate spool housing (5) and spool (2) from trimmer. Remove any old line remaining on spool.

Recommended line diameter is 2.4 mm (0.095 in.). Maximum length of line is 6 m (20 ft.). Thread half the length of the new line through eyelet of spool. Wind both ends of line on spool in the direction indicated by arrow on spool. Be careful not to allow the lines to cross over each other. Insert line ends through line guides (4) in housing while assembling spool (2), spring (3) and housing (5). Pull out each line to a length of approximately 10 cm (4 in.). Tighten knob (6) while making sure that spool locating teeth engage notches in housing.

Semi-Automatic Advance Trimmer

Refer to Fig. SO2 for an exploded view of semi-automatic, dual line (red and black) trimmer head used on some models. To extend line with engine stopped, pull down on lower half of trimmer head and rotate in a counterclockwise direction while pulling line out. To extend trimmer line with engine running, operate engine at full speed and tap the trimmer head on the ground. The line should automatically advance approximately 25 mm (1 in.) each time trimmer head is tapped on the ground.

To renew trimmer line, insert locking pin into hole in top of gear head. Unscrew lower part of trimmer head using an Allen wrench. Rotate nut (10) clockwise (left-hand threads) to loosen. Remove any old line remaining on spool (4). Trimmer head uses two 3 m (10 ft.) pieces of 2.4-3.3 mm (0.095-0.130 in.) diameter line. Insert end of each line

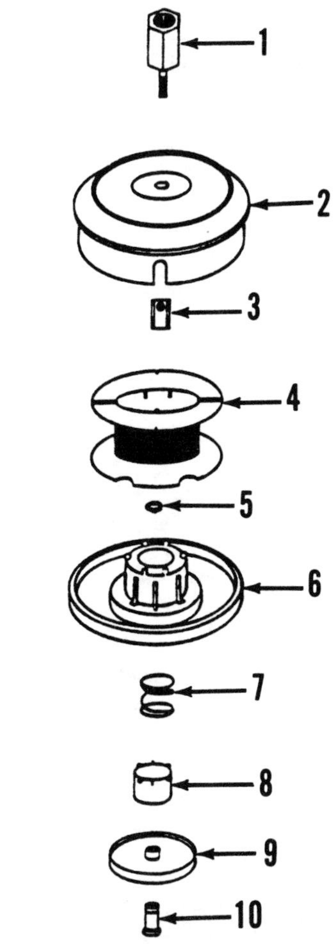

Fig. SO2—Exploded view of semi-automatic dual strand trimmer used on some models.

1. Shaft bolt
2. Case
3. Line guide
4. Spool
5. Snap ring
6. Cover
7. Spring
8. Outer drive
9. Button
10. Nut

into inner retainer of spool. Turn the spool over and wind both lines in the direction indicated by arrow on spool. Make certain that the lines are wound parallel and do not cross over each other. Leave at least 10 cm (4 in.) of line extending from spool, then clip each line into the retainer notches in the spool to prevent the line from unwinding. Thread line ends through line guides (3) and insert spool (4) into the housing (2). Pull lines outward to release them from retaining notches. Assemble cover (6), spring (7), drive (8) and button (9) and nut (10). Turn nut counterclockwise to tighten.

Semi-Automatic Advance Trimmer

Refer to Fig. SO3 for an exploded view of semi-automatic, dual line (solid red) trimmer used on some models. To extend line with engine stopped, push button (4) and pull line out of line guide to desired length. To extend line with engine running, operate engine at full rpm and tap button (4) on the ground. A measured amount of line will automatically be advanced each time button is tapped on the ground.

To renew trimmer line, push in on locking tabs and unsnap cover (5) from housing (1). Remove button (4) and spool (3). Remove any remaining line from spool. Recommended line diameter is 2.4 mm (0.095 in.) and length is 5 m (20 ft.). Fold line in half leaving one end 14 cm (5.5 in.) longer than the other (Fig. SO4). Hook new line into the slot in center of spool, then wind both ends of the line onto spool in direction of arrow (A). Note that one line is wound on one side of the spool center divider, while the other line is wound on the other side of the divider. Thread ends of line through line guides (2—Fig. SO3) and install spool (3) into the spool housing (1). Install the button (4) and snap the cover (5) into place. Trim line ends so they are equal length.

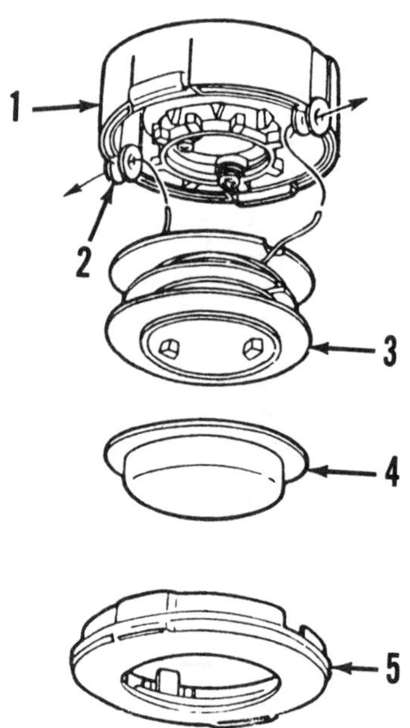

Fig. SO3—Exploded view of semi-automatic dual strand trimmer head used on some models.

1. Trimmer case
2. Line guide
3. Spool
4. Button
5. Cover

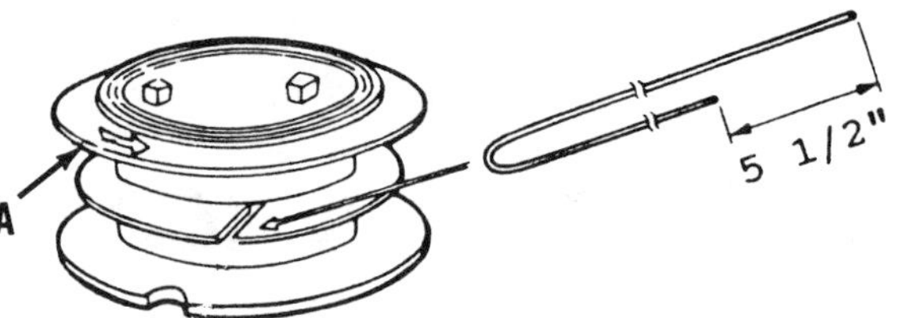

Fig. SO4—Fold new line in half and hook line in slot. Wind in direction of the arrow (A). Refer to text.

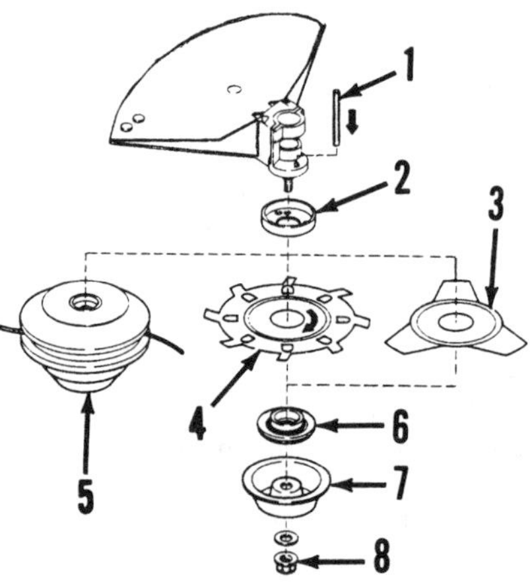

Fig. SO5—Exploded view of cutting blades available for some models.

1. Pin
2. Grass deflector plate
3. Ridged grass blade
4. Flexible grass blade
5. String trimmer head
6. Thrust washer
7. Cap
8. Nut

BLADE

Some models may be equipped with blades shown in Fig. SO5 and Fig. SO6. To remove blade, insert locking pin (1) to lock the drive shaft. Remove retaining nut (8) and withdraw blade. Note that retaining nut may have either left-hand threads or right-hand threads, depending on direction of blade rotation.

When installing blade, make certain that cutting edges point in direction of blade rotation. Install thrust washer (6) with cupped side towards the blade. Tighten nut (8) securely. Remove locking pin (1).

FLEXIBLE DRIVE SHAFT

Models equipped with a curved drive shaft housing use a flexible drive shaft. The drive shaft should be removed, cleaned and lubricated periodically. Drive shaft may be removed by separating drive shaft housing from the engine. Lubricate drive shaft with multipurpose grease.

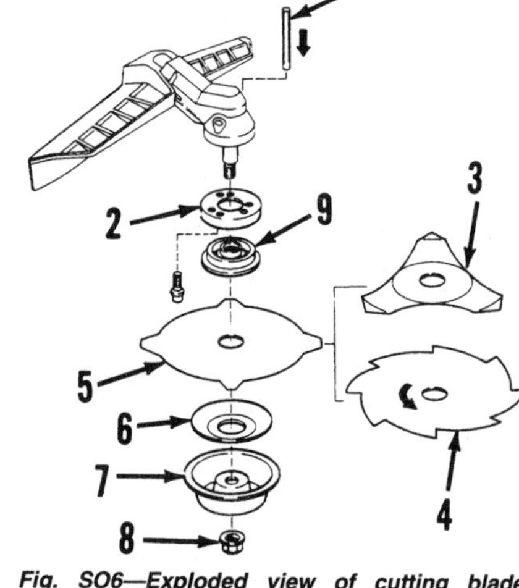

Fig. SO6—Exploded view of cutting blades available for some models.

1. Pin
2. Grass shield
3. Ridged grass blade
4. Eight edge blade
5. Four edge blade
6. Thrust washer
7. Support plate
8. Nut

SOLID DRIVE SHAFT

Models equipped with a straight drive shaft housing use a solid drive shaft supported in bushings in drive shaft housing. No regular maintenance is required. Note that drive shaft may be either splined or threaded into the clutch drum.

BEARING HEAD

Refer to Fig. SO7 for an exploded view of bearing head used on some models. Bearings (3 and 6) are sealed and require no regular maintenance.

To disassemble bearing head, remove trimmer head, drive shaft bolt (9), grass shield (8), cup washer (7) and safety shield (6) from bearing head. Remove bolts and separate bearing head housing (2 and 3). Remove arbor (4) and bearings. Clean, inspect and renew parts as necessary.

GEAR HEAD

Some models are equipped with gear head shown in Fig. SO8. Gear head lu-

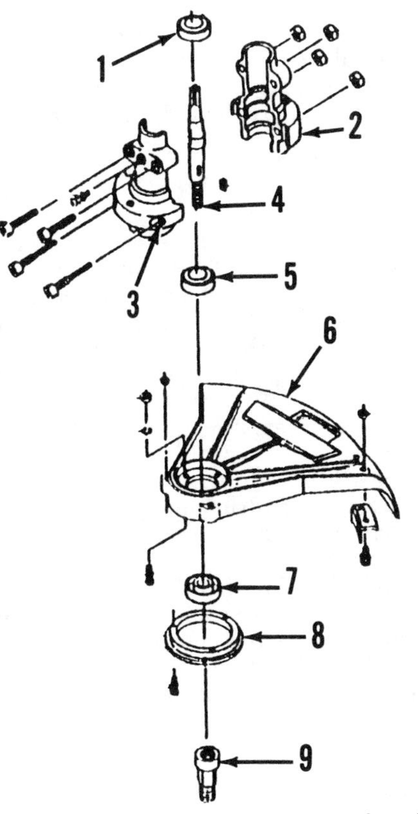

Fig. SO7—Exploded view of bearing head used on some models.

1. Bearing
2. Housing
3. Housing
4. Arbor
5. Bearing
6. Shield
7. Cup washer
8. Grass shield
9. Shaft bolt

Fig. SO8—Exploded view of gear head used on some models.

1. Snap ring
2. Snap ring
3. Bearing
4. Bearing
5. Input shaft & gear
6. Housing
7. Clamp bolt
8. Bolt
9. Check plug
10. Bearing
11. Gear
12. Arbor shaft
13. Bearing
14. Spacer
15. Snap ring
16. Seal
17. Cup washer

bricant level should be checked at 50-hour intervals of use. Remove check plug (9) from side of gear housing. If no grease is visible inside the housing, fill gear head housing approximately 2/3 full with multipurpose grease. Do not use a pressure grease gun to fill gear head as damage to bearing seals may occur.

To disassemble gear head shown in Fig. SO8, remove trimmer head or blade. Remove clamp bolts from gear head housing (6) and separate drive shaft tube from housing. Remove snap ring (2). Insert screwdriver or other suitable wedge in clamping split in housing (6) and carefully expand the housing. Pull input shaft (5) and bearings (3 and 4) from housing. Remove cup washer (17) and seal (16). Remove snap ring (15), then pull arbor shaft (12) from housing. If bearing (10) remains in housing, heat housing to approximately 140 degrees F (60 degrees C) and tap housing on wooden block to dislodge bearing from housing.

Clean, inspect and renew parts as needed. To reassemble, reverse the disassembly procedure. Fill gear head housing approximately 2/3 full with multipurpose grease.

To disassemble gear head shown in Fig. SO9, remove trimmer head or blade. Remove clamp bolts from gear head housing (5) and separate drive shaft tube from housing. Remove snap ring (2). Insert a screwdriver or suitable wedge tool into housing clamp split and carefully spread housing to remove input shaft (4) and bearings (3). Unbolt and remove grass cover (15) and safety shield (20). Remove seal (13) and snap ring (12). Use a suitable puller to remove arbor shaft (10). If bearing (7) remains in housing, heat housing to approximately 140 degrees F (60 degrees C) and tap housing on wooden block to dislodge bearing from housing.

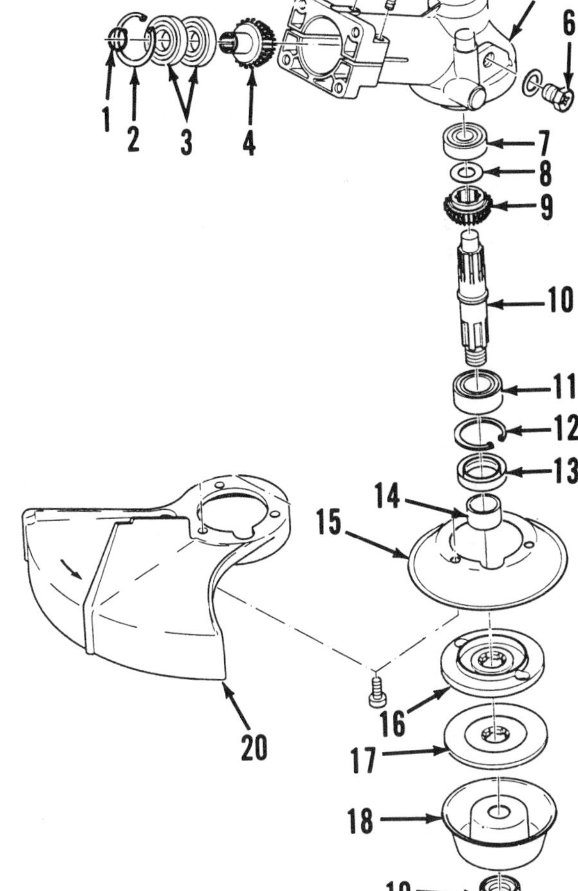

Fig. SO9—Exploded view of gear head used on some models.

1. Snap ring
2. Snap ring
3. Bearings
4. Input shaft & gear
5. Housing
6. Check plug
7. Bearing
8. Washer
9. Gear
10. Arbor shaft
11. Bearing
12. Snap ring
13. Seal
14. Spacer
15. Shield
16. Grass cover
17. Thrust washer
18. Support plate
19. Nut
20. Safety shield

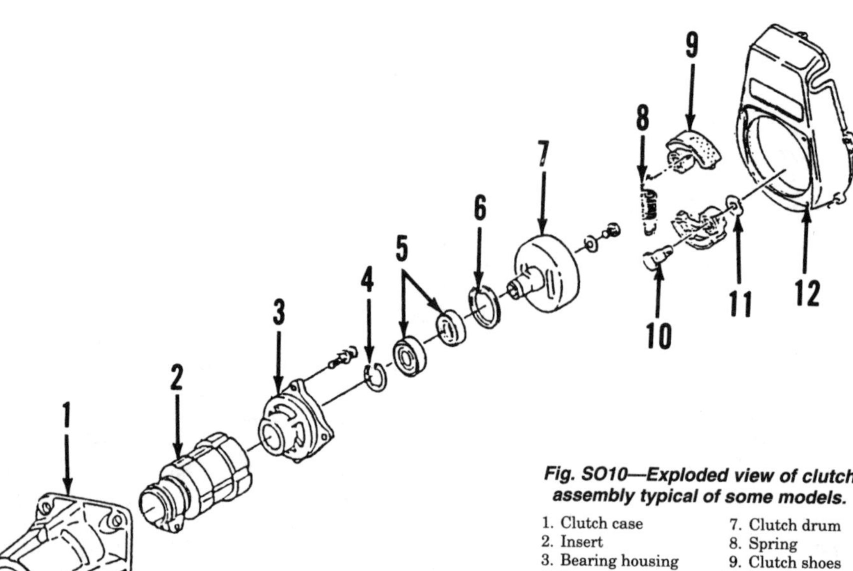

Fig. SO10—Exploded view of clutch assembly typical of some models.

1. Clutch case
2. Insert
3. Bearing housing
4. Snap ring
5. Bearings
6. Snap ring
7. Clutch drum
8. Spring
9. Clutch shoes
10. Shoulder bolt
11. Washer
12. Engine shroud

Clean, inspect and renew parts as needed. To reassemble, reverse the disassembly procedure. Fill gear head housing approximately 2/3 full with multipurpose grease.

CLUTCH

To remove clutch assembly, detach drive shaft tube from clutch housing. Remove screws attaching clutch case (1—Fig. SO10) to engine shroud (12). Separate clutch case with clutch drum (7) from engine. Unbolt and remove clutch shoes (9) from engine flywheel.

To disassemble clutch drum, reach through slots in drum and detach snap ring (6) from bearing carrier (3). Remove clutch drum and bearings (5) from carrier. Remove snap ring (4) and press bearings from clutch drum.

Inspect all parts for wear and renew as needed. When installing clutch shoes, note arrows on shoes indicating direction of rotation. Arrows must point in direction of crankshaft rotation.

STIHL

GASOLINE POWERED STRING TRIMMERS

Model	Engine Manufacturer	Engine Model	Displacement
FR106, FS106	Stihl	...	34.4 cc
FS36, FS40, FS44	Stihl	...	30.2 cc
FS48, FS52	Stihl	...	17.1 cc
FS50, FS51	Stihl	...	16.0 cc
FS56, FS60, FS62, FS62AVE, FS62AVRE, FS65, FS66, FS66AVE, FS66AVRE	Stihl	...	19.6 cc
FS80, FS81, FS81AVE, FS81AVRE	Stihl	...	22.5 cc
FS86AVE, FS86AVRE	Stihl	...	25.4 cc
FS90, FS96, FS150, FS151	Stihl	O15	32.0 cc
FS160	Stihl	...	29.8 cc
FS180, FS220	Stihl	...	35.2 cc
FS200	Stihl	O20	32.0 cc
FS202	Stihl	O20	35.0 cc
FS280	Stihl	...	39.0 cc
FS353	Stihl	O8S	56.0 cc
FS360	Stihl	...	51.7 cc
FS410	Stihl	O41	61.0 cc
FS420	Stihl	...	56.5 cc

ENGINE INFORMATION

The trimmer or brush cutter may be equipped with a two-stroke, air-cooled engine manufactured by Stihl. Refer to appropriate engine section in this manual for engine service information.

FUEL MIXTURE

Manufacturer recommends mixing regular or unleaded gasoline with a high-quality, two-stroke engine oil designed for air-cooled engines. Recommended fuel:oil ratio is 50:1 when using Stihl oil. Fuel:oil ratio should be 25:1 when using any other two-stroke oil.

STRING TRIMMER

Several types of string trimmer heads have been used. Some trimmers may be equipped with more than one type of trimmer head. Refer to Figs. SL10 through SL16 for an exploded view of trimmer head.

To extend trimmer line on manual trimmer heads (Figs. SL11 and SL12), stop engine and loosen lock knob (6) until lines may be pulled from spool. Pull lines out to desired length, then tighten knob.

To extend trimmer line on semi-automatic advance trimmer heads (Figs. SL10, SL13 and SL14), stop engine and push in on spool button and pull lines out to desired length. To advance trimmer line with engine running, operate engine at full rpm with trimmer head horizontal above the ground and tap trimmer head lightly against the ground. Each time head is tapped, a measured amount of line is advanced.

The trimmer heads shown in Figs. SL15 and SL16 automatically dispense line while engine is running without tapping trimmer head on ground.

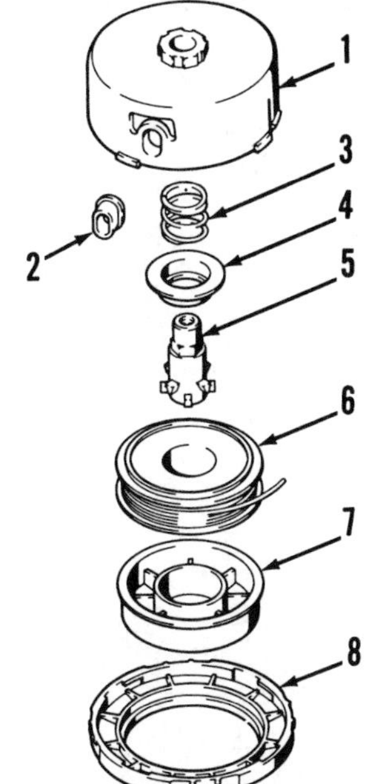

Fig. SL10—Exploded view of single-strand, semi-automatic advance trimmer head used on some models. Refill with 33 feet (10 m) of 0.080-in. (2.0 mm) diameter monofilament line.

1. Drum
2. Eyelet
3. Spring
4. Sleeve
5. Cam
6. Spool
7. Button
8. Cover

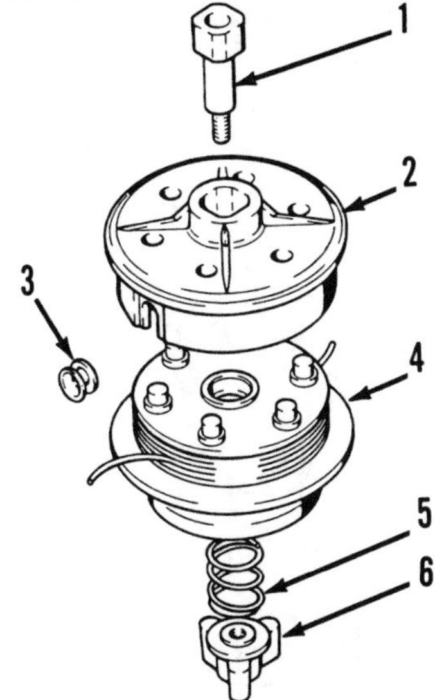

Fig. SL11—Exploded view of dual-strand, manual advance trimmer head used on some models. Refill with 17 feet (5.2 m) of 0.095-in. (2.4 mm) diameter line.

1. Adapter
2. Drum
3. Eyelet
4. Spool
5. Spring
6. Nut (L.H.)

Illustrations courtesy Stihl Inc.

To remove trimmer head, observe arrow on head when unscrewing head. Trimmer head, or head mounting nut if so equipped, has left-hand threads (turn clockwise to remove). Insert stop pin in bore at top of gear head to lock drive shaft when removing and installing trimmer head.

To install new line, remove trimmer head screw cap or push in on locking tabs and separate spool from trimmer drum. Remove any remaining old line from spool and clean all components. On most models, install new line by inserting end of line into hole in spool hub as far as possible. Note arrow on spool when winding new string on spool. On trimmer head shown in Fig. SL14, insert line in slots (T—Fig. SL14A) before installing spool.

When installing new line in trimmer head shown in Fig. SL15, route line around wire guide (2—Fig. SL15A). Extended line length should be 10-14 cm (4-5$^1/_2$ in.).

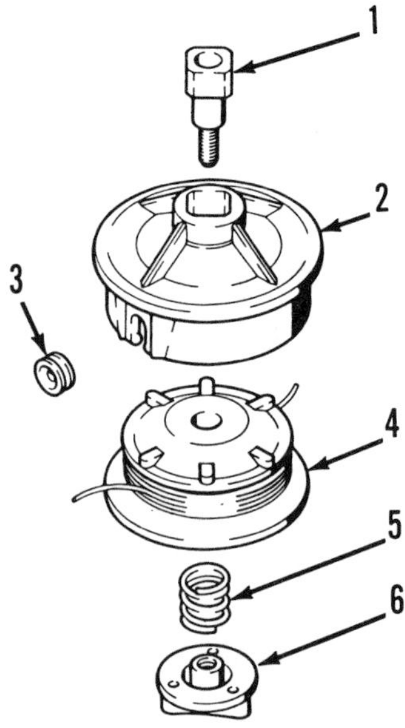

Fig. SL12—Exploded view of dual-strand, manual advance trimmer head used on some models. Refill with 33 feet (10 m) of 0.080-in. (2.0 mm) diameter line.

1. Adapter
2. Drum
3. Eyelet
4. Spool
5. Spring
6. Nut

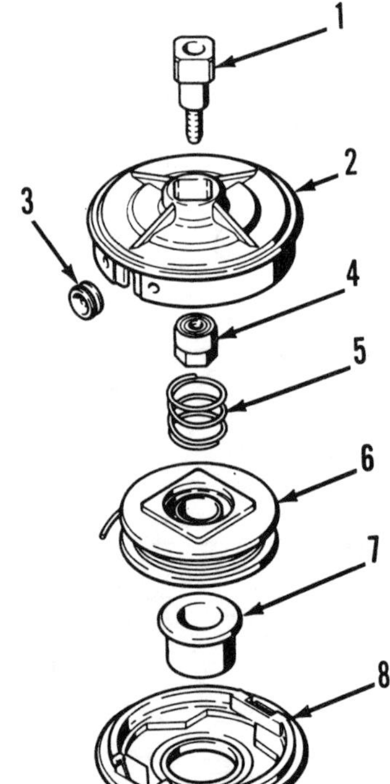

Fig. SL13—Exploded view of single-strand, semi-automatic advance trimmer head used on some models. Refill with 33 feet (10 m) of 0.080-in. (2.0 mm) diameter line.

1. Adapter
2. Drum
3. Eyelet
4. Nut
5. Spring
6. Spool
7. Button
8. Cover

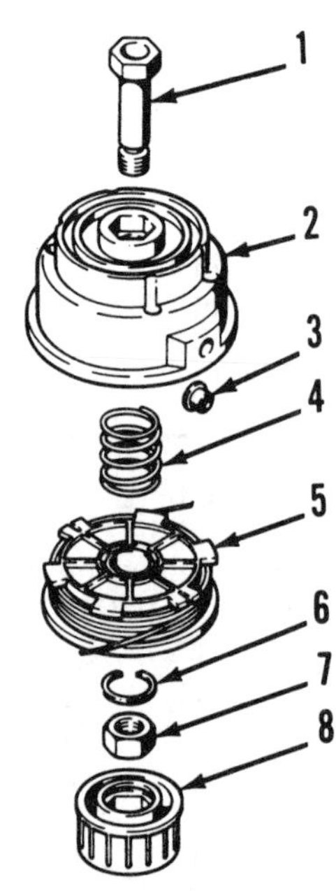

Fig. SL14—Exploded view of dual-strand, semi-automatic advance trimmer head used on some models. Refill with 25 feet (7.6 m) of 0.080-in. (2.0 mm) diameter line. Nut (7) has left-hand threads on some models. Adapter (1) is not used on some models.

1. Adapter
2. Drum
3. Eyelet
4. Spring
5. Spool
6. Snap ring
7. Nut
8. Button

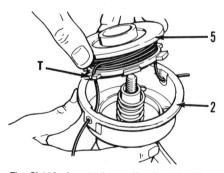

Fig. SL14A—Insert trimmer line in slots (T) on spool before installing spool (5) in drum (2) of trimmer head shown in Fig. SL14.

BLADE

A "Polycut" blade is available for some models. To install, refer to Fig. SL17. Note that "Polycut" head has left-hand threads and is self-tightening as trimmer is used. Base of trimmer head is marked to indicate minimum blade length. If blade length is less than indicated, renew blades.

A "Rotocut 200" (Fig. SL18) is available for some models. To install, place blade (3) on thrust plate (1). Install thrust washer (4) over shaft (2) and install cover (5). Install nut (6) (left-hand threads). A round pin may be inserted through hole in side of gear head to prevent head rotation during tightening.

Models with a gear head may be equipped with a variety of weed and grass blades (Fig. SL19). Heavy-duty

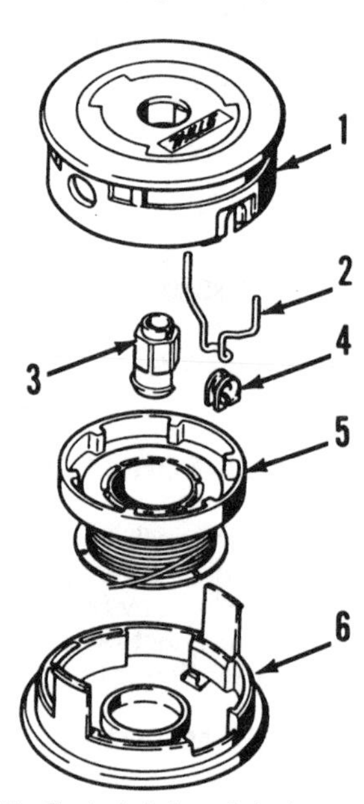

Fig. SL15—Exploded view of single-strand, automatic advance trimmer head used on some models. Refill with 25 feet (7.6 m) of 0.080-in. (2.0 mm) diameter line. Nut (3) has left-hand threads on some models.

1. Drum
2. Wire guide
3. Nut
4. Eyelet
5. Spool
6. Cover

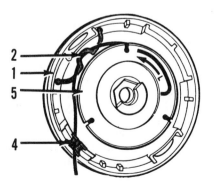

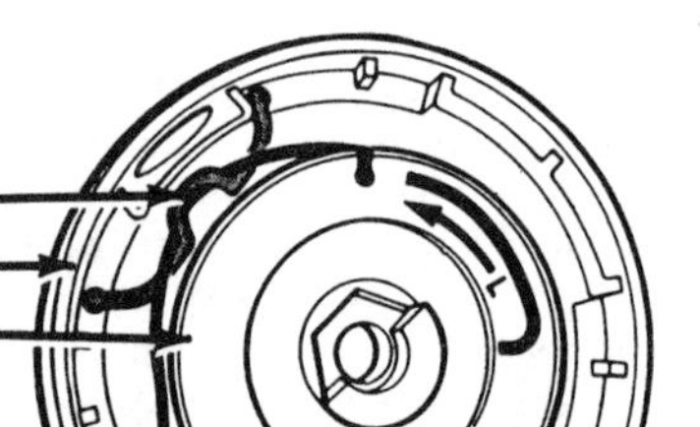

Fig. SL15A—Place trimmer line around wire guide (2) before passing line through eyelet (4) on trimmer head shown in Fig. SL15.

units may be equipped with a brush or saw blade (Fig. SL20). Blades are installed using procedure outlined for installation of "Rotocut 200" blade.

DRIVE SHAFT

Flexible Drive Shaft Models

The flexible drive shaft on models so equipped should be removed and cleaned after every 20 hours of operation. Lubricate shaft with lithium-based grease.

Solid Drive Shaft Models

Regular maintenance is not required for the solid drive shaft. If shaft is removed, lubricate shaft with lithium-based grease before installation.

The bushings in the drive shaft housing may be removed on some models. Check parts availability before attempting removal. Mark location of old bushings before removal. A recommended tool that may be used to pull out the bushings is a suitably sized tap that is threaded into the bushing. Early FS410 models were equipped with two bushings; later models are equipped with three bushings. Three bushings may be installed on early models by referring to Fig. SL21 for new bushing location. A 4.1 mm (0.016 in.) hole must be drilled in the housing at location shown for spring clip that retains bushing.

BEARING HEAD

All Models So Equipped

Model FS36 is equipped with flanged bushings (3—Fig. SL22) to support the

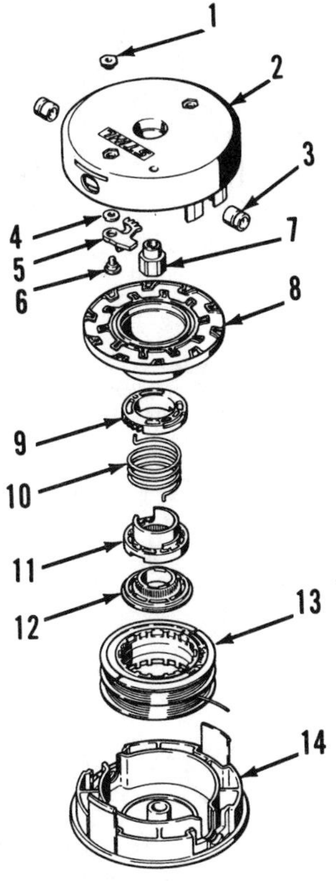

Fig. SL16—Exploded view of dual-strand, automatic advance trimmer head used on some models. Refill with 25 feet (7.6 m) of 0.095-in. (2.4 mm) diameter line.

1. Nut
2. Drum
3. Eyelet
4. Washer
5. Pawl
6. Screw
7. Nut
8. Index plate
9. Synchronizer
10. Spring
11. Adjuster
12. Ratchet
13. Spool
14. Cover

Fig. SL17—View of "Polycut" trimmer head available for some models.

1. Thrust plate
2. Shaft (L.H. threads)
3. Trimmer head

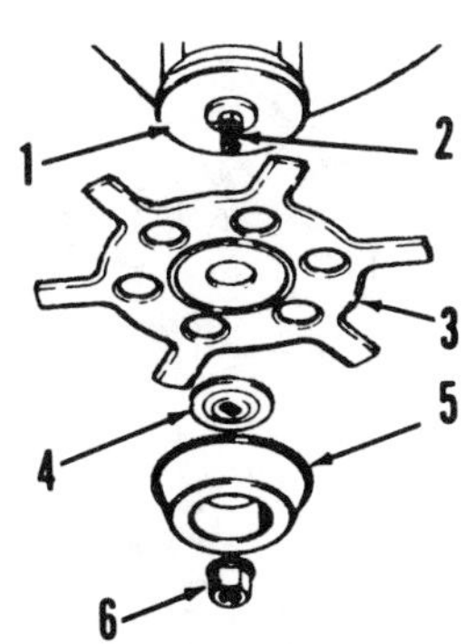

Fig. SL18—View of "Rotocut 200" blade available for some models.

1. Thrust plate
2. Shaft (L.H. threads)
3. Blade
4. Washer
5. Cover
6. Nut (L.H.)

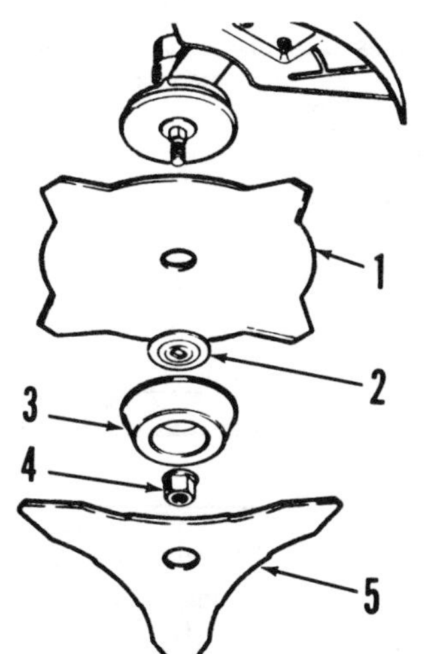

Fig. SL19—Exploded view of weed and grass blades available for some models.

1. Four-cutting-edge blade
2. Washer
3. Cover
4. Nut (L.H.)
5. Three-cutting-edge blade

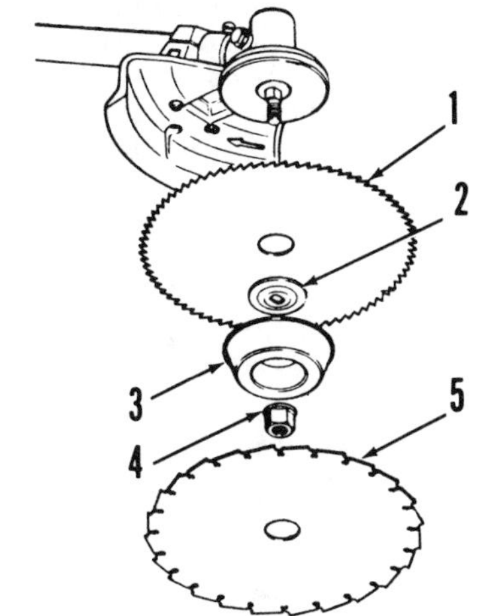

Fig. SL20—Exploded view of saw blades available for some models.

1. Saw blade
2. Washer
3. Cover
4. Nut (L.H.)
5. Chisel tooth saw blade

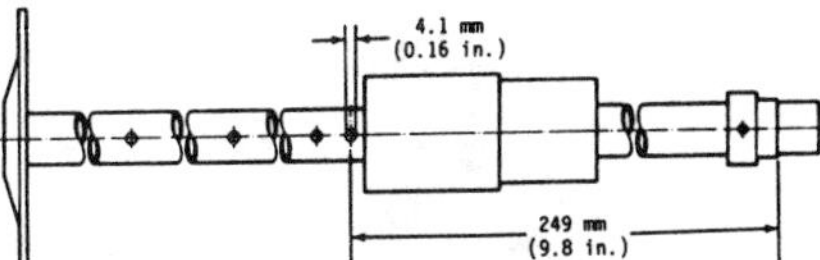

Fig. SL21—On Model FS410, install a third bushing in the drive shaft housing at the location shown. Refer to text.

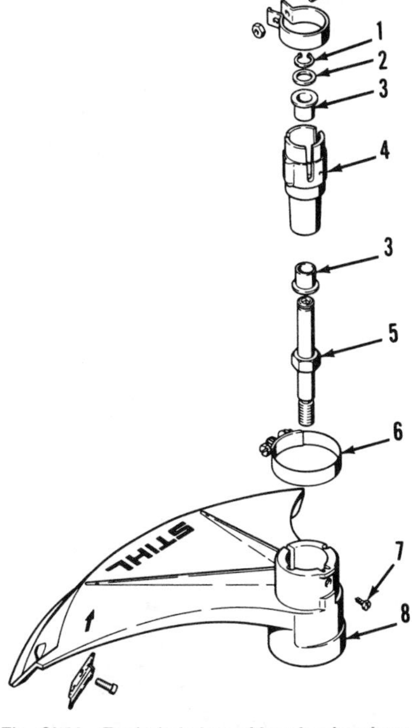

Fig. SL22—Exploded view of bearing head used on Model FS36.

1. Snap ring
2. Washer
3. Flanged bushing
4. Bearing housing
5. Arbor
6. Clamp
7. Locating screw
8. Deflector

arbor (5). Model FS40 is equipped with needle bearings (2—Fig. SL23) to support the arbor (5). All other models with a bearing head use ball bearings (5 and 7—Figs. SL24 or SL25) to support the arbor (4).

To disassemble, remove trimmer head and trimmer deflector from bearing head. Remove clamp screw and set screw from bearing housing and separate housing from drive tube. Remove snap ring from arbor shaft and pull shaft out of housing. Drive bearings from housing.

When reassembling, press new bearings into housing until they bottom against shoulder of housing. Align holes (H—Fig. SL26) on bearing housing and drive shaft housing. Align rib (R—Fig. SL27) on bearing housing with notch (N) in deflector.

GEAR HEAD

All Models So Equipped

Trimmer or brush cutter may be equipped with a one- or two-piece gear head housing. Refer to appropriate following service section.

ONE-PIECE HOUSING. Lubricant level should be checked after every 20 hours of operation. Remove fill plug in side of housing and add lubricant so housing is $^2/_3$ full. Recommended lubricant is lithium-based grease.

Refer to Figs. SL28 through SL31 for an exploded view of gear heads with a one-piece housing. To disassemble gear head, remove trimmer head or blade assembly. Remove clamp bolt (7) and

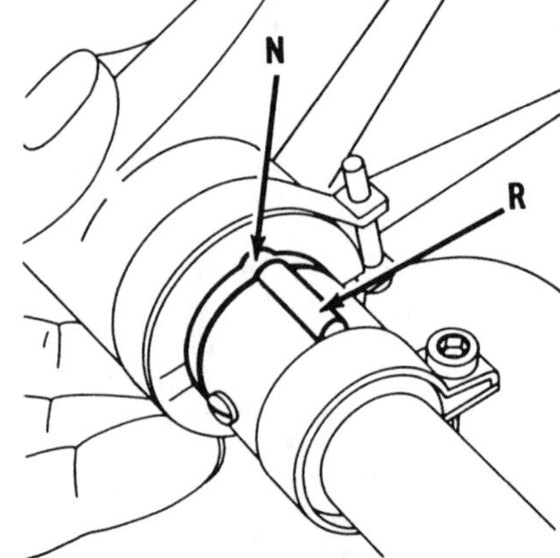

Fig. SL27—On Models FS36 and FS40, rib (R) on bearing housing must align with notch (N) in deflector shield.

Fig. SL23—Exploded view of bearing head used on Model FS40.

1. Washer
2. Needle bearing
3. Bearing housing
4. Washer
5. Arbor
6. Thrust plate

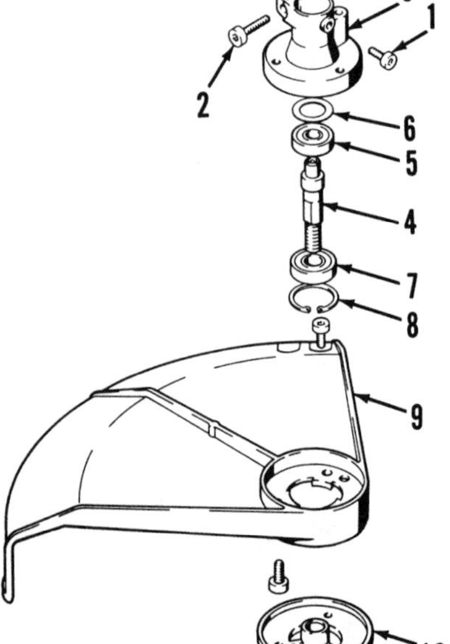

Fig. SL24—Exploded view of bearing head used on some models.

1. Locating screw
2. Clamp bolt
3. Housing
4. Arbor
5. Bearing
6. Washer
7. Bearing
8. Snap ring
9. Deflector
10. Thrust plate

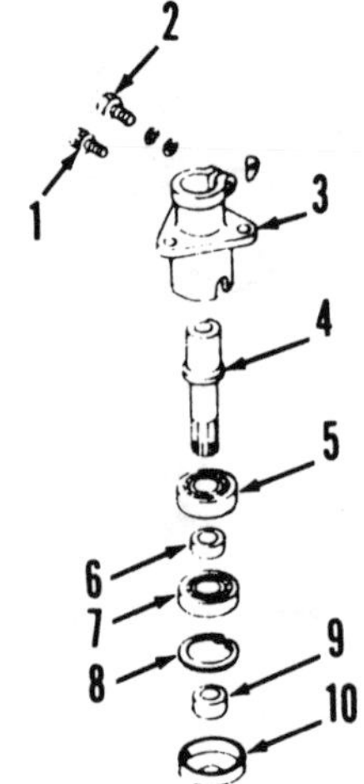

Fig. SL25—Exploded view of bearing head used on some models.

1. Locating screw
2. Clamp bolt
3. Housing
4. Arbor
5. Bearing
6. Spacer
7. Bearing
8. Snap ring
9. Spacer
10. Thrust plate

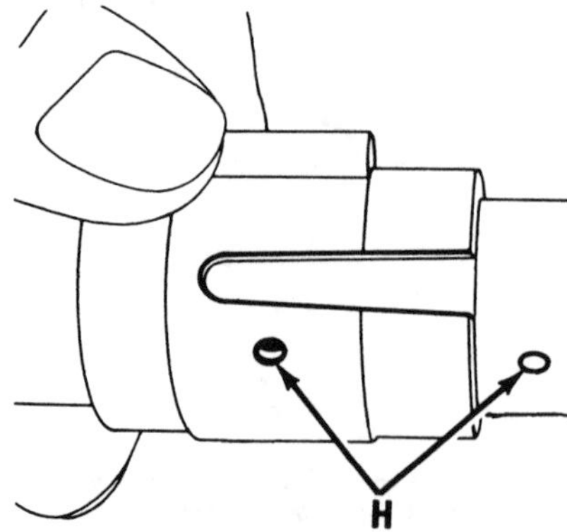
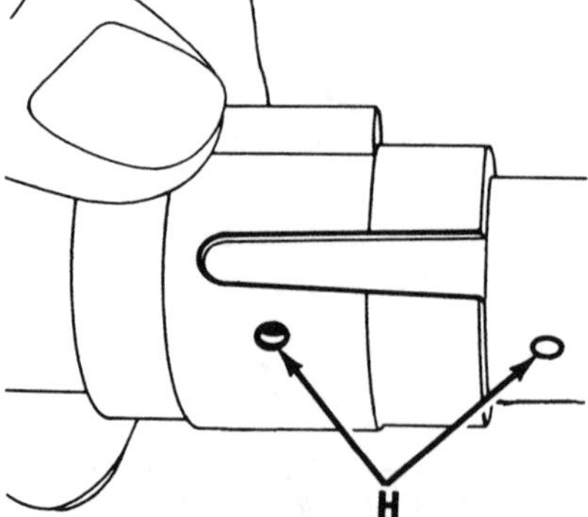

Fig. SL26—When attaching drive shaft housing and bearing housing, align holes (H) then install locating screw.

Fig. SL28—Exploded view of gear head with one-piece housing used on some models.

1. Snap ring
2. Snap ring
3. Shim
4. Bearing
5. Bearing
6. Input shaft
7. Clamp bolt
8. Locating screw
9. Check plug
10. Housing
11. Anti-wrap guard
12. Bearing
13. Shim
14. Output gear
15. Arbor
16. Bearing
17. Snap ring
18. Adapter
19. Thrust plate
20. Washer
21. Washer
22. Bolt

locating screw (8) if used. Separate gear head from drive shaft housing tube. Remove snap ring (1) and use a suitable puller to remove input shaft (6) and bearings as an assembly from housing (10). Remove snap ring (2) and press input shaft out of bearings as required. Remove snap ring (17) and use a suitable puller to remove arbor shaft (15) and bearing assembly. Press bearings from arbor shaft as necessary. It may be necessary to heat housing to approximately 140° C (280° F) to ease removal and installation of bearings. Some units are equipped with shims that allow adjustment of gear mesh and backlash.

TWO-PIECE HOUSING. Lubricant level should be checked after every 20 hours of operation. Remove fill plug (1—Fig. SL32) to check lubricant. Gear head should contain 40 cc (1.35 oz.) of SAE 90 gear lubricant.

To disassemble gear head, remove trimmer head or blade assembly. Remove clamp bolt and separate gear head from drive shaft housing tube. Remove screws and separate lower gear head housing (21) from upper gear head housing (2). Press arbor (14) and gear assembly out of the thrust plate and ball bearing. Remove snap ring (16). Heat housing to 280° F (140° C) and press bearing (18) out of housing. Remove seal (23). Press gear (15) off arbor. Remove the two locating screws (3). Heat housing to 280° F (140° C) and press input shaft (11) and bearing assembly out of housing. Remove snap rings and press bearings from input shaft as required. Remove needle bearing (13) only if bearing is to be renewed.

During gear head assembly, shims should be installed to provide a slight amount of gear backlash. Shafts should turn freely with no binding.

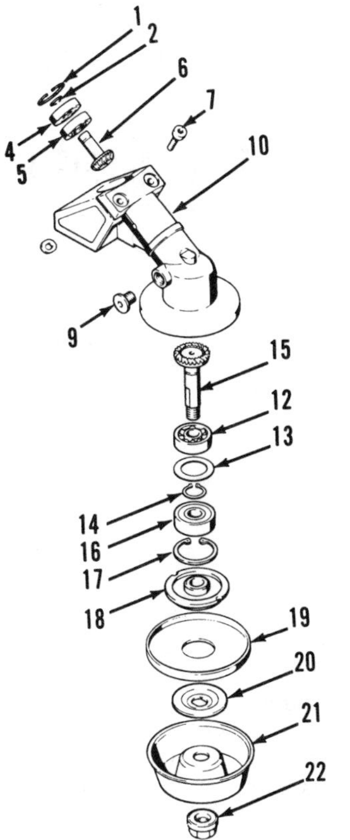

Fig. SL30—Exploded view of gear head with one-piece housing used on some models.

1. Snap ring
2. Snap ring
4. Bearing
5. Bearing
6. Input shaft
7. Clamp screw
9. Fill plug
10. Housing
12. Bearing
13. Washer
14. Snap ring
15. Arbor
16. Bearing
17. Snap ring
18. Thrust plate
19. Cover
20. Concave washer
21. Cup
22. Nut (L.H.)

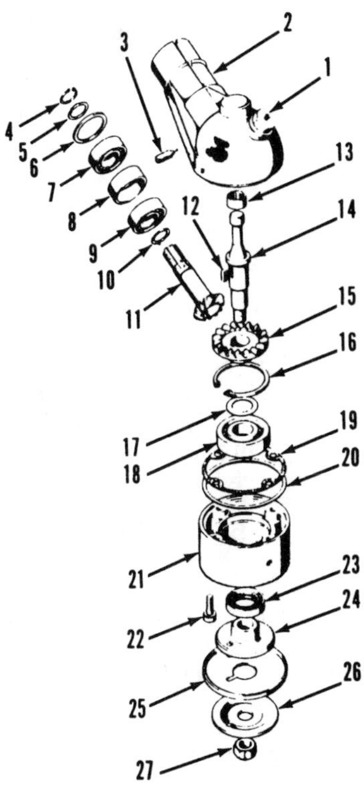

Fig. SL32—Exploded view of gear head with two-piece housing used on some models.

1. Fill plug
2. Housing
3. Locating screws
4. Snap ring
5. Shim
6. Shim
7. Bearing
8. Spacer
9. Bearing
10. Shim
11. Input shaft
12. Key
13. Needle bearing
14. Arbor
15. Gear
16. Snap ring
17. Shim
18. Bearing
19. Gasket
20. Shim
21. Housing
22. Bolt
23. Seal
24. Adapter
25. Thrust plate
26. Washer
27. Nut (L.H.)

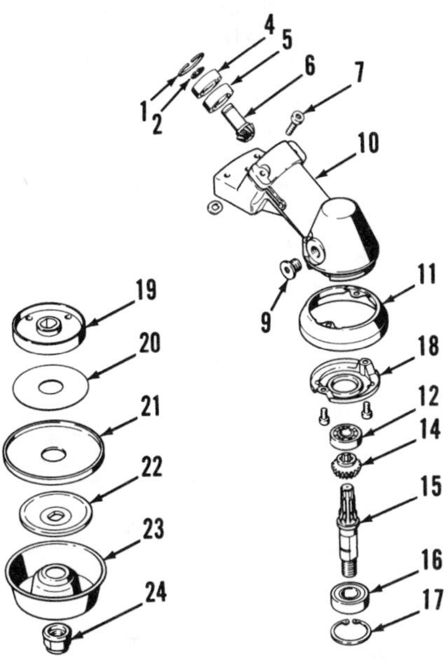

Fig. SL29—Exploded view of gear head with one-piece housing used on some models.

1. Snap ring
2. Snap ring
4. Bearing
5. Bearing
6. Input shaft
7. Clamp screw
9. Fill plug
10. Housing
11. Anti-wrap guard
12. Bearing
14. Gear
15. Arbor
16. Bearing
17. Snap ring
18. Cover plate
19. Thrust plate
20. Washer
21. Cover
22. Concave washer
23. Cup
24. Nut (L.H.)

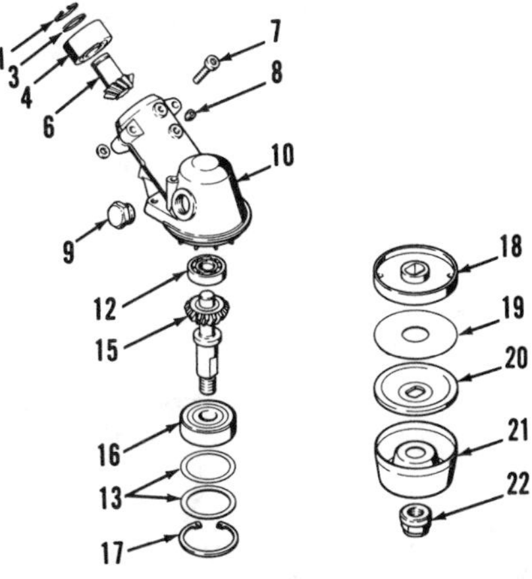

Fig. SL31—Exploded view of gear head with one-piece housing used on some models. Unscrew set screw (8) before removing bearing.

1. Snap ring
2. Washer
4. Bearing
6. Input shaft
7. Clamp screw
8. Locating screw
9. Fill plug
10. Housing
12. Bearing
13. Shims
15. Arbor
16. Bearing
17. Snap ring
18. Cover
19. Washer
20. Concave washer
21. Cup
22. Nut (L.H.)

STIHL

GASOLINE POWERED BLOWERS

Model	Engine Manufacturer	Engine Model	Displacement
BG17, SG17	Stihl	...	56.5 cc
BR320, SR320	Stihl	...	56.5 cc
BR400, SR400	Stihl	...	56.5 cc

ENGINE INFORMATION

These blowers are equipped with a two-stroke, air-cooled engine manufactured by Stihl. Refer to appropriate engine section in this manual for engine service information.

FUEL MIXTURE

Manufacturer recommends mixing regular or unleaded gasoline with a high-quality, two-stroke engine oil designed for air-cooled engines. Recommended fuel:oil ratio is 50:1 when using Stihl oil. Fuel:oil ratio should be 25:1 when using any other two-stroke oil.

FAN

The blower fan (3—Fig. SL1) is attached to the engine flywheel and is accessible after separating engine and blower assembly from back plate. Remove blower tube elbow from blower housing. Remove mounting screws from outer half of fan housing (5). Remove cap (1) on blower models or bellows on sprayer models. Separate blower housing halves (2 and 5). Remove fan mounting screws and remove fan.

To install fan, reverse removal procedure. Tighten fan retaining screws to 8 N·m (71 in.-lbs.).

SPRAYER PUMP

Models So Equipped

The sprayer pressure pump is mounted on blower housing outer case (5—Fig. SL1) and is driven by a coupling (1—Fig. SL2) on flywheel retaining nut. To remove pump, first remove engine and blower assembly from back plate. Disconnect hoses from pump housing base (11), remove mounting screws and remove pump assembly.

To disassemble, remove pump mounting screws and separate pump housing (7) from housing base (11). Remove retaining nut (9) and pull impeller (8) off pump shaft (2). Remove bearing retaining screws (3), then press shaft (2) and bearing (4) out of pump housing. Remove snap ring (5) and press shaft out of bearing. Drive seal (6) from housing.

When reassembling, install seal (6) with open side facing outward. Press into housing until bottomed against shoulder of housing. Heat bearing (4) to approximately 50° C (120° F) before pressing onto pump shaft. Press shaft and bearing assembly into pump housing until bottomed in housing.

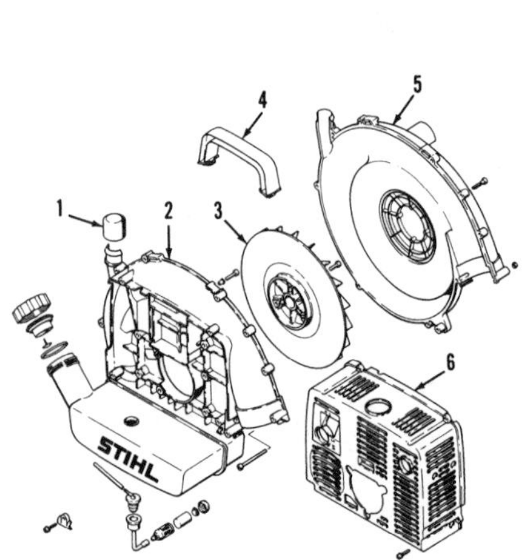

Fig. SL1—Exploded view of blower housing.
1. Cap
2. Blower inner case
3. Fan
4. Handle
5. Blower outer case
6. Engine shroud

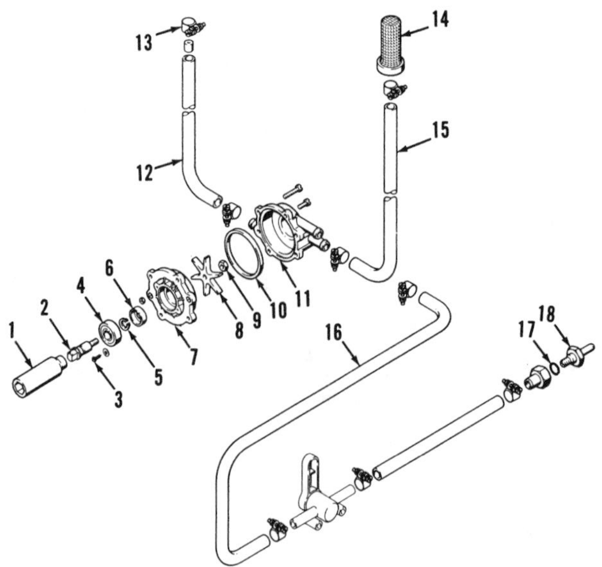

Fig. SL2—Exploded view of pressure pump used on mist/blower models.
1. Drive coupling
2. Pump shaft
3. Screw
4. Bearing
5. Snap ring
6. Seal
7. Pump housing
8. Impeller
9. Nut
10. Seal ring
11. Pump housing base
12. Return line
13. Restrictor
14. Strainer
15. Suction line
16. Pressure line
17. "O" ring
18. Metering jet

Illustrations courtesy Stihl Inc.

TANAKA

GASOLINE POWERED TRIMMERS

Models	Engine Make	Displacement
AST-5000	Tanaka	20.0 cc (1.22 cu. in.)
AST-7000	Tanaka	21.0 cc (1.28 cu. in.)
AST-7000N & AST-7000S	Tanaka	20.0 cc (1.22 cu. in.)
SUM-321	Tanaka	31.0 cc (1.86 cu. in.)
TBC-160 & TBC-162	Tanaka	16.0 cc (0.94 cu. in.)
TBC-202 & TBC-205	Tanaka	20.0 cc (1.22 cu. in.)
TBC-210	Tanaka	21.0 cc (1.28 cu. in.)
TBC-215	Tanaka	20.0 cc (1.22 cu. in.)
TBC-220	Tanaka	21.0 cc (1.28 cu. in.)
TBC-220SS, TBC-232 & TBC-240	Tanaka	22.6 cc (1.38 cu. in.)
TBC-250	Tanaka	24.8 cc (1.51 cu. in.)
TBC-265	Tanaka	26.0 cc (1.59 cu. in.)
TBC-300, TBC-322 & TBC-325	Tanaka	31.0 cc (1.86 cu. in.)
TBC-355	Tanaka	34.0 cc (2.07 cu. in.)
TBC-373	Tanaka	37.4 cc (2.28 cu. in.)
TBC-400, TBC-422C & TBC-425	Tanaka	40.0 cc (2.44 cu. in.)
TBC-500	Tanaka	46.0 cc (2.81 cu. in.)
TBC-501	Tanaka	50.2 cc (3.06 cu. in.)
TBC-2100 & TBC-2110	McCulloch	21.2 cc (1.29 cu. in.)
TBC-2500	Tanaka	24.8 cc (1.51 cu. in.)
TBC-2800	Tanaka	28.0 cc (1.71 cu. in.)
TBC-4000, TBC-4500 & TBC-5000	Tanaka	20.0 cc (1.22 cu. in.)
TPE-2110	McCulloch	21.2 cc (1.29 cu. in.)
TPE-250	Tanaka	24.8 cc (1.51 cu. in.)
TST-218	Tanaka	20.0 cc (1.22 cu. in.)

ENGINE INFORMATION

Two-stroke, air-cooled gasoline engines are used on all models. McCulloch engines are used on TBC-2100/2110 and TPE-2110 models and Tanaka (TAS) engines are used on other models. Identify the engine by manufacturer and displacement, then refer to the appropriate engine service section in this manual.

FUEL MIXTURE

Oil must be mixed with the fuel. A good quality oil designed for use in 2-stroke chain saw or trimmer engines should be mixed with regular or unleaded gasoline. Mix oil with gasoline at the ratio recommended by the oil manufacturer. If the recommended ratio is not known mix oil with gasoline at a fuel:oil ratio of 25:1.

STRING TRIMMER

The trimmer may be equipped with a manual advance or automatic advance trimmer head. Refer to following paragraphs.

Manual Advance Head

Refer to Fig. TA10 for view of dual strand, manual advance trimmer head used on some models. To extend line, loosen lock knob (6) until line can be pulled from housing. Pull line to desired length and tighten lock knob.

To install new line, remove lock knob (6), spring (5) and spool (4). Remove any remaining old line. Install new line on spool. Wind each end of new line in same direction around spool, being careful not to twist the lines. Wind line in direction indicated by arrow on spool, then insert line ends through line guides (3). Install spool, spring and lock knob.

Automatic Advance Head

Some models may be equipped with a dual strand, automatic advance trimmer head. The line is extended when the engine is accelerated or decelerated. Line will advance approximately 14 mm (1/2 in.) each time.

To install new line, press against tabs of drum (1—Fig. TA11) and separate cover (12) from drum. Disassemble trimmer head and remove any remaining old line and clean components. Note letter (L) on top of drum.

Illustrations courtesy Tanaka Ltd.

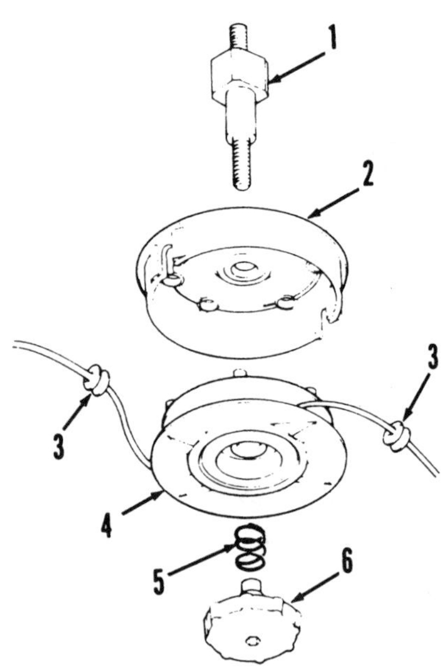

Fig. TA10—Exploded view of dual strand, manual advance trimmer head used on some models.

1. Drive shaft adapter
2. Drum
3. Eyelet
4. Spool
5. Spring
6. Lock knob

Fig. TA11—Exploded view of dual strand, automatic advance trimmer head used on some models. Note location of identifying letter (L).

1. Drum
2. Eyelet
3. Adapter
4. Washers
5. Spring
6. Hook
7. Line
8. Spool
9. Balls (4)
10. Slider
11. Washer
12. Cover

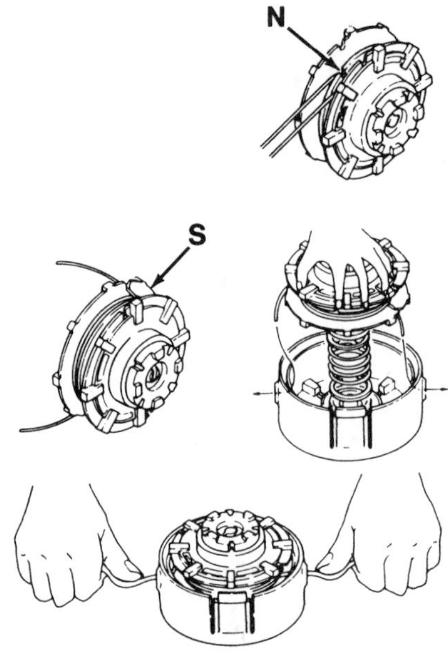

Fig. TA12—When installing new trimmer line, insert line in notch (N) on spool divider and wind both ends of line in direction indicated by arrow on spool. Refer to text.

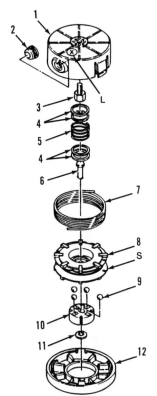

All trimmers can use line with diameter of 2.4 mm (0.095 in.) or 2.7 mm (.105 in.). Trimmer heads with letter L or LS on head also can use line with diameter of 3.3 mm (.130 in.).

Line length should be 12 m (39 ft.) if using 2.4 mm or 2.7 mm diameter line on trimmer heads marked with letter L or LS. Line length for 3.3 mm diameter line is 5.8 m (19 ft.). On trimmer heads marked with letter R, S, M or X, line length should be 6 m (20 ft.).

To install new line, hold ends of line together and insert looped end in notch (N—Fig. TA12). Wrap both ends of line around spool in same direction. Wind line around spool in direction indicated by arrow on spool being careful not to twist the lines. Insert each line into slots (S) on opposite sides of spool. There must be at least 100 mm (4 in.) of line extending from spool.

Reassemble trimmer head while passing line through eyelets (2—Fig. TA11). BE sure line is not trapped by lugs on spool. After assembly, pull out lines so they disengage from slots in spool. Trim lines to equal lengths of 50-100 mm (2-4 in.).

NOTE: If line length is less than 50 mm (2 in.), trimmer will not adjust line length properly and engine may overspeed.

Note that to remove trimmer head from shaft, head must be rotated counterclockwise on curved shaft models or clockwise (L.H. threads) on straight shaft models.

BLADE

Some models may be equipped with a four-edge cutting blade or a saw blade. Note that blade retaining screw on straight shaft models has left-hand threads. Be sure that all components fit properly and are centered.

DRIVE SHAFT

Curved Shaft Models

Models with a curved drive shaft housing are equipped with a flexible drive shaft. The drive shaft should be removed cleaned and lubricated after every 30 hours of operation.

Detach trimmer head assembly from drive shaft housing and remove shaft. Apply multipurpose grease to shaft. The drive shaft liner is available separately on some models.

Straight Shaft Models

Periodic maintenance is not required for the drive shaft on models with a straight drive shaft housing. If removed, apply mutlipurpose grease to shaft. The drive shaft rides in bushings that are renewable on some models.

Model TST-218 is equipped with a telescoping drive shaft. See Fig. TA13. The upper drive shaft (6) rides in ball bearings (8) and the lower drive shaft (15) rides in renewable bushings (14).

BEARING HEAD

Curved Shaft Models

The bearing head is equipped with sealed bearings and does not require periodic maintenance. Two types of bearing heads have been used. Early models are equipped with a snap ring (7—Fig. TA14) that retains bearings and arbor (5). No snap ring is used on later models (Fig. TA15).

To disassemble bearing head on early models, remove trimmer head. Remove clamp bolt (1—Fig. TA14) and locating screw (2) and separate bearing head from drive shaft housing tube.

Remove snap ring (7), then use a suitable puller to extract arbor (5) and bearing (6). Use a suitable puller and remove bearing (4). If required, press bearing (6) off arbor.

To reassemble, press bearing (4) into housing. Install arbor in bearing (4) and housing. Press bearing (6) onto arbor shaft and into housing until snap ring (7) can be installed.

To disassemble later style bearing head, remove trimmer head (13—Fig. TA15), cup washer (12), covers (10) and

Illustrations courtesy Tanaka Ltd.

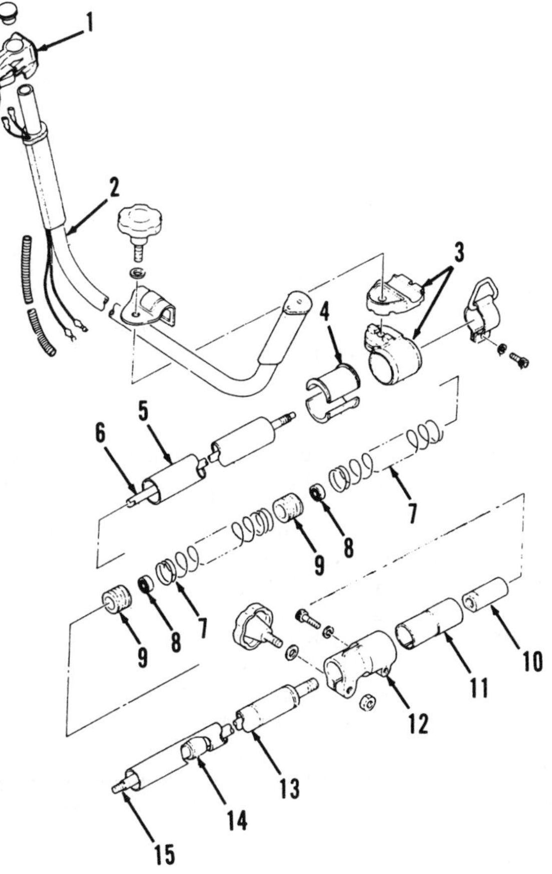

Fig. TA13—Exploded view of drive shaft housing used on Model TST-218.

1. Throttle trigger
2. Handle
3. Handle bracket
4. Spacer
5. Drive shaft housing
6. Upper drive shaft
7. Springs
8. Bearing
9. Bearing head
10. Drive shaft connector
11. Sleeve
12. Coupler
13. Housing
14. Bushing
15. Lower drive shaft

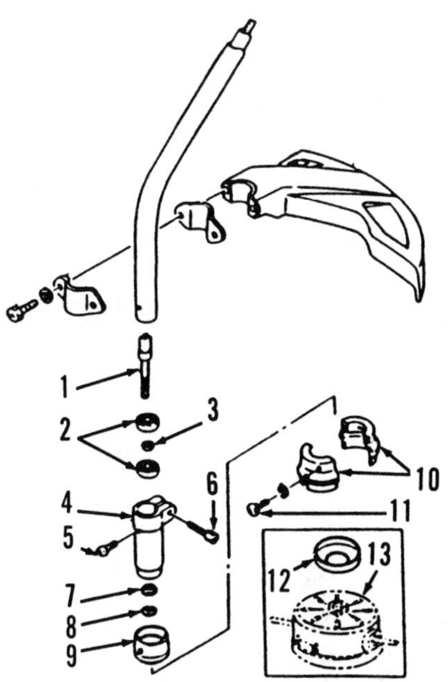

Fig. TA15—Exploded view of bearing head used on later models.

1. Arbor
2. Bearings
3. Spacer
4. Housing
5. Locating screw
6. Clamp bolt
7. Special washer
8. Special washer
9. Sleeve
10. Covers
11. Screw
12. Cup washer
13. Trimmer head

sleeve (9). Unscrew locating screw (5) and clamp screw (6) and separate bearing head (4) from drive shaft housing tube. Remove washers (7 and 8) and press or pull arbor (1) and bearings (2) from housing.

Inspect all parts and renew as needed. Reassemble by reversing disassembly sequence.

GEAR HEAD

Straight Shaft Models

The gear head should be lubricated after every 50 hours of operation. Remove trimmer head or blade and unscrew plug (7—Fig. TA16) from side of

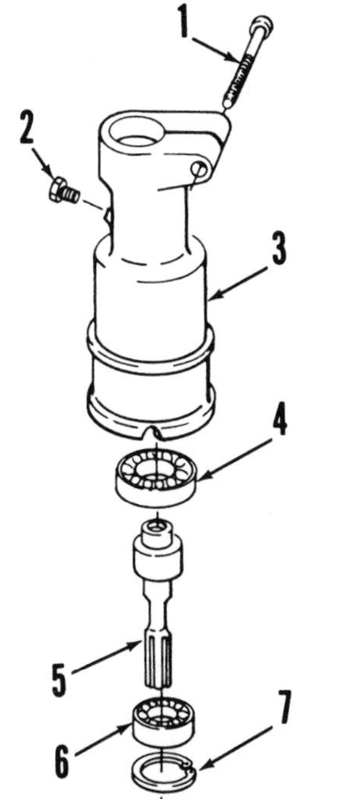

Fig. TA14—Exploded view of bearing head used on early models.

1. Clamp bolt
2. Locating screw
3. Housing
4. Bearing
5. Arbor
6. Bearing
7. Snap ring

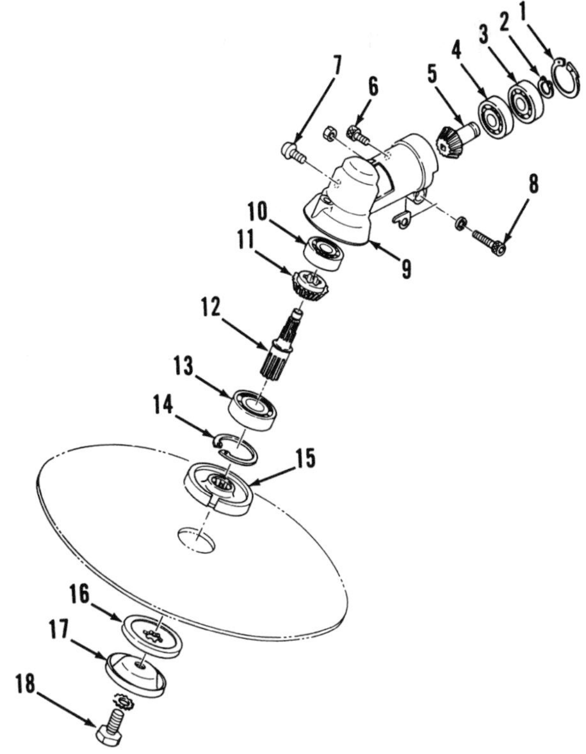

Fig. TA16—Exploded view of gear head. Early models may have a seal between snap ring (14) and bearing (13).

1. Snap ring
2. Snap ring
3. Bearing
4. Bearing
5. Input shaft
6. Locating screw
7. Fill plug
8. Clamp bolt
9. Housing
10. Bearing
11. Gear
12. Arbor
13. Bearing
14. Snap ring
15. Blade holder
16. Blade holder
17. Cup washer
18. Cap screw

Illustrations courtesy Tanaka Ltd.

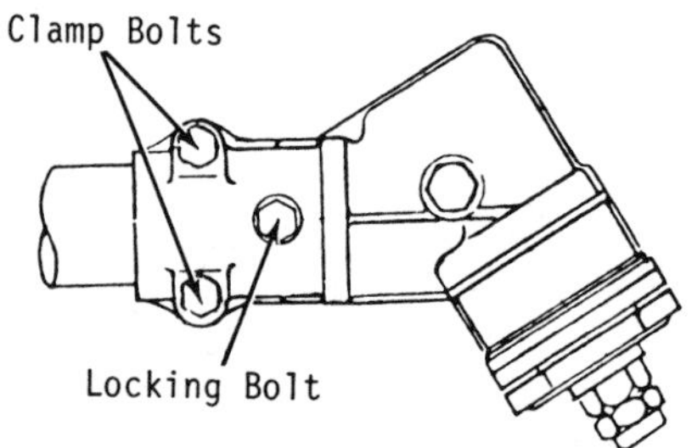

Fig. TA17—To separate gear head from drive shaft housing, remove clamp bolts and locking (head locating) bolt. Later models are equipped with only one clamp bolt.

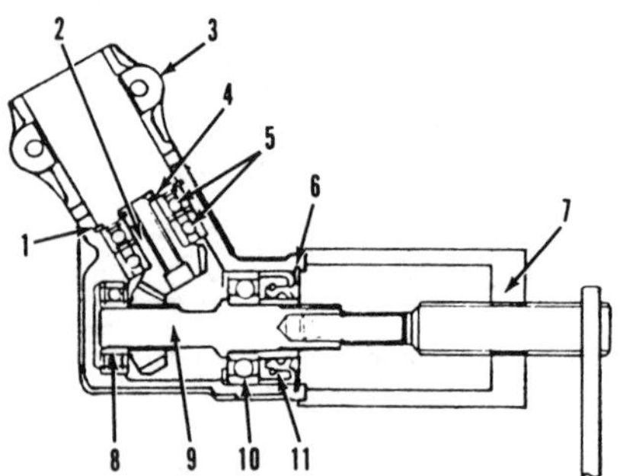

Fig. TA18—Install puller tool (7) as shown to remove arbor shaft (9) and bearing (10). Refer to text.

gear head. Inject multipurpose grease through opening until housing is approximately 2/3 full.

To disassemble gear head, first remove blade. Remove clamp bolt (Fig. TA17) and head locking bolt. Separate head from drive shaft and housing.

Detach snap ring (14—Fig. TA16). Install Tanaka puller 015-29339-000

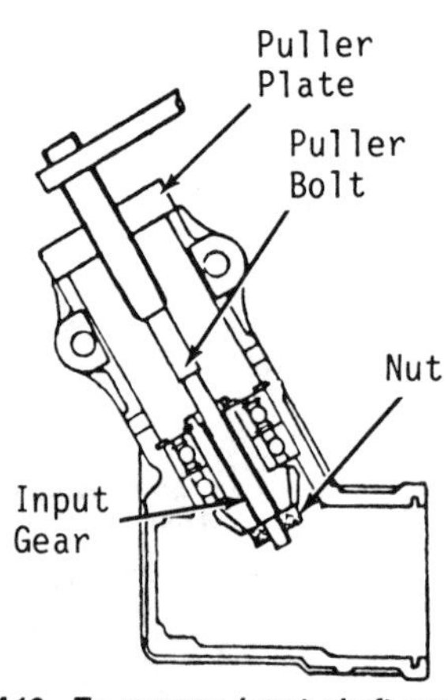

Fig. TA19—To remove input shaft and bearing assembly, install puller as shown. Refer to text.

shown in Fig. TA18, or other suitable puller, and withdraw arbor (9) with bearing (10). Detach snap ring (1). Install Tanaka puller 016-29373-000 shown in Fig. TA19 and withdraw input shaft and bearings as an assembly. Detach snap ring (2—Fig. TA16) and press shaft out of bearings. Heat housing, if necessary, and tap housing against a wood block to dislodge bearing (10).

Reassemble gear head by reversing disassembly procedure. Tanaka tool 031-29373-000 can be used to install bearing (10). Tanaka tool 032-29373-000 can be used to install input shaft and bearing assembly.

BATTERY

Some models are equipped with an electric starter. A battery pack of ni-cad batteries provides power to drive the

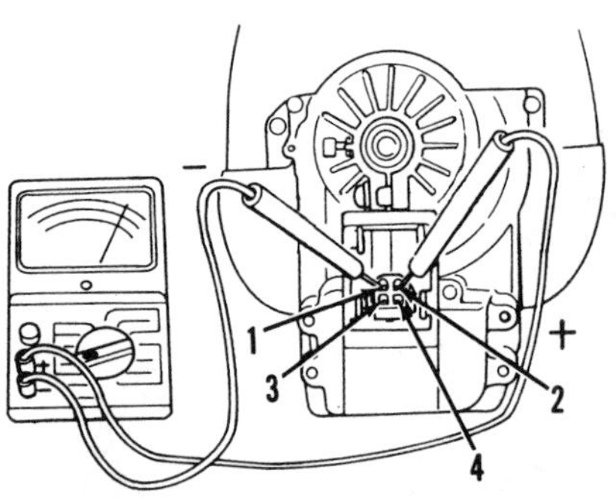

Fig. TA20—Check battery voltage by attaching tester to connector terminals as outlined in text.

starter. The battery pack should fully recharge using charger within 15 hours. To check for faulty battery pack, recharge battery pack, then disconnect four-wire connector leading to handlebar. With engine stopped, connect negative lead of a voltmeter to terminal (1—Fig. TA20) of female connector and positive lead to terminal (2). Battery voltage reading should be at least 4.8 volts on Model AST-5000 or 7.0 volts on Model AST-7000.

Refer to engine service section for information on remainder of electrical system.

STARTER

Refer to the appropriate ENGINE SERVICE section for service to the starter assembly.

CLUTCH

Refer to the appropriate ENGINE SERVICE section for clutch removal and service procedures.

TANAKA

GASOLINE POWERED BLOWERS

Model	Engine Manufacturer	Engine Model	Displacement
THB-300	Tanaka	...	31 cc
TBL-455	Tanaka	...	43 cc
TBL-500	Tanaka	...	43 cc

ENGINE INFORMATION

Tanaka (TAS) two-stroke, air-cooled gasoline engines are used on Tanaka blowers. Identify engine by displacement and refer to Tanaka engine service section in this manual.

FUEL MIXTURE

Oil must be mixed with the fuel. Recommended fuel is regular or unleaded gasoline. Do not use gasoline containing alcohol. Recommended oil is Tanaka or another high-quality oil designed for use in air-cooled, two-stroke engines. Mix oil with gasoline at ratio recommended on oil container. Otherwise, fuel:oil ratio should be 25:1.

BLOWER ASSEMBLY

To remove blower impeller (4—Figs. TA50 or TA51), first remove engine and blower assembly from frame on backpack models. On all models, remove tube clamps and remove blower tube (10) from blower case. On Models TBL-455 and TBL-500, remove air cleaner body (13—Fig. TA51) and air guide plate (15). On all models, remove blower case mounting screws and separate blower case halves (2 and 5). On Model THB-300, remove nut (3—Fig. TA50) and pull impeller and flywheel assembly (4) off crankshaft. On Models TBL-455 and TBL-500, remove screws (3—Fig. TA51) attaching impeller (4) to engine flywheel and remove impeller.

To remove engine from blower, first remove impeller as outlined above. Disconnect fuel line, throttle cable and stop switch wires. Remove engine cover and fuel tank. On Models TBL-455 and TBL-500, remove flywheel mounting nut and pull flywheel off crankshaft. On all models, remove engine mounting screws and separate engine from blower case.

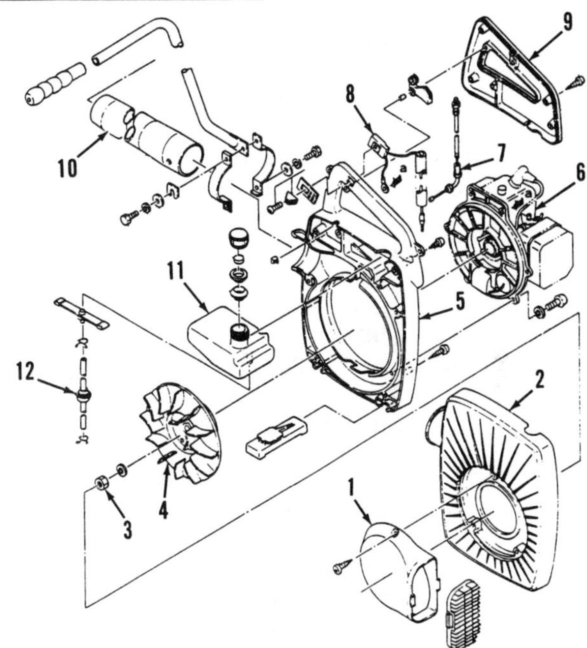

Fig. TA50—Exploded view of THB-300 blower.

1. Air intake housing
2. Blower case half
3. Nut
4. Impeller
5. Blower case half
6. Engine
7. Throttle cable
8. Stop switch
9. Handle
10. Blower pipe
11. Fuel tank
12. Fuel line

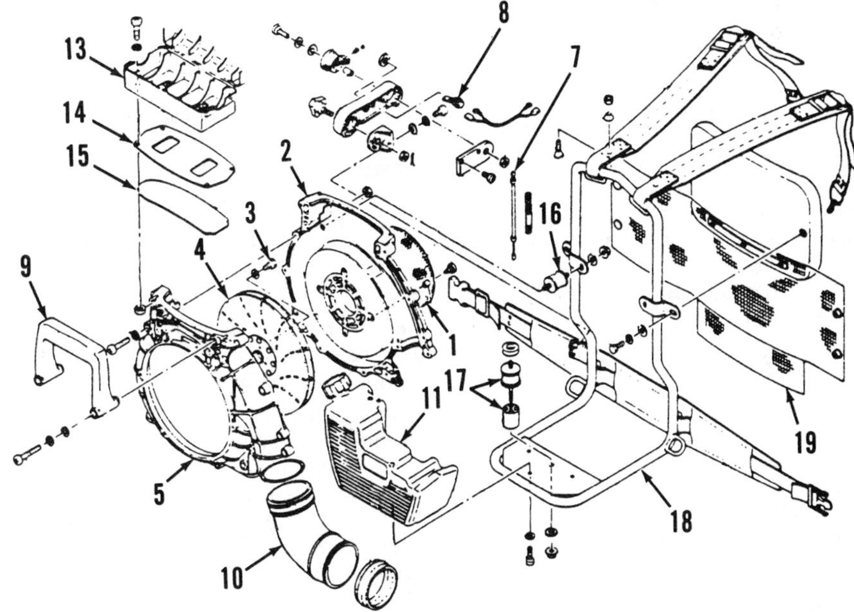

Fig. TA51—Exploded view of blower assembly used on Models TBL-455 and TBL-500.

1. Screen
2. Blower case half
3. Cap screw
4. Impeller
5. Blower case half
7. Throttle cable
8. Stop switch
9. Handle
10. Blower pipe
11. Fuel tank
13. Air cleaner body
14. Gasket
15. Air guide plate
16. Rubber cushion
17. Vibration damper
18. Back-pack frame
19. Cushion

Illustrations courtesy Tanaka Ltd.

TORO
GASOLINE POWERED TRIMMERS

Model	Engine Make	Displacement
30900	Kioritz	21.2 cc
30910	Kioritz	21.2 cc
30920	Kioritz	30.1 cc
51600	Kioritz	13.8 cc
51625	Kioritz	13.8 cc
51628	Mitsubishi	21.2 cc
51638	Mitsubishi	28.0 cc
51641 TC-1000	Mitsubishi	16.0 cc
51642 TC-2000	Mitsubishi	21.2 cc
51643-TC-3000	Mitsubishi	24.1 cc
51644 TC-4000	Mitsubishi	24.1 cc
51645 TC-5000	Mitsubishi	32.5 cc
51645	Mitsubishi	33.0 cc
51650	Mitsubishi	24.1 cc
51652 TC3105	Mitsubishi	21.0 cc
51653	Mitsubishi	28.0 cc
51660 TC3500	Mitsubishi	24.1 cc
51660	Mitsubishi	24.1 cc
51675 TC5010	Mitsubishi	33.0 cc
51700	Kioritz	21.2 cc
TC3510	Mitsubishi	24.1 cc
51903 Trimmer	...	31.0 cc
51906 Trimmer	...	31.0 cc
51908 Brush cutter	...	31.0 cc
51911 Trimmer	...	28.0 cc
51916 Trimmer	...	28.0 cc
51918 Brush cutter	...	28.0 cc
51920 Trimmer	...	26.2 cc
51926 Trimmer	...	26.2 cc

ENGINE INFORMATION

Engines may be manufactured as Kioritz, Maruyuma, Mitsubishi, IDC or Toro. Identify the engine by manufacturer and displacement and refer to the appropriate KIORITZ, MARUYUMA, MITSUBISHI, IDC or TORO Engine Service section of this manual.

STRING TRIMMER

Refer to Figs. TO10 through TO15 for an exploded view of string trimmer heads used. Not all heads will be covered in detail; however, the most widely used heads are covered. Service procedure for the remaining heads is similar.

Semi-Automatic Dual Strand Trimmer Head

To manually advance the trimmer line with the engine stopped, push the button in the center of spool (7—Fig. TO10) at the bottom of the head and pull the line. To extend the line with the engine running, operate the trimmer at maximum speed and tap the button on the ground. The line should extend a small amount automatically. If the line does not extend with the engine running, stop the engine and extend the line manually. If the line is broken inside the housing, it will be necessary to disassemble the unit and feed the line through the drum eyelet.

To remove and disassemble the string trimmer head, proceed as follows. Hold the drum firmly and turn spool in the direction shown in Fig. TO11 to remove slack. Twist with a hard snap until the plastic peg is between holes, then separate the spool from the drum.

Clean and inspect all parts for damage. If new line is installed, it should be 0.095 in. (2.41 mm) diameter. The spool will hold approximately 20 ft. (6 m) of line. Insert the line through the hole of the spool as shown in Fig. TO12 and pull the line through until it is the same length on both sides. Wrap both ends of the line on spool at the same time in the direction indicated by an arrow marked on the edge of the spool. Wind the line tightly and evenly from side to side and do not twist the lines.

Install spool while directing the ends of both lines through the eyelets in the housing. Align the pegs on drum with slots in the spool and push the spool into drum. Hold the drum firmly, then twist spool quickly in the direction shown in Fig. TO13 so peg enters the hole with a click and locks the spool in position. Trim the lines to the desired length before starting the engine.

Semi-Automatic Dual Strand Trimmer Head

To manually advance the trimmer line with the engine stopped, push the

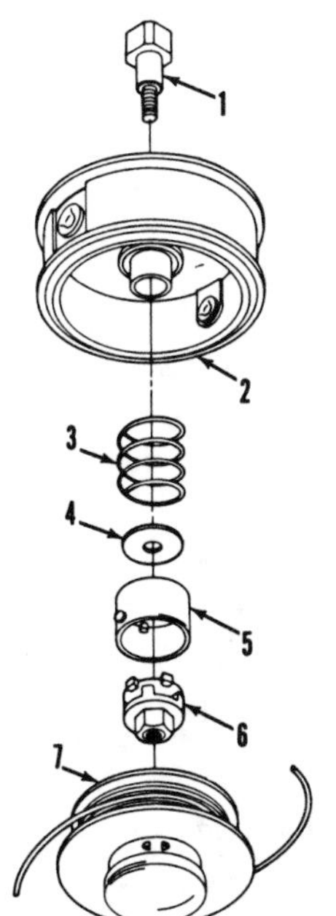

Fig. TO10—Exploded view of the dual strand semi-automatic line trimmer head used on some models.

1. Drive shaft adapter
2. Housing
3. Spring
4. Washer
5. Outer drive cam
6. Inner drive cam
7. Spool

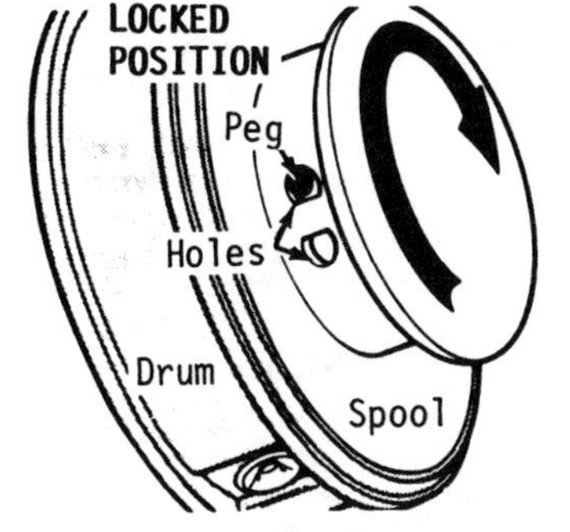

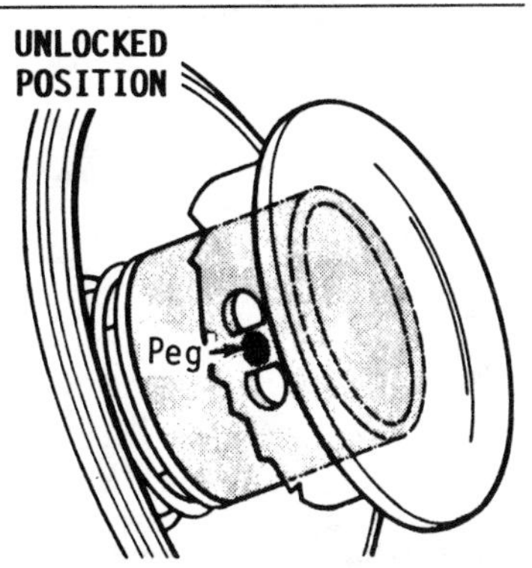

Fig. TO11—To remove spool, hold drum firmly and turn spool in direction shown until plastic peg is between holes as shown in lower view.

button in the center of spool (8—Fig. TO14) at the bottom of the head and pull the line. To extend the line with the engine running, operate the trimmer at maximum speed and tap the button on the ground. The line should extend a small amount automatically. If the line does not extend with the engine running, stop the engine and extend the line manually. If the line is broken inside the housing, it will be necessary to disassemble the unit and feed the line through the eyelet (2).

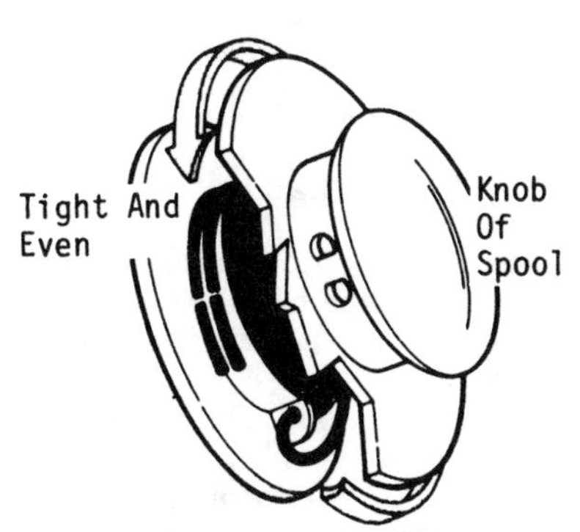

Fig. TO12—End of line must be inserted through hole on spool as shown in upper view. Wind line tightly in direction indicated by arrow on spool.

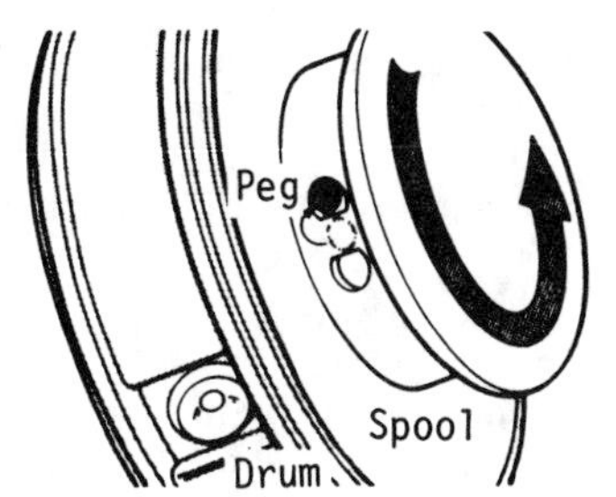

Fig. TO13—Hold drum firmly and twist in direction indicated to lock spool in position.

To remove and disassemble the string trimmer head, proceed as follows. Insert the widest possible screwdriver into the slot in spool cap and twist to "pop" the spool assembly off. Clean and inspect all parts for damage. Remove any remaining line if new line is being installed.

Line should be 0.095 in. (2.41 mm) diameter and the spool will hold approximately 20 ft. (6 m) of line. Insert the line through the hole of the spool and pull the line through until it is the same length on both sides. Wrap both ends of the line on spool at the same time in the direction indicated by an arrow marked on the spool. Wind the line tightly and evenly from side to side and do not twist the lines. Clip the ends of the lines in the two line slots (6). Insert the free ends of the line through line guides (2) and install the spool in housing (1). Pull on the ends of the line to release the lines from slots (6). Make sure the spool is securely latched.

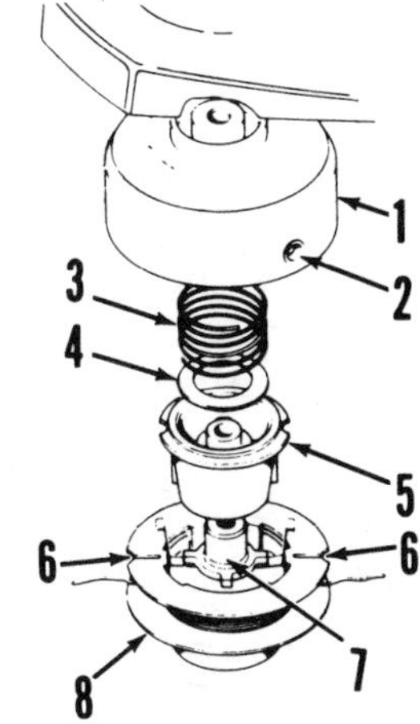

Fig. TO14—Exploded view of dual strand semi-automatic trimmer head used on some models.

1. Housing
2. Line guide
3. Spring
4. Washer
5. Outer drive cam
6. Line slots
7. Inner drive cam
8. Spool

Four Strand Fixed Trimmer

This trimmer head is fitted with two lengths of 0.130 in. (3.3 mm) monofilament line (6—Fig. TO15). The lines are secured to the trimmer head plate (2) by plate (3) and left-hand thread nut (4). When new, each line should be 14 in. (35.6 cm) long and lines should be clipped into the locking slots in the trimmer head. Install cotter pin (5) after tightening the nut (4).

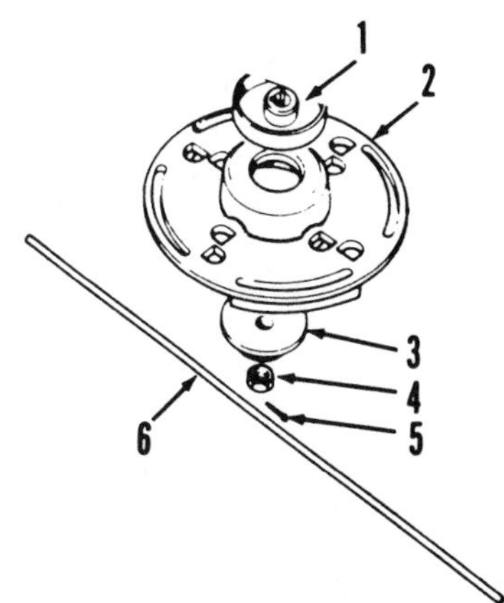

Fig. TO15—Exploded view of four strand fixed line trimmer head with 0.130 in. (3.3 mm) used on some models. Dual strand fixed line trimmer head with 0.105 in. (2.7 mm) line used on some models is similar.

1. Cup washer
2. Plate
3. Plate
4. Nut (L.H.)
5. Cotter pin

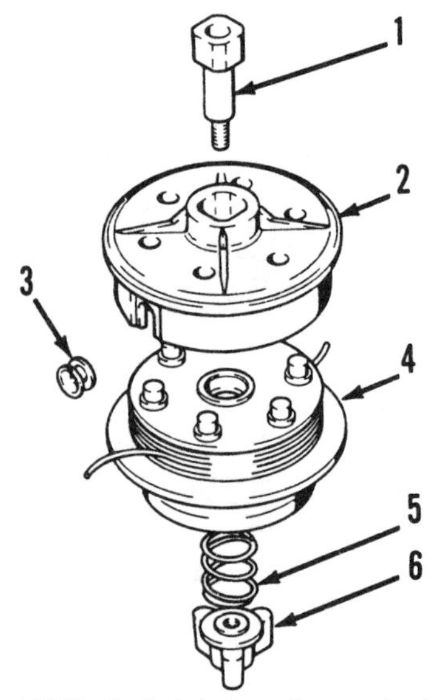

Fig. TO16—Exploded view of manual advance two strand trimmer head typical of the type used on some models.

1. Adapter
2. Drum
3. Line guide
4. Spool
5. Spring
6. Knob

Manual Advance Trimmer

To extend trimmer line, stop the engine and loosen the lock knob (6—Fig. TO16). Pull the spool (4) away from the drum (2) until the lines can be pulled to the desired length. Make certain the spool locating grommets engage the notches in the body (2). Tighten knob (8) securely.

To install new line, remove knob (6), spring (5) and spool (4). Clean and inspect all parts for damage. Insert the line through the hole of the spool and pull the line through until it is the same length on both sides. Wrap both ends of the line on spool at the same time in the direction indicated by an arrow marked on the edge of the spool. Wind the line tightly and evenly from side to side and do not twist the lines. Direct the ends of both lines through the eyelets (3) in the housing while installing the spool. Install spring (5) and tighten knob (6).

BLADE

Hard cutting blades are available for installation on certain models. Check the manufacturers recommendation for proper application. Some models should not be fitted with hard cutting blades. All of the available hard blades can be dangerous and should be selected and used with great care. Blades of different diameters should be matched to the specific model of the powerhead. A blade too small or too large will reduce the effectiveness of operation and may increase the chance for damage or injury. Sharpen each tooth following the original sharpening angle and tooth set. Sharpen all teeth evenly to maintain balance and do not file into the radius at the root.

To remove or install blade, insert a tool into hole in upper adapter and bearing head or gear head to prevent the drive shaft from turning. Remove nut, lower adapter and blade.

DRIVE SHAFT

Curved Drive Shaft

Some models are equipped with a flexible drive shaft located inside the curved housing. The drive shaft should be removed, inspected and lubricated at 50-hour intervals. The shaft (cable) can be withdrawn from either end of the housing. If the drive shaft cannot be easily withdrawn or turned, it may be necessary to install the housing as well as the drive shaft.

Coat the shaft lightly with multipurpose grease before installing. Reversing the drive shaft each time it is installed may extend the life of the shaft. Make sure both ends fully engage the adapters at the engine and the bearing head.

Straight Drive Shaft

Some models are equipped with a solid, straight drive shaft that is supported in five renewable bushings inside the housing. The manufacturer recommends removing, cleaning and lubricating the shaft after each 50-hours of use. The shaft should be perfectly straight and drive surfaces at the ends should not be rounded. Any discoloration or wear on the steel drive shaft indicates bushing wear.

If service parts are available the drive shaft bushings can be removed and new bushings installed. Mark the locations of the bushings within the housing before removing so that new bushings can be installed in the same locations.

BEARING HEAD

Models with a curved drive shaft housing may be equipped with the bearing head shown in Fig. TO17 or Fig. TO18. The bearing head shown is equipped with sealed bearings and will require no regular maintenance. Refer to the following procedure to disassemble the unit for service.

Remove the trimmer head and cup washer. Remove the locating screw and clamp screw (3 and 4—Fig. TO17 or 1 and 2—Fig. TO18). Pull the bearing head from the drive shaft and housing. Remove snap ring (10—Fig. TO17 or 8—Fig. TO18), then use a suitable puller or other suitable tool to remove the arbor shaft and bearings (6, 7 and 8—Fig. TO17 or 5, 7 and 9—Fig. TO18) from the housing. It may be necessary to heat the housing (5—Fig. TO17 or 3—Fig. TO18) before the bearings will move from the housing bores. Further disassembly will depend upon the extent of damage and availability of service parts.

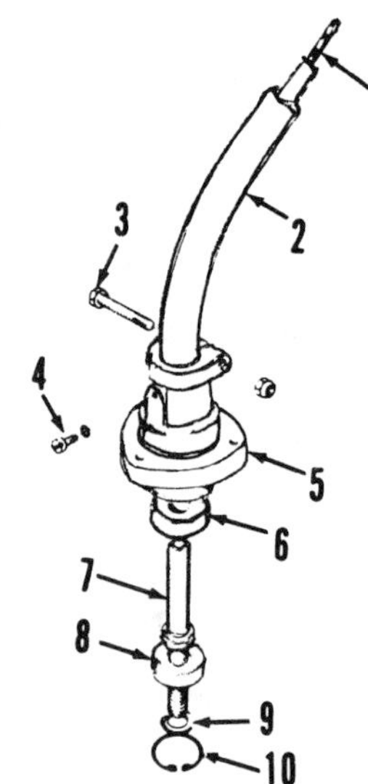

Fig. TO17—Exploded view of curved drive shaft housing and bearing head typical of some models.

1. Drive shaft
2. Drive shaft housing
3. Clamp bolt
4. Locating screw
5. Bearing housing
6. Bearing
7. Arbor shaft
8. Bearing
9. Spacer
10. Snap ring

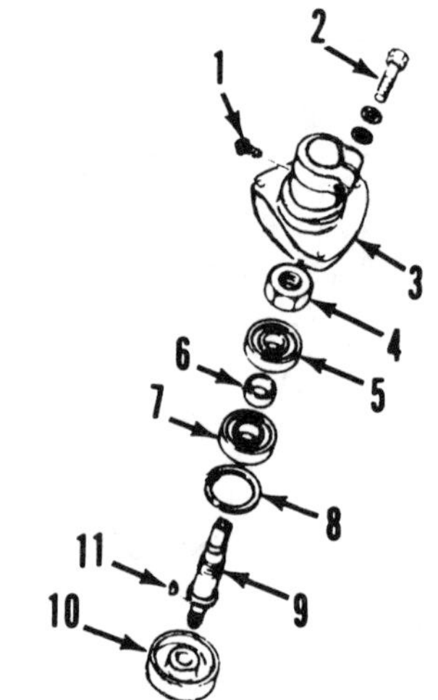

Fig. TO18—Exploded view of the bearing head used on some models. Refer also to the bearing head shown in Fig. TO17.

1. Locating screw
2. Clamp bolt
3. Bearing housing
4. Nut
5. Bearing
6. Spacer
7. Bearing
8. Snap ring
9. Arbor shaft
10. Cup washer
11. Pin

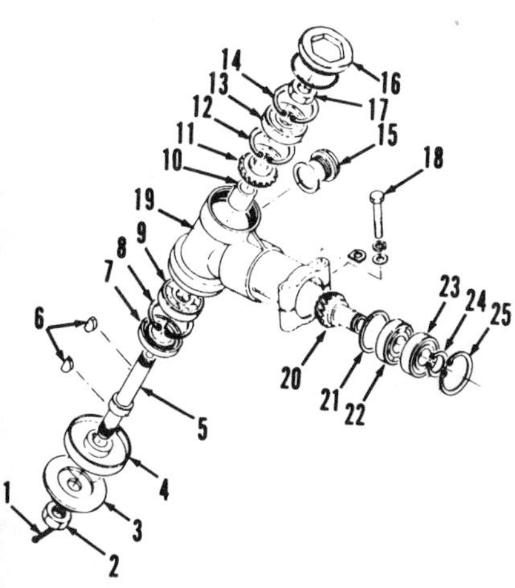

Fig. TO19—Exploded view of the gear head used on some models, including 30920.

1. Cotter pin
2. Nut
3. Adapter plate
4. Cup washer
5. Arbor shaft
6. Woodruff keys
7. Seal
8. Snap ring
9. Bearing
10. Spacer
11. Gear
12. Snap ring
13. Bearing
14. Snap ring
15. Level check plug
16. Plug
17. Nut
18. Clamp bolt
19. Housing
20. Gear
21. Spacer
22. Bearing
23. Bearing
24. Snap ring
25. Snap ring

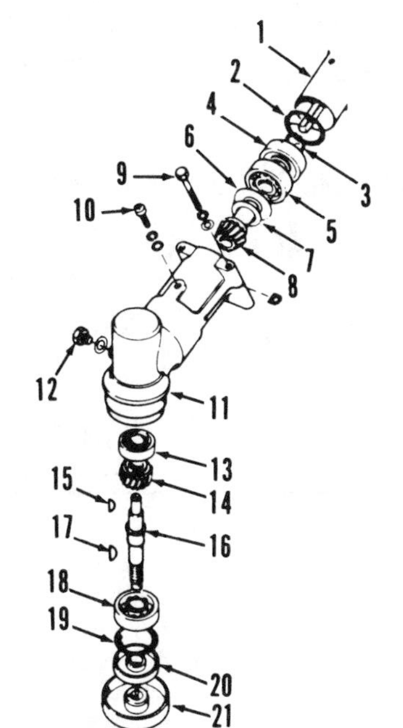

Fig. TO20—Exploded view of gear head typical of some models. Refer also to Fig. TO19 for another type.

1. Drive shaft housing
2. Snap ring
3. Snap ring
4. Bearing
5. Bearing
6. Spacer washer
7. Spacer washer
8. Input gear
9. Clamp bolt
10. Locating screw
11. Housing
12. Check plug
13. Bearing
14. Gear
15. Key
16. Arbor shaft
17. Key
18. Bearing
19. Snap ring
20. Seal
21. Cup washer

GEAR HEAD

The gear head should be lubricated after each 50 hours of operation. Remove trimmer or blade and fill plug (15—Fig. TO19 or 12—Fig. TO20). The housing should be 2/3 filled with grease. If necessary, add multipurpose grease into the opening for the fill plug. Do not overfill the housing.

To disassemble the gear head, first remove the trimmer or blade. Remove the locating screw and clamp screw (18—Fig. TO19 or 9 and 10—Fig. TO20), then pull the gear head from the end of the drive shaft housing. Remove snap ring (25—Fig. TO19 or 2—Fig. TO20), then use a suitable puller to pull the pinion and bearings (20, 22 and 23—Fig. TO19 or 4, 5 and 8—Fig. TO20) from the housing. It may be necessary to heat the housing and spread the clamping gap to facilitate removal.

CAUTION: Excessive force while spreading the clamp or excessive heat can damage the housing. Use caution when using either method.

Remove snap ring (24—Fig. TO19 or 3—Fig. TO20) and press bearings from pinion if renewal is required. Remove seal and snap ring (7 and 8—Fig. TO19 or 18 and 19—Fig. TO20).

On models shown in Fig. TO19, remove plug (16) and nut (17). Bump the arbor (5), gear (11) and upper bearing (13) from the housing. Use a suitable puller if necessary to remove bearing (9).

On models shown in Fig. TO20, withdraw arbor (16), gear (14) and bearings (13 and 18). If stuck in housing, bearings can usually be dislodged by heating the housing and bumping the housing against a wood block.

Inspect and clean components. Reassemble by reversing disassembly procedure.

ENGINE COVER

Some models are equipped with the partial engine cover shown in Fig. TO21. To remove the cover, remove decal (5) or cut along the seam in the middle of the decal. Remove the eight screws and lock knob (1) securing the halves of the cover together, then separate the halves. Note the positions of internal parts before completely separating the halves. Lift the stop switch (8) from the cover and detach the attached wires if necessary. Disconnect the throttle cable from the trigger (12) and remove the trigger (12) and return spring (13).

STARTER

Refer to the appropriate ENGINE SERVICE section for service to the starter assembly.

CLUTCH

Refer to the appropriate ENGINE SERVICE section for clutch removal and service procedures.

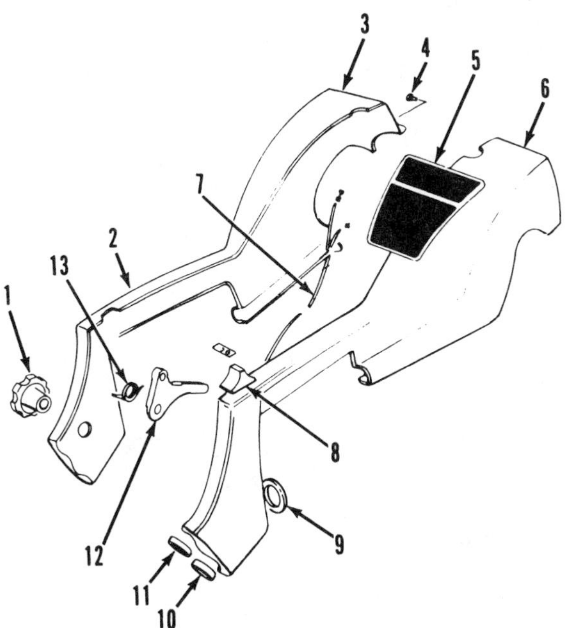

Fig. TO21—Exploded view of the engine cover used on Model 51625. Other models may be equipped with similar covers.

1. Lock knob
2. Screw
3. Cover half
4. Screw
5. Decal
6. Cover half
7. Engine stop wires
8. Engine stop switch
9. Grommet
10. Grommet
11. Grommet
12. Throttle trigger
13. Trigger return spring

TML (TRAIL)

GASOLINE POWERED STRING TRIMMERS

Model	Engine Manufacturer	Engine Model	Displacement
BC-35	TML	150528	35.0 cc
LT-35	TML	150528	35.0 cc

ENGINE INFORMATION

All Models

All models are equipped with a two-stroke air-cooled gasoline engine manufactured by TML (Trail). Refer to TML (TRAIL) ENGINE SERVICE section of this manual.

FUEL MIXTURE

All Models

Manufacturer recommends mixing regular grade (unleaded is an acceptable substitute) gasoline with a good quality two-stroke air-cooled engine oil at a ratio of 20:1. Do not use fuel containing alcohol.

STRING TRIMMER

All Models

Trimmer may be equipped with a single strand (Fig. TL10) or a dual strand (Fig. TL16) manual trimmer head. Refer to appropriate paragraph for model being serviced.

Fig. TL10—Exploded view of single strand manual trimmer head used on some models.

1. Adapter
2. Pin
3. Spool
4. Line
5. Spool cover
6. Line guide
7. Spring
8. Lock knob

Single Strand Trimmer Head. Refer to Fig. TL10 for an exploded view of the single strand trimmer head used on some models. To extend line, stop trimmer engine and wait until all head rotation has stopped. Pull down on spool cover (Fig. TL11) and rotate top in direction of arrow (Fig. TL12) while pulling line out of head. Procedure may have to be repeated until line end reaches mark on trimmer head (Fig. TL13) provided to gage correct line length.

To renew line, push in on spool cover (5-Fig. TL10) and unscrew knob (8). Refer to Fig. TL14. Remove knob (8-Fig. TL10), spring (7), spool cover (5) and spool (3). Remove any remaining line and clean spool and inside of spool cover. Insert the end of the new line into "V" shaped slot in spool (Fig. TL15). Wind line in direction indicated by arrow on spool. Insert line through line guide in spool cover and reinstall spool, spool cover, spring and knob.

Dual Strand Trimmer Head. Refer to Fig. TL16 for exploded view of the dual strand manual trimmer head used on some models. To extend line, stop trimmer engine and wait until all head rotation has stopped. Loosen knob (6). Pull each line end at the same time until each line is extended 6 inches (15 cm). Tighten knob (6).

To renew line, cut 15 feet (4.6 m) of 0.095 inch (2.4 mm) monofilament line. Remove lock knob (6) and remove lower housing (5) and spool (4). Remove any remaining old line. Clean all parts of trimmer head. Pull line guides (2) down (do not remove) and clean outside surfaces with a wet soapy cloth. Apply a few drops of oil into cavities after cleaning. Loop new line into two equal lengths and insert line ends through holes at center of spool. Pull line ends out until stopped by spool. Wind both ends onto spool in direction indicated

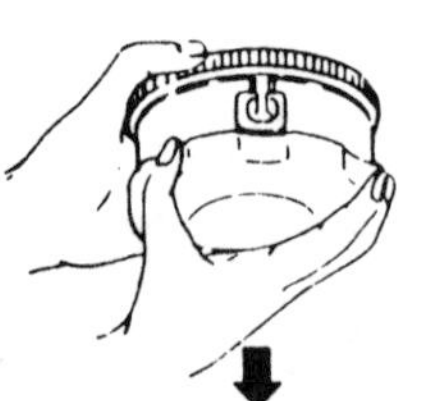

Fig. TL11—To extend line, pull down on spool cover and rotate. Refer to Fig. TL12.

Fig. TL12—Pull out line as cover is rotated. Refer to text.

Fig. TL13—Spool is marked to indicate correct line length.

Fig. TL14—To remove spool, push up on cover and remove lock knob. Refer to text.

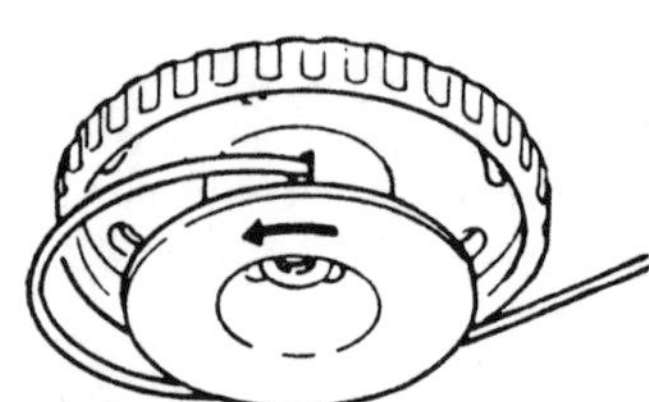

Fig. TL15—Wind new line on spool in direction indicated by arrow on spool.

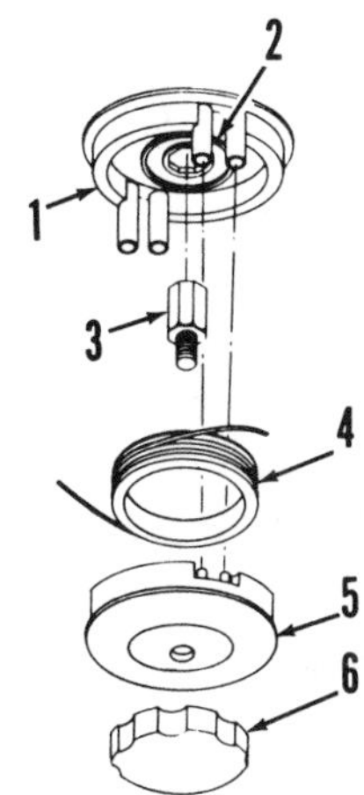

Fig. TL16—Exploded view of dual strand manual trimmer head used on some models.

1. Upper cover
2. Line guides
3. Adapter
4. Spool
5. Lower cover
6. Lock knob

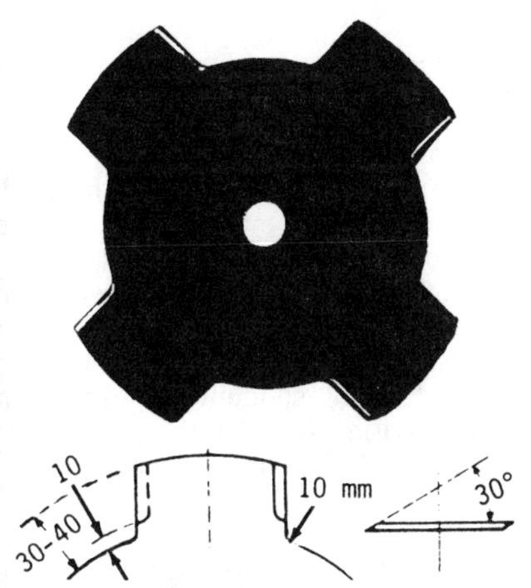

Fig. TL17—Some models may be equipped with a four cutting edge blade. Refer to illustration and text for sharpening procedure.

by arrow on spool. Insert line ends through line guides in upper cover and install spool, lower cover and lock knob.

BLADE

All Models

Trimmer may be equipped with a four cutting edge blade (Fig. TL17) or an eighty tooth saw blade (Fig. TL18). Blade should be installed with parts assembled in sequence shown in Fig. TL19.

To sharpen the four cutting edge blade, refer to Fig. TL17. Blade edge

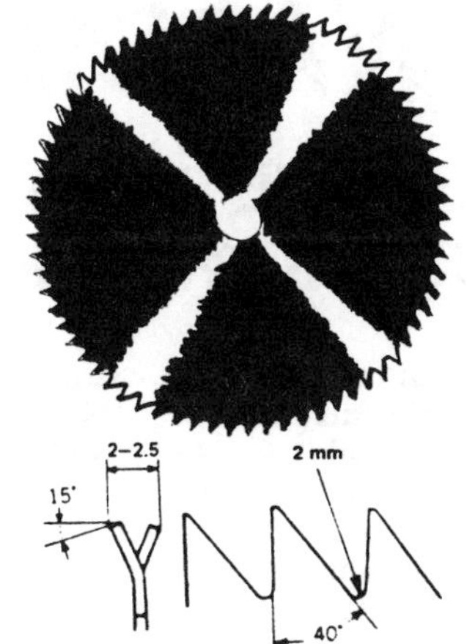

Fig. TL18—Some models may be equipped with an eighty tooth saw blade. Refer to illustration and text for sharpening procedure.

should have a length of 1.18-1.58 inch (30-40 mm). Do not grind the chamfered section of the blade root. Make certain the root of cutting blade remains chamfered to prevent cracking or breakage. Sharpen all teeth equally to maintain blade balance.

To sharpen the eighty tooth saw blade, refer to Fig. TL18. Maintain a 0.04-0.08 inch (1-2 mm) radius at the tooth root. Maintain a 0.08-0.09 inch (2-2.5 mm) tooth set. Sharpen all teeth equally to maintain blade balance.

DRIVE SHAFT

All Models

All models are equipped with a solid steel drive shaft (4-Fig. TL19) which is supported in drive shaft housing (1) in four renewable bushings (2). Drive shaft and bushings require no regular maintenance; however, before removing bushings (2), mark bushing locations in drive shaft housing. Install new bushings at old bushing locations. When installing drive shaft, lightly lubricate with SAE 30 oil prior to installation.

GEAR HEAD

All Models

All models are equipped with gear head shown in Fig. TL19. At 30 hour intervals of use, lubricate gear head by removing trimmer head or blade as-

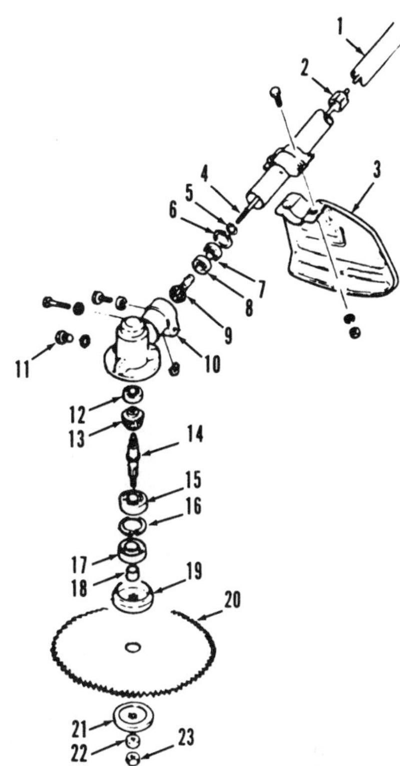

Fig. TL19—Exploded view of drive shaft housing and gear head assembly.

1. Drive shaft housing
2. Bushings
3. Shield
4. Drive shaft
5. Snap ring
6. Snap ring
7. Bearing
8. Bearing
9. Input shaft
10. Housing
11. Check plug
12. Bearing
13. Output gear
14. Arbor (output) shaft
15. Bearing
16. Snap ring
17. Seal
18. Spacer
19. Adapter
20. Blade
21. Adapter
22. Nut
23. Jam nut

sembly and check plug (11). Pump lithium base grease into gear head housing until grease appears at lower seal (17).

To disassemble gear head, separate gear head from drive shaft housing. Remove trimmer head or blade. Remove snap ring (6). Insert screwdriver or suitable wedge in gear head housing clamp split. Carefully expand housing and remove input shaft (9) and bearing assembly. Remove snap ring (5) and press bearings (8 and 7) from input shaft as necessary. Remove spacer (18) and seal (17). Remove snap ring (16). Use suitable puller to remove arbor shaft (14) and bearing assembly. Remove bearing (15) and gear (13) from arbor shaft as necessary. If bearing (12) stays in housing, heat housing to 140° F (60° C) and tap housing on wooden block to remove bearing.

WARDS

GASOLINE POWERED STRING TRIMMERS

Model	Engine Manufacturer	Engine Model	Displacement
2049	Tecumseh	AV520	85.0 cc
24206	Kioritz	....	16.0 cc
24207	Kioritz	....	21.2 cc
24369	Tecumseh	AV520	85.0 cc
XEC-24300	Kioritz	....	13.8 cc
XEC-24340	Kioritz	....	13.8 cc
XEC-24341	Kioritz	....	16.0 cc
XEC-24342	Kioritz	....	21.2 cc
XEC-24358	Kioritz	....	13.8 cc
XEC-24359	Kioritz	....	21.2 cc
XEC-24361	Kioritz	....	30.8 cc

ENGINE INFORMATION

All Models

Wards line trimmers and brush cutters may be equipped with Kioritz or Tecumseh two-stroke air-cooled gasoline engines. Identify engine model by engine manufacturer, trimmer model number or engine displacement. Refer to KIORITZ ENGINE SERVICE or TECUMSEH ENGINE SERVICE section of this manual.

FUEL MIXTURE

All Models

Manufacturer recommends mixing regular grade gasoline (unleaded is an acceptable substitute) with a good quality two-stroke air-cooled engine oil at a 25:1 ratio. Do not use fuel containing alcohol.

STRING TRIMMER

Models XEC-24359 And XEC-24361

Semi-Automatic Dual Strand Trimmer Head. Models XEC-24359 and XEC-24361 may be equipped with dual strand trimmer head as shown in Fig. WD10. To manually advance line with engine stopped, push in on button (7) and pull on each line. Procedure may have to be repeated to obtain desired line length. To extend line with engine running, operate trimmer at full operating rpm and tap button (7) on the ground. Line will automatically extend a measured amount.

To renew trimmer line, hold drum firmly and turn spool in direction shown in Fig. WD11 to remove slack. Twist with a hard snap until plastic peg is between holes. Pull spool out of drum. Remove old line from spool. Spool will hold aproximately 20 feet (6 m) of monofilament line. Insert one end of new line through hole on spool (Fig. WD12) and pull line through until line is the same length on both sides of hole. Wind both ends of line at the same time in direction indicated by arrow on spool. Wind tightly and evenly from side to side and do not twist line. Insert ends of line through line guide openings, align pegs on drum with slots in spool and push spool into drum. Hold drum firmly, twist spool suddenly in direction shown in Fig. WD13 until peg enters hole with a click and locks spool in posi-

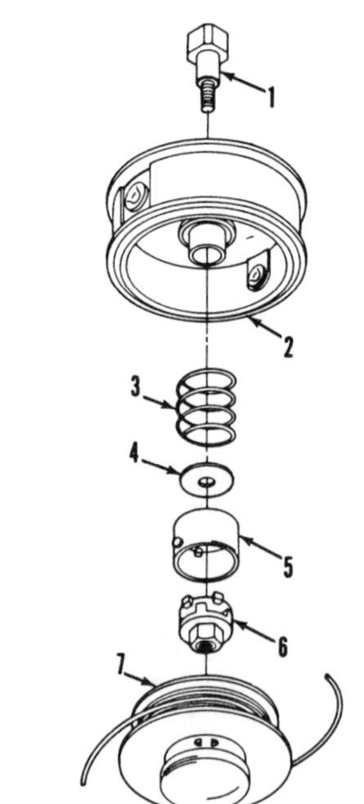

Fig. WD10—Exploded view of dual strand semi-automatic trimmer head used on some models.

1. Bolt
2. Drum
3. Spring
4. Washer
5. Outer drive
6. Inner cam
7. Spool

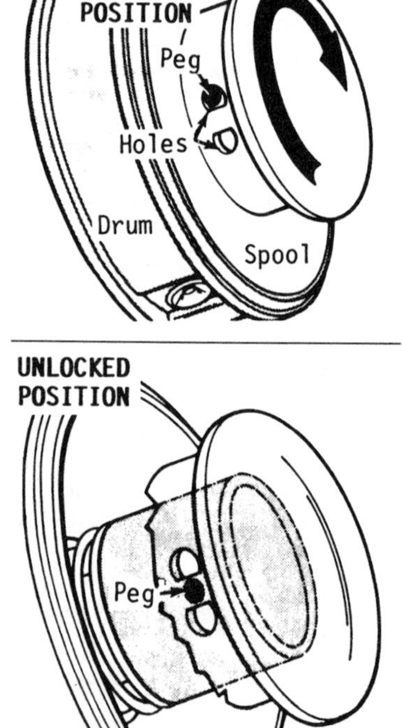

Fig. WD11—To remove spool, hold housing firmly and turn spool in direction shown to take up slack, then twist with a sudden snap until plastic peg is between holes as shown in lower view.

ion. Trim extending lines to correct lengths.

Manual Advance Dual Strand Trimmer Head. Models XEC-24359 and XEC-24361 may be equipped with manual advance dual strand trimmer head shown in Fig. WD14. To extend line, loosen lock knob (6) approximately one turn. Pull out the line on each side until line lengths are 6 inches (152 mm).

To renew line, remove slotted screw (8) and washer (7). Unscrew ball lock (6). Remove cover (5) and spring (3). Remove spool (4). Cut two 12 foot (4 m) lengths of 0.095 inch (2.4 mm) monofilament line. Insert one end of each line through the slot and into the locating hole on bottom side of spool. Line ends should extend approximately 1/4 inch (6.4 mm) through locating holes. Hold lines tight and wind in a counterclockwise direction using care not to cross the lines. Insert the end of each line into each slot leaving approximately 6 inches (152 mm) of line extending from spool. Place spool into drum and feed one line through each of the line guides. Install spring, cover, ball lock, washer and screw.

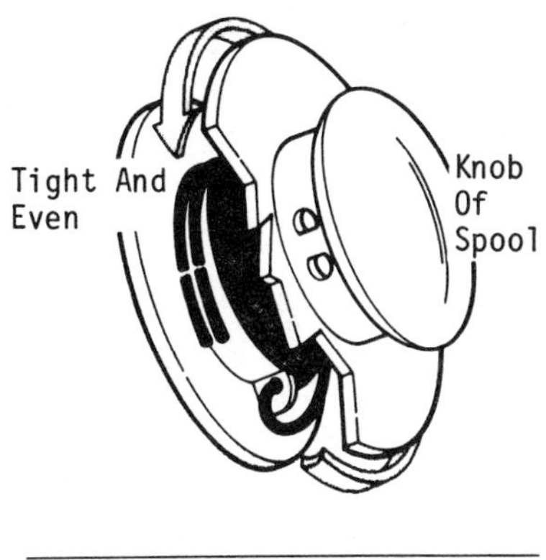

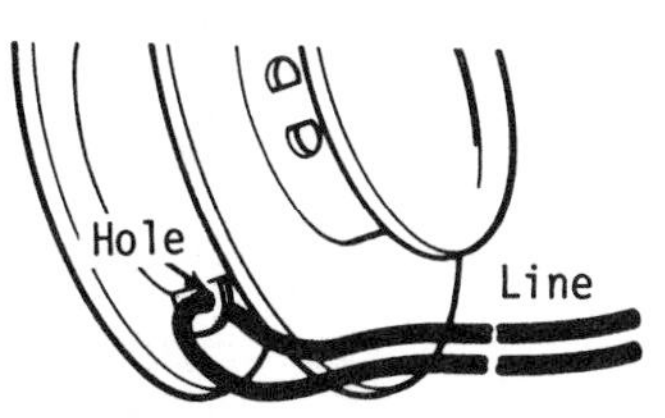

Fig. WD12—End of line must be inserted through hole on spool as shown in lower view. Wind line tightly in direction indicated by arrow on spool.

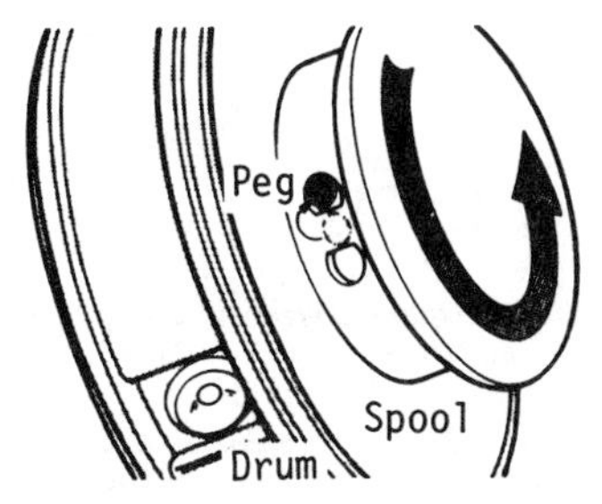

Fig. WD13—Hold drum firmly and twist suddenly to lock spool in position.

Models XEC-24300, XEC-24340, XEC-24341, XEC-24342, XEC-24358, 24206 And 24207

Models XEC-24300, XEC-24340, XEC-24341, XEC-24342, XEC-24358, 24206 and 24207 may be equipped with a semi-automatic single strand trimmer head shown in Fig. WD15. Line may be manually advanced with engine stopped by pushing in on housing (12) and pulling line out as required.

To renew line, remove cotter pin (13-Fig. WD15). Rotate housing (12) counterclockwise and remove housing and line spool (7). Remove foam pads (9 and 10) and any remaining old line. Clean spool and inner surface of outer housing (12). Check indexing teeth on spool and in housing. Cut off approximately 25 feet (7.6 mm) of 0.080 inch (2 mm) monofilament line and tape one end of line to spool (Fig. WD16). Wind line on spool in direction indicated by arrow on spool (Fig. WD17). Install foam pads (9 and 10) with line between them as shown in Fig. WD17. Insert line end through line guide (14-Fig. WD15) opening and install spool and housing. Push in on housing and rotate housing clockwise to lock in position, then install cotter pin (13).

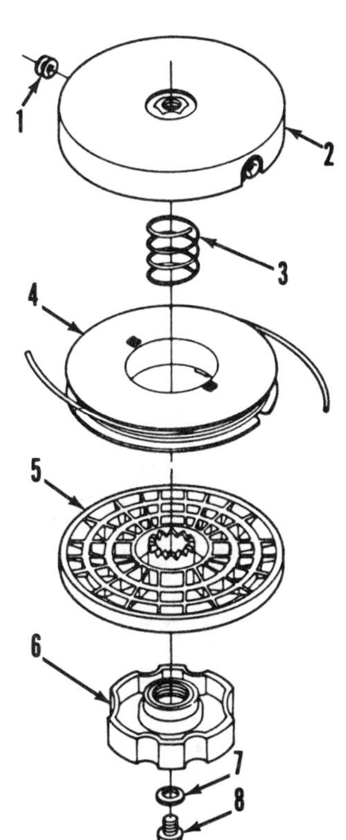

Fig. WD14—Exploded view of manual trimmer head used on some models. This head is no longer available.

1. Line guide
2. Hub
3. Spring
4. Spool
5. Cover
6. Ball lock
7. Washer
8. Screw

Models 2049 And 24369

Models 2049 and 24369 may be equipped with a four strand trimmer head shown in Fig. WD18.

To renew trimmer line, remove bolt (8) and cover (7). Remove spools (6) and remove any remaining old line. Clean inside of upper body. Wind new monofilament line on the four spools (6). Place spools (6) back in upper body (1), install springs (5) and install cover (7). Install bolt (8) and tighten securely.

BLADE

Models XEC-24359, XEC-24361, 2049 And 24369

Models XEC-24359, XEC-24361, 2049 and 24369 may be equipped with a 10

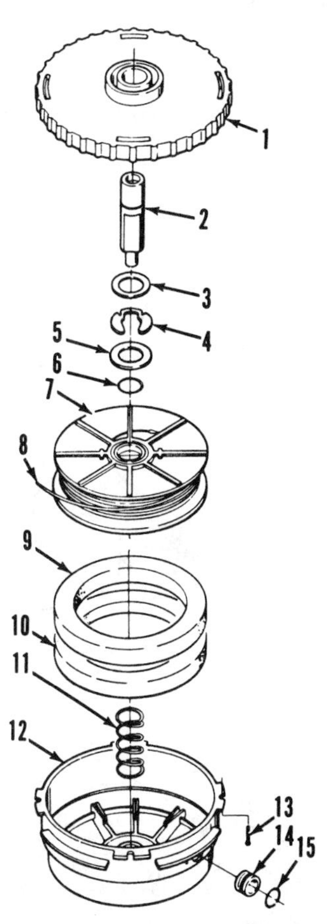

Fig. WD15—Exploded view of semi-automatic trimmer head used on some models.

1. Plate
2. Adapter
3. Washer
4. Retainer ring
5. Washer
6. Retainer ring
7. Spool
8. Line
9. Foam pad
10. Foam pad
11. Spring
12. Hub
13. Cotter pin
14. Line guide
15. Retainer

inch saw blade. When installing blade, make certain all adapter plates are centered and seated squarely against blade and tighten nut (left-hand thread) securely.

DRIVE SHAFT

Models 24206, 24207, XEC-24300, XEC-24340, XEC-24341, XEC-24342 And XEC-24358

Models 24206, 24207, XEC-24300, XEC-24340, XEC-24341, XEC-24342 and XEC-24358 are equipped with flexible drive shafts supported in a curved drive shaft housing. Drive shaft should be removed at 18 hour intervals of use, cleaned and lubricated with lithium base grease. Reverse positions of drive shaft ends (engine end now at trimmer head end) and install drive shaft in housing. Reversing drive shaft ends each time it is lubricated will extend drive shaft life.

Models 2049, 24369, XEC-24358 And XEC-24361

Models 2049, 24369, XEC-24358 and XEC-24361 are equipped with a solid drive shaft supported in a straight drive shaft housing tube. No regular maintenance is required; however, if drive shaft is removed, lubricate drive shaft with lithium base grease before reinstallation.

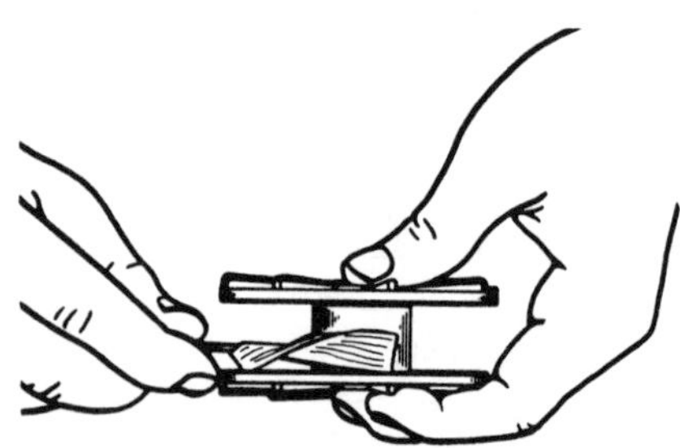

Fig. WD16—Tape one end of line to center of spool as shown.

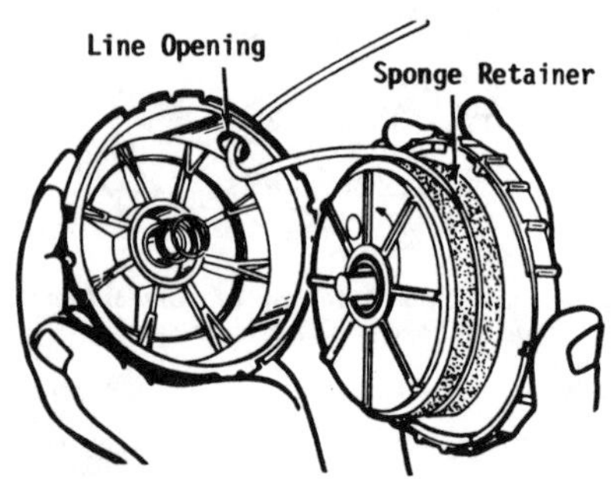

Fig. WD17—Foam pads are installed on spool with trimmer line between them.

BEARING HEAD

All Models So Equipped

Bearing heads used on all models except Models 2049 and 24369 are shown in Fig. WD19 or WD20. Bearing heads are equipped with sealed bearings and require no regular maintenance. To disassemble either bearing head, remove screw (1) and clamp screw (2). Remove adapter plate (10) and snap ring (8). Use suitable puller to remove bearing and arbor assemblies. Remove nut (4) and remove bearings and spacer as required.

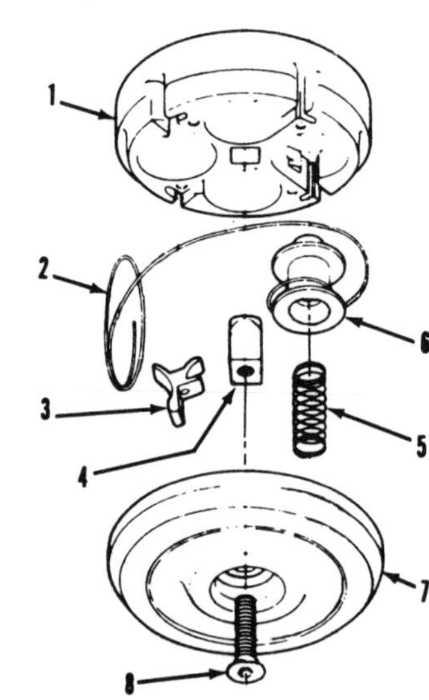

Fig. WD18—Exploded view of four strand trimmer head used on Models 2049 and 24369.

1. Upper housing
2. Line
3. Line retainer
4. Arbor post
5. Spring
6. Spools
7. Cover
8. Screw

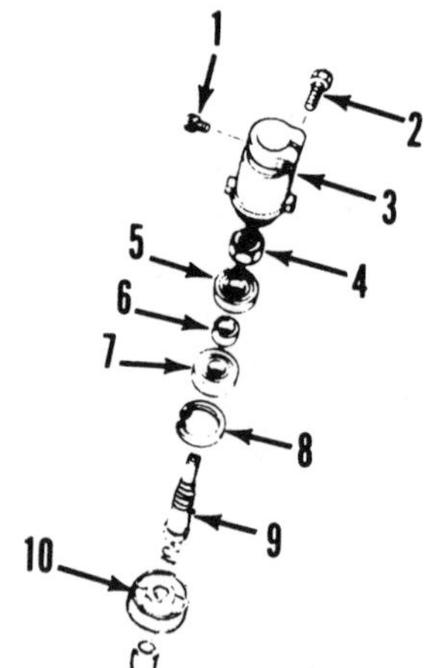

Fig. WD19—Exploded view of bearing head used on some models.

1. Screw
2. Clamp screw
3. Housing
4. Nut
5. Bearing
6. Spacer
7. Bearing
8. Snap ring
9. Shaft
10. Adapter plate & key

Bearing head used on Models 2049 and 24369 is shown in Fig. WD21. Bearing head is equipped with sealed bearings and requires no regular maintenance.

To disassemble bearing head, remove trimmer head or blade assembly. Re-

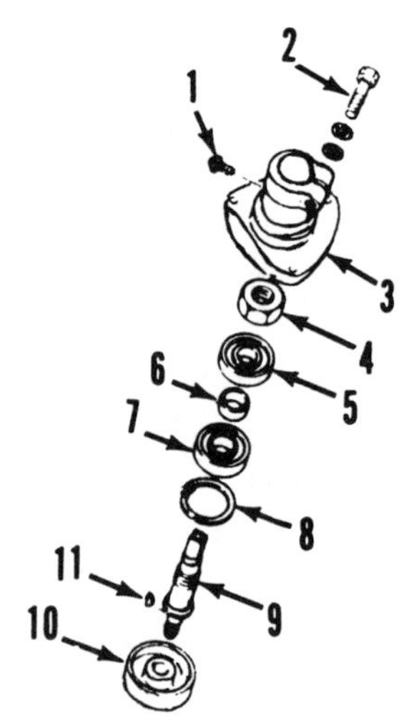

Fig. WD20—Exploded view of bearing head used on some models.

1. Screw
2. Clamp screw
3. Housing
4. Nut
5. Bearing
6. Spacer
7. Bearing
8. Snap ring
9. Shaft
10. Adapter
11. Key

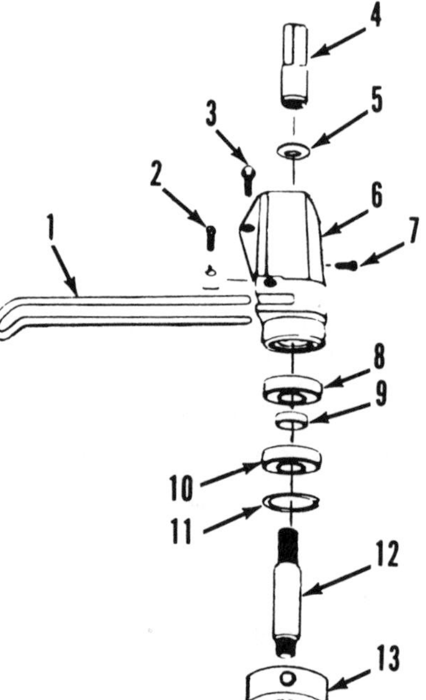

Fig. WD21—Exploded view of bearing head used on Models 2049 and 24369.

1. Wire bracket
2. Bolt
3. Bolt
4. Drive shaft adapter
5. Washer
6. Housing
7. Locating screw
8. Bearing
9. Spacer
10. Bearing
11. Snap ring
12. Arbor shaft
13. Cup washer

ove clamp bolt (3) and locating screw). Separate gear head from drive aft housing tube. Remove snap ring 1). Secure head assembly in a vise. ace a 1-3/8 inch wooden dowel with a '4 inch hole drilled through center over arbor shaft, against the square coupling end. Tap wooden dowel with a mallet to remove arbor shaft and bearing assembly. Disassemble bearings, coupling and arbor assembly as required.

To reassemble, place coupling (4) and washer (5) on arbor (12). Press one bearing onto arbor. Install assembly into housing. Install spacer (9) and press remaining bearing onto arbor and into housing. Install snap ring.

WEED EATER

ELECTRIC POWERED STRING TRIMMERS

Model	Volts	Amps	Cutting Swath	Line Diameter	Rpm
1208	120	2.0	8 in.	0.065 in.	N/A
1210	120	2.8	10 in.	0.065 in.	N/A
1214	120	3.5	14 in.	0.065 in.	N/A
1216	120	4.5	16 in.	0.080 in.	N/A

N/A—Rpm specifications not available.

ELECTRICAL REQUIREMENTS

All models require electrical circuits with 120-volt alternating current. Extension cord length should not exceed 00 feet (30.5 m). Make certain all circuits and connections are properly grounded at all times.

STRING TRIMMER

All Models

All models are equipped with a single strand semi-automatic trimmer head shown in Fig. WE1. Models 1208 and 210 are equipped with 35 feet (10.7 m) of 0.065 inch (1.6 mm) line, Model 1214 is equipped with 50 feet (15.2 m) of 0.065 inch (1.6 m) line and Model 1216 is equipped with 40 feet (12.2 m) of 0.080 inch (2.0 mm) line.

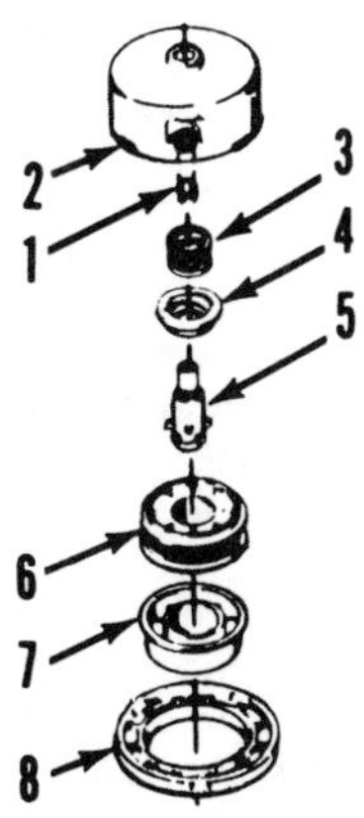

Fig. WE1—Exploded view of single strand semi-automatic trimmer head used on all models.

1. Line guide
2. Housing
3. Spring
4. Spring adapter
5. Drive cam
6. Spool
7. Button
8. Cover

To extend line with trimmer engine stopped, push in on button (7) while pulling on line end. Procedure may have to be repeated to obtain desired line length. To extend line with trimmer engine running, operate trimmer engine at full rpm and tap button (7) on the ground. Each time button (7) is tapped on the ground a measured amount of new line will be advanced.

To renew line, remove cover (8), button (7) and spool (6). Clean all parts thoroughly and remove any remaining old line from spool. Wind correct length and diameter line on spool in direction indicated by arrow on spool. Insert line end through line guide opening in housing (2) and install spool, button and cover.

Illustrations courtesy Poulan/Weed Eater

WEED EATER

GASOLINE POWERED STRING TRIMMERS

Model	Engine Manufacturer	Engine Model	Displacement
650, 657, 670	Tecumseh	AV520	85 cc
1000	Fuji	...	37.7 cc
1400, 1400T	Poulan	...	22.2 cc
1500	Poulan	...	26.2 cc
1600, 1600T	Poulan	...	26.2 cc
1700, 1700A	Poulan	...	26.2 cc
1740	Poulan	...	26.2 cc
1900	Poulan	...	26.2 cc
GTI-15, GTI-15T	Poulan	...	22 cc
GTI-16	Poulan	...	30 cc
GTI-16 Super	Poulan	...	30 cc
GTI-17	Poulan	...	26 cc
GTI-17XP	Poulan	...	30 cc
GTI-18, GTI-18K	Poulan	...	30 cc
GTI-19	Poulan	...	30 cc
HP-30	Poulan	...	30 cc
XR-20, XR-20T	Poulan	...	22.2 cc
XR-30	Poulan	...	26.2 cc
XR-50, XR-50A	Poulan	...	26.2 cc
XR-70	Poulan	...	26.2 cc
XR-75	Poulan	...	26.2 cc
XR-80, XR-80A	Poulan	...	28 cc
XR-85	Poulan	...	28 cc
XR-90	Poulan	...	28 cc
XR-95	Poulan	...	28 cc
XR-100	Poulan	...	26.2 cc
XR-105	Poulan	...	22.2 cc
XR-125	Poulan	...	22.2 cc
XT-20, XT-20T	Poulan	...	22 cc
XT-50	Poulan	...	30 cc
XT-85	Poulan	...	30 cc
XT-100	Poulan	...	30 cc
XT-125	Poulan	...	30 cc

ENGINE INFORMATION

The models in this section are equipped with a Fuji, Poulan or Tecumseh engine. Refer to appropriate engine service section for engine service information.

FUEL MIXTURE

Manufacturer recommends combining regular gasoline with Poulan/Weed Eater two-stroke engine oil mixed as indicated on container. Gasohol or other alcohol blended fuels are not approved by manufacturer.

STRING TRIMMER

Models 1400, 1500, 1600, 1700, 1740, XR-20, XR-30, XR-50, XR-70, XR-75, XR-80, XR-85 And XR-105

These models are equipped with the single strand, semi-automatic trimmer head shown in Figs. WE10 or WE11. Early type trimmer head (Fig. WE10) is identified by the adapter (1) that drives the trimmer head. Service procedure for both heads is similar.

To extend line with trimmer engine stopped, push in on button (7) while pulling on line end. Repeat procedure as needed to obtain desired line length. To extend line with trimmer engine running and head rotating, tap button (7) on ground. Each time button is tapped on ground, a measured amount of line is advanced.

To install new line, remove cover (8), button (7) and spool (6). Clean all parts thoroughly and remove any remaining old line from spool. Wind approximately 30 feet (9 m) of 0.080-in. (2 mm) diameter monofilament line on spool in direction indicated by arrow on spool. Insert line end through line guide opening in housing (2) and install spool, button and cover.

Models XR-90, XR-95, XR-100 And 1000

Models XR-90, XR-95, XR-100 and 1000 are equipped with the dual strand, manual trimmer head shown in Fig. WE12. To extend line, stop trimmer engine and push in on plate (8) while pulling each line out of housing (2).

To install new trimmer line, remove screw (9), plate (8), spring (6) and spool (7). Remove any remaining line from

Illustrations courtesy Poulan/Weed Eater

·ach side of spool. Clean spool, housing ınd plate. Insert ends of two new 0.095-n. (2.4 mm) diameter lines in holes lo-·ated within spool and wind lines in lirection indicated by arrow on spool. 'otal amount of installed line should not ·xceed spool diameter. Make certain line avers (3) are in position and install pool in housing with the "THIS SIDE N" instructions on spool toward inside f trimmer head. Install spring (6), cov-·r (8) and screw (9).

Models 650, 657 And 670

Models 650, 657 and 670 are equipped with the four strand trimmer head shown in Fig. WE13.

To install new line, remove screw (8) and cover (7). Remove spools (6) and remove any old line. Clean inside of head.

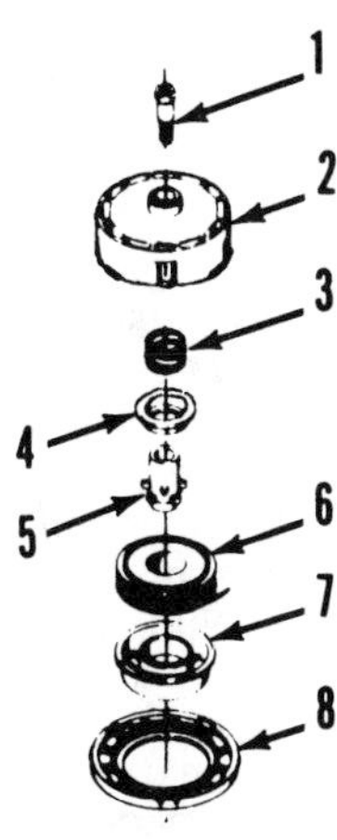

Fig. WE10—Exploded view of old style single strand, semi-automatic trimmer head used on early Models 1500, 1700, XR-30, XR-50, XR-70, XR-75, XR-80 and XR-85.

1. Drive shaft adapter
2. Housing
3. Spring
4. Spring adapter
5. Drive cam
6. Spool
7. Button
8. Cover

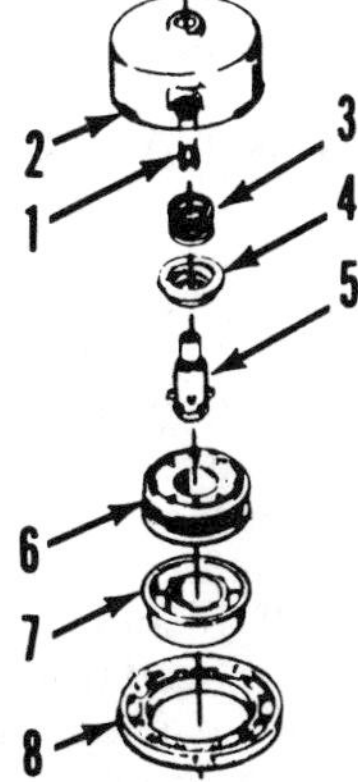

Fig. WE11—Exploded view of later style single strand, semi-automatic trimmer head used on Models 1400, 1600, 1740 and XR-20, and later Models 1500, 1700, XR-30, XR-50, XR-70, XR-75, XR-80 and XR-85.

1. Line guide
2. Housing
3. Spring
4. Spring adapter
5. Drive cam
6. Spool
7. Button
8. Cover

Wind new monofilament line on the four spools (6). Reassemble trimmer head.

Models GTI-15T, GTI-17XP, XT-20T And Some GTI-16, GTI-16 Super Models

Models GTI-15T, GTI-17XP, XT-20T and some GTI-16 and GTI-16 Super Models are equipped with the single strand, semi-automatic trimmer head shown in Fig. WE14.

To extend line with trimmer engine stopped, push in on button (4) while pulling on line end. Repeat procedure as needed to obtain desired line length. To extend line with trimmer engine running and head rotating, tap button (4) on ground. Each time button is tapped on ground, a measured amount of line is advanced.

To install new line, disengage tabs on cover (6) from housing (1). Remove old line and clean parts. Recommended line diameter is 0.080 inch (2 mm). Wind line around spool in direction indicated by arrow on spool.

Models 1400T, 1600T, GTI-15, GTI-17, XR-20, XR-20T And Some HP-30 Models

Models 1400T, 1600T, GTI-15, GTI-17, XR-20, XR-20T and some HP-30 models are equipped with the single strand, semi-automatic trimmer head shown in Fig. WE15.

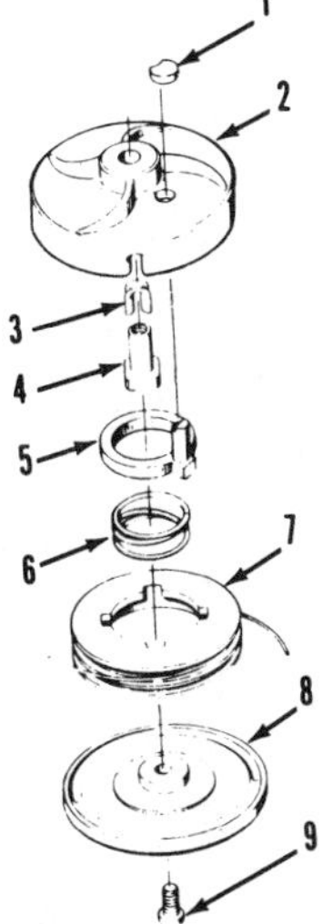

Fig. WE12—Exploded view of dual strand, manual trimmer head used on Models XR-90, XR-95, XR-100 and 1000.

1. Lock ring cap
2. Housing
3. Line guide
4. Drive shaft adapter
5. Lock ring
6. Spring
7. Spool
8. Cover
9. Screw

To extend line with trimmer engine stopped, push in on button (6) while pulling on line end. Repeat procedure as needed to obtain desired line length. To extend line with trimmer engine running and head rotating, tap button (6) on ground. Each time button is tapped on ground a measured amount of line is advanced.

To install new line, remove cover (7), button (6) and spool (5). Clean all parts thoroughly and remove any remaining old line from spool. Wind 0.080 inch (2 mm) diameter monofilament line on spool in direction indicated by arrow on spool. Insert line end through line guide opening in housing (1) and install spool, button and cover.

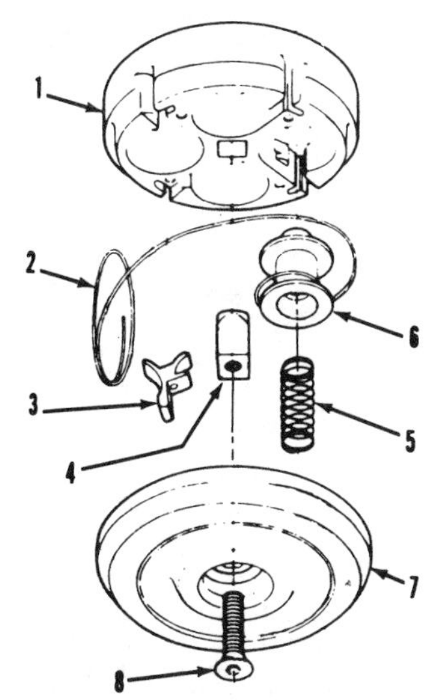

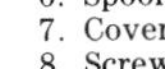

Fig. WE13—Exploded view of the four strand trimmer head used on Models 650, 657 and 670.

1. Upper housing
2. Line
3. Line retainer
4. Arbor post
5. Spring
6. Spool
7. Cover
8. Screw

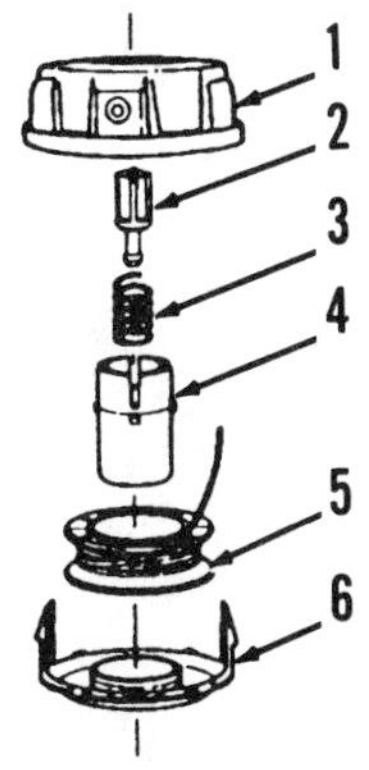

Fig. WE14—Exploded view of single strand, semi-automatic trimmer head used on Models GTI-15T, GTI-17XP and XT-20T, and some GTI-16 and GTI-16 Super models.

1. Housing
2. Adapter
3. Spring
4. Button
5. Spool
6. Cover

Illustrations courtesy Poulan/Weed Eater

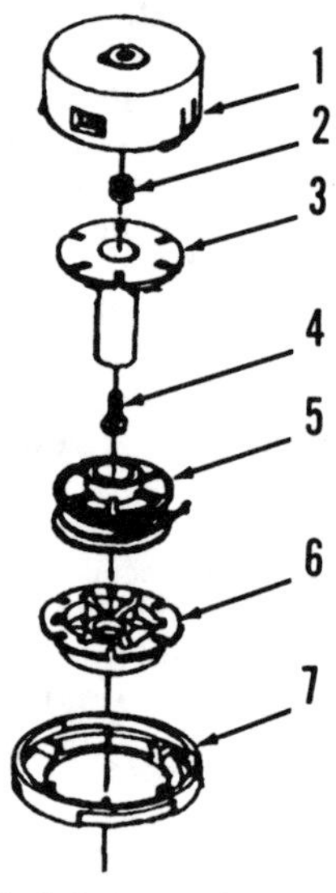

Fig. WE15—Exploded view of single strand, semi-automatic trimmer head used on Models 1400T, 1600T, GTI-15, GTI-17, XR-20, XR-20T and some HP-30 models.

1. Housing
2. Spring
3. Spool post
4. Screw
5. Spool
6. Button
7. Cover

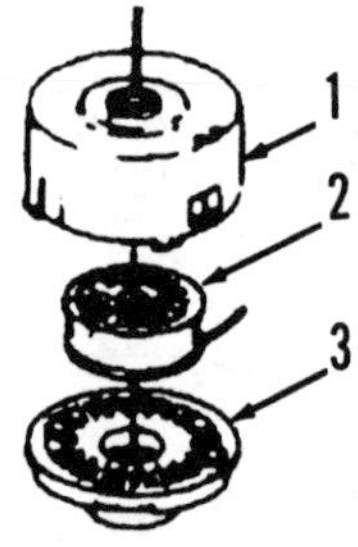

Fig. WE16—Exploded view of single strand, semi-automatic trimmer head used on Models 1700A, 1900, GTI-16, GTI-16 Super, GTI-18, GTI-18K, GTI-19, XR-50A, XR-80A, XR-125, XT-50, XT-85, XT-100, XT-125 and some HP-30 models.

1. Housing
2. Spool
3. Cover & button assy.

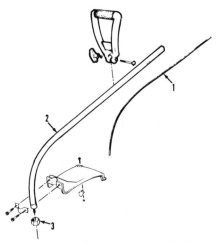

Fig. WE17—Exploded view of flexible drive shaft (1), drive shaft housing tube (2) and dust cover (3) used on Models 1400, 1400T, 1500, 1600, 1600T, 1740, GTI-15, GTI-15T, GTI-16, GTI-16 Super, GTI-17, GTI-17XP, HP-30, XR-20, XR-20T, XR-30, XR-50A, XT-20, XT-20T and XT-50.

Models 1700A, 1900, GTI-16, GTI-16 Super, GTI-18, GTI-18K, GTI-19, XR-50A, XR-80A, XR-125, XT-50, XT-85, XT-100, XT-125 And Some HP-30 Models

These models are equipped with the single strand, semi-automatic trimmer head shown in Fig. WE16.

To extend line with trimmer engine stopped, push in on button while pulling on line end. Repeat procedure as needed to obtain desired line length. To extend line with trimmer engine running and head rotating, tap button on ground. Each time button is tapped on ground, a measured amount of line is advanced.

To install new line, detach cover (3) from housing (1). Remove old line and clean parts. Recommended line diameter is 0.080 inch (2 mm). Wind line around spool in direction indicated by arrow on spool.

BLADE

Some models may be equipped with a blade. When installing blade, be sure all adapter plates are centered and seated squarely against blade. Blade nut has left-hand threads.

DRIVE SHAFT

Curved Shaft Models

Models with a curved drive shaft housing (2—Fig. WE17) are equipped with a flexible drive shaft (1). The drive shaft should be removed, cleaned and lubricated after every 20 hours of operation. Detach head assembly from drive shaft housing and remove shaft. Apply lithium-based grease to shaft.

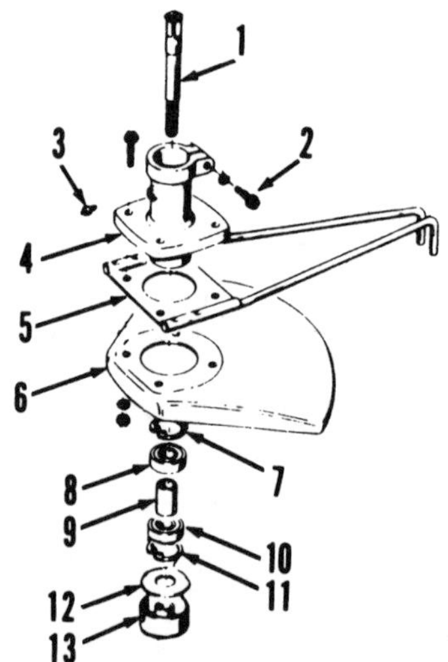

Fig. WE18—Exploded view of bearing head used on Models 1700, 1700A, 2600, 2610, GTI-18, GTI-18K, XR-50, XR-70, XR-75, XR-80, XR-80A, XR-85 and XT-85.

1. Drive shaft adapter
2. Clamp bolt
3. Locating screw
4. Housing
5. Bracket (if equipped)
6. Shield
7. Snap ring
8. Bearing
9. Spacer
10. Bearing
11. Snap ring
12. Washer
13. Drive disc

Straight Shaft Models

Periodic maintenance is not required for the drive shaft on models with a straight drive shaft housing. If removed apply lithium-based grease to shaft.

BEARING HEAD

Models 1400, 1400T, 1500, 1600, 1600T, 1740, GTI-15, GTI-15T, GTI-16, GTI-16 Super, GTI-17, GTI-17XP, HP-30, XR-20, XR-20T, XR-30, XR-50A, XT-20, XT-20T And XT-50

These models are equipped with a bearing head that is an integral part of the drive shaft housing tube (Fig. WE17). Regular maintenance is not required. Service parts are not available.

Models 1700, 1700A, 2600, 2610, GTI-18, GTI-18K, XR-50, XR-70, XR-75, XR-80, XR-80A, XR-85 And XT-85

These models are equipped with the bearing head shown in Fig. WE18. The bearing head is equipped with sealed bearings; regular maintenance is not required.

To disassemble bearing head, remove trimmer head or blade assembly. Remove clamp bolt (2) and locating screw (3). Separate bearing head assembly from drive shaft housing. Remove shield (6) and bracket (5), if so equipped. Remove cup washer (13) and washer (12). Carefully press drive shaft adapter (1) out of bearings. Remove snap rings (7 and 11). Press bearings (8 and 10) and spacer (9) out of housing.

Models 650, 657 And 670

Models 650, 657 and 670 are equipped with the bearing head shown in Fig. WE19. The bearing head is equipped with sealed bearings; regular maintenance is not required.

To disassemble bearing head, remove trimmer head or blade assembly. Remove clamp bolt (3) and locating screw (7). Separate gear head from drive shaft housing tube. Remove snap ring (11). Secure head assembly in a vise. Place a $1^3/_8$-in. wood dowel with a $^3/_4$-in. hole drilled through center over arbor (12), against the square coupling end. Tap wood dowel with a mallet to remove arbor and bearing assembly. Disassemble bearings, coupling and arbor assembly as required.

Illustrations courtesy Poulan/Weed Eater

To reassemble, place coupling (4) and washer (5) on arbor (12). Press one bearing onto arbor. Install assembly into housing. Install spacer (9) and press remaining bearing onto arbor and into housing. Install snap ring (11).

GEAR HEAD

All Models So Equipped

The gear head should be lubricated after every 10 hours of operation by injecting lithium-based grease through screw hole in side of gear head. Fill housing so it is approximately two-thirds full of grease.

The gear head on Models 1000, 1900, XR-105, XR-125, XT-100, XT-125 and XT-200 must be serviced as a unit assembly; individual components are not available.

Models XR-90, XR-95 and XR-100 are equipped with the gear head shown in Fig. WE20. To disassemble gear head, remove trimmer head or blade assembly. Remove clamp bolt and head locating screw and separate gear head from drive shaft housing tube. Remove cup washer (17) and spacer (14). Remove snap ring (2) and use a suitable puller to remove input shaft (5) and bearings as an assembly. Remove snap ring (1) and press bearings (3 and 4) from input shaft as required. Remove seal (16) and snap ring (15). Use a suitable puller to remove arbor (12) and bearing assembly. Press bearing (13) and gear (11) from shaft as required. If bearing (10) remains in housing (6), heat housing to 140° F (60° C) and tap housing on wood block to remove bearing.

ENGINE COVER

All Models So Equipped

Some models are equipped with the full engine cover shown in Fig. WE21. To remove engine cover, remove clamp bolt (8) and separate engine assembly from drive shaft housing. Remove the four 10-24 screws and separate housings (5) and (9) slightly. Disconnect ignition wire from module and separate fuel line so junction fitting stays with crankcase side of fuel line. Separate housings completely. Remove the three 8-24 screws from inner side of housing (5) and remove the air baffle. Remove the five 10-24 screws located under air baffle and separate housing (4) from housing (5). Remove fuel tank cap and remove fuel tank. Remove the four screws securing carburetor cover plate and remove carburetor cover. Disconnect spark plug, remove the four 10-24 screws at drive shaft housing side of cover (9), then remove cover.

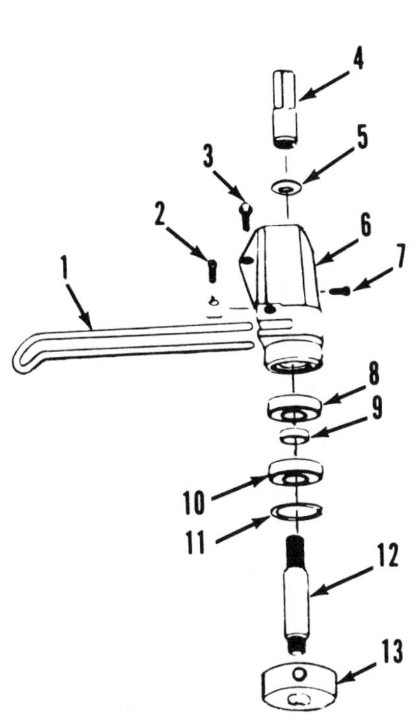

Fig. WE19—Exploded view of bearing head used on Models 650, 657 and 670.

1. Wire bracket
2. Screw
3. Bolt
4. Drive shaft adapter
5. Washer
6. Housing
7. Locating screw
8. Bearing
9. Spacer
10. Bearing
11. Snap ring
12. Arbor
13. Cup washer

Fig. WE20—Exploded view of gear head used on Models XR-90, XR-95 and XR-100.

1. Snap ring
2. Snap ring
3. Bearing
4. Bearing
5. Input shaft
6. Housing
7. Locating bolt
8. Clamp bolt
9. Check plug
10. Bearing
11. Gear
12. Arbor shaft
13. Bearing
14. Spacer
15. Snap ring
16. Seal
17. Cup washer

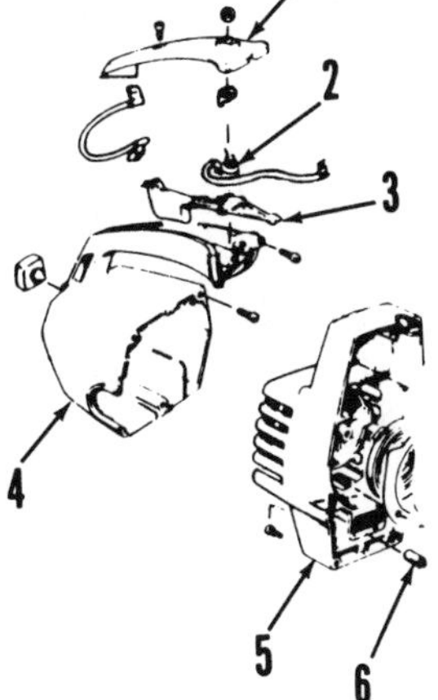

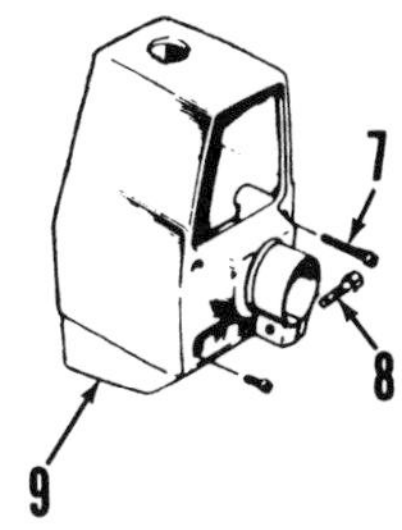

Fig. WE21—Exploded view of engine cover assembly used on some models.

1. Throttle housing cover
2. Ignition switch
3. Throttle trigger
4. Handle
5. Fan housing
6. Spacer
7. Screw
8. Clamp bolt
9. Cover

Illustrations courtesy Poulan/Weed Eater

WEED EATER

GASOLINE POWERED BLOWERS

Model	Engine Manufacturer	Engine Model	Displacement
920	Poulan	...	26.2 cc
925	Poulan	...	26.2 cc
940	Poulan	...	26.2 cc
960	Poulan	...	26.2 cc
1925	Poulan	...	26.2 cc
1960	Poulan	...	26.2 cc
GBI-20	Poulan	...	22 cc
GBI-22, GBI-22V	Poulan	...	22 cc
GBI-30V	Poulan	...	30 cc

ENGINE INFORMATION

The models in this section are equipped with a Poulan engine. Refer to appropriate engine service section for engine service information.

FUEL MIXTURE

Manufacturer recommends mixing regular gasoline with Poulan/Weed Eater two-stroke engine oil mixed as indicated on container. Gasohol or other alcohol-blended fuels are not approved by manufacturer.

FAN

To remove blower fan (11—Fig. WE40) on Models 920, 925, 940, 960, 1925 and 1960, remove tube clamp (9) from blower housing. Remove blower housing screws and separate blower housing halves (6 and 13). Remove fan mounting nut (12) and withdraw fan from drive shaft (4). When installing fan, tighten fan retaining nut to 19-20 N·m (14-15 ft.-lbs.).

To remove blower fan (7—Fig. WE41) on Models GBI-22, GBI-22V and GBI-30V, remove retaining screws from blower housing and separate blower housing halves (5 and 12). Remove fan retaining nut (11) and withdraw fan from end of crankshaft.

To remove blower fan (3—Fig. WE42) on Model GBI-20, remove screws from blower housing and separate outer blower housing (4) and recoil starter assembly from inner blower housing (2). Remove screws mounting fan (3) to flywheel (1) and remove fan.

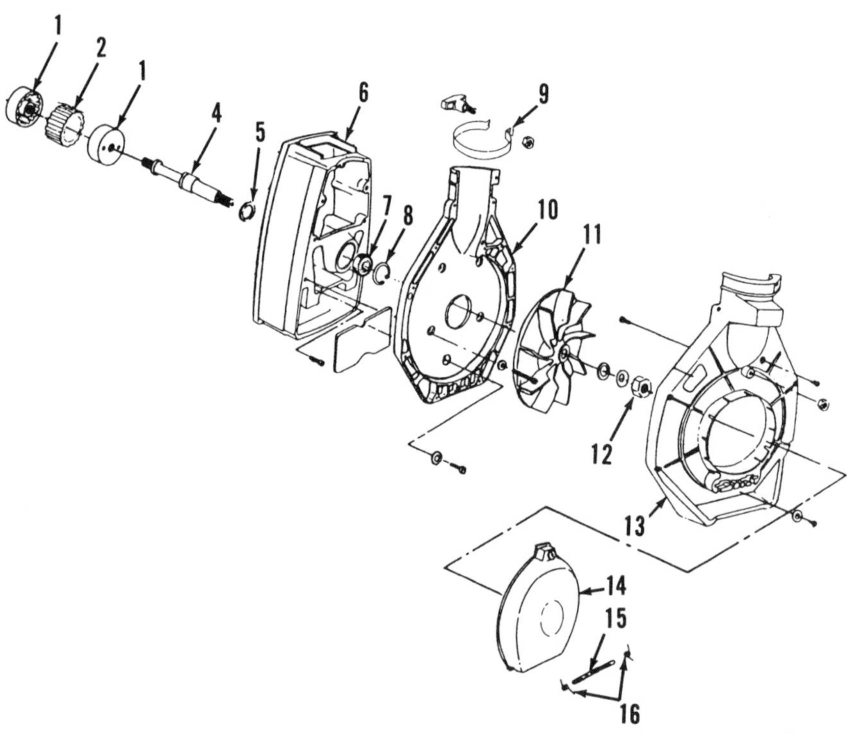

Fig. WE40—Exploded view of fan shroud assembly used on Models 920, 925, 940, 960, 1925 and 1960.

1. Shaft coupling
2. Coupling hub
4. Fan shaft
5. Washer
6. Shroud
7. Bearing
8. Snap ring
9. Clamp
10. Blower housing
11. Fan
12. Nut
13. Blower housing
14. Inlet door
15. Pivot pin
16. Springs

SHROUD BEARING

The fan shaft (4—Fig. WE40) on Models 920, 925, 940, 960, 1925 and 1960 is supported by a bearing (7) in the fan shroud (6). To remove bearing and drive shaft, first remove blower housing (10 and 13) and fan (11). Unbolt and remove fan shroud from engine. Detach snap ring (8), then heat shroud to 300° F (149° C) and remove bearing and shaft.

The fan end of crankshaft on Models GBI-22, GBI-22V and GBI-30V is supported by bearing (3—Fig. WE41) in starter housing (1). To remove bearing, first separate blower housing (5 and 12), fan (7) and starter housing (1) from engine. Press bearing out of starter housing.

Illustrations courtesy Poulan/Weed Eater

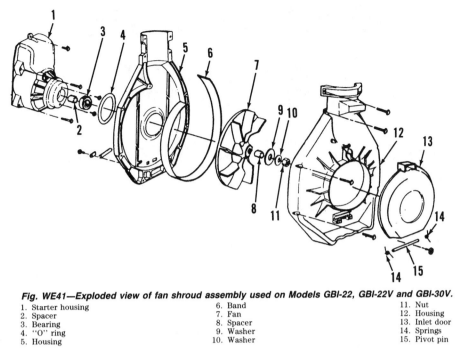

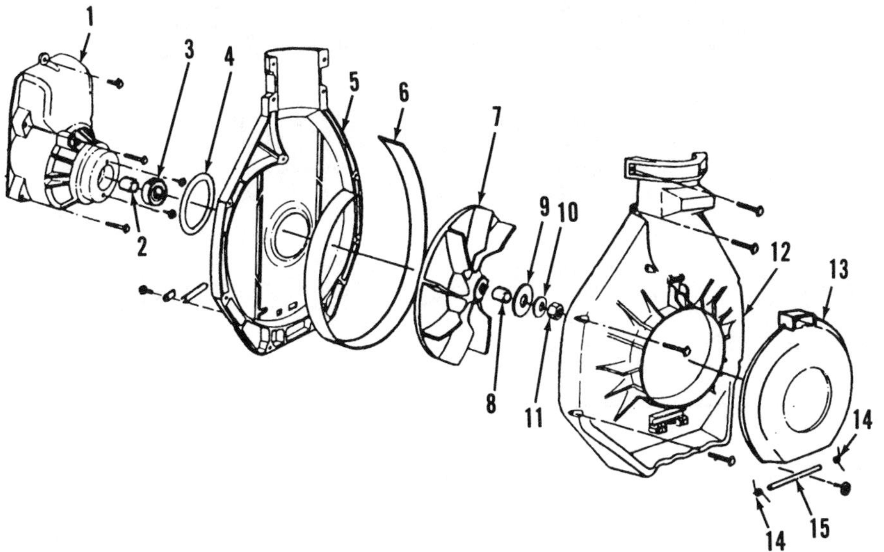

Fig. WE41—Exploded view of fan shroud assembly used on Models GBI-22, GBI-22V and GBI-30V.

1. Starter housing
2. Spacer
3. Bearing
4. "O" ring
5. Housing
6. Band
7. Fan
8. Spacer
9. Washer
10. Washer
11. Nut
12. Housing
13. Inlet door
14. Springs
15. Pivot pin

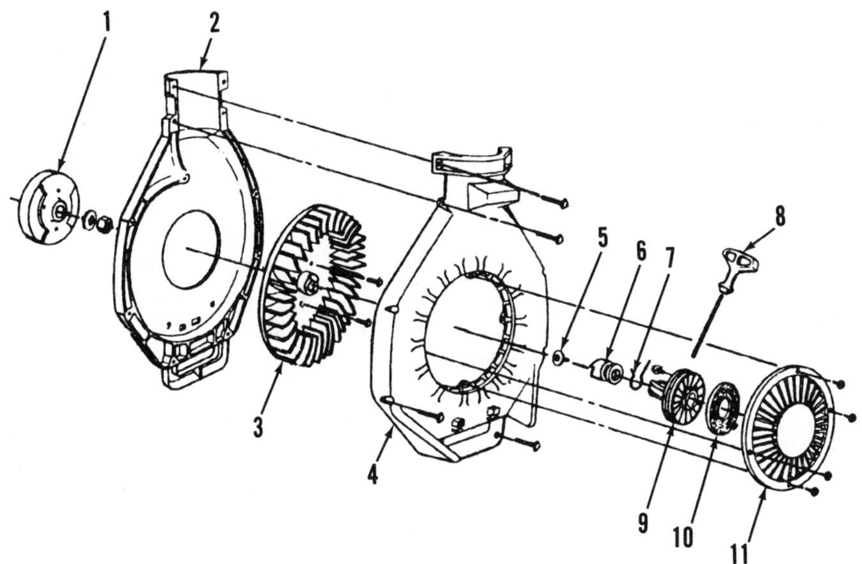

Fig. WE42—Exploded view of fan shroud assembly used on Model GBI-20.

1. Flywheel
2. Blower housing
3. Fan
4. Blower housing
5. Screw
6. Starter pinion
7. Spring
8. Rope handle
9. Starter pulley
10. Recoil spring
11. Pulley housing

Illustrations courtesy Poulan/Weed Eater

WESTERN AUTO

GASOLINE POWERED STRING TRIMMERS

Model	Engine Manufacturer	Engine Model	Displacement
95-2027-1	Kioritz	G2	16.0 cc
95-2028-9	Kioritz	H-1A	21.2 cc

ENGINE INFORMATION

All Models

All models are equipped with Kioritz two-stroke air-cooled engines. Identify engine model by trimmer model or engine displacement. Refer to KIORITZ ENGINE SERVICE section of this manual.

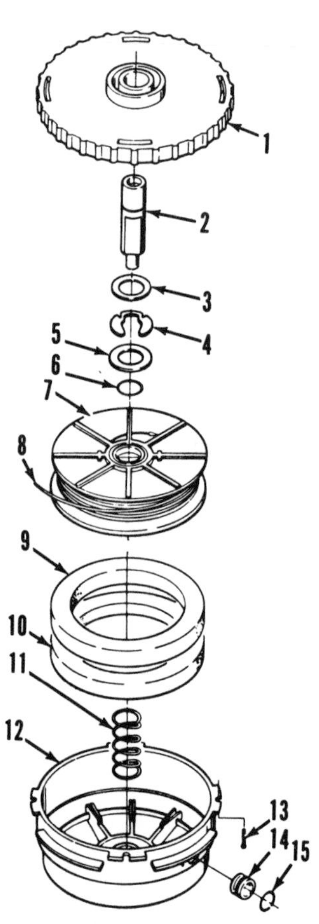

Fig. WA10—Exploded view of single strand semi-automatic trimmer head for Model 95-2027-1.

1. Cover
2. Drive shaft adapter
3. Washer
4. Retainer ring
5. Washer
6. Retainer ring
7. Spool
8. Line
9. Foam pad
10. Foam pad
11. Spring
12. Housing
13. Cotter pin
14. Line guide
15. Retainer

FUEL MIXTURE

All Models

Manufacturer recommends mixing regular grade gasoline (unleaded is an acceptable substitute) with a good quality two-stroke air-cooled engine oil at a 25:1 ratio. Do not use fuel containing alcohol.

STRING TRIMMER

Model 95-2027-1

Model 95-2027-1 is equipped with a single strand semi-automatic trimmer head shown in Fig. WA10. Line may be manually advanced with engine stopped by pushing in on housing (12) while pulling on line. Procedure may have to be repeated until desired line length is obtained. To advance line with engine running, operate trimmer engine at full rpm and tap housing (12) on the ground. Each time housing is tapped on the ground, a measured amount of trimmer line is advanced.

To renew trimmer line, remove cotter pin (13). Twist housing (12) counterclockwise and remove housing. Remove foam pads (9 and 10) and any remaining line from spool (7). Clean spool and inner area of housing. Cut off approximately 25 feet (7.6 m) of 0.080 inch (2 mm) monofilament line and tape one end of line to spool (Fig. WA11). Wind line on spool in direction indicated by arrow on spool (Fig. WA12). Install foam pads (9 and 10) so line is protruding from center of foam pads (Fig. WA12). Insert end of line through line guide and install spool, housing and spring. Push in on housing and twist housing to lock in position and install cotter pin (13—Fig. WA10).

Model 95-2028-9

Model 95-2028-9 is equipped with a single strand semi-automatic trimmer head shown in Fig. WA13. Line may be manually advanced with engine stopped by pushing in on housing (9) while pulling on line. Procedure may have to be repeated to obtain desired line length. To advance line with engine running, operate engine at full rpm and tap housing (9) on the ground. Each time housing is tapped on the ground, a measured amount of trimmer line will be advanced.

To renew trimmer line, remove cotter pin (10) and twist housing (9) counterclockwise to remove housing. Remove foam pad (6) and any remaining line on spool (3). Clean spool and inside of housing. Cut off approximately 25 feet (7.6 m) of 0.080 inch (2 mm) monofilament line and tape one end of line to spool (Fig. WA11). Wind line on spool in direction indicated by arrow on spool

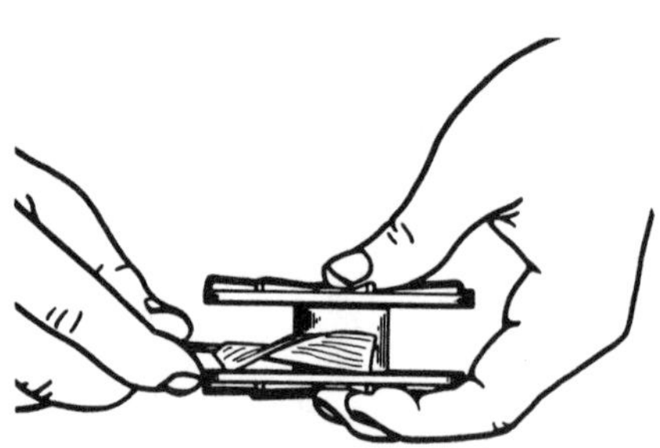

Fig. WA11—Tape new trimmer line end to center of spool as shown.

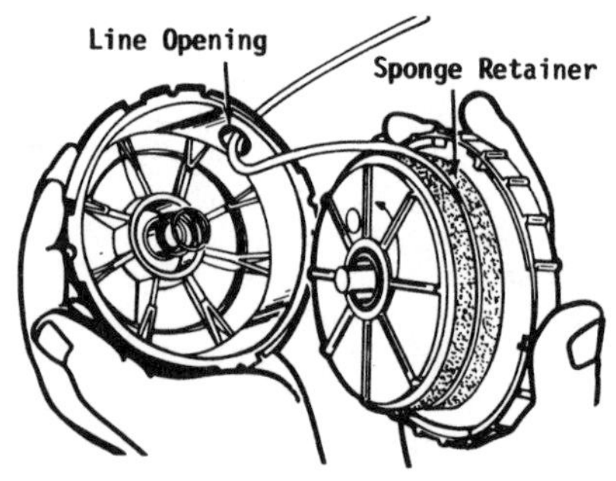

Fig. WA12—Install foam pads with line protruding from center of pads as shown. Wind line in direction indicated by arrow on spool.

Fig. WA14). Install foam pad with line end protruding from between foam pad and spool as shown in Fig. WA14. Insert line end through line guide and install housing and spring assembly on spool. Push in on housing and twist housing to lock into position. Install cotter pin through hole in housing and cover.

BLADE

Model 95-2028-9

Model 95-2028-9 may be equipped with a 60 tooth saw blade or an eight tooth weed and grass blade. To install blade with trimmer head removed, rotate cup washer (13–Fig. WA16) until hole in cup washer aligns with hole in gear head housing. Install a round tool into hole to prevent drive shaft turning. Install blade and lower adapter plate. Install and tighten nut. Install a new split pin in arbor to prevent nut loosening.

DRIVE SHAFT

All Models

All models are equipped with a flexible drive shaft enclosed in the drive shaft housing tube. Drive shaft has squared ends which engage adapters at each end. Drive shaft should be removed for maintenance at 50 hour intervals of use. Remove screw (4—Fig. WA15 or Fig. WA16) and bolt (3) at bearing head housing, then separate bearing head from drive shaft housing. Pull flexible drive shaft from housing. Lubricate drive shaft with lithium base grease and reinstall in drive shaft housing with end which was previously at clutch end at bearing head end. Reversing drive shaft ends extends drive shaft life. Make certain ends of drive shaft engage upper and lower square drive adapters when installing.

BEARING HEAD

Model 95-2027-1

Model 95-2027-1 is equipped with the bearing head shown in Fig. WA15. Bearing head is equipped with sealed bearings (7 and 9) and requires no regular maintenance. To disassemble bearing head, remove bolt (3) and screw (4) and separate bearing head from drive shaft housing tube. Remove trimmer head or blade assembly. Remove cup washer (13) and snap ring (10). Use a suitable puller to remove arbor shaft (11) and bearing assembly. Remove nut (6) and press bearings from arbor shaft as required.

Model 95-2028-9

Model 95-2028-9 is equipped with the bearing head shown in Fig. WA16. Bearing head is equipped with sealed bearings (7 and 9) and requires no regular maintenance. To disassemble bearing head, remove bolt (3) and screw (4) and separate bearing head from drive shaft housing tube. Remove trimmer head or blade assembly. Remove cup washer (13) and snap ring (10). Use suitable puller to remove arbor shaft (11) and bearing assembly. Remove nut (6) and press bearings from arbor shaft as required.

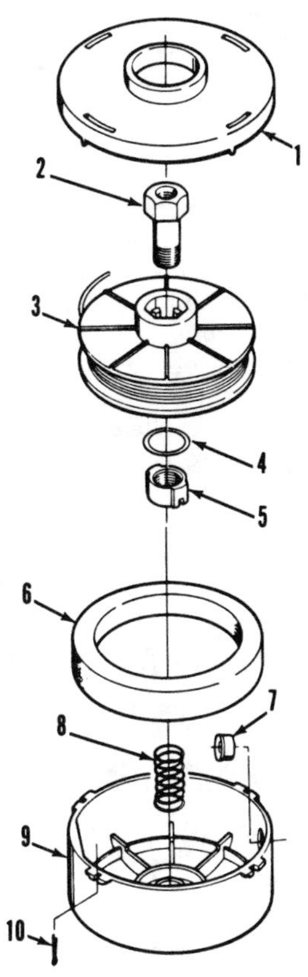

Fig. WA13—Exploded view of single strand semi-automatic trimmer head for Model 95-2028-9.

1. Cover
2. Drive shaft adapter
3. Spool
4. "O" ring
5. Drive adapter nut
6. Foam pad
7. Line guide
8. Spring
9. Housing
10. Cotter pin

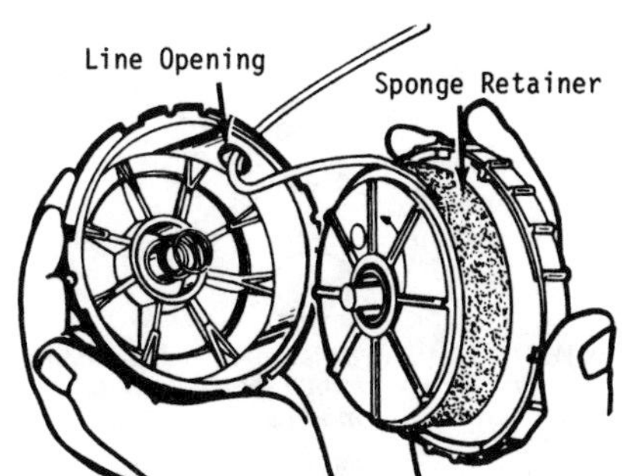

Fig. WA14—Install foam pad with line protruding from between pad and spool as shown. Wind line in direction indicated by arrow on spool.

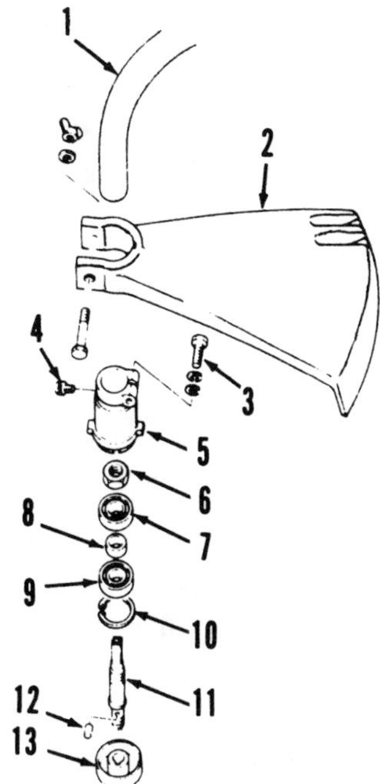

Fig. WA15—Exploded view of bearing head assembly used on Model 95-2027-1.

1. Drive shaft housing tube
2. Shield
3. Bolt
4. Screw
5. Housing
6. Nut
7. Bearing
8. Spacer
9. Bearing
10. Snap ring
11. Arbor (output) shaft
12. Pin
13. Cup washer

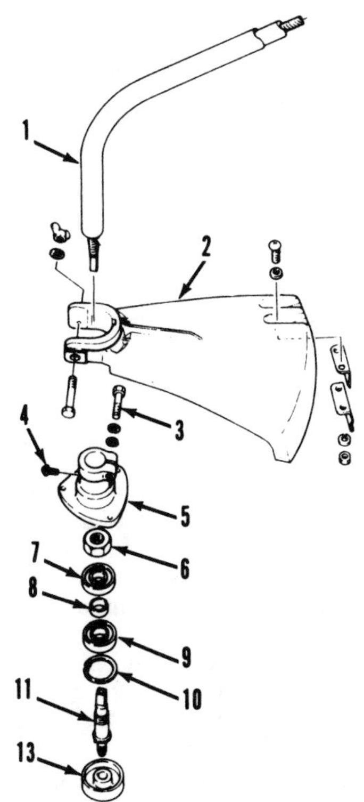

Fig. WA16—Exploded view of gear head assembly used on Model 95-2028-9. Refer to Fig. WA15 for legend.

WINDMILL BY VANDERMOLEN CORP.

GASOLINE POWERED TRIMMERS

Models	Engine Make	Engine Model	Displacement
L1840E/F/G	Kawasaki	TD18	18.4 cc (1.12 cu. in.)
L1845G	Kawasaki	TD18	18.4 cc (1.12 cu. in.)
L2035G	Kawasaki	....	20.3 cc (1.24 cu. in.)
L2815G	Kawasaki	....	28.1 cc (1.71 cu. in.)
L3335G/G1	Kawasaki	TD33	33.3 cc (2.03 cu. in.)
X3335E	Kawasaki	TD33	33.3 cc (2.03 cu. in.)

ENGINE INFORMATION

Engines manufactured by Kawasaki are used. Identify the engine by displacement and refer to the KAWASAKI Engine Service section of this manual.

FUEL MIXTURE

The manufacturer recommends mixing a good quality engine oil designed for use with air cooled two-stroke engines with regular or unleaded gasoline at a ratio of 25:1. Oil and gasoline should be mixed in a separate container before filling the equipment fuel tank.

STRING TRIMMER

Semi-Automatic Single Strand Trimmer Head

Refer to Fig. WM10 for the single line, semi-automatic string trimmer head typical of the type used on some models. To manually advance the trimmer line with the engine stopped, push the button (8) at the bottom of the spool and pull the line out to desired length. To extend the line with the engine running, operate the trimmer at maximum speed and tap the spool button on the ground. Line should extend a small amount automatically. If the line does not extend with the engine running, stop the engine and extend the line manually. If line is broken inside the housing, it will be necessary to disassemble the unit and feed the line through the eyelet (3) in the drum.

To disassemble, press the tab marked "PUSH," then twist the cover (9) to remove cover, button (8) and spool (6). Be careful not to lose the spring (5). Clean and inspect all parts for damage. A new eyelet (3) can be installed if worn.

If new line is installed, it should be 0.080 inch (2.0 mm) diameter and 15 feet (4.5 m) long. Insert end of line through the eye of the spool as shown in Fig. WM11 so approximately 1 inch (25 mm) extends past the eye. Wrap line on spool in same direction as arrow on spool. Wind the line tightly and evenly from side to side, taking care not to twist the line. Install spool while directing line end through the eyelet (3—Fig. WM10) in the housing. Make certain the words "THIS SIDE UP" on spool face up. Install the button and cover. The cover should snap into place when the locking tabs on cover and housing engage. Trim the line so approximately 6 inches (15 cm) extends from drum.

If the trimmer head retaining nut (4—Fig. WM10) must be removed, lock the shaft to prevent it from rotating by inserting a pin through the hole in the bearing head. The nut has left-hand thread.

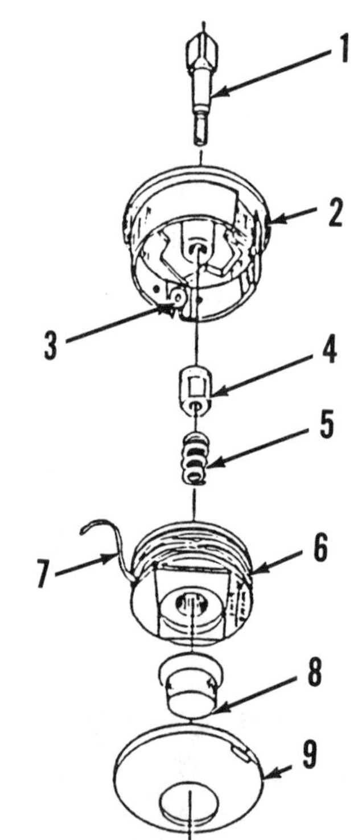

Fig. WM10—Exploded view of the semi-automatic single line string trimmer head used on some models.

1. Adapter
2. Housing
3. Eyelet (line guide)
4. Nut
5. Spring
6. Spool
7. Line
8. Button
9. Cover

Semi-Automatic Dual Strand Trimmer

Refer to Fig. WM12 for the dual line, semi-automatic string trimmer head typical of the type used on some models. To manually advance the trimmer lines with the engine stopped, push the button at the bottom of the spool (7) and pull both of the lines. To extend the lines with the engine running, operate the trimmer at maximum speed and tap the button on the ground. Both lines should extend a small amount

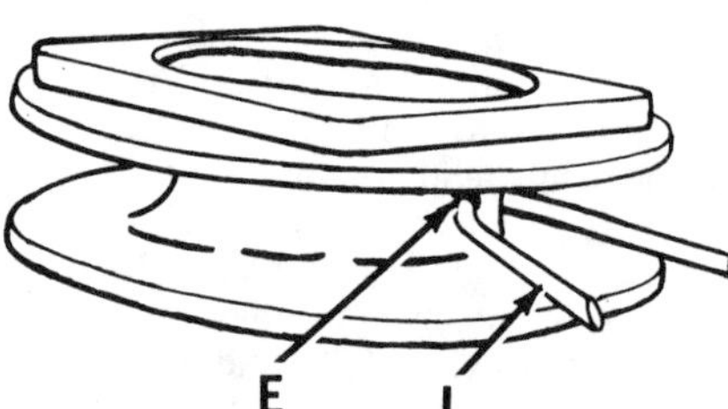

Fig. WM11—Insert the end of line (L) through the eye (E) of the spool as shown so approximately 1 inch (25 mm) extends past the eye.

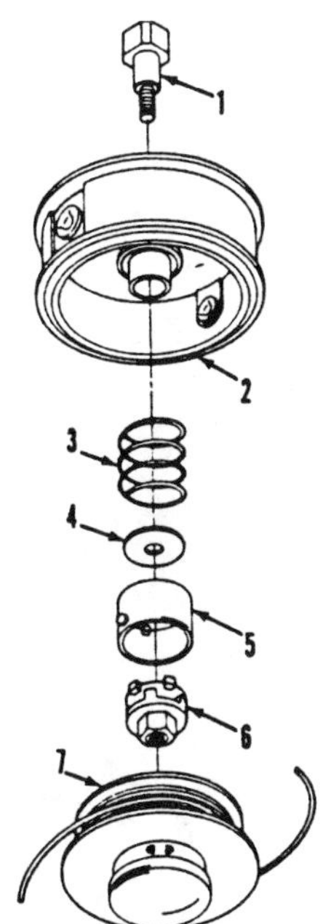

Fig. WM12—Exploded view of the semi-automatic dual line string trimmer head used on some models.

1. Adapter
2. Housing
3. Spring
4. Washer
5. Outer cam
6. Inner cam
7. Spool

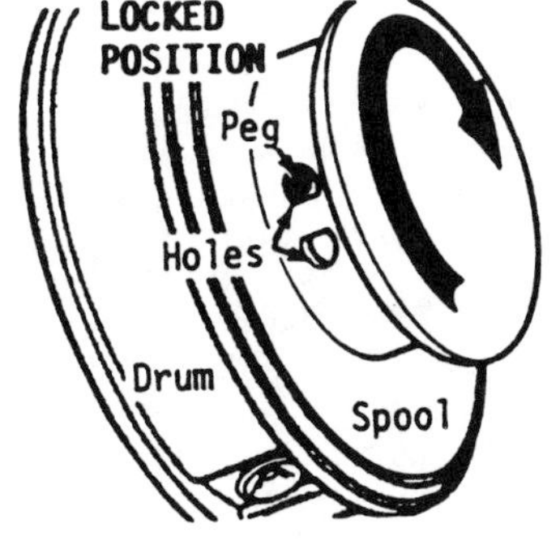

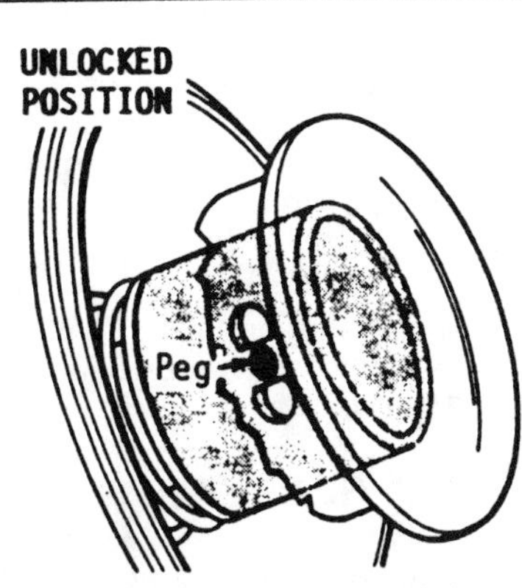

Fig. WM13—To remove the spool from the trimmer head shown in Fig. WM12, hold the drum firmly and turn the spool in the direction shown to take up slack, then twist with a sudden snap until the plastic peg is between the holes as shown in the lower view.

automatically. If the line does not extend with the engine running, stop the engine and extend the lines manually. If a line is broken inside the housing, it will be necessary to disassemble the unit and feed the line through the eyelet.

To remove and disassemble the string trimmer head, proceed as follows. Hold the drum firmly and turn spool in the direction shown in Fig. WM13 to remove slack. Twist with a hard snap until the plastic peg is between holes, then separate the spool from the drum.

Clean and inspect all parts for damage. New line should be the same diameter as originally installed by the manufacturer. Standard height spool will hold approximately 20 ft. (6 m) of 0.080 in. (2 mm) diameter line; 18 ft. of 0.095 in. (2.4 mm) diameter line; 15 ft. of 0.105 in. (2.7 mm) diameter line or 10 ft. of 0.130 in. (3.3 mm) diameter line. Do not overfill the spool.

Insert the line through the eye of the spool as shown in Fig. WM14 and pull the line through until it is the same length on both sides. Wrap both ends of the line on spool at the same time in clockwise direction as viewed from the top of spool. Wind the line tightly and evenly from side to side, but do not twist the lines.

Insert ends of line through line guide openings, being careful not to let the line slip out of the spool. Align the pegs on drum with slots in the spool and push the spool into drum. Hold the drum firmly, then twist spool in the direction shown in Fig. WM15 so peg enters the hole with a click and locks the spool in position. Trim the line ends to the recommended cutting length: 4 in. (101 mm) for 15-19 cc engine, 5 in. (127 mm) for 20-24 cc engine, 6 in. (152 mm) for 26-33 cc engine.

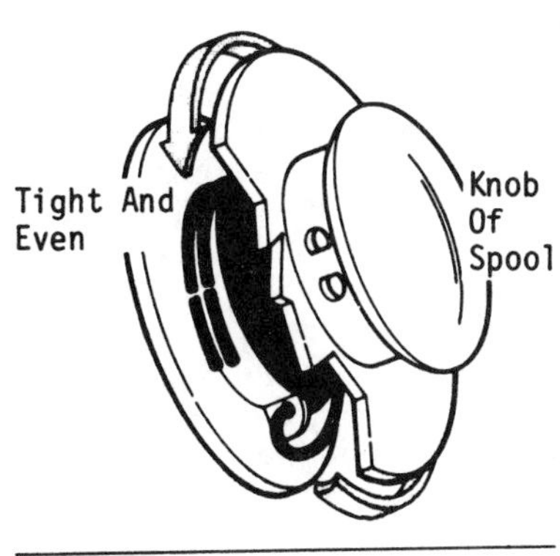

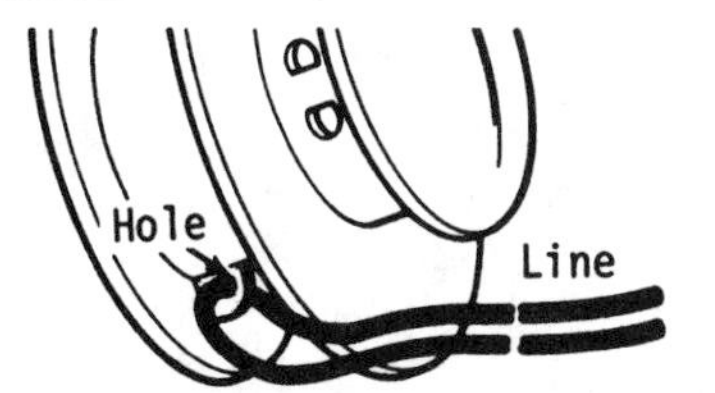

Fig. WM14—The end of the line must be inserted through the hole on spool as shown in the lower view. Wrap line tightly and evenly in the direction indicated by the arrow.

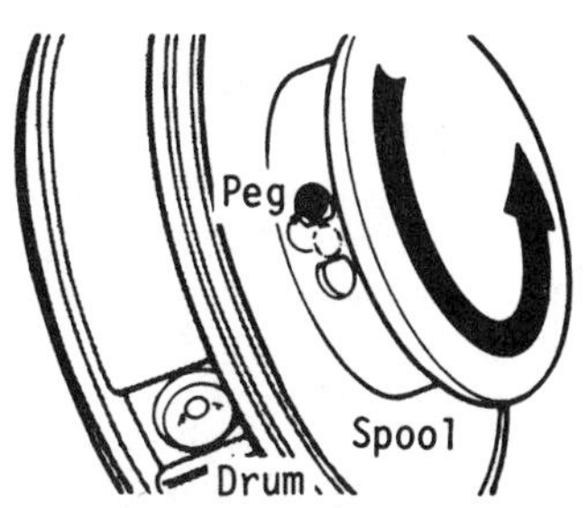

Fig. WM15—Hold the drum firmly and twist to lock the spool in position.

Manual Advance Trimmer

Refer to Fig. WM16 for an exploded view of the dual line trimmer head used on some models. To advance the trimmer line, shut off the engine and wait until all head rotation has stopped. Grasp lower ring of spool (6) and pull down to compress spring, then turn counterclockwise so spool grommets (5) engage next notch in housing (2). Pull each line (4) outward through eyelet (3). Repeat if necessary until line length is approximately 4 in. (101 mm) from the drum for models with 18.4 cc engines; 5 in. (127 mm) for models with 20.3 cc engines or 6 in. (152 mm) for models with 28.1-33 cc engines.

NOTE: If spring tension makes it difficult to disengage spool locating grommets from housing notches,

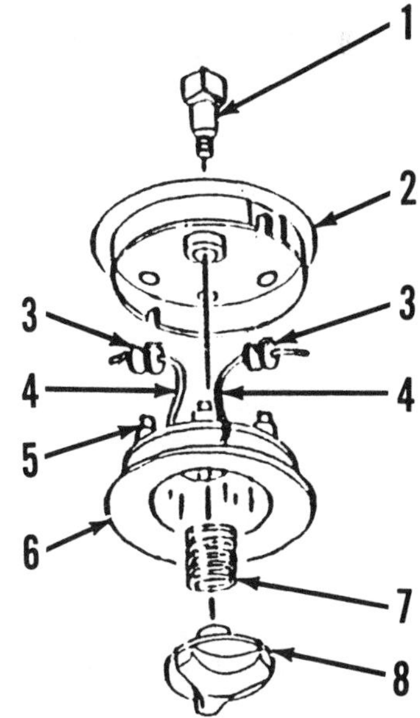

Fig. WM16— Exploded view of the dual strand manual advance trimmer head used on some models.

1. Nut
2. Housing
3. Eyelet
4. Trimmer line
5. Grommet
6. Spool
7. Spring
8. Nut

loosen knob (8) to relieve spring tension. The knob (8) and bolt (1) may have either left- or right-hand threads.

Make certain the locating grommets (5) engage the notches in the body (2). Tighten knob (8) securely.

To install new line, remove knob (8) and spring (7). Withdraw trimmer head. Separate spool (6) from the housing (2). Clean and inspect all parts for damage.

New line should be the same diameter as originally installed by the manufacturer. Standard height spool will hold approximately 20 ft. (6 m) of 0.080 in. (2 mm) diameter line; 18 ft. of 0.095 in. (2.4 mm) diameter line; 15 ft. of 0.105 in. (2.7 mm) diameter line or 10 ft. of 0.130 in. (3.3 mm) diameter line. "Low Profile" heads used on some models will hold about 25 percent less line. Do not overfill the spool.

Insert the new line through the hole of the spool and pull the line through until it is the same length on both sides. Wrap both ends of the line on spool at the same time in the direction indicated by an arrow marked on the edge of the spool. Wind the line tightly and evenly from side to side and do not twist the lines. Direct the ends of both lines through the eyelets (3) in the housing while inserting the spool(6) in the housing (2). Install spring (2) and tighten knob (1). Trim line ends to recommended cutting length: 4 in. (101 mm) for 15-19 cc engine, 5 in. (127 mm) for 20-24 cc engine, 6 in. (152 mm) for 26-33 cc engine.

BLADE

A variety of hard cutting blades including a "Combo Cutter" (Fig. WM17)

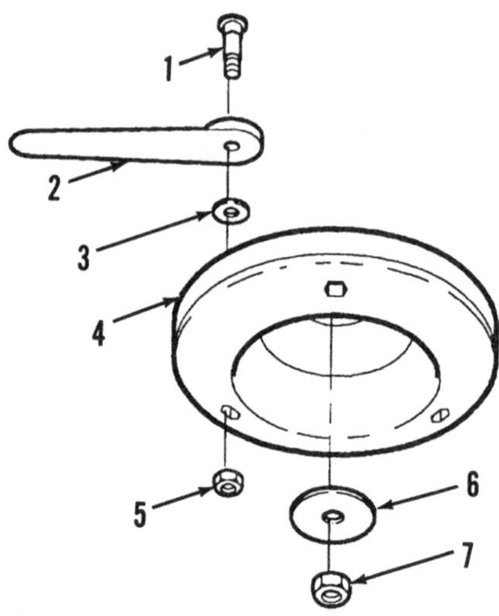

Fig. WM17—Combo Cutter trimmer head is available for installation on 3335G models.

1. Pivot bolt
2. Cutter blade
3. Washer
4. Hub
5. Nut
6. Washer
7. Nut

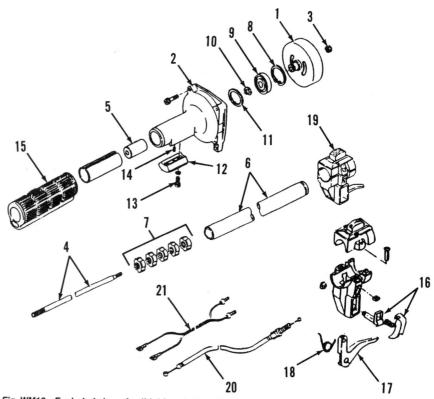

Fig. WM18—Exploded view of solid drive shaft and housing typical of some models including L3335G.

1. Clutch drum
2. Clutch housing
3. Nut
4. Drive shaft
5. Insert
6. Drive shaft housing
7. Bushings
8. Snap ring
9. Bearing
10. Snap ring
11. Thrust washer
12. AV mount
13. Screw
14. Spring pin (3x8 mm)
15. Grip
16. Throttle interlock
17. Throttle lever
18. Spring
19. Stop switch & throttle assy.
20. Throttle cable
21. Stop wires

that has three cutting blades are available and may be installed on some models. Hard blades can be dangerous and should be selected and used with great care. Blades of different diameters should be matched to the specific model of the powerhead. A blade too small or too large will reduce the effectiveness of operation and may increase the chance for damage or injury. Check with the manufacturer to determine approved application. Sharpen each tooth following the original sharpening angle and tooth set. Sharpen all teeth evenly to maintain balance.

To remove or install blade, insert a tool into hole in upper adapter and gear head to prevent the drive shaft from turning. Remove bolt, lower adapter and blade.

DRIVE SHAFT

These models are equipped with a straight, solid drive shaft (4—Fig. WM18 or Fig. WM19) that rides in bushings (7) within the drive shaft housing. Periodic drive shaft maintenance is not required, but if removed, the drive shaft should be cleaned, inspected and lubricated with multipurpose grease before installing.

To remove the drive shaft, first remove the gear head from the lower end of the drive shaft housing as follows. Remove gear head locating screw (4—Fig. 20) and shield (11). Pull the gear head from the end of the drive shaft housing, then pull the drive shaft from the housing.

Bushings (7—Fig. WM18 or Fig. WM19) are available separately and should be installed in their original locations. The drive shaft housing should be separated from the engine assembly as follows before removing the bushings. Detach the engine stop switch wire and the throttle cable. Remove the two retaining screws and pull the handle and drive shaft housing from the engine assembly.

When assembling, tighten the gear head locating screw and the clamp screw securely.

GEAR HEAD

The gear head should be lubricated after each 30 hours of operation. Remove trimmer or blade, then use a hand operated grease gun to inject multipurpose grease into fitting (F—Fig. WM20). Refer to (Fig. WM21). Old

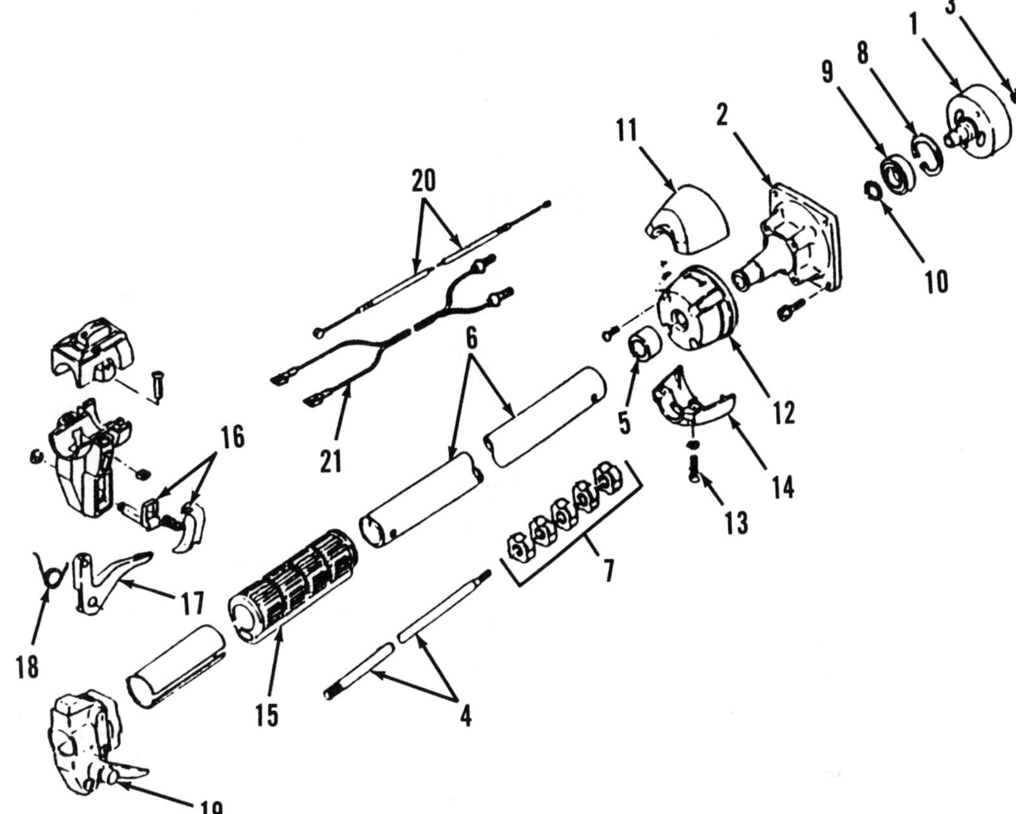

Fig. WM19—Exploded view of solid drive shaft and housing typical of some models including L2035G and L2815G.

1. Clutch drum
2. Clutch housing
3. Nut
4. Drive shaft
5. Bushing
6. Drive shaft housing
7. Bushings
8. Snap ring
9. Bearing
10. Snap ring
11. Clamp
12. Rubber mount
13. Socket screw
14. Clamp
15. Grip
16. Throttle interlock
17. Throttle lever
18. Spring
19. Stop switch & throttle assy.
20. Throttle cable
21. Stop wires

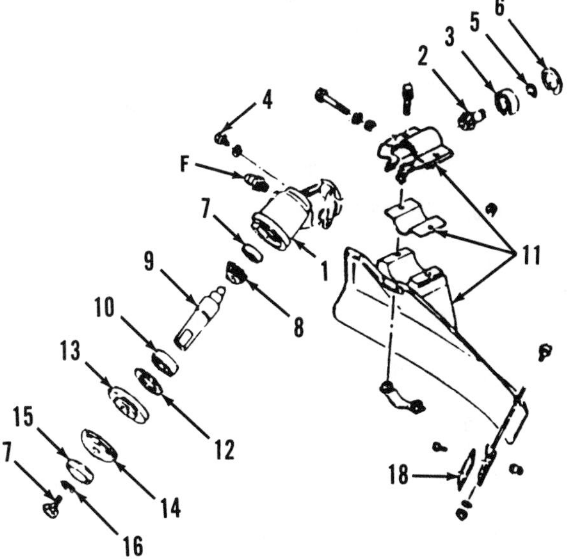

Fig. WM20—Exploded view typical of the gear head used on all models.

1. Housing
2. Pinion gear
3. Bearing
4. Screw
5. Snap ring
6. Snap ring
7. Bearing
8. Gear
9. Shaft
10. Sealed bearing
11. Shield
12. Snap ring
13. Upper clamp washer
14. Washer
15. Cup washer
16. Lockwasher
17. Screw
18. Cutter

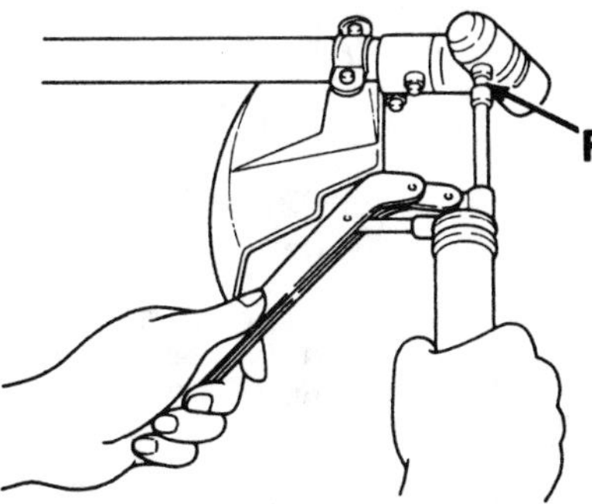

Fig. WM21—The gear housing should be 2/3 filled with lithium based multipurpose grease. Refer to text.

grease should be expelled from around the shaft (9—Fig. WM20) and damage could result if the trimmer head or blade is not removed before filling.

To disassemble the gear head, use a suitable tool to hold the shaft, then remove the trimmer or blade. Remove the locating and clamp screws, then pull the gear head from the end of the drive shaft housing. Remove snap ring (6), then use a suitable puller to pull the pinion (2) and bearing (3) from the housing. It may be necessary to heat the housing and spread the clamping gap to facilitate removal.

CAUTION: Excessive force while spreading the clamp or excessive heat can damage the housing. Use caution when using either method.

Remove snap ring (5) and press bearings from pinion if renewal is required. Remove snap ring (12), then withdraw shaft (9), gear (8) and bearings (7 and 10). If stuck in housing, bearing (7) can usually be dislodged by heating the housing and bumping the housing against a wood block.

Inspect and clean components. Reassemble by reversing disassembly procedure. Tighten the locating and clamp screws securely.

STARTER

Refer to the appropriate ENGINE SERVICE section for service to the starter assembly.

CLUTCH

Refer to the appropriate ENGINE SERVICE section for clutch removal and service procedures.

YARD PRO

GASOLINE POWERED STRING TRIMMERS

Model	Engine Manufacturer	Engine Model	Displacement
110	Poulan	...	26.2 cc
116	Poulan	...	28 cc
120, 120A	Poulan	...	26.2 cc
130, 130A	Poulan	...	28 cc
140	Poulan	...	26.2 cc
145	Poulan	...	28 cc
150	Poulan	...	28 cc
160	Poulan	...	28 cc

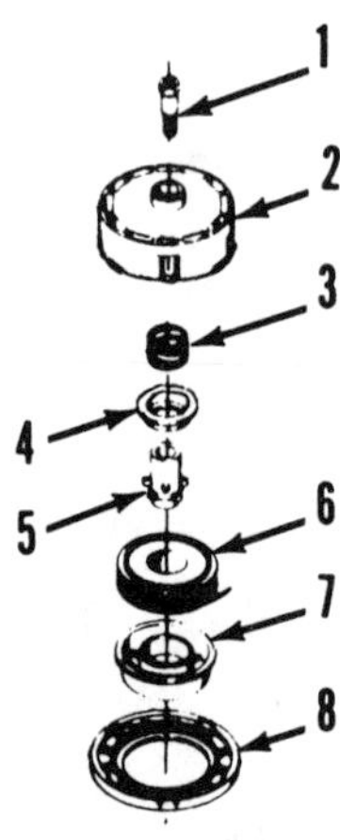

Fig. YP10—Exploded view of early style single strand, semi-automatic trimmer head used on early Models 110, 120, 130 and 140.

1. Drive shaft adapter
2. Housing
3. Spring
4. Spring adapter
5. Drive cam
6. Spool
7. Button
8. Cover

Fig. YP11—Exploded view of later style single strand, semi-automatic trimmer head used on Models 110, 120, 130 and 140.

1. Line guide
2. Housing
3. Spring
4. Spring adapter
5. Drive cam
6. Spool
7. Button
8. Cover

ENGINE INFORMATION

The models in this section are equipped with a Poulan engine. Refer to appropriate engine service section for engine service information.

FUEL MIXTURE

Manufacturer recommends mixing regular gasoline with Poulan/Weed Eater two-stroke engine oil mixed as indicated on container. Gasohol or other alcohol blended fuels are not approved by manufacturer.

STRING TRIMMER

Models 110, 120, 130 And 140

Models 110, 120, 130 and 140 are equipped with the single strand, semi-automatic trimmer head shown in Figs. YP10 or YP11. Early type trimmer head (Fig. YP10) is identified by the adapter (1) that drives the trimmer head. Service procedure for both heads is similar.

To extend line with trimmer engine stopped, push in on button (7) while pulling on line end. Repeat procedure as needed to obtain desired line length. To extend line with trimmer engine running and head rotating, tap button (7) on ground. Each time button is tapped on ground, a measured amount of line is advanced.

To install new line, remove cover (8), button (7) and spool (6). Clean all parts thoroughly and remove any remaining old line from spool. Wind approximately 30 feet (9 m) of 0.080-in. (2 mm) diameter monofilament line on spool in direction indicated by arrow on spool. Insert line end through line guide opening in housing (2) and install spool, button and cover.

Models 150 And 160

Models 150 And 160 are equipped with the dual strand, manual trimmer head shown in Fig. YP12. To extend line, stop trimmer engine and push in on plate (8) while pulling each line out of housing (2).

To install new trimmer line, remove screw (9), plate (8), spring (6) and spool (7). Remove any remaining line from each side of spool. Clean spool, housing and plate. Insert ends of two new 0.095-in. (2.4 mm) diameter lines in holes located within spool and wind lines in direction indicated by arrow on spool. Total amount of installed line should not exceed spool diameter. Make certain line

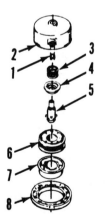

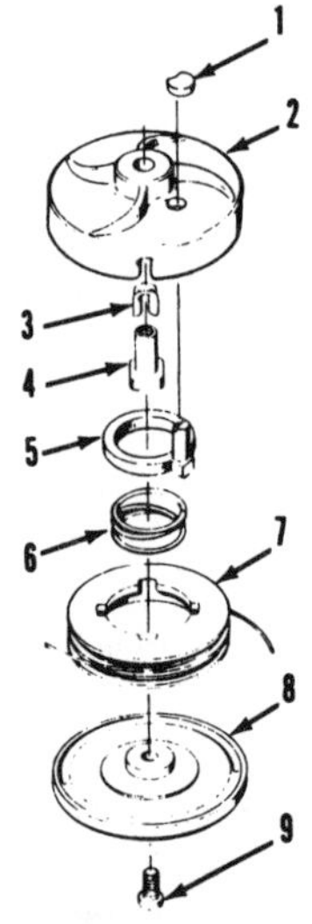

Fig. YP12—Exploded view of dual strand, manual trimmer head used on Models 150 and 160.

1. Lock ring cap
2. Housing
3. Line guide
4. Drive shaft adapter
5. Lock ring
6. Spring
7. Spool
8. Cover
9. Screw

savers (3) are in position and install spool in housing with the "THIS SIDE IN" instructions on spool toward inside of trimmer head. Install spring (6), cover (8) and screw (9).

Model 116

Model 116 is equipped with the single strand, semi-automatic trimmer head shown in Fig. YP13.

To extend line with trimmer engine stopped, push in on button (6) while pulling on line end. Repeat procedure as needed to obtain desired line length. To extend line with trimmer engine running and head rotating, tap button (6) on ground. Each time button is tapped on ground, a measured amount of line is advanced.

To install new line, remove cover (7), button (6) and spool (5). Clean all parts thoroughly and remove any remaining old line from spool. Wind 0.080-in. (2 mm) diameter monofilament line on spool in direction indicated by arrow on spool. Insert line end through line guide opening in housing (1) and install spool, button and cover.

Models 120A, 130A And 145

Models 120A, 130A and 145 are equipped with the single strand, semi-automatic trimmer head shown in Fig. YP14.

To extend line with trimmer engine stopped, push in on button while pulling on line end. Repeat procedure as needed to obtain desired line length. To extend line with trimmer engine running and head rotating, tap button on ground. Each time button is tapped on ground, a measured amount of line is advanced.

To install new line, detach cover (3) from housing (1). Remove old line and clean parts. Recommended line diameter is 0.080 inch (2 mm). Wind line around spool in direction indicated by arrow on spool.

BLADE

Some models may be equipped with a blade. When installing blade, be sure all adapter plates are centered and seated squarely against blade. Blade mounting nut has left-hand threads.

DRIVE SHAFT

Curved Shaft Models

Models with a curved drive shaft housing (2—Fig. YP15) are equipped with a flexible drive shaft (1). The drive shaft should be removed, cleaned and lubricated after every 20 hours of operation. Detach head assembly from drive shaft housing and remove shaft. Apply lithium-based grease to shaft.

Straight Shaft Models

Periodic maintenance is not required for the drive shaft on models with a straight drive shaft housing. If removed, apply lithium-based grease to shaft.

BEARING HEAD

Models 110, 116, 120 And 120A

Models 110, 116, 120 and 120A are equipped with a bearing head that is an integral part of the drive shaft housing tube (Fig. YP15). Regular maintenance is not required. Service parts are not available.

Models 130 And 130A

Models 130 and 130A are equipped with the bearing head shown in Fig. YP16. The bearing head is equipped with sealed bearings; regular maintenance is not required.

To disassemble bearing head, remove trimmer head or blade assembly. Remove clamp bolt (2) and locating screw (3). Separate bearing head assembly from drive shaft housing. Remove shield (6) and bracket (5), if so equipped. Remove cup washer (13) and washer (12). Carefully press drive shaft adapter (1) out of bearings. Remove snap rings (7 and 11). Press bearings (8 and 10) and spacer (9) out of housing.

To reassemble, reverse disassembly procedure.

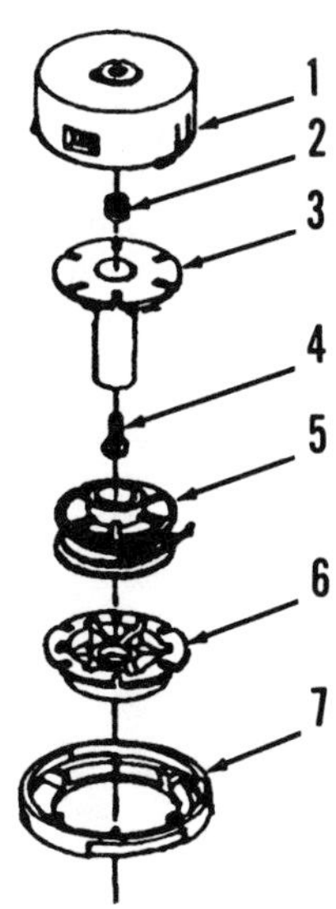

Fig. YP13—Exploded view of single strand, semi-automatic trimmer head used on Model 116.

1. Housing
2. Spring
3. Spool post
4. Screw
5. Spool
6. Button
7. Cover

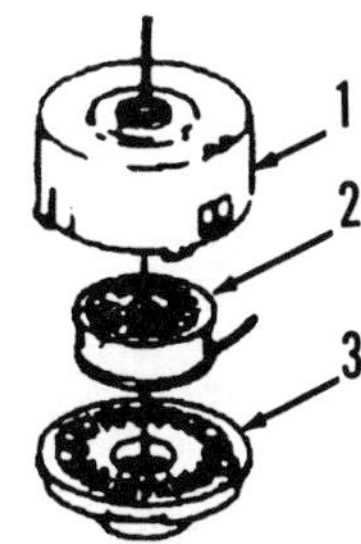

Fig. YP14—The single strand, semi-automatic trimmer head used on Models 120A, 130A and 145 consists of housing (1), spool (2) and cover (3). Line release button is located in cover.

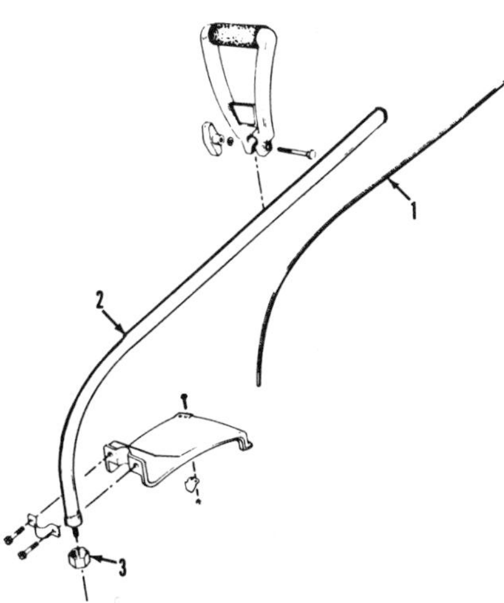

Fig. YP15—Exploded view of flexible drive shaft (1), drive shaft housing tube (2) and dust cover (3) used on Models 110, 116, 120 and 120A.

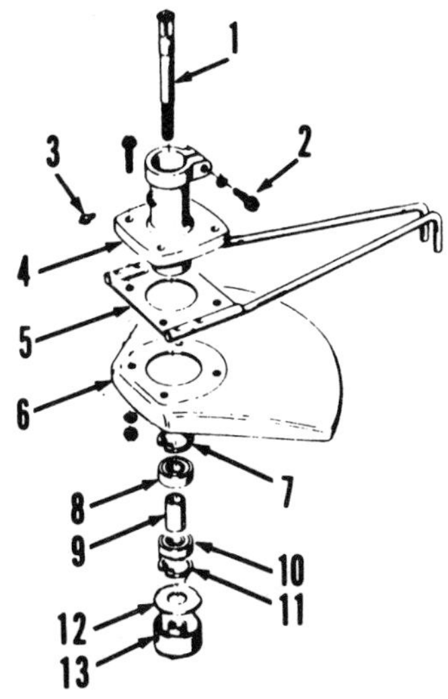

Fig. YP16—Exploded view of bearing head used on Models 130 and 130A.

1. Drive shaft adapter
2. Clamp bolt
3. Locating screw
4. Housing
5. Bracket (if equipped)
6. Shield
7. Snap ring
8. Bearing
9. Spacer
10. Bearing
11. Snap ring
12. Washer
13. Drive disc

GEAR HEAD

All Models So Equipped

The gear head should be lubricated after every 10 hours of operation by injecting lithium-based grease through screw hole in side of gear head. Fill housing so it is approximately two-thirds full of grease.

The gear head must be serviced as a unit assembly; individual components are not available.

ENGINE COVER

All Models So Equipped

Some models are equipped with the full engine cover shown in Fig. YP17. To remove engine cover, remove clamp bolt (8) and separate engine assembly from drive shaft housing. Remove the four 10-24 screws and separate housings (5) and (9) slightly. Disconnect ignition wire from module and separate fuel line so junction fitting stays with crankcase side of fuel line. Separate housings completely. Remove the three 8-24 screws from inner side of housing (5) and remove the air baffle. Remove the five 10-24 screws located under air baffle and separate housing (4) from housing (5). Remove fuel tank cap and remove fuel tank. Remove the four screws securing carburetor cover plate and remove carburetor cover. Disconnect spark plug, remove the four 10-24 screws at drive shaft housing side of cover (9), then remove cover.

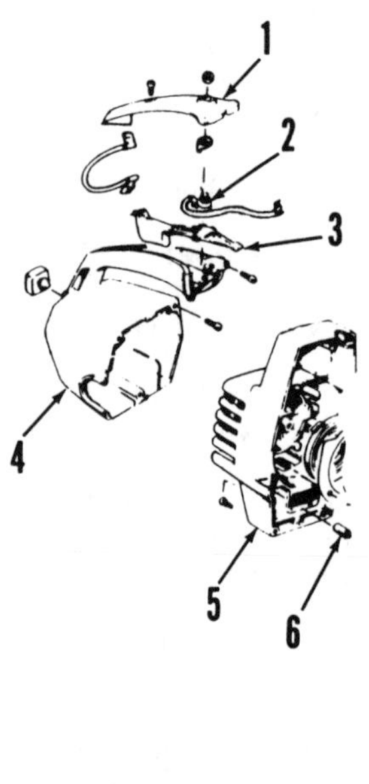

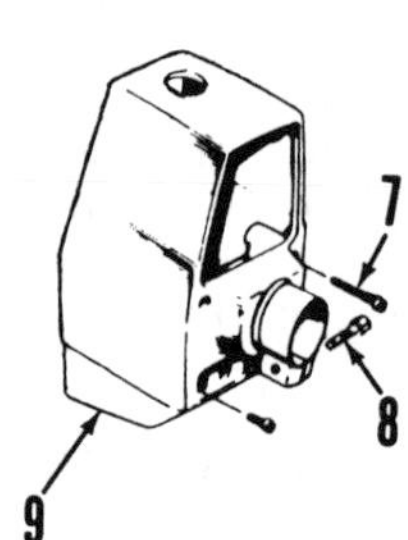

Fig. YP17—Exploded view of engine cover assembly used on some models.

1. Throttle housing cover
2. Ignition switch
3. Throttle trigger
4. Handle
5. Fan housing
6. Spacer
7. Screw
8. Clamp bolt
9. Cover

YAZOO

GASOLINE POWERED STRING TRIMMERS

Model	Engine Manufacturer	Engine Model	Displacement
YBC-16	Tanaka	....	16.0 cc
YBC-23	Tanaka	....	22.6 cc
YBC-31	Tanaka	....	30.5 cc

ENGINE INFORMATION

All Models

Yazoo line trimmers and brush cutters are equipped with Tanaka (TAS) two-stroke air-cooled engines. Engines may be identified by engine displacement. Refer to TANAKA (TAS) ENGINE SERVICE sections of this manual.

FUEL MIXTURE

All Models

Manufacturer recommends mixing regular grade gasoline (unleaded is an acceptable substitute) with a good quality two-stroke air-cooled engine oil at a 25:1 ratio. Do not use fuel containing alcohol.

STRING TRIMMER

All Models

Model YBC-16 is equipped with an eight blade plastic flexible blade with line trimmer head offered as an option. The dual strand manual trimmer head is standard on Models YBC-23 and YBC-31.

Refer to Fig. YA10 for an exploded view of the dual strand manual trimmer head available for most models. To extend line, stop trimmer engine and wait until all head rotation has stopped. Loosen lock knob (6) (left-hand thread) until line ends can be pulled from housing. Pull lines until desired length has been obtained. Correct line length is 3.4-4.7 inches (10-12 cm).

To renew line, remove lock knob (6) and housing (5). Remove any remaining line on spool (2) and clean spool and housing. Install new line on spool. Wind line in direction indicated by arrow on spool. New line diameter when wound on spool must not exceed spool diameter. Insert line ends through line guides (4) and reinstall housing and lock knob.

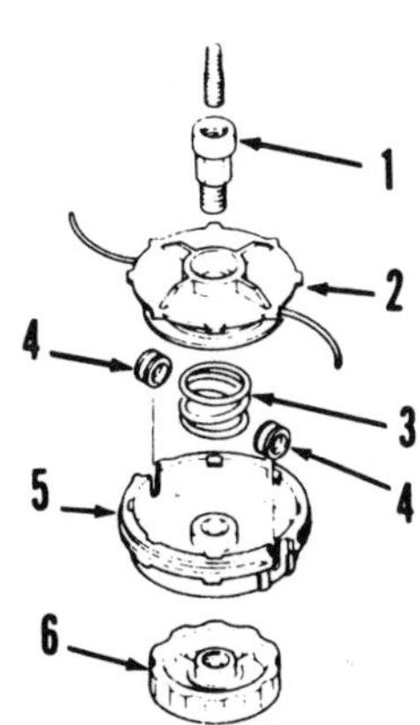

Fig. YA10—Exploded view of the dual strand manual trimmer head standard on most models.
1. Drive shaft adapter
2. Spool
3. Spring
4. Line guides
5. Housing
6. Lock knob

BLADE

Models YBC-23 And YBC-31

Models YBC-23 and YBC-31 may be equipped with a four cutting edge blade or a saw blade. To remove blade, rotate blade until hole (H-Fig. YA11) in guard is aligned with hole (H) in cup washer (2). Insert a round tool into aligned holes to prevent blade rotation. Remove bolt (7) (left-hand thread), washer (6), cover (5) and adapter (4). Remove blade (3). When installing blade, tighten bolt (7) to 250 in.-lbs. (28 N·m).

DRIVE SHAFT

Model YBC-16

Model YBC-16 is equipped with a flexible drive shaft enclosed in the drive shaft housing tube. Drive shaft has squared ends which engage adapters at each end. Drive shaft should be removed for maintenance at 20 hour intervals of use. To remove, separate drive shaft housing from engine, then pull drive shaft from housing. Clean drive shaft and lubricate with lithium base grease. Reinstall drive shaft in housing.

Models YBC-23 And YBC-31

Models YBC-23 and YBC-31 are equipped with a solid steel drive shaft supported in five renewable bushing assemblies located in drive shaft housing tube (Fig. YA12). Drive shaft requires no regular maintenance; however, if drive shaft has been removed, lubricate drive shaft with lithium base gease before reinstallation. To renew bushing assemblies, mark locations of old bushings on drive shaft housing, then remove all old bushings. Install new bushings with suitable driver at old bushing locations.

BEARING HEAD

Model YBC-16

Model YBC-16 is equipped with sealed bearing housing (3-Fig. YA13).

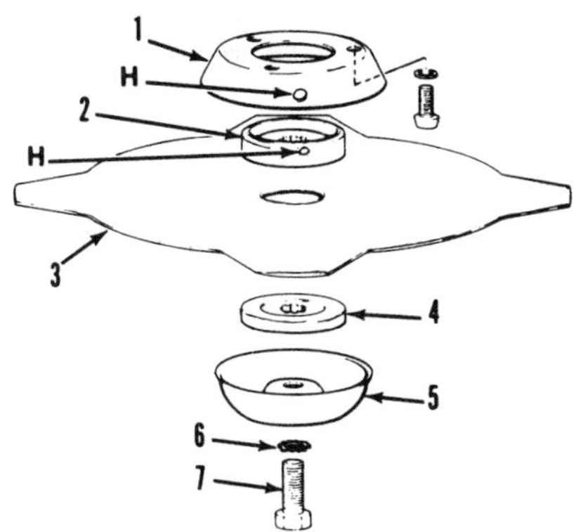

Fig. YA11—Exploded view of blade assembly available for Models YBC-23 and YBC-31.
1. Anti-wrap guard
2. Cup washer
3. Blade
4. Adapter plate
5. Cover
6. Washer
7. Bolt (LH)
H. Hole

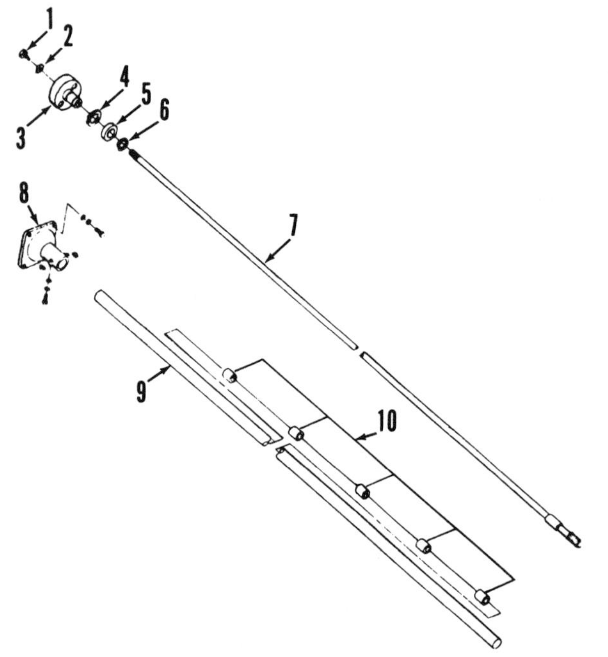

Fig. YA12—Exploded view of drive shaft and housing assembly used on Models YBC-23 and YBC-31.

1. Bolt
2. Washer
3. Clutch drum
4. Snap ring
5. Bearing
6. Snap ring
7. Drive shaft
8. Clutch housing
9. Drive shaft tube
10. Bushings

No regular maintenance is required and no service parts are available.

Fig. YA13—Bearing head assembly (3) is attached to drive shaft housing tube (1) by clamp (2). No service parts are available for bearing head.

GEAR HEAD

Models YBC-23 And YBC-31

Models YBC-23 and YBC-31 are equipped with the gear head shown in Fig. YA 14. Gear head lubricant level should be checked at 50 hour intervals of use by removing check plug (9). Gear head housing should be 2/3 full of lithium base grease. Do not use a pressure grease gun to install grease as bearing seal and housing damage will occur.

To disassemble gear head, remove trimmer head or blade assembly. Remove locating screw (7) and clamp bolt (8) and separate gear head from drive shaft housing. Remove spacer (16) and seal (15). Remove snap ring (14) and use a suitable puller to remove arbor shaft (12) and bearing assembly. If bearing (10) stays in housing, heat housing to 140° F (60° C) and tap housing on wooden block to remove bearing. Remove gear (11) from arbor shaft. Press bearing (13) from arbor shaft as required. Remove snap ring (1). Insert a screwdriver into clamp split in gear head housing and carefully expand housing. Remove input shaft (5) and bearing assembly. Remove snap ring (2) and press bearings (3 and 4) from input shaft as required.

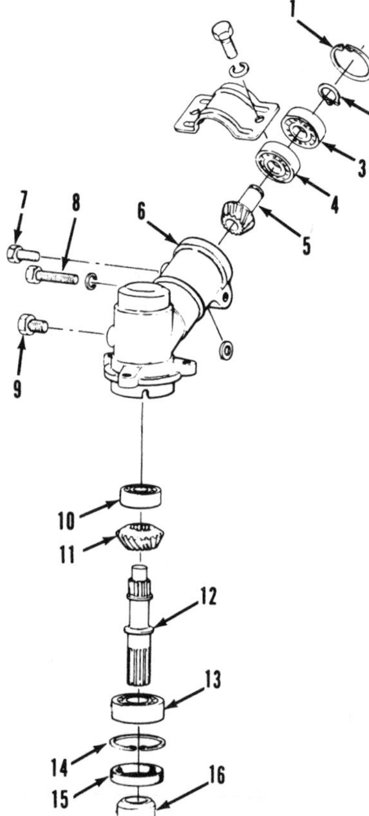

Fig. YA14—Exploded view of gear head used on Models YBC-23 and YBC-31.

1. Snap ring
2. Snap ring
3. Bearing
4. Bearing
5. Input shaft
6. Housing
7. Locating screw
8. Clamp bolt
9. Check plug
10. Bearing
11. Gear
12. Arbor (output) shaft
13. Bearing
14. Snap ring
15. Seal
16. Spacer

ALPINA
ENGINE SERVICE

Model	Bore	Stroke	Displacement
21	...	...	20.5 cc (1.25 cu. in.)
25	...	...	24.8 cc (1.5 cu. in.)
30	...	...	27.4 cc (1.67 cu. in.)
34	...	...	32.5 cc (1.98 cu. in.)
42	...	...	41.1 cc (2.5 cu. in.)
52	...	...	52.3 cc (3.19 cu. in.)

ENGINE INFORMATION

These two-stroke, air-cooled gasoline engines are used on Alpina trimmers and brush cutters.

MAINTENANCE

LUBRICATION. The engine is lubricated by oil mixed with the fuel. Refer to the appropriate trimmer or brush cutter service section for the amount and type of oil the manufacturer of the equipment recommends mixing with gasoline.

SPARK PLUG. The recommended spark plug is an NGK BM6A or equivalent and the electrode gap should be 0.024 in. (0.6 mm). Tighten the spark plug to 20 N·m (177 in.-lb.) torque.

CARBURETOR. The engine is equipped with a Walbro WT carburetor. The model number stamped on the carburetor will be required for ordering parts. Refer to Fig. AL101 for an exploded view typical of the carburetor.

Initial adjustment of the idle mixture screw (5) and the high-speed mixture screw (6) is 1-1/4 turns open. The settings of these mixture screws is critical to the operation of the engine. Final adjustment should be performed carefully to insure easy starting and maximum performance.

To adjust the mixture screws, first remove and clean the air filter, then reinstall it. Start the engine and allow it to run until it reaches normal operating temperature. If necessary, turn each of the mixture screws (5 and 6) clockwise until seated lightly, then back the screws out (counterclockwise) 1-1/4 turns to provide the initial adjustment so the engine can be started. Turn the idle speed stop screw (14) so the engine idles at just below clutch engagement rpm. Adjust the idle mixture needle (5) so the engine idles smoothly and accelerates without hesitation. Readjust the idle speed stop screw (14) if necessary to slow the idle speed. Adjust the high-speed mixture screw (6) to provide the best performance while operating at maximum speed under load. The high-speed mixture screw may be set slightly rich to improve performance under load. The engine may be damaged if the high-speed screw is set too lean.

To disassemble the carburetor, refer to Fig. AL101. Remove metering chamber cover (1) and fuel pump cover (17) for access to internal components. Remove metering lever (26) and fuel inlet valve (25). Remove fuel mixture screws (5 and 6). Remove fuel filter screens (10 and 20), check valve (4) and Welch plug (11).

Clean and inspect all components. If the unit has been improperly stored, passages may be clogged with deposits that are hard, solid and nearly transparent. Clean passages with suitable carburetor cleaning solvent and compressed air. Be careful not to damage the openings or sealing surfaces while cleaning. Check the condition of diaphragms (2 and 19) carefully. Install new diaphragms if hard (not flexible), torn or otherwise damaged. Examine the fuel inlet valve (25), spring (24) and lever (26). A new fuel inlet valve needle (25), and mixture screws (5 and 6) can be installed, but their seats cannot be serviced if damaged. Inspect the condition of the check valve (8) and filter screen (10).

Check the height of the metering lever as shown in Fig. AL102 using Walbro tool 500-13 or equivalent. End of metering lever should just touch the leg of the tool. If the tool is not available, the lever should be 0.060-0.070 in. (1.52-1.78 mm) below the surface for gasket (3—Fig. AL101). Carefully bend the lever if necessary to obtain the correct lever height. Inspect the primer bulb (15). Install a new bulb if hard, cracked or otherwise damaged.

IGNITION SYSTEM. The engine is equipped with a solid-state ignition system. The ignition module/coil is located under the cowling at the front of the engine. Two screws attach the ignition module/coil (17—Fig. AL103) to the engine's crankcase (18). When installing, set the air gap between the flywheel magnets and the legs of the ignition module as follows. Install the ignition module, but tighten the two screws only enough to hold it in place away from the flywheel. Insert 0.010-0.015 in. (0.254-0.381 mm) thick brass or plastic shim stock between the

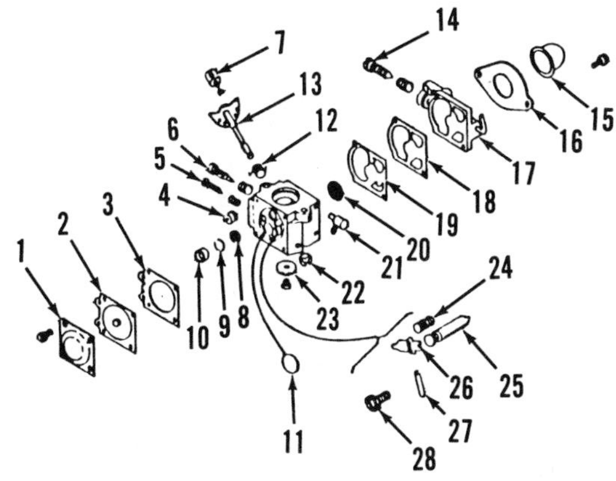

Fig. AL101—Exploded view of Walbro WT carburetor.

1. Metering chamber cover
2. Metering diaphragm
3. Gasket
4. Check valve
5. Low speed mixture screw
7. High speed mixture screw
8. Plug
9. Retainer
10. Screen
11. Weclch plug
12. Return spring
13. Throttle shaft
14. Idle speed screw
15. Primer bulb
16. Retainer
17. Fuel pump cover
18. Gasket
19. Fuel pump diaphragm
20. Filter screen
21. Fuel fitting
22. "E" ring
23. Throttle plate
24. Spring
25. Fuel inlet valve
26. Metering lever
27. Pin
28. Screw

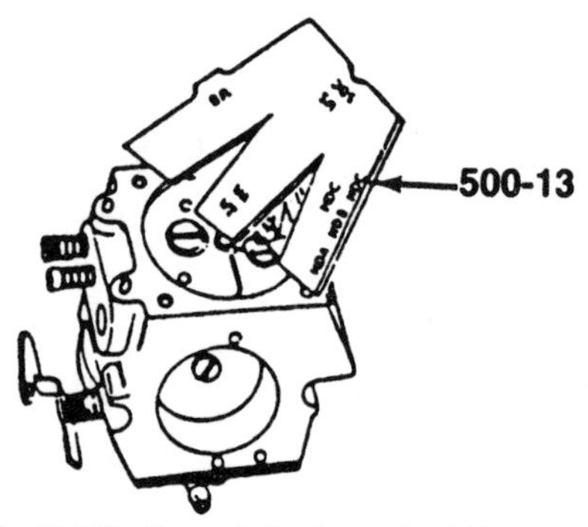

Fig. AL102—The metering lever should just touch the leg of the Walbro tool 500-13. If necessary, bend the lever to adjust the lever height

legs of the ignition module and the flywheel, then turn the flywheel until the flywheel magnets are near the module legs. Loosen the screws attaching the ignition module and press legs of the ignition module against the shim stock, then tighten the two attaching screws. Remove the shim stock, then turn the flywheel and check to be sure the flywheel does not hit the legs of the coil.

REPAIRS

PISTON, PIN AND RINGS. To remove the piston (25—Fig. AL103), separate the drive shaft housing from the engine. Remove air cleaner, carburetor, insulator (1 through 9) and ignition coil (17). Remove cover (31), muffler (30) and insulator (29). Remove the nuts attaching the cylinder, then pull the cylinder (27) straight up, off the piston. Remove the piston pin retaining rings (23), push the pin (24) out using a suitable pusher tool, then separate the piston from the connecting rod. Needle bearing (22) is located in the connecting rod.

Inspect the cylinder and piston for damage. The piston, rings and cylinder are available in standard size only.

Position the piston on the connecting rod so arrow on top of piston will be toward the exhaust port (muffler) side of cylinder. Lubricate the piston pin and bearing, then install the piston pin. Install new retaining rings (23) if bent or condition is otherwise questionable. Install the retaining rings with the gap toward the top or bottom or the piston.

Make sure the end of each piston ring surrounds the pin located in ring groove. Be careful to install the cylinder straight down over the piston. If the

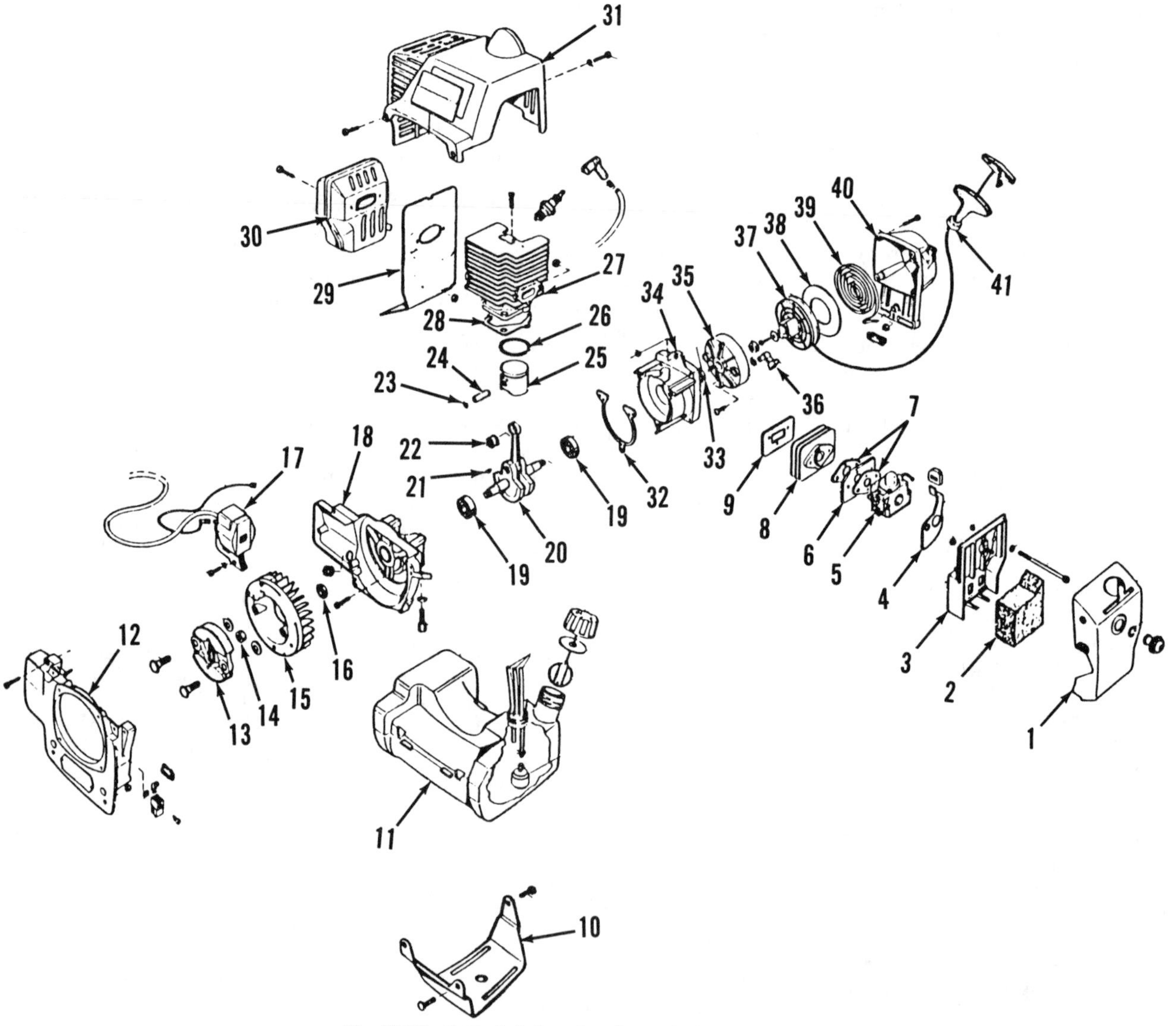

Fig. AL103—Exploded view of engine typical of all models.

1. Air filter cover
2. Air filter
3. Housing
4. Choke
5. Carburetor
6. Gaskets
7. Insulator plate
8. Insulator block
9. Gasket
10. Flange
11. Fuel tank
12. Cover
13. Clutch shoes
14. Nut
15. Flywheel
16. Seal
17. Ignition coil/module
18. Crankcase half
19. Main bearings
20. Crankshaft & connecting rod assy.
21. Woodruff key
22. Needle bearing
23. Retaining ring
24. Piston pin
25. Piston
26. Piston ring
27. Cylinder
28. Gasket
29. Heat deflector
30. Muffler
31. Cover
32. Gasket
33. Seal
34. Crankcase half
35. Pawl plate
36. Starter pawl
37. Pulley
38. Plate
39. Spring
40. Starter housing
41. Rope & handle

cylinder is turned, the ring can catch in a port and break the end of the ring.

CYLINDER. The piston, rings and cylinder are available in standard size only and the cylinder should not be bored oversize. Inspect the cylinder for any damage and install new parts as necessary. If the chrome plating is worn from the cylinder, a new cylinder should be installed.

CRANKSHAFT AND CONNECTING ROD. The crankshaft and connecting rod are available only as an assembly (20—Fig. AL103); individual components are not available.

Remove the spark plug and insert a piece of rope or a piston stop in the spark plug hole to prevent the crankshaft from turning. Remove the rewind starter and pawl plate (37). Remove the clutch (13) and the flywheel retaining nut (14). Use a suitable puller to remove the flywheel (15). Remove the cylinder and piston as described in PISTON, PIN AND RINGS paragraph. Remove the screws attaching the halves of the crankcase together and separate halves (18 and 34). Heat the crankcase if necessary to remove the main bearings (19) from the crankcase bores. If the bearings stay on the crankshaft, use a suitable puller to pull the bearings from the main journals.

The main bearing should turn smoothly with no perceptible play or ratcheting. Use a suitable tools to press new main bearings and seals into the crankcase bores. Lips of seals (16 and 33) should be toward inside of crankcase and should be lubricated before installing the crankshaft.

CLUTCH. Clutch shoes (12—Fig. AL104) are attached to the flywheel with pivot screws (11). The clutch drum of all models operates in bearings (8 or 19) located in the cover (5) or drive flange (18).

To remove the clutch drum from backpack models with flex drive, first press plunger (17) and separate the flexible shaft from drive flange (18). Remove the screws attaching the drive flange (18) from the engine. Hold the clutch drum (21) and unscrew drive adapter (16).

On other models, remove screws (6) and separate the clutch housing (5) and drive shaft from the engine. Remove screws (1 and 7) then remove cover (2), vibration isolator (3) and drive shaft from the clutch housing (5).

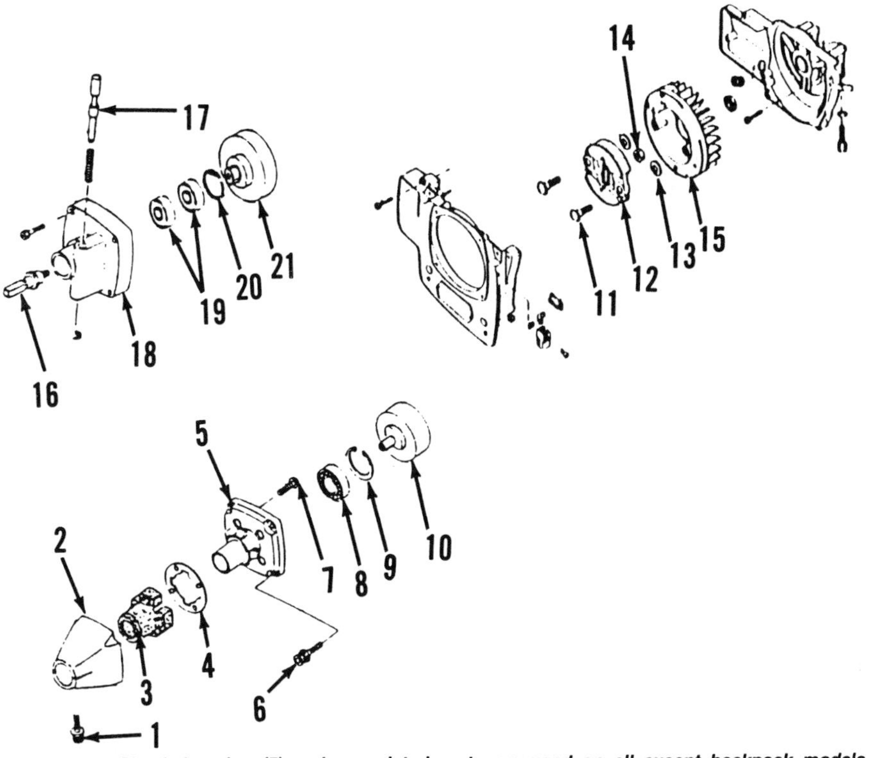

Fig. AL104—Clutch housing (5) and associated parts are used on all except backpack models. Backpack models are fitted with drive flange (18) and associated parts.

1. Locating screw
2. Cover
3. Vibration isolator
4. Plate
5. Clutch housing
6. Screw
7. Screw
8. Bearing
9. Snap ring
10. Clutch drum
11. Pivot screws
12. Clutch shoes & springs
13. Washers
14. Nut
15. Flywheel
16. Drive adapter
17. Release plunger
18. Drive flange
19. Bearings
20. Snap ring
21. Clutch drum

Press clutch drum (10 or 21) from the bearings (8 or 19). Remove snap ring (9 or 20), then use a suitable puller to remove bearings (8 or 19). It may be necessary to heat the housing to facilitate removal and installation of the bearings.

Inspect the clutch shoes (12) and drum (10 or 21) for excessive wear. Inspect the springs for evidence of overheating or other damage. Clutch (12) is available only as an assembly.

REWIND STARTER. Refer to Fig. AL105 for exploded view of rewind starter. To disassemble the starter, unbolt and remove the housing from the engine. Remove handle from the rope and allow the rope to wind into the starter. Remove center screw (6), then remove washer (7) and the rope pulley (8). Wear appropriate eyewear and gloves to protect against injury when removing the spring (9). The spring may unwind from the housing uncontrollably. If necessary for service, remove the pulley plate.

The rope must be the correct diameter and length for the starter to operate properly. If the rope is too large in diameter or too long, the rope may bind when trying to wind onto the pulley. When installing new rope, measure the length and diameter of the old rope, then install new rope that matches the original.

To assemble the starter, apply a small amount of light grease to the starter housing post, spring and the back of the pulley. Install the rewind spring so it is wound counterclockwise from the outer end. Attach the rope to the pulley, making sure the knot is fully nested in the pocket. Pull the rope tight and wind the rope counterclockwise as viewed from the pawl (engine) side. Install the pulley/rope and rotate slightly until the spring hooks into the pulley and the pulley drops into the housing. Guide the end of the rope through the housing and attach the handle.

When assembling or if the starter rope does not fully rewind, preload the recoil spring as follows. Hold the pulley to keep it from turning, then pull a small loop in the rope between the pulley and the inside of the housing. Hold the rope and wind the pulley to preload the pulley, allow the pulley to rewind the rope, then check operation. The spring should wind the rope around the pulley fully, but the spring must bind when the rope is fully extended. It should be possible to rotate the pulley at least 1/4 turn when the rope is pulled out completely. Complete the assembly by reversing the disassembly procedure when the spring preload is correctly set.

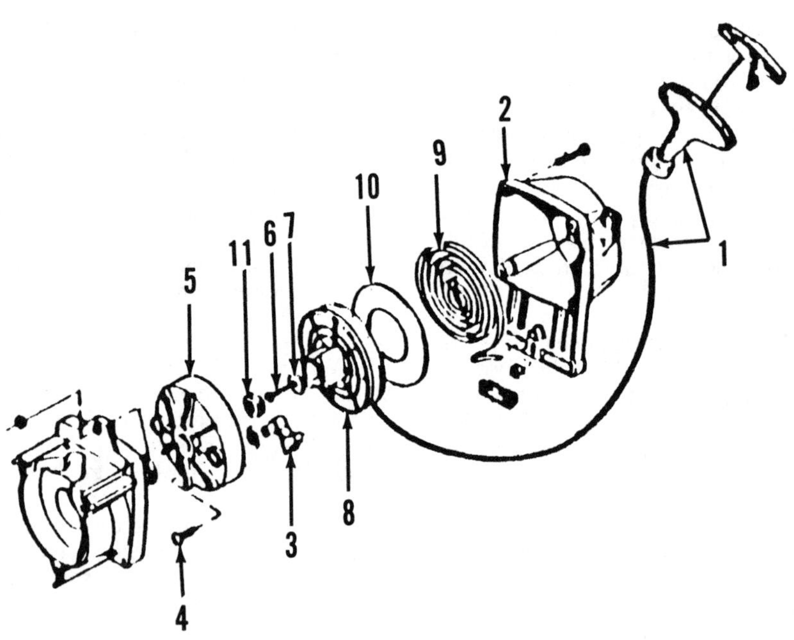

Fig. AL105—Exploded view of recoil starter.

1. Handle & rope
2. Housing
3. Pawl & spring
4. Pawl screw
5. Pawl plate
6. Screw
7. Washer
8. Pulley
9. Spring
10. Plate
11. Nut

DEERE

ENGINE SERVICE

Model	Bore	Stroke	Displacement
110	32 mm (1.26 in.)	26 mm (1.02 in.)	21.2 cc 1.29 cu. in.)
210, 220, 240, 250 & 260	32 mm (1.26 in.)	26 mm (1.02 in.)	21.2 cc (1.29 cu. in.)
300	32.2 mm (1.27 in.)	30 mm (1.18 in.)	24.4 cc (1.49 cu. in.)
350	35 mm (1.38 in.)	32 mm (1.26 in.)	30.8 cc (1.88 cu. in.)
450	40 mm (1.57 in.)	32 mm (1.26 in.)	40.2 cc (2.45 cu. in.)

ENGINE INFORMATION

These two-stroke, air-cooled engines are used on some Deere trimmers and brush cutters. Refer to Deere Trimmer section for engine application.

MAINTENANCE

LUBRICATION. The engine is lubricated by oil mixed with the fuel. Refer to the appropriate trimmer or brush cutter service section for the amount and type of oil the manufacturer of the equipment recommends mixing with gasoline.

SPARK PLUG. Recommended spark plug for Model 350 is a Champion CJ8 or equivalent. Recommended spark plug for other models is Champion CJ7Y or equivalent. Electrode gap should be 0.024-0.028 in. (0.6-0.7 mm). Tighten the spark plug securely to the torque listed in the TIGHTENING TORQUE paragraph.

CARBURETOR. Various types of carburetors have been used. Refer to the appropriate following section for carburetor service.

Walbro WA. Some engines are equipped with a Walbro WA diaphragm carburetor. Initial adjustment of idle mixture screw (18—Fig. JD101) is one turn out from a lightly seated position. Initial adjustment of high speed mixture screw (17) is 1-1/14 turns out. Final adjustments are performed with trimmer line at recommended length or blade installed.

Start and run engine until normal operating temperature is reached. Adjust idle speed screw to approximately 3000 rpm (trimmer head or blade should not rotate on models with a clutch). Adjust idle mixture screw so engine runs at maximum idle speed and accelerates without hesitation. Readjust idle speed as necessary. Operate unit at full throttle (no load) and adjust high speed mixture screw to obtain maximum engine rpm, then turn screw counterclockwise until engine just starts to "four-cycle."

When overhauling carburetor, refer to exploded view in Fig. JD101 and remove covers (1 and 28) for access to internal components. Remove circuit plate (10), diaphragms (2, 11 and 26), metering lever (6) and fuel inlet valve (7), fuel screen (24) and fuel mixture screws (17 and 18).

Clean carburetor using suitable solvent and compressed air. Do not use drills or wires to clean orifices. Examine fuel inlet valve and seat. Inlet valve is renewable, but carburetor body must be renewed if seat is excessively worn or damaged. Inspect mixture screws and seats. Renew carburetor body if seats are excessively worn or damaged.

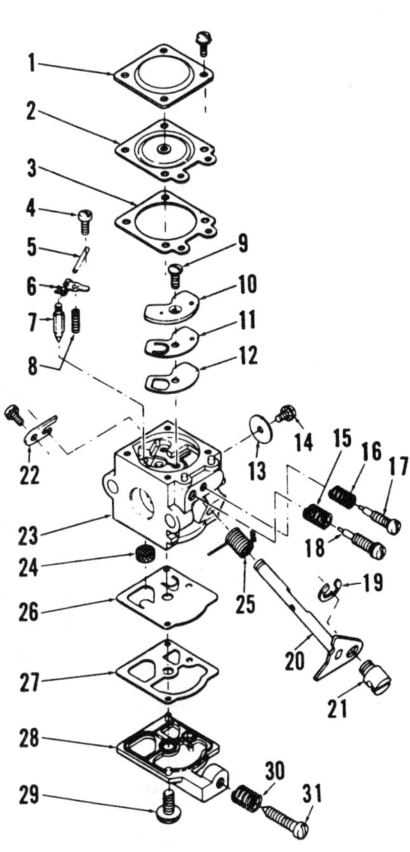

Fig. JD101—Exploded view of Walbro WA carburetor used on some models.

1. Cover
2. Metering diaphragm
3. Gasket
4. Screw
5. Pin
6. Metering lever
7. Fuel inlet valve
8. Spring
9. Screw
10. Circuit plate
11. Diaphragm
12. Gasket
13. Throttle plate
14. Screw
15. Spring
16. Spring
17. High speed mixture screw
18. Idle mixture screw
19. "E" clip
20. Throttle shaft
21. Swivel
22. Clip
23. Carburetor body
24. Inlet screen
25. Return spring
26. Fuel pump diaphragm
27. Gasket
28. Cover
29. Screw
30. Spring
31. Idle speed screw

Clean fuel screen. Inspect diaphragms for tears and other damage.

When reassembling, check metering lever height as shown in Fig. JD102 using Walbro tool 500-13. Metering lever should just touch leg on tool. Bend lever to obtain correct lever height.

Walbro WY and WYL. Some engines may be equipped with a Walbro WY or WYL carburetor. This is a

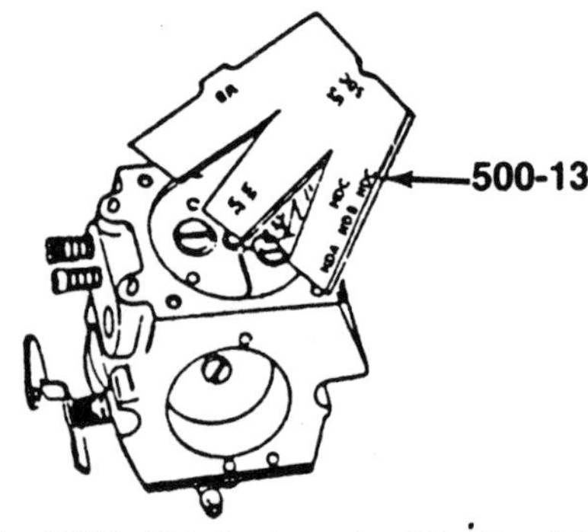

Fig. JD102—Metering lever should just touch leg of Walbro tool 500-13. Bend lever to obtain correct lever height.

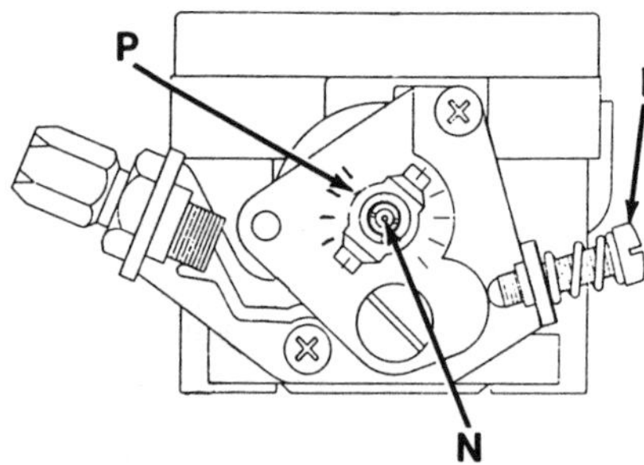

Fig. JD103—On Walbro WY or WYL carburetor, idle speed screw is located at (I), idle limiter plate is located at (P) and idle mixture needle is located a (N). A plug covers the idle mixture needle.

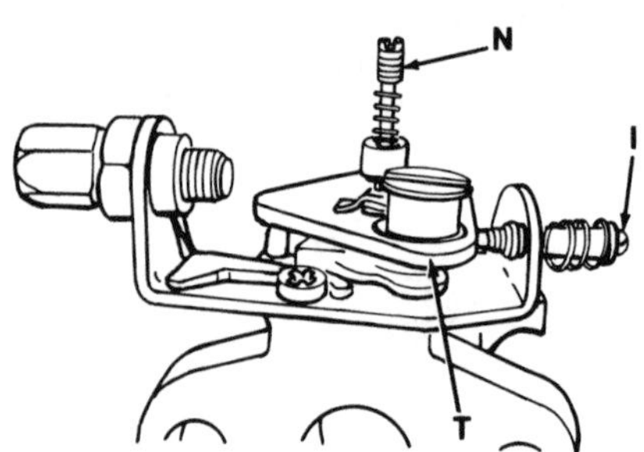

Fig. JD104—View of idle mixture needle (N) used on Walbro WY and WYL carburetor.

diaphragm-type carburetor that uses a barrel-type throttle rather than a throttle plate.

Idle fuel for the carburetor flows up into the throttle barrel where it is fed into the air stream. On some models, the idle fuel flow can be adjusted by turning an idle limiter plate (P—Fig JD103). Initial setting is in center notch. Rotating the plate clockwise will lean the idle mixture.

Inside the mixture plate is an idle mixture needle (N) that is preset at the factory. If removed, use the following procedure to determine correct position. Back out needle (N—Fig. JD104) until unscrewed. Screw in needle five turns on Model WY or 15 turns on Models WYL. Rotate idle mixture plate (P—Fig. JD103) to center notch. Run engine until normal operating temperature is attained. Adjust idle speed

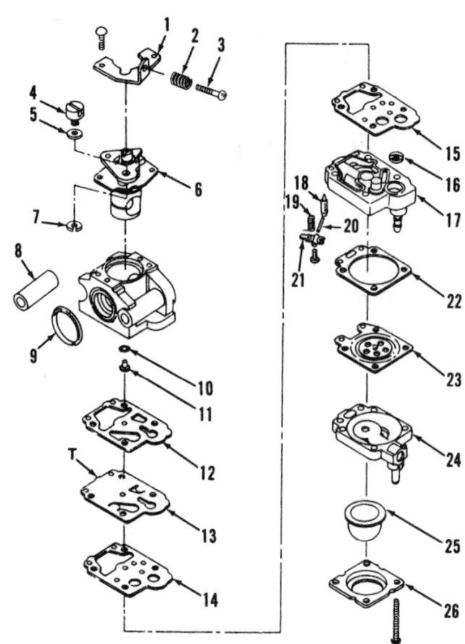

Fig. JD105—Exploded view of Walbro WY carburetor. Model WYL is similar.

1. Bracket
2. Spring
3. Idle speed screw
4. Swivel
5. Washer
6. Throttle barrel assy.
7. "E" ring
8. Sleeve
9. "O" ring
10. "O" ring
11. Main jet
12. Gasket
13. Fuel pump diaphragm
14. Fuel pump plate
15. Gasket
16. Fuel screen
17. Fuel pump body
18. Fuel inlet valve
19. Spring
20. Pin
21. Metering lever
22. Gasket
23. Metering diaphragm
24. Plate
25. Primer bulb
26. Cover

screw so trimmer head or blade does not rotate. Rotate idle mixture needle (N—Fig. JD104) and obtain highest rpm (turning needle clockwise leans the mixture), then turn needle 1/4 turn counterclockwise. Readjust idle speed screw. Note that idle mixture plate and needle are available only as an assembly with throttle barrel (6—Fig. JD105). The high speed mixture is controlled by a removable fixed jet (11—Fig. JD105).

To overhaul carburetor, refer to exploded view in Fig. JD105. Remove retainer (26), plate (24), diaphragm (23), fuel pump body (17), plate (14) and diaphragm (13). Remove bracket (1) and throttle barrel assembly (6).

On models with a plastic body, clean only with solvents approved for use with plastic. Do not use wire or drill bits to clean fuel passages. Do not disassemble throttle barrel assembly (6). Examine fuel inlet valve and seat. Inlet valve (18) is renewable, but fuel pump body (17) must be renewed if seat is excessively worn or damaged. Clean fuel screen (16). Inspect diaphragms for tears and other damage. When installing plates and gaskets (12 through 22), note that tabs (T) on ends will "stair-step" when correctly installed. Adjust metering lever height dimension

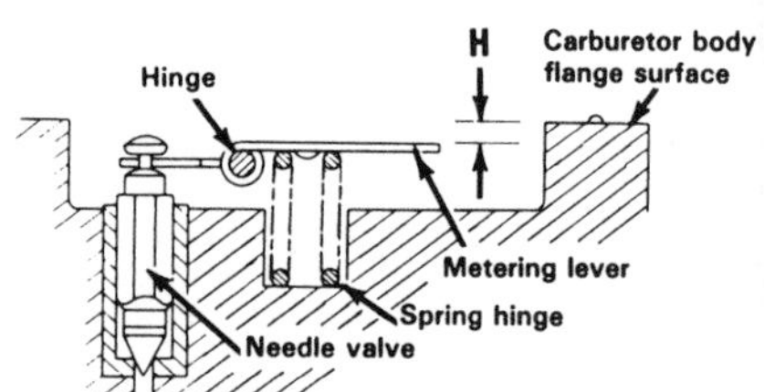

Fig. JD106—Metering lever height (H) must be set on diaphragm carburetors. Refer to text for specified height.

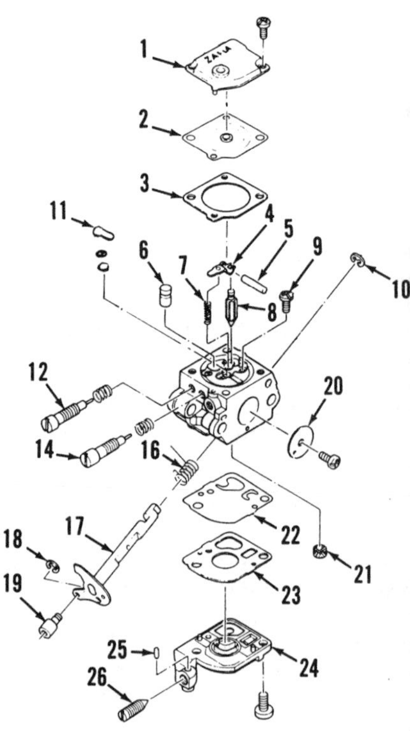

Fig. JD107—Exploded view of Zama C1U carburetor used on some models.

1. Cover
2. Metering diaphragm
3. Gasket
4. Metering lever
5. Pin
6. Nozzle
7. Spring
8. Fuel inlet valve
9. Screw
10. "E" ring
11. Welch plug
12. High speed mixture screw
14. Idle mixture screw
16. Spring
17. Throttle shaft
18. "E" ring
19. Swivel
20. Throttle plate
21. Fuel inlet screen
22. Fuel pump diaphragm
23. Gasket
24. Cover
25. Pin
26. Idle speed screw

(H—Fig. JD106) to obtain 1.5 mm (0.059 in.) between carburetor body surface and lever.

Zama C1U. Refer to Fig. JD107 for an exploded view of the Zama C1U carburetor used on some engines.

Initial setting of idle mixture screw (14) and high speed mixture screw (12) is 1-1/8 turns out from a lightly seated position. Final adjustment is performed with engine at normal operating temperature and trimmer line at normal length or blade installed.

Adjust idle speed stop screw to approximately 3000 rpm. Adjust idle mix-

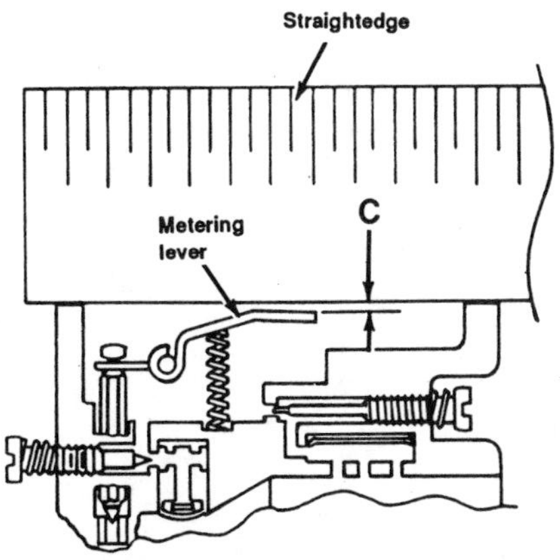

Fig. JD108—Metering lever should be bent so height (C) is 0-0.3 mm (0.0-0.012 in.) on Zama C1U carburetor.

ture screw (14) so engine idles smoothly and accelerates cleanly without hesitation. Operate unit at full throttle (no load) and adjust high speed mixture screw (12) to obtain maximum engine rpm, then turn screw counterclockwise until engine just starts to "four-cycle."

To disassemble carburetor, refer to Fig. JD107 and remove covers (1) and 24) for access to internal components. Remove diaphragms (2 and 22), metering lever (4) and fuel inlet valve (8) and fuel mixture screws (12 and 14). To remove Welch plug (11), pierce plug toward the end of the "tail" portion with a suitable punch, but use care not to damage underlying body metal.

Clean and inspect all components. Clean fuel channels using compressed air and solvent; do not use wires or drills to clean orifices. Inspect diaphragms (2 and 22) for defects that may affect operation. Examine fuel inlet valve (8) and seat. Inlet valve is renewable, but carburetor must be renewed if seat is damaged or excessively worn. Discard carburetor body if mixture screw seats are damaged or excessively worn.

When reassembling, apply sealant to outer edge of new Welch plug. Clearance (C—Fig. JD108) between metering lever and a straightedge placed across gasket surface of carburetor body should be 0-0.3 mm (0-0.012 in.). Bend metering lever as needed, being careful not to force inlet needle onto the seat.

IGNITION SYSTEM. All engines are equipped with an electronic ignition system that does not use breaker points. On some models including 450, the ignition module is separate from the ignition coil. On most models, the module is incorporated in the coil assembly.

Ignition can be considered satisfactory if a spark will jump across the 3 mm (1/8 in.) electrode gap of a test plug when the engine is turned with the recoil starter. If there is no spark, check the stop switch and connecting wire for shorts to ground. Ignition may be irregular at starting speeds if gap between the legs of the coil core and the flywheel magnets is too wide. Specified gap is 0.2-0.3 mm (0.008-0.012 in.). Refer to the IGNITION paragraphs in the REPAIRS section for testing the ignition coil.

REPAIRS

COMPRESSION PRESSURE. Cylinder compression pressure should be checked with the carburetor choke and throttle wide open. Check the compression pressure several times to make sure that indicated pressure is correct. For optimum performance, cylinder compression pressure should be as follows.

Models 110, 210, 220, 240,
260 & 300 . . . . 538 kPa (78 psi)
Model 250
Before serial No. 030101 . . . . 586 kPa (85 psi)
Serial No. 030101 and up . . . 538 kPa (78 psi)
Models 350 & 450. . . 689 kPa (100 psi)

TIGHTENING TORQUE. Recommended tightening torque values are as follows.

Carburetor
110, 210, 220, 240, 250, 260,
300 & 350. . . . . 4 N·m (35 in.-lb.)
Clutch hub
210, 240 & 260 . . . . 19 N·m (168 in.-lb.)
250 before serial number
030101 . . . . 13.6-15.8 N·m (121-140 in.-lb.)
450 . . . . 3.4-4.5 N·m (30-40 in.-lb.)
Clutch flange
450 . . . . 40-44 N·m (30-32 in.-lb.)
Clutch shoes
220 . . . . 7.8-9.7 N·m (69-86 in.-lb.)
250 after Serial number
030100 . . . . 7.8-9.7 N·m (69-86 in.-lb.)
300 . . . . 4.9-5.8 N·m (43-51 in.-lb.)
Crankcase
110, 210, 220, 240, 250,
260, 300 & 350 . . . . 3.6 N·m (32 in.-lb.)
Cylinder
110, 220, 250 & 300 . . . . 5.9 N·m (52 in.-lb.)
210, 240, 260 & 350 . . . . 3.9 N·m (35 in.-lb.)
450 . . . . 7.3-8.5 N·m (65-75 in.-lb.)
Flywheel
110 & 220 . . . . 18 N·m (160 in.-lb.)
250 after Serial No. 030100 . . 18 N·m (160 in.-lb.)
300 . . . . 10.7-12.7 N·m (95-112 in.-lb.)
Ignition module
110, 210, 240 & 260 . . . . 2 N·m (18 in.-lb.)
220 & 300. . . . . 3.6 N·m (32 in.-lb.)
250 before Serial No.030101. 2.2 N·m (19 in.-lb.)
250 after Serial No.030100 . . 3.6 N·m (32 in.-lb.)
350 & 450. . . . . 2.2 N·m (19 in.-lb.)
Spark plug. . . . . 16-17 N·m (130-150 in.-lb.)

IGNITION. If the ignition module is separate from the ignition coil, it must be replaced with one known to be good to determine its condition. The ignition coil can be tested using an ohmmeter.

Test models 110, 210, 220, 240, 250, 260, 300 and 300 with an integral module and coil using an accurate ohmmeter as follows. Detach the wire to the stop switch and attach one tester lead to the detached wire or the terminal of the coil. Ground the other lead of the tester and observe the resistance in ohms. Resistance should be within the following range.

Model	Resistance
100	1.0-1.5 ohms
210	1.0-2.0 ohms
220	160-240 ohms
240	1.5-2.5 ohms
250 with integral module	110-220 ohms
260	1.5-2.5 ohms
300	160-240 ohms
350 with integral module	70-132 ohms

For other models, test the ignition coil using an accurate ohmmeter. Compare the measured resistance with the following specifications.

Model	Primary winding	Secondary winding
250 w/separate coil	0-0.2 ohms	1,500-3,000 ohms
350 w/separate coil	0-0.2 ohms	500-1,500 ohms
450	0-0.22 ohms	1,350-3,300 ohms

PISTON, PIN AND RINGS. To remove the piston (4—Fig. JD109, Fig.

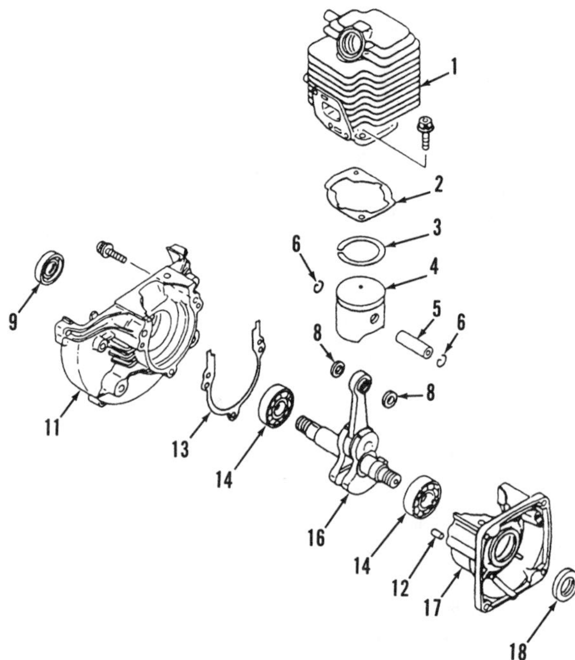

Fig. JD109—Exploded view engine typical of Models 110, 210, 240 and 260.

1. Cylinder
2. Gasket
3. Piston ring
4. Piston
5. Piston pin
6. Retaining rings
8. Washer
9. Seal
11. Crankcase half
12. Dowel pin
13. Gasket
14. Bearing
16. Crankshaft assy.
17. Crankcase half
18. Seal

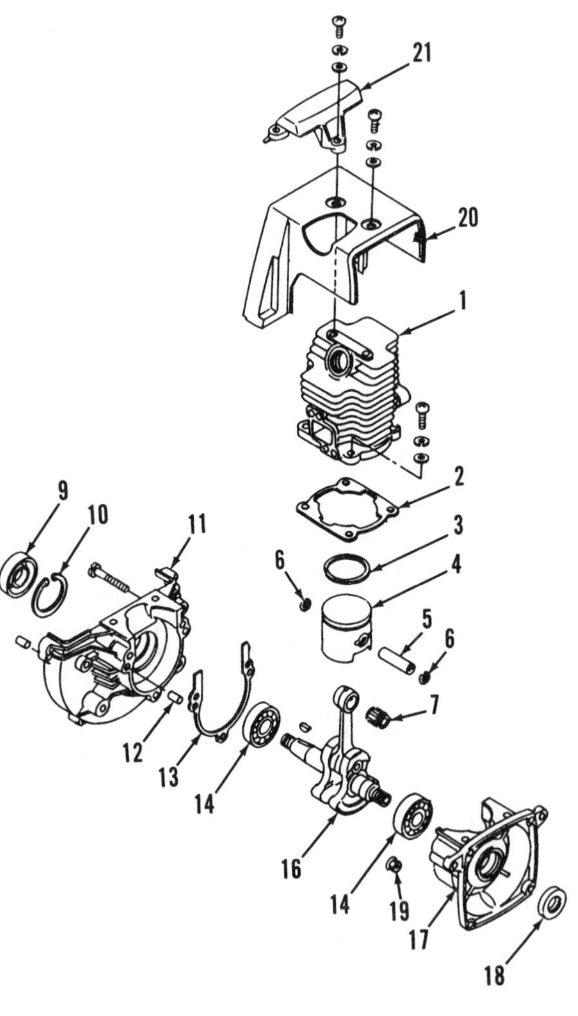

Fig. JD110—Exploded view of Model 220 and 300 engine. Model 250 engine after serial number 030100 is similar.

1. Cylinder
2. Gasket
3. Piston ring
4. Piston
5. Piston pin
6. Retaining rings
7. Bearing
9. Seal
10. Snap ring
11. Crankcase half
12. Dowel pin
13. Gasket
14. Bearing
16. Crankshaft assy.
17. Crankcase half
18. Seal
19. Plug
20. Cover
21. Guard

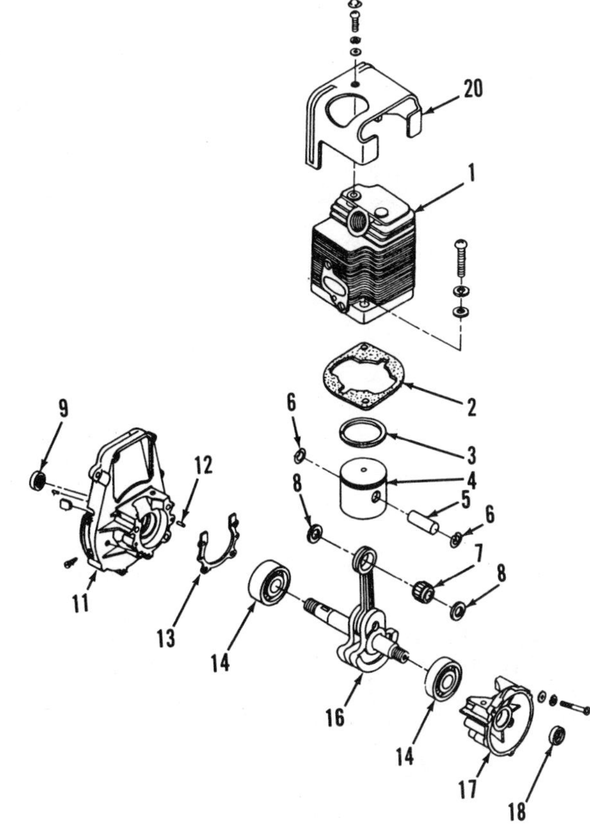

Fig. JD111—Exploded view of Model 250 engine before serial number 030101.

1. Cylinder
2. Gasket
3. Piston ring
4. Piston
5. Piston pin
6. Retaining rings
7. Bearing
8. Washer
9. Seal
11. Crankcase half
12. Dowel pin
13. Gasket
14. Bearing
16. Crankshaft assy.
17. Crankcase half
18. Seal
20. Cover

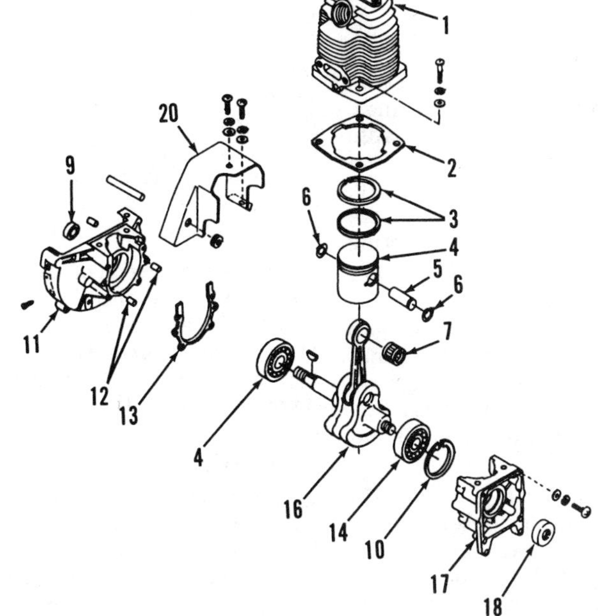

Fig. JD112—Exploded view of Model 350 and 450 engine.

1. Cylinder
2. Gasket
3. Piston ring
4. Piston
5. Piston pin
6. Retaining rings
7. Bearing
9. Seal
10. Snap ring
11. Crankcase half
12. Dowel pin
13. Gasket
14. Bearing
16. Crankshaft assy.
17. Crankcase half
18. Seal
20. Cover

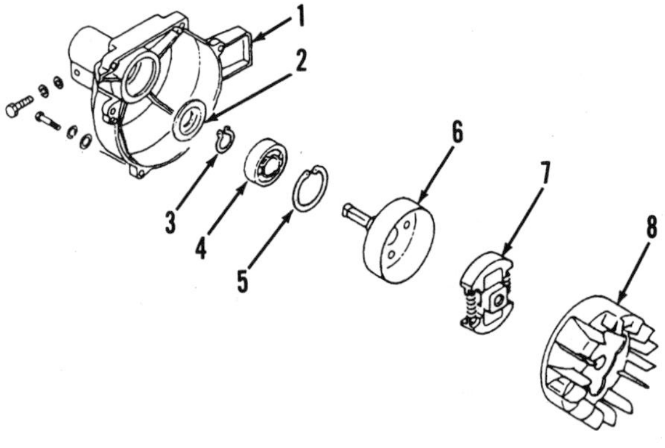

Fig. JD113—Exploded view of clutch used on Model 240. Clutch assembly (7) is also used on Model 210.

1. Housing
2. Washer
3. Snap ring
4. Bearing
5. Snap ring
6. Clutch drum
7. Clutch shoes & hub
8. Flywheel

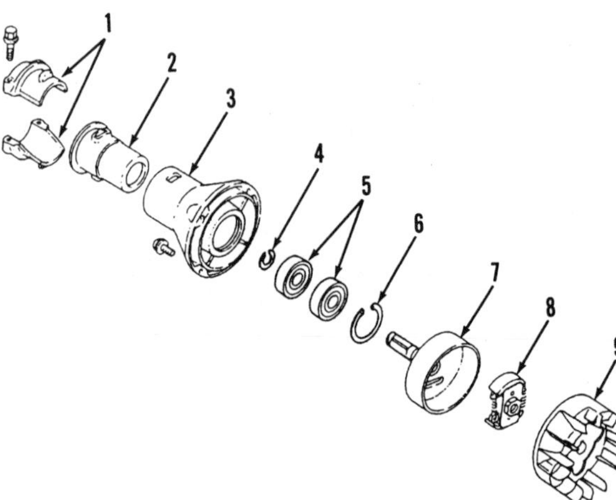

Fig. JD114—Exploded view of clutch used on Model 260.

1. Collar
2. Vibration isolator
3. Housing
4. Snap ring
5. Bearings
6. Snap ring
7. Clutch drum
8. Clutch shoes & hub
9. Flywheel

engine. Remove the cooling shroud and recoil starter. Remove the spark plug and insert a piece of rope or piston stop in the spark plug hole to prevent the engine from turning. Remove the clutch and the nut attaching the flywheel. Use a suitable puller to remove the flywheel. Remove the carburetor, muffler and ignition coil. Remove the screws attaching the cylinder, then pull the cylinder straight up, off the piston. Remove the piston pin retaining rings, push the pin out using a suitable pusher tool, then separate the piston from the connecting rod. On 110, 210, 240 and 260 models, thrust washers are located on both sides of the connecting rod and will be loose when the piston pin is removed.

Install a new cylinder if the end gap of a new ring exceeds 0.5 mm (0.02 in.). Ring side clearance in piston groove should not exceed 0.1 mm (0.004 in.). Piston and rings are available in standard size only.

Piston pin diameter is 8 mm (0.315 in.) for 220, 250 and 300 models; 10 mm (0.394 in.) for 350 and 450 models. Clearance between the piston pin and bore in piston should not exceed 0.03 mm (0.0012 in.). The pin should not be worn more than 0.013 mm (0.0005 in.).

Position the thrust washers (8—Fig. JD109 or Fig. JD111) on each side of the connecting rod of models so equipped. On all models, position the piston on the connecting rod so arrow on top of piston will be toward the exhaust port (muffler) side of cylinder. Lubricate the piston pin and bearing, then install the piston pin. Install new retaining rings (6—Fig. JD109, Fig. JD110, Fig. JD111 or Fig. JD112) if bent or condition is otherwise questionable. Install the retaining rings with the gap toward the top or bottom or the piston.

Make sure the end of each piston ring surrounds the pin located in ring groove. Be careful to install the cylinder straight down over the piston. If the cylinder is turned, the ring can catch in a port and break the end of the ring.

CYLINDER. The piston, rings and cylinder are available in standard size only and the cylinder should not be bored oversize. Inspect the cylinder for any damage and install new parts as necessary. If the chrome plating is worn from the cylinder, a new cylinde should be installed.

CRANKSHAFT, ROD ANI CRANKCASE. The crankshaft an connecting rod are available only as a assembly (16—Fig. JD109, Fig. JD110 Fig. JD111 or Fig. JD112); individua components are not available. The needle bearing (7—Fig. JD110, Fig. JD11 or Fig. JD112) is available separatel on some models.

To remove the crankshaft and connecting rod assembly, remove the cylinder and piston as described in PISTON PIN AND RINGS paragraph. Remove the screws attaching the halves of the crankcase together and separate halves. Heat the crankcase if necessar to remove the main bearings from the crankcase bores. If the bearings stay o the crankshaft, use a suitable puller t pull the bearings from the main journals. Some models may have a sna ring (10—Fig. JD110 or Fig. JD112) installed in the case bore.

The main bearing should turr smoothly with no perceptible play o ratcheting. Connecting rod side clearance should not exceed 0.45 mm (0.01 in.) for Model 300 or 0.4 mm (0.016 in. for other models.

Support the crankshaft at the mai bearings or journals and measure runout at the ends of the crankshaft Measured runout should not exceed 0.05 mm (0.002 in.).

Use a suitable tools to press new main bearings and seals into the crankcase bores. Lips of seals (9 and 18—Fig JD109, Fig. JD110, Fig. JD111 or Fig JD112) should be toward inside o crankcase and should be lubricated before installing the crankshaft.

CLUTCH. Most engines are equipped with a two- or three-shoe clutch. Refer to Fig. JD113, Fig. JD114, Fig. JD115, Fig. JD116, Fig. JD117 and Fig. JD118 for exploded views of the clutches used. The shoe assembly is located at the drive end of the crankshaft and mounted on the flywheel or drive flange. The clutch drum is operates in bearings located in the drive housing.

To remove the clutch drum, reach through slot and detach the snap ring, then pull the clutch drum and bearing from the housing. The drum and housing can be removed more easily if the housing is heated. On Model 210, the drum and housing are available only as a unit assembly and should not be disassembled.

The clutch hub, springs and shoes on Models 240 and 260 are available only as a unit assembly. Clutch shoes on all other models are available only as a set.

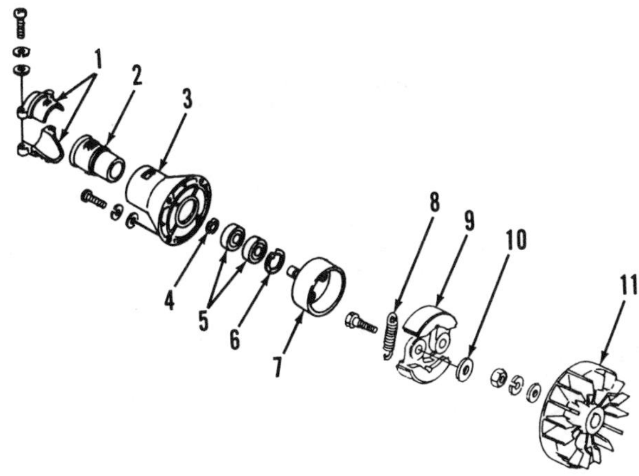

Fig. JD115—Exploded view of clutch used on Model 250 after serial number 030100 and Model 300. Model 220 is similar but is equipped with one bearing (5).

1. Collar
2. Vibration isolator
3. Housing
4. Snap ring
5. Bearings
6. Snap ring
7. Clutch drum
8. Clutch spring
9. Clutch shoes
10. Washer
11. Flywheel

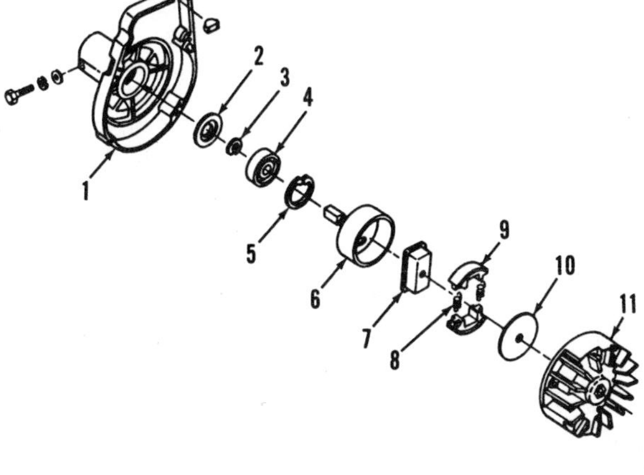

Fig. JD116—Exploded view of clutch used on Model 250 before serial number 030101.

1. Housing
2. Washer
3. Snap ring
4. Bearing
5. Snap ring
6. Clutch drum
7. Hub
8. Spring
9. Clutch shoe
10. Washer

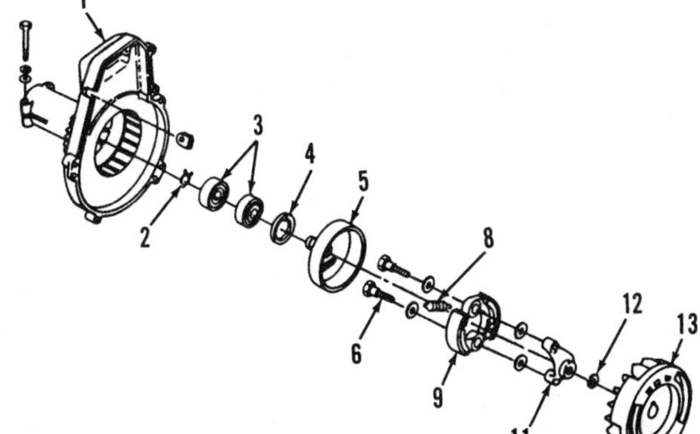

Fig. JD117—Exploded view of clutch used on Model 350.

1. Housing
2. Snap rings
3. Bearings
4. Snap ring
5. Clutch drum
6. Pivot screw
7. Washer
8. Spring
9. Clutch shoe
10. Washer
11. Hub
12. Lockwasher
13. Flywheel

as a unit assembly. Clutch shoes on all other models are available only as a set.

Maximum allowable clutch drum inside diameter is 51.5 mm (2.028 in.) for Models 210, 240, 250 and 260; 55.5 mm (2.185 in.) for Models 220 and 300; 63.5 mm (2.500 in.) for Model 350; 73.5 mm (2.894 in.) for Model 450.

On Model 450, tighten clutch flange (10—Fig. JD118) to 40-44 N•m (30-32 ft.-lb.) torque. Install the clutch so recessed portion of bore in hub (9) is toward flange (10). Tighten screws securing clutch hub and shoe assembly to flange to 3.4-4.5 N•m (30-40 in.-lb.) torque.

On Model 260 and early Model 250, install washer (2—Fig. JD113 or Fig. JD116) so concave side is toward bearing.

REWIND STARTER. Refer to Fig. JD119, Fig. JD120 or Fig. JD121 for an exploded view of typical starters. To disassemble starter, detach starter housing from engine. If rope is intact, remove handle and allow rope pulley to rotate slowly to relieve rewind spring tension. Unscrew center screw and remove rope pulley. Wear appropriate eye protection and gloves before detaching rewind spring from housing as spring may uncoil uncontrolled.

On models with removable pawl (4—Fig. JD119), install pawl in hole of pawl carrier (2). When installing pawl

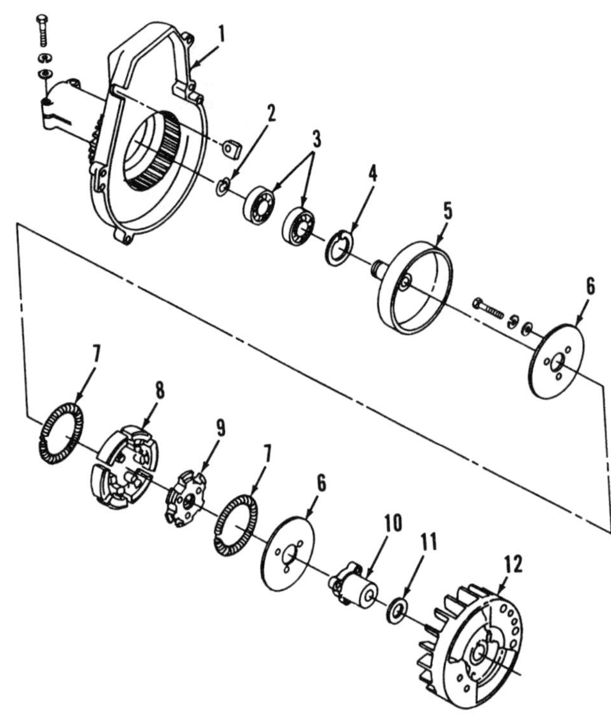

Fig. JD118—Exploded view of clutch used on Model 450.

1. Housing
2. Snap ring
3. Bearings
4. Snap ring
5. Clutch drum
6. Plate
7. Spring
8. Clutch shoe
9. Hub
10. Flange
11. Washer
12. Flywheel

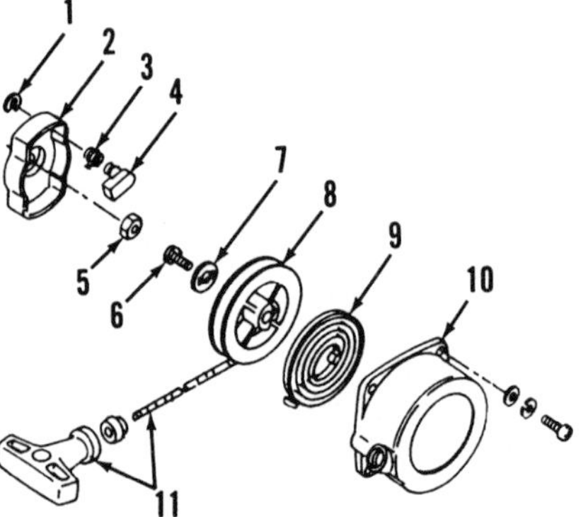

Fig. JD119—Exploded view of rewind starter used on Models 110, 220, 240, 260, 300 and Model 250 after serial number 030100.

1. "E" ring
2. Pawl carrier
3. Spring
4. Pawl
5. Nut
6. Screw
7. Washer
8. Pulley
9. Rewind spring
10. Starter housing
11. Rope & handle

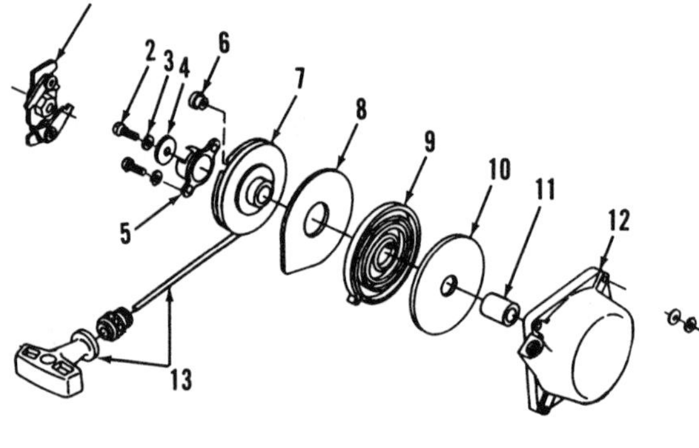

Fig. JD121—Exploded view of rewind starter used on Model 450.

1. Pawl carrier
2. Screw
3. Lockwasher
4. Washer
5. Flange
6. Retainer
7. Pulley
8. Plate
9. Rewind spring
10. Plate
11. Bushing
12. Starter housing
13. Rope & handle

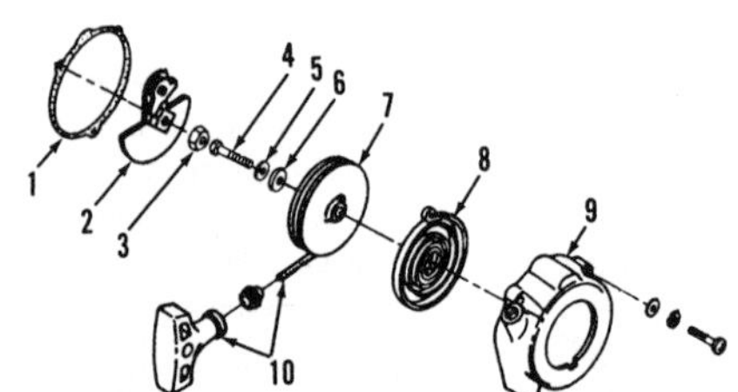

Fig. JD120—Exploded view of rewind starter used on Model 250 before serial number 030101.

1. Gasket
2. Pawl carrier
3. Nut
4. Screw
5. Lockwasher
6. Washer
7. Pulley
8. Rewind spring
9. Starter housing
10. Rope & handle

Tighten pawl carrier to 18 N·m (160 in.-lb.) on Models 350 or 450. On all other models, tighten pawl carrier retaining nut to 18 N·m (160 in.-lbs.).

To assemble starter, lubricate center post of housing and spring side with light grease. Rewind spring is installed with coils wrapped in a counterclockwise direction from outer end. Rope length is 850 mm (33.5 in.). Assemble starter while passing rope through housing rope outlet and attach rope handle to rope. Apply Loctite to center retaining screw.

To place tension on starter rope, pull rope out of housing. Engage rope in notch on pulley and turn pulley counterclockwise three turns. Hold pulley and disengage rope from pulley notch. Release pulley and allow rope to wind on pulley. Check starter operation. Rope handle should be held against housing by spring tension, but it must be possible to rotate pulley at least 1/2 turn against spring tension when rope is pulled out fully.

DEERE

ENGINE SERVICE

Model	Bore	Stroke	Displacement
2E	30 mm (1.18 in.)	30 mm (1.18 in.)	21.2 cc (1.29 cu. in.)
3E	35 mm (1.38 in.)	32.0 mm (1.26 in.)	30.8 cc (1.88 cu. in.)
4E	38 mm (1.50 in.)	35 mm (1.38 in.)	39.7 cc (2.42 cu. in.)
5E	40 mm (1.57 in.)	35 mm (1.38 in.)	44.0 cc (2.68 cu. in.)

ENGINE INFORMATION

These two-stroke, air cooled engines are used on some Deere blowers. Refer to Deere Blower section for engine application.

MAINTENANCE

LUBRICATION. Engine lubrication is obtained by mixing gasoline with an oil designed for two-stroke, air-cooled engines. Refer to BLOWER service section for manufacturer's recommended fuel: oil mixture ratio.

SPARK PLUG. Recommended spark plug for Model 4E engine is Champion CJ8 or equivalent. Recommended spark plug for all other models is Champion CJ7Y, or equivalent. Specified electrode gap is 0.6-0.7 mm (0.024-0.028 in.). Tighten spark plug to 16 N·m (142 in.-lb.).

CARBURETOR. All models are equipped with a variation of the Walbro WA diaphragm-type carburetor. Refer to Fig. JD201 and Fig. JD202. Initial adjustment of idle mixture screw (18—Fig. JD201 or Fig. JD202) is 7/8 turn out from a lightly seated position on Model 5E or 1-1/4 turns out on all other models. Initial adjustment of high-speed mixture screw (17) is 1-1/4 turns out on all models.

Final adjustments are performed with engine at operating temperature and running. Adjust idle speed screw to

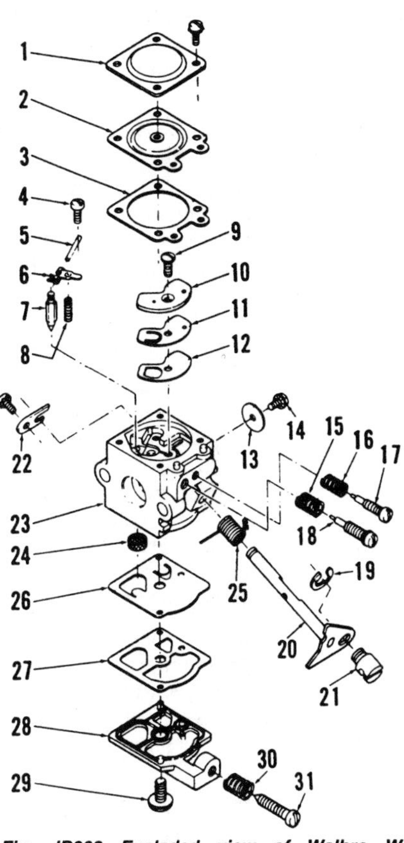

Fig. JD202—Exploded view of Walbro WA carburetor used on Model 4E.

1. Cover
2. Metering diaphragm
3. Gasket
4. Screw
5. Pin
6. Metering lever
7. Fuel inlet valve
8. Spring
9. Screw
10. Circuit plate
11. Check valve
12. Gasket
13. Throttle plate
14. Screw
15. Spring
16. Spring
17. High speed mixture needle
18. Idle mixture needle
19. "E" ring
20. Throttle shaft
21. Swivel
22. Throttle shaft clip
23. Carburetor body
24. Screen
25. Spring
26. Fuel pump diaphragm
27. Gasket
28. Cover
29. Screw
30. Spring
31. Idle speed screw

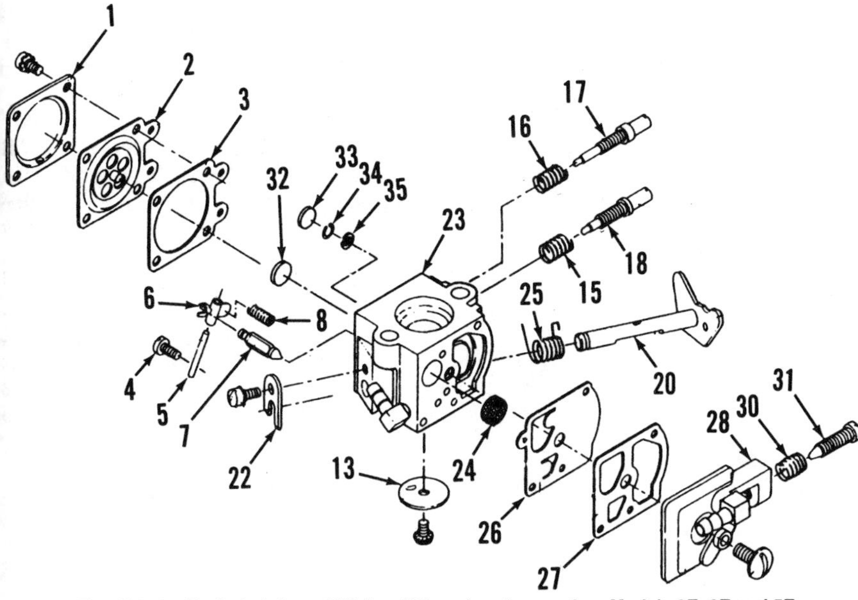

Fig. JD201—Exploded view of Walbro WA carburetor used on Models 2E, 3E and 5E.

1. Cover
2. Metering diaphragm
3. Gasket
4. Screw
5. Pin
6. Metering lever
7. Fuel inlet valve
8. Spring
13. Throttle plate
15. Spring
16. Spring
17. High speed mixture needle
18. Idle mixture needle
20. Throttle shaft
23. Retainer clip
24. Inlet screen
25. Spring
26. Fuel pump diaphragm
27. Gasket
28. Cover
30. Spring
31. Idle speed screw
32. Plug
33. Plug
34. Snap ring
35. Screen

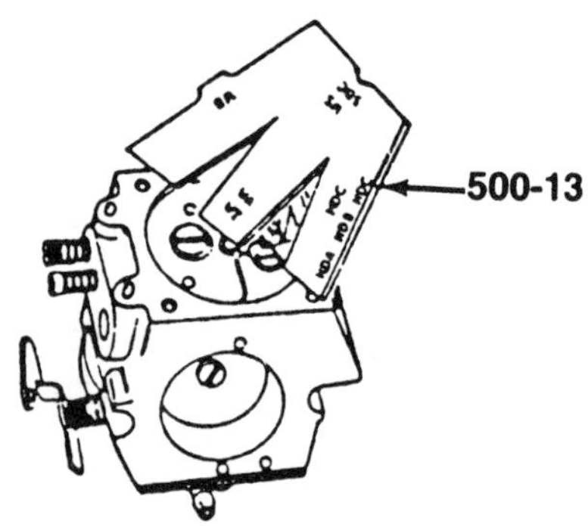

Fig. JD203—Metering lever should just touch leg of Walbro tool 500-13. Bend lever to obtain correct lever height.

approximately 2600 rpm. Adjust idle mixture screw so engine runs at maximum idle speed and accelerates without hesitation. Readjust idle speed. Operate unit at full throttle (no-load) and adjust high-speed mixture screw to obtain maximum engine rpm, then turn counterclockwise until engine just starts to "four-cycle."

When overhauling carburetor, refer to exploded view in Fig. JD201 or Fig. JD202 and remove covers (1 and 28) for access to internal components. Remove diaphragms, metering lever (6) and fuel inlet valve (7), fuel screen (24) and fuel mixture screws (17 and 18).

Clean carburetor using suitable solvent and compressed air. Do not use drills or wires to clean orifices. Examine fuel inlet valve and seat. Inlet valve is renewable, but carburetor body must be renewed if seat is excessively worn or damaged. Inspect mixture screws and seats. Renew carburetor body if seats are excessively worn or damaged. Clean fuel screen. Inspect diaphragms for tears and other damage.

When reassembling, check metering lever height as shown in Fig. JD203 using Walbro tool 500-13. Metering lever should just touch leg on tool. Bend lever to obtain correct lever height.

IGNITION SYSTEM. The engine is equipped with an electronic ignition system that used a separate ignition module and ignition coil. Ignition system performance is considered satisfactory if a spark will jump across a 3 mm (1/8 in.) electrode gap on a test spark plug. If no spark is produced, check on/off switch, wiring and ignition module air gap. Ignition module air gap should be 0.3-0.4 mm (0.012-0.016 in.). If switch, wiring and module air gap are satisfactory, but spark is not present, refer to REPAIRS section and check service specifications.

REPAIRS

COMPRESSION PRESSURE. For optimum performance, cylinder compression pressure should be 689 kPa (100 psi) on Models 2E and 5E, 640 kPa (93 psi) on Model 3E, or 586 kPa (85 psi) on Models 4E.

TIGHTENING TORQUE. Recommended tightening torque values are as follows:

Carburetor . . . . 4 N·m (35 in.-lb.)

Crankcase
- 4E . . . . 9-11 N·m (80-97 in.-lb.)
- All other models . . . . 3.6 N·m (32 in.-lb.)

Cylinder:
- 4E . . . . 9-11 N·m (80-97 in.-lb.)
- All other models . . . . 7.9 N·m (70 in.-lb.)

Fan:
- 2E . . . . 15-20 N·m (133-177 in.-lb.)
- 3E & 5E . . . . 30 N·m (22 ft.-lb.)
- 4E . . . . 3.5-4.0 N·m (31-35 in.-lb.)

Flywheel:
- 2E . . . . 12-14 N·m (106-124 in.-lb.)
- 4E . . . . 39.5-44 N·m (29-32 ft.-lb.)

Ignition module:
- 2E, 3E & 5E . . . . 2 N·m (18 in.-lb.)
- 4E . . . . 3.5-4.0 N·m (31-35 in.-lb.)

Spark plug . . . . 16 N·m (142 in.-lb.)

Starter pawl plate:
- 3E & 5E . . . . 18 N·m (159 in.-lb.)
- 4E . . . . 20-24 N·m (177-212 in.-lb.)

IGNITION. When checking for faulty ignition module, replace the ignition module with a module known to be good. If ignition is then satisfactory, module is faulty. To check the ignition coil, refer to following resistance specifications (values are in ohms). Primary resistance is not measured on Model 2E, substitute a known good coil if faulty ignition coil is suspected.

	Primary	Secondary
2E	1500-3000	
3E & 5E	0.0-0.05	1500-3000
4E	0.0-0.2	500-1500

PISTON, PIN AND RINGS. Refer to Fig. JD204, Fig. JD205 or Fig. JD206 for exploded view of engine assembly. Piston and rings are available in standard size only. To remove and install piston refer to CRANKSHAFT CONNECTING ROD AND CRANKCASE section.

Use a feeler gage to measure piston ring side clearance with new ring installed in piston ring groove. Maximum allowable piston ring side clearance is 0.1 mm (0.004 in.). Renew piston if clearance is excessive.

Renew piston pin of piston pin is worn more than 0.013 mm (0.0005 in.). Maximum allowable piston pin clearance is 0.03 mm (0.001 in.).

When installing piston, position piston on rod so arrow on piston crown is toward exhaust port. Be sure piston ring gap properly surrounds locating pin in ring groove.

CYLINDER. The cylinder is available only in standard size and cannot be bored. The cylinder bore is plated. Inspect cylinder for excessive wear and damage.

CRANKSHAFT, ROD AND CRANKCASE. Refer to Fig. JD204, Fig. JD205 or Fig. JD206 for exploded

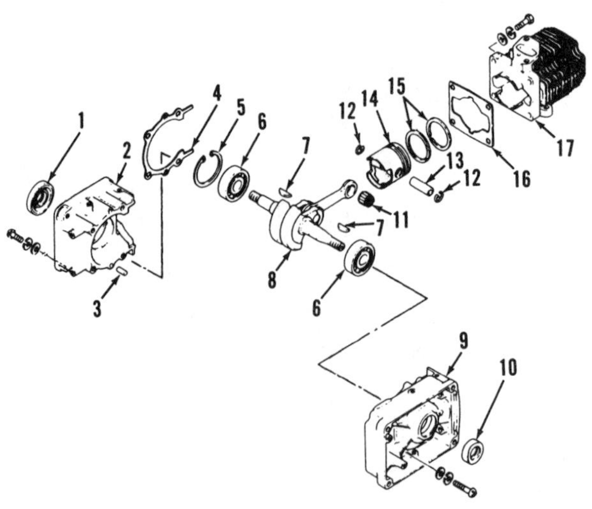

Fig. JD204—Exploded view of Model 2E engine.

1. Seal
2. Crankcase half
3. Dowel pin
4. Gasket
5. Snap ring
6. Bearing
7. Key
8. Crankshaft & connecting rod
9. Crankcase half
10. Seal
11. Bearing
12. Snap ring
13. Piston pin
14. Piston
15. Piston rings
16. Gasket
17. Cylinder

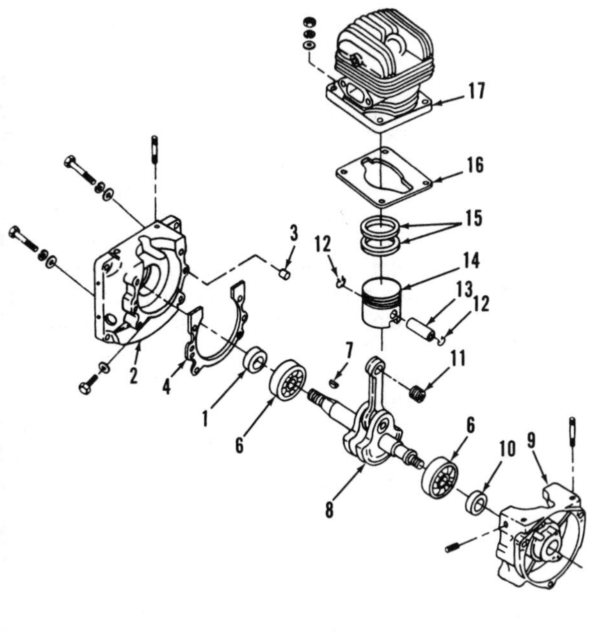

Fig. JD205—Exploded view of Model 4E engine. Refer to Fig. JD204 for parts identification.

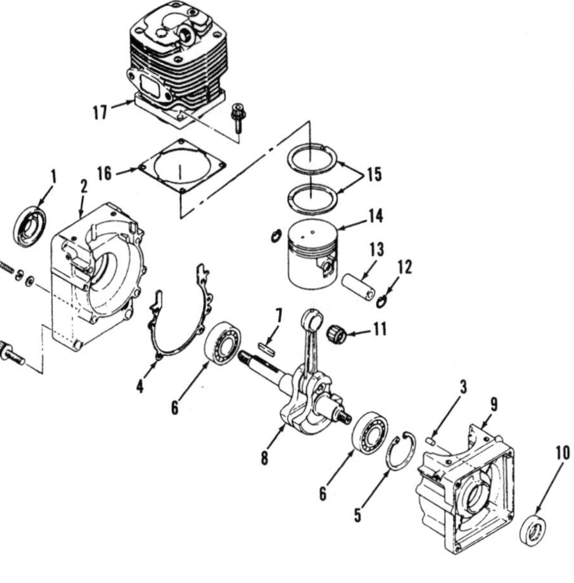

Fig. JD206—Exploded view of Models 5E engine. Model 3E engine is similar. Refer to Fig. JD204 for parts identification.

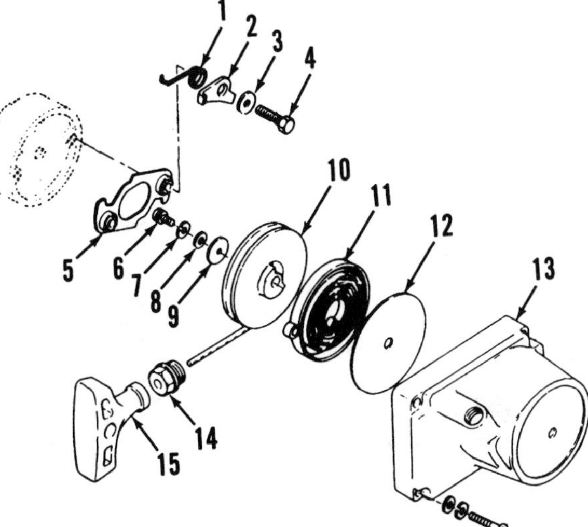

Fig. JD207—Exploded view of rewind starter used on Model 2E.

1. Spring
2. Pawl
3. Washer
4. Screw
5. Pawl carrier
6. Screw
7. Lockwasher
8. Washer
9. Washer
10. Pulley
11. Rewind spring
12. Plate
13. Starter housing
14. Rope guide
15. Rope handle

view of engine assembly. The crankshaft and connecting rod are a unit assembly; individual components are not available. The connecting rod small end is equipped with a renewable needle bearing on some models.

To remove crankshaft and connecting rod, unbolt and remove recoil starter, engine cover (if used), fuel tank, air cleaner, carburetor, muffler and ignition coil. Remove cylinder cover and back pack frame. Remove spark plug and place the end of a rope into cylinder to prevent crankshaft from turning. Remove nuts retaining fan and flywheel and remove both from crankshaft. Unbolt and separate crankcase from blower housing.

Scribe a line on the cylinder base and one of the crankcase halves to ensure correct reassembly, then unbolt and remove cylinder from crankcase. Remove piston pin retaining rings, then push piston pin out of piston and connecting rod. If piston pin cannot be removed by hand, use JDZ-23 piston pin tool, or similar tool, to push pin out of piston.

Remove crankcase screws and separate crankcase halves by tapping end of crankshaft with a rubber mallet. Some models are equipped with a snap ring next to one of the main bearings. The main bearings usually stay in the crankcase halves. If main bearings remain on crankshaft, use a suitable puller or press to remove main bearings.

Renew crankshaft assembly if rod big end side clearance exceeds 0.4 mm (0.016 in.). Maximum allowable crankshaft runout is 0.05 mm (0.002 in.) measured at crankshaft ends with crankshaft supported at main bearings.

When installing new main bearings, do not use any type of sealant between outer race of baring and crankcase bore. Lubricate all parts with 2-cycle engine oil during assembly. Be sure that crankshaft rotates freely after crankcase screws are tightened.

Piston must be installed with arrow on crown pointing toward exhaust side of engine. Be sure that piston ring end gaps are positioned around pins in piston ring groove. Compress piston rings with fingertips and slide cylinder over piston. Do not rotate cylinder when placing it over piston as ring gap may become disengaged from locating pin and damage cylinder.

Adjust air gap between ignition module laminations and flywheel magnets to 0.3-0.4 mm (0.012-0.016 in.). Complete reassembly by reversing disassembly procedure.

REWIND STARTER. Model 2E. Refer to Fig. JD207 for an exploded view of starter. To disassemble starter,

Fig. JD208—Assemble pawls (P) on Model 2E as shown.

detach starter housing from engine. If rope is not broken, remove rope handle and allow rope to wind into starter to relieve spring tension. Unscrew center screw (6) and remove rope pulley (10). Wear appropriate eye protection and gloves before detaching rewind spring from housing as spring may uncoil uncontrolled.

Install pawl assemblies as shown in Fig. JD208. Apply Loctite to threads of pawl screws and tighten to 3.4-4.5 N•m (30-40 in.-lb.). Prior to assembling starter, lubricate center post of housing and spring side with light grease. Rewind spring is installed with coils wrapped in a counterclockwise direction from outer end. Rope length is 850 mm (33.5 in.). Assemble starter while passing rope through housing rope outlet and attach rope handle to rope. Apply Loctite to center retaining screw.

To place tension on starter rope, pull rope out of housing. Engage rope in notch on pulley and turn pulley counterclockwise three turns. Hold pulley and disengage rope from pulley notch. Release pulley and allow rope to wind on pulley. Check starter operation. Rope handle should be held against housing by spring tension, but it must be possible to rotate pulley at least 1/2 turn against spring tension when rope is pulled out fully.

Model 3E. Refer to Fig. JD209 for an exploded view of starter. To disassemble starter, detach starter housing (13) from engine. If rope is not broken, remove rope handle and allow rope to wind into starter to relieve spring tension. Unscrew center screw (8) and remove rope pulley (10). Wear appropriate eye protection and gloves before detaching rewind spring from housing as spring may uncoil uncontrolled.

Pawl plate (6—Fig. JD209) and retaining nut (7) have left-hand threads. Install pawl assemblies (2) as shown in Fig. JD210. Apply Loctite to threads of pawl screws (4) and tighten to 3.5-4.5

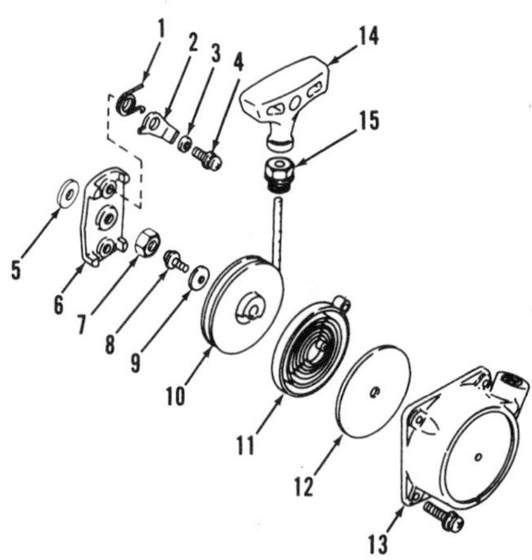

Fig. JD209—Exploded view of rewind starter used on Model 3E.

1. Spring
2. Pawl
3. Spacer
4. Screw
5. Washer
6. Pawl carrier
7. Nut
8. Screw
9. Washer
10. Pulley
11. Rewind spring
12. Plate
13. Starter housing
14. Rope handle
15. Rope guide

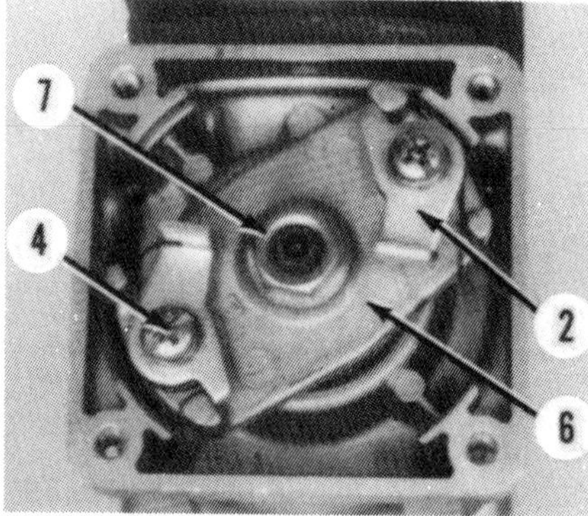

Fig. JD210—Assemble pawls on Model 3E as shown. Nut (7) and pawl carrier (6) have left-hand threads.

N•m (30-40 in.-lb.). Tighten pawl plate to 8-10 N•m (71-88 in.-lb.). Tighten retaining nut to 16-20 N•m (142-0177 in.-lb.).

Prior to assembling starter, lubricate center post of housing and spring side with light grease. Rewind spring is installed with coils wrapped in a clockwise direction from outer end. Rope length is 850 mm (33.5 in.). Assemble starter while passing rope through housing rope outlet and attach rope handle to rope. Apply Loctite to center retaining screw.

To place tension on starter rope, pull rope out of housing. Engage rope in notch on pulley and turn pulley clockwise three turns. Hold pulley and disengage rope from pulley notch. Release pulley and allow rope to wind on pulley. Check starter operation. Rope handle should be held against housing by spring tension, but it must be possible to rotate pulley at least 1/2 turn against spring tension when rope is pulled out fully.

Model 4E. Refer to Fig. JD211 for an exploded view of starter. To disassemble starter, detach starter housing (12) from engine. If rope is not broken, remove rope handle and allow rope to wind into starter to relieve spring tension. Unscrew center screw (4) and remove rope pulley (9). Wear appropriate eye protection and gloves before detaching rewind spring from housing as spring may uncoil uncontrolled.

Prior to assembling starter, lubricate center post of housing and side of spring with light grease. Rewind spring is installed with coils wrapped in a counterclockwise direction from outer end. Rope length is 950 mm (37.5 in.). Install pawl spring (7—Fig. JD212) on friction plate (5) so short end of spring engages tab (T) on plate. Install pawls (6) in pulley as shown in Fig. JD212. Tighten pawl plate to 8-10 N•m (71-88 in.-lb.). Position spring (8) over center post of starter housing. Be sure rope is located in notch (N). Install friction plate (5), placing long end of spring (7) into hole (H) in pulley. Apply Loctite to center retaining screw openings in fric-

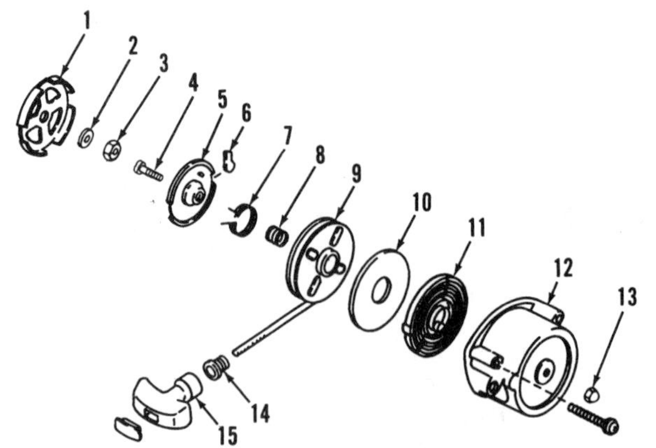

Fig. JD211—Exploded view of rewind starter used on Model 4E.

1. Pawl plate
2. Washer
3. Nut
4. Screw
5. Friction plate
6. Pawl
7. Spring
8. Spring
9. Pulley
10. Plate
11. Rewind spring
12. Starter housing
13. Acorn nut
14. Rope guide
15. Rope handle

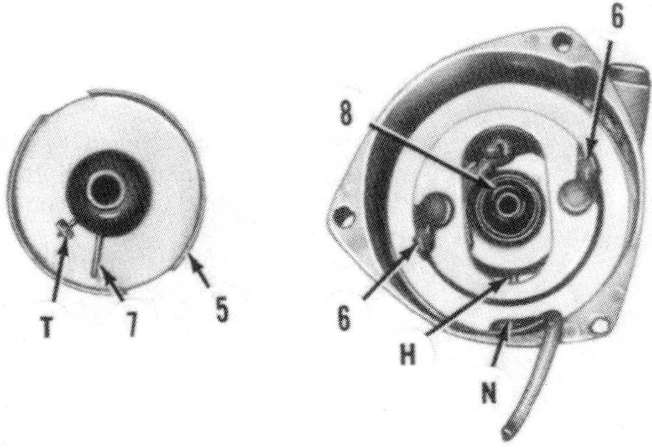

Fig. JD212—On Model 4E, insert short end of spring (7) in tab (T) on friction plate (5). Note installation of pawls (6) on pulley.

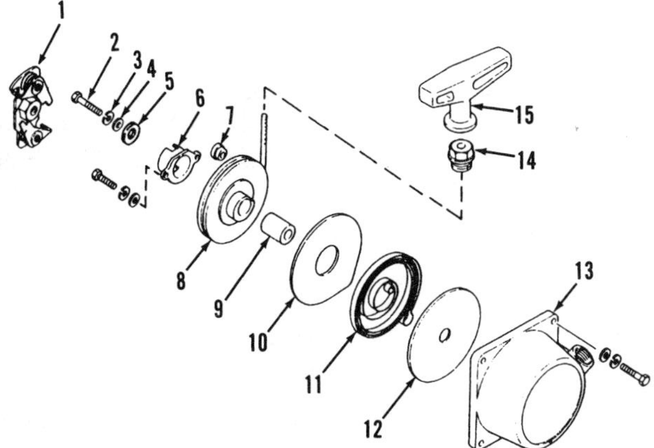

Fig. JD213—Exploded view of rewind starter used on Model 5E.

1. Pawl carrier
2. Screw
3. Lockwasher
4. Washer
5. Washer
6. Flange
7. Retainer
8. Pulley
9. Bushing
10. Plate
11. Rewind spring
12. Plate
13. Starter housing
14. Rope guide
15. Rope handle

tion plate, then install acorn nut (13—Fig. JD211).

To place tension on starter rope, pull rope out of housing. Engage rope in notch on pulley and turn pulley counterclockwise three turns. Hold pulley and disengage rope from pulley notch. Release pulley and allow rope to wind on pulley. Check starter operation. Rope handle should be held against housing by spring tension, but it must be possible to rotate pulley at least 1/2 turn against spring tension when rope is pulled out fully.

Model 5E. Refer to Fig. JD213 for a exploded view of starter. To disassemble starter, detach starter housing from engine. If rope is not broken, remove rope handle and allow rope to wind into starter to relieve spring tension. Unscrew center screw and remove rope pulley. Wear appropriate eye protection and gloves before detaching rewind spring from housing as spring may uncoil uncontrolled. Tighten pawl carrier to 18 N•m (160 in.-lb.).

Prior to assembling starter, lubricate center post of housing and spring side with length grease. Rewind spring is installed with coils wrapped in a clockwise direction from outer end. Rope length is 850 mm (33.5 in.). Assemble starter while passing rope through housing rope outlet and attach rope handle to rope. Apply Loctite to center retaining screw. To place tension on starter rope, pull rope out of housing. Engage rope in notch pulley and turn pulley clockwise three turns. Hold pulley and disengage rope from pulley notch. Release pulley and allow rope to wind on pulley.

Check starter operation. Rope handle should be held against housing by spring tension but it must be possible to rotate pulley at least 1/2 turn against spring tension when rope is pulled out fully.

DEERE
ENGINE SERVICE

Model	Bore	Stroke	Displacement
21C & 21S	32 mm (1.26 in.)	26 mm (1.02 in.)	21.2 cc (1.29 cu. in.)
25S	32.2 mm (1.268 in.)	30.0 mm (1.181 in.)	24.4 cc (1.49 cu. in.)
30S	36.0 mm (1.417 in.)	30.0 mm (1.181 in.)	30.5 cc (1.861 cu. in.)
38B	38.0 mm (1.496 in.)	33.0 mm (1.299 in.)	37.4 cc (2.284 cu. in.)

ENGINE INFORMATION

These two-stroke, air cooled engines are used on some Deere trimmers and brush cutters. Refer to Deere Trimmer section for engine application.

MAINTENANCE

LUBRICATION. The engine is lubricated by mixing oil with the gasoline fuel. John Deere 2-Cycle Engine Oil, 50:1 mix is recommended. Also approved for use are 2-cycle oils containing ashless-type additives and certified by BIA for Service TC-W, mixed at 32:1. Do not use automotive type oils.

SPARK PLUG. The recommended spark plug for normal application is Champion BPM7A, BPMR7A, CJ7Y, RCJ7Y or equivalent. The electrode gap should be 0-6-0.7 mm (0.024-0.028 in.). Tighten the spark plug securely to the torque listed in the TIGHTENING TORQUE paragraph.

CARBURETOR. The engines are equipped with the following Zama C1U series carburetors:

Models 21C and 21S . . Zama C1U-K19
Model 25S . . . . Zama C1U-K20
Model 30S . . . . Zama C1U-K21
Model 38B . . . . Zama C1U-K22

The manufacturer's name and model number is stamped on the carburetor. To remove carburetor, disconnect fuel line and throttle cable. Remove air cleaner assembly, mounting screws, carburetor and insulator. When installing, tighten insulator and carburetor mounting screws to 4.5 N•m (40 in.-lb.). Adjust throttle cable jam nuts so throttle lever contacts slow idle screw when throttle trigger is released. When throttle trigger is squeezed, carburetor throttle lever should be fully open. Note that additional adjustment can be obtained on Model 38B by loosening cable clamp on handlebar and sliding cable to lengthen or shorten wire cable.

Initial adjustment of the fuel mixture screws is as follows: Lightly seat slow idle speed mixture screw (15—Fig. JD301), then back out 1-1/8 turn for Models 21C, 21S and 25S or one turn for Models 30S and 38B. Lightly seat high speed mixture screw (17), then back out 1-1/8 turns for Models 21C and 21S; back out 1-1/4 turns for Model 30S; back out 1-1/8 turns for Model 38B. The settings of these mixture screws is critical to the operation of the engine. Final adjustment should be performed carefully to insure easy starting and maximum performance.

To adjust the mixture screws, first remove and clean the air filter, then reinstall it. If necessary, turn each of the mixture screws (15 and 17) clockwise until seated lightly, then back the screws out (counterclockwise) to recommended settings listed above to provide the initial adjustment so the engine can be started. Start the engine and allow it to run until it reaches normal operating temperature. Turn the idle speed stop screw (27) so the engine idles at about 2800-3000 rpm. Adjust the idle mixture needle (15) so the engine idles smoothly and accelerates without hesitation. Readjust the idle speed stop screw (27) if necessary to slow the idle speed. The trimmer head should not turn when the engine is idling. Adjust the high-speed mixture screw (17) until there is a slight "four-cycle" exhaust sound at full throttle with no load. This slightly rich mixture should provide the best performance while operating at maximum speed under load. The engine may be damaged if the high-speed screw is set too lean. Turning the high-speed mixture screw clockwise leans the mixture and turning it counterclockwise enriches the mixture.

To disassemble the carburetor, refer to Fig. JD301 and remove metering diaphragm cover (1) and primer pump

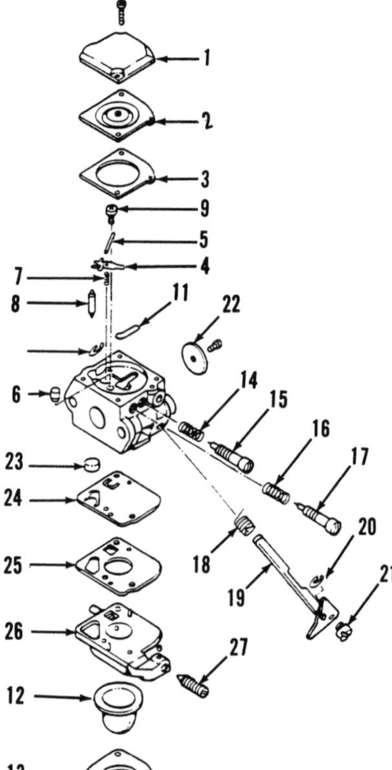

Fig. JD301—Exploded view of Zama carburetor typical of the type used.

1. Cover
2. Metering diaphragm
3. Gasket
4. Metering lever
5. Pin
6. Nozzle
7. Spring
8. Fuel inlet valve
9. Screw
10. "E" ring
11. Welch plug
12. Primer pump
13. Retainer
14. Spring
15. Low-speed mixture screw
16. Spring
17. High-speed mixture screw
18. Spring
19. Throttle shaft
20. "E" ring
21. Swivel
22. Throttle plate
23. Fuel inlet screen
24. Fuel pump diaphragm
25. Gasket
26. Cover
27. Idle speed screw

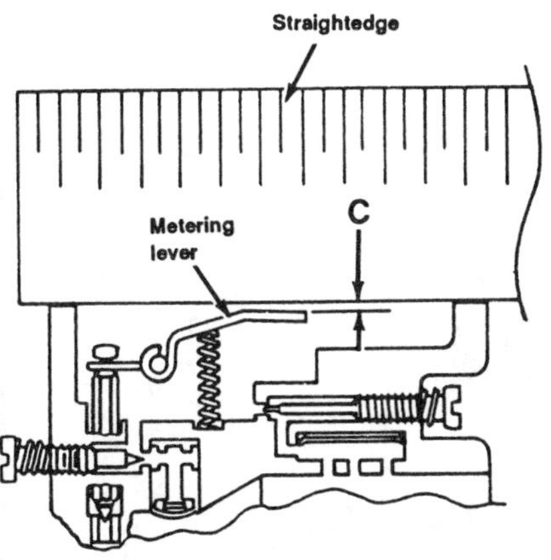

Fig. JD302—On Zama models, the metering lever should have 0-0.3 mm (0-0.012 in.) clearance when measured as shown.

housing (26). Remove metering lever (4), spring (7) and fuel inlet valve (8). Remove high and low speed mixture screws. Remove fuel inlet screen (23). It is not necessary to remove throttle shaft (19) and plate (22) unless wear or damage is evident.

Clean and inspect all components. If the unit has been improperly stored, passages may be clogged with deposits that are hard, solid and nearly transparent. Spray carburetor cleaner through all passages. Be careful not to damage the openings or sealing surfaces while cleaning. Check the condition of diaphragms (2 and 24) carefully. Renew diaphragm if hard (not flexible), torn or otherwise damaged. Examine the fuel inlet valve (8), spring (7) and lever (4). A new fuel inlet valve needle (8), and mixture screws (15 and 17) can be installed, but their seats cannot be serviced if damaged. To remove Welch plug (11), carefully pierce the plug near the end of the "tail" section, then pry the plug out. Do not insert the punch too deeply or the body and passages under the plug may be damaged. Apply sealant to outer edge of new plug, then press plug in until flush with metering chamber surface.

Check the height of the metering lever as shown in Fig. JD302. The clearance (C) between the metering lever and a straightedge positioned across the gasket surface of the carburetor body should be 0-0.012 in. (0-0.3 mm). Carefully bend the lever if necessary to obtain the correct lever height.

IGNITION SYSTEM. All engines are equipped with an electronic ignition system that does not use breaker points. On some models including 30S, the ignition module is separate from the ignition coil. On most models, the module is incorporated in the coil assembly.

Ignition can be considered satisfactory if a spark will jump across the 3 mm (1/8 in.) electrode gap of a test plug when the engine is turned with the recoil starter. If there is no spark, check the stop switch and connecting wire for shorts to ground. Ignition may be irregular at starting speeds if gap between the legs of the coil core and the flywheel magnets is too wide. Specified gap is 0.2-0.3 mm (0.008-0.012 in.). Refer to the IGNITION paragraphs in the REPAIRS section for testing the ignition coil.

REPAIRS

COMPRESSION PRESSURE. Cylinder compression pressure should be checked with the carburetor choke and throttle wide open. Check the compression pressure several times to make sure that indicated pressure is correct. For optimum performance, cylinder compression pressure should be as follows.

Models 21C & 21S . . 862 kPa (125 psi)
Model 25S. . . . . 538 kPa (78 psi)
Models 30S & 38B . . 689 kPa (100 psi)

TIGHTENING TORQUES. Recommend tightening torques are as follows.

Carburetor
21C & 21S . . . . 3.4-4.5 N•m (30-40 in.-lb.)
25S & 30S . . 3.4-4 N•m (30-35 in.-lb.)
38B . . . . 4-5 N•m (35-45 in.-lb.)
Carburetor insulator
21C, 21S, 25S, 30S & 38B. . . . . 4.5 N•m (40 in.-lb.)
Clutch shoes
21C & 21S . . . . 18-20 N•m (160-175 in.-lb.)
Crankcase
21C & 21S . . . . 3.4-4.5 N•m (30-40 in.-lb.)
25S & 30S . . 3.4-4 N•m (30-35 in.-lb.)
38B . . . . 8-9 N•m (70-80 in.-lb.)
Cylinder
21C & 21S . . . . 7.3-8.5 N•m (65-75 in.-lb.)
25S, 30S & 38B . . . . 8-9 N•m (70-80 in.-lb.)
Flywheel
21C & 21S . . . . 18-20 N•m (160-175 in.-lb.)
25S & 30S (clutch shoe hub) . . . 10.7-13 N•m (95-115 in.-lb.)
Flywheel cover
21C & 21S . . 2-2.5 N•m (17-22 in.-lb.)
25S & 30S . . 2.8-4 N•m (25-35 in.-lb.)
38B. . . . . 7-8.5 N•m (65-75 in.-lb.)
Ignition module
21C & 21S . . 2-2.5 N•m (17-22 in.-lb.)
25S. . . . . 3.4-4 N•m (30-35 in.-lb.)
30S . . . .
38B. . . . . 4-4.5 N•m (35-40 in.-lb.)
Muffler
21C & 21S . . . . 5.7-6.2 N•m (50-55 in.-lb.)
25S & 30S . . . . 3.4-4.0 N•m (30-35 in.-lb.)
38B . . . . 8-9 N•m (70-80 in.-lb.)
Muffler cover
25S, 30S & 38B . . . . 1.4-2 N•m (12-17 in.-lb.)
Pawl carrier
21C, 21S, 25S, 30S & 38B . . . . . 8-10 N•m (70-90 in.-lb.)
Pawl carrier lock nut
21C & 21S . . . . 16-20 N•m (140-175 in.-lb.)
25S, 30S & 38B . . . . 16-17.5 N•m (140-155 in.-lb.)
Spark plug. . . . . 16-17 N•m (130-150 in.-lb.)

IGNITION. The ignition primary windings and triggering components in the module can be tested by installing one known to be good to determine the condition of the original unit. If the condition is corrected by installing a good coil/module the original unit should be considered faulty. The ignition coil secondary winding can be tested using an accurate ohmmeter. Compare the measured resistance with the following specifications.

Model	Secondary winding
21C & 21S	1,000-2,000 ohms
25S	1,500-2,500 ohms
30S	9,000-11,000 ohms
38B	1,000-1,500 ohms

PISTON, PIN AND RINGS. To remove the piston (4—Fig. JD303, Fig. JD304, Fig. JD305 or Fig. JD306), separate the drive shaft housing from the engine. Remove covers and the recoil starter. Remove the spark plug and insert a piece of rope or a piston stop in the spark plug hole to prevent the crankshaft from turning. Remove the clutch and the nut attaching the flywheel. Use a suitable puller to remove the flywheel. Remove the carburetor, muffler and ignition coil. Remove the screws attaching the cylinder, then pull the cylinder (1) straight up, off the piston. Remove the piston pin retaining rings (6), push the pin (5) out using a suitable pusher tool, then separate the piston from the connecting rod. Thrust washers (8) are located on both sides of the connecting rod of most models. The thrust washers will be loose when the piston pin is removed.

Install a new cylinder if the end gap of a new ring exceeds 0.5 mm (0.02 in.). Ring side clearance in piston groove should not exceed 0.1 mm (0.004 in.). Piston and rings are available in standard size only.

Clearance between the piston pin and bore in piston should not exceed

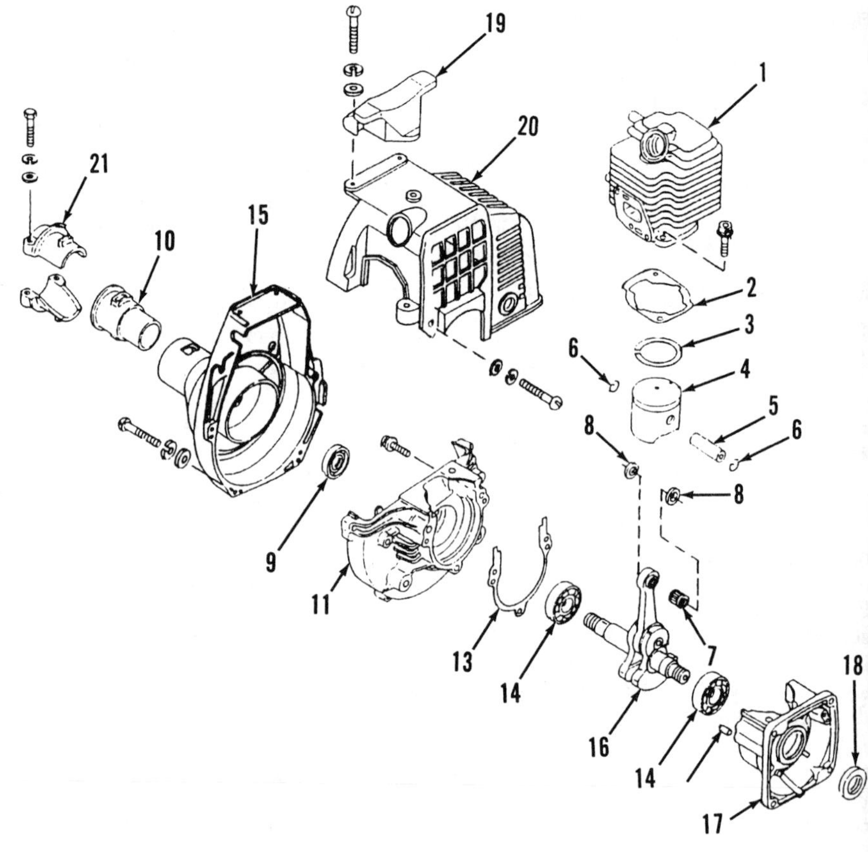

Fig. JD303—Exploded view of engine typical of 21C and 21S models.

1. Cylinder
2. Gasket
3. Piston ring
4. Piston
5. Piston pin
6. Retaining ring
7. Bearing
8. Thrust washers
9. Seal
10. Cushion
11. Crankcase half
12. Dowel pin
13. Gasket
14. Main bearings
15. Clutch cover
16. Crankshaft/connecting rod assy.
17. Crankcase half
18. Seal
19. Guard
20. Cover
21. Clamp adapter

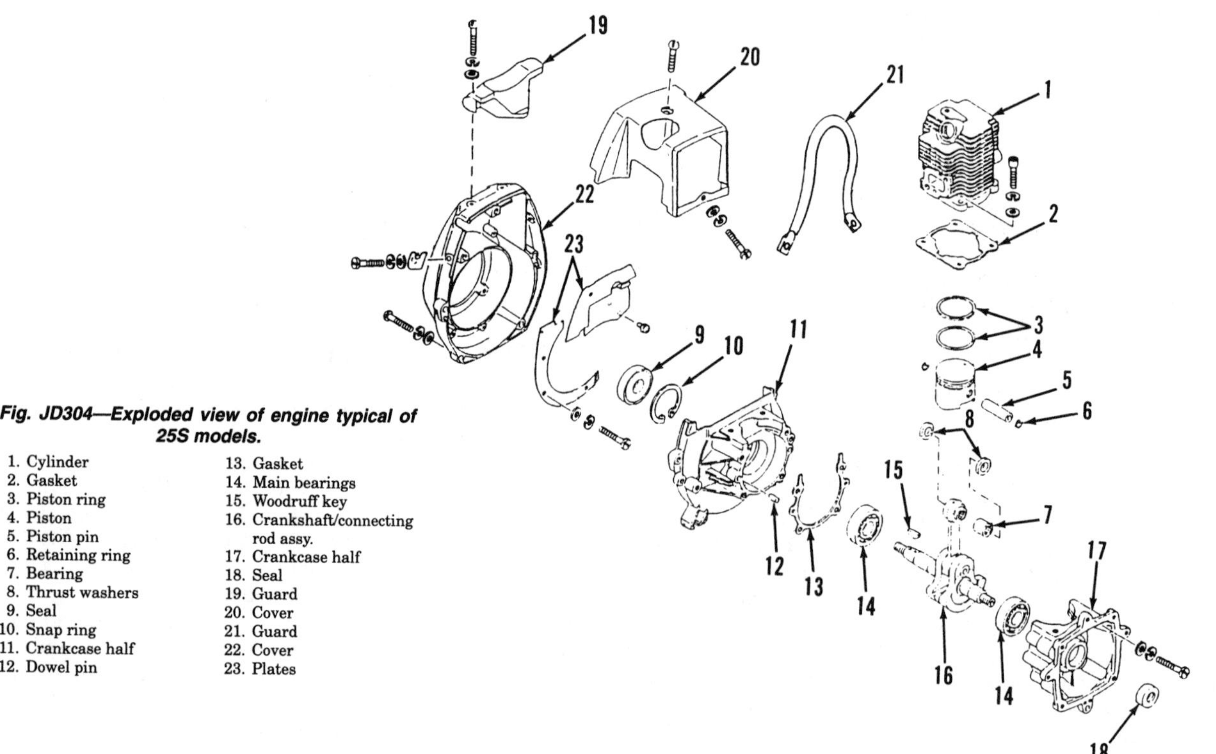

Fig. JD304—Exploded view of engine typical of 25S models.

1. Cylinder
2. Gasket
3. Piston ring
4. Piston
5. Piston pin
6. Retaining ring
7. Bearing
8. Thrust washers
9. Seal
10. Snap ring
11. Crankcase half
12. Dowel pin
13. Gasket
14. Main bearings
15. Woodruff key
16. Crankshaft/connecting rod assy.
17. Crankcase half
18. Seal
19. Guard
20. Cover
21. Guard
22. Cover
23. Plates

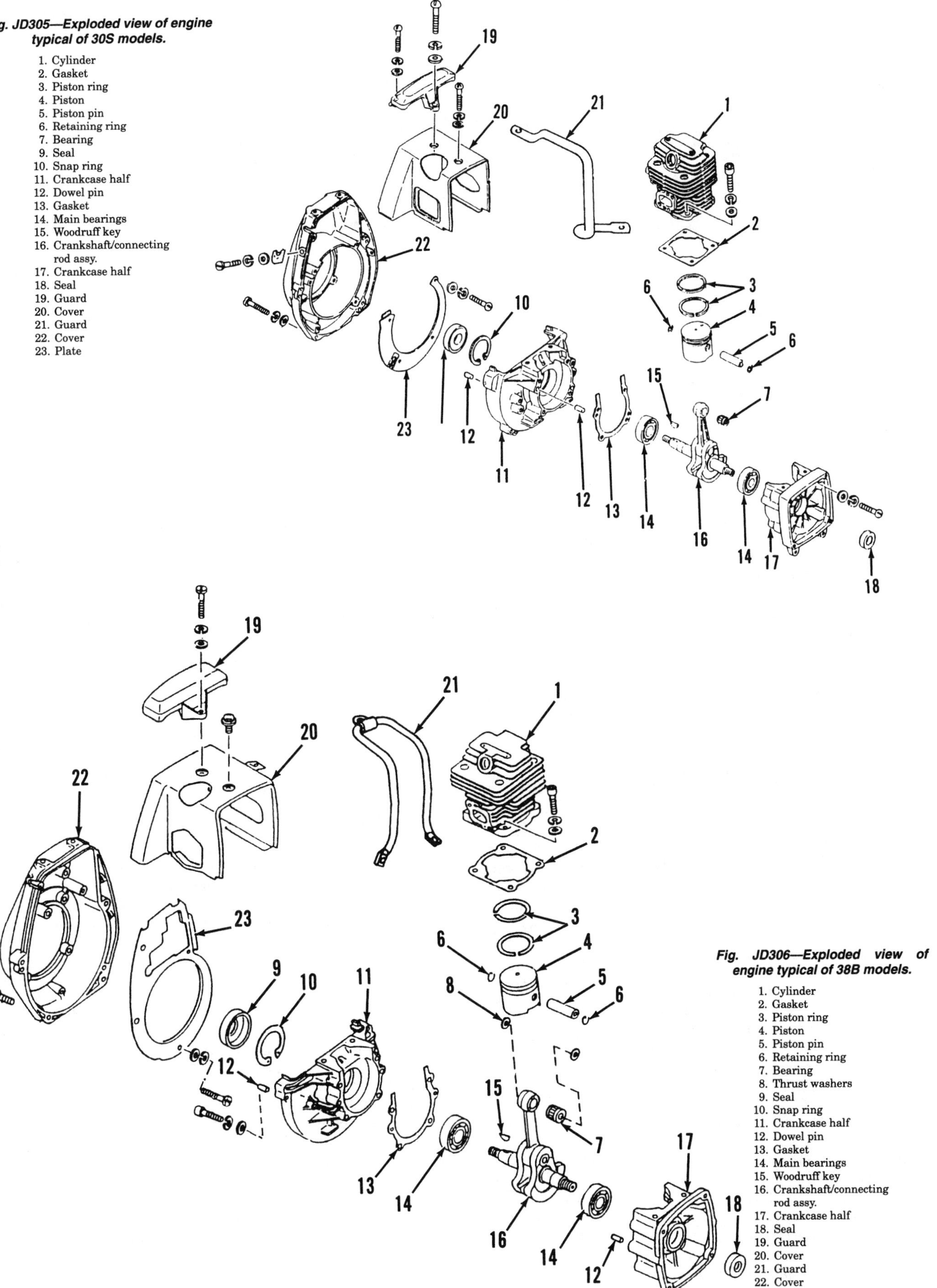

Fig. JD305—Exploded view of engine typical of 30S models.

1. Cylinder
2. Gasket
3. Piston ring
4. Piston
5. Piston pin
6. Retaining ring
7. Bearing
9. Seal
10. Snap ring
11. Crankcase half
12. Dowel pin
13. Gasket
14. Main bearings
15. Woodruff key
16. Crankshaft/connecting rod assy.
17. Crankcase half
18. Seal
19. Guard
20. Cover
21. Guard
22. Cover
23. Plate

Fig. JD306—Exploded view of engine typical of 38B models.

1. Cylinder
2. Gasket
3. Piston ring
4. Piston
5. Piston pin
6. Retaining ring
7. Bearing
8. Thrust washers
9. Seal
10. Snap ring
11. Crankcase half
12. Dowel pin
13. Gasket
14. Main bearings
15. Woodruff key
16. Crankshaft/connecting rod assy.
17. Crankcase half
18. Seal
19. Guard
20. Cover
21. Guard
22. Cover
23. Plate

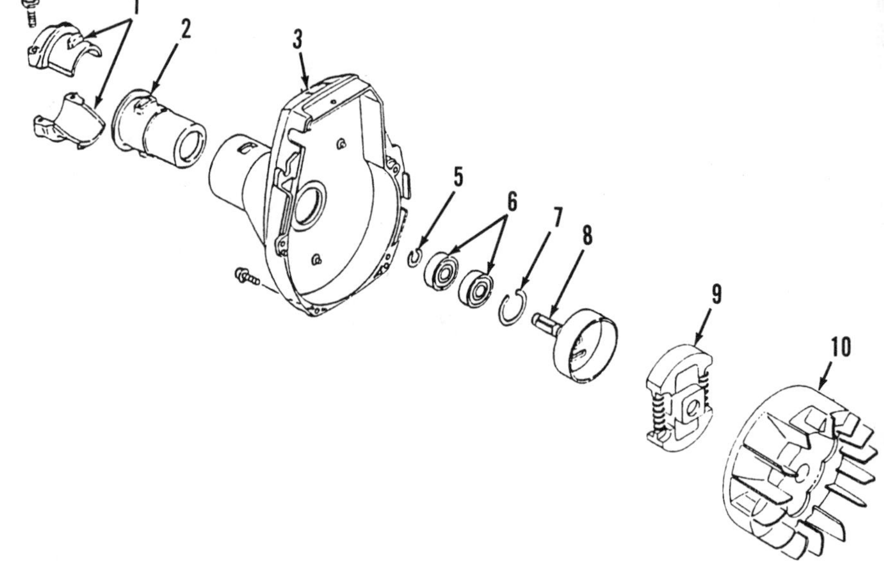

Fig. JD307—Exploded view of clutch typical of the type used on 21C and 21S models. The clutch (9) is available only as an assembly.

1. Clamp adapter
2. Cushion
3. Cover
5. Snap ring
6. Bearings
7. Snap ring
8. Clutch drum
9. Clutch shoes, hub & springs
10. Flywheel

0.03 mm (0.0012 in.). The pin should not be worn more than 0.013 mm (0.0005 in.).

Position the thrust washers (8—Fig. JD303, Fig. JD304 or Fig. JD306) on each side of the connecting rod. Position the piston on the connecting rod so arrow on top of piston will be toward the exhaust port (muffler) side of cylinder. Lubricate the piston pin and bearing, then install the piston pin. Install new retaining rings (6—Fig. JD303, Fig. JD304, Fig. JD305 or Fig. JD306) if bent or condition is otherwise questionable. Install the retaining rings with the gap toward the top or bottom or the piston.

Make sure the end of each piston ring surrounds the pin located in ring groove. Be careful to install the cylinder straight down over the piston. If the cylinder is turned, the ring can catch in a port and break the end of the ring.

CYLINDER. The piston, rings and cylinder are available in standard size only and the cylinder should not be bored oversize. Inspect the cylinder for any damage and install new parts as necessary. If the chrome plating is worn from the cylinder, a new cylinder should be installed.

CRANKSHAFT, ROD AND CRANKCASE. The crankshaft and connecting rod are available only as an assembly (16—Fig. JD303, Fig. JD304, Fig. JD305 or Fig. JD306); individual components are not available.

To remove the crankshaft and connecting rod assembly, remove the cylinder and piston as described in PISTON, PIN AND RINGS paragraph. Remove the screws attaching the halves of the crankcase together and separate halves. Heat the crankcase if necessary to remove the main bearings from the crankcase bores. If the bearings stay on the crankshaft, use a suitable puller to pull the bearings from the main journals. Some models may have a snap ring (10—Fig. JD304, Fig. JD305 or Fig. JD306) installed in the case bore.

The main bearing should turn smoothly with no perceptible play or ratcheting. Connecting rod side clearance should not exceed 0.4 mm (0.016 in.).

Support the crankshaft at the main bearings or journals and measure runout at the ends of the crankshaft. Measured runout should not exceed 0.05 mm (0.002 in.).

Use suitable tools to press new main bearings and seals into the crankcase bores. Lips of seals (9 and 18—Fig. JD303, Fig. JD304, Fig. JD305 or Fig. JD306) should be toward inside of crankcase and should be lubricated before installing the crankshaft.

CLUTCH. The shoe assembly of 21C and 21S models is located at the drive end of the crankshaft as shown in Fig. JD307. The drive hub of 21C and 21S models is threaded and also attaches the flywheel to the crankshaft. The shoes of 25S, 30S and 38B models are attached to the flywheel as shown in Fig. JD308. The clutch drum of all models operates in bearings located in the cover or drive flange.

To remove the clutch drum, first separate the drive shaft housing from the engine, then unbolt and remove the cover (3—Fig. JD307) or drive flange (4—Fig. JD308). On most models, the clutch drum has a hole so snap ring (7—Fig. JD307 or Fig. JD308) can be removed. It may be necessary to heat the housing until warm to touch to facilitate removal of the bearings from the housing as the bearings are a press fit. If the clutch drum is not slotted, remove snap ring (5). After removing the clutch drum, remove the remaining snap ring and bearings.

Inspect the clutch shoes (9) and drum (8) for excessive wear. Some clutch shoes are fitted with lining, while other shoes are not. Install new springs if overheated or otherwise damaged. Clutch (9—Fig. JD307) is available only as an assembly. The housing (3—Fig. JD307) or drive flange (4—Fig. JD308) should be heated when installing the bearings. Refer to TIGHTENING TORQUES paragraph when assembling.

REWIND STARTER. Refer to Fig. JD309 for exploded view of rewind starter. To disassemble the starter, unbolt and remove the housing from the engine. Remove handle from the rope and allow the rope to wind into the starter. Remove center screw (6), then remove washer (7) and the rope pulley (8). Wear appropriate eyewear and gloves to protect against injury when removing the spring (9). The spring may unwind from the housing uncontrollably. If necessary for service, remove the pulley plate.

The rope must be the correct diameter and length for the starter to operate properly. If the rope is too large in diameter or too long, the rope may bind

Fig. JD308—Exploded view of clutch typical of the type used on 25S, 30S and 38B models.

1. Clamp adapter
2. Cushion
3. Cover
4. Drive flange
5. Snap ring
6. Bearings
7. Snap ring
8. Clutch drum
9. Clutch shoes
10. Flywheel
11. Pivot screw
12. Washers
13. Springs
14. Flywheel retaining nut

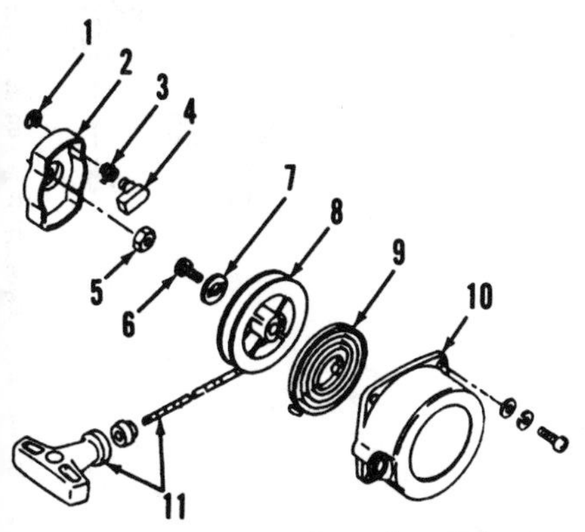

Fig. JD309—Exploded view of rewind starter typical of all models.

1. "E" ring
2. Pawl carrier
3. Spring
4. Pawl
5. Nut
6. Screw
7. Washer
8. Pulley
9. Rewind spring
10. Starter housing
11. Rope and handle

when trying to wind onto the pulley. When installing new rope, measure the length and diameter of the old rope, then install new rope that matches the original.

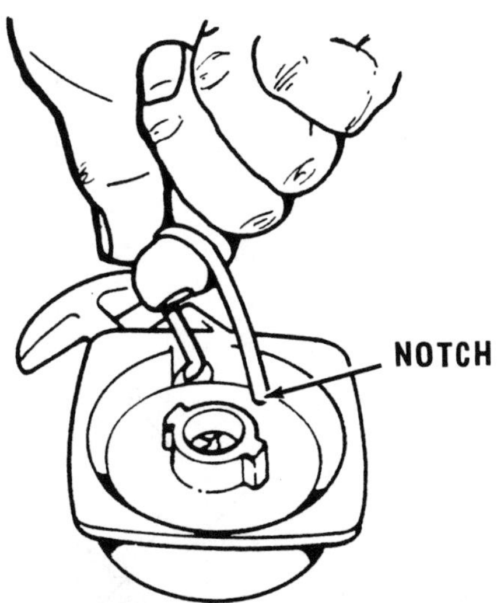

Fig. JD310—To set the preload of the starter recoil spring, pull a loop in the rope with the rope in the notch in the pulley, then wind the pulley as necessary. When the rope is released, it will pull out of the notch.

To assemble the starter, apply a small amount of light grease to the starter housing post, spring and the back of the pulley. Install the rewind spring so it is wound counterclockwise from the outer end. Attach the rope to the pulley, making sure the knot is fully nested in the pocket. Pull the rope tight and wind the rope counterclockwise as viewed from the pawl (engine) side. Install the pulley/rope and rotate slightly until the spring hooks into the pulley and the pulley drops into the housing. Guide the end of the rope through the housing and attach the handle.

When assembling or if the starter rope does not fully rewind, preload the recoil spring as follows. Hold the pulley to keep it from turning, then pull a small loop in the rope between the pulley and the inside of the housing. Hold the rope and wind the pulley to preload the pulley, allow the pulley to rewind the rope, then check operation. The spring should wind the rope around the pulley fully, but the spring must bind when the rope is fully extended. It should be possible to rotate the pulley at least 1/4 turn when the rope is pulled out completely. Complete the assembly by reversing the disassembly procedure when the spring preload is correctly set.

DOLMAR

ENGINE SERVICE

Model	Bore	Stroke	Displacement
3300	37.0 mm (1.46 in.)	31.0 mm (1.22 in.)	33.0 cc (2.01 cu. in.)
4000	40.0 mm (1.57 in.)	31.0 mm (1.22 in.)	39.0 cc (2.44 cu. in.)
4500	43.0 mm (1.69 in.)	31.0 mm (1.22 in.)	45.0 cc (2.74 cu. in.)

ENGINE INFORMATION

These two-stroke air-cooled gasoline engines are used on Dolmar string trimmers and brush cutters.

MAINTENANCE

LUBRICATION. The engine is lubricated by mixing oil with the gasoline fuel. Use only an oil designed for two-stroke, air-cooled engines. Refer to the TRIMMER SERVICE section for the type of oil and mixing ratio recommended by the equipment manufacturer.

SPARK PLUG. The recommended spark plug is a Champion RCJ6Y, NGK BPMR-7A or equivalent. The electrode gap should be 0.5-0.8 mm (0.020-0.030 in.). Tighten the spark plug to the torque listed in the TIGHTENING TORQUE paragraph.

CARBURETOR. The engine is equipped with a Walbro WT carburetor. The manufacturer's name and model number is stamped on the carburetor.

To remove carburetor, unbolt and remove engine shroud. Remove air filter assembly (2 and 3—Fig. D101) and stud nuts (5). Disconnect choke linkage (7), throttle cable and fuel line, then remove carburetor. When installing, tighten the attaching screws to the torque listed in the TIGHTENING TORQUE paragraph.

Refer to Fig. D102 for an exploded view typical of the carburetor. Initial adjustment of the low-speed mixture needle (13) and the high-speed mixture needle (14) is 1-1/4 turns open. The settings of these mixture needles is critical to the operation of the engine. Final adjustment should be performed carefully to insure easy starting and maximum performance.

To adjust the mixture needles, first remove and clean the air filter (3—Fig. D101), then reinstall it. Start the engine and allow it to run until it reaches normal operating temperature. If necessary, turn each of the mixture screws (13 and 14—Fig. D102) clockwise until seated lightly, then back the screws out

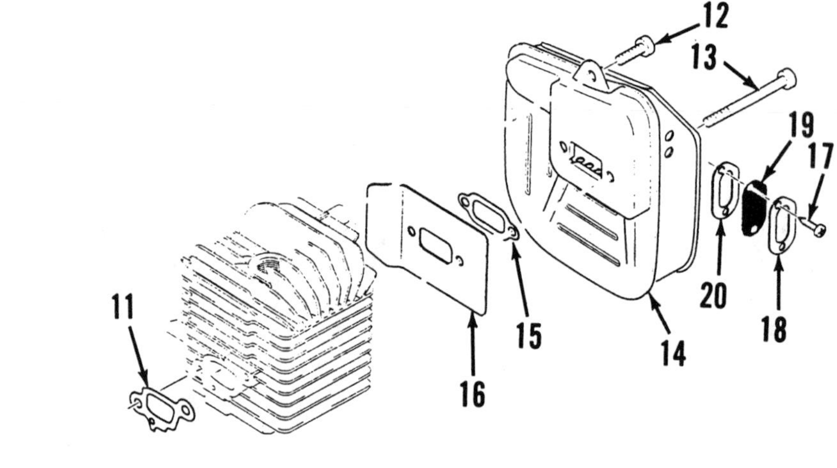

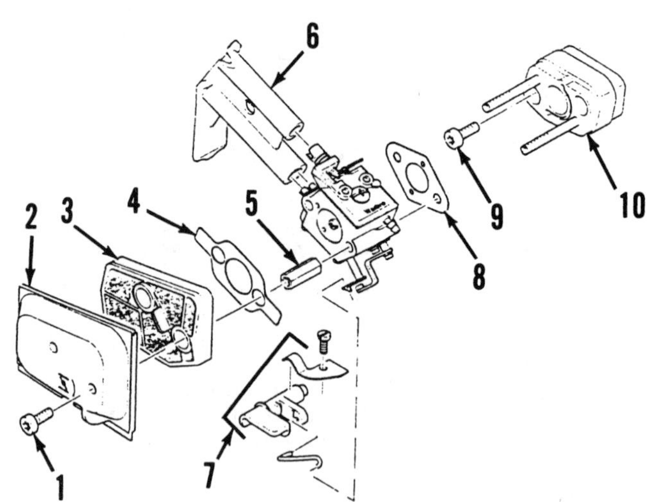

Fig. D101—View of carburetor and air filter.

1. Screw
2. Cover
3. Air filter
4. Gasket
5. Nuts
6. Adjusting guide
7. Choke linkage
8. Gasket
9. Screw
10. Adapter
11. Gasket
12. Short screw
13. Long screw
14. Muffler
15. Gasket
16. Heat shield
17. Screw
18. Cover
19. Screen
20. Gasket

Illustrations courtesy Echo Inc.

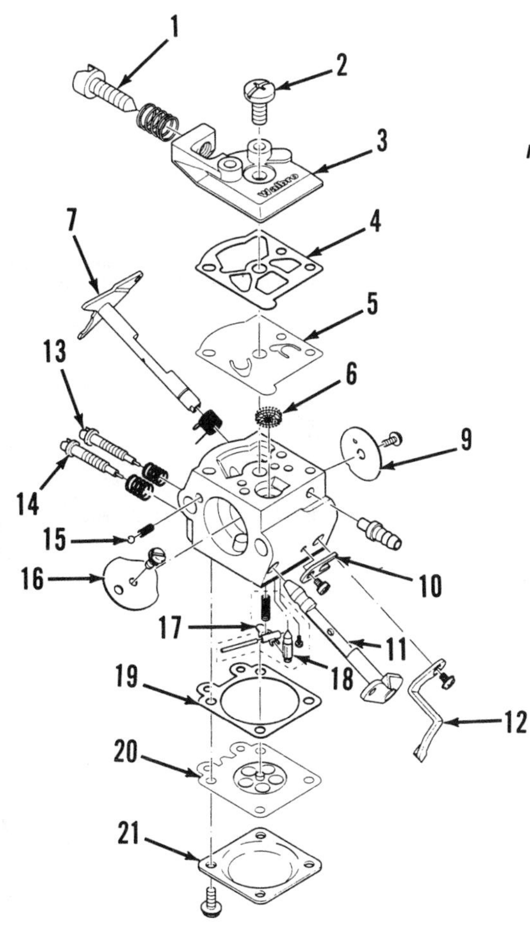

Fig. D102—Exploded view of typical Walbro WT carburetor.

1. Idle speed screw
2. Screw
3. Pump cover
4. Gasket
5. Pump diaphragm
6. Screen
7. Throttle shaft
9. Throttle plate
10. Shaft retainer clip
11. Choke shaft
12. Throttle lever
13. Low-speed mixture needle
14. High-speed mixture needle
15. Detent ball
16. Choke plate
17. Metering lever
18. Fuel inlet needle
19. Gasket
20. Metering diaphragm
21. Cover

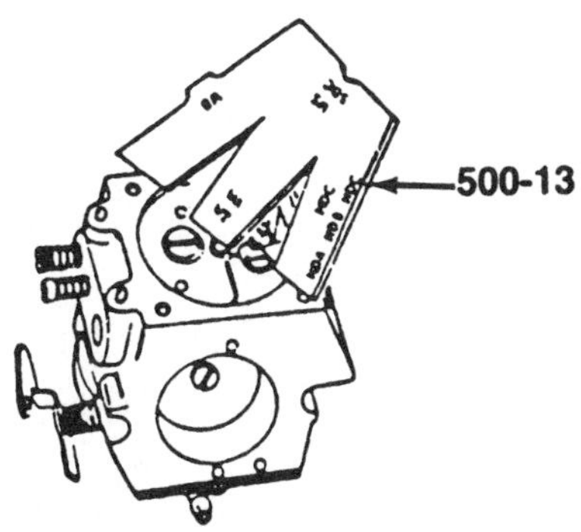

Fig. D103—The metering lever should just touch the leg of the Walbro tool 500-13. If necessary, bend the lever to adjust the lever height.

(counterclockwise) 1-1/4 turns to provide the initial adjustment so the engine can be started. Turn the idle speed stop screw (1) so the engine idles slowly, just below clutch engagement rpm. Adjust the low-speed mixture needle (13) so the engine idles smoothly and accelerates without hesitation. Readjust the idle speed stop screw (1) if necessary to slow the idle speed. The trimmer head should not turn when the engine is idling. Adjust the high-speed mixture needle (14) to provide the best performance while operating at maximum speed under load. The high-speed mixture needle may be set slightly rich to improve performance under load. The engine may be damaged if the high-speed screw is set too lean.

To disassemble the carburetor, refer to Fig. D102. Remove pump cover (3), gasket (4), pump diaphragm (5), and screen (6). Remove metering chamber cover (21) and diaphragm (20). Remove retaining screw, pin, metering lever (17), spring and fuel inlet valve (18). Remove low- and high-speed mixture screws (13 and 14). It is not necessary to remove throttle and choke shafts (7 and 11) unless wear or damage is evident. If choke is removed, be careful not to lose detent ball (15) and spring when shaft is withdrawn.

Clean and inspect all components. If the unit has been improperly stored, passages may be clogged with deposits that are hard, solid and nearly transparent. Blow carburetor cleaner through all passages. Be careful not to damage the openings or sealing surfaces while cleaning. Check the condition of diaphragms (5 and 20) carefully. Install new diaphragms if hard (not flexible), torn or otherwise damaged. Examine the fuel inlet valve (18), spring and metering lever (17). A new fuel inlet valve needle (18), and mixture needles (13 and 14) can be installed, but their seats cannot be serviced if worn or damaged. Inspect the condition of the filter screen (6) and clean or replace.

Check the height of the metering lever as shown in Fig. D103 using Walbro tool 500-13 or equivalent. End of metering lever should just touch the leg of the tool. If the tool is not available, the lever should be 1.52-1.78 mm (0.060-0.070 in.) below the surface for gasket (19—Fig. D102). Carefully bend the lever if necessary to obtain the correct lever height.

IGNITION SYSTEM. The engine is equipped with a solid-state ignition system. The ignition module/coil is located under the cowling at the front of the engine. Two screws attach the ignition module/coil to the engine's cylinder. When installing, set the air gap between the flywheel magnets and the legs of the ignition module as follows. Install the ignition module, but tighten the two screws only enough to hold it in place away from the flywheel. Insert 0.25 mm (0.010 in.) thick brass or plastic shim stock between the legs of the ignition module and the flywheel, then turn the flywheel until the flywheel magnets are near the module legs. Loosen the screws attaching the ignition module and press legs of the ignition module against the shim stock, then tighten the two attaching screws to the torque listed in the TIGHTENING TORQUE paragraph. Remove the shim stock, then turn the flywheel and check to be sure the flywheel does not hit the legs of the coil.

REPAIRS

TIGHTENING TORQUE. Recommended tightening torques are as follows.

Carburetor
- Attaching nuts............ 4-5 N•m (35-45 in.-lb.)
- Intermediate flange .... 5-6 N•m (45-55 in.-lb.)

Clutch housing
- First assembly.......... 10-11 N•m (85-95 in.-lb.)
- Second assembly .... 6-7 N•m (55-65 in.-lb.)

Clutch housing/Drive shaft clamp............. 9-11 N•m (78-95 in.-lb.)

Clutch pivot screws......... 7-9 N•m (65-78 in.-lb.)

Crankcase/Engine housing
- First assembly.......... 10-11 N•m (85-95 in.-lb.)

Illustrations courtesy Echo Inc.

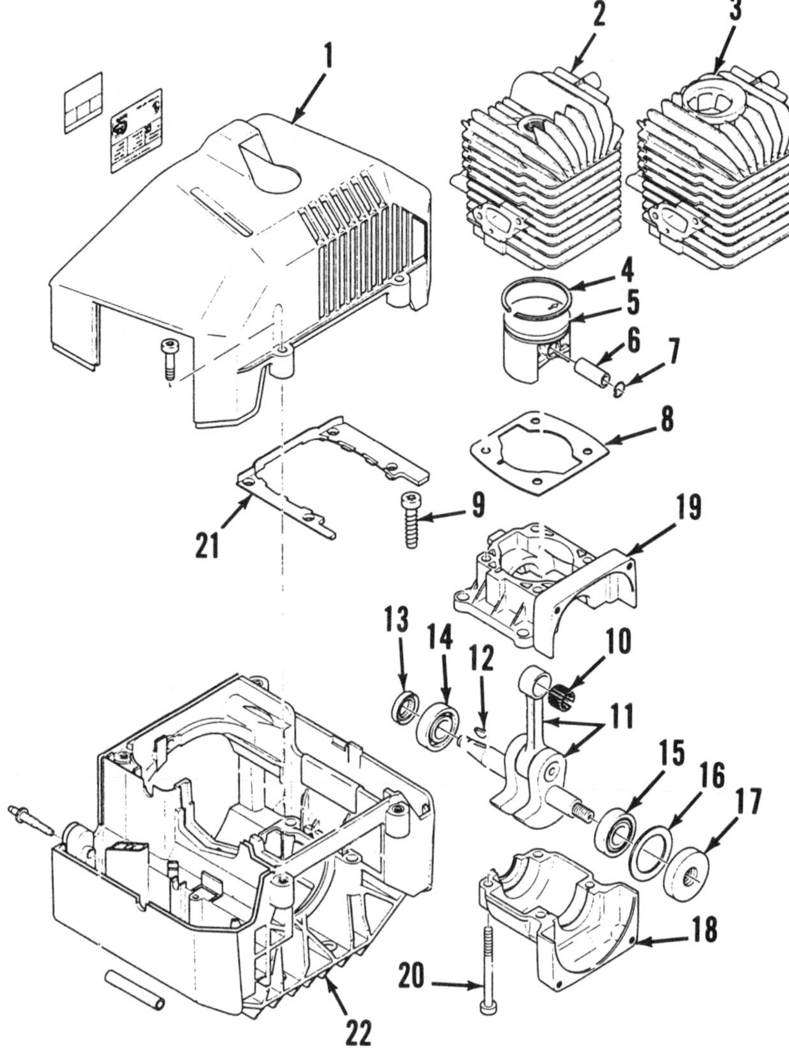

Fig. D104—View of the engine crankshaft, crankcase, cylinder and housing (22) separated.

1. Top cover
2. Cylinder (3300 and 4000)
3. Cylinder (4500)
4. Piston ring
5. Piston
6. Piston pin
7. Retaining ring
8. Cylinder base gasket
9. Screw
10. Needle bearing
11. Crankshaft and connecting rod
12. Woodruff key
13. Seal
14. Ball bearing
15. Ball bearing
16. Spacer
17. Seal
18. Crankcase lower half
19. Crankcase upper half
20. Screw
21. Air deflector
22. Housing

Second assembly	6-7 N•m (55-65 in.-lb.)
Cylinder	10-11 N•m (85-95 in.-lb.)
Flywheel	19-21 N•m (165-185 in.-lb.)
Handle	2 N•m (18 in.-lb.)
Ignition coil/module	7-9 N•m (65-78 in.-lb.)
Muffler	
M5x55	5-6 N•m (45-55 in.-lb.)
M5x16	7-9 N•m (65-78 in.-lb.)
Spark plug	14-16 N•m (137-146 in.-lb.)

CYLINDER, PISTON AND RING. The piston and ring can be inspected through the exhaust port after removing the muffler (14—Fig. D101). The cylinder, piston and ring (4 and 5—Fig. D104) are available in standard size only.

To remove the cylinder, remove the engine top cover (1), muffler (14—Fig. D102), carburetor, adapter (10) and spark plug. Remove the four cylinder attaching screws (20—Fig. D104), working through holes in the housing (22). Carefully lift the cylinder from the piston. Remove retaining rings (7), then remove the piston pin (6) to separate the piston from the connecting rod. Needle bearing (10) can be removed from the connecting rod bore.

The cylinder base gasket (8) is fitted to the air deflector (21). Remove the gasket and clean all residue from the cylinder, crankcase and air deflector. Push the gasket into the air deflector. Make sure the gasket is correctly positioned and seated before installing the cylinder.

Install the piston with the arrow on its top pointing toward the exhaust side. Install the retaining rings (7) with the opening either toward the top or bottom. Do not install the retaining rings with the gap at either side. Lubricate the piston, ring and cylinder, position the ring gap around the pin in the piston groove, then install the cylinder over the piston assembly. Tighten fasteners to the torque listed in the TIGHTENING TORQUE paragraph.

CRANKSHAFT AND CONNECTING ROD. The crankshaft and connecting rod (11—Fig. D104) assembly can be removed after first removing the flywheel and the cylinder as described in the appropriate paragraphs. Remove the four screws (9) that attach the crankcase to the housing (22). Carefully separate the halves of the crankcase (18 and 19) to remove the seals, bearings and crankshaft assembly.

Clean all parts carefully and inspect for damage. The crankshaft is available for service only as a pressed together assembly with the connecting rod. The connecting rod should always be coated with lubricant to prevent rust and should be covered to prevent dirt from entering the bearings. Do not remove the main bearings (14 and 15) unless new bearings are ready to be installed.

Lubricate the crankshaft bearings and shaft sealing surfaces with oil. Po-

Illustrations courtesy Echo Inc.

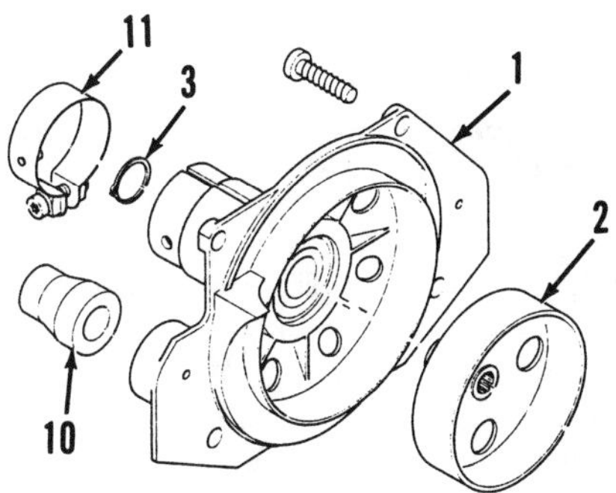

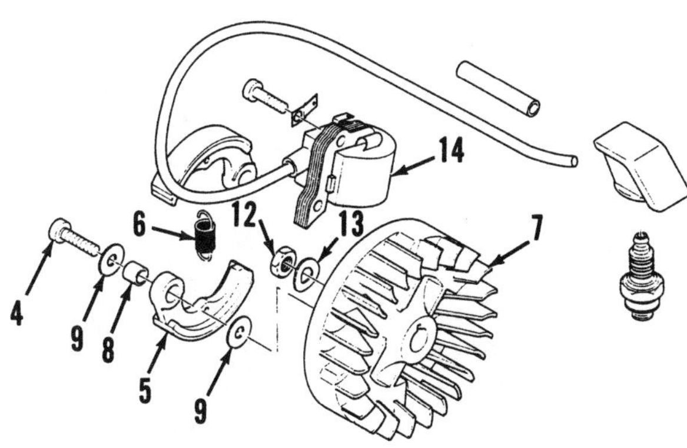

Fig. D105—Exploded view of the clutch assembly. Bearing and housing (1) is only available as an assembly.

1. Clutch housing and bearing assembly
2. Clutch drum
3. Snap ring
4. Screw
5. Clutch shoe
6. Spring
7. Flywheel
8. Bushing
9. Washers
10. Vibration insulators
11. Clamp
12. Nut
13. Lock washer
14. Ignition coil

sition the spacer (16) and seals (13 and 17) over the shaft with the lips of the seals toward the inside. Position the crankshaft in the lower case half and make sure the bearings (14 and 15), washer (16) and seals (13 and 17) are located correctly. Make sure the mating surfaces of the crankcase halves are clean and dry, coat the surfaces lightly and evenly with Loctite 510 or equivalent, then install the upper case half. Install and tighten the screws (9) to the torque listed in TIGHTENING TORQUE paragraph.

FLYWHEEL. Remove the clutch drum and clutch shoes as described in the TRIMMER SERVICE section. Remove the engine top cover, then unbolt and remove the ignition coil/module. Remove the flywheel retaining nut, then use the special puller (part No. 944.500.880) to pull the flywheel from the crankshaft.

Be sure the key (12—Fig. D104) is in place and the tapered surfaces of the flywheel and crankshaft are clean and dry before installing the flywheel. Tighten fasteners to the torque listed in TIGHTENING TORQUE paragraph.

CLUTCH. Refer to Fig. D105 and the TRIMMER SERVICE section for removal and service procedures. Inspect vibration isolators (10—Fig. D105) and install new units if damaged.

RECOIL STARTER. Refer to the TRIMMER SERVICE section for removal and service procedures.

ECHO

ENGINE SERVICE

Model	Bore	Stroke	Displacement
SRM-140D, SRM-DA, GT-140, GT-140A, GT-140B	26.0 mm (1.024 in.)	26.0 mm (1.024 in.)	13.8 cc (0.842 cu. in.)
GT-160, GT-160A, GT-160AE	28.0 mm (1.102 in.)	26.0 mm (1.024 in.)	16.0 cc (0.976 cu. in.)
SRM-200, SRM-200AE, SRM-200BE, SRM-200D, SRM-200DA, SRM-200DB, SRM-200E, SRM-201F, SRM-201FA, SRM-202D, SRM-202DA, SRM-202F, SRM-202FA, SRM-210E, SRM-210AE, GT-200, GT-200A, GT-200B, GT-200BE	32.2 mm (1.268 in.)	26.0 mm (1.024 in.)	21.2 cc (1.294 cu. in.)
SRM-300, SRM-302ADX	28.0 mm (1.102 in.)	37.0 mm (.457 in.)	30.1 cc (1.837 cu. in.)
SRM-300E, SRM-300AE	35.0 mm (1.378 in.)	32.0 mm (1.260 in.)	30.8 cc (1.880 cu. in.)
SRM-400E, SRM-400AE, SRM-402DE	40.0 mm (1.575 in.)	32.0 mm (1.260 in.)	40.2 cc (2.452 cu. in.)

ENGINE INFORMATION

These two-stroke air-cooled gasoline engines are used on Echo trimmers, cutters and other equipment.

MAINTENANCE

LUBRICATION. The engine is lubricated by mixing oil with the gasoline fuel. Use only an oil designed for two-stroke, air-cooled engines. Refer to the ECHO TRIMMER SERVICE section for the recommended type of oil and mixing ratio.

SPARK PLUG. The recommended spark plug for normal application is NGK BM6A or Champion CJ8 for all models except SRM-400 trimmers. NGK BPM7A or Champion CJ7Y spark plug is recommended for SRM-400 trimmers. The electrode gap should be 0.024-0.028 in. (0.6-0.7 mm) for all models. Tighten the spark plug securely to the torque listed in the TIGHTENING TORQUE paragraph.

CARBURETOR. Walbro WA, Walbro WT, Walbro WY, Walbro WYL and Zama C1U diaphragm carburetors and Keihin float type carburetors have been used. The manufacturer's name and model number are stamped on the carburetor. Refer to appropriate ECHO Equipment Section for carburetor application and initial needle setting. Refer to the following tuning and service information for the specific carburetor type used. When installing, tighten the attaching screws to the torque listed in the TIGHTENING TORQUE paragraph.

Walbro WA. Refer to appropriate Equipment Section for carburetor application and initial settings for mixture needles (17 and 18—Fig. EC1). For performing final mixture adjustments, the engine must be at normal operating temperature and running. On trimmer models, trimmer line should be at the maximum recommended length or blade installed. Adjust the idle speed by turning screw (31) until the engine is operating at slow idle speed. On models with clutch, idle speed should be slower than clutch engagement speed or about 2,500-3,000 rpm. Adjust the low-speed mixture needle so the engine runs smoothly at idle speed and accelerates without hesitation. If necessary, readjust idle speed. Operate the engine at full throttle (with no load) and adjust the high-speed mixture needle to obtain maximum rpm, then turn the needle counterclockwise until the engine just starts to slow because of the mixture being too rich (four-cycle).

When overhauling the carburetor, refer to Fig. EC1. Remove metering chamber cover (1) and fuel pump cover (28) for access to internal components. Remove circuit plate (10) and check valve (11). Remove metering lever (6) and fuel inlet valve (7). Remove fuel mixture screws (17 and 18).

Clean and inspect all components. If the unit has been improperly stored, passages may be clogged with deposits that are hard, solid and nearly transparent. Clean passages with suitable carburetor cleaning solvent and compressed air. Be careful not to damage the openings or sealing surfaces while cleaning. Examine the fuel inlet valve (7) and seat. Inlet valve can be replaced, but the seat is part of the carbu-

Illustrations courtesy Echo Inc.

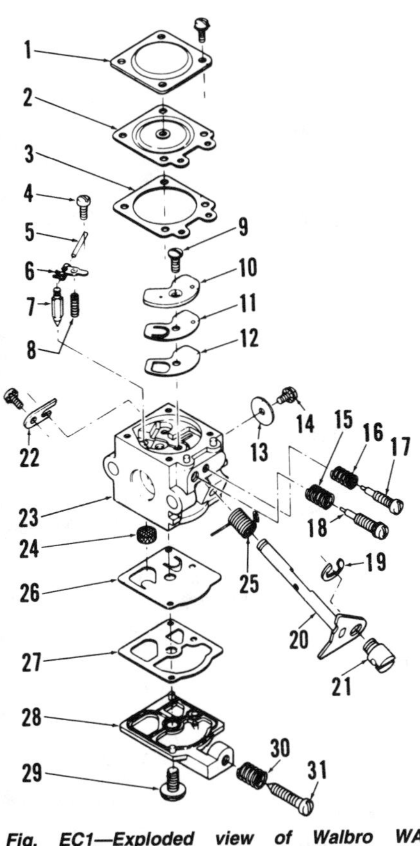

Fig. EC1—Exploded view of Walbro WA carburetor used on some models.

1. Cover
2. Metering diaphragm
3. Gasket
4. Metering lever screw
5. Pivot pin
6. Metering lever
7. Fuel inlet valve
8. Spring
9. Screw
10. Circuit plate
11. Check valve
12. Gasket
13. Throttle valve
14. Screw
15. Spring
16. Spring
17. High speed mixture needle
18. Idle mixture needle
19. "E" clip
20. Throttle shaft
21. Swivel
22. Throttle shaft clip
23. Body
24. Inlet screen
25. Return spring
26. Fuel pump diaphragm
27. Gasket
28. Cover
29. Screw
30. Spring
31. Idle speed screw

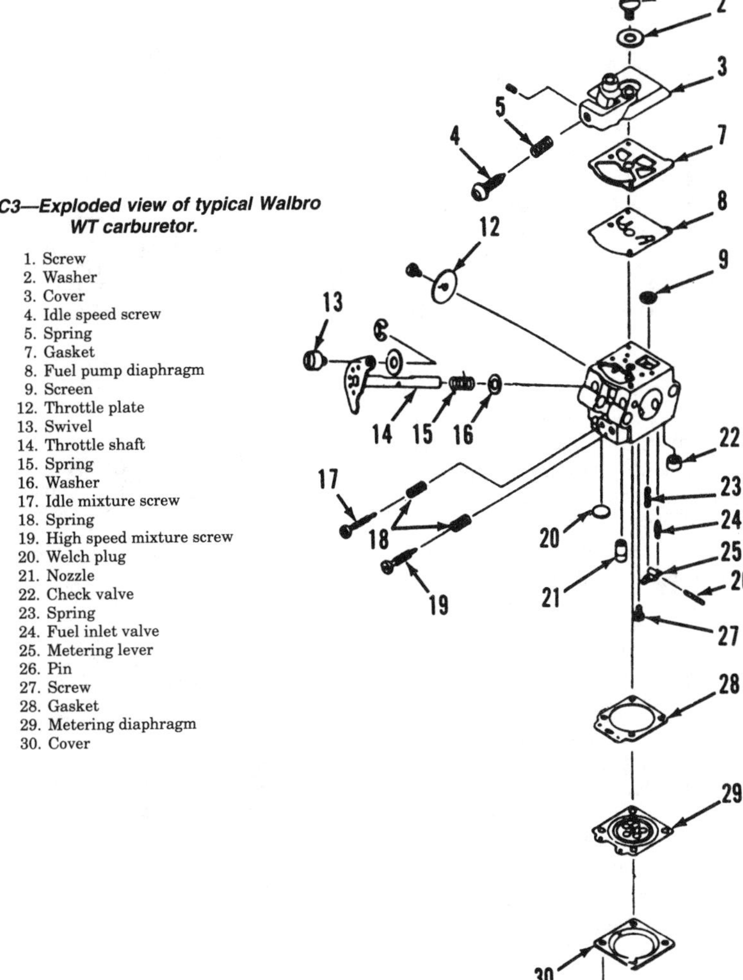

Fig. EC3—Exploded view of typical Walbro WT carburetor.

1. Screw
2. Washer
3. Cover
4. Idle speed screw
5. Spring
7. Gasket
8. Fuel pump diaphragm
9. Screen
12. Throttle plate
13. Swivel
14. Throttle shaft
15. Spring
16. Washer
17. Idle mixture screw
18. Spring
19. High speed mixture screw
20. Welch plug
21. Nozzle
22. Check valve
23. Spring
24. Fuel inlet valve
25. Metering lever
26. Pin
27. Screw
28. Gasket
29. Metering diaphragm
30. Cover

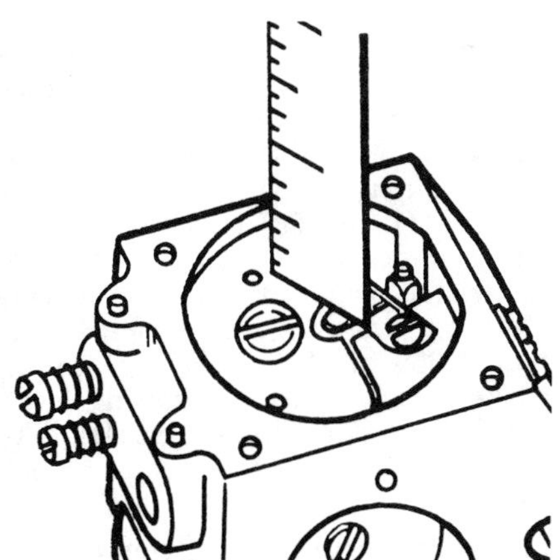

Fig. EC2—On Walbro WA carburetor, metering lever is correctly adjusted when its upper surface is flush with circuit plate.

retor body and cannot be serviced. Examine the mixture needles (17 and 18) and install new needles if damaged. Clean or replace fuel screen (24). Inspect diaphragms (2 and 26) for tears or other damage. The diaphragms must be flexible.

Check the height of the metering lever as shown in Fig. EC2. The lever should be just flush with the top of the circuit plate. The metering lever should just touch leg on the tool. Bend the lever carefully if necessary to obtain correct height.

Walbro WT. The manufacturer's name and model number are stamped on the carburetor. Refer to the appropriate ECHO Equipment Section for carburetor original application and initial settings for mixture needles. When installing, tighten the attaching screws to the torque listed in the TIGHTENING TORQUE paragraph.

Refer to Fig. EC3 for an exploded view typical of the carburetor. Initial adjustment of the low-speed mixture needle (17) and the high-speed mixture needle (19) is 1 turn open. The settings of these mixture needles is critical to the operation of the engine. Final adjustment should be performed carefully to insure easy starting and maximum performance.

To adjust the mixture needles, first remove, clean and reinstall the air filter. Start the engine and allow it to run until it reaches normal operating temperature. If necessary, turn each of the mixture screws (17 and 19) clockwise until seated lightly, then back the screws out (counterclockwise) the number of turns listed in the appropriate Equipment Section so the engine can be started. Turn the idle speed stop screw (4) so the engine idles slowly, just below clutch engagement rpm. Adjust the low-speed mixture needle (17) so the engine idles smoothly and accelerates without hesitation. Readjust the idle speed stop screw (4) if necessary to slow the idle speed. The trimmer head should not turn when the engine is idling. Adjust the high-speed mixture needle (19) to provide the best performance while operating at maximum speed under load. The high-speed mixture needle may be set slightly rich to improve performance under load. The engine may be damaged if the high-speed screw is set too lean.

To disassemble the carburetor, refer to Fig. EC3. Remove fuel pump cover (3) and metering chamber cover (30) for access to internal components. Remove metering lever (25), fuel inlet valve (24) and fuel inlet screen (9). Remove nozzle (21) and check valve seat (22). Welch plug (20) can be removed by prying out with a sharp punch. Use care not to damage carburetor casting when removing Welch plug. Remove fuel mixture screws (17 and 19).

Clean and inspect all components. If the unit has been improperly stored, passages may be clogged with deposits that are hard, solid and nearly transparent. Be careful not to damage the openings or sealing surfaces while cleaning. Check the condition of diaphragms (8 and 29) carefully. Install new diaphragms if hard (not flexible), torn or otherwise damaged. Examine the fuel inlet valve (24), spring (23) and lever (25). A new fuel inlet valve needle (24), and mixture needles (17 and 19) can be installed, but their seats cannot be serviced if damaged. Inspect the condition of the filter screen (9).

Check the height of the metering lever as shown in Fig. EC4 using Walbro tool 500-13 or equivalent. End of metering lever should just touch the leg of the tool. If tool is not available, the lever should be 1.52-1.78 mm (0.060-0.070 in) below surface for gasket (28—Fig. EC4). Carefully bend the lever if necessary to obtain correct lever height.

Walbro WY and WYL. These carburetors use a barrel type throttle rather than a throttle plate. Idle fuel for the

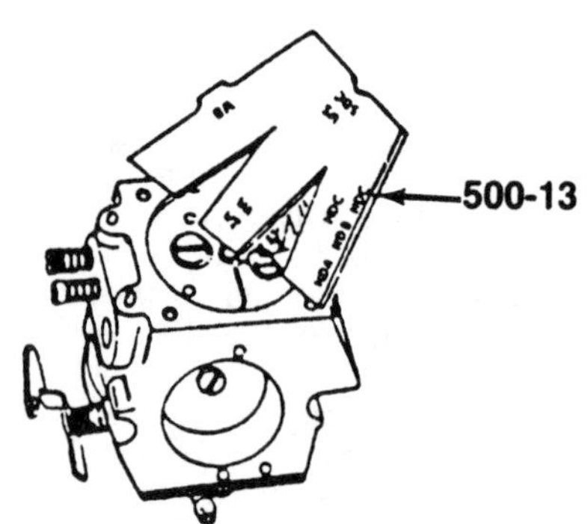

Fig. EC4—On Walbro WT carburetor, metering lever should just touch leg of Walbro tool 500-13. Bend lever to obtain correct lever height.

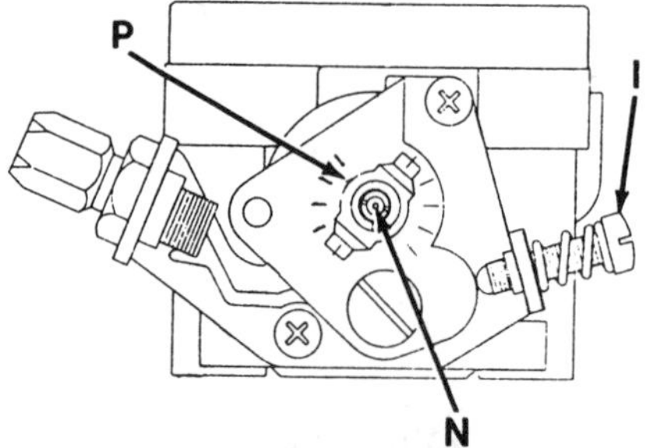

Fig. EC5—On Walbro WY or WYL carburetor, idle speed screw is located at (I), idle limiter plate is located at (P) and idle mixture needle is located at (N). A plug covers the idle mixture needle.

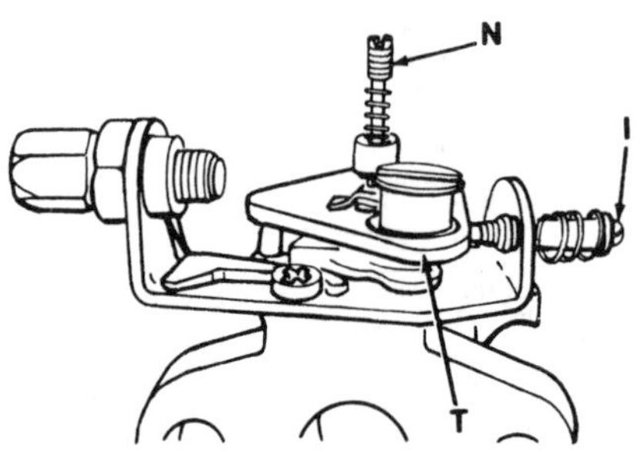

Fig. EC6—View of idle mixture needle (N) used on Walbro WY and WYL carburetor.

carburetor flows into the throttle barrel where it is fed into the air stream. Refer to appropriate Equipment Section for carburetor application and initial settings for mixture needle. The idle fuel flow can be adjusted by turning an idle limiter plate (P—Fig. EC5). Initial setting is in center notch. Rotating the plate clockwise will lean the idle mixture.

Inside the idle limiter plate is an idle mixture needle (N—Fig. EC6) that is preset at the factory. If removed, use the following procedure to determine correct position. Back out needle until unscrewed. Find the point where the threads of the idle mixture needle just start to engage, then turn the needle IN the number of turns specified in the Equipment Section. The needle does not contact a seat. Rotate idle mixture plate (P) to center notch.

For performing final mixture adjustment, the engine must be at normal operating temperature and running. On trimmer models, trimmer line should be at the maximum recommended length or blade installed. Adjust the idle speed by turning screw (3) until the engine is operating at slow idle speed. On models with clutch, idle speed should be slower than clutch engagement speed or about 2,500-3,000 rpm. Adjust the low-speed mixture needle so the engine runs smoothly at idle speed and accelerates without hesitation. If necessary, readjust idle speed. Rotate the idle mixture plate to the center

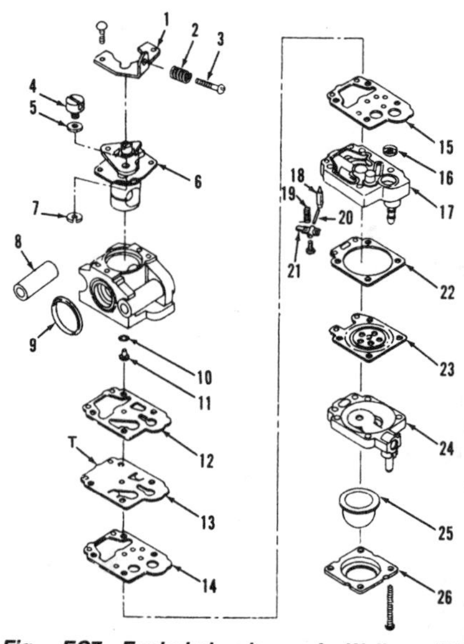

Fig. EC7—Exploded view of Walbro WY carburetor. Model WYL is similar.

1. Bracket
2. Spring
3. Idle speed screw
4. Swivel
5. Washer
6. Throttle barrel assy.
7. "E" ring
8. Sleeve
9. "O" ring
10. "O" ring
11. Main jet
12. Gasket
13. Fuel pump diaphragm
14. Fuel pump plate
15. Gasket
16. Fuel screen
17. Fuel pump body
18. Fuel inlet valve
19. Spring
20. Pin
21. Metering lever
22. Gasket
23. Metering diaphragm
24. Plate
25. Primer bulb
26. Cover

notch. The high-speed mixture is controlled by a removable fixed jet (11).

To overhaul the carburetor, refer to Fig. EC7. Remove retainer (26), plate (24), diaphragm (23), fuel pump body (17), plate (14) and diaphragm (13). Remove bracket (1) and throttle barrel assembly (6).

On models with a plastic body, clean only using solvents approved for use with plastic. Do not use wires or drills to clean orifices. Do not disassemble the throttle barrel assembly. The idle speed mixture needle is available only as an assembly with the throttle barrel. Examine the fuel inlet valve (18) and its seat. The inlet valve is renewable, but the seat is part of the fuel pump body (17). Clean fuel screen (16). Inspect diaphragms (13 and 23). Note that tabs on plates and gaskets (12 through 15) will "stair step" when correctly assembled. Metering lever (Fig. EC8) should be 1.5 mm (0.059 in.) below the surface for gasket (22). Bend the metering lever carefully to adjust the height (H), taking care not to force the needle against its seat.

Keihin Carburetor. Refer to Fig. EC9 for identification and exploded view of Keihin float type carburetor. To adjust idle speed, the engine must be at

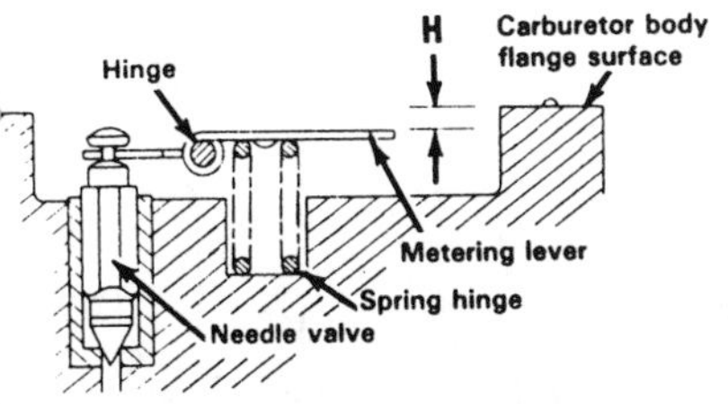

Fig. EC8—Metering lever height (H) must be set on diaphragm-type carburetors. Refer to text for specified height.

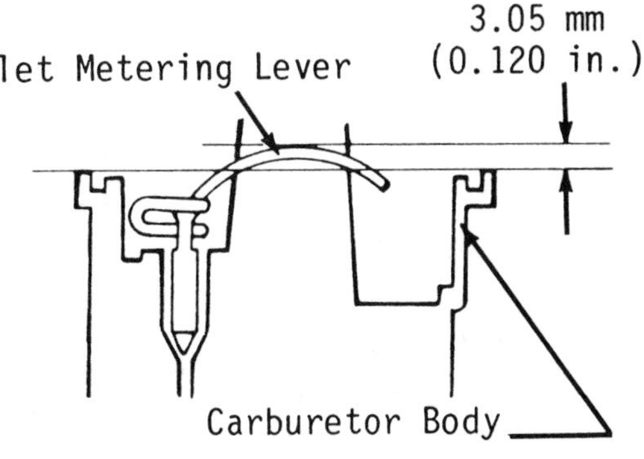

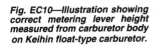

Fig. EC10—Illustration showing correct metering lever height measured from carburetor body on Keihin float-type carburetor.

normal operating temperature and running. Turn the idle speed screw (1) to obtain 2,500-3,000 rpm. This speed should be just below the clutch engagement rpm. Counterclockwise rotation of the screw lowers the engine speed. Clockwise rotation of the idle speed screw raises the throttle valve (29) increasing the engine idle speed.

To disassemble, remove bolt (12), fuel bowl (10), float (8), fuel inlet valve (5) and main jet (4). Clean all components using suitable carburetor cleaning solvent and compress air. Standard height of the metering lever is 3.05 mm (0.120 in.), measured from top of the float chamber rim as shown in Fig. EC10.

Fuel mixture adjustment at full load is accomplished by changing the position of "E" clip (27—Fig. EC9) on the jet needle (28). To enrich the fuel mixture, install the clip in a lower groove of the jet needle. To lean the mixture, install the clip in a higher groove. Refer to Fig. EC11.

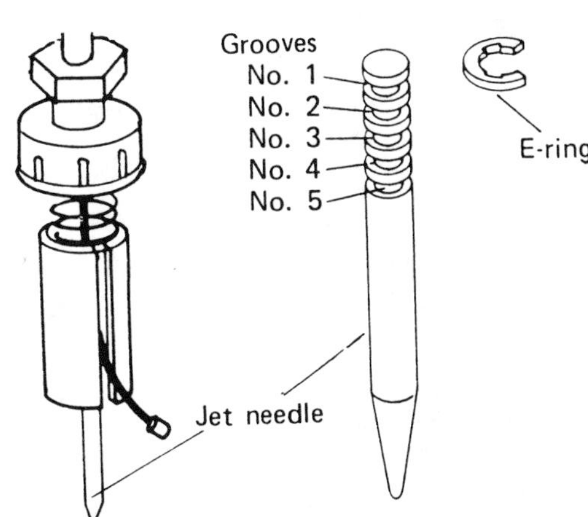

Fig. EC11—Illustration showing five grooves on jet needle of Keihin float-type carburetor. Placing "E" clip on number 1 groove leans high speed mixture. Grooves number 2 and 4 are standard mixture, groove number 5 enriches high speed mixture.

Zama C1U. Refer to appropriate Equipment Section for carburetor application and initial settings for mixture needles (12 and 14—Fig. EC12). The settings of these mixture screws is critical to the operation of the engine. Final adjustment should be performed carefully to insure easy starting and maximum performance.

To adjust the mixture screws, first remove and clean the air filter, then reinstall it. Start the engine and allow it to run until it reaches normal operating temperature. If necessary, turn each of the mixture screws (12 and 14) clockwise until seated lightly, then back the screws out (counterclockwise) the number of turns specified by the equipment manufacturer so the engine can be started. Turn the idle speed stop screw (26) so the engine idles at about 2500-3000 rpm. Adjust the idle mixture needle (14) so the engine idles smoothly and accelerates without hesitation. Readjust the idle speed stop screw (26) if necessary to slow the idle speed. If equipped with a clutch, the trimmer head should not turn when the engine is idling. Adjust the high speed mixture screw (12) to provide the best performance while operating at maximum speed under load. The high speed mixture screw may be set slightly rich to improve performance under load. The engine may be damaged if the high-speed screw is set too lean.

To disassemble the carburetor, refer to Fig. EC12. Remove metering chamber cover (1) and fuel pump cover (24) for access to internal components. Remove fuel inlet valve (8) and nozzle (6). Remove mixture adjusting screws (12 and 14). To remove the Welch plug (11), carefully pierce the plug near the end of the "tail" section, then pry the plug out. Do not insert the punch too deeply or the body and passages under the plug may be damaged. Apply sealant to outer edge of new plug before installing.

Clean and inspect all components. If the unit has been improperly stored, passages may be clogged with deposits that are hard, solid and nearly trans-

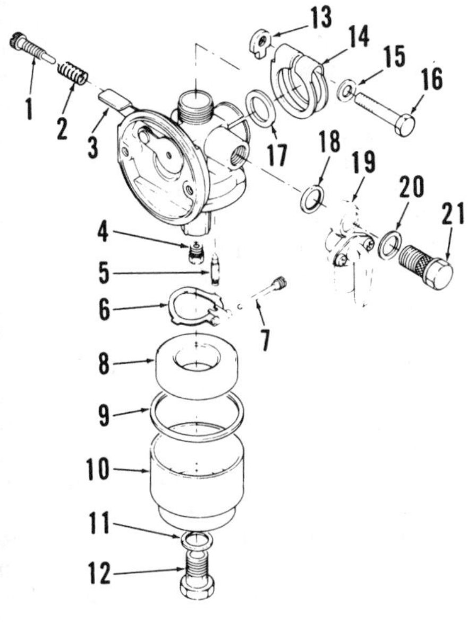

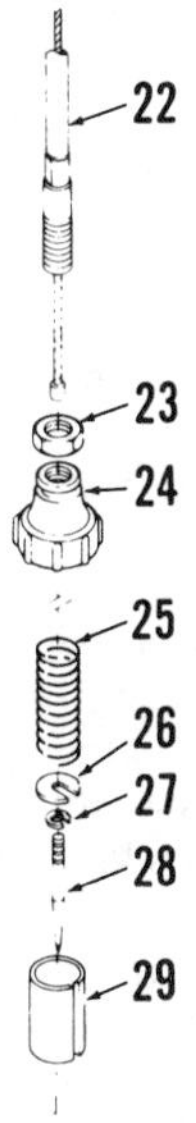

Fig. EC9—Exploded view of Keihin float type carburetor.

1. Idle speed screw
2. Spring
3. Choke shutter
4. Main jet
5. Fuel inlet valve
6. Float arm
7. Pivot pin
8. Float
9. Packing
10. Float bowl
11. Gasket
12. Holding bolt
13. Clip
14. Clamp
15. Washer
16. Bolt
17. Washer
18. Packing
19. Fuel shut-off
20. Packing
21. Banjo bolt
22. Throttle cable
23. Nut
24. Cover
25. Throttle spring
26. Spring seat
27. "E" clip
28. Jet needle
29. Throttle valve

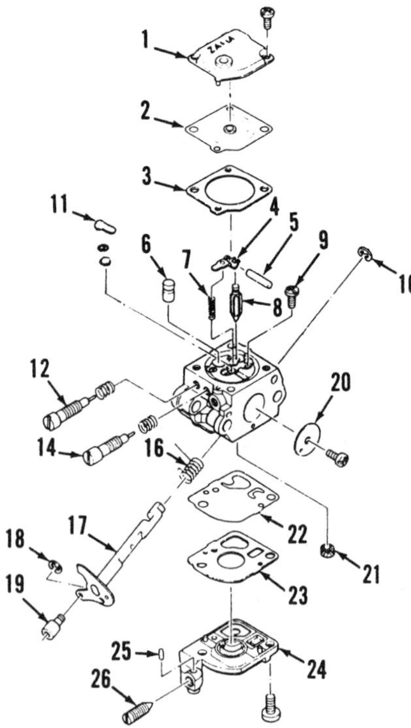

Fig. EC12—Exploded view of Zama C1U carburetor used on some models.

1. Cover
2. Metering diaphragm
3. Gasket
4. Metering lever
5. Pin
6. Nozzle
7. Spring
8. Fuel inlet valve
9. Screw
10. "E" ring
11. Welch plug
12. High speed mixture screw
14. Idle mixture screw
16. Spring
17. Throttle shaft
18. "E" ring
19. Swivel
20. Throttle plate
21. Fuel inlet screen
22. Fuel pump
23. Fuel pump diaphragm
23. Gasket
24. Cover
25. Pin
26. Idle speed screw

Straightedge

Metering lever

C

Fig. EC13—Metering lever should be bent so height (C) is 0-0.3 mm (0-0.012 in.) on Zama C1U carburetor.

parent. Be careful not to damage the openings or sealing surfaces while cleaning. Check the condition of diaphragms (2 and 22) carefully. Install new diaphragms if hard (not flexible), torn or otherwise damaged. Examine the fuel inlet valve (8), spring (7) and lever (4). A new fuel inlet valve needle (8), and mixture screws (12 and 14) can be installed, but their seats cannot be serviced if damaged.

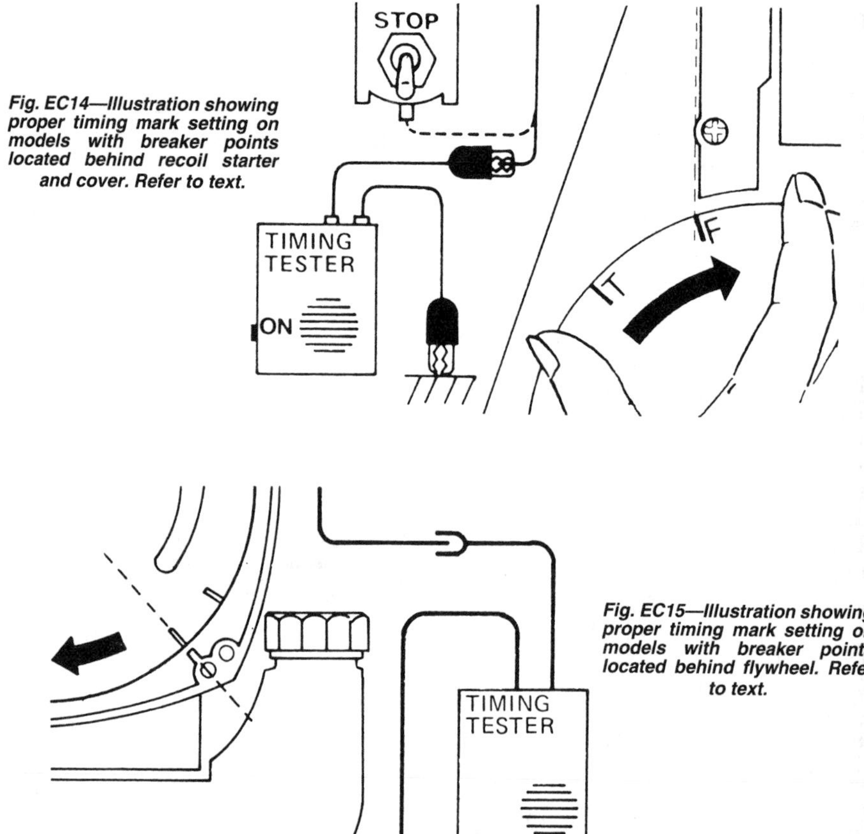

Fig. EC14—Illustration showing proper timing mark setting on models with breaker points located behind recoil starter and cover. Refer to text.

TIMING TESTER

Fig. EC15—Illustration showing proper timing mark setting on models with breaker points located behind flywheel. Refer to text.

Check the height of the metering lever as shown in Fig. EC13. The clearance (C) between the metering lever and a straightedge positioned across the gasket surface of the carburetor body should be 0-0.012 in. (0-0.3 mm). Carefully bend the lever if necessary to obtain the correct lever height.

IGNITION SYSTEM. Some early engines may be equipped with breaker point ignition system, but most models are equipped with a Capacitor Discharge Ignition (CDI) system that has no breaker points. The CDI module is located outside the flywheel and requires no regular maintenance. Refer to the appropriate following paragraphs for the model being serviced.

Breaker Point Ignition System. Breaker points may be located behind either the flywheel or the recoil starter. To inspect or service the breaker points, first remove the starter assembly. Refer to the following paragraphs for service.

If the breaker points are located behind the recoil starter pawl, unbolt and remove the lock nut and the starter pawl carrier. The lock nut and pawl carrier both have left hand threads.

If the breaker points are located under the flywheel, the opening in the flywheel will allow adjustment of the breaker point gap, but the flywheel must be removed to install new breaker points or condenser. If necessary, remove the retaining nut and use an appropriate puller to remove the flywheel.

To check and adjust the point gap and ignition timing, disconnect the stop switch wire and attach one lead from a timing tester (Echo 990510-00031 or equivalent) to the stop wire. Ground the other tester lead to the engine. Turn the flywheel in the normal direction and use the timing tester to determine the exact location where the breaker points **just** open.

On models with points located behind the starter pawl, the timing mark should be aligned with the edge of the coil leg as shown in Fig. EC14.

On models with points under the flywheel, the first mark on the flywheel should align with the timing mark on the crankcase as shown in Fig. EC15.

Adjust the breaker point gap as necessary to set the timing to the correct position. Setting the gap wider will advance the timing. Narrowing the gap will cause the points to open later, when the timing mark is closer to the Top Dead Center mark "T." When correctly set, the breaker point gap at maximum

Illustrations courtesy Echo Inc.

pening will be 0.3-0.4 mm (0.012-0.016 n.).

CD Ignition System. The CD ignition system has no moving parts except he flywheel magnets and should require no regular maintenance. The omponents may be affected by extreme eat or cold.

Ignition can be considered satisfacory if a spark will jump across the 3 nm (1/8 in.) electrode gap of a test plug vhen the engine is turned with the reoil starter. If there is no spark, check he stop switch and connecting wire for horts to ground. Ignition may be iregular at starting speeds if gap beween the legs of the coil core and the lywheel magnets is too wide. Refer to he IGNITION paragraphs in the REPAIRS section for setting the air gap and for testing the ignition coil.

CARBON. Exhaust ports in the cylnder and the muffler should be cleaned periodically to prevent loss of power due to carbon build-up. Remove the muffler cover and any baffles. Turn the flywheel until the piston is at Top Dead Center, then scrape any carbon from inside the muffler. Remove carbon from inside the ports using a wooden scraper. Be careful not to scratch the edges of the ports or the piston. Do not attempt to run the engine with any parts of the muffler missing.

REPAIRS

TIGHTENING TORQUES. Recommended tightening torque specifications are as follows.

Spark plug . . . . . . 17 N·m (150 in.-lb.)

Cylinder cover
- (as equipped) . . . . 1.5-1.9 N·m (13-17 in.-lb.)

Cylinder
- GT-160, GT-160A & GT-160AE, GT-200, GT-200BE & GTL-140. . 5.7-6.0 N·m (50-55 in.-lb.)
- SRM-140D, SRM-140DA, SRM-200 . . . . 5.7-6.0 N·m (50-55 in.-lb.)
- SRM-200D, SRM-200DA & SRM-200DB. . . . . 3-4 N·m (30-35 in.-lb.)
- SRM-200E, SRM-200AE & SRM-200FA, SRM-210E & SRM-210AE. . . . . 5.7-6.0 N·m (50-55 in.-lb.)
- SRM-202D, SRM-202DA & SRM-202FA . . . . 3-4 N·m (30-35 in.-lb.)
- SRM-300, SRM-300E, SRM-300E/1, SRM-300AE, SRM-300AE/1 . . . . 7-8 N·m (65-75 in.-lb.)
- SRM-302ADX . . . . 8-9 N·m (13-17 in.-lb.)
- SRM-400, SRM-400E, SRM-400AE & SRM-402DE . . . . 7-8 N·m (65-75 in.-lb.)

Crankcase
- GTL-140. . . . . 4.5-5.7 N·m (40-50 in.-lb.)
- SRM-140D, SRM-140DA. . . . . 4.5-5.7 N·m (40-50 in.-lb.)
- SRM-302ADX . . . . 4.5-5.7 N·m (40-50 in.-lb.)
- All Other Models. . . . . 4-5 N·m (35-45 in.-lb.)

Flywheel nut
- GT-140, GT-160 . . . . 8-10 N·m (70-80 in.-lb.)
- GT-160AE . . . . 14-16 N·m (120-140 in.-lb.)
- GTL-140. . . . . 20-24 N·m (175-210 in.-lb.)
- GT-200 . . . . . 8-10 N·m (70-80 in.-lb.)
- GT-200BE . . . . 14-16 N·m (120-140 in.-lb.)
- SRM-140D, SRM-140DA . 20-24 N·m (175-210 in.-lb.)
- SRM-200, SRM-200AE, SRM-200BE. . . . . 14-16 N·m (120-140 in.-lb.)
- SRM-200D, SRM-200DA, SRM-200DB, SRM-202DA & SRM-202FA. . . . . 20-24 N·m (175-210 in.-lb.)
- SRM-210E, SRM-210AE. . 14-16 N·m (120-140 in.-lb.)
- SRM-300, SRM-300E, SRM-300E/1 . . . . 20-24 N·m (175-210 in.-lb.)

IGNITION. Clearance (air gap) between the legs of the coil/module and the flywheel magnets should be 0.35-0.40 mm (0.014-0.016 in.) for models with breaker point ignition; 0.3 mm (0.012 in.) for models with CD ignition. If the gap is too wide, the ignition may be weak and the engine difficult to start. If the gap is too close, the coil and flywheel may bump into each other and cause extensive damage.

To check the air gap, first remove the fan cover, then turn the flywheel until the magnets are located under the legs of the coil. Use non-magnetic feeler gauge to measure the clearance between the coil legs and the flywheel magnets (Fig. EC16).

To change the air gap, loosen the two screws attaching the coil, then move the coil as required. Threads of the coil attaching screws should be coated with Loctite before tightening.

Resistance of the coil windings can be checked using an accurate ohmmeter. Resistance should be as follows.

Models With Breaker Points	Primary ohms	Secondary ohms
GT-140A, GT-140B, GT-160 & GT-160A	0.5-0.8	7-10
GTL-140	0.6-0.8	7-10
SRM-200D, SRM-200DA, SRM-200DB, SRM-202DA & SRM-202FA	0.5-0.6	5-6
SRM-202DB	...	5-6
GT-200	0.6-0.8	5-6
SRM-140D & SRM-140DA	0.6-0.8	8-10
SRM-200	0.5-0.7	6-9
GT-200A, GT-200B & SRM-302ADX	0.5-0.7	8-9.5
Models With CD Ignition		
Models with exciter lead	...	500-1,500
Models without exciter lead		1,500-3,000

PISTON, PIN AND RINGS. To remove the piston (36—Fig. EC17 or 17—Fig. EC18), separate the drive

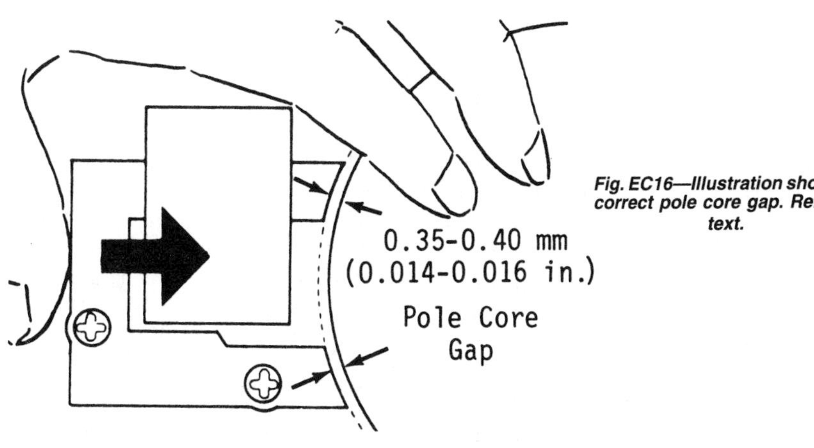

Fig. EC16—Illustration showing correct pole core gap. Refer to text.

Illustrations courtesy Echo Inc.

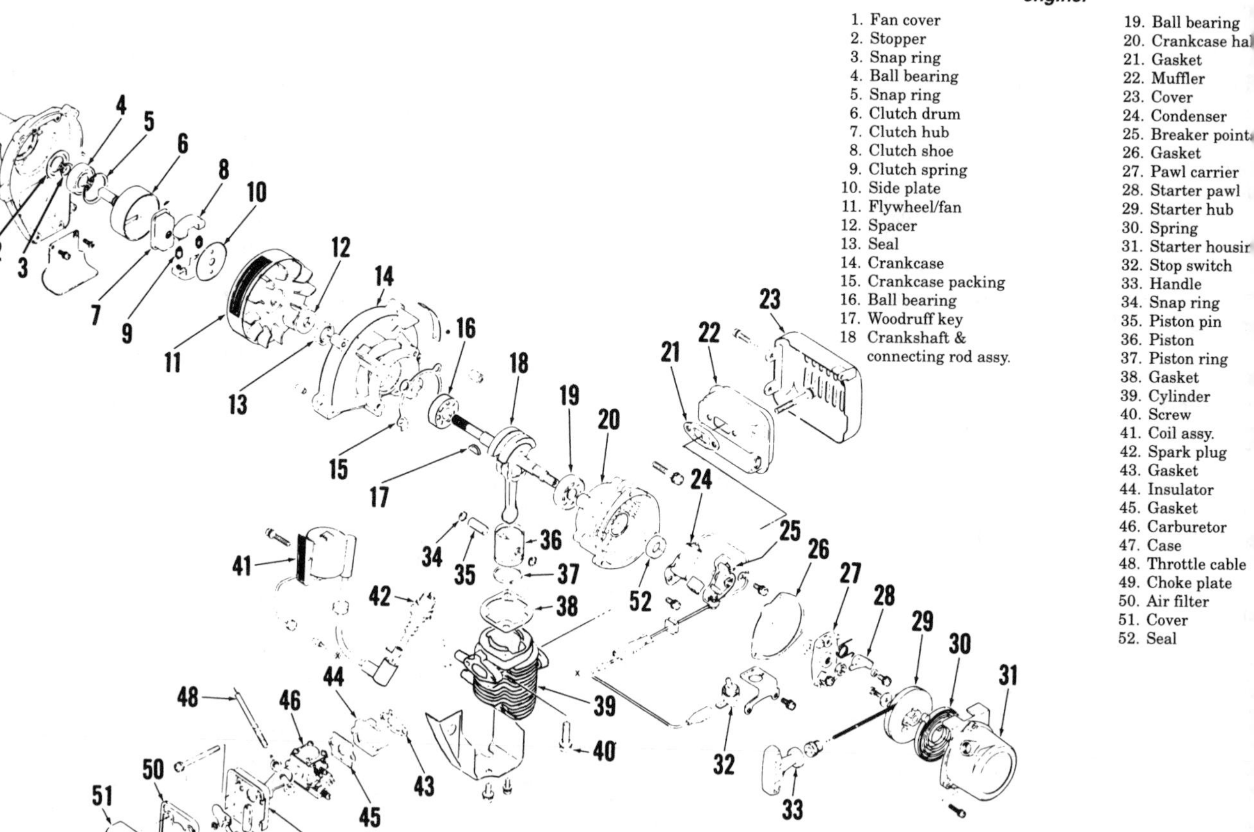

Fig. EC17—Exploded view of typical 140 serie engine.

1. Fan cover
2. Stopper
3. Snap ring
4. Ball bearing
5. Snap ring
6. Clutch drum
7. Clutch hub
8. Clutch shoe
9. Clutch spring
10. Side plate
11. Flywheel/fan
12. Spacer
13. Seal
14. Crankcase
15. Crankcase packing
16. Ball bearing
17. Woodruff key
18. Crankshaft & connecting rod assy.
19. Ball bearing
20. Crankcase ha
21. Gasket
22. Muffler
23. Cover
24. Condenser
25. Breaker point
26. Gasket
27. Pawl carrier
28. Starter pawl
29. Starter hub
30. Spring
31. Starter housir
32. Stop switch
33. Handle
34. Snap ring
35. Piston pin
36. Piston
37. Piston ring
38. Gasket
39. Cylinder
40. Screw
41. Coil assy.
42. Spark plug
43. Gasket
44. Insulator
45. Gasket
46. Carburetor
47. Case
48. Throttle cable
49. Choke plate
50. Air filter
51. Cover
52. Seal

shaft housing from the engine. Remove covers, carburetor, muffler and ignition coil. Remove the screws attaching the cylinder, then pull the cylinder straight up, off the piston. Remove the piston pin retaining rings, push the pin out using a suitable pusher tool, then separate the piston from the connecting rod. Make sure the needle bearings are not lost when separating the piston from the connecting rod.

The piston may be equipped with one or two rings. Ring(s) are pinned to prevent rotation in the groove(s). Standard ring side clearance in piston groove is 0.06 mm (0.0024 in.) for all models. If side clearance is 0.10 mm (0.004 in.) or more, install new ring(s) and/or piston.

Install a new pin if it is worn 0.02 mm (0.0008 in.) or more smaller than standard diameter. Install a new piston if the pin bore is enlarged more than 0.03 mm (0.0012 in.) larger than standard. Refer to the following for standard pin diameter and bore diameter in piston.

Models	Piston pin and bore standard diameter
SRM-140D	6.0 mm (0.2362 in.)
SRM-302ADX	9.0 mm (0.3543 in.)
SRM-300, SRM-300E, SRM-300AE, SRM-400AE, SRM400E & SRM-400DE	10 mm (0.3937 in.)
Other models	8.0 mm (0.3150 in.)

Install a new piston if the skirt diameter is 0.10 mm (0.004 in.) smaller than standard. Refer to the following for standard piston skirt diameter measured at right angles to the pin.

Cylinder bore diameter	Piston skirt standard diameter
26 mm (1.024 in.)	25.90 mm (1.020 in.)
28 mm (1.102 in.)	27.90 mm (1.101 in.)
32.2 mm (1.268 in.)	32.10 mm (1.264 in.)
35 mm (1.378 in.)	34.90 mm (1.374 in.)
40 mm (1.575 in.)	39.90 mm (1.571 in.)

Ring end gaps must be correctly positioned over the pins in the ring grooves when installing the piston. Attach the piston to the connecting rod with the arrow on top of piston toward the exhaust. Make sure the clips retaining the piston pin are completely seated in the piston pin bore grooves. The opening in the pin retaining clips should be either to the top or bottom. Be careful to install the cylinder straight down over the piston. If the cylinder is turned, the ring can catch in a port and break the end of the ring.

CYLINDER. The piston, rings and cylinder are available in standard size only and the cylinder should not be bored oversize. Inspect the cylinder for any damage and install new parts as necessary. If the chrome plating is worn from the cylinder, a new cylinder should be installed.

CRANKSHAFT AND CONNECTING ROD ASSEMBLY. The crankshaft and connecting rod are available only as an assembly (18—Fig. EC17 or 25—Fig. EC18); individual components are not available.

To remove the crankshaft and connecting rod assembly, remove the flywheel, rewind starter, cylinder and piston. Remove the pawl carrier (27—Fig. EC17) or fan (11—Fig. EC18). Remove the screws attaching the halves of the crankcase together and separate halves. Heat the crankcase if necessary to remove the main bearings from the crankcase bores. If the bear-

Illustrations courtesy Echo Inc.

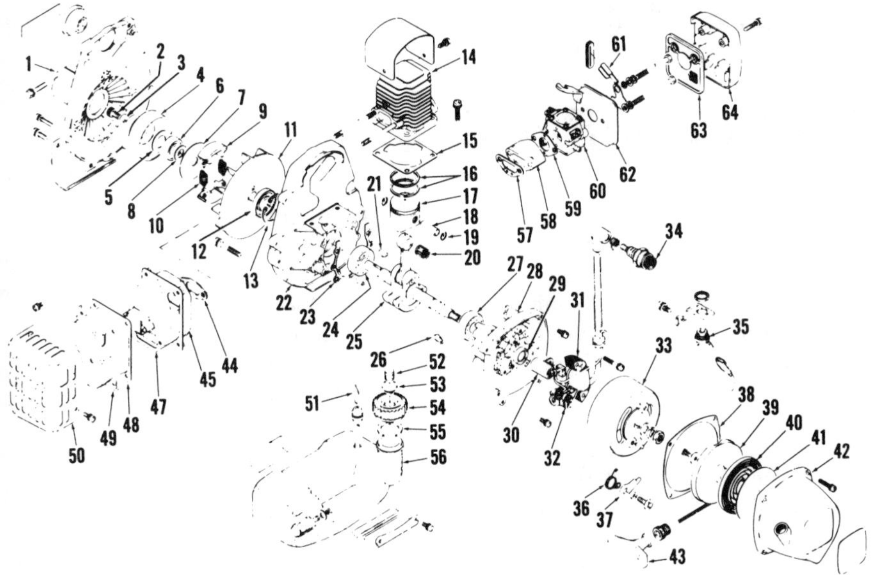

Fig. EC18—Exploded view of typical 200 series engine.

1. Fan cover
2. Bolt
3. Washer
4. Clutch drum
5. Spacer
6. Ball bearing
7. Plate
8. Spacer
9. Clutch shoe
10. Clutch spring
11. Fan
12. Seal
13. Snap ring
14. Cylinder
15. Gasket
16. Piston rings
17. Piston
18. Piston rings
19. Snap ring
20. Needle bearing
21. Woodruff key
22. Crankcase half
23. Packing
24. Ball bearing
25. Crankshaft & connecting rod assy.
26. Woodruff key
27. Ball bearing
28. Crankcase half
29. Seal
30. Sleeve
31. Coil assy.
32. Breaker points
33. Flywheel
34. Spark plug
35. Stop switch
36. Spring
37. Pawl
38. Gasket
39. Starter drum
40. Spring
41. Plate
42. Starter housing
43. Handle
44. Gasket
45. Case
47. Baffle
48. Gasket
49. Case
50. Cover
51. Fuel line
52. Vent
53. Check valve
54. Cap
55. Gasket
56. Fuel tank
57. Gasket
58. Insulator
59. Gasket
60. Carburetor
61. Choke plate
62. Case
63. Air filter
64. Cover

ings stay on the crankshaft, use a suitable puller to pull the bearings from the main journals. Some models may have a snap ring (13—Fig. EC18) installed in the case bore.

The main bearings should turn smoothly with no perceptible play or ratcheting. Connecting rod side clearance should be 0.55-0.60 mm (0.022-0.026 in.), but must not exceed 0.7 mm (0.028 in.) for GT-140, GT-140A, GT-140B, GTL-140, GT-160, GT-160A, GT-160AE, GT-200, GT-200A, GT-200B, GT-200BE, SRM-140D, SRM -140DA, 0.4 mm (0.016 in.). Connecting rod side clearance for other models should be 0.25-0.30 mm (0.010-0.012 in.), but must not exceed 0.40 mm (0.016 in.). If connecting rod side clearance is excessive, the connecting rod and crankshaft assembly should be renewed.

The piston pin should have very little noticeable clearance in the needle bearing located in the connecting rod. If play is excessive with a new piston pin or if the bearing is rough, install a new bearing. Be careful not to damage the connecting rod when removing and installing the bearing.

Support the crankshaft at the main bearings or journals and measure runout at the ends of the crankshaft. Maximum runout is 0.05 mm (0.002 in.).

New crankshaft seals and gaskets must be used when assembling. Use suitable tools to press new main bearings and seals into the crankcase bores. Lips of seals (13 and 52—Fig. EC17 or 12 and 29—Fig. EC18) should be toward inside of crankcase and should be lubricated before installing the crankshaft. Refer to TIGHTENING TORQUES paragraph for recommended torque values. Trim excess gasket material from the cylinder base of the crankcase before installing the base gasket and cylinder (38 and 39—Fig. EC17 or 14 and 15—Fig. EC18).

KIORITZ-ECHO SPECIAL TOOLS

The following special tools are available from Echo Central Service Distributors.

FLYWHEEL HOLDER

897712-06030...SRM-140, SRM-140DA
897712-07930............GTL-140
897501-03932..........SRM-200D, SRM-200DA, SRM-200DB, SRM202DA, SRM-202FA, SRM-302ADX
895115-00330... GT-160AE, GT-200BE, SRM-200, SRM-200E, SRM-200AE, SRM-200BE, SRM-201F, SRM-201FA, SRM-210E, SRM-210AE, SRM-300E, SRM-300AE, SRM-400E, SRM-400AE, SRM-402DD

MAGNETO SPANNER AND GAGE

895115-00330............All Models

BEARING WEDGE SET

897701-06030..........SRM-140D, SRM-140DA, GT-140A, GTL-140, GT-160, GT-160AE, GT-200, GT-200A, GT-200B, GT-200BE, SRM-200, SRM-200AE, SRM-200BE, SRM-200E, SRM-201F, SRM-201FA, SRM-202DA, SRM-202FA, SRM-210E, SRM-210AE, SRM-300E, SRM-300AE, SRM-400E, SRM-400AE
897701-02830..........SRM-200D, SRM-200DA, SRM-200DB, SRM-202DA, SRM-202FA, SRM-300

DRIVERS

897718-06030..........SRM-140D, SRM-140DA, SRM-200, SRM-200AE, SRM-200BE, SRM-200E, GT-140A, GT-140B, GT-160, GT-160A, GTL-140, GT-200, SRM-302ADX
897718-02830..........SRM-300E, SRM-300AE, SRM-400E, SRM-400AE, SRM-402DD

PISTON PIN TOOL

097702-06030............All Models

PRESSURE TESTER

990510-0020.............All Models

TIMING TESTER

990510-00031............All Models

Illustrations courtesy Echo Inc.

ECHO

ENGINE SERVICE

Model	Bore	Stroke	Displacement
2400	34.0 mm (1.339 in.)	26.0 mm (1.024 in.)	23.6 cc (1.440 cu. in.)
2500 & 2600	32.2 mm (1.268 in.)	30.0 mm (1.181 in.)	24.4 cc (1.489 cu. in.)
3100	36.0 mm (1.417 in.)	30.0 mm (1.181 in.)	30.5 cc (1.861 cu. in.)
3400 & 3600	38.0 mm (1.50 in.)	30.0 mm (1.18 in.)	34.0 cc (2.08 cu. in.)
3800	38.0 mm (1.496 in.)	33.0 mm (1.299 in.)	37.4 cc (2.284 cu. in.)
4600	42 mm (1.654 in.)	33 mm (1.299 in.)	45.7 cc (2.790 cu. in.)

ENGINE INFORMATION

These two-stroke air-cooled gasoline engines are used on Echo trimmers and brush cutters. To obtain the correct service parts, it is necessary to know the complete model number and the serial number of the equipment.

MAINTENANCE

LUBRICATION. The engine is lubricated by mixing oil with the gasoline fuel. Use only an oil designed for two-stroke, air cooled engines. Refer to the ECHO TRIMMER SERVICE section for the recommended type of oil and mixing ratio.

SPARK PLUG. The recommended spark plug for normal application is NGK BPM7A, Champion CJ7Y or equivalent. The electrode gap should be 0.024-0.028 in. (0.6-0.7 mm). Tighten the spark plug securely to the torque listed in the TIGHTENING TORQUE paragraph.

CARBURETOR. Walbro WA, Walbro WT, Walbro WY, Walbro WYL and Zama C1U diaphragm carburetors and Keihin float type carburetors have been used. The manufacturer's name and model number are stamped on the carburetor. Refer to appropriate ECHO Equipment Section for carburetor application and initial settings for mixture needles. Refer to the following tuning and service information for the specific carburetor type used. When installing, tighten the attaching screws to the torque listed in the TIGHTENING TORQUE paragraph.

Walbro WA. Refer to appropriate Equipment Section for carburetor application and initial settings for mixture needles (17 and 18—Fig. EC201). For performing final mixture adjustments, the engine must be at normal operating temperature and running. On trimmer models, trimmer line should be at the maximum recommended length or blade installed. Adjust the idle speed by turning screw (31) until the engine is operating at slow idle speed. On models with clutch, idle speed should be slower than clutch engagement speed or about 2,500-3,000 rpm. Adjust the low speed mixture needle so the engine runs smoothly at idle speed and accelerates without hesitation. If necessary, readjust idle speed. Operate the engine at full throttle (with no load) and adjust the high speed mixture needle to obtain maximum rpm, then turn the needle counterclockwise until the engine just starts to slow because of the mixture being too rich (four-cycle).

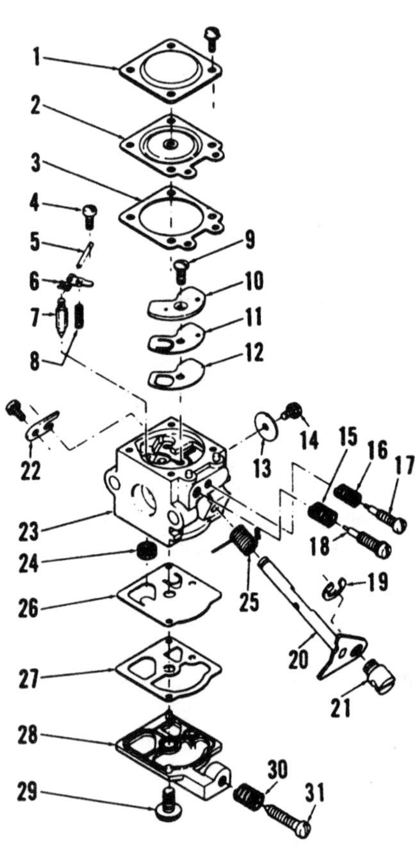

Fig. EC201—Exploded view of Walbro WA carburetor typical of the type used on some models.

1. Cover
2. Metering diaphragm
3. Gasket
4. Metering lever screw
5. Metering lever pin
6. Metering lever
7. Fuel inlet valve
8. Metering lever spring
9. Circuit plate screw
10. Circuit plate
11. Check valve
12. Gasket
13. Throttle valve
14. Shutter screw
15. Spring
16. Spring
17. High speed mixture needle
18. Low speed mixture needle
19. "E" clip
20. Throttle shaft
21. Swivel
22. Throttle shaft clip
23. Body
24. Inlet screen
25. Return spring
26. Fuel pump diaphragm
27. Gasket
28. Cover
29. Cover screw
30. Spring
31. Idle speed stop screw

When overhauling the carburetor, refer to Fig. EC201. Remove metering chamber cover (1) and fuel pump cover (28) for access to internal components. Remove metering lever (6), fuel inlet valve (7), circuit plate (10), check valve (11), fuel inlet screen (24) and mixture screws (17 and 18).

Clean and inspect all components. If the unit has been improperly stored,

Illustrations courtesy Echo Inc.

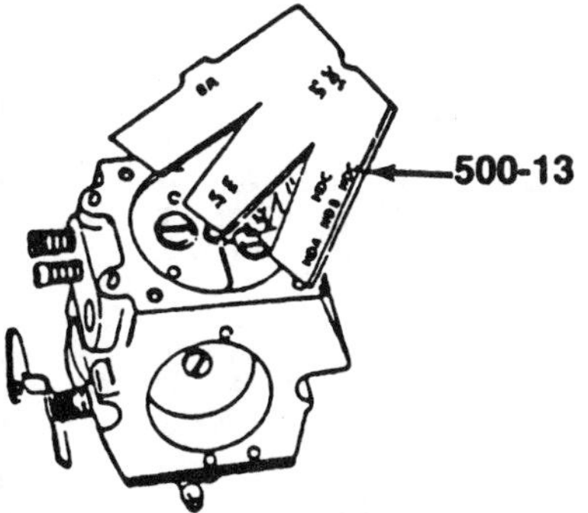

Fig. EC202—Metering lever should just touch leg of Walbro tool 500-13. Bend lever to obtain correct lever height.

passages may be clogged with deposits that are hard, solid and nearly transparent. Clean passages with suitable carburetor cleaning solvent and compressed air. Be careful not to damage the openings or sealing surfaces while cleaning. Examine the fuel inlet valve (7) and seat. Inlet valve can be replaced, but the seat is part of the carburetor body and cannot be serviced. Examine the mixture needles (17 and 18) and install new needles if damaged. Clean fuel screen (24). Inspect diaphragms (2 and 26) for tears or other damage. The diaphragms must be flexible.

Check the height of the metering lever as shown in Fig. EC202 using Walbro tool 500-13. The metering lever should just touch leg on the tool (lever should be just flush with the top of the circuit plate). Bend the lever carefully if necessary to obtain correct height.

Walbro WT. The manufacturer's name and model number are stamped on the carburetor. Refer to the appropriate Equipment Section for carburetor original application and initial settings for mixture needles. When installing, tighten the attaching screws to the torque listed in the TIGHTENING TORQUE paragraph.

Refer to Fig. EC203 for an exploded view typical of the carburetor. Initial adjustment of the low speed mixture needle (17) and the high speed mixture needle (19) is 1 turn open. The settings of these mixture needles is critical to the operation of the engine. Final adjustment should be performed carefully to insure easy starting and maximum performance.

To adjust the mixture needles, first remove, clean and reinstall the air filter. Start the engine and allow it to run until it reaches normal operating temperature. If necessary, turn each of the mixture screws (17 and 19) clockwise until seated lightly, then back the screws out (counterclockwise) the number of turns listed in the appropriate Equipment Section so the engine can be started. Turn the idle speed stop screw (4) so the engine idles slowly, just below clutch engagement rpm. Adjust the low speed mixture needle (17) so the engine idles smoothly and accelerates without hesitation. Readjust the idle speed stop screw (4) if necessary to slow the idle speed. The trimmer head should not turn when the engine is idling. Adjust the high speed mixture needle (19) to provide the best performance while operating at maximum speed under load. The high speed mixture needle may be set slightly rich to improve performance under load. The engine may be damaged if the high-speed screw is set too lean.

To disassemble the carburetor, refer to Fig. EC203. Remove fuel pump cover (3) and metering chamber cover (30) for access to internal components. Remove metering lever (25), fuel inlet valve (24) and fuel inlet screen (9). Remove nozzle (21) and check valve seat (22). Welch plug (20) can be removed by prying out with a sharp punch. Use care not to damage carburetor casting when removing Welch plug. Remove fuel mixture screws (17 and 19).

Clean and inspect all components. If the unit has been improperly stored, passages may be clogged with deposits that are hard, solid and nearly transparent. Be careful not to damage the openings or sealing surfaces while cleaning. Check the condition of dia-

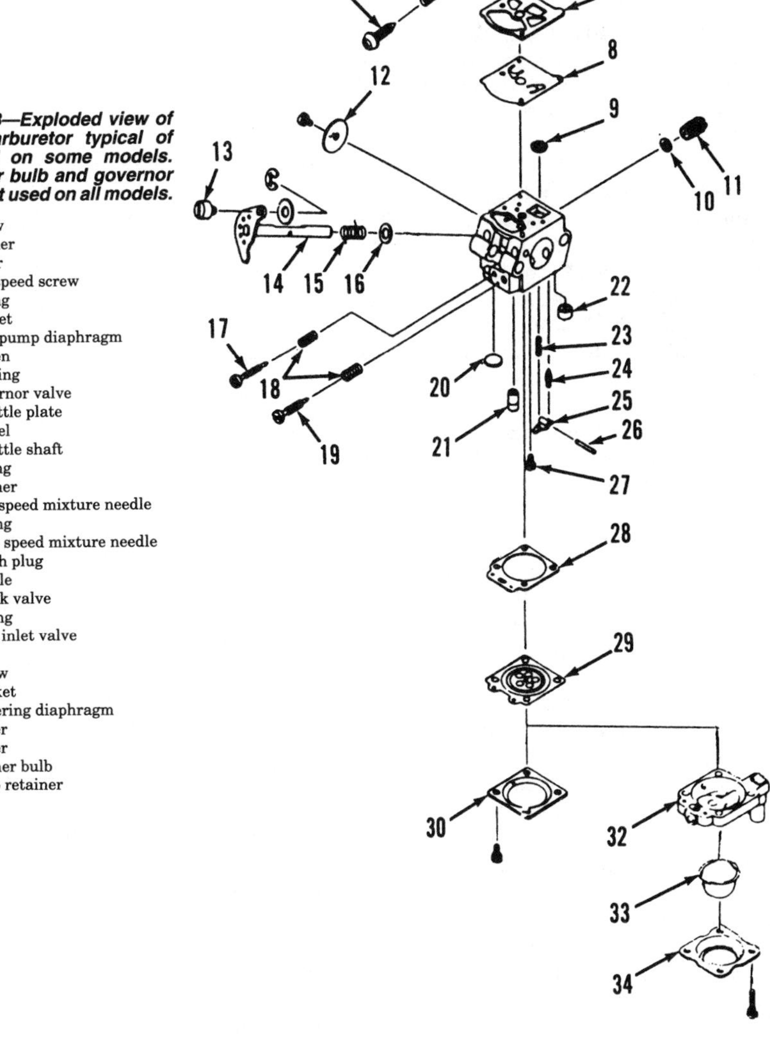

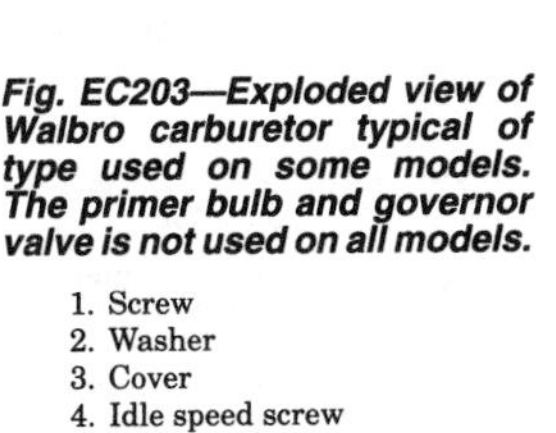

Fig. EC203—Exploded view of Walbro carburetor typical of type used on some models. The primer bulb and governor valve is not used on all models.

1. Screw
2. Washer
3. Cover
4. Idle speed screw
5. Spring
7. Gasket
8. Fuel pump diaphragm
9. Screen
10. "O" ring
11. Governor valve
12. Throttle plate
13. Swivel
14. Throttle shaft
15. Spring
16. Washer
17. Low speed mixture needle
18. Spring
19. High speed mixture needle
20. Welch plug
21. Nozzle
22. Check valve
23. Spring
24. Fuel inlet valve
26. Pin
27. Screw
28. Gasket
29. Metering diaphragm
30. Cover
32. Cover
33. Primer bulb
34. Bulb retainer

Illustrations courtesy Echo Inc.

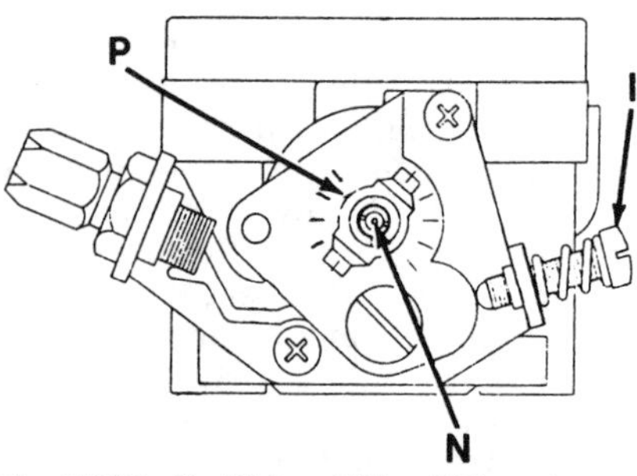

Fig. EC204—On Walbro WY or WYL carburetor, idle speed screw is located at (I), idle limiter plate is located at (P) and idle mixture needle is located at (N). A plug covers the idle mixture needle.

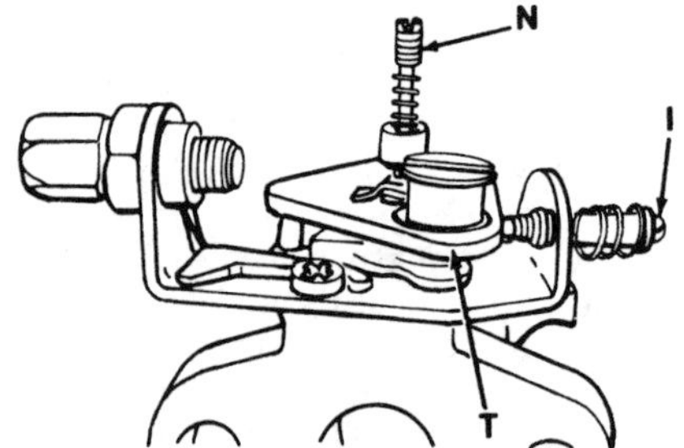

Fig. EC205—View of idle mixture needle used on Walbro WY and WYL carburetor.

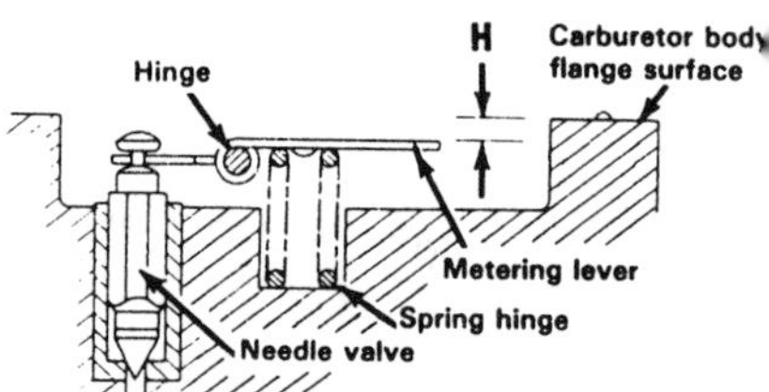

Fig. EC207—Metering lever height (H) must be set on diaphragm type carburetors. Refer to text for specified height.

phragms (8 and 29) carefully. Install new diaphragms if hard (not flexible), torn or otherwise damaged. Examine the fuel inlet valve (24), spring (23) and lever (25). A new fuel inlet valve needle (24), and mixture needles (17 and 19) can be installed, but their seats cannot be serviced if damaged. Inspect the condition of the filter screen (9).

Check the height of the metering lever as shown in Fig. EC202 using Walbro tool 500-13 or equivalent. End of metering lever should just touch the leg of the tool. If tool is not available, the lever should be 1.52-1.78 mm (0.060-0.070 in) below surface for gasket (28—Fig. EC203). Carefully bend the lever if necessary to obtain the correct lever height.

Walbro WY and WYL. These carburetors use a barrel type throttle rather than a throttle plate. Idle fuel for the carburetor flows into the throttle barrel where it is fed into the air stream. Refer to appropriate Equipment Section for carburetor application and initial settings for mixture needle. The idle fuel flow can be adjusted by turning an idle limiter plate (P—Fig. EC204). Initial setting is in center notch. Rotating the plate clockwise will lean the idle mixture.

Inside the idle limiter plate is an idle mixture needle (N—Fig. EC205) that is preset at the factory. If removed, use the following procedure to determine correct position. Find the point where the threads of the idle mixture needle just start to engage, then turn the screw **IN** the number of turns listed in the appropriate Equipment Section. The needle does not contact a seat. Rotate idle mixture plate (P) to center notch.

For performing final mixture adjustment, the engine must be at normal operating temperature and running. On trimmer models, trimmer line should be at the maximum recommended length or blade installed. Adjust the idle speed by turning screw (3) until the

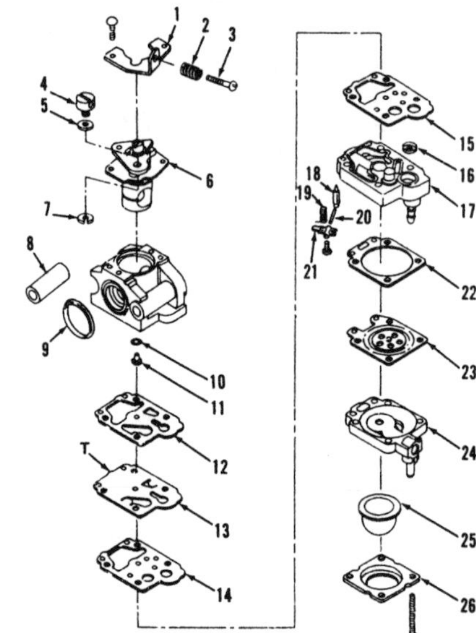

Fig. EC206—Exploded view of Walbro WY carburetor. Model WYL is similar.

1. Bracket
2. Spring
3. Idle speed screw
4. Swivel
5. Washer
6. Throttle barrel assy.
7. "E" ring
8. Sleeve
9. "O" ring
10. "O" ring
11. Main jet
12. Gasket
13. Fuel pump diaphragm
14. Fuel pump plate
15. Gasket
16. Fuel screen
17. Fuel pump body
18. Fuel inlet valve
19. Spring
20. Pin
21. Metering lever
22. Gasket
23. Metering diaphragm
24. Plate
25. Primer bulb
26. Cover

engine is operating at slow idle speed. On models with clutch, idle speed should be slower than clutch engagement speed or about 2,500-3,000 rpm. Adjust the low speed mixture needle so the engine runs smoothly at idle speed and accelerates without hesitation. If necessary, readjust idle speed. Rotate the idle mixture plate to the center notch. The high speed mixture is controlled by a removable fixed jet (11).

To overhaul the carburetor, refer to Fig. EC206. Remove retainer (26), plate (24), diaphragm (23), fuel pump body (17), plate (14) and diaphragm (13). Remove bracket (1) and throttle barrel assembly (6).

On models with a plastic body, clean only using solvents approved for use with plastic. Do not use wires or drills to clean orifices. Do not disassemble the throttle barrel assembly. The idle speed mixture needle is available only as an assembly with the throttle barrel. Examine the fuel inlet valve (18) and its seat. The inlet valve is renewable, but the seat is part of the fuel pump body (17). Clean fuel screen (16). Inspect diaphragms (13 and 23). Note that tabs on plates and gaskets (12 through 15) will "stair step" when correctly assembled. Metering lever (Fig. EC207) should be 1.5 mm (0.059 in.) below the surface for gasket (22). Bend the metering lever carefully to adjust the height (H), taking care not to force the needle against its seat.

Zama C1U. Refer to appropriate Equipment Section for carburetor application and initial settings for mixture needles (12 and 14—Fig. EC208). The settings of these mixture screws is critical to the operation of the engine. Final adjustment should be performed carefully to insure easy starting and maximum performance.

To adjust the mixture screws, first remove and clean the air filter, then reinstall it. Start the engine and allow it to run until it reaches normal operating temperature. If necessary, turn each of the mixture screws (12 and 14) clockwise until seated lightly, then back the screws out (counterclockwise) the number of turns specified so the engine can be started. Turn the idle speed stop screw (26) so the engine idles at about 2500-3000 rpm. Adjust the low speed mixture needle (14) so the engine idles smoothly and accelerates without hesitation. Readjust the idle speed stop screw (26) if necessary to slow the idle speed. If equipped with a clutch, the trimmer head should not turn when the engine is idling. Adjust the high speed mixture screw (12) to provide the best performance while operating at maximum speed under load. The high speed mixture screw may be set slightly rich to improve performance under load. The engine may be damaged if the high-speed screw is set too lean.

To disassemble the carburetor, refer to Fig. EC208. Remove metering cham-

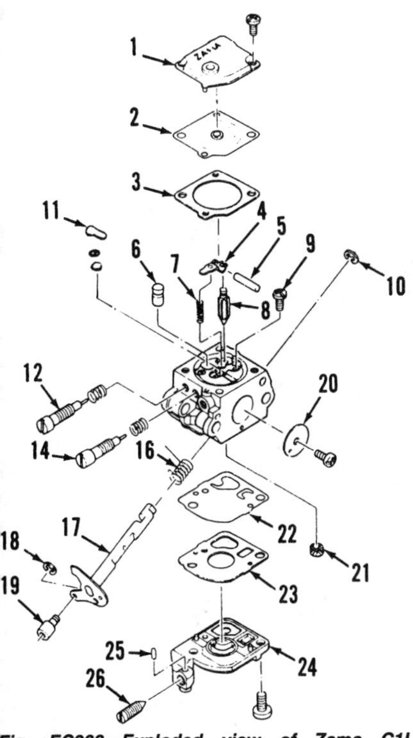

Fig. EC208—Exploded view of Zama C1U carburetor typical of the type used on some models.

1. Cover
2. Metering diaphragm
3. Gasket
4. Metering lever
5. Pin
6. Nozzle
7. Spring
8. Fuel inlet valve
9. Screw
10. "E" ring
11. Welch plug
12. High speed mixture screw
14. Low speed mixture screw
16. Spring
17. Throttle shaft
18. "E" ring
19. Swivel
20. Throttle plate
21. Fuel inlet screen
22. Fuel pump diaphragm
23. Gasket
24. Cover
25. Strainer
26. Idle speed screw

ber cover (1) and fuel pump cover (24) for access to internal components. Remove fuel inlet valve (8) and nozzle (6). Remove mixture adjusting screws (12 and 14). To remove the Welch plug (11), carefully pierce the plug near the end of the "tail" section, then pry the plug out. Do not insert the punch too deeply or the body and passages under the plug may be damaged. Apply sealant to outer edge of new plug before installing.

Clean and inspect all components. If the unit has been improperly stored, passages may be clogged with deposits that are hard, solid and nearly transparent. Be careful not to damage the openings or sealing surfaces while cleaning. Check the condition of diaphragms (2 and 22) carefully. Install new diaphragms if hard (not flexible), torn or otherwise damaged. Examine the fuel inlet valve (8), spring (7) and lever (4). A new fuel inlet valve needle (8), and mixture screws (12 and 14) can be installed, but their seats cannot be serviced if damaged.

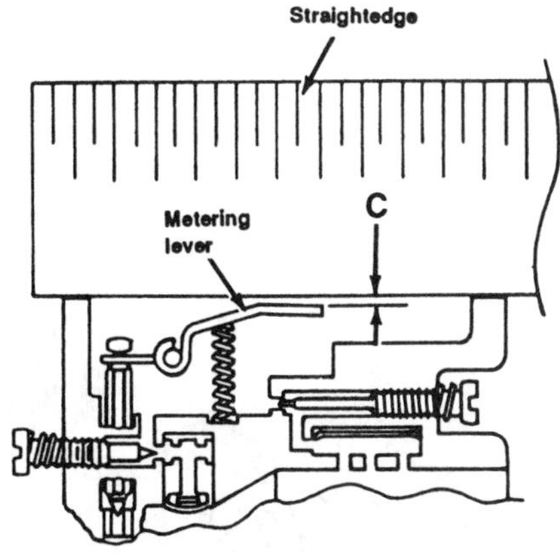

Fig. EC209—Metering lever should be bent so height (C) is 0-0.3 mm (0-0.012 in.) on Zama C1U carburetor.

Check the height of the metering lever as shown in Fig. EC209. The clearance (C) between the metering lever and a straightedge positioned across the gasket surface of the carburetor body should be 0-0.012 in. (0-0.3 mm). Carefully bend the lever if necessary to obtain the correct lever height.

IGNITION SYSTEM. All engines are equipped with an electronic ignition system that does not use breaker points. On some models, the ignition module is separate from the ignition coil; however, the module is incorporated in the coil assembly of most models.

Ignition can be considered satisfactory if a spark will jump across the 3 mm (1/8 in.) electrode gap of a test plug when the engine is turned with the recoil starter. If there is no spark, check the stop switch and connecting wire for shorts to ground. Ignition may be irregular at starting speeds if gap between the legs of the coil core and the flywheel magnets is too wide. Refer to the IGNITION paragraphs in the REPAIRS section for setting the air gap and for testing the ignition coil.

REPAIRS

COMPRESSION PRESSURE. For optimum performance, cylinder compression pressure should be 105 psi for 2400 models; 115 psi for 2500, 2600, 3100, 3800 and 4600 models; 135 psi for 3400 and 3600 models. Compression pressure should always be at least 75 percent of the optimum.

TIGHTENING TORQUE. Recommended tightening torque values are as follows.

Carburetor
- 2400 & 2500 . . . . 3.5-4.5 N•m (30-40 in.-lb.)
- 2600, 3100, 3400 & 3600. 3.0-4.5 N•m (25-40 in.-lb.)
- 3800 & 4600 . . 4-5 N•m (35-45 in.-lb.)

Carburetor insulator
- 2400 . . . . 3-4 N•m (25-35 in.-lb.)
- 2500 . . . . . 3.5-4.0 N•m (30-35 in.-lb.)
- 2600 . . . . . 7.5-8.5 N•m (65-75 in.-lb.)
- 3100, 3400 & 3600. . . . . 6-8 N•m (45-70 in.-lb.)
- 3800 & 4600 . . 4-5 N•m (35-45 in.-lb.)

Clutch hub
- 2400 . . . . 18-20 N•m (160-175 in.-lb.)

Clutch shoes
- 2500 . . . . 5-6 N•m (45-55 in.-lb.)
- 2600, 3100, 3400 & 3600. . . 7-11 N•m (60-95 in.-lb.)
- 3800 & 4600 . 8-10 N•m (70-80 in.-lb.)

Crankcase
- 2400 . . . . . 3.5-4.5 N•m (30-40 in.-lb.)
- 2500 . . . . . 3.5-4.0 N•m (30-35 in.-lb.)
- 2600 . . . . . 3.0-5.0 N•m (25-45 in.-lb.)
- 3100, 3400 & 3600. . . . . 7-11 N•m (60-95 in.-lb.)
- 3800 & 4600 . . 8-9 N•m (70-80 in.-lb.)

Cylinder
- 2400 . . . . . 7.5-8.5 N•m (65-75 in.-lb.)
- 2600, 3100, 3400 & 3600. . . 7-10 N•m (60-90 in.-lb.)
- 2500, 3800 & 4600. . . . . 8-9 N•m (70-80 in.-lb.)

Cylinder cover
- 2600 . . . . 3-4 N•m (25-35 in.-lb.)
- 3100, 3400 & 3600. . . . . 5-7 N•m (45-50 in.-lb.)

Fan cover
- 2400 . . . . . 2.0-2.5 N•m (20-25 in.-lb.)
- 2500 . . . . 3-4 N•m (25-35 in.-lb.)
- 2600 . . . . . 3.0-4.5 N•m (25-40 in.-lb.)
- 3100, 3400 & 3600. . . . . 7-11 N•m (60-95 in.-lb.)
- 3800 & 4600. . . . . 7.5-8.5 N•m (65-75 in.-lb.)

Flywheel
- 2500. . . . . . 11-13 N•m (95-115 in.-lb.)
- 2600, 3100, 3400 & 3600. . 18-23 N•m (155-200 in.-lb.)
- 3800 & 4600. . . . . 28-32 N•m (245-280 in.-lb.)

Ignition coil/module
- 2400 . . . . . 2.0-2.5 N•m (17-22 in.-lb.)
- 2500 . . . . . 3.5-4.0 N•m (30-35 in.-lb.)
- 2600 . . . . . 1.4-2.8 N•m (12-24 in.-lb.)
- 3100 & 3400 . 7-11 N•m (60-95 in.-lb.)
- 3600 . . . . 7-9 N•m (60-80 in.-lb.)
- 3800 & 4600. . . . . 3.5-4.0 N•m (30-35 in.-lb.)

Muffler
- 2400 & 2500. . . . . 5.5-6.5 N•m (50-55 in.-lb.)
- 2600, 3100, 3400 & 3600. . . 7-11 N•m (60-95 in.-lb.)
- 3800 & 4600 . . 8-9 N•m (70-80 in.-lb.)

Muffler cover
- 3100 & 3400 . . 5-8 N•m (45-70 in.-lb.)
- 3800 & 4600. . . . . 1.5-2.0 N•m (12-17 in.-lb.)

Spark plug. . . . . 15-17 N•m (130-150 in.-lb.)

Illustrations courtesy Echo Inc.

Starter center post
3400 & 3600. . . . . 2.5-3.5 N•m (22-30 in.-lb.)
Starter pawl carrier
2400 & 2500 . 8-10 N•m (70-90 in.-lb.)
2600 . . . . 20-24 N•m (175-210 in.-lb.)
3100,3400, 3600, 3800 & 4600 . . . . 8-10 N•m (70-90 in.-lb.)
Starter pawl carrier nut
2500 & 3100. . . . . 16-18 N•m (140-155 in.-lb.)
3400 & 3600. . . . . 16-20 N•m (140-175 in.-lb.)
3800 & 4600. . . . . 16-18 N•m (140-155 in.-lb.)
Starter housing
2600 . . . . . 1.4-2.8 N•m (12-24 in.-lb.)
3100, 3400 & 3600. . . . . . 1.5-2.5 N•m (13-22 in.-lb.)

IGNITION. The ignition primary windings and triggering components in the module can be tested by installing one known to be good to determine the condition of the original unit. If the condition is corrected by installing a good coil/module the original unit should be considered faulty. The ignition coil secondary winding can be tested using an accurate ohmmeter. Compare the measured resistance with the following specifications.

Model	Secondary winding
2400	1,500-2,500 ohms
2500	1,000-1,500 ohms
2600	2,000-2,600 ohms
3100, 3400 & 3600	11,000-15,000 ohms
3800 & 4600	1,000-1,500 ohms

Clearance (air gap) between the legs of the coil/module and the flywheel magnets should be 0.3 mm (0.012 in.). If the gap is too wide, the ignition may be weak and the engine difficult to start. If the gap is too close, the coil and flywheel may bump into each other and cause extensive damage.

To check the air gap, first remove the fan cover, then turn the flywheel until the magnets are located under the legs of the coil. Use non-magnetic feeler gauge to measure the clearance between the coil legs and the flywheel magnets.

To change the air gap, loosen the two screws attaching the coil, then move the coil as required. Threads of the coil attaching screws should be coated with Loctite before tightening.

PISTON, PIN AND RINGS. To remove the piston (4—Fig. EC210 or Fig. EC211), separate the drive shaft housing from the engine. Remove covers and the recoil starter. Remove the spark plug and insert the end of a rope or a piston stop in the spark plug hole to prevent the crankshaft from turning. Remove the clutch and the nut attaching the flywheel. Use a suitable puller to remove the flywheel. Remove the carburetor, muffler and ignition coil. Remove the screws attaching the cylinder, then pull the cylinder (1) straight up, off the piston. Remove the piston pin retaining rings (6), push the pin (5) out using a suitable pusher tool, then separate the piston from the connecting rod. Thrust washers (8) are located on both sides of the connecting rod of most models. The thrust washers will be loose when the piston pin is removed.

Install a new cylinder if the end gap of a new ring exceeds 0.5 mm (0.02 in.). Ring side clearance in piston groove should not exceed 0.1 mm (0.004 in.). Piston and rings are available in standard size only.

Clearance between the piston pin and bore in piston should not exceed 0.03 mm (0.0012 in.). The pin should not be worn more than 0.013 mm (0.0005 in.).

If so equipped, position the thrust washers (8) on each side of the connecting rod. Position the piston on the connecting rod so arrow on top of piston will be toward the exhaust port (muffler) side of cylinder. Lubricate the piston pin and bearing, then install the piston pin. Install new retaining rings (6) if bent or condition is otherwise questionable. Install the retaining rings with the gap toward the top or bottom of the piston.

Make sure the end of each piston ring surrounds the pin located in ring groove. Be careful to install the cylinder straight down over the piston. If the cylinder is turned, the ring can catch in a port and break the end of the ring.

CYLINDER. The piston, rings and cylinder are available in standard size only and the cylinder should not be bored oversize. Inspect the cylinder for any damage and install new parts as necessary. If the chrome plating is worn from the cylinder, a new cylinder should be installed.

CRANKSHAFT, ROD AND CRANKCASE. The crankshaft and connecting rod are available only as an assembly (16—Fig. EC210 or Fig. EC211); individual components are not available.

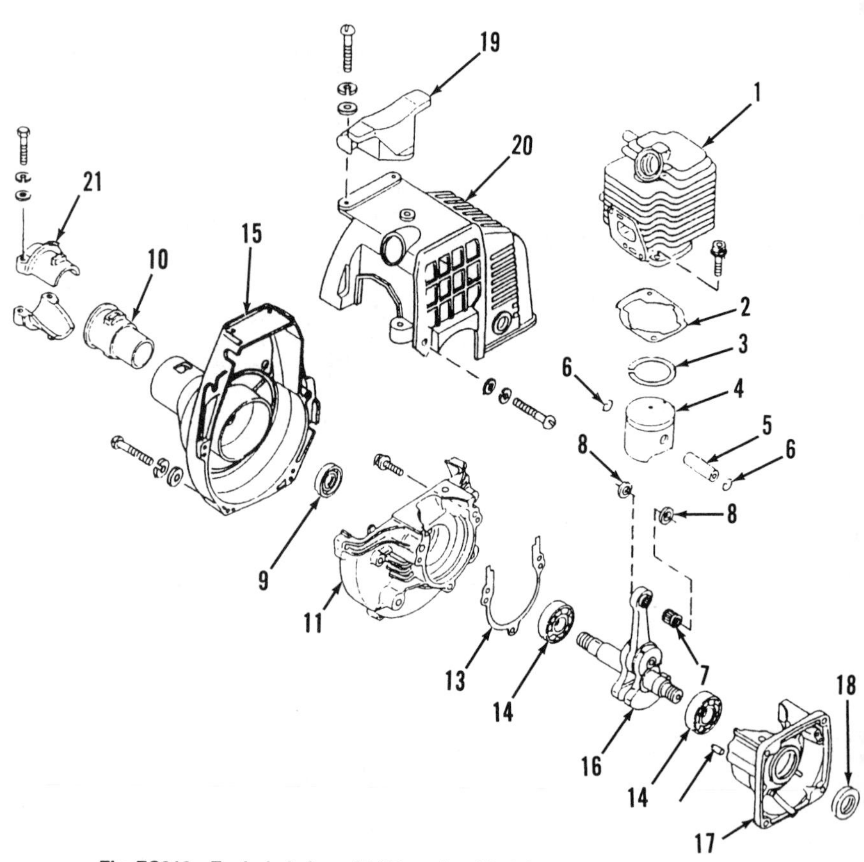

Fig. EC210—Exploded view of 2400 engine. Models 3100 and 3400 are similar.

1. Cylinder
2. Gasket
3. Piston ring
4. Piston
5. Piston pin
6. Retaining ring
7. Bearing
8. Thrust washers
9. Seal
10. Cushion
11. Crankcase half
12. Dowel pin
13. Gasket
14. Main bearings
15. Clutch cover
16. Crankshaft/connecting rod assy.
17. Crankcase half
18. Seal
19. Guard
20. Cover
21. Clamp adapter

Illustrations courtesy Echo Inc.

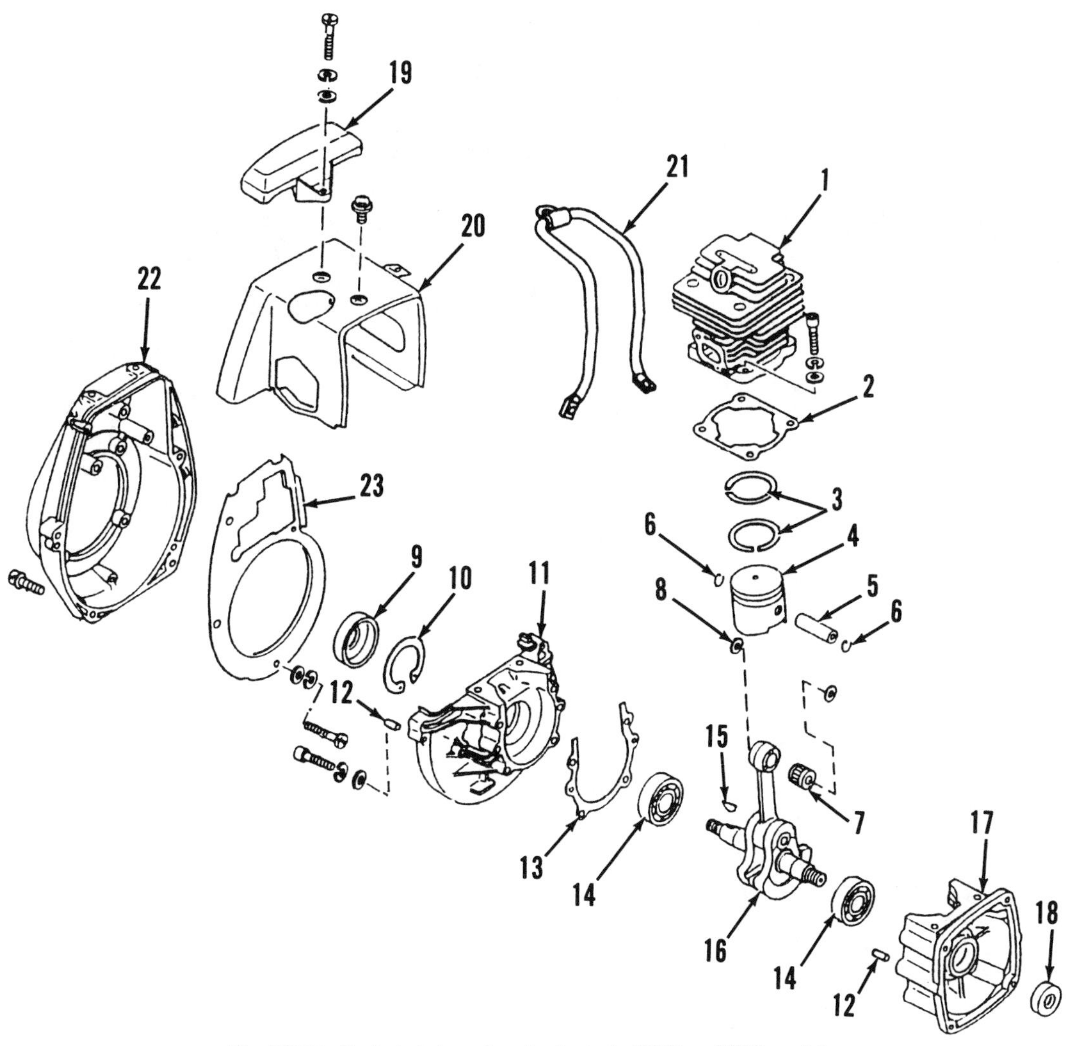

Fig. EC211—Exploded view of engine typical of 3800 and 4600 models.

1. Cylinder
2. Gasket
3. Piston ring
4. Piston
5. Piston pin
6. Retaining ring
7. Bearing
8. Thrust washers
9. Seal
10. Snap ring
11. Crankcase half
12. Dowel pin
13. Gasket
14. Main bearings
15. Woodruff key
16. Crankshaft/connecting rod assy.
17. Crankcase half
18. Seal
19. Guard
20. Cover
21. Guard
22. Cover
23. Plate

To remove the crankshaft and connecting rod assembly, remove the cylinder and piston as described in PISTON, PIN AND RINGS paragraph. Remove the screws attaching the halves of the crankcase together and separate halves. Heat the crankcase if necessary to remove the main bearings from the crankcase bores. If the bearings stay on the crankshaft, use a suitable puller to pull the bearings from the main journals. Some models may have a snap ring (10) installed in the case bore.

The main bearing should turn smoothly with no perceptible play or ratcheting. Connecting rod side clearance should not exceed 0.4 mm (0.016 in.).

Support the crankshaft at the main bearings or journals and measure runout at the ends of the crankshaft. Measured runout should not exceed 0.05 mm (0.002 in.). A shop experienced in servicing built-up crankshaft assemblies can align the shaft.

Use suitable tools to press new main bearings and seals into the crankcase bores. Lips of seals (9 and 18) should be toward inside of crankcase and should be lubricated before installing the crankshaft.

CLUTCH. The shoe assembly of 2400 models is located at the drive end of the crankshaft as shown in Fig. EC212. The drive hub of 2400 models is threaded and also attaches the flywheel to the crankshaft. The shoes of 2500, 2600, 3100, 3400, 3800 and 4600 models are attached to the flywheel as shown in Fig. EC213. The clutch drum of all models operates in bearings located in the cover or drive flange.

To remove the clutch drum, first separate the drive shaft housing from the engine, then unbolt and remove the cover (3—Fig. EC212) or drive flange (4—Fig. EC213). On most models, the clutch drum has a hole so snap ring (7—Fig. EC212 or Fig. EC213) can be removed. It may be necessary to heat the housing to facilitate removal of the bearings from the housing. If the clutch drum is not slotted, remove snap ring (5). After removing the clutch drum, remove the remaining snap ring and bearings.

Inspect the clutch shoes (9) and drum (8) for excessive wear. Some clutch shoes are fitted with lining, while other shoes are not. Install new springs if overheated or otherwise damaged. Clutch (9—Fig. EC212) is available only as an assembly. The housing (3—Fig. EC212) or drive flange (4—Fig.

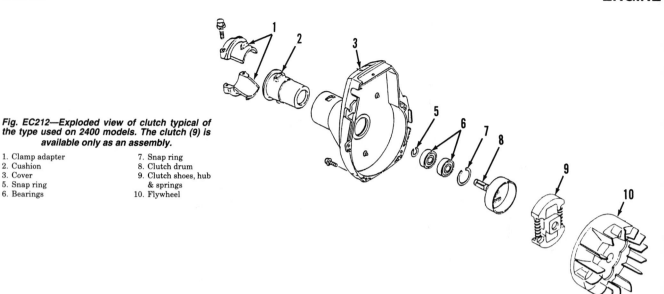

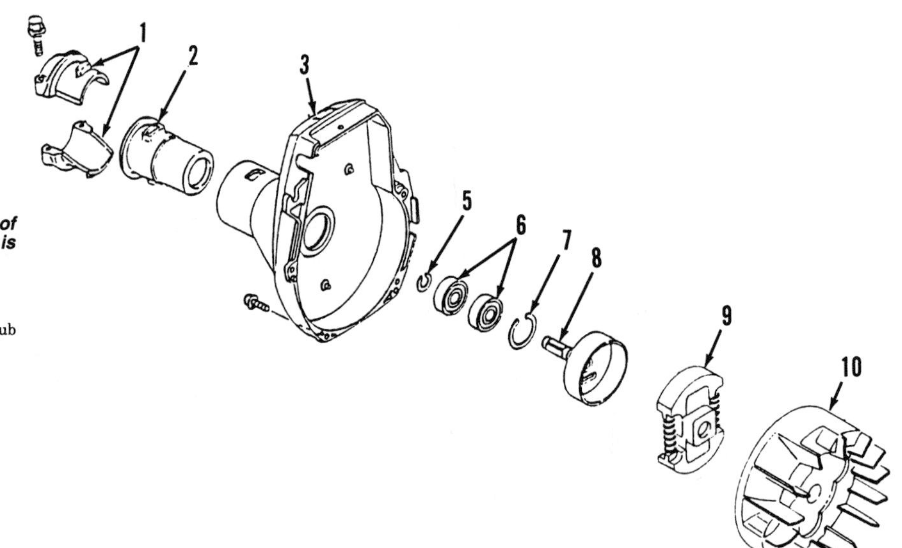

Fig. EC212—Exploded view of clutch typical of the type used on 2400 models. The clutch (9) is available only as an assembly.

1. Clamp adapter
2. Cushion
3. Cover
5. Snap ring
6. Bearings
7. Snap ring
8. Clutch drum
9. Clutch shoes, hub & springs
10. Flywheel

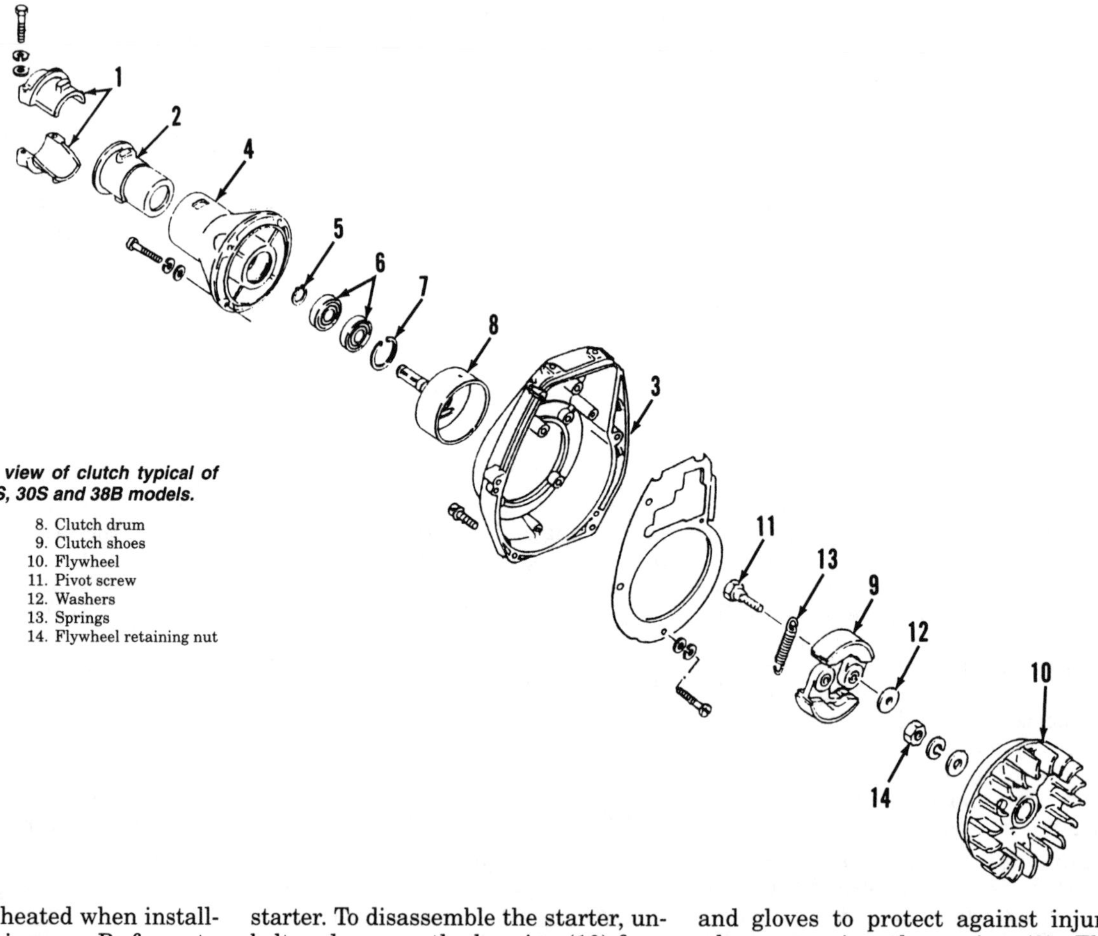

Fig. EC213—Exploded view of clutch typical of the type used on 25S, 30S and 38B models.

1. Clamp adapter
2. Cushion
3. Cover
4. Drive flange
5. Snap ring
6. Bearings
7. Snap ring
8. Clutch drum
9. Clutch shoes
10. Flywheel
11. Pivot screw
12. Washers
13. Springs
14. Flywheel retaining nut

EC213) should be heated when installing the bearings. Refer to TIGHTENING TORQUE paragraph when assembling.

RECOIL STARTER. Refer to Fig. EC214 for exploded view of rewind starter. To disassemble the starter, unbolt and remove the housing (10) from the engine. Remove handle from the rope and allow the rope to wind into the starter. Remove center screw (6), then remove washer (7) and the rope pulley (8). Wear appropriate eye protection and gloves to protect against injury when removing the spring (9). The spring may unwind from the housing uncontrollably. If necessary for service, remove the pulley plate.

The rope must be the correct diameter and length for the starter to operate

Illustrations courtesy Echo Inc.

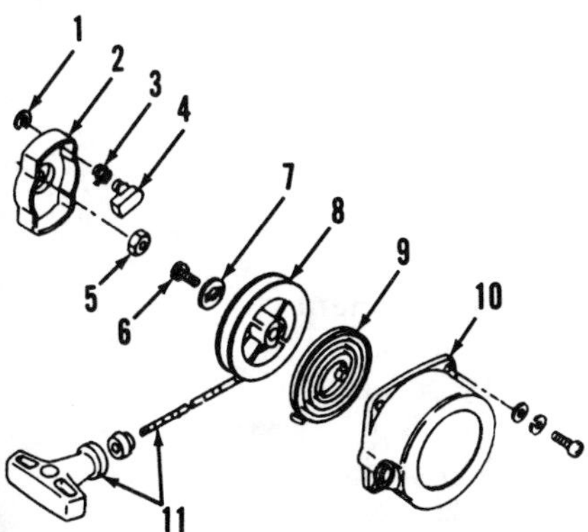

Fig. EC214—Exploded view of rewind starter typical of all models.

1. "E" ring
2. Pawl carrier
3. Spring
4. Pawl
5. Nut
6. Screw
7. Washer
8. Pulley
9. Rewind spring
10. Starter housing
11. Rope and handle

properly. If the rope is too large in diameter or too long, the rope may bind when trying to wind onto the pulley. When installing new rope, measure the length and diameter of the old rope, then install new rope that matches the original.

To assemble the starter, apply a small amount of light grease to the starter housing post, spring and the back of the pulley. Install the rewind spring so it is wound counterclockwise from the outer end. Attach the rope to the pulley, making sure the knot is fully nested in the pocket. Pull the rope tight and wind the rope counterclockwise as viewed from the pawl (engine) side. Install the pulley/rope and rotate slightly until the spring hooks into the pulley and the pulley drops into the housing. Guide the end of the rope through the housing and attach the handle.

When assembling or if the starter rope does not fully rewind, preload the recoil spring as follows. Hold the pulley to keep it from turning, then pull a small loop in the rope between the pulley and the inside of the housing. Hold the rope and wind the pulley to preload the pulley, allow the pulley to rewind the rope, then check operation. The spring should wind the rope around the pulley fully, but the spring must bind when the rope is fully extended. It should be possible to rotate the pulley at least 1/4 turn when the rope is pulled out completely. Complete the assembly by reversing the disassembly procedure when the spring preload is correctly set.

EFCO

ENGINE SERVICE

Model	Bore	Stroke	Displacement
200	32 mm (1.26 in.)	28 mm (1.10 in.)	22.5 cc 1.37 cu. in.)
220	32 mm (1.26 in.)	28 mm (1.10 in.)	22.5 cc 1.37 cu. in.)
260	34 mm (1.34 in.)	28 mm (1.10 in.)	25.4 cc (1.55 cu. in.)

ENGINE INFORMATION

The EFCO Model 200, 220 and 260 two-stroke, air-cooled gasoline engines are used on Jonsered and Olympyk string trimmers and brush cutters. The engine is equipped with a cantilever-type crankshaft that is supported in two ball bearings at the flywheel end. Refer to following section for other EFCO engine models.

MAINTENANCE

LUBRICATION. Engine lubrication is obtained by mixing gasoline with an oil designed for two-stroke, air-cooled engines. Refer to trimmer service section for manufacturer's recommended fuel: oil mixture ratio.

SPARK PLUG. Recommended spark plug is a Champion CJ7Y or equivalent. Specified electrode gap for all models is 0.6-0.7 mm (0.024-0.028 in.).

CARBURETOR. The engine is equipped with a Walbro WZ or WYK carburetor. These are diaphragm-type carburetors that use a barrel-type throttle rather than a throttle plate.

Idle fuel for the carburetor flows up into the throttle barrel where it is fed into the air stream. Idle fuel flow can be adjusted by turning idle limiter plate (P—Fig. EF101). Initial setting is in center notch. Rotating the plate clockwise will lean the idle mixture.

Inside the limiter plate is an idle mixture needle (N—Fig. EF102) that is preset at the factory (a plug covers the needle). If idle mixture needle is removed, use the following procedure to determine correct position. Back out needle (N) until unscrewed, then screw in needle six turns for WZ carburetor or 15 turns for WYK carburetor. Rotate idle mixture limiter plate (P—Fig. EF101) to center notch.

Run engine until normal operating temperature is attained. Adjust idle speed screw (I) so trimmer head or blade does not rotate. Rotate idle mixture needle (N—Fig. EF102) and obtain highest rpm (turning needle clockwise leans the mixture), then turn needle counterclockwise until rpm decreases 200-500 rpm. Readjust idle speed screw. Note that idle mixture limiter and needle are available only as an assembly with throttle barrel.

Fig. EF101—On Walbro WZ carburetor idle speed screw is located at (I), idle mixture limiter plate is located at (P) and idle mixture needle is located at (N). A plug covers the idle mixture needle.

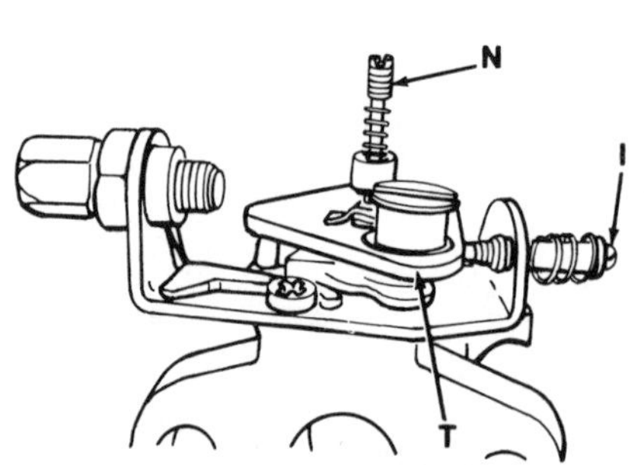

Fig. EF102—View of idle mixture needle (N). Refer to text for adjustment procedure.

Initial setting of high-speed mixture screw (23—Fig. EF103 or Fig. EF104) is 1 ½ turns out from a lightly seated position. Adjust high-speed mixture screw to obtaion highest engine speed. On Model 200 engine, turn high-speed screw counter-clockwise so engine rpm is 7400-7500 on a new engine or 7900-8000 on an engine that has run over 50 hours. On Model 220 and 260 engines, turn high-speed screw counterclockwise so engine rpm is 9000-9200 on a new engine or 9400-9500 on an engine that has run over 50 hours. Do not adjust mixture too lean as engine may be damaged.

To overhaul carburetor, refer to exploded view in Fig. EF103 or Fig. EF104 and note the following: Clean only with solvents approved for use with plastic. Do not disassemble throttle barrel assembly. Examine fuel inlet valve and seat. Inlet valve is renewable, but carburetor body must be renewed if seat is excessively worn or damaged. Inspect high-speed mixture screw and seat. Renew carburetor body if seat is excessively worn or damaged. Clean fuel screen. Inspect diaphragms for tears and other damage. When installing plates and gaskets (13, 14 and 15), note that tabs on edges will "stairstep" when correctly installed. Adjust metering lever height to obtain 1.5 mm (0.059 in.) between carburetor body surface and lever as shown in Fig. EF105.

IGNITION SYSTEM. The engine is equipped with an electronic ignition system. Ignition system performance is considered satisfactory if a spark will jump across a 3 mm (1/8 in.) electrode gap on a test spark plug. If no spark is produced, check on/off switch, wiring and ignition module air gap. Ignition mocule air gap should be 0.3 mm (0.012

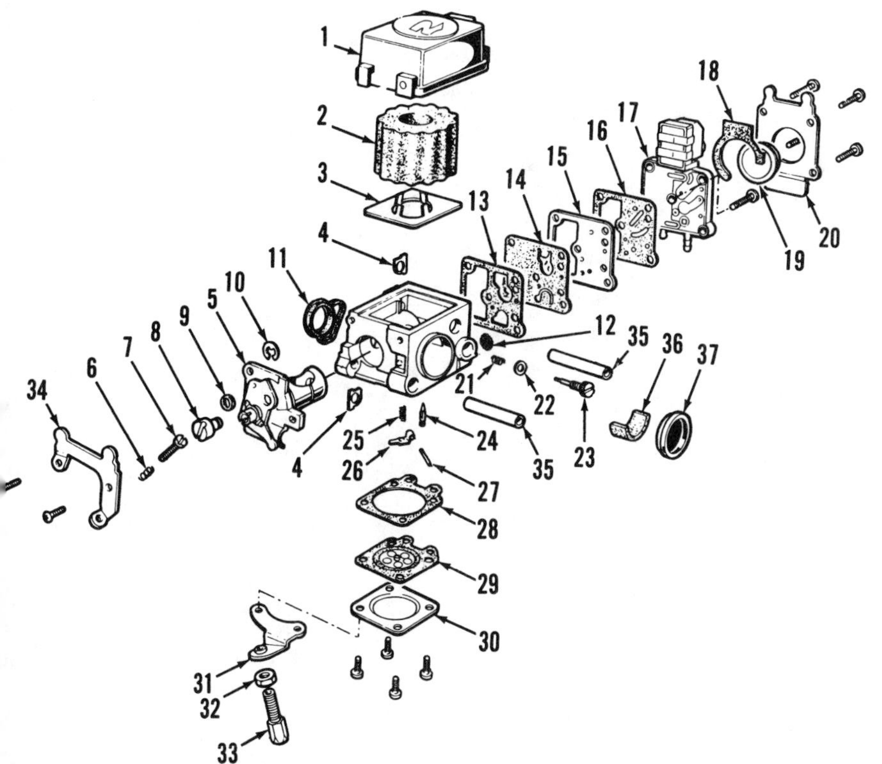

Fig. EF103—Exploded view of Walbro WZ carburetor.

1. Cover
2. Air cleaner element
3. Plate
4. Plate
5. Throttle barrel assy.
6. Spring
7. Idle speed screw
8. Swivel
9. Washer
10. "E" ring
11. Gasket
12. Screen
13. Gasket
14. Fuel pump diaphragm
15. Plate
16. Gasket
17. Fuel pump cover
18. Gasket
19. Primer bulb
20. Retainer
21. Spring
22. Washer
23. High-speed mixture screw
24. Fuel inlet valve
25. Spring
26. Metering lever
27. Pin
28. Gasket
29. Metering diaphragm
30. Cover
31. Bracket
32. Nut
33. Cable adjuster
34. Support
35. Sleeve
36. Seal
37. Cover

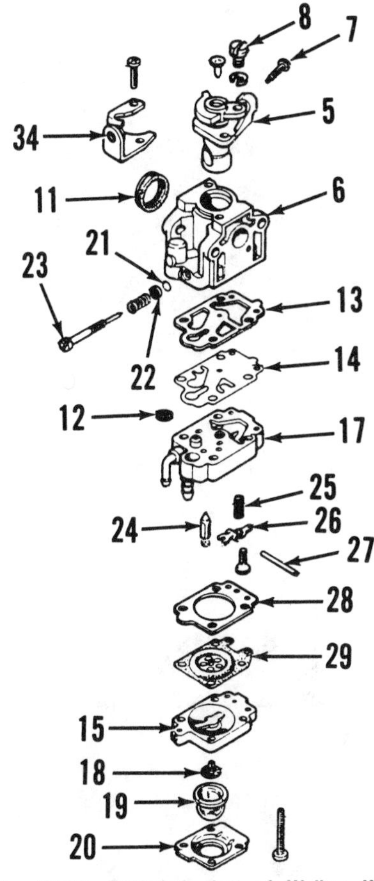

Fig. EF104—Exploded view of Walbro WYK carburetor.

5. Throttle barrel assy.
6. Carburetor body
7. Idle speed screw
8. Pivot
11. Gasket
13. Gasket
14. Fuel pump diaphragm
15. Primer plate
17. Fuel pump body
18. Check valve
19. Primer bulb
20. Retainer plate
21. "O" ring
22. Washer
23. High-speed mixture screw
24. Fuel inlet valve
25. Spring
26. Metering lever
27. Pivot pin
28. Gasket
29. Metering diaphragm
34. Bracket

in.). If switch, wiring and module air gap are satisfactory, but spark is not present, renew ignition module.

REPAIRS

TIGHTENING TORQUES. Recommended tightening torque specifications are as follows:

Clutch hub . . . . 18 Nm (160 in.-lbs.)

Crankcase. . . . . 6 Nm (53 in.-lbs.)

Crankpin . . . . 30 Nm (22 ft.-lbs.)

PISTON, CONNECTING ROD, RINGS AND CYLINDER. The cylinder and crankcase are one piece. To remove piston, the crankshaft must be removed. Disconnect ignition wires and throttle cable from engine. Unbolt and remove drive shaft assembly from engine. Remove spark plug and install a suitable tool or insert end of rope into spark plug hole to prevent crankshaft from turning. Remove clutch assembly from crankshaft. Remove muffler cover and flywheel shroud. Remove recoil starter assembly. Remove flywheel retaining nut and tap flywheel with a plastic mallet to loosen flywheel from crankshaft taper. Remove gas tank and tank bracket. Detach crankcase cover (17—Fig. EF106). Unscrew crankpin (11) on early models or detach snap ring (20) on later models. Remove bearing (10A) on later models. Position big end of rod so it is clear of crankshaft as shown in Fig. EF107, then press crankshaft out of crankcase. Withdraw rod and piston assembly from crankcase.

Inspect components for excessive wear and damage. Specified piston ring end gap is 0.15-0.35 mm (0.006-0.014 in.). Piston and cylinder are stamped with letter "A," "B" or "F," according to size. Install new piston or cylinder with same letter grade as discarded part.

Connecting rod bearings are available only with rod. Do not attempt to remove bearings from rod on early

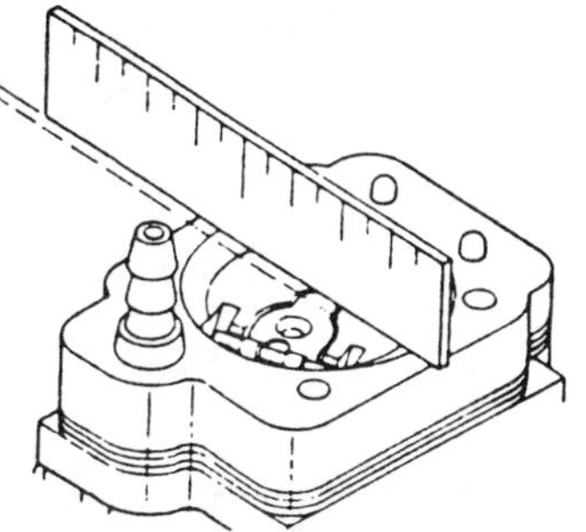

Fig. EF105—Metering lever height must be set on diaphragm-type carburetors. Refer to text for specified height.

models. On later models, big end bearing is removable, but small end bearing is not removable.

During assembly, note the following. Assemble piston on rod so closed end of piston pin is on same side as arrow on

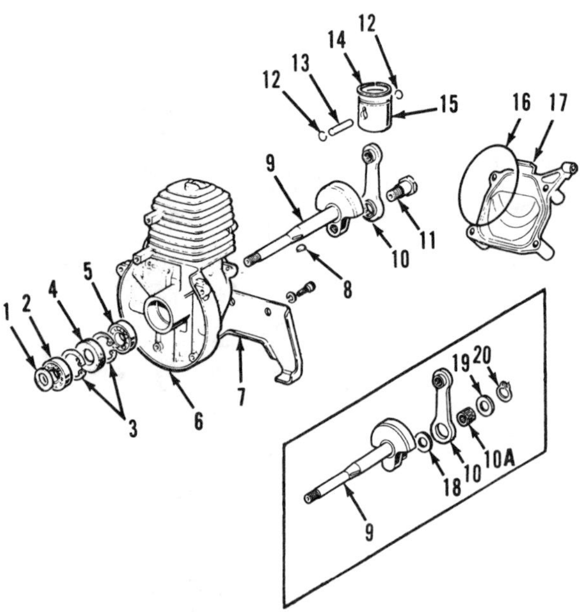

Fig. EF106—Exploded view of engine. Connecting rod assembly shown in box is used on later models.

1. Spacer
2. Bearing, sealed
3. Snap ring
4. Seal
5. Bearing, plain
6. Crankcase cylinder
7. Support
8. Key
9. Crankshaft
10. Connecting rod
10A. Bearing
11. Crankpin
12. Retaining rings
13. Piston pin
14. Piston
15. Piston ring
16. "O" ring
17. Cover
18. Washer
19. Washer
20. Snap ring

Fig. EF107—Connecting rod (10) must be positioned as shown so crankshaft (9) can be removed.

piston crown. Install piston and rod so arrow on piston crown points toward exhaust port. Be sure piston ring end gap properly surrounds locating pin in piston ring groove. Lubricate piston, cylinder and connecting rod bearing with oil Apply Loctite to threads of crankpin (11—Fig. EF106) on early models and tighten to 30 Nm (22 ft.-lbs.). On late models, install thrust washer (19) and snap ring (20). On all models, tighten crankcase cover screw to 6 Nm (53 in.-lbs.) Complete reassembly by reversing disassembly procedure.

CRANKSHAFT AND CRANKCASE. The crankshaft is a cantilever type that is supported by two bearings in the crankcase. To remove the crankshaft, remove flywheel and detach crankcase cover (17—Fig. EF106). Unscrew crankpin (11) on early models or detach snap ring (20) on later models. Remove bearing (10A) on later models. Position big end of rod so it is clear of crankshaft as shown in Fig. EF107. Press crankshaft out of crankcase. Drive or press bearings (2 and 5—Fig. EF106) and seal (4) out of crankcase while removing snap rings (3). Note depth of seal before removal as reference for installation of new seal, or use EFCO seal installation tool 4138347.

During assembly, note the following: Outer bearing (2) is sealed. Position bearings against snap rings. Apply Loctite to threads of crankpin (11—Fig. EF106) on early models and tighten to 30 Nm (22 ft.-lbs.). On late models, install thrust washer (19) and snap ring (20). On all models, tighten crankcase cover screws to 6 Nm (53 in.-lbs.).

CLUTCH. All models are equipped with a two-shoe clutch shown in Fig. EF108. Note that clutch hub (9) has left-hand threads (turn clockwise to remove). Minimum allowable thickness of clutch shoe lining is 0.8 mm (0.032 in.). Clutch shoes (8) are available only as a pair. Tighten clutch hub (9) to 18 Nm (160 in.-lbs.).

To disassemble clutch drum assembly, separate housing (2—Fig. EF109) from engine and drive shaft tube. On Models 220 and 260, the drive shaft must be unscrewed from the clutch drum. Detach snap ring (1) and press or drive clutch drum out of housing. Detach snap ring (5) and remove bearing (4). Reassemble by reversing disassembly procedure.

REWIND STARTER. The engine may be equipped with the starter

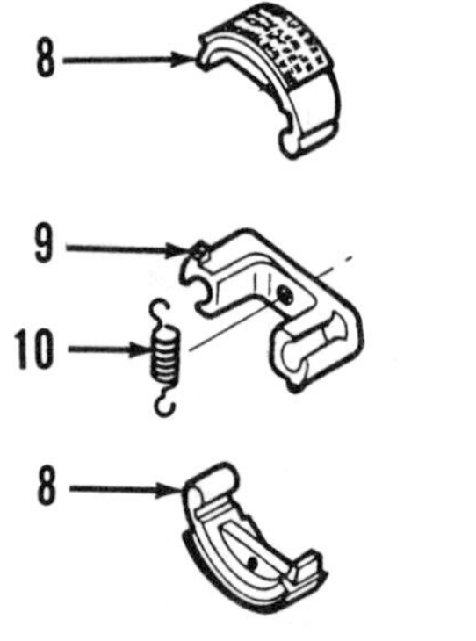

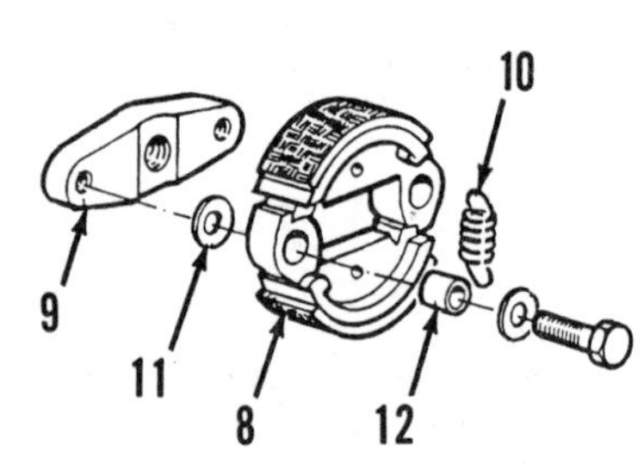

Fig. EF108—Exploded view of two different styles of clutch shoes.

8. Clutch shoes
9. Clutch hub
10. Return spring
11. Washer
12. Collar

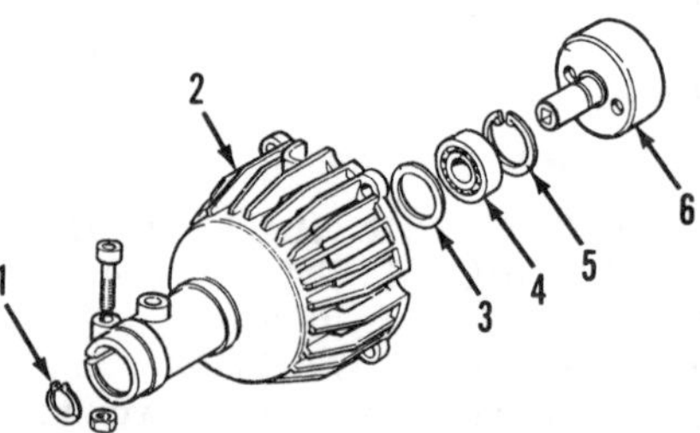

Fig. EF109—Exploded view of clutch drum and housing assembly. Washer (3) is absent on some models.

1. Snap ring
2. Housing
3. Washer
4. Bearing
5. Snap ring
6. Clutch drum

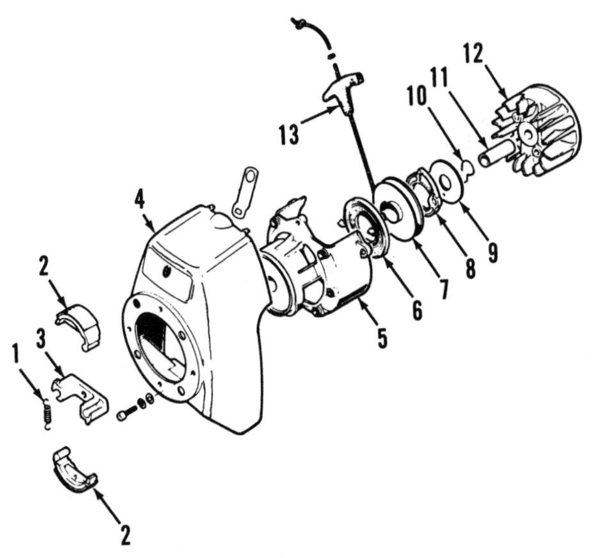

Fig. EF110—Exploded view of rewind starter used on some models. Refer also to Fig. EF111 for alternate-type of rewind starter.

1. Clutch spring
2. Clutch shoe
3. Clutch hub
4. Shroud
5. Starter housing
6. Rewind spring
7. Pulley
8. Pawl
9. Washer
10. Clip
11. Spacer
12. Flywheel
13. Rope handle

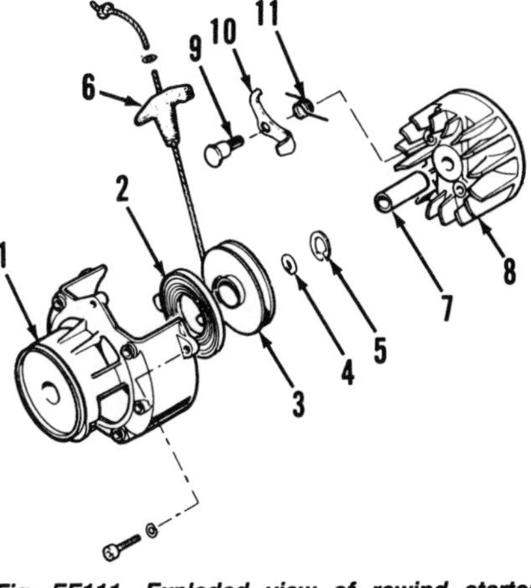

Fig. EF111—Exploded view of rewind starter used on some models.

1. Starter housing
2. Rewind spring
3. Pulley
4. Washer
5. Snap ring
6. Rope handle
7. Spacer
8. Flywheel
9. Stud
10. Pawl
11. Spring

shown in Fig. EF110 or EF111. To disassemble starter, remove clutch hub (3—Fig. EF110) and shroud (4). Note that clutch hub has left-hald threads. Remove starter housing. Detach rope handle and allow rope to wind into starter. On models so equipped, remove snap ring (5—Fig. EF111). Disassemble starter. Wear appropriate safety eyewear and gloves when working with or around rewind spring as spring may uncoil uncontrolled.

Before assembling starter, lubricate center post of housing and spring side of pulley with light grease. Install rewind spring in a counterclockwise direction from outer end. Assemble starter while pasing rope through housing rope outlet and attach rope handle to rope. To place tension on starter rope, rotate pulley counterclockwise so notch in pulley is aligned with rope outlet, then hold pulley to prevent pulley rotation. Pull rope back into housing while positioning rope in pulley notch. Turn rope pulley counterclockwise six turns. Allow pulley to turn clockwise until notch aligns with rope outlet. Disengage rope from notch then release pulley and allow rope to wind on pulley. Check starter operation. Rope handle should be held against housing by spring tension, but it must be possible to rotate pulley at least ¼ turn counterclockwise when rope is pulled out fully.

EFCO

ENGINE SERVICE

Model	Bore	Stroke	Displacement
300, 310 & 320	36 mm (1.42 in.)	30 mm (1.18 in.)	30.5 cc (1.86 cu. in.)
400, 410 & 420	40 mm (1.57 in.)	30 mm (1.18 in.)	37.7 cc (2.30 cu. in.)
450 & 460	40 mm (1.57 in.)	30 mm (1.18 in.)	37.7 cc (2.30 cu. in.)

ENGINE INFORMATION

These engines are used on some Jonsered and Olympyk string trimmers and brush cutters.

MAINTENANCE

LUBRICATION. Engine lubrication is obtained by mixing regular grade gasoline with an oil designed for two-stroke, air-cooled engines. Refer to trimmer service section for manufacturer's recommended fuel:oil mixture ratio.

SPARK PLUG. Recommended spark plug is a Champion CJ7Y or equivalent. Specified electrode gap for all models is 0.6-0.7 mm (0.024-0.028 in.).

CARBURETOR. The engine may be equipped with a Tillotson, Walbro or Zama diaphragm-type carburetor. The manufacturer's name and carburetor model number are stamped on the carburetor. Refer to following section for service information.

Tillotson HU53. To adjust carburetor, turn idle speed mixture screw (6—Fig. EF201) and high speed mixture screw (7) in (clockwise) until lightly seated, then turn each screw out 1-1/8 turns. Final adjustment is performed with engine at normal operating temperature. Trimmer line should be extended fully or blade assembly installed during adjustment.

Start engine and adjust idle mixture screw so engine idles smoothly and accelerates without hesitation. Adjust idle speed screw (22), if necessary, so that trimmer head does not rotate when engine is idling. Adjust high speed mixture screw (7) until there is a slight "four-cycle" exhaust sound at full throttle with no load. This slightly rich mixture should provide the best performance while operating at maximum speed under load. The engine may be damaged if the high speed screw is set too lean. Turning the high speed mixture screw clockwise leans the mixture and turning it counterclockwise enriches the mixture.

To disassemble carburetor, refer to Fig. EF201 and remove fuel pump cover (1) and metering chamber cover (19) for access to internal components. Remove pin (16), metering lever (15), spring (9) and fuel inlet valve (14). Remove check valve (13) and filter screen (10). Welch plug (8) can be removed by prying out with a sharp punch. Use care not to damage carburetor casting when removing Welch plug. Remove fuel mixture screws (6 and 7). It is not necessary to remove throttle plate (4) and shaft (11) unless wear or damage is evident.

Clean components using solvent and compressed air. Do not attempt to clean passages with drill bits or wire as carburetor calibration may be affected if passages are enlarged. Check diaphragms (3 and 18) for tears, cracks or other damage. Renew idle and high speed adjusting needles if needle points are grooved or broken. Carburetor must be renewed if needle seats are damaged. Inspect fuel inlet valve (14) and seat for wear or damage. Valve is renewable, but carburetor must be renewed if seat is damaged.

Reassemble carburetor by reversing disassembly procedure. Adjust metering lever (15) so lever is flush with diaphragm chamber floor as shown in Fig. EF202. Bend lever adjacent to spring (9) to obtain correct lever position.

Walbro WT. To adjust carburetor, turn idle mixture screw (17—Fig. EF203) and high speed mixture screw (16) in (clockwise) until lightly seated, then turn both screws out 1-1/8 turns. Final adjustment is performed with engine at normal operating temperature.

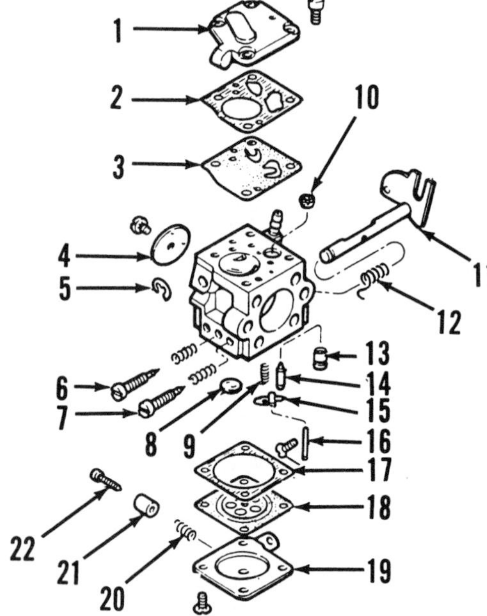

Fig. EF201—Exploded view of Tillotson Model HU carburetor used on some models.

1. Fuel pump cover
2. Gasket
3. Fuel pump diaphragm
4. Throttle plate
5. "E" ring
6. Idle mixture screw
7. High speed mixture screw
8. Welch plug
9. Spring
10. Filter screen
11. Throttle shaft
12. Return spring
13. Nozzle check valve
14. Fuel inlet valve
15. Metering lever
16. Pivot pin
17. Gasket
18. Metering diaphragm
19. Cover
20. Spring
21. Bushing
22. Idle speed screw

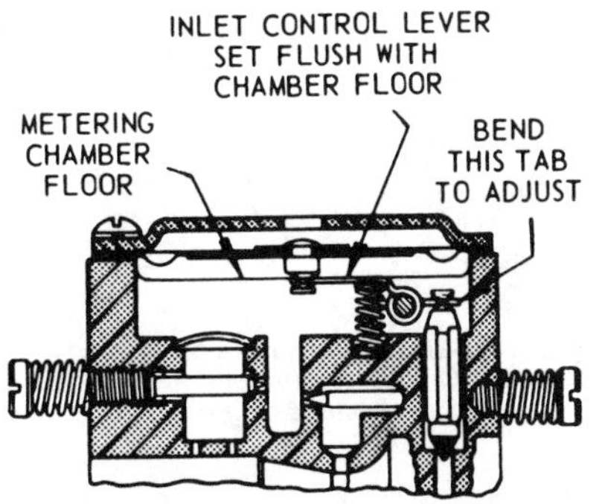

Fig. EF202—Diaphragm lever on Tillotson Model HU carburetor should be flush with diaphragm chamber floor as shown above.

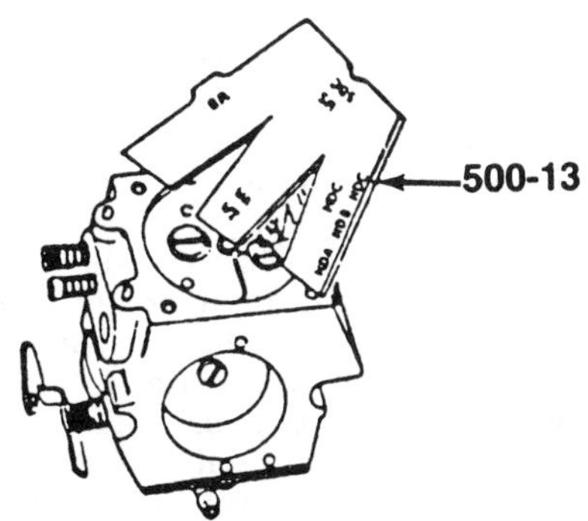

Fig. EF204—Metering lever should just touch leg of Walbro too No. 500-13. Bend lever to obtain correct lever height.

Trimmer line should be extended fully or blade assembly installed during adjustment.

Start engine and adjust idle mixture screw (17) so engine idles smoothly and accelerates without hesitation. Adjust the idle speed screw (1), if necessary, so that trimmer head does not rotate when engine is idling. Adjust the high speed mixture screw (16) until there is a slight "four-cycle" exhaust sound at full throttle with no load. This slightly rich mixture should provide the best performance while operating at maximum speed under load. The engine may be damaged if the high speed screw is set too lean. Turning the high speed mixture screw clockwise leans the mixture and turning it counterclockwise enriches the mixture.

To disassemble carburetor, refer to Fig. EF203 and remove fuel pump cover (2) and metering chamber cover (10) for access to internal components. Remove pivot pin (7), metering lever (8), spring (13) and fuel inlet valve (6). Remove filter screen (5), check valve (14) and fuel mixture screws (16 and 17). Welch plug (15) can be removed by prying out with a sharp punch. Use care not to damage carburetor casting when removing Welch plug. It is not necessary to remove throttle plate (18) and shaft (19) unless wear or damage is evident.

Clean components using solvent and compressed air. Do not attempt to clean passages with drill bits or wire as carburetor calibration may be affected if passages are enlarged. Check diaphragms (4 and 11) for tears, cracks or other damage. Install new diaphragms if hard (not flexible), torn or otherwise damaged. Renew idle and high speed mixture needles (16 and 17) if needle points are grooved or broken. Carburetor must be renewed if needle seats are damaged. Inspect fuel inlet valve (6) and seat for wear or damage. Valve is renewable, but carburetor must be renewed if seat is damaged.

Reassemble carburetor by reversing disassembly procedure. Check metering lever height as shown in Fig. EF204 using Walbro tool 500-13. Metering lever should just touch leg on tool. If tool is not available, the lever should be 1.52-1.78 mm (0.060-0.070 in) below surface for gasket (12—Fig. EF203). Bend lever to obtain correct lever height.

Walbro WZ. This is a diaphragm-type carburetor that uses a barrel-type throttle rather than a throttle plate.

ADJUSTMENT. Idle fuel for the carburetor flows up into the throttle barrel where it is fed into the air stream. The idle circuit is equipped with an outer idle limiter plate (P—Fig. EF205) for fine tune adjustment and an inner idle needle (N), which is preset at the factory, for the actual idle mixture setting. Note that for service, idle mixture limiter plate and mixture needle are available only as an assembly with the throttle barrel.

Initial setting of the outer idle limiter plate (P) is in the center notch. Rotating the plate clockwise will lean the idle mixture or rotating it counterclockwise will enrich the idle mixture. Adjust idle speed screw (I—Fig. EF205) so trimmer head or blade does not rotate.

The idle mixture needle (N—Fig. EF205) is located inside the idle limiter plate (a plug covers the needle). The needle is preset at the factory and should not require adjustment. If the needle (N—Fig. EF206) is removed, use the following procedure to determine correct position. Back out needle until unscrewed, then turn needle in (clockwise) six turns. Rotate idle mixture limiter plate (P—Fig. EF205) to center notch. Run engine until normal operating temperature is attained. Adjust idle speed screw (I) so trimmer head or blade does not turn. Rotate idle mixture needle (N) and obtain highest rpm (turning needle clockwise leans the mixture), then turn needle counterclockwise until rpm decreases 200-500 rpm. Readjust idle speed screw so trimmer head or blade does not rotate.

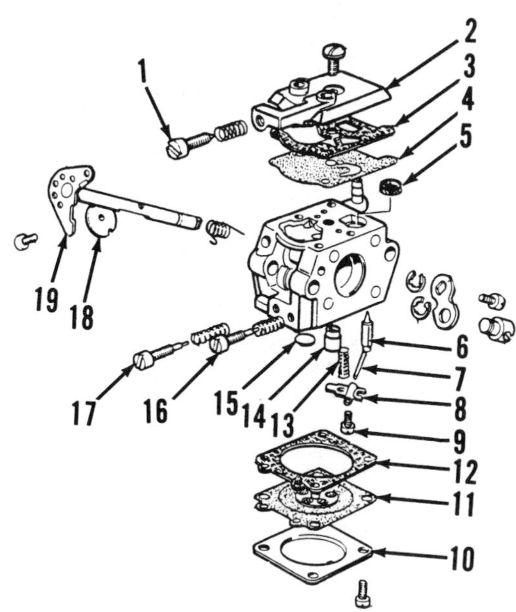

Fig. EF203—Exploded view of Walbro Model WT carburetor used on some models.

1. Idle speed screw
2. Fuel pump cover
3. Gasket
4. Fuel pump diaphragm
5. Filter screen
6. Fuel inlet valve
7. Pivot pin
8. Metering lever
9. Screw
10. Cover
11. Metering diaphragm
12. Gasket
13. Spring
14. Check valve
15. Welch plug
16. High speed mixture screw
17. Idle mixture screw
18. Throttle plate
19. Throttle shaft

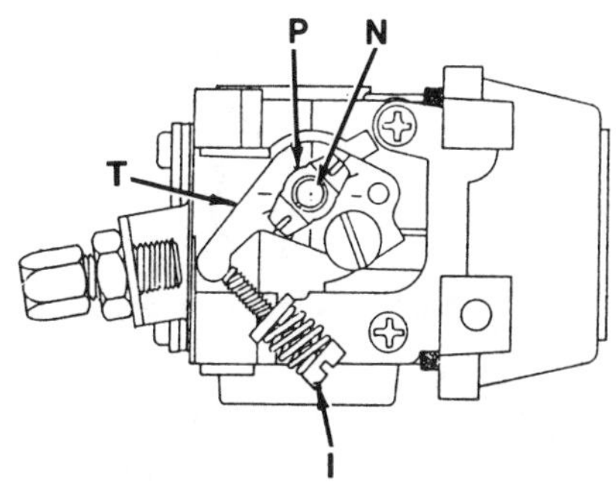

Fig. EF205—On Walbro WZ carburetor, idle speed screw is located at (I), idle mixture limiter plate is located at (S) and idle mixture needle is located at (N). A plug covers the idle mixture needle.

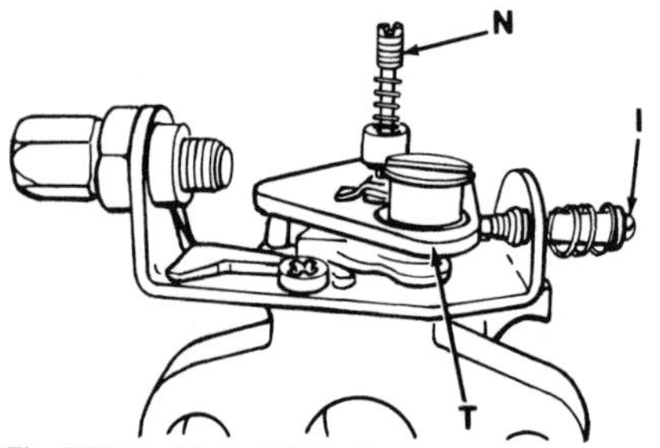

Fig. EF206—View of idle mixture needle (N). Refer to text for adjustment procedure.

Initial setting of high speed mixture screw (23—Fig. EF207) is 1-1/2 turns out from a lightly seated position. Turning the needle in (clockwise) leans the mixture or turning needle out enriches the mixture. Satisfactory high speed operation can normally be obtained by turning high speed mixture needle until there is a slight "four-cycle" exhaust sound at full throttle with no load. This slightly rich mixture should provide the best performance while operating at maximum speed under load. The engine may be damaged if the high-speed screw is set too lean.

OVERHAUL. To overhaul carburetor, refer to Fig. EF207 and remove air cleaner assembly (1-3), cover (30) and metering diaphragm (29). Remove pivot pin (27) metering lever (26), spring (25) and fuel inlet needle (24). Unbolt and remove retainer (20) and primer bulb (19). Remove fuel pump cover (17), gasket (16), plate (15), fuel pump diaphragm (14), gasket (13) and screen (12). Remove retainer (34) and withdraw throttle barrel (5). Remove high-speed mixture needle (23).

Clean only with solvents approved for use with plastic. Do not disassemble throttle barrel. Throttle barrel is available only as an assembly. Examine fuel inlet valve (24) and seat. Inlet valve may be renewed if worn or damaged, but seat is not serviceable and carburetor body must be renewed if seat is worn or damaged. Inspect high-speed mixture screw (23) and seat. Renew carburetor body if seat is excessively worn or damaged. Clean or renew fuel screen (12). Inspect diaphragms for tears and other damage.

When installing plates and gaskets (13, 14 and 15), note that tabs on edges

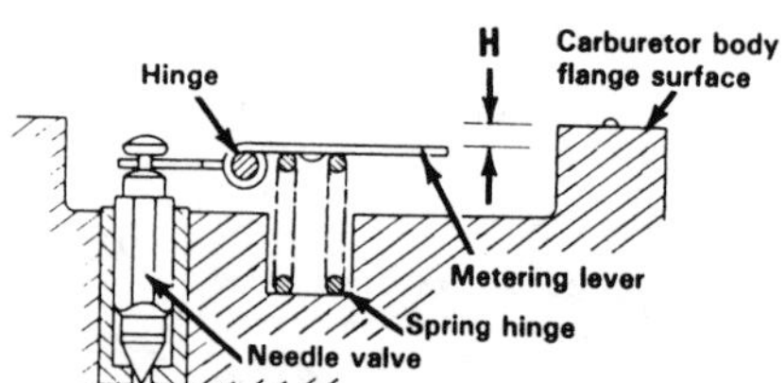

Fig. EF208—Metering lever height (H) must be set on diaphragm-type carburetors. Refer to text for specified height.

will "stair-step" when correctly installed. Adjust metering lever height to obtain 1.5 mm (0.060 in.) between carburetor body and lever as shown in Fig. EF208.

Zama C1Q and C1S. Refer to Fig. EF209 for an exploded view of typical Zama C1 carburetor. Some models are equipped with a fuel primer bulb (not shown). Depressing the bulb forces extra fuel into the air stream during starting.

Initial adjustment of idle mixture screw (14) and high speed mixture screw (16) is one turn out from a lightly seated position. Final adjustment is performed with engine at normal operating temperature. Trimmer line should be extended fully or blade installed during adjustment. Adjust idle mixture screw so engine idles smoothly and accelerates without hesitation. Adjust idle speed screw (1), if necessary, so that trimmer head or blade does not turn when engine is idling. Run engine

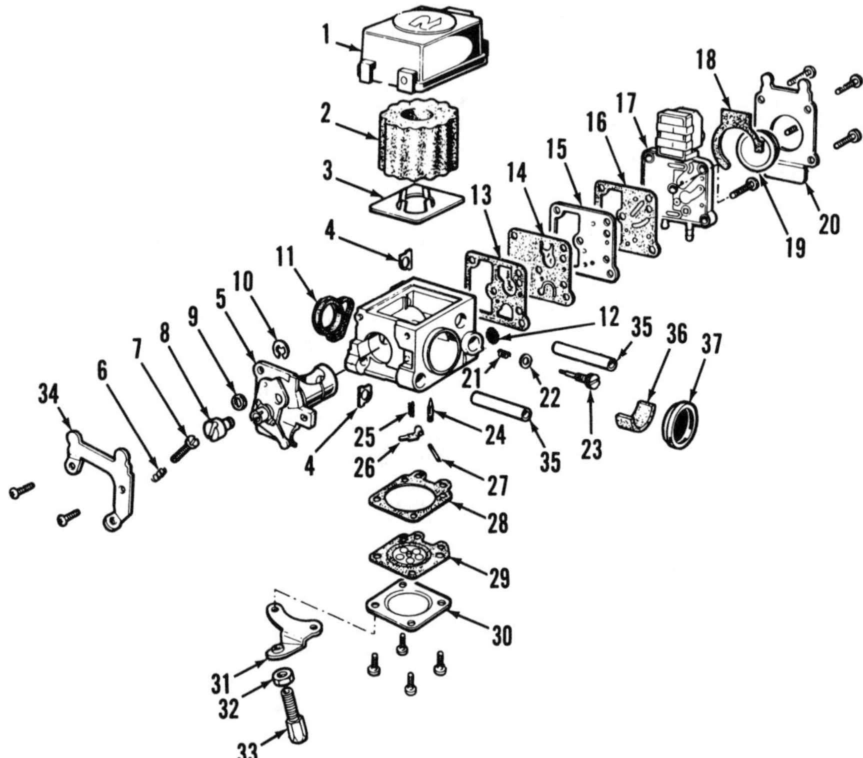
Fig. EF207—Exploded view of Walbro WZ carburetor used on some models.

1. Cover
2. Air cleaner element
3. Plate
4. Plate
5. Throttle barrel assy.
6. Spring
7. Idle speed screw
8. Swivel
9. Washer
10. "E" ring
11. Gasket
12. Screen
13. Gasket
14. Fuel pump diaphragm
15. Plate
16. Gasket
17. Fuel pump cover
18. Gasket
19. Primer bulb
20. Retainer
21. Spring
22. Washer
23. High speed mixture screw
24. Fuel inlet valve
25. Spring
26. Metering lever
27. Pivot pin
28. Gasket
29. Metering diaphragm
30. Cover
31. Bracket
32. Nut.
33. Cable adjuster
34. Support
35. Sleeve
36. Seal
37. Cover

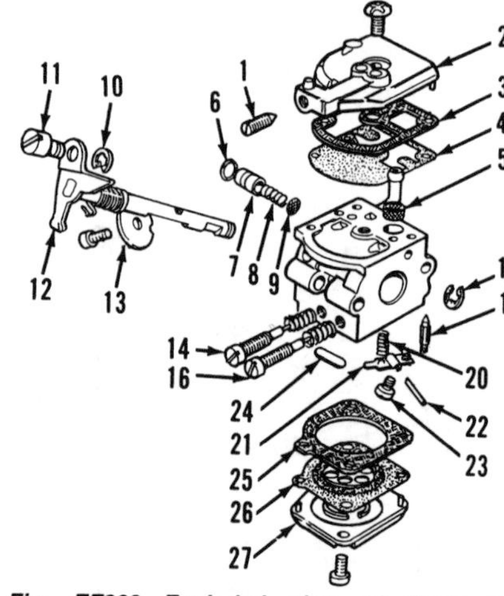
Fig. EF209—Exploded view of Zama C1S carburetor used on some models.

1. Idle speed screw
2. Cover
3. Gasket
4. Fuel pump diaphragm
5. Filter screen
6. "O" ring
7. Accelerator pump piston
8. Spring
9. Screen
10. Clip
11. Swivel
12. Throttle shaft
13. Throttle plate
14. Idle mixture screw
16. High speed mixture screw
18. "E" ring
19. Fuel inlet valve
20. Spring
21. Metering lever
22. Pivot pin
23. Screw
24. Welch plug
25. Gasket
26. Metering diaphragm
27. Cover

at full throttle and adjust high speed mixture screw so engine runs at highest speed (turning mixture screw clockwise leans the mixture), then turn high speed screw counterclockwise until rpm decreases 200-500 rpm. Do not adjust high speed mixture screw too lean as engine damage may result.

Some models are equipped with an accelerator pump that forces additional fuel into the carburetor bore when the throttle shaft is rotated. The pump piston (7—Fig. EF209) rests against a flat on the throttle shaft. Shaft rotation moves the piston against fuel in a passage.

To disassemble carburetor, refer to Fig. EF209 and remove fuel pump cover (2) and metering chamber cover (27) for access to internal components. Remove pivot pin (22), metering lever (21), spring (20) and fuel inlet valve (19). Remove idle mixture screw (14) and high speed mixture screw (16). Use a pin punch to pierce and pry out Welch plug (24).

Clean and inspect all components. If unit has been improperly stored, passages may be clogged with deposits that are hard, solid and nearly transparent. Spray carburetor cleaner through all passages. Be careful not to damage the openings or sealing surfaces while cleaning. Check the condition of diaphragms (4 and 26). Renew diaphragm if hard (not flexible), torn or otherwise damaged. Examine the fuel inlet valve (19) and mixture needles (14 and 16) for wear or damage. Inlet valve and mixture needles can be renewed, but their seats cannot be serviced if damaged.

To reassemble carburetor, reverse disassembly procedure. Note the two types of metering levers in Fig. EF210. Step-type lever should be adjusted so that clearance "A" is 0-0.3 mm (0-0.012 in.). Flat-type lever should be adjusted so that it is flush with metering chamber floor. Bend metering lever to adjust as needed.

IGNITION SYSTEM. The engine is equipped with an electronic ignition system. Ignition system performance is considered satisfactory if a spark will jump across a 3 mm (1/8 in.) electrode gap on a test spark plug. If no spark is produced, check on/off switch for proper operation and wiring for open circuit. If switch and wiring are satisfactory, check ignition module air gap. There should be 0.3 mm (0.012 in.) clearance between leg of module and flywheel magnet. If switch, wiring and module air gap are satisfactory but spark is not present, renew ignition module.

REPAIRS

TIGHTENING TORQUE. Recommended tightening torque specifications are as follows:

Clutch hub	25 N·m (220 in.-lbs.)
Crankcase	6 N·m (53 in.-lbs.)
Flywheel	15 N·m (132 in.-lbs.)

CYLINDER, PISTON, PIN AND RINGS. Crankcase and cylinder halves (1 and 12—Fig. EF211) must be split to remove piston (10). Refer to CONNECTING ROD, CRANKSHAFT AND CRANKCASE section for procedure. Remove retaining rings (8) and push pin (9) from piston to separate piston from connecting rod. If piston pin is a tight fit, heat may be applied to piston crown to make removal of pin easier. The piston may be equipped with one or two piston rings. Ring rotation is prevented by a locating pin in each piston ring groove.

Specified piston ring end gap is 0.15-0.35 mm (0.006-0.014 in.). Maximum allowable ring end gap is 1.0 mm (0.040 in.). To check piston ring groove wear, measure side clearance between top of ring and piston ring land. Renew piston if clearance exceeds 0.15 mm (0.006 in.). Renew cylinder if cylinder bore surface finish is worn away revealing the aluminum. Light scratches on piston skirt and cylinder can be polished out using emery cloth. An engine short block assembly is available for service.

When reassembling, install piston so arrow on piston crown points toward exhaust ports (Fig. EF212). Be sure that piston ring gaps are correctly indexed with locating pins in piston ring grooves. Lubricate piston and cylinder with two-cycle engine oil when installing cylinder.

CONNECTING ROD, CRANKSHAFT AND CRANKCASE. Crankcase and cylinder halves (1 and 12—Fig. EF211) must be split for access to crankshaft. Disconnect ignition wires and throttle cable from engine. Unbolt and remove clutch housing and drive shaft assembly. Remove engine from frame.

Remove spark plug and install piston locking tool or insert end of a rope into cylinder to prevent crankshaft from rotating. Unscrew clutch assembly from crankshaft. Remove recoil starter, fan cover and flywheel. Remove carburetor, gas tank, tank bracket, muffler cover and muffler. Remove screws from crankcase and separate crankcase and cylinder halves. Do not damage crankcase and cylinder mating surfaces. Lift crankcase, connecting rod and piston assembly from cylinder.

Remove snap rings (8), push out piston pin (9) and separate piston (10) from connecting rod. Use a puller to remove bearings (5) from crankshaft.

Connecting rod, crankpin and crankshaft are a pressed-together assembly and available only as a unit. Connecting rod big end rides on a roller bearing and should be inspected for excessive wear and damage. If rod, bearing or crankshaft is damaged, complete crankshaft and connecting rod assembly must be renewed. An engine short block assembly is also available for service.

There is no gasket between crankcase and cylinder halves. Apply a suitable liquid gasket maker to crankcase and cylinder mating surfaces when reassembling.

On early models, be sure snap rings (4—Fig. EF211) properly fit into grooves in cylinder half (12). On all models, seals (S—Fig. EF213) should not obstruct oil holes (H). On later models, seal (2—Fig. EF211) replaces seal (3) and snap ring (4). Edge of seal (2) must fit in groove in cylinder half. Tighten crankcase screws to 6 N.m (53 in.-lbs.).

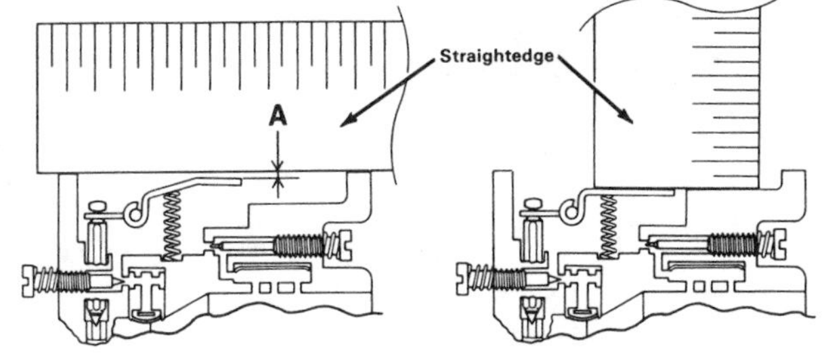

Fig. EF210—On Zama carburetors, note shape of metering lever and refer to drawing for correct metering lever height. Stepped type metering lever should be bent so height (A) is 0-0.3 mm (0.000-0.012 in.). Straight type metering lever should be flush with chamber floor as shown.

CLUTCH. All models are equipped with a two-shoe clutch shown in Fig. EF214 or Fig. EF215. Minimum allowable thickness of the shoe lining is 0.8 mm (0.032 in.). Clutch shoes are available only as a pair.

To disassemble the clutch drum assembly, separate the housing (2—Fig. EF214 or Fig. EF215) from the engine and drive shaft tube. On models with anti-vibration mount, separate the support (8—Fig. EF216) and shock absorber (9) from the housing (2). Remove snap ring (1—Fig. EF214 or Fig. EF215) and press or drive the clutch drum (7) from the housing and bearings (4). Bearings (4) can be pulled from the housing after removing snap ring (6). Reassemble by reversing the disassembly procedure.

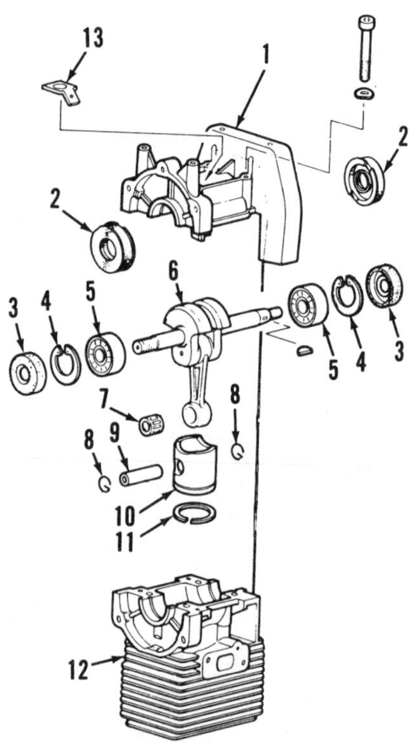

Fig. EF211—Exploded view of engine typical of all models. Flanged seal (2) replaces seal (3) and snap ring (4) on later models.

1. Crankcase half
2. Flanged seal
3. Seal
4. Snap ring
5. Bearing
6. Crankshaft & rod assy.
7. Bearing
8. Retaining rings
9. Piston pin
10. Piston
11. Piston ring
12. Cylinder

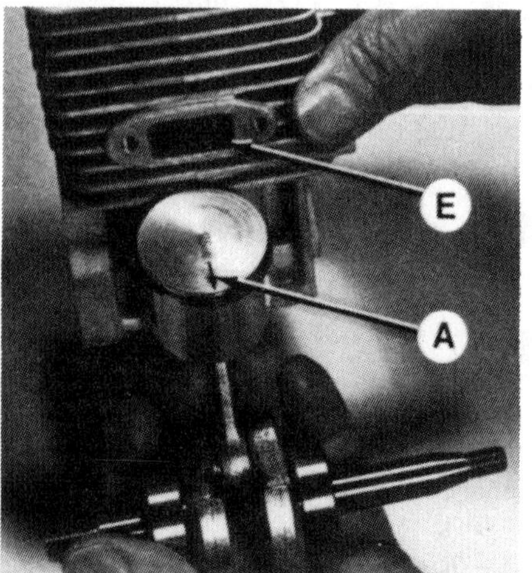

Fig. EF212—Piston must be installed with arrow (A) facing exhaust port side of cylinder.

REWIND STARTER. The engine is equipped with the starter shown in Fig. EF217 or Fig. EF218. To disassemble the starter, detach the rope handle and allow rope to wind onto the starter pulley. Unbolt and remove the starter

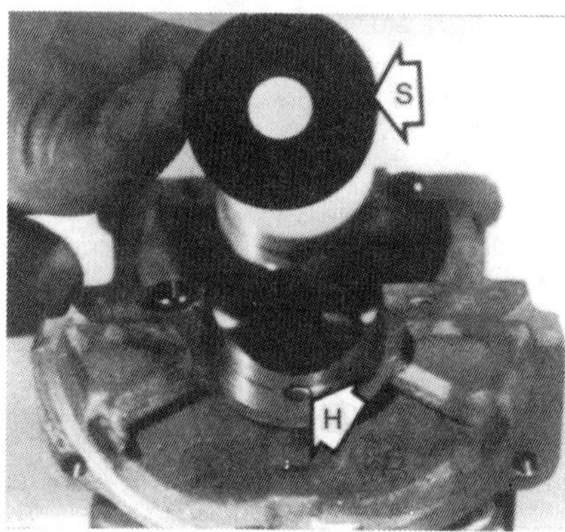

Fig. EF213—Seal (S) should not obstruct lubricating oil hole (H).

housing (10). Wear appropriate safety eyeware and gloves, then remove screw (6) and lift pulley (8) and rope from the housing. Be careful and remove the spring.

To assemble the starter, apply a small amount of light grease to the starter housing post, spring and the back of the pulley. Install the rewind spring in the housing so it is wound counterclockwise from the outer end. Attach the rope to the pulley, making sure the knot is fully nested in the pocket. Pull the rope tight while winding it on the pulley. Install the pulley/rope while rotating it slightly until the spring hooks into the pulley and the pulley drops into the housing. Guide the end of the rope through the housing and attach the handle.

When assembling or if the starter rope does not fully rewind, preload the recoil spring as follows. Hold the pulley to keep it from turning, then pull a

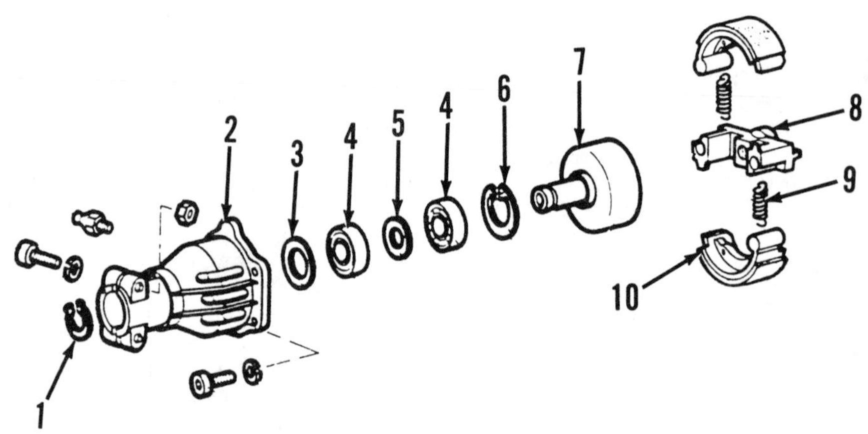

Fig. EF214—Exploded view of clutch assembly used on early models. Refer to Fig. EF215 for late style clutch assembly.

1. Snap ring
2. Housing
3. Washer
4. Bearings
5. Washer
6. Snap ring
7. Clutch drum
8. Clutch hub
9. Return spring
10. Clutch shoes

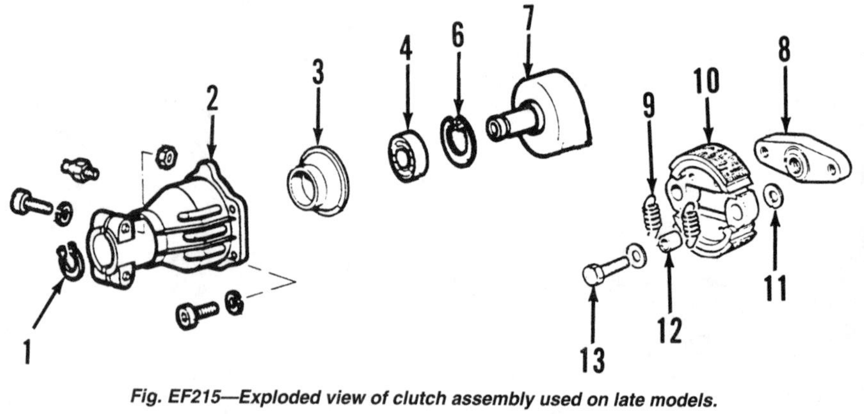

Fig. EF215—Exploded view of clutch assembly used on late models.

1. Snap ring
2. Housing
3. Spacer
4. Bearing
6. Snap ring
7. Clutch drum
8. Drive hub
9. Springs
10. Clutch shoes
11. Washer
12. Bushing
13. Cap screw

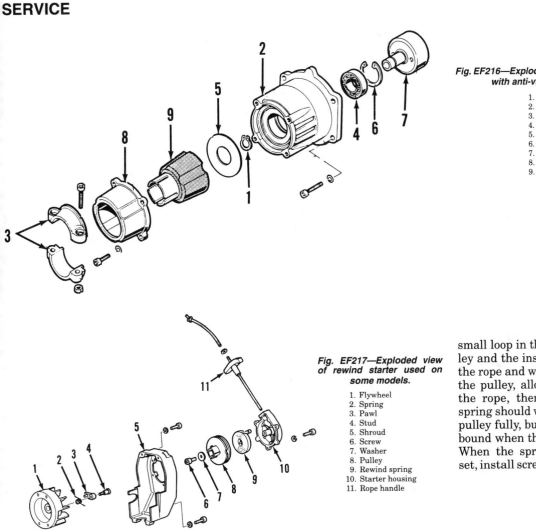

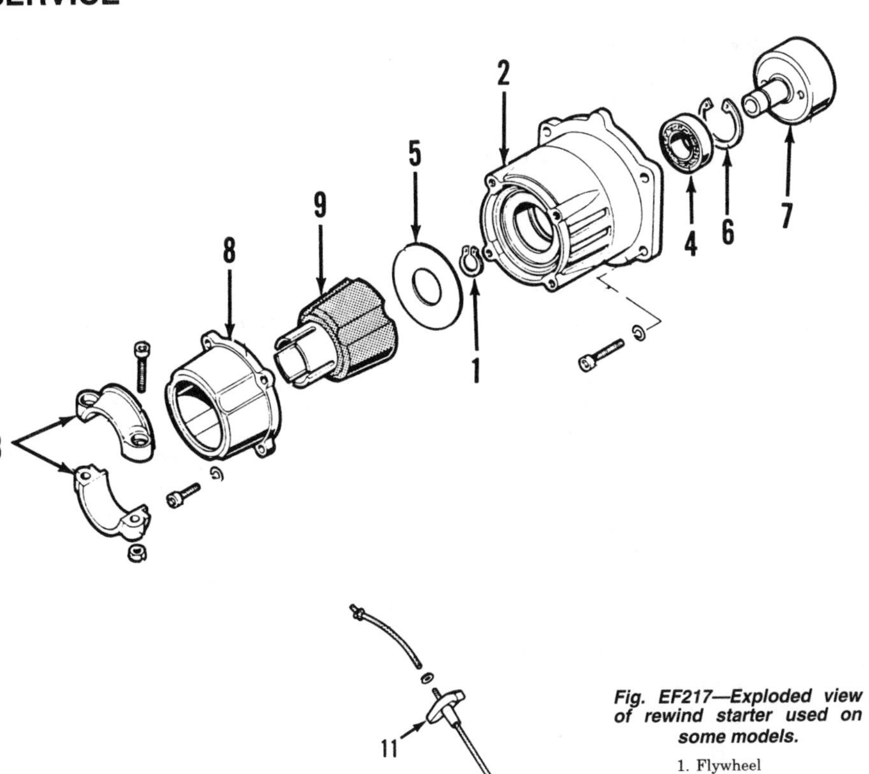

Fig. EF216—Exploded view of trimmers equipped with anti-vibration drive system.

1. Snap ring
2. Housing
3. Clamp
4. Bearing
5. Washer
6. Snap ring
7. Clutch drum
8. Support
9. Shock absorber

Fig. EF217—Exploded view of rewind starter used on some models.

1. Flywheel
2. Spring
3. Pawl
4. Stud
5. Shroud
6. Screw
7. Washer
8. Pulley
9. Rewind spring
10. Starter housing
11. Rope handle

small loop in the rope between the pulley and the inside of the housing. Hold the rope and wind the pulley to preload the pulley, allow the pulley to rewind the rope, then check operation. The spring should wind the rope around the pulley fully, but the spring must not be bound when the rope is fully extended. When the spring preload is correctly set, install screw and washer (6 and 7).

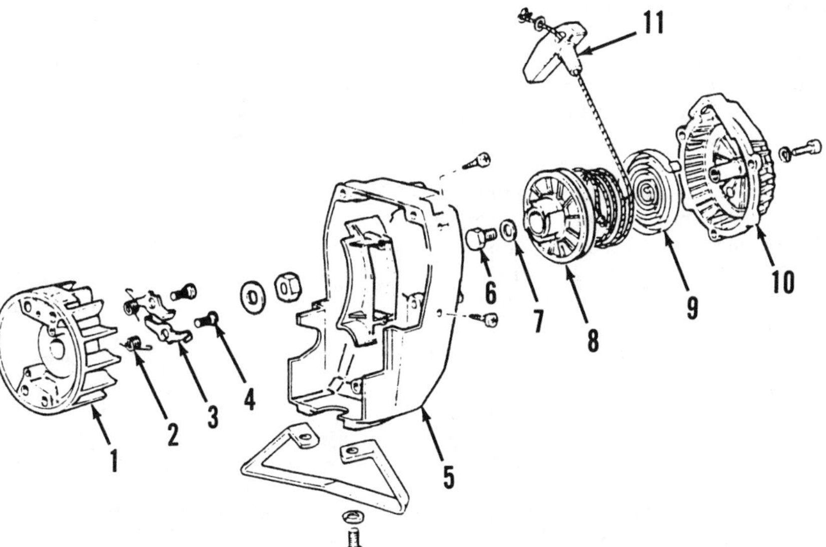

Fig. EF218—Exploded view of rewind starter used on late models.

1. Flywheel
2. Spring
3. Pawl
4. Screw
5. Shroud
6. Screw
7. Washer
8. Pulley
9. Rewind spring
10. Starter housing
11. Rope handle

EFCO

ENGINE SERVICE

Model	Bore	Stroke	Displacement
8300	34 mm (1.34 in.)	30 mm (1.18 in.)	27 cc (1.66 cu. in.)
8350 & 8355	38 mm (1.50 in.)	30 mm (1.18 in.)	35 cc (2.14 cu. in.)
8400 & 8405	40 mm (1.57 in.)	30 mm (1.18 in.)	38 cc (2.32 cu. in.)
8420 & 8425	40 mm (1.57 in.)	33 mm (1.3 in.)	42 cc (2.56 cu. in.)
8510 & 8515	44 mm (1.73 in.)	33 mm (1.3 in.)	51 cc (3.11 cu. in.)

ENGINE INFORMATION

These two-stroke, air-cooled gasoline engines are used on some Olympyk trimmer and brush cutter models.

MAINTENANCE

LUBRICATION. The engine is lubricated by mixing gasoline with an oil designed for two-stroke, air-cooled engines. Refer to trimmer service section for manufacturer's recommended fuel:oil mixture ratio.

SPARK PLUG. The recommended spark plug is a Champion DJ7Y or equivalent and the electrode gap should be 0.6-0.7 mm (0.024-0.028 in.).

CARBURETOR. The engine may be equipped with a Walbro WT or Zama C1Q diaphragm carburetor. Carburetor mixture adjustments should be performed with trimmer or brush cutter installed. Be sure the air filter is clean before adjusting. Refer to the following section for service information.

Walbro WT. Refer to Fig. EF301. Initial setting of the low- and high-speed mixture needles (15 and 16) is 1-1/4 turns open from lightly seated. The engine should be warmed to normal temperature when making final adjustments.

Start the engine and adjust idle speed screw (5) so trimmer head or blade does not turn. Adjust the low-speed mixture needle (16) to obtain the highest speed, then turn the needle 1/6 turn counterclockwise. Adjust idle speed screw (5) as necessary to slow the engine below clutch engagement speed. Operate the unit at full throttle and adjust the high-speed mixture needle (15) to obtain the maximum engine rpm, then turn the needle 1/6 turn counterclockwise. Do not adjust the mixture screws to obtain the highest rpm, because the mixture will be too lean and may result in engine damage.

Refer to Fig. EF301 when overhauling the carburetor. Remove retainer (1), fuel primer bulb (2), fuel pump cover (4) and metering chamber cover (25) for access to internal components. Remove metering lever (21) and fuel inlet valve (20). Remove fuel mixture needles (15 and 16), filter screen (8) and check valve (19).

Clean all passages using suitable carburetor cleaner and compressed air. Do not use drills or wires to clean passages as carburetor calibration could be upset if passages are enlarged. Examine the fuel inlet valve (20) and its seat. Inspect mixture needles (15 and 16) and their seats. If necessary, a new fuel inlet valve or adjustment needle can be installed, but the seats are integral with the carburetor body. Clean fuel screen (8). Inspect diaphragms (7 and 24) for tears or other damage. The diaphragms must be flexible with no holes or cracks.

Check the metering lever height with Walbro tool 500-13 as shown in Fig. EF302. Metering lever should just touch leg of the setting tool. If necessary, bend the lever to change height.

Zama C1Q. Refer to Fig. EF303. Initial setting of the low- and high-speed mixture needles (15 and 16) is one turn open from lightly seated. The engine should be warmed to normal temperature when making final adjustments.

Start the engine and adjust idle speed screw (4) so trimmer head or blade does not turn. Adjust the low-speed mixture needle (15) to obtain the highest idle speed, then check engine

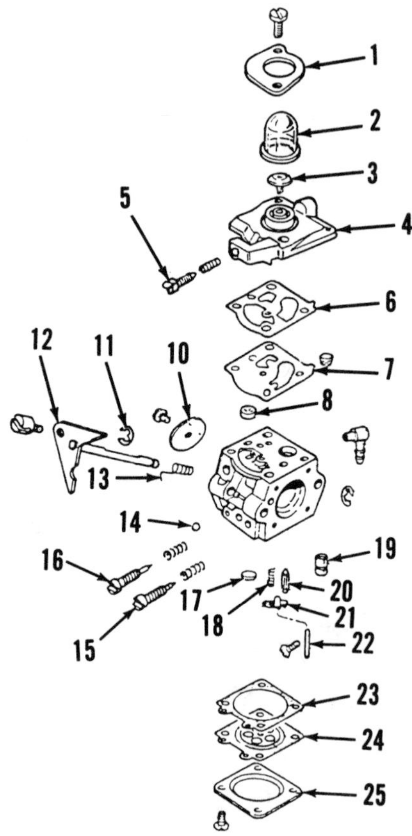

Fig. EF301—Exploded view of typical Walbro WT carburetor.

1. Retainer plate
2. Primer bulb
3. Check valve
4. Fuel pump cover
5. Idle speed screw
6. Gasket
7. Fuel pump diaphragm
8. Screen
9. Clip
10. Throttle plate
11. Clip
12. Throttle shaft
13. Return spring
14. Ball
15. High-speed mixture needle
16. Low-speed mixture needle
17. Welch plug
18. Spring
19. Check valve
20. Fuel inlet valve
21. Metering lever
22. Pin
23. Gasket
24. Metering diaphragm
25. Cover

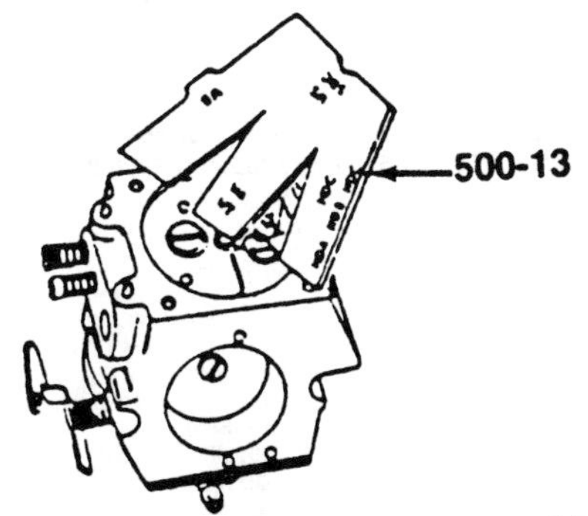

Fig. EF302—Metering lever should just touch leg of Walbro tool 500-13. Bend lever if necessary to change lever height.

acceleration. Turn the low-speed mixture needle counterclockwise to richen the mixture to provide smooth and fast acceleration. Adjust idle speed screw (4) as necessary to slow the engine below clutch engagement speed. Operate the unit at full throttle and adjust the high-speed mixture needle (16) to obtain the maximum engine rpm, then turn the needle counterclockwise until the engine speed slows to 9,500-9,600 rpm for a new engine or 10,300-10,500 rpm for an engine that has run more than 50 hours. Do not adjust the mixture screws to obtain the highest rpm, because the mixture will be too lean and may result in engine damage.

Refer to Fig. EF303 when overhauling the carburetor. Remove retainer (1), fuel primer bulb (2), fuel pump cover (3) and metering chamber cover (19) for access to internal components. Remove gaskets, diaphragms, fuel inlet needle (13), metering lever (14), fuel mixture screws (15 and 16) and filter screen (10).

Clean all parts using suitable carburetor cleaner and compressed air. Do not use drills or wires to clean fuel passages and carburetor calibration may be upset if passages are enlarged. Examine the fuel inlet valve (13) and its seat. Inspect mixture needles (15 and 16) and their seats. If necessary, a new fuel inlet valve or adjustment needle can be installed, but the seats are integral with the carburetor body. Clean fuel screen (10). Inspect diaphragms (8 and 18) for tears or other damage. The diaphragms must be flexible with no holes or cracks.

Assemble the carburetor by reversing the disassembly procedure. Note the two types of metering levers shown in Fig. EF304. Adjust clearance "A" for models with the bent lever to 0-0.03 mm (0-0.012 in.). Models with flat metering lever should be flush with the carburetor floor as shown in the right-side view. If necessary, bend the lever to change height.

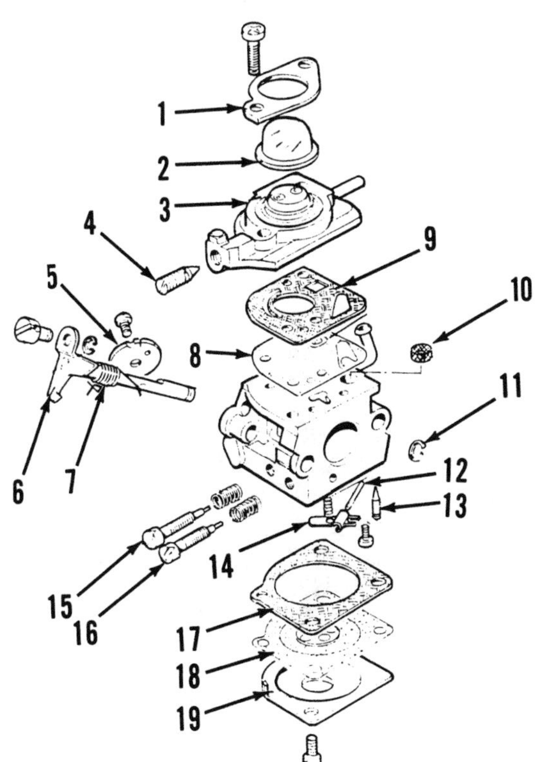

Fig. EF303—Exploded view of typical Zama C1 carburetor.

1. Retainer plate
2. Primer bulb
3. Fuel pump cover
4. Idle speed screw
5. Throttle plate
6. Throttle shaft
7. Return spring
8. Fuel pump diaphragm
9. Gasket
10. Screen
11. Clip
12. Pivot pin
13. Fuel inlet valve
14. Metering lever
15. Low-speed mixture needle
16. High-speed mixture needle
17. Gasket
18. Metering diaphragm
19. Cover

IGNITION SYSTEM. All engines are equipped with an electronic ignition system that does not use breaker points. On some models, the ignition module is separate from the ignition coil; however, the module is incorporated in the coil assembly of most models.

Ignition can be considered satisfactory if a spark will jump across the 3 mm (1/8 in.) electrode gap of a test plug when the engine is turned with the recoil starter. If there is no spark, check the stop switch and connecting wire for improper operation or faulty connections. Ignition may be irregular at starting speeds if gap between the legs of the coil core and the flywheel magnets is too wide.

Clearance (air gap) between the legs of the coil and the flywheel magnets should be 0.3 mm (0.012 in.). If the gap is too wide, the ignition may be weak and the engine difficult to start. If the gap is too close, the coil and flywheel may bump into each other and cause extensive damage. Use non-magnetic feeler gauge to measure the clearance. To change the air gap, loosen the two screws attaching the coil, then move the coil as required. Threads of the coil attaching screws should be coated with Loctite before tightening.

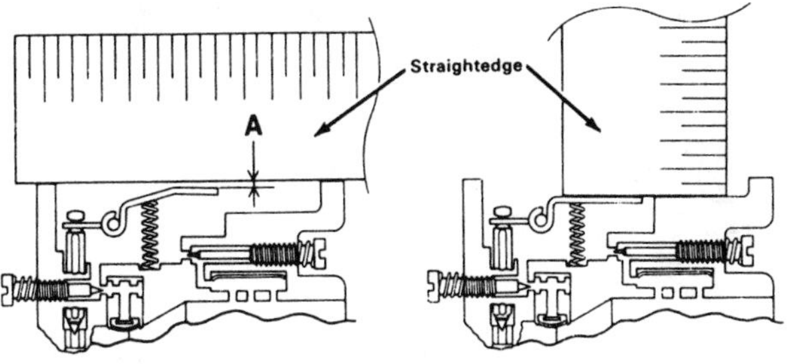

Fig. EF304—Compare shape of the metering lever with the illustration before checking the lever height. Stepped type lever shown on the left should be bent to height necessary to provide clearance (A) of 0-0.3 mm (0-0.012 in.). The straight type lever should be flush with chamber floor as shown on the right.

REPAIRS

CYLINDER, PISTON, PIN AND RINGS. To remove the piston (7—Fig. EF305 or Fig. EF306), separate the drive shaft housing from the engine. Remove air cleaner, carburetor and insulator. Remove cover (1), muffler (2) and insulator (3). Remove clutch cover (10—Fig. EF307 or Fig. EF308) with clutch drum (6) and ignition coil (2). Remove the screws attaching the cylinder, then pull the cylinder (4—Fig. EF305 or Fig. EF306) straight up, off the piston. Remove the piston pin retaining rings (8), push the pin (9) out using a

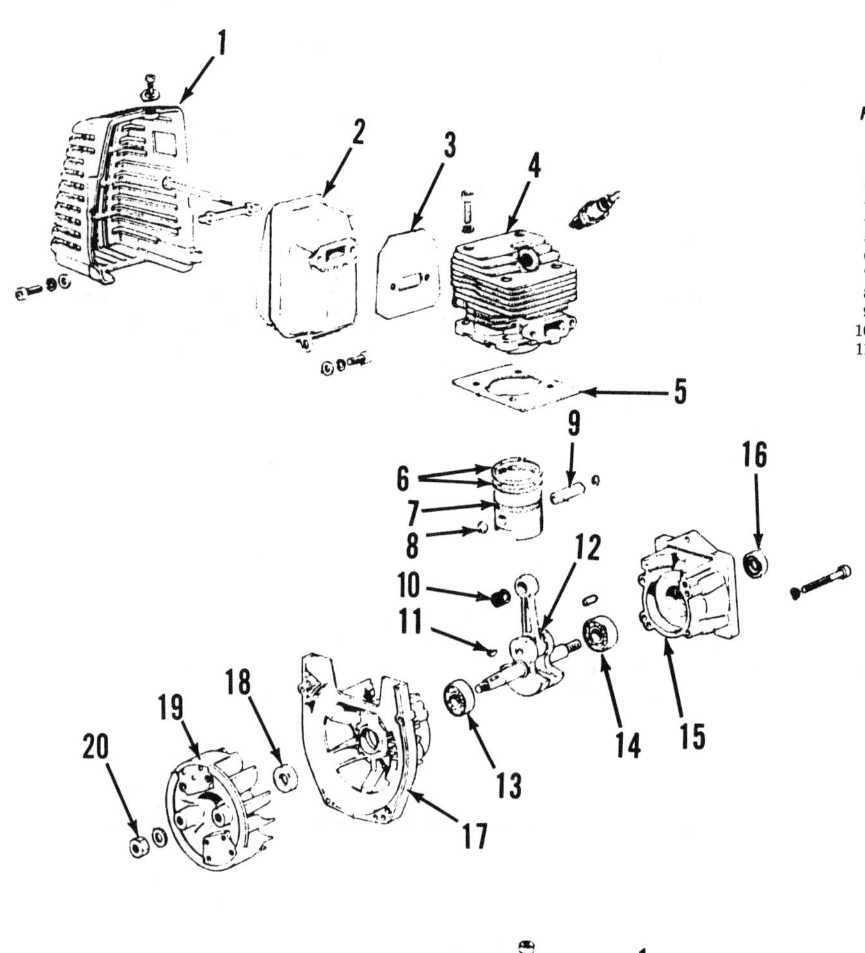

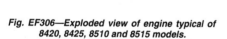

Fig. EF305—Exploded view of engine typical of 8300, 8350, 8355, 8400, 8400 and 8405 models.

1. Cover
2. Muffler
3. Heat insulator
4. Cylinder
5. Base gasket
6. Piston rings
7. Piston
8. Retaining ring
9. Piston pin
10. Needle bearing
11. Woodruff key
12. Crankshaft/connecting rod assy.
13. Main bearing
14. Main bearing
15. Crankcase half
16. Seal
17. Crankcase half
18. Seal
19. Flywheel
20. Nut

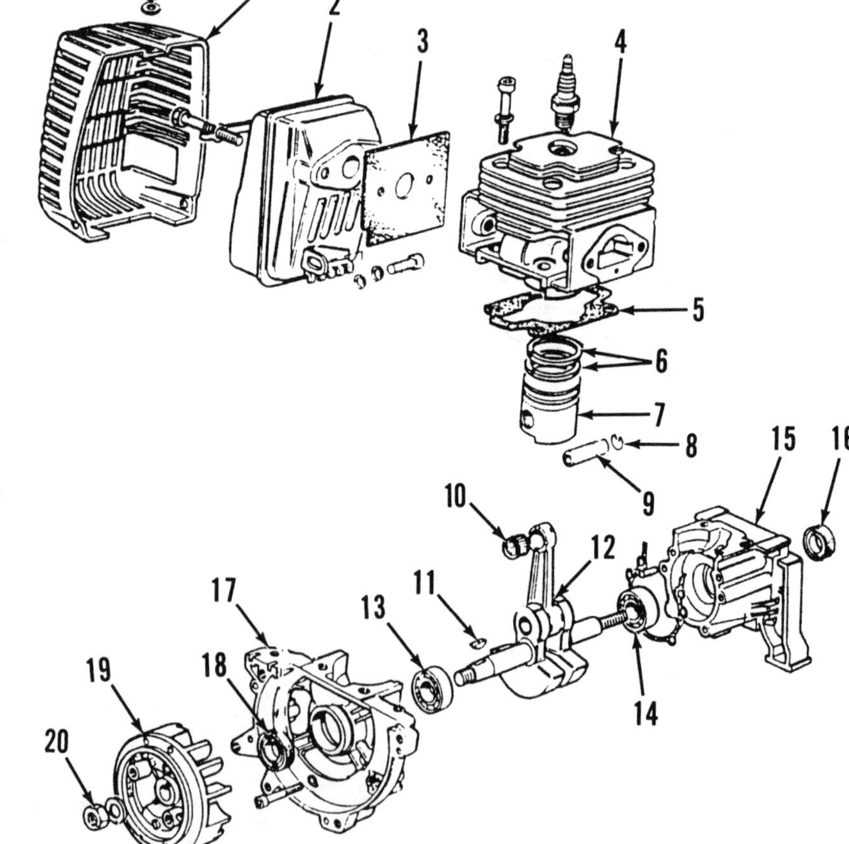

Fig. EF306—Exploded view of engine typical of 8420, 8425, 8510 and 8515 models.

1. Cover
2. Muffler
3. Heat insulator
4. Cylinder
5. Base gasket
6. Piston rings
7. Piston
8. Retaining ring
9. Piston pin
10. Needle bearing
11. Woodruff key
12. Crankshaft/connecting rod assy.
13. Main bearing
14. Main bearing
15. Crankcase half
16. Seal
17. Crankcase half
18. Seal
19. Flywheel
20. Nut

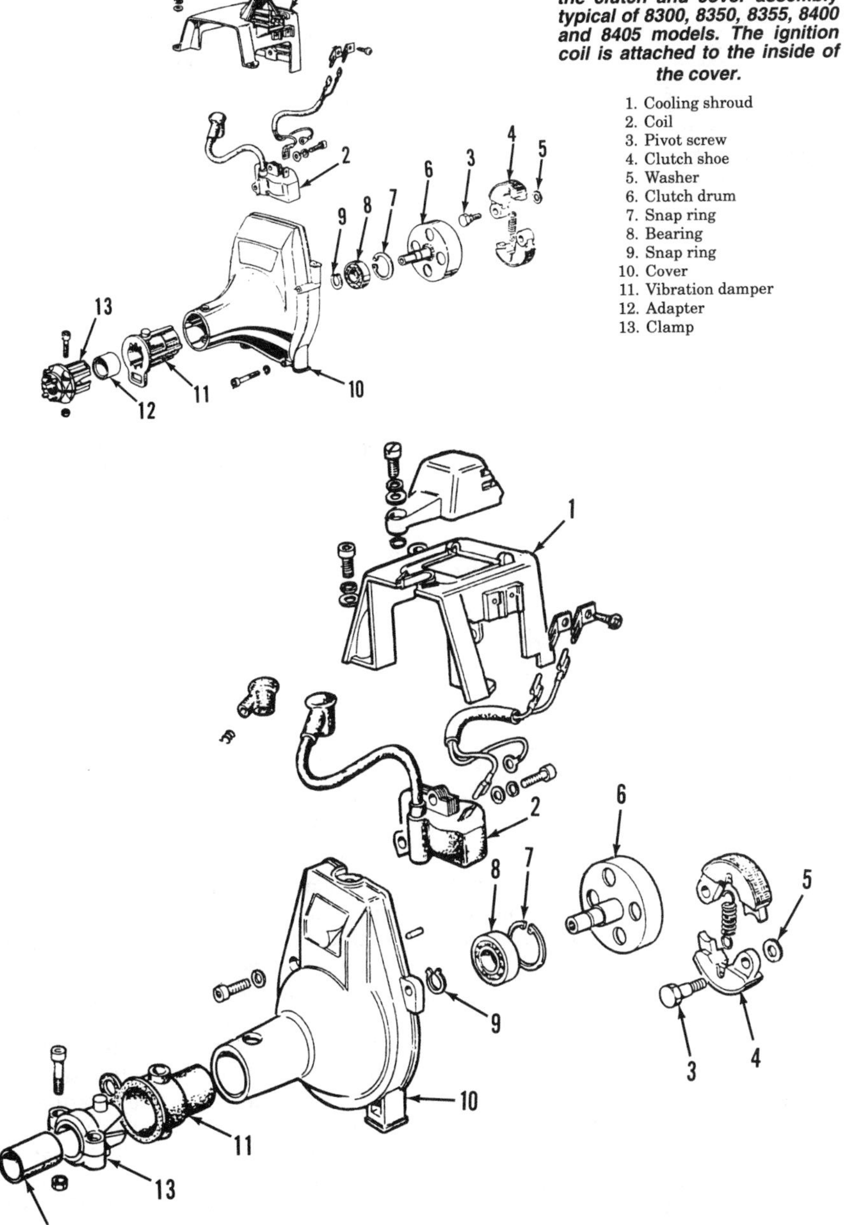

Fig. EF307—Exploded view of the clutch and cover assembly typical of 8300, 8350, 8355, 8400 and 8405 models. The ignition coil is attached to the inside of the cover.

1. Cooling shroud
2. Coil
3. Pivot screw
4. Clutch shoe
5. Washer
6. Clutch drum
7. Snap ring
8. Bearing
9. Snap ring
10. Cover
11. Vibration damper
12. Adapter
13. Clamp

Fig. EF308—Exploded view of clutch and cover typical of 8420, 8425, 8510 and 8515 models. The coil (2) is attached to the cover (10).

1. Cooling shroud
2. Coil
3. Pivot screw
4. Clutch shoe
5. Washer
6. Clutch drum
7. Snap ring
8. Bearing
9. Snap ring
10. Cover
11. Vibration damper
12. Adapter
13. Clamp

suitable pusher tool, then separate the piston (7) from the connecting rod. Needle bearing (10) is located in the connecting rod.

Inspect the cylinder and piston for damage. The piston, rings and cylinder are available in standard size only.

Position the piston on the connecting rod so arrow on top of piston will be toward the exhaust port (muffler) side of cylinder. Lubricate the piston pin and bearing, then install the piston pin. Install new retaining rings (8) if bent or condition is otherwise questionable. Install the retaining rings with the gap toward the top or bottom of the piston.

Make sure the end of each piston ring surrounds the pin located in ring groove. Be careful to install the cylinder straight down over the piston. If the cylinder is turned, the ring can catch in a port and break the end of the ring.

CYLINDER. The piston, rings and cylinder are available in standard size only and the cylinder should not be bored oversize. Inspect the cylinder for any damage and install new parts as necessary. If the chrome plating is worn from the cylinder, a new cylinder should be installed.

CRANKSHAFT AND CONNECTING ROD. The crankshaft and connecting rod are available only as an assembly (12—Fig. EF305 or Fig. EF306); individual components are not available.

To remove crankshaft assemby, remove the spark plug and insert a piece of rope or a piston stop in the spark plug hole to prevent the crankshaft from turning. Remove the rewind starter, nut (5—Fig. EF309 or Fig. EF310) and pawl plate (1). Remove the clutch (3, 4 and 5—Fig. EF307 or Fig. EF308) and the flywheel retaining nut (20—Fig. EF305 or Fig. EF306). Use a suitable puller to remove the flywheel. Remove the cylinder and piston as described in PISTON, PIN AND RINGS paragraph. Remove the screws attaching the halves of the crankcase together and separate halves (15 and 17). Heat the crankcase if necessary to remove the main bearings (13 and 14) from the crankcase bores. If the bearings stay on the crankshaft, use a suitable puller to pull the bearings from the main journals.

The main bearing should turn smoothly with no perceptible play or ratcheting. Use a suitable tools to press new main bearings and seals into the crankcase bores. Lips of seals (16 and 18) should be toward inside of crankcase and should be lubricated before installing the crankshaft.

CLUTCH. Clutch shoes (4—Fig. EF307 or Fig. EF308) are attached to the flywheel with pivot screws (3). The clutch drum of all models operates in bearing (8) located in the cover (10).

Remove screws from clamp (13) and separate the drive shaft from the cover. Remove attaching screws and separate the cover (10) from the engine. Inspect the vibration isolator (11) and replace if necessary.

Remove snap ring (7), then press clutch drum (6) and bearing (8) from the cover. Remove snap ring (9) and use a suitable puller to remove bearing if replacement is required. It may be necessary to heat the housing to facilitate removal and installation of the bearings.

Inspect the clutch shoes (4) and drum (6) for excessive wear. Inspect the spring for evidence of overheating or other damage.

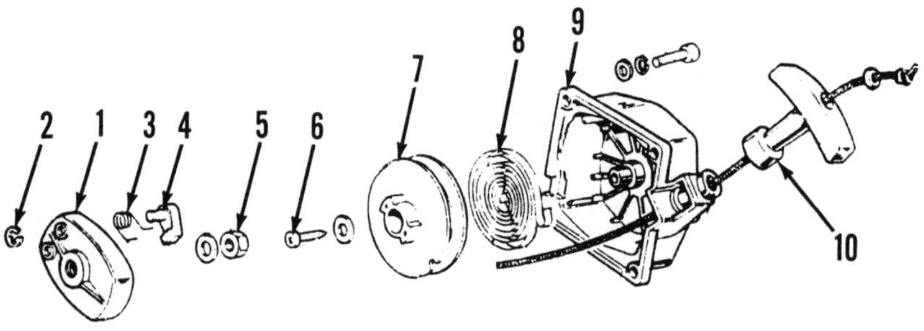

Fig. EF309—Exploded view of recoil start typical of 8300, 8350, 8355, 8400, 8400 and 840 models.

1. Plate
2. "E" ring
3. Spring
4. Pawl
5. Nut
6. Screw
7. Pulley
8. Spring
9. Housin
10. Handl

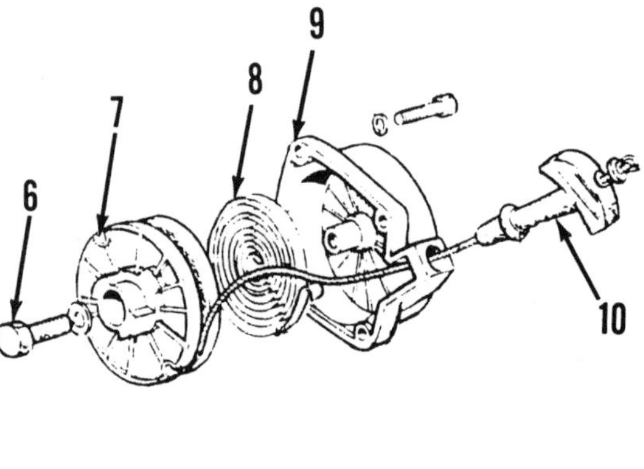

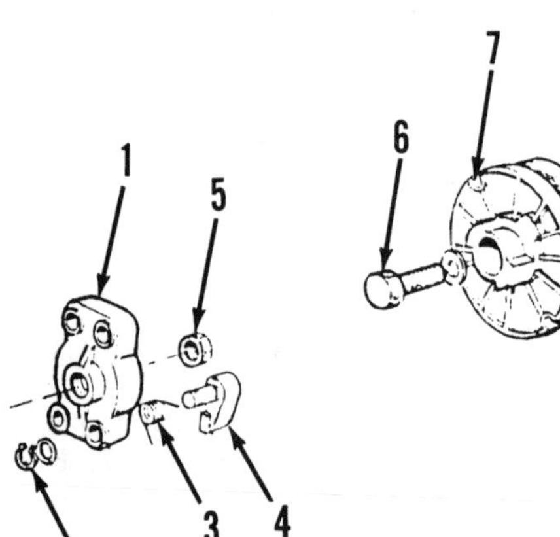

Fig. EF310—Exploded view of recoil starte typical of 8420, 8425, 8510 and 8515 models.

1. Plate
2. "E" ring
3. Spring
4. Pawl
5. Nut
6. Screw
7. Pulley
8. Spring
9. Housin
10. Handle

REWIND STARTER. Refer to Fig. EF309 or Fig. EF310 for exploded view of rewind starter. To disassemble the starter, unbolt and remove the housing from the engine. Remove handle from the rope and allow the rope to wind into the starter. Remove center screw (6), then remove washer and the rope pulley (7). Wear appropriate eyewear and gloves to protect against injury when removing the spring (8). The spring may unwind from the housing uncontrollably. If necessary for service, remove the pulley plate.

The rope must be the correct diameter and length for the starter to operate properly. If the rope is too large in diameter or too long, the rope may bind when trying to wind onto the pulley. When installing new rope, measure the length and diameter of the old rope, then install new rope that matches the original.

To assemble the starter, apply a small amount of light grease to the starter housing post, spring and the back of the pulley. Install the rewind spring so it is wound counterclockwise from the outer end. Attach the rope to the pulley, making sure the knot is fully nested in the pocket. Pull the rope tight and wind the rope counterclockwise as viewed from the pawl (engine) side. Install the pulley/rope and rotate slightly until the spring hooks into the pulley and the pulley drops into the housing. Guide the end of the rope through the housing and attach the handle.

When assembling or if the starter rope does not fully rewind, preload the recoil spring as follows. Hold the pulley to keep it from turning, then pull a small loop in the rope between the pulley and the inside of the housing. Hold the rope and wind the pulley to preload the pulley, allow the pulley to rewind the rope, then check operation. The spring should wind the rope around the pulley fully, but the spring must bind when the rope is fully extended. It should be possible to rotate the pulley at least 1/4 turn when the rope is pulled out completely. Complete the assembly by reversing the disassembly procedure when the spring preload is correctly set.

FUJI-ROBIN

ENGINE SERVICE

Model	Bore	Stroke	Displacement
EC01-A	28.0 mm (1.10 in.)	25.0 mm (0.98 in.)	15.4 cc (0.94 cu. in.)
EC01-E	28.0 mm (1.10 in.)	26.0 mm (1.02 in.)	16.0 cc (0.97 cu. in.)
EC02-E	31.5 mm (1.24 in.)	26 mm (1.02 in.)	20.3 cc (1.24 cu. in.)
EC02-EH	33 mm (1.30 in.)	26.0 mm (1.02 in.)	22.2 cc (1.35 cu. in.)
EC02-F	33 mm (1.30 in.)	30 mm (1.18 in.)	25.6 cc (1.56 cu. in.)
EC02-R	32 mm (1.26 in.)	28 mm (1.10 in.)	22.5 cc (1.37 cu. in.)
EC03	36 mm (1.42 in.)	30 mm (1.18 in.)	30.5 cc (1.86 cu. in.)
EC03-1R	36 mm (1.42 in.)	28 mm (1.19 in.)	28.0 cc (1.71 cu. in.)
EC03-2R	36 mm (1.42 in.)	30 mm (1.18 in.)	30.5 cc (1.86 cu. in.)
EC03-E	37 mm (1.46 in.)	32 mm (1.26 in.)	34.4 mm (2.10 cu. in.)
EC03-F	36 mm (1.42 in.)	30 mm (1.18 in.)	30.5 cc (1.86 cu. in.)
EC04-3R	40 mm (1.58 in.)	30 mm (1.18 in.)	37.7 cc (2.30 cu. in.)
EC04-E	40 mm (1.58 in.)	32 mm (1.26 in.)	40.2 cc (2.45 cu. in.)
EC05-M	44 mm (1.73 in.)	34 mm (1.34 in.)	51.7 cc (3.15 cu. in.)
EC022GA	...	...	21.7 cc (1.32 cu. in.)
EC025GA	...	...	24.5 cc (1.50 cu. in.)
...	33 mm (1.30 in.)	26 mm (1.02 in.)	22.2 cc (1.35 cu. in.)

ENGINE INFORMATION

Fuji two-stroke, air-cooled gasoline engines are used by several manufacturers of string trimmers, brush cutters and blowers.

MAINTENANCE

LUBRICATION. Engine lubrication is obtained by mixing gasoline with an oil designed for two-stroke, air-cooled engines. Refer to trimmer or blower Service Section for manufacturer's recommended fuel:oil mixture ratio.

SPARK PLUG. Recommended spark plug for Model EC03E and EC04E engines is NGK BPM7A or equivalent. Recommended spark plug for Model EC03-2R and EC04-3R engines is NGK B7HS or equivalent. Recommended spark plug for all other models is NGK BM7A or equivalent. Specified electrode gap is 0.6-0.7 mm (0.024-0.028 in.) for all engines.

CARBURETOR. Various carburetors have been used. The manufacturer's name and carburetor model number are stamped on the carburetor. Refer to appropriate following section.

Walbro WA. Some engines are equipped with a Walbro WA diaphragm-type carburetor. Initial adjustment of idle and high speed mixture screws is one turn out from a lightly seated position. Final adjustments are performed with trimmer line at recommended length or blade installed. Be sure engine air filter is clean before adjusting carburetor. Engine must be at operating temperature and running. Adjust idle speed screw (1—Fig. FJ101) so trimmer head or blade does not rotate. Adjust idle mixture screw (14) to obtain maximum idle speed possible, then turn idle mixture screw 1/6 turn counterclockwise. Readjust idle speed. Operate unit at full throttle and adjust high speed mixture screw (16) to obtain maximum engine rpm then turn high speed mixture screw 1/6 turn counterclockwise.

When overhauling carburetor, refer to exploded view in Fig. FJ101. Remove fuel pump cover (4) and metering chamber cover (32) for access to internal components. Remove circuit plate (28), check valve (27), metering lever (24), fuel inlet valve (21), and fuel mixture screws (14 and 16).

Clean and inspect all components. If the unit has been improperly stored, passages may be clogged with deposits that are hard, solid and nearly transparent. Clean passages with suitable carburetor cleaning solvent and compressed air. Be careful not to damage the openings or sealing surfaces while cleaning. Examine fuel inlet valve and seat. Inlet valve (21) is renewable, but carburetor body must be renewed if seat is excessively worn or damaged. Inspect mixture screws and seats. Renew carburetor body if seats are excessively worn or damaged. Clean fuel screen (17). Inspect diaphragms (6 and 31) for tears and other damage.

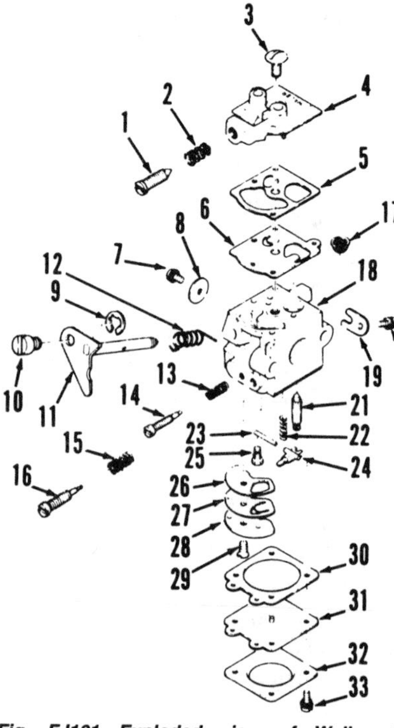

Fig. FJ101—Exploded view of Walbro WA carburetor used on some models.

1. Idle speed screw
2. Spring
3. Screw
4. Pump cover
5. Gasket
6. Fuel pump diaphragm
7. Screw
8. Throttle plate
9. "E" ring
10. Cable clamp
11. Throttle shaft
12. Spring
13. Spring
14. Idle mixture screw
15. Spring
16. High speed mixture screw
17. Screen
18. Body
19. Clip
20. Screw
21. Fuel inlet valve
22. Spring
23. Pin
24. Metering lever
25. Screw
26. Gasket
27. Check valve
28. Circuit plate
29. Screw
30. Gasket
31. Metering diaphragm
32. Cover
33. Screw

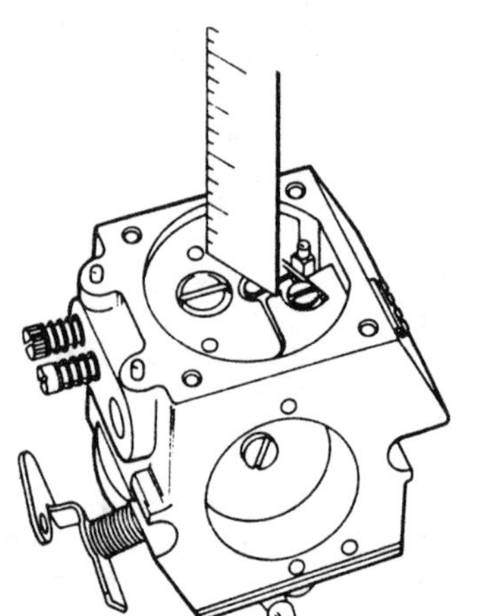

Fig. FJ102—On Walbro WA carburetor, metering lever should be flush with top of circuit plate.

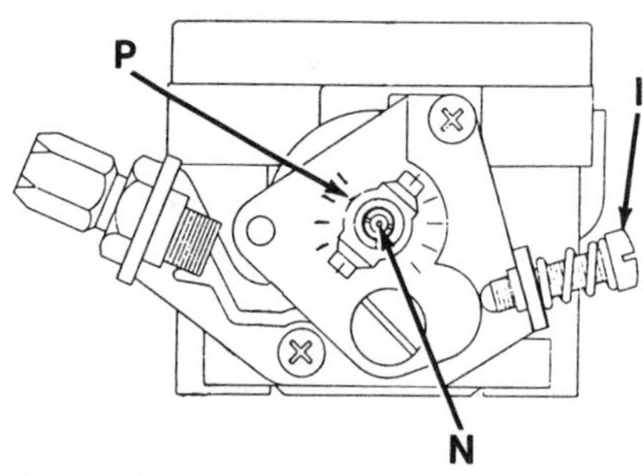

Fig. FJ103—On Walbro WY, WYJ and WYL carburetors, idle speed screw is located at (I), idle mixture plate is located at (P) and idle mixture needle is located at (N). A plug covers the idle mixture needle.

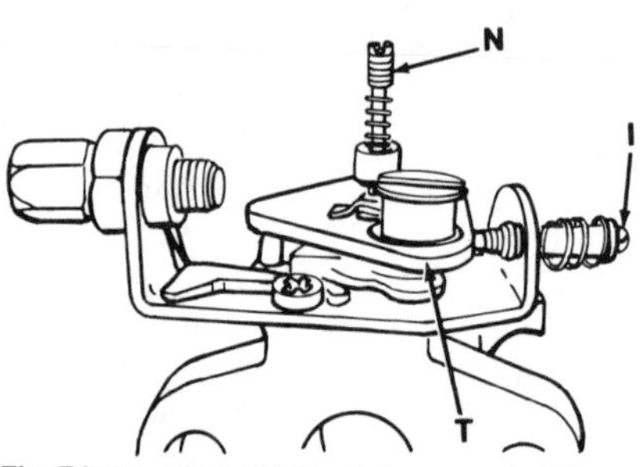

Fig. FJ104—View of idle mixture needle (N) used on Walbro WY, WYJ and WYL carburetors.

Check metering lever height as shown in Fig. FJ102. Upper surface of metering lever should be flush with top of circuit plate. Bend lever to obtain correct lever height.

Walbro WY, WYJ and WYL. Some engines may be equipped with a Walbro WY, WYJ or WYL carburetor. This is a diaphragm-type carburetor that uses a barrel-type throttle rather than a throttle plate. Idle fuel for the carburetor flows up into the throttle barrel where it is fed into the air stream. On some models, the idle fuel flow can be adjusted by turning an idle mixture limiter plate (P—Fig. FJ103). Initial setting is in center notch. Rotating the plate clockwise will lean the idle mixture. Inside the mixture plate is an idle mixture needle (N) that is preset at the factory and should not require adjustment.

If idle mixture needle is removed, use the following procedure to determine correct position. Back out needle (N—Fig. FJ104) until unscrewed. Screw in needle five turns on Model WY or 15 turns on Models WYJ and WYL. Rotate idle mixture plate (P—Fig. FJ103) to center notch. Run engine until normal operating temperature is attained. Adjust idle speed screw so trimmer head or blade does not rotate. Rotate idle mixture needle (N—Fig. FJ104) and obtain highest rpm (turning needle clockwise leans the mixture), then turn needle 1/4 turn counterclockwise. Readjust idle speed screw. Note that idle mixture plate and needle are available only as an assem-

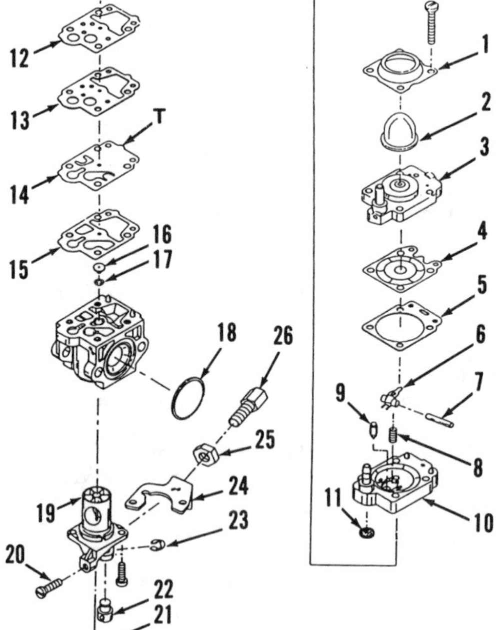

Fig. FJ105—Exploded view of Walbro WY carburetor. Models WYJ and WYL are similar.

1. Cover
2. Primer bulb
3. Plate
4. Metering diaphragm
5. Gasket
6. Metering lever
7. Pin
8. Spring
9. Fuel inlet valve
10. Fuel pump body
11. Fuel screen
12. Gasket
13. Fuel pump plate
14. Fuel pump diaphragm
15. Gasket
16. Main jet
17. "O" ring
18. "O" ring
19. Throttle barrel assy.
20. Idle speed screw
21. Plug
22. Swivel
23. "E" ring
24. Bracket
25. Nut
26. Adjuster

bly with throttle barrel (19—Fig. FJ105). The high speed mixture is controlled by a removable fixed jet (16—Fig. FJ105).

To overhaul carburetor, refer to exploded view in Fig. FJ105. Remove retainer (1), plate (3), diaphragm (4), fuel pump body (10), plate (13) and diaphragm (14). Remove throttle barrel assembly (19).

On models with a plastic body, clean only with solvents approved for use with plastic. Do not use wire or drill bits to clean fuel passages. Do not disassemble throttle barrel assembly (19). Examine fuel inlet valve and seat. Inlet valve (9) is renewable, but fuel pump body (10) must be renewed if seat is excessively worn or damaged. Clean fuel screen (11). Inspect diaphragms for tears and other damage. When installing plates and gaskets (10 through 15), note that tabs (T) on ends will "stair-step" when correctly installed. Adjust metering lever height dimension (D—Fig. FJ106) to obtain 1.5 mm (0.059 in.) between carburetor body surface and lever.

Walbro WZ. Some engines may be equipped with a Walbro WZ carburetor. This is a diaphragm-type carburetor that uses a barrel-type throttle rather than a throttle plate.

Idle fuel for the carburetor flows up into the throttle barrel where it is fed into the air stream. Idle fuel flow can be adjusted by turning idle mixture limiter plate (P—Fig. FJ107). Initial setting is in center notch. Rotating the plate clockwise will lean the idle mixture. Inside the mixture plate is an idle mixture needle (N—Fig. FJ104) that is preset at the factory (a plug covers the needle). If idle mixture needle is removed, use the following procedure to determine correct position. Back out needle (N) until unscrewed, then screw in needle six turns. Rotate idle mixture plate (P—Fig. FJ107) to center notch. Run engine until normal operating temperature is attained. Adjust idle speed screw so trimmer head or blade does not rotate. Rotate idle mixture needle (N—Fig. FJ104) and obtain highest rpm (turning needle clockwise leans the mixture), then turn needle counterclockwise until rpm decreases 200-500 rpm. Readjust idle speed screw. Note that idle mixture plate and needle are available only as an assembly with throttle barrel (24—Fig. FJ108).

Initial setting of high speed mixture screw (42—Fig. FJ108) is 1 1/2 turns out from a lightly seated position. Adjust high speed mixture screw to obtain highest engine speed, then turn screw 1/4 turn counterclockwise. Do not adjust mixture too lean as engine may be damaged.

To overhaul carburetor, refer to exploded view in Fig. FJ108. Remove air cleaner assembly (33-36). Remove retainer plate (2), cover (5), plate (7), diaphragm (8), cover (16), metering lever (12), fuel inlet valve (10) and throttle valve assembly (24).

Clean only with solvents approved for use with plastic. Do not use wire or drill bits to clean fuel passages as fuel delivery may be affected if passages are enlarged. Do not disassemble throttle barrel assembly (24). Examine fuel inlet valve and seat. Inlet valve (10) is renewable, but carburetor body must be renewed if seat is excessively worn or damaged. Inspect high-speed mixture screw and seat. Renew carburetor body if seat is excessively worn or damaged. Clean fuel screen. Inspect diaphragms for tears and other damage.

Adjust metering lever height dimension (D—Fig. FJ106) to obtain 1.5 mm (0.059 in.) between carburetor body surface and lever. When installing plates and gaskets (6 through 9—Fig. FJ108) note that tabs on outer edges will "stair-step" when correctly installed.

TK Series. Refer to Fig. FJ109 for an exploded view of the TK diaphragm-type carburetor used on some models. Initial setting for the idle mixture screw (18) is 3/4 turn open from a lightly seated position. Initial setting for the high speed mixture screw (21) is two turns open from a lightly seated position. Be sure engine air filter is clean before adjusting carburetor. Final adjustments are made with engine at normal operating temperature. Trimmer line must be fully extended or blade assembly installed on trimmer models. Adjust idle speed screw (17) so engine rpm is 2500-3000. Trimmer head or blade should not rotate. Adjust idle

Fig. FJ106—Bend metering lever (1) as needed so height dimension (D) is as specified in text.

1. Metering lever
2. Fuel inlet valve
3. Spring
4. Body

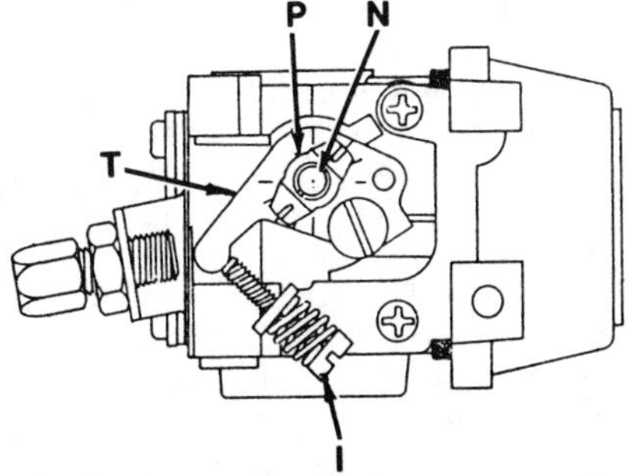

Fig. FJ107—On Walbro WZ carburetor, idle speed screw is located at (I), idle mixture plate is located at (P) and idle mixture needle is located at (N). A plug covers the idle mixture needle.

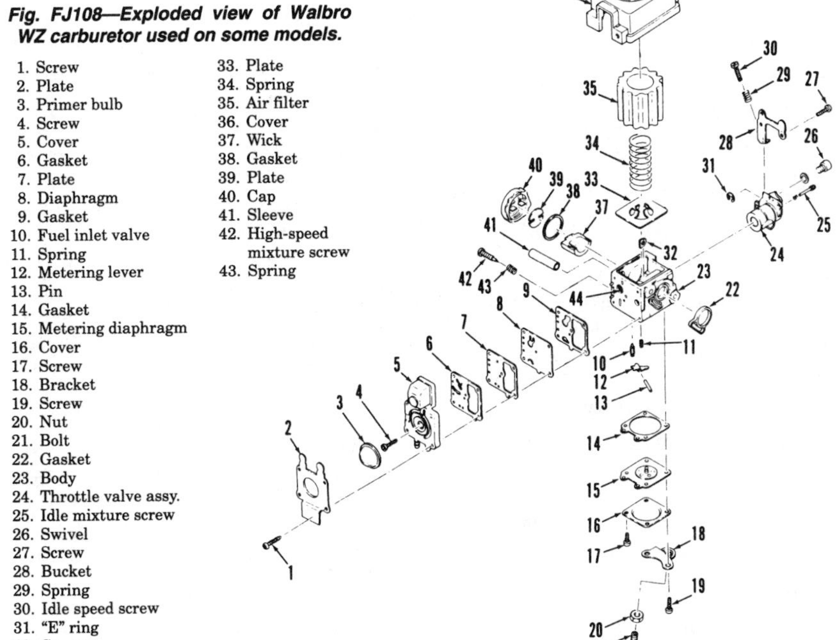

Fig. FJ108—Exploded view of Walbro WZ carburetor used on some models.

1. Screw
2. Plate
3. Primer bulb
4. Screw
5. Cover
6. Gasket
7. Plate
8. Diaphragm
9. Gasket
10. Fuel inlet valve
11. Spring
12. Metering lever
13. Pin
14. Gasket
15. Metering diaphragm
16. Cover
17. Screw
18. Bracket
19. Screw
20. Nut
21. Bolt
22. Gasket
23. Body
24. Throttle valve assy.
25. Idle mixture screw
26. Swivel
27. Screw
28. Bucket
29. Spring
30. Idle speed screw
31. "E" ring
32. Support
33. Plate
34. Spring
35. Air filter
36. Cover
37. Wick
38. Gasket
39. Plate
40. Cap
41. Sleeve
42. High-speed mixture screw
43. Spring

Fig. FJ109—Exploded view of TK diaphragm carburetor used on some models.

1. Air filter cover
2. Gasket
3. Screen
4. Bracket
5. Filter
6. Screen
7. Housing
8. Throttle valve
9. Fuel needle
10. Clip
11. Spring seat
12. Spring
13. Cap
14. Nut
15. Throttle cable adjuster
16. Spring
17. Idle speed screw
18. Idle mixture screw
19. Spring
20. Spring
21. High speed mixture
22. "O" ring
23. Tube
24. Body
25. Spring
26. Fuel inlet valve
27. Metering lever
28. Pin
29. Screw
30. Gasket
31. Metering diaphragm
32. Cover
33. Screw
34. Seal rings
35. Fuel pump plate
36. Gasket
37. Fuel pump diaphragm
38. Cover
39. Screw
40. Stud
41. Choke lever
42. Choke plate
43. Washer
44. Nut

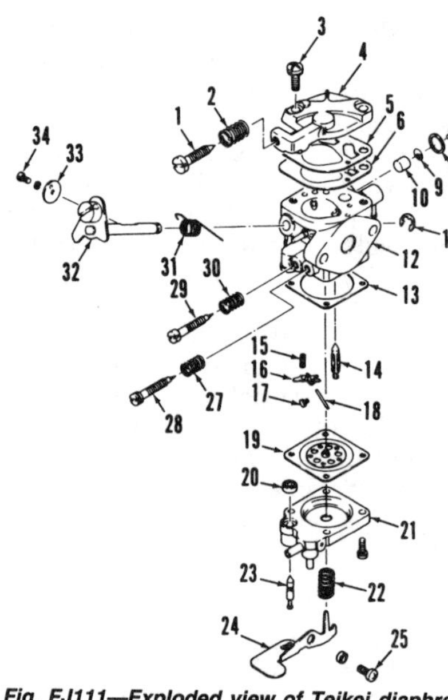

Fig. FJ111—Exploded view of Teikei diaphragm carburetor used on some models.

1. Idle speed screw
2. Spring
3. Screw
4. Fuel pump cover
5. Gasket
6. Diaphragm
7. Plug
8. "O" ring
9. Screen
10. Felt
11. "E" ring
12. Body
13. Gasket
14. Fuel inlet valve
15. Spring
16. Fuel inlet lever
17. Screw
18. Pin
19. Diaphragm
20. Seat
21. Cover
22. Spring
23. Plunger
24. Primer lever
25. Screw
27. Spring
28. High-speed mixture screw
29. Idle mixture screw
30. Spring
31. Spring
32. Throttle shaft
33. Throttle plate
34. Screw

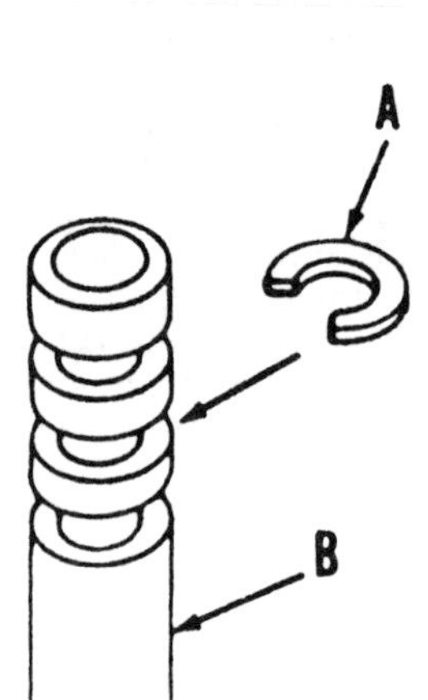

Fig. FJ110—Normal position for jet needle clip (A) is in the center groove of jet needle (B).

mixture screw (18) so engine accelerates cleanly without hesitation. If necessary, readjust idle speed screw. Operate engine at full throttle and adjust high speed mixture screw (21) to obtain maximum engine speed, then turn screw counterclockwise 1/6 turn to enrich fuel mixture slightly.

Midrange mixture is determined by the position of clip (10) on jet needle (9). There are three grooves in upper end of the jet needle and normal position of clip is in the middle groove. See Fig. FJ110. The mixture will be leaner if clip is installed in the top groove, or richer if clip is installed in the bottom groove. To overhaul, refer to Fig. FJ109 and remove air cleaner assembly (1-7), cover (32), metering lever (27), fuel inlet valve (26), cover (38), fuel pump (35-37), mixture screws (18 and 21) and throttle valve (8).

Clean and inspect all components. If the unit has been improperly stored, passages may be clogged with deposits that are hard, solid and nearly transparent. Clean passages with suitable carburetor cleaning solvent and compressed air. Be careful not to damage the openings or sealing surfaces while cleaning. Examine fuel inlet valve and seat. Inlet valve (26) is renewable, but carburetor body must be renewed if seat is excessively worn or damaged. Inspect mixture screws and seats. Renew carburetor body if seats are excessively worn or damaged. Inspect diaphragms (31 and 37) for tears and other damage.

Fuel inlet lever spring (25) free length should be 9.5 mm (0.35 in.). Metering lever height dimension (D—Fig. FJ106) should be 2.0 mm (0.08 in.). Carefully bend lever to obtain dimension.

Teikei. Some models may be equipped with the Teikei diaphragm carburetor shown in Fig. FJ111. Initial setting of idle mixture screw (29) is 1 1/4 turns out from a lightly seated position. Initial setting of high speed mixture screw (28) is 3/4 turn out. Be sure engine air filter is clean before adjusting carburetor. Final adjustment is performed with engine at normal operating temperature. Before final adjustment on trimmer models, cutter line should be at desired length or blade assembly installed. Adjust idle mixture screw (29) so engine idles smoothly and accelerates cleanly without hesitation. Adjust idle speed screw (1) so engine idles just below clutch engagement speed. Open throttle to wide open position and adjust high speed mixture needle beyond initial setting. Do not adjust high speed mixture screw too lean as engine may be damaged.

To overhaul, refer to Fig. FJ111 and remove fuel pump cover (4) and metering chamber cover (21) for access to internal components. Clean and inspect all components. If the unit has been improperly stored, passages may be clogged with deposits that are hard, solid and nearly transparent. Clean passages with suitable carburetor cleaning solvent and compressed air. Be careful not to damage the openings or sealing surfaces while cleaning.

Examine fuel inlet valve and seat. Inlet valve (14) is renewable, but carburetor body must be renewed if seat is excessively worn or damaged. Inspect ixture screws (28 and 29) and seats. enew carburetor body if seats are excessively worn or damaged. Inspect diahragms (6 and 19) for tears and other amage.

Metering lever height dimension)—Fig. FJ106) should be 2.0 mm (0.08 ı.). Carefully bend lever to obtain diıension.

Float-Type Carburetor. Some ıodels are equipped with the float-type arburetor shown in Fig. FJ112. If quipped with an idle mixture screw 8), initial setting is one turn out from a ghtly seated position. Jet needle clip 5) should be installed in second groove

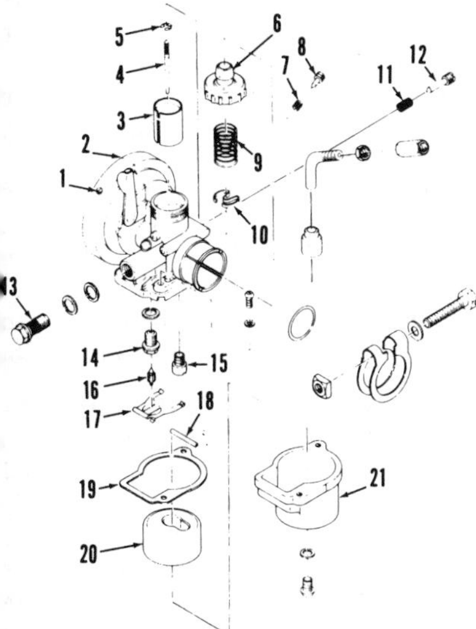

Fig. FJ112—Exploded view of float-type carburetor used on some models. Fitting (13) on some models may be equipped with a fuel shut-off valve.

1. Choke lever
2. Body
3. Throttle valve
4. Fuel inlet valve
5. Clip
6. Cap
7. Spring
8. Air screw
9. Spring
10. Spring seat
11. Spring
12. Idle speed screw
13. Fitting
14. Fuel inlet valve seat
15. Main jet
16. Fuel inlet valve
17. Float lever
18. Pin
19. Gasket
20. Float

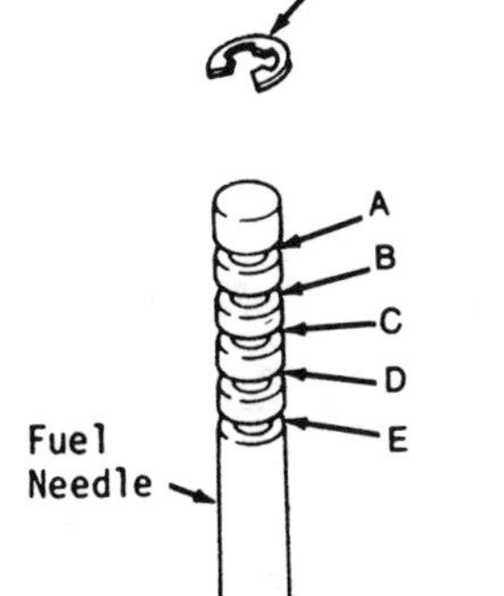

Fig. FJ113—Normal position of clip on jet needle is determined according to engine model. Refer to text.

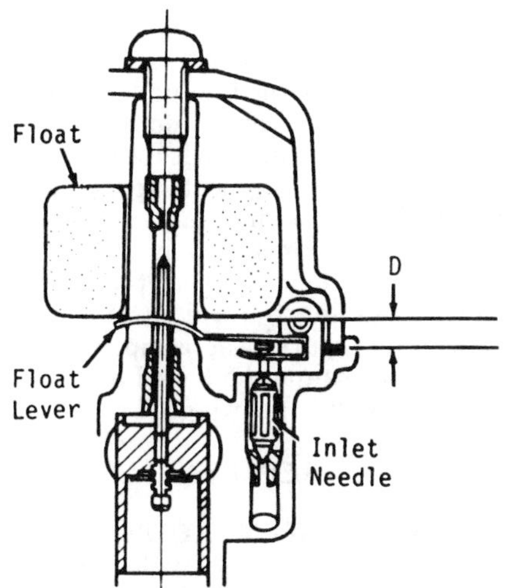

Fig. FJ114—Float level should be measured as shown. Refer to text for distance measurement.

(B—Fig. FJ113) on EC02 models or in the third groove (C) on EC03 and EC04 models.

Float level (D—Fig. FJ114) should be 3.5 mm (0.138 in.) from gasket surface at fuel inlet needle side and 3 mm (0.118 in.) from gasket surface at opposite side of float.

DPK Series. Some models are equipped with the DPK diaphragm-type carburetor shown in Fig. FJ115. Initial setting of high speed mixture screw (15) is 1 1/2 turns out from a lightly seated position. Perform final adjustment with trimmer line fully extended or blade assembly installed and engine at normal operating temperature. Be sure engine air filter is clean before adjusting carburetor. Operate engine at full throttle and turn high speed mixture screw (15) so engine runs smoothly at maximum speed, then back out screw 1/8 turn. Normal range of adjustment is 1-2 turns out. Adjust idle speed screw (12) so engine idles just below clutch engagement speed.

Midrange mixture is determined by the position of clip (7) on jet needle (8). There are three grooves in upper end of the jet needle and normal position of clip is in the middle groove. See Fig. FJ110. The mixture will be leaner if clip is installed in the top groove, or richer if clip is installed in the bottom groove.

To overhaul, refer to Fig. FJ115 and remove lever (3), throttle slide (9), mixture needles (12 and 15), fuel pump cover (18), metering chamber cover (26), metering lever (20) and fuel inlet valve (19).

Clean and inspect all components. If the unit has been improperly stored, passages may be clogged with deposits that are hard, solid and nearly transparent. Clean passages with suitable

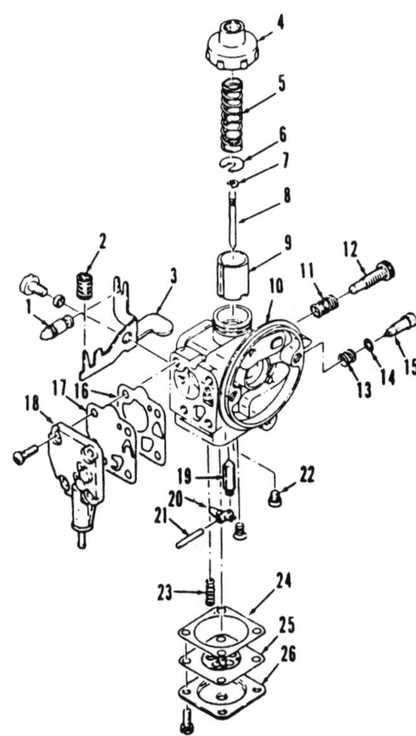

Fig. FJ115—Exploded view of DPK diaphragm-type carburetor used on some models.

1. Primer valve
2. Spring
3. Lever
4. Cap
5. Spring
6. Retainer
7. Clip
8. Jet needle
9. Throttle slide
10. Body
11. Spring
12. Idle speed screw
13. Spring
14. "O" ring
15. Main fuel mixture screw
16. Pump gasket
17. Pump diaphragm
18. Pump cover
19. Fuel inlet valve
20. Metering lever
21. Pin
22. Main jet
23. Spring
24. Gasket
25. Diaphragm
26. Cover

carburetor cleaning solvent and compressed air. Be careful not to damage the openings or sealing surfaces while cleaning. Examine mixture needles (12 and 15) and fuel inlet valve (19) for wear or damage and renew as necessary. Inspect diaphragms (17 and 25) for tears and other damage.

Metering lever height dimension (D—Fig. FJ106) should be 2.0-2.4 mm (0.08-0.09 in.). Carefully bend lever to obtain dimension.

IGNITION SYSTEM. Early engines are equipped with breaker point ignition and later models use electronic ignition system. Refer to the appropriate following paragraphs for servicing information.

Breaker Point Ignition System. The ignition condenser and breaker point set are located behind the flywheel. To adjust breaker point setting, remove flywheel and rotate crankshaft so breaker point contacts are at widest gap. Adjust gap to 0.35 mm (0.014 in.).

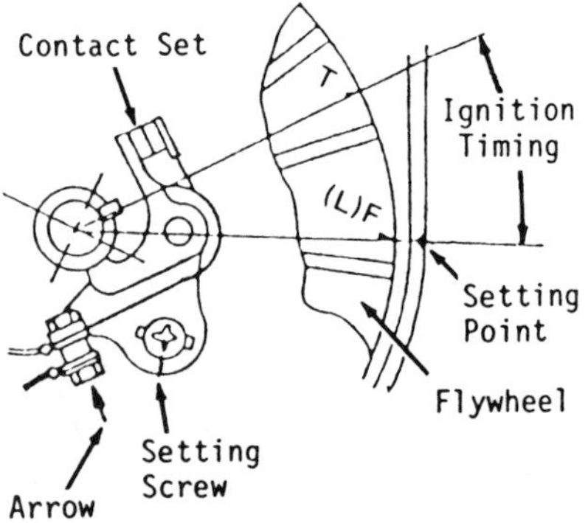

Fig. FJ116—View showing location of timing mark on flywheel and crankcase. Refer to text.

Ignition timing should be set at 26 degrees BTDC on EC01 engine or 25 degrees BTDC on EC02 engine. To check timing, rotate flywheel until the "F" mark cast on flywheel surface aligns with setting mark on crankcase (Fig. FJ116). Carefully remove flywheel and make certain contact set is just beginning to open.

Air gap between flywheel and ignition coil should be 0.5 mm (0.020 in.) for EC01 and EC02 engines or 0.2 mm (0.008 in.) for EC03 and EC04 engines.

Electronic Ignition System. Later models are equipped with an electronic ignition system that has no breaker points and requires little maintenance. The ignition system performance can be considered satisfactory if a spark will jump across a 3 mm (1/8 in.) electrode gap of a test plug. If the spark will not jump this gap, first check the OFF/ON stop switch for proper operation and the connecting wires for shorts. The air gap between the legs of the ignition coil/module and the magnets in the flywheel should be 0.2 mm (0.008 in.). If the air gap is too wide, the test plug may not indicate spark. If the air gap is correct and the stop wiring is not grounded, install a new ignition coil/module. Be sure to set the air gap when installing the coil/module, then recheck for spark. The components of the module cannot be tested except by replacing with a known good unit.

REPAIRS

TIGHTENING TORQUE. Recommended fastener torque values are as follows:

Crankcase
- EC02-E & EC02-EH (20.3 & 22.2 cc) models . 3.9-4.9 N•m (35-43 in.-lb.)
- EC03-1R, EC03-2R & EC04-3R. . . . . 4-7 N•m (35-62 in.-lb.)
- EC03-E, EC04-E & EC05-M . . . . 6.4-7.8 N•m (57-69 in.-lb.)
- Other (15.4, 16, 22.5 & 25.6 cc) models . . . . 4.1-4.7 N•m (35-62 in.-lb.)

Cylinder
- EC02-E & EC02-EH (20.3 & 22.2 cc) models . 6.4-7.8 N•m (57-69 in.-lb.)
- EC03-1R, EC03-2R & EC04-3R. . . . . 9-11 N•m (78-95 in.-lb.)
- EC03-E & EC04-E. . . . 10.8-12.7 N•m (96-112 in.-lb.)
- EC05-M . . . . 6.4-7.8 N•m (57-69 in.-lb.)
- Other (15.4, 16, 22.5 & 25.6 cc) models . . . . 4.1-4.7 N•m (35-62 in.-lb.)

Flywheel
- EC01-A & 16 cc models 11.8-13.7 N•m (104-121 in.-lb.)
- EC02-E, EC02-EH & EC02-F (20.3, 22.2 & 25.6 cc) models . . . . . 10.8-12.7 N•m (96-112 in.-lb.)
- EC02-R. . . . . 13.7-15.6 N•m (121-138 in.-lb.)
- EC03-1R, EC03-2R & EC04-3R. . . . . 14-18 N•m (124-159 in.-lb.)
- EC03-E & EC04-E. . . . . 9.8-13.7 N•m (87-121 in.-lb.)
- EC05-M . . . . 28.4-34.3 N•m (21-25 ft.-lb.)

Spark plug
- EC02-R. . . . . 21.6-29.4 N•m (191-260 in.-lb.)
- EC02-F & EC05-M . . . 14.7-24.5 N•m (130-217 in.-lb.)
- All other models . . . . . 14.7-19.6 N•m (130-173 in.-lb.)

PISTON, PIN AND RINGS. Refer to Fig. FJ117, Fig. FJ118 or Fig. FJ119. To remove the piston, first remove cooling shroud and recoil starter assembly. Remove the carburetor and muffler. Remove all screws attaching the cylinder to the crankcase and carefully pull the cylinder from the piston. Remove retaining rings, pull pin from the piston

Fig. FJ117—Exploded view of typical EC01-A engine. Series EC02, 16 cc and 22.2 cc engines are similar.

1. Housing
2. Rewind starter
3. Pulley
4. Spring
5. Ratchet
6. Brake spring
7. Plate
8. Screw
9. Nut
10. Flywheel
11. Ignition coil/module
12. Seal
13. Crankcase half
14. Gasket
15. Bearing
16. Key
17. Crankshaft assy.
18. Bearing
19. Crankcase half
20. Seal
21. Bearing
22. Retainer ring
23. Piston pin
24. Piston
25. Piston rings
26. Cylinder
27. Gasket

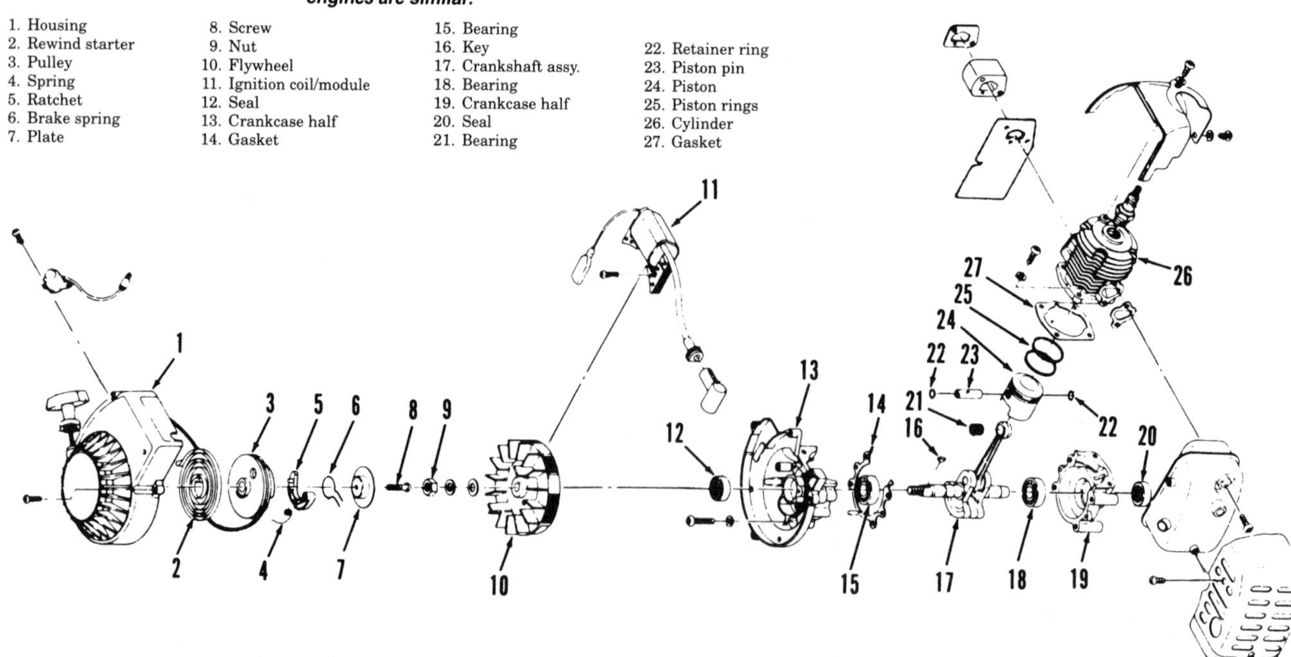

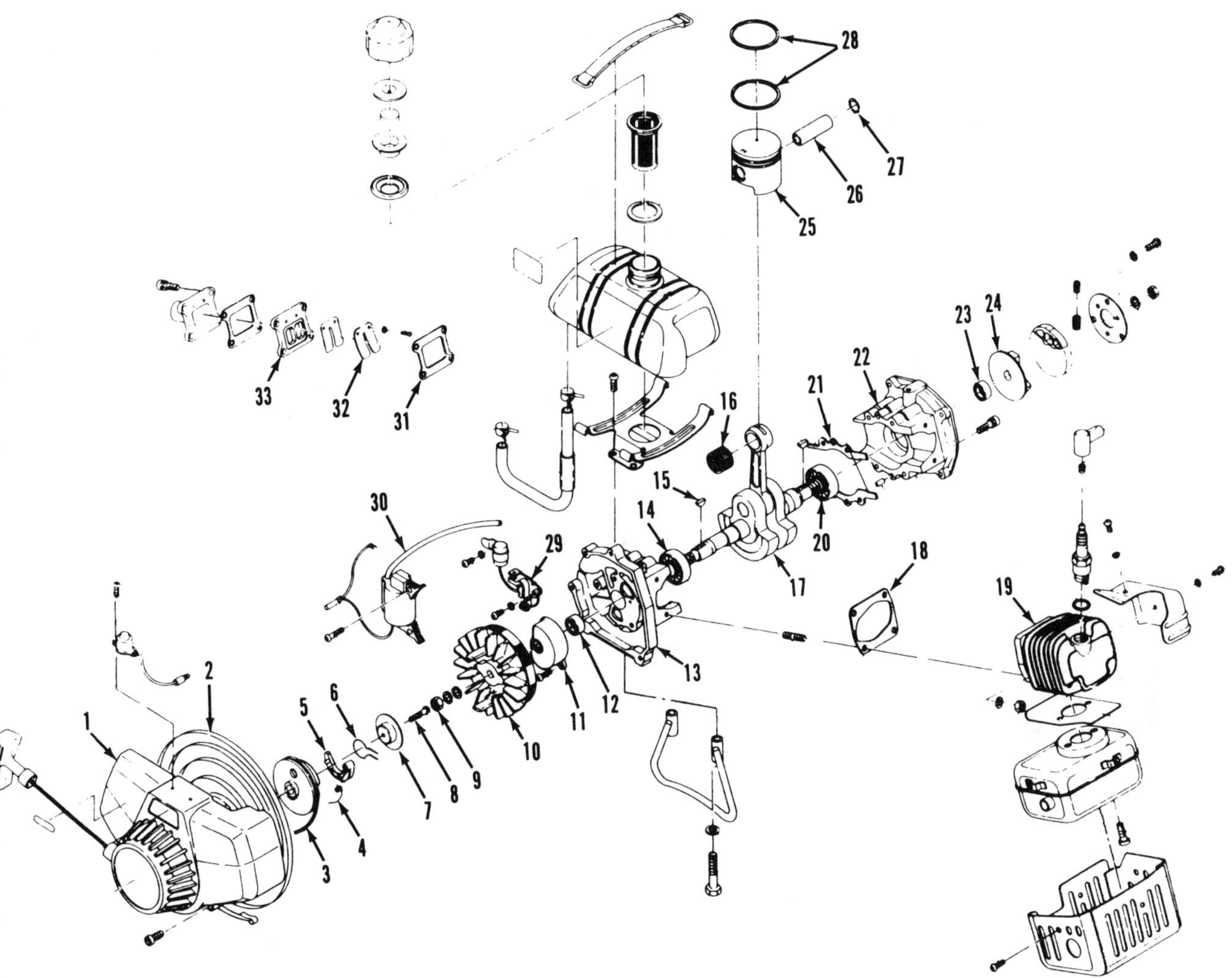

Fig. FJ118—Exploded view of typical Series EC04 engine. Series EC03 engines are similar.

1. Housing
2. Rewind spring
3. Pulley
4. Spring
5. Ratchet
6. Brake spring
7. Plate
8. Screw
9. Nut
10. Flywheel
11. Cover
12. Seal
13. Crankcase half
14. Bearing
15. Key
16. Bearing
17. Crankshaft assy.
18. Gasket
19. Cylinder
20. Bearing
21. Gasket
22. Crankcase half
23. Seal
24. Clutch retainer
25. Piston
26. Piston pin
27. Retainer ring
28. Piston rings
29. Breaker points
30. Ignition coil
31. Gasket
32. Reed backup plate
33. Reed plate

bore, then lift the piston from the connecting rod. If necessary, the piston pin bearing can be removed from the connecting rod.

The piston and rings are available in standard size only. Refer to the following standard piston diameters.

EC01-A & 16 cc models . . . . 28.00 mm (1.102 in.)
EC02-E . . . . 31.47 mm (1.239 in.)
EC02-EH & EC02-F (22.2 & 25.6 cc models) . 32.97 mm (1.298 in.)
EC02-R . . . . 31.99 mm (1.260 in.)
EC03-1R & EC03-2R . . . . . . 35.96 mm (1.416 in.)
EC03-E . . . . 36.98 mm (1.456 in.)
EC04-3R . . . . 39.94 mm (1.572 in.)
EC04-E . . . . 39.98 mm (1.574 in.)
EC05-M . . . . 43.96 mm (1.730 in.)

Install a new piston if the measured diameter is 0.05 mm (0.002 in.) smaller than the listed standard diameter. Ring end gap in the cylinder should be 0.1-0.3 mm (0.004-0.012 in.). If the gap of a new ring is greater than 1.0 mm (0.040 in.), the cylinder is excessively worn. If side clearance of a new ring in the piston groove exceeds 0.15 mm (0.006 in.), install a new piston.

The standard piston pin diameter and pin bore in the piston for models with 28, 31.5, 32 and 33 mm diameter piston is 8.00 mm (0.315 in.). Minimum allowable pin diameter is 7.99 mm (0.3146 in.) and the maximum allowable pin bore diameter in the piston is 8.02 mm (0.3157 in.).

The standard piston pin diameter and pin bore in the piston for models with 36 and 37 mm diameter piston is 10.00 mm (0.3937 in.). Minimum allowable pin diameter is 9.983 mm (0.3930 in.) and the maximum allowable pin bore diameter in the piston is 10.03 mm (0.3949 in.).

The standard piston pin diameter and pin bore in the piston for models with 40 and 44 mm diameter piston is 12.00 mm (0.4724 in.). Minimum allowable pin diameter is 11.983 mm (0.4718 in.) and the maximum allowable pin bore diameter in the piston is 12.03 mm (0.4736 in.).

When installing the piston, make sure the "M" mark on the top of piston is toward the flywheel end of the crankshaft.

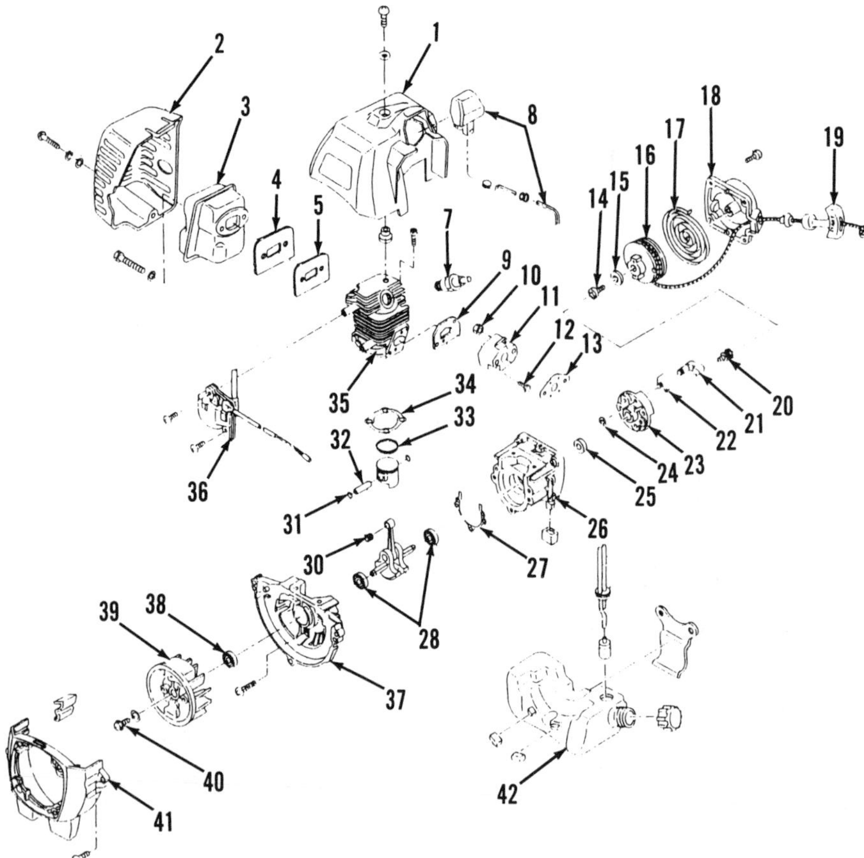

Fig. FJ119—Exploded view of engine typical EC022GA and EC025GA models.

1. Cylinder cover
2. Exhaust cover
3. Muffler
4. Heat shield
5. Gasket
6. Spacer
7. Spark plug
8. Spark plug cap
9. Gasket
10. Nut
11. Insulator block
12. Screw
13. Carburetor gasket
14. Screw
15. Washer
16. Pulley
17. Rewind spring
18. Housing
19. Handle
20. Screw
21. Starter pawl
22. Spring
23. Starter plate
24. "E" ring
25. Seal
26. Crankcase half
27. Gasket
28. Main bearings
29. Crankshaft & connecting rod
30. Needle bearing
31. Retaining ring
32. Piston pin
33. Piston ring
34. Cylinder base gask
35. Cylinder
36. Ignition coil/modul
37. Crankcase half
38. Seal
39. Flywheel
40. Screw
41. Housing
42. Fuel tank

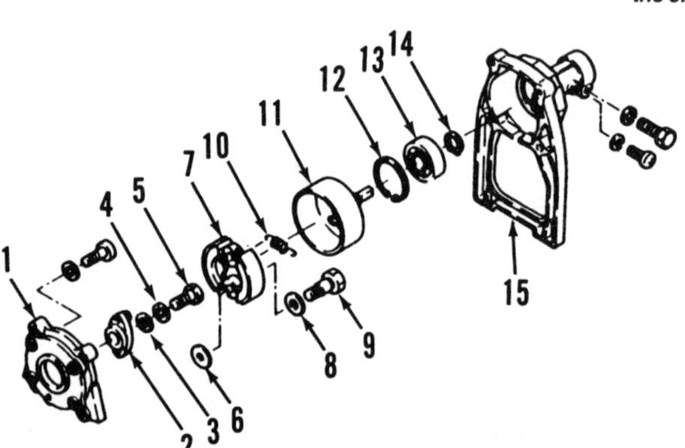

Fig. FJ120—Exploded view of the clutch used on some models.

1. Plate
2. Flange
3. Washer
4. Lockwasher
5. Screw
6. Washer
7. Clutch shoes
8. Washer
9. Screw
10. Spring
11. Clutch drum
12. Snap ring
13. Bearing
14. Snap ring
15. Clutch housing

CYLINDER. Inspect the cylinder for excessive wear or other damage. Install a new cylinder if clearance between the cylinder and a new piston exceeds the following limit.

EC01-A and 16 cc models. . . . 0.08 mm (0.003 in.)
EC02-E & EC02-EH. . . . . 0.10 mm (0.004 in.)
EC02-R . . . . 0.12 mm (0.0047 in.)
Other models. . . . . 0.18 mm (0.007 in.)

CRANKSHAFT, ROD AND CRANKCASE. The crankshaft and connecting rod are a unit assembly; individual components are not available. The connecting rod small end is equipped with a renewable needle bearing on some models.

To remove crankshaft assembly, remove fuel tank, muffler cover, muffler and carburetor. Remove spark plug and install locking bolt or end of a rope in spark plug hole to lock piston and connecting rod. Remove flywheel and clutch. Separate cylinder from crankcase and piston. Remove bolts retaining crankcase halves and separate crankcase being careful not to damage crankcase mating surfaces. Press main bearings off crankshaft as necessary. If main bearings remain in crankcase halves, heat crankcase slightly to aid in removal of bearings. Pry seals out o crankcase halves.

Renew crankshaft assembly if connection rod side clearance on crankshaft exceeds 0.7 mm (0.028 in.) Maximum allowable crankshaft runout is 0.1 mm (0.004 in.) measured at main bearing journals with crankshaft supported at ends. Maximum allowable crankshaft end play is 0.8 mm (0.031 in.).

REED VALVE. Some models are equipped with a reed valve induction system. Inspect reed valve petals and seats on reed valve plate (33—Fig. FJ118). Renew reed valve assembly if petals or seats are damaged.

CLUTCH. Most engines used on trimmers or brush cutters are equipped with a two-or three-shoe clutch. The shoe assembly is located at the drive end of the crankshaft and mounted on a flange or on the back side of the flywheel. The clutch drum rides in the drive housing. To remove the clutch drum (11—Fig. FJ120 or FJ121) or (6—Fig. FJ122), unbolt and remove clutch housing and drive tube from clutch housing. On models with slots in clutch face, reach through slot and de-

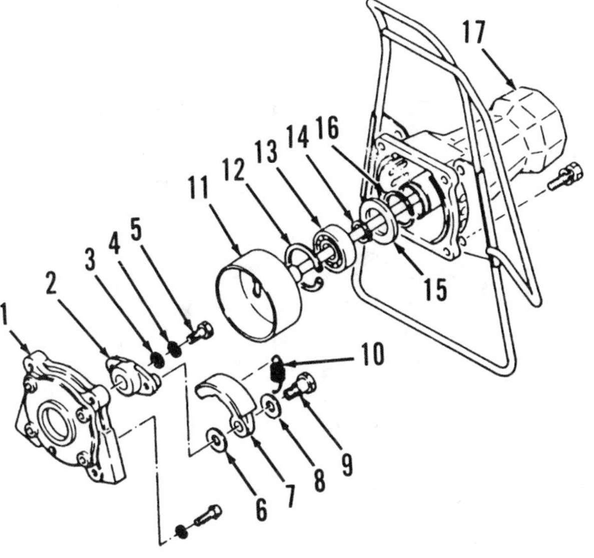

Fig. FJ121—Exploded view of clutch assembly with drive shaft attached to clutch drum (11).

1. Plate
2. Flange
3. Washer
4. Lockwasher
5. Screw
6. Washer
7. Clutch shoes
8. Washer
9. Screw
10. Spring
11. Clutch drum
12. Snap ring
13. Bearing
14. Snap ring
15. Washer
16. Snap ring
17. Clutch housing

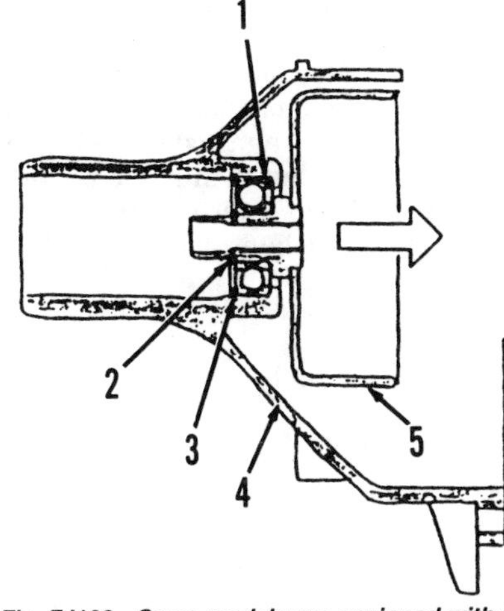

Fig. FJ123—Some models are equipped with the clutch drum assembly shown above.

1. Bearing
2. Snap ring
3. Snap ring
4. Clutch housing
5. Clutch drum

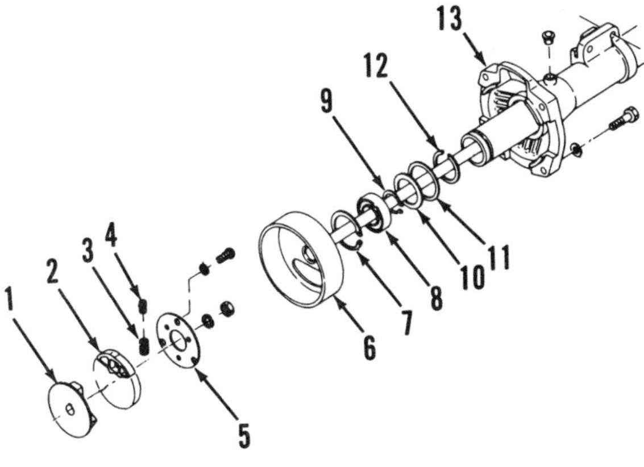

Fig. FJ122—Exploded view of the clutch used on some models. Notice that one inner spring (4) fits an inside outer spring (3) to hold each clutch shoe (2) on the hub (1).

1. Hub
2. Shoes
3. Outer spring
4. Inner spring
5. Plate
6. Clutch drum
7. Snap ring
8. Bearing
9. Snap ring
10. Spacer
11. Washer
12. Snap ring
13. Clutch housing

tach snap ring (12—Fig. FJ120 or FJ121) or (7—Fig. FJ122), then separate clutch drum and bearing (13—Fig. FJ120 or FJ121) or (8—Fig. FJ122) from clutch housing. Note that on some models, clutch drum and drive shaft must be removed as a unit.

On engines without slotted clutch drum, detach snap ring (2—Fig. FJ123) and press clutch drum shaft (5) out of bearing (1). Detach snap ring (3), heat clutch housing (4) and remove bearing. Reverse removal procedure to install clutch drum.

Inspect clutch shoes (7—Figs. FJ120 and FJ121) or (2—Fig. FJ122) for wear and renew as necessary. When installing shoes, note arrows on shoes indicating direction of rotation. Arrows must point in direction of crankshaft rotation.

REWIND STARTER. Refer to Fig. FJ124, Fig. FJ125 or Fig. FJ126 for exploded view of typical starter. To disassemble starter, detach starter housing from engine. Remove rope handle and allow rope to wind into starter. Unscrew center screw and remove rope pulley. Wear appropriate safety eye wear and gloves before detaching rewind spring from housing as spring may uncoil uncontrolled.

To assemble starter, lubricate center post of housing and spring side with light grease. Assemble starter while passing rope through housing rope outlet and attach rope handle to rope. To place tension on starter rope, pull rope out of housing. Engage rope in notch on

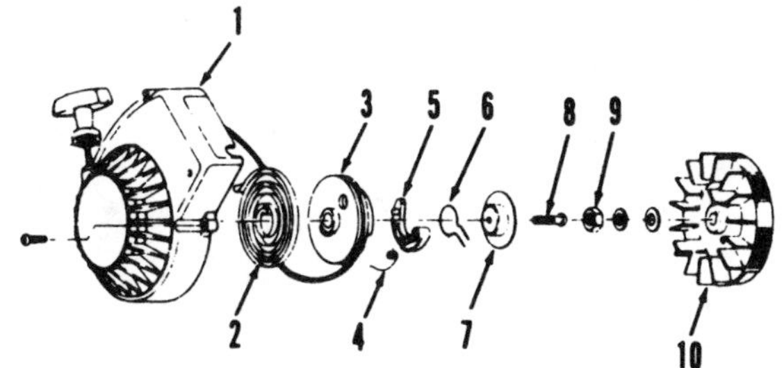

Fig. FJ124—Exploded view of rewind starter used on some models.

1. Starter housing
2. Rewind spring
3. Pulley
4. Spring
5. Ratchet
6. Brake spring
7. Plate
8. Screw
9. Nut
10. Flywheel

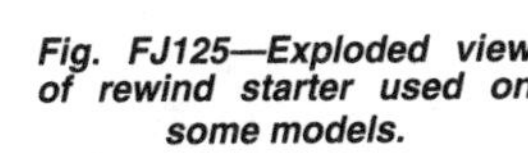

Fig. FJ125—Exploded view of rewind starter used on some models.

1. Starter housing
2. Rewind spring
3. Pulley
4. Spring
5. Ratchet
6. Brake spring
7. Plate
8. Screw
9. Nut
10. Flywheel

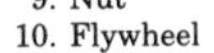

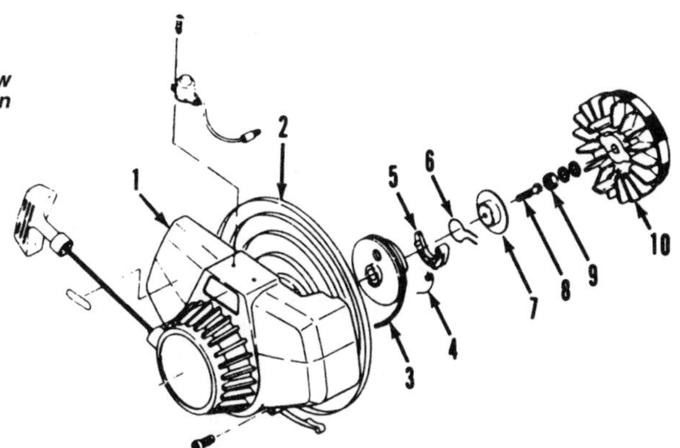

pulley and turn pulley against spring tension. Hold pulley and disengage rope from pulley notch. Release pulley. Check starter operation. Rope handle should be held against housing by spring tension, but it must be possible to rotate pulley at least 1/4 turn against spring tension when rope is pulled out fully.

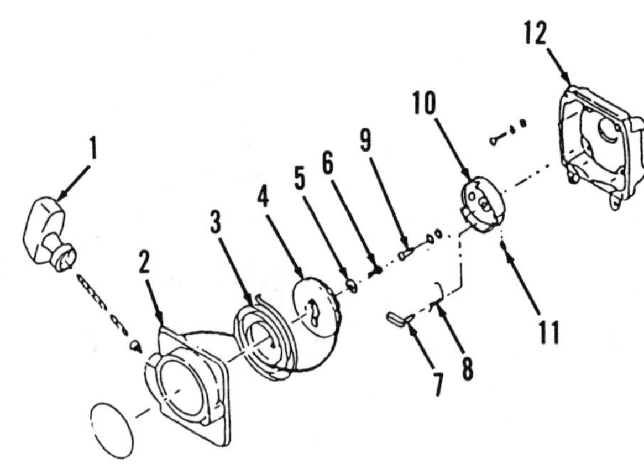

Fig. FJ126—Exploded view of rewind starter used on some models.

1. Rope handle
2. Starter housing
3. Rewind spring
4. Pulley
5. Washer
6. Screw
7. Pawl
8. Spring
9. Screw
10. Plate
11. "E" ring
12. Housing

HOMELITE

ENGINE SERVICE

Model	Bore	Stroke	Displacement
HB-280, HB-380	$1^{5}/_{16}$ in. (33.3 mm)	$1^{3}/_{16}$ in. (30.2 mm)	1.6 cu. in. (26.2 cc)
HB-480*, HB-680*	$1^{7}/_{16}$ in. (36.5 mm)	$1^{3}/_{16}$ in. (30.2 mm)	1.9 cu. in. (31.2 cc)
ST-80, ST-100, ST-120, ST-160, ST-160A, ST-165 ST-180, ST-260	$1^{5}/_{16}$ in. (33.3 mm)	$1^{3}/_{16}$ in. (30.2 mm)	1.6 cu. in. (26.2 cc)
ST-200, ST-210 ST-310	$1^{7}/_{16}$ in. (36.5 mm)	$1^{3}/_{16}$ in. (30.2 mm)	1.9 cu. in. (31.2 cc)

*Early Models HB-480 and HB-680 are equipped with 1.6 cu. in. (26.2 cc) displacement engine.

ENGINE INFORMATION

The Homelite two-stroke, air-cooled engines covered in this section are used on Homelite string trimmers, brush cutters and blowers.

MAINTENANCE

LUBRICATION. The engine on all models is lubricated by mixing oil with gasoline. Homelite oil is recommended and should be mixed at ratio designated on container. If Homelite oil is not used, manufacturer specifies that only oils designed for two-stroke engines with a fuel:oil ratio of 32:1 or more should be used.

An antioxidant fuel stabilizer (such as Sta-Bil) should be added to fuel if Homelite oil is not used. Homelite oil contains an antioxidant fuel stabilizer.

SPARK PLUG. Recommended spark plug is Champion DJ7J for Models ST-80, ST-100, ST-120, ST-200 and ST-210. Recommended spark plug for all other models is Champion DJ7Y. Spark plug electrode gap should be 0.025 inch (0.6 mm).

CARBURETOR. Various carburetors are used depending on equipment model. Refer to appropriate carburetor section below for service information.

Keihin. A Keihin float-type carburetor is used on some blower engines. Adjust idle speed so engine idles at 3350-3500 rpm. Idle mixture is not adjustable. High-speed mixture is controlled by removable fixed jet (14—Fig. HL40-1). Midrange mixture is determined by the position of clip (7) on jet needle (6). There are three grooves in upper end of the jet needle and normal position of clip is in the middle groove. The mixture will be leaner if clip is installed in the top groove, or richer if clip is installed in the bottom groove.

Overhaul of carburetor is evident after inspection and referral to Fig. HL40-1. Before removing carburetor from engine, unscrew cap (3) and withdraw throttle slide (8) assembly. When overhauling carburetor, refer to Fig. HL40-1 and note the following: Examine fuel inlet valve and seat. Inlet valve (13) is renewable. The inlet seat is not renewable and carburetor body (12) must be renewed if seat is excessively worn or damaged. When installing throttle slide, be sure groove in side of throttle slide indexes with pin in bore of carburetor body.

Walbro HDC. Initial setting of low speed mixture screw (10—Fig. HL40-2) is $1^{1}/_{2}$ turns out from a lightly seated position. Initial setting of high-speed mixture screw (11), on models so equipped, is $^{3}/_{4}$ turn out. Final adjustment is performed with engine running at normal operating temperature. Adjust idle speed screw (9) so engine idles at 2800-

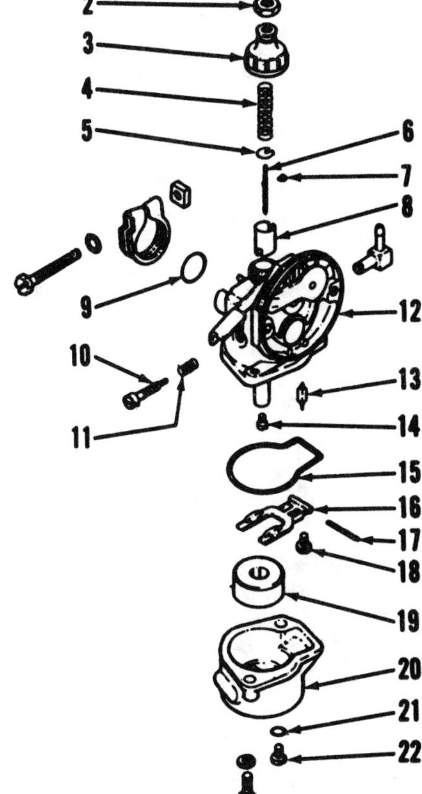

Fig. HL40-1—Exploded view of Keihin carburetor used on later Models HB-280, HB-380, HB-480 and HB-680.

1. Cable adjusting nut
2. Nut
3. Cap
4. Spring
5. Retainer
6. Jet needle
7. Clip
8. Throttle slide
9. "O" ring
10. Idle speed screw
11. Spring
12. Body
13. Fuel inlet valve
14. Main jet
15. Gasket
16. Float arm
17. Float pin
18. Screw
19. Float
20. Fuel bowl
21. Gasket
22. Drain screw

3200 rpm on Models ST-160, ST-160A, ST-165, ST-180 and ST-260, or just below

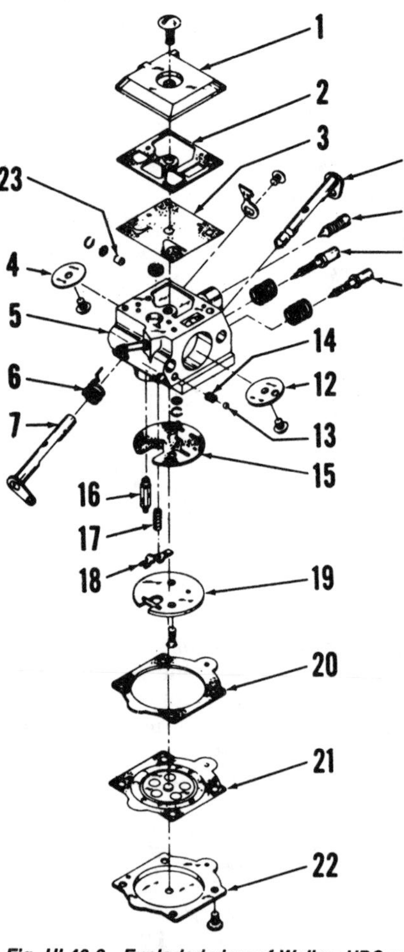

Fig. HL40-2—Exploded view of Walbro HDC carburetor. High-speed mixture screw (11) is absent on some models.

1. Cover
2. Gasket
3. Fuel pump diaphragm
4. Throttle plate
5. Body
6. Return spring
7. Throttle shaft
8. Choke shaft
9. Idle speed screw
10. Idle mixture screw
11. High-speed mixture screw
12. Choke plate
13. Detent ball
14. Spring
15. Gasket
16. Fuel inlet valve
17. Spring
18. Metering lever
19. Circuit plate
20. Gasket
21. Metering diaphragm
22. Cover
23. Limiting jet

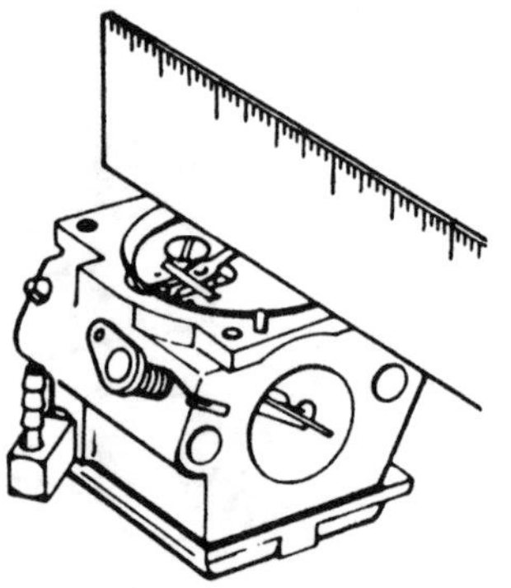

Fig. HL40-3—Tip of metering lever should be flush with body on Walbro HDC carburetor. Bend metering lever as needed.

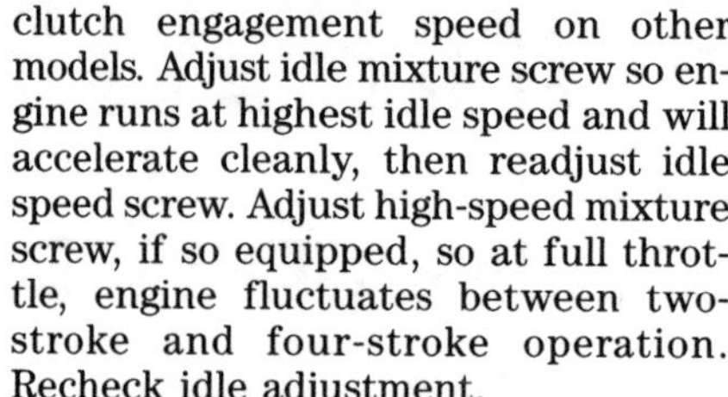

clutch engagement speed on other models. Adjust idle mixture screw so engine runs at highest idle speed and will accelerate cleanly, then readjust idle speed screw. Adjust high-speed mixture screw, if so equipped, so at full throttle, engine fluctuates between two-stroke and four-stroke operation. Recheck idle adjustment.

Carburetor disassembly and reassembly is evident after inspection of carburetor and referral to Fig. HL40-2. Some carburetors are equipped with an accelerator pump that uses a bladder to eject additional fuel through the main

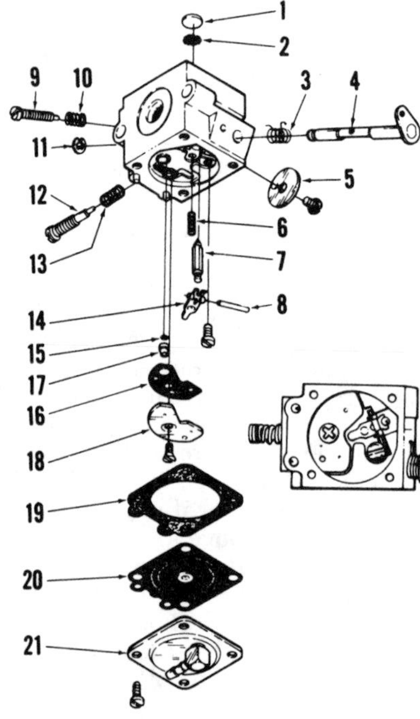

Fig. HL40-4—Exploded view of typical Walbro WA carburetor.

1. Welch plug
2. Screen
3. Spring
4. Throttle shaft
5. Throttle plate
6. Spring
7. Fuel inlet valve
8. Lever pin
9. High-speed mixture screw
10. Spring
11. Clip
12. Idle mixture screw
13. Spring
14. Metering lever
15. Screen
16. Gasket
17. Check valve
18. Circuit plate
19. Gasket
20. Metering diaphragm
21. Fuel inlet cover

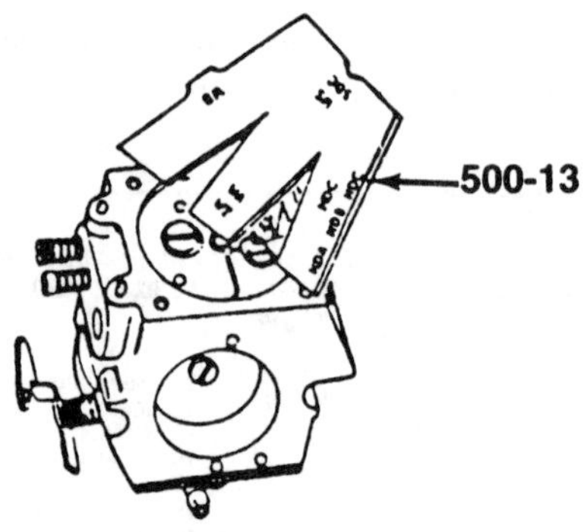

Fig. HL40-5—On Walbro WA carburetor, metering lever should just touch leg of Walbro tool 500-13. Bend lever to obtain correct lever height.

fuel orifice when needed. Clean and inspect all components. Inspect diaphragms (3 and 21) for defects that may affect operation. Examine fuel inlet valve and seat. Inlet valve (16) is renewable, but carburetor body must be renewed if seat is damaged or excessively worn. Wires or drill bits should not be used to clean passages as fuel flow may be altered. Discard carburetor body if mixture screw seats are damaged or excessively worn. Screens should be clean. Be sure choke and throttle plates fit shafts and carburetor bore properly. Apply Loctite to retaining screws. Adjust metering lever height so metering lever tip is flush with body as shown in Fig. HL40-3.

Walbro WA. Some engines are equipped with a Walbro WA diaphragm-type carburetor.

To adjust carburetor on trimmers, proceed as follows: Initial adjustment of idle mixture screw (12—Fig. HL40-4) is $1^1/_4$ turns out from a lightly seated position. Final adjustments are performed with trimmer line at recommended length or blade installed. Engine must be at operating temperature and running. Adjust idle speed screw so engine idles at 2800-3200 rpm on Models ST-80, ST-100 and ST-120. Adjust idle mixture screw so engine runs at highest idle speed and will accelerate cleanly, then readjust idle speed screw. High-speed mixture is not adjustable.

To adjust carburetor on blowers, proceed as follows: Initial adjustment of idle and high-speed mixture screws is one turn out. Adjust idle speed so engine idles at 3350-3500 rpm. Adjust idle mixture screw (12—Fig. HL40-4) so engine will accelerate cleanly. Adjust high speed mixture screw (9) so maximum engine rpm is 7200-7800 for HB-280, 7800-8600 for HB-480 and 7600-8400 for HB-680.

When overhauling carburetor, refer to exploded view in Fig. HL40-4. Examine fuel inlet valve and seat. Inlet valve (7) is renewable, but carburetor body must be renewed if seat is excessively worn or damaged. Inspect mixture screws and seats. Renew carburetor body if seats are excessively worn or damaged. Clean fuel screen. Inspect diaphragms for tears and other damage.

Check metering lever height as shown in Fig. HL40-5 using Walbro tool 500-13. Metering lever should just touch leg on tool. Bend lever to obtain correct lever height.

Zama C1S or C2S. Some engines are equipped with a Zama C1S or C2S diaphragm-type carburetor.

To adjust carburetor, proceed as follows: Initial adjustment of idle mixture

ꞏrew (13—Fig. HL40-6) is 1¹/₄ turns out ꞏom a lightly seated position. Final adꞏstments are performed with trimmer ꞏne at recommended length or blade inꞏalled. Engine must be at operating ꞏmperature and running. Adjust idle ꞏeed screw so engine idles at 2800-ꞏ200 rpm. Adjust idle mixture screw so ꞏngine runs at highest idle speed and ꞏill accelerate cleanly, then readjust ꞏle speed screw. High-speed mixture is ꞏot adjustable.

Carburetor disassembly and reassemꞏly is evident after inspection of carbuꞏetor and referral to Fig. HL40-6. On ꞏIodel C2S, do not lose detent ball when ꞏithdrawing choke shaft. Clean and inꞏpect all components. Inspect diꞏphragms (5 and 27) for defects that ꞏay affect operation. Examine fuel inꞏet valve and seat. Inlet valve (22) is ꞏenewable, but carburetor body must be ꞏenewed if seat is damaged or excessiveꞏy worn. Discard carburetor body if mixture screw seat is damaged or excessively worn. Clean fuel screen.

To reassemble carburetor, reverse disassembly procedure. Metering lever should be level with chamber floor as shown in Fig. HL40-7. Bend metering lever as needed.

IGNITION. Early Model ST-100 is equipped with a conventional breaker-point, flywheel magneto. Breaker point gap should be 0.015 inch (0.38 mm). Ignition timing is not adjustable. However, an incorrect breaker point gap setting will affect ignition timing.

A solid state ignition is used on all models except early ST-100 models. The ignition module is attached to the side of the engine cylinder. Ignition service is accomplished by replacing ignition components until the faulty component is located. Air gap between ignition module and flywheel is adjustable and should be 0.015 inch (0.38 mm). Loosen ignition module mounting screws and adjust module position to set air gap.

REPAIRS

TIGHTENING TORQUE VALUES. Tightening torque values are listed in following table:

Flywheel	100-150 in.-lbs. (11.3-16.9 N·m)
Spark plug	120-180 in.-lbs. (13.6-20.3 N·m)
Crankcase screws—socket head	45-55 in.-lbs. (5.1-6.2 N·m)

COMPRESSION PRESSURE. For optimum performance of all models, cylinder compression pressure should be 115-145 psi (792-1000 kPa) with engine at normal operating temperature. Engine should be inspected and repaired when compression pressure is 90 psi (621 kPa) or below.

CYLINDER, PISTON, PIN AND RINGS. The cylinder (6—Figs. HL40-8, HL40-9 or HL40-10) may be removed after unscrewing four screws in bottom of crankcase (19). Be careful when removing cylinder as crankshaft assembly will be loose in crankcase. Care should be

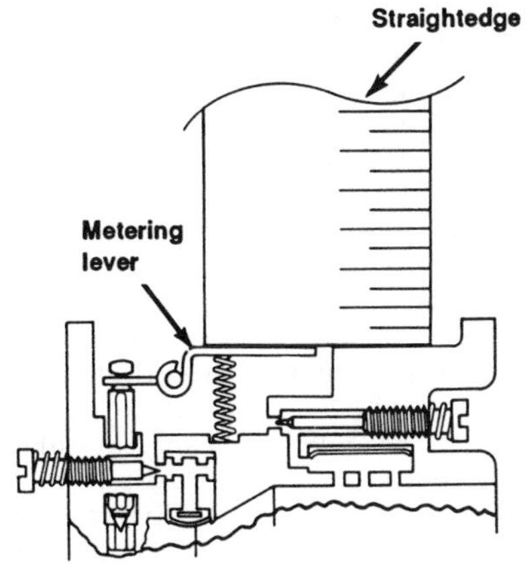

Fig. HL40-7—On Zama C1S and C2S carburetors, metering lever should be flush with metering chamber floor. Bend metering lever as needed.

Fig. HL40-6—Exploded view of typical Zama C1S carburetor. Model C2S is similar. Model C2S is equipped with a choke shaft and plate.

2. Fuel pump cover
3. Gasket
4. Plate
5. Fuel pump diaphragm
6. Screen
7. Body
8. Throttle plate
9. Throttle shaft
10. Spring
11. "E" ring
13. Idle mixture screw
15. Spring
16. Plug
20. Check valve
21. Spring
22. Fuel inlet valve
23. Metering lever
24. Pin
25. Metering disc
26. Gasket
27. Metering diaphragm
28. Cover

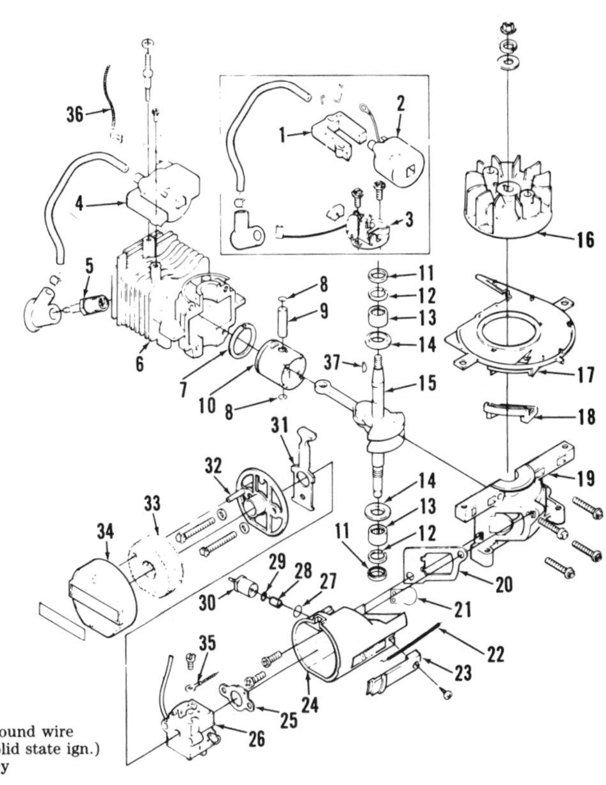

Fig. HL40-8—Exploded view of engine used on Models ST-80, ST-100 and ST-120. Early Model ST-100 trimmers are equipped with breaker point ignition shown in inset.

1. Coil core
2. Ignition coil
3. Breaker point assy.
4. Ignition module
5. Spark plug
6. Cylinder
7. Piston ring
8. Retaining rings
9. Piston pin
10. Piston
11. Seal
12. Seal spacer
13. Needle bearing
14. Thrust washer
15. Crankshaft
16. Flywheel
17. Air cover
18. Seal
19. Crankcase
20. Gasket
21. Reed valve petal
22. Throttle cable
23. Cable clamp
24. Carburetor housing
25. Gasket
26. Carburetor
27. "O" ring
28. Filter
29. Gasket
30. Fuel inlet
31. Choke
32. Filter support
33. Air filter
34. Cover
35. Ground wire (early ST-100)
36. Ground wire (solid state ign.)
37. Key

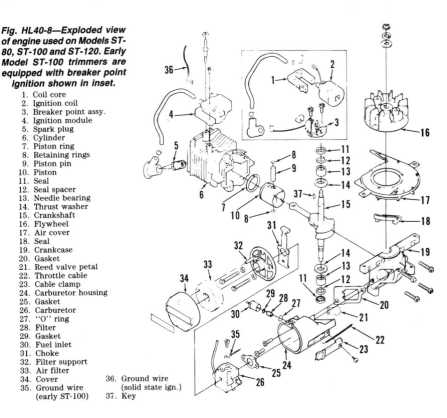

taken not to damage mating surfaces of cylinder and crankcase. Pry out piston pin retaining ring (8) and push piston pin (9) out of piston to separate piston from connecting rod.

Inspect piston and cylinder for wear, scoring or other damage and renew as necessary. Use a wooden scraper to remove carbon from cylinder ports. Cylinder and crankcase mating surfaces should be flat and free of nicks and scratches. Mating surfaces should be cleaned then coated with room temperature vulcanizing (RTV) silicone sealer before assembly.

Piston must be assembled to connecting rod so that piston ring end gap is located opposite exhaust port side of cylinder. Some pistons have a locating pin in piston ring groove, and piston ring end gap must index with the locating pin. Some pistons do not have a pin in the ring groove. On these models, piston and ring must be assembled to connecting rod so ring gap and notch in piston are located opposite exhaust port side of cylinder. Lubricate piston and cylinder with engine oil before installing piston in cylinder.

CRANKSHAFT AND CONNECTING ROD. The crankshaft and connecting rod are serviced as an assembly. To disassemble, first separate engine from string trimmer or blower unit. Remove carburetor and muffler. Remove spark plug and place end of a starter rope into cylinder to lock the piston and crankshaft. Remove flywheel retaining nut and pull flywheel off crankshaft. On trimmer models, remove clutch assembly from flywheel. On all models, remove screws attaching crankcase (19—Figs. HL40-8, HL40-9 or HL40-10) to cylinder (6). Tap crankcase with plastic mallet to break seal between mating surfaces, then separate crankcase from cylinder and remove crankshaft and connecting rod assembly. Pry out piston pin retaining ring, push piston pin out of piston and separate piston from connecting rod. Note that main bearing rollers are loose in their cages and may fall out when removed. To aid in their removal, wrap a piece of paper around crankshaft and slide bearings out over the paper. Remove the bearing and paper sleeve together to hold needle bearings in place.

Inspect crankshaft bearings (13) and renew if scored or worn. Crankshaft and connecting rod must be renewed as an assembly if worn or damaged.

Thrust washers (14) should be installed with shoulder to outside. Bearings are installed with lettered side facing outward. Lubricate seals (11) with oil and install onto crankshaft with lip to inside. Thoroughly clean crankcase and cylinder mating surfaces, then apply light coat of silastic sealant to mating surfaces. Assemble crankshaft, cylinder and crankcase, but do not tighten crankcase screws at this time. When properly assembled, outer surface of seals should be flush with cylinder and crankcase. Gently tap each end of crankshaft with a plastic hammer to establish end play in crankshaft. Tighten crankcase screws evenly to 50 in.-lbs. (5.6 N·m). Make certain that crankshaft does n bind when rotated.

REED VALVE. All models ar equipped with a reed valve inductio system. Reed petal (21—Figs. HL40- HL40-9 or HL40-10) is accessible afte removing carburetor and manifol spacer from crankcase. Renew reed pe al if cracked, bent or otherwise dan aged. Do not attempt to straighten bent reed petal. Seating surface for ree petal should be flat, clean and smooth When reassembling, apply a light co of silastic sealant to mating surface o manifold. Use grease to hold reed pet in place when manifold is assembled t crankcase.

CLUTCH. Models ST-200 and ST-21 are equipped with centrifugal clutche (29—Fig. HL40-9), which are accessibl after removing engine housing. Clutc hub (29) has left-hand threads. Inspec bushing (31) and renew if excessivel worn. Install clutch hub (29) while not ing "OUTSIDE" marked on side of hub

REWIND STARTER. Refer to blow er section for service of rewind starter used on blowers.

Fig. HL40-9—Exploded view of engine used on Models ST-160, ST-180, ST-200 and ST-210. Adapter (34) is used in place of clutch components (29, 30 and 31) on Models ST-160 and ST-180.

4. Ignition modul
5. Spark plug
6. Cylinder
7. Piston ring
8. Retaining ring
9. Piston pin
10. Piston
11. Seal
12. Seal spacer
13. Needle bearing
14. Thrust washer
15. Crankshaft
16. Flywheel
17. Key
18. Shroud
19. Crankcase
20. Gasket
21. Reed valve petal
22. Carburetor spacer
23. Air baffle
24. Gasket
25. Carburetor
26. Tubing
27. Filter support
28. Air filter
29. Clutch hub
30. Clutch drum
31. Bushing
32. Drive shaft
33. Drive tube
34. Adapter

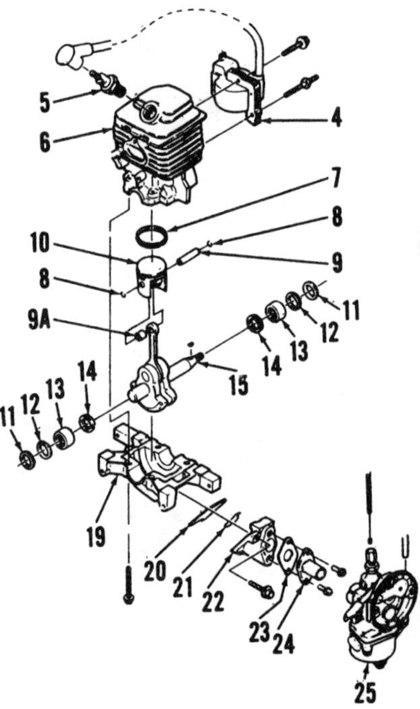

Fig. HL40-10—Typical exploded view of engine used on Model HB-280, HB-480 and HB-680 blowers. Bearing (9A) is only used on later Model HB-480 and HB-680.

4. Ignition module
5. Spark plug
6. Cylinder
7. Piston ring
8. Retaining ring
9. Piston pin
10. Piston
11. Seal
12. Seal spacer
13. Needle bearing
14. Thrust washer
15. Crankshaft
19. Crankcase
20. Gasket
21. Reed valve petal
22. Carburetor spacer
23. Gasket
24. Intake manifold
25. Carburetor

To service rewind starters on trimmers, remove starter housing (10—Figs. HL40-11 or HL40-12). Pull starter rope and hold rope pulley with notch in pulley adjacent to rope outlet. Pull rope back through outlet so that it engages notch in pulley and allow pulley to completely unwind. Unscrew pulley retaining screw (5) and remove rope pulley, being careful not to dislodge rewind spring in housing. Wear appropriate safety eyewear and gloves before detaching rewind spring from housing as spring may uncoil uncontrolled.

Rewind spring is wound in clockwise direction in starter housing. Rope is wound on rope pulley in clockwise direction as viewed with pulley in housing. To place tension on rewind spring, pass rope through rope outlet in housing and install rope handle. Pull rope out and hold rope pulley so notch on pulley is adjacent to rope outlet. Pull rope back through outlet between notch in pulley and housing. Turn rope pulley clockwise to place tension on spring. Pull rope out of notch, release pulley and allow rope to wind onto pulley. Check starter action. Do not place more tension on rewind spring than is necessary to draw rope handle up against housing.

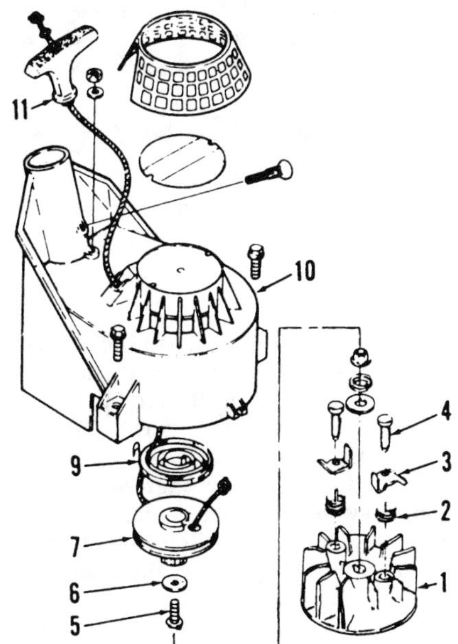

Fig. HL40-11—Exploded view of rewind starter used on Models ST-80, ST-100 and ST-120.

1. Flywheel
2. Spring
3. Pawl
4. Pawl pin
5. Screw
6. Washer
7. Rope pulley
9. Rewind spring
10. Housing
11. Rope handle

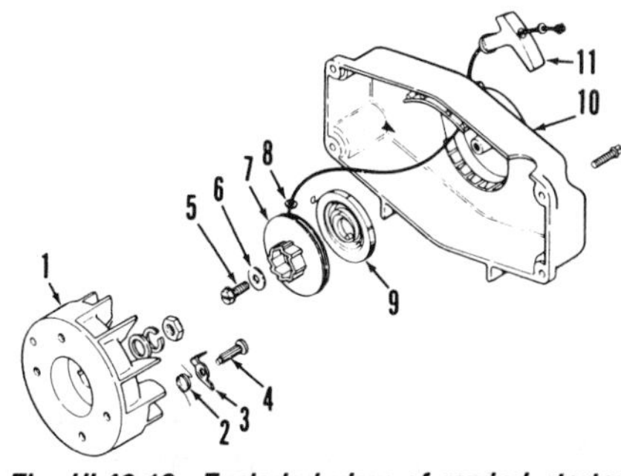

Fig. HL40-12—Exploded view of rewind starter used on Models ST-200 and ST-210.

1. Flywheel
2. Spring
3. Pawl
4. Pawl pin
5. Screw
6. Washer
7. Rope pulley
8. Nylon washer
9. Rewind spring
10. Housing
11. Rope handle

HOMELITE

ENGINE SERVICE

Model	Bore	Stroke	Displacement
ST-400	1¾ in. (44 mm)	1-1/8 in. (35 mm)	3.3 cu. in. (54 cc)

ENGINE INFORMATION

The 3.3 cu. in. (54 cc) displacement engine is used to power the ST-400 brushcutter.

MAINTENANCE

SPARK PLUG. Recommended spark plug is a Champion CJ6. Spark plug electrode gap should be 0.025 inch (0.6 mm).

CARBURETOR. Model ST-400 brushcutter is equipped with a Tillotson HS-207A carburetor.

To adjust carburetor, turn idle speed stop screw in until it just contacts throttle lever tab, then turn screw in ½-turn further. Turn idle and main fuel adjustment needles in gently until they just contact seats, then back each needle out one turn. With engine warm and running, adjust idle fuel needle so that engine runs smoothly, then adjust idle stop screw so that engine runs at 2600 rpm, or just below clutch engagement speed. Check engine acceleration and open idle fuel needle slightly if engine will not accelerate properly. Adjust main fuel needle under load so engine will neither slow down nor smoke excessively.

GOVERNOR. The engine is equipped with an air-vane type governor; refer to Fig. HL43-1.

To adjust governor using vibrating reed or electronic tachometer, proceed as follows: With engine warm and running and throttle trigger released, adjust position of cable nuts (see Fig. HL43-1A) on remote control cable so that engine slow idle speed is 2500 rpm, or just below clutch engagement speed. Then when throttle trigger is fully depressed, engine no-load speed should be 6300 rpm. To adjust maximum governed no-load speed, loosen screw (14—Fig. HL43-1) and move speed adjusting plate (13) as required to obtain no-load speed of 6300 rpm. When adjusting maximum no-load speed, be sure that governor link (26) is reconnected at hole "A" in carburetor throttle shaft lever. Governor spring (12) is connected to third hole away from hole "A" (two open holes between link and spring). Be sure that governor linkage moves smoothly throughout range of travel.

MAGNETO AND TIMING. All engines are equipped with a solid-state ignition (Fig. HL43-4). Ignition service is accomplished by replacing ignition components until faulty part is located. Air gap between ignition module (3) and flywheel is adjustable and should be 0.015 inch (0.4 mm). Loosen ignition module mounting screws and adjust module position to set air gap.

LUBRICATION. The engine is lubricated by mixing oil with regular gasoline. Recommended oil is Homelite

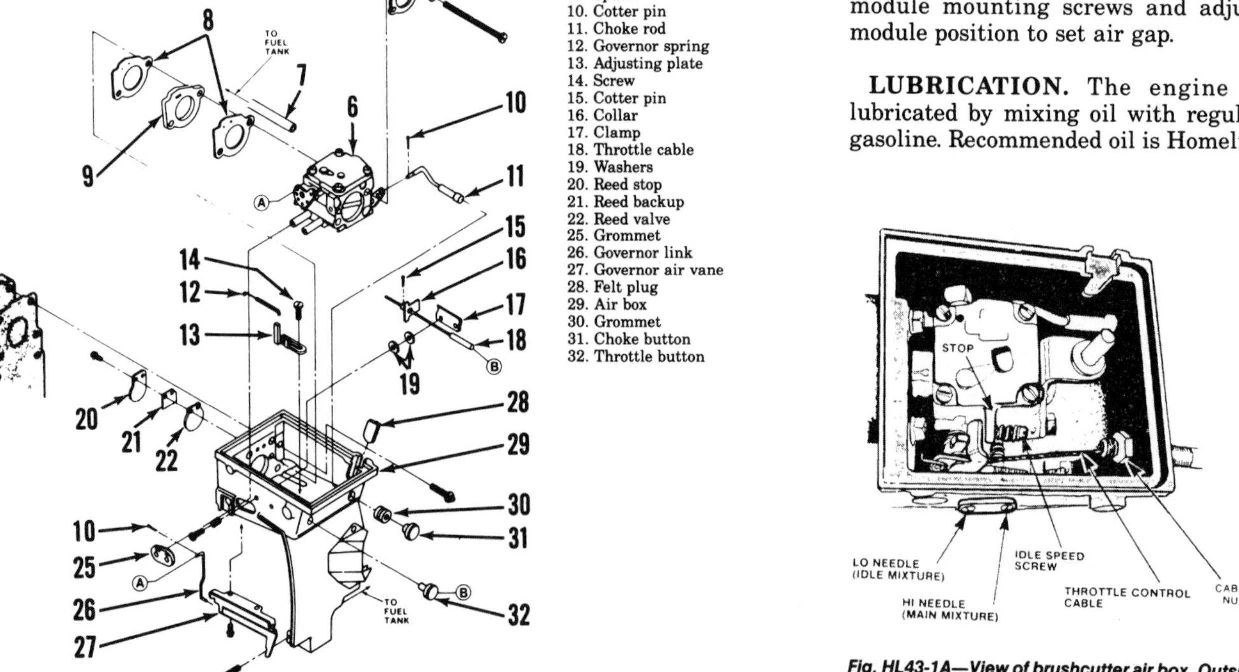

Fig. HL43-1—Exploded view of air box assembly on Model XL-12 engine.

1. Nut
2. Air filter cover
3. Retaining ring
4. Air filter element
5. Mounting bracket
6. Carburetor
7. Fuel line
8. Gasket
9. Spacer
10. Cotter pin
11. Choke rod
12. Governor spring
13. Adjusting plate
14. Screw
15. Cotter pin
16. Collar
17. Clamp
18. Throttle cable
19. Washers
20. Reed stop
21. Reed backup
22. Reed valve
25. Grommet
26. Governor link
27. Governor air vane
28. Felt plug
29. Air box
30. Grommet
31. Choke button
32. Throttle button

Fig. HL43-1A—View of brushcutter air box. Outside throttle cable nut is not shown.

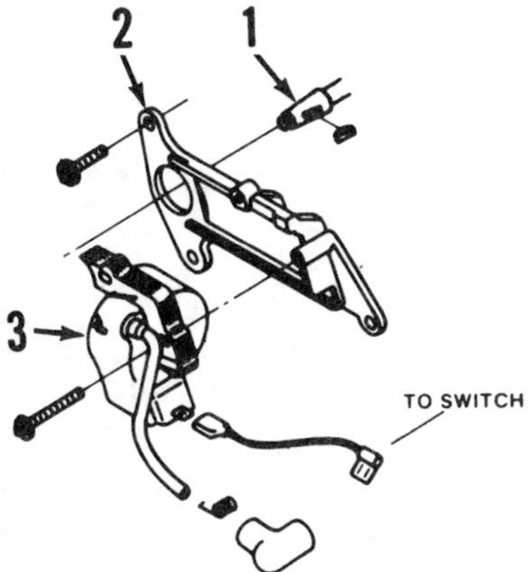

Fig. HL43-4—Exploded view of solid-state ignition.
1. Crankshaft
2. Stator plate
3. Ignition module

two-stroke oil mixed at ratio as designated on oil container. If Homelite oil is not available, a good quality oil designed for two-stroke engines may be used when mixed at a 16:1 ratio, however, an anti-oxidant fuel stabilizer (such as Sta-Bil) should be added to fuel mix. Anti-oxidant fuel stabilizer is not required with Homelite® oils as they contain fuel stabilizer so the fuel mix will stay fresh up to one year.

CARBON. Muffler, manifold and cylinder exhaust ports should be cleaned periodically to prevent loss of power through carbon build up. Remove muffler and scrape free of carbon. With muffler or manifold removed, turn engine so that piston is at top dead center and carefully remove carbon from exhaust ports with a wooden scraper. Be careful not to damage chamfered edges of exhaust ports or to scratch piston. Do not run engine with muffler removed.

REPAIRS

COMPRESSION PRESSURE. For optimum performance, cylinder compression pressure should be 130-155 psi (896-1069 kPa) with engine at normal operating temperature. Engine should be inspected and repaired when compression is 90 psi (621 kPa) or below.

CONNECTING ROD. Connecting rod and piston assembly can be removed after removing cylinder from crankcase. Refer to Fig. HL43-5. Be careful not to lose any of the 31 needle rollers when detaching rod from crankpin.

Renew connecting rod if bent or twisted, or if crankpin bearing surface is scored, burned or excessively worn. The caged needle roller piston pin bearing can be renewed by pressing old bearing out and pressing new bearing in with Homelite tool No. 23756. Press on lettered end of bearing cage only.

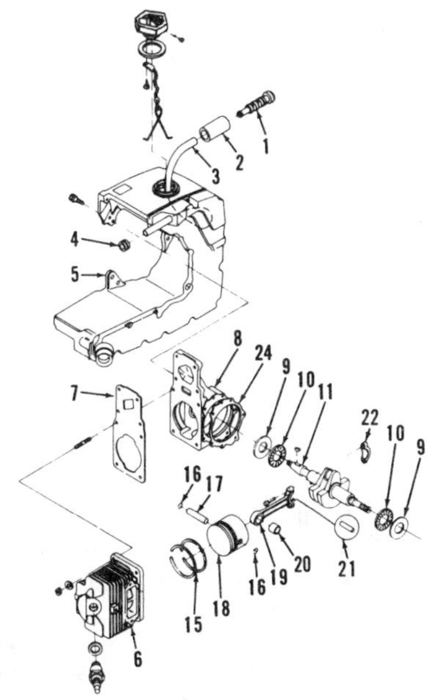

Fig. HL43-5—Exploded view of engine. Refer to Fig. HL43-5A for brushcutter drivecase.

1. Fuel pickup
2. Fuel filter
3. Fuel line
4. Grommet
5. Fuel tank
6. Cylinder
7. Gasket
8. Crankcase
9. Thrust washer
10. Thrust bearing
11. Crankshaft
15. Piston rings
16. Retaining ring
17. Piston pin
18. Piston
19. Connecting rod
20. Needle bearing
21. Crankpin rollers (31)
22. Rod cap
24. Gasket

It is recommended that the crankpin needle rollers be renewed as a set whenever engine is disassembled for service. When assembling connecting rod on crankshaft, stick 16 rollers in rod and 15 rollers in rod cap. Assemble rod to cap with match marks aligned, and with open end of piston pin towards flywheel side of engine. Wiggle the rod as cap retaining screws are being tightened to align the fractured mating surfaces of rod and cap.

PISTON, PIN AND RINGS. The piston is fitted with two pinned compression rings. Renew piston if scored, cracked or excessively worn, or if ring side clearance in top ring groove exceeds 0.0035 inch (0.09 mm).

Recommended piston ring end gap is 0.070-0.080 inch (1.8-2.0 mm); maximum allowable ring end gap is 0.085 inch (2.2 mm). Desired ring side clearance of groove is 0.002-0.003 inch (0.05-0.08 mm).

Piston, pin and rings are available in standard size only. Piston and pin are available in a matched set, and are not available separately.

Piston pin has one open and one closed end and may be retained in piston with snap rings or a Spirol pin. A wire retaining ring is used on exhaust side of piston on some models and should not be removed.

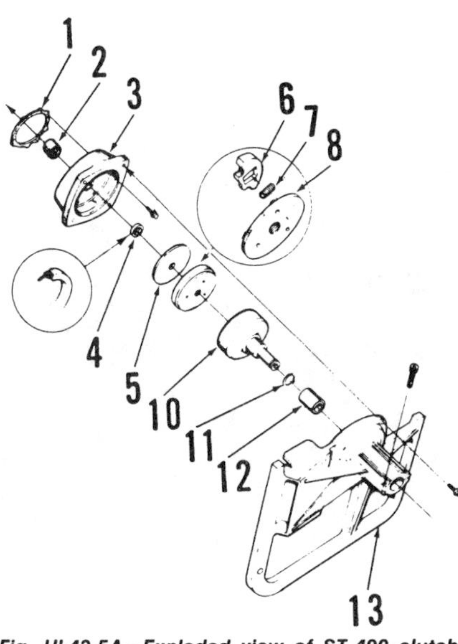

Fig. HL43-5A—Exploded view of ST-400 clutch assembly.

1. Gasket
2. Bearing
3. Drivecase
4. Seal
5. Cover
6. Clutch shoe
7. Spring
8. Clutch hub
10. Clutch drum
11. Snap ring
12. Bearing
13. Frame

To remove piston pin remove the snap ring at intake side of piston. On piston with Spirol pin at exhaust side, drive pin from piston and rod with slotted driver (Homelite tool No. A-23949). On all other models, insert a 3/16-inch pin through snap ring at exhaust side and drive piston pin out.

When reassembling, be sure closed end of piston pin is to exhaust side of piston (away from piston pin ring locating pin). Install Truarc snap ring with sharp edge out.

The cylinder bore is chrome plated. Renew the cylinder if chrome plating is worn away exposing the softer base metal.

CRANKCASE, BEARING HOUSING AND SEALS. CAUTION: Do not lose crankcase screws. New screws of the same length must be installed in place of old screws. Refer to parts book if correct screw length is unknown.

The crankshaft is supported in two caged needle roller bearings and crankshaft end play is controlled by a roller bearing and hardened steel thrust washer at each end of the shaft. Refer to Fig. HL43-5.

The needle roller main bearings and crankshaft seals in crankcase and drivecase can be renewed using Homelite tools Nos. 23757 and 23758. Press bearings and seals from crankcase or bearing housing with large stepped end of tool No. 23757, pressing towards outside of either case.

To install new needle bearings, use the shouldered short end of tool No. 23757 and press bearings into bores from inner

Fig. HL43-6—When installing flat reed valve, reed backup and reed stop, be sure reed is centered between two points indicated by black arrows.

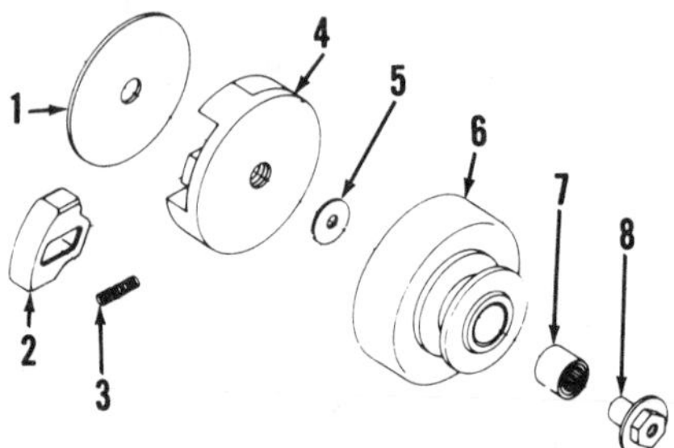

Fig. HL43-7—Exploded view of clutch used on saw engines.

1. Cover
2. Clutch shoe
3. Spring
4. Plate
5. Thrust washer
6. Clutch drum
7. Needle bearing
8. Nut

side of either case. Press on lettered end of bearing cage only.

To install new seals, first lubricate the seal and place seal on long end of tool No. 23758 so that lip of seal will be towards needle bearing as it is pressed into place.

To install crankshaft, lubricate thrust bearings (10) and place on shaft as shown. Place a hardened steel thrust washer to the outside of each thrust bearing. Insert crankshaft into crankcase being careful not to damage seal in crankcase. Place a seal protector sleeve (Homelite tool No. 23759) on crankshaft and gasket on shoulder of drivecase or pump housing. Lubricate seal protector sleeve, seal and needle bearing and mate drivecase or pump housing to crankshaft and crankcase. Use **NEW** retaining screws. Clean the screw threads and apply Loctite to threads before installing screws. Be sure the screws are correct length; screw length is critical. Tighten the screws alternately and remove seal protector sleeve from crankshaft.

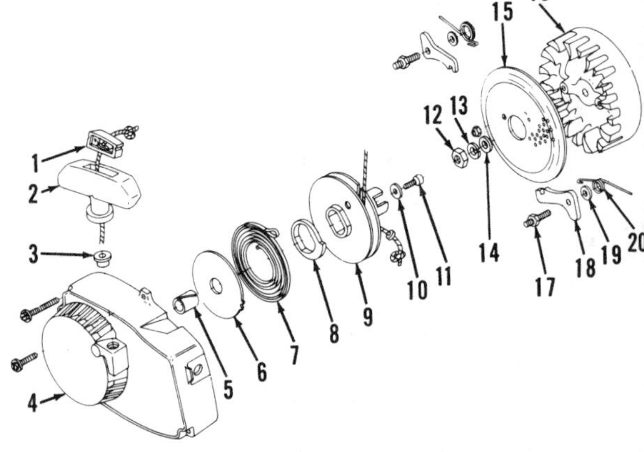

Fig. HL43-8—Exploded view of rewind starter.

1. Rope retainer
2. Handle
3. Bushing
4. Starter housing
5. Bushing
6. Washer
7. Rewind spring
8. Spring lock
9. Rope pulley
10. Washer
11. Screw
12. Nut
13. Lockwasher
14. Washer
15. Screen
16. Flywheel
17. Stud
18. Pawl
19. Washer
20. Spring

CLUTCH. To service clutch on ST-400 models, unscrew cap screws securing frame (13—Fig. HL43-5A) to drivecase (3) and separate brushcutting unit from engine. Remove snap ring (11) and clutch drum (10). Rotate clutch hub in counterclockwise direction to remove clutch assembly. Inspect clutch components and renew any which are damaged or excessively worn.

REWIND STARTER. To disassemble starter, refer to exploded view in Fig. HL43-8 and proceed as follows: Pull starter rope out fully, hold pulley (9) and place rope in notch of pulley. Let pulley rewind slowly. Hold pulley while removing screw (11) and washer (10). Turn pulley counterclockwise until disengaged from spring, then carefully lift pulley off starter post. Turn open side of housing down and rap housing sharply against top of work bench to remove spring. CAUTION: Be careful not to dislodge spring when removing pulley as spring could cause injury if it should uncoil rapidly.

Install new spring with loop in outer end over pin in blower housing and be sure spring is coiled in direction shown in Fig. HL43-8. Install pulley (9), turning pulley clockwise until it engages spring and secure with washer and screw. Insert new rope through handle and hole in blower housing. Knot both ends of the rope and harden the knots with cement. Turn pulley clockwise eight turns and slide knot in rope into slot and keyhole in pulley. Let starter pulley rewind slowly.

Starter pawl spring outer ends are hooked behind air vanes on flywheel in line with starter pawls when pawls are resting against flywheel nut. Pull starter rope slowly when installing blower housing so that starter cup will engage pawls.

HOMELITE

ENGINE SERVICE

Model	Bore	Stroke	Displacement
HK-18	1.14 in.	1.10 in.	1.12 cu. in
	(28.9 mm)	(27.9 mm)	(18.4 cc)
HK-24	1.26 in.	1.18 in.	1.47 cu. in.
	(32.0 mm)	(30.0 mm)	(24.1 cc)
HK-33	1.45 in.	1.22 in.	2.03 cu. in.
	(36.8 mm)	(30.9 mm)	(33.3 cc)

ENGINE INFORMATION

These engines are used as the power units for the Model HK-18, HK-24 and HK-33 Trimmer/Brushcutter.

MAINTENANCE

SPARK PLUG. Recommended spark plug is a Champion CJ8. Specified electrode gap is 0.025 inch (0.6 mm).

CARBURETOR. Initial setting for both mixture needles on Model HK-18 is one turn out from a lightly seated position. Initial setting of the high speed mixture needle on Models HK-24 and HK-33 is 1½ turns out from a lightly seated position. On all later models, the setting of the high speed mixture needle may be out as much as 2½ turns to obtain best performance.

After running engine so normal operating temperature is reached, run engine at wide open throttle (string must be at normal cutting length). Turn high speed mixture needle in so engine begins to run smoothly, then back out screw 1/8 turn. On Model HK-18, adjust idle mixture needle so engine idles smoothly and will accelerate without hesitation. Adjust idle speed screw on all models so engine idles just below clutch engagement speed (string head does not rotate).

On Models HK-24 and HK-33, midrange mixture is determined by the position of clip (7—Fig. HL45-1) on jet needle (8). There are three grooves located at the upper end of the jet needle (see Fig. HL45-2) and the normal position of clip (7) is in the middle groove. The mixture will be leaner if clip is installed in the top groove or richer if clip is installed in the bottom groove.

Model HK-18 is equipped with a Walbro WA series carburetor.

Models HK-24 and HK-33 are equipped with the slide-valve, diaphragm type carburetor shown in Fig. HL45-1. Carburetor is equipped with an integral fuel pump (16, 17 and 18). During servicing inspect fuel pump and metering diaphragms for pin holes, tears and other damage. Diaphragms should be flexible. Metal button must be tight on metering diaphragm. When assembling the carburetor note that the metering diaphragm lever should be flush with the

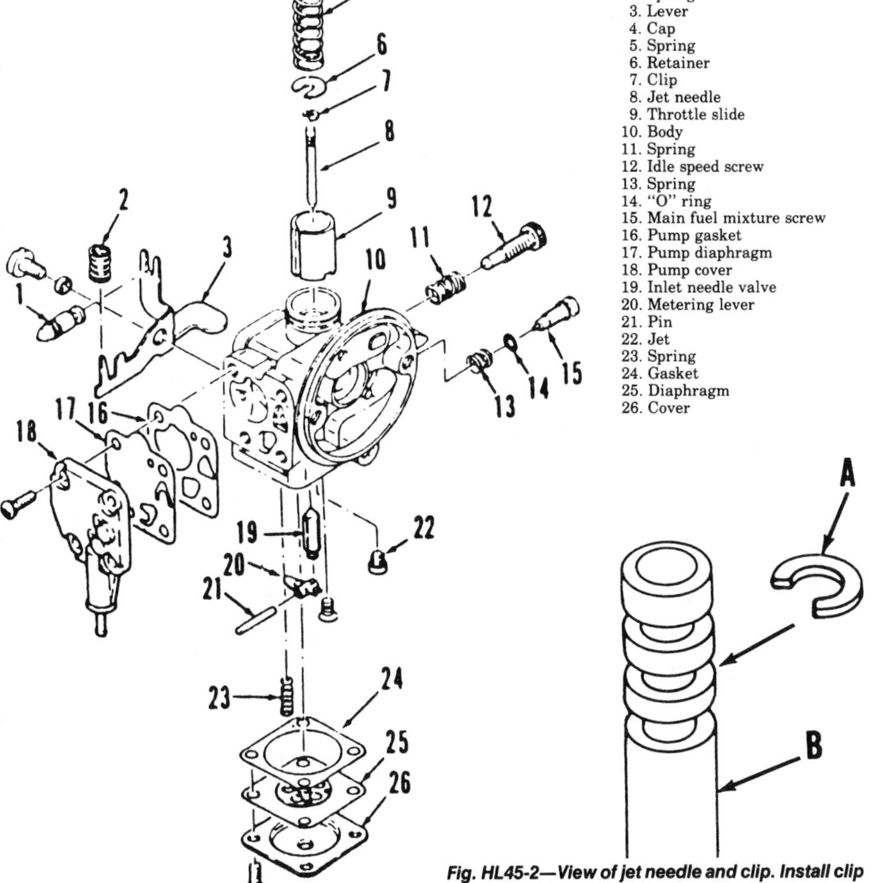

Fig. HL45-1—Exploded view of carburetor used on Models HK-24 and HK-33.

1. Tickler valve
2. Spring
3. Lever
4. Cap
5. Spring
6. Retainer
7. Clip
8. Jet needle
9. Throttle slide
10. Body
11. Spring
12. Idle speed screw
13. Spring
14. "O" ring
15. Main fuel mixture screw
16. Pump gasket
17. Pump diaphragm
18. Pump cover
19. Inlet needle valve
20. Metering lever
21. Pin
22. Jet
23. Spring
24. Gasket
25. Diaphragm
26. Cover

Fig. HL45-2—View of jet needle and clip. Install clip in middle groove for normal operation.

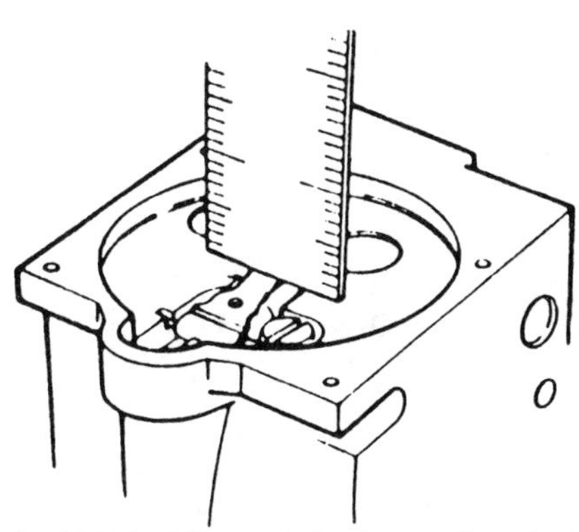

Fig. HL45-3—Adjust metering lever so lever just touches straightedge.

floor of cavity as shown in Fig. HL45-3. If necessary, adjust lever. Be sure retainer (6—Fig. HL45-1) is properly installed and secures jet needle and clip in throttle slide (9). Groove in side of throttle slide must engage pin in carburetor body when installing slide assembly.

IGNITION SYSTEM. All models use a transistorized ignition system consisting of a coil and an igniter. The flywheel-to-coil air gap is not adjustable.

The ignition system is operating satisfactorily if spark will jump across the 1/8 inch (3 mm) gap of a test spark plug (Homelite part JA-31316-4). If no spark is produced, check on/off switch and wiring.

The igniter may be tested with an ohmmeter as follows: Set ohmmeter to the R X 10K scale and connect the black ohmmeter lead to the igniter case and connect the red ohmmeter lead to the igniter lead tab. Ohmmeter needle should deflect from infinity to slightly more than zero ohms. Reverse the ohmmeter leads and the ohmmeter needle should again deflect from infinity to slightly more than zero ohms. The ohmmeter needle should not return all the way back to zero ohms after deflecting to infinity. Replace igniter if any faults are noted.

The coil may be tested wth an ohmmeter as follows: Set ohmmeter to the R X 1 scale and connect the red ohmmeter lead to the primary lead wire. Connect the black ohmmeter lead wire to the coil core. Specified resistance of the primary winding is 0.5 ohms for Model HK-18 and 0.6-0.7 ohms for Models HK-24 and HK-33. Connect the red ohmmeter lead to the spark plug wire and connect the black ohmmeter lead to the coil core. Specified resistance of the secondary coil winding is 0.97 ohms for Model HK-18 and 0.7-0.8 ohms for Models HK-24 and HK-33. Replace coil assembly if other test results are obtained.

REPAIRS

HOMELITE SPECIAL TOOLS. Special tools which will aid in servicing are as follows:

Tool No. and Description.
22828—Snap ring pliers.
JA-31316-4—Test spark plug.
94194—Compression gage.
94197—Carburetor tester.
17789—Carburetor repair tool kit.
94455—Alignment tool (for clutch drum removal).
A-98059—Flywheel puller.
98061-42—Tool kit (early models).
PR-24A—External snap ring pliers (Snap-On).
TM-30—Clutch head driver (Snap-On).

COMPRESSION PRESSURE. For optimum performance, compression pressure should be as follows with a hot engine and throttle and choke open. Crank engine until maximum pressure is observed on compression gage.

HK-18:
Low . . . . . 115 psi (793 kPa)
High . . . . . 145 psi (1000 kPa)

HK-24:
Low . . . . . 140 psi (965 kPa)
High . . . . . 170 psi (1172 kPa)

HK-33:
Low . . . . . 160 psi (1103 kPa)
High . . . . . 190 psi (1310 kPa)

A compression reading of 90 psi (620 kPa) or lower indicates a need for repairs.

TIGHTENING TORQUES. Engine tightening torques are listed below. All values are in inch-pounds (in.-lbs. × 0.113=N · m).

Air cleaner:
HK-24 & HK-33 . . . . . 14.5-17 in.-lbs.
Clutch pin to flywheel:
HK-18 & HK-24 . . . . . 69-85 in.-lbs.
HK-33 . . . . . 120-137 in.-lbs.
Crankcase . . . . . 30-34 in.-lbs.
Cylinder to crankcase:
HK-24 & HK-33 . . . . . 30-34 in.-lbs.
Flywheel:
HK-18 & HK-24 . . . . . 69-85 in.-lbs.
HK-33 . . . . . 120-137 in.-lbs.
Muffler . . . . . 34-39 in.-lbs.
Rope pulley . . . . . 120-137 in.-lbs.
Spark plug . . . . . 103-146 in.-lbs.

CRANKSHAFT AND CONNECTING ROD. Refer to Figs. HL45-5 and HL45-6 for exploded views. Crankshaft is pressed together at connecting rod journal, therefore crankshaft and

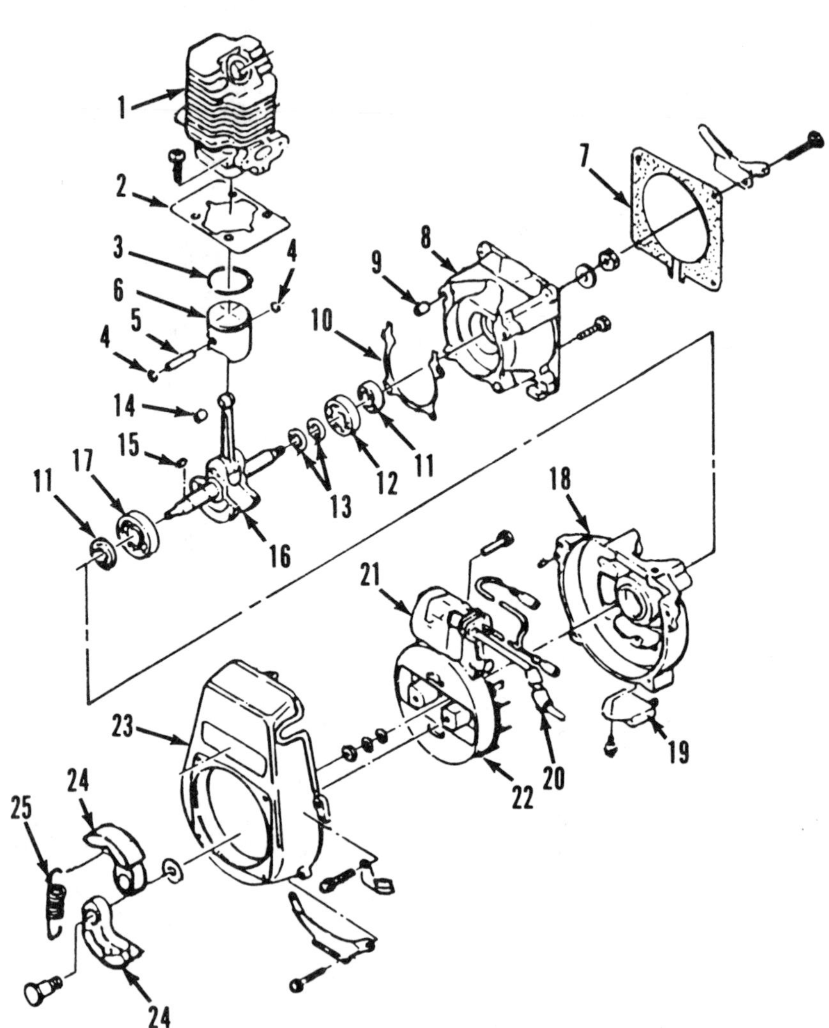

Fig. HL45-5—Exploded view of HK-18 engine assembly.

1. Cylinder
2. Gasket
3. Ring
4. Clip
5. Piston pin
6. Piston
7. Gasket
8. Crankcase
9. Dowel pin
10. Gasket
11. Seal
12. Bearing
13. Shims
14. Bushing
15. Woodruff key
16. Crankshaft & rod assy
17. Bearing
18. Crankcase
19. Igniter
20. Tube
21. Coil
22. Flywheel
23. Shroud
24. Clutch shoe
25. Clutch spring

connecting rod must be replaced as an assembly. Crankshaft is supported by ball bearings at both ends.

To remove crankshaft assembly, remove shroud and starter. On Model HK-18, unscrew starter pulley retaining nut and pry starter pulley off of crankshaft. On Models HK-24 and HK-33, the starter pulley is threaded onto crankshaft and is removed by unscrewing. On all models, remove flywheel, carburetor, muffler and cylinder. Split crankcase and remove crankshaft. Remove piston. Renew crankshaft assembly.

Inspect crankshaft assembly for damage and excessive wear. Be sure to inspect main bearings and roller bearing in small end of connecting rod.

Check crankshaft end play during reassembly. Crankshaft end play should be 0.002-0.010 inch (0.05-0.27 mm). Shims (13—Fig. HL45-5 or 21—Fig. HL45-6) are available in thicknesses of 0.004 inch (0.1 mm), 0.008 inch (0.2 mm), 0.016 inch (0.4 mm) and 0.024 inch (0.06 mm). To determine the correct shim pack thickness the following measurements must be taken: Magneto side of crankshaft half (dimension "A"); starter side of crankshaft half (dimension "B"); distance between outside edges of crankshaft counterweights (dimension "C"). Place a straightedge across gasket surface of magneto side of crankcase half. Measure the distance from the face of the outside bearing race to the bottom of the straightedge. This measurement is dimension "A". Place a straightedge across gasket surface of starter side of crankcase half. Measure the distance from the face of the outside bearing race to the bottom of the straightedge. This measurement is dimension "B". Using a vernier caliper, measure the distance between the machined surfaces of the crankshaft counterweights as shown in Fig. HL45-7. This measurement is dimension "C". Add dimensions "A" and "B", then deduct dimension "C". This will give the total thickness of the shim pack that will be needed. Refer to Table 1 for correct shim pack thickness. Shims must be installed on the starter side of crankshaft.

PISTON AND RINGS. Model HK-18 is equipped with one piston ring and Models HK-24 and HK-33 are equipped with two piston rings. Piston pin is retained in bore with two retaining rings.

Renew piston if scored, cracked, excessively worn or if side clearance in ring groove exceeds 0.027 inch (0.7 mm).

CYLINDER. Cylinder may be unbolted and removed from crankcase after shroud, muffler, carburetor and starter housing are removed.

Replace cylinder if scored, cracked or otherwise damaged. Use a crossing "X" pattern when retorquing cylinder retaining screws.

Fig. HL45-6—Exploded view of Models HK-24 and HK-33 engine assembly.

9. Pulley
10. Crankcase
11. Dowel pin
12. Gasket
13. Seal
14. Bearing
15. Cylinder
16. Gasket
17. Rings
18. Clips
19. Piston pin
20. Piston
21. Shims
22. Bushing
23. Woodruff key
24. Crankshaft & rod assy.
25. Dowel pin
26. Crankcase
27. Igniter
28. Coil
29. Tube
30. Flywheel
31. Shroud
32. Clutch shoe
33. Clutch spring

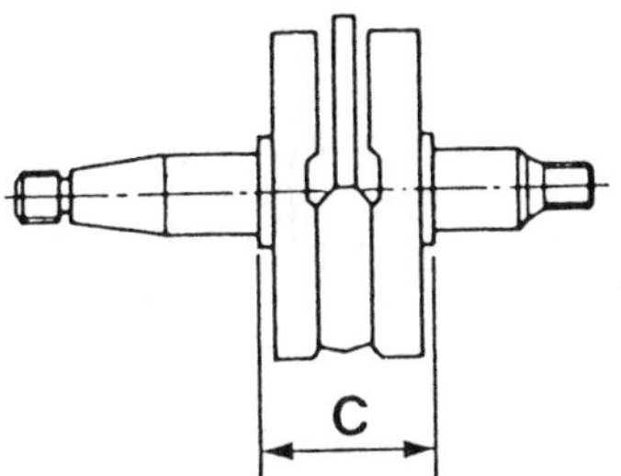

Fig. HL45-7—Measure distance (C) between machined surfaces of crankshaft couunterweights to determine crankshaft end play.

Fig. HL45-8—Lobes on clutch shoes should be in position shown when assembling clutch.

CLUTCH. Install clutch shoes onto flywheel with the lobes positioned as shown in Fig. HL45-8. Clutch will not engage if shoes are installed backwards. Shoes and clutch drum should be inspected for excessive wear or damage and replaced if necessary.

RECOIL STARTER. Model HK-18. Refer to Fig. HL45-9 for an exploded view of starter assembly. To disassemble starter, remove starter assembly from engine. Pull rope 6 inches (15.2 cm) out of housing (8). Align notch in pulley (5) with rope hole in housing. While holding pulley and rope hole in alignment, pull slack rope back through rope hole in side housing. Hold rope in notch while slowly allowing pulley to unwind relieving spring (6) tension.

Remove the center screw and washer, then slowly lift pulley off center post of housing. Do not dislodge rewind spring. Use care if spring must be removed. Do not allow spring to uncoil uncontrolled.

Inspect rope and spring. Lubricate center post of housing with light grease prior to reassembly. Reassembly is reverse of disassembly procedure. Wind all but 6 inches (15.2 cm) of rope onto pulley before installing pulley in starter housing. Wrap rope around pulley in a counterclockwise direction as viewed from pawl side of pulley. Press down on pulley while turning to engage pulley with spring hook. Install retaining screw and washer. Three prewinds counterclockwise are required on the rewind spring. After assembly, check for rewind spring bottoming out. With rope pulled all the way out of starter, pulley should still rotate, counterclockwise. If pulley will not rotate any further with rope pulled out, then release one prewind from spring and recheck.

Models HK-24 and HK-33. Refer to Fig. HL45-10 for an exploded view of starter assembly. To disassemble starter, first remove starter assembly from engine. Slide rope guide (8) out of starter housing (10) and slip rope (6) into slot on pulley. Hold rope in notch while slowly allowing pulley to unwind, relieving spring (7) tension.

Remove the center screw, retainer (1), pawl (2) and springs (3 and 4). Slowly lift pulley off starter housing post while using a small screwdriver to release pulley from spring hook. Use care if spring must be removed. Do not allow spring to uncoil uncontrolled.

Inspect rope, pawl and springs for breakage and excessive wear and replace as needed. Lubricate center post of housing with light grease prior to reassembly. Reassembly is reverse of disassembly procedure. Install spring in a counterclockwise direction from outer end. Wind all but 6 inches (15.2 cm) of rope onto pulley before installing pulley in starter housing. Wrap rope around pulley in a counterclockwise direction as viewed from pawl side of pulley. Press down on pulley while turning to engage pulley with spring hook. Reinstall retaining screw, retainer, pawl, pawl spring and loop spring. Make sure loop spring is installed properly as shown in Fig. HL45-11. Three prewinds counterclockwise are required on the rewind spring. Recheck to be sure pulley rewinds completely when released.

CLEARANCE "0" (Inch)	CLEARANCE "0" (mm)	SHIM NO.
−.004" to −.001"	−0.11 to +0.03	NONE
+.001" to +.005"	+0.03 to +0.13	.004"
+.005" to +.009"	+0.13 to +0.23	.008"
+.009" to +.013"	+0.23 to +0.33	.012"
+.013" to +.017"	+0.33 to +0.43	.016"
+.017" to +.021"	+0.43 to +0.53	.020"
+.021" to +.025"	+0.53 to +0.63	.024"

TABLE 1—Select shim to obtain specified end play.

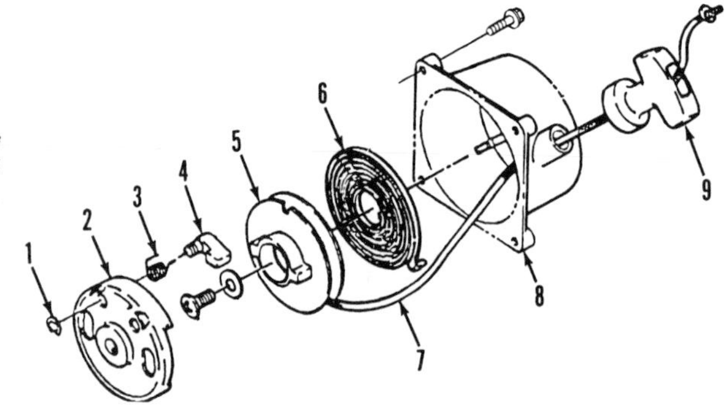

Fig. HL45-9—Exploded view of recoil starter used on Model HK-18.
1. "E" ring
2. Pulley
3. Spring
4. Pawl
5. Reel
6. Spring
7. Rope
8. Housing
9. Handle

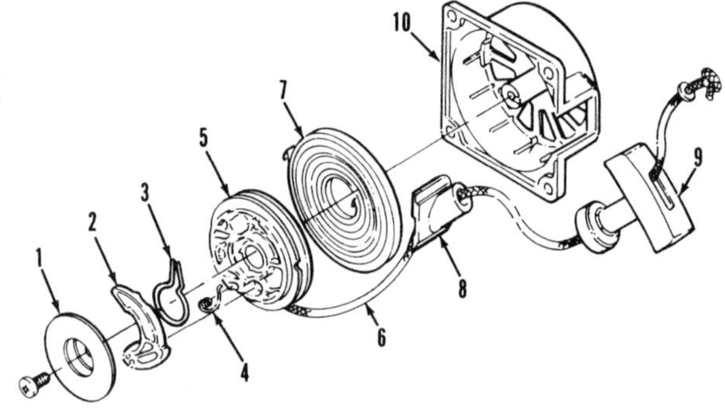

Fig. HL45-10—Exploded view of recoil starter used on Models HK-24 and HK-33.
1. Retainer
2. Pawl
3. Loop spring
4. Pawl spring
5. Pulley
6. Rope
7. Spring
8. Guide
9. Handle
10. Housing

Fig. HL45-11—Loop spring must be installed as shown.

HOMELITE

ENGINE SERVICE

Models	Bore	Stroke	Displacement
HLT-15, HB-100, ST-145, ST-155, ST-175, HB-180, ST-185, BP-250, ST-285, ST-385, ST-485, SX-135	33.3 mm (1.310 in.)	28.8 mm (1.134 in.)	25.0 cc (1.53 cu. in.)
HLT-16, HLT-17, HBC-18, HLT-18, HBC-30	36.5 mm (1.437 in.)	(28.8 mm) (1.133 in.)	(30.0 cc) (1.83 cu. in.)
PSE-3000, PLT-3200, PBC-3400, PLT-3400, PBC-3600	36.5 mm (1.437 in.)	(28.8 mm) (1.133 in.)	(30.0 cc) (1.83 cu. in.)
625, 725, 825	33.3 mm (1.310 in.)	28.8 mm (1.133 in.)	25.0 cc (1.53 cu. in.)
630, 730, 830	36.5 mm (1.437 in.)	28.8 mm (1.133 in.)	30.0 cc (1.83 cu. in.)

ENGINE INFORMATION

The Homelite two-stroke, air-cooled engines covered in this section are used on the Homelite string trimmers, brushcutters and blowers listed.

MAINTENANCE

LUBRICATION. The manufacturer recommends mixing Homelite 2-Cycle oil with regular or unleaded gasoline at the ratio indicated on the package. When using regular BIA certified TC-W oil, mix at a ratio of 32:1.

An antioxidant fuel stabilizer (such as Sta-Bil)should be added to the fuel if Homelite oil is not used. Homelite oil contains an antioxidant fuel stabilizer.

SPARK PLUG. Recommended spark plug is Champion DJ-7Y with electrode gap of 0.025 in. (0.6 mm). The manufacturer recommends that a new plug be installed each year. Tighten the plug to 120-180 in.-lb. (13.6-20.3 N.m) torque.

CARBURETOR. Walbro and Zama carburetors are used depending on equipment model. Refer to following appropriate carburetor section for service information.

Walbro WT To adjust carburetor on trimmer, proceed as follows: Turn idle mixture screw (12—Fig. HL46-1) and high speed mixture screw (14) counterclockwise until lightly seated, then turn each mixture screw counterclockwise 1-1/4 turns open. Run engine until normal operating temperature is reached.

Turn idle mixture screw clockwise until highest engine speed is reached, then turn screw counterclockwise 1/8 turn. Run engine at full throttle under load (trimmer line must be extended). Turn high speed mixture screw clockwise until highest engine speed is attained, then turn mixture screw counterclockwise 1/8 turn. Set idle speed screw so trimmer head or blade does not rotate when engine is idling.

To adjust carburetor on blower, turn idle mixture screw (12) and high speed mixture screw (14) clockwise until lightly seated, then turn each mixture screw counterclockwise one turn open. Final adjustment is performed with engine at normal operating temperature. Adjust idle mixture screw so engine accelerates cleanly without hesitation.

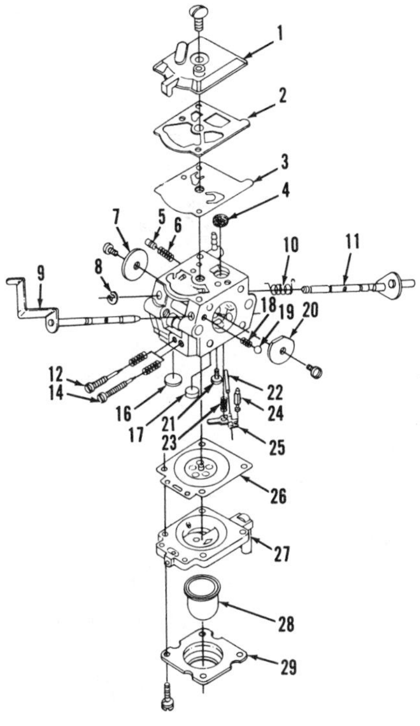

Fig. HL46-1—Exploded view of Walbro WT carburetor. Throttle shaft (11) is on opposite side shown on some models. Accelerator piston (5) and spring (6) are not used on all models.

1. Cover
2. Gasket
3. Fuel pump diaphragm
4. Screen
5. Accelerator piston
6. Spring
7. Throttle plate
8. "E" ring
9. Choke shaft
10. Spring
11. Throttle shaft
12. Idle mixture screw
14. High speed mixture screw
16. Welch plug
17. Nozzle
18. Spring
19. Detent ball
20. Choke plate
21. Screw
22. Pin
23. Spring
24. Fuel inlet valve
25. Metering lever
26. Metering diaphragm
27. Cover
28. Primer bulb
29. Bulb retainer

Run engine at full throttle and adjust high speed so engine runs at highest speed, then turn screw counterclockwise until engine speed begins to decrease. Adjust idle speed screw so engine idles smoothly.

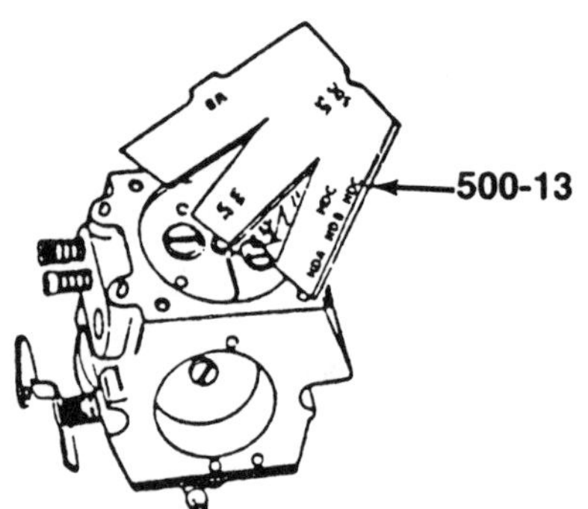

Fig. HL46-2—Metering lever should just touch leg of Walbro tool 500-13. Bend lever to obtain correct lever height.

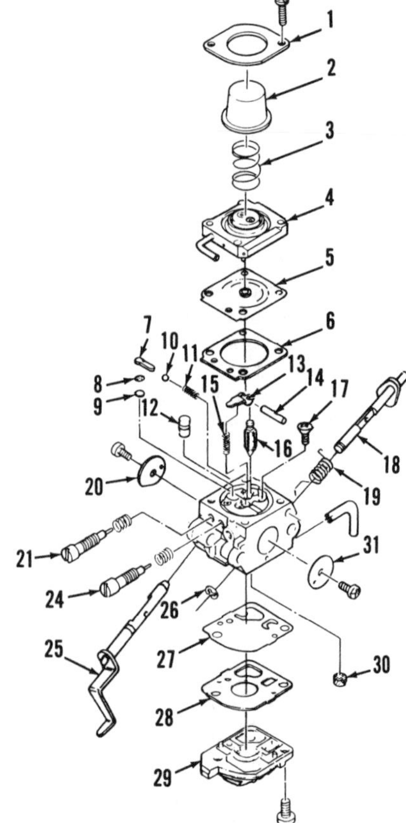

Fig. HL46-3—Exploded view of Zama C1U carburetor used on some models.

1. Cover
2. Primer bulb
3. Spring
4. Cover
5. Metering diaphragm
6. Gasket
7. Welch plug
8. Retainer
9. Screen
10. Detent ball
11. Spring
12. Nozzle
13. Metering lever
14. Pin
15. Spring
16. Fuel inlet valve
17. Screw
18. Throttle shaft
19. Spring
20. Choke plate
21. Idle mixture screw
24. High speed mixture screw
25. Choke shaft
26. "E" ring
27. Fuel pump diaphragm
28. Gasket
29. Fuel inlet screws
30. Cover
31. Fuel inlet screen

Some models are equipped with an accelerator pump that forces additional fuel into the carburetor bore when the throttle shaft is rotated. The pump piston (5—Fig. HL46-1) rests against a flat on the throttle shaft. Shaft rotation moves the piston against fuel in a passage.

To disassemble carburetor, refer to Fig. HL46-1 and remove cover (1) and retainer (29) for access to internal components. Remove metering lever (25), fuel inlet valve (24), screen (4), nozzle (17) and mixture screws (12 and 14). Welch plug (16) can be removed by prying out with a sharp punch. Use care not to damage carburetor casting when removing Welch plug. Do not lose detent ball (19) when withdrawing choke shaft (9). Accelerator pump piston (5) is released when throttle shaft (11) is withdrawn.

Clean and inspect all components. Do not use wire or drill bits to clean fuel passages as fuel flow may be altered. Check condition of diaphragms (3 and 26) carefully. Install new diaphragms if hard (not flexible), torn or otherwise damaged. Examine fuel inlet valve (24) and seat. Inlet valve is renewable, but carburetor body must be renewed if seat is damaged or excessively worn. Discard carburetor body if mixture screw seats are damaged or excessively worn. Clean or replace fuel screen (4).

To reassemble carburetor, reverse disassembly procedure. Check metering lever height as shown in Fig. HL46-2 using Walbro tool 500-13. Metering lever should just touch leg on tool If tool is not available, the lever should be 1.52-1.78 mm (0.060-0.070 in.) below the mounting surface for diaphragm (26). Bend lever to obtain correct lever height.

Zama. To adjust carburetor, turn idle mixture screw (21—Fig. HL46-3) and high speed mixture screw (24) in until lightly seated, then turn each mixture screw counterclockwise one turn open. Run engine until normal operating temperature is reached. Adjust idle mixture screw so engine idles smoothly and accelerates without hesitation. Run engine at full throttle under load (trimmer line must be extended). Turn high speed mixture screw clockwise until highest engine speed is attained, then turn mixture screw counterclockwise 1/8 turn. Set idle speed screw so trimmer head or blade does not rotate when engine is idling.

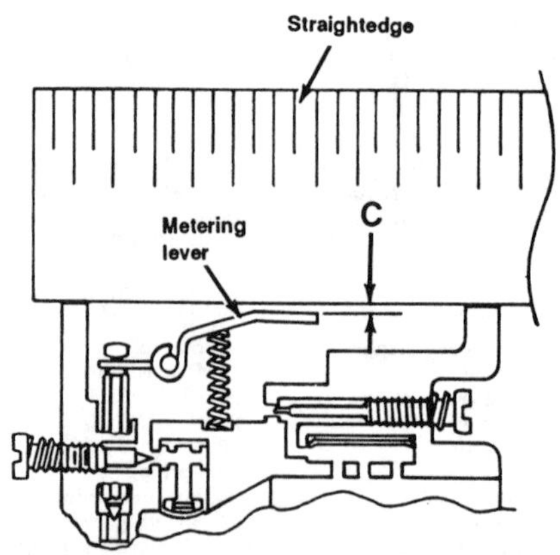

Fig. HL46-4—Metering lever on Zama carburetor should be bent so height (C) is 0-0.3 mm (0-0.012 in.).

To disassemble the carburetor, refer to Fig. HL46-3 and remove retainer (1) and cover (29) for access to internal components. Remove cover (4), diaphragms (5 and 27), metering lever (13), fuel inlet valve (16), retainer (8) and screen (9), nozzle (12) and fuel screen (30). Do not lose detent ball (10) when withdrawing choke shaft (25). To remove Welch plug (7), pierce the plug towards the end of the "tail" portion with a suitable punch. Do not insert punch too deeply as underlying body metal may be damaged. Apply suitable sealant to outer edge of new Welch plug.

Clean and inspect all components. Do not use wire or drill bits to clean fuel passages as calibration of carburetor may be affected. Examine the fuel inlet valve (16), mixture screws (21 and 24) and their seats for wear or damage. Valve and mixture screws are renewable, but carburetor body must be replaced if seats are damaged or excessively worn.

To reassemble carburetor, reverse disassembly procedure. Clearance (C—Fig. HL46-4) between metering lever and a straightedge placed across metering side of carburetor body should be 0-0.03 mm (0-0.012 in.). Bend metering lever as needed to obtain correct height.

IGNITION. A solid state ignition is used on all models. The ignition module is attached to the side of the engine cylinder. Ignition service is accomplished by replacing ignition components until the faulty component is located.

Air gap between ignition module and flywheel magnet is adjustable and should be 0.4 mm (0.015 in.). Loosen ignition module mounting screws and adjust module position to set air gap.

REPAIRS

TIGHTENING TORQUE VALUES. Tightening torque values are listed in the following table:

Air box cover . . . . 2.3-3.3 N•m (20-30 in.-lbs.)
Carburetor and air box . . . 3.3-4.5 N•m (30-40 in.-lbs.)
Clutch adapter shaft . . . 11.3-16.9 N•m (100-150 in.-lbs.)
Clutch. . . . . 9.0-11.3 N•m (80-100 in.-lbs.)
Crankcase cover . . . . 4.5-5.6 N•m (40-50 in.-lbs.)
Cylinder . . . . 6.2-7.3 N•m (55-65 in.-lbs.)
Drive adapter. . . . . 11.3-16.9 N•m (100-150 in.-lbs.)
Engine housing . . . . 4.5-5.6 N•m (40-50 in.-lbs.)
Heat dam. . . . . 4.5-5.6 N•m (40-50 in.-lbs.)
Ignition module . . . . 3.3-4.5 N•m (30-40 in.-lbs.)
Muffler . . . . 4.5-5.6 N•m (40-50 in.-lbs.)
Spark plug . . . . 13.6-20.3 N•m (120-180 in.-lbs.)

COMPRESSION PRESSURE. For optimum performance of all models, cylinder compression pressure should be 656-725 kPa (95-105 psi) with engine at normal operating temperature. Cold compression pressure should be 690-759 kPa (100-110 psi).

CYLINDER, PISTON, PIN AND RINGS. Refer to Fig. HL46-5 or Fig. HL46-6. Piston, bearings and connecting rod are serviced only as an assembly that is available only in standard size. The connecting rod has a caged roller bearing at both ends. The piston is equipped with a single piston ring.

To remove the cylinder (25), piston and connecting rod (22), remove the muffler (35), carburetor (30), fuel tank (33) and crankcase cover (27). Remove the screws attaching the cylinder, then lift the cylinder. Tilt the cylinder and piston slightly to release the connecting rod from the crankshaft crankpin. Withdraw the piston from the cylinder.

The cylinder bore has a hard chrome finish that cannot be resized or resurfaced. Inspect the cylinder bore for scoring, scratches, excessive wear or other damage. The piston, piston ring and cylinder are available in standard size only.

There is no piston ring locating pin in the piston ring groove. When installing the cylinder over the piston, locate the piston ring end gap toward the center of the exhaust port.

CRANKSHAFT AND CRANKCASE. Refer to Fig. HL46-5 or Fig. HL46-6. The crankshaft of all models is supported by two ball bearings (16 and 20). To remove the crankshaft, first re-

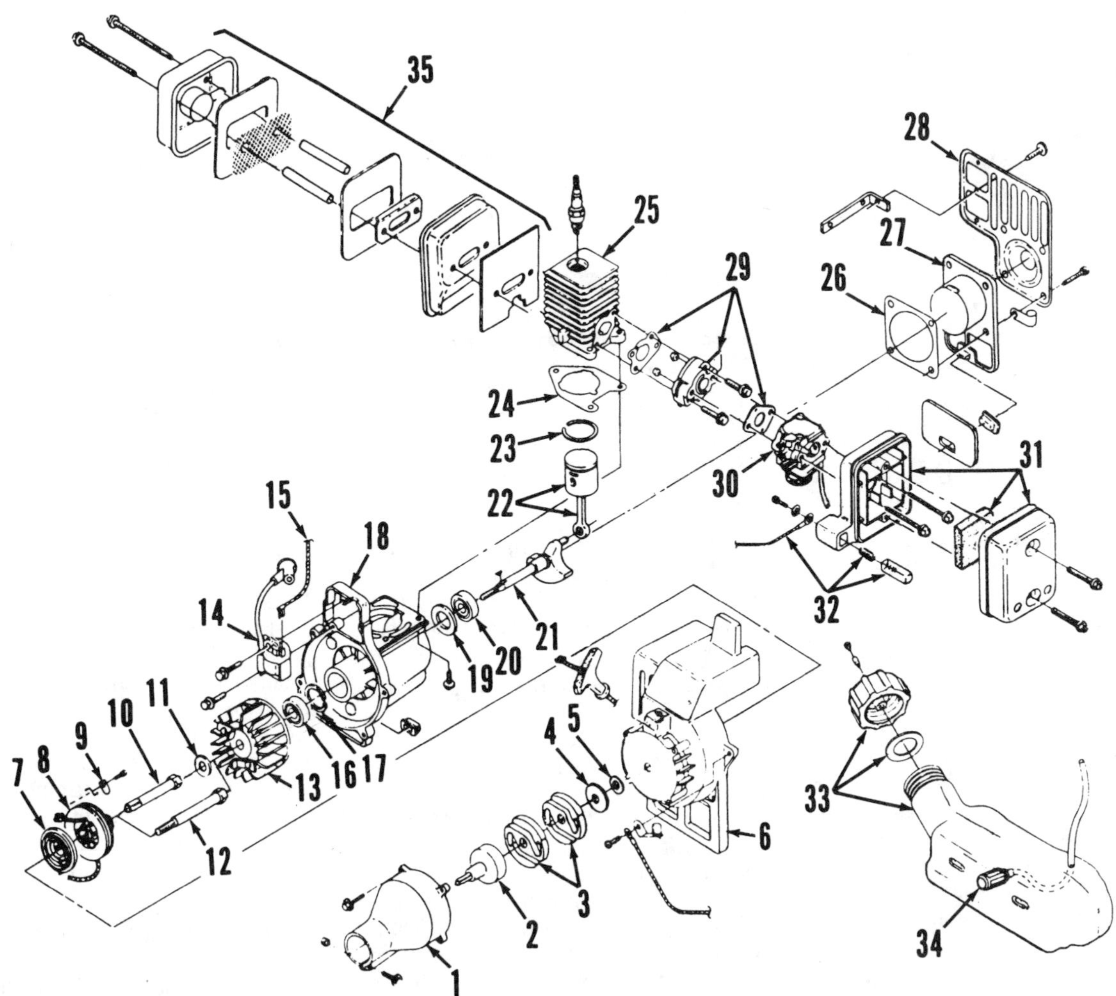

Fig. HL46-5—Exploded view typical of most trimmer engines. Blower engines are similar. The drive adapter (10) is used on models without clutch.

1. Tube adapter
2. Clutch drum
3. Clutch rotors
4. Washer
5. Washer
6. Engine housing
7. Rewind spring
8. Rope pulley
9. Retainer
10. Drive adapter
11. Washer
12. Clutch adapter
13. Flywheel
14. Ignition module
15. Wire to stop switch
16. Ball bearing
17. Snap ring
18. Crankcase
19. Seal
20. Ball bearing
21. Crankshaft
22. Piston & connecting rod assy.
23. Piston ring
24. Gasket
25. Cylinder
26. Gasket
27. Crankcase cover
28. Shield
29. Heat dam & gasket
30. Carburetor
31. Air filter & housing
32. Stop switch
33. Fuel tank
34. Fuel filter
35. Muffler assy.

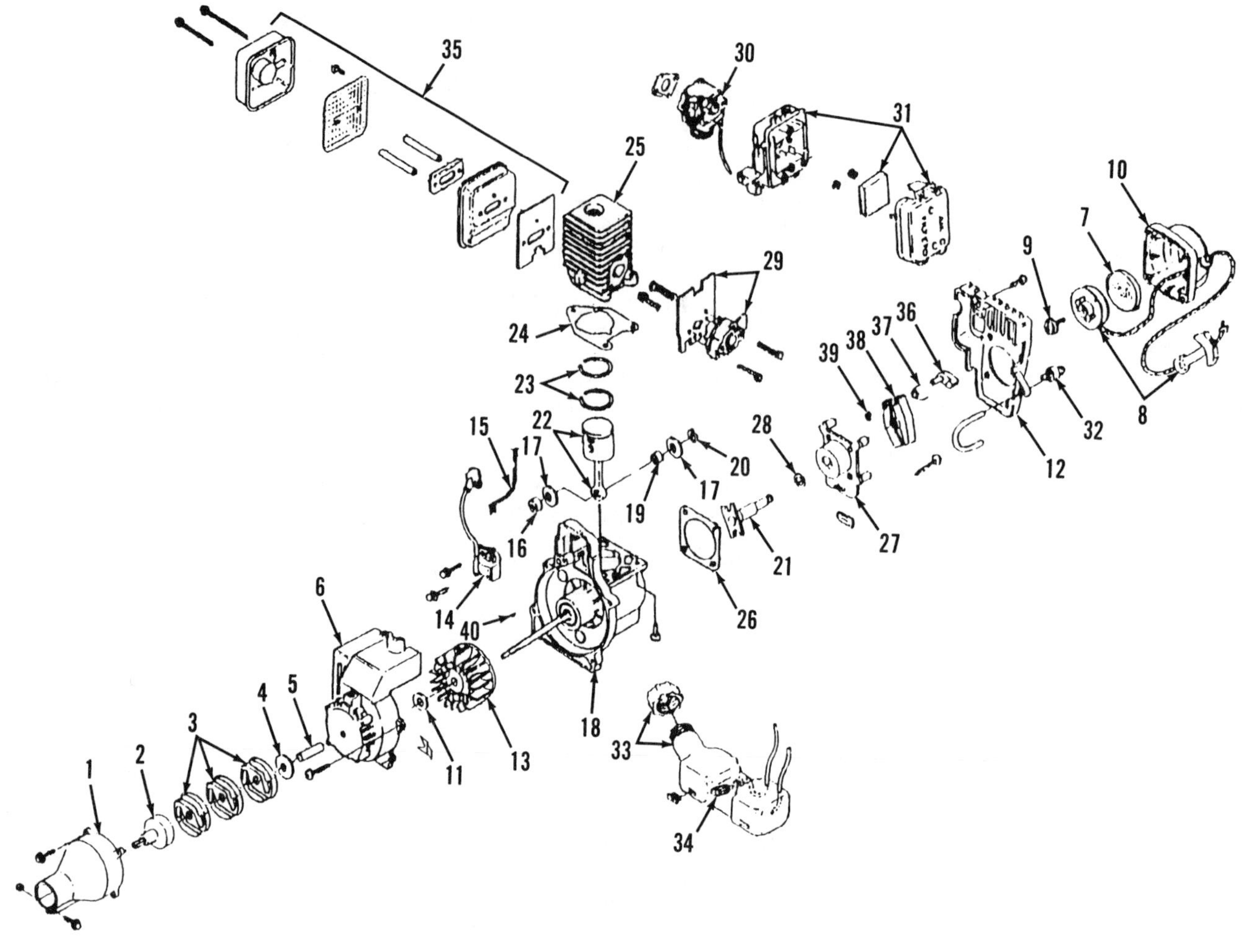

Fig. HL46-6—Exploded view of engine typical of PLT 3400 and PBC 3600.

1. Drive shaft housing adapter
2. Clutch drum
3. Clutch rotors
4. Washer
5. Spacer
6. Engine housing
7. Rewind spring
8. Rope, handle & pulley
9. Retaining screw
10. Starter housing
11. Washer
12. Engine cowling
13. Flywheel
14. Ignition coil/module
15. Wire to stop switch
16. Bearing spacer
17. Thrust washers
18. Crankshaft & crankcase
19. Needle bearing
20. Retaining ring
21. Starter shaft
22. Piston & connecting rod
23. Piston rings
24. Cylinder base gasket
25. Cylinder
26. Gasket
27. Crankcase cover
28. Spacer
29. Heat shield & dam
30. Carburetor
31. Air filter & housing
32. Primer bulb
33. Fuel tank
34. Fuel filter
35. Muffler
36. Starter pawl
37. Spring
38. Starter cup
39. Retaining ring
40. Woodruff key

move the flywheel (13), then remove the drive key from the crankshaft. On models with a rear starter, remove the starter assembly as described in the Equipment section of this book. On all models, remove the rear cover (27). Remove the cylinder as described in the CYLINDER, PISTON, PIN AND RINGS paragraphs of this section. Press the crankshaft out of the bearings toward the rear. Bearings (16 and 20) and seal (19) can be pressed or driven from the bore of the crankcase. Do not remove the bearings or seal unless new parts are available.

Install seal (19) with the spring loaded lip toward the rear (connecting rod). Press the seal into position until the front face of the seal is 16 mm (5/8 in.) from the outside face of the bearing bore. Press the sealed front bearing (16) into the bore until it is seated against snap ring (17). Lubricate the lip of seal (19), then press bearing (20) against the shoulder in the crankcase. Press the crankshaft into the bearings until seated against the inner bearing (20).

CLUTCH. Some trimmers are equipped with a clutch, while others are driven direct. The clutch may include two or three S-shaped rotors (3—Fig. HL46-5 or Fig. HL46-6). Each of the rotors must be unscrewed from the adapter (12—Fig. HL46-5) or crankshaft (Fig. HL46-6) one at a time. Attempting to remove two or more rotors at once may damage the threads on the adapter or the crankshaft. Rotors can be gripped while removing using Homelite tool (part No. A-93791) or equivalent. A rope may be inserted into the spark plug hole to hold the crankshaft while removing the clutch rotors.

FLYWHEEL. The flywheel of some models is held in place by a drive adapter (10—Fig. HL46-5) or clutch adapter (12). The flywheel of later models is retained by the clutch rotors (3—Fig. HL46-6), washer (11) and spacer (12). Remove the clutch from models so equipped. Remove the drive adapter or clutch adapter (10 or 12—Fig. HL46-5). Remove spacer (5—Fig HL46-6) and washer (11) from models so equipped. Bump the flywheel with a soft-faced mallet to dislodge the flywheel from the tapered surface. Remove the flywheel and the drive key.

When assembling, be sure to clean and dry the tapered surfaces of the crankshaft and flywheel. Install the drive key and tighten all of the fasteners to the torque listed in TIGHTENING TORQUE VALUES paragraph. Tighten the flywheel onto the crankshaft taper before installing the ignition coil/module. Be sure to set (adjust) the air gap between the flywheel magnets and the legs of the ignition coil/module.

STARTER. Refer to the BLOWER Service Section for service to the rewind starter used on blower models or to the TRIMMER Service Section for service to the electric starting system used on some models. Additional service information and procedures may be located in the appropriate TRIMMER service section. Refer to the appropriate following paragraphs for service to the Front Mounted rewind starter shown in Fig. HL46-5 or the Rear Mounted starter shown in Fig. HL46-6.

Front Mounted Starter. The starter pulley and spring (7 and 8—Fig. HL46-5) are contained in the engine housing (6). To service the starter on trimmers with clutches, first remove the clutch assembly (2, 3, 4 and 5), then remove the engine housing (6). Remove the rope handle and allow the rope to wind into the starter housing.

WARNING: Be careful when disassembling, because the rewind spring (7) may unwind uncontrollably and can cause injury. Wear appropriate eye protection and gloves when removing the pulley and spring.

Remove the screws attaching the pulley retainer to the engine housing and remove the pulley and rope (8). On some models the pulley will be retained by a plate, while on others models individual retainer tabs (9) are used. Remove, clean and inspect the spring (7). Inspect the pawls attached to the flywheel and service as necessary. Pawls may be available only as an assembly with the flywheel.

Lubricate the center post and the rewind spring lightly with grease before assembling. Attach the outer end of the spring (7) to the housing cavity and install by winding the spring in a clockwise direction. Rope length should be 42 in. (107 cm). The inner end of the rope should be attached to the pulley and the free end should be routed through the rope guide before attaching the handle to the outer end. Assemble the pulley on the center post. Pull a loop in the rope at the notch provided in starter pulley, then turn the pulley clockwise while holding the rope in the notch. Release the rope from the pulley notch and let the spring unwind slowly while winding the rope on the pulley. The spring should be preloaded enough to rewind the rope completely and should hold the starter handle against the guide, but the spring must not bind before the rope is fully extended. When the rope is fully extended, it should be possible to turn the pulley at least 1/4 turn before the spring binds.

Rear Mounted Starter. The starter pulley and spring (7 and 8—Fig. HL46-6) are contained in a housing (10) attached to the engine cover (12). To service the pulley and spring, unbolt and remove the housing from the engine cover. Remove the rope handle and allow the rope to wind into the starter housing.

WARNING: Be careful when disassembling, because the rewind spring (7) may unwind uncontrollably and can cause injury. Wear appropriate eye protection and gloves when removing the pulley and spring.

Remove the retaining screw (9) and remove the pulley and rope (8) from the housing. Remove, clean and inspect the spring (7). Inspect the pawl (36) and spring (37) located in the starter cup (38). If necessary, unscrew the starter cup from the starter shaft (21). Pawl and spring may be removed after removing the clip (39).

Lubricate the center post and the rewind spring lightly with grease before assembling. Attach the outer end of the spring (7) to the housing cavity and install by winding the spring in a counterclockwise direction. The inner end of the rope should be attached to the pulley and the free end should be routed through the rope guide before attaching the handle to the outer end. Assemble the pulley on the center post. Pull a loop in the rope at the notch provided in starter pulley, then turn the pulley counterclockwise while holding the rope in the notch. Release the rope from the pulley notch and let the spring unwind slowly while winding the rope on the pulley. The spring should be preloaded enough to rewind the rope completely and should hold the starter handle against the guide, but the spring must not bind before the rope is fully extended. When the rope is fully extended, it should be possible to turn the pulley at least 1/4 turn before the spring binds.

HOMELITE

ENGINE SERVICE

Models	Engine Bore	Engine Stroke	Displacement
HBC-38, PBC-3800, HBC-40 & PBC-4000 Pro	1.5625 in. (39.7 mm)	1.281 in. (32.5 mm)	2.46 cu. in. (40.0 cc)

ENGINE INFORMATION

The Homelite two-stroke, air-cooled engines covered in this section are used on the Homelite trimmers and brush cutters listed.

MAINTENANCE

LUBRICATION. The manufacturer recommends mixing Homelite 2-Cycle oil with regular or unleaded gasoline at the ratio indicated on the package. When using regular BIA certified TC-W oil, mix at a ratio of 32:1.

An antioxidant fuel stabilizer (such as Sta-Bil)should be added to the fuel if Homelite oil is not used. Homelite oil contains an antioxidant fuel stabilizer.

SPARK PLUG. Recommended spark plug for most application is Champion CJ-6Y with electrode gap of 0.025 in. (0.6 mm). The manufacturer recommends that a new plug be installed each year. Tighten the plug to 120-180 in.-lb. (13.6-20.3 N·m) torque.

CARBURETOR. Engines are equipped with a Walbro WT diaphragm carburetor or a Zama C1Q diaphragm carburetor. Refer to following sections for service.

Walbro WT. To adjust carburetor, turn idle mixture screw (12—Fig. HL47-1) and high speed mixture screw (14) 1-1/4 turns out from a lightly seated position. Start and run engine until normal operating temperature is reached.

Turn idle mixture screw clockwise until highest engine speed is reached, then turn screw counterclockwise 1/8 turn. Run engine at full throttle under load (trimmer line must be extended). Turn high speed mixture screw clockwise until highest engine speed is attained, then turn mixture screw counterclockwise 1/8 turn. Set idle speed screw so trimmer head or blade does not rotate when engine is idling.

To disassemble carburetor, refer to Fig. HL47-1 and remove cover (1) and retainer (29) for access to internal components. Remove metering lever (25), fuel inlet valve (24), screen (4), nozzle (17) and mixture screws (12 and 14). Welch plug (16) can be removed by prying out with a sharp punch. Use care not to damage carburetor casting when removing Welch plug. Do not lose detent ball (19) when withdrawing choke shaft (9). Accelerator pump piston (5) is released when throttle shaft (11) is withdrawn.

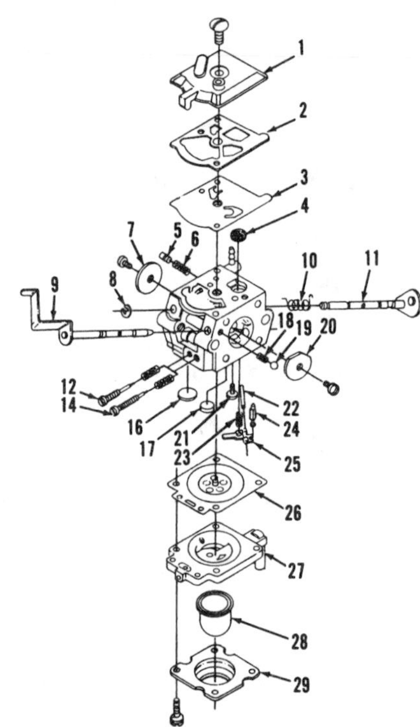

Fig. HL47-1—Exploded view of Walbro WT carburetor typical of some models. Throttle shaft (11) is on opposite side shown on some models. Accelerator piston (5) and spring (6) are not used on all models.

1. Cover
2. Gasket
3. Fuel pump diaphragm
4. Screen
5. Accelerator piston
6. Spring
7. Throttle plate
8. "E" ring
9. Choke shaft
10. Spring
11. Throttle shaft
12. Idle mixture screw
14. High speed mixture screw
16. Welch plug
17. Nozzle
18. Spring
19. Detent ball
20. Choke plate
21. Screw
22. Pin
23. Spring
24. Fuel inlet valve
25. Metering lever
26. Metering diaphragm
27. Cover
28. Primer bulb
29. Retainer

Clean and inspect all components. Do not use wire or drill bits to clean fuel passages as fuel flow may be altered. Check condition of diaphragms (3 and 26) carefully. Install new diaphragms if hard (not flexible), torn or otherwise damaged. Examine fuel inlet valve (24) and seat. Inlet valve is renewable, but carburetor body must be renewed if seat is damaged or excessively worn. Discard carburetor body if mixture screw seats are damaged or excessively worn. Clean or replace fuel screen (4).

To reassemble carburetor, reverse disassembly procedure. Check metering lever height as shown in Fig. HL47-2 using Walbro tool 500-13. Metering lever should just touch leg on tool. If tool is not available, the lever should be 1.52-1.78 mm (0.060-0.070 in.) below the mounting surface for diaphragm (26). Bend lever to obtain correct lever height.

Zama. To adjust carburetor, turn idle mixture screw (21—Fig. HL47-3) and high speed mixture screw (24) in until lightly seated, then turn each mixture

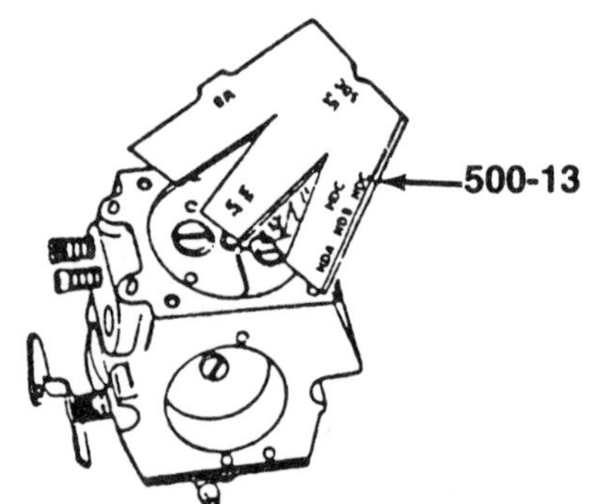

Fig. HL47-2—Metering lever should just touch leg of Walbro tool 500-13. Bend metering lever to obtain correct lever height.

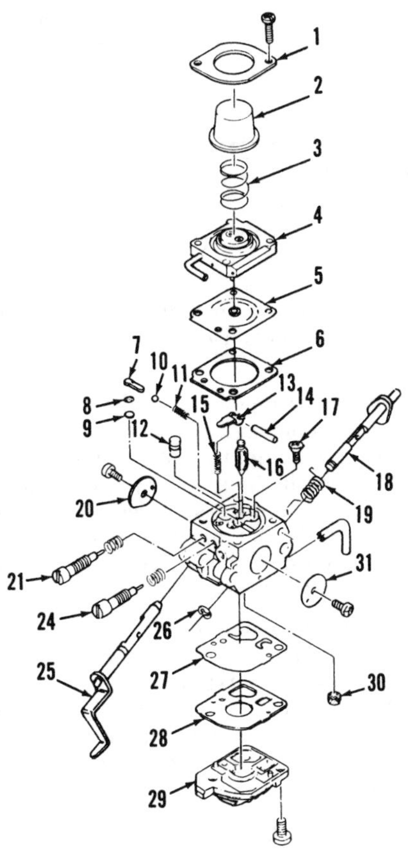

Fig. HL47-3—Exploded view of Zama C1Q carburetor typical of some models. Primer bulb (2) may not be used on all models.

1. Cover
2. Primer bulb
3. Spring
4. Cover
5. Metering diaphragm
6. Gasket
7. Welch plug
8. Retainer
9. Screw
10. Detent ball
11. Spring
12. Nozzle
13. Metering lever
14. Pin
15. Spring
16. Fuel inlet valve
17. Screw
18. Throttle shaft
19. Spring
20. Choke plate
21. Idle mixture screw
24. High speed mixture screw
25. Choke shaft
26. "E" ring
27. Fuel pump diaphragm
28. Gasket
29. Fuel inlet screen
30. Cover
31. Throttle plate

screw counterclockwise one turn open. Run engine until normal operating temperature is reached.

Adjust idle mixture screw so engine idles smoothly and accelerates without hesitation. Run engine at full throttle under load (trimmer line must be extended). Turn high speed mixture screw clockwise until highest engine speed is attained, then turn mixture screw counterclockwise 1/8 turn. Set idle speed screw so trimmer head or blade does not rotate when engine is idling.

To disassemble the carburetor, refer to Fig. HL47-3 and remove retainer (1) and cover (29) for access to internal components. Remove cover (4), diaphragms (5 and 27), metering lever (13), fuel inlet valve (16), retainer (8) and screen (9), nozzle (12) and fuel screen (30). Do not lose detent ball (10) when withdrawing choke shaft (25). To remove Welch plug (7), pierce the plug towards the end of the "tail" portion with a suitable punch. Do not insert punch too deeply as underlying body metal may be damaged. Apply suitable sealant to outer edge of new Welch plug.

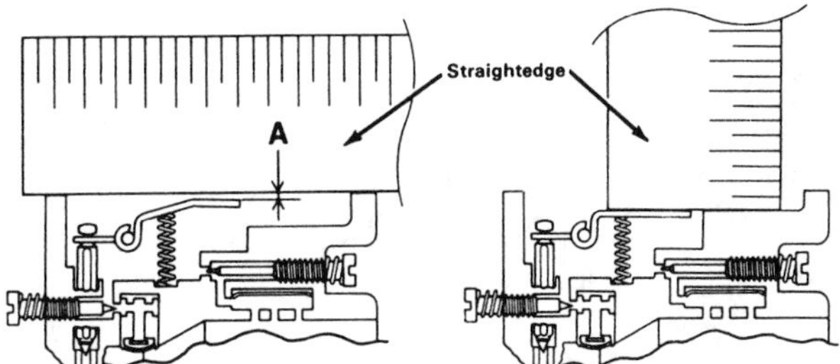

Fig. HL47-4—Compare shape of themetering lever with the illustration before checking the lver height. Stepped type lever shown on the left should be bent to height necessary to provide clearance (A) of 0.0.3 mm (0-0.012 in.). The straight type lever should be flush with chamber floor as shown on the right.

Clean and inspect all components. Do not use wire or drill bits to clean fuel passages as calibration of carburetor may be affected. Examine the fuel inlet valve (16), mixture screws (21 and 24) and their seats for wear or damage. Valve and mixture screws are renewable, but carburetor body must be replaced if seats are damaged or excessively worn.

Assemble the carburetor by reversing the disassembly procedure. Note the two tpyes of metering levers shown in Fig. HL47-4. Adjust clearance "A" for models with the bent lever to 0-0.03 mm (0-0.012 in.). Models with flat metering lever should be flush with the carburetor floor as shown in the right-side view. If necessary, bend the lever to change height.

IGNITION. A solid state ignition is used on all models. The ignition module is attached to the side of the engine cylinder. Ignition service is accomplished by replacing ignition components until the faulty component is located.

Air gap between ignition module and flywheel magnet is adjustable and should be 0.008-0.012 inch (0.2-0.3 mm). Loosen ignition module mounting screws and adjust module position to set air gap. Tighten ignition module retaining screws to 45-55 in.-lb. (5.1-6.2 N•m).

REPAIRS

TIGHTENING TORQUE VALUES. Recommended tightening torque values are as follows:

Carburetor	25-35 in.-lb. (2.8-3.9 N•m)
Clutch hub	150-200 in.-lb. (17-22.6 N•m)
Crankcase	60-80 in.-lb. (6.8-9.0 N•m)
Flywheel	200-250 in.-lb. (22.6-28.2 N•m)
Ignition module	45-55 in.-lb. (5.1-6.2 N•m)
Intake manifold	30-40 in.-lb. (3.4-4.5 N•m)
Spark plug	120-180 in.-lb. (13.6-20.3 N•m)

CYLINDER, PISTON, PIN AND RING. The cylinder (19—Fig. HL47-5) may be removed using the following procedure. Remove trimmer drive shaft and clutch unit from engine. Unbolt and remove starter housing (5), muffler shield (4), air shroud (1), fuel tank (2) and support pad (3). Remove muffler and carburetor from cylinder.

Insert starter rope or other suitable piston stop in cylinder to prevent crankshaft from turning. Remove flywheel nut and flywheel (14) from crankshaft. Remove flywheel shroud (13) and ignition module (20). Unscrew four screws in bottom of crankcase (10) and remove cylinder. Be careful when removing cylinder as crankshaft assembly will be loose in crankcase. Care should be taken not to damage mating surfaces of cylinder and crankcase.

Remove piston pin retaining rings (15). Push piston pin (16) out of piston (17) and separate piston from connecting rod.

The cylinder bore is chrome plated. Inspect cylinder bore and discard cylinder if chrome plating is worn away or if damaged. Cylinder can not be bored for oversize pistons.

The piston is equipped with a single piston ring (18). Oversize piston and ring are not available.

Piston is equipped with a piston ring locating pin in the piston ring groove. Install piston ring so end gap indexes with locating pin in ring groove.

To reassemble, reverse the disassembly procedure. Piston should be assembled to connecting rod so piston ring end gap faces intake port side of cylin-

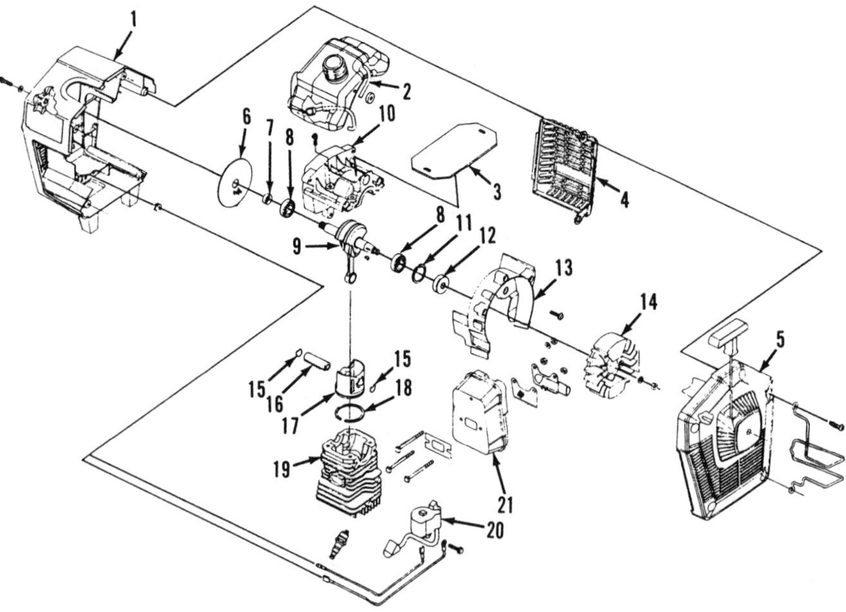

Fig. HL47-5—Exploded view of engine.

1. Shroud
2. Fuel tank
3. Plate
4. Muffler shield
5. Recoil starter housing
6. Crankcase plate
7. Seal
8. Bearing
9. Crankshaft & connecting rod assy.
10. Crankcase
11. Snap ring
12. Seal
13. Flywheel shroud
14. Flywheel
15. Retaining rings
16. Piston pin
17. Piston
18. Piston ring
19. Cylinder
20. Ignition module
21. Muffler

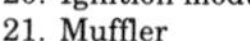

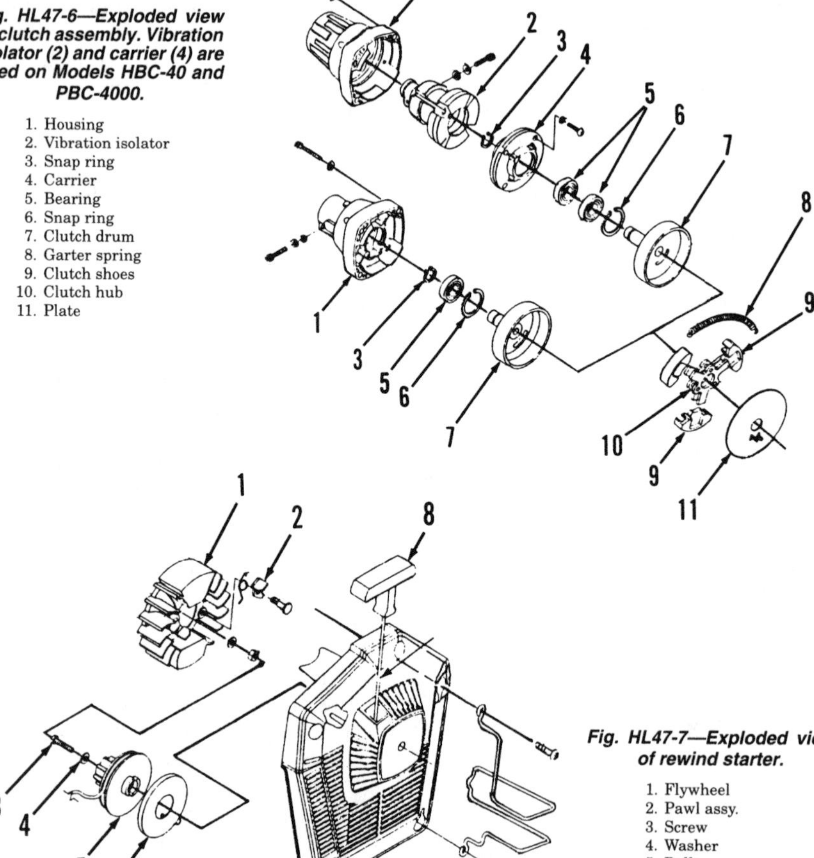

Fig. HL47-6—Exploded view of clutch assembly. Vibration isolator (2) and carrier (4) are used on Models HBC-40 and PBC-4000.

1. Housing
2. Vibration isolator
3. Snap ring
4. Carrier
5. Bearing
6. Snap ring
7. Clutch drum
8. Garter spring
9. Clutch shoes
10. Clutch hub
11. Plate

Fig. HL47-7—Exploded view of rewind starter.

1. Flywheel
2. Pawl assy.
3. Screw
4. Washer
5. Pulley
6. Rewind spring
7. Housing
8. Rope handle

der. Lightly lubricate cylinder and piston with engine oil before sliding cylinder over piston.

CONNECTING ROD, CRANKSHAFT AND CRANKCASE. Crankshaft assembly (9—Fig. HL47-5) is free after separating cylinder from crankcase as outlined in CYLINDER, PISTON, PIN AND RING section. Connecting rod, bearing and crankshaft are a unit assembly. Do not attempt to disassemble.

Inspect components and renew any that are damaged or excessively worn. When reassembling, install seals (7 and 12) with lip to inside. Cylinder and crankcase mating surfaces should be flat and free of nicks and scratches. Clean mating surfaces, then coat with a suitable sealer before assembly.

Bearings, seals and snap ring must be positioned correctly on crankshaft before final assembly. Snap ring (11—Fig. HL47-5) must engage groove in crankcase and cylinder. Tighten crankcase screws to 60-80 in.-lb. (6.8-9.0 N•m).

CLUTCH. Power is transmitted through the three-shoe clutch shown in Fig. HL47-6. To remove clutch drum (7), detach drive shaft and clutch housing (1) from engine. Detach snap ring (3). Separate clutch carrier (4) from housing. Reach through slot in clutch drum (7) and detach snap ring (6). Press clutch drum and bearing(s) out of housing or carrier.

Clutch shoes (9) are available only as a set. When assembling shoes, hook spring (8) ends together between any two shoes. Tighten clutch hub to 150-200 in.-lb. (17-22.6 N•m).

REWIND STARTER. To service rewind starter, remove starter housing (7—Fig. HL47-7). Pull starter rope and hold rope pulley with notch in pulley adjacent to rope outlet. Pull rope back through outlet so that it engages notch in pulley and allow pulley to completely unwind.

Unscrew pulley retaining screw (3) and remove rope pulley being careful not to dislodge rewind spring in housing. Wear appropriate eye protection and gloves before detaching rewind spring from housing as spring may uncoil uncontrolled.

Rewind spring is wound in counterclockwise direction in starter housing. Rope is wound on rope pulley in counerclockwise direction as viewed with pulley in housing.

To place tension on rewind spring, pass rope through outlet in housing and install rope handle. Pull rope out and hold rope pulley so notch on pulley is adjacent to rope outlet. Pull rope back through outlet between notch in pulley and housing. Turn rope pulley counterclockwise to place tension on spring. Pull rope out of notch, release pulley and allow rope to wind onto pulley.

Check starter action. Do not place more tension on rewind spring than is necessary to draw rope handle against housing.

HUSQVARNA

ENGINE SERVICE

Model	Bore	Stroke	Displacement
36	36 mm (1.42 in.)	32 mm (1.26 in.)	36 cc (2.20 cu. in.)
140	40 mm (1.57 in.)	32 mm (1.26 in.)	40 cc (2.44 cu. in.)
165	48 mm (1.89 in.)	36 mm (1.42 in.)	65 cc (3.96 cu. in.)
244	42 mm (1.65 in.)	32 mm (1.26 in.)	44 cc (2.68 cu. in.)
250	44 mm (1.73 in.)	32 mm (1.26 in.)	49 cc (3.0 cu. in.)

ENGINE INFORMATION

These engines are used on Husqvarna Series 36R, 140R, 165R, 165RX, 244R, 244RX and 250RX trimmers and brush cutters. Refer to adjoining Husqvarna engine sections for engine service information on other Husqvarna models.

MAINTENANCE

LUBRICATION. Engine lubrication is obtained by mixing gasoline with an oil designed for two-stroke, air-cooled engines. Refer to trimmer service section for manufacturer's recommended fuel:oil mixture ratio.

SPARK PLUG. Recommended spark plug is a Champion RCJ7Y or equivalent. Specified electrode gap for all models is 0.5 mm (0.020 in.).

CARBURETOR. All models are equipped with a Tillotson diaphragm-type carburetor (Figs. HQ101 and HQ102). Service and adjustment procedure is similar for both carburetors.

Initial adjustment of idle mixture screw (24) is one turn out from a lightly seated position. Initial adjustment of high-speed mixture screw (23) is $^3/_4$ turn out.

Final adjustments are made with trimmer line fully extended or blade assembly installed. Engine must be at operating temperature and running. Turn idle speed screw (11) in until trimmer head or blade just begins to rotate. Adjust idle mixture screw to obtain maximum idle speed, then turn idle mixture screw $^1/_6$ turn counterclockwise. Adjust idle speed screw until trimmer head or

Fig. HQ101—Exploded view of Tillotson carburetor used on some models.

1. Screw
2. Pump cover
3. Gasket
4. Fuel pump diaphragm
5. Welch plug
6. Screw
7. Clip
8. Body
9. Ball
10. Spring
11. Idle speed screw
12. Collar
13. Spring
14. Choke plate
15. Screw
16. Choke shaft
17. Spring
18. Throttle plate
19. Throttle shaft
20. Screw
21. Spring
22. Spring
23. High-speed mixture screw
24. Idle mixture screw
25. Screw
26. Pin
27. Gasket
28. Metering diaphragm
29. Cover
30. Screw
31. Metering lever
32. Fuel inlet valve
33. Spring
34. Welch plug
35. Welch plug
36. Retainer
37. Screen

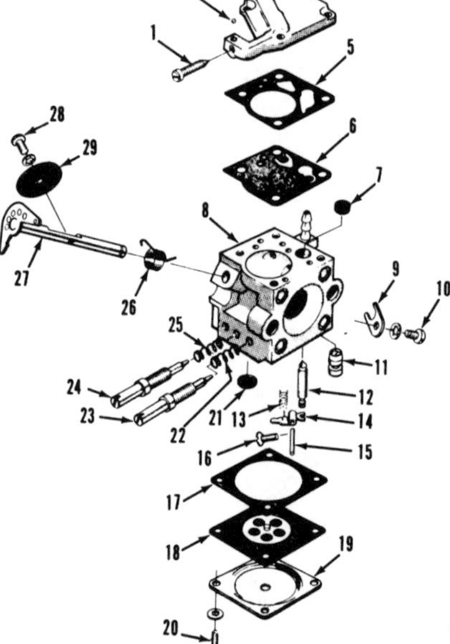

Fig. HQ102—Exploded view of Tillotson carburetor used on some models.

1. Idle speed screw
2. Ball
3. Screw
4. Pump cover
5. Gasket
6. Fuel pump diaphragm
7. Screen
8. Body
9. Clip
10. Screw
11. Check valve
12. Fuel inlet valve
13. Spring
14. Metering lever
15. Pin
16. Screw
17. Gasket
18. Metering diaphragm
19. Cover
20. Screw
21. Welch plug
22. Spring
23. High-speed mixture screw
24. Idle mixture screw
25. Spring
26. Spring
27. Throttle shaft
28. Screw
29. Throttle plate

Illustrations courtesy Husqvarna Forest & Garden

blade stops rotating (approximately 2500 rpm). Operate trimmer at full throttle and adjust high-speed mixture screw to obtain maximum engine rpm, then turn high-speed mixture 1/6 turn counterclockwise. Engine speed must not exceed 12,500 rpm.

Carburetor disassembly and reassembly is evident after inspection of carburetor and referral to Figs. HQ101 and HQ102. Clean and inspect all components. Wire or drill bits should not be used to clean passages as fuel flow may be altered if passages are enlarged. Inspect diaphragms for defects that may affect operation. Examine fuel inlet valve and seat. Inlet valve is renewable, but carburetor body must be renewed if seat is damaged or excessively worn.

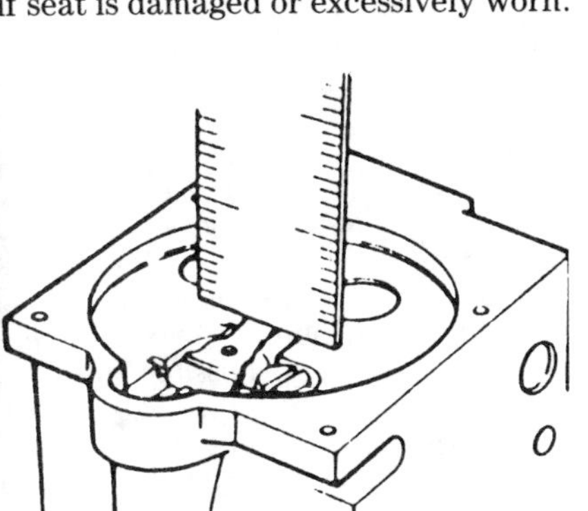

Fig. HQ103—Metering lever must be flush with carburetor body. Bend lever as needed.

Discard carburetor body if mixture screw seats are damaged or excessively worn. Screens should be clean. Be sure throttle plate fits shaft and carburetor bore properly. Apply Loctite to throttle plate retaining screws. Adjust metering lever height so metering lever tip is flush with body as shown in Fig. HQ103.

IGNITION SYSTEM. The engine is equipped with an electronic ignition system. Ignition system performance is considered satisfactory if a spark will jump across a 3 mm (1/8 in.) electrode gap on a test spark plug. If no spark is produced, check on/off switch, wiring and ignition module air gap. Air gap between ignition module and flywheel magnet should be 0.35-0.40 mm (0.014-0.016 in.). If switch, wiring and module air gap are satisfactory, but spark is not present, renew ignition module.

REPAIRS

CYLINDER, PISTON, PIN AND RINGS. The piston is accessible after removing cylinder. Remove piston pin retainers and use a suitable puller to extract pin from piston.

The piston is equipped with one piston ring. Ring rotation is prevented by a locating pin in each piston ring groove. Piston ring end gap should not exceed 0.6 mm (0.024 in.).

Piston and cylinder are coded by stamped letters on piston crown and top of cylinder. Code letters are "A," "B" and "C." Install piston in cylinder with a corresponding letter code.

Cylinder should be inspected and any aluminum transfer from piston (especially at exhaust port area) should be removed with fine emery cloth. Inspect cylinder for scoring or excessive wear and renew as necessary.

Lubricate piston and cylinder bore with oil prior to assembly. Install piston so arrow on piston crown points towards exhaust port. Be sure piston ring gaps are correctly indexed with locating pins in piston ring grooves when installing cylinder.

CRANKSHAFT, CONNECTING ROD AND CRANKCASE. Crankshaft, connecting rod and rod bearing are a unit assembly; individual components are not available. The crankshaft is supported by ball bearings at both ends. A renewable needle bearing is located in the small end of the connecting rod.

To remove crankshaft and connecting rod assembly, refer to Figs. HQ104 and HQ105. Remove cooling shroud, recoil starter assembly, muffler, carburetor

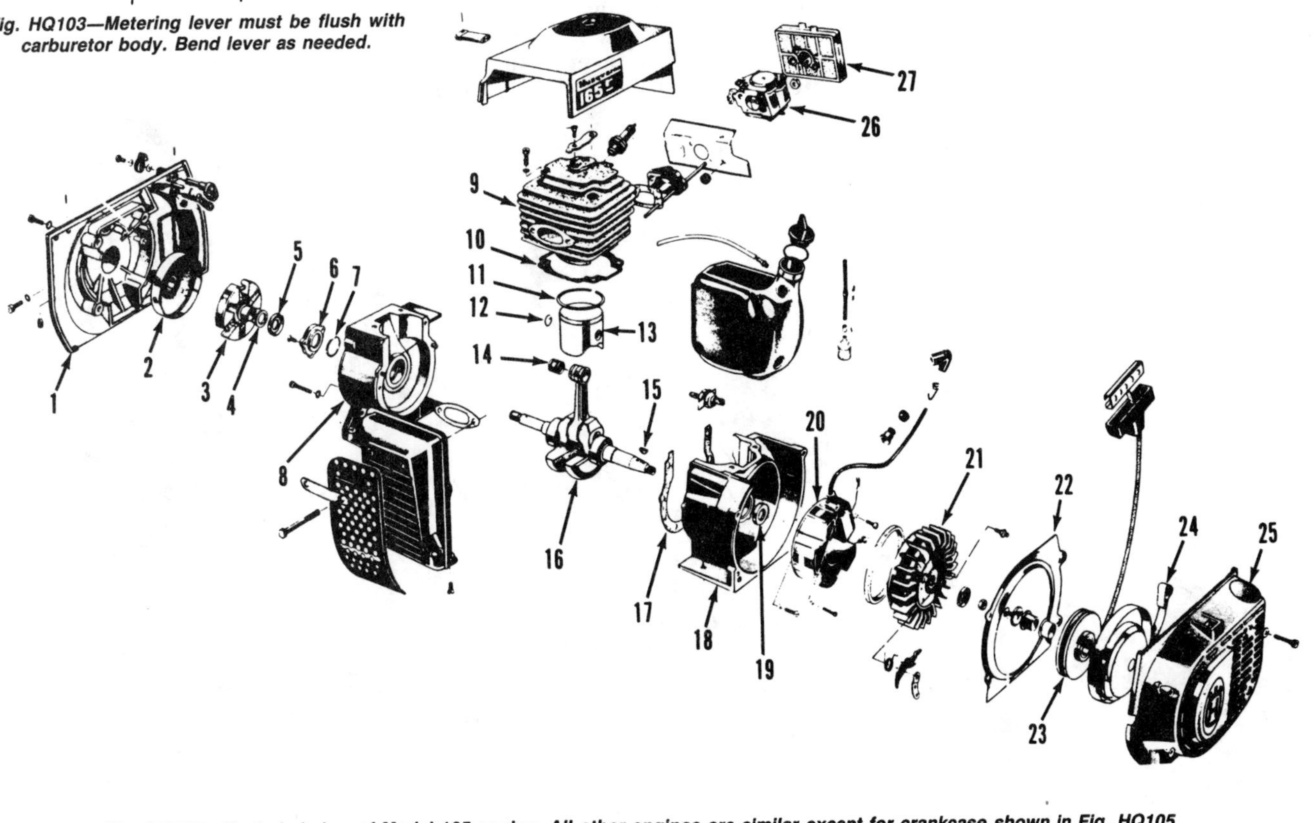

Fig. HQ104—Exploded view of Model 165 engine. All other engines are similar except for crankcase shown in Fig. HQ105.

1. Cover
2. Clutch drum
3. Clutch assy.
4. Shim
5. Seal
6. Seal plate
7. "O" ring
8. Crankcase half
9. Cylinder
10. Gasket
11. Piston ring
12. Retainer
13. Piston
14. Bearing
15. Key
16. Crankshaft assy.
17. Gasket
18. Crankcase half
19. Seal
20. Ignition system
21. Flywheel
22. Shroud
23. Pulley
24. Rewind spring
25. Cover
26. Carburetor
27. Air cleaner

Illustrations courtesy Husqvarna Forest & Garden

and flywheel. Remove centrifugal clutch assembly. Note that clutch hub assembly or clutch hub retaining nut has left-hand threads. Remove cylinder retaining bolts and carefully work cylinder away from crankcase and piston. Remove crankcase retaining bolts and carefully separate crankcase halves. Remove crankshaft and connecting rod assembly. It may be necessary to slightly heat crankcase halves to remove or install the ball bearing main bearings.

To reassemble engine, install ball bearings on crankshaft making certain they are seated against shoulders of crankshaft. Heat crankcase halves slightly and install crankshaft assembly making certain bearings seat completely in bearing bores. Tighten crankcase retaining bolts in a criss-cross pattern. Lubricate seals (5) and seal "O" ring (7) prior to installation.

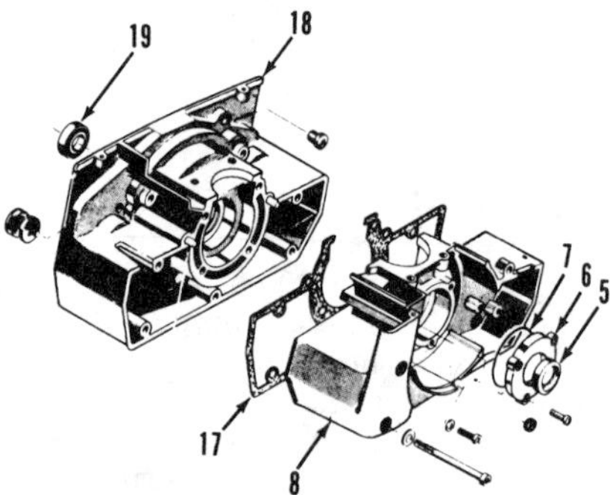

Fig. HQ105—Exploded view of crankcase assembly used on all engines except Model 165.

5. Seal
6. Seal plate
7. "O" ring
8. Crankcase half
17. Gasket
18. Crankcase half
19. Seal

CLUTCH. Refer to Figs. HQ106 or HQ107 for an exploded view of clutch. Clutch hub retaining nut (5—Fig. HQ106) has left-hand threads. On Model 165 engine, clutch hub (3—Fig. HQ107) has left-hand threads. Clutch hub, shoes and springs are available only as a unit assembly. Clutch drum bearings are not available separately, only with housing.

Early Model 140 engines were equipped with a clutch housing (1—Fig. HQ106) with a bearing bore to accept a 9 mm thick, 32 mm diameter bearing. Drive shaft used on these models has a 46 mm long shoulder that seats directly against bearing and requires no shim between bearing and drive shaft shoulder.

Late production engines are equipped with a 14 mm thick, 35 mm diameter bearing. Bearings on these models are retained in clutch housing (1) by a snap ring. The drive shaft used on these models has a 44 mm shoulder that the bearing seats against and a 2 mm shim is installed between the bearing and drive shaft shoulder. Do not attempt to interchange parts between early and late models.

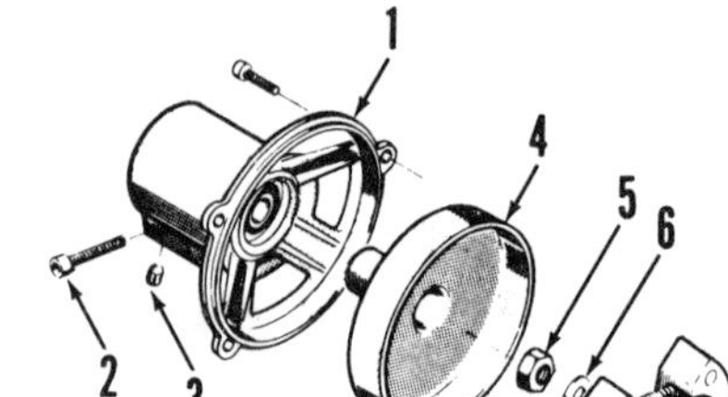

Fig. HQ106—Exploded view of clutch assembly used on all engines except Model 165.

1. Clutch housing
2. Clamp bolt
3. Locating screw
4. Clutch drum
5. Nut (L.H.)
6. Washer
7. Clutch assy.

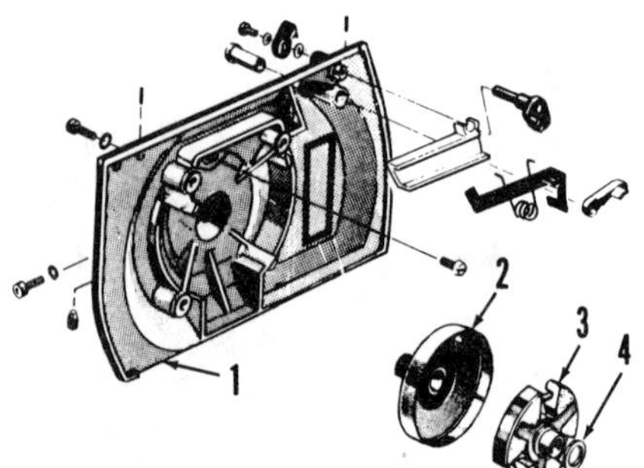

Fig. HQ107—Exploded view of clutch assembly used on Model 165 engine.

1. Cover
2. Clutch drum
3. Clutch assy.
4. Shim

REWIND STARTER. Refer to Figs. HQ108 or HQ109 for an exploded view of starter. To disassemble starter, detach starter housing from engine. Remove rope handle and allow rope to wind into starter. Unscrew center screw and remove rope pulley. Wear appropriate safety eyewear and gloves before detaching rewind spring from housing as spring may uncoil uncontrolled.

To assemble starter, lubricate center post of housing and spring side with light grease. Install rewind spring so coil windings are clockwise from outer end on Model 165 or counterclockwise on all other models. Assemble starter while passing rope through housing rope outlet and attach rope handle to rope. To place tension on starter rope, pull rope out of housing. Engage rope in notch on pulley and turn pulley two turns clockwise on Model 165 or counterclockwise on all other models to place tension on spring. Hold pulley and disengage rope from pulley notch. Release pulley and allow rope to wind on pulley. Check starter operation. Rope handle should be held against housing by spring tension, but it must be possible to rotate pulley at least an additional ½ turn when rope is pulled out fully.

It may be necessary to pull starter rope slightly as starter housing assembly is installed to engage flywheel starter pawls with pulley.

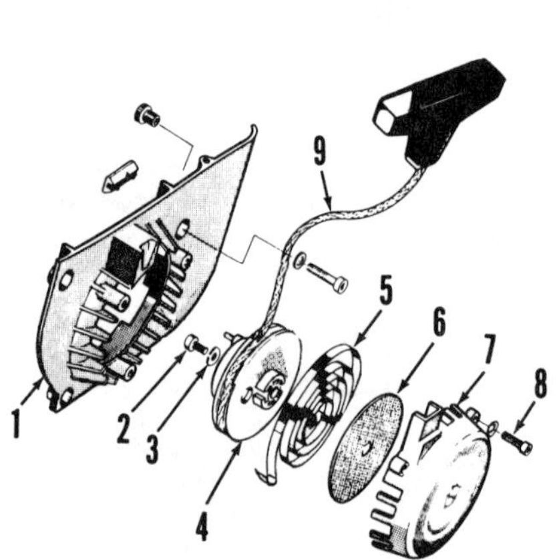

Fig. HQ108—Exploded view of rewind starter used on all engines except Model 165.

1. Cover
2. Screw
3. Washer
4. Pulley
5. Rewind spring
6. Plate
7. Housing
8. Screw
9. Rope

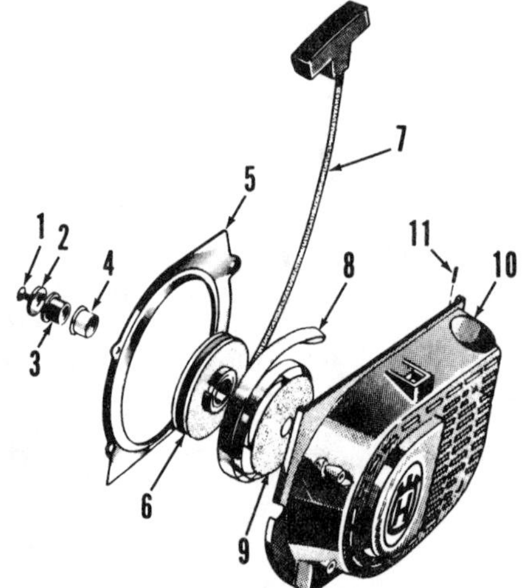

Fig. HQ109—Exploded view of rewind starter used on Model 165 engine.

1. Screw
2. Washer
3. Bearing
4. Bearing sleeve
5. Cover
6. Pulley
7. Rope
8. Rewind spring
9. Plate
10. Cover
11. Pin

Illustrations courtesy Husqvarna Forest & Garden

HUSQVARNA

ENGINE SERVICE

Model	Bore	Stroke	Displacement
18	28 mm (1.10 in.)	30 mm (1.18 in.)	18.5 cc (1.13 cu. in.)

ENGINE INFORMATION

This engine is used on Husqvarna Model 18RL trimmer. Refer to adjoining Husqvarna engine sections for engine service information on other Husqvarna models.

MAINTENANCE

LUBRICATION. Engine lubrication is obtained by mixing gasoline with an oil designed for two-stroke, air-cooled engines. Refer to trimmer service section for manufacturer's recommended fuel:oil mixture ratio.

SPARK PLUG. Recommended spark plug is a NGK BM6A or equivalent. Specified electrode gap for all models is 0.7 mm (0.028 in.).

CARBURETOR. The engine is equipped with a Walbro WT diaphragm-type carburetor. Refer to Fig. HQ201 for an exploded view of carburetor. Initial adjustment of idle mixture screw (13) and high-speed mixture screw (12) is one turn open. Final adjustment is performed with engine at normal operating temperature and cutter line at desired length. Turn idle speed screw (20) in until trimmer head or blade just begins to rotate. Adjust idle mixture screw so engine idles smoothly and accelerates cleanly without hesitation. Readjust idle speed screw so trimmer head or blade stops turning. Adjust high-speed mixture screw for best engine performance under load. Do not adjust high-speed mixture screw too lean as engine may be damaged.

Carburetor disassembly and reassembly is evident after inspection of carburetor and referral to Fig. HQ201. Clean and inspect all components. Inspect diaphragms (2 and 23) for defects that may affect operation. Examine fuel inlet valve and seat. Inlet valve (5) is renewable, but carburetor body must be renewed if seat is damaged or excessively worn. Discard carburetor body if mixture screw seats are damaged or excessively worn. Clean fuel screen (24).

Check metering lever height as shown in Fig. HQ202 using Walbro tool 500-13. Metering lever should just touch leg on tool. Bend lever to obtain correct lever height.

IGNITION SYSTEM. The engine is equipped with a breaker-point-type ignition system. The ignition condenser and breaker points are located behind the flywheel. To adjust breaker-point gap, the flywheel must be removed. Breaker-point gap should be 0.35 mm (0.014 in.). Points should be adjusted so points begin to open when match mark on flywheel aligns with "M" or "P" mark cast on crankcase.

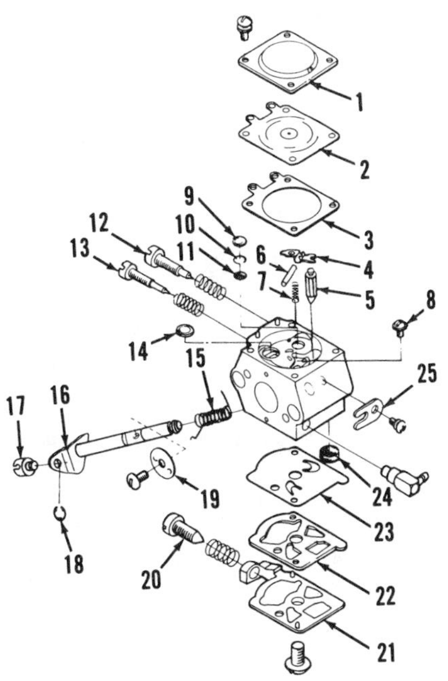

Fig. HQ201—Exploded view of Walbro WT carburetor.

1. Cover
2. Metering diaphragm
3. Gasket
4. Metering lever
5. Fuel inlet valve
6. Pin
7. Spring
8. Screw
9. Welch plug
10. Retainer
11. Screen
12. High-speed mixture screw
13. Idle mixture screw
14. Welch plug
15. Spring
16. Throttle shaft
17. Swivel
18. "E" ring
19. Throttle plate
20. Idle speed screw
21. Cover
22. Gasket
23. Fuel pump diaphragm
24. Fuel inlet screen
25. Retainer

REPAIRS

PISTON, PIN AND RINGS. The piston is equipped with two piston rings. Ring rotation is prevented by a locating pin in each piston ring groove.

Piston and rings are available only in standard diameter.

Install piston so arrow on piston crown points towards exhaust port. Be sure piston ring gaps are correctly indexed with locating pins in piston ring grooves when installing cylinder.

CYLINDER. The engine is equipped with a plated cylinder. Renew cylinder if bore is excessively worn, scored or otherwise damaged. Cylinder is available only in standard size.

CRANKSHAFT, CONNECTING ROD AND CRANKCASE. Crankshaft, connecting rod and rod bearing are a unit assembly; individual components are not available. The crankshaft is supported by ball bearings at both ends.

To remove crankshaft and connecting rod assembly (see Fig. HQ203), first disengage trimmer drive shaft from engine. Remove cooling shroud, recoil starter assembly, muffler, carburetor and flywheel. Remove centrifugal clutch assembly. Remove cylinder retaining bolts and work cylinder away from crankcase and piston. Remove crankcase retaining bolts and carefully separate crankcase halves. Remove crankshaft and connect-

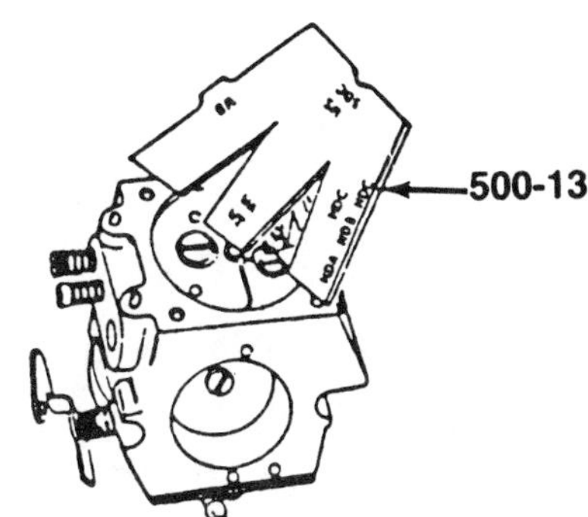

Fig. HQ202—Metering lever should just touch leg of Walbro tool 500-13. Bend lever to obtain correct lever height.

Illustrations courtesy Husqvarna Forest & Garden

ing rod assembly. It may be necessary to slightly heat crankcase halves to remove or install the ball bearing main bearings.

A renewable needle bearing is located in the small end of the connecting rod.

To install crankshaft, reverse removal procedure. Install seals with lip towards inside of crankcase.

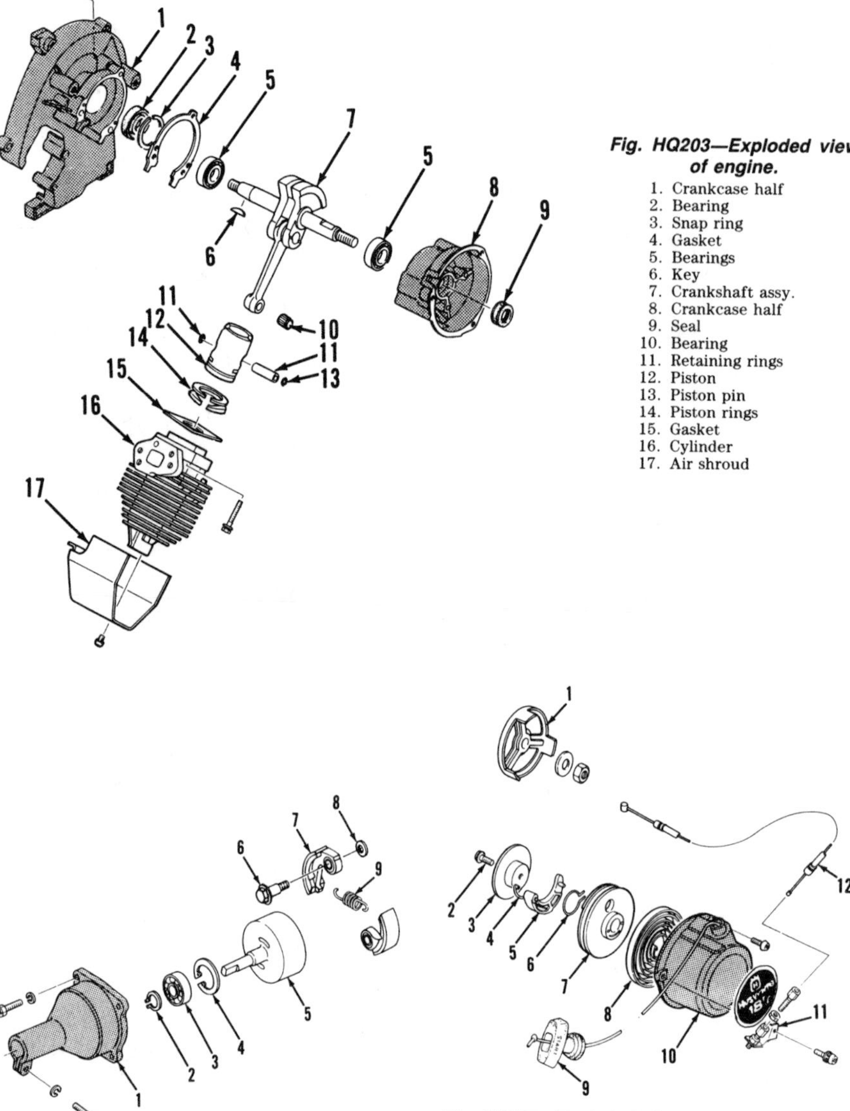

Fig. HQ203—Exploded view of engine.

1. Crankcase half
2. Bearing
3. Snap ring
4. Gasket
5. Bearings
6. Key
7. Crankshaft assy.
8. Crankcase half
9. Seal
10. Bearing
11. Retaining rings
12. Piston
13. Piston pin
14. Piston rings
15. Gasket
16. Cylinder
17. Air shroud

Fig. HQ204—Exploded view of clutch assembly.

1. Housing
2. Snap ring
3. Bearing
4. Snap ring
5. Clutch drum
6. Pivot screw
7. Clutch shoe
8. Washer
9. Spring

Fig. HQ205—Exploded view of rewind starter.

1. Plate
2. Screw
3. Friction washer
4. Spring
5. Pawl
6. Friction spring
7. Pulley
8. Rewind spring
9. Rope handle
10. Starter housing
11. Throttle cable bracket
12. Throttle cable

CLUTCH. The engine is equipped with a two-shoe clutch. The clutch shoe assembly is mounted on the flywheel. The clutch drum rides in the drive housing, which may be the fan housing on some engines.

To remove clutch drum, first unbolt and remove drive housing (1—Fig. HQ204) from engine. Reach through slot and detach snap ring (4), then press clutch drum (5) and bearing (3) out of housing. Heating housing will ease removal. Detach snap ring (2) and press clutch drum shaft out of bearing (3). Clutch shoes (7) are available only as a pair.

Reverse removal procedure to install clutch drum.

REWIND STARTER. Refer to Fig. HQ205 for an exploded view of starter. To disassemble starter, detach starter housing (10) from engine. Remove rope handle and allow rope to wind into starter. Unscrew center screw (2) and remove rope pulley (7). Wear appropriate safety eyewear and gloves before detaching rewind spring (8) from housing as spring may uncoil uncontrolled.

To assemble starter, lubricate center post of housing and spring side with light grease. Install rewind spring so coil windings are clockwise from outer end. Assemble starter while passing rope through housing rope outlet and attach rope handle to rope. To place tension on starter rope, pull rope out of housing. Engage rope in notch on pulley and turn pulley clockwise to place tension on spring. Hold pulley and disengage rope from pulley notch. Release pulley and allow rope to wind on pulley. Check starter operation. Rope handle should be held against housing by spring tension, but it must be possible to rotate pulley at least 1/2 turn clockwise when rope is pulled out fully.

HUSQVARNA

ENGINE SERVICE

Model	Bore	Stroke	Displacement
22	30 mm (1.18 in.)	30 mm (1.18 in.)	21.2 cc (1.29 cu. in.)
25	32 mm (1.26 in.)	30 mm (1.18 in.)	24.1 cc (1.47 cu. in.)
125	34 mm (1.34 in.)	28 mm (1.10 in.)	25.4 cc (1.55 cu. in.)
132	38 mm (1.50 in.)	28 mm (1.10 in.)	31.8 cc (1.94 cu. in.)

ENGINE INFORMATION

These engines are used on Husqvar-a Series 22, 25, 125 and 132 trimmers nd brush cutters. Refer to adjoining usqvarna engine sections for engine ervice information on other Husqvar-a models.

MAINTENANCE

LUBRICATION. Engine lubrication is btained by mixing gasoline with an oil esigned for two-stroke, air-cooled en-ines. Refer to trimmer service section or manufacturer's recommended uel:oil mixture ratio.

SPARK PLUG. Recommended spark lug is a NGK BM6A or equivalent on Iodel 22 and 25 engines, or a NGK BPM6Y on Model 125 and 132 engines. pecified electrode gap for all models is .6-0.7 mm (0.024-0.028 in.).

CARBURETOR. Later Model 22 and 5 engines are equipped with a Walbro VY diaphragm carburetor and Model 25 and 132 engines are equipped with Walbro WYK diaphragm carburetor. Early Model 22 and 25 engines are equipped with a slide-valve-type carbu-etor. Refer to following sections for service information.

Walbro WY and WYK. Both carbure-ors use a barrel-type throttle rather han a throttle plate. Idle fuel for the arburetor flows up into the throttle barrel where it is fed into the air stream. On some models, the idle fuel flow can be adjusted by turning an idle mixture limiter plate (P—Fig. HQ301). Initial set-ting is in center notch. Rotating the plate clockwise will lean the idle mix-ture. Inside the limiter plate is an idle mixture needle (N—Fig. HQ302) that is preset at the factory (a plug covers the needle). If removed, use the following procedure to determine correct posi-tion. Back out needle (N) until un-screwed. Screw in needle five turns on Model WY or 15 turns on Model WYK. Rotate idle mixture plate (P—Fig. HQ301) to center notch. Run engine un-til normal operating temperature is at-tained. Adjust idle speed screw (I) so en-gine idles at 3000 rpm. Rotate idle mixture needle (N—Fig. HQ302) and ob-tain highest rpm (turning needle clock-wise leans the mixture), then turn nee-dle ¹/₄ turn counterclockwise. Readjust idle speed screw. Note that idle mixture limiter plate and needle are available only as an assembly with throttle barrel.

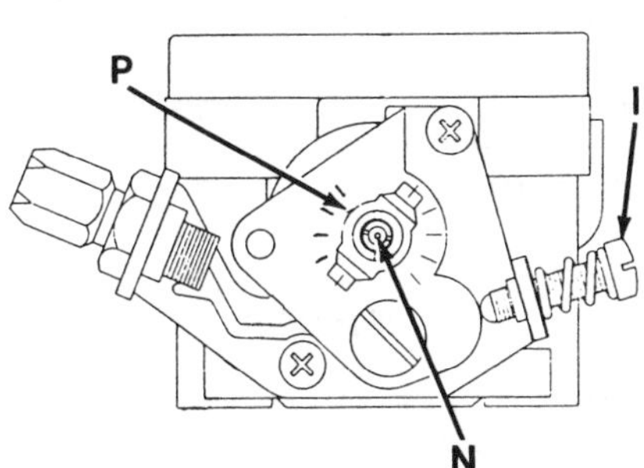

Fig. HQ301—On Walbro WY and WYK carburetors, idle speed screw is located at (I), idle mixture limiter plate is located at (P) and idle mixture nee-dle is located at (N). A plug covers the idle mix-ture needle.

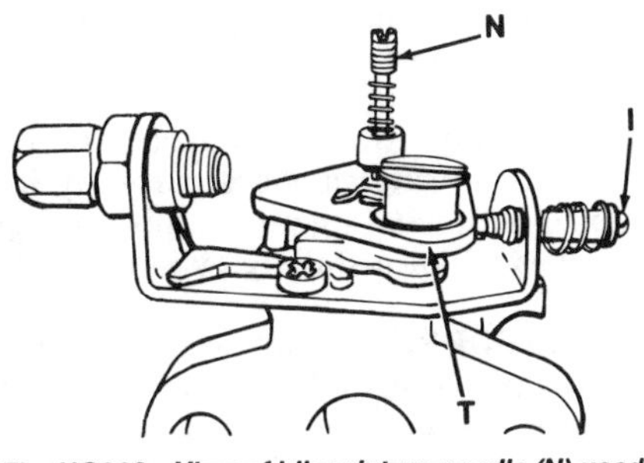

Fig. HQ302—View of idle mixture needle (N) used on Walbro WY and WYK carburetors.

High-speed mixture is controlled by a fixed main jet (20—Fig. HQ303).

To overhaul carburetor, refer to ex-ploded view in Fig. HQ303 and note the

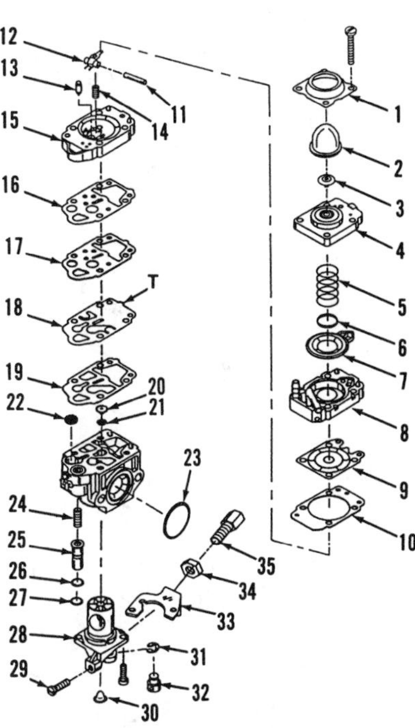

Fig. HQ303—Exploded view of Walbro WYK. Mod-el WY is similar.

1. Cover
2. Primer bulb
3. Check valve
4. Plate
5. Spring
6. Retainer
7. Start diaphragm
8. Start diaphragm body
9. Metering diaphragm
10. Gasket
11. Pin
12. Metering lever
13. Fuel inlet valve
14. Spring
15. Fuel pump body
16. Gasket
17. Fuel pump plate
18. Fuel pump diaphragm
19. Gasket
20. Main jet
21. "O" ring
22. Fuel screen
23. "O" ring
24. Spring
25. Start valve
26. "O" ring
27. "O" ring
28. Throttle barrel assy.
29. Idle speed screw
30. Plug
31. "E" ring
32. Swivel
33. Bracket
34. Nut
35. Adjuster

Illustrations courtesy Husqvarna Forest & Garden

following: On models with a plastic body, clean only with solvents approved for use with plastic. Do not use wire or drill bits to clean fuel passages. Do not disassemble throttle barrel assembly. Examine fuel inlet valve and seat. Inlet valve (13) is renewable, but fuel pump body (15) must be renewed if seat is excessively worn or damaged. Clean fuel screen (22). Inspect diaphragms for tears and other damage. When installing plates and gaskets (16 through 19), note that tabs (T) on ends will "stair-step" when correctly installed. Adjust metering lever height to obtain 1.5 mm (0.059 in.) between carburetor body surface and lever as shown in Fig. HQ304.

Slide-Valve Type Carburetor. The carburetor used on early Model 22 and

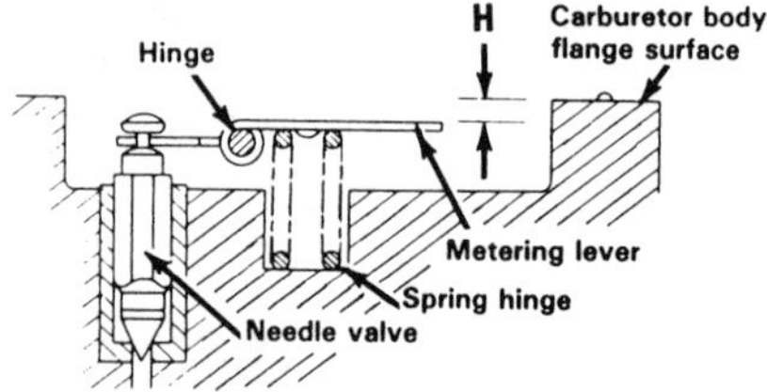

Fig. HQ304—Metering lever height (H) must be 1.5 mm (0.059 in.) on Walbro WY and WYK carburetors.

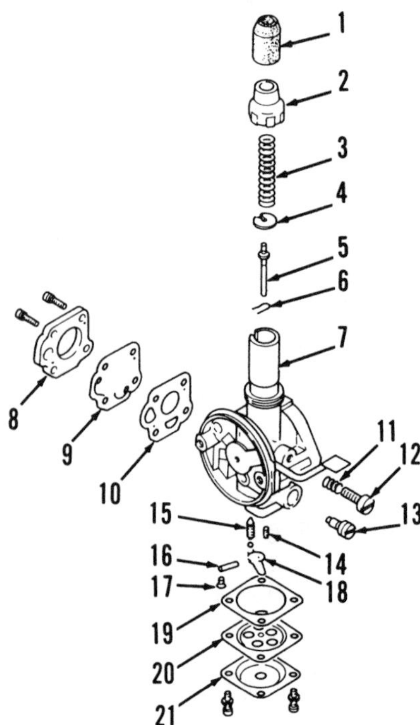

Fig. HQ305—Exploded view of slide-valve-type carburetor used on early Models 22 and 25.

1. Boot
2. Cap
3. Spring
4. Retainer
5. Jet needle
6. Clip
7. Throttle slide
8. Cover
9. Fuel pump diaphragm
10. Gasket
11. Spring
12. Idle speed screw
13. Mixture screw
14. Spring
15. Fuel inlet valve
16. Pin
17. Screw
18. Metering lever
19. Gasket
20. Metering diaphragm
21. Cover

25 engines is a diaphragm-type carburetor with a slide-valve-type throttle rather than a throttle plate. The carburetor has an integral fuel pump.

Fuel mixture is adjusted by turning mixture screw (13—Fig. HQ305). Midrange mixture is determined by the position of the clip (6) on jet needle (5). Normal position of clip is in the middle groove. The mixture will be leaner if clip is installed in the top groove, or richer if clip is installed in the bottom groove.

Before removing carburetor from engine, unscrew cap (2) and withdraw throttle slide (7) assembly. When overhauling carburetor, refer to Fig. HQ305 and note the following: Examine fuel inlet valve and seat. Inlet valve (15) is renewable, but carburetor body must be renewed if seat is excessively worn or damaged. Inspect mixture screw and seat. Renew carburetor body if seat is excessively worn or damaged. Inspect diaphragms for tears and other damage. When installing throttle slide (7), be sure groove in side of throttle slide indexes with pin in bore of carburetor body.

IGNITION SYSTEM. The engine is equipped with an electronic ignition system. All later models are equipped with a one-piece ignition module that includes the ignition coil. Early Models 22 and 25 are equipped with a two-piece ignition system.

The ignition system is considered satisfactory if a spark will jump across the 3 mm (1/8 in.) gap of a test spark plug. If no spark is produced, check on/off switch, wiring and ignition module/coil air gap. Air gap between ignition module/coil and flywheel magnet should be 0.3 mm (0.012 in.).

REPAIRS

PISTON, PIN AND RINGS. The piston is accessible after removing cylinder. Remove piston pin retainers and use a suitable puller to extract pin from piston.

The piston is equipped with two piston rings. Ring rotation is prevented by a locating pin in each piston ring groove.

Piston and rings are available only in standard diameter.

Install piston so arrow on piston crown points toward exhaust port. Be sure piston ring gaps are correctly indexed with locating pins in piston ring grooves when installing cylinder.

CYLINDER. The engine is equipped with a plated cylinder. Renew cylinder if bore is excessively worn, scored or otherwise damaged. Cylinder is available only in standard size.

CRANKSHAFT, CONNECTING RO AND CRANKCASE. Crankshaft, co necting rod and rod bearing are a un assembly; individual components a not available. The crankshaft is suppor ed by ball bearings at both ends. renewable needle bearing is located i the small end of the connecting rod.

To remove crankshaft and connecti rod assembly (see Fig. HQ306), sep rate engine from trimmer drive sha Remove cooling shroud, flywheel hou ing, recoil starter assembly, muffle carburetor and fuel tank. Remove nu retaining flywheel and recoil start pawl carrier to crankshaft and remov flywheel and pawl carrier. Remove cy inder mounting screws and work cyli der off crankcase and piston. Remov crankcase retaining bolts and separa crankcase halves. Remove cranksha and connecting rod asssembly. He crankcase if necessary to aid removal main bearings.

To reassemble engine, reverse disa sembly procedure. Install seals (14 an 18) with lip toward inside of crankcas

CLUTCH. The upper end of the driv shaft is threaded into the clutch drun hub on early models. To service clutch detach drive housing (4—Fig. HQ307 from engine. Clutch shoes (9) are avail able only as a set.

To service clutch drum (7), remov gear head from drive shaft housing. De tach drive shaft housing tube from driv housing (1). To remove clutch drum o models with a threaded drive shaft, in sert a tool through slot of clutch drun so it cannot rotate, then turn square en (trimmer end) of drive shaft so drum un screws from drive shaft. On models wit a removable drive shaft, reach throug slot in clutch drum and detach snap rin (6). If necessary, remove bearings (5 from housing.

REWIND STARTER. Refer to Figs HQ308 or HQ309 for an exploded view of starter. To disassemble starter, detach starter housing (9) from engine. Remove rope handle and allow rope to wind into starter. Unscrew center screw (5) and remove rope pulley (7). Wear appropriate safety eyewear and gloves before detaching rewind spring (8) from housing as spring may uncoil uncontrolled.

To assemble starter, lubricate center post of housing and spring side with light grease. Install rewind spring so coil windings are clockwise from outer end on Models 22 and 25 or counterclockwise on Models 125 and 132. Assemble starter while passing rope through housing rope outlet and attach rope handle to rope. To place tension on starter rope, pull rope out of housing. Engage rope in notch on pulley and turn pulley

Illustrations courtesy Husqvarna Forest & Garden

o place tension in spring. Hold pulley nd disengage rope from pulley notch. elease pulley and allow rope to wind n pulley. Check starter operation. Rope handle should be held against housing by spring tension, but it must be possible to rotate pulley an additional $^1/_2$ turn when rope is pulled out fully.

ig. HQ306—Exploded view of engine. Model 125 and 132 engines are equipped with a nap ring in crankcase half (16) to locate bearing (12).

1. Muffler
2. Cylinder
3. Spacer block
4. Carburetor
5. Gasket
6. Piston rings
7. Piston
8. Piston pin
9. Retaining ring
10. Needle bearing
11. Crankshaft & connecting rod assy.
12. Bearings
13. Crankcase half
14. Seal
15. Dowel pin
16. Crankcase half
17. Flywheel
18. Seal
19. Nut
20. Flywheel housing

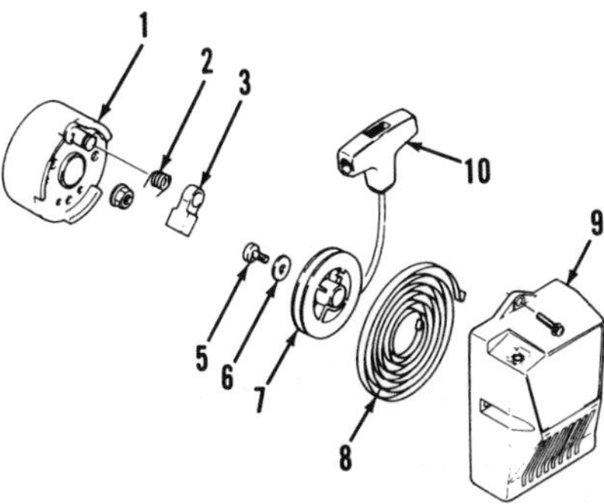

Fig. HQ308—Exploded view of rewind starter used on Models 22 and 25.

1. Pawl carrier
2. Spring
3. Pawl
5. Screw
6. Washer
7. Pulley
8. Rewind spring
9. Starter housing
10. Rope handle

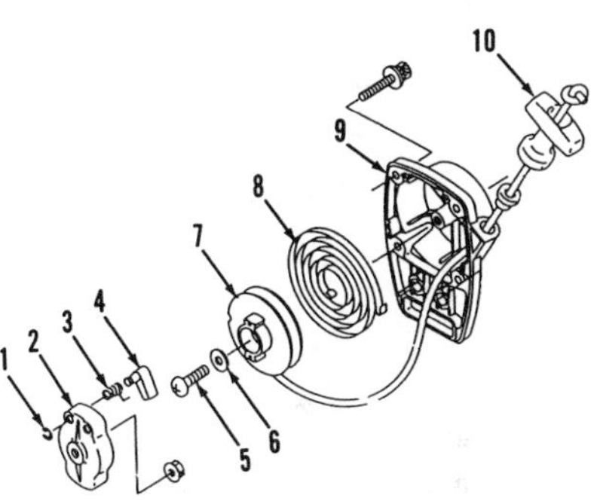

Fig. HQ309—Exploded view of rewind starter used on Models 125 and 132.

1. "E" ring
2. Pawl carrier
3. Spring
4. Pawl
5. Screw
6. Washer
7. Pulley
8. Rewind spring
9. Starter housing
10. Rope handle

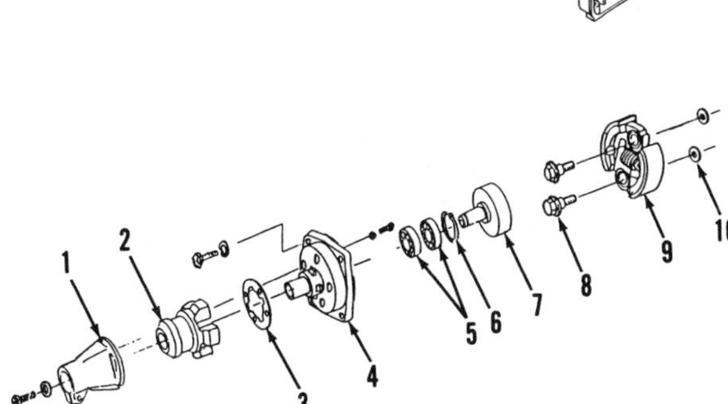

ig. HQ307—Exploded view of clutch. Drive housing assembly (1, 2, 3 and 4) is one piece on some models.

1. Housing
2. Vibration isolator
3. Plate
4. Housing
5. Bearings
6. Snap ring
7. Clutch drum
8. Pivot screw
9. Clutch assy.
10. Washer

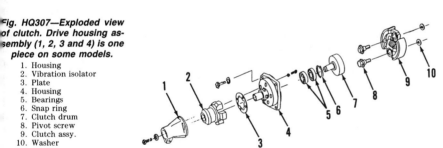

Illustrations courtesy Husqvarna Forest & Garden

HUSQVARNA

ENGINE SERVICE

Model	Bore	Stroke	Displacement
26	....	....	26 cc (1.29 cu. in.)
32	....	....	32 cc (1.95 cu. in.)

ENGINE INFORMATION

These engines are used on Husqvarna Model 26LC, 26RLC, 32LC, 32R, 32RL and 32RLC trimmers. Refer to adjoining Husqvarna engine sections for engine service information on other Husqvarna models.

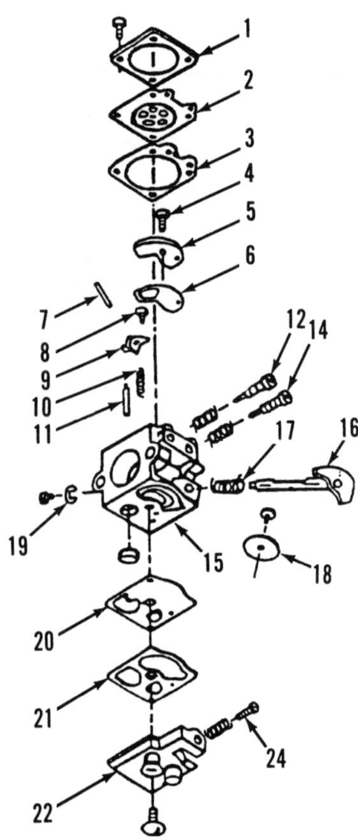

Fig. HQ401—Exploded view of Walbro WA carburetor.

1. Cover
2. Metering diaphragm
3. Gasket
4. Screw
5. Circuit plate
6. Gasket
7. Pin
8. Screw
9. Metering lever
10. Spring
11. Fuel inlet valve
12. High-speed mixture screw
14. Idle mixture screw
15. Carburetor body
16. Throttle shaft
17. Spring
18. Throttle plate
19. "E" ring
20. Screen
21. Fuel pump diaphragm
22. Gasket
23. Cover
24. Idle speed screw

MAINTENANCE

LUBRICATION. Engine lubrication is obtained by mixing gasoline with an oil designed for two-stroke, air-cooled engines. Refer to trimmer service section for manufacturer's recommended fuel:oil mixture ratio.

SPARK PLUG. Recommended spark plug is a Champion CJ14 or equivalent. Specified electrode gap for all models is 0.63 mm (0.025 in.).

CARBURETOR. The engine is equipped with a Walbro WA diaphragm-type carburetor. Initial adjustment of idle and high-speed mixture screws is one turn out from a lightly seated position. Final adjustments are performed with trimmer line at recommended length or blade installed. Engine must be at operating temperature and running. Adjust idle speed screw (24—Fig. HQ401) so trimmer head or blade does not rotate (approximately 3000 rpm). Adjust idle mixture screw (14) so engine idles smoothly and accelerates without hesitation. Readjust idle speed as necessary. Operate unit at full throttle and adjust high-speed mixture screw (12) to obtain maximum engine rpm, then turn high-speed mixture screw $^1/_6$ turn counterclockwise. Do not adjust high-speed mixture too lean as engine may be damaged.

When overhauling carburetor, refer to exploded view in Fig. HQ401. Examine fuel inlet valve and seat. Inlet valve (11) is renewable, but carburetor body must be renewed if seat is excessively worn or damaged. Inspect mixture screws and seats. Renew carburetor body if seats are excessively worn or damaged. Clean fuel screen (20). Inspect diaphragms for tears and other damage.

Check metering lever height as shown in Fig. HQ402. Metering lever should be flush with circuit plate. Bend lever to obtain correct lever height.

IGNITION SYSTEM. The engine is equipped with an electronic ignition system. Ignition system performance i considered satisfactory if a spark wi jump across a 3 mm ($^1/_8$ in.) electrode ga on a test spark plug. If no spark is prc duced, check on/off switch, wiring an ignition module air gap. Air gap be tween ignition module and flywhee magnet should be 0.25-0.36 mm (0.010 0.014 in.). If switch, wiring and modul air gap are satisfactory, but spark is nc present, renew ignition module.

REPAIRS

PISTON, PIN AND RING. The pisto (7—Fig. HQ403) is accessible afte removing cylinder (10). Remove pisto pin retainers (5) and use a suitabl puller to extract pin (6) from piston.

The piston is equipped with a singl piston ring (8). Ring rotation is prevent ed by a locating pin in the piston rin groove. Piston is available in standar size only.

Be sure piston ring end gap is correct ly indexed with locating pin in pisto ring groove when installing cylinder.

CYLINDER. The cylinder is availabl in standard size only. Renew cylinder i damaged or excessively worn.

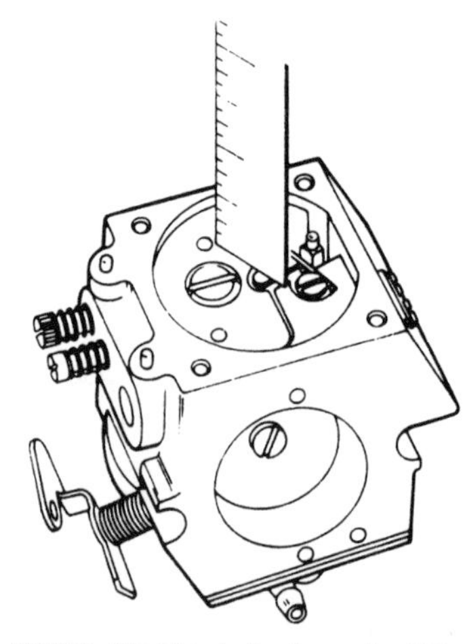

Fig. HQ402—Tip of metering lever should be flush with circuit plate. Bend metering lever as needed.

Illustrations courtesy Husqvarna Forest & Garde

CRANKSHAFT AND CONNECTING ROD. The crankshaft (13—Fig. HQ403) is supported at flywheel end only by two ball bearings (15 and 18). The stamped steel connecting rod (11) has a caged roller bearing at both ends. Connecting rod and bearings are serviced only as an assembly.

To remove crankshaft and connecting rod, first separate engine from trimmer drive shaft housing. Remove clutch housing, recoil starter assembly, flywheel housing, muffler and carburetor. Remove spark plug and place a piston locking tool or end of a rope in spark plug hole to lock piston and connecting rod. Remove flywheel nut and withdraw flywheel from crankshaft. Remove fuel tank and crankcase shroud assembly (1). Remove cylinder retaining screws and work cylinder off crankcase and piston. Remove connecting rod (11) from crankpin. Detach snap ring (19) and carefully press crankshaft out of bearings. Drive or press bearings out of crankcase, remove snap rings (16) and remove seal (17).

When reinstalling crankshaft, install seal (17) in bearing bore of crankcase so cupped side of seal is toward inside of crankcase. Outer main bearing (18) has a single shielded side that must be out toward flywheel side of engine after installation. Press bearings (15 and 18) in until seated against snap rings. Install spacer (14) on crankshaft main bearing journal and press crankshaft into main bearings.

REED VALVE. A reed valve (3—Fig. HQ403) is located on the inner face of the crankcase cover. Inspect reed petal and discard if torn, broken, creased or otherwise damaged.

CLUTCH. The engine is equipped with a two-shoe clutch (10—Fig. HQ404). Clutch hub, shoes and spring are available only as a unit assembly. The clutch drum is contained in housing (13). Drum and housing are available only as a unit assembly.

REWIND STARTER. Refer to Fig. HQ404 for an exploded view of rewind starter. To disassemble starter, detach clutch housing (13) and starter housing (8) from engine. Remove rope handle (14) and allow rope to wind into starter. Unscrew pulley retainer (7) and remove rope pulley (5). Wear appropriate safety eyewear and gloves before detaching rewind spring (6) from housing as spring may uncoil uncontrolled.

To assemble starter, lubricate center post of housing and spring side with light grease. Install rewind spring so coil windings are clockwise from outer end. Rope length should be 107 cm (42 in.). Assemble starter while passing rope through housing rope outlet and attach rope handle to rope. To place tension on starter rope, pull rope out of housing. Engage rope in notch on pulley and turn pulley clockwise to place tension on rewind spring. Hold pulley and disengage rope from pulley notch. Release pulley and allow rope to wind on pulley. Check starter operation. Rope handle should be held against housing by spring tension, but it must be possible to rotate pulley at least $^{1}/_{4}$ turn clockwise when rope is pulled out fully.

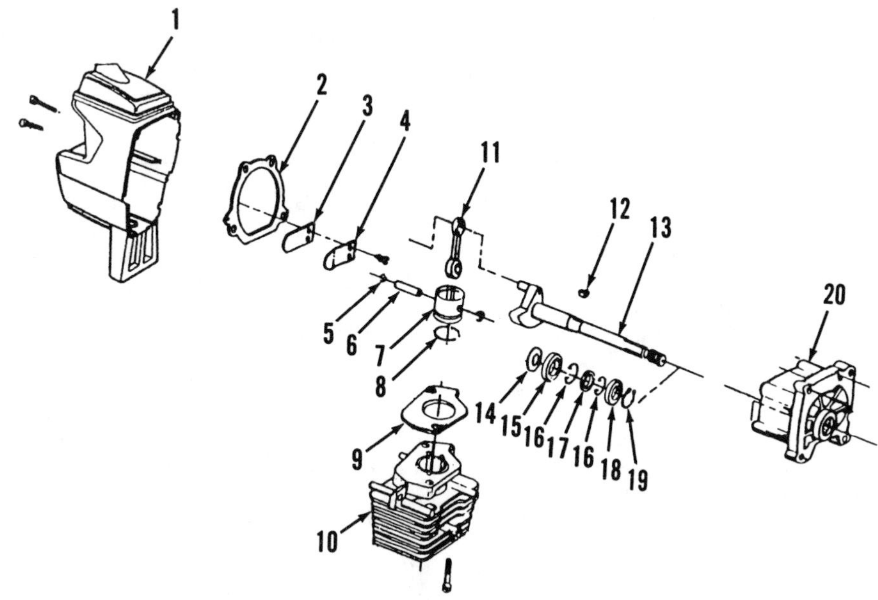

Fig. HQ403—Exploded view of engine.

1. Cover
2. Gasket
3. Reed petal
4. Backup plate
5. Retaining ring
6. Piston pin
7. Piston
8. Piston ring
9. Gasket
10. Cylinder
11. Connecting rod
12. Key
13. Crankshaft
14. Spacer
15. Bearing
16. Snap ring
17. Seal
18. Bearing
19. Snap ring
20. Crankcase

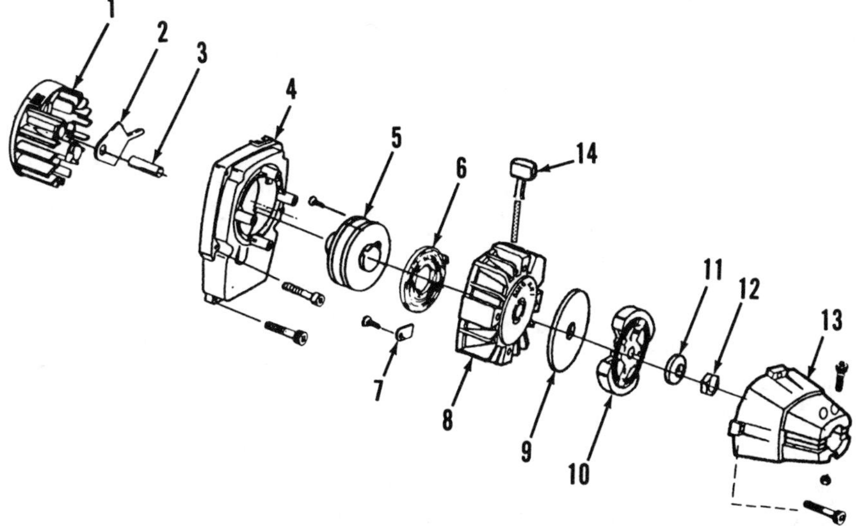

Fig. HQ404—Exploded view of clutch and rewind starter assemblies. Counterweight (2) is not used on all models.

1. Flywheel
2. Counterweight
3. Spacer
4. Shroud
5. Pulley
6. Rewind spring
7. Retainer
8. Starter housing
9. Plate
10. Clutch assy.
11. Belleville washer
12. Nut
13. Housing
14. Rope handle

HUSQVARNA

ENGINE SERVICE

Model	Bore	Stroke	Displacement
39	40 mm (1.57 in.)	32 mm (1.26 in.)	40 cc (2.4 cu. in.)
240	42 mm (1.65 in.)	32 mm (1.26 in.)	44 cc (2.7 cu. in.)
245	42 mm (1.65 in.)	32 mm (1.26 in.)	44 cc (2.7 cu. in.)

ENGINE INFORMATION

These engines are used on Husqvarna Model 39R, 240R, 245R and 245RX trimmers and brush cutters. Refer to adjoining Husqvarna engine sections for engine service information on other Husqvarna models.

MAINTENANCE

LUBRICATION. Engine lubrication is obtained by mixing gasoline with an oil designed for two-stroke, air-cooled engines. Refer to trimmer service section for manufacturer's recommended fuel:oil mixture ratio.

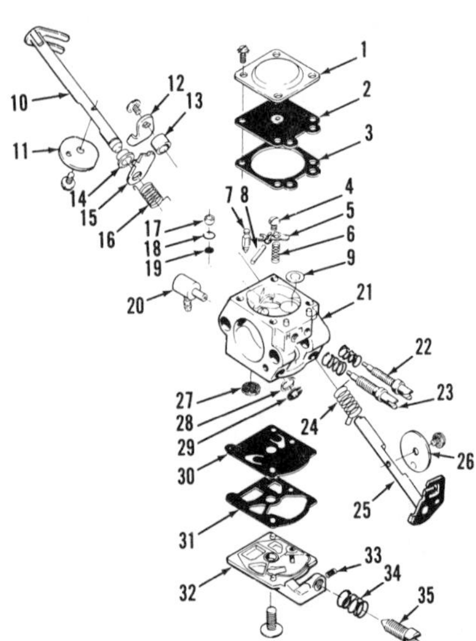

Fig. HQ501—Exploded view of typical Walbro WT carburetor.

1. Cover
2. Metering diaphragm
3. Gasket
4. Screw
5. Metering lever
6. Spring
7. Fuel inlet valve
8. Pin
9. Welch plug
10. Choke shaft
11. Choke plate
12. Arm
13. Spacer
14. Spacer
15. Lever
16. Spring
17. Welch plug
18. Retainer
19. Screen
20. Fuel fitting
21. Carburetor body
22. Idle mixture screw
23. High-speed mixture screw
24. Spring
25. Throttle shaft
26. Throttle plate
27. Fuel inlet screen
28. Washer
29. "E" ring
30. Fuel pump diaphragm
31. Gasket
32. Cover
33. Screw
34. Spring
35. Idle speed screw

SPARK PLUG. Recommended spark plug is a Champion RCJ7Y or equivalent. Specified electrode gap for all models is 0.5 mm (0.020 in.).

CARBURETOR. All models are equipped with a Walbro WT diaphragm carburetor. Initial adjustment of idle mixture screw (22—Fig. HQ501) and high-speed mixture screw (23) is one turn out from a lightly seated position. Final adjustments are performed with trimmer line at recommended length or blade installed. Engine must be at operating temperature and running. Adjust idle speed screw (35) to approximately 2500 rpm (trimmer head or blade should not rotate). Adjust idle mixture screw so engine runs at maximum idle speed and accelerates without hesitation. Readjust idle speed. Operate unit at full throttle and adjust high-speed mixture screw to obtain maximum engine rpm, then turn counterclockwise until engine starts to four-cycle. Engine speed must not exceed 12,500 rpm.

Carburetor disassembly and reassembly is evident after inspection of carburetor and referral to Fig. HQ501. Clean and inspect all components. Inspect diaphragms (2 and 30) for defects that may affect operation. Examine fuel inlet valve and seat. Inlet valve (7) is renewable, but carburetor body (21) must be renewed if seat is damaged or excessively worn. Discard carburetor body if mixture screw seats are damaged or excessively worn. Clean fuel screen (27).

Check metering lever height as shown in Fig. HQ502 using Walbro tool 500-13. Metering lever should just touch leg on tool. Bend lever to obtain correct lever height.

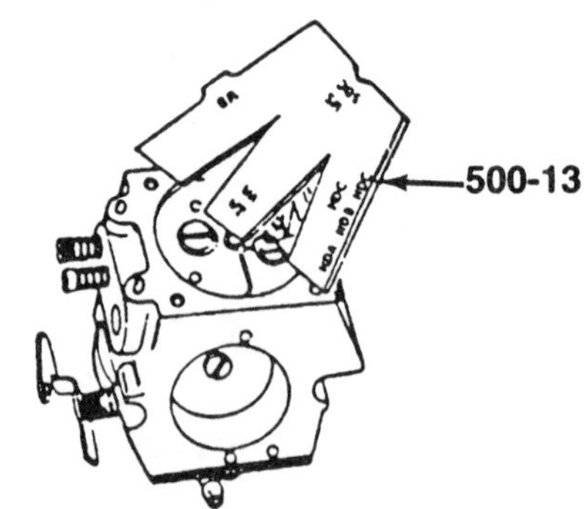

Fig. HQ502—Metering lever should just touch leg of Walbro tool 500-13. Bend lever to obtain correct lever height.

IGNITION SYSTEM. The engine is equipped with an electronic ignition system. Ignition system performance is considered satisfactory if a spark will jump across a 3 mm (1/8 in.) electrode gap on a test spark plug. If no spark is produced, check on/off switch, wiring and ignition module air gap. Air gap between ignition module and flywheel magnet should be 0.3 mm (0.012 in.). If switch, wiring and module air gap are satisfactory, but spark is not present, renew ignition module.

REPAIRS

PISTON, PIN AND RING. The piston (3—Fig. HQ503) is accessible after removing cylinder (1). Remove piston pin retainers (5) and use a suitable puller to extract pin (4) from piston.

Piston and piston ring are available only in standard size.

Install piston on connecting rod so arrow on piston crown will point toward exhaust port when the cylinder is installed.

The piston is equipped with a single piston ring. Piston ring rotation is prevented by a locating pin in the piston ring groove. Make certain ring end gap is correctly positioned around locating pin before installing piston in cylinder.

CYLINDER. Inspect cylinder and renew if scratched, scored or otherwise damaged. Cylinder is available in standard size only with a fitted piston.

Illustrations courtesy Husqvarna Forest & Garden

CRANKSHAFT, CONNECTING ROD AND CRANKCASE. Crankshaft and connecting rod are a unit assembly. Crankshaft main bearings (9—Fig. HQ503) are supported in interlocking bearing carriers (7).

To remove crankshaft and connecting rod, first separate engine from trimmer drive shaft. Remove engine cover, fuel tank and recoil starter assembly. Remove spark plug and install a piston locking tool in spark plug hole to prevent crankshaft from turning. Remove clutch housing and clutch assembly. Remove nut retaining flywheel and remove flywheel from crankshaft. Remove cylinder mounting screws and separate cylinder (1) from crankcase (11) and piston. Remove piston pin retainers (5), piston pin (4) and piston (3) from connecting rod. Remove main bearing carrier mounting screws and withdraw crankshaft and connecting rod from crankcase. Withdraw bearing carriers (7), seals (8) and bearings (9) from crankshaft ends.

When assembling engine, install seals (8) so lip is toward bearing. Make sure mating surfaces of bearing carriers (7), lower crankcase (11) and cylinder (1) are clean and dry. Place a thin bead of a suitable form-in-place gasket compound onto sealing areas of lower crankcase (11) and cylinder (1). Tighten cylinder screws to 11 N·m (97 in.-lbs.). Make sure crankshaft rotates freely.

CLUTCH. The upper end of the drive shaft is threaded into the clutch drum hub (2—Fig. HQ504). To service clutch, detach drive housing (1) from engine. Clutch shoes and hub (3) are available only as a unit assembly.

To service clutch drum, remove gear head from drive shaft housing. Detach drive shaft housing tube from drive housing. Hold drive shaft while unscrewing clutch drum. Housing and bearing are available only as a unit assembly.

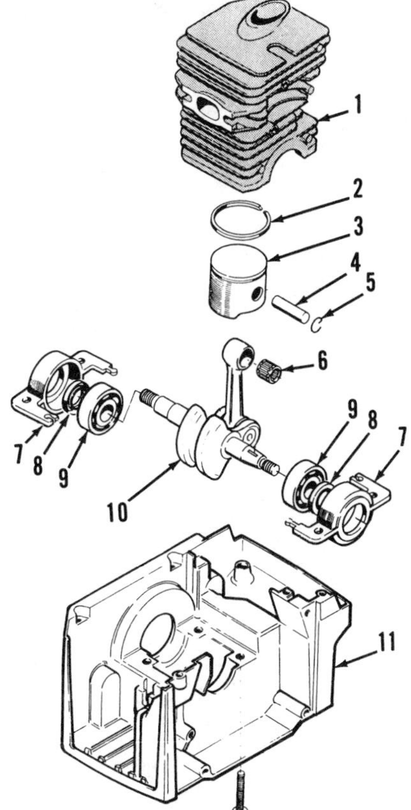

Fig. HQ503—Exploded view of engine.

1. Cylinder
2. Piston ring
3. Piston
4. Piston pin
5. Retaining ring
6. Bearing
7. Bearing carrier
8. Seal
9. Main bearings
10. Crankshaft & connecting rod assy.
11. Crankcase

REWIND STARTER. Refer to Fig. HQ505 for an exploded view of rewind starter. To disassemble starter, detach starter housing (9) from engine. Remove rope handle and allow rope to wind into starter. Unscrew center screw (5) and remove rope pulley (7). Wear appropriate safety eyewear and gloves before detaching rewind spring (8) from housing as spring may uncoil uncontrolled.

To assemble starter, lubricate center post of housing and spring side with light grease. Install rewind spring so coil windings are clockwise from outer end. Assemble starter while passing rope through housing rope outlet and attach rope handle to rope. To place tension on starter rope, pull rope out of housing. Engage rope in notch on pulley and turn pulley two turns clockwise to place tension on rewind spring. Hold pulley and disengage rope from pulley notch. Release pulley and allow rope to wind on pulley. Check starter operation. Rope handle should be held against housing by spring tension, but it must be possible to rotate pulley at least $^1/_2$ turn clockwise when rope is pulled out fully.

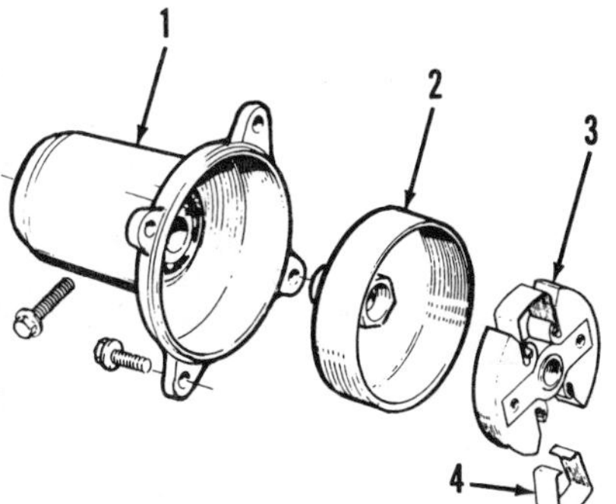

Fig. HQ504—Exploded view of clutch assembly.

1. Housing
2. Clutch drum
3. Clutch assy.
4. Spring

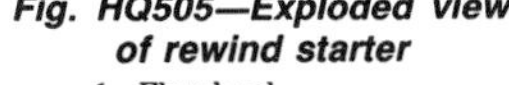
Fig. HQ505—Exploded view of rewind starter

1. Flywheel
2. Spring
3. Pawl
4. Pin
5. Screw
6. Washer
7. Pulley
8. Rewind spring
9. Starter housing
10. Rope handle

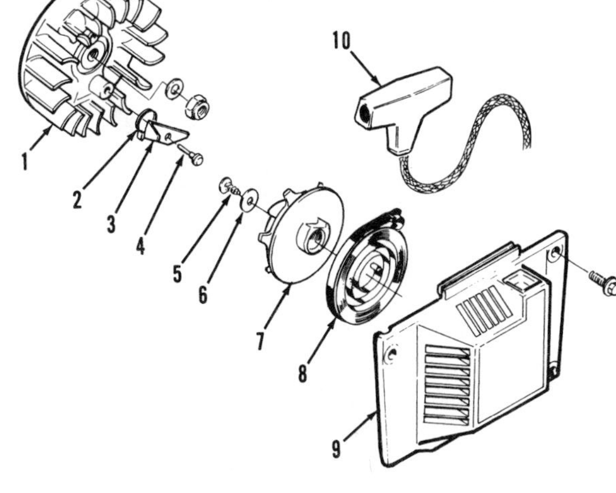

IDC

ENGINE SERVICE

Model	Bore	Stroke	Displacement
A28	33.27 mm (1.31 in.)	31.75 mm (1.25 in.)	28.5 cc (1.7 cu. in.)
A31	34.8 mm (1.37 in.)	31.75 mm (1.25 in.)	31.0 cc (1.9 cu. in.)

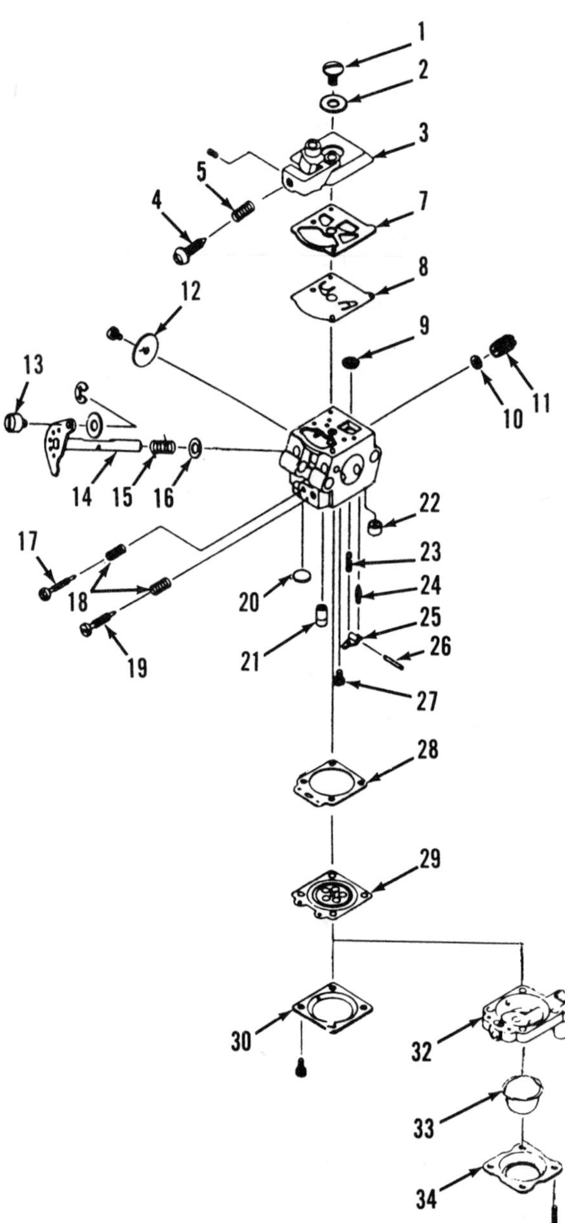

Fig. ID101—Exploded view of Walbro WT carburetor. Model WTA is similar. The governor valve (11) and primer (33) are not used on all models.

1. Screw
2. Washer
3. Cover
4. Idle speed screw
5. Spring
7. Gasket
8. Fuel pump diaphragm
9. Screen
10. "O" ring
11. Governor valve
12. Throttle plate
13. Swivel
14. Throttle shaft
15. Spring
16. Washer
17. Low-speed mixture screw
18. Spring
19. High-speed mixture screw
20. Welch plug
21. Nozzle
22. Check valve
23. Spring
24. Fuel inlet valve
25. Metering lever
26. Pin
27. Screw
28. Gasket
29. Metering diaphragm
30. Cover
32. Cover
33. Primer bulb
34. Bulb retainer

ENGINE INFORMATION

These two-stroke, air cooled gasoline engines are used by several equipment manufacturers. The engine is equipped with a cantilever-type crankshaft that is supported in two ball bearings at the flywheel end.

MAINTENANCE

LUBRICATION. The engine is lubricated by mixing oil with the gasoline fuel. Use only an oil designed for two-stroke, air cooled engines. Refer to the equipment manufacturer's recommended type of oil and mixing ratio.

SPARK PLUG. The recommended spark plug is a Champion DJ8J or equivalent and the electrode gap should be 0.025 in. (0.635 mm). Tighten the spark plug securely to the torque listed in the TIGHTENING TORQUE paragraph.

CARBURETOR. The engine may be equipped with a Walbro or Zama carburetor. The manufacturer's name and model number are stamped on the carburetor. Refer to the appropriate following paragraphs for service information. When installing, tighten the attaching screws to the torque listed in the TIGHTENING TORQUE paragraph.

Walbro WT and WTA. Refer to Fig. ID101 for an exploded view typical of the carburetor. Initial adjustment of the idle mixture screw (17) and the high-speed mixture screw (19) is 1-1/4 turns open. The settings of these mixture screws is critical to the operation of the engine. Final adjustment should be performed carefully to insure easy starting and maximum performance.

To adjust the mixture screws, first remove and clean the air filter, then reinstall it. Start the engine and allow it to run until it reaches normal operating temperature. If necessary, turn each of the mixture screws (17 and 19) clockise until seated lightly, then back the crews out (counterclockwise) 1-1/4 urns to provide the initial adjustment the engine can be started. Turn the lle speed stop screw (4) so the engine lles at about 2800-3000 rpm. Adjust he idle mixture needle (17) so the engine idles smoothly and accelerates ithout hesitation. Readjust the idle peed stop screw (4) if necessary to slow he idle speed. If equipped with a lutch, the trimmer head should not urn when the engine is idling. Adjust he high-speed mixture screw (19) to rovide the best performance while operating at maximum speed under load. he high-speed mixture screw may be et slightly rich to improve performance under load. The engine may be amaged if the high-speed screw is set oo lean.

To disassemble the carburetor, refer o Fig. ID101 and remove cover (3 and 0) for access to internal components. emove diaphragms (8 and 29), fuel creen (9), mixture screws (17 and 19), ozzle (21), check valve (22), metering ever (25) and fuel inlet valve (24). Velch plug (20) can be removed by iercing the plug with a sharp pointed unch. Be careful not to insert punch oo deeply as underlying body metal nay be damaged.

Clean and inspect all components. If he unit has been improperly stored, assages may be clogged with deposits hat are hard, solid and nearly transparent. Be careful not to damage the penings or sealing surfaces while leaning. Check the condition of diahragms (8 and 29) carefully. Install ew diaphragms if hard (not flexible), orn or otherwise damaged. Examine he fuel inlet valve (24), spring (23) and ever (25). A new fuel inlet valve needle 24), and mixture screws (17 and 19) an be installed, but their seats cannot e serviced if damaged. Inspect the condition of the check valve (22) and filter creen (9).

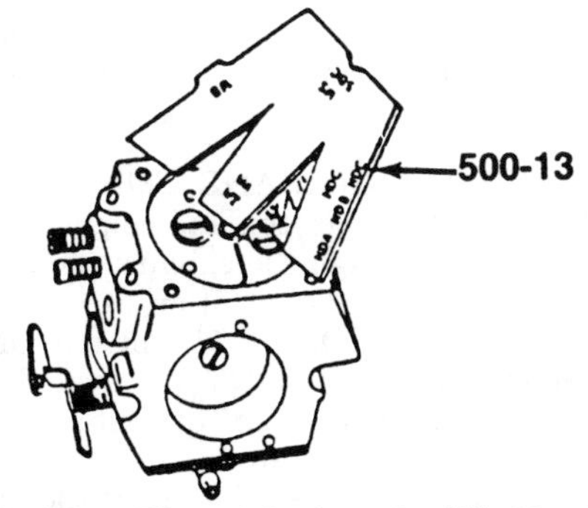

Fig. ID102—The metering lever should just touch the leg of the Walbro tool 500-13. If necessary, bend the lever to adjust the lever height.

Check the height of the metering lever as shown in Fig. ID102 using Walbro tool 500-13 or equivalent. End of metering lever should just touch the leg of the tool. If the tool is not available, the lever should be 0.060-0.070 in. (1.52-1.78 mm) below the surface for gasket (28—Fig. ID101). Carefully bend the lever if necessary to obtain the correct lever height.

Some carburetors may be equipped with a governor valve (11—Fig. ID101) that enriches the mixture at high-speed to prevent over speeding. The governor valve, if installed, cannot be adjusted.

Some carburetors are equipped with a primer bulb (33). Install a new bulb if hard, cracked or otherwise damaged.

Zama C1U. Refer to Fig. ID103 for an exploded view typical of the carburetor. Initial adjustment of the idle mixture screw (17) and the high-speed mixture screw (15) is 1-1/4 to 1-1/2 turns open. The settings of these mixture screws is critical to the operation of the engine. Final adjustment should be performed carefully to insure easy starting and maximum performance.

To adjust the mixture screws, first remove and clean the air filter, then reinstall it. Start the engine and allow it to run until it reaches normal operating temperature. If necessary, turn each of the mixture screws (15 and 17) clockwise until seated lightly, then back the screws out (counterclockwise) 1-1/4 turns to provide the initial adjustment so the engine can be started. Turn the idle speed stop screw (28) so the engine idles at about 2800-3000 rpm. Adjust the idle mixture needle (17) so the engine idles smoothly and accelerates without hesitation. Readjust the idle speed stop screw (28) if necessary to slow the idle speed. If equipped with a clutch, the trimmer head does not turn when the engine is idling. Adjust the high-speed mixture screw (15) to provide the best performance while operating at maximum speed under load. The high-speed mixture screw may be set slightly rich to improve performance under load. The engine may be damaged if the high-speed screw is set too lean.

To disassemble the carburetor, refer to Fig. ID103 and remove covers (1 and 26) for access to internal components. Remove diaphragms (2 and 24), metering lever (4), fuel inlet valve (8), nozzle (6) and mixture screws (15 and 17). Welch plug (12) can be removed by piercing the plug towards the end of the "tail" portion with a suitable sharp pointed punch. Be careful not to insert punch too deeply as underlying body metal may be damaged, ruining the carburetor casting.

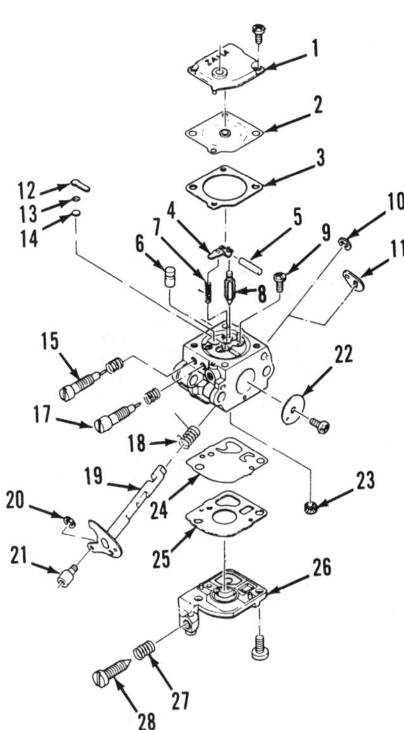

Fig. ID103—Exploded view of the Zama C1U carburetor used on some models.

1. Cover
2. Metering diaphragm
3. Gasket
4. Metering lever
5. Pin
6. Nozzle
7. Spring
8. Fuel inlet valve
9. Screw
10. "E" ring
11. Arm
12. Welch plug
13. Retainer
14. Screen
15. High speed mixture screw
17. Low speed mixture screw
18. Spring
19. Throttle shaft
20. "E" ring
21. Swivel
22. Throttle plate
23. Fuel inlet screen
24. Fuel pump diaphragm
25. Gasket
26. Cover
27. Spring
28. Idle speed screw

Clean and inspect all components. If the unit has been improperly stored, passages may be clogged with deposits that are hard, solid and nearly transparent. Be careful not to damage the openings or sealing surfaces while cleaning. Check the condition of diaphragms (2 and 24) carefully. Install new diaphragms if hard (not flexible), torn or otherwise damaged. Examine the fuel inlet valve (8), spring (7) and lever (4). A new fuel inlet valve needle (8), and mixture screws (15 and 17) can be installed, but their seats cannot be serviced if damaged. Apply suitable sealant to the new Welch plug (12) before installing.

Check the height of the metering lever as shown in Fig. ID104. The clearance (C) between the metering lever and a straightedge positioned across the gasket surface of the carburetor body should be 0-0.012 in. (0-0.3 mm). Carefully bend the lever if necessary to obtain the correct lever height.

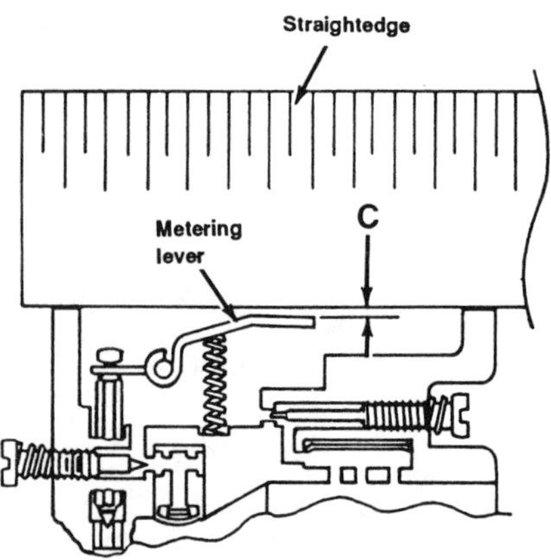

Fig. ID104—On Zama models, the metering lever should have 0-0.3 mm (0-0.012 in.) clearance when measured as shown.

IGNITION SYSTEM. The engine is equipped with a solid-state ignition system. The ignition module/coil is located under the cowling at the front of the engine. Two screws attach the ignition module/coil to the engine's cylinder. When installing, set the air gap between the flywheel magnets and the legs of the ignition module as follows. Install the ignition module, but tighten the two screws only enough to hold it in place away from the flywheel. Insert 0.010-0.015 in. (0.254-0.381 mm) thick brass or plastic shim stock between the legs of the ignition module and the flywheel, then turn the flywheel until the flywheel magnets are near the module legs. Loosen the screws attaching the ignition module and press legs of the ignition module against the shim stock, then tighten the two attaching screws to the torque listed in the TIGHTENING TORQUE paragraph. Remove the shim stock, then turn the flywheel and check to be sure the flywheel does not hit the legs of the coil.

REPAIRS

COMPRESSION PRESSURE. The compression pressure should be 90-120 psi (621-828 kPa) for optimum pressure. Check compression pressure with the engine warm and both throttle and choke open fully.

TIGHTENING TORQUE. Recommended tightening torque values are as follows.

Air filter . . . . 15-25 in.-lb. (1.7-2.8 N·m)
Carburetor
  Attaching screws . . . . 35-40 in.-lb. (3.9-4.5 N·m)
  Choke plate attaching screw . . . . 35-40 in.-lb. (3.9-4.5 N·m)
  Throttle wire swivel screw 9-12 in.-lb. (1.0-1.4 N·m)
Clutch
  Cover attaching screws . . 35-40 in.-lb. (3.9-4.5 N·m)
  Drum . . . . 38-44 in.-lb. (4.3-5.0 N·m)
  Rotor (hub) . . . . 150-160 in.-lb. (16.9-18 N·m)
Crankcase
  Cylinder attaching screws . . . . 110-120 in.-lb. (12.4-13.5 N·m)
  Cover (blower models) . . . . 67 in.-lb. (7.5 N·m)
Crankshaft
  Extension nut (blower models) . . . . 150-160 in.-lb. (16.9-18 N·m)
Drive shaft housing
  Clamp screw . . . . 70-80 in.-lb. (7.9-9 N·m)
  Locking (fitting) screw . . 15-20 in.-lb. (1.7-2.3 N·m)
Fan shroud . . . . 110-120 in.-lb. (12.4-13.5 N·m)
Flywheel
  Blower models . . . . 150-160 in.-lb. (16.9-18 N·m)
  Trimmer models without clutch . . . . . . 150-160 in.-lb. (16.9-18 N·m)
Ignition
  Module/coil . . . . 28-35 in.-lb. (3.2-3.9 N·m)
  Slide switch to cover . . . . . 7-12 in.-lb. (0.8-1.4 N·m)
  Slide switch to starter housing . . . . 10-15 in.-lb. (1.1-1.7 N·m)
  Stop wire to starter hsg. . 10-15 in.-lb. (1.1-1.7 N·m)
  Toggle switch nut . . . . . . 25-35 in.-lb. (2.8-3.9 N·m)
Muffler
  Exhaust tube . . . . 15-25 in.-lb. (1.7-2.8 N·m)
  Heat shield . . . . 15-25 in.-lb. (1.7-2.8 N·m)
  Muffler attaching screws
    Before S/N 809000000 . . . . 56 in.-lb. (6.3 N·m)
    S/N 809000000 and above . . . . 80-90 in.-lb. (90-10.1 N·m)
Reed valve backup plate . . 15-20 in.-lb. (1.7-2.3 N·m)
Reed plate attaching screws . . . . 35-40 in.-lb. (3.9-4.5 N·m)
Shroud extension (engine stand) . . . . 25-35 in.-lb. (2.8-3.9 N·m)
Spark plug . . . . 190-210 in.-lb. (21.4-23.6 N·m)
Starter housing . . . . 35-40 in.-lb. (4.1-4.5 N·m)
Starter pulley retainer . . . 20-30 in.-lb. (2.3-3.4 N·m)

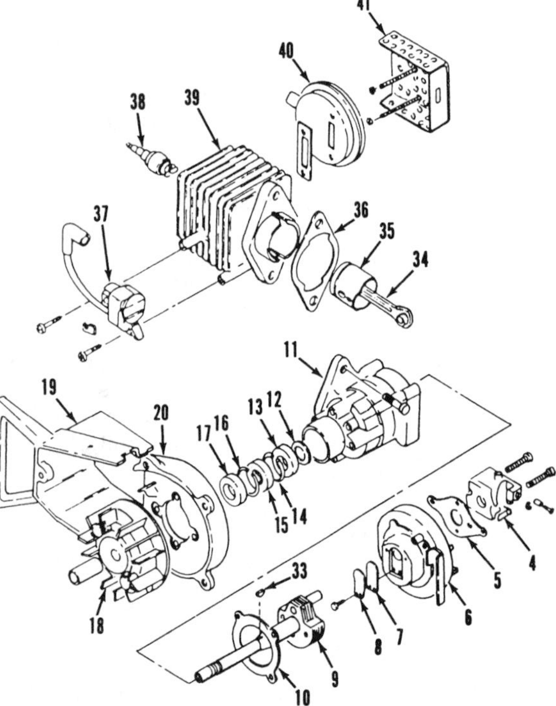

Fig. ID105—Exploded view of engine typical of type used on Model 200 and 210 blowers.

4. Carburetor
5. Gasket
6. Crankcase cover
7. Reed petal
8. Reed backup
9. Crankshaft
10. Gasket
11. Crankcase
12. Thrust washer
13. Inner bearing
15. Seal
16. Snap rings
17. Sealed bearing
18. Flywheel
20. Cover
33. Woodruff key
34. Connecting rod
35. Piston
36. Gasket
37. Ignition module
39. Cylinder
40. Muffler
45. Reed block

PISTON, RING AND CONNECTING ROD. The piston and ring can be inspected through the exhaust port after removing the muffler (40—Fig. ID105 or Fig. ID106). The piston and connecting rod (34 and 35) are available for service only as an assembly and should not be separated.

To remove the piston, remove the engine shrouds (covers), muffler and cylinder (39). Remove the carburetor

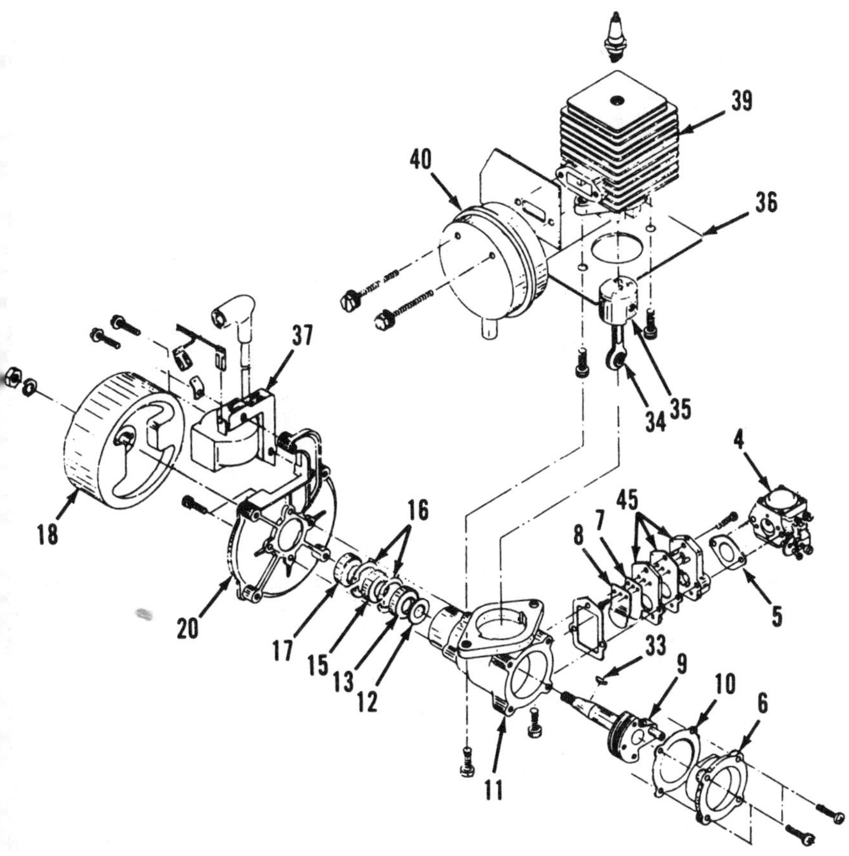

Fig. ID106—Exploded view of engine typical of most models.

4. Carburetor
5. Gasket
6. Crankcase cover
7. Reed petal
8. Reed backup
9. Crankshaft
10. Gasket
11. Crankcase
12. Thrust washer
13. Inner bearing
14. Snap ring
15. Seal
16. Snap ring
17. Sealed bearing
18. Flywheel
19. Shroud
20. Cover
33. Key
34. Connecting rod
35. Piston
36. Gasket
37. Ignition module
38. Spark plug
39. Cylinder
40. Muffler
45. Reed valve

(4—Fig. ID105) from the rear of the engine of all except 200 and 210 blower models. Unbolt and remove the crankcase rear cover (6—Fig. ID105 or Fig. ID106). Slide the connecting rod to the rear and lift the piston and connecting rod from the engine.

The piston is equipped with one ring. The ring of models before serial number 910045201 is 0.46 in. (1.16 mm) thick. The ring of engines with serial number 910045201 and higher is 0.052 in. (1.23 mm) thick. For all models, side clearance of the ring in the piston groove should not exceed 0.005 in. (0.127 mm). The ends of the ring should have 0.085 in. (2.159 mm) gap in the cylinder bore. The piston and cylinder are only available in standard sizes.

Assemble the piston and cylinder as follows. Lubricate the piston and cylinder, then align the ring gap with the pin in the piston groove. Compress the piston ring with your fingers and insert the piston into the cylinder bore. On 200 and 210 blower models, the longer side of the piston skirt should be on the same side of the cylinder as the exhaust port. On all other models, make sure the ring gap and pin in the groove is away from the exhaust port.

For engines installed on **trimmers and cultivators**, install the cylinder base gasket (36—Fig. ID105 or Fig. ID106) with the longer straight side of the gasket on the same side of the cylinder as the exhaust port. For engines used on 200 and 210 blowers, install the gasket on the cylinder with the small notch on the same side as the exhaust port. For engines used on 280, 300BV, 310, and 310BV blowers and blower/vacs, install the gasket on the cylinder base with the longer flat side of the gasket **away** from the exhaust port side.

Position the cylinder/piston on the crankcase with the following orientation. For engines installed on all models **except** 200 and 210 blowers, the cylinder exhaust port should be on the same side as the large open end of the crankcase for the cover (6—Fig. ID105). On engines for 200 and 210 blowers, the exhaust port should be on the side opposite the crankcase opening for the reed valve (45—Fig. ID106).

Lubricate the connecting rod bearing and the crankpin, then install the cylinder/piston/connecting rod/cylinder base gasket while sliding the connecting rod over the crankshaft crankpin. Make sure that parts are still aligned as previously described, then install the screws attaching the cylinder to the crankcase. Tighten the screws to the torque listed in the TIGHTENING TORQUE paragraph.

CYLINDER. The cylinder and piston are available in standard size only. Check both the piston and cylinder for wear or damage. It is suggested that both be renewed if either is worn or damaged excessively. Refer to the PISTON, RING AND CONNECTING ROD paragraph for removal and installation procedures.

CRANKSHAFT AND CONNECTING ROD. The crankshaft (9—Fig. ID105 or Fig. ID106) is supported in two ball bearings (13 and 17) at the flywheel end. The crankshaft and bearings can be checked for damage after removing the cylinder, piston and connecting rod as described in the PISTON, RING AND CONNECTING ROD paragraphs.

The condition of the two ball bearings that support the crankshaft can be checked by turning the crankshaft after removing the cylinder, piston and connecting rod. The crankshaft should rotate smoothly and should not show any signs of damage or roughness.

The connecting rod is fitted with a roller bearing that rides on the crankpin. The connecting rod bearings are available only as an assembly with the connecting rod and piston. Inspect the crankpin for any scoring or other signs of damage. If the crankpin is damaged, a new connecting rod and crankshaft should both be installed.

To remove the crankshaft, first remove the flywheel, fuel tank and shrouds. Do not forget to remove the flywheel drive key from the crankshaft. Remove the cylinder, piston and connecting rod as described in the PISTON, RING AND CONNECTING ROD paragraphs. Press the crankshaft from the crankcase and bearings. Use a bearing puller that grips the inner race to pull the sealed outer bearing (17). Use a puller to remove the unsealed inner bearing (13). On early models so equipped, remove the snap rings (14 and 16). Remove the seal (15).

Pack the sealed outer bearing (17) with grade 2 lithium-base bearing grease. Clean any grease from the surfaces that contact the crankshaft and crankcase. Press outer bearing into the crankcase bore, with the seal to the outside, until the bearing is flush with the crankcase. Press the seal (15) into the bore with the spring loaded lip toward the inside, until the seal is 0.400 in. (10.16 mm) from the inside surface of the crankcase as shown at A—Fig. ID107. Lubricate the lips of the seal with two-stroke engine oil after installing.

Position the thrust washer (12) on the crankshaft, then clean any grease or oil from the surfaces of the bearing (13) that contact the crankshaft and

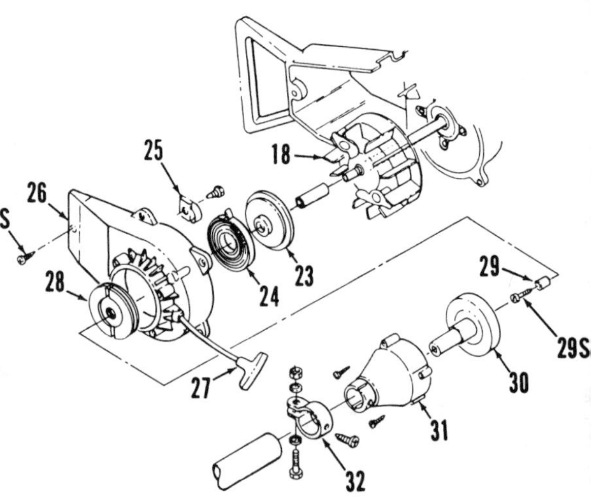

Fig. ID109—Exploded view of the clutch rewind starter and flywheel used on some models. Screw (29S) is trapped inside drum (30) by spacer (29).

18. Flywheel
23. Pulley
24. Rewind starter
25. Retainer
26. Cover
27. Starter rope
28. Clutch hub
29. Spacer
29S. Screw
30. Clutch drum
31. Clutch housing
32. Clamp

crankcase. Press the inner bearing (13) onto the crankshaft until it just contacts the thrust washer lightly. Support the inner race of the bearing while pressing it onto the crankshaft.

Clean the outer race of the bearing (13) and the bore in the crankcase, then press the crankshaft and inner bearing into the crankcase until the clearance between the crankshaft and crankcase is 0.030 in. (0.762 mm) as shown at B—Fig. ID107. The clearance can be measured with a feeler gauge through the opening for the cylinder and connecting rod. Turn the crankshaft and check to be sure that it turns freely.

Install the piston, cylinder and connecting rod as described in the PISTON, RING AND CONNECTING ROD paragraphs.

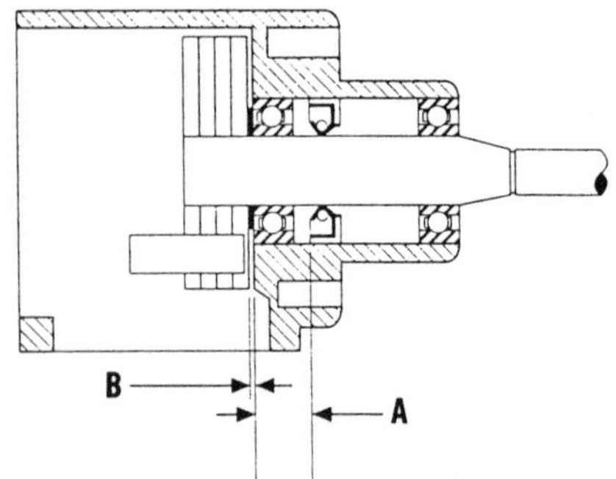

Fig. ID107—Install seal to the depth "A" of 0.400 in. (10.16 mm). When the crankshaft and bearing is pressed into the crankshaft, clearance "B" should be 0.030 in. (0.762 mm).

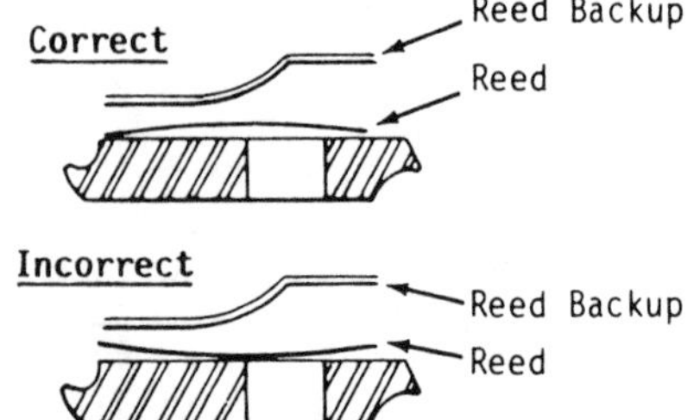

Fig. ID108—The reed valve must be assembled as shown.

REED VALVE. The reed valve assembly is attached to the crankcase cover (6—Fig. ID105) of engines used for all models except 200 and 210 blowers. The reed valve assembly (7, 8 and 45—Fig. ID106) is attached to the side of the crankcase of engines for 200 and 210 blowers. On all models, install the reed pedal and backup plate as shown in Fig. ID108.

CLUTCH. To remove the clutch, separate the drive shaft housing and drive shaft from the engine, then remove the clutch housing (31—Fig. ID109). Hold the flywheel using the special tool (part No. 612470) or equivalent and remove the screw (29S) from the center of the clutch drum. Loctite was applied to the threads of screw (29S) of early models and the screw may be difficult to remove. Later models are equipped with a Torx screw at this location. The clutch drum can be removed after removing the center screw.

Unscrew the clutch rotor (hub) using special tool (part No. 147337) or equivalent, then remove the clutch (28) and spacer sleeve. When assembling, tighten screws and clutch rotor to the torque listed in TIGHTENING TORQUE paragraph.

REWIND STARTER. Refer to Fig. ID109, Fig. ID110 or Fig. ID111 for an exploded view of the rewind starter. On cultivator or trimmer models, separate the drive shaft and housing from the engine. On blower models, the blower must be removed. On models with clutch, the clutch assembly must be removed before removing the starter and housing.

To disassemble the removed starter, remove the handle and allow the rope to wind into the starter. Unscrew the pulley retaining screw (8—Fig. ID110)

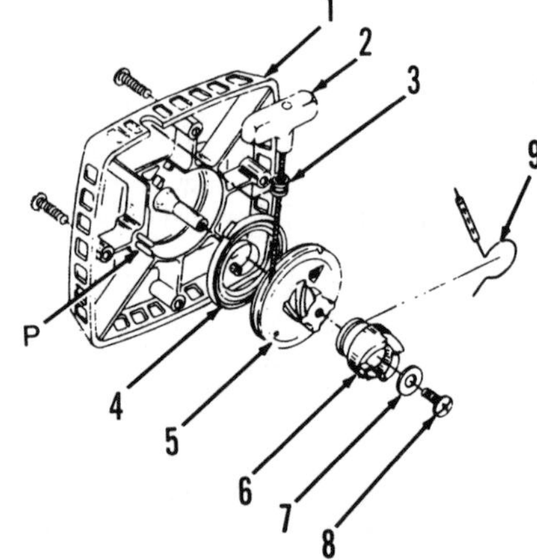

Fig. ID110—Exploded view of rewind starter used on some models. Note that long end of spring (9) must fit between pegs (P) on housing.

1. Starter housing
2. Rope handle
3. Rope guide
4. Rewind spring
5. Pulley
6. Ratchet
7. Washer
8. Screw
9. Spring

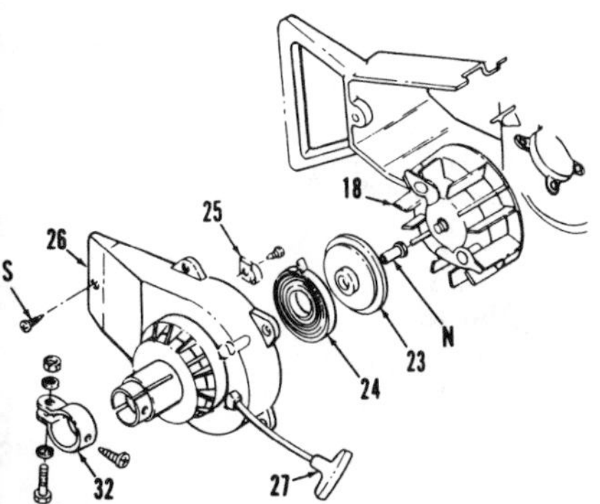

Fig. ID111—Exploded view of rewind starter and drive adapter used on direct drive models. Crankshaft is different than models with clutch. Flywheel is retained by nut (N).

18. Flywheel
23. Pulley
24. Rewind spring
25. Retainer
26. Starter housing
27. Rope handle
32. Clamp

or the screw and retainer (25—Fig. ID112). Wear appropriate safety eye ware and gloves, then remove the pulley and rope. On most models, the spring is contained in a removable housing that can be lifted from the housing. Be careful that the spring does not uncoil uncontrolled.

To assemble the starter, apply a small amount of Mobile grease HP or equivalent to the starter housing post, spring and the back of the pulley. Install the rewind spring so it is wound clockwise from the outer end. Attach the rope to the pulley (23—Fig. ID109, 5—Fig. ID110 or 23—Fig. ID111), making sure the knot is fully nested in the pocket. Pull the rope tight and wind the rope clockwise as viewed from the pawl (engine) side. Install the pulley/rope and rotate slightly until the spring hooks into the pulley and the pulley drops into the housing. Guide the end of the rope through the housing and attach the handle.

When assembling or if the starter rope does not fully rewind, preload the recoil spring as follows. Hold the pulley to keep it from turning, then pull a small loop in the rope between the pulley and the inside of the housing (26—Fig. ID109, 1—Fig. ID110 or 26—Fig. ID111). Hold the rope and wind the pulley to preload the pulley, allow the pulley to rewind the rope, then check operation. The spring should wind the rope around the pulley fully, but the spring must not be bound when the rope is fully extended. When the spring preload is correctly set, install the retainer (25—Fig. ID112).

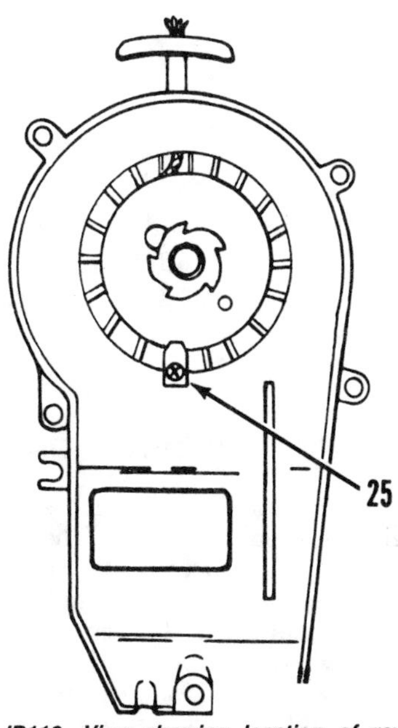

Fig. ID112—View showing location of rewind starter pulley retainer (25) used on some models.

IDC
ENGINE SERVICE

Model	Bore	Stroke	Displacement
AC-1	32.51 mm (1.28 in.)	31.75 mm (1.25 in.)	26.2 cc (1.6 cu. in.)

ENGINE INFORMATION

This four-stroke, air-cooled gasoline engine is used by RYOBI. The valves are operated by a cam located in the crankcase via push rods and rocker arms. The cantilever-type crankshaft is supported in bearings at the flywheel end. The crankshaft and bearings are not available as service parts and should not be removed.

MAINTENANCE

LUBRICATION. The engine is lubricated by 3.4 fl. oz. (100 ml) of oil contained in the engine crankcase. Use SAE 30 oil designed for use in four-stroke engines with API service class SF, SG or SH. Check the oil level before each use and change the oil after each 25 hours of operation. The oil should be changed after the first 10 hours of operation of a new engine or after the engine is rebuilt. The oil should also be changed before storing the unit for an extended time.

A dipstick (Fig. ID1) is attached to the fill plug. To check the oil level, make sure the engine has cooled and the oil has had time to return to the crankcase. Position the unit with engine level and the drive shaft straight. Remove the fill plug, wipe the plug dry with a clean cloth, then reinstall and tighten the plug. Remove the plug and observe the level of the oil on the dipstick. Oil level should be maintained at the top of the dipstick.

Change the engine oil as follows. Be sure to catch and discard the oil in a safe and approved method. Start the engine and allow it to run until it reaches normal operating temperature. Stop the engine, remove the oil fill plug, then tip the unit and pour all of the oil from the opening (Fig. ID1). Be sure to allow all of the oil to drain and be removed.

Refill the crankcase with 3.4 fl. oz. (100 ml) of RYOBI Four-Cycle Engine Oil or a good quality SAE 30 oil designated API service class SG, SF or SH. Be sure the O-ring is installed on the fill plug and tighten the plug securely.

FUEL. The fuel tank should be filled with fresh regular or unleaded gasoline only. Do not mix oil with the fuel. The use of oxygenated (alcohol blended) gasoline is discouraged, but if used it should be as fresh as possible. Never use oxygenated fuel that has been stored 60 days or longer. Drain the fuel tank and run the engine until it stops before storing the unit. The manufacturer also recommends mixing 0.8 fl. oz. (23 ml) of STA-BIL or an equivalent fuel additive with each gallon of oxygenated gasoline. Always mix additives with the gasoline in a separate container; never in the fuel tank.

The fuel pickup line inside the tank is fitted with a filter that is weighted to keep the pick up at the lowest part of the tank. The filter and pickup can be fished from the tank through the filler opening if replacement is required.

SPARK PLUG. The recommended spark plug is a Champion RDZ19H or equivalent and the electrode gap should be 0.025 in. (0.635 mm). Tighten the spark plug securely to the torque listed in the TIGHTENING TORQUE paragraph.

CARBURETOR. The engine is equipped with a Walbro carburetor. The manufacturer's model number is stamped on the carburetor. The carburetor can be removed after removing the air filter cover and filter (Fig. ID2). The throttle cable is attached to the third hole from the top of the carburetor throttle lever. When installing, tighten the attaching screws to the torque listed in the TIGHTENING TORQUE paragraph.

Refer to Fig. ID3 for an exploded view typical of the carburetor. Initial adjustment of the low-speed mixture screw and the high-speed mixture screw (Fig. ID4) is 1 turn open for units with serial number prior to 407000001 or 1-1/8 turns for units with serial number 407000001 and greater. The settings of these mixture screws is critical to the operation of the engine. Final adjustment should be performed carefully to

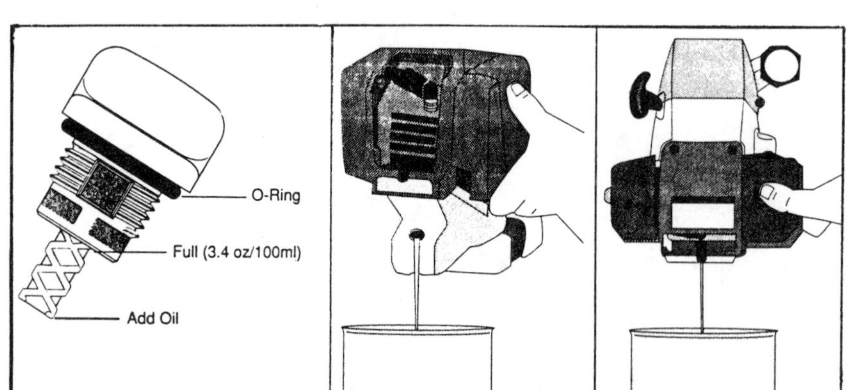

Fig. ID1—The oil level dipstick is attached to the filler plug. Make sure the "O" ring is installed on the plug.

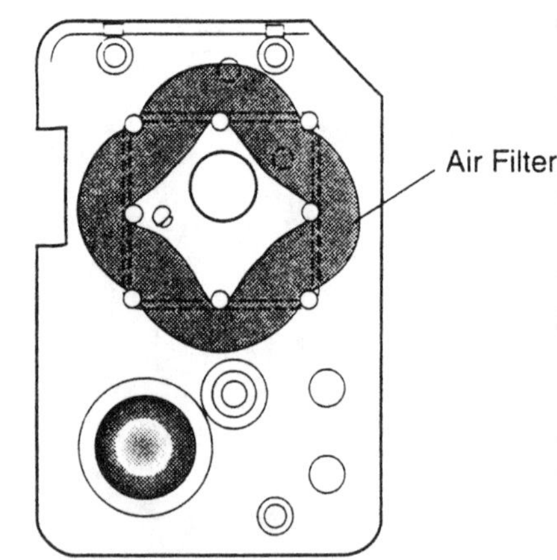

Fig. ID2—The air filter should be located as shown between the 8 posts.

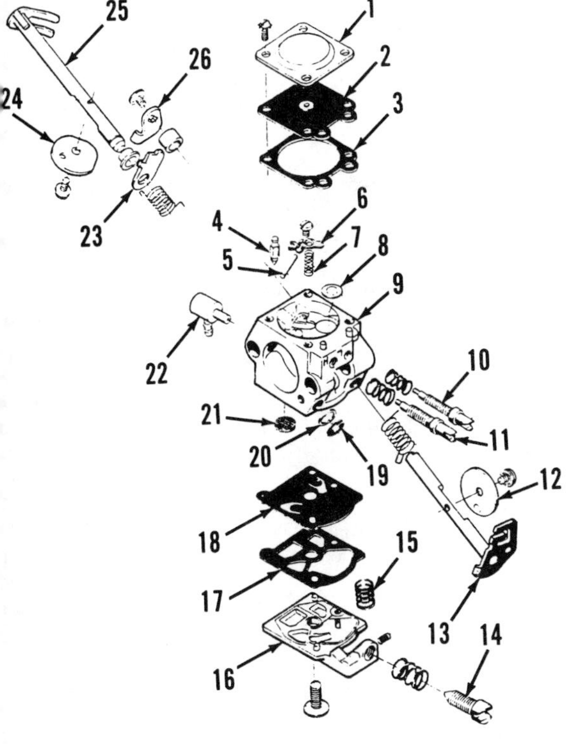

Fig. ID3—Exploded view of Walbro carburetor typical of the type used.

1. Cover
2. Metering diaphragm
3. Gasket
4. Fuel inlet valve
5. Pin
6. Metering lever
7. Spring
8. Welch plug
9. Carburetor body
10. Low-speed mixture screw
11. High-speed mixture screw
12. Choke plate
13. Choke shaft
14. Idle speed stop screw
15. Spring
16. Cover
17. Gasket
18. Fuel pump diaphragm
19. Retainer
20. Washer
21. Fuel screen
22. Fuel inlet fitting
23. Throttle lever
24. Throttle plate
25. Throttle shaft
26. Cam

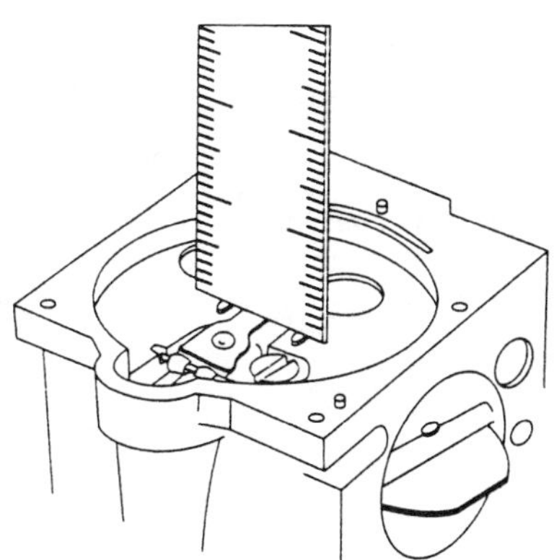

Fig. ID5—Use a straightedge placed between the two projections as shown to measure the height of the fuel control lever. Refer to the text.

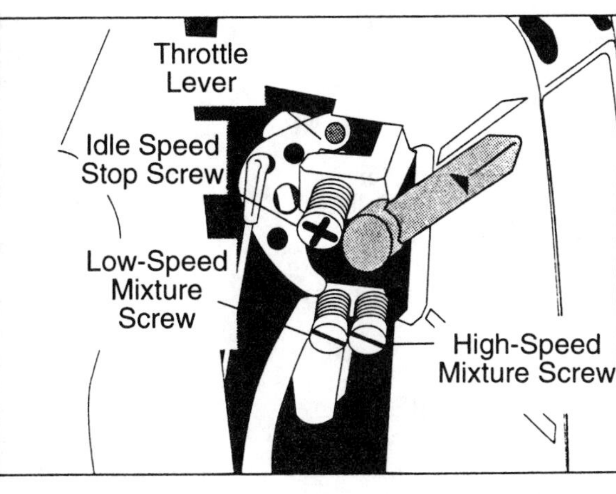

Fig. ID4—Adjust the low-speed mixture, high-speed mixture and idle speed as described in the text.

insure easy starting and maximum performance.

To adjust the mixture screws, first remove and clean the air filter, then reinstall it. Start the engine and allow it to run until it reaches normal operating temperature. If necessary, turn each of the mixture screws (Fig. ID4) clockwise until seated lightly, then back the screws out (counterclockwise) to initial setting as described above to provide the initial adjustment so the engine can be started.

Turn the idle speed stop screw so the engine idles slow enough the clutch does not engage the trimmer or other attachment. Turning the mixture screws clockwise leans the fuel:air mixture and turning screws counterclockwise enriches the mixture.

Adjust the idle mixture needle so the engine idles smoothly and accelerates without hesitation. Readjust the idle speed stop screw if necessary to slow the idle speed. Adjust the high-speed mixture screw to provide the best performance while operating at maximum speed under load. The high-speed mixture screw may be set slightly rich to improve performance under load. The engine may be damaged if the high-speed screw is set too lean.

To disassemble the carburetor, refer to Fig. ID3 and remove covers (1 and 16) for access to internal components. Remove diaphragms (2 and 18), fuel metering lever (6), fuel inlet valve (4) and fuel mixture needles (10 and 11). In order to thoroughly clean carburetor internal passages it is recommended that Welch plug (8) and fuel screen (21) be removed.

Clean and inspect all components. If the unit has been improperly stored, passages may be clogged with deposits that are hard, solid and nearly transparent. Be careful not to damage the openings or sealing surfaces while cleaning. Do not use drill bits or wire to clean fuel ports and passages. Check the condition of diaphragms (2 and 18) carefully. Install new diaphragms if hard (not flexible), torn or otherwise damaged. Examine the fuel inlet valve (4), spring (7) and lever (6). A new fuel inlet valve needle (4), and mixture screws (10 and 11) can be installed, but their seats cannot be serviced if damaged. Inspect the condition of the filter screen (21) and clean or replace. Apply a suitable sealant to outer edge of new Welch plug prior to installing.

To check the height of the metering lever, place a straightedge across the two projections on either side of the lever as shown in Fig. ID5. End of metering lever should be 0.060-0.070 in. (1.52-1.78 mm) below the straightedge. Carefully bend the lever if necessary to obtain the correct lever height.

Install a new primer bulb if hard, cracked or otherwise damaged. Attach the lines to the proper fittings of the primer as indicated in Fig. ID6. If necessary, the primer bulb can be removed from the air filter base after squeezing the mounting tabs on the front of the bulb assembly.

VALVE CLEARANCE ADJUSTMENT. The clearance between the rocker arms and valves should be checked and adjusted, if necessary, after each 50 hours of operation.

Unbolt and remove the engine cover, then remove the valve cover. Remove the spark plug and turn the engine flywheel until the piston is at the top of the cylinder on the compression stroke. At this position, the rocker arms for

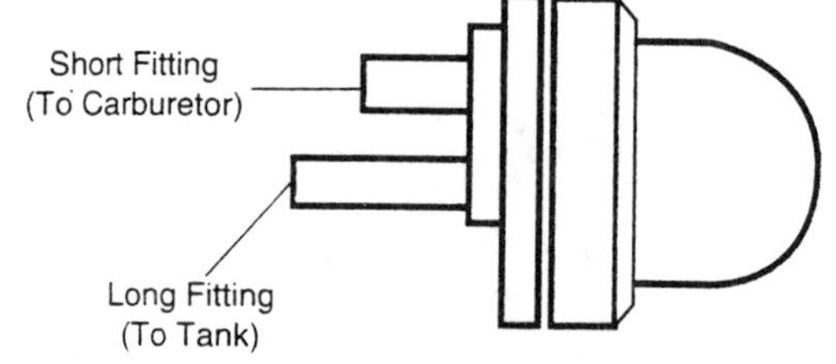

Fig. ID6—The primer bulb is fitted with a check valve and hoses should be attached properly as shown.

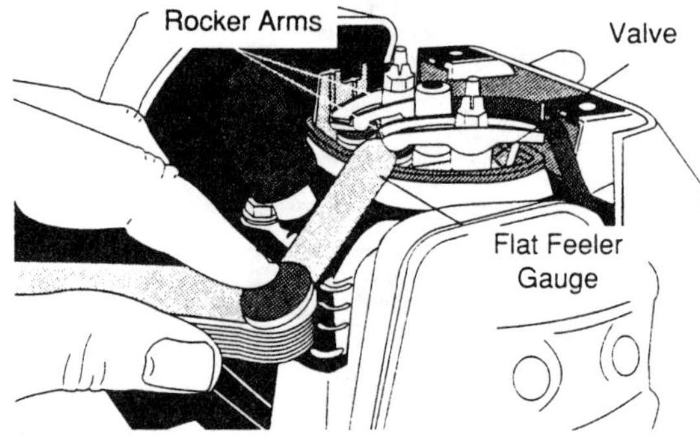

Fig. ID7—Refer to the text when measuring the valve clearance. The clearance is indicated by the thickest feeler gauge that can be inserted between the valve and rocker arm without forcing.

both valves should be loose and both valves closed. If either valve is open (tight), turn the flywheel one complete turn and recheck. Measure the clearance between the rocker arm and valve stem using a feeler gauge as shown in Fig. ID7.

The correct clearance is 0.003-0.006 in. (0.076-0.152 mm). Clearance is changed by turning the adjusting nut at the center of the rocker arm. Turning the nut counterclockwise increases rocker arm to valve clearance. Be very careful to adjust the clearance correctly.

Reinstall the valve cover using a new gasket. Tighten the center screw to the torque listed in the TIGHTENING TORQUE paragraph. Attach the breather hose and install the engine cover, tightening the screws to the torque listed in the TIGHTENING TORQUE paragraph.

SPARK ARRESTER SCREEN. The exhaust outlet of the muffler is fitted with a spark arrester screen which should be removed and cleaned every 50 hours of operation. The spark arrester and screen is held in place with one screw. If the screen cannot be cleaned, install a new screen. Do not operate the unit with the screen removed. Tighten the attaching screw to the torque listed in the TIGHTENING TORQUE paragraph.

IGNITION SYSTEM. The engine is equipped with a solid-state ignition system. The ignition module/coil is located under the cowling at the front of the engine. Two screws attach the ignition module/coil to the engine's cylinder.

When installing, set the air gap between the flywheel magnets and the legs of the ignition module as follows. Install the ignition module, but tighten the two screws only enough to hold it in place away from the flywheel. Insert 0.008-0.012 in. (0.20-0.30 mm) thick brass or plastic shim stock between the legs of the ignition module and the flywheel, then turn the flywheel until the flywheel magnets are near the module legs. Loosen the screws attaching the ignition module and press legs of the ignition module against the shim stock, then tighten the two attaching screws to 30-40 in.-lb. (2.8-3.3 N•m). Remove the shim stock, then turn the flywheel and check to be sure the flywheel does not hit the legs of the coil.

REPAIRS

Many of the nuts, washers and screws used to assemble these engines are special and should not be interchanged with other similar parts.

COMPRESSION PRESSURE. The compression pressure should be 115-125 psi (793-862 kPa) for optimum performance. Check compression pressure with the engine warm and both throttle and choke open fully. Low pressure may indicate leaking valves, leaking head gasket or worn piston and rings. Carbon buildup will be indicated by higher pressures.

TIGHTENING TORQUE. Recommended tightening torque values are as follows.

Air filter . . . . 25-30 in.-lb.
(2.8-3.3 N•m)
Cam bracket . . . . 15-20 in.-lb.
(1.7-2.2 N•m)
Carburetor and mounting insulator
Attaching screws . . . . 30-35 in.-lb.
(3.3-3.9 N•m)
Clutch
Cover attaching screws . . 35-45 in.-lb.
(3.9-5.0 N•m)
Rotor (hub) . . . . 140-150 in.-lb.
(15.8-16.9 N•m)
Cylinder attaching screws 35-45 in.-lb.
(3.9-5.0 N•m)
Cylinder head attaching
nuts . . . . 35-45 in.-lb.
(3.9-5.0 N•m)
Drive shaft housing
Locking (fitting) screw . . 15-20 in.-lb.
(1.7-2.2 N•m)
Engine covers
Front . . . . 15-20 in.-lb.
(1.7-2.2 N•m)
Rear . . . . 30-35 in.-lb.
(3.3-3.9 N•m)
Top . . . . 20-25 in.-lb.
(2.5-3.0 N•m)
Fan housing . . . . 40-45 in.-lb.
(4.5-5.0 N•m)
Fuel tank bracket . . . . 25-35 in.-lb.
(2.8-3.3 N•m)
Grip (handle)
Throttle and switch
retainer . . . . 15-20 in.-lb.
(1.7-2.2 N•m)
Upper to lower . . . . 20-25 in.-lb.
(2.2-2.8 N•m)
Ignition
Module/coil . . . . 30-40 in.-lb.
(3.3-4.4 N•m)
Muffler
Attaching screws . . . . 40-45 in.-lb.
(4.5-5.0 N•m)
Spark arrester screw . . . . 15-20 in.-lb.
(1.7-2.2 N•m)
Oil pan . . . . 35-45 in.-lb.
(3.9-4.9 N•m)
Rocker arm cover . . . . 20-30 in.-lb.
(2.2-3.3 N•m)
Spark plug . . . . 100-110 in.-lb.
(11.2-13.5 N•m)

DISASSEMBLY. Many of the components can be removed and serviced without complete disassembly of the engine. However, following the sequence listed will be helpful if complete disassembly is required. Drain fuel from the tank and oil from the crankcase. If the drive shaft and housing is fitted with a coupling, separate the engine and upper drive shaft from the lower part of the drive shaft and equipment. Remove the six Torx T-25 screws attaching the upper part of the grip (6—Fig. ID8), then separate and remove the top half. The vibration isolator will hold the halves of the grip together requiring the grip to be pried apart.

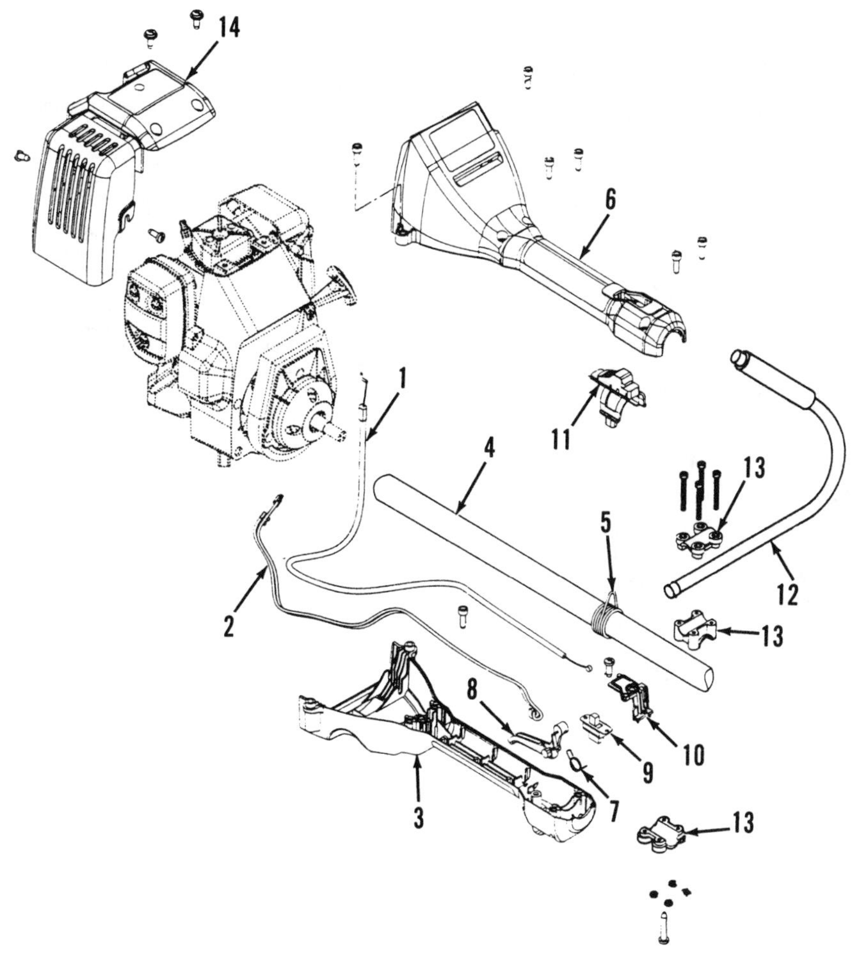

Fig. ID8—Exploded view of the grip and throttle trigger assembly.

1. Throttle cable
2. Engine stop wires
3. Grip lower housing
4. Drive shaft housing
5. Shoulder strap attachment
6. Grip upper housing
7. Throttle return spring
8. Throttle trigger
9. Engine stop switch
10. Trigger & switch retainer
11. Engine stop switch slider
12. J handle
13. Clamp assembly
14. Top cover

Observe the location of the throttle cable (1) and stop switch wires (2) to help you position these in the correct location when assembling. Detach the throttle cable and stop switch wires, then press the rear of the handle (3) down to remove it from the vibration isolator.

Remove the air filter cover, air filter, air filter base and carburetor (1, 2, 3 and 6—Fig. ID9). Detach the fuel lines from the primer bulb (4). Unbolt and remove the top cover (14—Fig. ID8) from the engine. Remove the two screws attaching the carburetor mount isolator (8—Fig. ID9), then remove the isolator and gasket. Remove the intake baffle plate (9).

Unbolt and remove the muffler (14), being careful not to lose the trapped 5 mm nut for the upper rear screw located near the spark plug. Do not attempt to remove the heat shield (16) from between the muffler and the cylinder until other parts trapping it are removed. If the gasket (15) is removed from the exhaust port, be careful not to damage the cylinder head.

Remove the three screws attaching the clutch housing (2—Fig. ID10), then remove the clutch drum (3), housing (2) and vibration isolator (4). If necessary, the drive spring (1) can be removed from the clutch drum. Turn the flywheel until the starter pawls are located at 12 o'clock and 6 o'clock and install the flywheel holding tool (part No. 180919). Use the clutch tool (part No. 180918) to turn the clutch rotor counterclockwise and remove the clutch (5).

Unbolt and remove the starter assembly from the front cover and withdraw the spacer (18—Fig. ID9) from the crankshaft. Remove the screws attaching the fuel tank bracket (16—Fig. ID10), then remove the fuel tank. Remove the four attaching screws from the front cover (17—Fig. ID9). Detach the stop switch wires when the cover is withdrawn sufficiently. Unbolt and remove the ignition module (19). Bump the flywheel with a soft-faced mallet to dislodge the flywheel from the tapered surface. Remove the flywheel and the drive key (20 and 21).

Remove the screw (1—Fig. ID11) from the center of the rocker arm cover, then remove the cover (2) and gasket (5). Remove the adjusting nuts (6) from both rocker arms, then remove the rocker arms (8) and pivots (7). Rocker arms, pivots and push rods (9) are identical for both valves, but should be installed in their original location. Keep each rocker arm with its push rod and pivot, marking each indicating its location on the intake valve or exhaust valve.

Remove the four retaining nuts and the special hardened washers attaching the cylinder head. Do not lose or mix these washers with other similar washers. Use needle nose pliers to remove the push rod guides (12) from the cylinder studs. Lift the cylinder head from the cylinder and remove gasket (18) and "O" rings (17). Do not attempt to separate the rocker box from the cylinder head. Remove the two screws (20) attaching the cylinder to the crankcase. Lift the cylinder (19) carefully, supporting the piston as the cylinder is raised. Slide the connecting rod to the rear and lift it from the crankshaft and crankcase. Remove the two screws attaching the cam bracket (22) to the crankcase and remove the cam gear (24), bracket and cam followers (23). **The crankshaft should not be removed from**

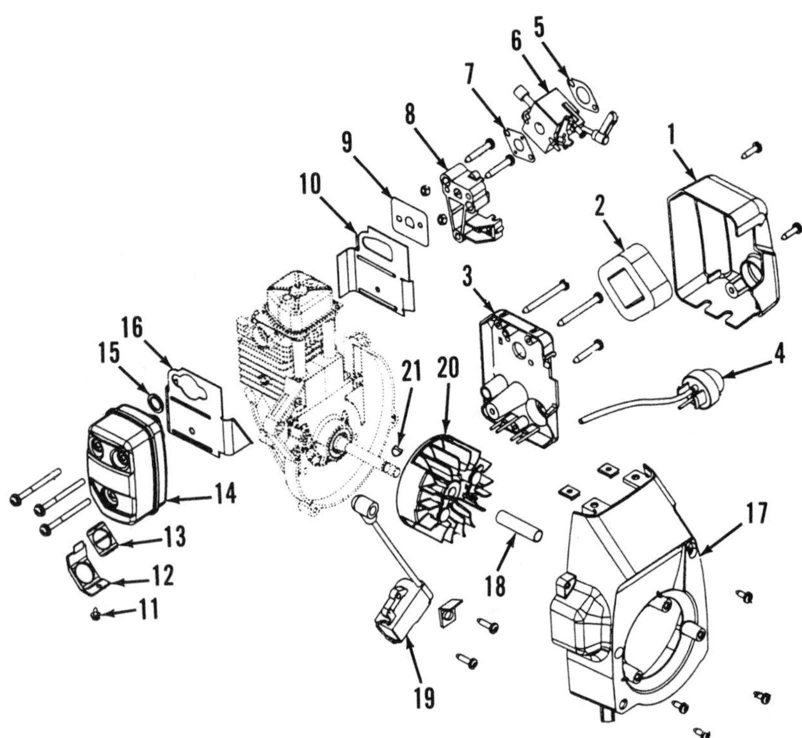

Fig. ID9—View of the intake, exhaust and ignition systems.

1. Air filter cover
2. Air filter foam
3. Air filter base
4. Primer bulb
5. Gasket
6. Carburetor
7. Gasket
8. Carburetor mount insulator
9. Gasket
10. Intake side baffle
11. Screw
12. Cover
13. Exhaust screen
14. Muffler
15. Gasket
16. Exhaust side baffle
17. Front cover
18. Spacer
19. Ignition module
20. Flywheel
21. Flywheel key

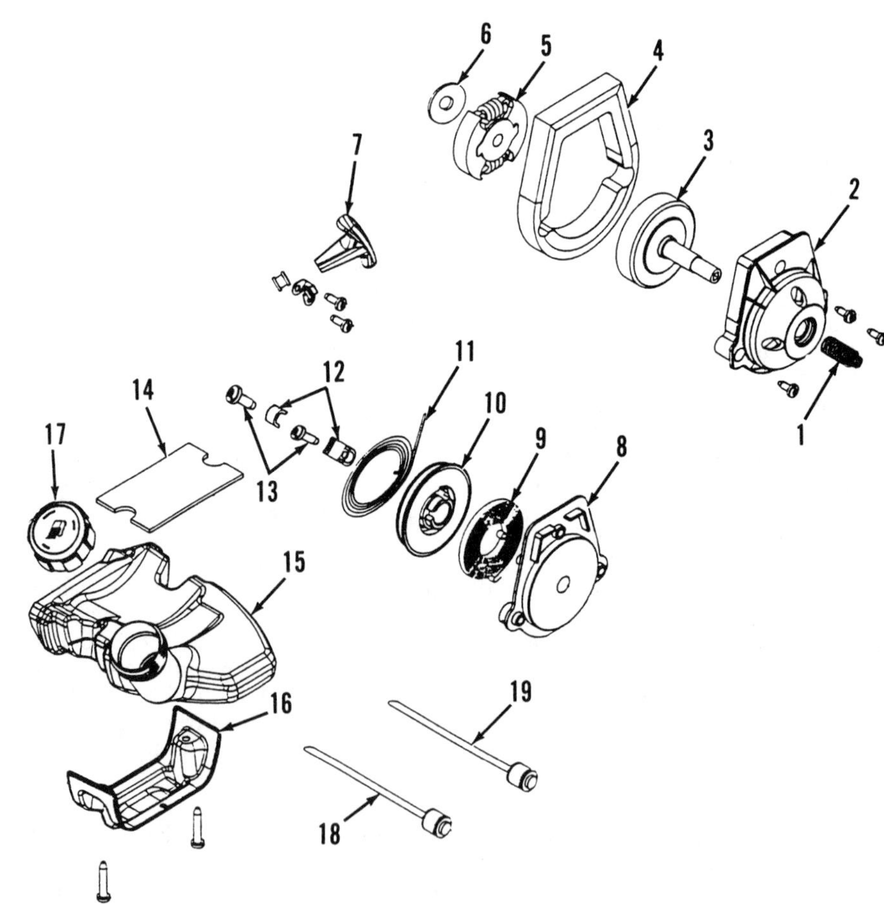

Fig. ID10—View of the clutch, starter and fuel tank.

1. Compression spring
2. Clutch housing
3. Clutch drum
4. Vibration isolator
5. Clutch rotor and shoes
6. Washer
7. Starter handle
8. Starter housing
9. Rewind spring
10. Starter pulley
11. Rope
12. Retainers
13. Screws
14. Tank pad
15. Fuel tank
16. Bracket
17. Cap
18. Pickup line and filter
19. Fuel return line

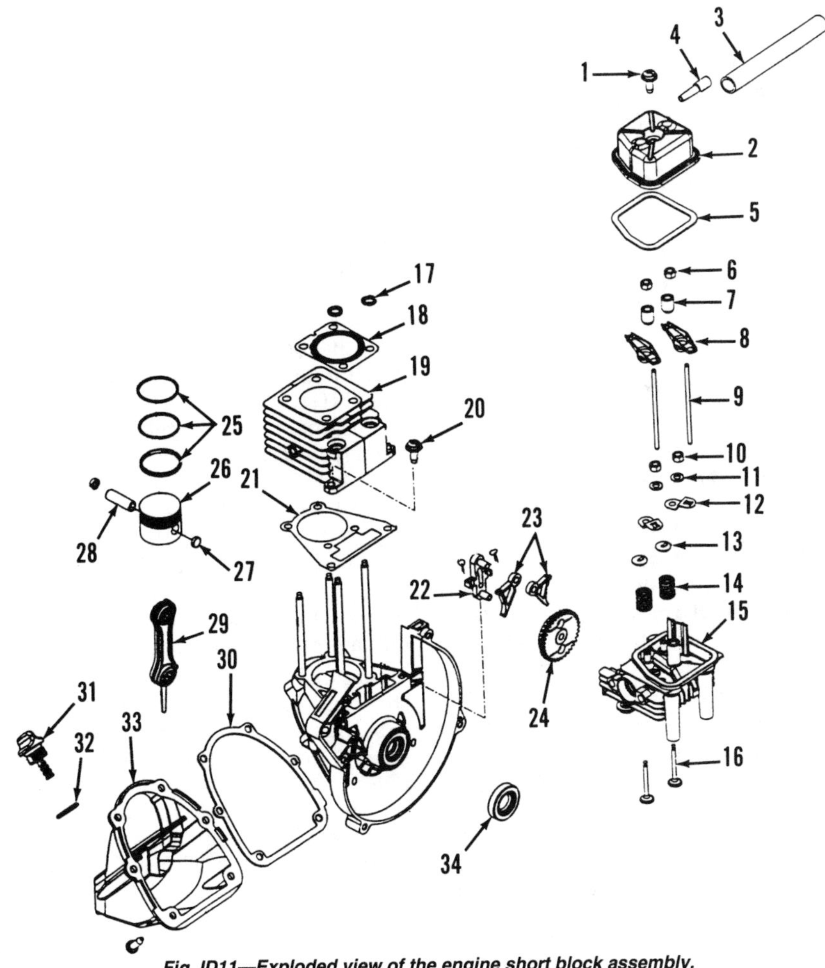

Fig. ID11—Exploded view of the engine short block assembly.

1. Screw
2. Rocker arm cover
3. Breather hose
4. Breather assembly
5. Gasket
6. Retaining and adjusting nuts
7. Rocker arm pivots
8. Rocker arms
9. Push rods
10. Retaining nuts
11. Washers
12. Push rod guides
13. Valve spring retainers
14. Valve springs
15. Cylinder head
16. Valves
17. "O" rings
18. Head gasket
19. Cylinder
20. Screws
21. Base gasket
22. Cam bracket
23. Cam followers
24. Cam and gear
25. Piston rings
26. Piston
27. Button plugs
28. Piston pin
29. Connecting rod
30. Gasket
31. Filler plug
32. "O" ring
33. Oil pan
34. Oil seal

the crankcase. The oil pan (33) can be unbolted from the rear of the crankcase if required. The lip type crankshaft oil seal (34) can be removed from the front of the crankcase if renewal is required.

REASSEMBLY. Reassemble in the reverse of disassembly procedure. Refer to the individual service paragraphs for additional assembly instructions. Tighten fasteners to the torque listed in the TIGHTENING TORQUE paragraph.

When assembling the halves of the grip (3 and 6—Fig. ID8), first install and assemble the lower grip, throttle trigger, return spring (7), engine stop switch (9) and retainer (10). Make sure the wires (2) and throttle cable (1) are routed properly.

Install the drive shaft and housing (4) so the hole in the upper end engages the locating screw in the lower grip half (3). Wrap masking tape around the drive shaft and lower grip to hold the parts together while installing the upper half of the grip. Install the slide (11), then install the upper half of the grip (6). Soap and water can be used to lubricate the vibration isolator making installation of the grips easier. Make sure that all parts fit together properly before installing the six attaching screws. When the halves of the grip fit together properly and the controls operate properly, cut the masking tape and install the six screw. Tighten fasteners to the torque listed in the TIGHTENING TORQUE paragraph. Make sure the engine is serviced with oil before starting.

CYLINDER HEAD AND VALVES. Clean the cylinder head and make sure to remove all gasket residue, but be careful to prevent damaging any surface while cleaning. Check all of the gasket surfaces for scratches or nicks. Inspect the small EGR (exhaust gas recirculation) hole between the intake and exhaust passages in the cylinder head.

The valves and seats cannot be serviced except by installing new parts. Check the valves for proper sealing. It should be possible to compress the valve springs with your fingers, then press the retainer (13—Fig. ID11) to the side and remove the retainer, spring (14) and valve (16).

Clean the gasket surfaces of the cylinder and head thoroughly, but do not nick, scratch or otherwise damage the surfaces while cleaning. Install new "O" rings (17), making sure they are seated correctly and not damaged or twisted, then lubricate the installed "O" rings with new oil.

Install a new cylinder head gasket (18) with the notch toward the spark plug side of the cylinder. The domed side of the cylinder head gasket should be toward the top. Make sure the studs and the bores for the studs inside the rocker arm compartment are clean and dry, then install the cylinder head and valves over the studs. Seal the two cylinder head studs inside the rocker arm compartment with RTV sealer, then install the push rod guides (12) over the studs. Install the four special hardened washers (11) and retaining nuts (10). Tighten the retaining nuts evenly in a crossing pattern to 35-40 in.-lb. (3.9-4.5 N•m).

Lubricate the push rods (9) with engine oil, then insert the rods into the push rod tubes until seated in the cam followers. Lubricate the rocker arms and pivots (7 and 8), then install the retaining/adjusting nuts (6). Refer to the VALVE CLEARANCE ADJUSTMENT paragraphs when installing these nuts.

The breather (4) should be inserted into the end of hose (3), then insert the hose through the hole in rocker arm cover (2) from the inside until the hose is securely wedged in the cover. Install the rocker arm cover using a new gasket (5) and tighten the retaining screw (1) to the torque listed in the TIGHTENING TORQUE paragraph.

PISTON, RINGS AND CONNECTING ROD. Rings (25—Fig. ID11) should not be removed from the piston (26) unless new rings are available for installation. Check the side clearance of the rings in the grooves. Clearance should not exceed 0.004 in. (0.107 mm).

The piston pin buttons (27) and piston pin (28) can be removed, separating the piston from the connecting rod (29). Inspect the crankpin for any scoring or other signs of damage. The crankshaft

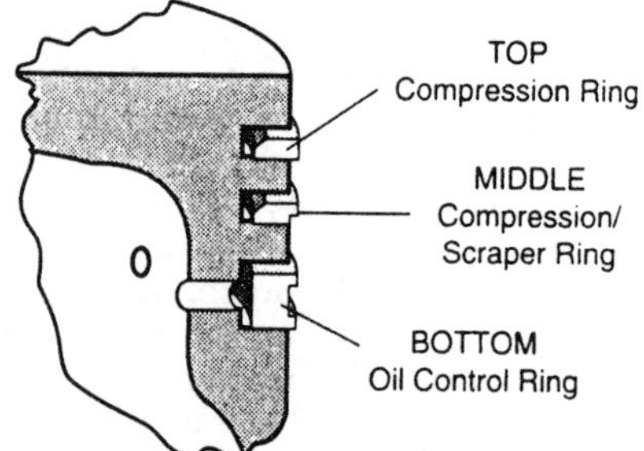

Fig. ID12—Install the piston rings in the grooves as shown. The chamfer on the inside of the rings should be toward the top of the piston. The ring with the groove on the outer diameter should be installed in the middle groove with the outer groove down.

is not available for service. If the crankpin is damaged, a new short block should be installed.

Clean the ring grooves in the piston, but be very careful not to nick or gouge the piston. Refer to Fig. ID12 and install the rings in the piston grooves as follows. Lubricate the new rings with clean oil before installing. Install the bottom oil control ring first, followed by the middle (compression/scraper ring). The middle ring should be installed as shown in Fig. ID12, with the inside chamfer to the top and the cut-away outer edge to the bottom. Install the top ring with the chamfered inner edge to the top as shown. Spread the ring gap only enough to install the ring over the piston. Be careful not to damage either the ring or the piston when installing. Install the piston pin buttons (27—Fig. ID11) with the smooth side out.

Lubricate the connecting rod bearing and the crankpin, then install the piston/connecting rod. The connecting rod should be installed on the crankshaft crankpin with the **markings on the needle bearing toward the front** (crankshaft counterweight). Slide the connecting rod over the crankshaft crankpin. Position the rings with the end gaps as shown in Fig. ID13 before installing the cylinder. Refer to the CYLINDER paragraph for installation of the cylinder.

CAM BRACKET, GEAR AND FOLLOWERS. The cam bracket

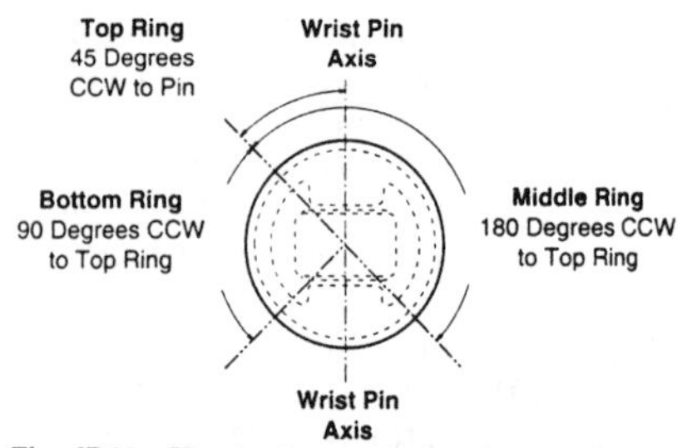

Fig. ID13—The end gap of the rings should be located as shown when installing the cylinder over the piston and rings.

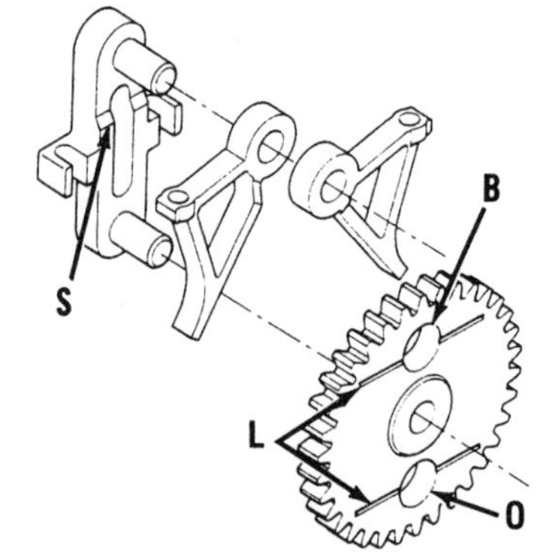

Fig. ID14—Refer to the text when assembling and installing the cam bracket, gear and followers.

(22—Fig. ID11) is attached to the crankcase with two screws. If removed, the cam gear (24) must be correctly timed to the position of the crankshaft. Cleaning and inspection may be accomplished without removing the bracket, gear and followers, but if removed, the gear must be timed to the crankshaft. Inspect all parts for cracks, damaged teeth, broken parts or other damage.

Assemble the bracket, gear and followers (Fig. ID14) as follows. Lubricate parts, then install the followers on the longer post, which is indicated by the step (S). Install the gear on the lower post, guiding the followers over the cam. Turn the gear until the blocked hole (B) is to the top and open hole (O) is down. The lines (L) should be parallel with the mounting surface of the bracket.

To install and time the cam to the crankshaft, proceed as follows. Turn the crankshaft until the crankpin is at the top of its stroke. The crankpin should be centered between the two marks on the crankcase inside the bore for the cylinder. Insert the bracket, gear and followers assembly into the crankcase with the blocked hole (B) still to the top and the open hole (O) down. Make sure the lines (L) remain parallel with the cylinder mounting surface of the crankcase when the bracket is seated. Install and tighten the two screws attaching the cam bracket to the torque listed in the TIGHTENING TORQUE paragraph.

CYLINDER. The cylinder and piston are available in standard size only. Check the piston and cylinder for wear or damage. It is suggested that both be renewed if either is worn or damaged excessively. Be sure that all gasket surfaces are cleaned thoroughly, but do not nick, scratch or otherwise damage the cylinder while cleaning. Lubricate the cylinder, piston and rings thoroughly before installing the cylinder.

Install the cam bracket, gear and followers assembly as previously described. Install the piston, rings and connecting rod as previously described. Carefully install the cylinder base gasket (21—Fig. ID11). Lubricate the cylinder bore with new oil. Check to be sure the ring end gaps are located as shown in Fig. ID13, press the rings carefully into their grooves and hold the piston pin buttons (27—Fig. ID11) in place while installing the cylinder over the piston. Install the two cylinder retaining screws to the torque listed in the TIGHTENING TORQUE paragraph. Install the cylinder head as previously described.

MUFFLER. Make sure the exhaust side baffle (16—Fig. ID9) is in place. Remove the old gasket (15) and clean the cylinder head carefully, being careful not to nick, scratch or otherwise damage the cylinder head.

Install a new gasket, then position the muffler. Install the lower screw first, but do not tighten until the other screws are installed. The 5 mm nut must be held in place in the slot nearest the spark plug while installing the upper screw. Tighten fittings to the torque listed in the TIGHTENING TORQUE paragraph.

CLUTCH. To remove clutch assembly, remove the six Torx T-25 screws attaching the upper part of the grip (6—Fig. ID8), then separate and remove the top half. The vibration isolator will hold the halves of the grip together, requiring the grip to be pried apart.

Observe the location of the throttle cable (1) and stop switch wires (2) to help you position these in the correct location when assembling. Detach the throttle cable and stop switch wires, then press the rear of the handle (3) down to remove it from the vibration isolator.

Remove the three screws attaching the clutch housing (2—Fig. ID15), then remove the clutch drum (3), housing (2) and vibration isolator (4). If necessary, the drive spring (1) can be removed from the clutch drum. Turn the flywheel until the starter pawls are located at 12 o'clock and 6 o'clock and install the flywheel holding tool (part No. 180919). Use the clutch tool (part No. 180918) to turn the clutch rotor counterclockwise and remove the clutch (5).

Inspect clutch drum (3—Fig. ID15) and rotor (5) for wear or damage and renew as necessary. When installing clutch, be sure that spacer (6) is in-

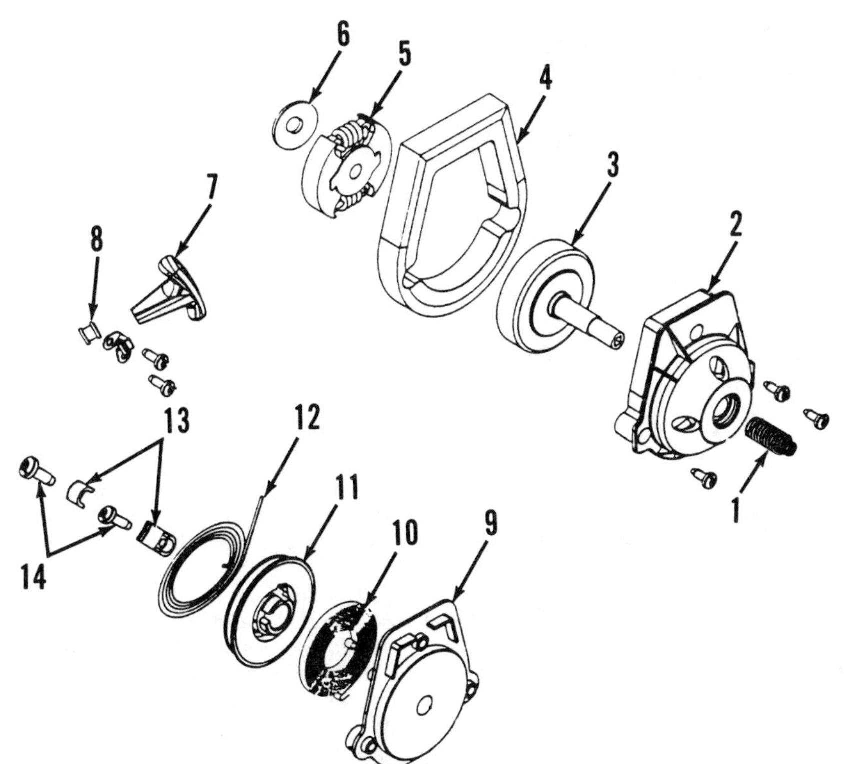

Fig. ID15—Exploded view of clutch assembly and rewind starter.

1. Spring
2. Clutch housing
3. Clutch drum
4. Isolator
5. Clutch rotor
6. Spacer
7. Rope handle
8. Guide eyelet
9. Starter housing
10. Rewind spring
11. Starter pulley
12. Rope
13. Retainers
14. Screws

stalled on crankshaft. Tighten clutch rotor to 140-150 in.-lb. (15.8-16.9 N•m).

REWIND STARTER. Refer to Fig. ID15 for an exploded view of typical rewind starter. To service starter, first remove the upper handle and the clutch assembly as previously outlined. Unbolt and remove starter housing from engine.

Remove the rope handle and allow the rope to wind into the starter. Remove the two screws (14—Fig. ID15) and retainers (13). Removing starter pulley (11). Use caution when removing rewind spring (10) as the spring may unwind uncontrollably causing injury. Wear appropriate safety eye wear and gloves before removing the recoil spring from the housing. Drop the starter housing in a trash container or on the floor to release the spring from the housing. A replacement rewind spring comes prewound and contained in a spring retainer.

When installing new rewind spring, be sure that spring windings are clockwise (open end of spring inner hook is to the left). Grasp spring with needle nose pliers and remove spring retainer. Position spring in starter housing with spring hook installed into groove in housing, then release the needle nose pliers holding the spring. Lubricate the center post and spring side of pulley with small amount of grease.

If replacing starter rope, insert rope through hole in pulley and tie a single knot approximately 1/2 in. (12.7 mm) from end of rope. Pull the knot into pocket in the pulley. Hold pulley with pawl teeth towards you, then wrap rope around pulley in clockwise direction. Thread the rope through the guide eyelet (8), then attach the handle (7). Install the pulley over the center post of the housing while making sure the pulley engages the end of the rewind spring. Wind the pulley one full turn to preload the rewind spring. Install pulley retainers (13) and screws (14).

JONSERED

ENGINE SERVICE

Model	Bore	Stroke	Displacement
GR26	34 mm (1.34 in.)	28 mm (1.10 in.)	25.4 cc (1.55 cu. in.)
GR32	35 mm (1.38 in.)	32 mm (1.26 in.)	30.8 cc (1.88 cu. in.)
GR36 & BP40	38 mm (1.5 in.)	32 mm (1.26 in.)	36.3 cc (2.2 cu. in.)

ENGINE IDENTIFICATION

These two-stroke, air-cooled, gasoline engines are used on some Jonsered trimmers and brush cutters.

MAINTENANCE

LUBRICATION. The engine is lubricated by oil mixed with the fuel. Refer to the appropriate trimmer or brush cutter service section for the amount and type of oil the equipment manufacturer recommends mixing with gasoline.

SPARK PLUG. Recommended spark plug for is a Champion RCJ7Y, NGK BPMR7A or equivalent. Electrode gap should be 0.5 mm (0.020 in.).

CARBURETOR. Walbro WT235 carburetor is used. To adjust, turn the low speed mixture needle (20—Fig. J101) clockwise until lightly seated, then back the screw out 1-1/4 turns. Turn the high speed mixture needle (19) clockwise until lightly seated, then back the needle out 1-1/4 turns. The housing around the mixture needles is marked "H" for the high speed needle and "L" for the low speed needle. If equipped with limiter caps (21), a special screwdriver is needed to adjust the mixture needles.

Start and run engine until normal operating temperature is reached. Adjust the idle mixture needle until the engine idles smoothly and accelerates cleanly without hesitation. Run the engine at full throttle (no load) and adjust the high speed needle until the engine runs with a slight "four-cycle" sound. For optimum setting, a tachometer should be used to check maximum engine speed. Maximum recommended rpm is 10,800 rpm for Model GR32 and 11,000 rpm for all other models. Maximum recommended speed should not be exceeded. Do not set either mixture needle too lean. If the low speed mixture needle is too lean it will not operate properly. If either needle is too lean, the engine can be damaged. Set the idle speed stop screw (16) so the engine idles about 2,500 rpm. On models with clutch, the engine should idle slowly enough that the clutch remains disengaged.

To remove carburetor, remove air cleaner housing. Remove two screws retaining carburetor and remove carburetor and carburetor cover. Disconnect fuel line and throttle cable.

To disassemble the carburetor, refer to Fig. J101 and remove covers (5 and 15) for access to internal components. Remove diaphragms (6 and 13), metering lever (8) and fuel inlet valve (10), Welch plug (9), fuel screen (12) and mixture needles (19 and 20).

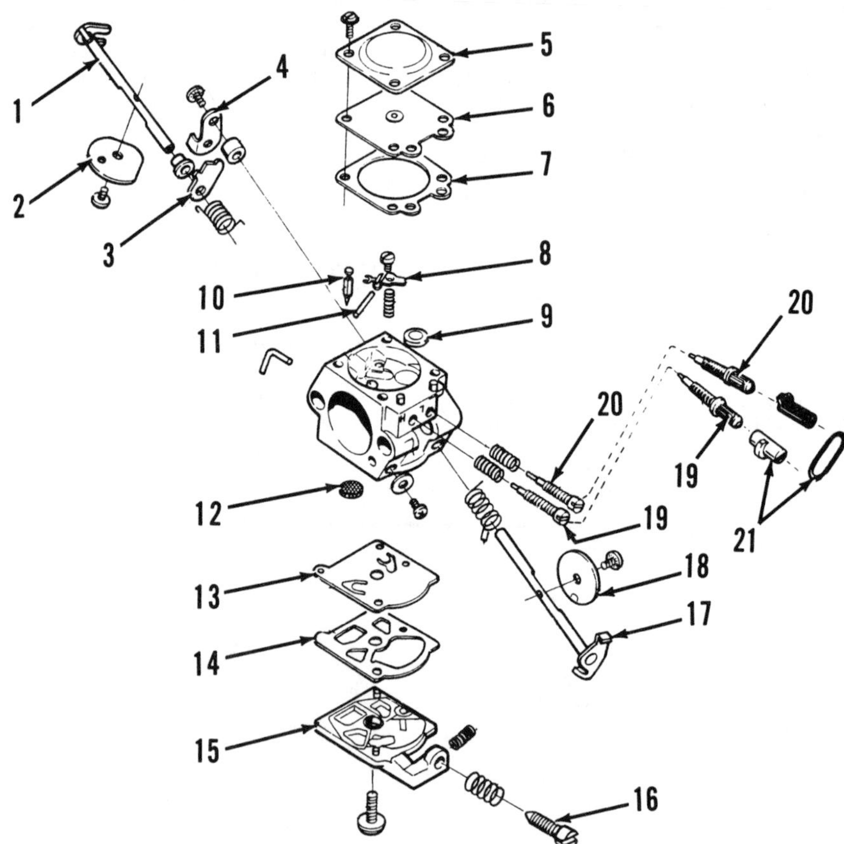

Fig. J101—Exploded view of Walbro WT carburetor typical of all models. Some models may not be equipped with limiter caps (21).

1. Choke shaft
2. Choke plate
3. Fast idle cam
4. Throttle lever
5. Cover
6. Metering diaphragm
7. Gasket
8. Metering lever
9. Welch plug
10. Fuel inlet valve
11. Pin
12. Fuel screen
13. Fuel pump diaphragm
14. Gasket
15. Cover
16. Idle speed stop screw
17. Throttle shaft
18. Throttle plate
19. High speed mixture needle
20. Low speed mixture needle
21. Limiter caps

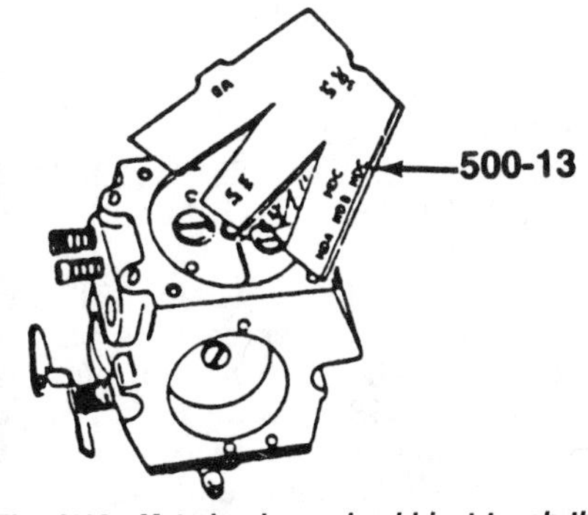

Fig. J102—Metering lever should just touch the leg of Walbro tool 500-13. Bend lever if necessary to obtain correct lever height.

Clean and inspect all components. If the unit has been improperly stored, passages may be clogged with deposits that are hard, solid and nearly transparent. Be careful not to damage the openings or sealing surfaces while cleaning. Check the condition of diaphragms (6 and 13) carefully. Install new diaphragms if hard (not flexible), torn or otherwise damaged. Examine the fuel inlet valve (10), spring and lever (8). A new fuel inlet valve needle (10), and mixture screws (19 and 20) can be installed, but their seats cannot be serviced if damaged. Clean or replace the filter screen (12).

When reassembling, apply a thin coat of sealant around edge of new Welch plug. Check the height of the metering lever as shown in Fig. J102 using Walbro tool 500-13 or equivalent. Carefully bend the lever if necessary to obtain the correct lever height.

IGNITION SYSTEM. The engine is equipped with an electronic ignition system that does not use breaker points. The module is incorporated in the coil assembly.

Ignition can be considered satisfactory if a spark will jump across the 3 mm (1/8 in.) electrode gap of a test plug when the engine is turned with the recoil starter. If there is no spark, check the stop switch and connecting wire for shorts to ground. Ignition may be irregular at starting speeds if gap between the legs of the coil core and the flywheel magnets is too wide.

The ignition module/coil is located under the fan housing at the front of the engine. Two screws attach the ignition module/coil. When installing, set the air gap between the flywheel magnets and the legs of the ignition module as follows. Install the ignition module, but tighten the two screws only enough to hold it in place away from the flywheel. Insert 0.3 mm thick brass or plastic shim stock between the legs of the ignition module and the flywheel, then turn the flywheel until the flywheel magnets are near the module legs. Loosen the screws attaching the ignition module and press legs of the ignition module against the shim, then tighten the two attaching screws. Remove the shim stock, then turn the flywheel and check to be sure the flywheel does not hit the legs of the coil.

REPAIRS

PISTON, PIN, RING AND CYLINDER. To remove the piston, separate the drive shaft housing from the engine and remove the clutch assembly as outlined in the STRING TRIMMER Service Section. Remove the recoil starter, ignition coil and spark plug. Insert a piece of rope or piston stop in the spark plug hole to prevent the engine from turning, then remove the clutch and the nut attaching the flywheel. Use a suitable puller to remove the flywheel. Remove the carburetor and muffler. Be careful not to lose the small plastic ring (5—Fig. J103) and pull the intake pipe (6) out, away from the cylinder. Remove the screws (7) attaching the cylinder, then pull the cylinder (11) straight up, off the piston. Remove the piston pin retaining rings (15), push the pin (14) out using a suitable pusher tool, then separate the piston (13) from the connecting rod. If necessary to remove the main bearings and seals (18 and 19), use suitable pullers and install new components when assembling.

The piston, ring and cylinder are available in standard size only and the cylinder should not be bored oversize. Inspect the cylinder for any damage and install new parts as necessary. If the chrome plating is worn from the cyl-

Fig. J103—Exploded view of engine typical of all models.

1. Screw
2. Air cleaner
3. Choke lever
4. Carburetor
5. Plastic ring
6. Intake pipe
7. Crankcase screws
8. Support
9. Crankcase half
10. Heat shield
11. Cylinder
12. Piston ring
13. Piston
14. Piston pin
15. Retaining clip
16. Pin bearing
17. Crankshaft assy.
18. Seal assy.
19. Main bearing

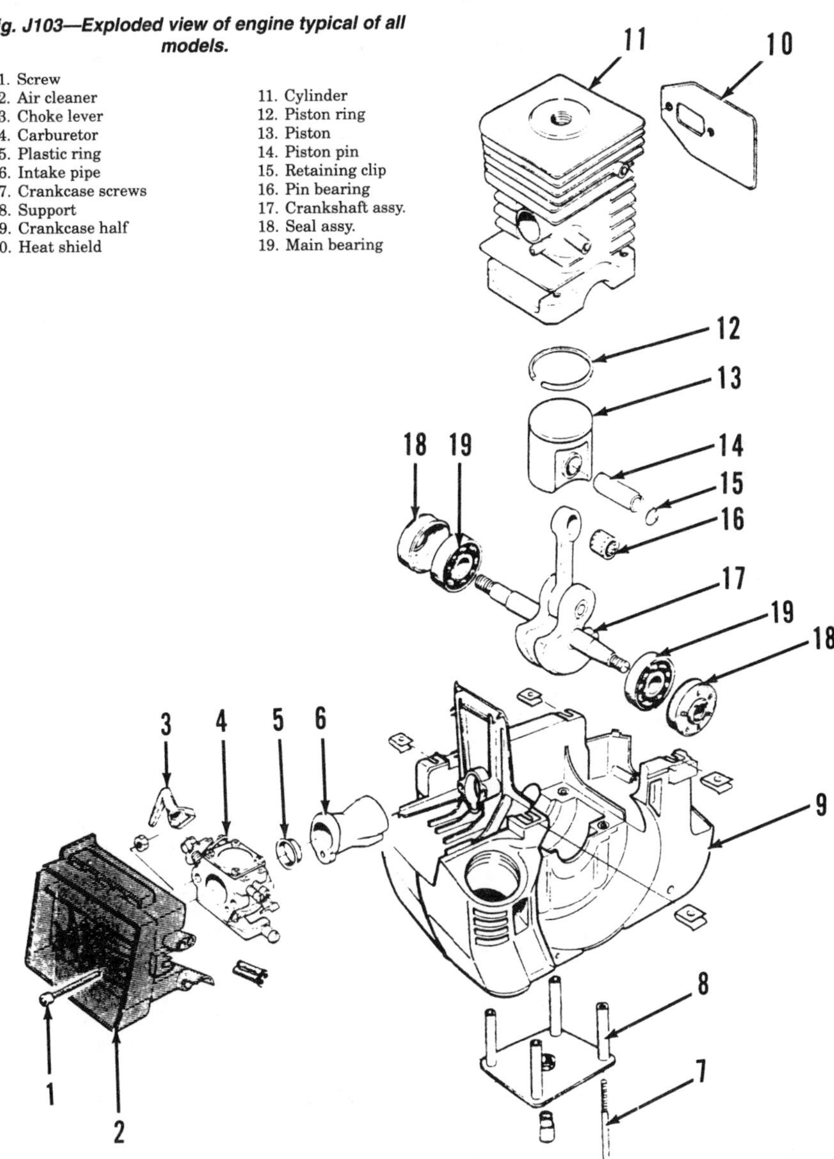

inder, a new cylinder should be installed. Clean sealer from the cylinder base and the lower half of the crankcase. Check the intake pipe (6) for cracking and make sure that ring (5) is not cracked or lost.

Install the piston on the connecting rod so arrow on top of piston will be toward the exhaust port (muffler) side of cylinder. Lubricate the piston pin and bearing, then install the piston pin. If removed, install new retaining rings (15). Install the retaining rings with the gap toward the top or bottom of the piston.

Insert the intake pipe (6) through the hole in the crankcase, but pull the pipe out far enough to allow the cylinder to be installed. Lubricate the connecting rod lower bearing, cylinder bore, piston and ring. Make sure the ends of the piston ring surround the pin located in ring groove. Apply a thin unbroken 1-1.5 mm line of sealer (part No. 503 26 70-01) to the base of the cylinder, then carefully slide the cylinder over the piston. Be careful to install the cylinder straight down over the piston. If the cylinder is twisted, the ring can catch in a port and break the end of the ring. If so equipped, install spacer (8). Install screws (7) and tighten in a crossing pattern evenly to 11 N•m torque.

NOTE: Screws (7) should be tightened to 11 N•m torque again after assembly is complete and engine has run for 2-3 minutes, then allowed to cool.

Slide the intake pipe (6) in, against the cylinder and make sure plastic ring (5) is correctly positioned, then install the carburetor and air cleaner housing (2).

CRANKSHAFT AND CONNECTING ROD. The crankshaft and connecting rod are available only as an assembly (17—Fig. J103); individual components are not available. A shop experienced in servicing built-up crankshaft assemblies can align the shaft.

To remove the crankshaft and connecting rod assembly, remove the cylinder and piston as described in PISTON PIN, RING AND CYLINDER paragraphs.

The main bearings should turn smoothly with no perceptible play or ratcheting. The main bearings (19) fit inside seals (18). Use suitable tools to press new main bearings and seals onto the crankshaft. Lubricate lips of seals (18) with engine oil before installing over the crankshaft.

Refer to PISTON, PIN, RING AND CYLINDER paragraphs for installing these parts.

CLUTCH. Refer to the Trimmer section for clutch removal and service procedures.

REWIND STARTER. Refer to the Trimmer section for service to the recoil starter.

JONSERED

ENGINE SERVICE

Model	Bore	Stroke	Displacement
GR41	40 mm (1.58 in.)	32 mm (1.26 in.)	40.2 cc (2.5 cu. in.)
RS44	42 mm (1.65 in.)	32 mm (1.26 in.)	44.3 cc (2.7 cu. in.)
GR50	44 mm (1.73 in.)	32 mm (1.26 in.)	48.7 cc (2.97 cu. in.)

ENGINE IDENTIFICATION

These two-stroke, air-cooled, gasoline engines are used on some Jonsered trimmers and brush cutters.

MAINTENANCE

LUBRICATION. The engine is lubricated by oil mixed with the fuel. Refer to the appropriate trimmer or brush cutter service section for the amount and type of oil the manufacturer the equipment recommends mixing with gasoline.

SPARK PLUG. Recommended spark plug for all models is a Champion RCJ7Y, NGK BPMR7A or equivalent. Electrode gap should be 0.5 mm (0.020 in.).

CARBURETOR. Walbro WT99 carburetor is used. To adjust, turn the low speed mixture needle (14—Fig. J121) clockwise until lightly seated, then back the screw out 1-1/4 turns. Turn the high speed mixture needle (15) clockwise until lightly seated, then back the needle out 1-1/4 turns. The grommet (9) around the mixture needles is marked "H" for the high speed needle and "L" for the low speed needle.

Start and run engine until normal operating temperature is reached. Adjust the idle mixture needle until the engine idles smoothly and accelerates cleanly without hesitation. Run the engine at full speed (no load) and adjust the high speed needle until the engine runs at the highest speed with a slight "four-cycle" sound. For optimum setting it is recommended that a tachometer be used to check engine rpm. Recommended maximum speed is 12,500 rpm. Recommended maximum speed should not be exceeded. Do not set either mixture needle too lean. If the low speed mixture needle is too lean it will not accelerate properly. If either mixture needle is set too lean, the engine can be damaged. Set the idle speed stop screw (23—Fig. J122) so the engine idles about 2,500 rpm. The engine should idle slowly enough that the clutch remains disengaged.

To remove carburetor, remove air cleaner housing (1—Fig. J121) and filter element (2). Remove two screws retaining carburetor and remove filter bracket (4) and carburetor. Disconnect fuel line and throttle cable.

To disassemble the carburetor, refer to Fig. J122 and remove covers (6 and 21) for access to internal components. Remove diaphragms (7 and 19), metering lever (11) and fuel inlet valve (9), Welch plug (13), fuel screen (18) and mixture needles (14 and 15).

Clean and inspect all components. If the unit has been improperly stored, passages may be clogged with deposits that are hard, solid and nearly transparent. Be careful not to damage the openings or sealing surfaces while cleaning. Check the condition of diaphragms (7 and 19) carefully. Install new diaphragms if hard (not flexible), torn or otherwise damaged. Examine the fuel inlet valve (9), spring (12) and lever (11). A new fuel inlet valve needle (9), and mixture screws (14 and 15) can be installed, but their seats cannot be serviced if damaged. Inspect the condition of the filter screen (18) and clean or replace screen.

When resembling, apply a thin coat of sealant around edge of new Welch plug. Install Welch plug using a suitable punch with a diameter larger than the plug to avoid deforming the plug. Check the height of the metering lever

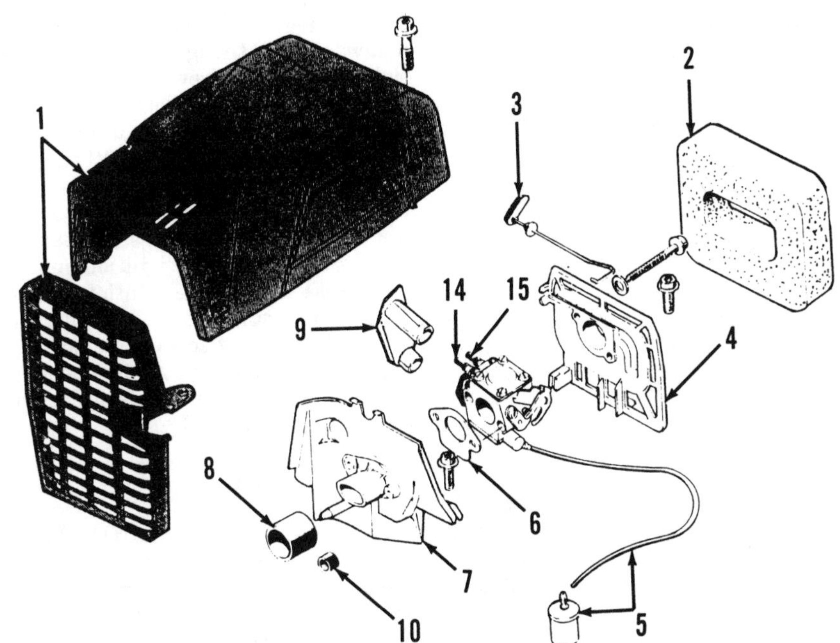

Fig. J121—View of typical covers, carburetor and air filter.

1. Covers
2. Air filter
3. Choke knob
4. Filter bracket
5. Fuel filter & hose
6. Gasket
7. Inlet housing
8. Inlet connector
9. Mixture needle grommet
10. Impulse channel
14. Low speed needle
15. High speed needle

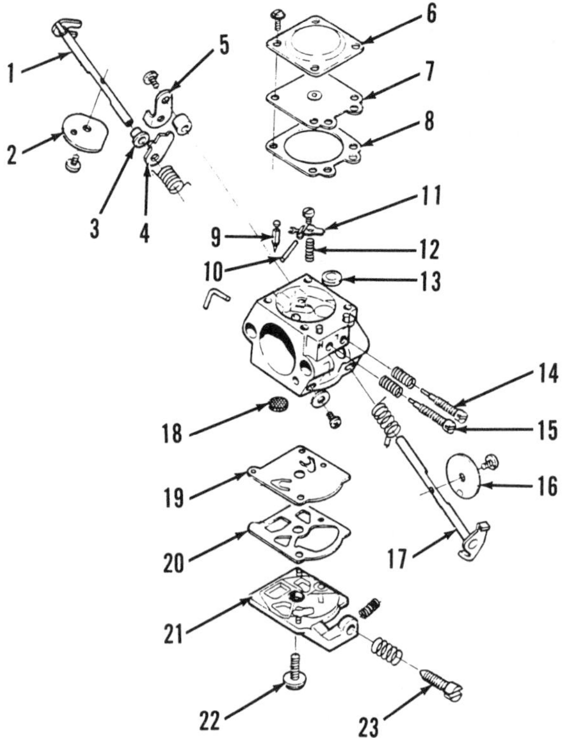

Fig. J122—Exploded view of typical Walbro WT carburetor.

1. Choke shaft
2. Choke plate
3. Spacer
4. Cam
5. Throttle lever
6. Cover
7. Metering diaphragm
8. Gasket
9. Fuel inlet valve
10. Pin
11. Metering lever
12. Spring
13. Welch plug
14. Low speed mixture needle
15. High speed mixture needle
16. Throttle plate
17. Throttle shaft
18. Fuel screen
19. Fuel pump diaphragm
20. Gasket
21. Cover
22. Screw
23. Low idle stop screw

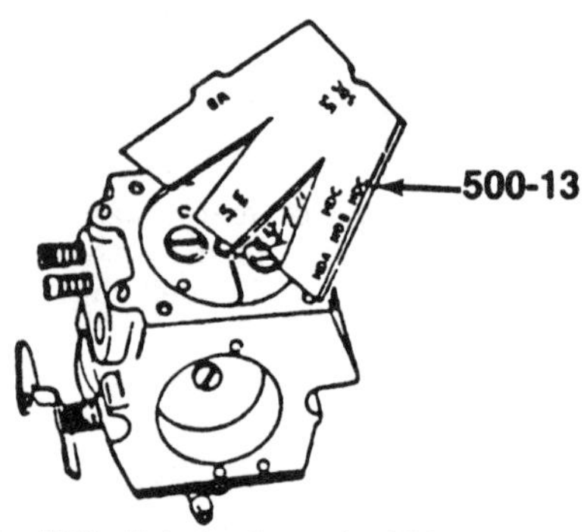

Fig. J123—Metering lever should just touch the leg of Walbro tool 500-13. Bend lever if necessary to obtain correct lever height.

as shown in Fig. J123 using Walbro tool 500-13 or equivalent. Carefully bend the lever if necessary to obtain the correct lever height.

Make certain that inlet connector (8—Fig. J121) and impulse channel (10) are in good condition and in proper position when installing carburetor. Install new components if either is damaged.

IGNITION SYSTEM. The engine is equipped with an electronic ignition system that does not use breaker points. The module is incorporated in the coil assembly.

Ignition can be considered satisfactory if a spark will jump across the 3 mm (1/8 in.) electrode gap of a test plug when the engine is turned with the recoil starter. If there is no spark, check the stop switch and connecting wire for shorts to ground. Ignition may be irregular at starting speeds if gap between the legs of the coil core and the flywheel magnets is too wide.

The ignition module/coil is located under the fan housing at the front of the engine. Two screws attach the ignition module/coil. When installing, set the air gap between the flywheel magnets and the legs of the ignition module as follows. Install the ignition module, but tighten the two screws only enough to hold it in place away from the flywheel. Insert 0.3 mm thick brass or plastic shim stock between the legs of the ignition module and the flywheel, then turn the flywheel until the flywheel magnets are near the module legs. Loosen the screws attaching the ignition module and press legs of the ignition module against the shim stock, then tighten the two attaching screws. Remove the shim stock, then turn the flywheel and check to be sure the flywheel does not hit the legs of the coil.

REPAIRS

PISTON, PIN, RING AND CYLINDER. To remove the piston, separate the drive shaft housing from the engine and remove the clutch drum assembly. Remove the recoil starter, ignition coil and spark plug. Insert a piece of rope or piston stop in the spark plug hole to prevent the engine from turning, then remove the clutch shoes/hub assembly and the nut attaching the flywheel. Use a suitable puller to remove the flywheel. Remove covers (1—Fig. J121), air cleaner (2), carburetor, intake housing (7) and muffler (1—Fig. J124). Remove the screws (5) attaching the cylinder, then pull the cylinder (8) straight up, off the piston. Remove the piston pin retaining rings (13), push the pin (12) out using a suitable pusher tool, then separate the piston (10) from the connecting rod. If necessary to remove the main bearings and seals (14, 15, 16, 18, 19 and 20), use suitable pullers and install new components when assembling.

The piston, ring and cylinder are available in standard size only and the cylinder should not be bored oversize. Inspect the cylinder for any damage and install new parts as necessary. If the chrome plating is worn from the cylinder, a new cylinder should be installed. Clean sealer from the cylinder base and the lower half of the crankcase (25). Check the intake connector (8) for cracking or other damage.

Install the piston on the connecting rod so arrow on top of piston will be toward the exhaust port (muffler) side of cylinder. Lubricate the piston pin and bearing, then install the piston pin. If removed, install new retaining rings (13). Install the retaining rings with the gap toward the top or bottom of the piston.

Lubricate the connecting rod lower bearing, cylinder bore, piston and ring. Make sure the ends of the piston ring surround the pin located in ring groove. Apply a thin unbroken 1-1.5 mm line of sealer (part No. 503 26 70-01) to the base of the cylinder, then carefully slide the cylinder over the piston. Be careful to install the cylinder straight down over the piston. If the cylinder is twisted, the ring can catch in a port and break the end of the ring. Install screws (5) and tighten in a crossing pattern evenly to 11 N·m torque.

NOTE: Screws (5) should be tightened to 11 N·m torque again after assembly is complete and engine has run for 2-3 minutes, then allowed to cool.

When assembling, be sure impulse channel (10—Fig. J121) is in place in cylinder. Install a new impulse channel if lost or damaged. Slide the intake connector (8), onto the cylinder, then install the carburetor and air cleaner housing.

CRANKSHAFT AND CONNECTING ROD. The crankshaft and connecting rod are available only as an

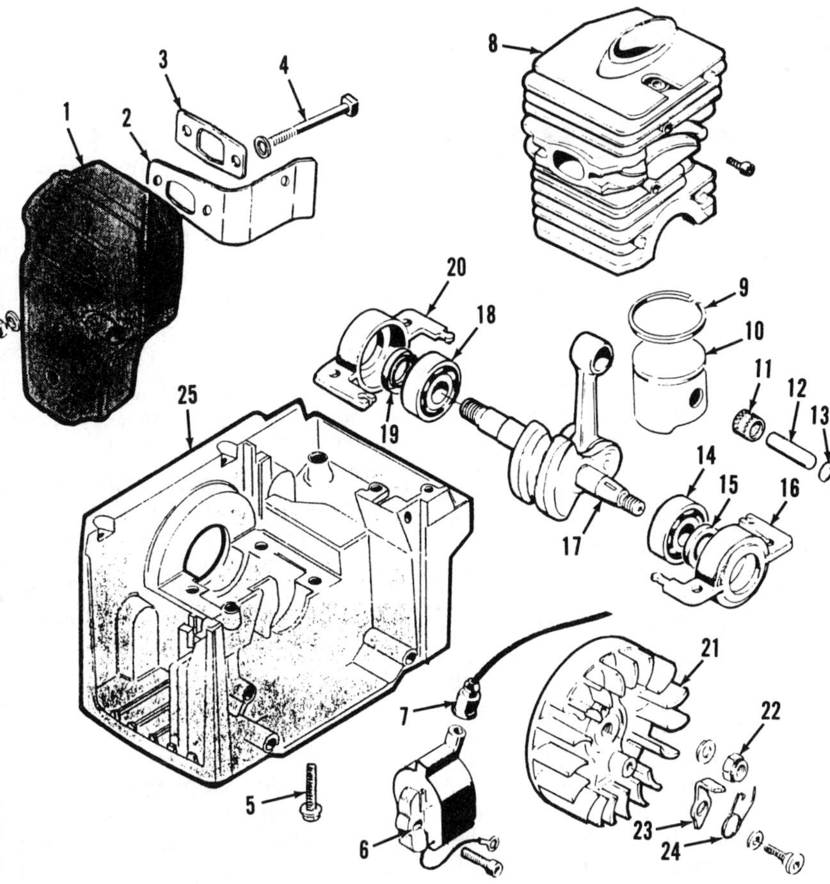

Fig. J124—Exploded view of engine typical of all models.

1. Muffler
2. Bracket
3. Gasket
4. Bolts
5. Screws
6. Ignition coil/module
7. Spark plug wire
8. Cylinder
9. Piston ring
10. Piston
11. Needle bearing
12. Piston pin
13. Retaining clip
14. Main bearing
15. Seal
16. Retainer half
17. Crankshaft & connecting rod assy.
18. Main bearing
19. Seal
20. Retainer half
21. Flywheel
22. Nut
23. Starter pawl
24. Spring
25. Crankcase lower half

assembly (17—Fig. J124); individual components are not available. A shop experienced in servicing built-up crankshaft assemblies can align the shaft.

To remove the crankshaft and connecting rod assembly, remove the cylinder and piston as described in PISTON, PIN, RING AND CYLINDER paragraphs. Lift the crankshaft, connecting rod, main bearings, seal and retainers (14 through 20) as an assembly from the crankcase.

The crankshaft should turn smoothly inside main bearings with no perceptible play or ratcheting. The main bearings (14 and 18) and seals (15 and 19) fit inside retainer halves (16 and 20). Twist retainers to separate the interlocking ends. A screwdriver or similar tool can be used to pull the retainers from the main bearings. Use suitable tools to remove and install new main bearings and seals. Lubricate lips of seals with engine oil before installing over the crankshaft. Make sure that tabs of retainer halves (16 and 20) are properly interlocked while assembling.

Refer to PISTON, PIN, RING AND CYLINDER paragraphs for installing these parts.

CLUTCH. Refer to the Trimmer section for clutch removal and service procedures.

REWIND STARTER. Refer to the Trimmer section for service to the recoil starter.

JONSERED

ENGINE SERVICE

Model	Bore	Stroke	Displacement
RS51	45 mm (1.77 in.)	32 mm (1.26 in.)	50.8 cc (3.1 cu. in.)

ENGINE IDENTIFICATION

These two-stroke, air-cooled, gasoline engines are used on some Jonsered trimmers and brush cutters.

MAINTENANCE

LUBRICATION. The engine is lubricated by oil mixed with the fuel. Refer to the appropriate trimmer or brush cutter service section for the amount and type of oil the manufacturer the equipment recommends mixing with gasoline.

SPARK PLUG. Recommended spark plug is a Champion RCJ7Y, NGK BPMR7A or equivalent. Electrode gap should be 0.5 mm (0.020 in.).

CARBURETOR. Walbro HDA86A carburetor is used. To adjust, turn the low speed mixture needle (14—Fig. J141) clockwise until lightly seated, then back the needle out 1-1/4 turn. Turn the high speed mixture needle (13) clockwise until lightly seated, then back the needle out 1-1/4 turn. The housing (8) around the mixture needles is marked "H" for the high speed needle and "L" for the low speed needle.

Start and run engine until normal operating temperature is reached. Adjust the idle mixture needle until the engine idles smoothly and accelerates cleanly without hesitation. Run the engine at full speed (no load) and adjust the high speed needle until the engine runs at the highest speed with a slight "four-cycle" sound. For optimum setting it is recommended that a tachometer be used to check engine rpm. Recommended maximum speed is 13,500 rpm. Recommended maximum speed should not be exceeded. Do not set either mixture needle too lean. If the low speed mixture needle is too lean it will not accelerate properly. If either needle is too lean, the engine can be damaged. Set the idle speed stop screw (15—Fig. J142) so the engine idles about 2,500 rpm. The engine should idle smoothly, but slowly enough that the clutch remains disengaged.

To disassemble the carburetor, refer to Fig. J142 and remove covers (1 and 26) for access to internal components. Remove diaphragms (2 and 24), metering lever (8) and fuel inlet valve (7), Welch plug (10), fuel screen (23) and fuel mixture needles (13 and 14).

Clean and inspect all components. If the unit has been improperly stored, passages may be clogged with deposits that are hard, solid and nearly transparent. Be careful not to damage the openings or sealing surfaces while cleaning. Check the condition of diaphragms (2 and 24) carefully. Install new diaphragms if hard (not flexible), torn or otherwise damaged. Examine the fuel inlet valve (7), spring (6) and lever (8). A new fuel inlet valve needle (7), and mixture screws (13 and 14) can be installed, but their seats cannot b[e] serviced if damaged. Inspect the condi[tion] of the filter screen (23).

When reassembling, apply thin coa[t] of sealant around edge of new Welc[h] plug (10). Install the plug using a suit[able] punch with a diameter larger tha[n] the plug to avoid deforming the plug. The metering lever should be flush wit[h] the body surface when measured with [a] straightedge as shown in Fig. J143. Carefully bend the lever if necessary t[o] obtain the correct lever height.

IGNITION SYSTEM. The engine i[s] equipped with an electronic ignitio[n] system that does not use breake[r] points. The module is incorporated i[n] the coil assembly.

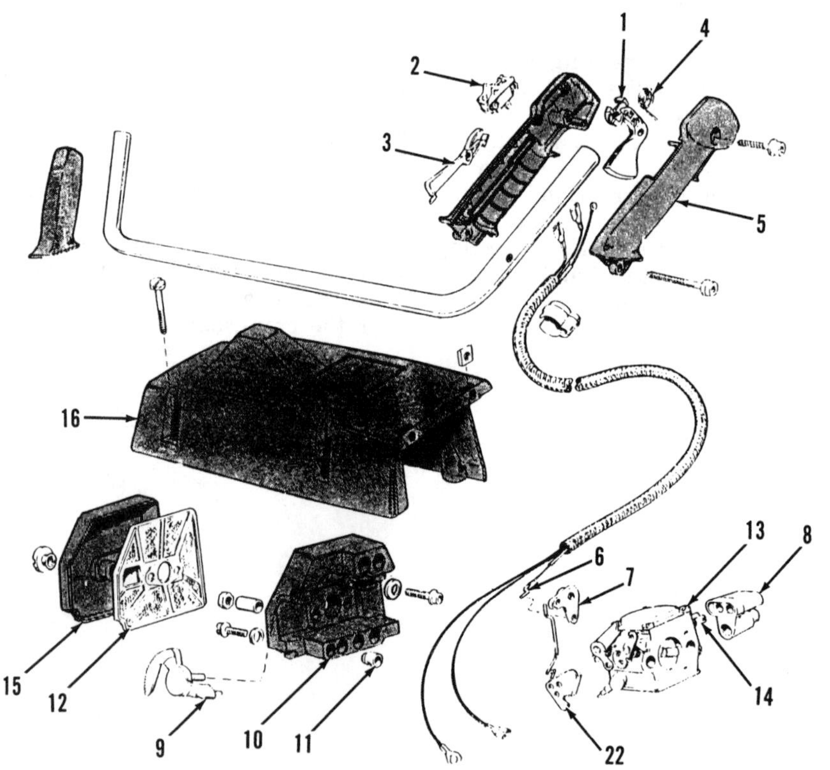

Fig. J141—Partially exploded view of typical air filter, carburetor and engine controls.

1. Throttle trigger
2. Engine stop switch
3. Throttle interlock
4. Spring
5. Hand grip
6. Throttle cable
7. Bellcrank
8. Needle cover
9. Choke lever
10. Inlet housing
11. Spacer
12. Air filter
13. High speed mixture needle
14. Low speed mixture needle
15. Filter cover
16. Cover

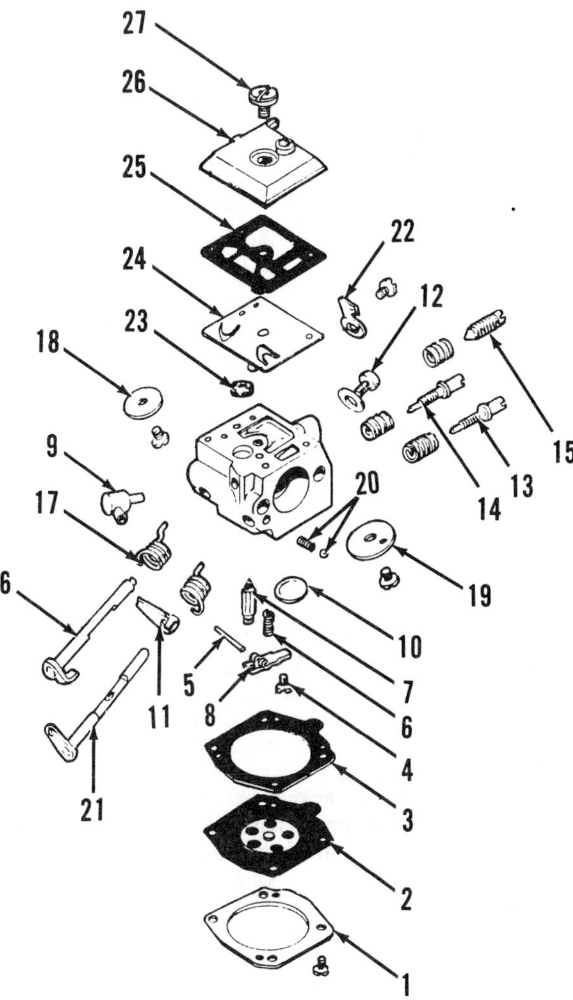

Fig. J142—Exploded view of carburetor typical of the Walbro HDA model used.

1. Cover
2. Metering diaphragm
3. Gasket
4. Screw
5. Pin
6. Spring
7. Fuel inlet valve
8. Metering lever
9. Fuel inlet fitting
10. Welch plug
11. Choke lever
12. Retainer
13. High speed mixture needle
14. Low speed mixture needle
15. Idle speed stop screw
16. Throttle shaft
17. Return spring
18. Throttle plate
19. Choke plate
20. Choke detent
21. Choke shaft
22. Throttle lever
23. Screen
24. Fuel pump diaphragm
25. Gasket
26. Cover
27. Screw & gasket

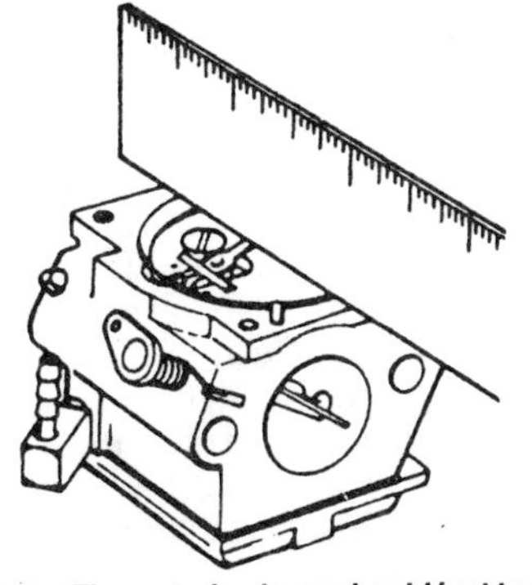

Fig. J143—The metering lever should just touch a straightedge placed across the carburetor body.

Ignition can be considered satisfactory if a spark will jump across the 3 mm (1/8 in.) electrode gap of a test plug when the engine is turned with the recoil starter. If there is no spark, check the stop switch and connecting wire for shorts to ground. Ignition may be irregular at starting speeds if gap between the legs of the coil core and the flywheel magnets is too wide.

The ignition module/coil is located under the fan housing at the front of the engine. Two screws attach the ignition module/coil. When installing, set the air gap between the flywheel magnets and the legs of the ignition module as follows. Install the ignition module, but tighten the two screws only enough to hold it in place away from the flywheel. Insert 0.3 mm (0.012 in.) thick brass or plastic shim stock between the legs of the ignition module and the flywheel, then turn the flywheel until the flywheel magnets are near the module legs. Loosen the screws attaching the ignition module and press legs of the ignition module against the shim stock, then tighten the two attaching screws. Remove the shim stock, then turn the flywheel and check to be sure the flywheel does not hit the legs of the coil.

REPAIRS

PISTON, PIN AND RINGS. The piston and ring can be inspected through the exhaust port after removing the muffler (7—Fig. J144). The piston and ring (11 and 13) are available in standard size only.

To remove the cylinder, remove the engine covers, muffler (7), carburetor, adapter (4) and spark plug. Remove the cylinder attaching screws, working through holes in the cylinder (9). Carefully lift the cylinder from the piston. Remove retaining rings (12), then remove the piston pin (14) to separate the piston from the connecting rod. Needle bearing (15) can be removed from the

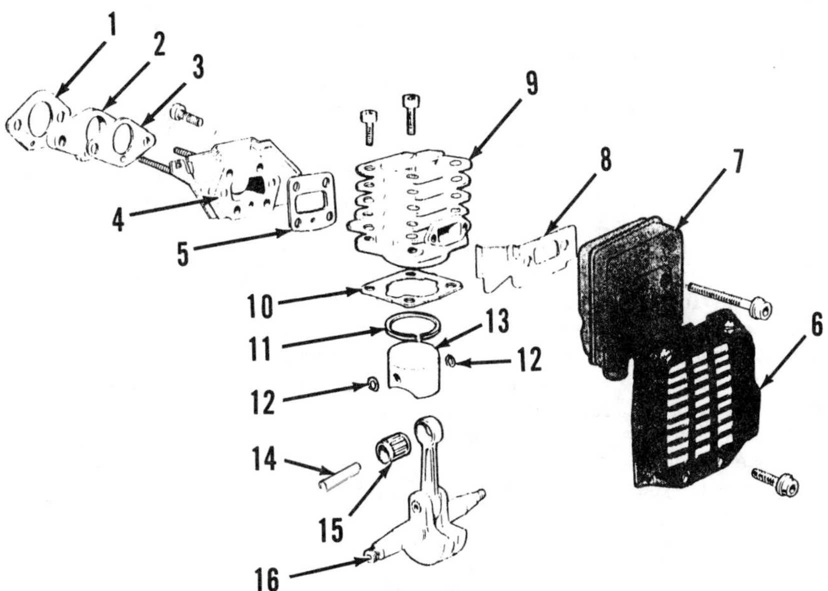

Fig. J144—Exploded view of the cylinder, piston and related parts.

1. Gasket
2. Insulator
3. Gasket
4. Adapter
5. Gasket
6. Heat shield
7. Muffler
8. Gasket/baffle
9. Cylinder
10. Cylinder base gasket
11. Piston ring
12. Retainer rings
13. Piston
14. Piston pin
15. Needle bearing
16. Crankshaft & connecting rod assy.

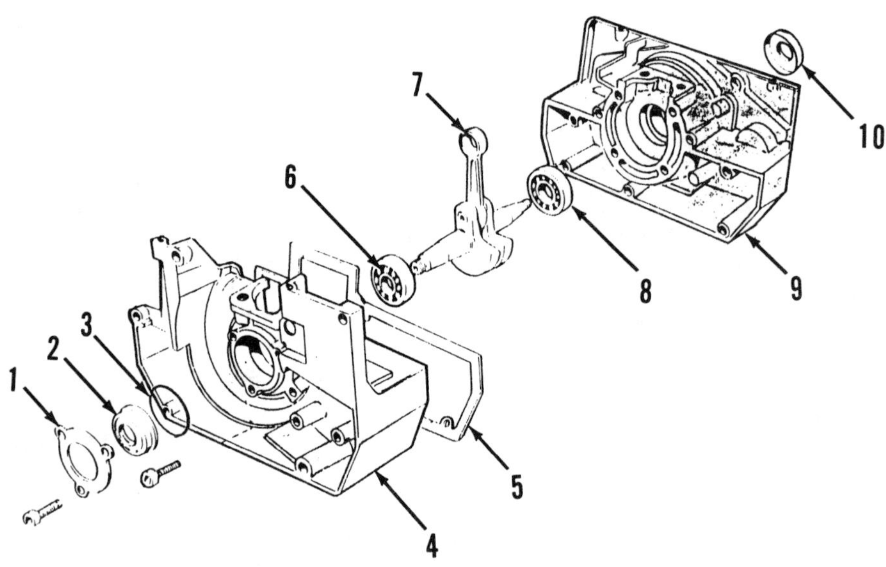

Fig. J145—Exploded view of the crankcase assembly.

1. Retainer
2. Seal
3. "O" ring
4. Crankcase half
5. Gasket
6. Main bearing
7. Crankshaft & connecting rod assy.
8. Main bearing
9. Crankcase half
10. Seal

connecting rod bore. Remove the cylinder base gasket (10) and clean all residue from the cylinder and crankcase.

Install the piston with the arrow on its top pointing toward the exhaust side. Lubricate the piston pin (14) and bearing (15), then install the piston pin. If removed, install new retaining rings (12) with the gap toward the top or bottom of the piston. Do not install the retaining rings with the gap at either side. Lubricate the piston, ring and cylinder, position the ring gap around the pin in the piston groove, then install the cylinder over the piston assembly. Be careful to install the cylinder straight down over the piston. If the cylinder is twisted, the ring can catch in a port and break the end of the ring.

CYLINDER. Inspect the cylinder for any damage and install new parts as necessary. If the chrome plating is worn from the cylinder, a new cylinder should be installed.

CRANKSHAFT SEALS. Seals (2 and 10—Fig. J145) can be removed and replaced without separating the crankcase halves. To remove the seal from the ignition side, first remove the flywheel. Remove screws attaching the retainer (1), then use a screwdriver or similar tool to pull the retainer and seal (2) from the case. Use a new "O" ring (3) when assembling. Seal (10) can be removed from the output side after removing the clutch assembly. Use a seal puller (part No. 504 91 40-01 or equivalent) to extract the seal from the crankcase. Install seals (2 and 10) with the lips toward the inside.

CRANKSHAFT AND CONNECTING ROD. The crankshaft and connecting rod assembly (7—Fig. J145) assembly can be removed after first removing the clutch, flywheel and cylinder. Remove crankshaft seals as described in the preceding CRANKSHAFT SEALS paragraph. Remove the nine screws that attach the crankcase halves together, then carefully pull each crankcase half from the end of the crankshaft. **Do not** pry the case halves apart. A special "C" clamp type extractor tool (part No. 502 51 61-01) is available which has fingers that grip the inside of the crankcase and uses a jack screw to push against the end of the crankshaft.

Clean all parts carefully and inspect for damage. The crankshaft is available for service only as a pressed together assembly with the connecting rod. The crankshaft and connecting rod should always be coated with lubricant to prevent rust and should be covered to prevent dirt from entering the bearings. Do not remove the main bearings (6 and 8) unless new bearings are ready to be installed. Support the crankcase sufficiently when removing or installing the main bearings.

Lubricate the crankshaft bearings and shaft sealing surfaces with oil. Heat the clutch side crankcase half (9) to 150 degrees C (300 degrees F), then install the crankshaft and main bearings in the case half. Make sure the end of the crankshaft **without** a Woodruff key slot is toward the clutch side (9). Make sure the bearing is fully seated. Use grease to hold gasket (5) in position against the case half (9). Heat the ignition side crankcase half (4) to 150 degrees C, then install the crankcase half over the crankshaft. Make sure the crankshaft and main bearings are fully seated and the gasket is properly positioned, then install the nine screws attaching the halves together. Check to be sure the crankshaft rotates freely in the main bearings. Correct problems before continuing assembly. If the shaft seems tight, bump the ends of the shaft lightly with a soft hammer and check for free rotation. After the halves are assembled, trim the gasket flush with the surface which contacts the cylinder base. Lubricate the main bearings and seal surfaces of the crankshaft with engine oil before installing the shaft seals.

CLUTCH. Refer to the Trimmer section for clutch removal and service procedures.

REWIND STARTER. Refer to the Trimmer section for service to the recoil starter.

KAWASAKI

ENGINE SERVICE

Model	Bore	Stroke	Displacement
KE18 & TD18	28.9 mm (1.14 in.)	27.9 mm (1.10 in.)	18.4 cc (1.12 cu. in.)
20	...	...	20.3 cc (1.24 cu. in.)
KE24 & TD24	32.0 mm (1.26 in.)	30.0 mm (1.18 in.)	24.4 cc (1.47 cu. in.)
28	...	...	28.1 cc (1.71 cu. in.)
TD33	36.8 mm (1.45 in.)	30.9 mm (1.22 in.)	33.3 cc 2.03 cu. in.)
TD40	40.0 mm (1.57 in.)	32.0 mm (1.26 in.)	40.2 cc (2.45 cu. in.)

ENGINE INFORMATION

Kawasaki two-stroke air-cooled gasoline engines are used by several manufacturers of string trimmers and brush cutters.

MAINTENANCE

LUBRICATION. The engine is lubricated by mixing oil with the gasoline fuel. Use only an oil designed for two-stroke, air cooled engines. Refer to the appropriate TRIMMER SERVICE section for the recommended type of oil and mixing ratio.

SPARK PLUG. The recommended spark plug for normal application is NGK B7S or equivalent and the electrode gap should be 0.6 mm (0.025 in.) for all models. Tighten the spark plug to the torque listed in the TIGHTENING TORQUE paragraph.

CARBURETOR. Engines may be equipped with a DPK (Fig. KA10) or Walbro (Fig. KA13) diaphragm carburetor. A Kehin float type carburetor (Fig. KA15) has also been used. The manufacturer's name and model number is stamped on the carburetor. Refer to the following tuning and service information for the specific carburetor type used.

DPK Series. Initial setting of the main fuel mixture needle (15—Fig. KA10) is 1-1/2 turns open from a lightly seated position. Make final adjustments with the trimmer line at the proper length or blade assembly installed. Engine should be at normal operating temperature and running. Operate engine at wide open throttle (no load) and turn the main fuel mixture needle until the engine runs the smoothest, then back the needle OUT 1/8 turn. The normal setting range is 1-2 turns out from lightly seated.

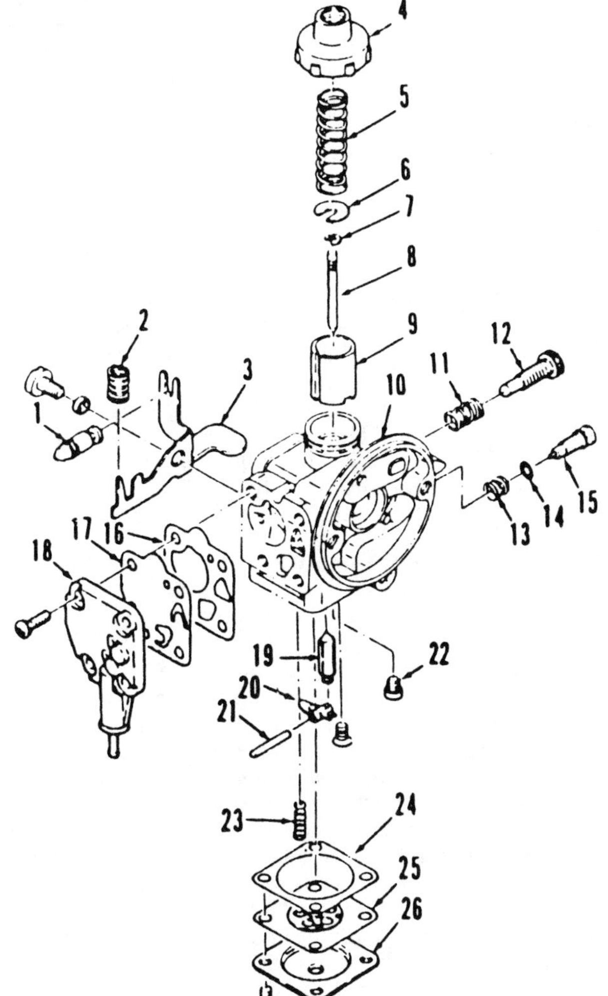

Fig. KA10—Exploded view of DPK diaphragm type carburetor used on some models.

1. Tickler valve
2. Spring
3. Lever
4. Cap
5. Spring
6. Retainer
7. Clip
8. Jet needle
9. Throttle slide
10. Body
11. Spring
12. Idle speed stop screw
13. Spring
14. "O" ring
15. Main fuel mixture needle
16. Pump gasket
17. Pump diaphragm
18. Pump cover
19. Inlet needle valve
20. Metering lever
21. Pin
22. Jet
23. Spring
24. Gasket
25. Diaphragm
26. Cover

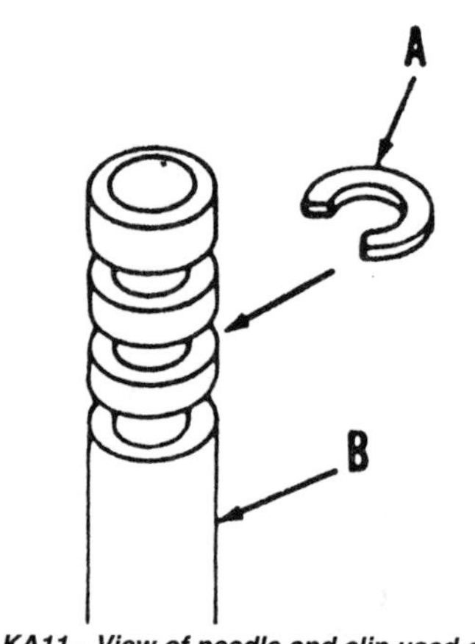

Fig. KA11—View of needle and clip used on DPK series carburetor. Install clip (A) in middle groove for normal operation.

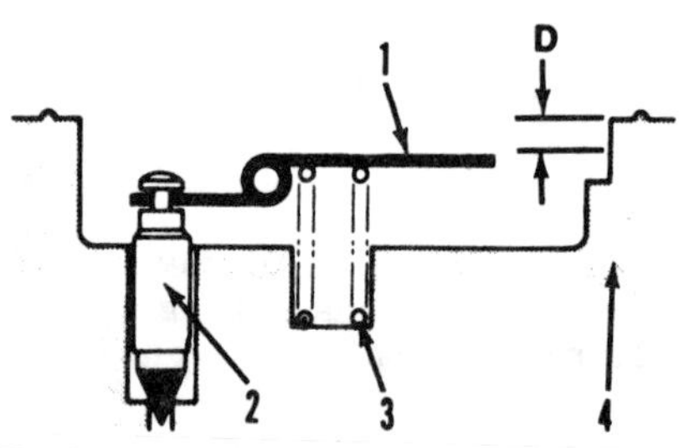

Fig. KA12—Dimension "D" should be 2.1-2.4 mm (0.08-0.09 in.).

1. Fuel lever
2. Fuel needle
3. Spring
4. Carburetor body

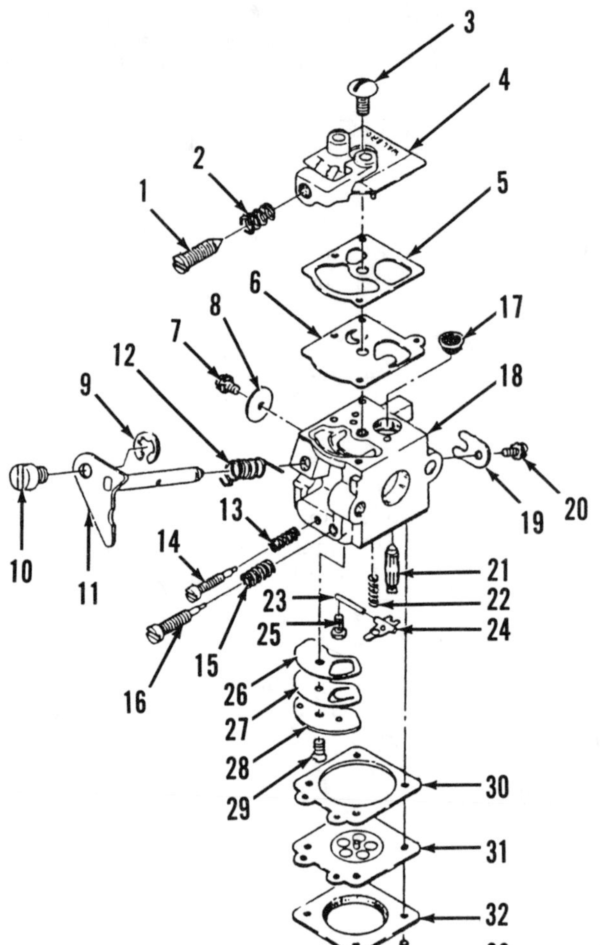

Fig. KA13—Exploded view of Walbro WA diaphragm type carburetor used on some models.

1. Idle speed stop screw
2. Spring
3. Screw
4. Pump cover
5. Gasket
6. Pump diaphragm
7. Screw
8. Throttle plate
9. "E" clip
10. Cable clamp
11. Throttle shaft
12. Spring
13. Spring
14. Low speed needle
15. Spring
16. High speed mixture needle
17. Fuel screen
18. Body
19. Clip
20. Screw
21. Fuel inlet needle
22. Spring
23. Pin
24. Fuel lever
25. Screw
26. Gasket
27. Check valve
28. Circuit plate
29. Screw
30. Gasket
31. Metering diaphragm
32. Cover
33. Screw

Adjust the idle speed screw (12) so the engine idles just below (slower than) clutch engagement speed.

Midrange mixture is determined by the position of clip (7) on the jet needle (8). There are three grooves located at the upper end of the jet needle (Fig. KA11) and the normal position of clip (A) is in the center groove of the jet needle (B). The mixture will be leaner if clip is installed in the top groove or richer if the clip is installed in the bottom groove.

To overhaul, refer to Fig. KA10 and remove lever (3), throttle slide (9), mixture needles (12 and 15), fuel pump cover (18), metering chamber cover (26), metering lever (20) and fuel inlet valve (19).

Clean and inspect all components. If the unit has been improperly stored, passages may be clogged with deposits that are hard, solid and nearly transparent. Clean passages with suitable carburetor cleaning solvent and compressed air. Be careful not to damage the openings or sealing surfaces while cleaning. The carburetor is equipped with an integral fuel pump (16, 17 and 18—Fig. KA10). During service, inspect the fuel pump and metering diaphragms for tears, holes (no matter how small) or any other damage. The diaphragms must be flexible and the metal button must be tight on the metering diaphragm (25). Examine mixture needles (12 and 15) and fuel inlet valve (19) for wear or damage and renew as necessary.

When assembling the carburetor notice that metering lever should be 2.1-2.4 mm (0.08-0.09 in.) below the carburetor body (D—Fig. KA12). Carefully bend lever to obtain dimension.

Walbro WA. Refer to Fig. KA13. Initial setting for both metering needles (14 and 16) should be 1 turn out from lightly seated. For performing final mixture adjustments, the engine must be at normal operating temperature and running. On trimmer models, trimmer line should be at the maximum recommended length or blade installed. Adjust the idle speed by turning screw (1) until the engine is operating at slow idle speed (slower than clutch engagement speed). Adjust the low-speed mixture needle (14) so the engine runs smoothly at idle speed and accelerates without hesitation. If necessary, readjust idle speed. Operate the engine at full throttle (with no load) and adjust the high-speed mixture needle to obtain maximum rpm, then turn the needle (16) counterclockwise until the engine just starts to slow because of the mixture being too rich (four-cycle).

To overhaul the carburetor, refer to Fig. KA13 and remove covers (4 and 32) for access to internal components. Remove metering lever (24) and fuel inlet valve (21), circuit plate (28) and check valve (27), fuel screen (17) and mixture needles (14 and 16).

Clean and inspect all components. If unit has been improperly stored, passages may be clogged with deposits that are hard, solid and nearly transparent. Clean passages with suitable carburetor cleaning solvent and compressed air. Be careful not to damage the openings or sealing surfaces while cleaning. Examine the fuel inlet valve (21) and seat. Inlet valve can be replaced, but the seat is part of the carburetor body and cannot be serviced. Examine the mixture needles (14 and 16) and install new needles if damaged. Clean fuel screen (17). Inspect diaphragms (6, 27 and 31) for tears or other damage. The diaphragms must be flexible.

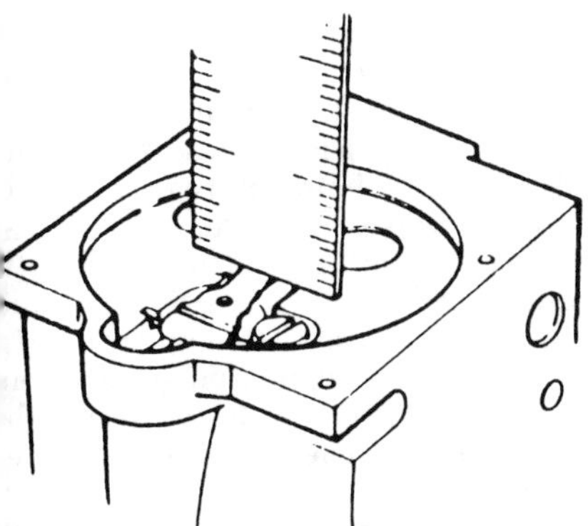

Fig. KA14—Metering valve lever should be flush with carburetor body on Walbro WA carburetor.

When reassembling, check the height of the metering lever as shown in Fig. KA14. The lever should be just flush with the top of the circuit plate. The metering lever should just touch leg on the tool. Bend the lever carefully if necessary to obtain correct height.

Kehin Float. Refer to Fig. KA15. Adjustment of the float type carburetor is limited to float level and position of the "E" clip (6).

To adjust float level, remove float bowl assembly (25) and invert the carburetor throttle body as shown in Fig. KA16. Distance (D—Fig. KA16) from the float to the bowl gasket should be 2.5 mm (0.09 in.). If necessary, bend the float lever (22—Fig. KA15) carefully to obtain the correct float level.

Install "E" clip in the center groove (C—Fig. KA17) of the fuel needle. Install the clip in a higher groove position (A or B) for leaner mixture or install the clip in a lower groove position to enrich the mixture.

IGNITION SYSTEM. Some early models may be equipped with a breaker point ignition; while later models are fitted with a solid state breakerless ignition. Refer to the appropriate following paragraphs for service.

Breaker Point Ignition. The breaker point set and condenser are attached to crankcase behind the recoil starter pulley. To adjust the point gap, remove recoil starter assembly. Rotate the flywheel so that points are at maximum opening and measure the gap. Point gap should be 0.3-0.4 mm (0.012-0.016 in.). Refer to Fig. KA18 and loosen the setting screw, then use a screwdriver to move the plate as required. Tighten the screw and recheck the gap between the points.

To adjust ignition timing, rotate flywheel until the "F" mark (line stamped on blades) is aligned with the crankcase mark (Fig. KA19). Ignition points should just begin to open when the flywheel and crankcase marks align. If timing is incorrect, adjust the breaker point gap as previously described to correct the timing.

Solid State (Breakerless) Ignition. The solid state ignition system has no moving parts except the flywheel magnets and should require no

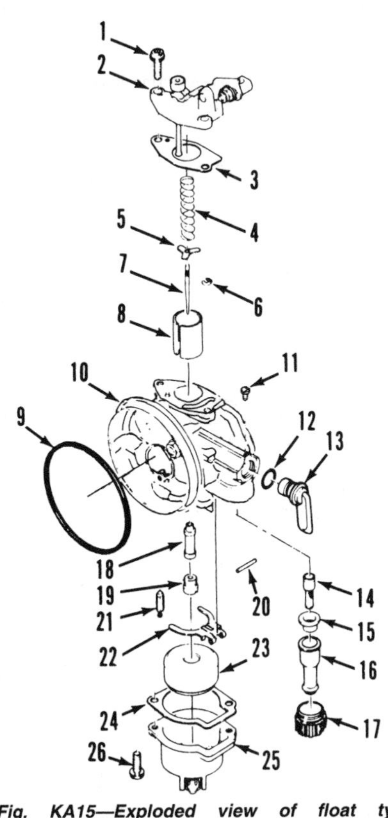

Fig. KA15—Exploded view of float type carburetor used on some models.

1. Screw
2. Cover
3. Gasket
4. Spring
5. Spring seat
6. Clip
7. Fuel needle
8. Slide
9. Gasket
10. Body
11. Screw
12. "O" ring
13. Shut-off valve
14. Strainer
15. Gasket
16. Fitting
17. Nut
18. Jet
19. Jet
20. Pin
21. Fuel inlet needle
22. Float hinge
23. Float
24. Gasket
25. Fuel bowl
26. Screw

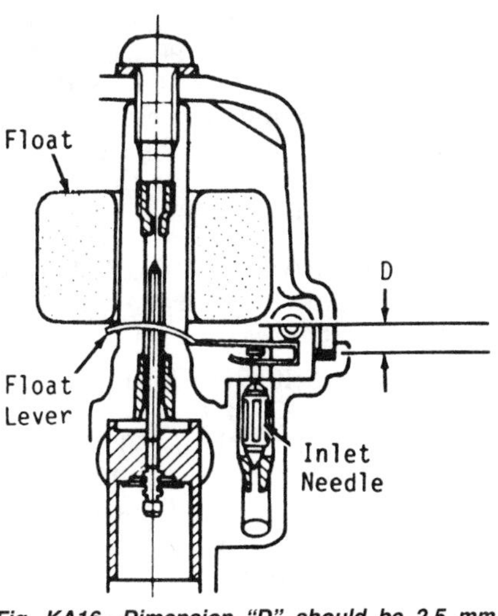

Fig. KA16—Dimension "D" should be 2.5 mm (0.09 in.) for correct float level setting.

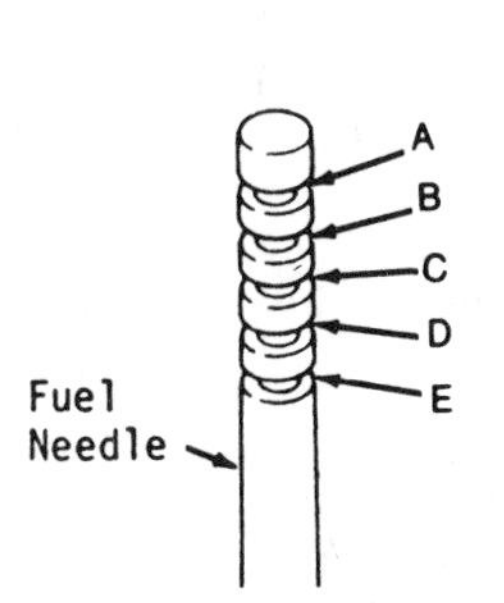

Fig. KA17—Refer to text for correct placement of fuel clip for model being serviced.

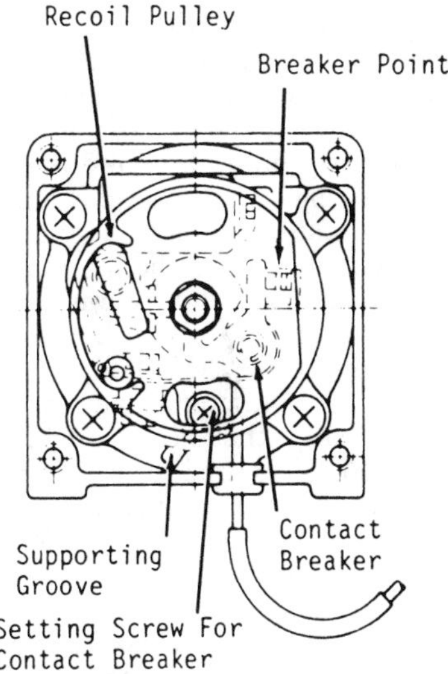

Fig. KA18—View showing location of breaker point ignition components used on some early models.

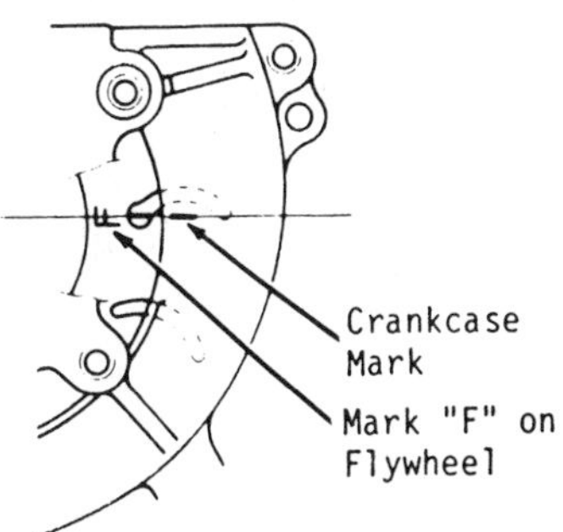

Fig. KA19—To adjust ignition timing on breaker point models, align "F" timing mark on flywheel with timing mark on crankcase.

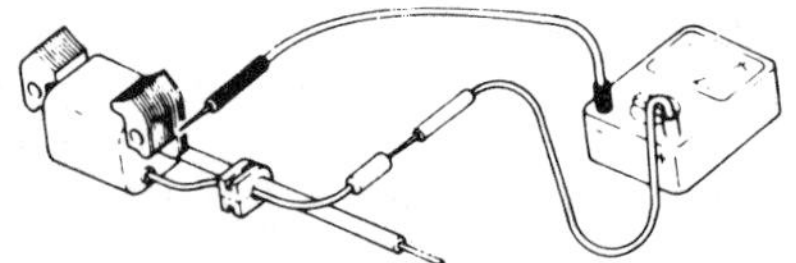

Fig. KA20—The ignition coil primary winding can be checked using an ohmmeter on some models. Refer to text.

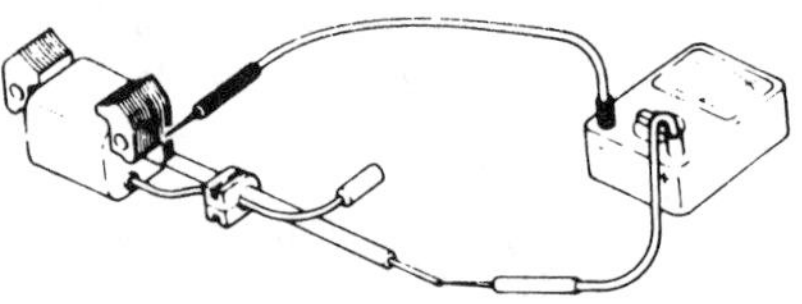

Fig. KA21—The ignition coil secondary winding can be checked using an ohmmeter on some models. Refer to text.

regular maintenance. The components may be affected by extreme heat or cold.

Ignition can be considered satisfactory if a spark will jump across the 3 mm (1/8 in.) electrode gap of a test plug when the engine is turned with the recoil starter. If there is no spark, check the stop switch and connecting wire for shorts to ground. Ignition may be irregular at starting speeds if gap between the legs of the coil core and the flywheel magnets is too wide.

The ignition coil of some models may be tested with an accurate ohmmeter as follows. Attach the red (+) ohmmeter lead to the primary lead and the black (-) lead to the coil core as shown in Fig. KA20. Measured resistance of the primary winding should be 0.5 ohms for 18.4 cc engines, 0.6-0.7 ohms for 24.1 and 33.3 cc engines or 0.9 ohms for 40.2 cc engines. Attach the red (+) ohmmeter lead to the spark plug wire and the black (-) lead to the coil core as shown in Fig. KA21. Measured resistance of the secondary winding should be 9.7 ohms for 18.4 cc engines, 7-8 ohms for 24.1 and 33.3 cc engines or 11.5 ohms for 40.2 cc engines.

The igniter of some models may be tested with an ohmmeter as follows. Attach the black (-) ohmmeter lead to the case of the igniter, then touch the red (+) lead to the igniter lead tab as shown in Fig. KA22 while observing the ohmmeter. Reverse the ohmmeter leads and recheck. The ohmmeter should momentarily deflect from infinity to slightly more than zero ohms. The ohmmeter needle should not return all the way to zero. Install an igniter that is known to be good to verify a faulty unit.

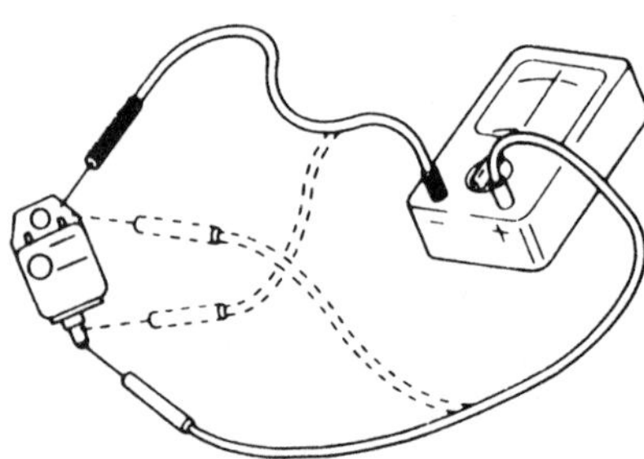

Fig. KA22—On some models, ignition igniter can be checked using an ohmmeter. Refer to text for correct test connection sequence.

CARBON. Exhaust ports in the cylinder and the muffler should be cleaned periodically to prevent loss of power due to carbon build-up. Remove the muffler cover and any baffles. Turn the flywheel until the piston is at Top Dead Center, then scrape any carbon from inside the muffler. Remove carbon from inside the ports using a wooden scraper. Be careful not to scratch the edges of the ports or the piston. Do not attempt to run the engine with any parts of the muffler missing.

REPAIRS

COMPRESSION PRESSURE. For optimum performance, compression pressure should be 793-1,000 kPa (115-145 psi) for 18.4 cc (1.12 cu. in.) engines; 965-1,172 kPa (140-170 psi) for 24.1 cc (1.47 cu. in.) engines; 1,103-1,310 kPa (160-190 psi) for 33.3 cc (2.03 cu. in.) engines. Crank the engine until maximum pressure is observed after it has reached operating temperature and with the throttle and choke both wide open.

TIGHTENING TORQUE. Recommended tightening torque specifications are as follows.

Clutch pivot bolt to flywheel:
KE18, TD18, KE24 &
TD24 . . . . . . 8-10 N•m (69-85 in.-lb.)
TD33 & TD40 . . . . 13-14 N•m (120-137 in.-lb.)

Crankcase:
KE18, TD18, KE24,
TD24 & TD33 . . . . 3-4 N•m (30-34 in.-lb.)
TD40 . . . . 5-7 N•m (52-61 in.-lb.)

Cylinder to crankcase:
KE18, TD18, KE24,
TD24 & TD33 3-4 N•m (30-34 in.-lb.)
TD40 . . . . 7-9 N•m (61-78 in.-lb.)

Flywheel:
KE18, TD18, KE24 &
TD24 . . . . . . 8-10 N•m (69-85 in.-lb.)
TD33 & TD40 . . . . 30-34 N•m (260-304 in.-lb.)

Spark plug:
All models . . . . 12-16 N•m (103-146 in.-lb.)

Ignition System. Clearance (air gap) between the legs of the coil/module and the flywheel magnets should be 0.35-0.40 mm (0.014-0.016 in.) for models with breaker points; 0.3 mm (0.012 in.) for models with solid state ignitio If the gap is too wide, the ignition m be weak and the engine difficult start. If the gap is too close, the coil ar flywheel may bump into each other a cause extensive damage.

To check the air gap, first remove t fan cover, then turn the flywheel un the magnets are located under the le of the coil. Use non-magnetic feel gauge to measure the clearance b tween the coil legs and the flywhe magnets.

To change the air gap, loosen the tw screws attaching the coil, then mo the coil as required. Threads of the c attaching screws should be coated wit Loctite before tightening.

CRANKSHAFT AND CONNEC ING ROD. Refer to Fig. KA23 for a exploded view of the crankshaft an crankcase typical of all models exce TD40 which is shown in Fig. KA24. T crankshaft of all models is pressed t gether at the connecting rod journa The connecting rod, rod bearing an crankshaft must be replaced as an a

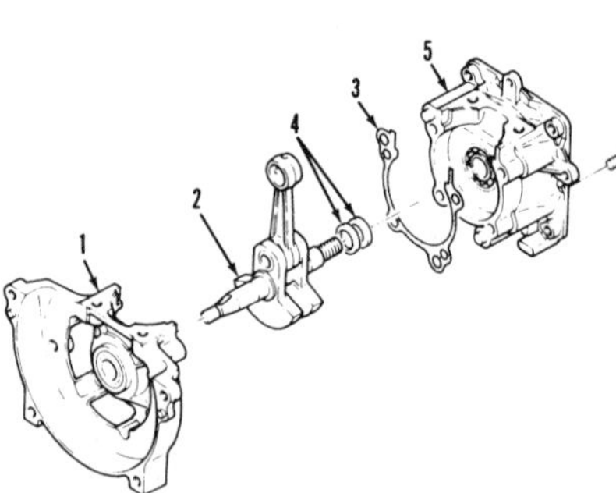

Fig. KA23—Exploded view of crankshaft an connecting rod assembly used on 18.4, 20.3, 24. 28.1 and 33.3 cc engines.

1. Crankshaft half
2. Crankshaft & connecting rod assy.
3. Gasket
4. Shims
5. Crankcase ha

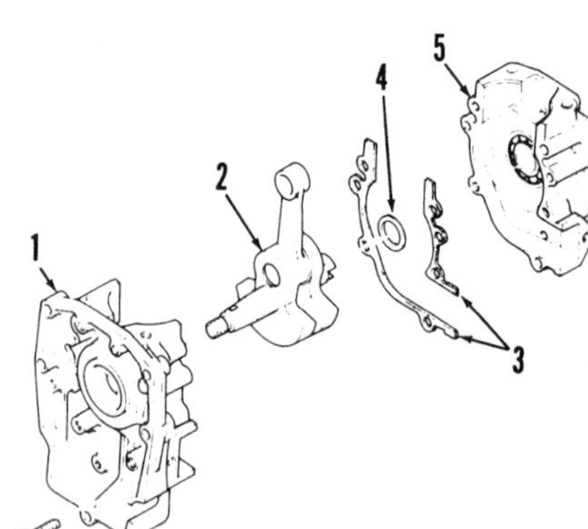

Fig. KA24—Exploded view of crankshaft an connecting rod assembly used on 40.2 cc engine

1. Crankcase half
2. Crankshaft & connecting rod assy.
3. Gaskets
4. Shim
5. Crankcase half

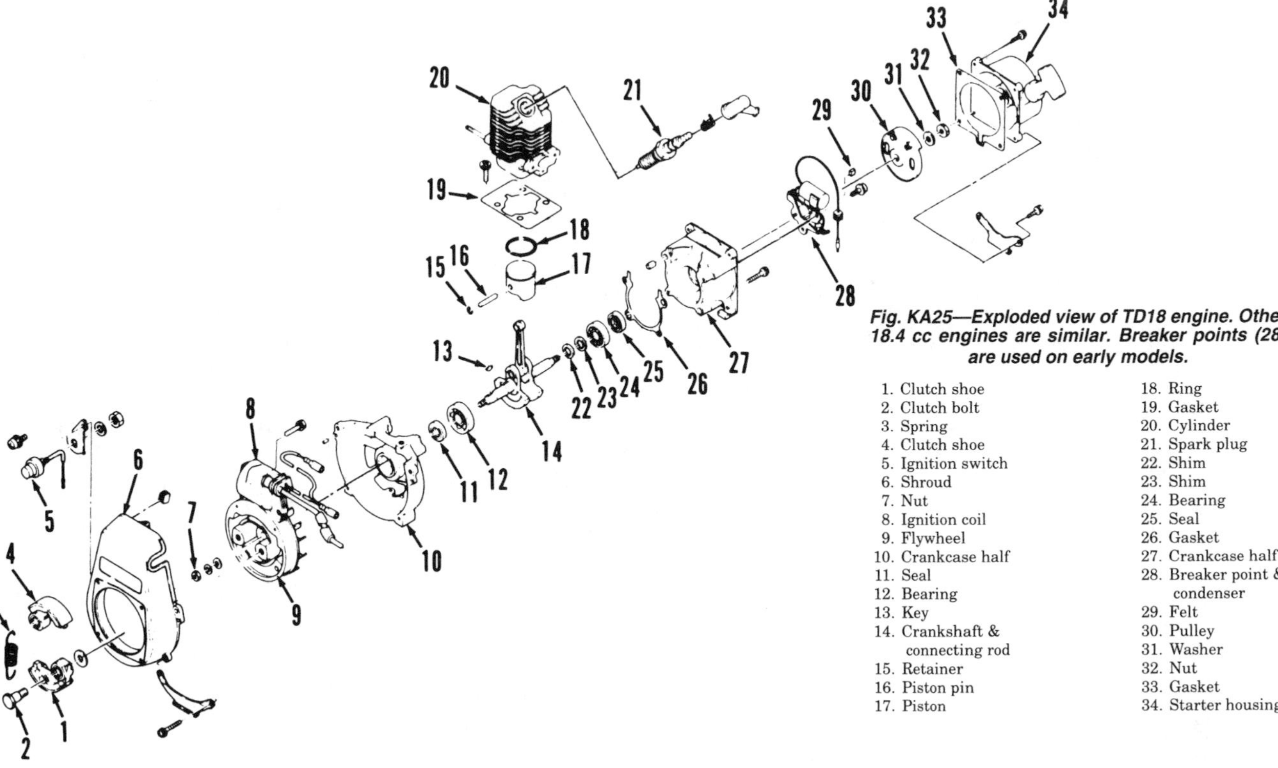

Fig. KA25—Exploded view of TD18 engine. Other 18.4 cc engines are similar. Breaker points (28) are used on early models.

1. Clutch shoe
2. Clutch bolt
3. Spring
4. Clutch shoe
5. Ignition switch
6. Shroud
7. Nut
8. Ignition coil
9. Flywheel
10. Crankcase half
11. Seal
12. Bearing
13. Key
14. Crankshaft & connecting rod
15. Retainer
16. Piston pin
17. Piston
18. Ring
19. Gasket
20. Cylinder
21. Spark plug
22. Shim
23. Shim
24. Bearing
25. Seal
26. Gasket
27. Crankcase half
28. Breaker point & condenser
29. Felt
30. Pulley
31. Washer
32. Nut
33. Gasket
34. Starter housing

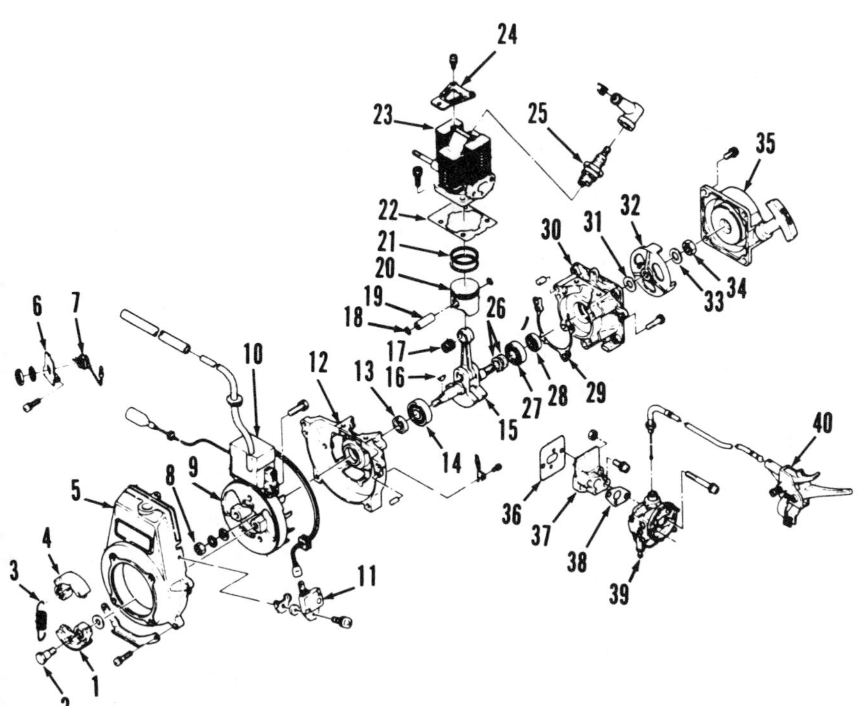

Fig. KA26—Exploded view of TD24 and TD33 engine. Other 20.3, 24.4, 28.1 and 33.3 cc engines are similar.

1. Clutch shoe
2. Clutch belt
3. Spring
4. Clutch shoe
5. Shroud
6. Bracket
7. Ignition switch
8. Nut
9. Flywheel
10. Ignition coil
11. Igniter
12. Crankcase half
13. Seal
14. Bearing
15. Crankshaft & connecting rod
16. Key
17. Bearing
18. Retainer
19. Piston pin
20. Piston
21. Rings
22. Gasket
23. Cylinder
24. Retainer
25. Spark plug
26. Shims
27. Bearing
28. Seal
29. Gasket
30. Crankcase half
31. Washer
32. Pulley
33. Washer
34. Nut
35. Starter housing
36. Gasket
37. Insulator
38. Gasket
39. Carburetor
40. Throttle trigger assy.

sembly. The crankshaft is supported by ball bearings at both ends. Refer to Fig. KA25 for exploded view typical of 18.4, 20.3 and 28.1 cc engines; to Fig. KA26 for exploded view typical of 24.1 and 33.3 cc engines; or to Fig. KA27 for exploded view of 40.2 cc engines.

To remove crankshaft assembly refer to the appropriate exploded view. Remove the engine cooling shrouds, covers and the recoil starter assembly. On models so equipped, remove the retaining nut (32—Fig. KA25 or 34—Fig. KA26), then remove the starter pulley (30—Fig. KA25 or 32—Fig. KA26). The starter pulley of some models including KE24, TD24 and TD33 is threaded onto the crankshaft and must be unscrewed. Remove the flywheel, carburetor, muffler and cylinder from all models.

Inspect the crankshaft assembly including the connecting rod, rod bearings and main bearings for damage and install parts as necessary.

Crankshaft end play must be correctly set using shims when assembling the crankshaft and crankcase. Shims (4—Fig. KA23) for 18.4, 20.3, 24.1, 28.1 and 33.3 cc engines are available in the thicknesses listed in Fig. KA28. Shims (4—Fig. KA24) for TD40 (40.2 cc) models are available in thicknesses listed in the chart shown in Fig. KA29. Shims thicknesses, dimensions and clearances are listed in millimeters only.

On 18.4, 20.3, 24.1, 28.1 and 33.3 cc engines, correct crankshaft end play is 0.05-0.268 mm. Refer to Fig. KA30 and

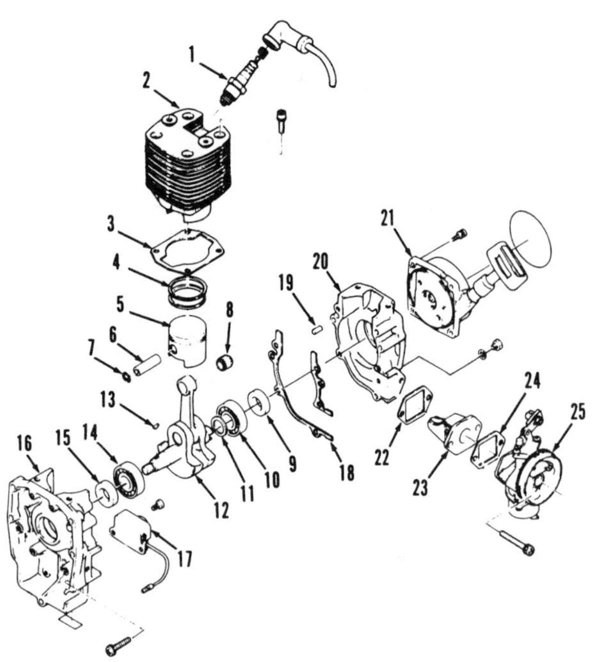

Fig. KA27—Exploded view of TD40 engine.

1. Spark plug
2. Cylinder head
3. Gasket
4. Rings
5. Piston
6. Piston pin
7. Retainer ring
8. Bearing
9. Seal
10. Bearing
11. Shim
12. Crankshaft & connecting rod
13. Key
14. Bearing
15. Seal
16. Crankcase half
17. Igniter
18. Gaskets
19. Dowel pin
20. Crankcase half
21. Starter housing
22. Gasket
23. Insulator
24. Gasket
25. Carburetor

Shim No.	Shim Thickness (mm)
①	0.1
②	0.2
③	0.4
④	0.6

Clearance (D)	Shim No.
-0.11~under +0.03	None
+0.03~under +0.13	①
+0.13~under +0.23	②
+0.23~under +0.33	②+①
+0.33~under +0.43	③
+0.43~under +0.53	③+①
+0.53~under +0.63	④

Fig. KA28—Refer to text for procedure to determine correct shim thickness and number. Note all dimensions are in millimeters.

measure dimensions "A," "B" and "C." Make certain that gasket is installed on one surface when measuring the distance ("A" or "B") from the main bearing inner race to the center of the crankcase. Add dimensions "A" and "B," then subtract the measured distance "C" from the sum of "A" and "B." The result is the end play or "Clearance (D)" listed in Fig. KA28. Refer to the chart in Fig. KA28 to select the correct combination of shims to install. Tighten the crankcase screws to the torque specified in the TIGHTENING TORQUE paragraph in a criss-cross pattern. Trim the gasket after the crankcase halves are secure.

On TD40 model, the correct crankshaft end play is 0.045-0.305 mm. Refer to Fig. KA31 and measure dimensions "A," "B" and "C." The gasket must be included in **one** of the measurements either "A" or "B" from the main bearing inner race to the center of the crankcase. Add dimensions "A" and "B," then subtract the measured distance "C" from the sum of "A" and "B." The result is the end play or "Clearance (D) listed in Fig. KA29. Refer to the chart in Fig. KA29 to select the correct combination of shims to install. Tighten the crankcase screws to the torque specified in the TIGHTENING TORQUE paragraph using the order shown in Fig. KA32. Trim the gasket after the crankcase halves are secure.

PISTON, PIN AND RINGS. The piston may have either one or two rings depending upon model. Rings are located in the groove(s) by pin (Fig. KA33) to prevent rotation. The piston pin needle bearing is installed in the connecting rod bore of all models except KE18 and TD18. The piston pin of KE18 and TD18 models rides directly in the connecting rod bore.

To remove piston, remove the covers and recoil starter assembly. Remove carburetor and muffler. Remove screw attaching the cylinder to the crankcase then carefully lift the cylinder awa from the crankcase and piston. Remov rings (3 and 6—Fig. KA34) and pres pin (5) from the piston pin bore. If s equipped, remove bearing (7) from th connecting rod bore.

When attaching the piston to con necting rod, arrow on the piston crow should point toward the flywheel. Th

Shim No.	Shim Thickness (mm)
①	0.1
②	0.2
③	0.4
④	0.6

TA 40	TA 51
Clearance (D)	Thickness Of Shim
-0.10~-0.09	None
-0.08~0.01	①
0.02~0.13	②
0.14~0.22	①+②
0.23~0.34	③
0.35~0.43	①+②
0.44~0.54	④
0.55~0.64	①+④
0.65~0.76	②+④
0.77~0.84	①+②+⑥

Fig. KA29—Refer to text for procedure t determine correct shim thickness and numbe Note all dimensions are in millimeters.

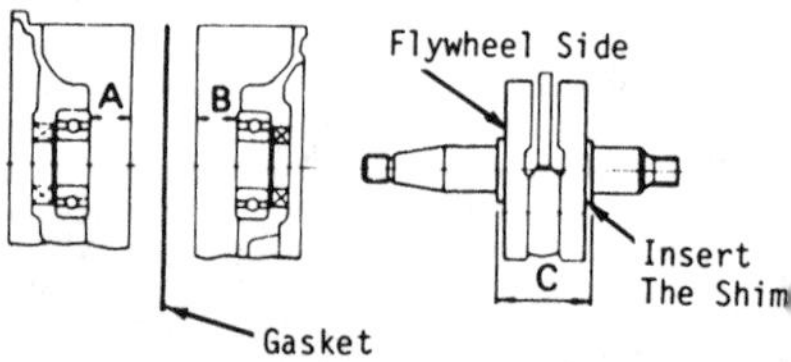

Fig. KA30—Illustration showing measuremen locations to determine correct thickness an number of shims required on 18.4, 20.3, 24.4, 28. and 33.3 cc engines.

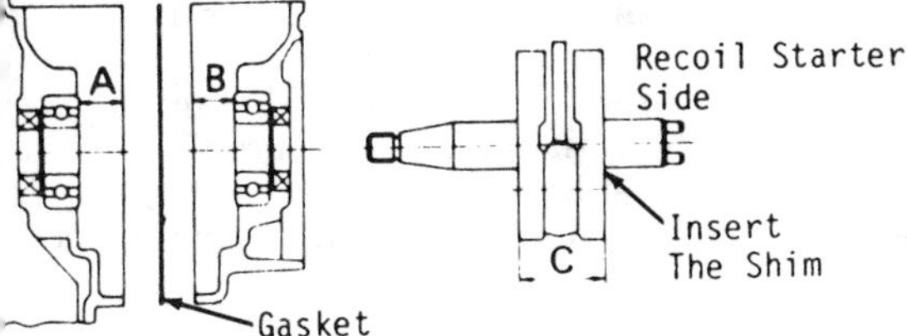

Fig. KA31—Illustration showing measurement locations to determine correct thickness and number of shims required on 40.2 cc engines.

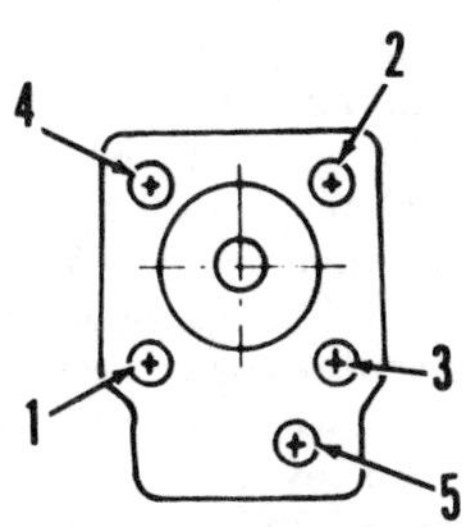

Fig. KA32—Tighten crankcase bolts in sequence shown to specified torque.

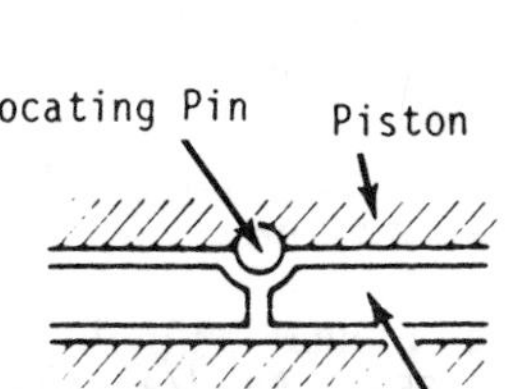

Fig. KA33—Piston ring or rings on all models are held in position by locating pins.

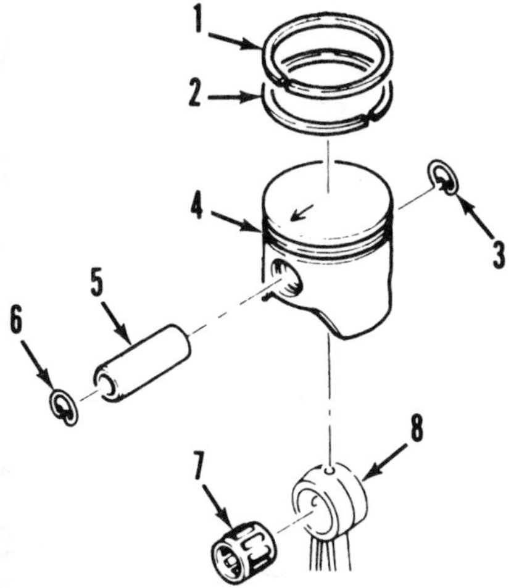

Fig. KA34—Exploded view of typical piston assembly. Some models are equipped with one ring only and connecting rod is not equipped with needle bearing (7).

1. Top ring
2. Second ring
3. Retainer
4. Piston
5. Piston pin
6. Retainer
7. Needle bearing
8. Connecting rod

piston pin must move smoothly in the pin bearing.

Correct piston ring end gap is 0.7 mm (0.03 in.). Correct ring groove clearance for top ring is 0.17 mm (0.007 in.) and 0.15 mm (0.006 in.) for the second ring.

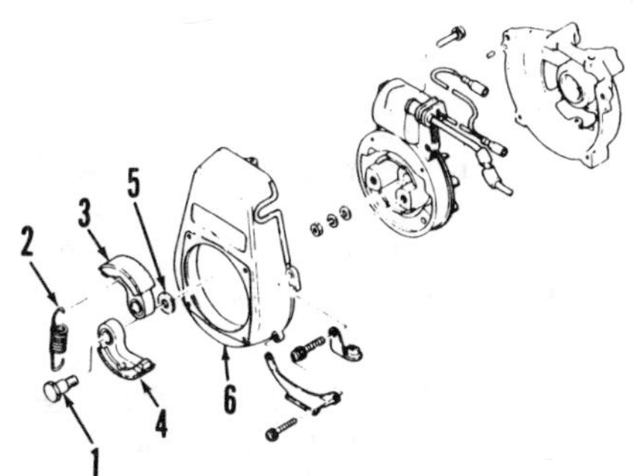

Fig. KA35—Exploded view of clutch shoe arrangement typical of most models.

1. Clutch pin (bolt)
2. Clutch spring
3. Clutch shoe
4. Clutch shoe
5. Washer
6. Shroud

Correct piston to cylinder clearance is 0.15 mm (0.006 in.).

CYLINDER. To remove the cylinder, first remove the covers, recoil starter assembly, carburetor and muffler. Remove screws attaching the cylinder to the crankcase, then carefully lift the cylinder away from the crankcase and piston. Inspect the cylinder and install a new cylinder if scored, cracked or if piston to cylinder clearance exceeds 0.15 mm (0.006 in.).

CLUTCH. Refer to Fig. KA35 for an exploded view of typical clutch shoe installation. Tighten clutch pivot bolts (1) to the torque listed in TIGHTENING TORQUE paragraph. If clutch engages at low idle speed, the spring (2) may be damaged. Clutch shoes, spring and drum should be inspected for excessive wear or damage any time the clutch drum is removed. Renew parts as required.

RECOIL STARTER. Several types of recoil starter have been used. Refer to the appropriate following paragraphs for service.

Models KE18 And TD18. Refer to Fig. KA36 for an exploded view of the starter assembly. To disassemble, unbolt and remove the unit from the engine. Relieve spring tension as follows. Pull the handle until the rope is out of the housing about 6 in. (15 cm) and align the notch in pulley (5) with the hole in housing for the rope. Hold the pulley to keep the spring from rewinding rope and pull slack in rope back, forming a loop between the pulley notch and the housing. Hold the loop in the rope and allow the pulley to unwind the spring (6) slowly.

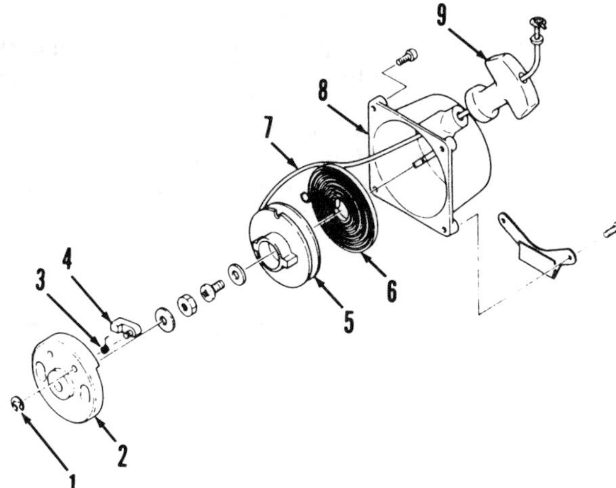

Fig. KA36—Exploded view of recoil starter used on 18.4 cc engines.

1. "E" ring
2. Pawl carrier
3. Spring
4. Pawl
5. Pulley
6. Spring
7. Rope
8. Housing
9. Handle

Remove the center screw and washer, then lift pulley (5) from the center post. Do not disturb the rewind spring (6). Use care when removing the spring. Do not allow the spring to unwind uncontrolled.

Inspect rope and spring. Lubricate the center post of housing with light grease prior to assembly. Install spring (6) in housing (8) beginning at the outside and winding in a clockwise direction. Wind all but about 6 in. (15 cm) of rope onto pulley (5), then assemble the pulley on the center post. Press the pulley into housing while making sure the center of pulley engages the recoil spring hook. Install the center retaining screw and washer. Insert the end of the rope through the hole in housing

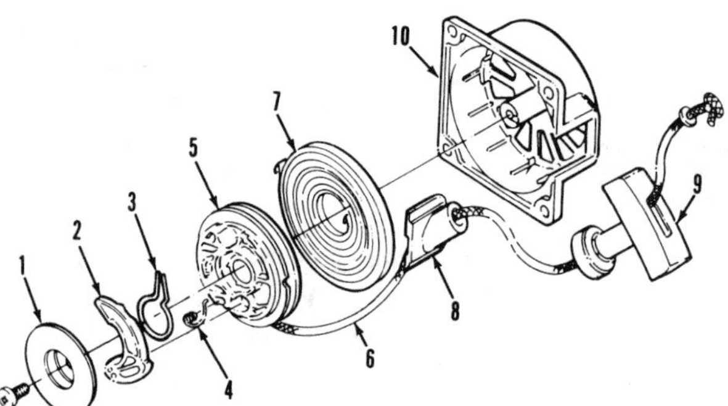

Fig. KA37—Exploded view of recoil starter used on 20.3, 24.4, 28.1, 33.3 and 40.2 cc engines.

1. Retainer
2. Pawl
3. Loop spring
4. Pawl spring
5. Pulley
6. Rope
7. Spring
8. Guide
9. Handle
10. Housing

Fig. KA38—Loop spring must be installed as shown.

and install the handle. Pull a loop in the rope between the notch in the pulley and the housing, then preload the rewind spring three turns clockwise. Check the preload by pulling the rope all the way out. The pulley should be able to turn further clockwise when the rope is fully extended. Be sure the spring does not bind with the rope extended, but the rope handle should be pulled against the housing when released.

Models KE24, TD24, TD33 And TD40. Refer to Fig. KA37 for an exploded view of the starter assembly. To disassemble, unbolt and remove the unit from the engine. Relieve spring tension as follows. Pull the handle until the rope is out of the housing about 6 in. (15 cm) and align the notch in pulley (5) with the hole in housing for the rope. Hold the pulley to keep the spring from rewinding rope, then pull slack in rope back, forming a loop between the pulley notch and the housing. Hold the loop in the rope and allow the pulley to unwind the spring (7) slowly. Remove the center screw, retainer (1), pawl (2) and springs (3 and 4). Lift the pulley slowly from the housing post, while using a small screwdriver to slide the spring hook from the pulley. Use care if the spring must be removed from the housing. Do not allow the spring to uncoil uncontrolled.

Inspect rope, pawl and springs for breakage or excessive wear. Install new parts as necessary. Lubricate the center post of the housing with light grease before assembling. Install spring (7) in housing (10) beginning at the outside and winding in a clockwise direction. Wind all but about 6 in. (15 cm) of rope onto pulley (5), then assemble the pulley on the center post. Press the pulley into housing while making sure the center of pulley engages the recoil spring hook. Install the loop spring (3), pawl (2) and pawl spring (4). Install the center screw, retainer (1) and pawl (2). Make sure the loop spring is installed properly as shown in Fig. KA38. Insert the end of the rope through the guide (8) and install the handle. Preload the rewind spring three turns clockwise, then slide the guide (8) into housing. Check the preload by pulling the rope all the way out. The pulley should be able to turn further clockwise when the rope is fully extended. Be sure the spring does not bind with the rope extended, but the rope handle should be pulled against the housing when released.

KIORITZ
ENGINE SERVICE

Model	Bore	Stroke	Displacement
Kioritz	26.0 mm (1.02 in.)	26.0 mm (1.02 in.)	13.8 cc (0.84 cu. in.)
Kioritz	28.0 mm (1.10 in.)	26.0 mm (1.02 in.)	16.0 cc (0.98 cu. in.)
Kioritz	32.2 mm (1.27 in.)	26.0 mm (1.02 in.)	21.2 cc (1.29 cu. in.)
Kioritz	28.0 mm (1.10 in.)	37.0 mm (1.46 in.)	30.1 cc (1.84 cu. in.)
Kioritz	40.0 mm (1.56 in.)	32.0 mm (1.26 in.)	40.2 cc (2.45 cu. in.)

ENGINE INFORMATION

Kioritz two-stroke air-cooled gasoline engines are used by several manufacturers of string trimmers and brush cutters.

MAINTENANCE

SPARK PLUG. Recommended spark plug is a Champion CJ8, or equivalent. Specified electrode gap for all models is 0.6-0.7 mm (0.024-0.28 in.).

CARBURETOR. Kioritz engines may be equipped with a Walbro diaphragm type carburetor with a built in fuel pump (Fig. KZ50) or a Zama diaphragm type carburetor (Fig. KZ52). Refer to appropriate paragraph for model being serviced.

Walbro Diaphragm Type Carburetor. Initial adjustment of fuel mixture needles from a lightly seated position is 1¹/₈ turn open for low speed mixture needle (18—Fig. KZ50) and 1¹/₄ turn open for high speed mixture needle (17).

Final adjustments are made with trimmer line at recommended length. Engine should be at operating temperature and running. Turn idle speed screw (31) to obtain 2500-3000 rpm, or just below clutch engagement speed. Adjust low speed mixture needle (18) to obtain consistent idling and smooth acceleration. Readjust idle speed screw (31) as required. Open throttle fully and adjust high speed mixture needle (17) to obtain highest engine rpm, then turn high speed mixture needle counterclockwise 1/8 turn.

To disassemble carburetor, remove the four screws retaining cover (1) to carburetor body. Remove cover (1), diaphragm (2) and gasket (3). Remove screw (4), pin (5), fuel inlet lever (6), spring (8) and fuel inlet needle (7). Remove screw (9) and remove circuit plate (10), check valve (11) and gasket (12). Remove screw (29), cover (28), gasket (27) and diaphragm (26). Remove inlet screen (24). Remove high and low speed mixture needles and springs. Remove throttle plate (13) and shaft (20) as required.

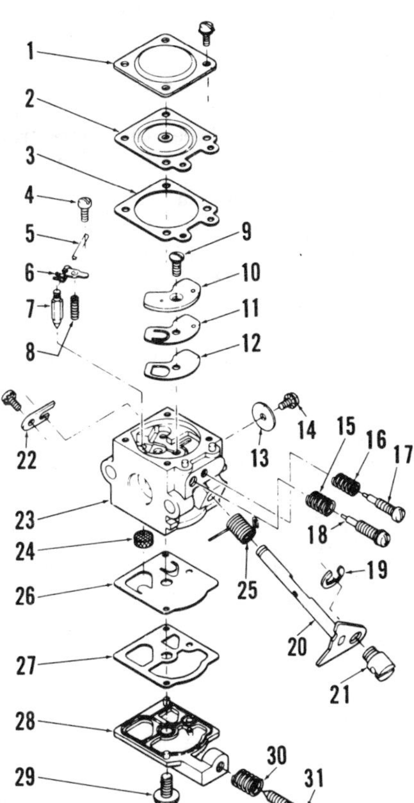

Fig. KZ50—Exploded view of Walbro carburetor used on some models.

1. Cover
2. Metering diaphragm
3. Gasket
4. Metering lever screw
5. Metering lever pin
6. Metering lever
7. Fuel inlet valve
8. Metering lever spring
9. Circuit plate screw
10. Circuit plate
11. Check valve
12. Gasket
13. Throttle valve
14. Shutter screw
15. Spring
16. Spring
17. High speed mixture needle
18. Idle mixture needle
19. "E" clip
20. Throttle shaft
21. Swivel
22. Throttle shaft clip
23. Body
24. Inlet screen
25. Return spring
26. Fuel pump diaphragm
27. Gasket
28. Cover
29. Cover screw
30. Spring
31. Idle speed screw

Carefully inspect all parts. Diaphragms should be flexible and free of cracks or tears. When reassembling, fuel inlet lever (6) should be flush with carburetor body (Fig. KZ51). Carefully bend fuel inlet lever to obtain correct setting.

Zama Diaphragm Type Carburetor. Initial adjustment of low speed (16—Fig. KZ52) and high speed (17) mixture needles is one turn open from a lightly seated position.

Final adjustments are made with trimmer line at recommended length. Engine should be at operating temperature and running. Turn idle speed screw (27) to obtain 2500-3000 rpm, or just below clutch engagement speed. Adjust low speed mixture needle (16) to obtain consistent idling and smooth acceleration. Readjust idle speed screw (27) as required. Open throttle fully and adjust high speed mixture needle (17) to obtain highest engine rpm, then turn high speed mixture needle counterclockwise 1/8 turn.

To disassemble carburetor, remove screw (26), pump cover (25), gasket (24) and diaphragm (23). Remove fuel inlet screen (22). Remove the two screws (1)

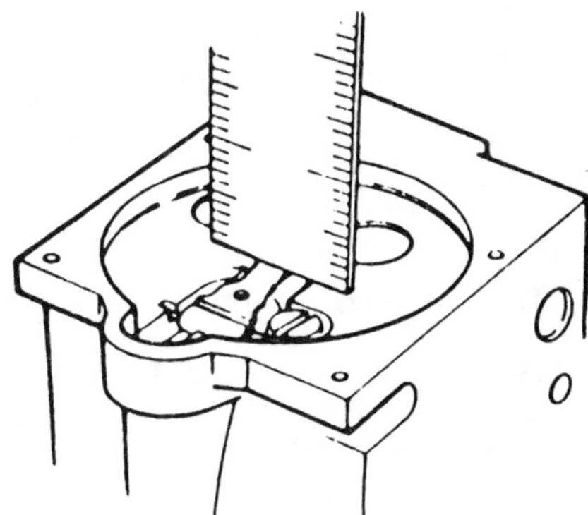

Fig. KZ51—Fuel inlet lever should be flush with carburetor body.

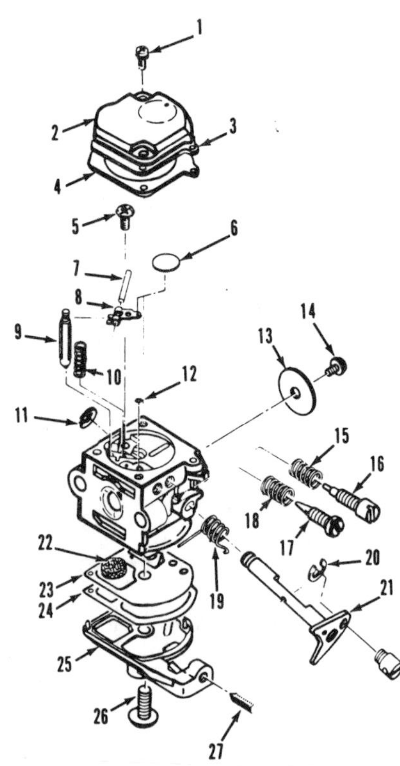

Fig. KZ52—Exploded view of Zama diaphragm carburetor used on some models.

1. Screw
2. Cover
3. Diaphragm
4. Gasket
5. Screw
6. Fuel metering lever disc
7. Pin
8. Fuel inlet lever
9. Fuel inlet needle
10. Spring
11. "E" ring
12. Disc
13. Throttle plate
14. Screw
15. Spring
16. Low speed mixture needle
17. High speed mixture needle
18. Spring
19. Spring
20. "E" ring
21. Throttle shaft
22. Screen
23. Diaphragm
24. Gasket
25. Cover
26. Screw
27. Idle speed screw

and remove cover (2), diaphragm (3) and gasket (4). Remove screw (5), pin (7), metering disc (6), fuel inlet lever (8), fuel inlet needle (9) and spring (10). Remove fuel mixture needles and springs. Remove "E" clip (11), throttle plate (13) and throttle shaft (21) as required.

Inspect all parts for wear or damage. Diaphragms should be flexible with no cracks or wrinkles. Fuel inlet lever (8) with metering disc (6) removed, should be flush with carburetor fuel chamber floor (Fig. KZ51).

IGNITION SYSTEM. Engines may be equipped with a magneto type ignition with breaker points and condenser or a CDI (capacitor-discharge) ignition system which requires no regular maintenance and has no breaker points. Ignition module (CDI) is located outside of flywheel. Refer to appropriate paragraph for model being serviced.

Breaker Point Ignition System. Breaker points may be located behind recoil starter or behind flywheel. Note location of breaker points and refer to following paragraphs for service.

To inspect or service magneto ignition with **breaker points and condenser located behind recoil starter and cover,** first remove fan cover. Refer to Fig. KZ53 and check pole gap between flywheel and ignition coil laminations. Gap should be 0.35-0.40 mm (0.014-0.016 in.). To adjust pole gap, loosen two retaining screws in coil (threads of retaining screws should be treated with Loctite or equivalent), place correct gage between flywheel and coil laminations. Pull coil to flywheel by hand as shown, then tighten screws and remove feeler gage.

Breaker points are accessible after removal of starter case, nut and pawl carrier. Nut and pawl carrier both have left-hand threads.

To adjust point gap and ignition timing, disconnect stop switch wire from stop switch. Connect one lead from a timing tester (Kioritz 990510-00031) or equivalent to stop switch wire. Ground remaining timing tester lead to engine body. Position flywheel timing mark as shown in Fig. KZ54 and set breaker point gap to 0.3-0.4 mm (0.012-0.014 in.). Rotate flywheel and check timing with timing tester. Readjust as necessary. Be accurate when setting breaker point gap. A gap greater than 0.4 mm (0.014 in.) will advance timing; a gap less than 0.3 mm (0.012 in.) will retard timing.

With point gap and flywheel correctly set, timing will be 23° BTDC.

To inspect or service magneto ignition with **breaker points and condenser located behind flywheel,** first remove starter case. Disconnect wire from stop switch and connect to timing tester (Kioritz 990510-00031) or equivalent. Ground remaining lead from timing tester to engine body. Position flywheel timing mark as shown in Fig. KZ55. If timing is not correct, loosen retaining screw on breaker point through flywheel slot openings. Squeeze screwdriver in crankcase groove to adjust point gap. Breaker point gap should be 0.3-0.4 mm (0.012-0.016 in.) with flywheel at TDC.

If breaker points require renewal, flywheel must be removed. When installing breaker points note that stop lead (black) from condenser must pass under coil. White wire from coil must pass between condenser bracket and oiler felt. Push wire down to avoid contact with flywheel.

Ignition coil air gap between coil and flywheel should be 0.4 mm (0.016 in.). Retaining screws should be treated with Loctite or equivalent.

Be accurate when setting breaker point gap. A gap greater than 0.4 mm (0.016 in.) will advance timing; a gap less than 0.3 mm (0.012 in.) will retard timing.

With point gap and flywheel correctly set, timing will be 30° BTDC. Tighten flywheel nut.

Primary and secondary ignition coil resistance may be checked with an ohmmeter without removing coil.

To check primary coil resistance, connect ohmmeter to disconnected ignition coil primary lead and ground remaining lead to engine. Primary coil resistance should register 0.5-0.8 ohms.

To check secondary coil resistance, connect one lead of ohmmeter to spark plug cable and remaining lead to ground on engine. Secondary coil resistance should register 5-10 ohms.

CD Ignition System. CD ignition system requires no regular maintenance and has no moving parts except for magnets cast in flywheel.

Ignition timing is fixed at 30° BTDC and clearance between CDI module laminations and flywheel should be 0.3 mm (0.012 in.). To check ignition timing, refer to Fig. KZ56. If timing is not correct, CDI module must be renewed.

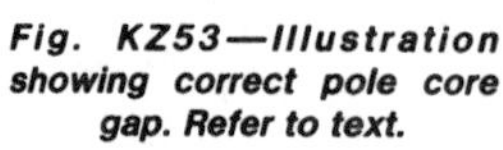

Fig. KZ53—Illustration showing correct pole core gap. Refer to text.

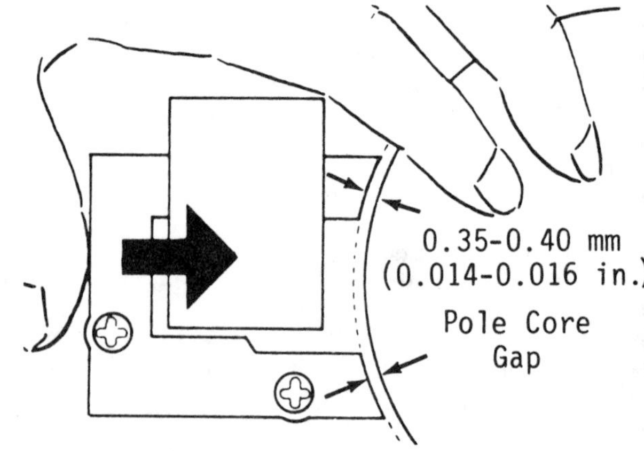

Ignition coil may be checked by con-
ıcting one ohmmeter lead to spark
.ug cable and remaining lead to coil
·imary lead; ohmmeter should regis-
ır 0.0-0.2 ohms for all models. Connect
ımmeter lead to coil primary lead
ed) wire and remaining ohmmeter
ad to either the coil exciter lead
grounded wire), if so equipped, or to
ıil laminations. Ohmmeter should reg-
ter 0.5-1.5k ohms for models with
ксiter lead or 1.5-3.0k ohms for re-
ıaining models. Connect one ohmmet-
· lead to exciter lead, of models so equipped, and remaining ohmmeter lead to coil laminations; ohmmeter should register 120-200 ohms.

CARBON. Muffler and cylinder exhaust ports should be cleaned periodically to prevent loss of power due to carbon build-up. Remove muffler cover and baffle plate and scrape muffler free of carbon. With muffler cover removed, position engine so piston is at top dead center and carefully remove carbon from exhaust ports with wooden scraper. Be careful not to damage the edges of exhaust ports or to scratch piston. Do not attempt to run engine without muffler baffle plate or cover.

LUBRICATION. Engine lubrication is obtained by mixing a good quality two-stroke air-cooled engine oil with gasoline. Refer to TRIMMER SERVICE section for fuel/oil mixture ratio recommended by trimmer manufacturer.

REPAIRS

COMPRESSION PRESSURE. For optimum performance, minimum compression pressure should be 621 kPa (90 psi). Compression test should be performed with engine cold and throttle and choke plates at wide open positions.

TIGHTENING TORQUES. Recommended tightening torque specifications are as follows:

Spark plug:
All models . . . . 14-15 N·m (168-180 in.-lbs.)
Cylinder cover:
All models so equipped 1.5-1.9 N·m (13-17 in.-lbs.)
Cylinder:
13.8, 16.0 & 21.2 cc engine . . . .5.7-6.0 N·m (50-55 in.-lbs.)
All other engines . . . .7.0-8.0 N·m (65-75 in.-lbs.)
Crankcase:
All models . . . . .4.5-5.7 N·m (40-50 in.-lbs.)

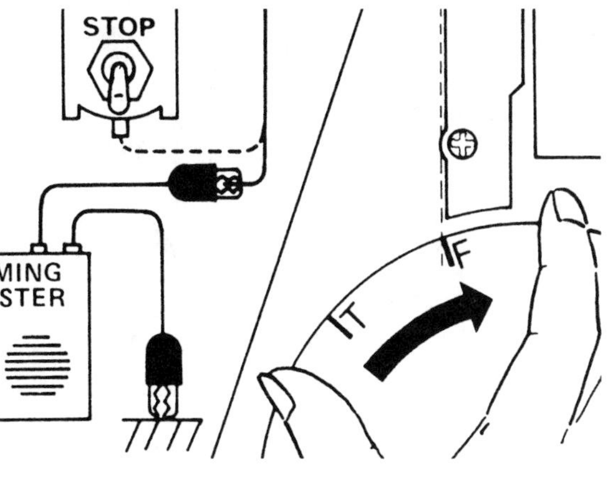

Fig. KZ54—Illustration showing proper timing mark setting for engines with breaker points located behind recoil starter and cover. Refer to text.

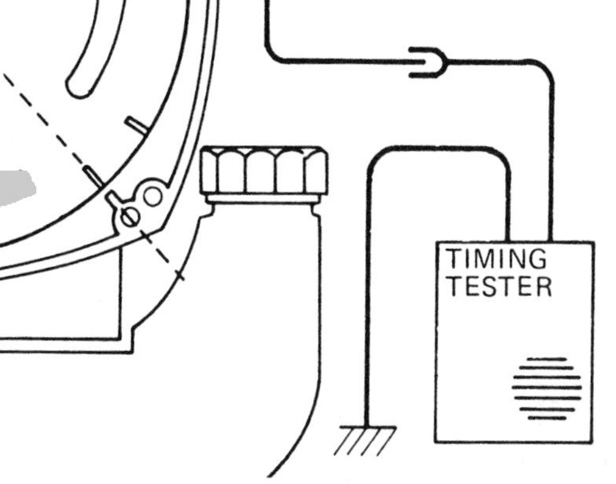

Fig. KZ55—Illustration showing proper timing mark setting for engines with breaker points located behind flywheel. Refer to text.

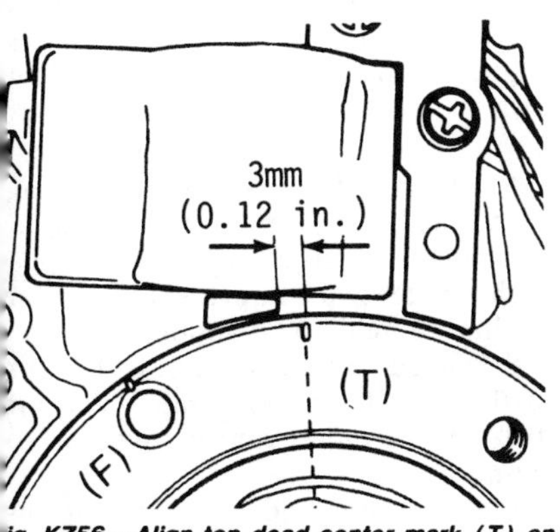

ig. KZ56—Align top dead center mark (T) on ywheel with laminations as shown to check timing on models with CD ignition. Refer to text.

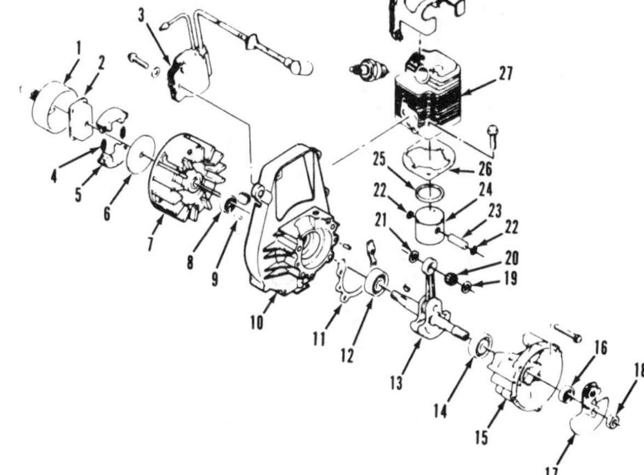

Fig. KZ57—Exploded view of engine similar to the 13.8, 16.0 and 21.2 cc (0.84, 0.98 and 1.29 cu. in.) displacement engines.

1. Clutch drum
2. Hub
3. Ignition module
4. Clutch springs
5. Clutch shoes
6. Plate
7. Flywheel
8. Seal
9. Key
10. Crankcase
11. Gasket
12. Bearing
13. Crankshaft & connecting rod assy.
14. Bearing
15. Crankcase cover
16. Seal
17. Ratchet assy.
18. Nut
19. Thrust washer
20. Bearing
21. Thrust washer
22. Retainer
23. Piston pin
24. Piston
25. Ring
26. Gasket
27. Cylinder

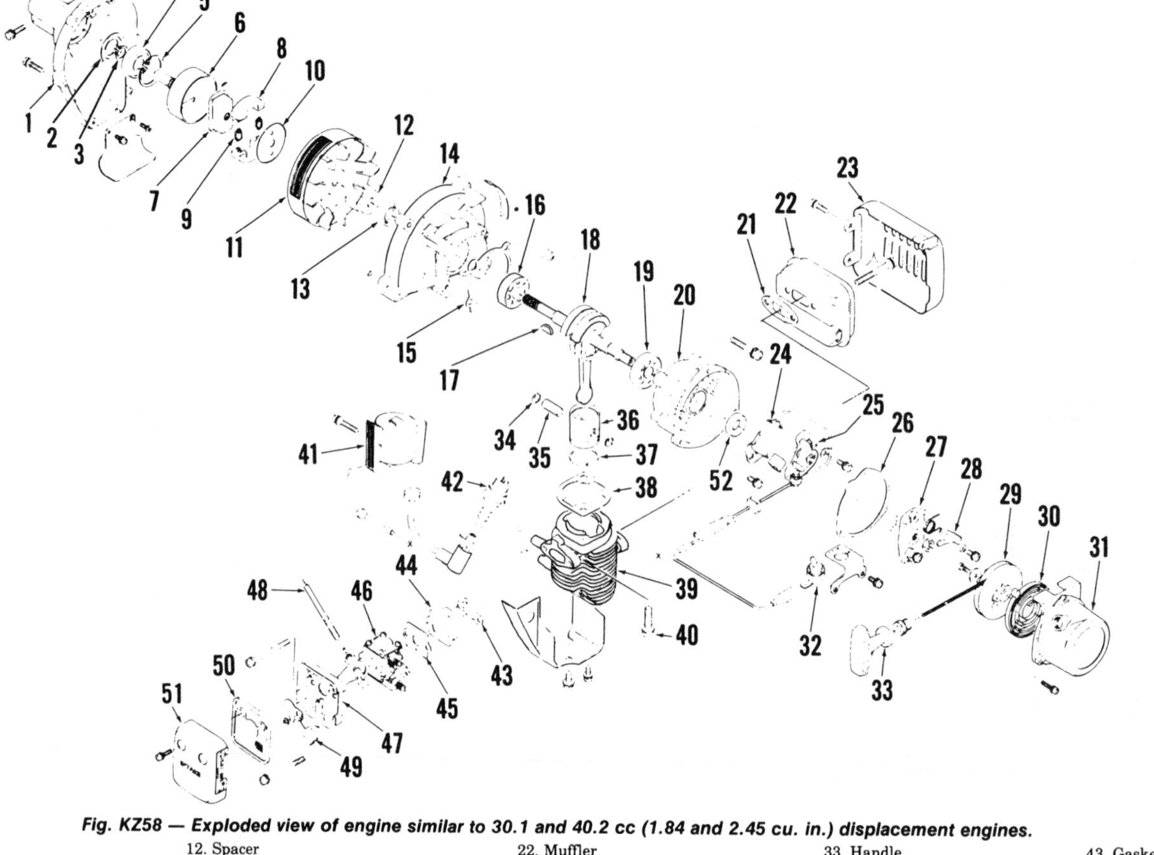

Fig. KZ58 — Exploded view of engine similar to 30.1 and 40.2 cc (1.84 and 2.45 cu. in.) displacement engines.

1. Fan cover
2. Stopper
3. Snap ring
4. Ball bearing
5. Snap ring
6. Clutch drum
7. Clutch hub
8. Clutch shoe
9. Clutch spring
10. Side plate
11. Flywheel/fan
12. Spacer
13. Seal
14. Crankcase
15. Crankcase packing
16. Ball bearing
17. Woodruff key
18. Crankshaft/connecting rod assy.
19. Ball bearing
20. Crankcase half
21. Gasket
22. Muffler
23. Cover
24. Condenser
25. Breaker points
26. Gasket
27. Pawl carrier
28. Pawl
29. Starter hub
30. Spring
31. Starter housing
32. Stop switch
33. Handle
34. Snap ring
35. Piston pin
36. Piston
37. Piston ring
38. Gasket
39. Cylinder
40. Screw
41. Coil assy.
42. Spark plug
43. Gasket
44. Insulator
45. Gasket
46. Carburetor
47. Case
48. Throttle cab
49. Choke shut
50. Air filter
51. Cover
52. Seal

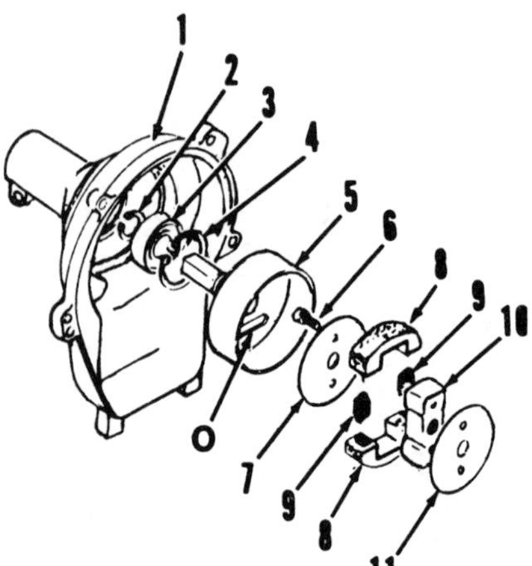

Fig. KZ59—Exploded view of clutch assembly.

O. Opening
1. Clutch housing
2. Snap ring
3. Bearing
4. Snap ring
5. Clutch drum
6. Screw
7. Plate
8. Clutch shoes
9. Clutch springs
10. Hub
11. Plate

CRANKSHAFT AND CONNECTING ROD. The crankshaft and connecting rod are serviced as an assembly only and crankshaft and connecting rod are not available separately.

To remove crankshaft and connecting rod assembly remove fan housing and clutch assembly. Remove carburetor, muffler and fuel tank. Remove starter assembly, flywheel and ignition module. Carefully remove cylinder (27—Fig. KZ57). Remove retaining rings (22) and use a suitable piston pin puller to remove pin (23). Note thrust washers (19 and 21) are installed on some engines and will fall when piston pin and piston are removed. Separate crankcase halves and remove crankshaft and connecting rod assembly. Carefully press ball bearings (12 and 14) off crankshaft as required. If bearings remain in crankcase, it may be necessary to heat crankcase halves slightly to remove bearings.

Inspect all parts for wear or damag Standard connecting rod side clearanc on crankpin journal is 0.55-0.60 mı (0.022-0.026 in.). If side clearance is 0. mm (0.028 in.) or more, crankshaft an connecting rod assembly must be re newed. Crankcase runout should no exceed 0.05 mm (0.002 in.). It may b necessary to heat crankcase halve slightly to install ball bearings (12 an 14).

PISTON, PIN AND RINGS. Ring are pinned to prevent ring rotation o all models. Piston may be equippe with one or two compression rings ac cording to model and application.

Standard ring end gap is 0.3 mı (0.012 in.). If ring end gap is 0.5 mn (0.02 in.) or more, renew rings and/o cylinder.

Standard ring side clearance in pis ton groove is 0.06 mm (0.0024 in.). I ring side clearance is 0.10 mm (0.004 in.

or more, renew ring and/or piston.

When installing piston, rings must be correctly positioned over pins in ring grooves. Install piston on connecting rod with arrow on top of piston towards exhaust side of engine. Make certain piston pin retaining rings are correctly seated in piston pin bore of piston. Use care when installing piston into cylinder that cylinder does not rotate.

CYLINDER. The cylinder bore has a chrome plated surface and must be renewed if plating is worn through or scored excessively. Worn spots will appear dull and may be easily scratched while chrome plating will be bright and much harder.

CLUTCH. Refer to Fig. KZ59 for an exploded view of centrifugal clutch assembly used on 13.8, 16.0 and 21.2 cc (0.84, 0.98 and 1.29 cu. in.) engines. Snap ring (4) is removed from snap ring bore through opening (O) in clutch drum. Drive clutch drum (5) out and remove snap ring (2). Remove ball bearing (3). Check shoes for wear or oil, check clutch springs for fatigue and renew parts as necessary. If removal of clutch hub is necessary, it is screwed on crankshaft with left-hand threads.

To remove clutch from all other engines, remove fan cover. Remove screw retaining clutch drum to crankshaft. Remove ball bearing from clutch drum. Check shoes for wear or oil, check clutch springs for fatigue and renew parts as necessary.

KOMATSU

ENGINE SERVICE

Model	Bore	Stroke	Displacement
G1E	28 mm (1.10 in.)	28 mm (1.10 in.)	17.2 cc (1.05 cu. in.)
G2E	34 mm (1.36 in.)	28 mm (1.10 in.)	25.4 cc (1.55 cu. in.)

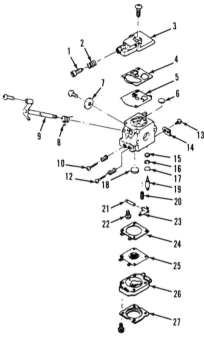

Fig. KU10—Exploded view of typical Walbro WA carburetor. Some models are equipped with a remote purge bulb that connects to plate (26).

1. Idle speed screw
2. Spring
3. Cover
4. Gasket
5. Fuel pump diaphragm
6. Inlet screen
7. Throttle plate
8. Spring
9. Throttle shaft
10. Idle mixture screw
12. High-speed mixture screw
13. Screw
14. Retainer
15. Check valve screen
16. Snap ring
17. Welch plug
18. Welch plug
19. Fuel inlet valve
20. Spring
21. Pin
22. Screw
23. Metering lever
24. Gasket
25. Metering diaphragm
26. Plate
27. Cover

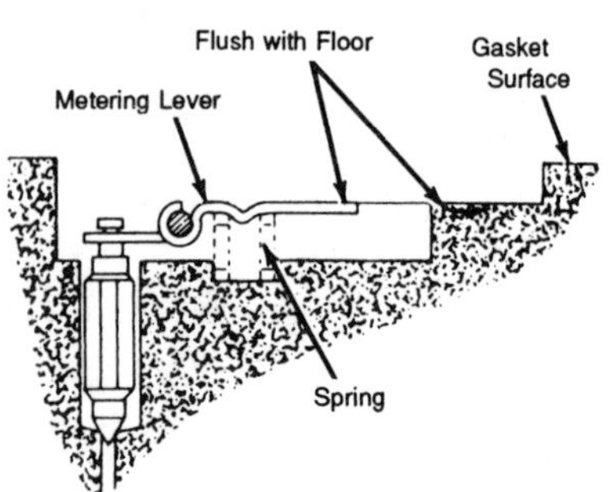

Fig. KU11—Metering lever should be flush with chamber floor as shown.

ENGINE INFORMATION

The Komatsu G1E and G2E two-stroke, air-cooled gasoline engines are used by several manufacturers of string trimmers and brush cutters. The engines are equipped with cantilever-type crankshafts that are supported in two ball bearings at the flywheel end. Refer to following sections for other Komatsu engine models.

MAINTENANCE

LUBRICATION. Engine lubrication is obtained by mixing gasoline with an oil designed for two-stroke, air-cooled engines. Refer to trimmer or blower service section for manufacturer's recommended fuel:oil mixture ratio.

SPARK PLUG. Recommended spark plug is a Champion RCJ8 or equivalent. Specified electrode gap for all models is 0.6-0.7 mm (0.024-0.028 in.). Tighten spark plug to 19.5-21.6 N·m (173-191 in.-lbs.).

CARBURETOR. The engine is equipped with a Walbro WA diaphragm-type carburetor. Some models are equipped with a remote air purge bulb that is connected to plate (26—Fig. KU10). Operating the air purge bulb (may be called a primer) fills the carburetor with fuel for faster fuel movement during starting.

Initial adjustment of idle mixture screw (10) is $1\frac{1}{4}$ turns out from a lightly seated position on trimmers and brush cutters, or $1\frac{1}{2}$ turns out on blowers. Initial adjustment of high-speed mixture screw (12) is one turn out on trimmers and brush cutters, or $1\frac{1}{2}$ turns out on blowers.

Final adjustments are performed with trimmer line at recommended length or blade installed. Engine must be at operating temperature and running. Be sure engine air filter is clean before adjusting carburetor.

Turn idle speed screw (1) in until trimmer head or blade just begins to rotate, or to 2700 rpm on blowers. Adjust idle mixture screw (10) to obtain maximum idle speed possible, then turn idle mixture screw $\frac{1}{6}$ turn counterclockwise. Readjust idle speed. Operate unit at full throttle and adjust high-speed mixture screw (12) to obtain maximum engine rpm, then turn high-speed mixture screw $\frac{1}{6}$ turn counterclockwise.

When overhauling carburetor, refer to exploded view in Fig. KU10. Examine fuel inlet valve and seat. Inlet valve (19) is renewable, but carburetor body must be renewed if seat is excessively worn or damaged. Inspect mixture screws and seats. Renew carburetor body if seats are excessively worn or damaged. Clean fuel inlet screen (6). Inspect diaphragms (5 and 25) for tears and other damage.

Metering lever (23) should be flush with chamber floor as shown in Fig. KU11. Bend lever to obtain correct lever height.

IGNITION SYSTEM. The engine is equipped with an electronic ignition system. The ignition system is considered satisfactory if a spark will jump across the 3 mm ($\frac{1}{8}$ in.) gap of a test spark plug. If no spark is produced check on/off switch, wiring and clearance between ignition module and flywheel. Ignition module air gap should be 0.25 mm (0.010 in.). If switch, wiring and module air gap are satisfactory but spark is not present, renew ignition module. Tighten ignition module retaining screws to 2.0-2.4 N·m (18-21 in.-lbs.). Apply Loctite to screws.

REPAIRS

COMPRESSION PRESSURE. For optimum performance, compression pressure should be 586 kPa (85 psi) and not less than 393 kPa (57 psi). Compression pressure should be checked with engine at operating temperature and with throttle and choke wide open.

TIGHTENING TORQUES. Recommended tightening torques are as follows:

Clutch shaft . . . . 12.0-13.6 N·m (140-160 in.-lbs.)
Crankcase cover. . . . . 2.9-3.3 N·m (26-34 in.-lbs.)
Crankpin screw . . . . 3.0-3.8 N·m (35-45 in.-lbs.)
Cylinder . . . . 5.9-6.8 N·m (53-60 in.-lbs.)
Flywheel . . . . 13.7-15.7 N·m (122-139 in.-lbs.)
Ignition module . . . . 2.0-2.4 N·m (18-21 in.-lbs.)
Spark plug . . . . 19.7-24.5 N·m (175-215 in.-lbs.)

PISTON, PIN AND RINGS. To remove piston, first remove fan housing, cylinder shroud, muffler and ignition module. Unscrew two retaining screws and remove cylinder by pulling straight up, otherwise the piston and ring may be damaged. Ring rotation is prevented by a locating pin in the piston ring groove. Remove piston pin retainers and use a suitable puller to remove piston pin. Remove piston from connecting rod.

Specified piston skirt diameter is 27.93 mm (1.099 in.) with a wear limit of 27.80 mm (1.094 in.). Specified piston ring groove width is 1.40 mm (0.055 in.) with a wear limit of 1.52 mm (0.059 in.). Piston ring end gap should be 0.10-0.25 mm (0.004-0.010 in.) and no more than 0.5 mm (0.019 in.). Specified piston ring width is 1.10 mm (0.043 in.) with a wear limit of 1.00 mm (0.039 in.). Specified piston ring thickness is 1.44 mm (0.057 in.) with a wear limit of 1.30 mm (0.051 in.).

The piston pin rides directly in connecting rod and piston. Specified piston pin diameter is 7.993 mm (0.315 in.) with a wear limit of 7.98 mm (0.314 in.).

Piston and ring are available in standard size only.

Install piston on rod so arrow on piston crown points toward exhaust port (Fig. KU12). Install piston pin so closed end is toward exhaust port. Be sure piston ring gap is correctly indexed with locating pin in piston ring groove when installing cylinder. Tighten cylinder retaining screws to 5.9-6.8 N·m (53-60 in.-lbs.).

CYLINDER. The cylinder bore is chrome plated. Renew cylinder if bore is excessively worn or bore surface is cracked, flaking or otherwise damaged. Specified cylinder bore is 28.01 mm (1.102 in.) with a wear limit of 28.07 mm (1.105 in.). Tighten cylinder retaining screws to 5.9-6.8 N·m (53-60 in.-lbs.).

CRANKSHAFT AND CONNECTING ROD. The crankshaft is supported at flywheel end only by two ball bearings. To remove crankshaft and connecting rod, remove fan housing (5—Fig. KU13) and recoil starter assembly, cooling shroud (4) and ignition module (3). Disconnect fuel line and remove fuel tank. Remove air filter assembly (35), carburetor (31), muffler cover (1) and muffler (2). Remove flywheel retaining nut and pull flywheel (9) off crankshaft. Remove cylinder mounting bolts and pull cylinder (27) straight off piston. Remove piston pin retaining rings (22), then tap piston pin (23) out of piston and remove piston (24). Remove crankcase cover mounting screws and carefully separate crankcase cover (30) from crankcase (11). Remove connecting rod retaining screw (21), noting that screw has left-hand threads. Remove washer (20), thrust washers (16) and connecting rod (17) from crankpin, being careful not to lose 13 loose bearing rollers (18). To separate crankshaft (15) from crankcase, heat crankcase to 100° C (212° F) and press out crankshaft. Remove bearings (10 and 13) and oil seal (12) from crankcase.

Specified connecting rod big end diameter is 15.64 mm (0.616 in.) with a wear limit of 15.80 mm (0.622 in.). Specified connecting rod small end diameter is 8.05 mm (0.317 in.) with a wear limit of 8.20 mm (0.322 in.).

Specified crankpin diameter is 9.547 mm (0.376 in.) with a wear limit of 9.53 mm (0.375 in.). Specified crankshaft main bearing journal diameter is 12.009 mm (0.473 in.) with a wear limit of 11.99 mm (0.472 in.).

Minimum rod bearing (18) roller diameter is 2.98 mm (0.117 in.) and minimum allowable length is 6.50 mm (0.256 in.).

Fig. KU12—Install piston so arrow on piston crown points toward exhaust port.

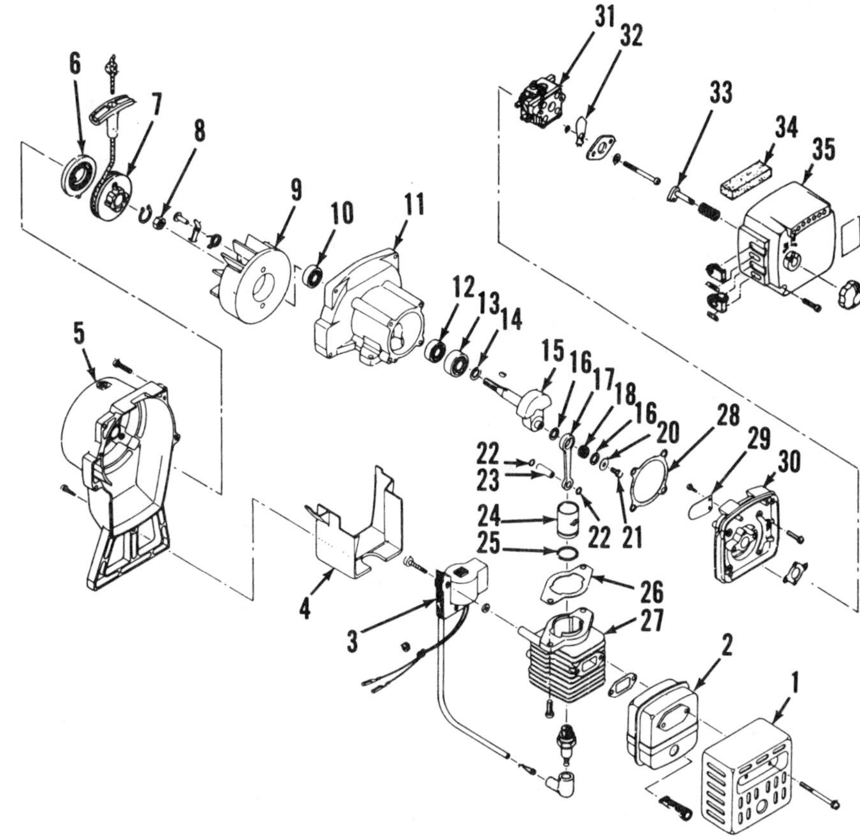

Fig. KU13—Exploded view of engine.

1. Muffler guard
2. Muffler
3. Ignition module
4. Cylinder shroud
5. Fan housing
6. Rewind spring
7. Pulley
8. Nut
9. Flywheel
10. Bearing
11. Crankcase
12. Seal
13. Bearing
14. Washer
15. Crankshaft
16. Thrust washers
17. Connecting rod
18. Needle bearing
20. Washer
21. Screw (L.H.)
22. Retaining rings
23. Piston pin
24. Piston
25. Piston ring
26. Gasket
27. Cylinder
28. Gasket
29. Reed valve
30. Crankcase cover
31. Carburetor
32. Choke plate
33. Choke shaft
34. Air filter element
35. Air cleaner cover

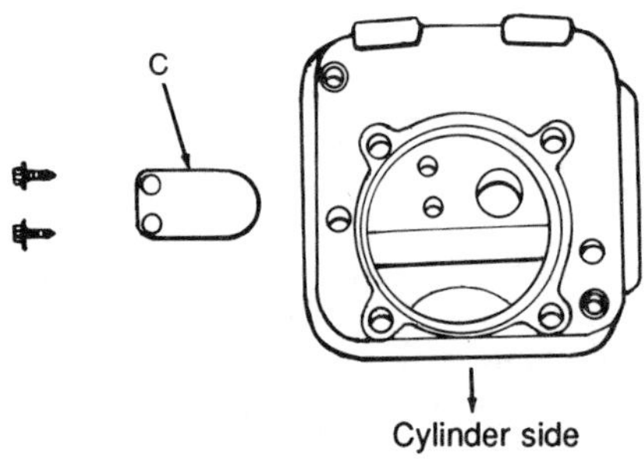

Fig. KU14—Install reed valve (C) so cut-off corner is toward cylinder side of crankcase cover.

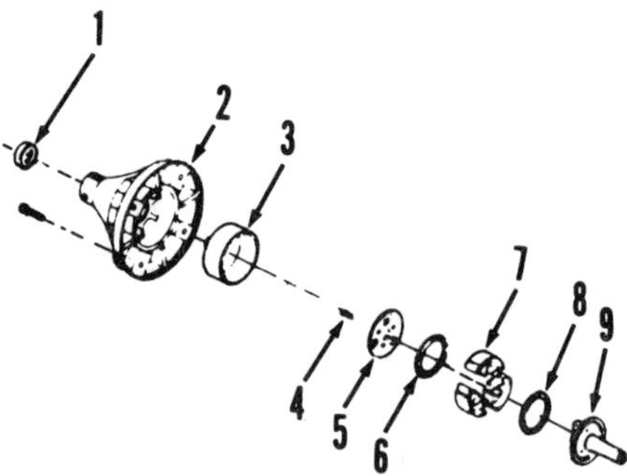

Fig. KU15—Exploded view of clutch assembly used on some models.

1. Spacer
2. Clutch housing
3. Clutch drum
4. Screw
5. Plate
6. Spring
7. Clutch shoes
8. Spring
9. Clutch shaft

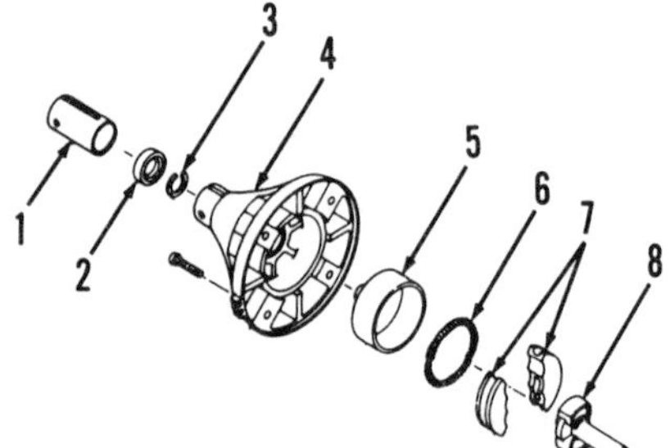

Fig. KU16—Exploded view of clutch assembly used on some models.

1. Sleeve
2. Spacer
3. Snap ring
4. Clutch housing
5. Clutch drum
6. Spring
7. Clutch shoes
8. Clutch shaft

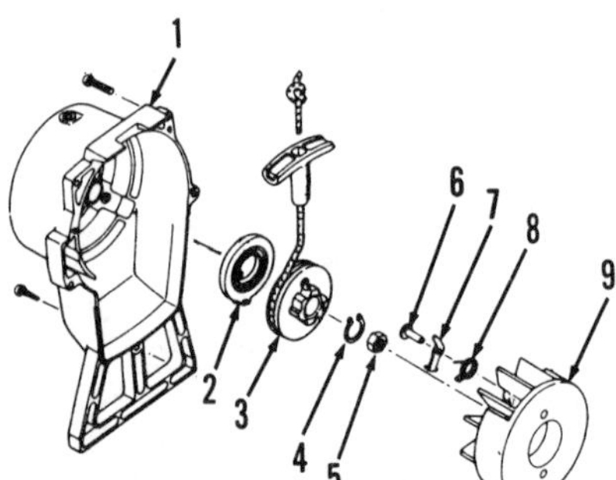

Fig. KU17—Exploded view of rewind starter used on trimmer engines. Pawl components (6, 7 and 8) are available only as an assembly on flywheel.

1. Housing
2. Rewind spring
3. Pulley
4. Snap ring
5. Nut
6. Post
7. Pawl
8. Spring
9. Flywheel

To assemble crankshaft, install spacer (14) and press bearing (13) onto crankshaft. Install seal (12) in crankcase so lip will be toward inside of engine. Heat crankcase to 100°C (212°F) and install bearing (10) with numbered side out. Install crankshaft and bearing in crankcase.

When installing connecting rod on crankpin, be sure 13 bearing rollers (18) are in place. Note that crankpin screw (21) has left-hand threads. Tighten crankpin screw to 3.0-3.8 N·m (35-45 in.-lbs.

REED VALVE. A reed valve (29—Fig. KU13) is located on the inside of the crankcase cover (30). Renew reed valve if cracked, broken or warped. Install reed valve so cut-off corner (C—Fig. KU14) is toward cylinder side of cover.

CLUTCH. Two clutch designs have been used. See Figs. KU15 and KU16. Clutch shoes are available only as a set. On models so equipped, be sure hole in side of sleeve (1—Fig. KU16) is aligned with hole in clutch housing. Tighten clutch shaft (8) to 12.0-13.6 N·m (140-160 in.-lbs.)

REWIND STARTER. Trimmers. Refer to Fig. KU17 for an exploded view of rewind starter used on trimmers. To disassemble starter, detach starter housing (1) from engine. Remove rope handle and allow rope to wind into starter. Remove snap ring (4) and remove rope pulley (3). Wear appropriate safety eyewear and gloves before detaching rewind spring (2) from housing as spring may uncoil uncontrolled.

To assemble starter, lubricate center post of housing and spring side with light grease. Install rewind spring so coil windings are clockwise from outer end. Assemble starter while passing rope through housing rope outlet and attach rope handle to rope. To place tension on starter rope, pull rope out of housing. Engage rope in notch on pulley and turn pulley four turns clockwise. Hold pulley and disengage rope from pulley notch. Release pulley and allow rope to wind on pulley. Check starter operation. Rope handle should be held against housing by spring tension, but it must be possible to rotate pulley at least $^1/_4$ turn clockwise when rope is pulled out fully.

Blowers. The rewind starter on engines used on blowers is located between the flywheel and the crankcase. Rewind spring case (1—Fig. KU18) is attached to the crankcase. To disassemble starter, the engine must be removed from blower housing. Push rope outlet into housing then pass rope handle through opening. Remove engine. Remove fan (9) and flywheel (6). Either remove rope handle or insert rope in rope pulley notch and allow rewind spring to unwind. Wear appropriate safety eyewear and gloves before detaching pulley (3) from rewind spring (2) as spring may uncoil uncontrolled. Note that hub of spring case (1) is slotted. Push in fingers of hub and disengage pulley from hub; rewind spring will be free when pulley is separated from spring.

To assemble starter, lubricate hub of spring case and spring side with light grease. Wind spring in case in a counterclockwise direction from outer end. Rope length should be 90 cm ($35^1/_2$ in.). Assemble spring case and pulley, but do not install on engine. To place tension on starter rope, pull rope out, engage rope in notch on pulley and turn pulley $2^1/_2$ turns counterclockwise. Hold pulley and disengage rope from pulley notch. Release pulley and allow rope to wind on pulley. It should be possible to turn pulley 2 more turns counterclockwise with rope fully extended. Install spring case on crankcase being sure notches on spring case and ribs on crankcase are aligned. Reassemble blower and check starter operation.

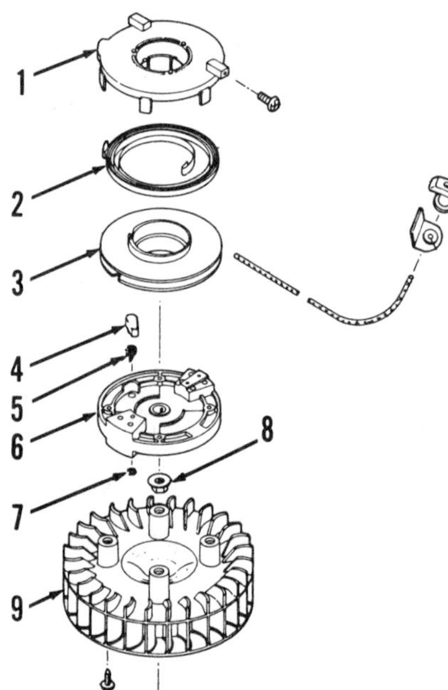

Fig. KU18—Exploded view of rewind starter used on blower engines.

1. Spring case
2. Rewind spring
3. Pulley
4. Pawl
5. Spring
6. "E" ring
7. Flywheel
8. Nut
9. Fan

KOMATSU/ZENOAH

ENGINE SERVICE

Model	Bore	Stroke	Displacement
G2D & G2KC	32 mm (1.26 in.)	28 mm (1.10 in.)	22.5 cc (1.37 cu. in.)
G2K	34 mm (1.34 in.)	28 mm (1.10 in.)	25.4 cc (1.55 cu. in.)
G3K	36 mm (1.42 in.)	33 mm (1.23 in.)	33.6 cc (2.05 cu. in.)
G4K	40 mm (1.58 in.)	33 mm (1.23 in.)	41.5 cc (2.53 cu. in.)
G23L	32 mm (1.26 in.)	28 mm (1.10 in.)	22.5 cc (1.37 cu. in.)
G26L	34 mm (1.34 in.)	28 mm (1.10 in.)	25.4 cc (1.55 cu. in.)
Blower	40 mm (1.58 in.)	33 mm (1.23 in.)	41.5 cc (2.53 cu. in.)

ENGINE INFORMATION

Komatsu/Zenoah two-stroke, air-cooled gasoline engines are used by several manufacturers to power string trimmers, brush cutters, blowers, hedge trimmers and other equipment. The engines in this section are piston ported and the carburetor is attached to the cylinder intake port. Refer to the preceding KOMATSU/ZENOAH Engine Service section for other Komatsu/Zenoah engines.

MAINTENANCE

LUBRICATION. Engine lubrication is obtained by mixing gasoline with an oil designed for two-stroke, air-cooled engines. Refer to trimmer or blower service section for manufacturer's recommended fuel:oil mixture ratio.

SPARK PLUG. Recommended spark plug for most applications is Champion RCJ-6Y. Electrode gap for all models should be 0.6-0.7 mm (0.024-0.028 in.). Tighten spark plug to 15-22 N.m (130-191 in.-lb.) torque.

CARBURETOR. Various brands of carburetors have been used. Refer to the appropriate following section for carburetor service.

Walbro HDA. The Walbro HDA is used on some blower engines. Initial setting of idle mixture screw (5—Fig. KU51) is 1-1/4 turns out on HDA-26B carburetor and 1-3/8 turns out on HDA-70 carburetor. Initial setting of high speed mixture screw (4) is fully closed. Note: Priming system will not operate properly if high speed mixture screw is open.

Final adjustment is performed with engine running at normal operating temperature. All blower tubing must be attached. Adjust idle speed stop screw (1) so engine idles at 2000 rpm. Adjust idle mixture screw to obtain highest idle speed, then turn screw counterclockwise until engine rpm decreases 200-400 rpm. Engine should idles smoothly and accelerate without hesitation. Readjust idle speed stop screw to 2000 rpm. Run engine at full throttle. If engine speed exceeds 8000 rpm, open high speed mixture screw no more than 1/4 turn.

To disassemble carburetor, refer to Fig. KU51 and remove covers (7 and 23) for access to internal components. Remove diaphragms (9 and 22), metering lever (18) and fuel inlet valve (15), fuel mixture screws (4 and 5), fuel inlet screen (10) and Welch plug (16).

Clean and inspect all components. Inspect diaphragms for defects that may affect operation. Examine fuel inlet valve and seat. Inlet valve (15) is renewable, but carburetor body must be renewed if seat is damaged or excessively worn. Discard carburetor body if mixture screw seats are damaged or ex-

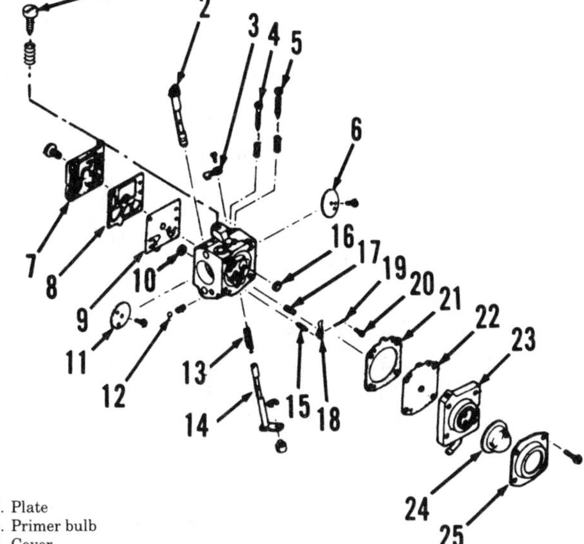

Fig. KU51—Exploded view of Walbro HDA diaphragm carburetor. All components may not be used on all models. Choke shaft (2) is on same side as throttle shaft (14) on some models.

1. Idle speed screw
2. Choke shaft
3. Throttle stop
4. High speed mixture screw
5. Low speed mixture screw
6. Throttle plate
7. Pump cover
8. Gasket
9. Pump diaphragm
10. Inlet screen
11. Choke plate
12. Choke detent ball
13. Spring
14. Throttle shaft
15. Fuel inlet valve
16. Welch plug
17. Spring
18. Metering lever
19. Pin
20. Screw
21. Gasket
22. Metering diaphragm
23. Plate
24. Primer bulb
25. Cover

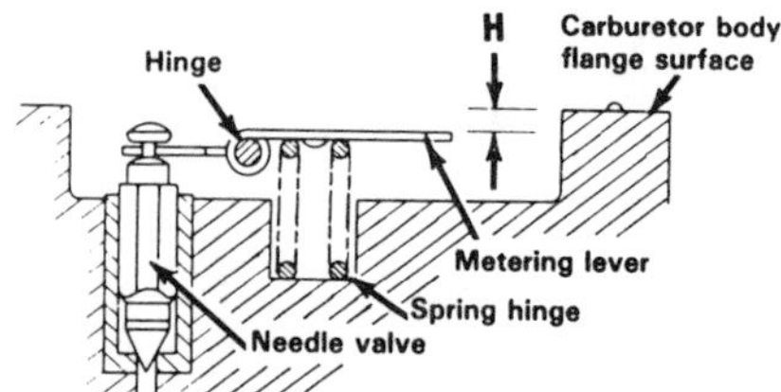

Fig. KU52—Metering lever height (H) must be set on diaphragm type carburetors. Refer to text for specified height.

cessively worn. Clean or renew fuel screen (10). If throttle or choke shaft was removed, apply Loctite to throttle or choke plate retaining screws.

When reassembling, apply thin bead of sealant to outer edge of new Welch plug. Adjust metering lever height to obtain 0.13 mm (0.005 in.) between carburetor body surface and lever as shown in Fig. KU52.

Walbro WY, WYJ and WYK. Some engines may be equipped with a Walbro WY, WYJ or WYK carburetor. This is a diaphragm type carburetor that uses a barrel-type throttle rather than a throttle plate.

Idle fuel for the carburetor flows up into the throttle barrel where it is fed into the air stream. On some models, the idle fuel flow can be adjusted by turning an idle mixture limiter plate (P—Fig. KU53). Initial setting is in center notch. Rotating the plate clockwise will lean the idle mixture. Inside the limiter plate is an idle mixture needle (N—Fig. KU54) that is preset at the factory (a plug covers the needle). If removed, use the following procedure to determine correct position. Back out needle (N) until completely unscrewed. Screw in needle 5 turns on Model WY or 15 turns on Models WYJ and WYK. Rotate idle mixture plate (P—Fig. KU53) to center notch. Run engine until normal operating temperature is attained. Adjust idle speed screw (I) so engine idles at 2300 rpm on Model G4K engines or 2900 rpm on other models. Rotate idle mixture needle (N—Fig. KU54) and obtain highest rpm (turning needle clockwise leans the mixture), then turn needle 1/4 turn counterclockwise. Readjust idle speed screw. Note that idle limiter plate and needle are available only as an assembly with the throttle barrel (25—Fig. KU55).

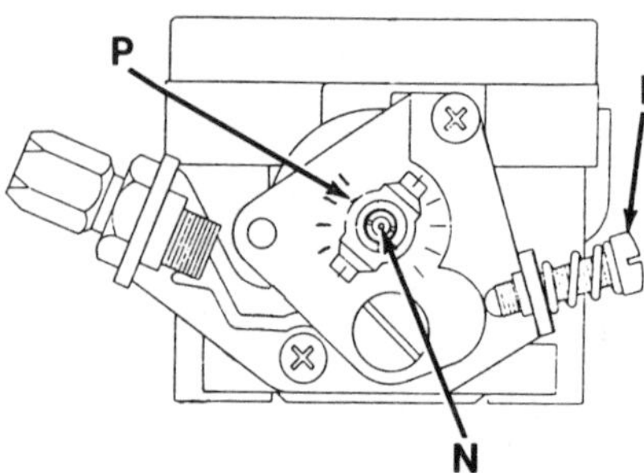

Fig. KU53—On Walbro WY carburetor, idle speed screw is located at (I), idle mixture limiter plate is located at (P) and idle mixture needle is located at (N). A plug covers the idle mixture needle.

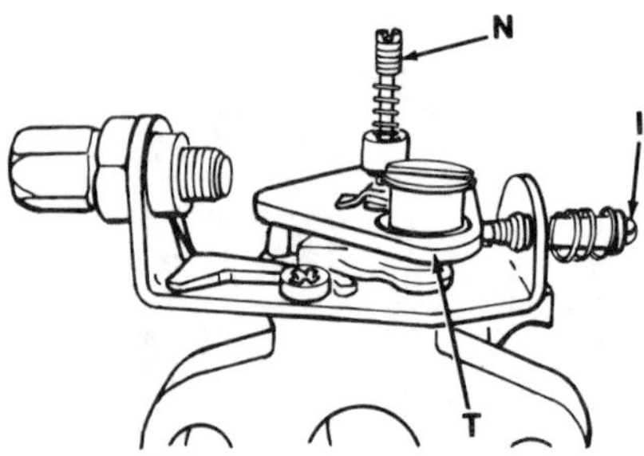

Fig. KU54—View of idle mixture needle (N) used on Walbro WY carburetor.

Most models are equipped with a removable fixed jet (16—Fig. KU55), however, some WYK models may be equipped with an adjustable high speed mixture screw (22). Initial setting of the high speed mixture screw is 1-1/2 turn out from a lightly seated position. Adjust screw to obtain best performanc with engine under load. Do not adjus mixture too lean as engine may be dam aged.

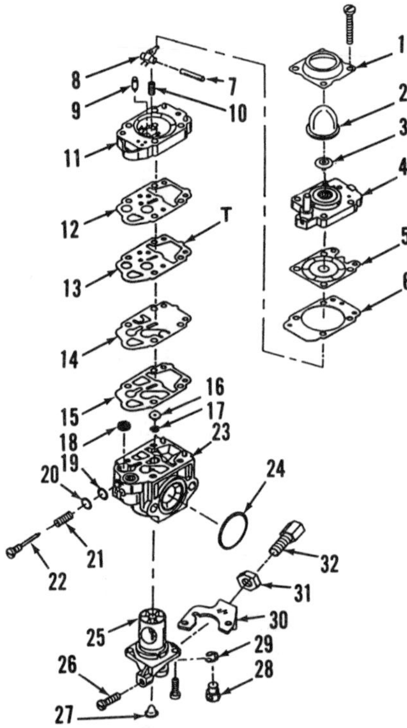

Fig. KU55—Exploded view of Walbro WYK carburetor. Models WY and WYJ are similar.

1. Cover
2. Primer bulb
3. Check valve
4. Plate
5. Metering diaphragm
6. Gasket
7. Pin
8. Metering lever
9. Fuel inlet valve
10. Spring
11. Fuel pump body
12. Gasket
13. Fuel pump plate
14. Fuel pump diaphragm
15. Gasket
16. Main jet
17. "O" ring
18. Fuel screen
19. "O" ring
20. Washer
21. Spring
22. High speed mixture screw
23. Body
24. "O" ring
25. Throttle barrel assy.
26. Idle speed screw
27. Plug
28. Swivel
29. "E" ring
30. Bracket
31. Nut
32. Cable adjuster

To overhaul carburetor, refer to exploded view in Fig. KU55 and remove cover (1), plate (4), fuel pump body (11 diaphragms (5 and 14) and gaskets. Remove screws retaining throttle barre (25) and withdraw throttle barrel fron carburetor body. Do not disassembl throttle barrel.

On models with a plastic body, clea only with solvents approved for us with plastic. Examine fuel inlet valv (9) and seat. Inlet valve is renewable but fuel pump body (11) must be re newed if seat is excessively worn o damaged. Clean fuel inlet screen (18) Inspect diaphragms for tears and othe damage.

When reassembling carburetor, not that tabs (T) on ends of plates and gas kets (12 through 15) will "stair-step" when correctly installed. Adjust meter ing lever height to obtain 1.5 mm (0.05 in.) between carburetor body surfac and lever as shown in Fig. KU52.

Nikki Carburetor. The Nikki car buretor used on some models is a dia phragm type carburetor that has ar integral fuel pump. When depressed, a lever attached to the metering dia phragm cover forces the metering dia phragm up thereby opening the fuel inlet valve. With the lever depressed actuating the primer bulb at the fuel tank forces additional fuel into the carburetor to aid starting. Note that there is a check valve in the fuel tank pickup that functions with the primer pump.

Initial setting for high speed mixture screw (13—Fig. KU56) is 2-1/2 turns out. Midrange mixture is determined by the position of the clip on jet needle (6). There are three grooves in upper end of the jet needle (Fig. KU57) and normal position of clip is in the middle groove. Installing clip in top groove will lean the mixture, or installing clip in bottom groove will enrich the mixture.

Before removing carburetor from engine, unscrew cap (2—Fig. KU56) and withdraw throttle slide (7) assembly.

When overhauling carburetor, refer to Fig. KU56 and remove fuel pump cover (8), metering chamber cover (21) and throttle components (1 through 7).

Examine fuel inlet valve (14) and seat. Inlet valve is renewable, but carburetor must be renewed if seat is excessively worn or damaged. Inspect mixture screw and seat. Renew carburetor if seat is excessively worn or dam-

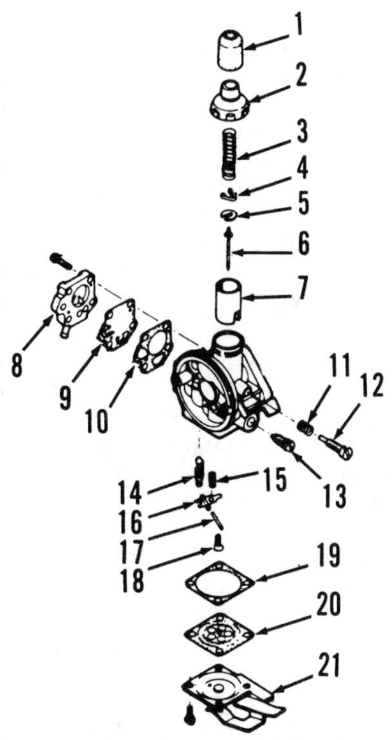

Fig. KU56—Exploded view of Nikki carburetor.

1. Cover
2. Cap
3. Spring
4. Retainer
5. Clip
6. Throttle slide
7. Fuel pump cover
8. Fuel pump diaphragm
9. Gasket
10. Spring
11. Idle speed screw
12. High speed mixture screw
13. Fuel inlet valve
14. Spring
15. Metering lever
16. Pin
17. Screw
18. Gasket
19. Metering diaphragm
20. Cover

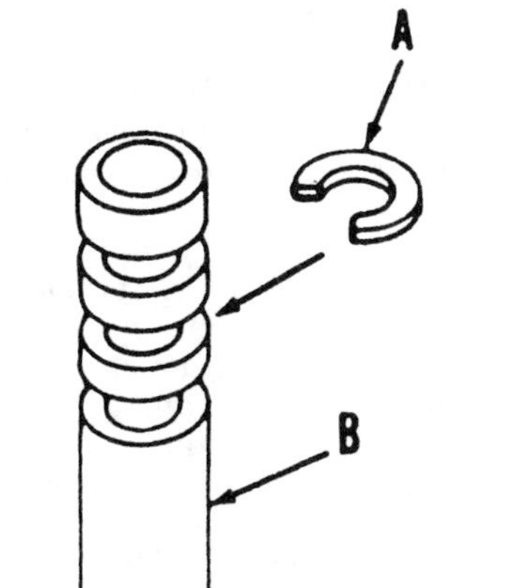

Fig. KU57—Midrange fuel mixture is determined by position of jet needle clip (A) on jet needle (B). Normal position is center groove.

aged. Inspect diaphragms for tears and other damage.

When reassembling, adjust metering lever height to obtain 1.6 mm (0.063 in.) between carburetor body surface and lever as shown in Fig. KU53. When installing throttle slide, be sure groove in side of throttle slide (7—Fig. KU56) indexes with pin in bore of carburetor body.

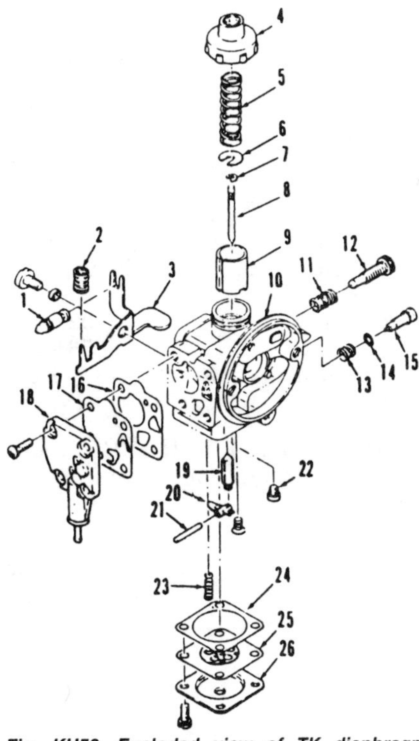

Fig. KU58—Exploded view of TK diaphragm carburetor used on some models.

1. Enrichment valve
2. Spring
3. Enrichment lever
4. Cap
5. Spring
6. Retainer
7. Clip
8. Jet needle
9. Throttle slide
10. Body
11. Spring
12. Idle speed screw
13. Spring
14. "O" ring
15. High speed mixture screw
16. Gasket
17. Fuel pump diaphragm
18. Cover
19. Fuel inlet valve
20. Metering lever
21. Pin
22. Needle jet
23. Spring
24. Gasket
25. Metering diaphragm
26. Cover

TK Diaphragm Carburetor. The TK diaphragm carburetor is equipped with an integral diaphragm-type fuel pump. Operating enrichment lever (3—Fig. KU58) opens enrichment valve (1) for additional fuel when starting engine.

Adjust idle speed screw (12) so engine idles just below clutch engagement speed. Initial setting of high speed mixture screw (15) is 1-1/2 turns out from a lightly seated position. Perform final adjustments with trimmer line at proper length or blade installed and engine at operating temperature. Be sure engine air filter is clean before adjusting carburetor.

Operate engine at wide-open throttle and turn high speed mixture screw in so engine begins to run smoothly, then back out screw 1/8 turn. Normal range of adjustment is 1-2 turns out from a lightly seated position. Midrange mixture is determined by the position of clip (7—Fig. KU58) on jet needle (8). There are three grooves in upper end of the jet needle (Fig. KU57) and normal position of clip is in the middle groove. Installing clip in top groove will lean the mixture, or installing clip in bottom groove will enrich the mixture.

Before removing carburetor from engine, unscrew cap (4—Fig. KU58) and withdraw throttle slide (9) assembly.

When overhauling carburetor, refer to Fig. KU58 and remove throttle assembly (4 through 9), covers (18 and 26), diaphragms (17 and 25) and fuel mixture screw (15).

Clean all parts with suitable solvent and compressed air. Examine fuel inlet valve (19) and seat. Inlet valve is renewable, but carburetor must be renewed if seat is worn or damaged. Inspect diaphragms for tears and other damage.

When reassembling, adjust metering lever height to obtain 1.4-1.7 mm (0.055-0.067 in.) between carburetor body surface and lever as shown in Fig. KU52. When installing throttle slide, be sure that groove in side of throttle slide (9—Fig. KU58) indexes with pin in bore of carburetor body.

TK Float Carburetor. Refer to Fig. KU59 for an exploded view of carburetor. Idle mixture is not adjustable. High speed mixture is controlled by removable fixed jet (12). Midrange mixture is determined by the position of clip (3) on jet needle (4). There are three grooves in upper end of the jet needle (Fig. KU57) and normal position of clip is in the middle groove. Installing clip in top groove will lean the mixture, or installing clip in bottom groove will enrich mixture.

Before removing carburetor from engine, unscrew cap and withdraw throttle slide (5—Fig. KU59) assembly. When overhauling carburetor, refer to Fig. KU59 and note the following: examine fuel inlet valve (7) and seat. The inlet valve is renewable, but carburetor must be renewed if valve seat is worn or damaged.

When reassembling, be sure that groove in side of throttle slide (5) indexes with pin in bore of carburetor body.

IGNITION SYSTEM. The engine is equipped with an electronic ignition system. Model G2KC is equipped with a one-piece ignition module that includes the ignition coil. On all other models, a two-piece ignition system is used. On blower engines, the ignition module is adjacent to the flywheel and the ignition coil is attached to the blower housing. On other two-piece systems, the ignition coil is adjacent to the flywheel and the ignition module is mounted on the crankcase.

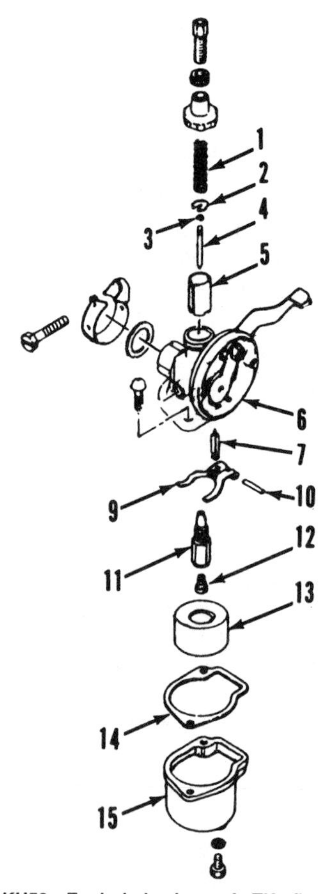

Fig. KU59—Exploded view of TK float-type carburetor.

1. Spring
2. Seat
3. Clip
4. Jet needle
5. Throttle slide
6. Body
7. Fuel inlet valve
9. Float lever
10. Pin
11. Needle jet
12. Main jet
13. Float
14. Gasket
15. Fuel bowl

The ignition system is considered satisfactory if a spark will jump across the 3 mm (1/8 in.) gap of a test spark plug. If no spark is produced, check on/off switch, wiring and air gap between ignition module/coil and flywheel magnet. Air gap on early Models G2D and G2K should be 0.3 mm (0.012 in.). Ignition module air gap on blower engine should be 0.3-0.4 mm (0.012-0.016 in.). Ignition module/coil air gap on all other models should be 0.4 mm (0.016 in.). On models with the ignition coil attached to the inside of the fan cover, it is necessary to remove the cylinder to set the air gap. Refer to REPAIRS section for ignition coil specifications.

REPAIRS

COMPRESSION PRESSURE. Refer to the following desired compression pressures.

G2D models . . . . 490 kPa (71 psi)
Minimum . . . . 297 kPa (43 psi)
G2K models . . . . 586 kPa (85 psi)
Minimum . . . . 393 kPa (57 psi)
G2KC models . . . . 441 kPa (64 psi)
Minimum . . . . 294 kPa (43 psi)
G3K models . . . . 686 kPa (99 psi)
Minimum . . . . 490 kPa (71 psi)
Early G4K models . . . 586 kPa (85 psi)
Minimum . . . . 393 kPa (57 psi)
Later G4K models . . . 686 kPa (99 psi)
Minimum . . . . 490 kPa (71 psi)
G23L &
G26L models . . . . . 638 kPa (92.5 psi)
Minimum. . . . . . . 392 kPa (56.9 psi)
Blower models . . . . . . 490 kPa (71 psi)
Minimum . . . . 343 kPa (50 psi)

TIGHTENING TORQUE. Recommended tightening torque values are as follows.

Carburetor
22.5 cc models . . . . 1.9-2.9 N•m (17-26 in.-lb.)
Other models. . . . . 2.9-4.4 N•m (26-39 in.-lb.)
Clutch shoe
G2D model. . . . . 4.9-6.6 N•m (43-52 in.-lb.)
Other 22.5 & 25.4 cc models. 5-8 N•m (43-69 in.-lb.)
33.6 & 41.5 cc models . . . . 11-17 N•m (96-148 in.-lb.)
Crankcase halves
22.5 & 25.4 cc models . . . 3.5-4.5 N•m (30-39 in.-lb.)
33.6 & 41.5 cc models . . . . . . 5-8 N•m (43-69 in.-lb.)
Cylinder
22.5 & 25.4 cc models . . . . . . 6-8 N•m (52-69 in.-lb.)
33.6 & 41.5 cc models . . . . . . 5-8 N•m (43-69 in.-lb.)
Flywheel (rotor)
22.5, 25.4 &
33.6 cc models (M8). . . . . 12-18 N•m (104-156 in.-lb.)
41.5 cc models (M10). . . . . 20-30 N•m (174-260 in.-lb.)
Ignition module
G2D models. . . . . 1.9-2.5 N•m (17-26 in.-lb.)
G2K, G3K & G4K models
Blower engines . . . . 1.4-1.8 N•m (12-16 in.-lb.)
Other models . . . . 2.5-4 N•m (22-35 in.-lb.)
Spark plug. . . . . 15-22 N•m (130-191 in.-lb.)

IGNITION SYSTEM. On some models the ignition module is separate from the ignition coil. On other models, the module is included with the coil assembly. On some models the ignition module is attached to the fan housing; while on most models, the module is attached to the cylinder or crankcase.

Air gap (clearance) between the coil shoes and the flywheel (rotor) magnets should be carefully set at 0.3-0.5 mm (0.012-0.020 in.). A special tool (part No. 1400-96210) is available for setting the location on models with coil attached to the fan housing. If the special tool is not available, the coil can be positioned on the fan housing to provide the correct air gap using a feeler gauge after removing the cylinder.

Refer to the following table for some ignition coil resistance specifications in ohms.

Model	Primary	Secondary
G2D	0.70-0.80	5,500-7,500
G2K		
Early	0.43-0.63	5,355-7,245
Later	0.48-0.58	5,355-7,245
G2KC	0.44-0.59	4,560-6,840
G3K		
Early	0.48-0.58	5,355-7,245
Later	0.57-0.77	3,520-5,280
G4K		
Early	0.43-0.63	5,675-6,930
Later	0.48-0.58	5,355-7,245
Latest	0.57-0.77	3,520-5,280
G23L & G26L	0.57-0.77	3,520-5,280
Blower engines	0.11-0.15	1,600-2,400

To check the ignition module, the manufacturer recommends using an accurate ohmmeter to check the resistance of a module that is known good, then comparing the resistance of the two modules. Variance in the readings of ohmmeters can lead to misleading resistance tests. If an ohmmeter is not available, replace the suspected unit with a unit that is known to be good.

PISTON, PIN AND RINGS. The piston is equipped with two piston rings. The rings are prevented from rotating by a pin located in each ring groove.

To remove the piston, first remove air cleaner, carburetor, muffler, cylinder cover and fan housing. Remove the cylinder mounting screws and pull the cylinder straight off piston. Remove retaining rings (6—Fig. KU60) and push piston pin (5) from the piston using a suitable pin removal tool. Be careful not to apply side thrust to the connecting rod while removing piston pin. Thrust washers (7) around the pin control connecting rod thrust and will be loose when the piston pin is removed.

The piston and rings are available only in standard diameter.

Piston to cylinder clearance should be 0.060 mm (0.0023 in.) for G2D

G2D
Piston diameter . . . . 32.0 mm (1.260 in.)
Minimum limit. . . . . 31.9 mm (1.256 in.)

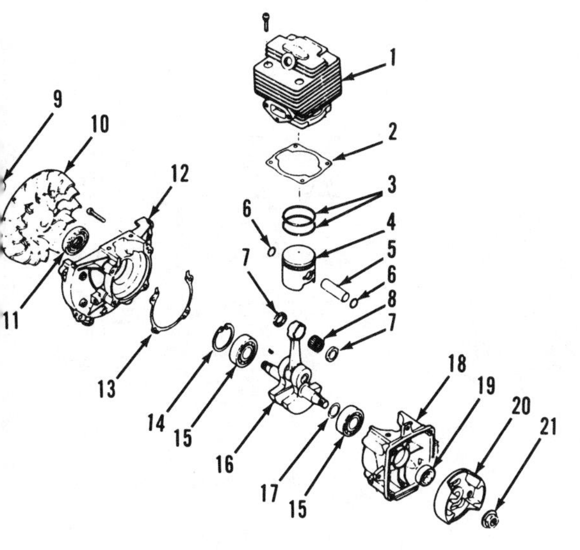

Fig. KU60—Exploded view of typical engine assembly.

1. Cylinder
2. Gasket
3. Piston rings
4. Piston
5. Piston pin
6. Retaining rings
7. Thrust washers
8. Bearing
9. Nut
10. Flywheel
11. Seal
12. Crankcase half
13. Gasket
14. Snap ring
15. Bearings
16. Crankshaft & connecting rod
17. Shim
18. Crankcase half
19. Seal
20. Starter plate
21. Nut

Piston-cylinder clearance . . 0.060 mm (0.0023 in.)
Maximum limit . . . . 0.2 mm (0.010 in.)
Piston pin diameter . . . . 8.0 mm (0.315 in.)
Minimum limit . . . . 7.98 mm (0.314 in.)
Pin bore in piston . . . . 8.0 mm (0.315 in.)
Maximum limit . . . . 8.04 mm (0.317 in.)
Ring groove width . . . . 1.5 mm (0.059 in.)
Maximum limit . . . . 1.6 mm (0.063 in.)

G2KC
Piston diameter . . . . 32.0 mm (1.260 in.)
Minimum limit . . . . 31.9 mm (1.256 in.)
Piston-cylinder clearance . . . . 0.025-0.065 mm (0.0010-0.0025 in.)
Maximum limit . . . . 0.2 mm (0.010 in.)
Piston pin diameter . . . . 8.0 mm (0.315 in.)
Minimum limit . . . . 7.98 mm (0.314 in.)
Pin bore in piston . . . . 8.0 mm (0.315 in.)
Maximum limit . . . . 8.04 mm (0.317 in.)
Ring groove width . . . . 1.5 mm (0.059 in.)
Maximum limit . . . . 1.6 mm (0.063 in.)

G2K
Piston diameter . . . . 34.0 mm (1.338 in.)
Minimum limit . . . . 33.86 mm (1.333 in.)
Piston-cylinder clearance . . 0.060 mm (0.0023 in.)
Maximum limit . . . . 0.2 mm (0.010 in.)
Ring groove width . . . . 1.5 mm (0.059 in.)
Maximum limit . . . . 1.6 mm (0.063 in.)

G3K
Piston diameter . . . . 36.0 mm (1.417 in.)
Minimum limit . . . . 35.86 mm (1.412 in.)
Piston-cylinder clearance . . 0.045 mm (0.0018 in.)
Maximum limit . . . . 0.2 mm (0.010 in.)
Piston pin diameter . . . . 9.0 mm (0.354 in.)
Minimum limit . . . . 8.98 mm (0.353 in.)
Pin bore in piston . . . . 9.0 mm (0.354 in.)
Maximum limit . . . . 9.04 mm (0.356 in.)
Ring groove width . . . . 1.5 mm (0.059 in.)
Maximum limit . . . . 1.6 mm (0.063 in.)

G4K & Blower engine
Piston diameter . . . . 40.0 mm (1.575 in.)
Minimum limit . . . . 39.86 mm (1.569 in.)
Piston-cylinder clearance . . 0.045 mm (0.0018 in.)
Maximum limit . . . . 0.2 mm (0.010 in.)
Piston pin diameter . . . . 11.0 mm (0.433 in.)
Minimum limit . . . . 10.98 mm (0.432 in.)
Pin bore in piston . . . . 11.0 mm (0.433 in.)
Maximum limit . . . . 11.04 mm (0.435 in.)

Fig. KU61—When installing piston, arrow on piston crown must point toward exhaust port.

Ring groove width . . . . 1.55 mm (0.061 in.)
Maximum limit . . . . 1.65 mm (0.065 in.)

Ring end gap should be 0.1-0.3 mm (0.004-0.012 in.) for all models. A new cylinder should be installed if the end gap of a new ring exceeds 0.7 mm (0.028 in.). The piston ring width should be 1.5 mm (0.059 in.) for all models and the minimum width is 1.4 mm (0.055 in.).

Install the piston with arrow on top of piston pointing toward the exhaust port. See Fig. KU61. Be sure piston ring end gaps are correctly aligned with the locating pins in the grooves when installing the cylinder. Lubricate cylinder bore, piston and rings with oil before installing the cylinder. Position the cylinder so it can be installed straight down over the piston, compress the rings with your fingers or suitable ring compressor tool, then slide the cylinder over the piston and rings. If the cylinder is twisted while installing, rings can catch in the ports and break.

CYLINDER. The cylinders with chrome plated bores are available in standard size only and cannot be resized. Pull straight up on the cylinder when removing. If the cylinder is twisted when removing, the rings can catch in the cylinder ports and break. Refer to the following for standard cylinder bore diameter.

G2D, G2KC . . . . 32.0 mm (1.260 in.)
G2K . . . . 34.0 mm (1.338 in.)
G3K . . . . 36.0 mm (1.417 in.)
G4K . . . . 40.0 mm (1.575 in.)
G23L . . . . 32.0 mm (1.260 in.)
G26L . . . . 34.0 mm (1.338 in.)
Blower . . . . 40.0 mm (1.575 in.)

Install new cylinder if plating is worn through or damaged. When assembling, refer to the TIGHTENING

TORQUE paragraph for recommended torque values.

CRANKSHAFT, CONNECTING ROD AND CRANKCASE. Crankshaft, connecting rod and bearings are a unit assembly; individual components are not available. The crankshaft is supported by ball bearings at both ends. Thrust washers (7—Fig. KU60) control connecting rod thrust.

To remove the crankshaft and connecting rod assembly, separate the engine from the drive unit. Remove the fuel tank, air cleaner, carburetor, muffler, fan housing and starter assembly. Remove the clutch assembly (if so equipped). Remove flywheel retaining nut (9) and pull flywheel from crankshaft. Remove the flywheel drive key the crankshaft. Remove starter pulley nut (21) and use a suitable puller to remove the pulley from the crankshaft. Remove cylinder mounting screws and lift the cylinder straight off the piston. Remove piston pin retaining washers (6), push the piston pin (5) from the piston, then remove the piston (4), thrust washers (7) and needle bearing (8). Remove the screws attaching the crankcase halves together, then tap one end of the crankshaft lightly to separate the crankcase halves. Remove the crankshaft (16). Pry seals (11 and 19) from the crankcase halves. Press old bearings (15) from case or shaft if new bearings are being installed.

Support ends of the crankshaft between lathe centers and measure runout at the main bearing journals. Measured runout should not exceed 0.07 mm (0.0028 in.). A shop experienced in servicing built-up crankshaft assemblies can align the shaft.

Use suitable tools to press new main bearings and seals into the crankcase bores. Lips of seals (11 and 19) should be toward inside of crankcase and should be lubricated before installing the crankshaft. Cut excess material from gasket (13) after assembling the crankcase.

Crankshaft end play should be 0.1-0.3 mm (0.004-0.012 in.) and is adjusted by adding or removing shims (17). End play should not exceed 0.4 mm (0.016 in.). End play resulting from worn bearings cannot be corrected by installing shims.

Refer to the TIGHTENING TORQUE paragraph for recommended torque values when assembling.

CLUTCH. Refer to Fig. KU62 for an exploded view of typical clutch assembly. The clutch shoes are attached to a clutch plate of G2D models. Shoes are attached to the flywheel of other models. To remove the clutch, disconnect the throttle cable and separate the engine from the drive housing. It may be necessary to use a suitable puller to remove the clutch plate or flywheel.

Clutch shoes are available only in pairs. Install components on clutch bolts as shown in Fig. KU63. Note position of washers. Open ends of clutch spring hooks should face inward. Install clutch shoes with arrows (Fig. KU64) facing outward. Apply a light coat of grease to the bushing portion of the clutch bolts, but be careful not to use too much grease or get grease on the friction surfaces of the shoes.

Refer to Fig. KU65 for drawing of clutch drum and bearing assembly typical of all models except G2KC. To remove the clutch drum, work through slots in the face of the clutch drum to dislodge snap ring. Press against drum shaft to push the drum and bearings from the housing. Do not attempt to remove the drum by prying or pressing against the drum.

The clutch drum can be removed from G2KC models so equipped after removing the snap ring from the end of shaft.

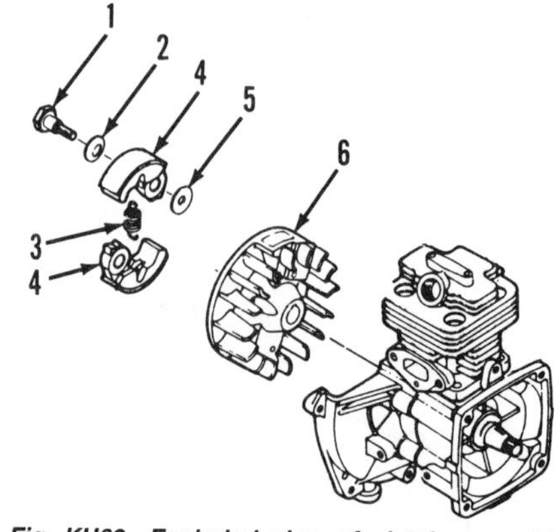

Fig. KU62—Exploded view of clutch assembly typical of most models.

1. Clutch bolt
2. Spring washer
3. Spring
4. Clutch shoes
5. Washer
6. Flywheel

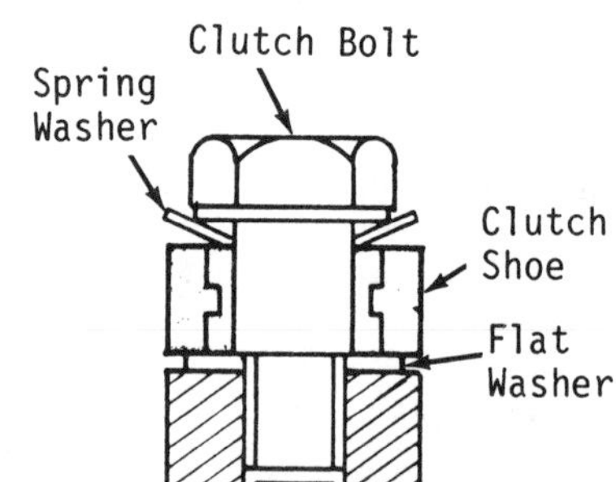

Fig. KU63—Assemble bolt, washers and clutch shoe as shown.

Fig. KU64—Install clutch shoes so arrows on shoes are visible.

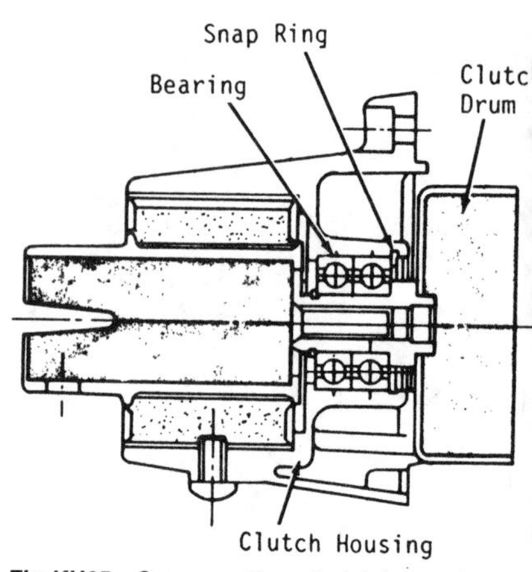

Fig KU65—Cross section of clutch housing and drum assembly typical of most models.

REWIND STARTER. Refer to Fig. KU66 for exploded views of rewind starters used. To disassemble the starter, unbolt and remove the housing (1) from the engine. Remove handle from the rope and allow the rope to wind into the starter. Remove center screw (10) and remove the rope pulley (3). Wear appropriate eye protection and gloves to protect against injury when removing the spring (2). The spring may unwind from the housing uncontrollably. If necessary to remove the pulley plate (9), use a suitable puller.

The rope must be the correct diameter and length for the starter to operate properly. If the rope is too large in diameter or too long, the rope may bind when trying to wind onto the pulley. When installing new rope, measure the length and diameter of the old rope, then install new rope that matches the original. Refer to the equipment service section for some starter rope applications.

To assemble the starter, apply a small amount of light grease to the

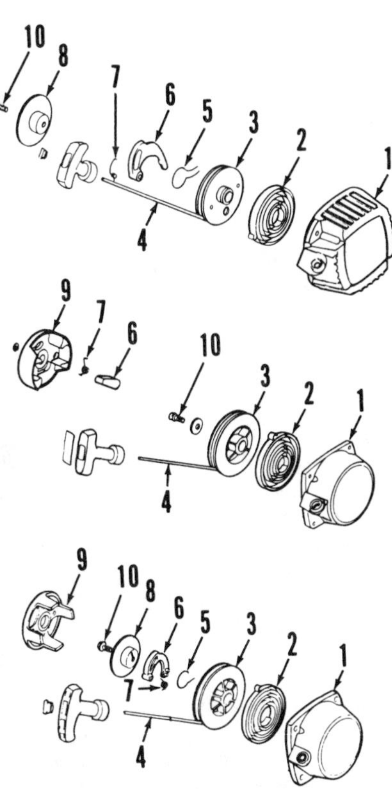

Fig. KU66—Exploded view of the rewind starter assemblies typical of those used.

1. Housing
2. Rewind spring
3. Pulley
4. Rope
5. Friction spring
6. Ratchet
7. Spring
8. Friction plate
9. Starter plate
10. Screw

Fig. KU67—Starter ratchet must be installed in pulley hole marked "R."

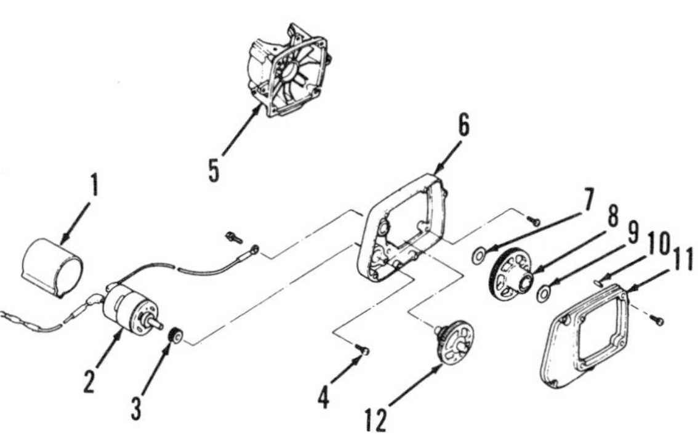

Fig. KU68—Exploded view of the electric starter assembly installed on some backpack blower models.

1. Cover
2. Starter motor
3. Pinion
4. Screw
5. Crankcase half
6. Gear case
7. Washer
8. Gear
9. Washer
10. Dowel
11. Cover
12. Gear

starter housing post, spring and the back of the pulley. Install the rewind spring so it is wound counterclockwise from the outer end. Attach the rope to the pulley (3—Fig. KU66), making sure the knot is fully nested in the pocket. Pull the rope tight and wind the rope counterclockwise as viewed from the pawl (engine) side. Install the pulley/rope and rotate slightly until the spring hooks into the pulley and the pulley drops into the housing. Guide the end of the rope through the housing and attach the handle.

When assembling or if the starter rope does not fully rewind, preload the recoil spring as follows. Hold the pulley to keep it from turning, then pull a small loop in the rope between the pulley and the inside of the housing (1). Hold the rope and wind the pulley to preload the pulley, allow the pulley to rewind the rope, then check operation. The spring should wind the rope around the pulley fully, but the spring must not bind when the rope is fully extended. It should be possible to rotate the pulley at least 1/4 turn when the rope is pulled out completely. Complete the assembly by reversing the disassembly procedure when the spring preload is correctly set.

On models with starter ratchet (6—Fig. KU66), the ratchet should be installed in the hole marked "R" as shown in Fig. KU67. The spring (7—Fig. KU66) should hold the ratchet out lightly.

ELECTRIC STARTER. Blowers may be equipped with an electric starter as shown in Fig. KU68. A battery pack is used to power the starter and a generating coil located near the flywheel provides charging current when the engine is running. The starter motor is serviced only as an assembly.

McCULLOCH

ENGINE SERVICE

Model	Bore	Stroke	Displacement
McCulloch	35.0 mm (1.38 in.)	25.4 mm (1.02 in.)	25.0 cc (1.52 cu. in.)

ENGINE INFORMATION

This two-stroke, air-cooled engine with a **rear mounted recoil starter** is used on trimmers, brush cutters, water pumps and blower/vacs made by McCulloch and other manufacturers.

MAINTENANCE

LUBRICATION. The engine is lubricated by mixing oil with the gasoline. Manufacturer recommends mixing regular or unleaded gasoline with a high-quality two-stroke engine oil designed for air-cooled engines. Recommended fuel:oil ratio is 40:1 when using McCulloch Custom Lubricant. Fuel:oil ratio should be 20:1 when using any other two-stroke oil, regardless of recommended ratio on oil container. Use only an oil designed for two-stroke, air-cooled engines.

SPARK PLUG. The recommended spark plug is a Champion DJ8J or equivalent and the electrode gap should be 0.63 mm (0.025 in.). Tighten the spark plug securely to the torque listed in the TIGHTENING TORQUE paragraph.

CARBURETOR. The engine may be equipped with a Walbro or Zama carburetor. Carburetors installed on trimmers that are designed for brush cutting blades have a governor valve (14—Fig. MC101 or 30—Fig. MC103) that limits the engine speed to approximately 6,500 rpm. When operating properly, the governed carburetor may have tendency to "hunt" or raise/lower the rpm during normal operation. The governor is not adjustable. Do not substitute a different carburetor, especially on governed models.

The manufacturer's name and model number is stamped on the carburetor. Refer to the appropriate following paragraphs for service information. When installing, tighten the attaching screws to the torque listed in the TIGHTENING TORQUE paragraph.

Walbro WA Series. Refer to Fig. MC101 for an exploded view typical of the carburetor. Initial setting for the low speed needle (23) and high speed needle is 1 1/4 turns open from lightly seated position. The settings of these mixture screws is critical to the operation of the engine. Final adjustment should be performed carefully to insure easy starting and maximum performance.

To adjust the mixture screws, first remove and clean the air filter, then reinstall it. Start the engine and allow it to run until it reaches normal operatin temperature. The initial setting of th mixture needles should allow the en gine to start.

Turn the idle speed stop screw (21) s the engine idles just slightly slowe than clutch engagement speed or at th slowest speed that the engine will con tinue to run. Adjust the low speed mix ture needle (23) so the engine idle smoothly and accelerates without hesi tation. The engine may accelerate bet ter if the idle mixture is set slightl rich. Readjust the idle speed stop screv (21) if necessary to slow the idle speed The trimmer or cutter head should no turn when the engine is idling.

To adjust the high speed mixtur screw (24), operate engine at full throt tle under operating load. Turn hig speed mixture screw to obtain mixture-rich four-cycle engine sound then turn mixture screw clockwise t lean the mixture until two-cycle engin sound is just obtained. The high-spee mixture screw may be set slightly ric to improve performance under load The engine may be damaged if th high-speed screw is set too lean.

To disassemble the carburetor, refe to Fig. MC101 and remove covers (1 and 19) for access to internal compo nents. Remove circuit plate (5), meter ing lever (10) and fuel inlet valve (11) fuel mixture screws (23 and 24) and fuel screen (16).

Clean and inspect all components. I the unit has been improperly stored, passages may be clogged with deposits that are hard, solid and nearly transparent. Be careful not to damage the openings or sealing surfaces while cleaning. Check the condition of diaphragms (2 and 17) carefully. Install new diaphragms if hard (not flexible), torn or otherwise damaged. Examine the fuel inlet valve (11), spring (12) and lever (10). A new fuel inlet valve needle (11), and mixture screws (23 and 24) can be installed, but their seats cannot be serviced if damaged. Make sure that tips of the adjusting needles are not

Fig. MC101—Exploded view of typical Walbro Model WA carburetor. Governor valve (14) is not used on some carburetors.

1. Cover
2. Metering diaphragm
3. Gasket
4. Screw
5. Circuit plate
6. Check valve
7. Gasket
8. Screw
9. Pin
10. Metering lever
11. Fuel inlet valve
12. Spring
13. "E" ring
14. Governor valve
15. Body
16. Fuel screen
17. Fuel pump diaphragm
18. Gasket
19. Cover
20. Spring
21. Idle speed screw
22. Throttle plate
23. Low speed mixture screw
24. High speed mixture screw
25. "E" ring
26. Throttle shaft
27. Swivel
28. Spring

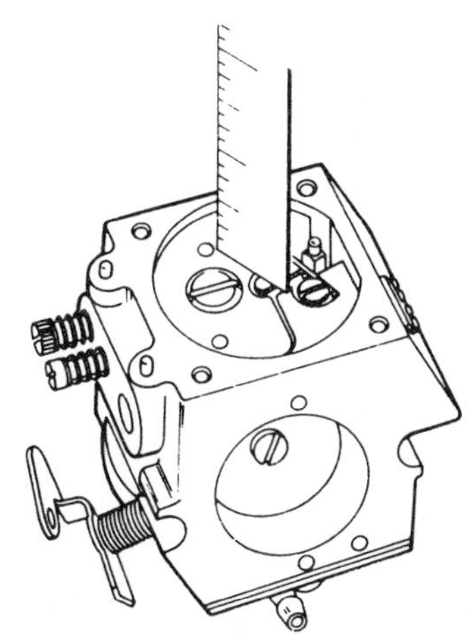

Fig. MC102—Metering lever should be flush with circuit plate as shown in Walbro WA carburetor. Bend lever to obtain correct lever height.

bent, broken or nicked. Clean the filter screen (16) and inspect its condition.

Check the height of the metering lever using with a straightedge as shown in Fig. MC102. The end of metering lever should be flush with the circuit plate. Carefully bend the lever if necessary to obtain the correct lever height.

Walbro WT. Refer to Fig. MC103 for an exploded view typical of the carburetor. Initial adjustment of the idle mixture screw (15) and the high speed mixture screw (14) is 1-1/4 turns open. The settings of these mixture screws is critical to the operation of the engine. Final adjustment should be performed carefully to insure easy starting and maximum performance.

To adjust the mixture screws, first remove and clean the air filter, then reinstall it. Start the engine and allow it to run until it reaches normal operating temperature. If necessary, turn each of the mixture screws (14 and 15) clockwise until seated lightly, then back the screws out (counterclockwise) 1-1/4 turn to provide the initial adjustment so the engine can be started. Turn the idle speed stop screw (24) so the engine idles at low speed.

Adjust the idle mixture needle (15) so the engine idles smoothly and accelerates without hesitation. Readjust the idle speed stop screw (24) if necessary to slow the idle speed. If equipped with a clutch, the trimmer head should not turn when the engine is idling.

Adjust the high speed mixture screw (14) to provide the best performance while operating at maximum speed under load. Make sure the trimmer line is at its maximum length when setting the high-speed mixture. Turn the mixture screw until a mixture-rich four-cycle sound is noticed, then turn mixture screw clockwise until two-cycle engine sound is just obtained. The engine may be damaged if the high speed screw is set too lean.

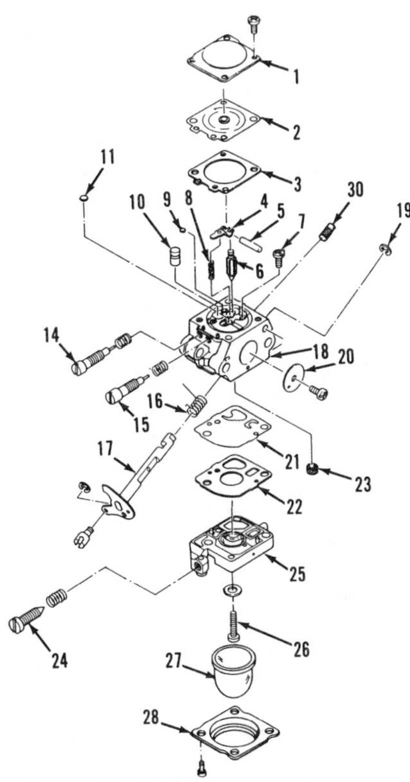

Fig. MC103—Exploded view of typical Walbro WT carburetor. Some models are not equipped with a governor valve (30).

1. Cover
2. Metering diaphragm
3. Gasket
4. Metering lever
5. Pin
6. Fuel inlet valve
7. Screw
8. Spring
9. Welch plug
10. Check valve
11. Welch plug
14. High speed mixture screw
15. Low speed mixture screw
16. Spring
17. Throttle shaft
18. Carburetor body
19. "E" ring
20. Throttle plate
21. Fuel pump diaphragm
22. Gasket
23. Fuel inlet screen
24. Idle speed screw
25. Cover
26. Screw
27. Primer bulb
28. Cover
30. Governor valve

To disassemble the carburetor, refer to Fig. MC103 and remove covers (1 and 28) for access to internal components. Remove metering lever (4) and fuel inlet valve (6), fuel mixture screws (14 and 15) and Welch plug (9).

Clean and inspect all components. If the unit has been improperly stored, passages may be clogged with deposits that are hard, solid and nearly transparent. Be careful not to damage the openings or sealing surfaces while cleaning. Check the condition of diaphragms (2 and 21) carefully. Install new diaphragms if hard (not flexible), torn or otherwise damaged. Examine the fuel inlet valve (6), spring (8) and lever (4). A new fuel inlet valve needle (6), and mixture screws (14 and 15) can be installed, but their seats cannot be serviced if damaged. Inspect the condition of the check valve (10) and filter screen (23).

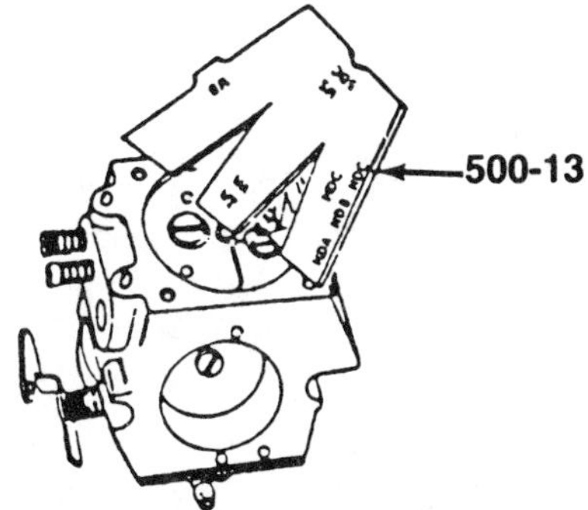

Fig. MC104—Metering lever should just touch leg of Walbro tool 500-13. Bend lever to obtain correct lever height.

Check the height of the metering lever as shown in Fig. MC104 using Walbro tool 500-13 or equivalent. End of metering lever should just touch the leg of the tool. Carefully bend the lever if necessary to obtain the correct lever height.

Some carburetors may be equipped with a governor valve (30—Fig. MC103) that enriches the mixture at high-speed to prevent overspeeding. The governor valve, if installed, cannot be adjusted.

Some carburetors are equipped with a primer bulb (27). Install a new bulb if hard, cracked or otherwise damaged.

Zama C1S or C1U. Refer to Fig. MC105 or Fig. MC106 for typical exploded views. Initial adjustment of the idle mixture screw (19) and the high speed mixture screw (18) is 1 to 1-1/4 turns open. The settings of these mixture screws is critical to the operation of the engine. Final adjustment should be performed carefully to insure easy starting and maximum performance.

To adjust the mixture screws, first remove and clean the air filter, then reinstall it. Start the engine and allow it to run until it reaches normal operating temperature. If necessary, turn each of the mixture screws (18 and 19) clockwise until seated lightly, then back the screws out (counterclockwise) 1 to 1-1/4 turns to provide the initial adjustment so the engine can be started. Turn the idle speed stop screw (20 or 20A) so the engine idles at slow speed.

Adjust the idle mixture needle (19) so the engine idles smoothly and accelerates without hesitation. Readjust the idle speed stop screw (20 or 20A) if necessary to slow the idle speed. If equipped with a clutch, the trimmer head should not turn when the engine is idling.

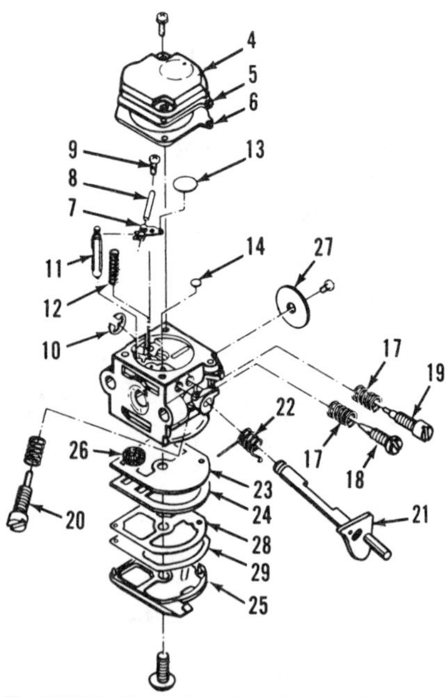

Fig. MC105—Exploded view of typical Zama C1S carburetor.

4. Cover
5. Metering diaphragm
6. Gasket
7. Fuel metering lever
8. Pin
9. Screw
10. "E" ring
11. Fuel inlet valve
12. Spring
13. Disk
14. Welch plug
17. Spring
18. High speed mixture screw
19. Low speed mixture screw
20. Idle speed screw
21. Throttle shaft
22. Spring
23. Fuel pump diaphragm
24. Retainer
25. Pump cover
26. Screen
27. Throttle plate
28. Gasket
29. Surge diaphragm

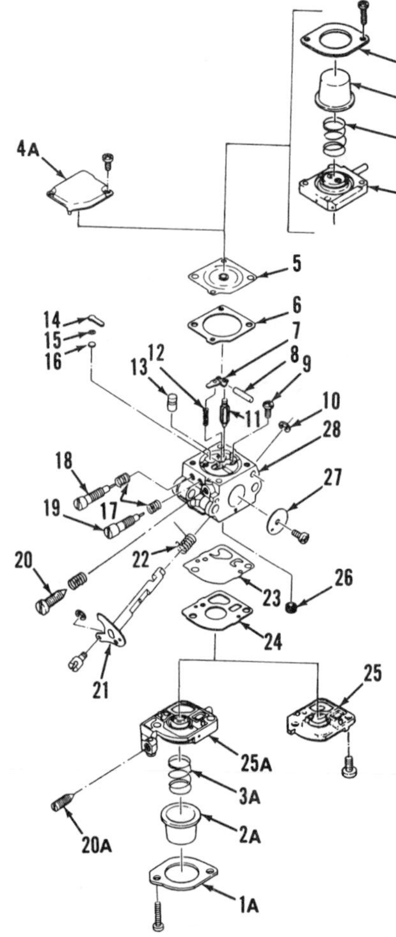

Fig. MC106—Exploded view of typical Zama C1U carburetor. Primer bulb assembly may be located as shown by parts (1, 2, 3 and 4) or (1A, 2A, 3A and 25 A) depending on application. On later models, or on models with a replacement primer bulb, spring (3 or 3A) is not used.

1. Cover
1A. Cover
2. Primer bulb
2A. Primer bulb
3. Spring
3A. Spring
4. Primer base
4A. Cover
5. Metering diaphragm
6. Gasket
7. Metering lever
8. Pin
9. Screw
10. "E" ring
11. Fuel inlet valve
12. Spring
13. Check valve nozzle
14. Welch plug
15. Retainer
16. Check valve
17. Spring
18. High speed mixture screw
19. Low speed mixture screw
20. Idle speed screw
21. Throttle shaft
22. Spring
23. Fuel pump diaphragm
24. Gasket
25. Cover
25A. Primer base
26. Fuel inlet screen
27. Throttle plate
28. Carburetor body

Adjust the high speed mixture screw (18) to provide the best performance while operating at maximum speed under load. Make sure the trimmer line is at its maximum length when setting the high-speed mixture. Turn the mixture screw until a mixture-rich four-cycle sound is noticed, then turn mixture screw clockwise until two-cycle engine sound is just obtained. The engine may be damaged if the high speed screw is set too lean.

To disassemble the carburetor, refer to Fig. MC105 or Fig. MC106 and remove metering chamber cover and fuel pump cover for access to internal components. Remove metering lever and fuel inlet valve, fuel mixture screws and Welch plug. Exercise care when removing either type of Welch plug (14—Fig. MC105 or Fig. MC106). Pierce the round plug (14—Fig. MC105) in the center, but do not insert punch to deeply and damage the underlying body material. To remove the Welch plug (14—Fig. MC106), carefully pierce the plug near the end of the "tail" section, then pry the plug out. Do not insert the punch too deeply or the body and passages under the plug may be damaged. Apply sealant (such as "Seal All" or clear finger nail polish) to the new plug when installing.

Clean and inspect all components. If the unit has been improperly stored, passages may be clogged with deposits that are hard, solid and nearly transparent. Be careful not to damage the openings or sealing surfaces while cleaning. Check the condition of diaphragms carefully. Install new diaphragms if hard (not flexible), torn or otherwise damaged. Examine the fuel inlet valve, spring and metering lever. A new fuel inlet valve needle and fuel mixture screws can be installed, but their seats cannot be serviced if damaged.

Note the shape of the metering lever and compare with the types shown in Fig. MC107. The clearance (A) between the stepped type metering lever (on the left) and a straightedge positioned across the gasket surface of the carburetor body should be flush to no more than 0.012 in. (0.03 mm) clearance. For models with straight type metering lever, the end of the lever should be flush with the chamber floor as shown in the view on the right. Carefully bend the lever if necessary to obtain the correct lever height.

IGNITION SYSTEM. The engine is equipped with a solid state electronic ignition system. Ignition components are contained in the module with the ignition coil (28—Fig. MC108). Ignition performance is considered satisfactory if a spark will jump across a 3 mm (1/8 in.) gap of a test plug. If no spark is produced, check the on/off switch, wiring and ignition module air gap. The solid-state electrical components are affected and may be easily damaged by heat. If insulators are installed, make sure they are reinstalled and in good condition.

Different ignition system coil/modules (28) and flywheels (6) have been used and these two components must be properly matched to each other and to the engine application for correct operation. On late models, the coil/module may be either black or cream colored

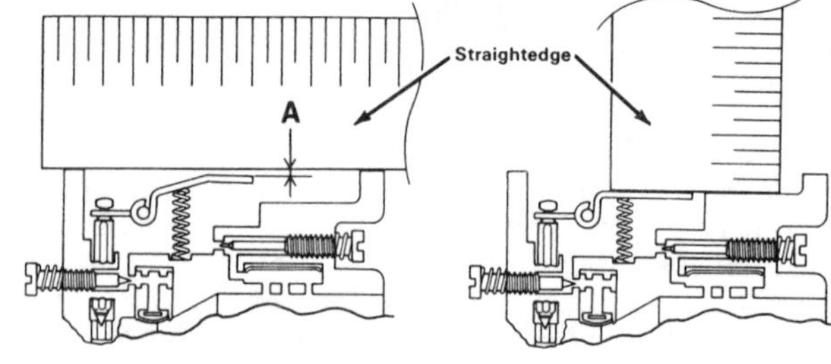

Fig. MC107—Note shape of metering lever and refer to drawing for correct metering lever height for Zama carburetors. Stepped-type metering lever should be bent so height (A) is 0-0.3 mm (0-0.012 in.). Straight-type metering lever should be flush with chamber floor as shown.

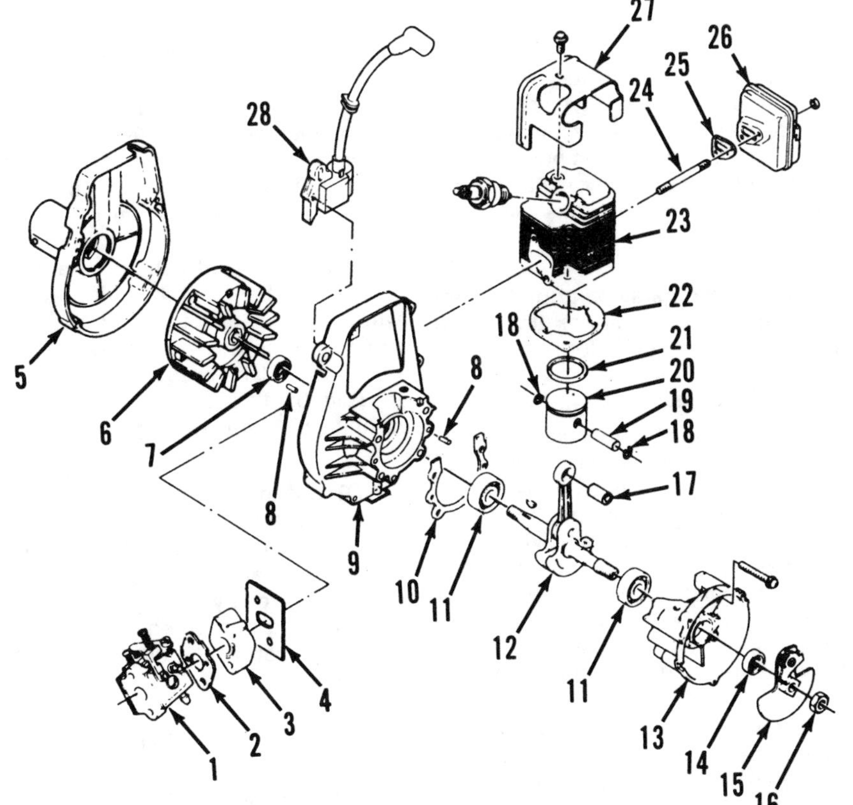

Fig. MC108—Exploded view of typical McCulloch engine. Cylinder (3) is rotated 180 degrees on some models, depending upon application.

1. Carburetor
2. Gasket
3. Insulator
4. Gasket/insulator shield
5. Fan housing
6. Flywheel
7. Seal
8. Pins
9. Crankcase
10. Gasket
11. Bearings
12. Crankshaft & connecting rod
13. Crankcase cover
14. Seal
15. Ratchet assy.
16. Nut
17. Bearing
18. Retainer
19. Piston pin
20. Piston
21. Piston pin
22. Gasket
23. Cylinder
24. Stud
25. Gasket
26. Muffler
27. Cylinder cover
28. Ignition coil/module

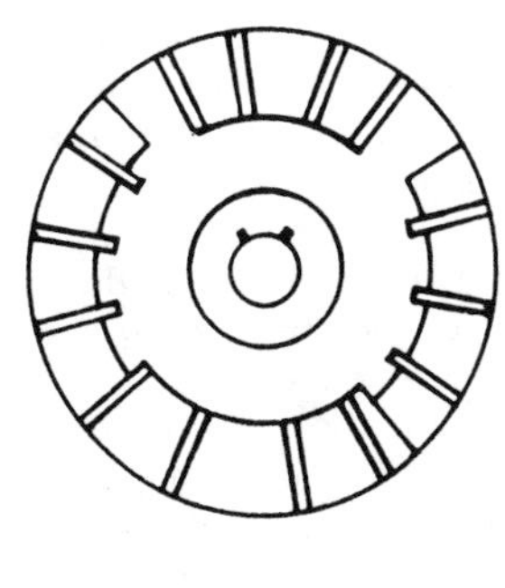

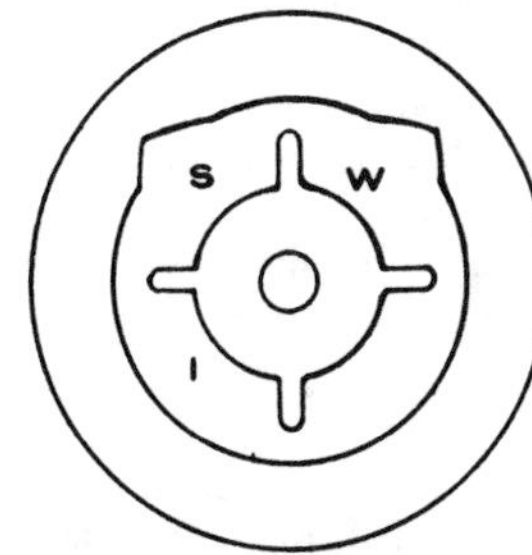

Fig. MC109—Early model flywheels may have two keyways. Engage "S" keyway if ignition module is black, or engage "W" keyway if ignition module is orange.

and the flywheel will be marked "FL", "S" or "W." A flywheel marked "S" must be used with a black ignition coil/module. If the flywheel is marked "FL" or "W," install a cream ignition coil/module.

Some early models may be equipped with an orange or black ignition module and the replacement flywheel may have two keyways. If equipped with a black ignition coil/module, engage the flywheel keyway marked "S" with the Woodruff key in the crankshaft. If equipped with an orange ignition coil/module, use the flywheel keyway marked "W." See Fig. MC109.

When installing the ignition coil/module (28—Fig. MC108), set the air gap between the flywheel magnets and the legs of the ignition coil as follows. Install the ignition coil, but tighten the two screws only enough to hold it in place away from the flywheel. Insert 0.010-0.012 in. (0.254-0.304 mm) thick brass or plastic shim stock between the legs of the coil and the flywheel, then turn the flywheel until the flywheel magnets are near the coil legs. Loosen the screws attaching the ignition coil and press coil against the shim stock, then tighten the two attaching screws to the torque listed in the TIGHTENING TORQUE paragraph. Remove the shim stock, then turn the flywheel and check to be sure the flywheel does not hit the legs of the coil.

REPAIRS

COMPRESSION PRESSURE. For optimum performance, compression pressure should be above 85 psi (586 kPa) for all models. Compression test should be performed with the engine at operating temperature and both throttle and choke (if so equipped) wide open. Low compression pressure can be caused by damaged rings and cylinder.

TIGHTENING TORQUE. Recommended tightening torque values are as follows:

Carburetor . . . . 25-30 in.-lb. (2.8-3.4 N•m)
Clutch drum . . . . 150-168 in.-lb. (17.0-19.0 N•m)
Crankcase halves . . . . 35-43 in.-lb. 4.0-4.8 N•m)
Cylinder attaching screws 71-81 in.-lb. (8.0-9.1 N•m)
Cylinder shroud screw . . . 15-26 in.-lb. (1.7-2.9 N•m)
Direct drive adapter . . . 150-168 in.-lb. (17.0-19.0 N•m)
Fan housing
attaching screws . . . . 12-16 in.-lb. (1.4-1.8 N•m)
Fan housing/drive shaft
Clamp screws (Alum. housing) . 35-42 in.-lb. (4.0-4.7 N•m)
Clamp screws (plastic housing) . . . . 25-30 in.-lb. (2.8-3.4 N•m)
Flywheel/Clutch nut . . . 150-168 in.-lb. (17.0-19.0 N•m)
Ignition coil . . . . 12-16 in.-lb. (1.4-1.8 N•m)
Muffler
Attaching nuts . . . . 41-50 in.-lb. (4.6-5.6 N•m)
Shield to starter . . . . 12-16 in.-lb. (1.4-1.8 N•m)
Spark plug . . . . 108-135 in.-lb. (12.2-15.2 N•m)
Starter
Drum attaching screws . . 18-21 in.-lb. (2.0-2.3 N•m)

PISTON, PIN AND RING. The piston and ring can be inspected through the exhaust port after removing the muffler (26—Fig. MC108). The piston is equipped with one ring that is prevented from rotating by a pin installed in the groove in the piston. Standard ring side clearance in the piston groove is 0.06 mm (0.0024 mm).

To remove the piston, remove the cylinder as described in CYLINDER paragraph. Clean the piston top and locate the arrow on the top of the piston. The arrow should point toward the engine's exhaust port and muffler. Remove both retaining rings (18), then use a suitable tool (part No. 215439 or equivalent) to remove the piston pin. Be prepared to catch the needle rollers when the pin is removed. Early models may have 8 caged rollers; later models are fitted with 21 loose needle rollers.

The piston and cylinder are only available in standard sizes. The cylinder bore of some engines is hard chrome plated and the piston must be unplated. The cylinder bore of other models is unplated and the piston must be hard chrome plated.

NOTE: Never install an unplated piston in an unplated cylinder or a plated piston in a plated cylinder.

The piston pin diameter is 8 mm (0.315 in.) for 21.2 cc displacement engines with chrome plated pistons. Piston pin diameter is 9 mm (0.354 in.) for 21.2 cc engines with unplated pistons.

Assemble the piston, pin and ring as follows: Grease the pin bore in the connecting rod lightly and, if so equipped, install the 21 loose needle rollers. The arrow on the top of piston must point toward the exhaust side of engine (port). Depending upon application, the piston and cylinder may be installed with the exhaust 180 degrees from the direction shown in Fig. MC108.

Install the pin retaining ring in the side of piston nearest the flywheel. Position the piston over the connecting rod, aligning the pin bores, then install the piston pin. Install the remaining retaining ring (18) and check the piston for smooth freedom of movement. The gap in the pin retaining rings (18) should be either directly on top or directly on the bottom. Lubricate the piston with the appropriate 2-stroke oil and install the piston ring in the groove. Refer to the CYLINDER paragraph for installation of the cylinder.

CYLINDER. To remove the cylinder, remove the engine top shroud (27—Fig. MC108), muffler (26) and carburetor (1). Remove the two screws attaching the cylinder to the crankcase, then lift the cylinder straight up away from the engine. Support the piston and connecting rod as the cylinder is removed to keep them from being damaged. Refer to the PISTON, PIN AND RING paragraphs for servicing these parts.

The piston and cylinder are only available in standard sizes. The cylinder bore of some engines is hard chrome plated and the piston must be unplated. The cylinder bore of other models is unplated and the piston must be hard chrome plated.

NOTE: Never install an unplated piston in an unplated cylinder or a plated piston in a plated cylinder.

The piston pin diameter is 8 mm (0.315 in.) for 21.2 cc displacement engines with chrome plated pistons. Piston pin diameter is 9 mm (0.354 in.) for 21.2 cc engines with unplated pistons.

Install new piston and cylinder if plating is worn through, scored or otherwise damaged. Areas where the hard chrome plating is worn will appear dull and can be easily scratched, while the chrome plating will be bright and much harder.

Carbon can be removed from the cylinder ports if carefully done using plastic or wood tools only. Do not scratch, gouge or otherwise remove any metal while cleaning the carbon. Remove all of the old cylinder base gasket from the cylinder and the crankcase before assembling. Avoid scratching or gouging the soft aluminum surfaces.

When assembling, position the cylinder base gasket on the crankcase. Lubricate the piston and cylinder lightly with the appropriate 2-stroke oil. Align the ring gap with the pin in the piston groove. Compress the piston ring with your fingers and carefully install the cylinder **straight** down. Do not twist the cylinder when installing, because the ring will catch in a port and break.

CRANKSHAFT, CONNECTING ROD AND CRANKCASE. Refer to Fig. MC108. The crankshaft and connecting rod are available only as an assembly. The pieces of the crankshaft are pressed together with connecting rod and correct alignment is critical. Dropping, pounding or any attempt to separate the crankshaft will damage the crankshaft assembly. The crankshaft seals (7 and 14) can be removed without removing the crankshaft using a screw type puller that fits over the crankshaft.

To remove the crankshaft and connecting rod assembly, first remove cylinder and piston as described in the CYLINDER paragraphs and the PISTON, PIN AND RING paragraphs. If so equipped, remove the clutch assembly from the flywheel as described in the CLUTCH paragraphs.

Remove the drive adapter from direct drive models. Hold the flywheel to lift the engine slightly off the work bench, then tap the flywheel on the side without magnets to loosen the flywheel. Remove the Woodruff key from the crankshaft. Remove the fuel tank and starter assemblies. Remove nut (16) and the starter ratchet (15). Remove the screws that attach the crankcase halves together, hold the half that is toward the rear (starter) and strike the projections on the front (magneto) half to separate. The crankcase halves are located by two dowel pins and the crankshaft main bearings.

NOTE: It may be necessary to heat the crankcase around the main bearing areas before the crankcase halves can be separated. Attempting to separate the halves by prying may damage the sealing surfaces of the case halves or disturb the alignment of the crankshaft.

Remove the crankshaft seals (7 and 14—Fig. MC108) and main bearings (11) if new seals and bearings are being installed. Use an appropriate puller to remove the main bearings. Clean the crankcase halves and crankshaft main journals, then carefully inspect all sealing surfaces for nicks, gouges or other damage.

Inspect and if necessary repair all surfaces of the crankshaft and crankcase that contact the main bearings for nicks, gouges or other condition that would interfere with smooth operation of the bearings. Inspect the Woodruff key and keyways in the crankshaft and in flywheel for any damage. Install new parts as necessary.

Inspect the mating tapers on crankshaft and in flywheel for damage. Inspect the connecting rod for evidence of overheating, excessive looseness or roughness. Inspect the threaded ends of the crankshaft for damaged threads.

Ball type main bearings are installed on some models, while other models are equipped with needle roller main bearings. If new main bearing is being installed, heat the crankcase half and use a bearing driver that contacts the outer race. Press the bearing into its bore until the distance from the inner side of the bearing is 11 mm (0.433 in.) from the mating surface of the crankcase half.

Fill the open cavity of the new seal with light grease, then press the seal into its bore until the outer (closed) side of the seal is flush with the crankcase.

Clean the mating surfaces of the crankcase halves and assemble using a ew gasket between the halves. Protect e seal from damage and insert the ankshaft into the magneto side ankcase half. Tap the crankshaft ghtly if necessary to make sure it is ated against the main bearing. In- all the rear (starter) half of the case er the crankshaft and carefully slide e halves together. When the case alves are nearly together, tap the ankcase with a soft-faced hammer to ake sure the cases are fully seated. stall and tighten the screws that join ankcase halves to the torque listed in IGHTENING TORQUE paragraph. urn the crankshaft and check for any ughness.

Make sure the mating tapers of the ankshaft and flywheel are clean and ry, then install the Woodruff key in the ankcase keyway. Refer to PISTON, IN AND RINGS and CYLINDER aragraphs for installing these compo- ents. Install the flywheel and tighten he clutch or direct drive adapter to the orque listed in TIGHTENING ORQUE paragraph. Install the clutch ssembly as described in the CLUTCH aragraph. Install the starter ratchet ssembly (15) hand tight, then install ck nut (16) to the torque listed in IGHTENING TORQUE paragraphs. omplete assembly by reversing disas- embly.

CLUTCH. Some models are quipped with the two-shoe clutch hown in Fig. MC110. With clutch ousing (1) removed, press against the haft end of drum (5) to dislodge the earing (4) and drum from housing. Re- move snap ring (3) and press bearing rom the drum.

Unscrew clutch hub (6) from the rankshaft for access to the clutch hoes (7) and springs (8). Springs are available as a pair. Clutch shoes are available as an assembly with the hub and springs.

When assembling, note that washer (2) is installed with the concave side to- ward snap ring (3). Oil outside of bear- ing (4) lightly and press the drum and bearing assembly into the housing until seated.

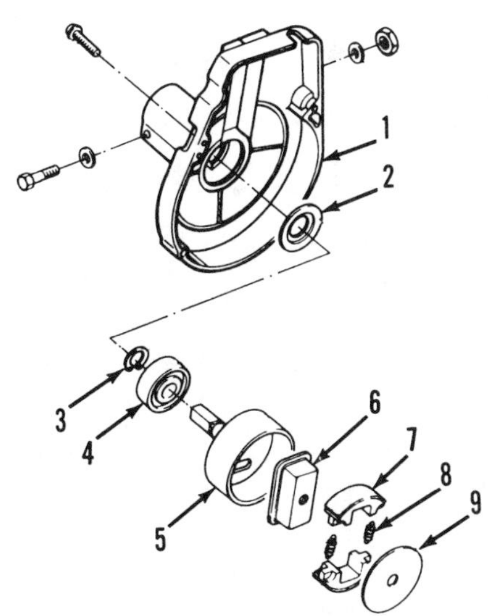

Fig. MC110—Exploded view of clutch assembly typical of some models.

1. Housing
2. Washer
3. Snap ring
4. Bearing
5. Clutch drum
6. Clutch hub
7. Clutch shoes
8. Clutch springs
9. Washer

REWIND STARTER. Refer to Fig. MC111 for an exploded view of the re- wind starter. To disassemble, first re- move starter from the engine. Pull rope handle (6) a few inches, then continue to pull until a notch in the pulley (3) is aligned with the location that rope is unwinding from the pulley. Hold the pulley in this position and place the rope in the notch. Pull slack in the rope and allow the pulley to unwind.

Wear appropriate eye protection and gloves to prevent injury. Place a shop towel around the pulley, remove screw (1) and lift pulley from the housing. Spring (4) should remain in the starter housing (5), but may unwind uncontrol- lably from the housing any time the pulley is removed. If the spring is to be removed from the housing, position the housing so the spring side is down against the floor, then tap the housing to dislodge the spring.

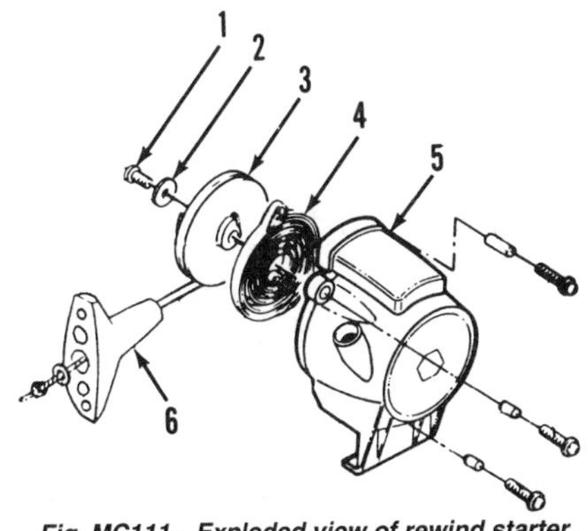

Fig. MC111—Exploded view of rewind starter.

1. Screw
2. Washer
3. Pulley
4. Rewind spring
5. Starter housing
6. Rope handle

If broken, install a new rewind spring (4). Do not attempt to repair broken ends of the spring. The nylon rope should be 0.13 in. (2.77 mm) diameter and 32.5-33.5 in. long. Rope that is too large in diameter or too long may cause the starter pulley to bind before the rope is wound onto the pulley.

Before assembling the starter, lubri- cate the center post of housing and spring side of pulley with light grease. Attach the end of spring (4) to the hous- ing and wind spring in clockwise direc- tion until it is installed in the housing. Attach the rope to the pulley (3), mak- ing sure the knot is completely nested in the notch of pulley. Wind the rope onto the pulley, insert the free end through the housing guide and install the handle (6). Install the pulley (3) se- cure with screw (1) and washer (2).

To put tension on the rope, put the rope nearest the pulley in the notch in the pulley, then form a small loop in the rope. Rotate the pulley counterclock- wise to preload the spring, then let the spring pull the rope onto the pulley. Check the starter operation. The rope handle should be held against the hous- ing, but should not cause the spring to bind. Check for binding by pulling the rope out fully, then attempting to turn the pulley an additional 1/4 turn. If the pulley cannot be turned, remove some preload to prevent spring breakage.

McCULLOCH

ENGINE SERVICE

Model	Bore	Stroke	Displacement
McCulloch	32.2 mm (1.27 in.)	25.4 mm (1.02 in.)	21.2 cc (1.29 cu. in.)

This engine is used on McCulloch Models EAGER BEAVER SUPER, EAGER BEAVER SUPER-SL, MAC 65 and MAC 65-SL.

ENGINE INFORMATION

The McCulloch engine covered in this section is a two-stroke, air-cooled, single-cylinder engine.

MAINTENANCE

LUBRICATION. Engine lubrication is obtained by mixing gasoline with an oil designed for two-stroke, air-cooled engines. Refer to service section for trimmer for manufacturer's recommended fuel:oil mixture ratio.

SPARK PLUG. Recommended spark plug is a Champion DJ8J or equivalent. Specified electrode gap for all models is 0.63 mm (0.025 in.). Tighten spark plug to 11.9-14.6 N·m (105-130 in.-lbs.).

CARBURETOR. All models are equipped with a diaphragm-type carburetor manufactured by Walbro. Models MAC 65 and EAGER BEAVER SUPER are equipped with a Walbro Model WA, while Models MAC 65-SL and EAGER BEAVER SUPER-SL are equipped with a Walbro Model WT. Refer to following sections for carburetor service.

Fig. MC201—Exploded view of typical Walbro Model WA carburetor.

1. Cover
2. Metering diaphragm
3. Gasket
4. Screw
5. Circuit plate
6. Check valve
7. Gasket
8. Screw
9. Metering lever pin
10. Metering lever
11. Fuel inlet valve
12. Spring
13. Screw
14. Retainer
15. Body
16. Inlet screen
17. Fuel pump diaphragm
18. Gasket
19. Cover
20. Spring
21. Idle speed screw
22. Throttle plate
23. Spring
24. Idle mixture screw
25. Spring
26. High-speed mixture screw
27. "E" ring
28. Spring
29. Throttle shaft

Walbro Model WA. Refer to Fig. MC201 for an exploded view of carburetor. Initial adjustment of idle mixture screw (24) and high-speed mixture screw (26) is one turn open. Final adjustment is performed with engine at normal operating temperature and cutter line at desired length. Adjust idle speed screw (21) to obtain desired idle speed. Adjust low-speed mixture screw (24) so engine idles smoothly and accelerates cleanly without hesitation. Adjust high-speed mixture screw (26) for best engine performance under load. Do not adjust high-speed mixture screw too lean as engine may be damaged.

When overhauling carburetor, refer to exploded view in Fig. MC201. Examine fuel inlet valve and seat. Inlet valve (11) is renewable, but carburetor body (15) must be renewed if seat is excessively worn or damaged. Inspect mixture screws and seats. Renew carburetor body if seats are excessively worn or damaged. Clean fuel screen (16). Inspect diaphragms (2, 6 and 17) for tears and other damage. Circuit plate (5) must be flat.

Metering lever (10) should be flush with circuit plate (5) as shown in Fig. MC202. Bend lever to obtain correct lever height.

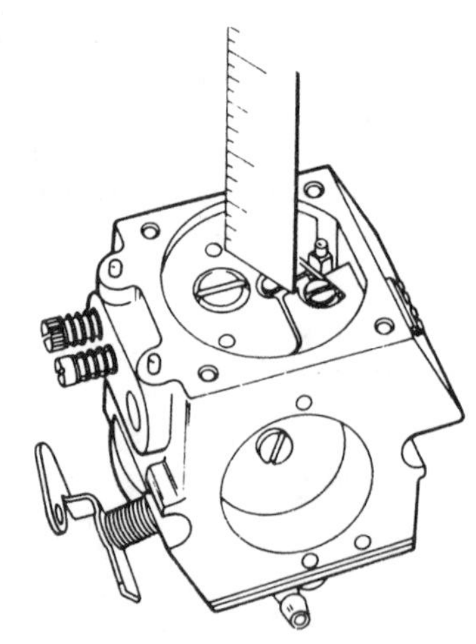

Fig. MC202—Metering lever should be flush with circuit plate (5) as shown on Walbro WA carburetor. Bend lever to obtain correct lever height.

Walbro Model WT. Refer to Fig. MC203 for an exploded view of carburetor. Initial adjustment of idle mixture screw (14) and high-speed mixture screw (16) is one turn open. Final adjustment is performed with engine at normal operating temperature and cutter line at desired length. Adjust idle speed screw (25) to obtain desired idle speed. Adjust low-speed mixture screw (14) so engine idles smoothly and accelerates cleanly without hesitation. Adjust high-speed mixture screw (16) for best engine performance under load. Do not adjust high-speed mixture screw too lean as engine may be damaged.

Carburetor disassembly and reassembly is evident after inspection of carburetor and referral to Fig. MC203. Clean and inspect all components. Inspect diaphragms (2 and 21) for defects that may affect operation. Examine fuel inlet valve and seat. Inlet valve (7) is renewable, but carburetor body must be renewed if seat is damaged or excessively worn. Discard carburetor body if mixture screw seats are damaged or excessively worn. Clean fuel screen (23).

Check metering lever height as shown in Fig. MC204 using Walbro tool 500-13. Metering lever should just touch leg on tool. Bend lever to obtain correct lever height.

Illustrations courtesy McCulloch Corp.

IGNITION SYSTEM. The engine is quipped with an electronic ignition ystem. Ignition system performance is onsidered satisfactory if a spark will ımp across a 3 mm (1/8 in.) electrode gap n a test spark plug. If no spark is produced, check on/off switch, wiring and gnition module air gap. Air gap beween ignition module and flywheel nagnet should be 0.3 mm (0.012 in.). If witch, wiring and module air gap are atisfactory, but spark is not present, reew ignition module.

REPAIRS

TIGHTENING TORQUES. Recomnended tightening torque specifications re as follows:

Crankcase . . . . 4.0-4.8 N·m (35-43 in.-lbs.)
Crankshaft nut . . . . 17.0-19.0 N·m (150-168 in.-lbs.)
Cylinder . . . . 8.0-9.1 N·m (71-81 in.-lbs.)
Spark plug . . . . 12.2-15.2 N·m (108-135 in.-lbs.)

PISTON, PIN AND RING. The piston (6—Fig. MC205) is accessible after removing cylinder (3). Remove piston pin retainers (9) and use a suitable puller to extract pin (7) from piston.

Install piston on connecting rod so arrow on piston crown will point toward exhaust port when the cylinder is installed.

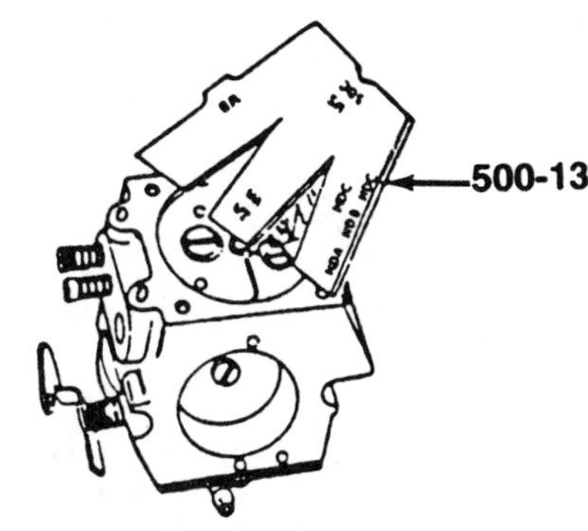
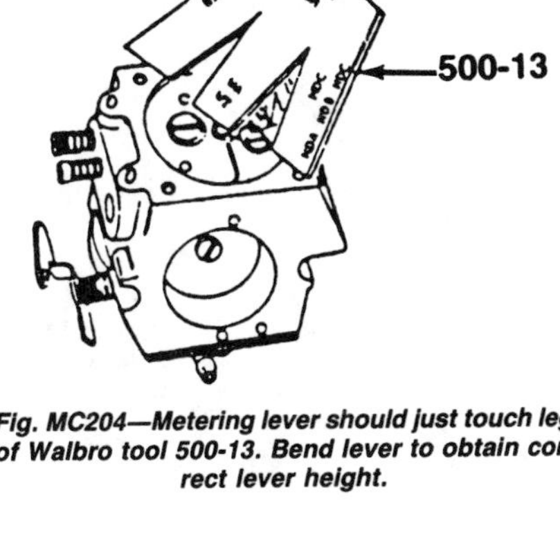

Fig. MC204—Metering lever should just touch leg of Walbro tool 500-13. Bend lever to obtain correct lever height.

The piston is equipped with a single piston ring (5). Piston ring rotation is prevented by a locating pin in the piston ring groove. Make certain ring end gap is correctly positioned around locating pin before installing piston in cylinder.

Standard piston diameter is 32.1 mm (1.268 in.). If piston diameter is 32.08 mm (1.263 in.) or less, renew piston. Oversize pistons are not available.

Standard piston pin bore diameter is 8.0 mm (0.315 in.). If piston pin bore diameter is 8.03 mm (0.316 in.) or more, renew piston.

Standard piston pin diameter is 8.0 mm (0.315 in.). If piston pin diameter is 7.98 mm (0.3142 in.) or less, renew piston pin.

Standard ring side clearance in piston groove is 0.06 mm (0.0024 in.). If ring side clearance is 0.10 mm (0.004 in.) or more, renew piston.

CYLINDER. Inspect cylinder and renew if scratched, scored or otherwise damaged. Cylinder is available in standard size only.

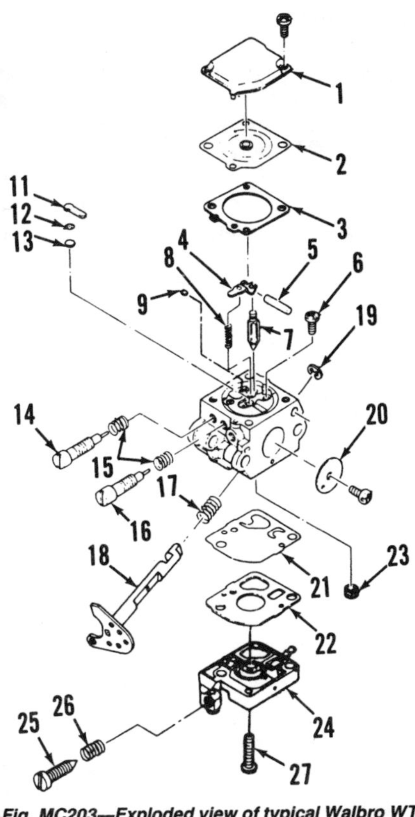

Fig. MC203—Exploded view of typical Walbro WT carburetor.

1. Cover
2. Metering diaphragm
3. Gasket
4. Metering lever
5. Pin
6. Screw
7. Fuel inlet valve
8. Spring
9. Welch plug
11. Welch plug
12. Retainer
13. Screen
14. Idle mixture screw
15. Spring
16. High-speed mixture screw
17. Spring
18. Throttle shaft
19. "E" ring
20. Throttle plate
21. Fuel pump diaphragm
22. Gasket
23. Fuel inlet screen
24. Cover
25. Idle speed screw
26. Spring
27. Screw

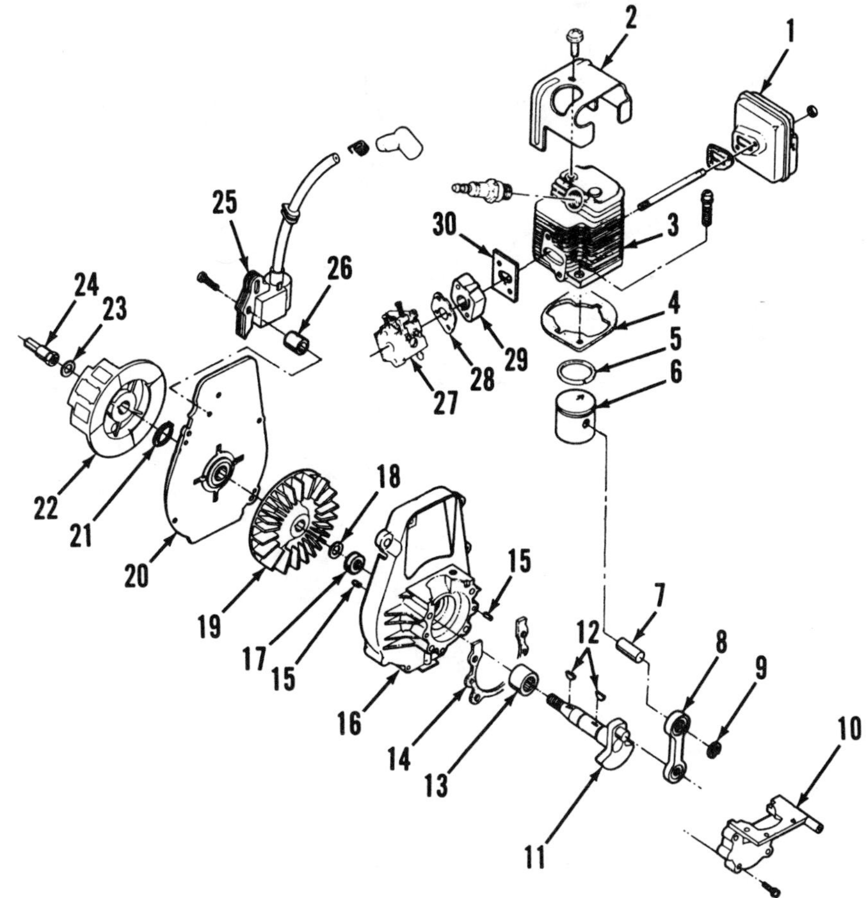

Fig. MC205—Exploded view of engine.

1. Muffler
2. Cylinder cover
3. Cylinder
4. Gasket
5. Piston ring
6. Piston
7. Piston pin
8. Connecting rod
9. Snap rings (2)
10. Crankcase cover
11. Crankshaft
12. Keys
13. Main bearing
14. Gasket
15. Dowel pin
16. Crankcase
17. Seal
18. Washer
19. Fan
20. Bearing housing
21. Snap ring
22. Flywheel
23. Washer
24. Coupling
25. Ignition module
26. Spacer
27. Carburetor
28. Gasket
29. Insulator
30. Gasket/insulator shield

Illustrations courtesy McCulloch Corp.

CRANKSHAFT AND CONNECTING ROD. The engine is equipped with a half-crankshaft (11—Fig. MC205) that is supported by bearing (13) and a sealed bearing in bearing plate (20).

To remove crankshaft and connecting rod, remove recoil starter housing, fuel tank, carburetor (27), muffler (1), cylinder cover (2) and spark plug. Install a piston stop tool or insert end of a rope through spark plug hole to lock piston and crankshaft. Remove coupling (24) and pull flywheel (22) off crankshaft. Remove ignition module (25) and spacer (26). Remove cylinder mounting screws and pull cylinder (3) from piston. Remove retaining rings (9) and separate piston pin (7) and piston (6) from connecting rod. Remove snap ring (21) and bearing plate (20). Remove fan (19) from crankshaft. Remove crankcase cover (10) from crankcase (16) and withdraw crankshaft and connecting rod from crankcase. Press main bearing (13) and seal (17) from crankcase.

Bearing plate (20) is available only as an assembly. Bearings in connecting rod (8) are not available separately. Inspect components for damage and excessive wear and renew as needed.

Fig. MC206—Exploded view of rewind starter.

1. Stop button
2. Spring
3. Stop switch wire
4. Rope handle
5. Rope outlet
6. Starter housing
7. Rewind spring
8. Pulley
9. Retainer
10. Screw
11. Trigger housing
12. Throttle cable guide
13. Throttle trigger
14. Throttle cable

REWIND STARTER. The engine is equipped with the rewind starter shown in Fig. MC206. To disassemble starter, disconnect throttle cable (14) and detach trigger housing (11) from starter housing (6). Disconnect stop switch wire (3) from engine. Separate starter housing from engine. Remove rope handle (4) and allow rope to wind into starter. Wear appropriate safety eyewear and gloves when working with or around rewind spring (7) as spring may uncoil uncontrolled. Remove screw (10) and pulley retainer (9) and remove starter pulley (8). Spring (7) should remain in starter housing (6). If spring must be removed from housing, position housing so spring side is down and against floor, then tap housing to dislodge spring.

Before assembling starter, lubricate center post of housing and side of spring with light grease. Assemble starter while passing rope through housing rope outlet and attach rope handle to rope. To place tension on starter rope, rotate pulley clockwise so notch in pulley is aligned with rope outlet, then hold pulley to prevent pulley rotation. Pull rope back into housing while positioning rope in pulley notch. Turn rope pulley clockwise until spring is tight. Allow pulley to turn counterclockwise until notch aligns with rope outlet. Disengage rope from notch then release pulley and allow rope to wind on pulley. Check starter operation. Rope handle should be held against housing by spring tension, but it must be possible to rotate pulley at least $^1/_4$ turn clockwise when rope is pulled out fully.

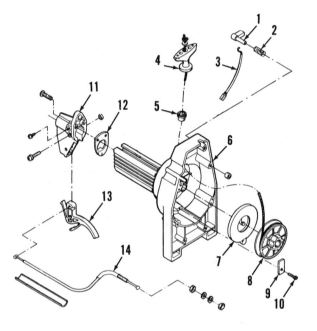

McCULLOCH

ENGINE SERVICE

Model	Bore	Stroke	Displacement
McCulloch	...	...	30 cc (1.83 cu. in.)
McCulloch	...	...	38 cc (2.32 cu. in.)

These engines are used on McCulloch Models PRO SCAPER III, IV and V.

ENGINE INFORMATION

The McCulloch engines covered in this section are two-stroke, air-cooled, single-cylinder engines.

MAINTENANCE

LUBRICATION. Engine lubrication is obtained by mixing gasoline with an oil designed for two-stroke, air-cooled engines. Refer to trimmer service section for manufacturer's recommended fuel:oil mixture ratio.

SPARK PLUG. Recommended spark plug is a Champion RDJ8J or equivalent. Specified electrode gap for all models is 0.63 mm (0.025 in.). Tighten spark plug to 11.9-14.6 N·m (105-130 in.-lbs.).

CARBURETOR. All models are equipped with a Tillotson diaphragm-type carburetor. Refer to Fig. MC301 for an exploded view of carburetor.

Initial adjustment of low-speed mixture screw (13) is one turn open from a lightly seated position. Final adjustment is made with engine running at normal operating temperature. Adjust idle speed screw (17) to obtain desired idle speed. String trimmer head or blade should not turn when engine is running at idle speed. Adjust low-speed mixture screw so engine idles smoothly and accelerates cleanly without hesitation.

Disassembly is evident after inspection of unit and referral to Fig. MC301. Clean fuel screen (21). Inspect spring (7) and renew if stretched or damaged. Inspect diaphragms (2 and 20) for tears, cracks and other damage. Renew mixture screws if tips are broken or grooved. Carburetor body must be renewed if mixture screw seats are damaged or excessively worn. Fuel inlet valve seat in carburetor body is not renewable; body must be renewed if seat is damaged or excessively worn.

Check height of metering lever (4) when assembling carburetor. Lever must be flush with chamber floor as shown in Fig. MC302. Bend lever adjacent to spring to obtain correct lever position.

IGNITION SYSTEM. The engine is equipped with an electronic ignition system. Ignition system performance is considered satisfactory if a spark will jump across a 3 mm (1/8 in.) electrode gap on a test spark plug. If no spark is produced, check on/off switch, wiring and ignition module air gap. Air gap between ignition module and flywheel magnet should be 0.25-0.30 mm (0.010-0.012 in.). If switch, wiring and module air gap are satisfactory, but spark is not present, renew ignition module.

REPAIRS

PISTON, PIN AND RINGS. Piston (5—Fig. MC303) is accessible after removing cylinder (2) from crankcase. Remove retaining rings (7) and push piston pin (6) out of piston. Separate piston from connecting rod.

The piston is fitted with two compression rings (4). A locating pin in each piston ring groove prevents ring rotation. Make certain that piston ring gaps are correctly positioned around locating pins when installing cylinder and that ring end gaps face exhaust port side of cylinder.

The piston pin (6) rides in a needle bearing (8) in the connecting rod small end. Bearing is available separately from rod.

Piston is available in standard size only.

CYLINDER. The cylinder bore is chrome plated. Renew cylinder if plating in bore is worn through, scored or otherwise damaged. Worn spots will appear dull and may be easily scratched, while chrome plating will be bright and much harder.

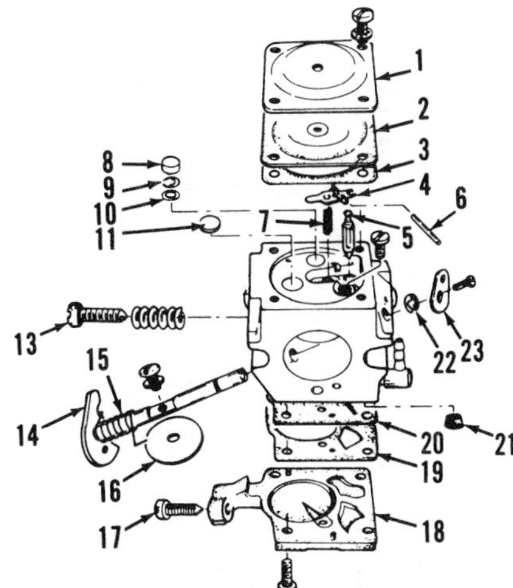

Fig. MC301—Exploded view of Tillotson HU carburetor.

1. Cover
2. Metering diaphragm
3. Gasket
4. Metering lever
5. Fuel inlet valve
6. Pin
7. Spring
8. Welch plug
9. Retainer
10. Screen
11. Welch plug
13. Idle mixture screw
14. Throttle shaft
15. Spring
16. Throttle plate
17. Idle speed adjust screw
18. Cover
19. Gasket
20. Fuel pump diaphragm
21. Screen
22. "E" ring
23. Arm

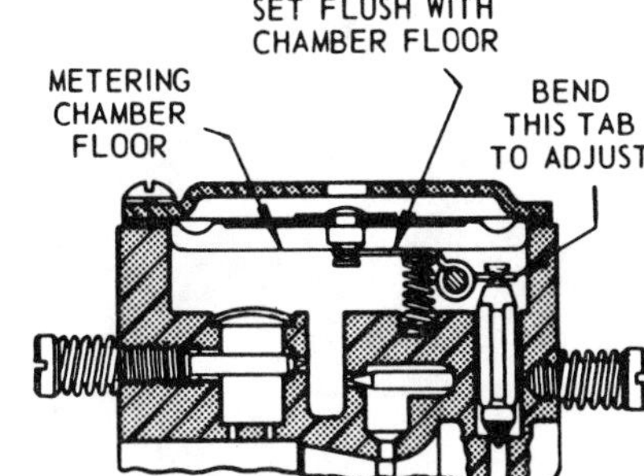

Fig. MC302—Metering lever should be flush with chamber floor as shown above.

Illustrations courtesy McCulloch Corp.

CRANKSHAFT AND CONNECTING ROD. The crankshaft and connecting rod are serviced as an assembly; individual components are not available.

To remove crankshaft assembly, first separate engine from trimmer drive shaft housing. Remove recoil starter assembly, muffler, fuel tank and carburetor. Remove spark plug and install a piston locking tool or insert end of a rope through spark plug hole to lock piston and crankshaft. Remove nuts (9 and 20) and withdraw clutch assembly (11—Fig. MC303) and flywheel (19) from crankshaft. Unbolt and remove cylinder (2). Remove retaining rings (7) and piston pin (6) to separate piston from connecting rod. Carefully separate crankcase halves (13 and 17) and remove crankshaft assembly from crankcase. Remove main bearings (15) and seals (12 and 18) as necessary.

To install crankshaft and connecting rod, reverse the removal procedure.

REED VALVE. All models are equipped with a reed valve induction system. Inspect reed valve petals and seats on reed valve plate (22—Fig. MC303). Renew reed valve assembly if petals or seats are damaged.

CLUTCH. Individual components for the clutch (11—Fig. MC303) are not available. Clutch must be serviced as a unit assembly.

REWIND STARTER. To disassemble starter, remove starter housing (8—Fig. MC304) from crankcase. Slide pinion (4) forward and detach spring (5). Pull starter rope and hold rope pulley with notch in pulley adjacent to rope outlet of housing. Pull rope back through rope outlet so it engages notch in pulley and allow pulley to completely unwind. Remove screw (1), washers (2 and 3) and pinion (4). Detach rope handle and remove pulley (6) while being careful not to dislodge rewind spring (7) in housing (8). Wear appropriate safety eyewear and gloves when working with or around rewind spring (7) as spring may uncoil uncontrolled.

Install rewind spring (7) in housing so coil direction is counterclockwise from outer end. Assemble starter while passing rope through housing rope outlet and attach rope handle to rope. To place tension on starter rope, rotate pulley counterclockwise so notch in pulley is aligned with rope outlet, then hold pulley to prevent pulley rotation. Pull rope back into housing while positioning rope in pulley notch. Turn rope pulley counterclockwise until spring is tight. Allow pulley to turn clockwise until notch aligns with rope outlet. Disengage rope from notch, then release pulley and allow rope to wind on pulley. Check starter operation. Do not place more tension on rewind spring than is necessary to draw rope handle up against housing. Install spring (5) and check starter action.

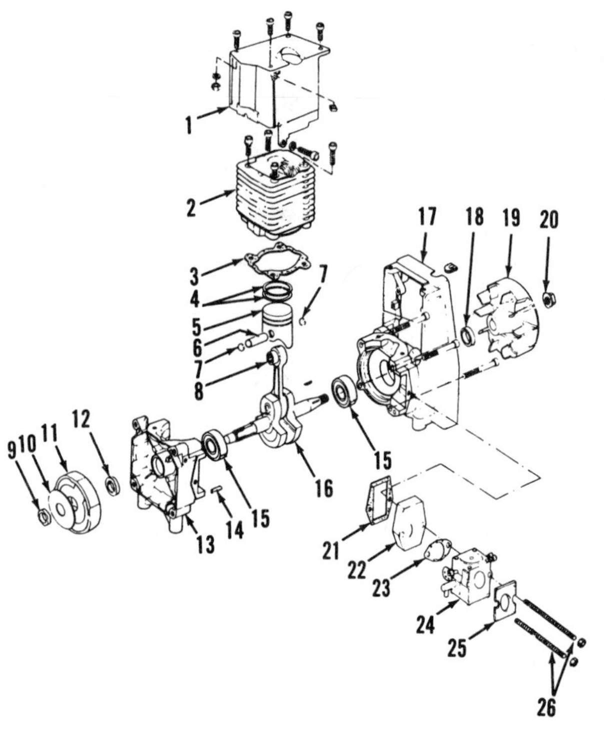

Fig. MC303—Exploded view of engine.

1. Cylinder cover
2. Cylinder
3. Gasket
4. Piston rings
5. Piston
6. Piston pin
7. Retaining rings
8. Bearing
9. Nut
10. Washer
11. Clutch assy.
12. Seal
13. Crankcase half
14. Dowel pin
15. Bearing
16. Crankshaft & rod assy.
17. Crankcase half
18. Seal
19. Flywheel
20. Nut
21. Gasket
22. Reed valve
23. Gasket
24. Carburetor
25. Gasket
26. Studs

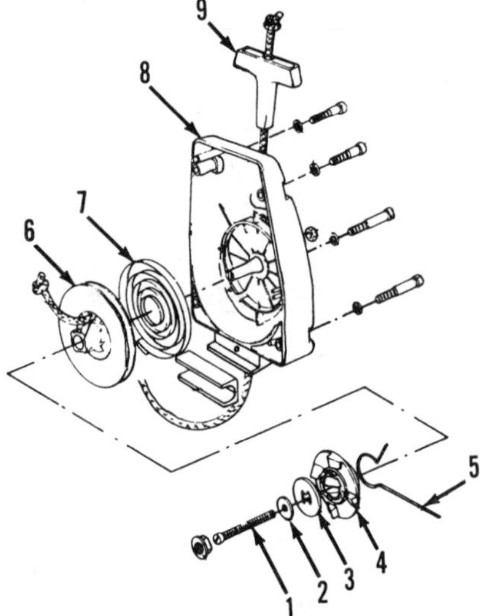

Fig. MC304—Exploded view of rewind starter.

1. Screw
2. Washer
3. Washer
4. Pinion
5. Spring
6. Pulley
7. Rewind spring
8. Housing
9. Rope handle

Illustrations courtesy McCulloch Corp.

MITSUBISHI

ENGINE SERVICE

Model	Bore	Stroke	Displacement
T110	30 mm (1.18 in.)	30 mm (1.18 in.)	21.2 cc (1.29 cu. in.)
TMX-21	30 mm (1.18 in.)	30 mm (1.18 in.)	21.2 cc (1.29 cu. in.)
T140	32 mm (1.26 in.)	30 mm (1.18 in.)	24.1 cc (1.47 cu. in.)
TM-24	32 mm (1.26 in.)	30 mm (1.18 in.)	24.1 cc (1.47 cu. in.)
T180	36 mm (1.42 in.)	32 mm (1.26 in.)	32.5 cc (1.98 cu. in.)
T200	39 mm (1.54 in.)	34 mm (1.34 in.)	40.6 cc (2.48 cu. in.)

ENGINE INFORMATION

Mitsubishi two-stroke, air-cooled gasoline engines are used by several manufacturers of string trimmers, brush cutters and blowers.

MAINTENANCE

LUBRICATION. Engine lubrication is obtained by mixing gasoline with an oil designed for two-stroke, air-cooled engines. Refer to equipment service section for manufacturer's recommended fuel:oil mixture ratio.

SPARK PLUG. Recommended spark plug is a NGK BM6A or equivalent. Specified electrode gap for all models is 0.6 mm (0.024 in.).

CARBURETOR. Various types of carburetors have been used. Refer to the appropriate following section for carburetor service.

Walbro WY and WYJ. Some engines may be equipped with a Walbro WY or WYJ carburetor. This is a diaphragm-type carburetor that uses a barrel-type throttle rather than a throttle plate.

Idle fuel for the carburetor flows up into the throttle barrel where it is fed into the air stream. On some models, the idle fuel flow can be adjusted by turning an idle mixture limiter plate (P—Fig. MI51). Initial setting is in center notch. Rotating the plate clockwise will lean the idle mixture. Inside the limiter plate is an idle mixture needle (N—Fig. MI52) that is preset at the factory. If removed, use the following procedure to determine correct position. Back out needle (N) until unscrewed. Screw in needle 5 turns on Model WY or 15 turns on Model WYJ. Rotate idle mixture plate (P—Fig. MI51) to center notch. Run engine until normal operating temperature is attained. Adjust idle speed screw (I) so trimmer head or blade does not rotate. Rotate idle mixture needle (N—Fig. MI52) and obtain highest rpm (turning needle clockwise leans the mixture), then turn needle $^1/_4$ turn counterclockwise. Readjust idle speed screw. Note that idle mixture plate and needle are available only as an assembly with throttle barrel.

The high-speed mixture is controlled by a removable fixed jet (16—Fig. MI53).

To overhaul carburetor, refer to exploded view in Fig. MI53 and note the following: On models with a plastic body, clean only with solvents approved for use with plastic. Do not disassemble throttle barrel assembly. Examine fuel inlet valve and seat. Inlet valve (9) is renewable, but fuel pump body (11) must be renewed if seat is excessively worn or damaged. Clean fuel screen (18). Inspect diaphragms for tears and other damage. When installing plates and gaskets (12 through 15) note that tabs (T) on ends will "stairstep" when correctly installed. Adjust metering lever height to obtain 1.5 mm (0.059 in.) between carburetor body surface and lever as shown in Fig. MI54.

Throttle Slide-Type Carburetor. Some models are equipped with the diaphragm carburetor shown in Fig. MI55. A throttle slide (11—Fig. MI56) is used in place of a throttle plate.

Initial adjustment of high-speed mixture screw (4—Fig. MI55) is $2^1/_2$ turns out from a lightly seated position. Final adjustment is performed with trimmer line fully extended or blade assembly installed. Engine should be at operating temperature and running. Operate trimmer at full throttle and adjust high-speed mixture screw to obtain maximum engine output with smooth acceleration. Turning mixture screw counterclockwise enriches mixture.

Normal position of jet needle clip (6—Fig. MI56) is in the center groove on jet needle (7). When installing metering diaphragm lever, adjust metering lever height to obtain 0.5 mm (0.020 in.) be-

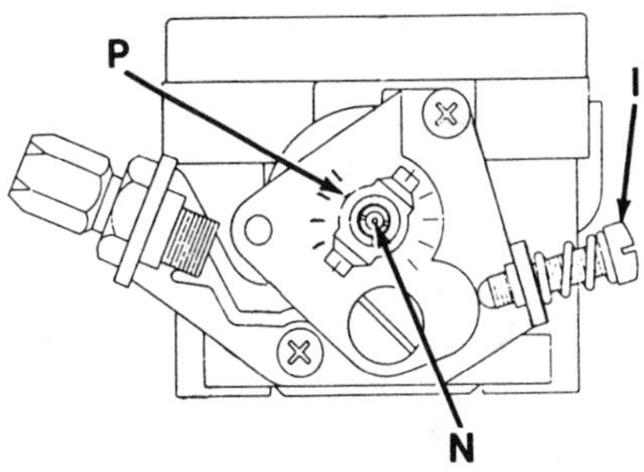

Fig. MI51—On Walbro WY or WYJ carburetor, idle speed screw is located at (I), idle mixture limiter plate is located at (P) and idle mixture needle is located at (N). A plug covers the idle mixture needle.

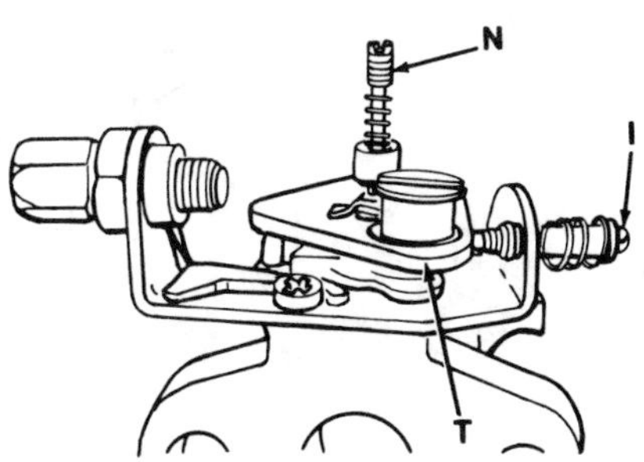

Fig. MI52—View of idle mixture needle (N) used on Walbro WY and WYJ carburetors.

tween carburetor body surface and lever as shown in Fig. MI54.

IGNITION SYSTEM. Models T110, T140, T180, TMX-21, TM-24 and later Model T200 are equipped with an electronic ignition system. Early Model T200 is equipped with a breaker-point-type ignition system.

Ignition system performance is considered satisfactory if a spark will jump across a 3 mm (1/8 in.) electrode gap on a test spark plug. If no spark is produced, check on/off switch, wiring and ignition module air gap. Air gap on models with an ignition module should be 0.3-0.4 mm (0.012-0.016 in.). If switch, wiring and module air gap are satisfactory, but spark is not present, renew ignition module.

Breaker points and condenser on early Model T200 are located behind flywheel. Breaker point gap should be 0.28-0.38 mm (0.011-0.015 in.). Air gap between ignition coil and flywheel should be 0.41-0.50 mm (0.016-0.020 in.). Points should be adjusted so points begin to open as match mark on flywheel aligns with "M" or "P" mark cast on crankcase.

REPAIRS

CYLINDER, PISTON, PIN AND RINGS. The piston is accessible after removing cylinder. Remove piston pin retainers and use a suitable puller to extract pin from piston.

The piston is equipped with two piston rings. Ring rotation is prevented by a locating pin in each piston ring groove. Piston is available in standard size only.

Standard piston ring end gap is 0.1-0.3 mm (0.004-0.012 in.) for all models. If ring end gap exceeds 0.7 mm (0.028 in.), renew rings and/or cylinder.

CRANKSHAFT, CONNECTING ROD AND CRANKCASE. See Fig. MI57 for an exploded view of the T200 engine. Crankshaft, connecting rod and rod bearing are a unit assembly; individual components are not available. The crankshaft is supported by ball bearings at both ends. A renewable needle bearing is located in the small end of the connecting rod.

To remove crankshaft, separate the engine from trimmer drive shaft or blower housing. Remove all cooling shrouds and rewind starter assembly. Remove muffler and carburetor. Remove ignition module or coil. Remove flywheel and clutch (if used) from crankshaft. Remove all cylinder retaining bolts, then carefully separate cylinder from crankcase. Cylinder should be pulled straight off piston with no twisting motion. Remove all crankcase retaining bolts, separate crankcase halves

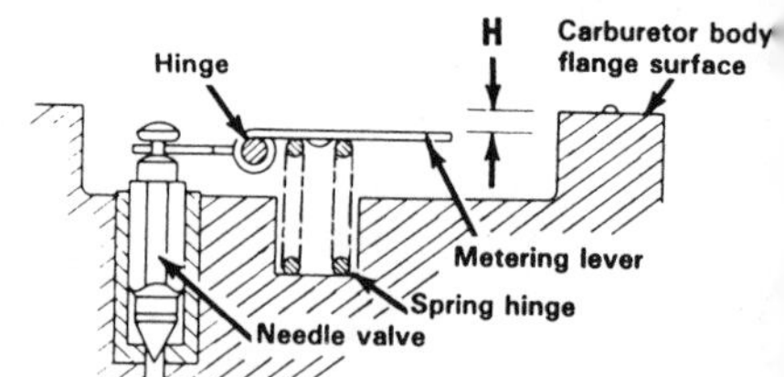

Fig. MI54—Metering lever height (H) must be set on diaphragm-type carburetors. Refer to text for specified height.

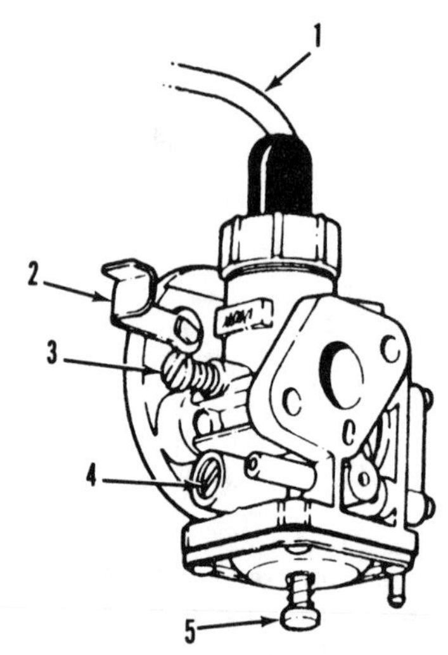

Fig. MI55—View of slide-valve-type diaphragm carburetor used on some models.

1. Throttle cable
2. Choke lever
3. Idle speed screw
4. High-speed mixture screw
5. Primer button

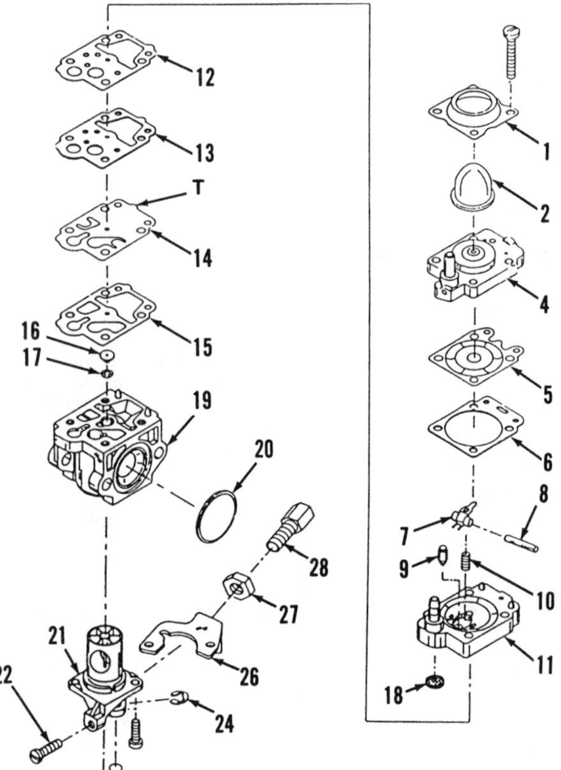

Fig. MI53—Exploded view of Walbro WYJ. Model WY is similar.

1. Cover
2. Primer bulb
4. Plate
5. Metering diaphragm
6. Gasket
7. Metering lever
8. Pin
9. Fuel inlet valve
10. Spring
11. Fuel pump body
12. Gasket
13. Fuel pump plate
14. Fuel pump diaphragm
15. Gasket
16. Main jet
17. "O" ring
18. Fuel screen
19. Body
20. "O" ring
21. Throttle barrel assy.
22. Idle speed screw
23. Plug
24. "E" ring
25. Swivel
26. Bracket
27. Nut
28. Adjuster

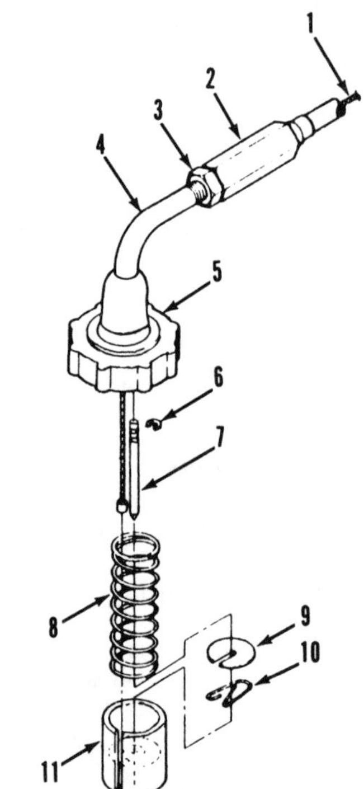

Fig. MI56—Exploded view of throttle slide assembly.

1. Inner throttle cable
2. Cable adjusting nut
3. Jam nut
4. Housing
5. Cap
6. Clip
7. Jet needle
8. Spring
9. Spring seat
10. Spring seat retainer
11. Throttle slide

and remove crankshaft. Heat crankcase if necessary to aid removal of main bearings.

Side clearance at rod big end should be 0.16-0.35 mm (0.006-0.014 in.) for all models. Standard crankshaft main bearing journal diameter is 12 mm (0.472 in.) for Models T110, T140, T180, TMX-21 and TM-24 and 15 mm (0.591 in.) for Model T200. If diameter is 0.05 mm (0.002 in.) less than standard diameter, renew crankshaft.

CLUTCH. Refer to Fig. MI58 for an exploded view of centrifugal clutch used on most models. All models are equipped with two clutch shoes and one clutch spring. The clutch drum is connected to the drive shaft. On some models the drive shaft is threaded into the clutch drum.

Clutch shoes are available only as a set. Install clutch shoes so side marked "M" is visible.

Refer to Figs. MI59 and MI60 for exploded view of typical clutch drum assemblies. Reach through slot in clutch drum to detach snap ring (4—Fig. MI59 or 8—Fig. MI60) and remove drum and bearing from housing. Inside diameter of clutch drum is 54-56 mm (2.13-2.20 in.) for Models T110, T140, TMX-21 and TM-24, and 76-78 mm (2.99-3.07 in.) for Models T180 and T200.

REWIND STARTER. Refer to Figs. MI61 or MI62 for an exploded view of starter. To disassemble starter, detach starter housing from engine. Remove rope handle and allow rope to wind into starter. Unscrew center screw and remove rope pulley. Wear appropriate safety eyewear and gloves before

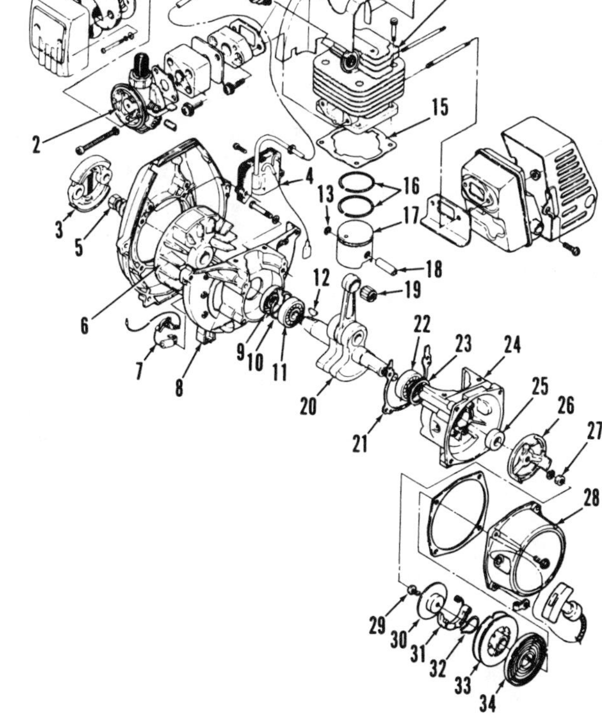

Fig. MI57—Exploded view of T200 engine. Other models are similar. Snap ring (10) is not used on all models. Points and condenser (7) are used on early models.

1. Air cleaner assy.
2. Carburetor
3. Clutch assy.
4. Ignition coil
5. Nut
6. Flywheel
7. Points & condenser
8. Crankcase
9. Seal
10. Snap ring
11. Bearing
12. Key
13. Retainer
14. Cylinder
15. Gasket
16. Piston rings
17. Piston
18. Piston pin
19. Bearing
20. Crankshaft assy.
21. Gasket
22. Bearing
23. Shim
24. Crankcase
25. Seal
26. Pulley
27. Nut
28. Housing
29. Screw
30. Friction plate
31. Pawl
32. Brake spring
33. Pulley
34. Rewind spring

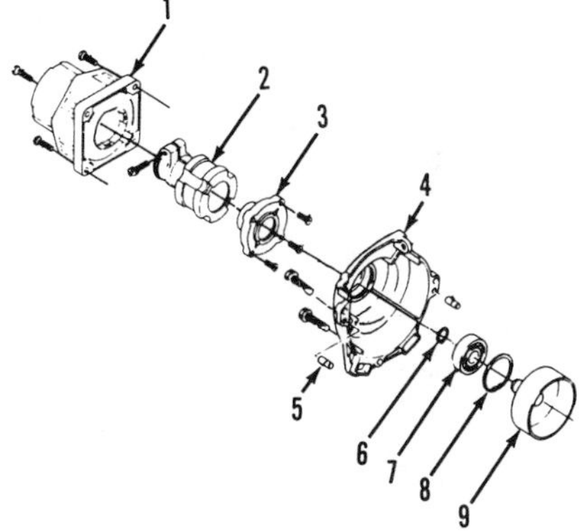

Fig. MI60—Exploded view of clutch drum assembly used on some models.

1. Housing
2. Vibration isolator
3. Support
4. Housing
5. Dowel pin
6. Snap ring
7. Bearing
8. Snap ring
9. Clutch drum

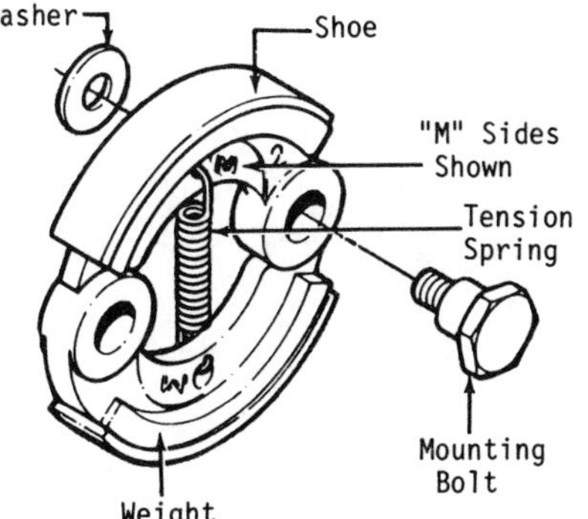

Fig. MI58—Exploded view of clutch shoe assembly used on some models.

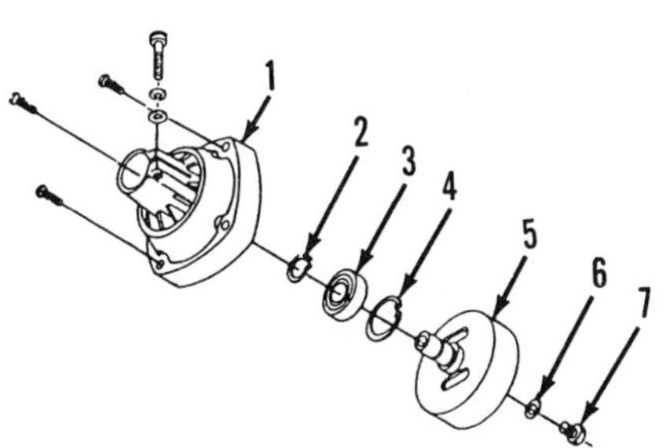

Fig. MI59—Exploded view of clutch drum assembly used on some models.

1. Housing
2. Snap ring
3. Bearing
4. Snap ring
5. Clutch drum
6. Washer
7. Screw

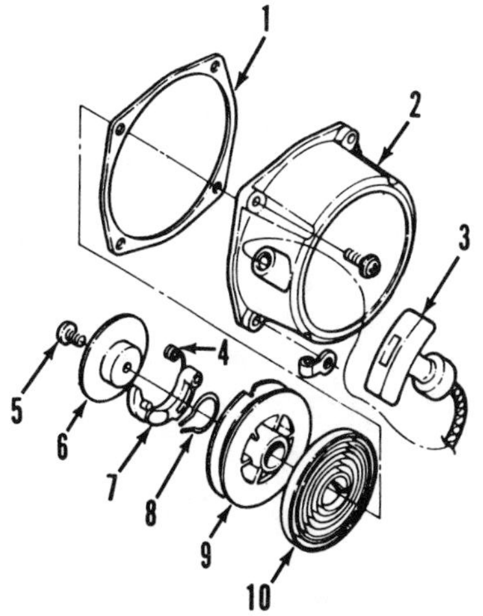

Fig. MI61—Exploded view of rewind starter used on some models.

1. Gasket
2. Housing
3. Rope handle
4. Spring
5. Screw
6. Friction plate
7. Pawl
8. Brake spring
9. Pulley
10. Rewind spring

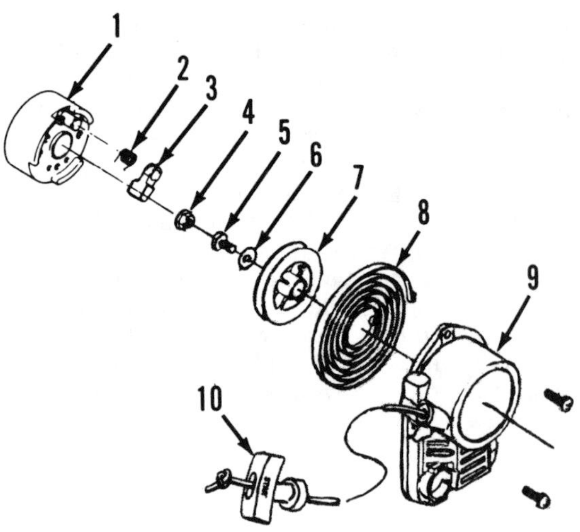

Fig. MI62—Exploded view of rewind starter used on some models.

1. Flywheel
2. Spring
3. Pawl
4. Nut
5. Screw
6. Washer
7. Pulley
8. Rewind spring
9. Housing
10. Rope handle

detaching rewind spring from housing as spring may uncoil uncontrolled.

To assemble starter, lubricate center post of housing and spring side with light grease. Install rewind spring so coil windings are counterclockwise from outer end. Assemble starter while passing rope through housing rope outlet and attach rope handle to rope. To place tension on starter rope, pull rope out of housing. Engage rope in notch on pulley and turn pulley counterclockwise. Hold pulley and disengage rope from pulley notch. Release pulley and allow rope to wind on pulley. Check starter operation. Rope handle should be held against housing by spring tension, but it must be possible to rotate pulley at least $^1/_4$ turn counterclockwise when rope is pulled out fully.

PISTON POWERED PRODUCTS

ENGINE SERVICE

Model	Bore	Stroke	Displacement
31 cc	1.37 in. (34.8 mm)	1.25 in. (31.8 mm)	1.9 cu. in. (31 cc)

ENGINE INFORMATION

Engine serial number decal is located on aluminum crankcase plate as shown in Fig. P10. Engines are equipped with Walbro diaphragm type carburetor. Cylinder head and cylinder is a single cast unit which may be separated from crankcase.

MAINTENANCE

SPARK PLUG. Recommended spark plug is a Champion DJ8J, or equivalent. Specified electrode gap is 0.025 inch (0.51 mm).

AIR CLEANER. Engine air filter should be cleaned and re-oiled at 10 hour intervals of normal use. If operating in dusty conditions, clean and re-oil more frequently.

To remove air filter, remove the two air filter housing retaining screws (S—Fig. P11) and lift filter housing from engine. Remove foam element (1) and clean housing and carburetor compartment thoroughly. Wash element in mild solution of detergent and water. Rinse thoroughly, wrap element in a dry cloth and squeeze water out. Allow element to air dry. Re-oil element with SAE 30 engine oil and squeeze excess oil out. Install element in housing and install housing on engine.

CARBURETOR. The "all position" Walbro diaphragm type carburetor is equipped with an idle speed adjustment screw and a low speed mixture needle. High speed mixture is controlled by a fixed jet. All adjustment procedures must be performed with trimmer line at proper length or blade installed.

Initial adjustment of low speed mixture needle (21—Fig. P14) is 1-1/2 turns open from a lightly seated position. To initially adjust idle speed screw (4), turn idle speed screw out counterclockwise until throttle lever contacts boss on carburetor, then turn screw in clockwise direction until screw just contacts throttle lever. Turn screw clockwise two full turns from this position.

Final carburetor adjustment is made with engine running and at operating temperature. Operate engine at idle speed (adjust idle speed screw in 1/8 turn increments as necessary) and turn low speed mixture needle slowly clockwise until engine falters. Note this position and turn low speed mixture needle counterclockwise until engine begins to run unevenly. Note this position and set low speed mixture needle halfway between first (lean) and last (rich) positions. Squeeze throttle trigger. If engine falters or hesitates on acceleration, turn low speed mixture needle counterclockwise 1/16 turn and repeat acceleration test. Continue until smooth acceleration is obtained. Adjust idle speed as necessary to maintain idle speed just below clutch engagement speed.

To disassemble carburetor, refer to Fig. P14. Remove the four screws (18) and remove diaphragm cover (17), diaphragm (16) and gasket (15). Remove screw (14) and carefully lift metering valve (12) and pin (13) from carburetor.

SERIAL NO. 40128548

Fig. P10—View showing engine serial number location.

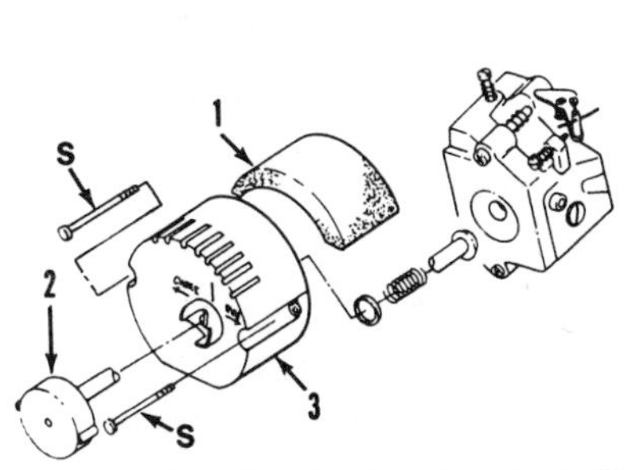

Fig. P11—View showing location of air filter retaining screws (S). Foam pad (1) is used as air filter element. Refer to text for cleaning procedure.

1. Air filter
2. Choke knob
3. Air filter housing

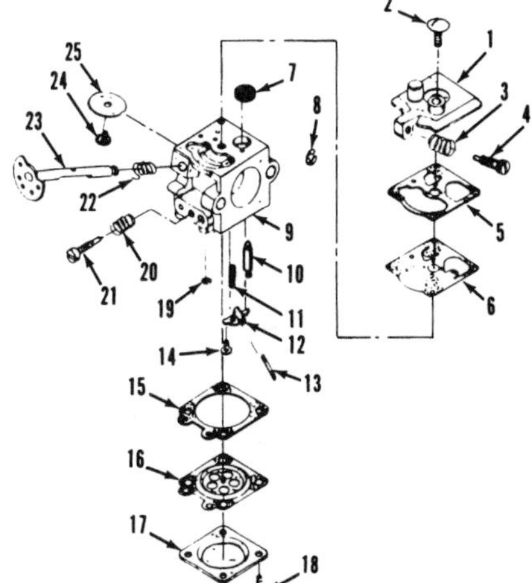

Fig. P14—Exploded view of Walbro diaphragm type carburetor.

1. Cover
2. Screw
3. Spring
4. Idle speed screw
5. Gasket
6. Diaphragm
7. Screen
8. "E" clip
9. Body
10. Fuel inlet needle
11. Spring
12. Fuel inlet lever
13. Pin
14. Screw
15. Gasket
16. Diaphragm
17. Cover
18. Screw
19. Welch plug
20. Spring
21. Low speed mixture needle
22. Spring
23. Throttle shaft
24. Screw
25. Throttle plate

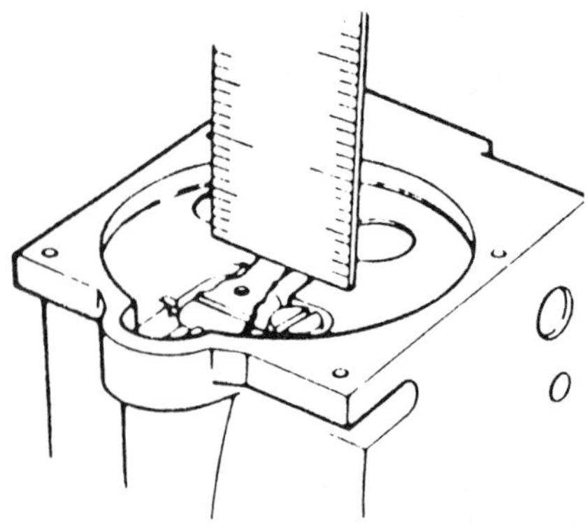

Fig. P15—Metering lever (fuel inlet lever) must be flush with fuel chamber floor as shown. Carefully bend lever to obtain correct adjustment.

Use care not to lose spring (11). Remove screw (2), cover (1), gasket (5), pump diaphragm (6), screen (7), low speed mixture needle (21) and spring (20). Remove screw (24) and throttle plate (25). Remove "E" clip (8) and throttle shaft (23). Welch plugs (19) may be removed as necessary and if new plugs are available.

Clean all metallic parts in a good quality carburetor cleaner. Rinse with clean water and use compressed air to dry. Metering lever should be flush with carburetor body (Fig. P15). Gently bend metering lever to obtain correct adjustment. Diaphragm is installed with rivet head toward metering valve lever.

IGNITION SYSTEM. Ignition module for the solid state ignition system is mounted on cylinder (37—Fig. P17). To service the module, remove the five screws retaining rewind starter assembly to engine and note location of the single screw with lag type threads. On some models, it will be necessary to remove plastic engine cover and fuel tank. Air gap between module and flywheel is 0.010-0.015 inch (0.25-0.38 mm).

LUBRICATION. Engine is lubricated by mixing gasoline with a good quality two-stroke air-cooled engine oil. Refer to TRIMMER SERVICE section for correct fuel/oil ratio recommended by trimmer manufacturer.

CARBON. Muffler and exhaust ports should be cleaned after every 50 hours of operation if engine is operated continuously at full load. If operated at light or medium load, the cleaning interval can be extended to 100 hours.

REPAIRS

COMPRESSION PRESSURE. For optimum performance cylinder compression pressure should be 90-120 psi (621-828 kPa). Compression pressure should be checked with engine at operating temperature and throttle and choke valves wide open.

TIGHTENING TORQUES. Recommended tightening torque specifications are as follows:

Crankcase plate to crankcase . . . . 120 in.-lbs. (13 N·m)

Cylinder to crankcase . . . 120 in.-lbs. (13 N·m)

Carburetor . . . . 40 in.-lbs. (4 N·m)

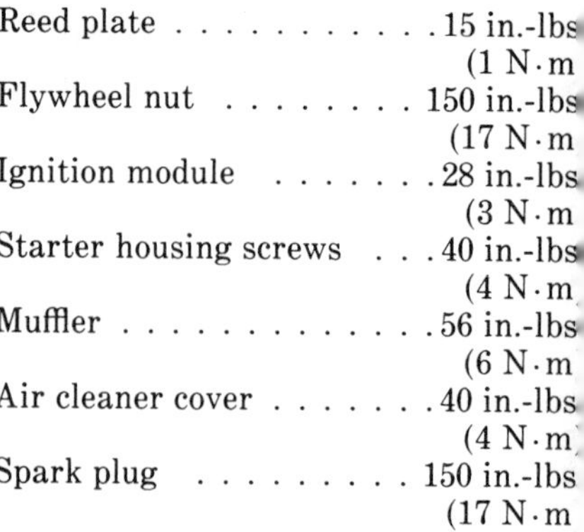

Reed plate . . . . 15 in.-lbs (1 N·m

Flywheel nut . . . . 150 in.-lbs (17 N·m

Ignition module . . . . 28 in.-lbs (3 N·m

Starter housing screws . . . 40 in.-lbs (4 N·m

Muffler . . . . 56 in.-lbs (6 N·m

Air cleaner cover . . . . 40 in.-lbs (4 N·m

Spark plug . . . . 150 in.-lbs (17 N·m

CRANKSHAFT. Cantilevered design crankshaft (9—Fig. P17) is supported on flywheel side by two ball bearing type main bearings (13 and 17). Crankshaft must be a press fit in ball bearing type main bearings. Connecting rod is a slip fit on stub crankpin journal. Crankpin journal must be smooth, round and free from scores or damage.

To remove crankshaft, from models equipped with clutch, first remove clutch housing (31—Fig. P18). Unscrew the clutch drum retaining screw (29S) located at bottom of squared drive shaft adapter hole of clutch drum (30) then remove drum. Threads of the slotted head screw are coated with thread locking material and may be difficult to remove. Unscrew clutch hub assembly (28) and shoes from end of crankshaft. On all models, remove the five screws retaining rewind starter housing (26—Fig. P18 or P18A), then remove housing. Note location of the single screw with lag type threads (S). Disconnect spark plug and remove stand assembly (19—Fig. P17). Remove flywheel retaining nut from direct drive models. Remove flywheel (18) and key (33) from all models. Remove fuel tank assembly and fuel line. Remove the three muffler

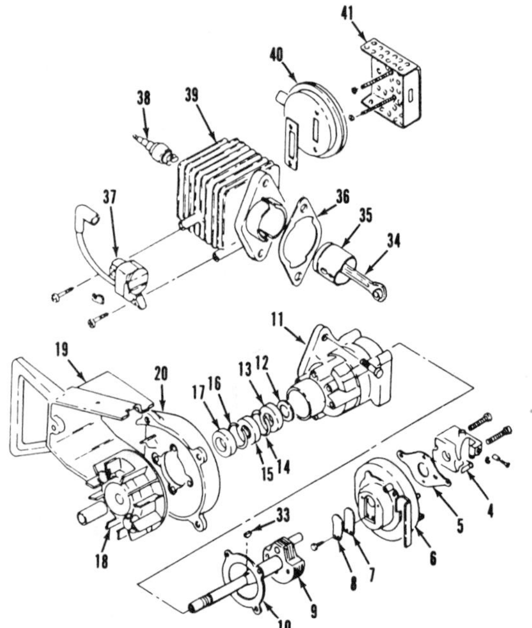

Fig. P17—Exploded view of Piston Powered Product engine.

4. Carburetor
5. Gasket
6. Crankcase plate
7. Reed plate
8. Reed backup
9. Crankshaft
10. Gasket
11. Crankcase
12. Thrust washer
13. Bearing
14. Snap ring
15. Seal
16. Snap ring
17. Bearing
18. Flywheel
19. Shroud
20. Cover
33. Key
34. Connecting rod
35. Piston
36. Gasket
37. Ignition module
38. Spark plug
39. Cylinder
40. Muffler
41. Muffler guard

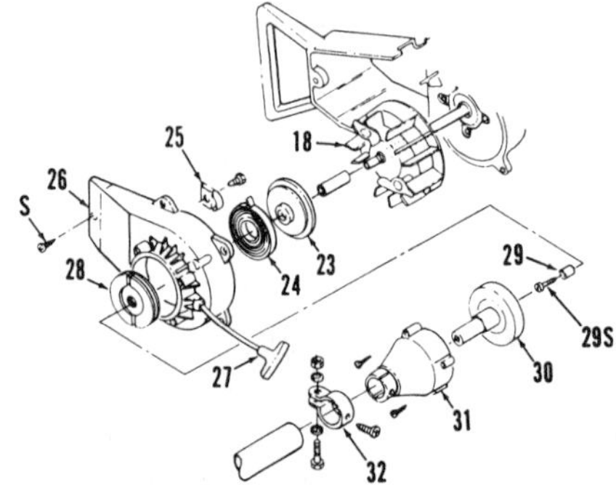

Fig. P18—Exploded view of the clutch, rewind starter and flywheel used on some models. Screw (29S) is trapped in drum (30) by spacer (29).

23. Pulley
24. Rewind spring
25. Retainer
26. Cover
27. Handle
28. Clutch hub assy.
29. Spacer
30. Clutch drum
31. Clutch housing
32. Clamp

ıounting screws and muffler assembly. emove air cleaner housing. Remove ıe two carburetor mounting screws, arburetor (4) and gasket (5). Remove ıe four crankcase plate mounting :rews and crankcase plate assembly ;). Remove the two cylinder mounting :rews and carefully work cylinder (39) way from piston. Rotate crankshaft ntil crankpin is at cylinder side of rankcase and slide connecting rod off rankpin to remove connecting rod and iston assembly. Remove the four crews retaining crankcase cover (20) to rankcase and remove cover. Careful-y press crankshaft (9—Fig. P17) out of earings in crankcase (11). Remove hrust washer (12) from crankshaft. rive bearings (13 and 17) from crank-ase housing, remove snap rings (14 and 6) and drive seal (15) out of crankcase ıousing.

To install crankshaft, assemble seal 15) in bearing bore of crankcase 0.875 nch (22.23 mm) from flywheel side of rankcase. Press against flat surface of eal so that cupped side of seal enters rankcase first. Install snap rings (14 nd 16). One main bearing (17) has a ingle shielded side which must be out oward flywheel side of engine after in-tallation. Press bearings (13 and 17) in ıntil seated against snap rings. Install hrust washer (12) on crankshaft main earing journal and press crankshaft nto main bearings. Rotate crankshaft ıntil crankpin is at cylinder side and nstall connecting rod and piston as-embly with cut-out portion of piston kirt toward crankshaft counterweight Fig. P21). Install gasket (36—Fig. P17) ınd crankcase cover (20), then tighten crews to specified torque (Fig. P19). Make certain ring gap is correctly posi-ioned at ring locating pin and carefully work cylinder (39—Fig. P17) over pis-on until seated against crankcase. Tighten screws to specified torque. In-stall fuel tank and rubber tank mounts (as equipped). Install crankcase plate assembly, carburetor, air cleaner and muffler. Install key (33) and flywheel (18), tightening flywheel nut to speci-fied torque. Install rewind starter as-sembly and clutch (as equipped).

PISTON, RINGS AND CON-NECTING ROD. Piston and connect-ing rod are serviced as an assembly only. Stamped steel connecting rod uti-lizes caged needle bearings at piston pin and crankpin journal end. Caged bear-ings are not available separately. Pis-ton ring on single ring piston has a locating pin in ring groove. Piston ring side clearance must not exceed 0.005 inch (0.13 mm). Piston ring width is 0.052 inch (1.32 mm). Piston ring end gap must not exceed 0.085 inch (2.16 mm). Piston standard diameter is 1.375-1.3805 inch (34.93-35.05 mm). Pis-ton skirt is cut-out on crankshaft coun-terweight side to provide clearance.

CYLINDER. Cylinder must be smooth and free of scratches or flaking. Clean carbon carefully as necessary. Standard cylinder bore diameter is 1.3790-1.3805 inches (35.03-35.05 mm). Check cylinder size by installing a new piston ring squarely in cylinder and measuring ring end gap. If ring end gap exceeds 0.085 inch (2.16 mm), renew cylinder.

CRANKCASE, BEARINGS AND SEAL. Seal (15—Fig. P17) is pressed into crankcase bearing bore 0.875 inch (22.23 mm) from flywheel side. Press seal from flat surface of seal and into bearing bore from flywheel side of crankcase. Install snap rings (14 and 16) and press main bearings in until seated against snap rings. Note one main bearing has a shielded side that must be out toward flywheel side of crankcase.

REED VALVE. Crankcase plate (6—Fig. P17) utilizes a single reed (7) and reed back-up plate (8) held in position by two screws. Reed and reed back-up plate must be installed as shown in Fig. P20.

POSITION OF REED CURVE

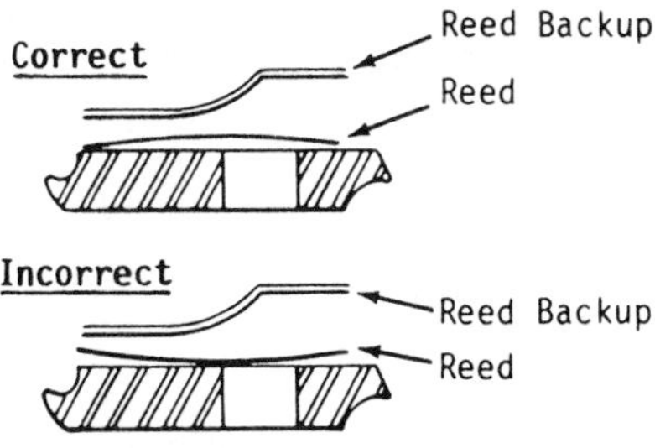

Fig. P20—Reed must be installed as shown.

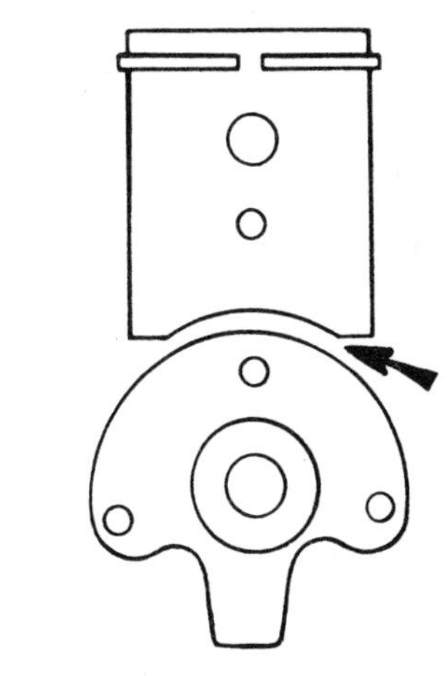

Fig. P21—Piston skirt is cut out on one side to clear crankshaft counterweight.

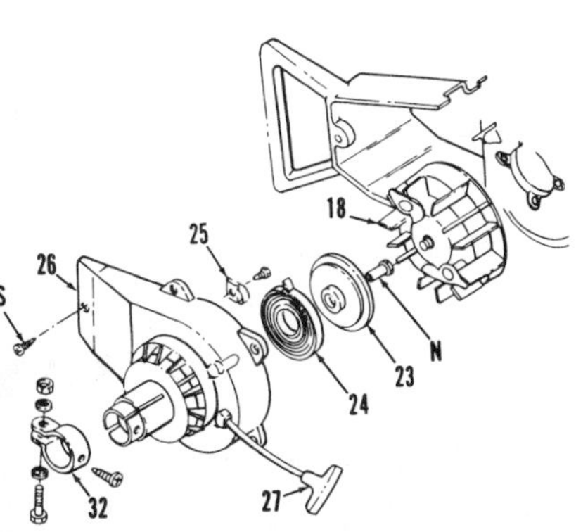

ig. P18A—Exploded view of rewind starter and rive adapter used on direct drive models. Crank-haft is different than models with clutch and fly-vheel is retained by nut (N). Refer to Fig. P18 for legend.

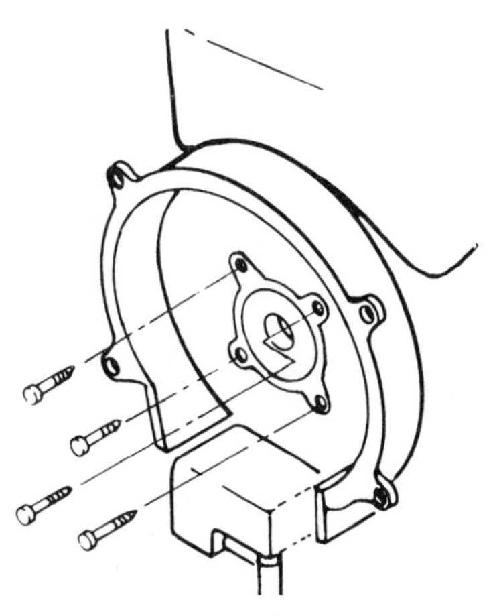

Fig. P19—Tighten screws in crankcase cover in a criss-cross pattern.

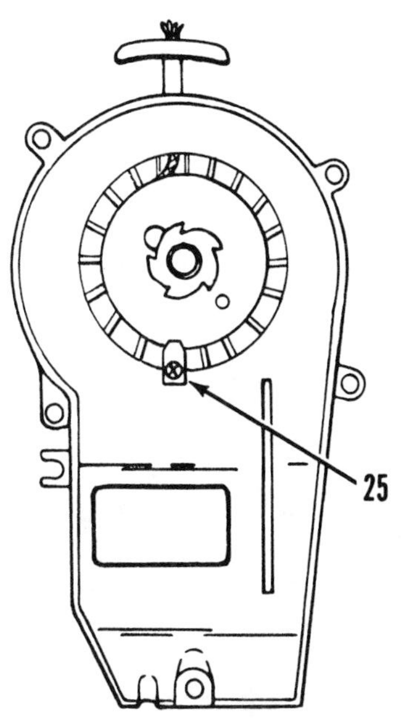

Fig. P22—View showing location of rewind starter pulley retainer (25). Refer to text.

REWIND STARTER. Rewind starter dogs and springs are attached to flywheel assembly. To disassemble rewind starter, remove handle (27—Fig. P18 or P18A) and allow rope to wind onto rope pulley until all spring tension is removed. Remove retainer screw and retainer (25—Fig. P22), then carefully lift out pulley. CAUTION: Rewind spring will uncoil rapidly and come out of rewind housing. Use care during this procedure. Before reassembly, lightly coat rewind spring and inner side of pulley with grease. Wind rope entirely onto pulley. Maximum length of rope is 33 inches (89 cm). Hook outer hook on spring to spring retainer in rewind housing and carefully begin coiling spring inside housing using housing and thumb to trap spring coils. With spring wound in housing, place pull on top of spring and use a hooked wi to work spring into position so pull will slip all the way down into housi and engage spring. Wind spring ju tight enough to provide tension to ho handle against rewind housing ar push rope through rope hole in housin Install handle and tie knot to retai rope in handle.

POULAN

ENGINE SERVICE

Model	Bore	Stroke	Displacement
Poulan	...	...	22.2 cc (1.35 cu. in.)
Poulan	...	...	26.2 cc (1.60 cu. in.)
Poulan	...	...	28 cc (1.72 cu. in.)

ENGINE INFORMATION

These engines are used on Poulan, Weed Eater and Yard Pro trimmers and blowers. Refer to adjoining Poulan engine section for engine service information on other Poulan engine models.

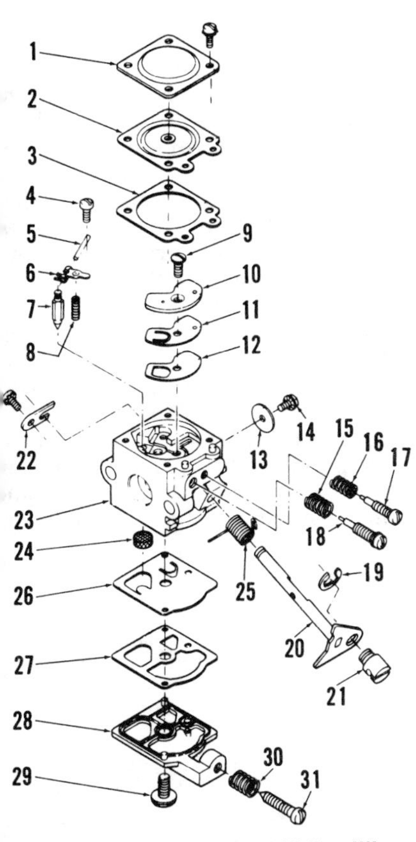

Fig. PN50—Exploded view of Walbro WA carburetor.

1. Cover
2. Metering diaphragm
3. Gasket
4. Screw
5. Pin
6. Metering lever
7. Fuel inlet valve
8. Spring
9. Screw
10. Circuit plate
11. Check valve
12. Gasket
13. Throttle plate
14. Screw
15. Spring
16. Spring
17. High-speed mixture screw
18. Idle mixture screw
19. "E" clip
20. Throttle shaft
21. Swivel
22. Clip
23. Body
24. Inlet screen
25. Return spring
26. Fuel pump diaphragm
27. Gasket
28. Cover
29. Screw
30. Spring
31. Idle speed screw

MAINTENANCE

LUBRICATION. Engine lubrication is obtained by mixing gasoline with an oil designed for two-stroke, air-cooled engines. Refer to trimmer or blower service section for manufacturer's recommended fuel:oil mixture ratio.

SPARK PLUG. Recommended spark plug is a Champion CJ14 for trimmer engines or a Champion CJ8 for blower engines. Specified electrode gap for all models is 0.6-0.65 mm (0.024-0.026 in.).

CARBURETOR. The engine is equipped with a Walbro WA diaphragm-type carburetor. Some models are equipped with a primer system that uses a plunger pump to force fuel into the intake passage prior to starting.

Initial adjustment of idle and high-speed mixture screws is 3/4 to 1 1/4 turns out from a lightly seated position (blower engine carburetor is not equipped with an idle mixture screw). Final adjustments are performed with trimmer line at recommended length or blade installed on trimmer models. Engine must be at operating temperature and running. Adjust idle speed screw (31—Fig. PN50) so engine idles at approximately 3000 rpm (on trimmers with a clutch, trimmer head or blade should not rotate). On trimmer engines, adjust idle mixture screw (18) so engine idles smoothly and accelerates without hesitation. Readjust idle speed. Operate unit at full-throttle and adjust high-speed mixture screw (17) to obtain maximum engine rpm, then turn high-speed mixture screw counterclockwise until engine just begins to run rough.

When overhauling carburetor, refer to exploded view in Fig. PN50. Examine fuel inlet valve and seat. Inlet valve (7) is renewable, but carburetor body must be renewed if seat is excessively worn or damaged. Inspect mixture screws and seats. Renew carburetor body if seats are excessively worn or damaged. Clean fuel screen (24). Inspect diaphragms (2, 11 and 26) for tears and other damage.

Check metering lever height as shown in Fig. PN51. Metering lever should be flush with circuit plate. Bend lever to obtain correct lever height.

IGNITION SYSTEM. The engine is equipped with an electronic ignition system. Ignition system performance is considered satisfactory if a spark will jump across a 3 mm (1/8 in.) electrode gap on a test spark plug. If no spark is produced, check on/off switch, wiring and ignition module air gap. Air gap between ignition module and flywheel magnet should be 0.25-0.36 mm (0.010-0.014 in.). If switch, wiring and module air gap are satisfactory, but spark is not present, renew ignition module.

REPAIRS

COMPRESSION PRESSURE. For optimum performance, compression pressure should be 621 kPa (90 psi). Compression pressure should be checked with engine at operating temperature and with throttle and choke wide-open.

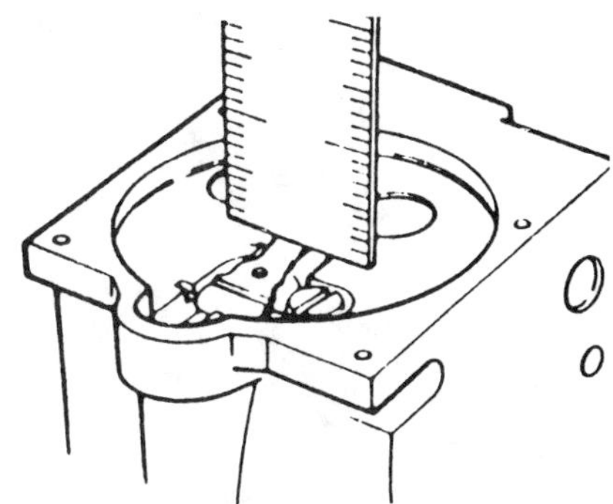

Fig. PN51—Metering lever should be flush with carburetor body.

Illustrations courtesy Poulan/Weed Eater

TIGHTENING TORQUES. Recommended tightening torques are as follows:

Clutch drum . . . . 3.4-4.0 N·m (30-35 in.-lbs.)
Clutch hub . . . . 18-20 N·m (156-180 in.-lbs.)
Crankcase . . . . 5.1-5.7 N·m (45-50 in.-lbs.)
Cylinder . . . . 7.0-7.3 N·m (60-65 in.-lbs.)
Flywheel . . . . 18-20 N·m (156-180 in.-lbs.)
Ignition module . . . . 3.4-4.0 N·m (30-35 in.-lbs.)
Spark plug . . . . 14-15 N·m (124-134 in.-lbs.)

PISTON, PIN AND RINGS. The piston is equipped with a single piston ring. A locating pin in the piston ring groove prevents ring rotation.

The piston is accessible after separating cylinder from crankcase. Remove both piston pin retaining rings (25—Fig. PN52). Use suitable piston pin removal tool (No. 31069) while applying heat to top of piston to remove piston pin (26) from piston. If pin removal tool is not available, use a press to press pin from piston. Do not attempt to drive the pin out of piston.

Standard ring end gap is 0.3 mm (0.012 in.). Standard ring side clearance in piston groove is 0.06 mm (0.0024 in.). If ring side clearance is 0.10 mm (0.004 in.) or more, renew piston.

When installing piston, ring ends must be correctly positioned around locating pin in piston ring groove. Install piston on connecting rod so piston ring locating pin will be positioned as shown in Fig. PN53. Closed end of piston pin must be toward exhaust side of engine. Apply heat to top of piston when installing piston pin. Apply engine oil to piston and cylinder prior to assembly. Do not rotate cylinder when installing cylinder over piston.

CYLINDER. The cylinder bore is chrome plated. Renew cylinder if plating in bore is worn through, scored or otherwise damaged. Worn spots will appear dull and may be easily scratched, while chrome plating will be bright and much harder.

CRANKSHAFT AND CONNECTING ROD. The crankshaft and connecting rod are serviced as an assembly; individual components are not available.

To remove crankshaft and connecting rod assembly, separate engine assembly from engine covers, fuel tank and cooling shrouds. Remove carburetor (7—Fig. PN52), fuel lines and carburetor housing (8). Remove muffler. Remove flywheel and ignition module. Remove drive shaft coupling or clutch hub from crankshaft. Remove cylinder retaining screws and slide cylinder off piston. Remove piston pin retainers (25) and use suitable piston pin removal tool to push pin out of piston. Remove mounti screws from crankcase halves and se arate crankcase halves. Remove cran shaft and connecting rod assembly (1 and thrust washers (16 and 19). U tools 31033 and 31087 to remove bea ings (15 and 20) and seals (13 and 2 from crankcase halves.

The piston pin bushing (23) in co necting rod is renewable. Use servic tools 31069, 31077 and 31092, or equiv lent tools, to remove bushing. Side bearing with numbers should face awa from flywheel side of crankshaft.

Install main bearings using tools 310 and 31088. Numbered side of bearin must be toward inside of crankcase ha Install seals using tools 31033 and 310 with seal lip toward bearing.

Install washers (16 and 19) so shou der is toward crankcase. Apply seale 30054 to mating surfaces of crankcas halves prior to assembly. Tighten cran case screws evenly to 5.1-5.7 N·m (45-5 in.-lbs.).

REED VALVE. A reed valve (11—Fi PN52) is located on the inner face of th carburetor housing (8). Inspect reed pe al and discard if torn, broken, crease or otherwise damaged. Sharp edge of re taining screw washer must be again reed petal. Tip of reed petal should b flat against housing surface; maximu allowable standoff is 0.13 mm (0.005 in.

CLUTCH. A two-shoe clutch (Fi PN54) is used on some engines. Befor removing clutch drum (1), be sure to ur screw hidden screw in center of clutc drum shaft. Unscrew the clutch hub b inserting a suitable spanner wrench i holes of clutch shoes. Clutch shoes an hub are available only as a unit assem

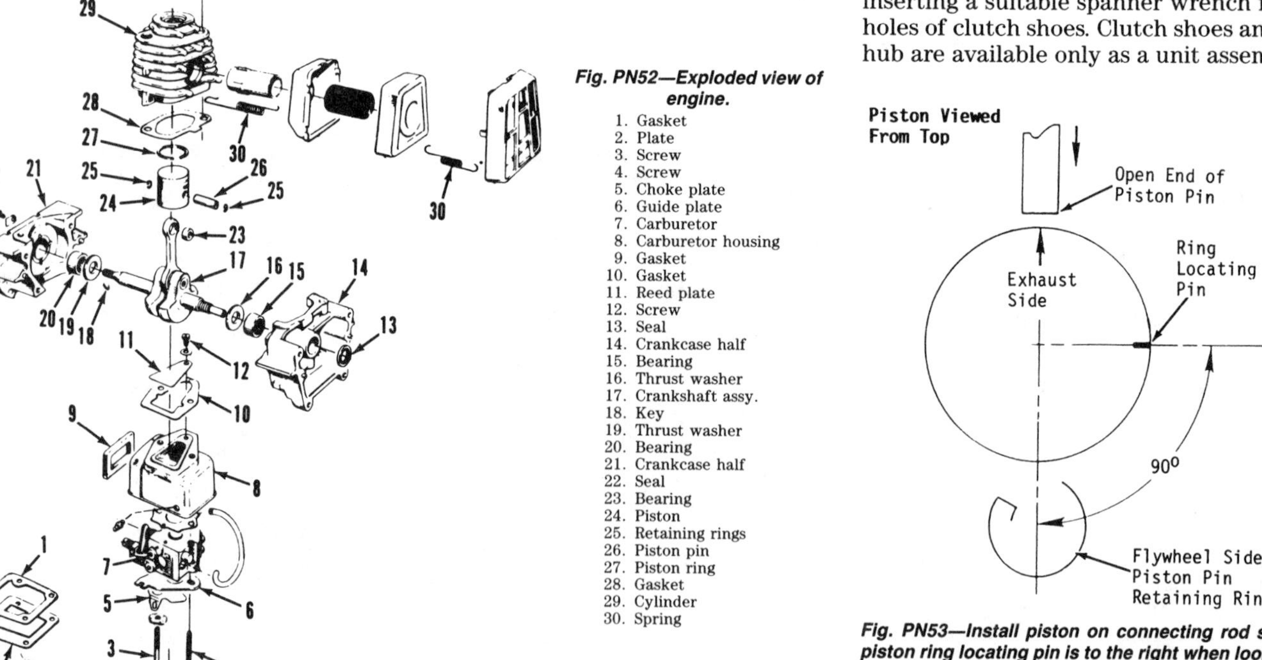

Fig. PN52—Exploded view of engine.

1. Gasket
2. Plate
3. Screw
4. Screw
5. Choke plate
6. Guide plate
7. Carburetor
8. Carburetor housing
9. Gasket
10. Gasket
11. Reed plate
12. Screw
13. Seal
14. Crankcase half
15. Bearing
16. Thrust washer
17. Crankshaft assy.
18. Key
19. Thrust washer
20. Bearing
21. Crankcase half
22. Seal
23. Bearing
24. Piston
25. Retaining rings
26. Piston pin
27. Piston ring
28. Gasket
29. Cylinder
30. Spring

Fig. PN53—Install piston on connecting rod s piston ring locating pin is to the right when look ing toward exhaust side of engine. Closed end o piston pin must be toward exhaust side after in stallation.

Illustrations courtesy Poulan/Weed Eat

bly. On models with two washers, install washer 15377 between hub and crankcase and washer 15381 between hub and drum as shown in Fig. PN54.

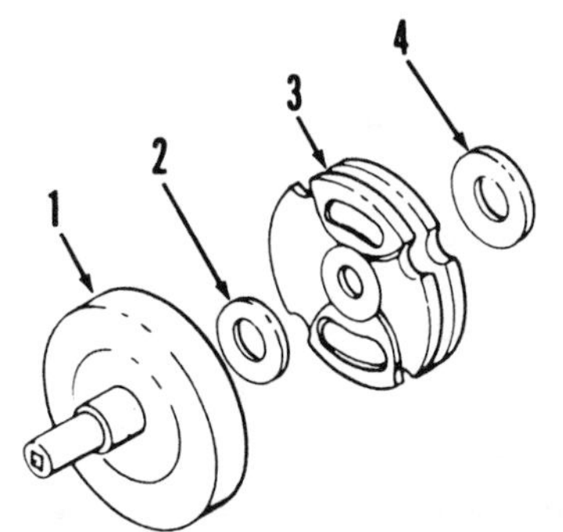

Fig. PN54—Exploded view of clutch assembly used on some models. Note location of thrust washers. Clutch drum is retained by a screw located in shaft of clutch drum (1).

1. Clutch drum
2. Thrust washer (15381)
3. Clutch hub & shoe assy.
4. Thrust washer (15377)

REWIND STARTER. Refer to Fig. PN55 for an exploded view of rewind starter. To disassemble starter, detach starter housing from engine. Remove rope handle and allow rope to wind into starter. Remove screw (6) and rope pulley. Wear appropriate safety eyewear and gloves before detaching rewind spring from housing as spring may uncoil uncontrolled.

To assemble starter, lubricate center post of housing and spring side with light grease. Install rewind spring (3) so coil windings are counterclockwise from outer end. Rope length should be 86 cm (34 in.). Assemble starter while passing rope through housing rope outlet and attach rope handle to rope. To place tension on starter rope, pull rope out of housing. Engage rope in notch on pulley and turn pulley three turns counterclockwise. Hold pulley and disengage rope from pulley notch. Release pulley and allow rope to wind on pulley. Check starter operation. Rope handle should be held against housing by spring tension, but it must be possible to rotate pulley at least $^1/_2$ turn counterclockwise when rope is pulled out fully.

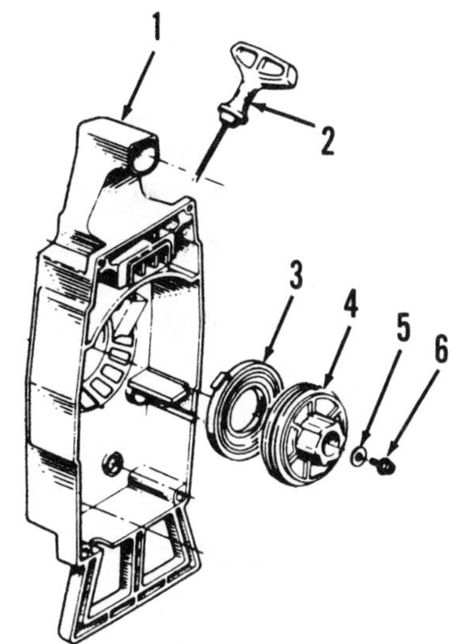

Fig. PN55—Exploded view of rewind starter.

1. Housing
2. Rope handle
3. Rewind spring
4. Pulley
5. Washer
6. Screw

POULAN

ENGINE SERVICE

Model	Bore	Stroke	Displacement
Poulan	...	...	22 cc (1.34 cu. in.)
Poulan	...	...	26 cc (1.59 cu. in.)
Poulan	...	...	30 cc (1.83 cu. in.)

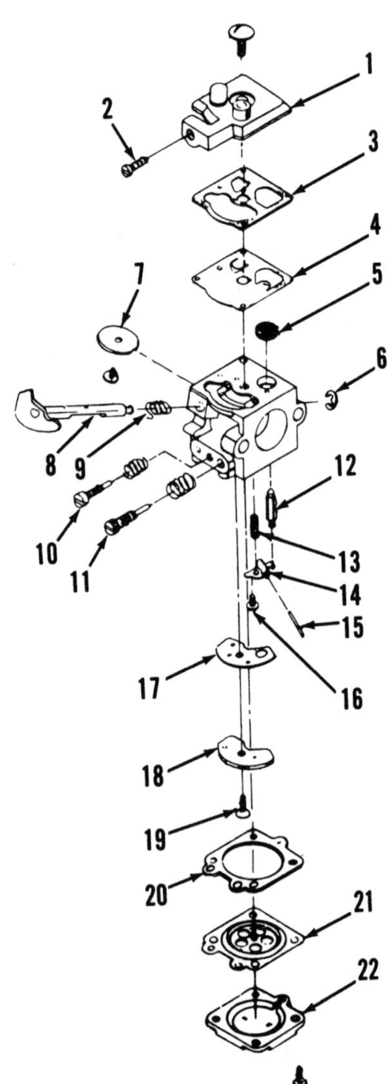

Fig. PN101—Exploded view of Walbro WA carburetor.

1. Cover
2. Idle speed screw
3. Gasket
4. Fuel pump diaphragm
5. Screen
6. "E" ring
7. Throttle plate
8. Throttle shaft
9. Spring
10. Idle mixture screw
11. High-speed mixture screw
12. Fuel inlet valve
13. Spring
14. Metering lever
15. Pin
16. Screw
17. Gasket
18. Circuit plate
19. Screw
20. Gasket
21. Metering diaphragm
22. Cover

ENGINE INFORMATION

These engines are used on Poulan and Weed Eater trimmers and blowers. Refer to adjoining Poulan engine section for engine service information on other Poulan engine models.

MAINTENANCE

LUBRICATION. Engine lubrication is obtained by mixing gasoline with an oil designed for two-stroke, air-cooled engines. Refer to trimmer service section for manufacturer's recommended fuel:oil mixture ratio.

SPARK PLUG. Recommended spark plug is a Champion CJ14 or equivalent. Specified electrode gap for all models is 0.635 mm (0.025 in.).

CARBURETOR. The engine is equipped with a Walbro WA diaphragm-type carburetor. Initial adjustment of idle and high-speed mixture screws is one turn out from a lightly seated position (blower engine carburetor is not equipped with an idle mixture screw). Final adjustments are performed with trimmer line at recommended length or blade installed on trimmer engines. Engine must be at operating temperature and running. Adjust idle speed screw (2—Fig. PN101) so engine idles at approximately 3000 rpm (on trimmers with a clutch, trimmer head or blade should not rotate). On trimmer engines, adjust idle mixture screw (10) so engine idles smoothly and accelerates without hesitation. Readjust idle speed. Operate unit at full-throttle and adjust high-speed mixture screw (11) to obtain maximum engine rpm, then turn high-speed mixture screw counterclockwise until engine just begins to run rough.

When overhauling carburetor, refer to exploded view in Fig. PN101. Examine fuel inlet valve and seat. Inlet valve (12) is renewable, but carburetor body must be renewed if seat is excessively worn or damaged. Inspect mixture screws and seats. Renew carburetor body if seats are excessively worn or damaged. Clean fuel screen (5). Inspect diaphragms (4 and 21) for tears and other damage.

Check metering lever height as shown in Fig. PN102. Metering lever should be flush with circuit plate. Bend lever to obtain correct lever height.

IGNITION SYSTEM. The engine is equipped with an electronic ignition system. Ignition system performance is considered satisfactory if a spark will jump across a 3 mm (1/8 in.) electrode gap on a test spark plug. If no spark is produced, check on/off switch, wiring and ignition module air gap. Air gap between ignition module and flywheel magnet should be 0.25-0.36 mm (0.010-0.014 in.). If switch, wiring and module air gap are satisfactory, but spark is not present, renew ignition module.

REPAIRS

PISTON, PIN AND RING. The piston (22—Fig. PN103) is accessible after removing cylinder (25) from crankcase (17). Remove piston pin retainers (19) and use a suitable puller to extract pin (20) from piston.

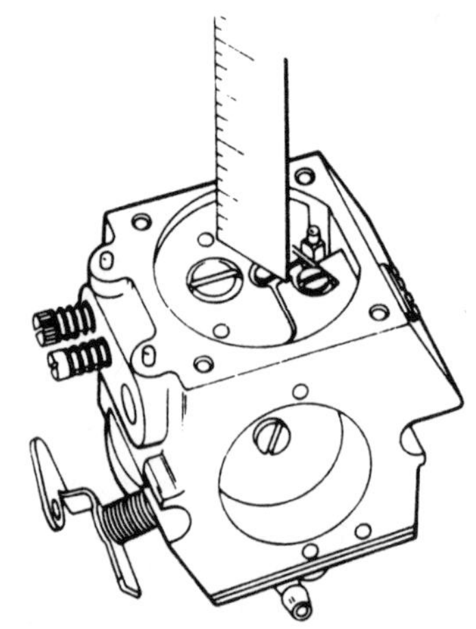

Fig. PN102—Tip of metering lever should be flush with circuit plate. Bend metering lever as needed.

The piston is equipped with a single piston ring. Ring rotation is prevented by a locating pin in the piston ring groove. Piston is available in standard size only.

Be sure piston ring end gap is correctly indexed with locating pin in piston ring groove when installing cylinder. Lubricate piston and cylinder bore with oil prior to reassembly.

CYLINDER. The cylinder is available in standard size only. Renew cylinder if damaged or excessively worn.

CRANKSHAFT AND CONNECTING ROD. The crankshaft (10—Fig. PN103) is supported at flywheel end only by two ball bearings (12 and 15). The stamped steel connecting rod (21) has a caged roller bearing at both ends. Connecting rod and bearings are serviced only as an assembly.

To remove crankshaft and connecting rod, separate engine assembly from engine covers, fuel tank and cooling shrouds. Remove carburetor and muffler. Remove spark plug and insert piston stop tool in spark plug hole or insert end of a rope through plug hole to lock piston and crankshaft. Remove flywheel retaining nut and remove flywheel from crankshaft. Remove cylinder mounting screws and slide cylinder off piston. Unbolt and remove reed block (6) from crankcase (17). Separate connecting rod from crankpin. Detach snap ring (16) and carefully press crankshaft out of bearings. Drive or press bearings (12 and 15) out of crankcase, remove snap rings (13) and remove seal (14).

When reinstalling crankshaft, install seal (14) in bearing bore of crankcase so cupped side of seal is toward inside of crankcase. Outer main bearing (15) has a single shielded side that must be out toward flywheel side of engine after installation. Press bearings (12 and 15) in until seated against snap rings. Install spacer (11) on crankshaft main bearing journal and press crankshaft into main bearings.

REED VALVE. A reed valve (8—Fig. PN103) is located on the inner face of the reed block (6). Inspect reed petal and discard if torn, broken, creased or otherwise damaged.

CLUTCH. Some engines may be equipped with a two-shoe clutch (10—Fig. PN104). Clutch hub, shoes and spring are available only as a unit assembly. The clutch drum is contained in housing (13). Drum and housing are available only as a unit assembly.

REWIND STARTER. Refer to Figs. PN104, PN105 or PN106 for an exploded view of rewind starter. To disassemble starter, detach starter housing from engine. Remove rope handle and allow rope to wind into starter. Unscrew pulley retainer or pulley retaining screw and remove rope pulley. Wear appropriate safety eyewear and gloves before

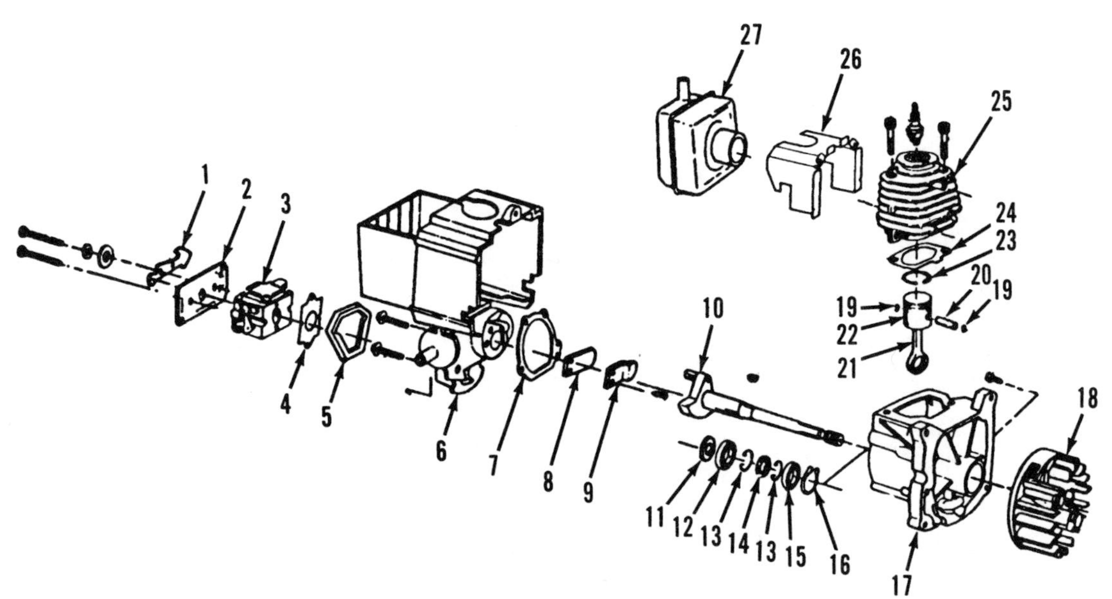

Fig. PN103—Exploded view of engine.

1. Choke shutter
2. Plate
3. Carburetor
4. Gasket
5. Seal
6. Reed block
7. Gasket
8. Reed valve
9. Reed stop
10. Crankshaft
11. Spacer
12. Inner bearing
13. Snap rings
14. Seal
15. Outer bearing
16. Snap ring
17. Crankcase
18. Flywheel
19. Retaining rings
20. Piston pin
21. Connecting rod
22. Piston
23. Piston ring
24. Gasket
25. Cylinder
26. Air baffle
27. Muffler

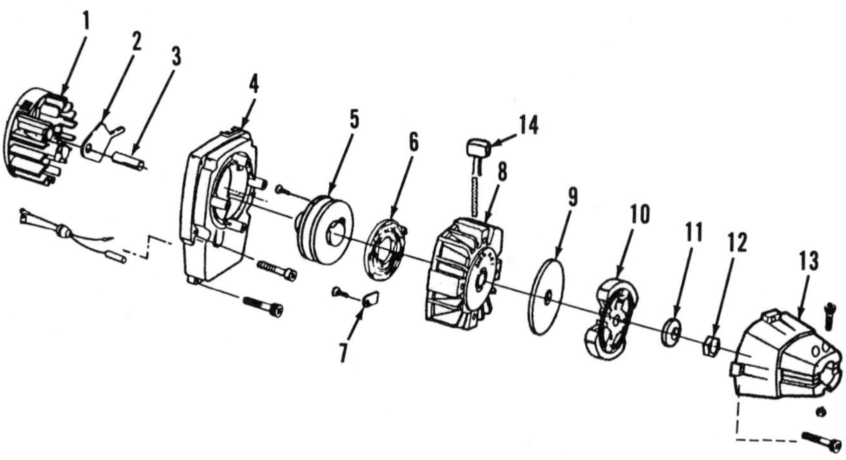

Fig. PN104—Exploded view of clutch and rewind starter assemblies used on trimmers. Counterweight (2) is not used on all models.

1. Flywheel
2. Counterweight
3. Spacer
4. Shroud
5. Starter pulley
6. Rewind spring
7. Retainer
8. Starter housing
9. Plate
10. Clutch assy.
11. Belleville washer
12. Nut
13. Housing
14. Rope handle

detaching rewind spring from housing as spring may uncoil uncontrolled.

To assemble starter, lubricate center post of housing and spring side with light grease. Install rewind spring so coil windings are counterclockwise from outer end. Rope length should be 107 cm (42 in.). Assemble starter while passing rope through housing rope outlet and attach rope handle to rope. To place tension on starter rope, pull rope out of housing. Engage rope in notch on pulley and turn pulley counterclockwise to place tension on rewind spring. Hold pulley and disengage rope from pulley notch. Release pulley and allow rope to wind on pulley. Check starter operation. Rope handle should be held against housing by spring tension, but it must be possible to rotate pulley at least an additional $^1/_4$ turn when rope is pulled out fully.

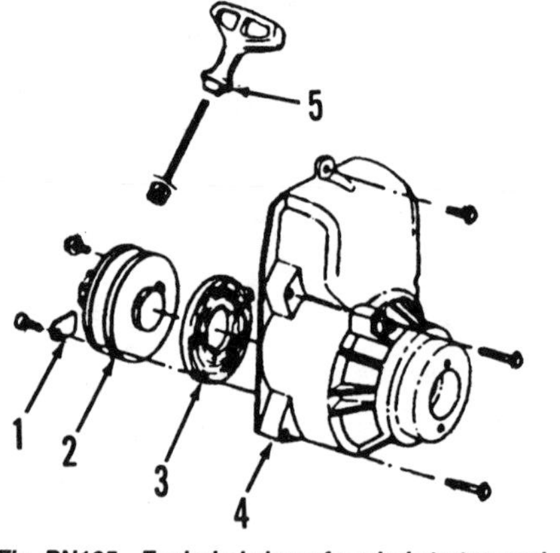

Fig. PN105—Exploded view of rewind starter used on some blower engines.

1. Retainer
2. Starter pulley
3. Rewind spring
4. Housing
5. Rope handle

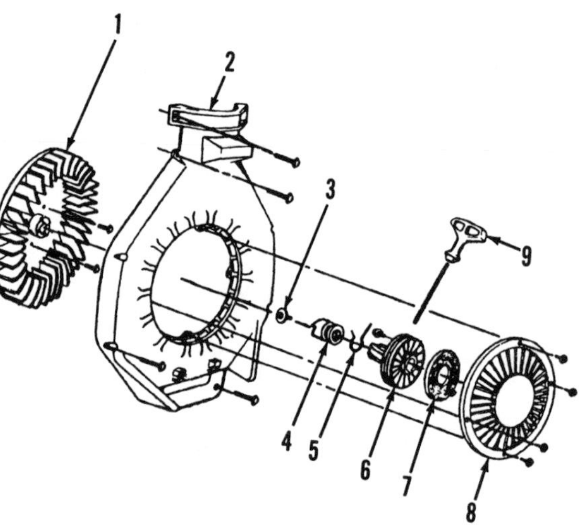

Fig. PN106—Exploded view of rewind starter used on some blower engines.

1. Blower fan
2. Blower housing
3. Screw
4. Ratchet
5. Spring
6. Starter pulley
7. Rewind spring
8. Housing
9. Rope handle

Illustrations courtesy Poulan/Weed Eater

SACHS-DOLMAR

ENGINE SERVICE

Model	Bore	Stroke	Displacement
Sachs-Dolmar	37.0 mm (1.46 in.)	31.0 mm (1.22 in.)	33.0 cc (2.01 cu. in.)
Sachs-Dolmar	40.0 mm (1.57 in.)	31.0 mm (1.22 in.)	40.0 cc (2.44 cu. in.)

ENGINE INFORMATION

Sachs-Dolmar two-stroke air-cooled asoline engines are used on Sachs-Dolar string trimmers and brush cut-ers.

MAINTENANCE

SPARK PLUG. Recommended park plug is a NGK BM7 A, or equiva-ent. Specified electrode gap for all odels is 0.6-0.7 mm (0.024-0.028 in.).

CARBURETOR. All models are quipped with a Walbro WT series dia-hragm type carburetor with a built in uel pump (Fig. SD50).

Initial setting of low (26) and high 25) speed mixture needles is two turns pen from a lightly seated position.

Final adjustments are made with rimmer line at recommended length or lade assembly installed. Engine hould be at operating temperature and unning. Adjust low speed mixture nee-lle (26) so that engine idles and acceler-ates smoothly. Adjust idle speed screw 1) to obtain 2900-3000 engine rpm, or ust below idle speed. Use an accurate ligital tachometer and adjust high speed mixture needle (25) to obtain 10,800-11,000 engine rpm. Recheck en-gine idle speed and acceleration.

IGNITION SYSTEM. All models are equipped with an electronic ignition system. Ignition system is considered satisfactory if spark will jump across the 3 mm (1/8 in.) gap of a test spark plug. If no spark is produced, check on/off switch and wiring. If switch and wiring are satisfactory and spark is not present, renew ignition module.

Air gap between ignition module and flywheel should be 0.2-0.3 mm (0.008-0.010 in.).

LUBRICATION. All models are lubricated by mixing gasoline with a good quality two-stroke air-cooled gasoline engine oil. Refer to TRIMMER SERVICE section for correct fuel/oil mixture ratio recommended by trimmer manufacturer.

REPAIRS

TIGHTENING TORQUES. Recommended tightening torque specifications are as follows:

Carburetor	10 N·m (7.0 ft.-lbs.)
Clutch nut	25 N·m (18.5 ft.-lbs.)
Flywheel	20 N·m (15.0 ft.-lbs.)
Spark plug	15 N·m (11.0 ft.-lbs.)
Cylinder bolts	6 N·m (4.5 ft.-lbs.)
Crankcase bolts	6 N·m (4.5 ft.-lbs.)
Muffler bolts	10 N·m (7.0 ft.-lbs.)

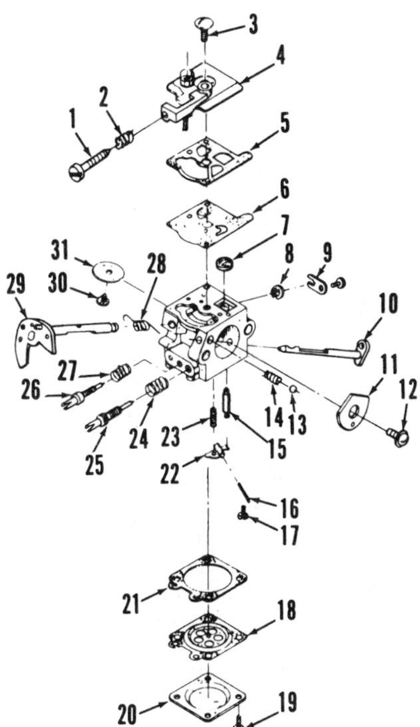

Fig. SD50—Exploded view of Walbro WT diaphragm type carburetor used on all models.

1. Idle speed screw
2. Spring
3. Screw
4. Pump cover
5. Gasket
6. Diaphragm
7. Screen
8. "E" ring
9. Clip
10. Choke shaft
11. Choke plate
12. Screw
13. Ball
14. Spring
15. Fuel inlet needle
16. Pin
17. Screw
18. Diaphragm
19. Screw
20. Cover
21. Gasket
22. Fuel inlet lever
23. Spring
24. Spring
25. High speed mixture needle
26. Low speed mixture needle
27. Spring
28. Spring
29. Throttle shaft
30. Screw
31. Throttle plate

CRANKSHAFT AND CONNECTING ROD. To remove crankshaft, remove all covers and shrouds. Remove clutch, ignition system, fuel tank, clutch flange and cylinder. Use care when separating cylinder from crankcase and pull cylinder straight off piston. Remove crankcase retaining screws and carefully separate crankcase halves. The manufacturer does not recommend separating connecting rod (12–Fig. SD52) from crankshaft (14) or removing the 12 connecting rod needle bearings (13). Remove seals (7 and 19) and snap rings (8 and 18). Heat crankcase until needle bearings (9 and 17) can be easily removed.

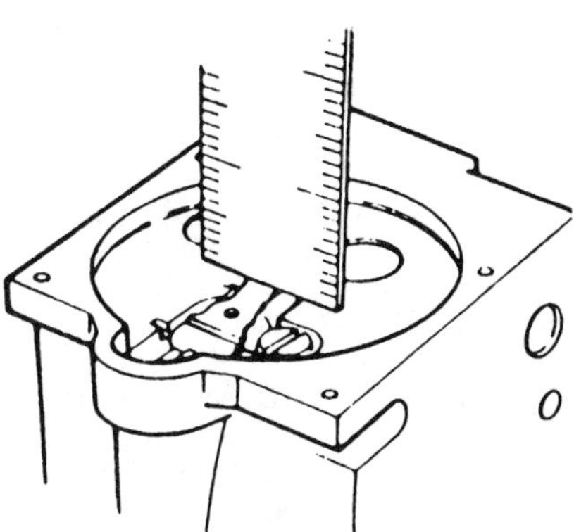

Fig. SD51—Fuel inlet lever must be flush with carburetor body. Carefully bend fuel inlet lever to adjust.

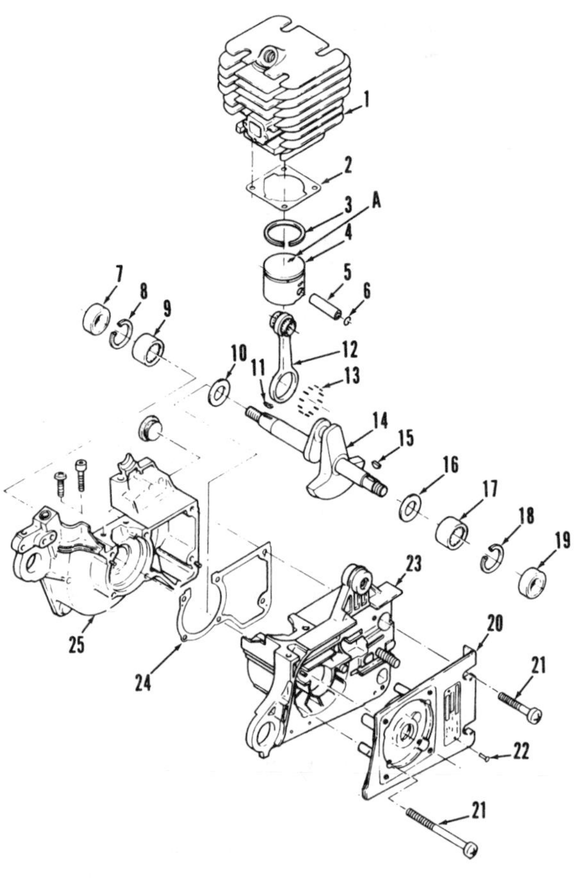

Fig. SD52—Exploded view of engine crankcase, crankshaft and cylinder assembly.

A. Arrow
1. Cylinder
2. Gasket
3. Ring
4. Piston
5. Piston pin
6. Retaining ring
7. Seal
8. Snap ring
9. Main bearing
10. Shim
11. Key
12. Connecting rod
13. Needle bearings
14. Crankshaft
15. Key
16. Shim
17. Main bearing
18. Snap ring
19. Seal
20. Clutch flange
21. Bolts
22. Rivet
23. Crankcase half
24. Gasket
25. Crankcase

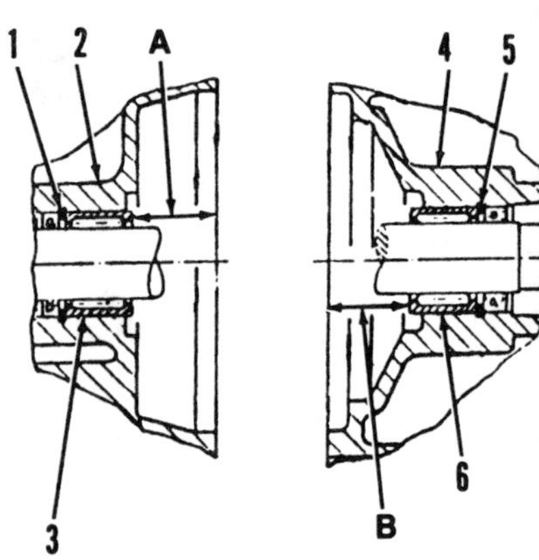

Fig. SD53—Cross-section view of main bearing installed in crankcase. Refer to text.

A. 16 mm (0.63 in.)
B. 15.7 mm (0.62 in.)
1. Snap ring
2. Crankcase half (clutch side)
3. Main bearing
4. Crankcase ha
5. Snap ring
6. Main bearing

To install needle bearings, heat crankcase until bearings can be installed in crankcase housings. Bearing cage is hardened on one side marked "xxx". If bearing cage edge is not marked, test with a file. Hardened side of bearing is installed toward crankshaft counterweight. Note that bearing (3—Fig. SD53) is installed 16 mm (0.63 in.) from gasket surface and bearing (6) is installed 15.7 mm (0.62 in.) from gasket surface. Bearing cages should not contact snap rings (1 and 5). Depth of main bearings and thickness of shims (10 and 16—Fig. SD52) control crankshaft end play. Correct crankshaft end play is 0.2-0.6 mm (0.79-2.36 in.). Vary shim (10 and 16) thickness or change position of bearing (9 or 17) in crankcase bearing bores as required to obtain correct crankshaft end play.

PISTON, PIN AND RINGS. The single ring aluminum piston is equipped with a locating pin in ring groove to prevent ring rotation. To remove piston, refer to CRANKSHAFT AND CONNECTING ROD paragraphs to remove cylinder. Remove retaining rings (6—Fig. SD52). Use a suitable piston pin puller to remove piston pin (5). Remove piston (4).

Make certain ring end gap is correctly positioned at locating pin before installing piston in cylinder. Arrow (A) on piston top must point toward exhaust side of engine after installation on connecting rod.

CYLINDER. To remove cylinder assembly refer to the CRANKSHAFT AND CONNECTING ROD paragraphs. Inspect cylinder for scoring or excessive wear and renew if damaged.

CLUTCH. Engines may be equipped with one of the clutch assemblies shown in Fig. SD54. To disassemble, remove snap ring (4) through opening (O) in clutch drum. Press drum assembly from clutch housing. Remove all necessary snap rings and remove bearings as required.

REWIND STARTER. Rewind starter assembly shown in Fig. SD55 is used on all models. To disassemble, remove fan housing and flywheel (8). Carefully remove brake spring (6) and snap ring (7). Remove starter pawl ratchet (4). Remove pulley (3), starter rope and handle (5), rewind spring (2) and disc (1) as an assembly keeping disc (1) and pulley (3) tight together during removal to prevent rewind spring from unwinding. Carefully allow tension of rewind spring to be released.

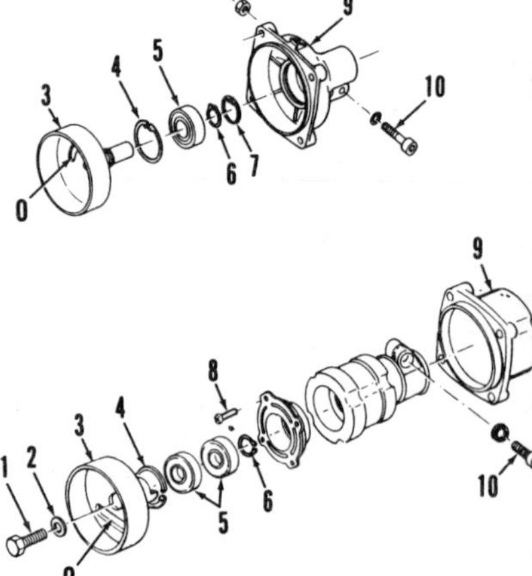

Fig. SD54—Exploded view of the centrifuga clutch assemblies.

O. Opening
1. Bolt
2. Washer
3. Clutch drum
4. Snap ring
5. Bearings
6. Snap ring
7. Snap ring
8. Screw
9. Clutch housin
10. Clamp bolt

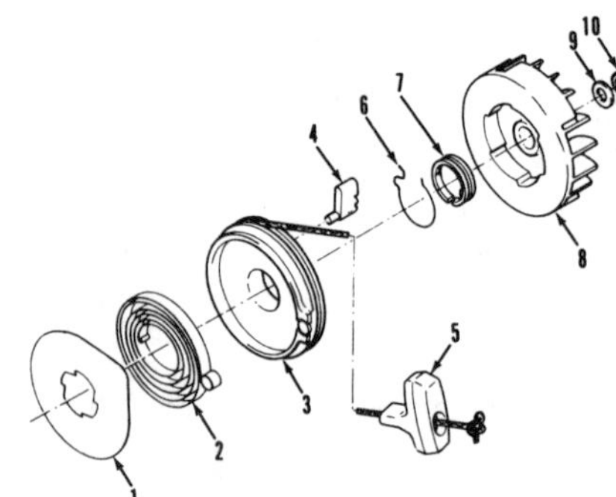

Fig. SD55—Exploded view of the rewind starte assembly.

1. Disc
2. Rewind spring
3. Pulley
4. Ratchet
5. Rope & handle assy.
6. Brake sprin
7. Snap ring
8. Flywheel
9. Washer
10. Nut

Illustrations courtesy Dolmar USA, Inc.

SHINDAIWA

ENGINE SERVICE

Model	Bore	Stroke	Displacement
S18	30.0 mm (1.18 in.)	26.0 mm (1.02 in.)	18.4 cc (1.1 cu. in.)
S20	30.0 mm (1.18 in.)	28.0 mm (1.10 in.)	19.8 cc (1.21 cu. in.)
S21	31.0 mm (1.22 in.)	28.0 mm (1.10 in.)	21.1 cc (1.29 cu. in.)
S230	32.0 mm (1.26 in.)	28.0 mm (1.10 in.)	22.5 cc (1.37 cu. in.)
S25, S30 & S250	32.0 mm (1.26 in.)	30.0 mm (1.18 in.)	24.1 cc (1.47 cu. in.)
S27	34.0 mm (1.34 in.)	30.0 mm (1.18 in.)	27.2 cc (1.7 cu. in.)
S35	36.0 mm (1.42 in.)	33.0 mm (1.30 in.)	33.6 cc (2.05 cu. in.)
S40	39.0 mm (1.54 in.)	33.0 mm (1.30 in.)	39.4 cc (2.40 cu. in.)
S45	40.0 mm (1.57 in.)	33 mm (1.30 in.)	41.5 cc (2.6 cu. in.)

ENGINE INFORMATION

These two-stroke, air-cooled engines are used on trimmers and brush cutters made by Shindaiwa and other manufacturers. Refer to the TRIMMER SERVICE Section for additional service.

MAINTENANCE

LUBRICATION. The engine is lubricated by mixing oil with the fuel. Use only oil designed for two-stroke, air-cooled engines. Refer to the TRIMMER SERVICE section for the type of oil and mixing ratio recommended by the equipment manufacturer.

SPARK PLUG. The recommended spark plug is a Champion CJ8 or equivalent and the electrode gap should be 0.024 in. (0.6 mm). Tighten the spark plug securely to the torque listed in the TIGHTENING TORQUE paragraph.

CARBURETOR. All models are fitted with TK or Walbro diaphragm carburetors. Refer to Table 1 for original application. Walbro WA carburetor has butterfly type throttle (8 and 9—Fig. SH45). Walbro WY, WYL, WYM and WZ models have rotary type throttle (24—Fig. SH47 or Fig. SH48). TK carburetors (DPK, DP, DPV, DPW, PC, WYP) used on these models have slide type throttle (8—Fig. SH51, Fig. SH52 or Fig. SH53).

Walbro WA Series. Refer to Fig. SH45 for an exploded view typical of the carburetor. Initial setting for the low-speed and high-speed mixture needles (17 and 18) is 1-1/8 turns open from lightly seated. The settings of these mixture screws is critical to the operation of the engine. Final adjustment should be performed carefully to insure easy starting and maximum performance.

To adjust the mixture screws, first remove and clean the air filter, then reinstall it. Start the engine and allow it to run until it reaches normal operating

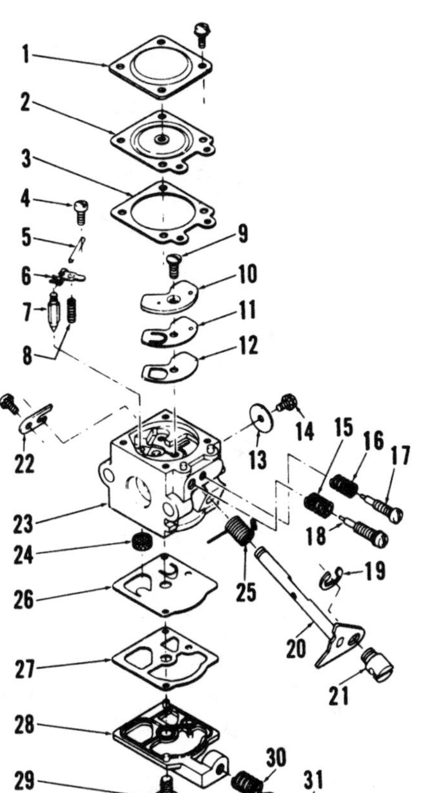

Fig. SH45—Exploded view of Walbro WA diaphragm carburetor used on some models.

1. Cover
2. Metering diaphragm
3. Gasket
4. Screw
5. Pin
6. Metering lever
7. Fuel inlet valve
8. Spring
9. Screw
10. Circuit plate
11. Check valve
12. Gasket
13. Throttle plate
14. Screw
15. Spring
16. Spring
17. Low speed mixture screw
18. High speed mixture screw
19. "E" clip
20. Throttle shaft
21. Swivel
22. Throttle shaft clip
23. Body
24. Fuel screen
25. Return spring
26. Fuel pump diaphragm
27. Gasket
28. Cover
29. Screw
30. Spring
31. Idle speed screw

temperature. The initial setting of the mixture needles should allow the engine to start. Turn the idle speed stop screw (31) so the engine idles just slightly slower than clutch engagement speed or at the slowest speed that the engine will continue to run.

Adjust the low-speed mixture needle (17) so the engine idles smoothly and accelerates without hesitation. The engine may accelerate better if the idle mixture is set slightly rich. Readjust the idle speed stop screw (31) if necessary to slow the idle speed. The trimmer or cutter head should not turn when the engine is idling.

Adjust the high-speed mixture screw (18) to provide the best performance while operating at maximum speed under load. The high-speed mixture screw may be set slightly rich to improve performance under load. The engine may be damaged if the high-speed screw is set too lean.

To disassemble the carburetor, refer to Fig. SH45 and remove covers (1 and 28) for access to internal components. Remove circuit plate (10), metering lever (6) and fuel inlet valve (7), mixture screws (17 and 18) and fuel screen (24).

Clean and inspect all components. If the unit has been improperly stored, passages may be clogged with deposits that are hard, solid and nearly transparent. Be careful not to damage the openings or sealing surfaces while cleaning. Check the condition of diaphragms (2, 11 and 26) carefully. Install new diaphragms if hard (not flexible), torn or otherwise damaged. Examine the fuel inlet valve (7), spring (8) and lever (6). A new fuel inlet valve needle (7) and mixture screws (17 and 18) can be installed, but their seats cannot be serviced if damaged. Clean the filter screen (24) and inspect its condition.

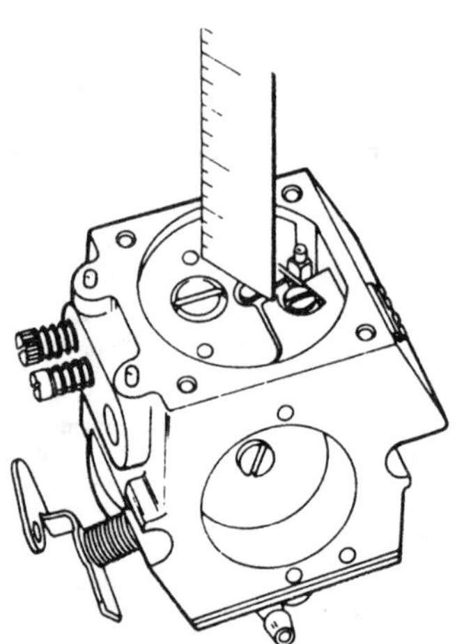

Fig. SH46—Metering lever should be flush with circuit plate on Walbro WA carburetor. Bend the lever if necessary to obtain correct lever height.

Check the height of the metering lever as shown in Fig. SH46. Upper surface of the lever should be aligned with surface of circuit plate. Carefully bend the lever if necessary to obtain the correct lever height.

If so equipped, inspect the primer bulb and install a new bulb if hard, cracked or otherwise damaged.

Walbro WY and WZ Series. Refer to Fig. SH47 or Fig. SH48 for a typical exploded view. Recommended initial setting for the low speed mixture needle (25—Fig. SH48) and the high speed mixture needle (42) is listed in Table 1 at the end of this section. Mixtures indicated as N/A are not adjustable. The low speed mixture needle (N—Fig. SH49) is set at the factory. The mixture needle is covered by a plug and should not be removed. If low speed mixture needle setting is disturbed, the needle is adjusted by counting the turns IN (clockwise) after threads of the needle just engage. The needle does not contact a seat. The high speed jet (17—Fi SH47) is not removable on all models.

To adjust the mixture screws, firs make certain that the air filter is clea Start the engine and allow it to run ur til it reaches normal operating tem perature. The initial setting of th mixture needles should allow the er gine to start. Turn the idle speed sto screw (20—Fig. SH47 or 30—Fig SH48) so the engine idles just slightl slower than clutch engagement spee or at the slowest speed that the engin will continue to run.

If so equipped, adjust the low spee mixture needle so the engine idle smoothly and accelerates without hesi tation. The engine may accelerate bet ter if the idle mixture is set slightl rich. Readjust the idle speed stop screv (20—Fig. SH47 or 30—Fig. SH48) i necessary to slow the idle speed. Th trimmer or cutter head should not tur when the engine is idling.

To disassemble the carburetor, refe to Fig. SH47 or Fig. SH48 and remove

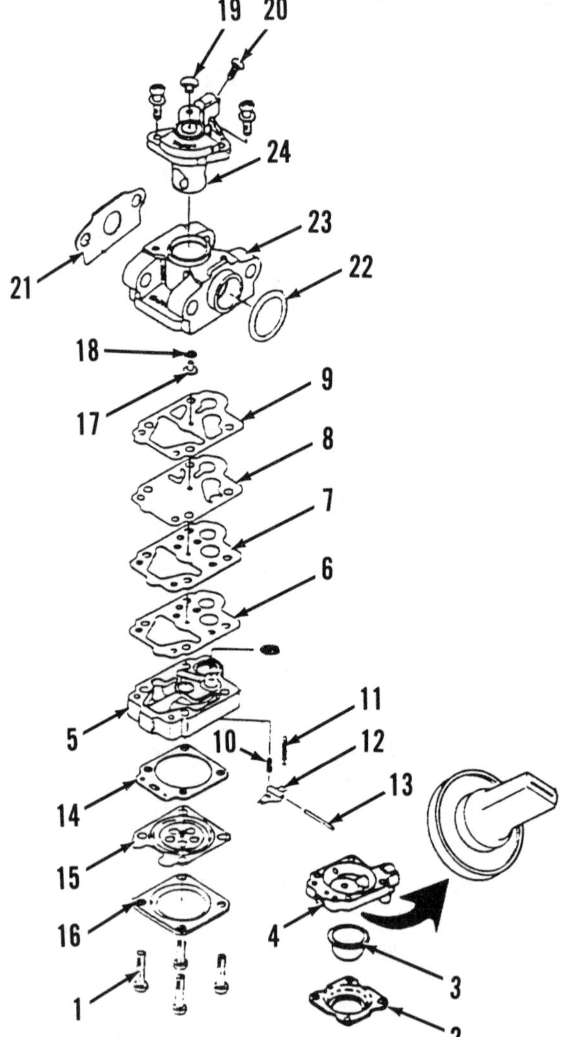

Fig. SH47—Exploded view o Walbro WY carburetor used on some models.

1. Screw
2. Plate
3. Primer bulb
4. Cover with check valve
5. Metering body
6. Gasket
7. Gasket
8. Fuel pump diaphragm
9. Gasket
10. Fuel inlet needle
11. Spring
12. Fuel inlet lever
13. Pin
14. Gasket
15. Metering diaphragm
16. Cover without primer
17. Main jet
18. "O" ring
19. Low-speed mixture needle cover
20. Idle speed screw
21. Gasket
22. "O" ring
23. Body
24. Throttle valve assy.

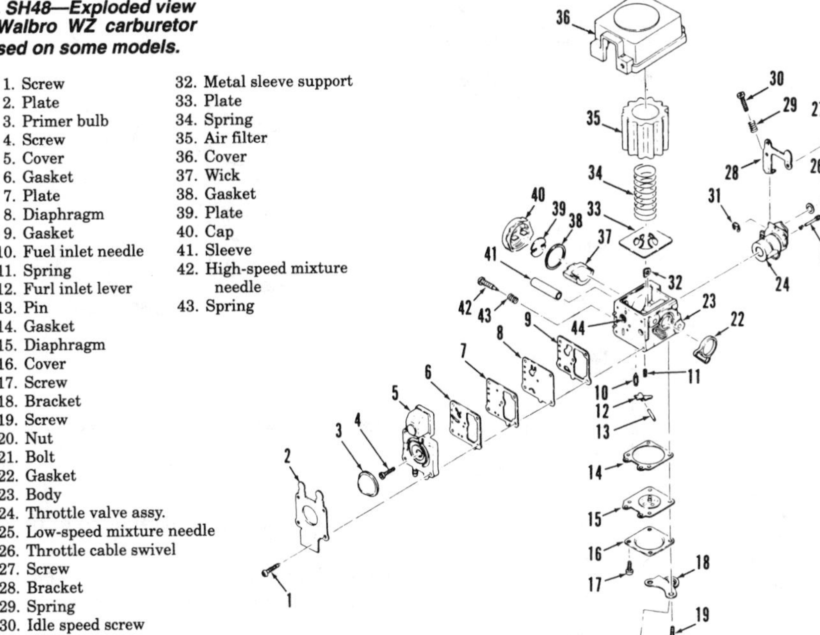

Fig. SH48—Exploded view of Walbro WZ carburetor used on some models.

1. Screw
2. Plate
3. Primer bulb
4. Screw
5. Cover
6. Gasket
7. Plate
8. Diaphragm
9. Gasket
10. Fuel inlet needle
11. Spring
12. Furl inlet lever
13. Pin
14. Gasket
15. Diaphragm
16. Cover
17. Screw
18. Bracket
19. Screw
20. Nut
21. Bolt
22. Gasket
23. Body
24. Throttle valve assy.
25. Low-speed mixture needle
26. Throttle cable swivel
27. Screw
28. Bracket
29. Spring
30. Idle speed screw
31. "E" ring
32. Metal sleeve support
33. Plate
34. Spring
35. Air filter
36. Cover
37. Wick
38. Gasket
39. Plate
40. Cap
41. Sleeve
42. High-speed mixture needle
43. Spring

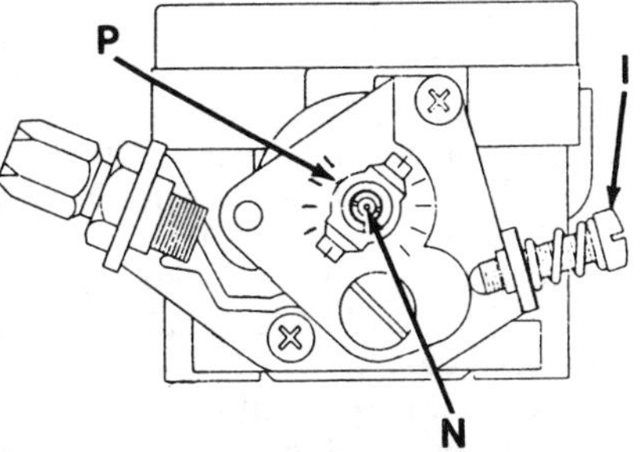

Fig. SH49—Metering lever height can be measured by placing a straightedge across the small pads in the carburetor body as shown, then measuring the gap with a feeler gauge.

cover (16) and plate (5). Remove screws retaining throttle barrel assembly (24) and withdraw throttle barrel from carburetor body.

Clean and inspect all components. Use caution if using commercial carburetor cleaner to prevent the harsh cleaner from causing damage. If the unit has been improperly stored, passages may be clogged with deposits that are hard, solid and nearly transparent. Be careful not to damage the openings or sealing surfaces while cleaning. Check the condition of diaphragms (8 and 15) carefully. Install new diaphragms if hard (not flexible), torn or otherwise damaged. Examine the fuel inlet valve (10), spring (11) and lever (12). New fuel inlet valve needle (10) and mixture adjustment needles (if so equipped) can be installed, but their seats cannot be serviced if damaged.

Some carburetors are equipped with a primer bulb (3). Install a new bulb if hard, cracked or otherwise damaged.

Check the height of the metering lever using Walbro tool 500-13. End of metering lever should just touch the leg of the tool. If tool is not available, use a straightedge and feeler gauge to measure the lever height as shown in Fig. SH50. Refer to Table 1 for sorrect lever height. Carefully bend the lever to obtain the correct lever height.

Fig. SH50—Place a straightedge across carburetor body to check metering lever height.

TK Series. Refer to Fig. SH51, Fig. SH52 or Fig. SH53 for typical exploded views of the types used. All models are not equipped with a low speed mixture need (21–Fig. SH51). If so equipped, refer to Table 1 at the end of this section for recommended initial setting. The idle mixture needle controls the idle air and tuning the needle clockwise reduces the amount of air, enriching the idle mixture. Recommended initial setting for the high speed mixture needle (18–Fig. SH51, Fig. SH52 or Fig. SH53) is listed in Table 1. Mixtures in Table 1 indicated as N/A are not adjustable. Leakage around the seal (14–Figure. SH53) will lean the mixture causing engine damage.

Clip (10–Fig. SH51, Fig. SH52 or Fig. SH53) should be installed in the center groove of the needle (9). The po-

Fig. SH51—Exploded view of TK diaphragm carburetor with choke (42) typical of one type used. Refer Fig. SH52 and Fig. SH53 for other similar TK models.

1. Air filter cover
2. Gasket
3. Screen
4. Bracket
5. Filter
6. Screen
7. Housing
8. Throttle valve
9. Fuel needle
10. Clip
11. Spring seat
12. Spring
13. Cap
14. Nut
15. Throttle cable adjuster
16. Spring
17. Idle speed screw
18. High-speed mixture needle
19. Spring
20. Spring
21. Low-speed mixture needle
22. "O" ring
23. Tube
24. Body
25. Spring
26. Fuel inlet needle
27. Fuel inlet lever
28. Pin
29. Screw
30. Gasket
31. Metering diaphragm
32. Cover
33. Screw
34. Sealing rings
35. Fuel pump plate
36. Gasket
37. Fuel pump diaphragm
38. Fuel pump cover
39. Screws
40. Stud
41. Choke lever
42. Choke plate
43. Washer
44. Nut

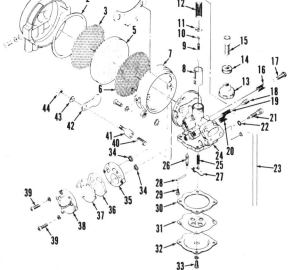

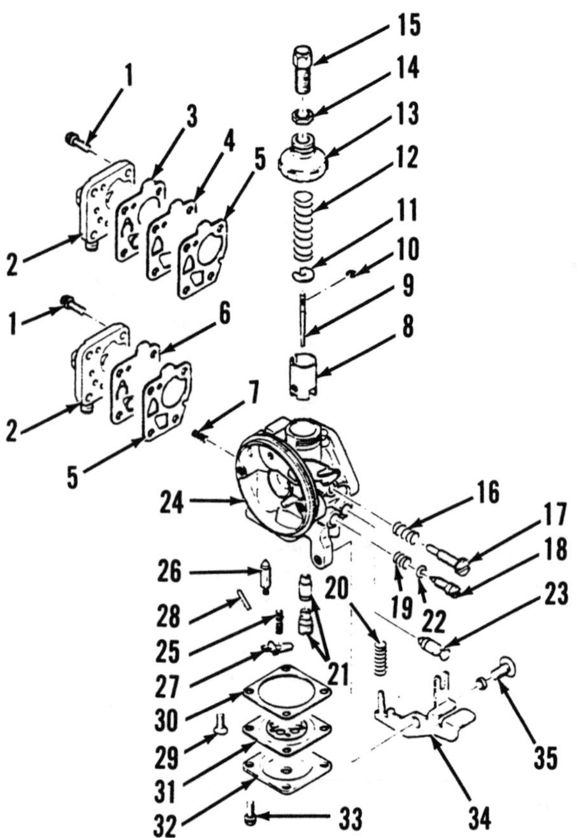

Fig. SH52—Exploded view of TK diaphragm carburetor with integral primer (23) typical of one type used. Gaskets and diaphragms (3, 4, 5 & 6) are not the same for all models. Refer also to Fig. SH51 and Fig. SH53 for other TK models.

1. Screws
2. Cover
3. Gasket with check valves
4. Fuel pump diaphragm
5. Gasket
6. Gasket
7. Check valve
8. Throttle valve
9. Fuel needle
10. Clip
11. Spring seat
12. Spring
13. Cap
14. Nut
15. Throttle cable adjuster
16. Spring
17. Idle speed screw
18. High-speed mixture needle
19. Spring
20. Primer spring
21. Needle jet assy.
22. "O" ring
23. Priming valve
24. Body
25. Spring
26. Fuel inlet needle
27. Fuel inlet lever
28. Pin
29. Screw
30. Gasket
31. Metering diaphragm
32. Cover
33. Screw
34. Priming lever
35. Pivot screw

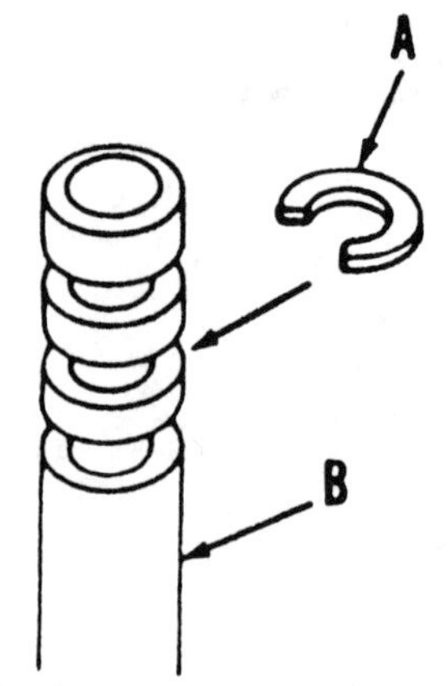

Fig. SH54—Fuel needle clip should be installed in the center groove.

sition of the clip controls the midrange mixture. Positioning the clip in a groove closer to the top will lean the mixture or closer to the bottom will enrich the mixture.

To disassemble the carburetor, remove screw (15—Fig. SH53) or unscrew cap (13—Fig. SH51 or Fig. SH52), then withdraw the throttle assembly. To disengage the cable from the throttle slide (8—Fig. SH51, Fig. SH52 or Fig. SH53), squeeze the slide and cap together compressing spring (12). Push the cable to the side allowing it to be withdrawn from the throttle slide. Complete the remainder of disassembly using Fig. SH51, Fig. SH52 or Fig. SH53 as a guide.

Clean and inspect all parts for wear or other damage. Inspect the fuel inlet needle (26) and install a new needle if the tip is worn or grooved. Compare the spring (25) with a new spring and install a new spring if it is questionable. Diaphragms should be soft and flexible with no rips or tears.

Install the fuel valve, spring and metering lever (27). Measure the lever height using a straightedge and feeler gauge as shown in Fig. SH50. Refer to Table 1 for setting height. Be very careful if it is necessary to bend the lever to correct the lever height. Install the clip (10—Fig. SH51, Fig. SH52 or Fig. SH53) in the center groove of the needle as shown in Fig. SH54.

On models with primer shown in Fig. SH52, tension of spring (20) should close the primer valve (23). If the primer lever (34—Fig. SH52) is made of red plastic, do not attempt to bend the lever. If necessary, metal primer levers can be bent at the location shown in Fig. SH55.

IGNITION SYSTEM. These engines are equipped with a transistorized (TCI) ignition system. On some models, the TCI igniter parts are potted

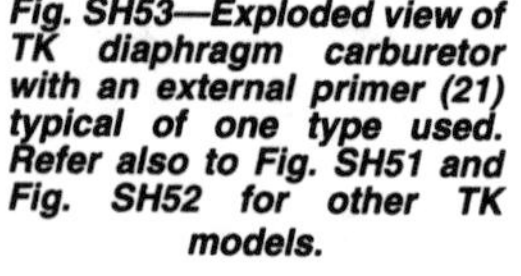

Fig. SH53—Exploded view of TK diaphragm carburetor with an external primer (21) typical of one type used. Refer also to Fig. SH51 and Fig. SH52 for other TK models.

1. Screws
2. Cover
3. Gasket with check valves
4. Fuel pump diaphragm
5. Gasket
6. Cover
7. Check valve assy.
8. Throttle valve
9. Fuel needle
10. Clip
11. Spring seat
12. Spring
13. Cap
14. Seal
15. Screw
16. Spring
17. Idle speed screw
18. High-speed mixture needle
19. Spring
20. Gasket
21. Primer bulb assy.
22. "O" ring
23. Hose
24. Body
25. Spring
26. Fuel inlet needle
27. Fuel inlet lever
28. Pin
29. Screw
30. Gasket
31. Metering diaphragm
32. Cover
33. Screw

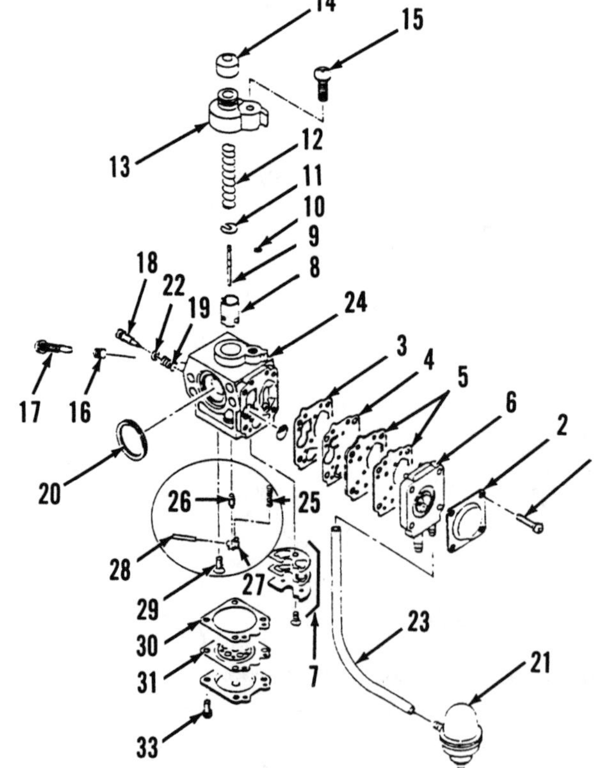

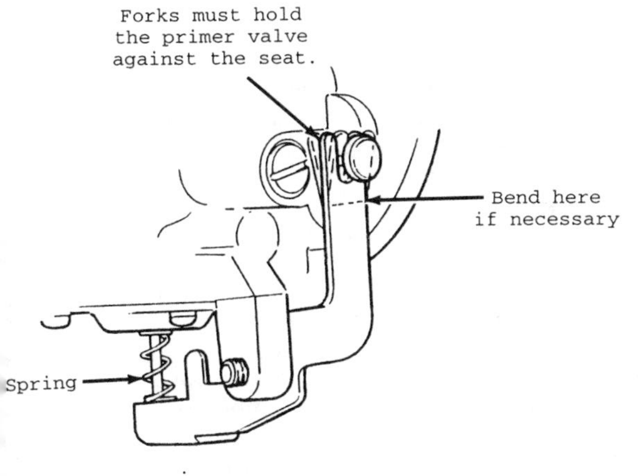

Fig. SH55—The primer valve should be held against its seat by the spring and lever. If the lever is made of plastic, do not attempt to bend it.

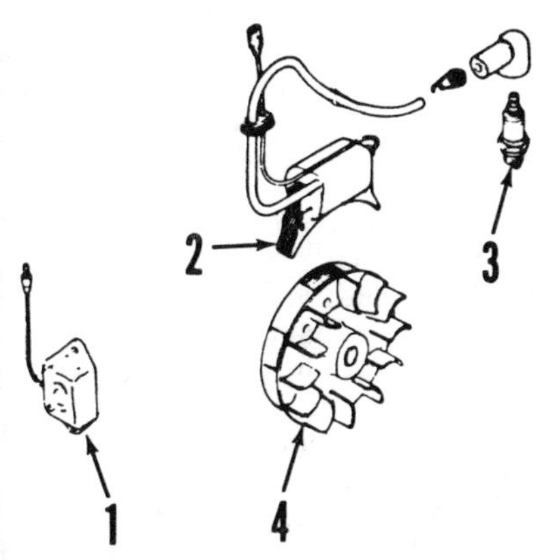

Fig. SH56—Exploded view of ignition system components.

1. Igniter
2. Coil
3. Spark plug
4. Flywheel (rotor)

in a separate metal or plastic case (1—Fig. SH56). On other models, the igniter components are combined with the ignition coil (2).

The solid-state electrical components are easily damaged by heat. If insulators are installed between the separate igniter unit or the coil, make sure these insulators are reinstalled and in good condition. When installing, set the air gap between the flywheel magnets and the legs of the ignition coil as follows. Install the ignition coil, but tighten the two screws only enough to hold it in place away from the flywheel. Insert 0.012-0.014 in. (0.30-0.35 mm) thick brass or plastic shim stock between the legs of the coil and the flywheel, then turn the flywheel until the flywheel magnets are near the coil legs. Loosen the screws attaching the ignition coil and press coil against the shim stock, then tighten the two attaching screws to the torque listed in the TIGHTENING TORQUE paragraph. Remove the shim stock, then turn the flywheel and check to be sure the flywheel does not hit the legs of the coil.

REPAIRS

COMPRESSION PRESSURE. For optimum performance, compression pressure should be above 85 psi (586 kPa) for all models. Compression test should be performed with the engine at operating temperature and both throttle and choke (if so equipped) wide open. The cylinders are hard-chrome plated and cannot be bored to a larger size.

TIGHTENING TORQUE. Recommended tightening torque values are as follows.

Carburetor attaching screws . . . . 35-44 in.-lb. (4-5 N•m)

Carburetor adapter to cylinder
- F-18, T-18, F-20, T-20, BP-35, C-35, B-40, C-230 and T-230 . . . . 35-44 in.-lb. (4-5 N•m)*
- C-25, T-25, C-27, T-27, B-45, RC-45, C-250 and T-250 . 44-52 in.-lb. (5-6 N•m)*

Clutch shoe . . . . 60-90 in.-lb. (7-10 N•m)

Crankcase halves
- BP-35, C-35 and B-40 . . . 60-70 in.-lb. (7-8 N•m)
- B-45 and RC-45. . . . . 60-70 in.-lb. (7-8 N•m)*
- Other models. . . . . 44-60 in.-lb. (5-7 N•m)

Cylinder to crankcase
- BP-35, C-35, B-40, B-45 and RC-45. . . . . 60-70 in.-lb. (7-8 N•m)***
- Other models. . . . . 44-60 in.-lb. (5-7 N•m)***

Cylinder cover . . . . 13-22 in.-lb. (1.5-2.2 N•m)

Starter hub/crankshaft
- BP-35, C-35, B-40, B-45 and RC-45. . . . . . 105-120 in.-lb. (12-14 N•m)
- Other models. . . . . 104-122 in.-lb. (12-14 N•m)

Flywheel
- BP-35, C-35, B-40, B-45 and RC-45. . . . . . 175-218 in.-lb. (20-25 N•m)
- Other models. . . . . 104-122 in.-lb. (12-14 N•m)

Ignition coil
- BP-35, C-35, B-40, B-45 and RC-45. . . . . 44-52 in.-lb. (5-6 N•m)*
- Other models. . . . . 35-44 in.-lb. (4-5 N•m)*

Muffler
- F-18 and T-18 . . . . 52-70 in.-lb. (6-8 N•m)**
- C-250, T-250, C-25, T-25 and C-27 . . . . 52-70 in.-lb. (6-8 N•m)*
- F-20, T-20, C-230 and T-230. . . . . 44-60 in.-lb. (5-7 N•m)**
- BP-35, C-35 and B-40 . . . 80-90 in.-lb. (9-10 N•m)**
- B-45 and RC-45. . . . . . . 90-105 in.-lb. (10-12 N•m)**

Spark plug. . . . . 148-160 in.-lb. (17-19 N•m)

Starter housing
- F-18 and T-18 . . . . 13-22 in.-lb. (1.5-2.5 N•m)*
- C-25, T-25, C-27, T-27, C-250 and T-250 . . . . 26-35 in.-lb. (3-4 N•m)*
- BP-35, C-35, B-40, B-45 and RC-45. . . . . 26-44 in.-lb. (3-5 N•m)

Starter hub
- F-18, T-18, F-20, T-20, C-25, T-25, C-27, T-27, C-230, T-230, C-250 and T-250. . . . . 104-122 in.-lb. (12-14 N•m)*
- BP-35, C-35, B-40, B-45 and RC-45. . . . . . 105-120 in.-lb. (12-14 N•m)

* Coat threads with Three Bond 1401 or equivalent locking agent.
** Coat threads with Three Bond 1360 or equivalent locking agent.
*** Coat threads with Three Bond Liquid Screw Lock or equivalent.

PISTON, PIN AND RINGS. The piston is equipped with two rings. The rings are prevented from rotating by a pin installed in each groove of the piston. Make certain the ring end gaps are aligned with the locating pins before the cylinder is installed over the piston and rings.

Before removing the piston, refer to the CYLINDER paragraphs and remove the cylinder. Clean the piston top and locate the arrow cast onto the crown. The arrow should point toward the engine's exhaust port and muffler.

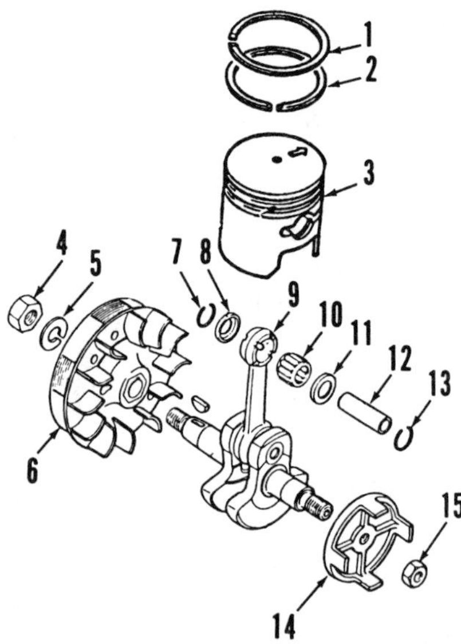

Fig. SH57—Exploded view of the crankshaft and connecting rod assembly.

1. Top ring
2. Second ring
3. Piston
4. Nut
5. Washer
6. Flywheel
7. Retainer
8. Thrust washer
9. Connecting rod & crankshaft assy.
10. Bearing
11. Thrust washer
12. Piston pin
13. Retainer
14. Starter drive hub
15. Nut

Remove both retaining rings (13—Fig. SH57) and press the pin from the piston. The pin should be a tight fit in the piston. When disassembling, note the location of the thrust washers (8 and 11). These thrust washers control connecting rod end play.

Remove rings from the piston and clean all parts thoroughly, being careful not to damage parts by harsh cleaning. It is suggested that new piston rings (1 and 2) and pin retaining rings (7 and 13) be installed if these parts are removed from the piston. Inspect the cylinder bore, piston and rings for scuffing or evidence of other damage. Side clearance of each ring in the piston groove should not exceed 0.008 in. (0.20 mm). Clearance between the piston and cylinder should not exceed 0.00118-0.00472 in. (0.03-0.12 mm). It is recommended that a new piston and cylinder be installed at the same time.

Inspect the piston pin (12), bearing (10), thrust washers (8 and 11) and connecting rod for evidence of overheating, scuffing or other damage. Install new parts as required.

Before installing new rings in the piston grooves, insert the ring into the cylinder bore. Use the bottom of the piston to square the ring in the cylinder and measure the gap between the ends of the ring with a feeler gauge. Gap should not exceed 0.0028 in. (0.07 mm). The standard end gap with new parts is 0.0008 in. (0.02 mm). If the gap is excessive with a new piston ring, install a new cylinder.

Make sure the arrow on the top of the piston points toward the exhaust side of the engine when the piston is installed. The ends of the rings will catch in the exhaust port if the piston is installed incorrectly. New pin retaining rings (7 and 13) should be installed if removed. Install the piston pin retaining rings (7 and 13) with the opening either toward the top or bottom of the piston. If the retaining ring comes out of the groove, the piston, rings and cylinder will be extensively damaged.

When assembling the piston to the connecting rod, install one of the retaining rings (7 or 13) in the piston. Install the piston pin part way into the piston from the side without the retaining ring. Lubricate the bearing (10) and thrust washers (8 and 11), then position the bearing and thrust washers in the connecting rod. Position the piston over the connecting rod and bearing with the arrow on top of piston pointing toward the exhaust side of the engine. Press the piston pin through the thrust washers, bearing, connecting rod and piston. Stop pressing the pin when it contacts the previously installed retainer ring. Install the remaining pin retaining ring (7 or 13) with the opening either to the top or bottom of the piston. Install the piston rings in the piston grooves and make sure the ends of the rings are aligned with the locating pins. Manufacturer's marks on the side of ring (if present) should be toward the top. Lubricate the piston and rings before installing the cylinder.

CYLINDER. To remove the cylinder, remove any interfering cowling, spark plug, carburetor and muffler. Remove the four screws attaching the cylinder to the crankcase, then pull the cylinder **straight up** away from the piston. Be careful to prevent dirt, broken parts or other items from falling into the opened crankcase. Do not damage the piston and connecting rod as the cylinder is lifted off.

The hard-chrome cylinder bore cannot be repaired. If the cylinder is damaged, install a new cylinder. It is recommended that a new piston and cylinder be installed at the same time so the new part will not be worn prematurely by the remaining old part. Refer to the PISTON, PIN AND RINGS paragraphs for inspection procedures.

Carbon can be removed from the cylinder ports if carefully done using plastic or wood tools only. Do not scratch, gouge or otherwise remove any metal while cleaning the carbon. Remove all of the old cylinder base gasket from the cylinder and the crankcase before assembling. Avoid scratching or gouging the soft aluminum surfaces. Baked on gasket material can be softened using commercial paint remover or gasket removal solvent.

Install the cylinder base gasket against the crankcase. The gasket must be installed **DRY**. Lubricate the cylinder, piston and rings before installing. Make sure the ends of the rings are aligned with the locating pins. Compress the rings with the proper size and type of ring compressor or with your fingers and carefully install the cylinder **straight** down. Do not twist the cylinder when installing, because the rings will catch in the ports and break. Coat the cylinder base screws with Three Bond Liquid Screw Lock or equivalent, then install and tighten the retaining screws to the torque listed in TIGHTENING TORQUE paragraph.

CRANKSHAFT, CONNECTING ROD AND CRANKCASE. Refer to Fig. SH57. The crankshaft and connecting rod are available only as an assembly. The pieces of the crankshaft are pressed together with connecting rod and correct alignment is critical. Dropping, pounding or any attempt to separate the crankshaft will damage the crankshaft assembly. The crankshaft seals can be removed without removing the crankshaft using a screw type puller (part No. 22150-96600) that fits over the crankshaft.

To remove the crankshaft and connecting rod assembly, first remove cylinder and piston as described in the CYLINDER paragraphs and the PISTON, PIN AND RINGS paragraphs. Remove the clutch assembly from the flywheel as described in the CLUTCH paragraphs, then use a puller that attaches to the threaded holes in the flywheel to remove the flywheel. Remove the Woodruff key from the crankshaft. Do not attempt to remove the flywheel by striking the crankshaft or flywheel. Remove the screws that attach the crankcase halves together, hold the half that is toward the rear (starter) and strike the projections on the front (magneto) half to separate. The crankcase halves are located by two dowel pins and the crankshaft main bearings.

NOTE: It may be necessary to heat the crankcase around the main bearing areas before the crankcase halves can be separated. Attempting to separate the halves by prying may damage the sealing surfaces of the case halves or disturb the alignment of the crankshaft.

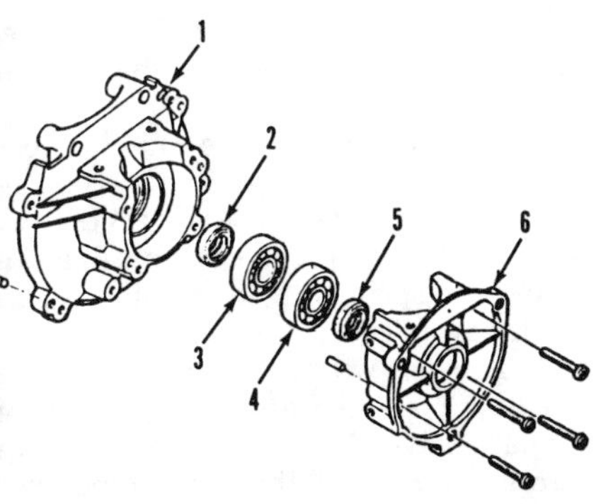

Fig. SH58—Exploded view of the crankcase assembly.

1. Crankcase half (magneto)
2. Seal
3. Main bearing
4. Main bearing
5. Seal
6. Crankcase half (starter)

Fig. SH59—Exploded views of 2-shoe, 3-shoe and 4-shoe clutches.

1. Shoulder bolt
2. Shoe
3. Thrust washer
4. Spring
5. Spring
6. Shoulder bolt
7. Shoe
8. Thrust washer
9. Screw
10. Allen bolt
11. Plate
12. Spring
13. Shoe
14. Clutch hub

Remove the crankshaft seals (2 and 5—Fig. SH58) and main bearings (3 and 4) if new seals and bearings are being installed. Use an appropriate puller to remove the main bearings. Clean the crankcase halves and crankshaft main journals, then carefully inspect all sealing surfaces for nicks, gouges or other damage. Inspect and if necessary repair all surfaces of the crankshaft and crankcase that contact the main bearings for nicks gouges or other condition that would interfere with smooth operation of the bearings. Inspect the Woodruff key and keyway in the crankshaft and in flywheel for any damage. Install new parts as necessary.

Inspect the mating tapers on crankshaft and in flywheel for damage. Inspect the connecting rod for evidence of overheating, excessive looseness or roughness. Inspect the threaded ends of the crankshaft for damaged threads. Install the crankshaft between lathe centers and measure crankshaft runout with a dial indicator at the main bearings. Measured runout should be less than 0.0008 in. (0.02 mm). If runout exceeds 0.0028 in. (0.07 mm), install a new crankshaft and connecting rod assembly.

If new main bearing is being installed, heat the crankcase half and use a bearing driver that contacts the outer race to press bearing until it just bottoms in bore. Allow the crankcase and bearing to cool and check the bearing for smooth rotation.

Fill the open cavity of the new seal with light grease, then press the seal into its bore until the outer (closed) side of the seal is flush with the crankcase. If the outside of seal case is rubber coated, the seal should be assembled dry. Apply a light coat of Three Bond 1304 or equivalent to the outside of seal case if it is not coated.

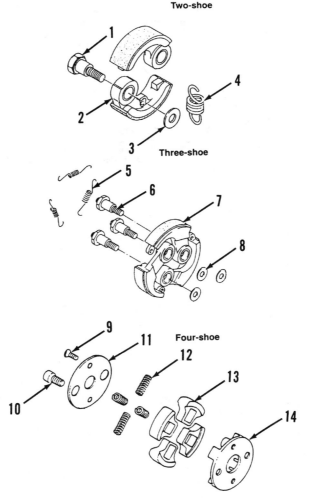

Clean the mating surfaces of the crankcase halves with acetone or other similar cleaner, then coat surfaces lightly and evenly with Three Bond Liquid Gasket or equivalent high-temperature liquid gasket. Be careful that sealer does not enter bearings, threaded holes or other unwanted areas. Protect the seal from damage and insert the crankshaft into the magneto side crankcase half. Tap the crankshaft lightly if necessary to make sure it is seated against the main bearing. Install the rear (starter) half of the case over the crankshaft and carefully slide the halves together. When the case halves are nearly together, tap the crankcase with a soft-faced hammer to make sure the cases are fully seated. Coat threads of screws that join crankcase halves with Three Bond Liquid Screw Lock. Install the screws and tighten to the torque listed in TIGHTENING TORQUE paragraphs. Turn the crankshaft and check for any roughness.

Make sure the mating tapers of the crankshaft and flywheel are clean and dry, then install the Woodruff key in the crankcase keyway. Install the flywheel and tighten the retaining nut to the torque listed in TIGHTENING TORQUE paragraphs. Refer to PISTON, PIN AND RINGS and CYLINDER paragraphs for installing these components. Install the clutch assembly as described in the CLUTCH paragraphs.

CLUTCH. Refer to Fig. SH59. A two shoe clutch is used on F-18, T-18, C-20, F-20, T-20, F-21, C-25, T-25, C-27, T-27, BP-35, C-230, F-230, T-230, C-250 and T-250 models. A three shoe clutch is used on B-45 and RC-45. A four shoe clutch is used on B-40 models. Model C-35 may be equipped with two, three or four shoe clutch.

To remove the clutch assembly, first remove the fan cover. On models with two shoes, remove the shoulder bolts (1). Do not lose the washers (3). Inspect the holes in shoes for spring (4) and bolts (1). Install new parts as necessary. The clutch shoes can be installed as either trailing shoe or leading shoe orientation as shown in Fig. SH60. Installation as leading shoe will result in faster engagement with the least amount of slippage, especially at slower engine speeds. There may be slight chatter during initial engagement. When shoes are installed as trailing shoe, engagement will be smoother, but slippage resulting in faster wear may occur at slower engine speeds. For most applications, shoes should be installed as leading shoe shown on the right in Fig. SH60.

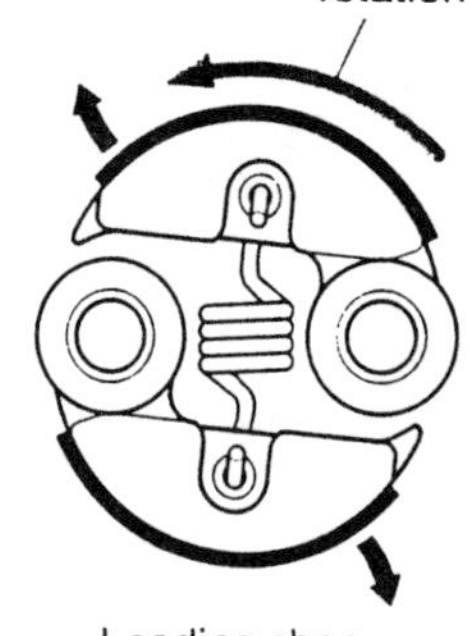

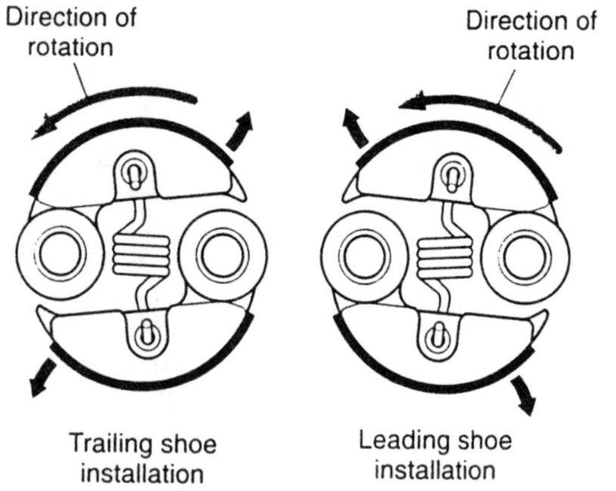

Fig. SH60—Clutches with two-shoes can be assembled with trailing shoes as shown at the left or with leading shoes as shown at the right. Refer to the text.

On models with three clutch shoes remove the clutch springs (5), then remove the shoulder bolts (6). Do not lose the washers (8). Inspect the holes in shoes for springs (5) and bolts (6). Install new parts as necessary.

On models with four clutch shoes, remove the flywheel and fan, then use an impact driver to remove the two countersunk screws (9) that attach the cover plate (11). After removing the cover plate, use an Allen wrench and remove the screws (10) attaching the clutch body (14) to the flywheel.

REWIND STARTER. Refer to the Trimmer Service Section for servicing the rewind starter.

Table 1

Model	Carb. Make	Carb. Model	Idle Mixture	Main Mixture	Lever Height
S-18					
(early)	Walbro	WY	7-8**	...	1.4-1.6 mm (0.054-0.064 in.)
(late)	TK	WYP-DPK8W	N/A	1 1/2*	2.1 mm (0.083 in.)
S-20					
Brushcutter (C-20)					
(early)	Walbro	WZ8C	...	...	1.4-1.6 mm (0.054-0.064 in.)
(late)	TK	DPV10W	N/A	1 3/4-2 1/4*	2.1 mm (0.083 in.)
Curved shaft trimmer (F-20)	Walbro	WA 135	1 1/8*	1 1/8*	1.4-1.6 mm (0.054-0.064 in.)
Trimmer with gear case (T-20)					
(early)	Walbro	WZ8C	5-6**	1 1/2*	1.4-1.6 mm (0.054-0.064 in.)
(late)	TK	DPV10W	N/A	1 3/4-2 1/4*	2.1 mm (0.083 in.)
S-21	Walbro	WY24B	N/A	N/A	1.4-1.6 mm (0.054-0.064 in.)
S-25					
Brushcutter (C-25)	TK	DP10W	0-1/2*	1 1/2-2 1/2*	1.4 mm (0.055 in.)
Trimmer with gearcase (T-25)	TK	DP10W	0-1/2*	2 1/4-2/3/4*	1.4 mm (0.055 in.)
S-27					
Trimmer with gearcase (T-27)	TK	DPV10W	0-1/2*	2 1/4-2/3/4*	1.4 mm (0.055 in.)
Brushcutter (C-27)	TK	DPV10W	0-1/2*	1 3/4-2 1/4*	1.4 mm (0.055 in.)
S-35					
Backpack (BP-35)	TK	PC10HW	N/A	N/A	3 mm (0.120 in.)
Brushcutter (C-35)	TK	DPV11W	0-1/2*	1 3/4-2 1/4*	2.1 mm (0.083 in.)
S-40					
Brushcutter (B-40)	TK	DPW13	0-3/4*	2 1/2-3*	1.4 mm (0.055 in.)
S-45					
Brushcutter (B-45)	TK	DPW12	0-3/4*	2 1/2-3*	1.4 mm (0.055 in.)
Brushcutter (RC-45)	TK	DPV1W1E	1/4*	2 1/4*	2.1 mm (0.083 in.)
S-230	Walbro	WYL-19	12-13**	Jet	1.4-1.6 mm (0.054-0.064 in.)
S-250	TK	DP-N10W	N/A	1 3/4-2 1/4*	2.1 mm (0.083 in.)

* Turns OUT (counterclockwise) from lightly seated position.
** Turns IN (clockwise) from initial thread engagement. Screw does not contact a seat.

STIHL

ENGINE SERVICE

Model	Bore	Stroke	Displacement
015	38.0 mm (1.50 in.)	28.0 mm (1.10 in.)	32.0 cc (1.96 cu. in.)

ENGINE INFORMATION

Stihl 015 series engines are used on Stihl string trimmers and brushcutters. Refer to following sections for other Stihl engine models.

MAINTENANCE

SPARK PLUG. Recommended spark plug for 015 series engine is a Bosch WKA175T6, or equivalent. Specified electrode gap should be 0.5 mm (0.020 in.).

CARBURETOR. A Walbro Model HDC diaphragm carburetor is used on 015 series engine. Initial adjustment of idle and high speed mixture needles from a lightly seated position is 3/4 turn open. Adjust idle speed screw until engine idles just below clutch engagement speed. Final adjustment should be made with engine at operating temperature and running. Adjust high speed mixture needle to obtain optimum performance with trimmer line at recommended length or blade assembly installed. Adjust idle mixture needle to obtain smooth idle and good acceleration.

Refer to Fig. SL50 for an exploded view of Walbro Model HDC carburetor. Use caution when disassembling carburetor not to lose ball (13) and spring (14) as choke shaft is removed.

Clean and inspect all parts. Inspect diaphragms for defects which may affect operation. Examine fuel inlet needle and seat. The needle is renewable, but carburetor body must be renewed if needle seat is excessively worn or damaged. Sharp objects should not be used to clean orifices or passages as fuel flow may be altered. Compressed air should not be used to clean main nozzle as check valve may be damaged. A check valve repair kit is available to renew a damaged valve. Fuel mixture needles must be renewed if grooved or broken. Inspect mixture needle seats in carburetor body and renew body if seats are damaged or excessively worn. Screens should be clean.

To reassemble carburetor, reverse disassembly procedure. Fuel metering lever should be flush with a straightedge laid across carburetor body as shown in Fig. SL51. Make certain lever spring correctly contacts locating dimple on lever before measuring lever height. Carefully bend lever to obtain correct height.

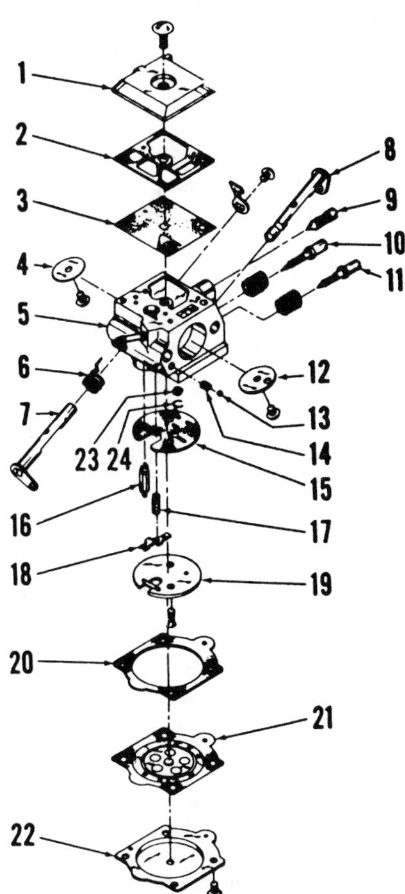

Fig. SL50—Exploded view of Walbro Model HDC diaphragm type carburetor.

1. Pump cover
2. Gasket
3. Fuel pump diaphragm & valves
4. Throttle plate
5. Body
6. Return spring
7. Throttle shaft
8. Choke shaft
9. Idle speed screw
10. Idle mixture needle
11. High speed mixture needle
12. Choke plate
13. Choke friction ball
14. Spring
15. Gasket
16. Fuel inlet valve
17. Spring
18. Diaphragm lever
19. Circuit plate
20. Gasket
21. Metering diaphragm
22. Cover
23. Check valve screen
24. Retainer

IGNITION SYSTEM. Model 015 engine may be equipped with a conventional flywheel magneto ignition system or a breakerless transistor ignition system. Refer to the appropriate paragraph for model being serviced.

Flywheel Magneto Ignition. Ignition breaker point gap should be 3.5-4.0 mm (0.014-0.016 in.). Ignition timing is not adjustable except by adjusting breaker point gap. Ignition timing should occur when piston is 2.2 mm (0.09 in.) BTDC. Magneto edge gap ("E" gap) shown in Fig. SL52 should be 3.0-7.5 mm (0.12-0.29 in.). Magneto edge gap may be adjusted slightly by loosening flywheel nut and rotating flywheel on crankshaft as there is a small clearance between flywheel groove and crankshaft key.

Air gap between ignition coil and flywheel should be 0.5 mm (0.020 in.). Ignition coil windings may be checked using an ohmmeter. Primary winding should have 0.8-1.3 ohms resistance and secondary winding should have 7200-8800 ohms.

Transistor Ignition System. Some models are equipped with a Bosch breakerless transistor ignition system. Ignition should occur when piston is 2.2 mm (0.087 in.) BTDC. Ignition timing may be adjusted slightly by loosening

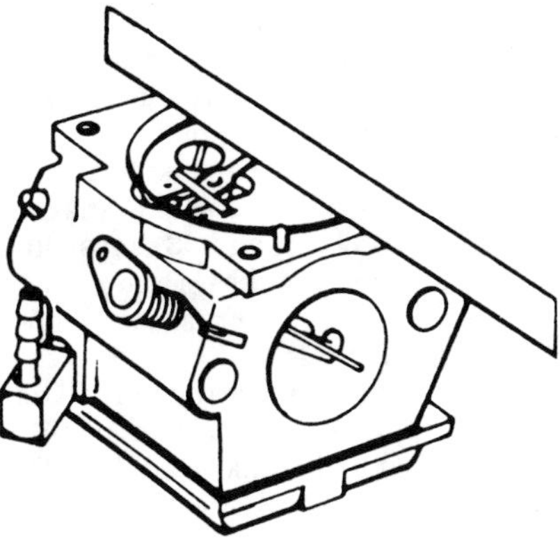

Fig. SL51—Diaphragm lever should just touch a straightedge placed across carburetor body as shown.

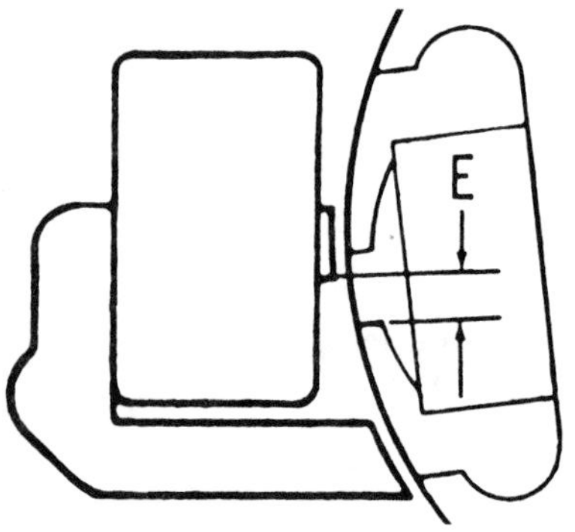

Fig. SL52—Magneto edge gap (E) should be 3.0-7.5 mm (0.12-0.29 in.).

flywheel nut and rotating flywheel on crankshaft as there is a small clearance between flywheel groove and crankshaft key.

Recommended air gap between ignition coil armature legs and flywheel is 0.15-0.2 mm (0.006-0.008 in.). Loosen ignition coil mounting screws and move ignition coil to adjust air gap.

LUBRICATION. The engine is lubricated by mixing gasoline with a good quality two-stroke air-cooled engine oil. Refer to TRIMMER SERVICE section for correct fuel/oil mixture ratio recommended by trimmer manufacturer.

REPAIRS

CRANKSHAFT AND SEALS. The crankshaft is supported in needle bearings (10 and 12—Fig. SL53) held between the cylinder and front crankcase half. Care should be taken when removing cylinder as crankshaft will be loose in crankcase and connecting rod may slide off bearing rollers (7) allowing them to fall into crankcase.

Large diameter needle bearing (10), retaining ring (9) and seal (8) on later models must be installed on flywheel end of crankshaft while smaller diameter bearing retaining ring and seal must be installed on clutch end. Some models are also equipped with thrust washers (T) located between crankshaft bearings and crankshaft. Bearings, retaining rings and seals on early models have the same outer diameter and may be installed on either end of crankshaft. Retaining rings (9 and 13) must fit in ring grooves of crankcase and cylinder. Tighten cylinder-to-crankcase screws to 7 N·m (60 in.-lbs.).

Before reassembling crankcase halves, apply a light coat of nonhardening sealant to crankcase mating surfaces.

CONNECTING ROD. To remove connecting rod, remove crankshaft as

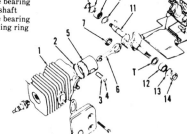

Fig. SL53—Exploded view of engine. Thrust washers (T) are used on late models.

T. Thrust washer
1. Cylinder
2. Piston ring
3. Piston pin
4. Pin retainer
5. Piston
6. Connecting rod
7. Bearing rollers (12)
8. Oil seal
9. Retaining ring
10. Needle bearing
11. Crankshaft
12. Needle bearing
13. Retaining ring
14. Oil seal
15. Crankcase
16. Gasket
17. Handle assy.
18. Oil pick-up

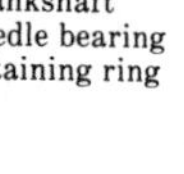

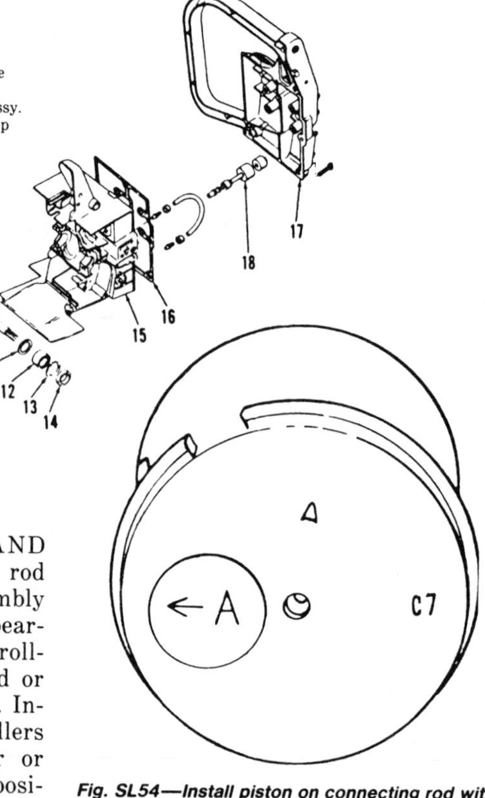

outlined in CRANKSHAFT AND SEALS paragraphs. Connecting rod (6—Fig. SL53) is a one-piece assembly supported on crankpin by 12 loose bearing rollers. Make certain bearing rollers are not lost as connecting rod or crankshaft is removed or handled. Inspect connecting rod, bearing rollers and crankpin for excessive wear or damage. Hold bearing rollers in position with heavy grease during reassembly. Make certain all twelve bearing rollers are in position before assembling crankcase.

CYLINDER, PISTON, PIN AND RINGS. Cylinder and front crankcase are one-piece. Crankshaft and bearings are loose when the cylinder is removed. Care must be taken not to damage mating surfaces of crankcase halves during disassembly.

Cylinder head is integral with cylinder. Piston is equipped with a single piston ring and the piston pin rides directly in the piston and small end of connecting rod. Cylinder bore is chrome plated and should be inspected for damage or excessive wear. Cylinder (1—Fig. SL53) and front crankcase half (15) are available only as a complete assembly.

Piston pin (3) must be installed with closed end of pin toward "A" side of piston crown shown in Fig. SL54 and piston must be installed with "A" side toward exhaust port in cylinder. Piston and piston pin are available in standard sizes only.

Refer to CRANKSHAFT AND SEALS paragraphs for assembly of crankcase and cylinder.

REWIND STARTER. Refer to Fig. SL55 for exploded view of pawl type rewind starter used on all models. Care should be taken if it is necessary to remove rewind spring (3) to prevent spring from uncoiling uncontrolled.

Fig. SL54—Install piston on connecting rod with "A" on piston crown towards exhaust port in cylinder.

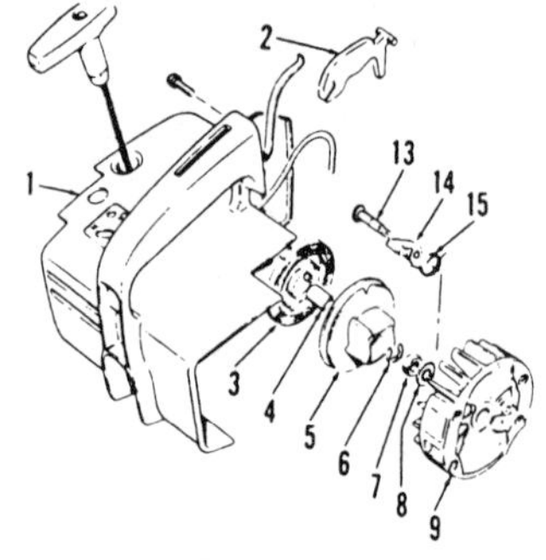

Fig. SL55—Exploded view of rewind starter.

1. Rear housing
2. Trigger interlock
3. Rewind spring
4. Bushing
5. Rope pulley
6. "E" ring
7. Flywheel nut
8. Washer
9. Flywheel
13. Stud
14. Pawl
15. Spring

Rewind spring must be wound in clockwise direction in housing. Wind starter rope in clockwise direction around rope pulley (5) as viewed with pulley installed in starter housing. Turn rope pulley 3-4 turns in clockwise direction before passing rope through rope outlet to place tension on rewind spring. To check spring tension, pull starter rope to full length. It should be possible to rotate rope pulley in clockwise direction with rope fully extended.

Starter pawl studs (13) are driven into flywheel. To renew pawl stud or spring, remove flywheel, then drive stud out of flywheel. Apply "Loctite" to stud before installation.

Illustrations courtesy Stihl Inc.

STIHL

ENGINE SERVICE

Model	Bore	Stroke	Displacement
O20*	38.0 mm (1.50 in.)	28.0 mm (1.10 in.)	32.0 cc (1.96 cu. in.)
O41	44.0 mm (1.73 in.)	40.0 mm (1.57 in.)	61.0 cc (3.72 cu. in.)

* Some O20 engines have a displacement of 35.0 cc (2.13 cu. in.).

ENGINE INFORMATION

Stihl O20 and O41 series engines are sed on Stihl string trimmers and rushcutters. Refer to preceding and ollowing sections for other Stihl enine models.

MAINTENANCE

SPARK PLUG. Recommended park plug for all models is a Bosch VSR6F, or equivalent. Specified elecrode gap should be 0.5 mm (0.020 in.).

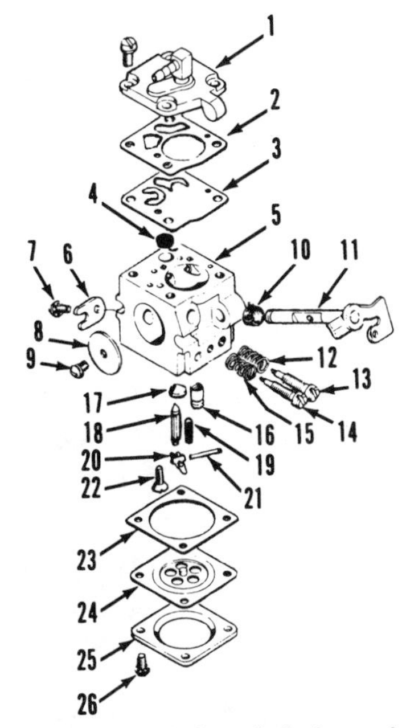

Fig. SL60—Exploded view of diaphragm type carburetor used on all models.

1. Pump cover
2. Gasket
3. Diaphragm
4. Screen
5. Body
6. Clip
7. Screw
8. Throttle plate
9. Screw
10. Spring
11. Throttle shaft
12. Spring
13. High speed mixture needle
14. Low speed mixture needle
15. Spring
16. Check valve
17. Welch plug
18. Fuel inlet needle
19. Spring
20. Fuel inlet lever
21. Pin
22. Screw
23. Gasket
24. Diaphragm
25. Cover
26. Screw

CARBURETOR. A diaphragm type carburetor is used on all models (Fig. SL60). Initial adjustment of low and high speed mixture needles for O20 engine is 1-1/4 turns open from a lightly seated position. Initial adjustment of O41 engine low and high speed mixture needles from a lightly seated position is 1-1/4 turns open for low speed mixture needle and 7/8 turn open for the high speed mixture needle.

To disassemble carburetor, refer to Fig. SL60. Clean filter screen (4). Welch plugs (18 and 24—Fig. SL61) may be removed by drilling plug with a suitable size drill bit, then pry out as shown in Fig. SL62. Care must be taken not to drill into carburetor body.

Inspect inlet lever spring (19—Fig. SL60) and renew if stretched or damaged. Inspect diaphragms for tears, cracks or other damage. Renew low and high speed mixture needles if needle points are grooved or broken. Carburetor body must be renewed if needle seats are damaged. Fuel inlet needle has a rubber tip which seats directly on a machined orifice in carburetor body. Inlet needle or carburetor body should be renewed if worn excessively.

Adjust position of inlet control lever so lever is flush with diaphragm chamber floor as shown in Fig. SL63. Bend lever adjacent to spring to obtain correct position.

IGNITION SYSTEM. Engine may be equipped with a conventional magneto type ignition system, a Bosch capacitor discharge ignition system or a Sems transistorized ignition system. Refer to the appropriate paragraph for model being serviced.

Magneto Ignition System. Ignition breaker point gap should be set at 3.5-4.0 mm (0.014-0.016 in.). Ignition timing is adjusted by loosening stator mounting screws and rotating stator plate. Ignition timing should occur when piston is 2.0-2.3 mm (0.08-0.087 in.) BTDC for O20 engine or 2.4-2.6 mm (0.095-0.102 in.) BTDC for O41 engine.

Ignition coil air gap should be 4-6 mm (0.16-0.24 in.) for O20 engine or 0.2-0.3 mm (0.008-0.012 in.) for O41 engine.

Ignition coil primary and secondary windings may be checked using an ohmmeter. Primary winding resistance should register 1.5-1.9 ohms for O20 engine, 1.9-2.5 ohms for O41 engine with Bosch date code 523 or 1.2-1.7

18 24

Fig. SL61—View showing location of Welch plugs (18 and 24).

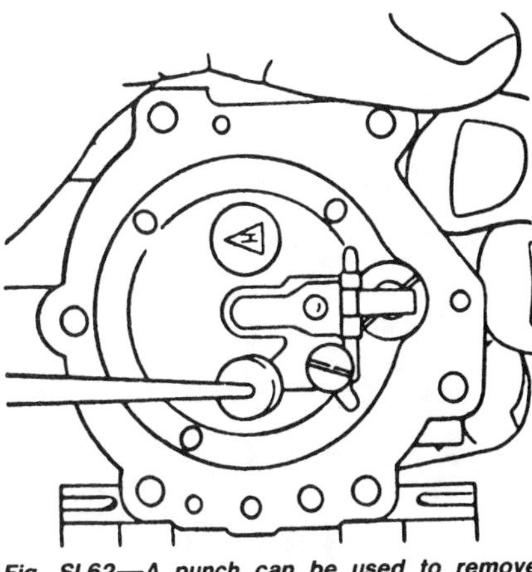

Fig. SL62—A punch can be used to remove Welch plugs after drilling a hole in plug. Refer to text.

Illustrations courtesy Stihl Inc.

ohms for O41 engine with Bosch date code 524.

Bosch Breakerless Ignition System. Ignition module air gap should be 0.2-0.3 mm (0.008-0.012 in.). Ignition should occur when piston is 2.5 mm (0.098 in.) BTDC.

Sems Breakerless Ignition System. Ignition module air gap should be 0.2-0.3 mm (0.008-0.012 in.). Ignition should occur when piston is 2.5 mm (0.098 in.) BTDC.

Ignition module primary and secondary windings may be checked using an ohmmeter. Primary winding resistance should be 0.4-0.5 ohms. Secondary winding resistance should be 2.7-3.3k ohms.

LUBRICATION. All Models are lubricated by mixing gasoline with a good quality two-stroke air-cooled engine oil. Refer to TRIMMER SERVICE section for correct fuel/oil mixture ratio recommended by trimmer manufacturer.

REPAIRS

TIGHTENING TORQUES. Recommended tightening torque specifications are as follows:

Clutch nut . . . . 39 N·m (29 ft.-lbs.)
Clutch hub . . . . 34 N·m (25.3 ft.-lbs.)
Clutch hub carrier (O20) . . . 28 N·m (21 ft.-lbs.)
Flywheel nut:
O20 . . . . 24 N·m (18 ft.-lbs.)
O41 . . . . 35 N·m (26 ft.-lbs.)

CRANKSHAFT AND SEALS. All models are equipped with a split type crankcase from which cylinder may be removed separately (Fig. SL64 and SL65). It may be necessary to heat crankcase halves slightly to remove main bearings if they remain in crankcase during disassembly.

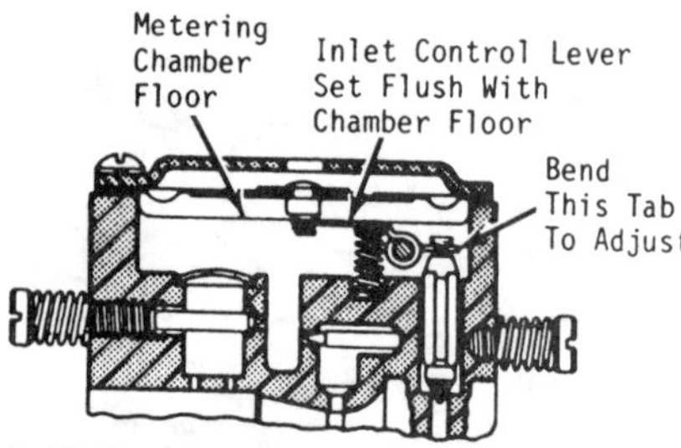

Fig. SL63—Diaphragm lever should be flush with fuel chamber floor as shown.

CONNECTING ROD. The connecting rod and crankshaft are considered an assembly and individual parts are not available separately. Do not remove connecting rod from crankshaft.

Connecting rod big end rides on a roller bearing and should be inspected for excessive wear or damage. If rod, bearing or crankshaft is damaged, complete crankshaft and connecting rod assembly must be renewed.

CYLINDER, PISTON, PIN AND RINGS. The aluminum alloy piston is equipped with two piston rings. The floating piston pin is retained in the piston with a snap ring at each end. The pin bore of the piston is unbushed; t connecting rod has a caged needle roll piston pin bearing.

Cylinder bore and cylinder head a cast as one-piece. The cylinder assem bly is available only with a fitted pi ton. Pistons and cylinders are groupe into different size ranges with approx mately 0.0005 mm (0.0002 in.) diffe ence between each range. Each group marked with letters "A" to "E". Lett "A" denotes smallest size with "E being largest. The code letter i stamped on the top of the piston and o the top of the cylinder. The code lett of the piston and the cylinder must b the same for proper fit of a new pisto

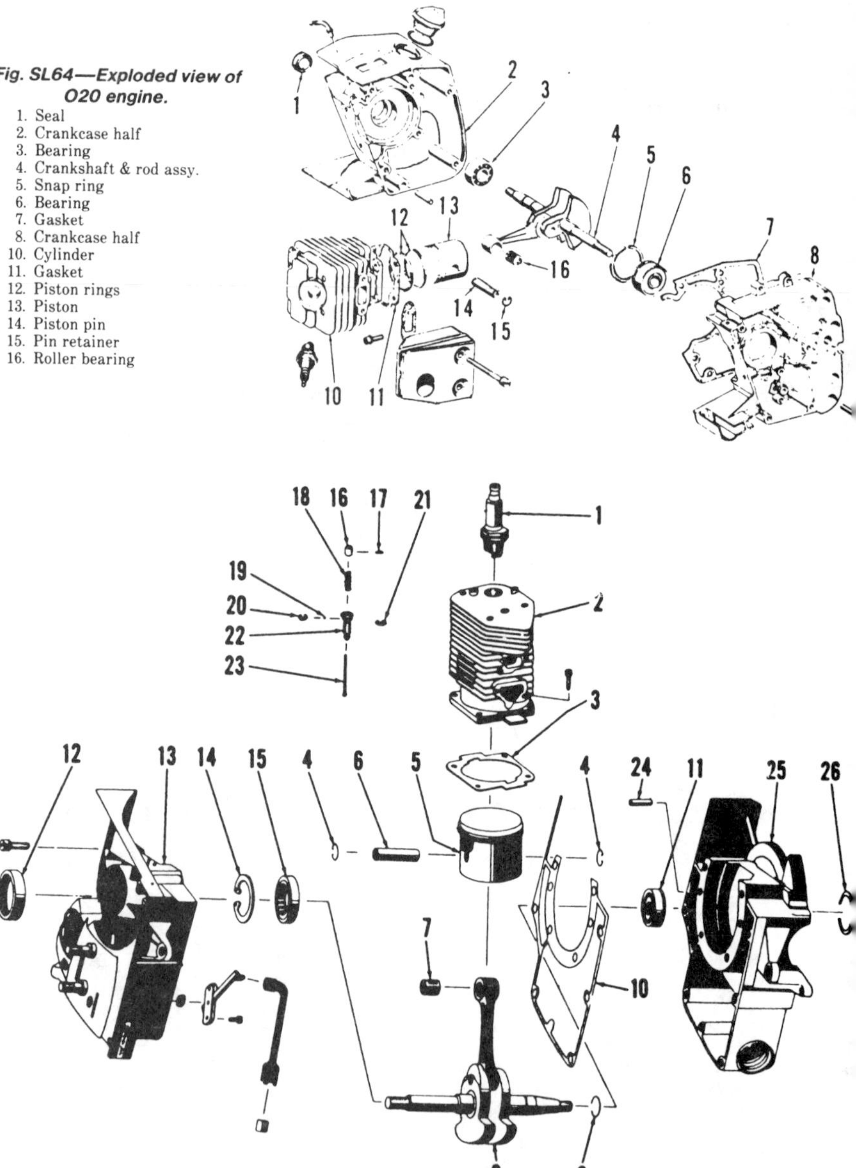

Fig. SL64—Exploded view of O20 engine.

1. Seal
2. Crankcase half
3. Bearing
4. Crankshaft & rod assy.
5. Snap ring
6. Bearing
7. Gasket
8. Crankcase half
10. Cylinder
11. Gasket
12. Piston rings
13. Piston
14. Piston pin
15. Pin retainer
16. Roller bearing

Fig. SL65—Exploded view of O41 engine.

1. Spark plug
2. Cylinder
3. Head gasket
4. Snap ring
5. Piston
6. Piston pin
7. Bearing
8. Crankshaft & rod assy.
9. Snap ring
10. Gasket
11. Bearing
12. Seal
13. Crankcase half
14. Snap ring
15. Bearing
16. Knob
17. Pin
18. Spring
19. Pin
20. Spring
21. Tab washer
22. Housing
23. Plunger
24. Pin
25. Crankcase half
26. Snap ring

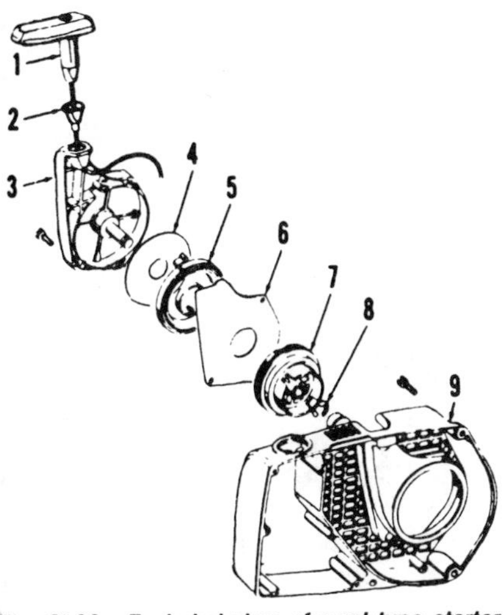

Fig. SL66—Exploded view of pawl type starter used on O20 engine.

1. Rope handle
2. Bushing
3. Housing
4. Washer
5. Rewind spring
6. Cover
7. Rope pulley
8. "E" ring
9. Fan housing

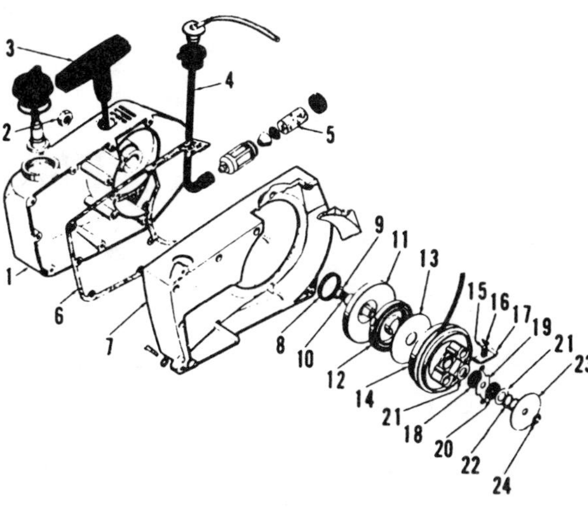

Fig. SL67—Exploded view of typical rewind starter used on O41 engine.

1. Fuel tank
2. Nut
3. Rope handle
4. Fuel pick-up
5. Filter
6. Gasket
7. Fan cover
8. Felt ring
9. Spring washer
10. Pulley shaft
11. Cover
12. Rewind spring
13. Washer
14. Rope pulley
15. Spring
16. Spring retainer
17. Friction shoe
18. Slotted washer
19. Brake lever
20. Slotted washer
21. Washer
22. Spring
23. Washer
24. "E" ring

in a new cylinder. However, new pistons are available for installation in used cylinders. Used cylinders with code letters "A" or "B" may use piston with code letter "A". Used cylinder with code letters "A", "B" or "C" may use piston with code letter "B". Used cylinder with code letters "B", "C" or "D" may use piston with code letter "C". Used cylinder with code letters "C", "D" or "E" may use piston with code letter "D". Used cylinder with code letters "D" or "E" may use piston with code letter "E".

Cylinder bore on all models is chrome plated. Cylinder should be renewed if chrome plating is flaking, scored or worn away.

To reinstall piston on connecting rod, install one snap ring in piston. Lubricate the piston pin needle bearing with motor oil, then slide bearing into pin bore of connecting rod. Install piston on rod so that arrow on piston crown points toward exhaust port. Push piston pin in far enough to install second snap ring.

After piston and rod assembly is attached to crankshaft, rotate crankshaft to top dead center and support piston with a wood block that will fit between piston skirt and crankcase when cylinder gasket is in place. A notch should be cut in the wood block so that it will fit around the connecting rod. Lubricate piston and rings with motor oil, then compress rings with compressor that can be removed after cylinder is pushed down over piston. On some models it may be necessary to remove the cylinder and install an additional gasket between the cylinder and crankcase if piston strikes top of cylinder.

REWIND STARTER. Friction shoe type and pawl type starters have been used. Refer to Fig. SL66 for an exploded view of starter assembly used on O20 engine and to Fig. SL67 for an exploded view of starter assembly used on O41 engine. Refer to Fig. SL68 for proper method of assembly of friction shoe plates to starter brake lever on O41 engine starter.

To place tension on rope of starter shown in Fig. SL66 for O20 engine, pull starter rope, then hold rope pulley to prevent spring from rewinding rope on pulley. Pull rope back through rope outlet and wrap two additional turns of rope on pulley without moving pulley. Release pulley and allow rope to rewind. Rope handle should be pulled against housing, but spring should not be completely wound when rope is pulled to greatest length.

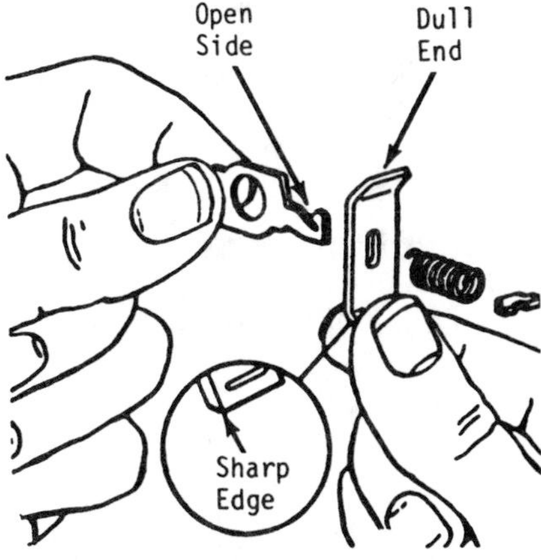

Fig. SL68—Illustration showing proper method of assembly of friction shoe plates to starter brake lever.

To place tension on O41 engine starter rope, pull rope out of handle until notch in pulley is adjacent to rope outlet, then hold pulley to prevent rope from rewinding. Pull rope back through outlet and out of notch in pulley. Turn rope pulley two turns clockwise and release rope back through notch. Check starter operation. Rope handle should be held against housing by spring tension, but spring should not be completely wound when rope is pulled to greatest length.

STIHL

ENGINE SERVICE

Model	Bore	Stroke	Displacement
O8S	47.0 mm (1.85 in.)	32.0 (1.26 in.)	56.0 cc (3.39 cu. in.)

ENGINE INFORMATION

Stihl O8S series engines are used on Stihl string trimmers and brushcutters. Refer to preceding sections for other Stihl engine models.

MAINTENANCE

SPARK PLUG. Recommended spark plug for O8S engine is a Bosch W175T7, or equivalent. Specified electrode gap should be 0.5 mm (0.020 in.).

CARBURETOR. O8S engine is equipped with a Tillotson diaphragm type carburetor. Initial adjustment of idle and high speed mixture needles is one turn open from a lightly seated position.

Final adjustments are made with trimmer line at recommended length or blade assembly installed. Engine should be at operating temperature and running. Adjust low speed mixture needle and idle speed screw until engine idles just below clutch engagement speed. Adjust high speed mixture needle to obtain optimum performance under load. Do not adjust high speed mixture needle too lean as engine may be damaged.

To disassemble carburetor, refer to Fig. SL70. Remove and clean filter screen (4). Welch plugs (18 and 24—Fig. SL71) can be removed by drilling plug with a suitable size drill bit, then pry out as shown in Fig. SL72. Care must be taken not to drill into carburetor body.

Inspect inlet lever spring (19—Fig. SL70) and renew if stretched or damaged. Inspect diaphragms for tears, cracks or other damage. Renew idle and high speed mixture needles if needle points are grooved or broken. Carburetor body must be renewed if needle seats are damaged. Fuel inlet needle has a rubber tip which seats directly on a machined orifice in carburetor body. Inlet needle or carburetor body should be renewed if worn excessively.

Inlet control lever should be adjusted so that control lever is flush with fuel chamber floor as shown in Fig. SL73. Carefully bend lever adjacent to spring to obtain correct position.

Fig. SL70—Exploded view of diaphragm type carburetor.

1. Pump cover
2. Gasket
3. Diaphragm
4. Screen
5. Body
6. Clip
7. Screw
8. Throttle plate
9. Screw
10. Spring
11. Throttle shaft
12. Spring
13. High speed mixture needle
14. Low speed mixture needle
15. Spring
16. Check valve
17. Welch plug
18. Fuel inlet needle
19. Spring
20. Fuel inlet lever
21. Pin
22. Screw
23. Gasket
24. Diaphragm
25. Cover
26. Screw

GOVERNOR. Model O8S is equipped with an air vane type governor. The governor linkage is attached to the carburetor choke shaft lever. Maximum speed is controlled by the air vane governor closing the choke plate.

Governed speed is adjusted by changing the tension of the governor spring. The adjusting plate is mounted to the engine behind the starter housing as shown in Fig. SL74. After maximum governed speed is adjusted at factory, position of spring is secured by a lead seal. If necessary to readjust governor, new position of governor spring should be sealed or wired securely. Maximum no load governed speed is 8000 rpm.

IGNITION SYSTEM. OS8 engine is equipped with a conventional magneto type igntion system.

Coil air gap should be 0.5 mm (0.020 in.). Ignition breaker point gap should be 3.5-4.0 mm (0.014-0.016 in.). Ignition timing is adjusted by loosening stator mounting screws and rotating stator plate. Ignition should occur when piston is 1.9-2.1 mm (0.075-0.083 in.) BTDC.

Coil primary and secondary windings may be checked using an ohmmeter. Primary winding resistance should be 1.9-2.5 ohms for Bosch coil with date code 523 or 1.2-1.7 ohms for Bosch coil with date code 524. Secondary winding resistance should be 5.0-6.7k ohms for

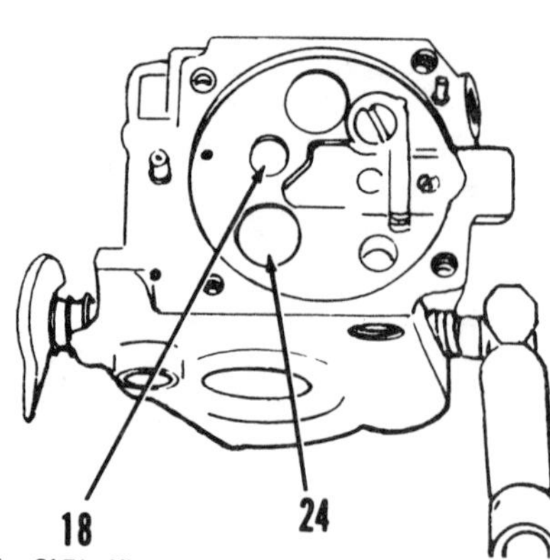

Fig. SL71—View showing location of Welch plugs (18 and 24).

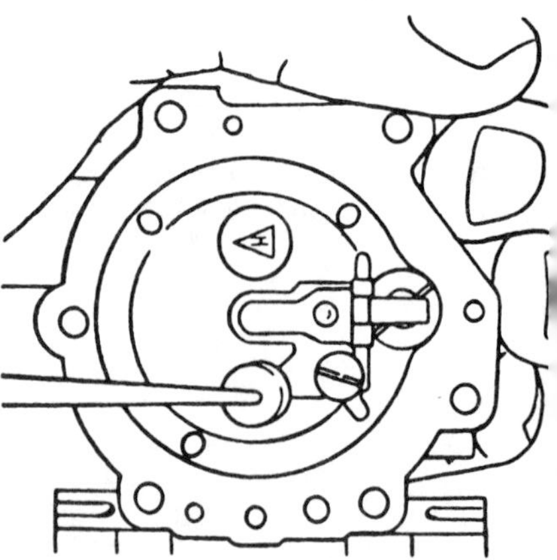

Fig. SL72—A punch can be used to remove Welch plugs after drilling a hole in plug. Refer to text.

Illustrations courtesy Stihl Inc.

Bosch coil with date code 523 or 5.0-6.7k ohms for Bosch coil with date code 524.

LUBRICATION. All Models are lubricated by mixing gasoline with a good quality two-stroke air-cooled engine oil. Refer to TRIMMER SERVICE section for correct fuel/oil mixture ratio recommended by trimmer manufacturer.

REPAIRS

TIGHTENING TORQUES. Recommended tightening torque specifications are as follows:

Clutch nut	34 N·m (25 ft.-lbs.)
Flywheel nut	29 N·m (21.7 ft.-lbs.)
Spark plug	24 N·m (18 ft.-lbs.)
Cylinder screws	10 N·m (7.2 ft.-lbs.)

CRANKSHAFT AND SEALS. All models are equipped with a split type crankcase from which cylinder may be removed separately (Fig. SL75). Crankshaft is supported at both ends in ball type main bearings and crankshaft end play is controlled by shims (11) installed between the bearing (10) and shoulders on the crankshaft on early models, or between bearing and crankcase on later models. Shims are available in a variety of thicknesses. Correct crankshaft end play is 0.2-0.3 mm (0.0008-0.012 in.). It may be necessary to heat crankcase halves slightly to remove main bearings if they remain in crankcase during disassembly.

CONNECTING ROD. The connecting rod and crankshaft are considered an assembly and individual parts are not available separately. Do not remove connecting rod from crankshaft.

Connecting rod big end rides on a roller bearing and should be inspected for excessive wear or damage. If rod, bearing or crankshaft is damaged, complete crankshaft and connecting rod assembly must be renewed.

CYLINDER, PISTON, PIN AND RINGS. The aluminum alloy piston is equipped with two piston rings. The floating piston pin is retained in the piston with a snap ring at each end. The pin bore of the piston is unbushed; the connecting rod has a caged needle roller piston pin bearing.

Cylinder bore and cylinder head are cast as one-piece. The cylinder is available only with a fitted piston. Pistons and cylinders are grouped into different size ranges with approximately 0.0005 mm (0.0002 in.) difference between each range. Each group is marked with letters "A" to "E". Letter "A" denotes smallest size with "E" being largest. The code letter is stamped on the top of the piston and on the top of the cylinder on all models. The code letter of the piston and the cylinder must be the same for proper fit of a new piston in a new cylinder. However, new pistons are available for installation in used cylinders. Used cylinders with code letters "A" or "B" may use piston with code letter "A". Used cylinder with code letters "A", "B" or "C" may use piston with code letter "B". Used cylinder with code letters "B", "C" or "D" may use piston with code letter "C". Used cylinder with code letters "C", "D" or "E" may use piston with code letter "D". Used cylinder with code letters "D" or "E" may use piston with code letter "E".

Cylinder bore on all models is chrome plated. Cylinder should be renewed if chrome plating is flaking, scored or worn away.

To reinstall piston on connecting rod, install one snap ring in piston. Lubricate the piston pin needle bearing with motor oil, then slide bearing into pin bore of connecting rod. Install piston on rod so that arrow on piston crown points toward exhaust port. Push piston pin in far enough to install second snap ring.

After piston and rod assembly is attached to crankshaft, rotate crankshaft to top dead center and support piston with a wood block that will fit between piston

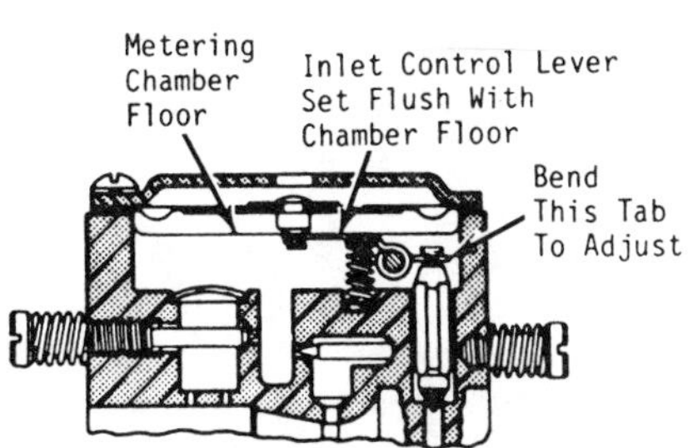

Fig. SL73—Diaphragm lever should be flush with fuel chamber floor as shown.

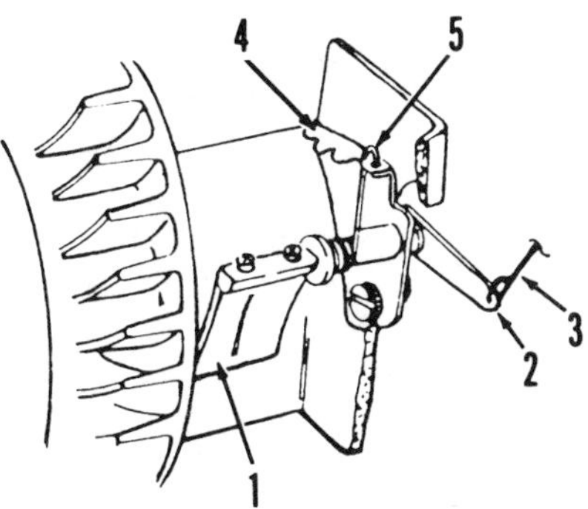

Fig. SL74—View of air vane type governor.

1. Air vane
2. Lever
3. Throttle link
4. Notched plate
5. Governor spring

Fig. SL75—Exploded view of O8S engine.

1. Spark plug
2. Cylinder
3. Head gasket
4. Snap ring
5. Piston pin
6. Piston
7. Crankcase half
8. Seal
9. Snap ring
10. Ball bearing
11. Shim
12. Gasket
13. Dowel pin
14. Crankcase half
15. Washer
16. Bearing
17. Crankshaft & rod assy.

Illustrations courtesy Stihl Inc.

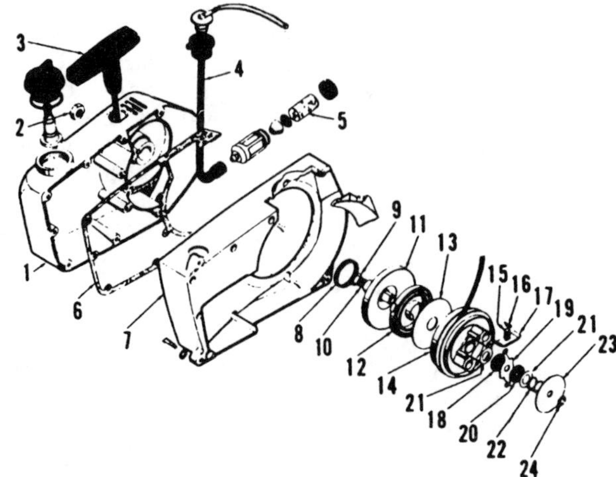

Fig. SL76—Exploded view of pawl type starter.

1. Fuel tank
2. Nut
3. Rope handle
4. Fuel pick-up
5. Filter
6. Gasket
7. Fan cover
8. Felt ring
9. Spring washer
10. Pulley shaft
11. Cover
12. Rewind spring
13. Washer
14. Rope pulley
15. Spring
16. Spring retainer
17. Friction shoe
18. Slotted washer
19. Brake lever
20. Slotted washer
21. Washer
22. Spring
23. Washer
24. "E" ring

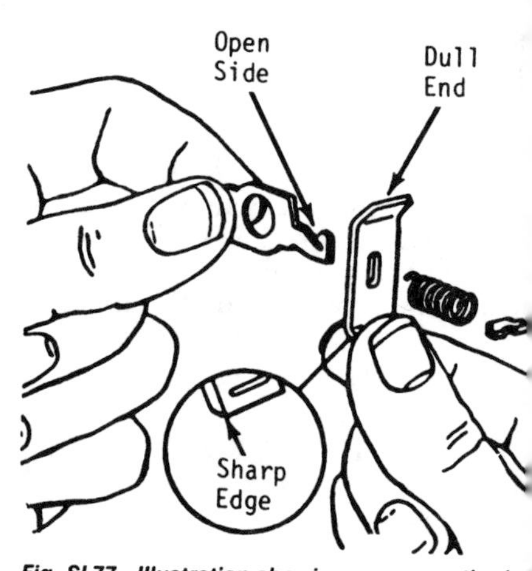

Fig. SL77—Illustration showing proper method of assembly of friction shoe plates to starter brake lever.

skirt and crankcase when cylinder gasket is in place. A notch should be cut in the wood block so that it will fit around the connecting rod. Lubricate piston and rings with motor oil, then compress rings with compressor that can be removed after cylinder is pushed down over piston. On some models it may be necessary to remove the cylinder and install an additional gasket between the cylinder and crankcase if piston strikes top of cylinder.

REWIND STARTER. O8S engine is equipped with a pawl type rewind starter assembly similar to Fig. SL76.

To place tension on engine starter rope, pull rope out of handle until notch in pulley is adjacent to rope outlet, then hold pulley to prevent rope from rewinding. Pull rope back through outlet and out of notch in pulley. Turn rope pulley two turns clockwise and release rope back through notch. Check starter operation. Rope handle should be held against housing by spring tension, but spring should not be completely wound when rope is pulled to greatest length.

Refer to Fig. SL77 for correct assembly of starter shoes on brake lever. Make certain assembly is installed as shown in exploded views and leading edges of friction shoes are sharp or shoes may not properly engage drum.

STIHL

ENGINE SERVICE

Model	Bore	Stroke	Displacement
Stihl	34.8 mm (1.37 in.)	31.8 mm (1.25 in.)	30.2 cc (1.9 cu. in.)

This engine is used on Stihl Models FS36, FS40 and FS44.

ENGINE INFORMATION

The Stihl engine covered in this section is a two-stroke, air-cooled, single-cylinder engine.

MAINTENANCE

LUBRICATION. Engine lubrication is obtained by mixing gasoline with an oil designed for two-stroke, air-cooled engines. Refer to trimmer or blower service section for manufacturer's recommended fuel:oil mixture ratio.

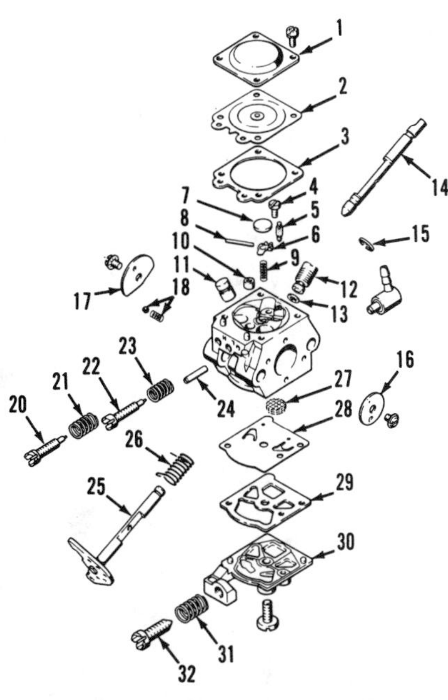

Fig. SL101—Exploded view of Walbro WT diaphragm carburetor.

1. Cover
2. Metering diaphragm
3. Gasket
4. Screw
5. Fuel inlet valve
6. Metering lever
7. Welch plug
8. Pin
9. Spring
10. Check valve
11. Fuel nozzle
12. Governor valve
13. "O" ring
14. Choke shaft
15. "E" ring
16. Throttle plate
17. Choke plate
18. Detent ball & spring
20. High-speed mixture screw
21. Spring
22. Idle speed mixture screw
23. Spring
24. Tube
25. Throttle shaft
26. Spring
27. Screen
28. Fuel pump diaphragm
29. Gasket
30. Fuel pump cover
31. Spring
32. Idle speed screw

SPARK PLUG. Recommended spark plug is AC CSR45, NGK BMR6A or equivalent. Specified electrode gap is 0.7-0.8 mm (0.028-0.031 in.). Tighten spark plug to 19 N·m (168 in.-lbs.).

CARBURETOR. The engine is equipped with a Walbro WT diaphragm-type carburetor. Refer to Fig. SL101 for an exploded view of carburetor. Initial adjustment of idle mixture screw (22) and high-speed mixture screw (20) is one turn open. Final adjustment is performed with engine at normal operating temperature and cutter line at desired length. Be sure air cleaner is clean before performing adjustments.

Adjust idle speed screw (32) clockwise until trimmer head begins to rotate, then turn screw counterclockwise one half turn. Trimmer head must not rotate when engine is at idle speed. Adjust idle mixture screw so engine idles smoothly and accelerates cleanly without hesitation. Readjust idle speed screw if necessary. Adjust high-speed mixture screw for best engine performance under load. Do not adjust high-speed mixture screw too lean as engine may be damaged.

Carburetor disassembly and reassembly is evident after inspection of carburetor and referral to Fig. SL101. Do not lose detent ball (18) when withdrawing choke shaft. Clean and inspect all components. Inspect diaphragms (2 and 28) for defects that may affect operation. Examine fuel inlet valve and seat. Inlet valve (5) is renewable, but carburetor body must be renewed if seat is damaged or excessively worn. Discard carburetor body if mixture screw seats are damaged or excessively worn. Clean fuel screen (27).

Press nozzle (11) into body until inner face is flush with bore as shown in Fig. SL102. Install choke plate (C) as shown in Fig. SL103. Install throttle plate (T) so hole (H) is toward metering chamber as shown in Fig. SL104. Apply Loc-

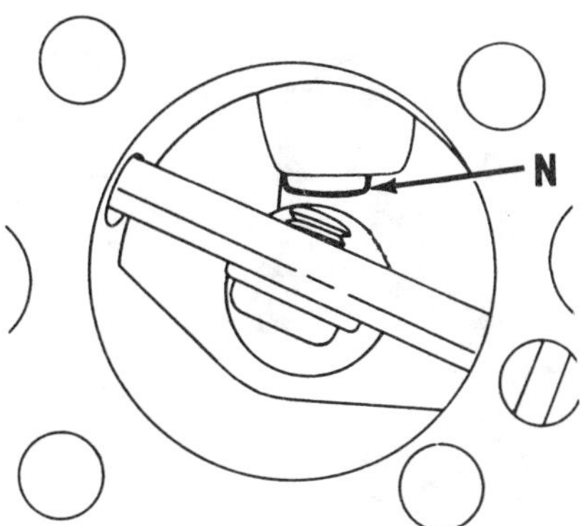

Fig. SL102—Install fuel nozzle (N) so inner face is flush with venturi bore.

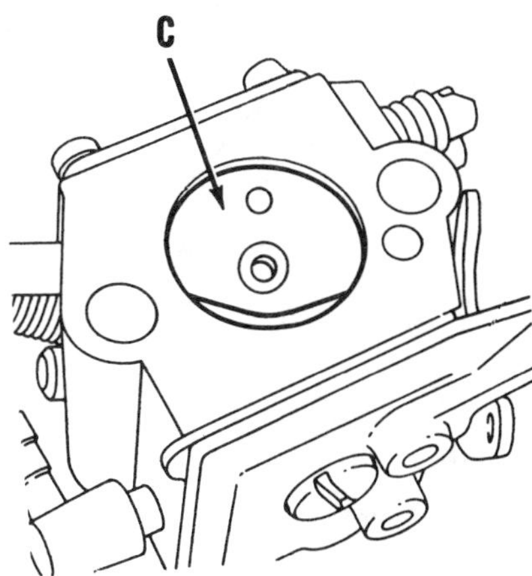

Fig. SL103—View showing correct installation of choke plate (C).

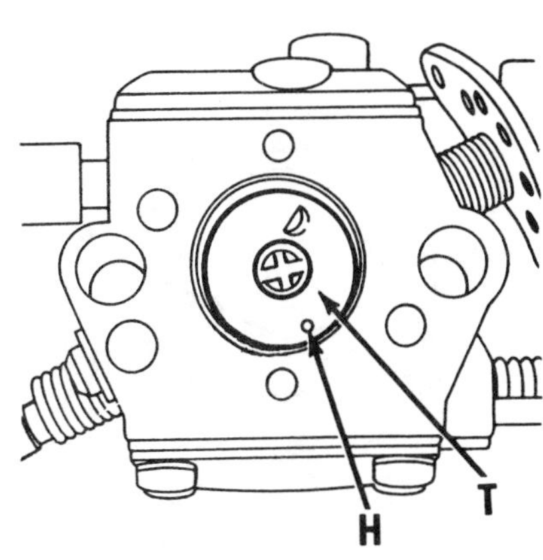

Fig. SL104—View showing correct installation of throttle plate (T). Hole (H) in plate must point toward metering chamber cover.

Illustrations courtesy Stihl Inc.

tite to choke and throttle plate retaining screws. Check metering lever height as shown in Fig. SL105 using Walbro tool 500-13. Metering lever should just touch leg on tool. Bend lever to obtain correct lever height. Install cover (1) so hole (H) is towards fuel inlet side of carburetor as shown in Fig. SL106.

The carburetor is equipped with a governor valve (12—Fig. SL101) that enriches the mixture at high speed to prevent overspeeding. The governor valve is not adjustable.

IGNITION SYSTEM. The engine is equipped with an electronic ignition system. Ignition system performance is considered satisfactory if a spark will jump across a 3 mm (1/8 in.) electrode gap on a test spark plug. If no spark is produced, check on/off switch, wiring and ignition module air gap. Air gap between ignition module and flywheel magnet should be 0.1-0.5 mm (0.004-0.020 in.). If switch, wiring and module air gap are satisfactory, but spark is not present, renew ignition module.

Tighten ignition module screws to 3.5 N•m (31 in.-lbs.).

Ignition timing should be 1.3-1.9 mm (0.05-0.07 in.) before top dead center at 6000 rpm. Ignition timing is not adjustable.

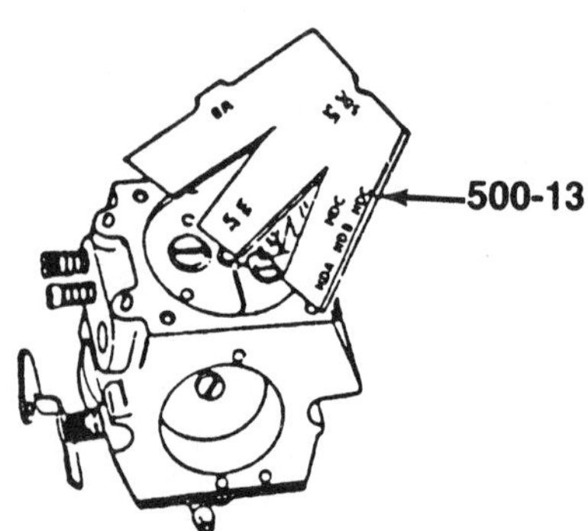

Fig. SL105—Leg of Walbro tool 500-13 should just touch metering lever.

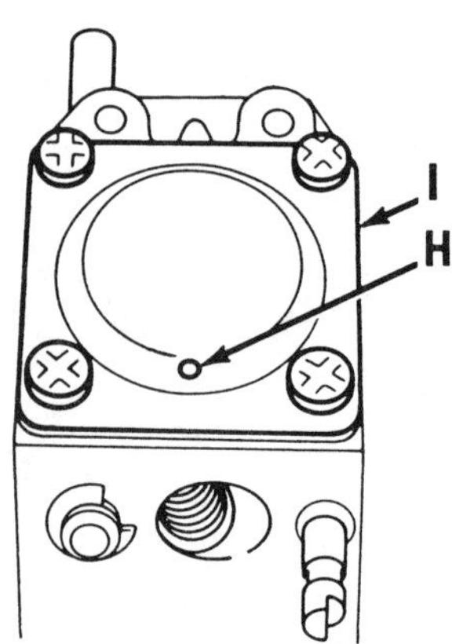

Fig. SL106—Install cover (1) so hole (H) is toward fuel inlet.

REPAIRS

TIGHTENING TORQUES. Recommended tightening torques values are as follows:

Carburetor	3.5 N•m (31 in.-lbs.)
Clutch hub	17 N•m (150 in.-lbs.)
Crankcase cover	5.5 N•m (49 in.-lbs.)
Cylinder	14 N•m (124 in.-lbs.)
Ignition module	3.5 N•m (31 in.-lbs.)
Muffler	6.5 N•m (57 in.-lbs.)
Spark plug	19 N•m (168 in.-lbs.)

PISTON, RINGS AND CONNECTING ROD. Piston and connecting rod (15—Fig. SL107) are serviced only as a unit assembly. The stamped steel connecting rod is equipped with a non-renewable roller bearing in the big end. Piston ring rotation is prevented by a locating p in the piston ring groove (Fig. SL108 Oversize pistons and piston rings are n available.

To remove piston and connecting ro assembly, first remove engine shrou fuel tank, carburetor and muffler. R move cylinder mounting screws and pu cylinder off piston. Unbolt and remov crankcase cover/reed block assemb (1—Fig. SL107). Pull connecting rod o crankshaft pin and remove piston an connecting rod assembly.

When installing piston and rod o crankpin, be sure cutaway portion piston skirt is toward crankshaft cou terweight (see Fig. SL109).

CYLINDER. The engine is equippe with a cylinder that has an impregna ed bore. Inspect cylinder for excessiv wear, scoring and other damage. Th cylinder is available only with a pisto and rod assembly.

When installing cylinder, be sure pis ton ring end gap properly surround

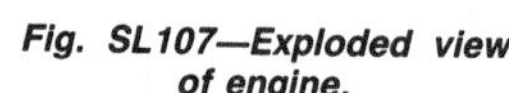

Fig. SL107—Exploded view of engine.

1. Crankcase cover
2. Reed valve
3. Reed stop
4. Gasket
5. Crankshaft
6. Key
7. Thrust washer
8. Bearing
9. Snap ring
10. Crankcase
11. Seal
12. Snap ring
13. Bearing
14. Shroud
15. Piston & rod assy.
16. Piston ring
17. Gasket
18. Cylinder

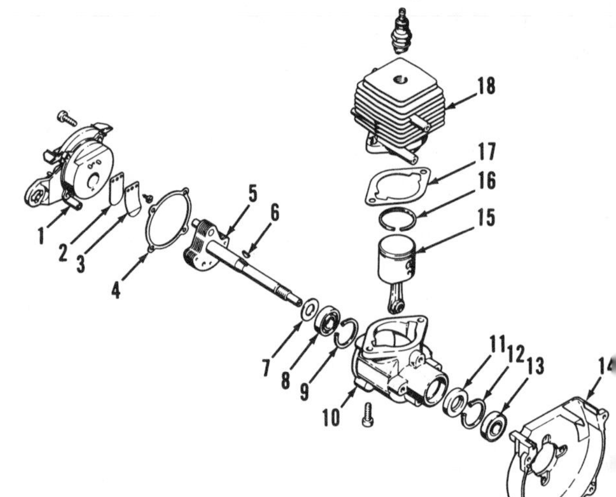

Fig. SL108—A pin prevents piston ring from rotating in ring groove. Ring end gap must be positioned around pin as shown.

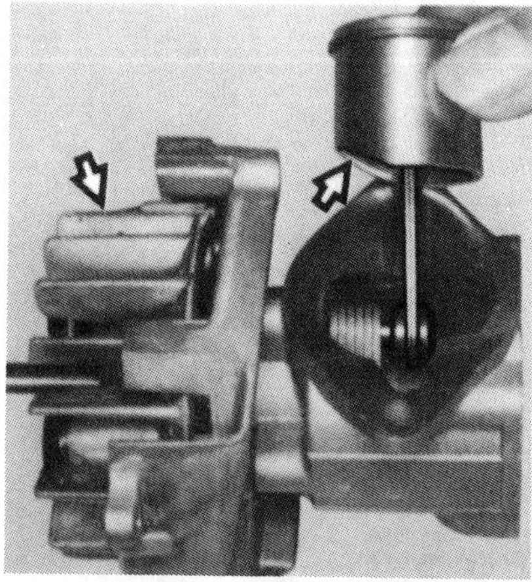

Fig. SL109—Piston skirt is cut away on one side to clear crankshaft counterweight and must be installed as shown.

Illustrations courtesy Stihl Inc.

locating pin in piston ring groove (Fig. SL108). Lubricate piston and cylinder bore with oil prior to assembly. The lower section of cylinder is tapered so piston ring is automatically compressed as cylinder is pushed over the piston.

CRANKSHAFT AND CRANKCASE. The crankshaft (5—Fig. SL107) is a cantilever design that is supported by two ball bearings (8 and 13).

To remove crankshaft, separate clutch housing and drive tube from engine. Be sure to unscrew hidden screw in center of clutch drum shaft and remove clutch drum. Use a suitable spanner wrench to unscrew clutch hub from crankshaft. See CLUTCH section. Remove crankcase cover (1), cylinder and piston. Remove flywheel and key from crankshaft. Press crankshaft out of main bearings. Heat crankcase to 212° F (100° C) to aid removal of bearings from crankcase.

When assembling crankcase, install snap ring (9) then install seal (4) so seal is against snap ring with lip toward inside of crankcase. Note that bearing (8) is open on both sides and that bearing should be pressed against snap ring (9). Install snap ring (12) and press bearing (13) against snap ring so shielded side faces outward. Install thrust washer (7) on crankshaft, then press crankshaft into main bearings. Install piston and rod assembly on crankshaft. Be sure cutaway portion of piston skirt is toward crankshaft counterweight (see Fig. SL109). Tighten crankcase cover screws to 5.5 N·m (49 in.-lbs.).

REED VALVE. A reed valve (2—Fig. SL107) is located on the inner face of the crankcase cover (1). Inspect reed petal and discard if torn, broken, creased or otherwise damaged.

CLUTCH. A two-shoe clutch (Fig. SL110) is used. The clutch hub (4) is threaded onto the crankshaft and retains the flywheel. Before removing clutch drum (5), be sure to unscrew hidden screw in center of clutch drum shaft. Unscrew the clutch hub by inserting a suitable spanner wrench in holes of clutch shoes. Clutch springs are available and must be renewed as a pair. Clutch shoes and hub are available only as a unit assembly. Install clutch on crankshaft so "OFF" on side of clutch hub is visible.

REWIND STARTER. Refer to Fig. SL111 for an exploded view of rewind starter. To disassemble starter, detach starter housing from engine. Remove rope handle and allow rope to wind into starter. Remove snap ring (5) and remove rope pulley (7). Wear appropriate safety eyewear and gloves before detaching rewind spring (8) from housing (9) as spring may uncoil uncontrolled.

To assemble starter, lubricate center post of housing and spring side with light grease. Install rewind spring so coil windings are clockwise from outer end. Rope length should be 96 cm (38 in.). Assemble starter while passing rope through housing rope outlet and attach rope handle to rope. To place tension on starter rope, pull rope out of housing. Engage rope in notch on pulley and turn pulley four turns clockwise. Hold pulley and disengage rope from pulley notch. Release pulley and allow rope to wind on pulley. Check starter operation. Rope handle should be held against housing by spring tension, but it must be possible to rotate pulley at least 1/2 turn clockwise when rope is pulled out fully.

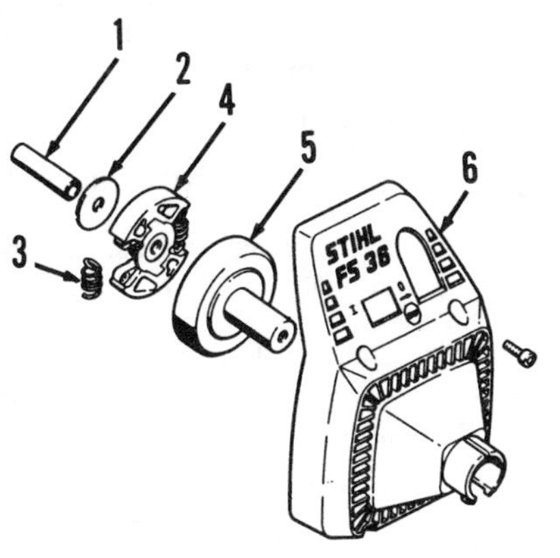

Fig. SL110—Exploded view of clutch assembly.
1. Spacer
2. Washer
3. Clutch spring
4. Clutch shoe & hub assy.
5. Clutch drum
6. Clutch housing

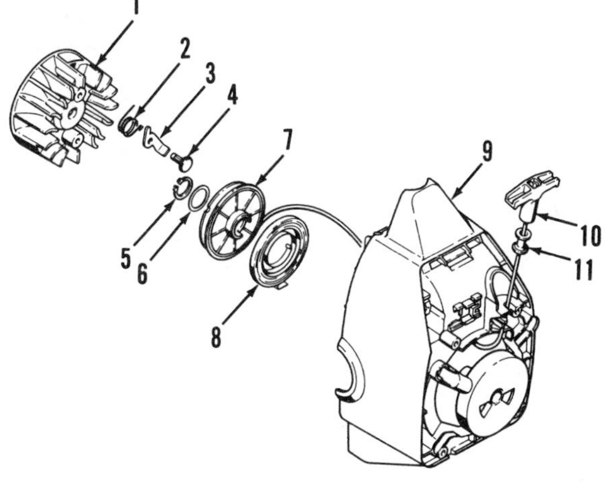

Fig. SL111—Exploded view of rewind starter.
1. Flywheel
2. Spring
3. Pawl
4. Stud
5. Snap ring
6. Washer
7. Spool
8. Rewind spring
9. Starter housing
10. Rope handle
11. Rope guide

STIHL
ENGINE SERVICE

Model	Bore	Stroke	Displacement
Stihl	29 mm (1.14 in.)	26 mm (1.02 in.)	17.1 cc (1.04 cu. in.)
Stihl	31 mm (1.22 in)	26 mm (1.02 in.)	19.6 cc (1.20 cu. in.)
Stihl	30 mm (1.18 in.)	28 mm (1.10 in.)	19.8 cc (1.21 cu. in.)
Stihl	32 mm (1.26 in.)	28 mm (1.10 in.)	22.5 cc (1.37 cu. in.)
Stihl	34 mm (1.36 in.)	28 mm (1.10 in.)	25.44 cc (1.55 cu. in.)
Stihl	37 mm (1.46 in.)	32 mm (1.26 in.)	34.4 cc (2.10 cu. in.)

These engines are used on Stihl Models FS48,FS52, FS56, FS60, FS62, FS62AVE, FS62AVRE, FS65, FS66, FS66AVE, FS66AVRE, FS80, FS81, FS81AVE, FS81AVRE, FS86AVE, FS86AVRE, FR106 and FS106.

ENGINE INFORMATION

The Stihl engines covered in this section are two-stroke, air-cooled, single-cylinder engines.

MAINTENANCE

LUBRICATION. Engine lubrication is obtained by mixing gasoline with an oil designed for two-stroke, air-cooled engines. Refer to trimmer or blower service section for manufacturer's recommended fuel:oil mixture ratio.

SPARK PLUG. Recommended spark plug is NGK BMR7A or equivalent. Specified electrode gap is 0.6 mm (0.024 in.). Tighten spark plug to 20 N·m (177 in.-lbs.).

CARBURETOR. Engines with 34.4 cc displacement are equipped with a Zama C1Q carburetor. All other engines are equipped with a Walbro WT carburetor. Refer to following sections for service information.

Walbro WT. Refer to Fig. SL201 for an exploded view of carburetor. Initial adjustment of idle mixture screw (11) and high-speed mixture screw (13) is one turn open. Final adjustment is performed with engine at normal operating temperature and cutter line at desired length. Be sure engine air filter is clean before performing carburetor adjustments.

Turn idle speed screw (34) clockwise until trimmer head rotates, then turn counterclockwise one half turn. Trimmer head must not rotate when engine is at idle speed. Adjust idle mixture screw so engine idles smoothly and accelerates cleanly without hesitation. Readjust idle speed screw if necessary. Open throttle to wide-open position and adjust high-speed mixture screw (13). Engine speed must not exceed 10,000 rpm. If an accurate tachometer is not available, do not adjust high-speed mixture needle beyond initial setting. Do not adjust high-speed mixture screw too lean as engine may be damaged.

The carburetor is equipped with an accelerator pump that forces additional fuel into the carburetor bore when the throttle shaft is rotated. The pump piston (26—Fig. SL201) rests against a flat on the throttle shaft. Shaft rotation moves the piston against fuel in a passage.

Carburetor disassembly and reassembly is evident after inspection of carburetor and referral to Fig. SL201. Do not lose detent ball (15) when withdrawing choke shaft. Accelerator pump piston (26) is released when throttle shaft is withdraw. Clean and inspect all components. Inspect diaphragms (2 and 30) for defects that may affect operation. Ex

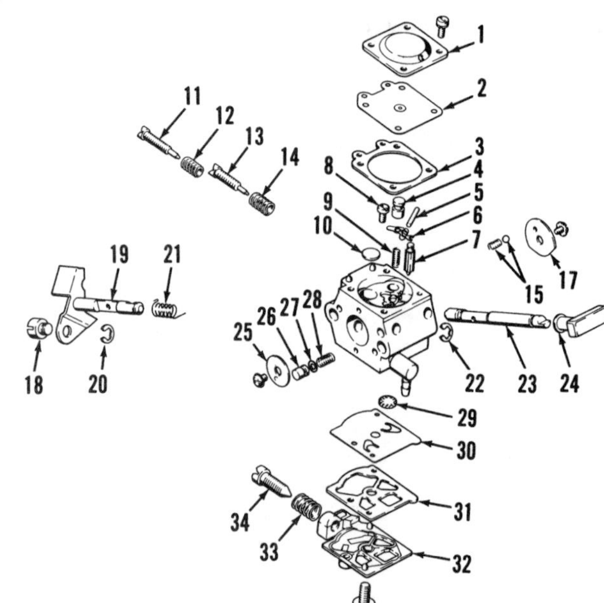

Fig. SL201—Exploded view of Walbro WT carburetor.

1. Cover
2. Metering diaphragm
3. Gasket
4. Nozzle
5. Pin
6. Metering lever
7. Fuel inlet valve
8. Screw
9. Spring
10. Welch plug
11. Idle mixture screw
12. Spring
13. High-speed mixture screw
14. Spring
15. Detent ball & spring
17. Choke plate
18. Swivel
19. Throttle shaft
20. "E" ring
21. Spring
22. "E" ring
23. Choke shaft
24. Handle
25. Throttle plate
26. Accelerator piston
27. "O" ring
28. Spring
29. Screen
30. Fuel pump diaphragm
31. Gasket
32. Cover
33. Spring
34. Idle speed screw

amine fuel inlet valve and seat. Inlet valve (7) is renewable, but carburetor body must be renewed if seat is damaged or excessively worn. Discard carburetor body if mixture screw seats are damaged or excessively worn. Clean fuel screen (29).

Press nozzle (4) into body until inner face is flush with venturi bore as shown in Fig. SL202. Install choke plate as shown in Fig. SL203. Install throttle plate so hole is toward metering chamber cover as shown in Fig. SL204. Apply Loctite to choke and throttle plate retaining screws. Check metering lever height as shown in Fig. SL205 using Walbro tool 500-13. Metering lever should just touch leg on tool. Bend lever to obtain correct lever height. Install cover (1—Fig. SL201) so hole is toward fuel inlet side of carburetor as shown in Fig. SL206.

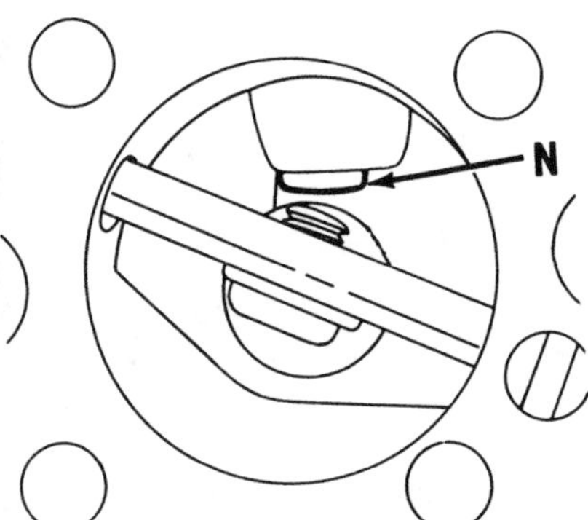

Fig. SL202—Install fuel nozzle (N) so inner face is flush with venturi bore.

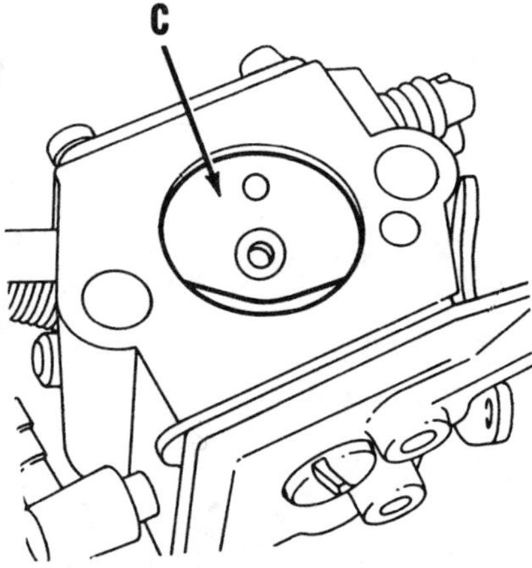

Fig. SL203—View showing correct installation of choke plate (C).

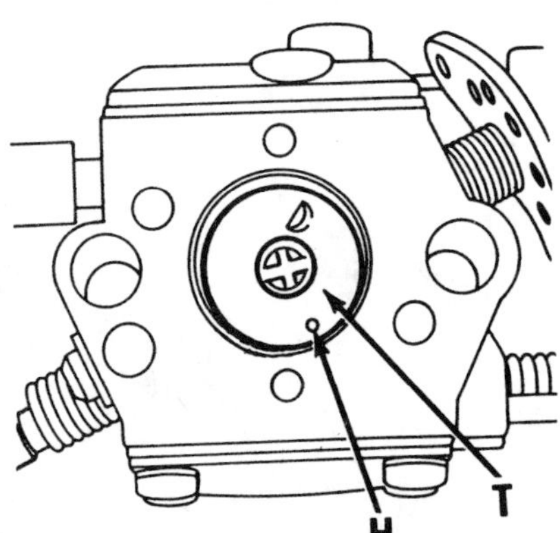

Fig. SL204—View showing correct installation of throttle plate (T). Hole (H) in plate should face metering chamber cover.

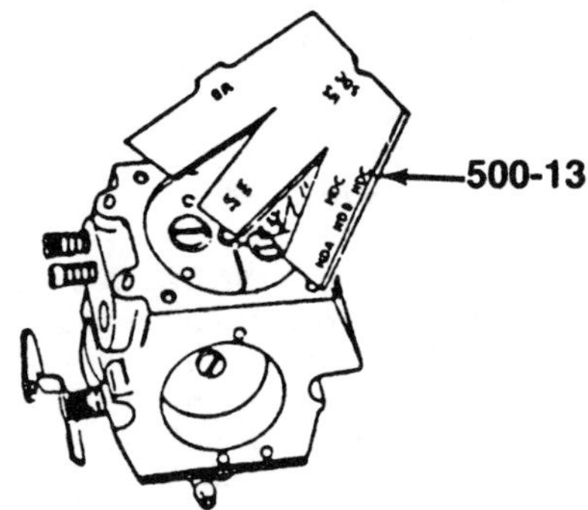

Fig. SL205—Leg of Walbro tool 500-13 should just touch metering lever.

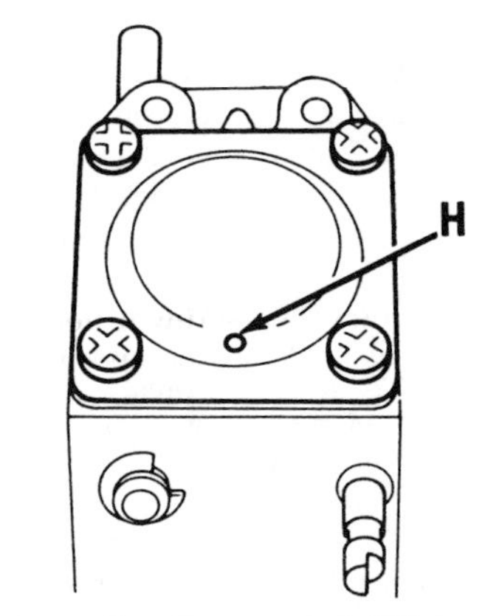

Fig. SL206—Install cover so hole (H) is toward fuel inlet.

Zama C1Q. Refer to Fig. SL207 for an exploded view of carburetor. Initial adjustment of idle mixture screw (12) and high-speed mixture screw (13) is 1 turn out from a lightly seated position.

Final adjustment is performed with engine at normal operating temperature. Be sure that air cleaner is clean before attempting to adjust carburetor. Before final adjustment on trimmer models, cutter line should be desired length. Turn idle speed screw (16) until cutting tool begins to rotate, then turn screw back out one half turn. Tool must not rotate when engine is at idle speed. Adjust idle mixture screw (12) so engine idles smoothly and accelerates cleanly without hesitation. Readjust idle speed screw if necessary. Open throttle to wide-open position and adjust high-speed mixture screw (13). Engine speed must not exceed 10,000 rpm. If an accurate tachometer is not available, do not adjust high-speed mixture needle beyond initial setting. Do not adjust high-speed mixture screw too lean as engine may be damaged.

Carburetor disassembly and reassembly is evident after inspection of carburetor and referral to Fig. SL207. Do not lose detent ball (18) when withdrawing choke shaft. Clean and inspect all components. Inspect diaphragms (2 and 29) for defects that may affect operation.

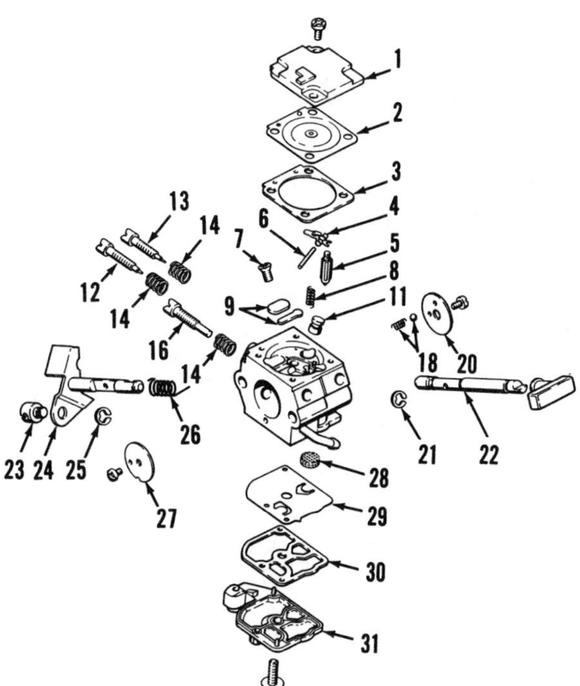

Fig. SL207—Exploded view of Zama C1Q carburetor.

1. Cover
2. Metering diaphragm
3. Gasket
4. Metering lever
5. Fuel inlet valve
6. Pin
7. Screw
8. Spring
9. Welch plugs
11. Nozzle
12. Idle mixture screw
13. High-speed mixture screw
14. Springs
16. Idle speed screw
18. Detent ball & spring
20. Choke plate
21. "E" ring
22. Choke shaft
23. Swivel
24. Throttle shaft
25. "E" ring
26. Spring
27. Throttle plate
28. Screen
29. Fuel pump diaphragm
30. Gasket
31. Cover

Illustrations courtesy Stihl Inc.

Examine fuel inlet valve and seat. Inlet valve (5) is renewable, but carburetor body must be renewed if seat is damaged or excessively worn. Discard carburetor body if mixture screw seats are damaged or excessively worn. Clean fuel screen (28).

To reassemble carburetor, reverse disassembly procedure. Metering lever should be level with chamber floor as shown in Fig. SL208. Bend metering lever as needed.

IGNITION SYSTEM. Some engines are equipped with a one-piece ignition module that includes the ignition coil. On other engines, a two-piece ignition system is used with the ignition coil adjacent to the flywheel and the ignition module mounted on the crankcase.

Ignition coil air gap should be 0.2-0.5 mm (0.008-0.020 in.) on Models FS52, FS62, FS66, FS81, FS86.

REPAIRS

PISTON, PIN AND RINGS. The piston (5—Fig. SL209) is equipped with two piston rings (3). Ring rotation is prevented by a locating pin in each piston ring groove (Fig. SL210). Piston and rings are available only in standard diameter.

To remove piston, first remove fan housing, engine cover, carburetor and muffler. Remove cylinder mounting screws and pull cylinder off the piston. Pry piston pin retainers (4—Fig. SL209) from piston and push piston pin (6) out of piston. Hold piston securely when removing pin to avoid applying side force to connecting rod. Remove piston and needle bearing (12) from connecting rod.

When reassembling, heat piston to about 60° C (140° F) to ease installation of piston pin. Install piston on connecting rod so mark on piston crown points toward exhaust port. Be sure piston ring gaps are correctly indexed with locating pins in piston ring grooves as shown in Fig. SL210. Lubricate piston and cylinder with oil prior to assembly. Use suitable clamping strap to compress piston rings. Align cylinder so it is correctly positioned on crankcase, then push cylinder straight down over piston. Tighten cylinder mounting screws evenly to 5 N·m (44 in.-lbs.).

Straightedge

Metering lever

Fig. SL208—Metering lever should be level with chamber floor. Bend metering lever as needed.

CYLINDER. The engine is equipped with a cylinder that has an impregnated bore. Renew cylinder if bore is excessively worn, scored or otherwise damaged. Cylinder is available only in standard size with a piston.

CRANKSHAFT, CONNECTING ROD AND CRANKCASE. Crankshaft, connecting rod and rod bearing are a unit assembly; individual components are not available. The crankshaft is supported by ball bearings at both ends.

To remove crankshaft, first remove spark plug and install a piston locking screw in spark plug hole to lock piston and crankshaft. Separate engine from clutch housing. Remove clutch assembly and flywheel from crankshaft. Remove recoil starter housing and unscrew locknut and starter pawl carrier (17.1 cc, 19.6 cc and 19.8 cc engines have left-hand threads) from end of crankshaft. Remove muffler, carburetor, fuel tank and ignition unit. Remove mounting screws from crankcase halves (9 and 15—Fig. SL209). Use a plastic hammer to tap crankshaft out of main bearings and crankcase halves. Remove oil seals (8). Heat crankcase to approximately 130° C (235° F) to aid removal and installation of bearings (10) in crankcase.

Install seals (8—Fig. SL209) with lip toward inside of crankcase. Shims (11) are available in thicknesses of 0.1 and 0.2 mm to adjust crankshaft end play. Maximum allowable end play is 0.3 mm (0.012 in.). There is no gasket between crankcase halves. Apply a suitable gasket sealer to crankcase half mating surfaces.

CLUTCH. The engine is equipped with a two-shoe clutch. The clutch shoe assembly is mounted on the flywhee (1—Fig. SL211). The clutch drum (8 rides in the drive housing (11), whic

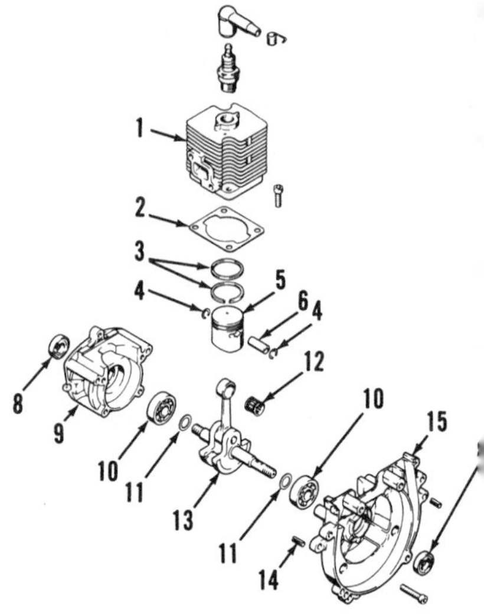

Fig. SL209—Exploded view of engine.

1. Cylinder
2. Gasket
3. Piston rings
4. Retaining rings
5. Piston
6. Piston pin
8. Seal
9. Crankcase half
10. Bearing
11. Shim
12. Bearing
13. Crankshaft assy
14. Dowel pin
15. Crankcase half

Fig. SL210—Piston ring end gaps must be positioned around locating pins in ring grooves as shown.

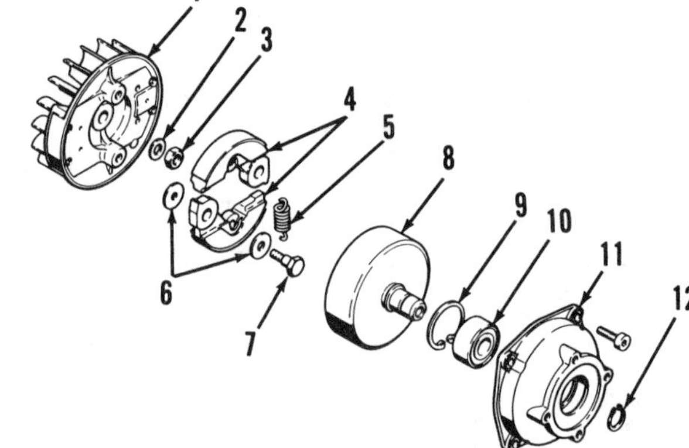

Fig. SL211—Exploded view of clutch assembly. On some models, the face of drum (8) is slotted to allow access to snap ring (9).

1. Flywheel
2. Washer
3. Nut
4. Clutch shoes
5. Spring
6. Washer
7. Shoulder bolt
8. Clutch drum
9. Snap ring
10. Bearing
11. Housing
12. Snap ring

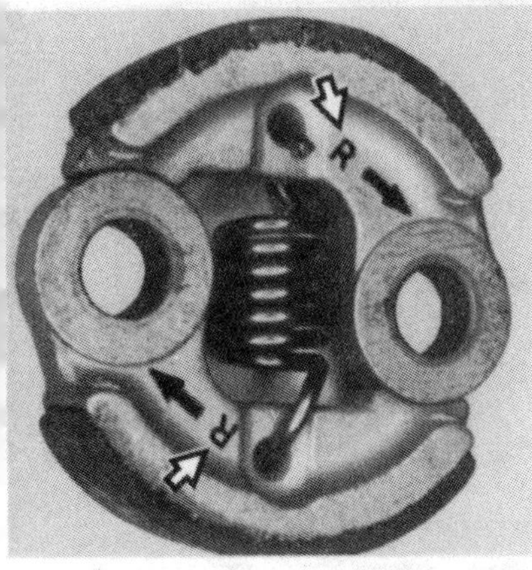

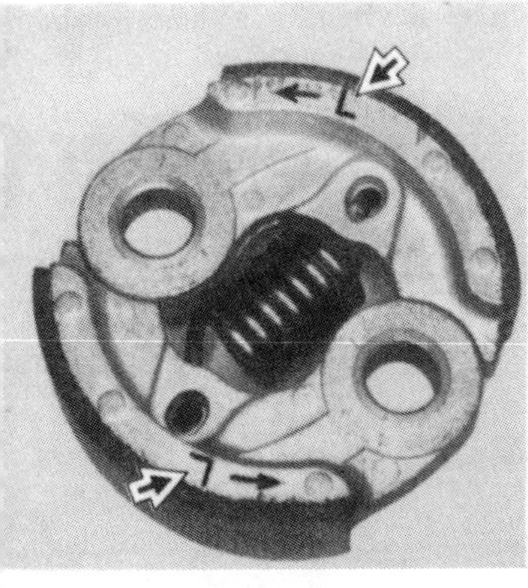

Fig. SL212—Install clutch shoes so "L" or "R" on shoe is visible, depending on direction of crankshaft rotation.

may be the fan housing on some engines.

To remove clutch drum on models with slots in clutch face, reach through slot and detach snap ring (9), then press clutch drum and bearing (10) out of housing. Heating housing will ease removal. On other engines, detach snap ring (12) and press clutch drum shaft out of bearing (10). Detach snap ring (9), heat housing to approximately 280° F (140° C) and remove bearing (10). Reverse removal procedure to install clutch drum.

Clutch shoes (4) are available as a pair. Prior to removing clutch shoes, note whether side marked "R" or "L" (Fig. SL212) faces outward so that shoes may be reinstalled in same position. Tighten clutch mounting screws to 8 N·m (6 ft.-lbs.).

REWIND STARTER. Refer to Figs. SL213 or SL214 for an exploded view of starter. To disassemble starter, detach starter housing (4) from engine. Remove rope handle and allow rope to wind into starter. Unscrew center screw (8) and remove rope pulley (6). Wear appropriate safety eyewear and gloves before detaching rewind spring (5) from housing as spring may uncoil uncontrolled.

To remove starter plate (12), unscrew retaining nut (8) then unscrew plate from crankshaft. Note that nut and plate have left-hand threads on 17.1 cc, 19.6 cc and 19.8 cc engines. Before removing pawl (10) from starter plate, note whether pawl is located in hole marked "R" or "L" so it can be reinstalled in same position (Fig. SL215 or SL216).

To assembly starter, install pawl (10) in hole marked "R" (Fig. SL215) or "L" (Fig. SL216) in starter plate. Legs of torsion spring (11) must locate against carrier plate and pawl as shown. Lubricate center post of housing and spring side with light grease. Install rewind spring so coil windings are positioned as shown in Figs. SL213 or SL214. Assemble starter while passing rope through housing rope outlet and attach rope handle to rope. To place tension on starter rope, pull rope out of housing. Engage rope in notch on pulley and rotate pulley against spring tension seven turns. Hold pulley and disengage rope from pulley notch. Release pulley and allow rope to wind on pulley. Check starter operation. Rope handle should be held against housing by spring tension, but it must be possible to rotate pulley at least an additional 1/2 turn when rope is pulled out fully.

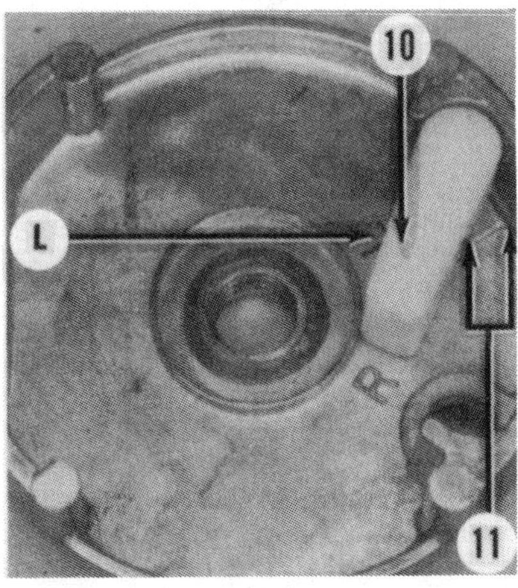

Fig. SL215—On 17.1 cc, 19.6 cc and 19.8 cc engines, install pawl (10) in starter plate hole marked "L." Be sure that legs of spring (11) are against pawl and plate as shown.

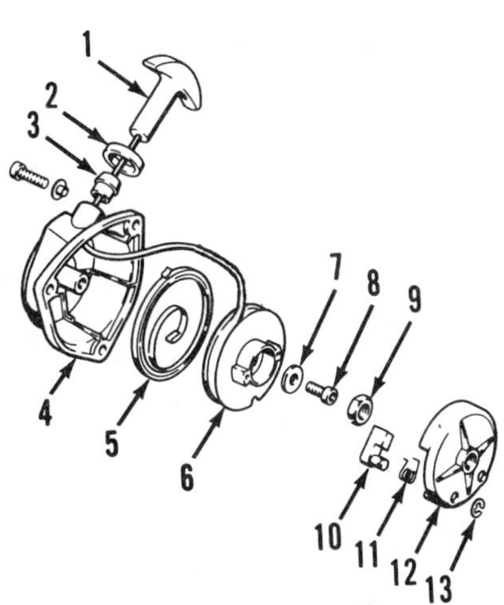

Fig. SL213—Exploded view of rewind starter used on 17.1 cc, 19.6 cc and 19.8 cc engines. Nut (9) and plate (12) have left-hand threads.

1. Rope handle
2. Cover
3. Rope guide
4. Starter housing
5. Rewind spring
6. Pulley
7. Washer
8. Screw
9. Nut
10. Pawl
11. Spring
12. Carrier plate
13. "E" ring

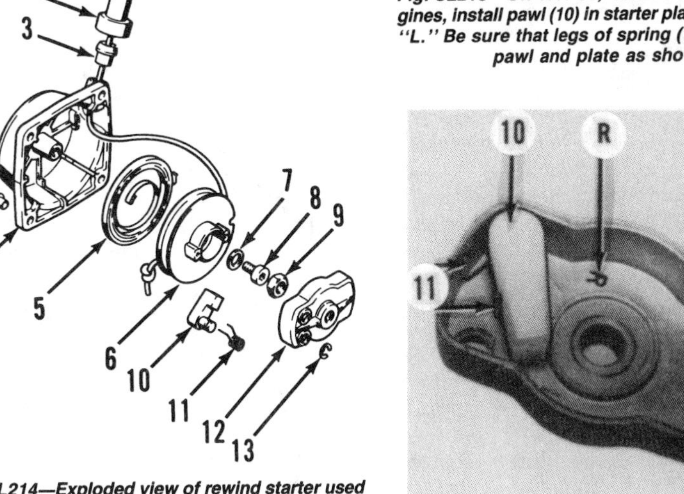

Fig. SL214—Exploded view of rewind starter used on 22.5 cc, 25.4 cc and 34.4 cc engines.

1. Rope handle
3. Rope guide
4. Starter housing
5. Rewind spring
6. Pulley
7. Washer
8. Screw
9. Nut
10. Pawl
11. Spring
12. Carrier plate
13. "E" ring

Fig. SL216—On 22.5 cc, 25.4 cc and 34.4 cc engines, install pawl (10) in starter plate hole marked "R." Note position of spring (11).

Illustrations courtesy Stihl Inc.

STIHL

ENGINE SERVICE

Model	Bore	Stroke	Displacement
Stihl	28 mm (1.10 in.)	26 mm (1.02 in.)	16.0 cc (0.96 cu. in.)

This engine is used on Stihl Models FS50 and FS51.

ENGINE INFORMATION

The Stihl engine covered in this section is a two-stroke, air-cooled, single-cylinder engine.

MAINTENANCE

LUBRICATION. Engine lubrication is obtained by mixing gasoline with an oil designed for two-stroke, air-cooled engines. Refer to trimmer or blower service section for manufacturer's recommended fuel:oil mixture ratio.

SPARK PLUG. Recommended spark plug is a NGK BMR6 or equivalent. Specified electrode gap for all models is 0.6-0.7 mm (0.024-0.028 in.).

CARBURETOR. The engine is equipped with a Teikei diaphragm-type carburetor. Refer to Fig. SL301 for an exploded view of carburetor.

Initial adjustment of fuel mixture needles from a lightly seated position is $1\frac{1}{4}$ turns open for the idle mixture screw and $\frac{3}{4}$ turn open for the high-speed mixture screw. Final adjustments are performed with trimmer line at recommended length or blade assembly installed. Engine must be at operating temperature and running. Be sure engine air filter is clean before performing carburetor adjustments.

Operate trimmer engine at full throttle and adjust high-speed mixture needle to obtain 9000 rpm. If an accurate tachometer is not available, do not adjust high-speed mixture needle beyond initial setting. Operate trimmer engine at idle speed and adjust idle mixture screw until a smooth idle is obtained and engine does not hesitate during acceleration. Adjust idle speed screw so engine idles just below clutch engagement speed.

Carburetor overhaul is evident after inspection and referral to Fig. SL301. Clean all parts in suitable solvent. Examine fuel inlet valve and seat. Inlet valve (14) is renewable, but carburetor body must be renewed if seat is excessively worn or damaged. Inspect mixture screws and seats. Renew carburetor body if seats are excessively worn or damaged. Inspect diaphragms (6 and 19) for tears and other damage.

The metering lever (16) must be 2.0 mm (0.08 in.) below gasket surface as shown in Fig. SL302.

IGNITION SYSTEM. The engine is equipped with an electronic ignition system. The ignition system is considered satisfactory if a spark will jump across the 3 mm ($\frac{1}{8}$ in.) gap of a test spark plug. If no spark is produced, check on/off switch, wiring and ignition module air gap. Ignition module air gap should be 0.2-0.3 mm (0.008-0.010 in.). The cylinder must be removed for access to module and flywheel so air gap can be set. Tighten ignition module retaining screws to 2.0 N·m (18 in.-lbs.). If switch, wiring and module air gap are satisfactory, but spark is not present, renew ignition module.

REPAIRS

TIGHTENING TORQUES. Recommended tightening torques are as follows:

Clutch shoe	8 N·m (71 in.-lbs.)
Crankcase cover	3.5 N·m (31 in.-lbs.)
Crankpin screw	2.0 N·m (18 in.-lbs.)
Cylinder	4.0 N·m (35 in.-lbs.)
Flywheel	15.0 N·m (133 in.-lbs.)
Ignition module	2.0 N·m (18 in.-lbs.)

FLYWHEEL. Note that flywheel nut has left-hand threads. Tighten nut to 15.0 N·m (133 in.-lbs.).

PISTON, PIN AND RINGS. To remove piston, remove muffler, carburetor and cylinder cover. Unscrew two retaining screws and remove cylinder by pulling straight up. Remove piston pin retain

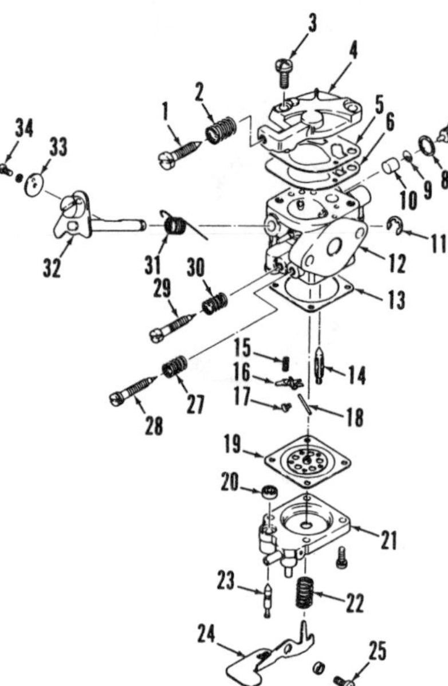

Fig. SL301—Exploded view of Teikei diaphragm carburetor.

1. Idle speed screw
2. Spring
3. Screw
4. Pump cover
5. Gasket
6. Diaphragm
7. Plug
8. "O" ring
9. Screen
10. Felt
11. "E" ring
12. Body
13. Gasket
14. Fuel inlet valve
15. Spring
16. Metering lever
17. Screw
18. Pin
19. Diaphragm
20. Seat
21. Cover
22. Spring
23. Plunger
24. Primer lever
25. Screw
27. Spring
28. High-speed mixture screw
29. Idle mixture screw
30. Spring
31. Spring
32. Throttle shaft
33. Throttle plate
34. Screw

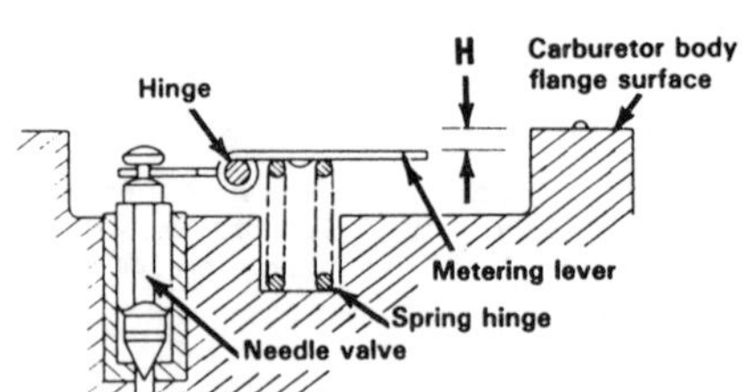

Fig. SL302—Height (H) of metering lever should be 2.0 mm (0.08 in.).

Illustrations courtesy Stihl Inc

s and use a suitable puller to remove ston pin. Hold piston securely when moving pin to avoid applying side rce to connecting rod. Remove piston om connecting rod.

Piston and ring are available in stanard size only.

ig. SL303—Install piston on rod so arrow on piston crown points toward exhaust port.

ig. SL304—Piston ring end gaps must be positioned around locating pins in ring grooves as shown.

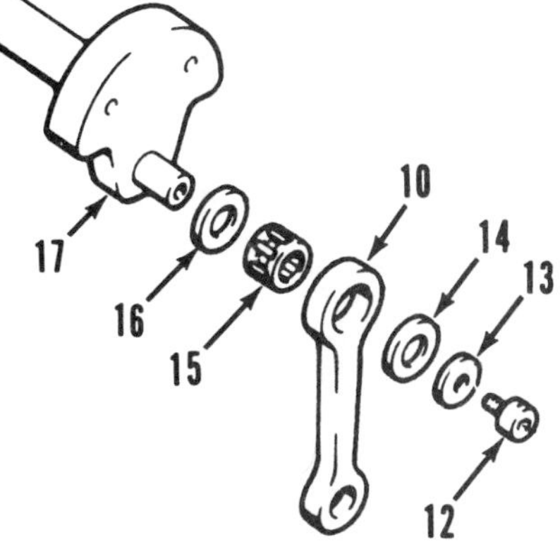

ig. SL305—Exploded view of connecting rod and crankshaft assembly.

10. Connecting rod
12. Screw
13. Washer
14. Shim
15. Bearing
16. Shim
17. Crankshaft

When reassembling, heat piston to about 60° C (140° F) to ease installation of piston pin. Install piston on connecting rod so arrow on piston crown points toward exhaust port (Fig. SL303). Be sure piston ring gaps are correctly indexed with locating pins in piston ring grooves as shown in Fig. SL304. Lubricate piston and cylinder with oil prior to assembly. Use suitable clamping strap to compress piston rings. Align cylinder so it is correctly positioned on crankcase, then push cylinder straight down over piston. Tighten cylinder retaining screws to 4.0 N·m (35 in.-lbs.).

CYLINDER. The cylinder bore is chrome plated. Renew cylinder if bore is excessively worn or bore surface is cracked, flaking or otherwise damaged. Tighten cylinder retaining screws to 4.0 N·m (35 in.-lbs.).

CRANKSHAFT AND CONNECTING ROD. The crankshaft is supported at flywheel end by two ball bearings. To remove crankshaft, disconnect throttle cable and remove fan housing mounting screws. Hold starter rope handle while removing fan housing and trimmer drive tube. Turn flywheel and recoil starter rope to release tension of rewind spring. Remove spark plug and install locking screw in spark plug hole to lock piston and crankshaft. Unbolt and remove clutch assembly from flywheel. Remove flywheel nut (left-hand threads) and pull flywheel off crankshaft. Remove snap ring, rope pulley and rewind spring housing. Remove muffler, carburetor, cylinder and piston. Remove fuel tank and fuel tank bracket. Remove crankcase cover. Install piston pin in small end of connecting rod and position a wooden block on top of crankcase to prevent crankshaft from turning. Remove connecting rod retaining screw (12—Fig. SL305), washer (13) and shim (14). Remove connecting rod (10), needle bearing (15) and second shim (16) from crankpin. Remove snap ring (10—Fig. SL306) and shim (9) from end of crankshaft (1). Use plastic mallet to tap crankshaft out of main bearings. Heat crankcase to 212° F (100° C) and tap lightly on wood block to remove bearings (3 and 8) from crankcase. Remove snap rings (4 and 7) and press oil seal (6) out of crankcase.

When installing crankshaft in crankcase and main bearings, vary thickness of shims (2 and 9—Fig. SL306) to obtain 0.1-0.3 mm (0.004-0.012 in.) end play. Install shim (16—Fig. SL305) on crankpin. Apply Loctite 242 to connecting rod retaining screw (12). Tighten crankpin screw to 2.0 N·m (18 in.-lbs.). Tighten crankcase cover screws to 3.5 N·m (31 in.-lbs.).

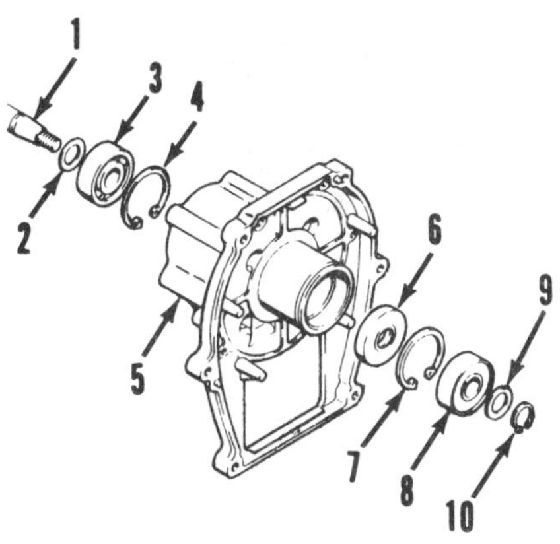

Fig. SL306—Exploded view of main bearing assembly.

1. Crankshaft
2. Shim
3. Bearing
4. Snap ring
5. Crankcase half
6. Seal
7. Snap ring
8. Bearing
9. Shim
10. Snap ring

REED VALVE. A reed valve is located on the inside of the crankcase cover. Renew reed valve if cracked, broken or warped.

CLUTCH. The engine is equipped with a two-shoe clutch. The clutch shoe assembly is mounted on the flywheel. The clutch drum rides in the fan housing.

To remove clutch drum, remove fan housing mounting screws. Hold tension on starter rope while removing fan housing and trimmer drive tube from engine. Remove clamp screw and locating screw from fan housing and pull drive tube out of housing. Reach through slot in drum and detach snap ring (1—Fig. SL307), then press clutch drum and bearing (3) out of fan housing. Reverse removal procedure to install clutch drum. Rotate starter rope pulley three turns clockwise to pretension starter rewind spring before installing fan housing.

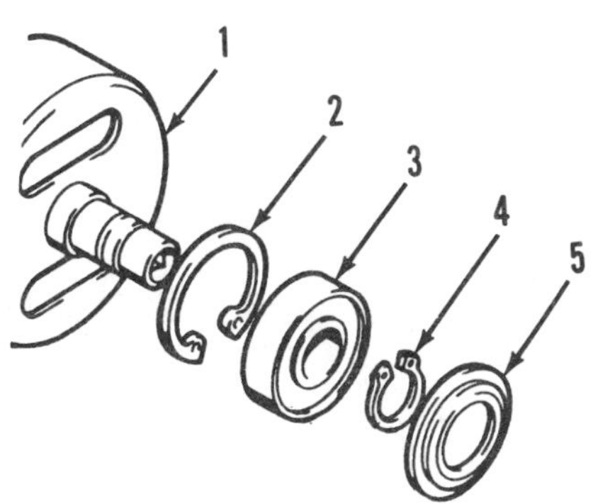

Fig. SL307—Exploded view of clutch drum and bearing assembly.

1. Clutch drum
2. Snap ring
3. Bearing
4. Snap ring
5. Washer

Clutch shoes are available as a pair. Install clutch shoes so sides marked "R" are visible as shown in Fig. SL308. Tighten clutch shoe screws to 8 N·m (71 in.-lbs.).

REWIND STARTER. The starter is located between the flywheel and the crankcase. The rewind spring is contained in a case that is attached to the crankcase. To remove starter assembly, remove fan housing from engine. Remove spark plug and install locking tool in spark plug hole to lock piston and crankshaft. Remove flywheel nut (left-hand threads) and pull flywheel off crankshaft. Remove starter pawls (1—Fig. SL309) and torsion springs (2) from flywheel if necessary. Pawls and springs must be renewed in pairs. Remove snap ring retaining rope pulley and remove pulley. Remove rewind spring housing mounting screws and remove spring and housing as an assembly.

When reassembling, position rope pulley on spring housing so that spring loop engages slot in pulley as shown in Fi SL310. Rope length should be 70 c (27½ in.) long. Wind rope around pu ley in a clockwise direction as viewe from flywheel side of pulley. Place te sion on rewind spring before engagin flywheel with pulley. Rotate rope rot and flywheel three turns clockwise t pretension starter spring, then insta fan housing. When properly installe rope handle should be held again housing by spring tension.

Fig. SL308—Install clutch shoes so "R" on shoe is visible.

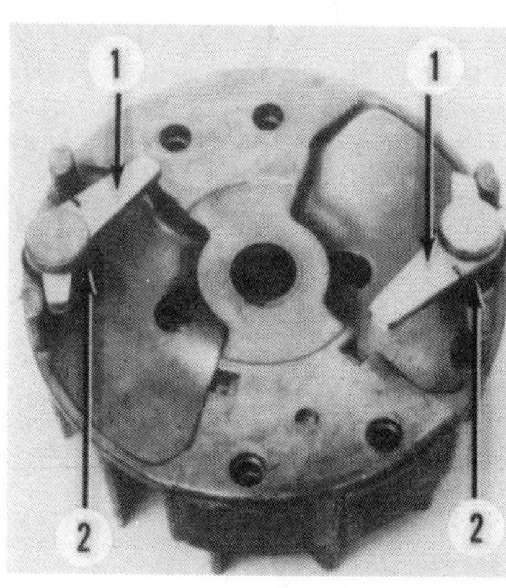

Fig. SL309—Starter pawls (1) are located on back side of flywheel.

Fig. SL310—Starter rewind spring loop must en gage slot in rope pulley.

Illustrations courtesy Stihl In

STIHL

ENGINE SERVICE

Model	Bore	Stroke	Displacement
Stihl	35 mm (1.38 in.)	31 mm (1.22 in.)	29.8 cc (1.82 cu. in.)
Stihl	38 mm (1.50 in.)	31 mm (1.22 in.)	35.2 cc (2.15 cu. in.)
Stihl	40 mm (1.57 in.)	31 mm (1.22 in.)	39.0 cc (2.38 cu. in.)

These engines are used on Stihl Models FS160, FS180, FS220 and FS280.

ENGINE INFORMATION

The Stihl engines covered in this section are two-stroke, air-cooled, single-cylinder engines.

MAINTENANCE

LUBRICATION. Engine lubrication is obtained by mixing gasoline with an oil designed for two-stroke, air-cooled engines. Refer to trimmer service section for manufacturer's recommended fuel:oil mixture ratio.

SPARK PLUG. Recommended spark plug is NGK BPMR7A or equivalent. Specified electrode gap is 0.5 mm (0.020 in.). Tighten spark plug to 20 N·m (177 in.-lbs.).

CARBURETOR. The engine is equipped with a Zama C1S diaphragm-type carburetor. Refer to Fig. SL401 for an exploded view of carburetor. Initial adjustment of idle mixture screw (15) and high-speed mixture screw (16) is one turn out from a lightly seated position. Final adjustment is performed with engine at normal operating temperature. Be sure engine air filter is clean. Before final adjustment on trimmer models, cutter line should be desired length.

Adjust idle mixture screw (15) so engine idles smoothly and accelerates cleanly without hesitation. Adjust idle speed screw (27) so engine idles just below clutch engagement speed. Open throttle to wide-open position and adjust high-speed mixture screw (16). Engine speed must not exceed 12,500 rpm. If an accurate tachometer is not available, do not adjust high-speed mixture screw beyond initial setting. Do not set high-speed adjustment screw too lean as engine damage may result. The ignition system on engines with 39 cc displacement has an engine speed limiting circuit that prevents engine speeds in excess of 13,200 rpm.

Carburetor disassembly and reassembly is evident after inspection of carburetor and referral to Fig. SL401. Do not lose detent ball (12) when withdrawing choke shaft. Clean and inspect all components. Inspect diaphragms (2 and 23) for defects that may affect operation. Examine fuel inlet valve and seat. Inlet valve (6) is renewable, but carburetor body must be renewed if seat is damaged or excessively worn. Discard carburetor body if mixture screw seats are damaged or excessively worn. Clean fuel screen (22).

Metering lever should be level with chamber floor as shown in Fig. SL402. Bend metering lever as needed.

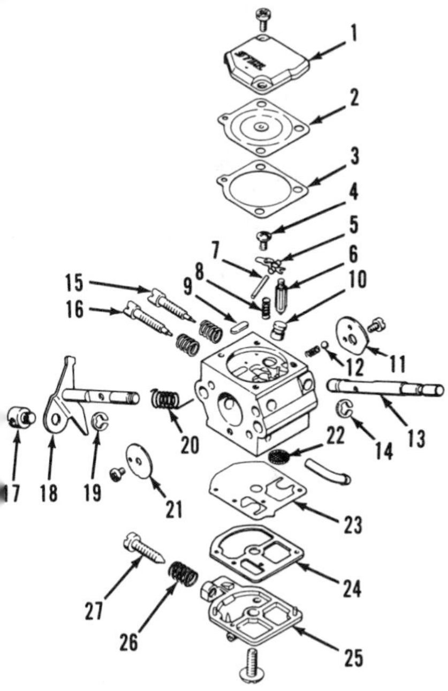

Fig. SL401—Exploded view of Zama C1S carburetor.

1. Cover
2. Metering diaphragm
3. Gasket
4. Screw
5. Metering lever
6. Fuel inlet valve
7. Pin
8. Spring
9. Welch plug
10. Nozzle
11. Choke plate
12. Detent ball
13. Choke shaft
14. "E" ring
15. Idle mixture screw
16. High-speed mixture screw
17. Swivel
18. Throttle shaft
19. "E" ring
20. Spring
21. Throttle plate
22. Screen
23. Fuel pump diaphragm
24. Gasket
25. Cover
26. Spring
27. Idle speed screw

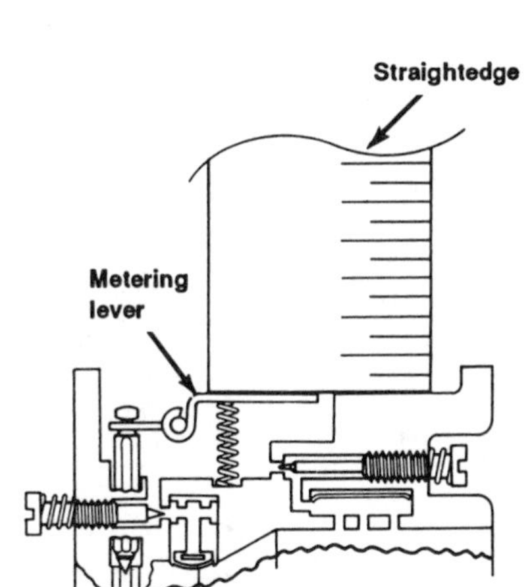

Fig. SL402—Metering lever should be level with chamber floor. Bend metering lever as needed.

IGNITION SYSTEM. Engines with 39 cc displacement are equipped with an ignition coil and a separate ignition module. On all other engines the ignition module and ignition coil are a molded assembly.

Air gap between ignition module/coil and flywheel magnet should be 0.15-0.25 mm (0.006-0.010 in.). Tighten module/coil retaining screws to 3.0 N·m (26 in.-lbs.).

The ignition system on engines with 39 cc displacement incorporates an engine speed limiter that prevents engine speed from exceeding 13,200 rpm.

Ignition coil primary windings resistance should be 0.8-1.3 ohms, and secondary windings resistance should be 7200-8800 ohms.

REPAIRS

TIGHTENING TORQUES. Recommended tightening torques are as follows:

Carburetor . . . . 4 N·m (35 in.-lbs.)
Clutch shoe . . . . 12 N·m (106 in.-lbs.)
Crankcase . . . . 8.5 N·m (75 in.-lbs.)
Cylinder . . . . 8 N·m (71 in.-lbs.).
Flywheel . . . . 24 N·m (212 in.-lbs.)
Ignition module . . . . 3 N·m (26 in.-lbs.)
Spark plug . . . . 20 N·m (177 in.-lbs.)
Starter cup . . . . 10 N·m (88 in.-lbs.)

INTAKE MANIFOLD. The intake manifold clamp must be positioned so the clamp opening is 70 degrees from vertical as shown in Fig. SL403. When inserting manifold through tank assembly, wrap a string around manifold flange as shown in Fig. SL404. Place ends of string through intake opening in fuel tank housing and pull string while pressing tank housing against manifold during assembly so flange on manifold does not fold back.

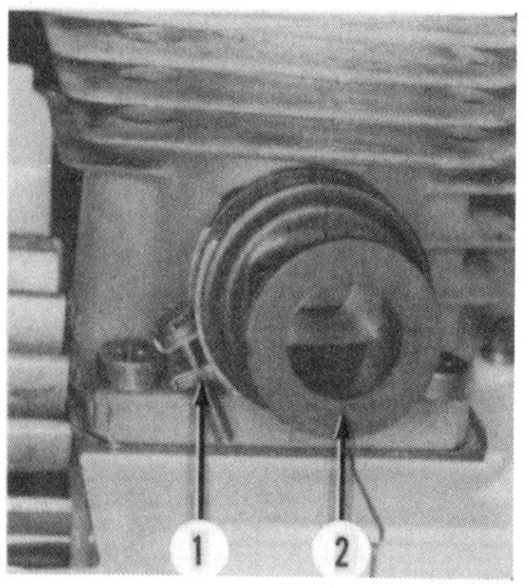

Fig. SL403—Position clamp (1) on intake manifold (2) so gap at clamp ends is 70 degrees from vertical as shown.

Fig. SL404—Wind a string around flange of intake manifold and pull string through opening in tank housing during installation of housing.

PISTON, PIN AND RINGS. The piston is equipped with two piston rings. Ring rotation is prevented by a locating pin in each piston ring groove. Piston and rings are available only in standard diameter.

To remove piston, remove engine shroud, muffler, air cleaner and carburetor. Remove metal sleeve from rubber intake manifold tube. Remove throttle cable clamp and disconnect ignition wires at spade terminals. Unbolt and remove clutch housing and trimmer drive shaft from engine. Remove rewind starter assembly. Remove fuel tank housing mounting screws, push manifold tube out of tank housing and remove housing from engine. Remove cylinder mounting screws and pull cylinder off piston. Pry piston pin retaining rings (6—Fig. SL405) from piston (4). Push piston pin (5) out of piston. If piston pin is stuck, lightly tap pin out of piston while holding piston securely to avoid applying side force to connecting rod. Remove piston and needle bearing (7) from connecting rod.

When reassembling, heat piston to about 60° C (140° F) to ease installation of piston pin. Install piston on connecting rod so arrow (Fig. SL406) on piston crown points toward exhaust port. Be sure piston ring gaps are correctly indexed with locating pins in piston ring grooves as shown in Fig. SL407. Lubr cate piston and cylinder bore with oi

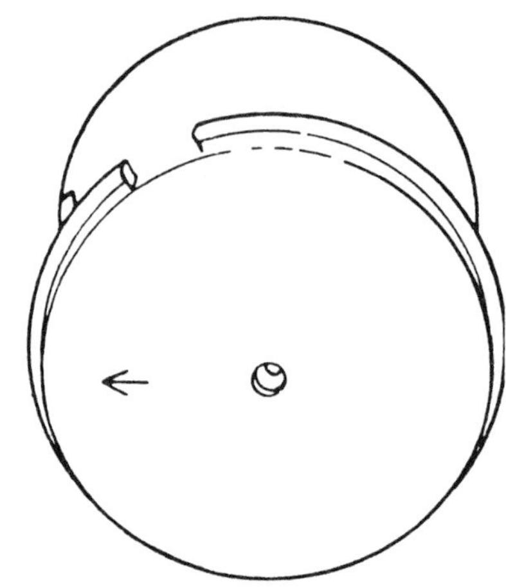

Fig. SL406—Install piston so arrow points towar exhaust port.

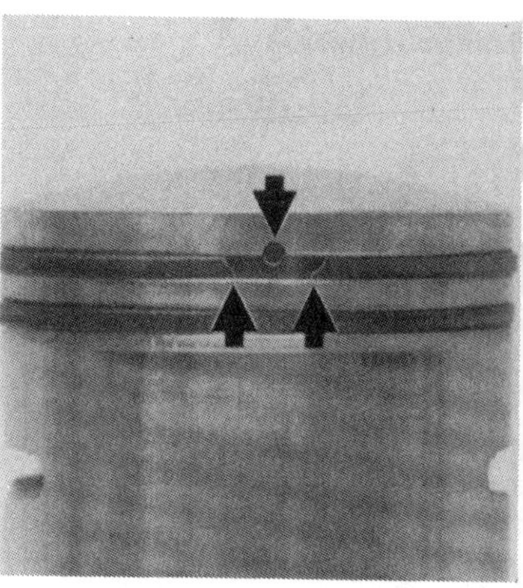

Fig. SL407—Piston ring end gaps must be positioned around locating pins in ring grooves as shown.

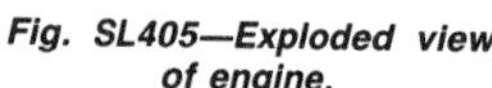

Fig. SL405—Exploded view of engine.

1. Cylinder
2. Gasket
3. Piston rings
4. Piston
5. Piston pin
6. Retaining ring
7. Bearing
8. Seal
9. Snap ring
10. Crankcase half
11. Dowel pin
12. Bearing
13. Crankshaft assy.
14. Key
15. Gasket
16. Crankcase half
17. Seal
18. Support

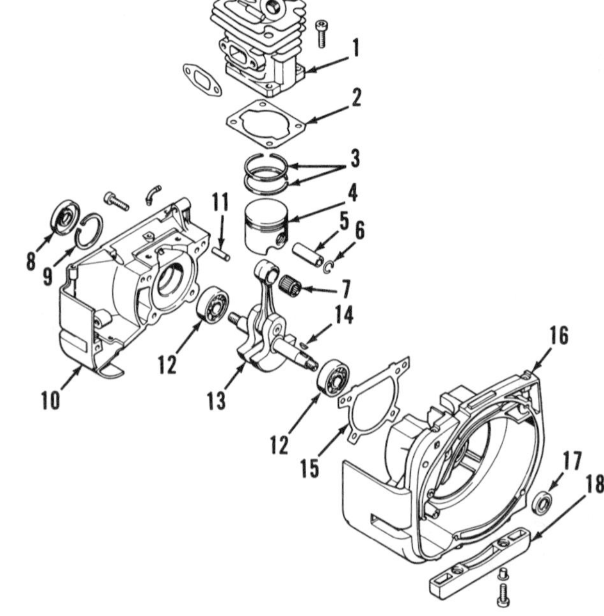

Illustrations courtesy Stihl Inc.

Use a suitable clamping strap to compress piston rings. Align cylinder so it is correctly positioned on crankcase, then push cylinder straight down over piston. Complete installation by reversing removal procedure.

CYLINDER. The engine is equipped with a cylinder that has an impregnated bore. Renew cylinder if bore is excessively worn, scored or otherwise damaged. Cylinder is available only in standard size with a piston. Tighten cylinder screws to 8 N·m (71 in.-lbs.).

CONNECTING ROD, CRANKSHAFT AND CRANKCASE. The crankshaft is supported by ball bearings at both ends. Connecting rod, crankpin and crankshaft are a pressed-together assembly and available only as a unit.

To remove crankshaft assembly, remove cylinder as previously outlined. Position a piece of wood between bottom of piston skirt and crankcase to prevent crankshaft from turning. Remove clutch assembly from flywheel. Remove flywheel mounting nut and pull flywheel from crankshaft using a suitable puller tool. Remove ignition module and trigger unit, if so equipped. Remove starter cup locknut, then unscrew starter cup from crankshaft. Remove piston pin and piston from connecting rod. Remove crankcase retaining screws and press crankshaft out of starter side crankcase half (10—Fig. SL405) first and then out of flywheel side crankcase half (16). Pry out seals (8 and 17) and remove snap ring (9). Heat crankcase halves to approximately 150° C (300° F), then tap lightly against wood block to remove main bearings (12).

Connecting rod big end rides on a roller bearing and should be inspected for excessive wear and damage. If rod, bearing or crankshaft is damaged, complete crankshaft and connecting rod assembly must be renewed.

When installing main bearings, heat crankcase halves to approximately 150° C (300° F) and seat bearing against snap ring (9—Fig. SL405) or against shoulder of crankcase half (16). It may be necessary to use a soldering iron to heat main bearing inner race to ease insertion of crankshaft. Install oil seals so lip is toward inside of crankcase. Tighten crankcase screws to 8.5 N·m (75 in.-lbs.).

CLUTCH. The engine is equipped with a two-shoe clutch. The clutch shoe assembly is mounted on the flywheel (1—Fig. SL408). The clutch drum (8) rides in the drive housing (11).

To remove clutch drum, first remove engine shroud and air cleaner assembly. Disconnect throttle cable and remove throttle cable clamp. Disconnect ignition wires at spade terminals. Unbolt and remove clutch housing and trimmer drive tube from engine. Detach snap ring (12) and press clutch drum shaft out of bearing (10). Detach snap ring (9) and press bearing (10) from housing. Reverse removal procedure to install clutch drum.

Clutch shoes are available as a pair. Install clutch shoes so arrows on shoes point in a counterclockwise direction as shown in Fig. SL409. Install clutch spring (6) so, when assembly is mounted on flywheel, the spring hook ends will be toward flywheel (1).

REWIND STARTER. Refer to Fig. SL410 for an exploded view of rewind starter. To disassemble starter, detach starter housing (3) from engine. Remove rope handle and allow rope to wind into starter. Detach retaining clip (8) and remove rope pulley (5). Wear appropriate safety eyewear and gloves before detaching rewind spring (4) from housing as spring may uncoil uncontrolled. To remove starter cup (10), unscrew retaining nut (9) then unscrew cup from crankshaft.

Rope length should be 96 cm ($37^3/_4$ in.). Wind rewind spring in counterclockwise direction from outer end. Note that clip (8) retains pulley (5) and pawl (6) and that peg on pawl must be inside clip as shown in Fig. SL411. Closed end of clip (C—Fig. SL411) points

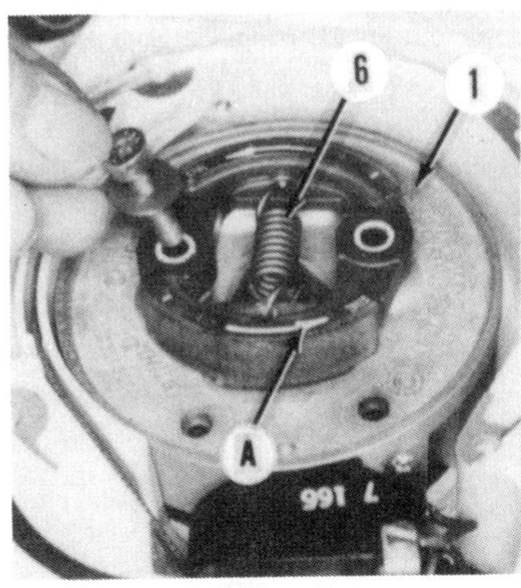

Fig. SL409—Install clutch shoes so arrow (A) points in counterclockwise direction. Hook ends of spring (6) must be toward flywheel (1).

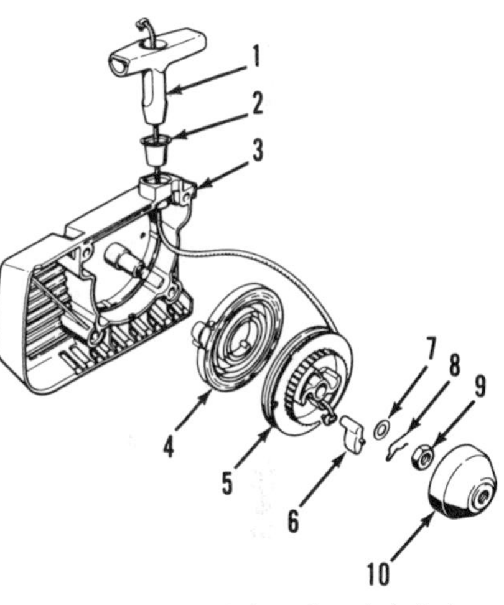

Fig. SL410—Exploded view of rewind starter.
1. Handle
2. Rope outlet
3. Starter housing
4. Rewind spring
5. Pulley
6. Pawl
7. Washer
8. Clip
9. Nut
10. Starter cup

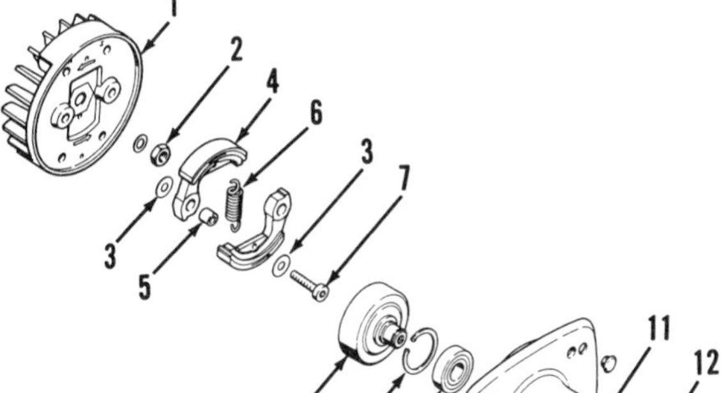

Fig. SL408—Exploded view of clutch assembly.
1. Flywheel
2. Nut
3. Washer
4. Clutch shoe
5. Bushing
6. Spring
7. Screw
8. Clutch drum
9. Snap ring
10. Bearing
11. Drive housing
12. Snap ring

Fig. SL411—Closed end of clip (C) should point in a counterclockwise direction and peg on pawl must be positioned inside the clip.

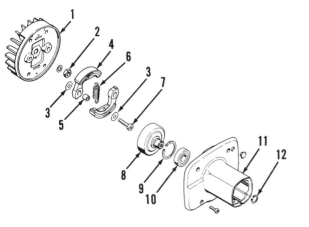

Illustrations courtesy Stihl Inc.

in a counterclockwise direction when installed correctly. Assemble starter while passing rope through housing rope outlet and attach rope handle to rope. To place tension on starter rope, pull rope out of housing. Engage rope in notch on pulley and turn pulley counterclockwise seven turns. Hold pulley and disengage rope from pulley notch. Release pulley and allow rope to wind on pulley. Check starter operation. Rope handle should be held against housing by spring tension, but it must be possible to rotate pulley at least $^1/_2$ turn counterclockwise when rope is pulled out fully.

Tighten starter cup to 10 N·m (7 ft.lbs.) and locknut to 24 N·m (18 ft.lbs.)

Illustrations courtesy Stihl Inc.

STIHL

ENGINE SERVICE

Model	Bore	Stroke	Displacement
Stihl	44 mm (1.73 in.)	34 mm (1.34 in.)	51.7 cc (3.16 cu. in.)
Stihl	46 mm (1.81 in.)	34 mm (1.34 in.)	56.5 cc (3.45 cu. in.)

These engines are used on Stihl Models BG17, BR320, BR400, FS360, FS420, SG17, SR320 and SR400.

ENGINE INFORMATION

The Stihl engines covered in this section are two-stroke, air-cooled, single-cylinder engines.

MAINTENANCE

LUBRICATION. Engine lubrication is obtained by mixing gasoline with an oil designed for two-stroke, air-cooled engines. Refer to trimmer or blower service section for manufacturer's recommended fuel:oil mixture ratio.

SPARK PLUG. Recommended spark plug is NGK BPMR7A or equivalent. Specified electrode gap is 0.5 mm (0.020 in.). Tighten spark plug to 25 N·m (221 in.-lbs.).

CARBURETOR. The engine is equipped with a Walbro HD diaphragm carburetor. Refer to Fig. SL501 for an exploded view of carburetor. Initial setting of idle mixture screw and high-speed mixture screw is one turn out from a lightly seated position. Final adjustment is performed with engine at normal operating temperature. Be sure that air filter is clean before adjusting carburetor.

Fig. SL501—Exploded view of Walbro HD carburetor.

1. Cover
2. Metering diaphragm
3. Gasket
4. Screw
5. Pin
6. Spring
7. Fuel inlet valve
8. Metering lever
9. Nozzle
10. Welch plug
11. "O" ring
12. Governor
13. High-speed mixture screw
14. Idle mixture screw
15. Idle speed screw
16. Throttle shaft
17. Spring
18. Throttle plate
19. Choke plate
20. Detent ball
21. Choke shaft
22. Throttle lever
23. Screen
24. Fuel pump diaphragm
25. Gasket
26. Cover

To perform final adjustment on trimmer and brush cutters, proceed as follows. Cutter line should be desired length. Adjust idle mixture screw (14—Fig. SL501) so engine idles smoothly and accelerates cleanly without hesitation. Adjust idle speed screw (15) so engine idles just below clutch engagement speed. Open throttle to wide-open position and adjust high-speed mixture screw (13). Engine must not exceed 12,500 rpm. If an accurate tachometer is not available, do not adjust high-speed mixture screw beyond initial setting. Do not set high-speed adjustment screw too lean as engine damage may result. The carburetor on trimmer or brush cutter engines with 56.5 cc displacement is equipped with a governor valve (12) that enriches the mixture at high-speed to prevent overspeeding.

To perform final adjustment on blowers, proceed as follows. Adjust idle mixture screw (14—Fig. SL501) so engine idles smoothly and accelerates cleanly without hesitation. Open throttle to wide-open position and adjust high-speed mixture screw (13) to obtain highest engine speed, then turn high-speed mixture screw counterclockwise until engine speed drops 150 rpm. Do not set adjustment screw too lean as engine damage may result.

Carburetor disassembly and reassembly is evident after inspection of carburetor and referral to Fig. SL501. On models so equipped, do not lose detent ball (20) when withdrawing choke shaft. Clean and inspect all components. Wires or drill bits should not be used to clean passages as fuel flow may be altered. Inspect diaphragms (2 and 24) for defects that may affect operation. Examine fuel inlet valve and seat. Inlet valve (7) is renewable, but carburetor body must be renewed if seat is damaged or excessively worn. Discard carburetor body if mixture screw seats are damaged or excessively worn. Screen should be clean.

Press nozzle (9) into body until inner face is flush with venturi wall as shown in Fig. SL502. Install throttle plate so holes (H—Fig. SL503) are toward fuel pump cover. Install choke plate so notch (N—Fig. SL504) is toward fuel pump cover. The metering lever should be

Fig. SL502—Install nozzle (arrow) so face is flush with carburetor bore.

flush with body surface as shown in Fig. SL505. Bend metering lever as needed.

IGNITION SYSTEM. The engine is equipped with a one-piece, solid state ignition system. The ignition module and ignition coil are a molded assembly.

Ignition coil air gap should be 0.2-0.3 mm (0.008-0.012 in.) on trimmers and brush cutters, and 0.15-0.25 mm (0.006-0.010 in.) on blowers. Tighten ignition coil retaining screws to 8.0 N·m (71 in.-lbs.). Ignition timing should be 2.4-3.0 mm (0.095-0.118 in.) BTDC on trimmers and brush cutters. Ignition timing on blowers should be 2.2-2.9 mm (0.08-0.11 in.) BTDC. Ignition timing is not adjustable.

Ignition coil primary windings resistance on trimmers and brush cutters should be 0.7-1.0 ohm, and secondary windings resistance should be 7700-10,300 ohms.

Ignition coil primary windings resistance on blowers should be 0.8-1.3 ohms, and secondary windings resistance should be 7200-8800 ohms.

REPAIRS

TIGHTENING TORQUES. Recommended tightening torques are as follows:

Carburetor:
- Trimmer . . . . .5 N·m (44 in.-lbs.)
- Blower . . . . .4.5 N·m (40 in.-lbs.)

Clutch shoe . . . . .12 N·m (106 in.-lbs.)

Crankcase . . . . .8 N·m (71 in.-lbs.)

Cylinder . . . . .8 N·m (71 in.-lbs.)

Flywheel:
- Trimmer . . . . .30 N·m (22 ft.-lbs.)
- Blower . . . . .25 N·m (221 in.-lbs.)

Ignition module . . . . .8 N·m (71 in.-lbs.)

Spark plug . . . . .25 N·m (221 in.-lbs.)

Starter cup . . . . .15 N·m (133 in.-lbs.)

Starter cup nut . . . . .25 N·m (221 in.-lbs.)

INTAKE MANIFOLD. The intake manifold clamp on trimmers and brush cutters must be positioned so the clamp screw is parallel to the cylinder fins as shown in Fig. SL506. Tighten screw so opening between clamp ends is 8-9 mm ($^{5}/_{16}$-$^{3}/_{8}$ in.). When inserting manifold through tank assembly, wrap a string around manifold and thread ends of string through opening in tank housing. Pull string while pushing tank housing against manifold so flange on manifold does not fold back.

PISTON, PIN AND RINGS. The piston is equipped with two piston rings. Ring rotation is prevented by a locating pin in each piston ring groove. Piston and rings are available only in standard diameter.

To remove piston, remove engine shrouds, carburetor and muffler. On trimmer and brush cutter models, disconnect throttle cable and ignition wires from engine. Unbolt and remove clutch housing and drive tube from engine. Remove fuel tank housing. On blower models, remove power unit from support frame. On all models, remove cylinder mounting screws and pull cylinder off piston. Pry retaining rings (6—Fig. SL507) from piston and push piston pin (5) out of piston. If pin is stuck, tap lightly with a brass drift while holding piston securely to avoid applying side thrust to connecting rod. Remove piston and needle bearing (7) from connecting rod.

Install piston on connecting rod so arrow (Fig. SL508) on piston crown points toward exhaust port. Heat the piston to approximately 60° C (140° F) to ease installation of piston pin. Be sure piston ring gaps are correctly indexed with locating pins in piston ring grooves as shown in Fig. SL509. Lubricate piston and cylinder bore with oil. Use a suitable clamping strap to compress piston rings. Align cylinder so it is correctly positioned on crankcase, then push cylinder straight down over piston. Complete installation by reversing removal procedure.

CYLINDER. The engine is equipped with a cylinder that has an impregnated bore. Renew cylinder if bore is excessively worn, scored or otherwise damaged. Cylinder is available only in standard size with a piston. Tighten cylinder screws to 8 N·m (71 in.-lbs.).

CONNECTING ROD, CRANKSHAFT AND CRANKCASE. The crankshaft (14—Fig. SL507) is supported by ball bearings (13) at both ends. Connecting rod, crankpin and crankshaft are a pressed-together assembly and available only as a unit.

To remove crankshaft assembly, first separate engine from clutch housing

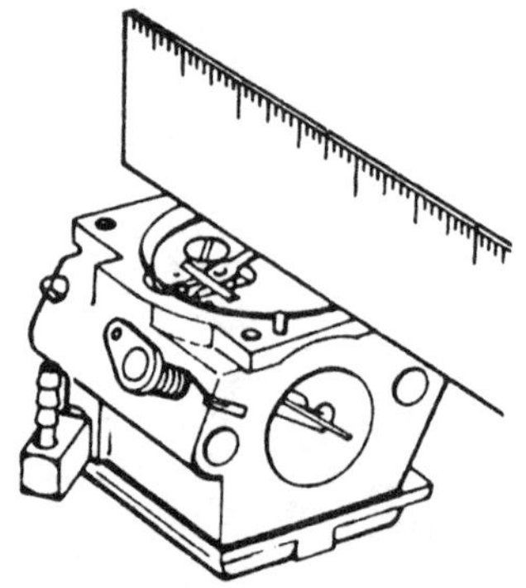

Fig. SL505—The metering lever should just touch a straightedge laid across the carburetor body. Bend lever as needed.

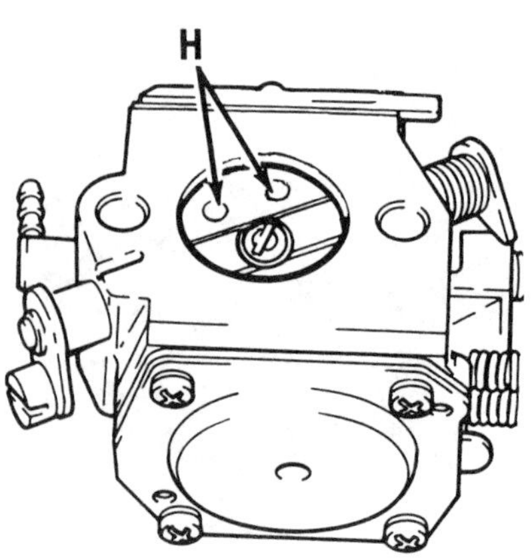

Fig. SL503—Install throttle plate so holes (H) are toward fuel pump cover.

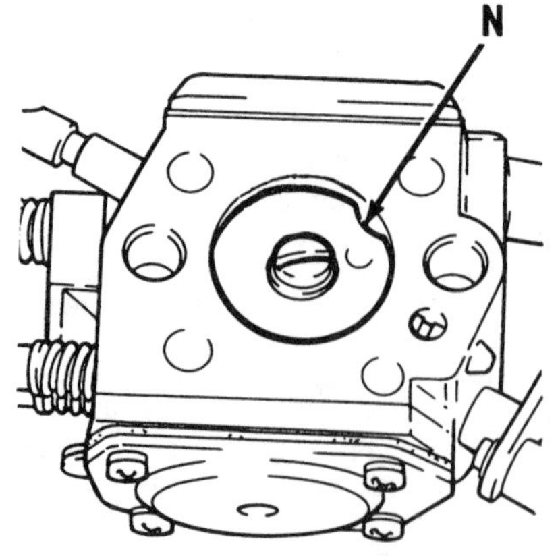

Fig. SL504—Install choke plate so notch (N) is toward fuel pump cover.

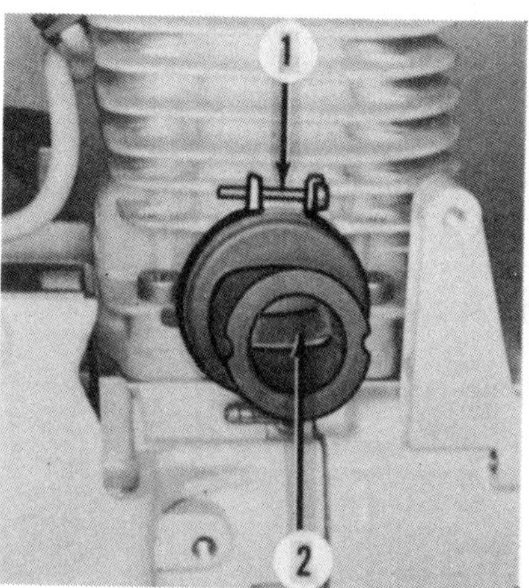

Fig. SL506—Install intake manifold clamp on trimmers and brush cutters so clamp screw (1) is parallel to cylinder fins as shown.

and drive tube on trimmer and brush cutter models, or from blower housing on blower models. Remove cylinder as outlined above. Position a piece of wood between bottom of piston skirt and crankcase to prevent piston and crankshaft from moving. Remove clutch assembly (trimmers and brush cutters) and flywheel (all models). A suitable puller will be required to remove flywheel. Unscrew starter cup locknut, then unscrew starter cup from crankshaft. Remove piston from connecting rod. Remove screws securing the crankcase halves and press crankshaft out of first one crankcase half and then the other half. Pry out oil seals (8 and 16) and remove snap ring (12). Press bearings (13) from crankcase halves (9 and 15).

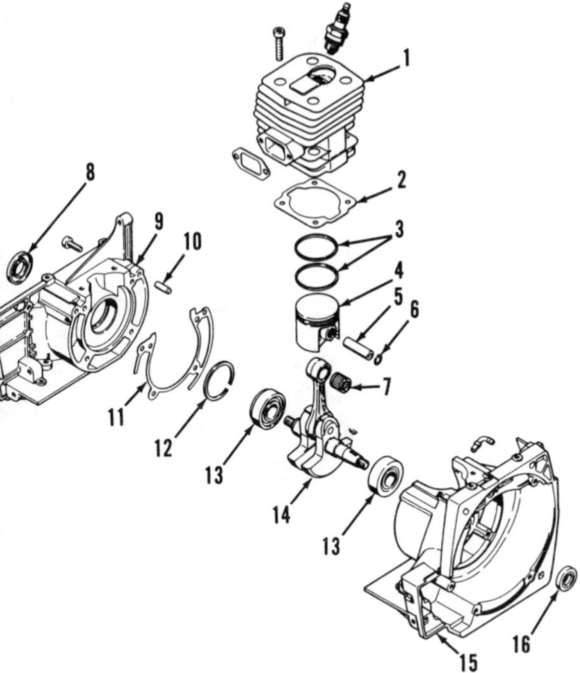

Fig. SL507—Exploded view of engine used on trimmers and brush cutters. Blower engine is similar.

1. Cylinder
2. Gasket
3. Piston rings
4. Piston
5. Piston pin
6. Retaining ring
7. Bearing
8. Seal
9. Crankcase half
10. Dowel pin
11. Gasket
12. Snap ring
13. Bearings
14. Crankshaft assy.
15. Crankcase half
16. Seal

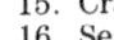

Connecting rod big end rides on a roller bearing and should be inspected for excessive wear and damage. If rod, bearing or crankshaft is damaged, complete crankshaft and connecting rod assembly must be renewed.

When installing main bearings, heat crankcase halves to approximately 80° C (180° F) and seat bearing against snap ring (12—Fig. SL507) or against shoulder of crankcase half (15). Install bearing with shouldered side toward snap ring (12). It may be necessary to heat main bearing to ease insertion of crankshaft. Install oil seals so lip is toward inside of crankcase. Tighten crankcase screws to 8 N·m (71 in.-lbs.).

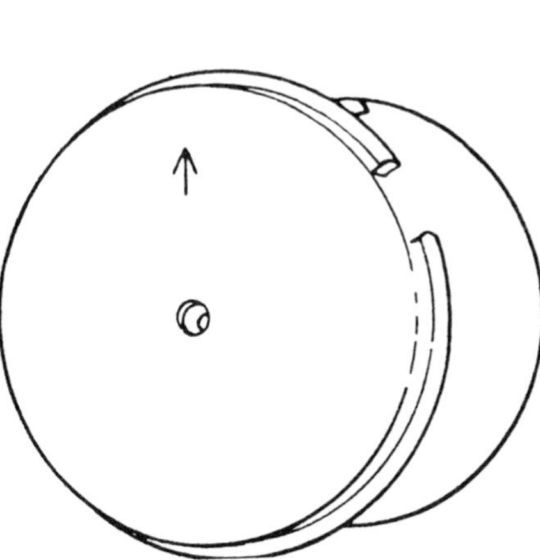

Fig. SL508—Install piston on connecting rod so arrow points toward exhaust port.

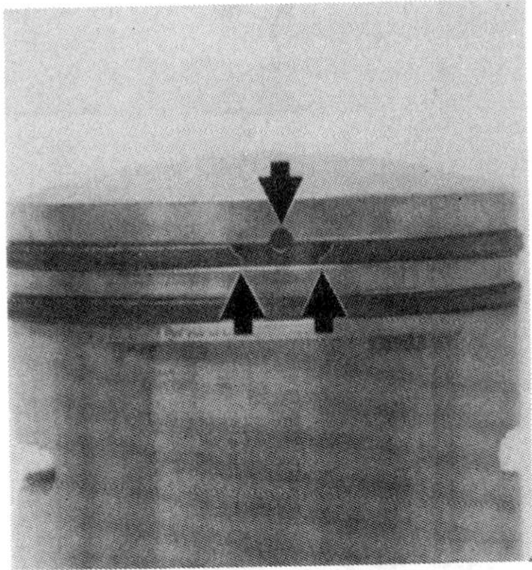

Fig. SL509—Piston ring end gaps must be positioned around locating pins in ring grooves as shown.

CLUTCH. The engine on trimmers and brush cutters is equipped with a two-shoe clutch. The clutch shoe assembly is mounted on the flywheel (1—Fig. SL510). The clutch drum (9) rides in the clutch housing (11).

To remove clutch drum, disconnect throttle cable and ignition wires from engine. Remove clutch housing mounting screws and remove clutch housing and drive tube as an assembly. Remove clutch housing clamp bolt and set screw and withdraw drive tube from housing. Detach snap ring (13) and press clutch drum shaft out of bearing (12). Detach snap ring (10) and remove bearing (12). Reverse removal procedure to install clutch drum.

Clutch shoes (3) are available as a pair. Install clutch shoes so arrows on shoes point in a counterclockwise direction as shown in Fig. SL511. Install clutch spring (5) so when assembly is mounted on flywheel the spring hook ends will be toward flywheel.

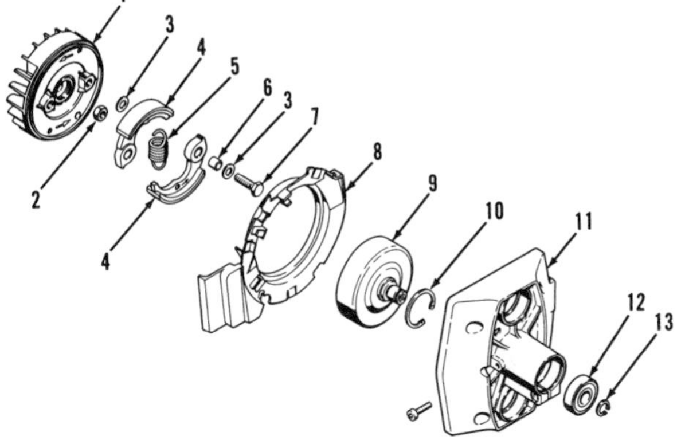

Fig. SL510—Exploded view of clutch assembly used on trimmers and brush cutters.

1. Flywheel
2. Nut
3. Washers
4. Clutch shoes
5. Spring
6. Bushing
7. Screw
8. Flywheel cover
9. Clutch drum
10. Snap ring
11. Drive housing
12. Bearing
13. Snap ring

REWIND STARTER. Refer to Fig. SL512 for an exploded view of rewind starter. To disassemble starter, detach starter housing (3) from engine. Remove rope handle and allow rope to wind into starter. Detach retaining clip (8) and remove rope pulley (5). Wear appropriate safety eyewear and gloves before detaching rewind spring (4) from housing as spring may uncoil uncontrolled.

To remove starter cup (10), unscrew locknut (9), then unscrew cup from crankshaft.

Rope length should be 96 cm ($37^3/_4$ in.). Wind rewind spring in counterclockwise direction from outer end. Note that clip (8) retains pulley and pawl (6) and that peg on pawl must be inside clip as shown in Fig. SL513. Closed end of clip (Fig. SL513) points in a counterclockwise direction when installed correctly. Assemble starter while passing rope through housing rope outlet and attach rope handle to rope. To place tension on starter rope, pull rope out of housing. Engage rope in notch on pulley and turn pulley counterclockwise seven turns. Hold pulley and disengage rope from pulley notch. Release pulley and allow rope to wind on pulley. Check starter operation. Rope handle should be held against housing by spring tension, but it must be possible to rotate pulley at least $^1/_2$ turn counterclockwise when rope is pulled out fully.

Tighten starter cup to 10 N·m (88 in.-lbs.) and locknut to 25 N·m (18 ft.-lbs.).

Fig. SL511—Install clutch shoes so arrows point in counterclockwise direction. Hook ends of spring (5) must be toward flywheel.

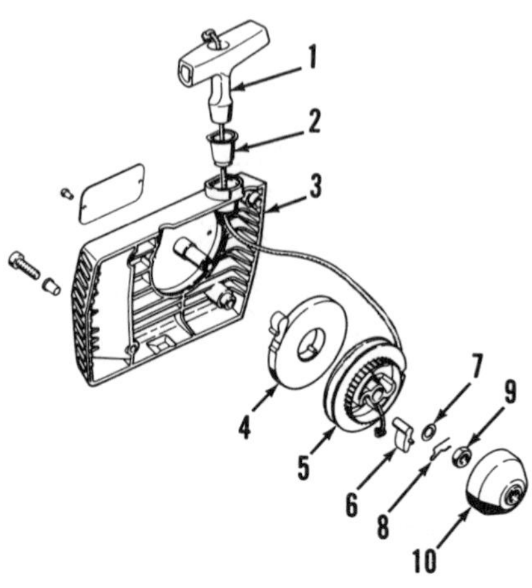

Fig. SL512—Exploded view of rewind starter used on trimmers and brush cutters. Starter on blowers is similar.

1. Handle
2. Rope outlet
3. Starter housing
4. Rewind spring
5. Pulley
6. Pawl
7. Washer
8. Clip
9. Nut
10. Starter cup

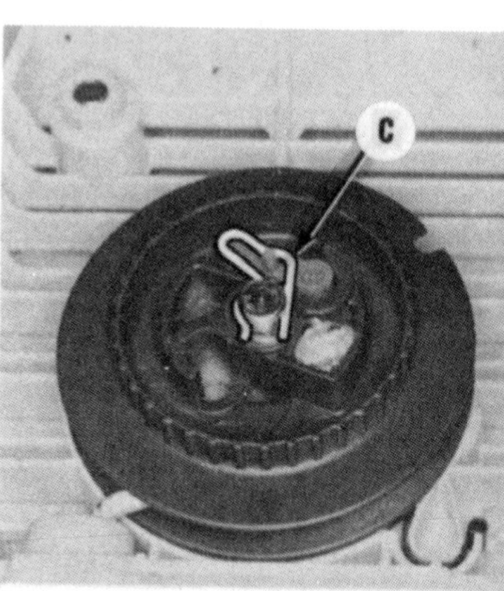

Fig. SL513—Closed end of starter clip (arrow) should point in a counterclockwise direction. Pawl pin must be located inside the clip.

Illustrations courtesy Stihl Inc.

TANAKA (TAS)

ENGINE SERVICE

Model	Bore	Stroke	Displacement
TBC-160 & TBC-162	27.0 mm (1.06 in.)	28.0 mm (1.10 in.)	16.0 cc (0.94 cu. in.)
AST-7000N, AST-7000S, TBC-202, TBC-205, TBC-215 & TST-218	30.0 mm (1.18 in.)	28.0 mm (1.10 in.)	20.0 cc (1.22 cu. in.)
AST-7000, TBC-210 & TBC-220	31.0 mm (1.22 in.)	28.0 mm (1.10 in.)	21.0 cc (1.28 cu. in.)
TBC-220SS, TBC-232 & TBC-240	31.0 mm (1.22 in.)	30.0 mm (1.18 in.)	22.6 cc (1.38 cu. in.)
TBC-250, TBC-2500 & TPE-250	[[ ]] mm ([ ] in.)	[[ ]] mm ([ ] in.)	24.8 cc (1.51 cu. in.)
TBC-265	33.0 mm (1.30 in.)	30.0 mm (1.18 in.)	26.0 cc (1.59 cu. in.)
TBC-2800	[ ] mm ([ ] in.)	30.0 mm (1.18 in.)	28.0 cc (1.71 cu. in.)
SUM-321, TBC-300, TBC-322 & TBC-325	36.0 mm (1.42 in.)	30.0 mm (1.18 in.)	31.0 cc (1.86 cu. in.)
TBC-355	38.0 mm (1.50 in.)	30.0 mm (1.18 in.)	34.0 cc (2.07 cu. in.)
TBC-373	38.0 mm (1.50 in.)	33.0 mm (1.30 in.)	37.4 cc (2.28 cu. in.)
TBC-400, TBC-422C & TBC-425	40.0 mm (1.57 in.)	32.0 mm (1.26 in.)	40.0 cc (2.44 cu. in.)
TBL-455 & TBL-500	38.0 mm (1.50 in.)	38.0 mm (1.50 in.)	43.0 cc (2.62 cu. in.)
TBC-500	39.0 mm (1.53 in.)	38.0 mm (1.50 in.)	46.0 cc (2.81 cu. in.)
TBC-501	41.0 mm (1.61 in.)	38.0 mm (1.50 in.)	50.2 cc (3.06 cu. in.)

ENGINE INFORMATION

These two-stroke, air-cooled engines are used on some Tanaka string trimmers, brush cutters and blowers as well as equipment of other manufacturers. Refer to other Tanaka engine section for service information on other Tanaka engines used on some models.

MAINTENANCE

LUBRICATION. Engine lubrication is obtained by mixing gasoline with an oil designed for two-stroke, air-cooled engines. Refer to trimmer or blower service section for manufacturer's recommended fuel:oil mixture ratio.

SPARK PLUG. Electrode gap should be 0.6 mm (0.024 in.) for all models. The recommended spark plug for most models is NGK BPM-6A or BPM-7A, but certain applications are fitted with other spark plugs. Champion CJ-6 is originally installed in TBC-355 and Champion CJ-8 is used in TBC-400 models.

CARBURETOR. Various types of carburetors have been used. Refer to the appropriate following section for carburetor service.

Walbro HDA. The Walbro HDA is used on some engines. Initial setting of idle and high-speed mixture screws is 1-1/8 turns out from a lightly seated position. Final adjustment is performed with engine running at normal operating temperature. Be sure engine air filter is clean before adjusting carburetor.

Adjust idle speed screw (9—Fig. TA101) so engine idles at 2500 rpm. Adjust idle mixture screw (10) to obtain highest idle speed, then turn screw 1/8-1/4 turn counterclockwise and readjust idle speed screw to 2500 rpm. Adjust high-speed mixture screw (11) to obtain highest engine speed at full throttle, then turn screw 1/8-1/4 turn

Illustrations courtesy Tanaka Ltd.

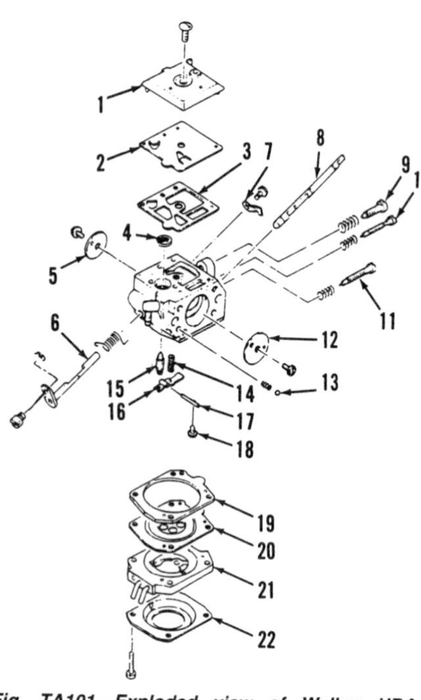

Fig. TA101—Exploded view of Walbro HDA carburetor.

1. Cover
2. Fuel pump diaphragm
3. Gasket
4. Screen
5. Throttle plate
6. Throttle shaft
7. Throttle stop
8. Choke shaft
9. Idle speed screw
10. Idle mixture screw
11. High speed mixture screw
12. Choke plate
13. Detent ball
14. Spring
15. Fuel inlet valve
16. Metering lever
17. Pin
18. Screw
19. Gasket
20. Metering diaphragm
21. Plate
22. Cover

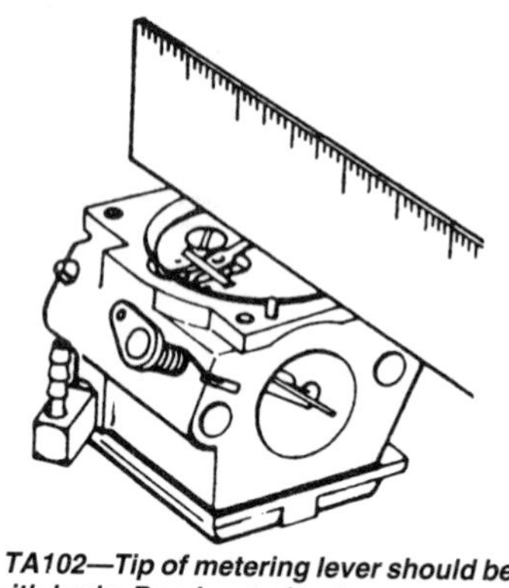

Fig. TA102—Tip of metering lever should be flush with body. Bend metering lever as needed.

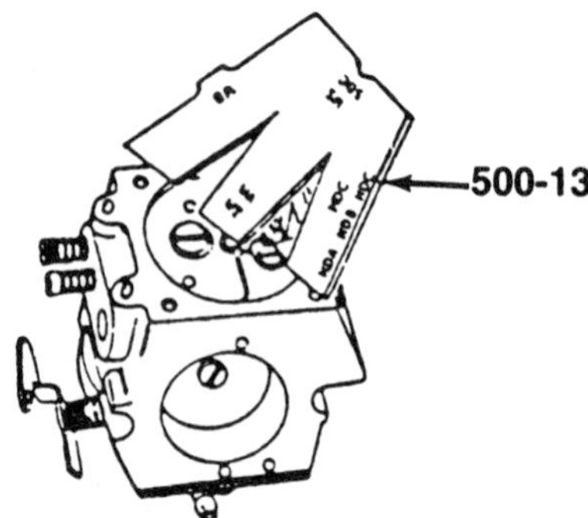

Fig. TA104—Metering lever should just touch leg of Walbro tool 500-13. Bend lever to obtain correct lever height.

counterclockwise. Do not adjust high-speed mixture screw too lean as engine may be damaged.

To disassemble carburetor, refer to Fig. TA101 and remove covers (1 and 22) for access to internal components. Remove diaphragms (2 and 20), fuel screen (4), metering lever (16), fuel inlet valve (15) and fuel mixture screws (9 and 10).

Clean and inspect all components. Wires or drill bits should not be used to clean passages as fuel flow may be altered. Inspect diaphragms (2 and 20) for defects that may affect operation. Examine fuel inlet valve and seat. Inlet valve (15) is renewable, but carburetor body must be renewed if seat is damaged or excessively worn. Discard carburetor body if mixture screw seats are damaged or excessively worn. Screens should be clean. Be sure throttle plate fits shaft and carburetor bore properly. Apply Loctite to throttle plate retaining screws.

Adjust metering lever height so meter lever tip is flush with body as shown in Fig. TA102.

Walbro WA. Some engines are equipped with a Walbro WA diaphragm-type carburetor. Initial adjustment of idle and high-speed mixture screws is 1-1/4 turns out from a lightly seated position. Final adjustments are performed with trimmer line at recommended length or blade installed. Engine must be at operating temperature and running. Be sure engine air filter is clean before adjusting carburetor.

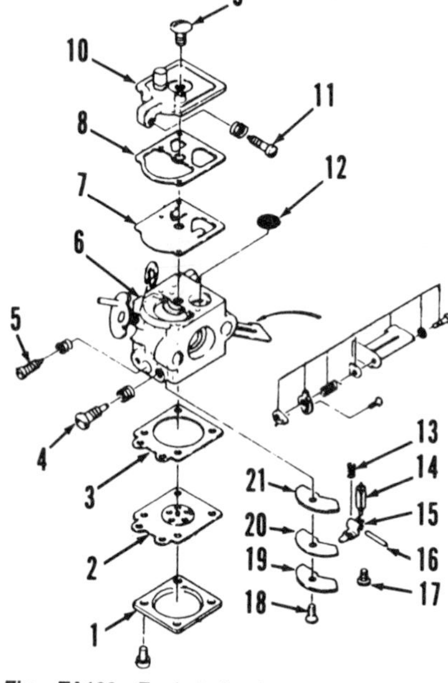

Fig. TA103—Exploded view of Walbro WA carburetor.

1. Cover
2. Diaphragm
3. Gasket
4. High speed mixture screw
5. Idle mixture screw
6. Body
7. Fuel pump diaphragm
8. Gasket
9. Screw
10. Cover
11. Idle speed screw
12. Screen
13. Spring
14. Fuel inlet valve
15. Metering lever
16. Pin
17. Screw
18. Screw
19. Circuit plate
20. Diaphragm
21. Gasket

Adjust idle speed screw (11—Fig. TA103) so trimmer head or blade does not rotate. Adjust idle mixture screw (5) to obtain maximum idle speed possible, then turn idle mixture screw 1/6 turn counterclockwise. If necessary, readjust idle speed screw so trimmer head or blade does not rotate at idle speed.

Operate unit at full throttle and adjust high-speed mixture screw (4) to obtain maximum engine rpm, then turn high-speed mixture screw counterclockwise until a very slight four-cycling exhaust sound is heard.

When overhauling carburetor, refer to exploded view in Fig. TA103 and remove covers (1 and 10) for access to internal components. Remove diaphragms (2 and 7), circuit plate (19), metering lever (15) and fuel inlet valve (14), fuel screen (12) and fuel mixture screws (4 and 5).

Clean and inspect all components. Examine fuel inlet valve and seat. Inlet valve (14) is renewable, but carburetor body must be renewed if seat is excessively worn or damaged. Inspect mixture screws and seats. Renew carburetor body if seats are excessively worn or damaged. Clean fuel screen. Inspect diaphragms for tears and other damage.

Check metering lever height as shown in Fig. TA104 using Walbro tool 500-13. Metering lever should just touch leg on tool. Bend lever to obtain correct lever height.

Walbro WY and WYJ. Some engines may be equipped with a Walbro WY or WYJ carburetor. This is a diaphragm-type carburetor that uses a barrel-type throttle rather than a throttle plate.

Idle fuel for the carburetor flows up into the throttle barrel where it is fed into the air stream. On some models, the idle fuel flow can be adjusted by turning an idle mixture limiter plate (P—Fig. TA105). Initial setting is in center notch. Rotating the plate clockwise will lean the idle mixture.

Inside the limiter plate is an idle mixture needle (N—Fig. TA106) that is preset at the factory. Removal of idle mixture needle is not recommended. If removed, use the following procedure to determine correct position. Back out

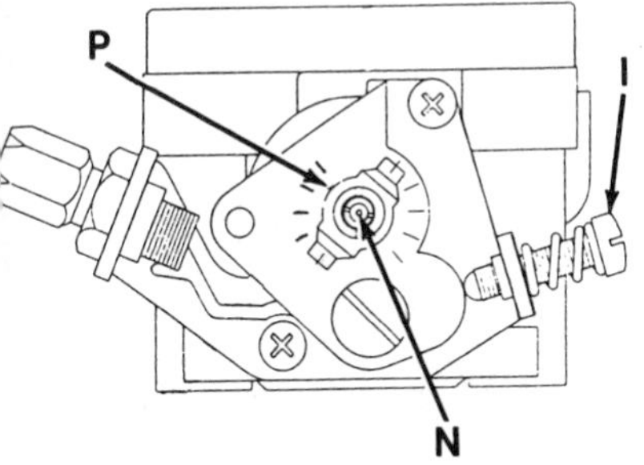

Fig. TA105—On Walbro WY or WYJ carburetor, idle speed screw is located at (I), idle mixture limiter plate is located at (P) and idle mixture needle is located at (N). A plug covers the idle mixture needle.

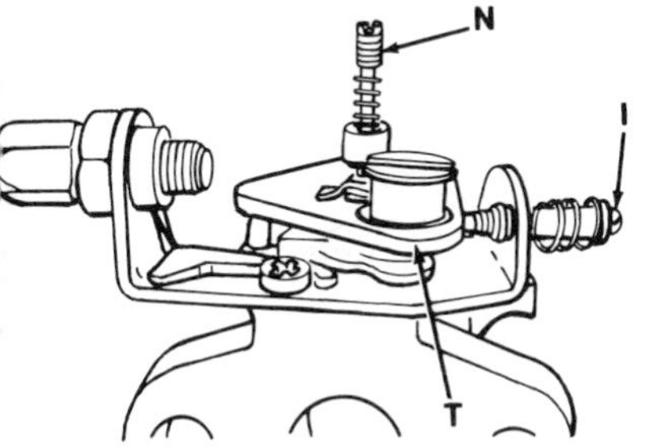

Fig. TA106—View of idle mixture needle (N) used on Walbro WY carburetor.

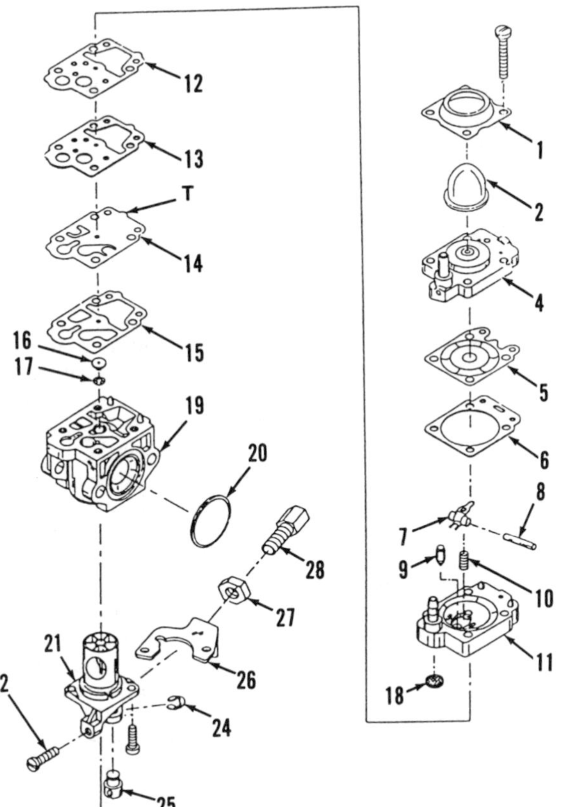

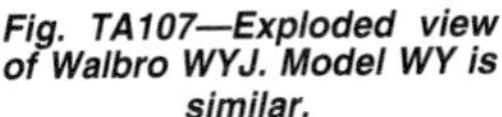

Fig. TA107—Exploded view of Walbro WYJ. Model WY is similar.

1. Cover
2. Primer bulb
4. Plate
5. Metering diaphragm
6. Gasket
7. Pin
8. Metering lever
9. Fuel inlet valve
10. Spring
11. Fuel pump body
12. Gasket
13. Fuel pump plate
14. Fuel pump diaphragm
15. Gasket
16. Main jet
17. "O" ring
18. Fuel screen
19. Body
20. "O" ring
21. Throttle barrel assy.
22. Idle speed screw
23. Plug
24. "E" ring
25. Swivel
26. Bracket
27. Nut
28. Adjuster

needle (N) until unscrewed. Screw in needle five turns on Model WY or 15 turns on Model WYJ. Rotate idle mixture plate (P—Fig. TA105) to center notch.

Run engine until normal operating temperature is attained. Adjust idle speed screw so trimmer head or blade does not rotate. Rotate idle mixture needle (N—Fig. TA106) and obtain highest rpm (turning needle clockwise leans the mixture), then turn needle 1/4 turn counterclockwise. Readjust idle speed screw. Note that idle mixture plate and needle are available only as an assembly with throttle barrel (21—Fig. TA107).

The high-speed mixture is controlled by a removable fixed jet (16—Fig. TA107).

To overhaul carburetor, refer to exploded view in Fig. TA107 and note the following: On models with a plastic body, clean only with solvents approved for use with plastic. Do not use wire or drill bits to clean fuel passages as fuel flow may be altered. Do not disassemble throttle barrel assembly (21). Examine fuel inlet valve and seat. Inlet valve (9) is renewable, but fuel pump body (11) must be renewed if seat is excessively worn or damaged. Clean fuel screen. Inspect diaphragms for tears and other damage. When installing plates and gaskets (12 through 15) note that tabs (T) on ends will "stair step" when correctly installed.

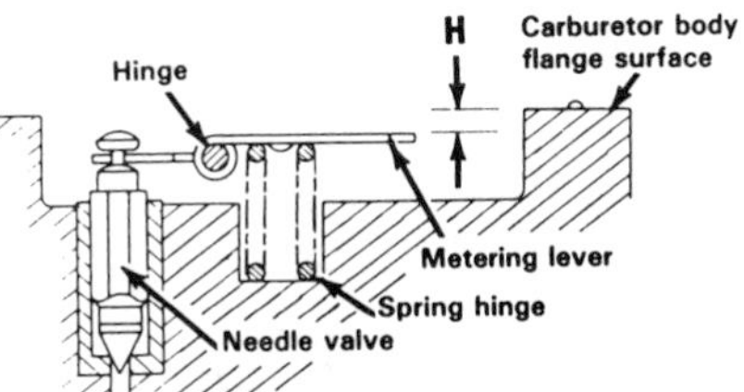

Fig. TA108—Metering lever height (H) must be set on diaphragm-type carburetors. Refer to text for specified height.

Adjust metering lever height to obtain 1.5 mm (0.059 in.) between carburetor body surface and lever as shown in Fig. TA108.

Walbro WZ. Some engines may be equipped with a Walbro WZ carburetor. This is a diaphragm-type carburetor that uses a barrel-type throttle rather than a throttle plate.

Idle fuel for the carburetor flows up into the throttle barrel where it is fed into the air stream. Idle fuel flow can be adjusted by turning idle mixture limiter plate (P—Fig. TA109). Initial setting is in center notch. Rotating the plate clockwise will lean the idle mixture.

Inside the limiter plate is an idle mixture needle (N—Fig. TA106) that is preset at the factory (a plug covers the needle). Removal of idle mixture needle

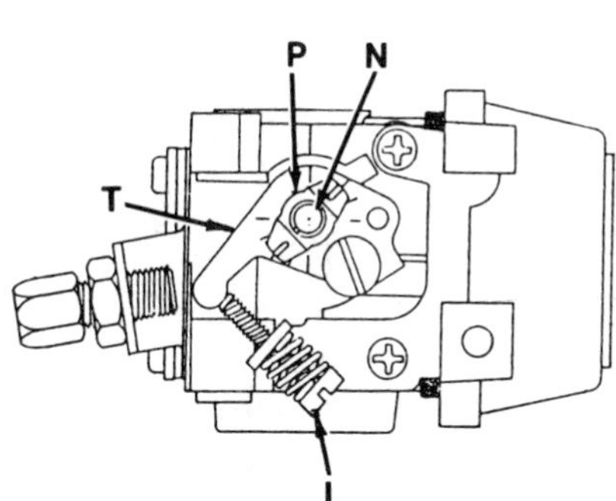

Fig. TA109—On Walbro WZ carburetor, idle speed screw is located at (I), idle mixture limiter plate is located at (P) and idle mixture needle is located at (N). A plug covers the idle mixture needle.

is not recommended. If idle mixture needle is removed, use the following procedure to determine correct position. Back out needle (N) until unscrewed, then screw in needle six turns. Rotate idle mixture plate (P—Fig. TA109) to center notch.

Run engine until normal operating temperature is attained. Adjust idle speed screw so trimmer head or blade does not rotate. Rotate idle mixture needle (N—Fig TA106) and obtain highest rpm (turning needle clockwise leans the mixture), then turn needle counterclockwise until rpm decreases 200-500 rpm. Readjust idle speed

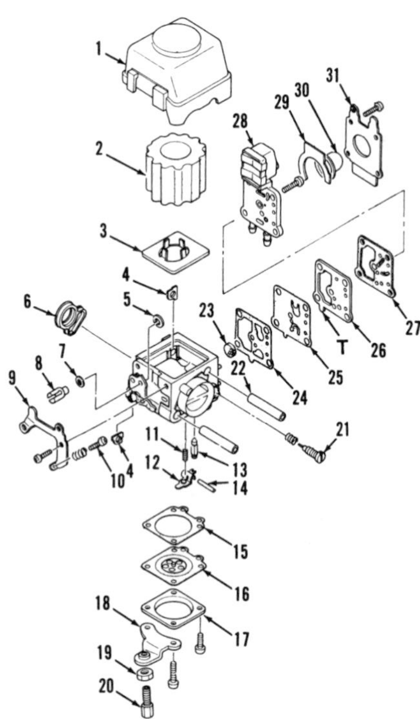

Fig. TA110—Exploded view of Walbro WZ carburetor.

1. Cover
2. Air cleaner element
3. Plate
4. Plate
5. Stop ring
6. Gasket
7. Thrust washer
8. Swivel
9. Bracket
10. Idle speed screw
11. Spring
12. Metering lever
13. Fuel inlet valve
14. Pin
15. Gasket
16. Metering diaphragm
17. Cover
18. Bracket
19. Nut
20. Cable adjuster
21. High peed mixture screw
22. Sleeve
23. Screen
24. Gasket
25. Fuel pump diaphragm
26. Plate
27. Gasket
28. Fuel pump cover
29. Gasket
30. Primer bulb
31. Retainer

screw. Note that idle mixture plate and needle are available only as an assembly with throttle barrel.

Initial setting of high-speed mixture screw (21—TA110) is 1-1/2 turns out from a lightly seated position. Adjust high-speed mixture screw to obtain highest engine speed, then turn screw 1/4 turn counterclockwise. Do not adjust mixture too lean as engine may be damaged.

To overhaul carburetor, refer to exploded view in Fig. TA110 and note the following: Clean only with solvents approved for use with plastic. Do not disassemble throttle barrel assembly. Examine fuel inlet valve and seat. Inlet valve (13) is renewable, but carburetor body must be renewed if seat is excessively worn or damaged. Inspect high-speed mixture screw and seat. Renew carburetor body if seat is excessively worn or damaged. Clean fuel screen. Inspect diaphragms for tears and other damage. When installing plates and gaskets (24, 25 and 26) note that tabs (T) on ends will "stair step" when correctly installed.

Adjust metering lever height to obtain 1.5 mm (0.059 in.) between carburetor body surface and lever as shown in Fig. TA108.

Float-Type Carburetor. Two different float-type carburetors have been used (see Fig. TA111 and Fig. TA112). Service procedure for both carburetors is similar.

Idle mixture is not adjustable. Idle speed may be adjusted by turning adjusting screw (17). High-speed mixture is controlled by removable fixed jet (9). Midrange mixture is determined by the position of clip (4) on jet needle (5). There are three grooves in upper end of the jet needle and normal position of clip is in the middle groove. The mixture will be leaner if clip is installed in the top groove, or richer if clip is installed in the bottom groove.

Before removing carburetor from engine, unscrew cap (1) and withdraw throttle slide (6) assembly. When overhauling carburetor, refer to Fig. TA111 or Fig. TA112 and note the following: Examine fuel inlet valve and seat. Inlet valve (10) is renewable on all models.

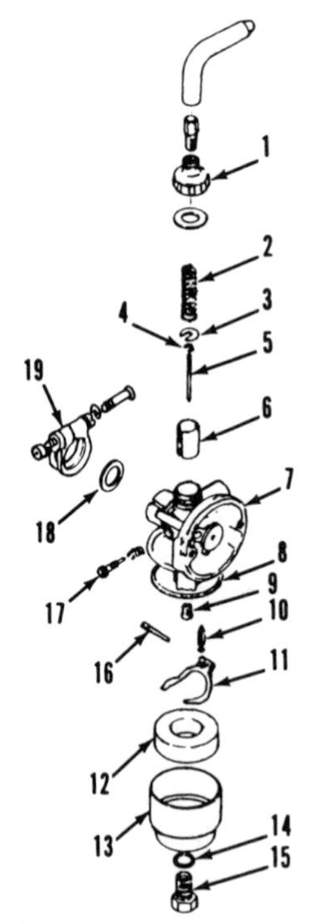

Fig. TA111—Exploded view of float-type carburetor used on some models.

1. Cap
2. Spring
3. Seat
4. Clip
5. Jet needle
6. Throttle slide
7. Body
8. Gasket
9. Main jet
10. Fuel inlet valve
11. Float lever
12. Float
13. Float bowl
14. Gasket
15. Screw
16. Pin
17. Idle speed screw
18. Gasket
19. Clamp

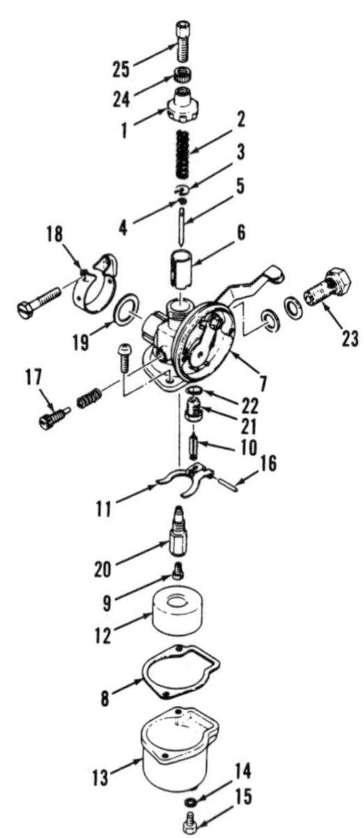

Fig. TA112—Exploded view of float-type carburetor used on some models.

1. Cap
2. Spring
3. Seat
4. Clip
5. Jet needle
6. Throttle slide
7. Body
8. Gasket
9. Main jet
10. Fuel inlet valve
11. Float lever
12. Float
13. Float bowl
14. Gasket
15. Screw
16. Pin
17. Idle speed screw
18. Clamp
19. Gasket
20. Nozzle
21. Fuel inlet valve seat
22. "O" ring
23. Fuel inlet bolt
24. Nut
25. Cable adjuster

Inlet seat (21) is renewable on some models. On some models the inlet seat is not renewable and carburetor body (7) must be renewed if seat is excessively worn or damaged. When installing throttle slide, be sure groove in side of throttle slide (6) indexes with pin in bore of carburetor body.

Rotary-Type Carburetor. Refer to Fig. TA113 for an exploded view of the rotary-type carburetor used on some models.

Idle mixture is not adjustable. High speed mixture is controlled by removable fixed jet (9). Midrange mixture is determined by the position of clip (4) on jet needle (5). There are three grooves in upper end of the jet needle and normal position of clip is in the middle groove. Installing clip in the top groove leans the mixture. Installing clip in the bottom groove will enrich the mixture.

Before removing carburetor from engine, unscrew cap (1) and withdraw throttle slide (6) assembly. When over-

Illustrations courtesy Tanaka Ltd.

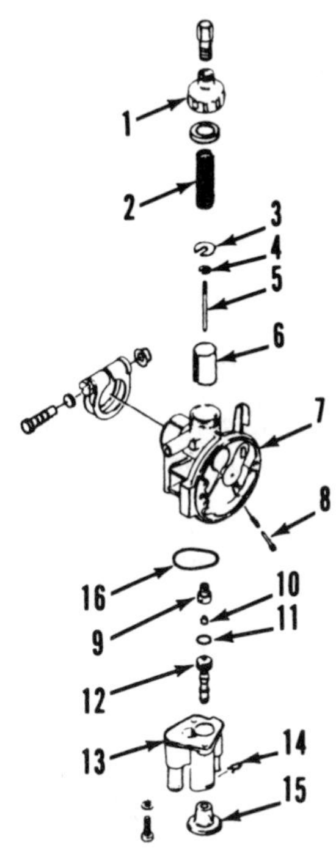

Fig. TA113—Exploded view of rotary-type carburetor used on some models.

Cap
Spring
Seat
Clip
Jet needle
Throttle slide
Body
Mixture screw
9. Main jet
10. Cap
11. "O" ring
12. Check valve
13. Reservoir
14. Clip
15. Rubber cap
16. Gasket

auling carburetor, refer to Fig. TA113 and note the following: Remove reservoir (13), clip (14) and rubber cap (15). Pull check valve (12) out of reservoir. Remove check valve cap (10) and "O" ring (11).

Inspect components and renew if damaged or excessively worn. When installing throttle slide, be sure groove in side of throttle slide (6) indexes with pin in bore of carburetor body.

IGNITION SYSTEM. The engine may be equipped with a breaker-point type ignition system or a solid-state type ignition system. Refer to appropriate following paragraphs for service information.

Breaker-Point Ignition System. The ignition condenser and breaker-points are located behind the flywheel. To adjust or renew breaker-points, the flywheel must be removed. Breaker-point gap should be 0.35 mm (0.014 in.).

Ignition timing is adjusted by moving magneto stator plate. Breaker-points should open when "M" mark of flywheel is aligned with reference mark on crankcase (see Fig. TA114).

On models with external ignition coil, air gap between coil legs and flywheel should be 0.35 mm (0.014 in.). On models with ignition coil on stator plate

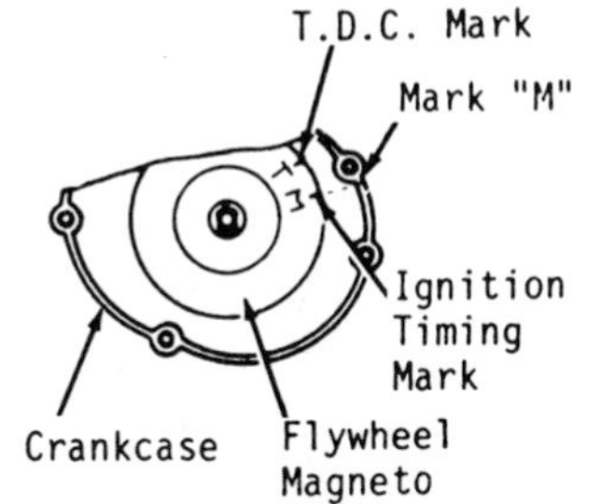

Fig. TA114—On models with breaker-points, align "M" mark on flywheel magneto with mark on crankcase as shown.

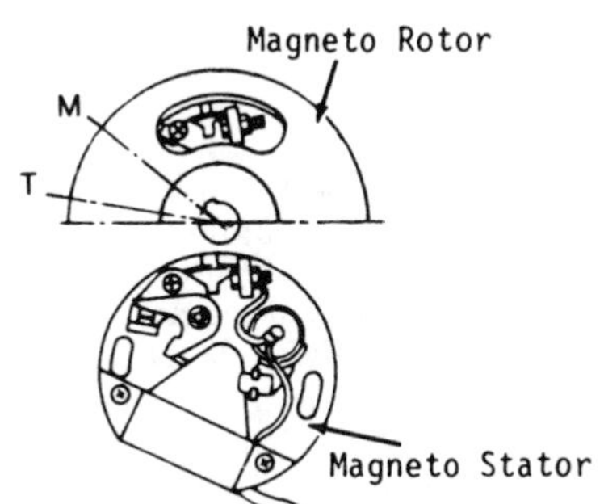

Fig. TA115—On models with ignition coil on stator plate, the metal core legs of the ignition coil should be flush with outer edge of the stator plate.

(Fig. TA115), the metal core legs of the ignition coil should be flush with outer edge of the stator plate.

Solid-State Ignition System. All later models are equipped with a solid-state ignition system. The engine may be equipped with a one-piece ignition module that includes the ignition coil, or a two-piece ignition system that consists of a separate ignition module and ignition coil. The ignition coil or module may be mounted on the blower housing, crankcase or cylinder.

The ignition system is considered satisfactory if a spark will jump across the 3 mm (1/8 in.) gap of a test spark plug. If no spark is produced, check on/off switch, wiring and ignition module/coil air gap. Air gap between flywheel magnet and ignition module/coil should be 0.25-0.35 mm (0.010-0.014 in.).

REPAIRS

PISTON, PIN AND RINGS. The piston is equipped with two piston rings. Ring rotation is prevented by a locating pin in each piston ring groove. Piston and rings are available only in standard diameter.

To remove piston, remove engine cover, starter housing and fuel tank. Remove air cleaner, carburetor and muffler. Remove cylinder mounting screws and pull cylinder off piston. Remove retaining rings (5—Fig. TA116),

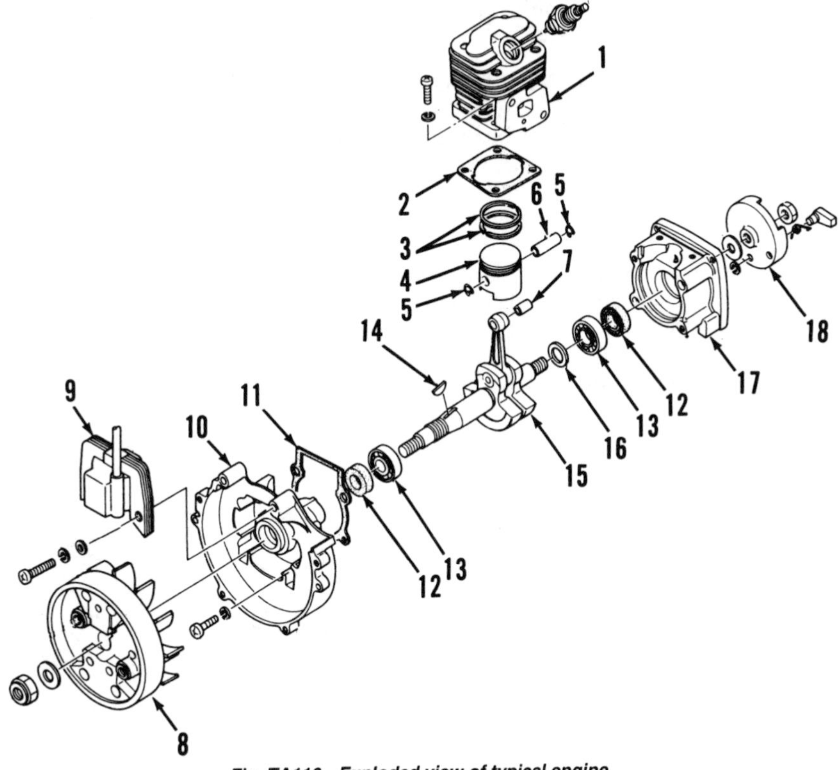

Fig. TA116—Exploded view of typical engine.

1. Cylinder
2. Gasket
3. Piston rings
4. Piston
5. Piston pin
6. Retaining rings
7. Needle bearing
8. Flywheel
9. Ignition coil
10. Crankcase half
11. Gasket
12. Seal
13. Bearings
14. Key
15. Crankshaft assy.
16. Shim
17. Crankcase half
18. Starter pulley

Illustrations courtesy Tanaka Ltd.

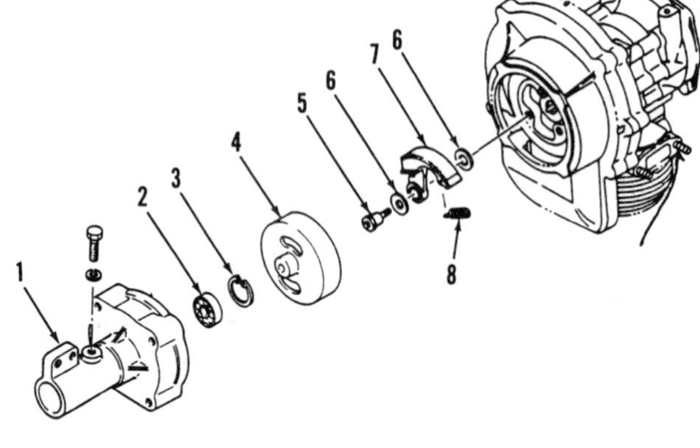

Fig. TA117—Exploded view of clutch assembly used on some models.

1. Housing
2. Bearing
3. Snap ring
4. Clutch drum
5. Shoulder screw
6. Washers
7. Clutch shoe
8. Spring

then use a suitable pin puller to push piston pin (6) out of piston. Remove piston (4) and bearing (7) from connecting rod.

Install piston so arrow on piston crown points toward exhaust port. On 50.2 cc engine, install piston so shaped portion of crown is toward intake. Lubricate piston and cylinder bore with oil. Be sure piston ring gaps are correctly indexed with locating pins in piston ring grooves when installing cylinder.

CYLINDER. Some engines are equipped with a chrome plated cylinder. Renew cylinder if bore is excessively worn, scored or otherwise damaged. Cylinder is available only in standard size.

CRANKSHAFT, CONNECTING ROD AND CRANKCASE. Crankshaft, connecting rod and rod bearing are a unit assembly; individual components are not available. The crankshaft is supported by ball bearings at both ends.

To remove crankshaft and connecting rod assembly, separate engine from trimmer drive housing. Remove engine cover, starter housing, fuel tank, air cleaner, carburetor and muffler. Remove spark plug and install the end of a starter rope in spark plug hole to lock piston and crankshaft. Remove nuts attaching flywheel and starter pulley to crankshaft. Use suitable puller to remove flywheel.

Remove cylinder mounting screws and pull cylinder off piston. Remove crankshaft keys and crankcase retaining bolts. Carefully tap on one end of crankshaft to separate crankcase halves. Remove crankshaft and connecting rod assembly from crankcase. Use suitable puller to push piston pin from piston and separate piston from crankshaft. If main bearings (13) remain in crankcase, heat crankcase halves slightly to aid bearing removal. Drive seals (12) out of crankcase halves.

A renewable needle bearing (7) is located in the small end of the connecting rod. Maximum allowable side clearance at rod big end is 0.5 mm (0.020 in.).

Install seals (12—Fig. TA116) with lip toward inside of crankcase. On some engines, shims (16) are available to adjust crankshaft end play. Maximum allowable crankshaft end play is 0.1 mm (0.004 in.).

CLUTCH. 50.2 cc Engine. Trimmers with a 50.2 cc engine are equipped with the clutch shown in Fig. TA11 The upper end of the drive shaft threaded into the clutch drum hub.

To service clutch, disconnect thrott cable and stop switch wires from e gine. Detach drive housing (1) from e gine. To service clutch drum (4), remov gear head from drive shaft housing. I sert a tool through slot of clutch dru so it cannot rotate, then turn squa end (trimmer end) of drive shaft s drum unscrews from drive shaft. D tach snap ring (3) then force drive sha and bearing out toward large end drive housing.

Clutch shoes (7) are available only a set. Clutch springs are available onl as a set.

All Other Engines. The engine equipped with a two-shoe clutch (Fi TA118). The clutch shoe assembly (1 is mounted on the flywheel. The clutc drum (6) rides in the drive housing (1 which may be the fan housing on som engines.

To remove clutch drum, first discor nect throttle cable and stop switc wires from engine. Separate trimme drive housing assembly from engin On models with slots in clutch fac reach through slot and detach sna ring (5—Fig. TA118), then press clutc drum (6) and bearing (4) out of housin Heating housing will ease removal.

On other engines, detach carrie (3—Fig. TA119) from drive housing (1 and press drum and bearing assembl out of carrier. Detach snap ring (4) an press clutch drum shaft out of bearing (5). Reverse removal procedure to in stall clutch drum.

Clutch shoes are available only as pair.

REWIND STARTER. Refer to Figs TA120, TA121 or TA122 for an explode view of starter. To disassemble starte detach starter housing from engine. Re move rope handle and allow rope t wind into starter. Unscrew cente

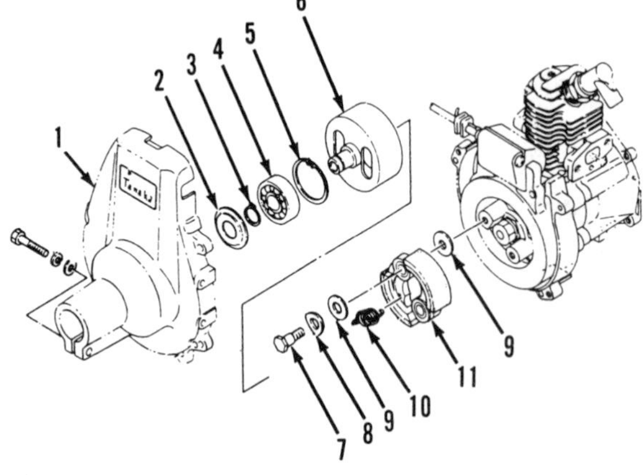

Fig. TA118—Exploded view of clutch assembly used on some models.

1. Clutch housing
2. Washer
3. Snap ring
4. Bearing
5. Snap ring
6. Clutch drum
7. Shoulder screw
8. Wave washer
9. Washer
10. Spring
11. Clutch shoe

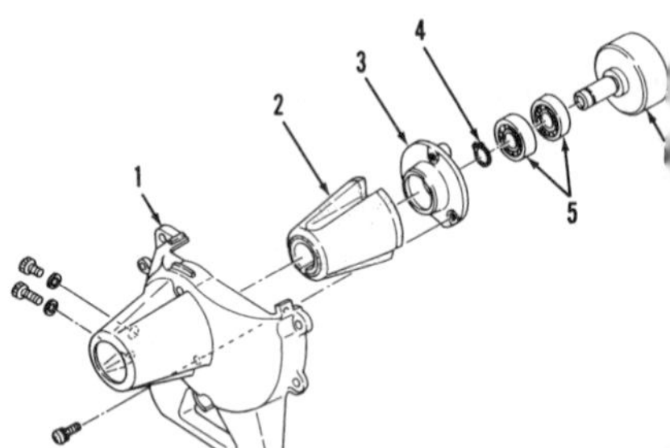

Fig. TA119—Exploded view of clutch drum an bearing assembly used on some models.

1. Housing
2. Isolator
3. Carrier
4. Snap ring
5. Bearings
6. Clutch drum

Illustrations courtesy Tanaka Ltd

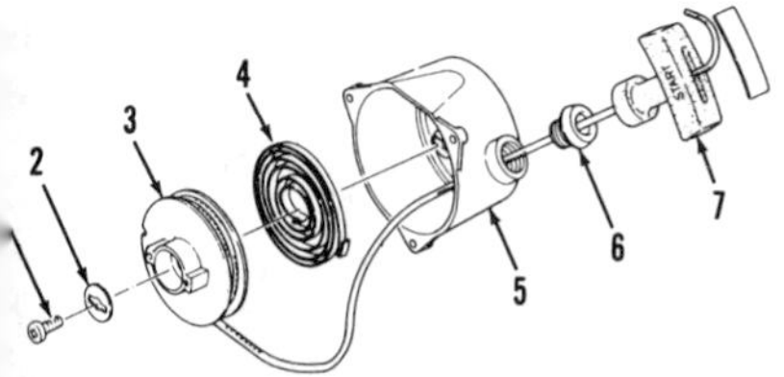

Fig. TA120—Exploded view of rewind starter used on some models.

Screw
Washer
Pulley
Rewind spring
5. Housing
6. Rope guide
7. Handle

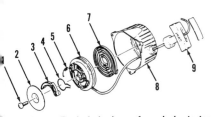

Fig. TA121—Exploded view of rewind starter used on some models.

Handle
Housing
Rewind spring
Pulley
Pawl
6. Washer
7. Friction plate
8. Washer
9. Screw

Fig. TA122—Exploded view of rewind starter used on some models.

Screw
2. Plate
3. Pawl
4. Friction spring
5. Spring
6. Pulley
7. Rewind spring
8. Housing
9. Handle

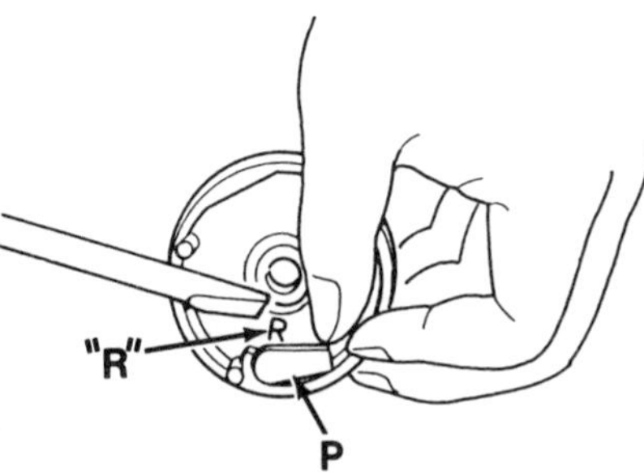

Fig. TA123—Install pawl (P) in hole marked "R".

screw and remove rope pulley. Wear appropriate safety eye protection and gloves before detaching rewind spring from housing as spring may uncoil uncontrolled.

To assemble starter, lubricate center post of housing and spring side with light grease. Install rewind spring so coil windings are counterclockwise from outer end (clockwise on Tanaka Models TBC-160, TBC-202 and TBC-210). Assemble starter while passing rope through housing rope outlet and attach rope handle to rope.

To place tension on starter rope, pull rope out of housing. Engage rope in notch on pulley and turn pulley counterclockwise (clockwise on Tanaka Models TBC-160, TBC-202 and TBC-210). Hold pulley and disengage rope from pulley notch. Release pulley and allow rope to wind on pulley.

Check starter operation. Rope handle should be held against housing by spring tension, but it must be possible to rotate pulley at least 1/4 turn counterclockwise (clockwise on Tanaka Models TBC-160, TBC-202 and TBC-210) when rope is pulled out fully.

On engines with a plate attached to the crankshaft that carries a pawl, install pawl (P—Fig. TA123) in hole marked "R".

ELECTRIC STARTER. An electric starter may be fitted to some 20 or 21 cc engines. Refer to Fig. TA124 for a diagram of the starter components. A battery pack of 1.2v/1.2AH nicad batteries provides power to the starting motor. A relay is used to energize the starter when the start button is depressed. The batteries are charged by a circuit located on the ignition coil. A rectifier converts alternating current to direct current for battery charging. The batteries can also be charged using 120v line current and a transformer as outlined in the Trimmer Section.

To check the starter motor operation, remove the spark plug, disconnect four-wire connector to the handle and use a jumper wire to connect terminals (1 and 4—Fig. TA125) of the female connector. Starter motor should spin, but if it does not, check the relay. If the starter motor runs, but does not turn the engine, check the drive gears.

To further check the relay, remove cover (1—Fig. TA124) and connect voltmeter leads to the motor terminals. Connect a jumper between terminals (1 and 4—Fig. TA125). If voltage is not indicated on the meter, install a new relay. If battery voltage is indicated at the starter motor terminals, but the motor does not turn, the motor is faulty.

To check the engine charging system, run the engine and disconnect the two-wire connector from the battery pack and the four-wire connector from the handlebar. Check voltage at terminals (1 and 2—Fig. TA125) of the female connector by attaching the negative lead from a voltmeter to terminal (1) and positive test lead to terminal (2). With the engine running at 6,000 rpm, the voltmeter should indicate more than 1.1 volts. If voltage is less than 1.1 volts, check the wiring harness for an open circuit. Check air gap (clearance)

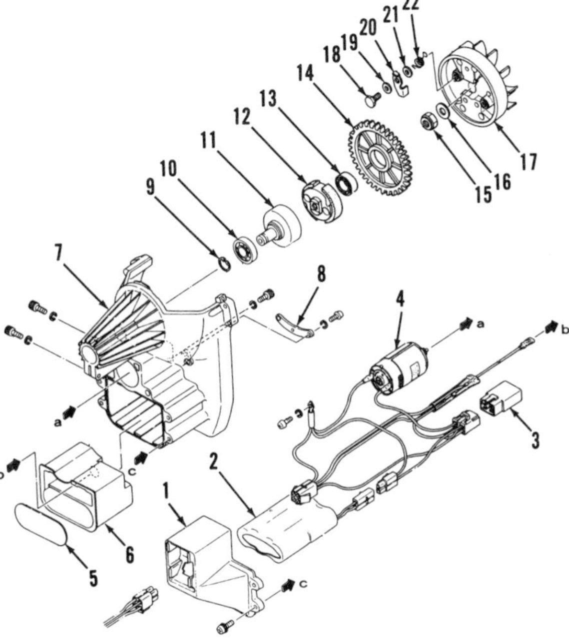

Fig. TA124—Exploded view of electric starter components on 21 cc engine. Components on 20 cc engine are similar.

1. Cover
2. Battery pack
3. Relay
4. Starter motor
5. Cushion
6. Case
7. Housing
8. Bracket
9. Snap ring
10. Bearing
11. Clutch drum
12. Clutch assy.
13. Bearing
14. Gear
15. Nut
16. Washer
17. Flywheel
18. Screw
19. Washer
20. Pawl
21. Washer
22. Spring

between the flywheel magnet and the legs of the coil. If an open circuit is not located and the air gap is correct, install a new ignition coil.

To check the wiring harness, stop the engine and detach the four-wire connector at the engine fan cover. Attach the negative test lead from a voltmeter to terminal (1—Fig. TA125) and the positive test lead to terminal (4). Battery voltage should be indicated on the tester. Attach the negative test lead from the voltmeter to terminal (1) and the positive test lead to terminal (3). The voltmeter should not indicate any voltage. If the wiring harness fails ei-

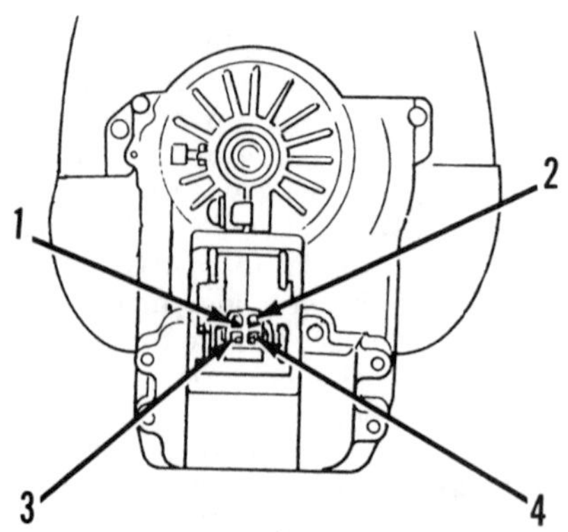

Fig. TA125—Tests may be performed on starter electrical system by attaching tester to connector terminals as outlined in text.

ther of these tests, repair or renew th wiring harness.

To check the battery pack, first re charge the unit. With the engin stopped, detach the four-wire connecto from the handlebar. Attach the nega tive lead from a voltmeter to the termi nal (1) of the female connector. Attac the positive test lead to terminal (2 Battery voltage should be at least 4. volts for 20 cc engine or 7.0 volts for 2 cc engine.

Components of the starter motor ar not available and unit must be service as an assembly.

TANAKA (TAS)

ENGINE SERVICE

Model	Bore	Stroke	Displacement
Tanaka	30 mm (1.18 in.)	28 mm (1.10 in.)	20.0 cc (1.22 cu. in.)

These engines are used on Tanaka Models AST-5000, TBC-4000, TBC-4500 and TBC-5000.

ENGINE INFORMATION

These Tanaka two-stroke, air-cooled gasoline engines are used on Tanaka Models AST-5000, TBC-4000, TBC-4500 and TBC-5000. Tanaka trimmer AST-5000 is equipped with an electric starter.

MAINTENANCE

LUBRICATION. Engine lubrication is obtained by mixing gasoline with an oil designed for two-stroke, air-cooled engines. Refer to trimmer service section for manufacturer's recommended fuel:oil mixture ratio.

SPARK PLUG. Recommended spark plug is NGK BPM6A or equivalent. Electrode gap should be 0.6 mm (0.024 in.).

CARBURETOR. Various types of carburetors have been used. Refer to the appropriate following section for carburetor service.

Walbro WY, WYJ and WYL. Some engines may be equipped with a Walbro WY, WYJ or WYL carburetor. This is a diaphragm-type carburetor that uses a barrel-type throttle rather than a throttle plate.

Idle fuel for the carburetor flows up into the throttle barrel where it is fed into the air stream. On some models, the idle fuel flow can be adjusted by turning an idle mixture limiter plate (P—Fig. TA201). Initial setting is in center notch. Rotating the plate clockwise will lean the idle mixture. Inside the limiter plate is an idle mixture needle (N—Fig. TA202) that is preset at the factory. If removed, use the following procedure to determine correct position. Back out needle (N) until unscrewed. Screw in needle five turns on Model WY or 15 turns on Models WYJ and WYL. Rotate idle mixture plate (P—Fig. TA201) to center notch. Run engine until normal operating temperature is attained. Adjust idle speed screw so trimmer head or blade does not rotate. Rotate idle mixture needle (N—Fig. TA202) and obtain highest rpm (turning needle clockwise leans the mixture), then turn needle 1/4 turn counterclockwise. Readjust idle speed screw. Note that idle mixture plate and needle are available only as an assembly with throttle barrel (18—Fig. TA203).

The high-speed mixture is controlled by a removable fixed jet (14—Fig. TA203).

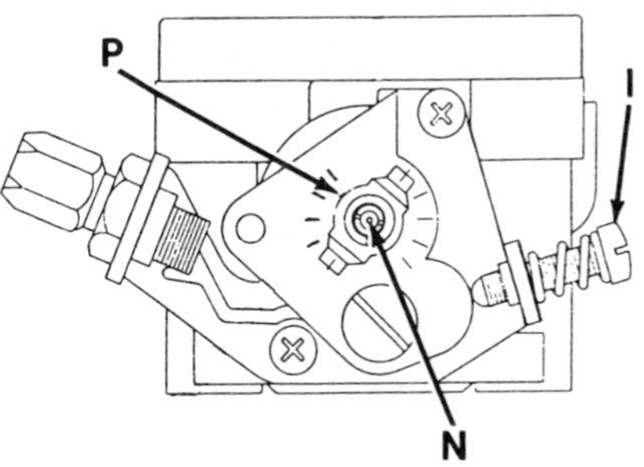

Fig. TA201—On Walbro WY, WYJ or WYL carburetor, idle speed screw is located at (I), idle mixture limiter plate is located at (P) and idle mixture needle is located at (N). A plug covers the idle mixture needle.

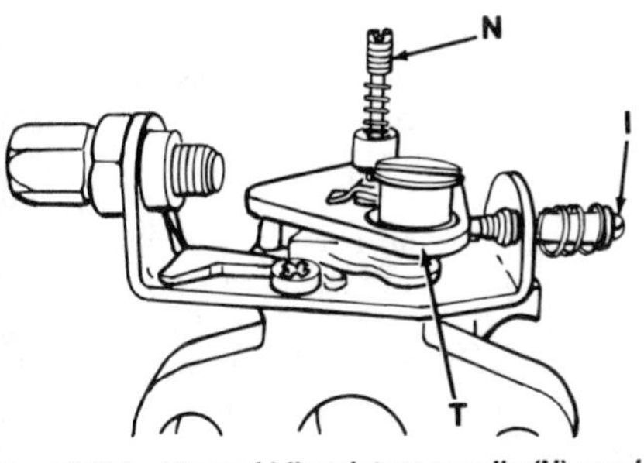

Fig. TA202—View of idle mixture needle (N) used on Walbro WY, WYJ and WYL carburetors.

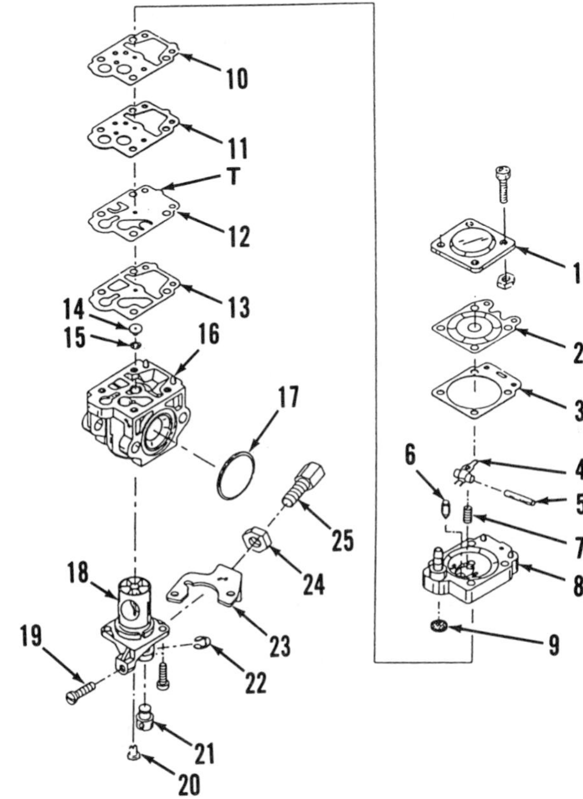

Fig. TA203—Exploded view of Walbro WYJ. Models WY and WYL are similar.

1. Cover
2. Metering diaphragm
3. Gasket
4. Metering lever
5. Pin
6. Fuel inlet valve
7. Spring
8. Fuel pump body
9. Fuel screen
10. Gasket
11. Fuel pump plate
12. Fuel pump diaphragm
13. Gasket
14. Main jet
15. "O" ring
16. Body
17. "O" ring
18. Throttle barrel assy.
19. Idle speed screw
20. Plug
21. Swivel
22. "E" ring
23. Bracket
24. Nut
25. Cable adjuster

Illustrations courtesy Tanaka Ltd.

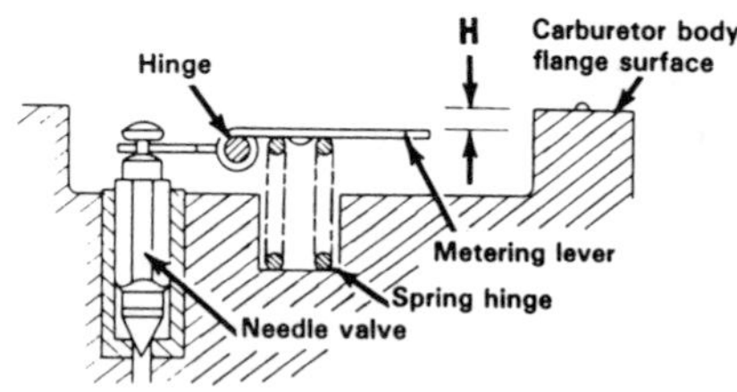

Fig. TA204—Metering lever height (H) must be set on diaphragm-type carburetors. Refer to text for specified height.

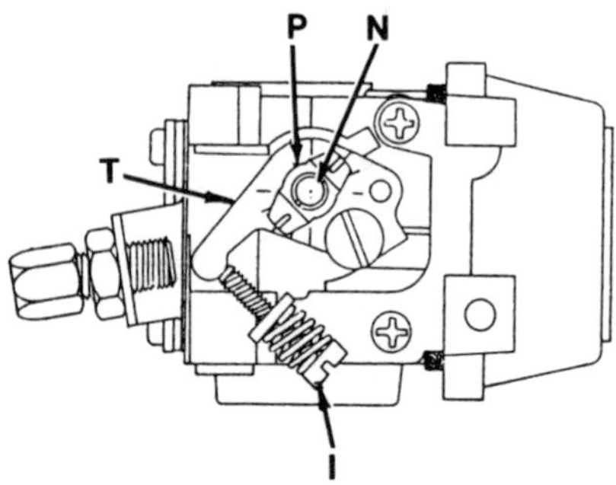

Fig. TA205—On Walbro WZ carburetor, idle speed screw is located at (I), idle mixture limiter plate is located at (P) and idle mixture needle is located at (N). A plug covers the idle mixture needle.

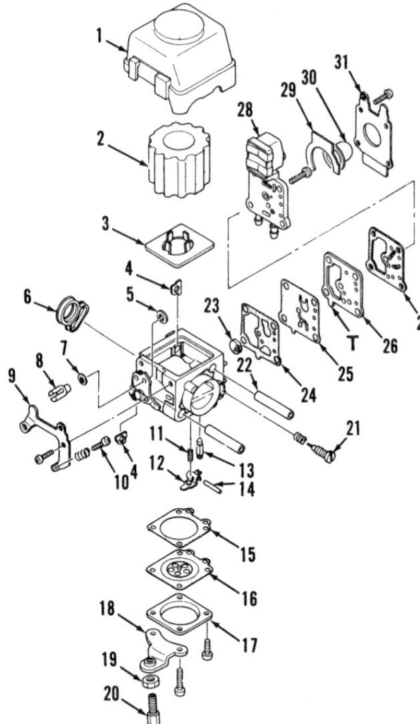

Fig. TA206—Exploded view of Walbro WZ carburetor.

1. Cover
2. Air cleaner element
3. Plate
4. Plate
5. Stop ring
6. Gasket
7. Thrust washer
8. Swivel
9. Bracket
10. Idle speed screw
11. Spring
12. Metering lever
13. Fuel inlet valve
14. Pin
15. Gasket
16. Metering diaphragm
17. Cover
18. Bracket
19. Nut
20. Cable adjuster
21. High-speed mixture screw
22. Sleeve
23. Screen
24. Gasket
25. Fuel pump diaphragm
26. Plate
27. Gasket
28. Fuel pump cover
29. Gasket
30. Primer bulb
31. Retainer

To overhaul carburetor, refer to exploded view in Fig. TA203 and note the following: On models with a plastic body, clean only with solvents approved for use with plastic. Do not disassemble throttle barrel assembly (18). Examine fuel inlet valve and seat. Inlet valve (6) is renewable, but fuel pump body (8) must be renewed if seat is excessively worn or damaged. Clean fuel screen. Inspect diaphragms for tears and other damage. When installing plates and gaskets (10 through 13), note that tabs (T) on ends will "stairstep" when correctly installed. Adjust metering lever height to obtain 1.5 mm (0.059 in.) between carburetor body surface and lever as shown in Fig. TA204.

Walbro WZ. Some engines may be equipped with a Walbro WZ carburetor. This is a diaphragm-type carburetor that uses a barrel-type throttle rather than a throttle plate.

Idle fuel for the carburetor flows up into the throttle barrel where it is fed into the air stream. Idle fuel flow can be adjusted by turning idle mixture limiter plate (P—Fig. TA205). Initial setting is in center notch. Rotating the plate clockwise will lean the idle mixture. Inside the limiter plate is an idle mixture needle (N—Fig. TA202) that is preset at the factory (a plug covers the needle). If idle mixture needle is removed, use the following procedure to determine correct position. Back out needle (N) until unscrewed, then screw in needle six turns. Rotate idle mixture plate (P—Fig. TA205) to center notch. Run engine until normal operating temperature is attained. Adjust idle speed screw so trimmer head or blade does not rotate. Rotate idle mixture needle (N—Fig. TA202) and obtain highest rpm (turning needle clockwise leans the mixture), then turn needle counterclockwise until rpm decreases 200-500 rpm. Readjust idle speed screw. Note that idle mixture plate and needle are available only as an assembly with throttle barrel.

Initial setting of high-speed mixture screw (21—Fig. TA206) is $1^1/_2$ turns out from a lightly seated position. Adjust high-speed mixture screw to obtain highest engine speed, then turn screw $^1/_4$ turn counterclockwise. Do not adjust mixture too lean as engine may be damaged.

To overhaul carburetor, refer to exploded view in Fig. TA206 and note the following: Clean only with solvents approved for use with plastic. Do not disassemble throttle barrel assembly. Examine fuel inlet valve and seat. Inlet valve is renewable, but carburetor body must be renewed if seat is excessively worn or damaged. Inspect high-speed mixture screw and seat. Renew carburetor body if seat is excessively worn or damaged. Clean fuel screen. Inspect diaphragms for tears and other damage. When installing plates and gaskets (24, 25 and 26), note that tabs (T) on ends will "stairstep" when correctly installed. Adjust metering lever height to obtain 1.5 mm (0.059 in.) between carburetor body surface and lever as shown in Fig. TA204.

IGNITION SYSTEM. The engine is equipped with an electronic ignition system. Ignition system performance is considered satisfactory if a spark will jump across a 3 mm ($^1/_8$ in.) electrode gap on a test spark plug. If no spark is produced, check on/off switch, wiring and ignition module air gap. Ignition module air gap should be 0.3 mm (0.012 in.). If switch, wiring and module air gap are satisfactory, but spark is not present, renew ignition module.

REPAIRS

PISTON, PIN AND RINGS. The piston is accessible after removing cylinder. Remove piston pin retainers (5—Fig. TA207) and use a suitable puller to extract pin from piston.

Piston and ring are available only in standard diameter.

Install piston on connecting rod so arrow on piston crown will point toward exhaust port when the cylinder is installed.

The piston is equipped with a single piston ring. Piston ring rotation is prevented by a locating pin in the piston ring groove. Make certain ring end gap is correctly positioned around locating pin before installing piston in cylinder.

CYLINDER. The cylinder bore is chrome plated. Renew cylinder if plating in bore is worn through, scored or otherwise damaged. Cylinder is available only in standard size.

CRANKSHAFT AND CONNECTING ROD. The engine is equipped with a half-crankshaft (13—Fig. TA207) that is supported by bearing (15) in crankcase (18) and a bearing (8—Fig. TA208) in fan housing (9).

To remove crankshaft and connecting rod, remove engine cover. Separate engine from trimmer drive housing. Unscrew clutch (7—Fig. TA208) from crankshaft. Unbolt and remove fan housing (9) and fuel tank. Remove flywheel mounting nut and pull flywheel (19—Fig. TA207) off crankshaft. Remove ignition coil, carburetor and muffler. Remove cylinder mounting screws and withdraw cylinder. Remove crankshaft key (14) and crankcase retaining bolts,

Illustrations courtesy Tanaka Ltd.

hen separate crankcase cover (8) from rankcase half (18). Remove snap ring 9), thrust washer (10), connecting rod 11) and bearing (12) from crankpin. Tap rankshaft (13) out of crankcase half.)rive seal (16) and bearing (15) from rankcase bore.

Crankcase is available only as an as-embly. Bearings in connecting rod are available separately. Inspect compo-ents for damage and excessive wear and renew as needed.

CLUTCH. Some models are equipped with the two-shoe clutch assembly shown in Fig. TA208. With drive hous-ng (3) separated from engine, press against shaft end of drum (6) to dislodge bearing (5) and drum from housing. Re-move snap ring (4) and press bearing off drum shaft. Unscrew clutch (7) from rankshaft. Clutch shoes, hub and springs are available only as an as-sembly.

REWIND STARTER. Engines With-out Electric Start. Refer to Fig. TA208 for an exploded view of rewind starter. To disassemble starter, detach starter housing (9) from engine. Remove rope handle and allow rope to wind into starter. Detach snap ring on engines so equipped, or unscrew pulley retainer (10), and remove rope pulley (12). Wear appropriate safety eyewear and gloves before detaching rewind spring (11) from housing as spring may uncoil uncon-trolled.

To assemble starter, lubricate center post of housing and spring side with light grease. Install rewind spring so coil windings are clockwise from outer end. Assemble starter while passing rope through housing rope outlet and attach rope handle to rope. To place tension on starter rope, pull rope out of housing. Engage rope in notch on pulley and turn pulley clockwise to place tension on spring. Hold pulley and disengage rope from pulley notch. Release pulley and allow rope to wind on pulley. Check starter operation. Rope handle should be held against housing by spring tension, but it must be possible to rotate pulley at least 1/4 turn clockwise when rope is pulled out fully.

Engines With Electric Start. Refer to Fig. TA209 for an exploded view of starter. To disassemble starter, detach starter housing (14) from engine. Remove rope handle and allow rope to wind into starter. Unscrew center screw (7) and remove rope pulley (12). Wear appropriate safety eyewear and gloves before detaching rewind spring (13) from housing as spring may uncoil uncontrolled.

To assemble starter, lubricate center post of housing and spring side with light grease. Install rewind spring so coil windings are counterclockwise from outer end. Assemble starter while passing rope through housing rope outlet and attach rope handle to rope. To place tension on starter rope, pull rope out of housing. Engage rope in notch on pulley and turn pulley counterclockwise. Hold pulley and disengage rope from pulley notch. Release pulley and allow rope to wind on pulley. Check starter operation. Rope handle should be held against housing by spring tension, but it must be possible to rotate pulley at least 1/4 turn counterclockwise when rope is pulled out fully.

ELECTRIC STARTER. Some engines may be equipped with an electric starter. Refer to Fig. TA210 for a diagram of starter components. A battery pack of four 1.2v/1.2AH nicad batteries provides power to the starter motor. A relay is used to energize the starter when the start button is depressed. The batteries are charged by a circuit off the ignition coil. A rectifier converts alternating current to direct current for battery charging. The batteries can also be charged using 120v line current and a transformer as outlined in trimmer section.

To check motor operation, remove spark plug, disconnect four-wire connector to handle and use a jumper wire to connect terminals (1 and 4—Fig. TA211) of female connector. Starter motor should run; if not, check relay. If motor runs, but engine does not run, check drive gears. To check relay, remove cover (14—Fig. TA210) and connect voltmeter test leads to motor terminals. Connect jumper wire between terminals (1 and 4—Fig. TA211). If no voltage is indicated at motor terminals, renew wiring harness; relay is not available separately. If battery voltage is indicated at motor terminals, but motor does not turn, motor is faulty.

To check engine charging system, run engine and disconnect two-wire connector to battery pack and four-wire connector to handlebar. Check voltage at terminals (1 and 2—Fig. TA211) of female connector by connecting voltmeter negative lead to terminal (1) and positive lead to terminal (2). With engine running at 6000 rpm, tester should indicate more than 1.1 volts. If voltage is lower than 1.1 volts, check wiring harness for open circuit. Check air gap be-

Fig. TA207—Exploded view of engine. Some engines are not equipped with snap ring (9) and thrust washer (10).

1. Cylinder
2. Gasket
3. Piston ring
4. Piston
5. Retaining rings
6. Piston pin
7. Bearing
8. Crankcase half
9. Snap ring
10. Thrust washer
11. Connecting rod
12. Bearing
13. Crankshaft
14. Key
15. Bearing
16. Seal
17. Gasket
18. Crankcase half
19. Flywheel

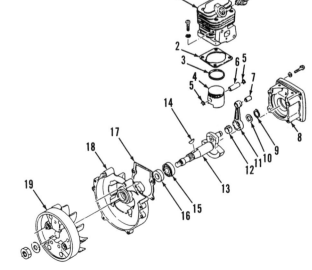

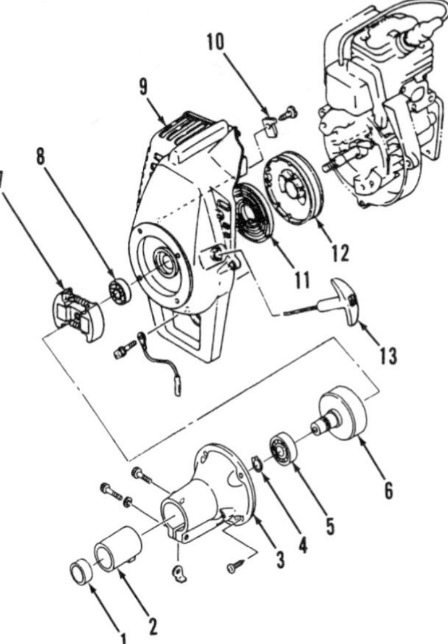

Fig. TA208—Exploded view of clutch and rewind starter assemblies used on engines not equipped with an electric starter. The clutch assembly is similar on all engines.

1. Collar
2. Rubber sleeve
3. Housing
4. Snap ring
5. Bearing
6. Clutch drum
7. Clutch assy.
8. Bearing
9. Starter housing
10. Retainer
11. Rewind spring
12. Pulley
13. Rope handle

Illustrations courtesy Tanaka Ltd.

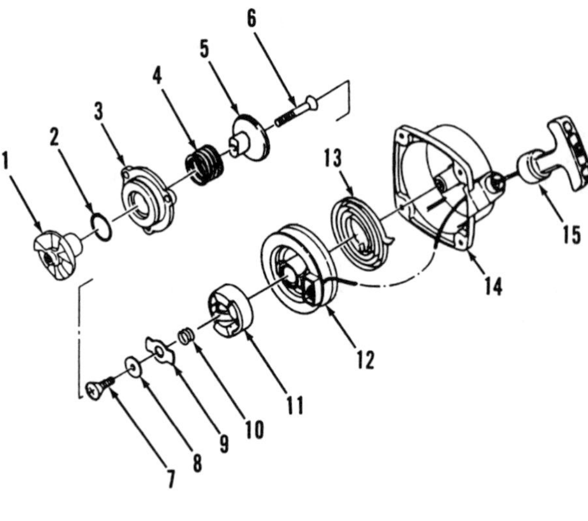

Fig. TA209—Exploded view of rewind starter used on engines with an electric starter.

1. Dog flange
2. "O" ring
3. Holder
4. Spring
5. Driver
6. Screw
7. Screw
8. Washer
9. Friction plate
10. Spring
11. Pawl
12. Pulley
13. Rewind spring
14. Starter housing
15. Rope handle

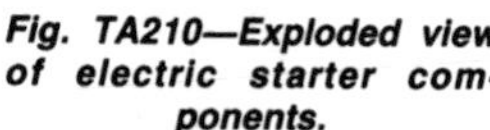

Fig. TA210—Exploded view of electric starter components.

1. Housing
2. Snap ring
3. Bearing
4. Clutch drum
5. Clutch assy.
6. Washer
7. Bearing
8. Housing
9. Gear
10. Bearing
11. Snap ring
13. Starter motor
14. Cover
15. Battery case
16. Relay
17. Battery pack
18. Cover

tween flywheel magnet and ignition coil. If both items are satisfactory, renew ignition coil.

To check wiring harness, shut off engine and disconnect four-wire connector. Connect voltmeter negative test lead to terminal (1—Fig. TA211) and positive lead to terminal (4). Battery voltage should be indicated on tester. Connect negative test lead to terminal (1) and positive test lead to terminal (3). There should be no voltage indicated on tester. Renew harness if either of these tests are failed.

To check battery pack, recharge battery pack then disconnect four-wire connector at handlebar. With engine stopped, connect negative lead of a voltmeter to terminal (1) of female connector and positive tester lead to terminal (2). Battery voltage reading should be at least 4.8 volts.

Starter motor (13—Fig. TA210) must be serviced as a unit assembly; components are not available.

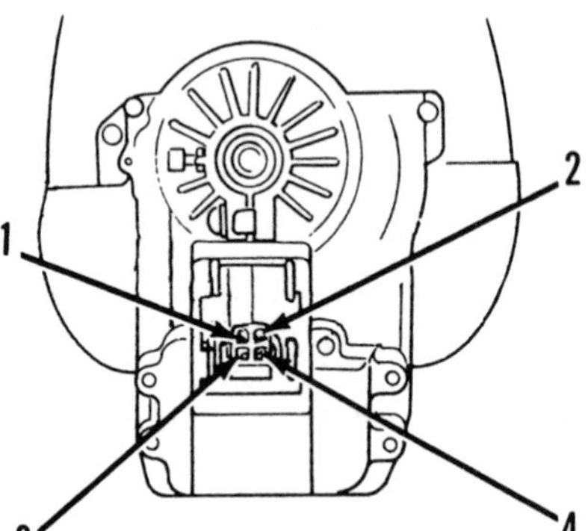

Fig. TA211—Tests may be performed on starter electrical system by attaching tester to connector terminals as outlined in text.

TECUMSEH

ENGINE SERVICE

Model	Bore	Stroke	Displacement
TC200	1.4375 in. (36.51 mm)	2.250 in. (57.15 mm)	2.0 cu. in. (32.8 cc)

ENGINE INFORMATION

Engine type and model numbers are stamped into blower housing base as indicated in Fig. T9. Always furnish engine model and type number when ordering parts. Tecumseh TC200 engine is used by several manufacturers of string trimmers and brushcutters.

MAINTENANCE

SPARK PLUG. Recommended spark plug is a Champion RCJ-8Y, or equivalent. Specified electrode gap is 0.030 inch (0.76 mm).

AIR CLEANER. Air cleaner element should be removed and cleaned at eight hour intervals of use. Polyurethane element may be washed in a mild detergent and water solution and squeezed until all dirt is removed. Rinse thoroughly. Wrap in clean dry cloth and squeeze until completely dry. Apply engine oil to element and squeeze out excess. Clean air cleaner body and cover and dry thoroughly.

CARBURETOR. Tecumseh TC200 engines used on string trimmers are equipped with diaphragm type carburetor with a single idle mixture needle. Initial adjustment of idle mixture needle is one turn open from a lightly seated position.

Final carburetor adjustment is made with engine at operating temperature and running. Operate engine at idle speed and turn idle mixture needle slowly clockwise until engine falters. Note this position and turn idle mixture needle counterclockwise until engine begins to run unevenly. Note this position and turn adjustment screw until it is halfway between first (lean) and last (rich) positions.

To disassemble carburetor, refer to Fig. T11. Remove idle speed stop screw (9) and spring. Remove pump cover (10), gasket (11) and diaphragm (12). Remove cover (1), diaphragm (2) and gasket (3). Carefully remove pin (15), metering lever (4), inlet needle valve (5) and spring (6). Remove screws retaining throttle plate to throttle shaft (8). Remove screws retaining choke plate to choke shaft (14). Remove "E" clip from throttle shaft and choke shaft and remove shafts. Remove all nonmetallic parts, idle mixture needle, fuel inlet screen and fuel inlet (13). Remove all Welch plugs.

Clean and inspect all parts. Do not allow parts to soak in cleaning solvent longer than 30 minutes.

To reassemble, install fuel inlet needle, metering lever spring and pin. Metering lever hooks onto the inlet needle and rests on the metering spring. Entire assembly is held in place by metering lever pin screw. Tip of metering lever must be 0.060-0.070 inch (1.52-1.78 mm) from the face of carburetor body (Fig. T12).

Install diaphragm gasket so tabs of gaskets align with the bosses on the carburetor body. After gasket is in place, install the diaphragm again aligning tabs to bosses. The head of the rivet in the diaphragm must be toward the carburetor body. Check the atmospheric vent hole in the diaphragm cover to make certain it is clean. Install cover on carburetor.

Install pump diaphragm with the corner holes aligning with the same holes in the carburetor body. Align pump gasket in the same manner and place pump cover onto carburetor.

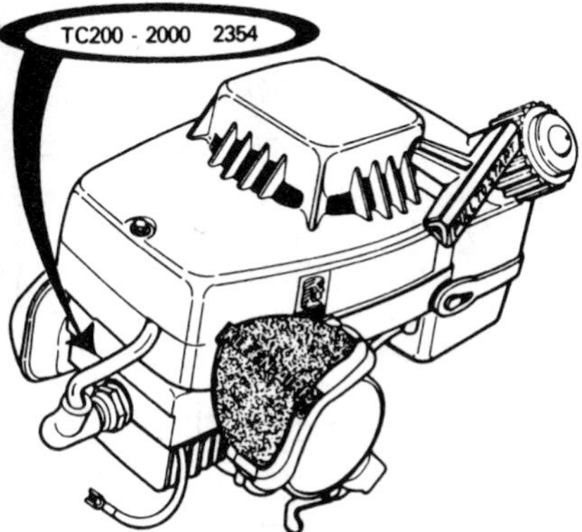

Fig. T9—Engine model and type number is stamped into blower housing base.

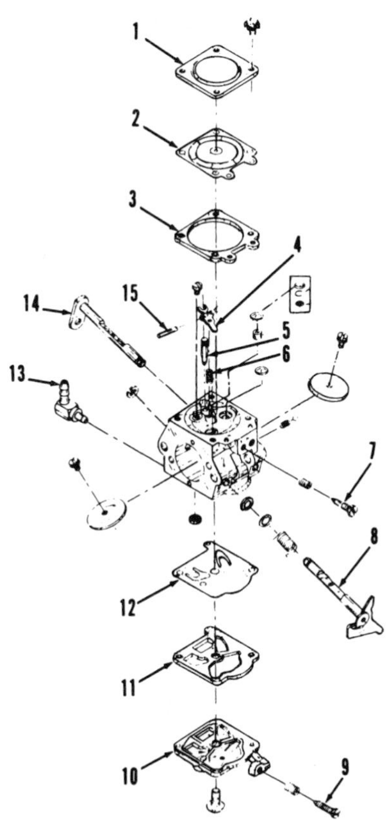

Fig. T11—Exploded view of diaphragm type carburetor used on TC200 engine.

1. Cover
2. Diaphragm
3. Gasket
4. Metering lever
5. Inlet needle valve
6. Spring
7. Idle mixture needle
8. Throttle shaft
9. Idle speed screw
10. Cover
11. Gasket
12. Diaphragm
13. Fuel inlet
14. Choke shaft
15. Pin

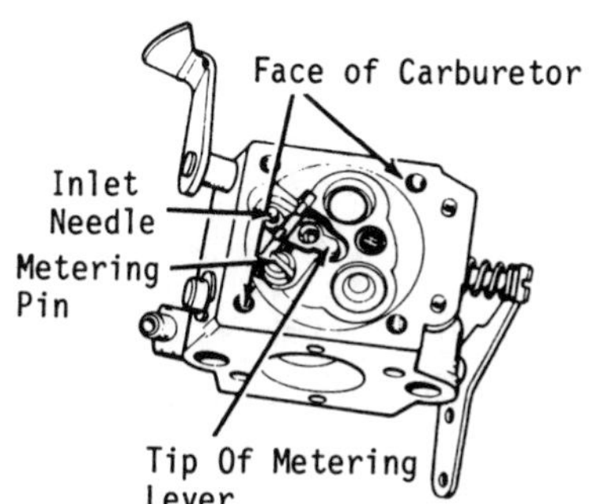

Fig. T12—Tip of metering valve lever should be 0.060-0.070 inch (1.52-1.78 mm) from the face of carburetor body.

Illustrations courtesy Tecumseh Products company

Numbers on throttle plate should face to the outside when throttle is closed. Apply a small amount of Loctite grade 609 to fuel inlet before installation.

IGNITION SYSTEM. All Model TC200 engines are equipped with a solid state ignition module located outside the flywheel. Correct air gap between laminations of module and magnets of flywheel is 0.012 inch (0.30 mm). Use Tecumseh gage part number 670297.

GOVERNOR ADJUSTMENT. Model TC200 engine is equipped with an air vane type governor. Refer to ENGINE REPAIRS paragraphs for adjustment procedure.

LUBRICATION. Engine is lubricated by mixing gasoline with a good quality two-stroke air-cooled engine oil. Refer to TRIMMER SERVICE section for correct fuel/oil mixture ratio recommended by trimmer manufacturer.

CARBON. Muffler and exhaust ports should be cleaned after every 50 hours of operation if engine is operated continuously at full load. If operated at light or medium load, the cleaning interval can be extended to 100 hours.

REPAIRS

TIGHTENING TORQUES. Recommended tightening torque specifications are as follows:

Crankcase cover to crankcase	70-100 in.-lbs. (8-11 N·m)
Cylinder to crankcase	60-75 in.-lbs. (7-8 N·m)
Carburetor	20-32 in.-lbs. (2.3-3.6 N·m)
Flywheel nut	180-240 in.-lbs. (20-27 N·m)
Ignition module	30-40 in.-lbs. (3.4-4.5 N·m)
Starter retainer screw	45-55 in.-lbs. (5.1-6.2 N·m)

CRANKSHAFT. To remove crankshaft, drain fuel tank, remove tank strap and disconnect fuel line at carburetor. Disconnect and remove spark plug. Remove the three screws retaining blower housing and rewind starter assembly and remove housing. Remove the two screws retaining ignition module. Use strap wrench to hold flywheel. Use flywheel puller (670299) to remove flywheel. Remove air cleaner assembly with carburetor, spacer, gaskets and screen. Mark and remove governor link from carburetor throttle lever. Remove the three 5/16 inch cap screws, then separate blower housing base from crankcase. Attach engine holder tool (670300) with the three blower housing base screws. Place tool in a bench vise. Remove muffler springs using tool fabricated from a 12 inch piece of heavy wire with a ¼ inch hook made on one end. Remove the four cylinder retaining nuts or Torx bolts, then pull cylinder off squarely and in line with piston. Use caution so rod does not bend. Install seal protector (670206) at magneto end of crankshaft and seal protector (670263) at pto end of crankshaft. Remove crankcase cover screws, then carefully separate crankcase cover from crankcase. Rotate crankshaft to top dead center and withdraw crankshaft through crankcase cover opening while sliding connecting rod off crankpin and over crankshaft. Refer to Fig. T18. Use care not to lose any of the 23 crankpin needle bearings which will be loose. Flanged side of connecting rod (Fig. T19) must be toward pto side of engine after installation. Handle connecting rod carefully to avoid bending.

Standard crankpin journal diameter is 0.5985-0.5990 inch (15.202-15.215 mm). Standard crankshaft pto side main bearing journal diameter is 0.6248-0.6253 inch (15.870-15.880 mm). Standard crankshaft magneto side main bearing journal diameter is 0.4998-0.5003 inch (12.69-12.71 mm). Crankshaft end play should be 0.004-0.012 inch (0.10-0.30 mm).

To install crankshaft, clean mating surfaces of crankcase, cylinder and crankcase cover. Avoid scarring or burring mating surfaces.

Crankshaft main bearing in crankcase of early model engines did not have a retaining ring as shown in Fig. T20. Retaining ring was installed as a running change in late model engines. To install new caged bearing in crankcase, place bearing on installation tool (670302) with the numbered side of bearing away from tool. Press bearing into crankcase until tool is flush with crankcase housing. Install retaining ring (as equipped). Place seal for magneto side onto seal installation tool (670301) so metal case of seal enters tool first. Press seal in until tool is flush with crankcase. Use the same procedure to install bearing and seal in crankcase cover using bearing installation tool (670304) and seal installation tool (670303).

New crankpin needle bearings are on bearing strips. Heavy grease may be used to retain old bearings on crankpin journal as required. During reassembly, connecting rod must not be forced onto crankpin journal as rod failure or bending will result. Apply Loctite 515 to mating surfaces of crankcase during reassembly and use seal protectors when installing lip seals over ends of crankshaft. When installing cylinder over piston, install a wooden block with a slot cut out for connecting rod under piston to provide support and prevent connecting rod damage. Exhaust ports in cylinder are on the same side of engine as muffler resting boss. Make certain cylinder is correctly positioned, stagger ring end gaps and compress rings using a suitable ring compressor which can be removed after cylinder is installed over piston. Install cylinder and push cylinder onto crankcase studs to expose 1-2 threads of studs. Install the four nuts onto exposed threads of studs, then push cylinder further down to capture nuts on studs. Tighten nuts or Torx bolts in a criss-cross pattern to specified torque.

Install muffler using fabricated tool to install springs. Install blower housing

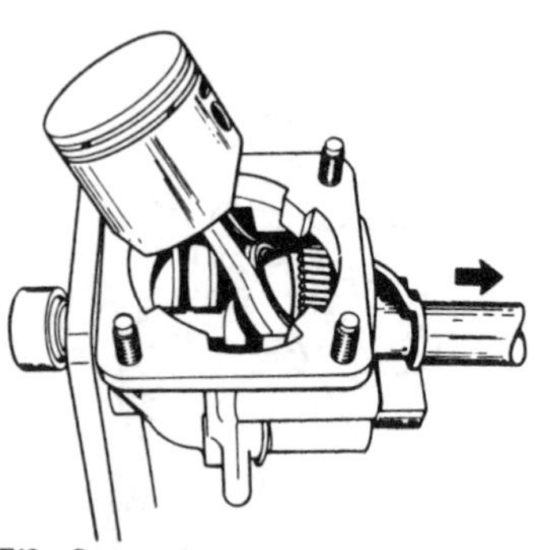

Fig. T18—Connecting rod must be carefully worked over crankpin during crankshaft removal. Do not lose the 23 loose crankpin needle bearings.

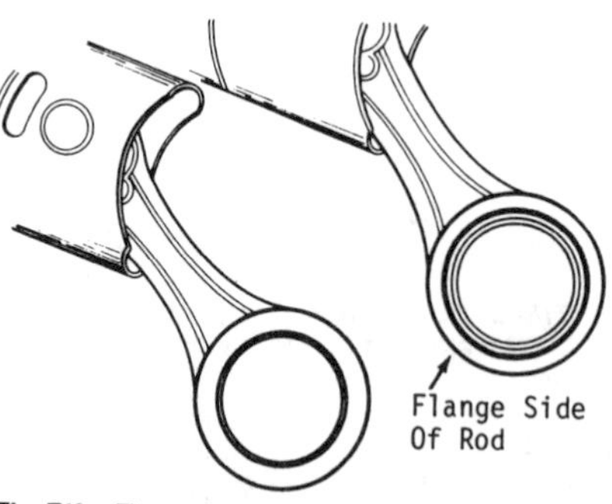

Fig. T19—Flanged side of connecting rod must face pto side of engine after installation.

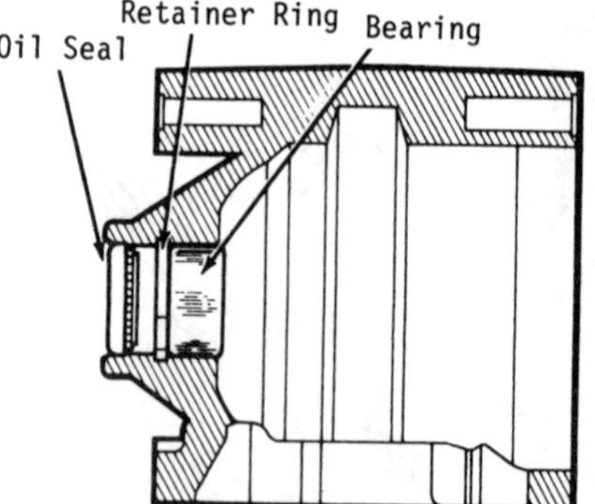

Fig. T20—Early Model TC200 engines did not have retaining ring shown. Retaining ring was installed as a running change in late model engines.

base and tighten the three screws to specified torque.

Refer to Fig. T26 to install governor air vane assembly. Speed adjustment lever is held in place by inserting screw into the blower housing base. Long end of governor spring hooks into the notch on neck of air vane. Short end hooks into the hole in speed adjustment lever. To decrease governed speed of engine, bend speed adjusting lever towards spark plug end of engine. To increase governed speed of engine, bend lever in the opposite direction. Throttle link is inserted into hole in the neck of the air vane and the hole closest to the throttle shaft in throttle plate.

Install carburetor, spacer, gaskets, screen and air cleaner body on engine. Tighten screws to specified torque. Install and adjust ignition module. Install blower housing/rewind starter assembly and tighten screws to specified torque. Install fuel tank.

PISTON, RINGS AND CONNECTING ROD. Standard piston diameter is 1.4327-1.4340 inch (36.39-36.42 mm). Standard width of both ring grooves is 0.050-0.051 inch (1.27-1.29 mm). Standard piston ring width is 0.46-0.47 inch (11.7-11.9 mm). Standard ring end gap is 0.004-0.014 inch (0.10-0.36 mm).

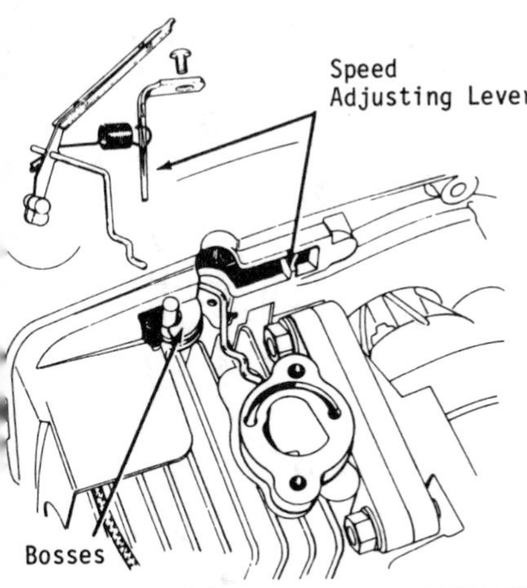

Fig. T26—View of air vane governor assembly used on Model TC200 engines. Refer to text.

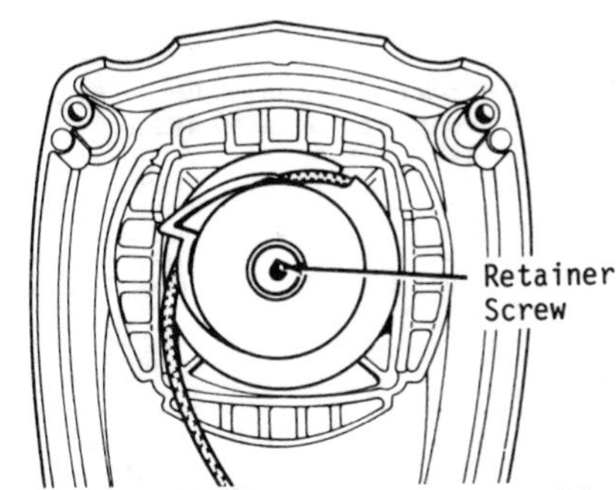

Fig. T27—View showing rewind starter retaining screw.

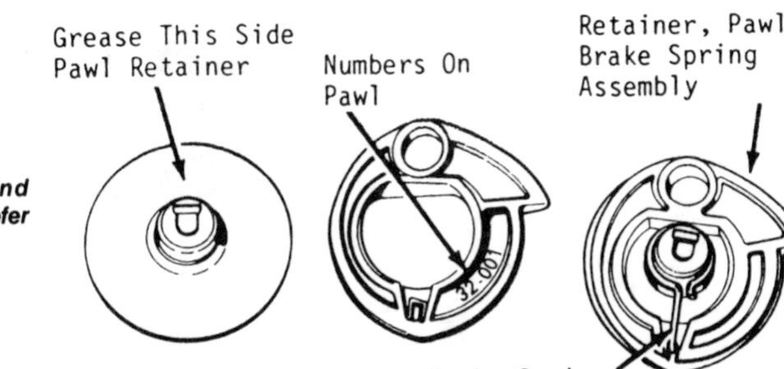

Fig. T28—View of rewind starter pawl and retainer. Refer to text.

CYLINDER. Cylinder must be smooth and free of scratches or flaking. Clean carbon carefully as necessary. Standard bore size is 1.4375 inches (36.513 mm).

TECUMSEH SPECIAL TOOLS. Tecumseh special tools are available to aid in engine disassembly and reassembly are listed by use and tool part number.

FLYWHEEL PULLER 670299
AIR GAP GAGE 670297
ENGINE HOLDER..........670300
SEAL PROTECTOR
(MAG. END)..............670206
SEAL PROTECTOR
(PTO END)...............670263
SEAL INSTALLER
(MAG END) 670301
SEAL INSTALLER
(PTO END)...............670303
BEARING INSTALLER
(MAG END) 670302
BEARING INSTALLER
(PTO END)...............670304

REWIND STARTER. The rewind starter assembly is incorporated into blower housing. Blower housing design varies according to engine model and specification number. To release rewind spring tension, remove staple in starter handle and slowly let spring tension release by winding rope onto rope sheave. Remove the 5/16 inch retainer screw (Fig. T27). Remove pawl retainer and pawl (Fig. T28) and extract starter pulley. Use caution not to pull rewind spring out of housing at this time. Uncoiling spring can be very dangerous. If rewind spring is damaged or weak, use caution when removing spring from housing.

To reassemble, grease center post of housing and portion of housing where rewind spring will rest. Grip rewind spring firmly with needlenose pliers ahead of spring tail. Insert spring and hook tail into housing as shown in Fig. T29. Make certain spring is seated in housing before removing needlenose pliers from spring. Grease top of spring. Insert starter rope into starter pulley and tie a knot in end of rope. With neck of starter pulley up, wind starter rope in a counterclockwise rotation. Place end of rope in notch of pulley and place pulley in housing. Press down on pulley and rotate until pulley attaches to rewind spring. Refer to Fig. T30. Lubricate pawl retainer with grease and place the pawl, numbers up, onto retainer. Place brake spring on center of retainer with tab locating into pawl (Fig. T28). Tab on pawl retainer must align with notch in center post of housing and locating hole in pawl must mesh with boss on starter pulley (Fig. T31). Install retainer screw (Fig. T27) and torque to specified torque. Use starter rope to wind spring a minimum of 2 turns counterclockwise and a maximum of 3 turns. Feed starter rope through starter grommet and secure starter handle with a knot.

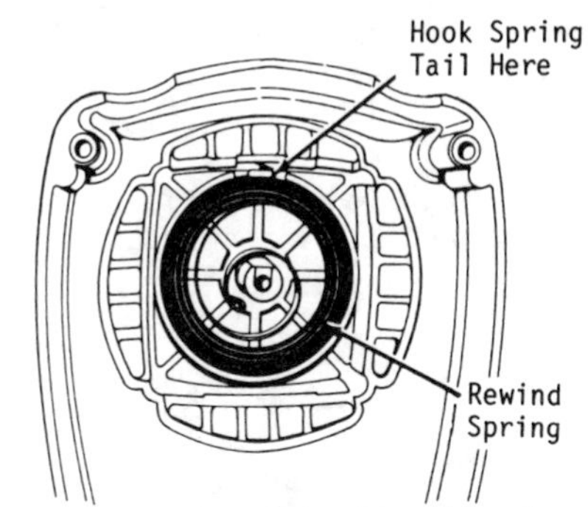

Fig. T29—View of rewind spring and housing.

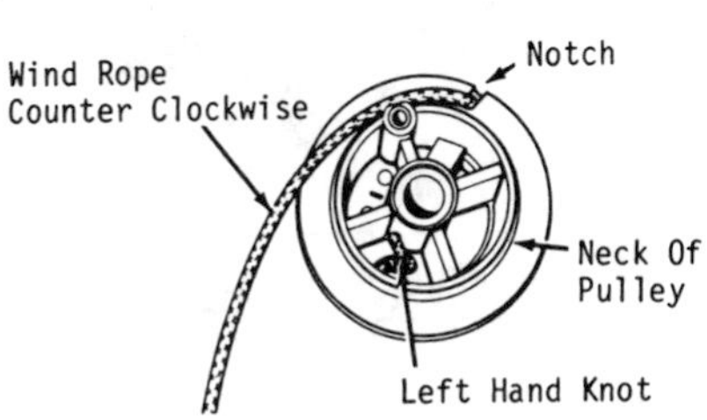

Fig. T30—View showing rewind starter rope as shown and as outlined in text.

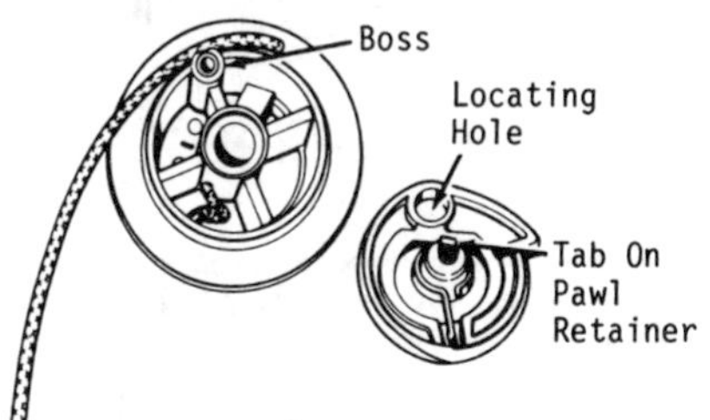

Fig. T31—Boss must engage locating hole on pawl retainer. Refer to text.

TECUMSEH

ENGINE SERVICE

Model	Bore	Stroke	Displacement
AV520	2.09 in. (53 mm)	1.50 in. (38 mm)	5.2 cu. in. (85 cc)

ENGINE INFORMATION

Engine type and model number tags will be at one of a number of locations. Refer to Fig. T50. Always furnish engine model and type number when ordering parts. Model AV520 engines used on string trimmers and brushcutters are equipped with a diaphragm type carburetor and utilize a ball bearing type main bearing at magneto side and a needle type main bearing at pto side.

MAINTENANCE

SPARK PLUG. Recommended spark plug is a Champion RJ-17M, or equivalent. Specified electrode gap is 0.030 inch (0.76 mm).

AIR CLEANER. Refer to Fig. T51 for an exploded view of air cleaner used on most models. Polyurethane element may be washed in a mild detergent and water solution and squeezed until all dirt is removed. Rinse thoroughly. Wrap in clean dry cloth, then squeeze until completely dry. Apply engine oil to element and squeeze out excess. Clean air cleaner body and cover and dry thoroughly.

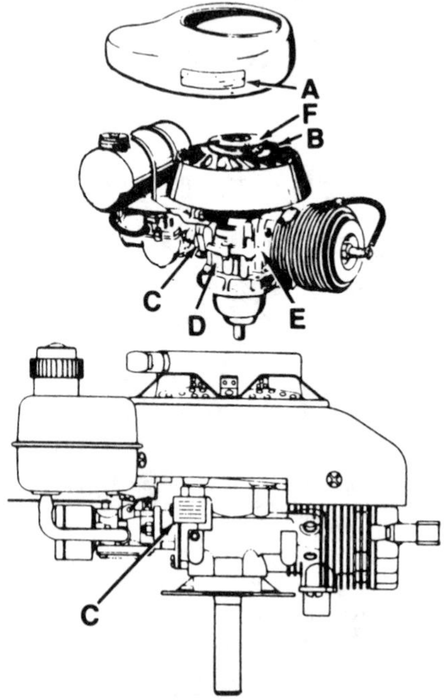

Fig. T50—The engine serial number and type number may be found at one of the locations indicated above.

A. Nameplate on air shroud
B. Model & type number plate
C. Metal tab on crankcase
D. Stamped on crankcase
E. Stamped on cylinder flange
F. Stamped on starter pulley

CARBURETOR. Tecumseh Model AV520 engine is equipped with a diaphragm type carburetor shown in Fig. T52. Most models are equipped with carburetor shown utilizing fixed high speed metering and adjustable low speed mixture needle; however, some models may be equipped with both low speed and high speed mixture needles. Carburetor model number is stamped on carburetor flange (Fig. T53).

Initial adjustment of low speed and high speed (as equipped) mixture needles is one turn open from a lightly seated position.

Final carburetor adjustment is made with engine at operating temperature and running. Operate engine at idle speed and turn low speed mixture needle slowly clockwise until engine falters. Note this position and turn low speed mixture needle counterclockwise until engine begins to falter. Note this position and turn mixture needle until it is halfway between first (lean) and last (rich) positions. Operate engine at rated governed speed with trimmer line at correct length or brush blade installed and use the same procedure to adjust the high speed mixture needle (as equipped) as used for the low speed mixture needle. Make adjustments on high speed mixture needle in 1/8 turn increments.

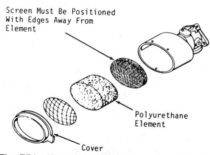

Screen Must Be Positioned With Edges Away From Element

Polyurethane Element

Cover

Fig. T51—View of air cleaner most commonly used on these engines. Refer to text for service procedures.

To disassemble carburetor, refer to Fig. T52. Remove throttle (29) and choke (8) plates and shafts. Remove low

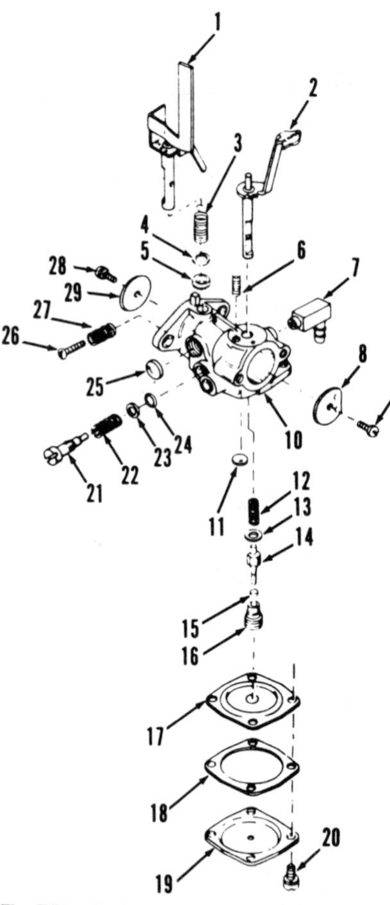

Fig. T52—Exploded view of diaphragm type carburetor used on Model AV520.

1. Throttle shaft
2. Choke shaft
3. Return spring
4. Steel washer
5. Felt washer
6. Choke positioning spring
7. Fuel fitting
8. Choke plate
9. Screw
10. Carburetor body
11. Welch plug
12. Valve spring
13. Gasket
14. Inlet needle
15. Neoprene seat
15. Neoprene seat
16. Seat fitting
17. Diaphragm
18. Gasket
19. Cover
20. Screw
21. Idle mixture needle
22. Spring
23. Washer
24. "O" ring
25. Welch plug
26. Idle speed screw
27. Spring
28. Screw
29. Throttle plate

Illustrations courtesy Tecumseh Products Co.

peed mixture needle, remove "O" ring n mixture needle and note design of crew. If equipped with high speed mix- ure needle, remove needle and discard "O" ring. Drill an off center hole in idle uel chamber Welch plug (25), then pry ut with suitable tool. Remove the four crews (20) retaining diaphragm cover 19) and remove cover, gasket (18) and iaphragm (17). Early type inlet needle eat fitting (16) is slotted and may be emoved using a screwdriver. Late style nlet needle seat fitting (16) must be emoved using a thin wall 9/32 inch ocket. Inlet needle is spring loaded. Jse care when removing not to lose spring (12). Remove and discard neo- prene needle seat (15) located in inlet needle seat fitting (16). Remove fuel inlet fitting (7). Note presence of filter screen in fuel inlet fitting. Drill off cen- ter hole in Welch plug (11) and remove plug.

Make certain all "O" rings and non- metallic parts are removed, then soak carburetor parts in clean carburetor cleaner for 30 minutes. Rinse in clean water and use compressed air to dry. To reassemble, make certain fuel inlet fit- ting filter screen is clear and press fit- ting partially in, apply Loctite 515 to exposed portion of fitting and press fit- ting in until seated. Refer to Fig. T54 and install new Welch plugs (11 and 25–Fig. T52). Install spring (12), needle (14), gasket (13), seat (15) and fitting (16). Make certain new diaphragm is the same style as the old diaphragm which was removed. Diaphragm rivet head must always be toward inlet needle valve (Fig. T55). Refer to Fig. T56 to determine installation location of diaphragm and gasket, then install in proper sequence. Install cover (19–Fig. T52). Place new "O" rings on fuel mix- ture needles and install needles until they are lightly seated, then back out one turn. Install choke shaft (2) and in- stall choke plate (8) with flat of choke plate toward fuel inlet side of carburetor and mark on face of choke plate parallel with choke shaft. Install throttle shaft (1) and install throttle plate with short line stamped in plate to top of car- buretor, parallel with throttle shaft, and facing out when throttle is closed.

IGNITION SYSTEM. Model AV520 engines may be equipped with a magne- to type ignition system or a solid state ignition system. Refer to appropriate paragraph for model being serviced.

Magneto Ignition. Coil (12–Fig. T57), condenser (15) and breaker point assembly (6) are located behind fly- wheel (1). To renew breaker points and condenser, remove rewind starter as- sembly (1–Fig. T60) and blower hous- ing (6). Remove nut (2), washer (3), starter cup (4) and screen (5). Use fly- wheel puller set (670215) to remove fly- wheel. DO NOT use knock off tool as main bearing damage will occur. Re- move clip retainer (2–Fig. T57), cover (3) and gasket (4). Disconnect wiring from breaker point assembly (6), re- move screw (7) and lift out breaker point assembly. Remove screw (14) and lift out condenser. Install new condens- er and breaker point assembly. Place one drop of engine oil on lubricating felt (9). Rotate engine until breaker point cam (5) opens breaker point set to maximum opening. Adjust breaker point plate until point gap is 0.020 inch

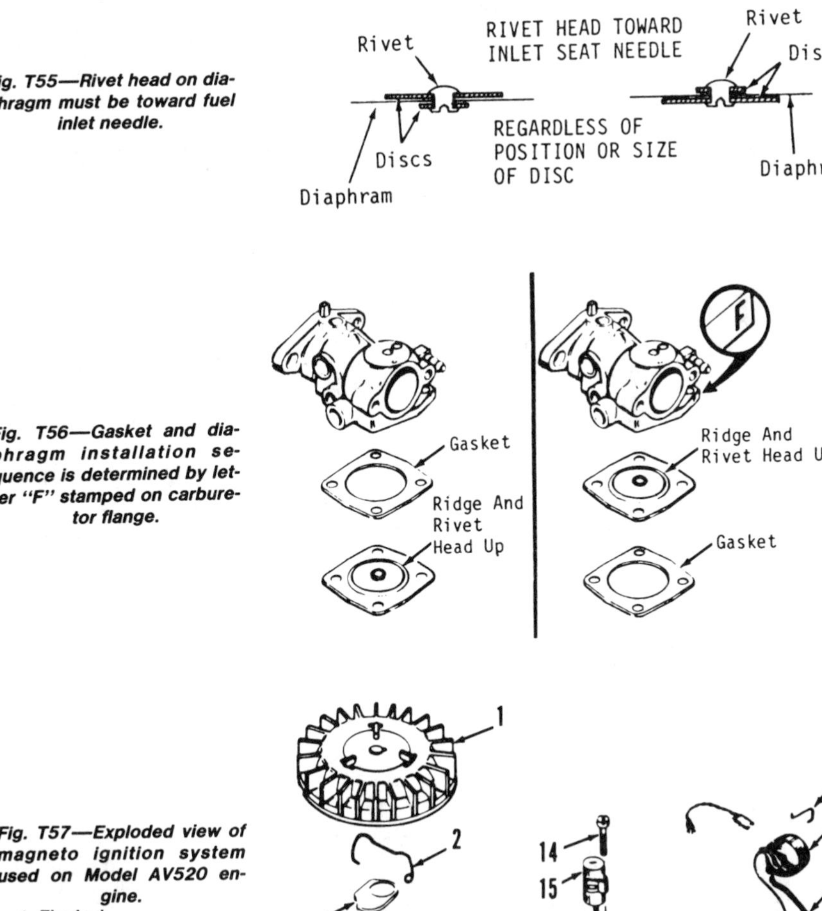

Fig. T55—Rivet head on diaphragm must be toward fuel inlet needle.

Fig. T56—Gasket and diaphragm installation sequence is determined by letter "F" stamped on carburetor flange.

Fig. T57—Exploded view of magneto ignition system used on Model AV520 engine.

1. Flywheel
2. Retainer
3. Cover
4. Gasket
5. Cam
6. Breaker points
7. Screw
8. Breaker point plate
9. Lubricating felt
10. Stator assy.
11. Spark plug lead
12. Coil
13. Coil locking clip
14. Screw
15. Condenser

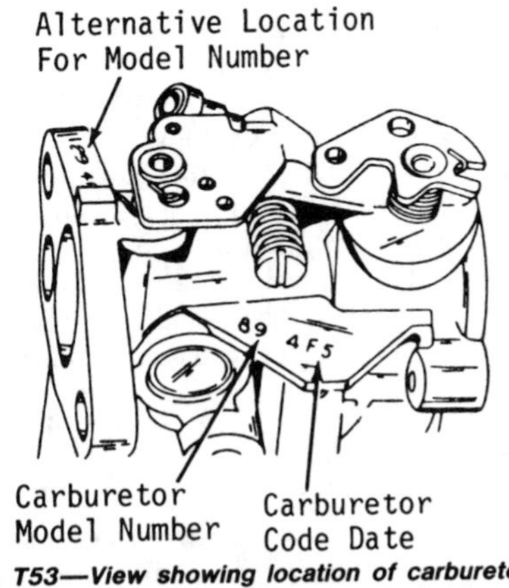

Fig. T53—View showing location of carburetor identification number on Tecumseh diaphragm type carburetor.

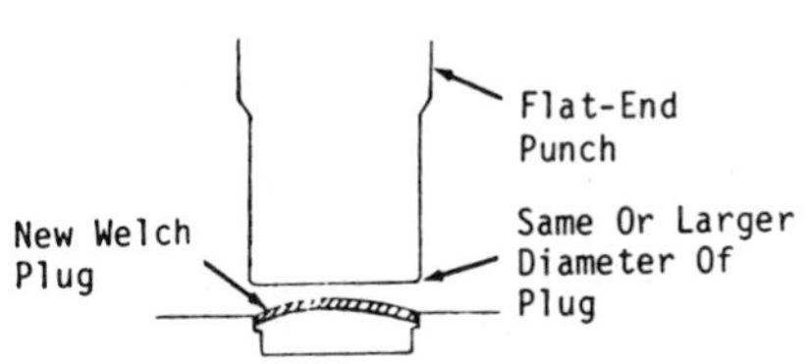

Fig. T54—Use a flat punch the same diameter or larger to install new Welch plugs.

(0.51 mm). Tighten screw (7) to maintain setting. Stator assembly should be positioned so ignition breaker points just open when piston top is 0.070 inch (1.78 mm) before top dead center with points correctly gapped. Correct air gap between coil and flywheel is 0.015 inch (0.38 mm).

Solid-State Ignition. The Tecumseh solid-state ignition system does not use ignition points. The system's only moving part is the rotating flywheel with the charging magnets. As the flywheel magnet passes position (1A—Fig. T58), a low-voltage ac current is induced into input coil (2). The current passes through rectifier (3), which converts it to dc current. Then, it travels to the capacitor (4) where it is stored. The flywheel rotates approximately 180 degrees to position (1B). As it passes trigger coil (5), it induces a small electric charge into the coil. This charge passes through resistor (6) and turns on the SCR (silicon-controlled rectifier) switch (7). With SCR switch closed, the low-voltage current stored in capacitor

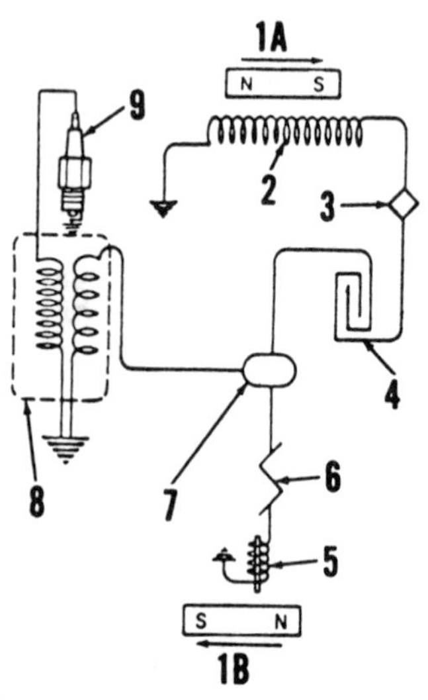

Fig. T58—Diagram of Tecumseh solid state ignition system. Items (3, 4, 5, 6 and 7) are encased in magneto assembly.

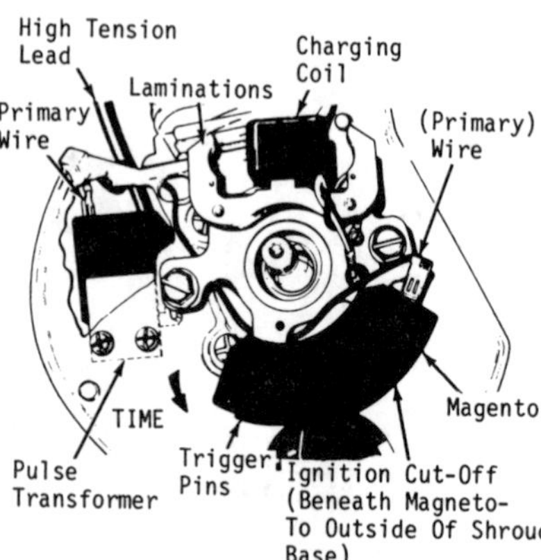

Fig. T59—View showing location of solid state ignition system component parts.

(4) travels to the pulse transformer (8). The voltage is stepped up instantaneously and the current is discharged across the electrodes of spark plug (9), producing a spark.

If system fails to produce a spark at spark plug, first make certain air gap between coil and flywheel is 0.005-0.008 inch (0.13-0.20 mm). Check the high-tension lead (Fig. T59). If condition of the high-tension lead is questionable, renew the pulse transformer and high-tension lead assembly. Check the condition of primary wire. Renew primary wire if insulation is faulty. The ignition charging coil (magneto), electronic triggering system and mounting plate are available only as an assembly. If necessary to renew this assembly, place the unit in position on the engine. Start the retaining screws, turn the mounting plate counterclockwise as far as possible, then tighten retaining screws to 5-7 ft.-lbs. (7-10 N·m).

GOVERNOR ADJUSTMENT. Model AV520 engine is equipped with an air vane type governor located on throttle shaft. Idle speed stop screw (26 Fig. T52) should be set to allow engine to idle at 2600 rpm. High speed stop screw (47—Fig. T60) should be set to limit engine maximum rpm to 4600-4800 rpm.

LUBRICATION. Engine is lubricated by mixing gasoline with a good quality two-stroke air-cooled engine oil. Refer to TRIMMER SERVICE section for correct mixture ratio recommended by trimmer manufacturer.

CARBON. Muffler and exhaust ports should be cleaned after every 50 hours of operation if engine is operated continuously at full load. If operated at light or medium load, the cleaning interval can be extended to 100 hours.

REPAIRS

TIGHTENING TORQUES. Recommended tightening torque specifications are as follows:

Crankcase base to crankcase	70-80 in.-lbs. (8-10 N·m)
Cylinder head	80-100 in.-lbs. (10-11 N·m)
Connecting rod	70-80 in.-lbs. (8-10 N·m)
Flywheel nut	264-324 in.-lbs. (30-37 N·m)
Ignition module	30-40 in.-lbs. (3.4-4.5 N·m)
Reed valve plate	50-60 in.-lbs. (6-7 N·m)
Rewind retainer screw	65-75 in.-lbs (7-8 N·m

CRANKSHAFT AND BEARINGS To remove crankshaft and main bearings, remove rewind starter assembl (1—Fig. T60), blower housing (6) an fuel tank. Remove muffler, nut (2 washer (3), starter cup (4) and scree (5). Note location and condition of ai vane governor. Use flywheel puller se (670215) to remove flywheel. DO NO use knock off tool to remove flywheel Remove ignition system componen parts. Remove carburetor assembly (40 and reed plate assembly (38). Remove cylinder head (30) and gasket (29). Remove the two connecting rod cap screws and carefully remove connecting ro cap (19). Use care not to lose the connecting rod needle bearings (18). Pusl connecting rod and piston assembly ou of cylinder. Remove piston pin retaining ring (24). Heat piston top slowly until piston pin (23) can be easily pushed out. Caged bearing (21) can be pressed out. Remove the four ca screws retaining base (13) plate to block and tap base plate to break gasket bond. Remove base plate/crankshaft assembly as a unit. If ball bearing main is noisy or damaged, slowly heat bearing area of base plate until ball bearing can be easily removed. Press bearing off of crankshaft. Insert tip of ice pick or similar tool into location shown in Fig. T61, then remove the wire retainer (10–Fig. T60). Remove retainer plate (11) and seal (12). Repeat procedure to remove wire retainer (34), retainer plate (35) and seal (36) in block. Press caged needle bearing (27) out of block.

Standard crankpin journal diameter is 0.8442-0.8450 inch (21.443-21.463 mm). Standard crankshaft pto side main bearing journal diameter is 0.9998-1.0003 inch (25.395-25.407 mm). Standard crankshaft magneto side main bearing journal diameter is 0.6691-0.6695 inch (16.995-17.005 mm). There should be zero crankshaft end play.

When installing ball bearing on magneto end of crankshaft, place a 1/4-in. (6.35 mm) dot of Loctite 609 in two places, 180 degrees apart, on crankshaft main bearing journal and press ball bearing into position. It may be necessary to heat base slightly when installing crankshaft so ball bearing will slip into bearing bore easily.

To install caged needle bearing in pto side of crankcase, heat crankcase slightly and press bearing into bearing bore.

To install crankshaft, install caged needle bearing and seal in cylinder block/crankcase assembly as outlined. Install ball bearing on crankshaft. In-

Illustrations courtesy Tecumseh Products Co.

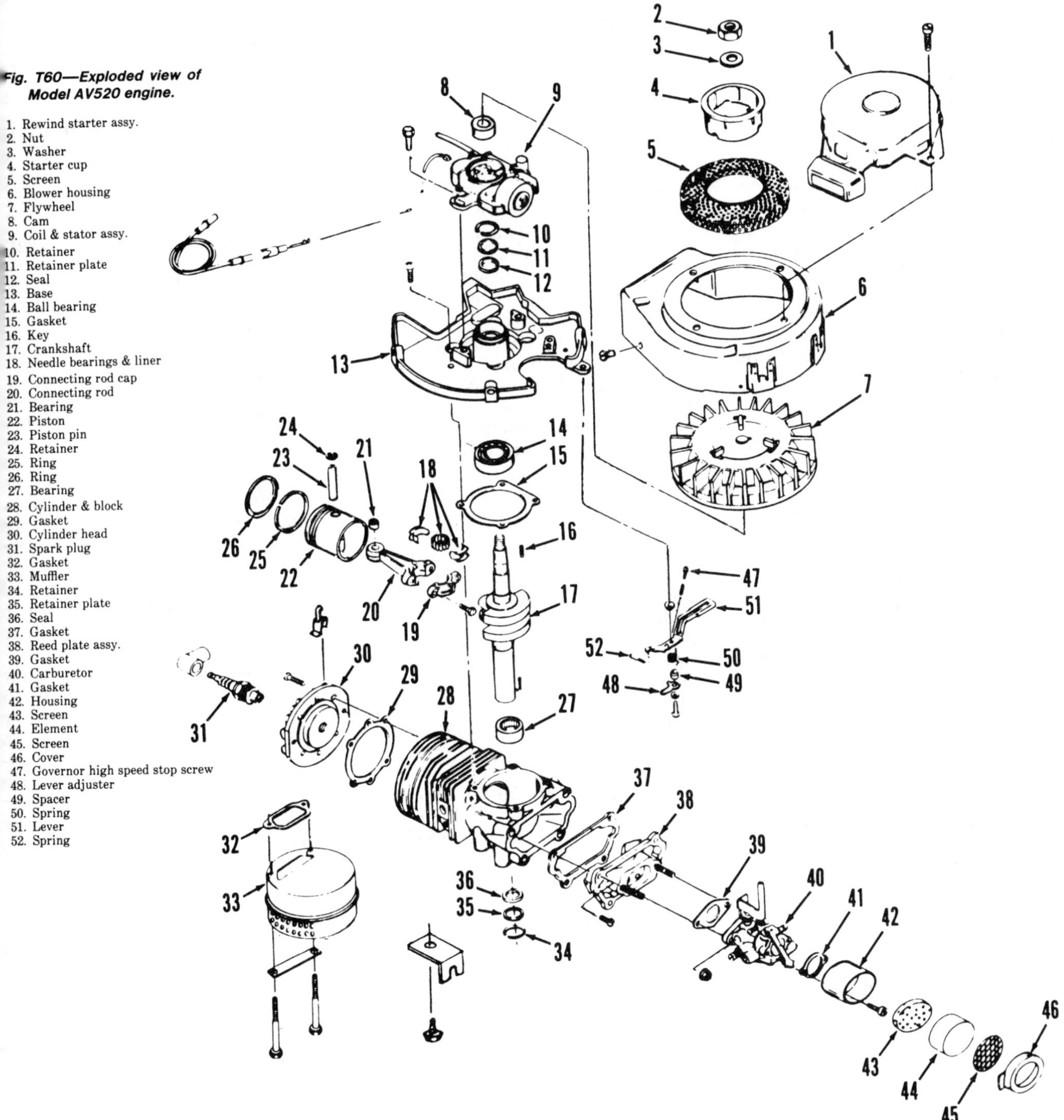

Fig. T60—Exploded view of Model AV520 engine.

1. Rewind starter assy.
2. Nut
3. Washer
4. Starter cup
5. Screen
6. Blower housing
7. Flywheel
8. Cam
9. Coil & stator assy.
10. Retainer
11. Retainer plate
12. Seal
13. Base
14. Ball bearing
15. Gasket
16. Key
17. Crankshaft
18. Needle bearings & liner
19. Connecting rod cap
20. Connecting rod
21. Bearing
22. Piston
23. Piston pin
24. Retainer
25. Ring
26. Ring
27. Bearing
28. Cylinder & block
29. Gasket
30. Cylinder head
31. Spark plug
32. Gasket
33. Muffler
34. Retainer
35. Retainer plate
36. Seal
37. Gasket
38. Reed plate assy.
39. Gasket
40. Carburetor
41. Gasket
42. Housing
43. Screen
44. Element
45. Screen
46. Cover
47. Governor high speed stop screw
48. Lever adjuster
49. Spacer
50. Spring
51. Lever
52. Spring

stall seal in base plate. Slightly heat base plate (13—Fig. T60) and install crankshaft and ball bearing assembly in base plate. Make certain to use seal protectors or tape to prevent seal damage. Place a thin bead of silicon type sealer to base plate gasket. Install crankshaft through caged needle bearing in cylinder block/crankcase assembly and carefully work crankshaft through seal and bearing until base plate contacts cylinder block/crankcase assembly. Use seal protector or tape to prevent seal damage. Install the four base plate retaining screws and tighten to specified torque. Install rings on piston and connecting rod assembly, stagger ring end gaps. Install needle bearing connecting rod bearings on crankshaft journal and remove paper backing on new bearings or use heavy grease on used bearings to retain in position. Compress rings and carefully install piston and connecting rod assembly into cylinder and crankcase. Install connecting rod cap and tighten screws to specified torque. Place a thin bead of silicon sealer to reed plate gasket and install gasket and reed plate. Tighten screws to specified torque. Install carburetor and air cleaner assembly. Install ignition system components and adjust as required. Continue to reverse disassembly procedure for reassembly.

PISTON, PIN AND RINGS. Standard piston diameter is 2.0870-2.0880 inch (53.010-53.035 mm). Upper and lower ring groove width is 0.0645-0.0655 inch (1.638-1.763 mm). Standard piston ring width is 0.0615-0.0625 inch (1.562-1.587 mm). Standard ring end gap is 0.006-0.016 inch (0.15-0.40 mm). If rings are beveled on inner edge, beveled edge is installed toward top of piston (Fig.

T64). Stagger ring end gaps around circumference of piston.

An offset piston is used on some models and is identified by a "V" or "1111" hash marks stamped into top of piston. The older version piston arrowhead is 90° from a line of the piston pin bore. Newer version piston arrowhead points in a line parallel to the piston bore. Refer to Fig. T62. Newer version wrist pin bore diameter is smaller at the arrowhead side. Piston which is not offset will have no markings on piston top and may be installed on connecting rod either way. Refer to CONNECTING ROD paragraphs for correct piston to connecting rod installation procedure.

Standard piston pin diameter is 0.4997-0.4999 inch (12.692-12.697 mm).

CONNECTING ROD. The steel connecting rod used on Model AV520 is equipped with a caged needle bearing at piston pin bore and with loose needle bearings at crankpin bore. New crankpin bore needle bearings are held in place by a waxed strip. Use heavy grease to retain old crankpin bore needle bearings in place. When installing new caged bearing in piston pin bore, press on lettered side of bearing. Offset piston is installed on connecting rod so that match marks on connecting rod will be toward magneto side when installed in crankcase. When assembling piston to connecting rod, "V" or "1111" hash marks will be to the left side of connecting rod with connecting rod match marks up (Fig. T62). Piston with no marks on top may be installed either way. To install piston on connecting rod, heat piston in oil until oil just begins to smoke. Install piston pin as shown in Fig. T63. Piston pin must slide into piston easily. Do not force.

CYLINDER, BLOCK AND CRANKSHAFT SEALS. Standard cylinder bore diameter is 2.093-2.094 inches (53.16-53.18 mm). Maximum clearance between piston and cylinder bore is 0.005-0.007 inch (0.13-0.18 mm). If clearance between piston and cylinder exceeds 0.007 inch (0.18 mm), or cylinder bore is scratched or scored, renew cylinder.

It is important to exercise extreme care when renewing crankshaft seals to prevent their being damaged during installation. If a protector sleeve is not available, use tape to cover any splines, keyways, shoulders or threads over which the seal must pass during installation. Seals should be installed with channel groove of seal toward inside (center) of engine.

REED VALVES. Model AV520 engines are equipped with reed type inlet valve (38—Fig. T60). Reed petals should not stand out more than 0.010 inch (0.2 mm) from the reed plate and must not be bent, distorted or cracked. The reed plate must be smooth and flat.

TECUMSEH SPECIAL TOOLS. Tecumseh special tools available to aid in engine disassembly and reassembly are listed by use and tool part number.

FLYWHEEL PULLER 67021
BALL BEARING DRIVER . . .67025
DIAL INDICATOR 67024

REWIND STARTER. The rewind starter assembly (1—Fig. T60) is riveted to blower housing (6) during production. If rewind starter must be renewed, note position on blower housing and cut rivets and bolt new unit to blower housing.

To disassemble rewind starter, remove handle (1—Fig. T65) and allow spring to slowly unwind in housing. Remove retainer screw (10), retainer cup (9), starter dog (8), dog spring (6) and brake spring (7). Lift pulley and spring assembly from rewind housing. Turn spring and keeper assembly to remove.

To reassemble rewind starter, apply a light coat of grease to rewind spring and place rewind spring and keeper assembly into pulley. Turn to lock into position. Place pulley into starter housing. Install brake spring, starter dog and dog return spring. Replace retainer cup and retainer screw. Tighten screw to specified torque.

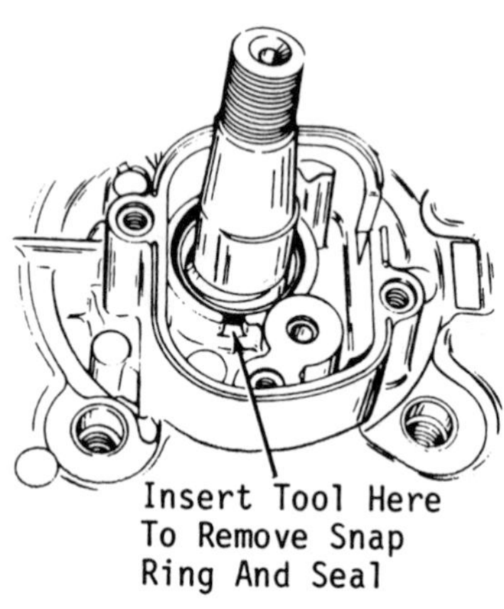

Fig. T61—Wire retainer ring must be removed to remove retainer plate and seal. Refer to text.

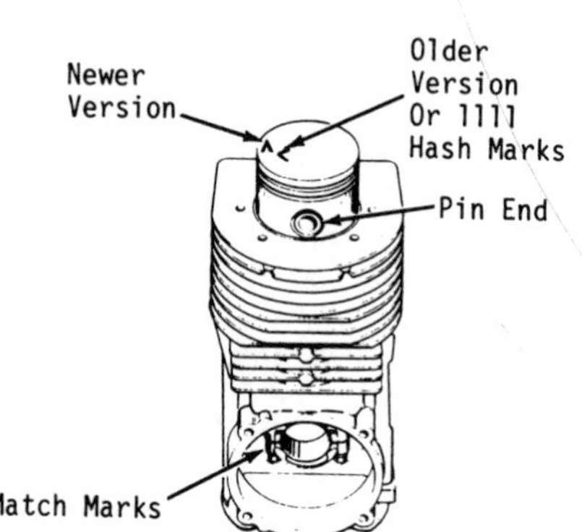

Fig. T62—View showing correct installation of connecting rod and piston assembly.

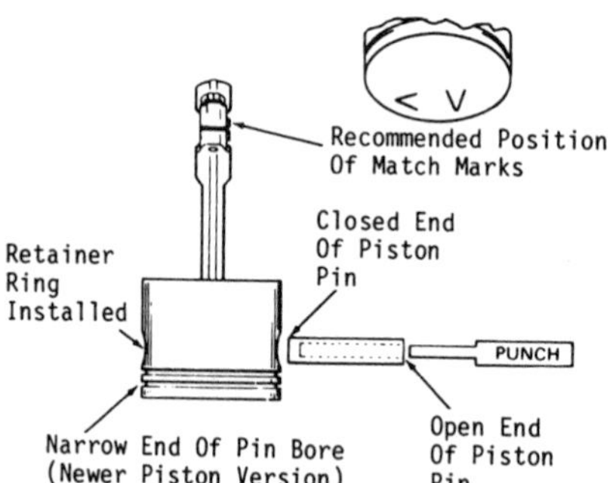

Fig. T63—View showing correct procedure for piston pin installation. Refer to text.

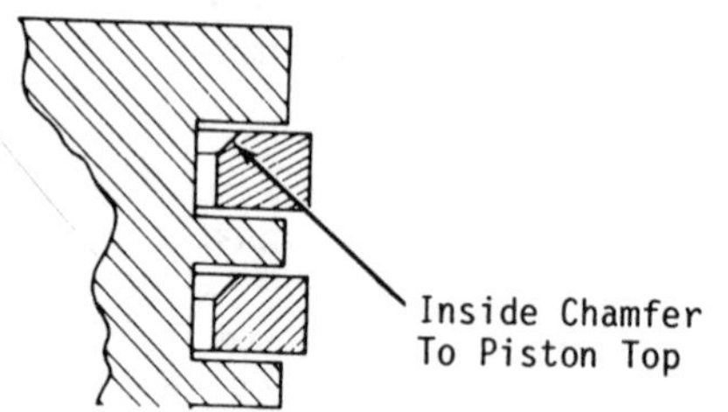

Fig. T64—If inner ring edge is beveled, beveled side is installed toward top of piston.

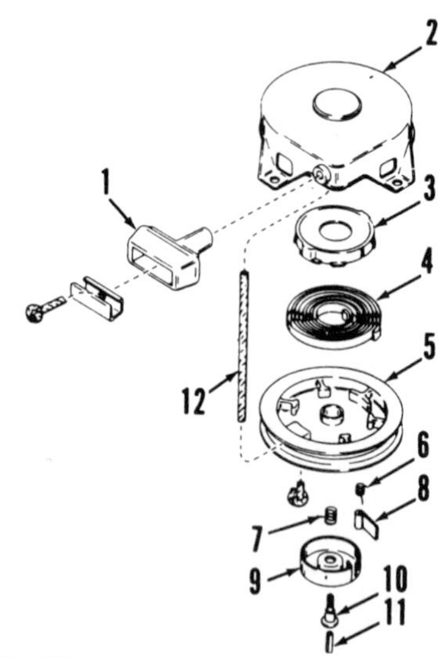

Fig. T65—Exploded view of rewind starter assembly.

1. Handle
2. Housing
3. Keeper
4. Spring
5. Pulley
6. Dog spring
7. Brake spring
8. Dog
9. Retainer
10. Screw
11. Centering pin
12. Rope

Illustrations courtesy Tecumseh Products Co.

TML (TRAIL)

ENGINE SERVICE

Model	Bore	Stroke	Displacement
150528	1.44 in. (36.5 mm)	1.28 in. (32.5 mm)	2.1 cu. in. (35 cc)

ENGINE INFORMATION

TML (Trail) two-stroke air-cooled gasoline engine is used on TML trimmers and brush cutters. The die cast aluminum cylinder is an integral part of one crankcase half. The crankshaft is supported in caged roller bearings at each end. Engine is equipped with a one piece connecting rod which rides on roller bearings.

MAINTENANCE

SPARK PLUG. Recommended spark plug is a Champion CJ6, or equivalent. Specified electrode gap is 0.025 inch (0.6 mm).

CARBURETOR. TML engine is equipped with a Walbro diaphragm type carburetor (Fig. TL1). Initial adjustment of low speed mixture needle (12) is 1-1/4 turns open from a lightly seated position. Initial adjustment of high speed mixture needle (13) is 1-1/16 turns open from a lightly seated position.

Final carburetor adjustment is made with trimmer line at recommended length, engine at operating temperature and running. Turn low speed mixture needle (12) clockwise until engine falters. Note this position and turn low speed mixture needle counterclockwise until engine falters. Note this position and turn low speed mixture needle until it is halfway between first (lean) and last (rich) positions. Adjust idle speed screw (3) until engine idles at 2500-3000 rpm, or just below clutch engagement speed. Operate engine at full rpm and adjust high speed mixture needle (13) using the same procedure outlined for low speed mixture needle. Turn high speed mixture needle in 1/8 turn increments. A properly adjusted carburetor will give high rpm with some unburned residue from muffler.

To disassemble carburetor, remove pump cover retaining screw (1), pump cover (2), diaphragm (5) and gasket (4). Remove inlet screen (6). Remove the four metering cover screws (27), metering cover (26), diaphragm (25) and gasket (24). Remove screw (20), pin (19), fuel lever (18), spring (17) and fuel inlet needle (16). Remove screw (23), circuit plate (22) and gasket (21). Remove high and low speed mixture needles and springs. Remove throttle plate (8) and throttle shaft (9) as required.

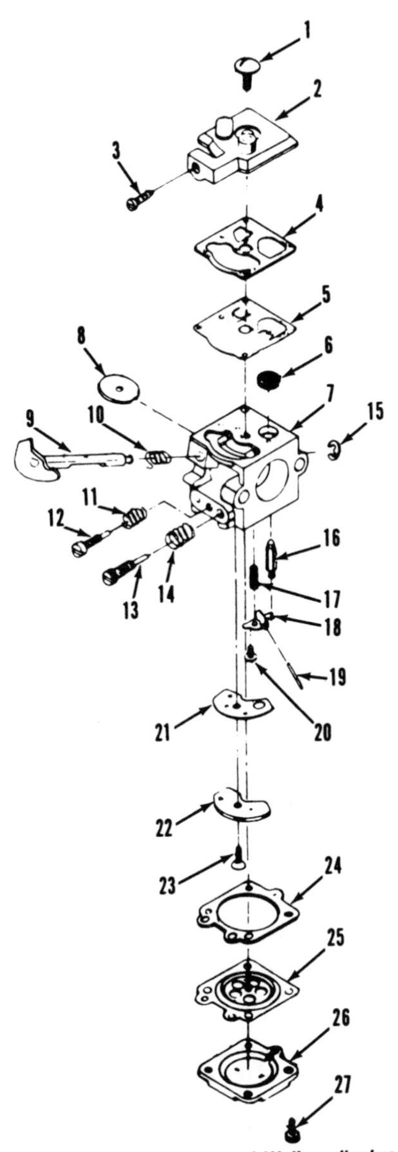

Fig. TL1—Exploded view of Walbro diaphragm type carburetor.

1. Screw
2. Pump cover
3. Idle screw
4. Gasket
5. Pump diaphragm
6. Inlet screen
7. Body
8. Throttle plate
9. Throttle shaft
10. Spring
11. Spring
12. Low speed mixture needle
13. High speed mixture needle
14. Spring
15. "E" clip
16. Fuel inlet needle
17. Spring
18. Fuel inlet lever
19. Pin
20. Screw
21. Gasket
22. Circuit plate
23. Screw
24. Gasket
25. Metering diaphragm
26. Cover
27. Screw

Clean parts thoroughly and inspect all diaphragms for wrinkles, cracks or tears. Diaphragms should be flexible and soft. Fuel inlet lever (18) should be flush with carburetor body (Fig. TL2).

IGNITION SYSTEM. Engine is equipped with a solid state ignition system. Ignition system is considered satisfactory if spark will jump across the 3 mm (1/8 in.) gap of a test spark plug. If no spark is produced, check on/off switch, wiring and air gap. If switch, wiring and air gap are satisfactory, install a new ignition module (11—Fig. TL3).

Correct air gap for ignition module is 0.015 inch (0.38 mm). If ignition module screws are loosened or removed, apply Loctite 242 thread locking compound to screw threads prior to installation. Timing is not adjustable.

LUBRICATION. Manufacturer recommends mixing gasoline with a good quality two-stroke, air-cooled engine oil. Refer to TRIMMER SERVICE section for correct fuel/oil mixture ratio recommended by trimmer manufacturer.

CARBON. Muffler and exhaust ports should be cleaned after every 50 hours of operation if engine is operated continuously at full load. If operated at light or medium load, the cleaning interval can be extended to 100 hours.

REPAIRS

COMPRESSION PRESSURE. For optimum performance, compression pressure for a cold engine with throttle and choke wide open should be 120-140 psi (827-965 kPa). Minimum acceptable

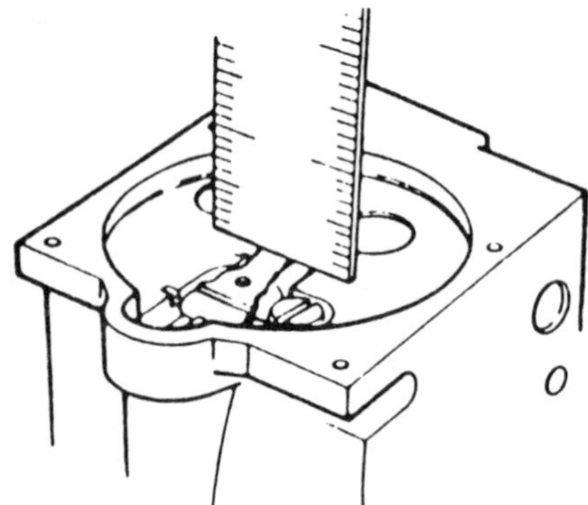

Fig. TL2—Fuel inlet valve lever should be flush with carburetor surface.

compression pressure for a cold engine is 90 psi (620 kPa).

TIGHTENING TORQUES. Recommended tightening torque specifications are as follows:

Crankcase cover	70 in.-lbs. (8 N·m)
Flywheel nut	175 in.-lbs. (20 N·m)
Ignition module	25 in.-lbs. (3 N·m)
Carburetor	30 in.-lbs. (3.4 N·m)

CRANKSHAFT AND BEARINGS. Crankshaft (17—Fig. TL3) is supported at each end in caged needle bearings clamped in bearing bores at crankcase split. To remove crankshaft, remove all cooling shrouds, recoil starter assembly, fuel tank, muffler and carburetor. Remove nut, flywheel and clutch. Remove the crankcase retaining bolts (20), then remove crankcase cover (19). Carefully remove crankshaft, pulling piston out of cylinder as crankshaft is removed. When handling crankshaft, hold connecting rod toward counterweight side to prevent the 11 connecting rod needle bearings from falling out. Remove all seals, bearings and thrust washers. Work connecting rod off small end of crankshaft using care to catch the 11 connecting rod needle bearings (18).

To reassemble, coat connecting rod needle bearings with heavy grease and install all 11 bearings on crankshaft connecting rod journal. Work connecting rod over small end of crankshaft and over bearings. Thrust washers are installed with chamfered side toward crankshaft web. Seals are installed with spring side toward the inner side of crankcase. Apply a thin coat of silicon sealer around crankcase mating edges and install crankcase cover. Make certain all bearings and seals are correctly positioned in crankcase bearing bores. Tighten crankcase cover bolts to specified torque.

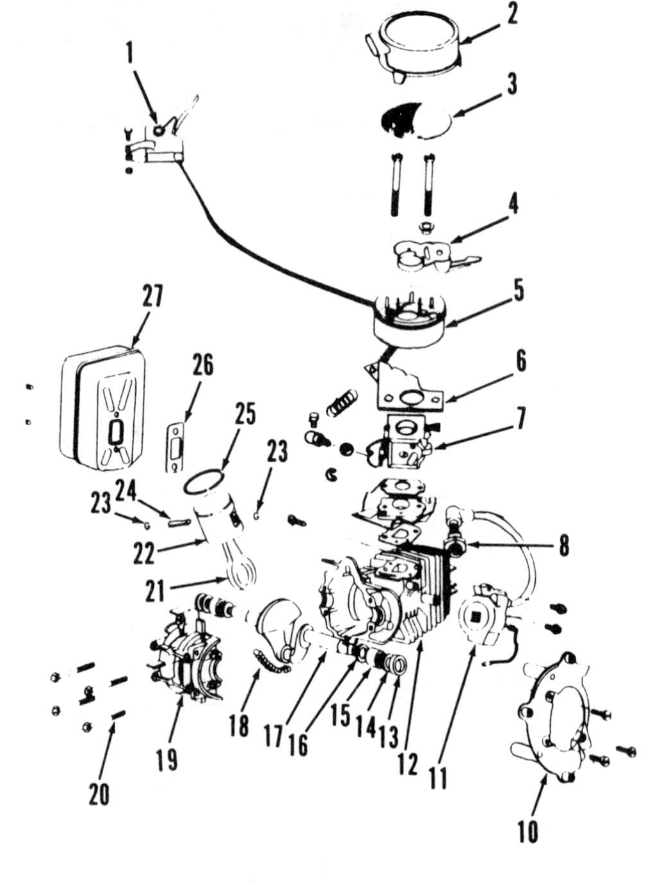

Fig. TL3—Exploded view of 150528 engine.

1. Throttle cable assy.
2. Air cleaner cover
3. Filter
4. Choke
5. Housing
6. Bracket
7. Carburetor
8. Spark plug
9. Flywheel
10. Base plate
11. Ignition module
12. Cylinder/crankcase
13. Seal
14. Retaining ring
15. Bearing
16. Thrust washer
17. Crankshaft
18. Needle bearings (11)
19. Crankcase cover
20. Crankcase cover bolts
21. Connecting rod
22. Piston
23. Retaining ring
24. Piston pin
25. Ring
26. Gasket
27. Muffler

PISTON, PIN AND RING. A single ring aluminum piston is used. Piston is equipped with a locating pin in piston ring groove to prevent ring from turning. To remove piston, refer to CRANKSHAFT AND BEARING paragraphs. After connecting rod has been removed, remove retaining rings (23—Fig. TL3) and press piston pin from piston. Remove piston.

Inspect piston for scratches, scoring or excessive wear. Renew piston as required.

CONNECTING ROD. The one piece connecting rod rides on 11 needle bearings at crankshaft journal. Piston pin rides directly in connecting rod piston pin bore. To remove connecting rod, refer to CRANKSHAFT AND BEARINGS paragraphs.

CYLINDER. The die-cast aluminum cylinder has a chrome plated bore and is an integral part of one crankcase half. To remove cylinder, refer to CRANKSHAFT AND BEARINGS paragraphs. Cylinder should be renewed if it is scored, chrome is flaking off or aluminum is showing. If in doubt as to whether a spot is where aluminum is showing, try to scratch the area carefully. Aluminum will scratch easily and chrome plating will not.

TORO

ENGINE SERVICE

Model	Bore	Stroke	Displacement
AC-1	1.28 in. (32.51 mm)	1.25 in. (31.75 mm)	1.6 cu. in. (26.2 cc)

ENGINE INFORMATION

This four-stroke, air-cooled gasoline engine is used on some Toro models. The valves are operated by a cam located in the crankcase via push rods and rocker arms. The cantilever-type crankshaft is supported in bearings at the flywheel end. The crankshaft and bearings are not available as service parts and should not be removed.

MAINTENANCE

LUBRICATION. The engine is lubricated by 3.4 fl. oz. (100 ml) of oil contained in the engine crankcase. Use SAE 30 oil designed for use in four-stroke engines with API service class SF, SG or SH. Check the oil level before each use and change the oil after each 25 hours of operation. The oil should be changed after the first 10 hours of operation of a new engine or after the engine is rebuilt. The oil should also be changed before storing the unit for an extended time.

A dipstick (Fig. TO101) is attached to the fill plug. To check the oil level, make sure the engine has cooled and the oil has had time to return to the crankcase. Position the unit with engine level and the drive shaft straight. Remove the fill plug, wipe the plug dry with a clean cloth, then reinstall and tighten the plug. Remove the plug and observe the level of the oil on the dipstick. Oil level should be maintained at the top of the dipstick.

Change the engine oil as follows. Be sure to catch and discard the oil in a safe and approved method. Start the engine and allow it to run until it reaches normal operating temperature. Stop the engine, remove the oil fill plug, then tip the unit and pour all of the oil from the opening. Be sure to allow all of the oil to drain and be removed. Refill the crankcase with 3.4 fl. oz. (100 ml) of TORO Four-Cycle Engine Oil or a good quality SAE 30 oil designated API service class SG, SF or SH. Be sure the O-ring is installed on the fill plug and tighten the plug securely.

FUEL. The fuel tank should be filled with fresh regular or unleaded gasoline only. Do not mix oil with the fuel. The use of oxygenated (alcohol blended) gasoline is discouraged, but if used it should be as fresh as possible. Never use oxygenated fuel that has been stored 60 days or longer. Drain the fuel tank and run the engine until it stops before storing the unit. The manufacturer also recommends mixing 0.8 fl. oz. (23 ml) of Toro Gas Conditioner/Stabilizer, STA-BIL or an equivalent fuel additive with each gallon of oxygenated gasoline. Always mix additives with the gasoline in a separate container; never in the fuel tank.

The fuel pickup line inside the tank is fitted with a filter that is weighted to keep the pick up at the lowest part of the tank. The filter and pickup can be fished from the tank through the filler opening if replacement is required.

SPARK PLUG. The recommended spark plug is a Champion RDZ19H or equivalent and the electrode gap should be 0.025 in. (0.635 mm). Tighten the spark plug securely to the torque listed in the TIGHTENING TORQUE paragraph.

CARBURETOR. The engine is equipped with a Walbro carburetor. The manufacturer's model number is stamped on the carburetor. The carburetor can be removed after removing the air filter cover and filter (Fig. TO102). The throttle cable is attached to the third hole from the top of the carburetor throttle lever. When installing, tighten the attaching screws to the torque listed in the TIGHTENING TORQUE paragraph.

Refer to Fig. TO103 for an exploded view typical of the carburetor. Initial adjustment of the low-speed mixture screw and the high-speed mixture screw (Fig. TO104) is 1-1/8 turns open. The settings of these mixture screws is critical to the operation of the engine. Final adjustment should be performed carefully to insure easy starting and maximum performance.

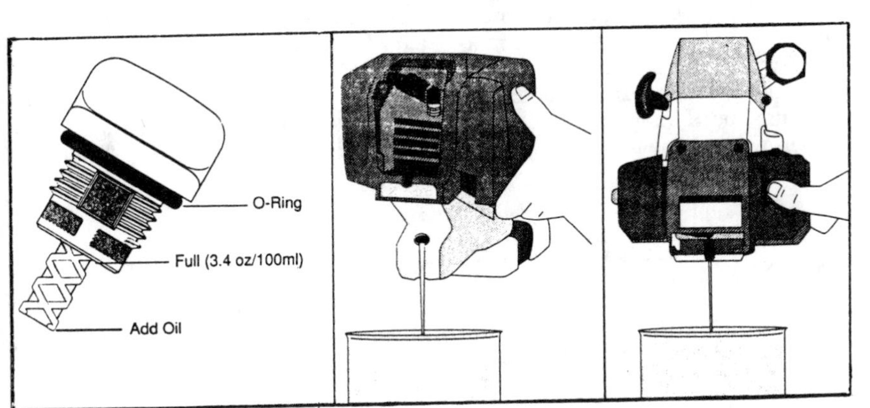

Fig. TO101—The oil level dipstick is attached to the filler plug. Make sure the "O" ring is installed on the plug.

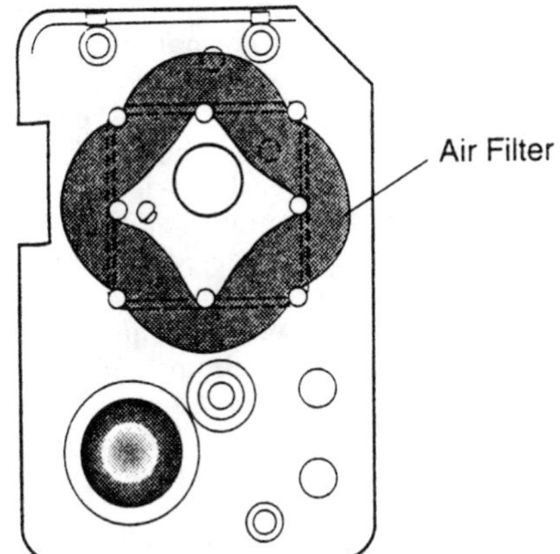

Fig. TO102—The air filter should be located as shown between the 8 posts.

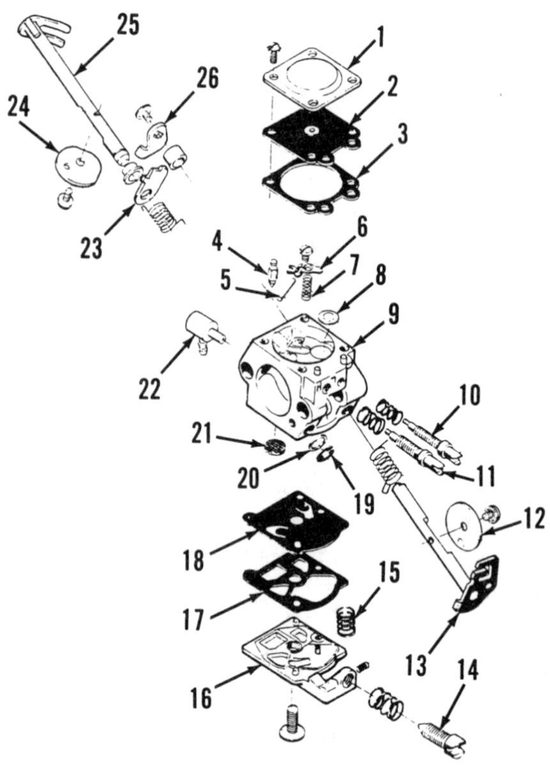

Fig. TO103—Exploded view of Walbro carburetor typical of the type used.

1. Cover
2. Metering diaphragm
3. Gasket
4. Fuel inlet valve
5. Pin
6. Metering lever
7. Spring
8. Welch plug
9. Carburetor body
10. Low-speed mixture screw
11. High-speed mixture screw
12. Choke plate
13. Choke shaft
14. Idle speed stop screw
15. Spring
16. Cover
17. Gasket
18. Fuel pump diaphragm
19. Retainer
20. Washer
21. Fuel screen
22. Fuel inlet fitting
23. Throttle lever
24. Throttle plate
25. Throttle shaft
26. Cam

Fig. TO105—Use a straightedge placed between the two projections as shown to measure the height of the fuel control lever. Refer to the text.

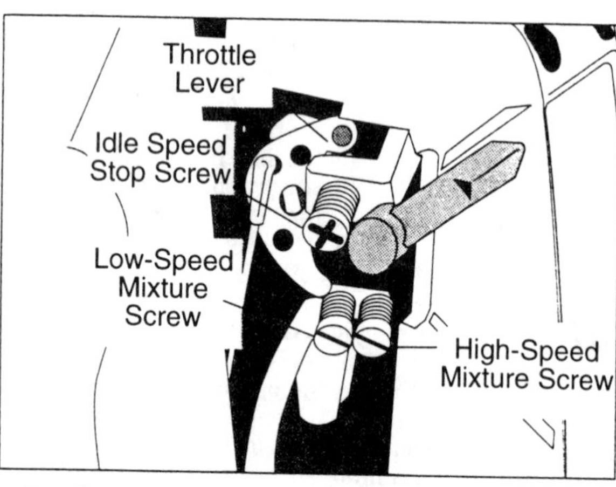

Fig. TO104—Adjust the low-speed mixture, high-speed mixture and idle speed as described in the text.

To adjust the mixture screws, first remove and clean the air filter, then reinstall it. Start the engine and allow it to run until it reaches normal operating temperature. If necessary, turn each of the mixture screws (Fig. TO104) clockwise until seated lightly, then back the screws out (counterclockwise) 1-1/8 turns to provide the initial adjustment so the engine can be started.

Turn the idle speed stop screw so the engine idles slow enough the clutch does not engage the trimmer or other attachment. Turning the mixture screws clockwise leans the fuel:air mixture and turning screws counterclockwise enriches the mixture.

Adjust the idle mixture needle so the engine idles smoothly and accelerates without hesitation. Readjust the idle speed stop screw if necessary to slow the idle speed. Adjust the high-speed mixture screw to provide the best performance while operating at maximum speed under load. The high-speed mixture screw may be set slightly rich to improve performance under load. The engine may be damaged if the high-speed screw is set too lean.

To disassemble the carburetor, refer to Fig. TO103 and remove covers (1 and 16) for access to internal components. Remove diaphragms (2 and 18), fuel metering lever (6), fuel inlet vlave (4) and fuel mixture needles (10 and 11). In order to thoroughly clean carburetor internal passages it is recommended that Welch plug (8) and fuel screen (21) be removed.

Clean and inspect all components. If the unit has been improperly stored, passages may be clogged with deposits that are hard, solid and nearly transparent. Be careful not to damage the openings or sealing surfaces while cleaning. Check the condition of diaphragms (2 and 18) carefully. Install new diaphragms if hard (not flexible), torn or otherwise damaged. Examine the fuel inlet valve (4), spring (7) and lever (6). A new fuel inlet valve needle (4), and mixture screws (10 and 11) can be installed, but their seats cannot be serviced if damaged. Inspect the condition of the filter screen (21).

To check the height of the metering lever, place a straightedge across the two projections on either side of the lever as shown in Fig. TO105. End of metering lever should be 0.060-0.070 in. (1.52-1.78 mm) below the straightedge. Carefully bend the lever if necessary to obtain the correct lever height.

Install a new primer bulb if hard, cracked or otherwise damaged. Attach the lines to the proper fittings of the primer as indicated in Fig. TO106. If

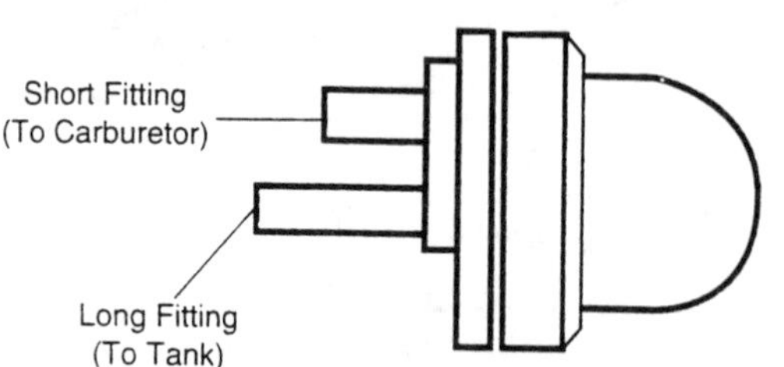

Fig. TO106—The primer bulb is fitted with a check valve and hoses should be attached properly as shown.

necessary, the primer bulb can be removed from the air filter base after squeezing the mounting tabs on the front of the bulb assembly.

VALVE CLEARANCE ADJUSTMENT. The clearance between the rocker arms and valves should be checked and adjusted, if necessary, after each 50 hours of operation.

Unbolt and remove the engine cover, then remove the valve cover. Remove the spark plug and turn the engine flywheel until the piston is at the top of the cylinder on the compression stroke. At this position, the rocker arms for both valves should be loose and both valves closed. If either valve is open (tight), turn the flywheel one complete turn and recheck. Measure the clearance between the rocker arm and valve stem using a feeler gauge as shown in Fig. TO107.

The correct clearance is 0.003-0.006 in. (0.076-0.152 mm). Clearance is changed by turning the adjusting nut at the center of the rocker arm. Be very careful to adjust the clearance correctly.

Reinstall the valve cover using a new gasket. Tighten the center screw to the torque listed in the TIGHTENING TORQUE paragraph. Attach the breather hose and install the engine cover, tightening the screws to the torque listed in the TIGHTENING TORQUE paragraph.

SPARK ARRESTER SCREEN. The exhaust outlet of the muffler is fitted with a spark arrester screen which should be removed and cleaned every 50 hours of operation. The spark arrester and screen is held in place with one screw. If the screen cannot be cleaned, install a new screen. Do not operate the unit with the screen removed. Tighten the attaching screw to the torque listed in the TIGHTENING TORQUE paragraph.

IGNITION SYSTEM. The engine is equipped with a solid-state ignition system. The ignition module/coil is located under the cowling at the front of the engine. Two screws attach the ignition module/coil to the engine's cylinder.

When installing, set the air gap between the flywheel magnets and the legs of the ignition module as follows. Install the ignition module, but tighten the two screws only enough to hold it in place away from the flywheel. Insert 0.008-0.012 in. (0.201-0.305 mm) thick brass or plastic shim stock between the legs of the ignition module and the flywheel, then turn the flywheel until the flywheel magnets are near the module legs. Loosen the screws attaching the ignition module and press legs of the ignition module against the shim stock, then tighten the two attaching screws to the torque listed in the TIGHTENING TORQUE paragraph. Remove the shim stock, then turn the flywheel and check to be sure the flywheel does not hit the legs of the coil.

REPAIRS

Many of the nuts, washers and screws used to assemble these engines are special and should not be interchanged with other similar parts.

COMPRESSION PRESSURE. The compression pressure should be 115-125 psi (793-862 kPa) for optimum performance. Check compression pressure with the engine warm and both throttle and choke open fully. Low pressure may indicate leaking valves, leaking head gasket or worn piston and rings. Carbon buildup will be indicated by higher pressures.

TIGHTENING TORQUE. Recommended tightening torque values are as follows.

Air filter	25-30 in.-lb. (2.8-3.3 N·m)
Cam bracket	15-20 in.-lb. (1.7-2.2 N·m)
Carburetor and mounting insulator	
Attaching screws	30-35 in.-lb. (3.3-3.9 N·m)
Clutch	
Cover attaching screws	35-45 in.-lb. (3.9-5.0 N·m)
Rotor (hub)	140-150 in.-lb. (15.8-16.9 N·m)
Cylinder attaching screws	35-45 in.-lb. (3.9-5.0 N·m)
Cylinder head attaching nuts	35-45 in.-lb. (3.9-5.0 N·m)
Drive shaft housing	
Locking (fitting) screw	15-20 in.-lb. (1.7-2.2 N·m)
Engine covers	
Top	15-20 in.-lb. (1.7-2.2 N·m)
Rear	30-35 in.-lb. (3.3-3.9 N·m)
Side	20-25 in.-lb. (2.5-3.0 N·m)
Fan housing	40-45 in.-lb. (4.5-5.0 N·m)
Fuel tank bracket	25-35 in.-lb. (2.8-3.3 N·m)
Grip (handle)	
Throttle and switch retainer	15-20 in.-lb. (1.7-2.2 N·m)
Upper to lower	20-25 in.-lb. (2.2-2.8 N·m)
Ignition	
Module/coil	30-40 in.-lb. (3.3-4.4 N·m)
Muffler	
Attaching screws	40-45 in.-lb. (4.5-5.0 N·m)
Spark arrester screw	15-20 in.-lb. (1.7-2.2 N·m)
Oil pan	35-45 in.-lb. (3.9-4.9 N·m)
Rocker arm cover	20-30 in.-lb. (2.2-3.3 N·m)
Spark plug	100-110 in.-lb. (11.2-12.3 N·m)

DISASSEMBLY. Many of the components can be removed and serviced without complete disassembly of the engine. However, following the sequence listed will be helpful if complete disassembly is required.

Drain fuel from the tank and oil from the crankcase. If the drive shaft and housing is fitted with a coupling, separate the engine and upper drive shaft from the lower part of the drive shaft and equipment. Remove the six Torx T-25 screws attaching the upper part of the grip (6—Fig. TO108), then separate and remove the top half. The vibration isolator will hold the halves of the grip together requiring the grip to be pried apart.

Observe the location of the throttle cable (1) and stop switch wires (2) to help you position these in the correct location when assembling. Detach the

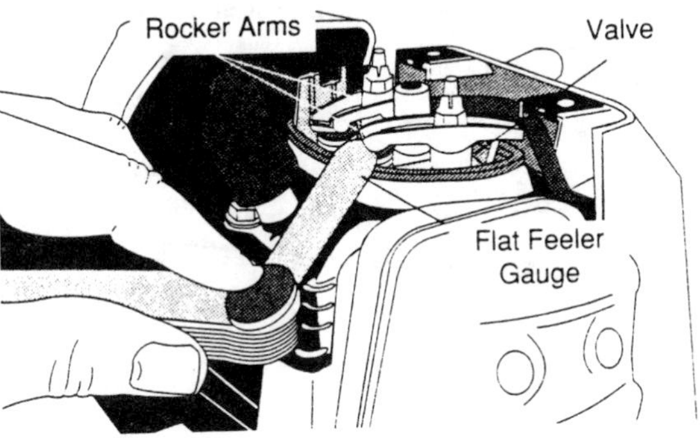

Fig. TO107—Refer to the text when measuring the valve clearance. The clearance is indicated by the thickest feeler gauge that can be inserted between the valve and rocker arm without forcing.

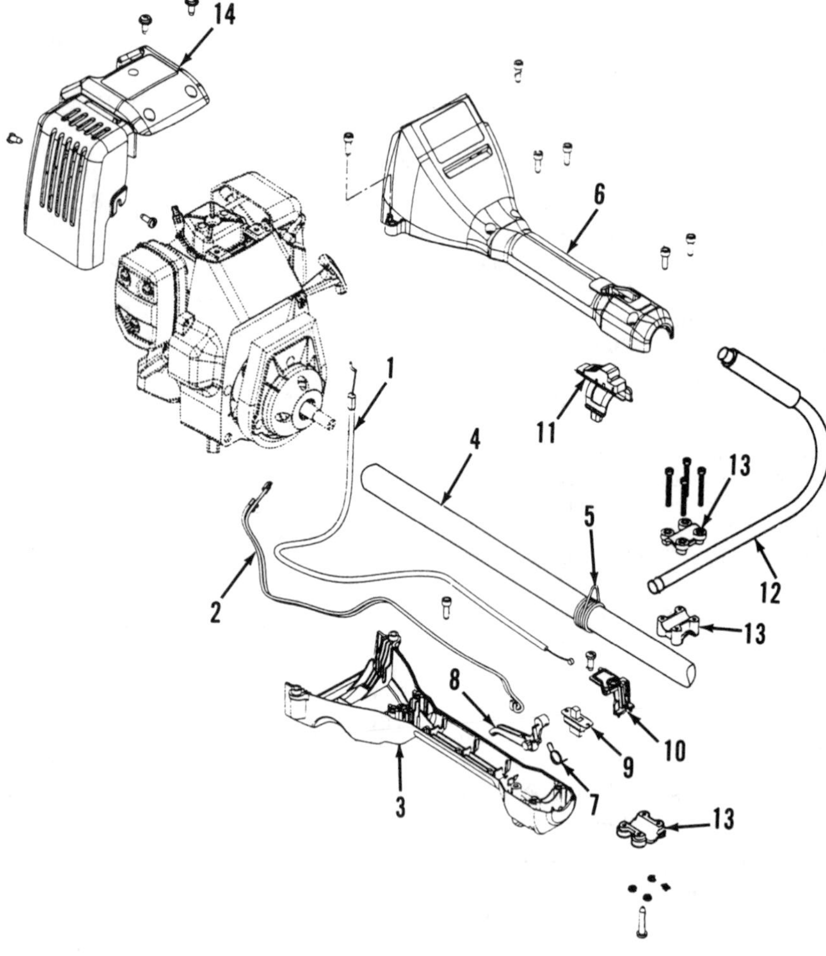

Fig. TO108—Exploded view of the grip and throttle trigger assembly.

1. Throttle cable
2. Engine stop wires
3. Grip lower housing
4. Drive shaft housing
5. Shoulder strap attachment
6. Grip upper housing
7. Throttle return spring
8. Throttle trigger
9. Engine stop switch
10. Trigger & switch retainer
11. Engine stop switch slider
12. J handle
13. Clamp assembly
14. Top cover

throttle cable and stop switch wires, then press the rear of the handle (3) down to remove it from the vibration isolator.

Remove the air filter cover , air filter, air filter base and carburetor (1, 2, 3 and 6—Fig. TO109). Detach the fuel lines from the primer bulb (4). Unbolt and remove the top cover (14—Fig. TO108) from the engine. Remove the two screws attaching the carburetor

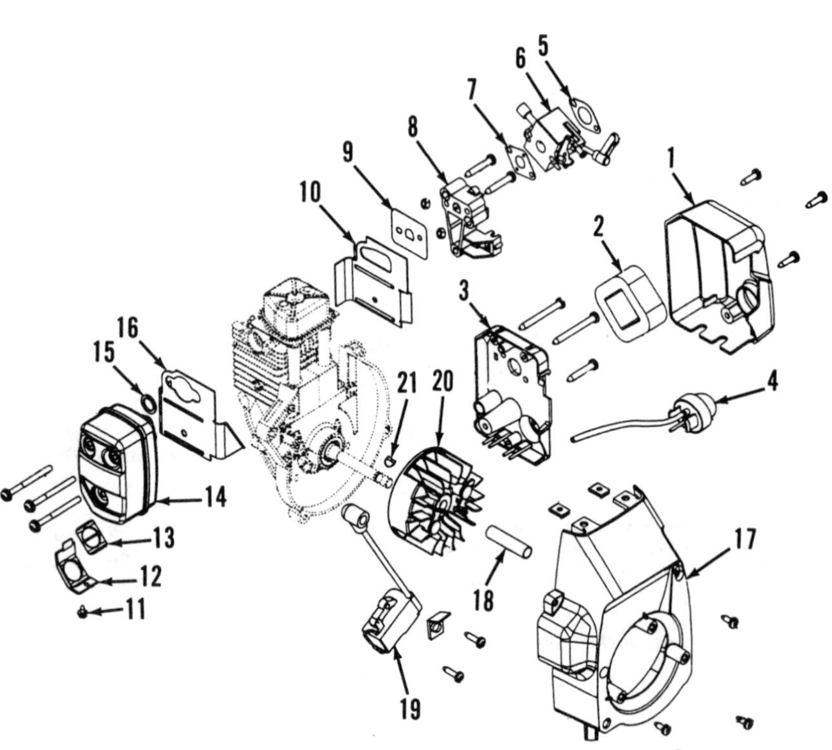

Fig. TO109—View of the intake, exhaust and ignition systems.

1. Air filter cover
2. Air filter foam
3. Air filter base
4. Primer bulb
5. Gasket
6. Carburetor
7. Gasket
8. Carburetor mount insulator
9. Gasket
10. Intake side baffle
11. Screw
12. Cover
13. Exhaust screen
14. Muffler
15. Gasket
16. Exhaust side baffle
17. Front cover
18. Spacer
19. Ignition module
20. Flywheel
21. Flywheel key

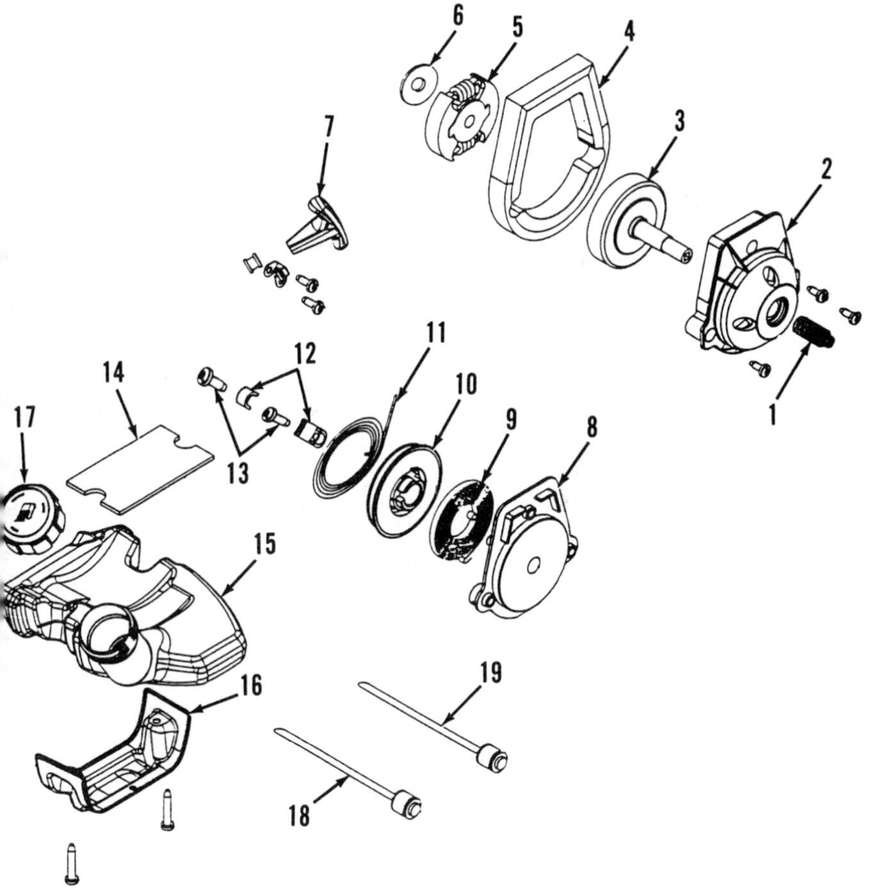

Fig. TO110—View of the clutch, starter and fuel tank.

1. Compression spring
2. Clutch housing
3. Clutch drum
4. Vibration isolator
5. Clutch rotor & shoes
6. Washer
7. Starter handle
8. Starter housing
9. Starter spring
10. Starter pulley
11. Rope
12. Starter pawls
13. Screws
14. Tank pad
15. Fuel tank
16. Bracket
17. Cap
18. Pickup line & filter
19. Fuel return line

mount isolator (8—Fig. TO109), then remove the isolator and gasket. Remove the intake baffle plate (9).

Unbolt and remove the muffler (14), being careful not to lose the trapped 5 mm nut for the upper rear screw located near the spark plug. Do not attempt to remove the heat shield (16) from between the muffler and the cylinder until other parts trapping it are removed. If the gasket (15) is removed from the exhaust port, be careful not to damage the cylinder head.

Remove the three screws attaching the clutch housing (2—Fig. TO110), then remove the clutch drum (3), housing (2) and vibration isolator (4). If necessary, the drive spring (1) can be removed from the clutch drum. Turn the flywheel until the starter pawls are located at 12 o'clock and 6 o'clock and install the flywheel holding tool (part No. 180919). Use the clutch tool (part No. 180918) to turn the clutch rotor counterclockwise and remove the clutch (5).

Unbolt and remove the starter assembly from the front cover and withdraw the spacer (18—Fig. TO109) from the crankshaft. Remove the screws attaching the fuel tank bracket (16—Fig. TO110), then remove the fuel tank. Remove the four attaching screws from the front cover (17—Fig. TO109). Detach the stop switch wires when the cover is withdrawn sufficiently. Unbolt and remove the ignition module (19). Bump the flywheel with a soft-faced mallet to dislodge the flywheel from the tapered surface. Remove the flywheel and the drive key (20 and 21).

Remove the screw (1—Fig. TO111) from the center of the rocker arm cover, then remove the cover (2) and gasket (5). Remove the adjusting nuts (6) from both rocker arms, then remove the rocker arms (8) and pivots (7). Rocker arms, pivots and push rods (9) are identical for both valves, but should be installed in their original location. Keep each rocker arm with its push rod and pivot, marking each indicating its location on the intake valve or exhaust valve.

Remove the four retaining nuts and the special hardened washers attaching the cylinder head. Do not lose or mix these washers with other similar washers. Use needle nose pliers to remove the push rod guides (12) from the cylinder studs. Lift the cylinder head from the cylinder and remove gasket (18) and "O" rings (17). Do not attempt to separate the rocker box from the cylinder head. Remove the two screws (20) attaching the cylinder to the crankcase. Lift the cylinder (19) carefully, supporting the piston as the cylinder is raised.

Slide the connecting rod to the rear and lift it from the crankshaft and crankcase. Remove the two screws attaching the cam bracket (22) to the crankcase and remove the cam gear (24), bracket and cam followers (23). **The crankshaft should not be removed from the crankcase.** The oil pan (33) can be unbolted from the rear of the crankcase if required. The lip type crankshaft oil seal (34) can be removed from the front of the crankcase if renewal is required.

REASSEMBLY. Reassemble in the reverse of disassembly procedure. Refer to the individual service paragraphs for additional assembly instructions. Tighten fasteners to the torque listed in the TIGHTENING TORQUE paragraph.

When assembling the halves of the grip (3 and 6—Fig. TO108), first install and assemble the lower grip, throttle trigger, return spring (7), engine stop switch (9) and retainer (10). Make sure the wires (2) and throttle cable (1) are routed properly.

Install the drive shaft and housing (4) so the hole in the upper end engages the locating screw in the lower grip half (3). Wrap masking tape around the drive shaft and lower grip to hold the parts together while installing the upper half of the grip. Install the slide (11), then install the upper half of the grip (6). Soap and water can be used to lubricate the vibration isolator making installation of the grips easier. Make sure that all parts fit together properly before installing the six attaching screws. When the halves of the grip fit together properly and the controls operate properly, cut the masking tape and install the six screw. Tighten fasteners to the torque listed in the TIGHTENING TORQUE paragraph. Make sure the engine is serviced with oil before starting.

CYLINDER HEAD AND VALVES. Clean the cylinder head and make sure

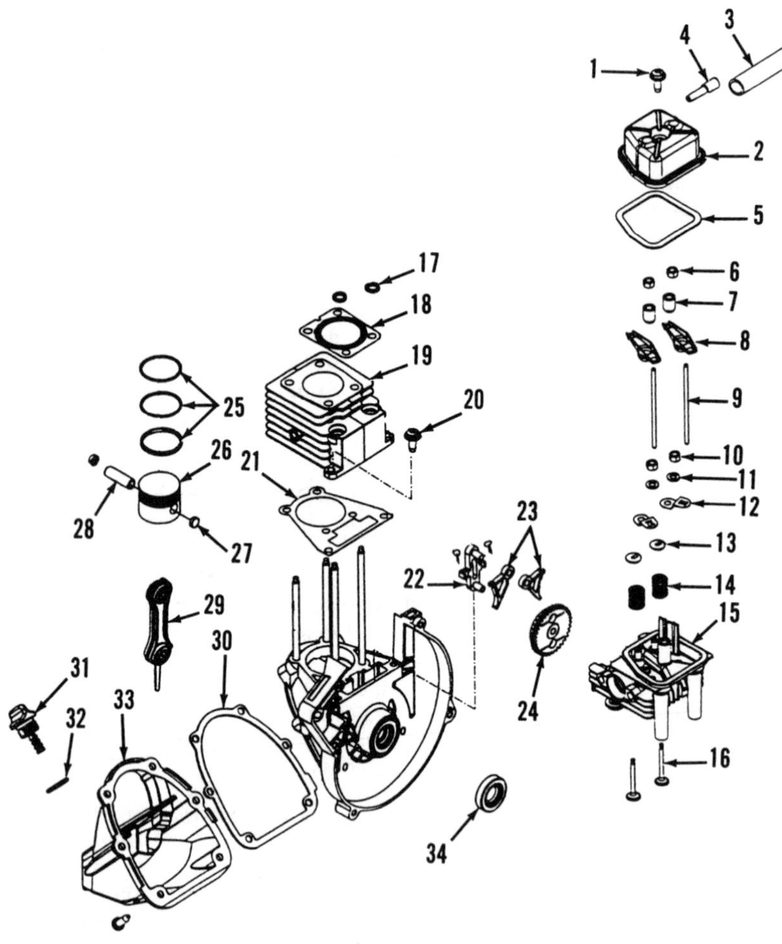

Fig. TO111—Exploded view of the engine sho block assembly.

1. Screw
2. Rocker arm cover
3. Breather hose
4. Breather assembly
5. Gasket
6. Retaining & adjusting nuts
7. Rocker arm pivots
8. Rocker arms
9. Push rods
10. Retaining nuts
11. Washers
12. Push rod guides
13. Valve spring retainers
14. Valve springs
15. Cylinder head
16. Valves
17. "O" rings
18. Head gasket
19. Cylinder
20. Screws
21. Base gasket
22. Cam bracket
23. Cam followers
24. Cam and gear
25. Piston rings
26. Piston
27. Button plugs
28. Piston pin
29. Connecting ro
30. Gasket
31. Filler plug
32. "O" ring
33. Oil pan
34. Oil seal

to remove all gasket residue, but be careful to prevent damaging any surface while cleaning. Check all of the gasket surfaces for scratches or nicks. Inspect the small EGR (exhaust gas recirculation) hole between the intake and exhaust passages in the cylinder head.

The valves and seats cannot be serviced except by installing new parts. Check the valves for proper sealing. It should be possible to compress the valve springs with your fingers, then press the retainer (13—Fig. TO111) to the side and remove the retainer, spring (13) and valve (16).

Clean the gasket surfaces of the cylinder and head thoroughly, but do not nick, scratch or otherwise damage the surfaces while cleaning. Install new "O" rings (19), making sure they are seated correctly and not damaged or twisted, then lubricate the installed "O" rings with new oil.

Install a new cylinder head gasket (18) with the notch toward the spark plug side of the cylinder. The domed side of the cylinder head gasket should be toward the top. Make sure the studs and the bores for the studs inside the rocker arm compartment are clean and dry, then install the cylinder head and valves over the studs. Seal the two cylinder head studs inside the rocker arm compartment with RTV sealer, then install the push rod guides (12) over the studs. Install the four special hardened washers (11) and retaining nuts (10). Tighten the retaining nuts in a crossing pattern to the torque listed in the TIGHTENING TORQUE paragraph.

Lubricate the push rods with engine oil, then insert into the push rod tubes until seated in the cam followers. Lubricate the rocker arms and pivots (7 and 8), then install the retaining/adjusting nuts (6). Refer to the VALVE CLEARANCE ADJUSTMENT paragraphs when installing these nuts.

The breather (4) should be inserted into the end of hose (3), then insert the hose through the hole in rocker arm cover (2) from the inside until the hose is securely wedged in the cover. Install the rocker arm cover using a new gasket (5) and tighten the retaining screw (1) to the torque listed in the TIGHTENING TORQUE paragraph.

PISTON, RINGS AND CONNECTING ROD. Rings (25—Fig. TO111) should not be removed from the piston (26) unless new rings are available for installation. Check the side clearance of the rings in the grooves. Clearance should not exceed 0.005 in. (0.127 mm).

The piston pin buttons (27) and piston pin (28) can be removed, separating the piston from the connecting rod (29). Inspect the crankpin for any scoring or other signs of damage. The crankshaft is not available for service. If the crankpin is damaged, a new short block should be installed.

Clean the ring grooves in the piston, but be very careful not to nick or gouge the piston. Refer to Fig. TO112 and install the rings in the piston grooves as follows. Lubricate the new rings with clean oil before installing. Install the bottom oil control ring first, followed by the middle (compression/scraper ring). The middle ring should be installed as shown in Fig. TO112, with the inside chamfer to the top and the cut-away outer edge to the bottom. Install the top ring with the chamfered inner edge to the top as shown. Spread the ring gap only enough to install the ring over the piston. Be careful not to damage either

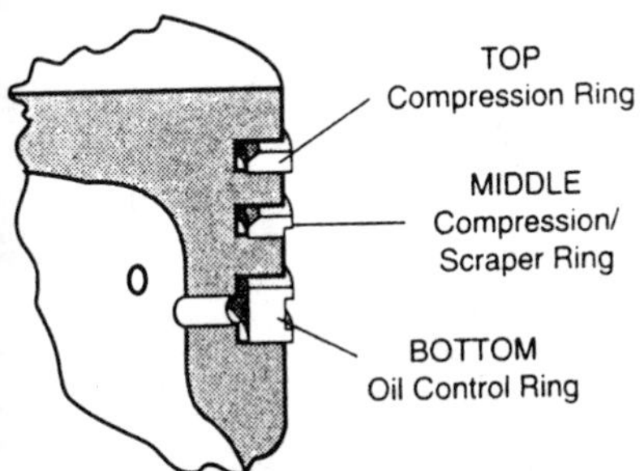

Fig. TO112—Install the piston rings in the grooves as shown. The chamfer on the inside of the rings should be toward the top of the piston. The ring with the groove on the outer diameter should be installed in the middle groove with the outer groove down.

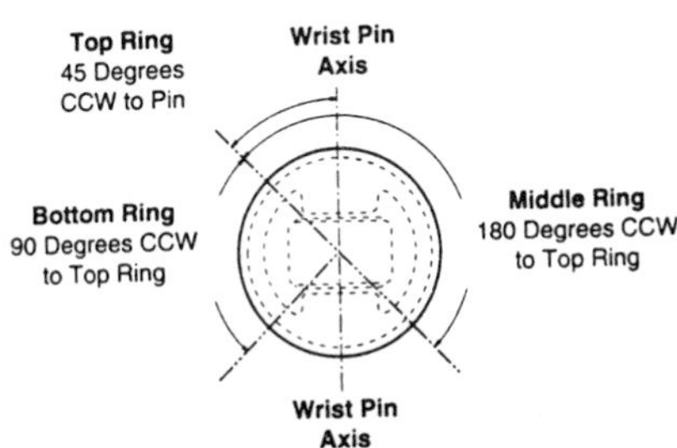

Fig. TO113—The end gap of the rings should be located as shown when installing the cylinder over the piston and rings.

the ring or the piston when installing. Install the piston pin buttons (27—Fig. TO111) with the smooth side out.

Lubricate the connecting rod bearing and the crankpin, then install the piston/connecting rod. The connecting rod should be installed on the crankshaft crankpin with the **markings on the needle bearing toward the front** (crankshaft counterweight). Slide the connecting rod over the crankshaft crankpin.

Position the rings with the end gaps as shown in Fig. TO113 before installing the cylinder. Refer to the CYLINDER paragraph for installation of the cylinder.

CAM BRACKET, GEAR AND FOLLOWERS. The cam bracket (22—Fig. TO111) is attached to the crankcase with two screws. If removed, the cam gear (24) must be correctly timed to the position of the crankshaft. Cleaning and inspection may be accomplished without removing the bracket, gear and followers, but if removed, the gear must be timed to the crankshaft. Inspect all parts for cracks, damaged teeth, broken parts or other damage.

Assemble the bracket, gear and followers (Fig. TO114) as follows. Lubricate parts, then install the followers on the longer post, which is indicated by the step (S). Install the gear on the lower post, guiding the followers over the cam. Turn the gear until the

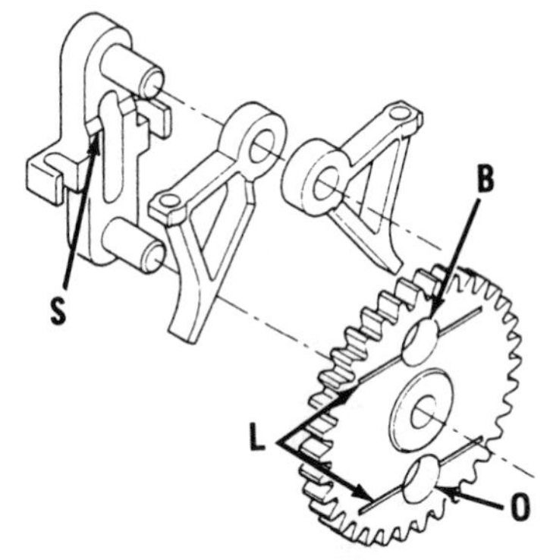

Fig. TO114—Refer to the text when assembling and installing the cam bracket, gear and followers.

blocked hole (B) is to the top and open hole (O) is down. The lines (L) should be parallel with the mounting surface of the bracket.

To install and time the cam to the crankshaft, proceed as follows. Turn the crankshaft until the crankpin is at the top of its stroke. The crankpin should be centered between the two marks on the crankcase inside the bore for the cylinder. Insert the bracket, gear and followers assembly into the crankcase with the blocked hole (B) still to the top and the open hole (O) down. Make sure the lines (L) remain parallel with the cylinder mounting surface of the crankcase when the bracket is seated. Install and tighten the two screws attaching the cam bracket to the torque listed in the TIGHTENING TORQUE paragraph.

CYLINDER. The cylinder and piston are available in standard size only. Check the piston and cylinder for wear or damage. It is suggested that both be renewed if either is worn or damaged excessively. Be sure that all gasket surfaces are cleaned thoroughly, but do not nick, scratch or otherwise damage the cylinder while cleaning. Lubricate the cylinder, piston and rings thoroughly before installing the cylinder.

Install the cam bracket, gear and followers assembly as described. Install the piston, rings and connecting rod as described. Carefully install the cylinder base gasket (21—Fig. TO111). Lubricate the cylinder bore with new oil. Check to be sure the ring end gaps are located as shown in Fig. TO113, press the rings carefully into their grooves and hold the piston pin buttons (27—Fig. TO111) in place while installing the cylinder over the piston. Install the two cylinder retaining screws to the torque listed in the TIGHTENING TORQUE paragraph. Install the cylinder head as previously described.

MUFFLER. Make sure the exhaust side baffle (16—Fig. TO109) is in place. Remove the old gasket (15) and clean the cylinder head carefully, being careful not to nick, scratch or otherwise damage the cylinder head.

Install a new gasket, then position the muffler. Install the lower screw first, but do not tighten until the other screws are installed. The 5 mm nut must be held in place in the slot nearest the spark plug while installing the upper screw. Tighten fittings to the torque listed in the TIGHTENING TORQUE paragraph.

CLUTCH. To remove clutch assembly, remove the six Torx T-25 screws attaching the upper part of the grip (6—Fig. ID8), then separate and remove the top half. The vibration isolator will hold the halves of the grip together, requiring the grip to be pried apart.

Observe the location of the throttle cable (1) and stop switch wires (2) to help you position these in the correct location when assembling. Detach the throttle cable and stop switch wires, then press the rear of the handle (3) down to remove it from the vibration isolator.

Remove the three screws attaching the clutch housing (2—Fig. ID15), then remove the clutch drum (3), housing (2) and vibration isolator (4). If necessary, the drive spring (1) can be removed from the clutch drum. Turn the flywheel until the starter pawls are located at 12 o'clock and 6 o'clock and install the flywheel holding tool (part No. 180919). Use the clutch tool (part No. 180918) to turn the clutch rotor counterclockwise and remove the clutch (5).

Inspect clutch drum (3—Fig. ID15) and rotor (5) for wear or damage and renew as necessary. When installing clutch, be sure that spacer (6) is installed on crankshaft. Tighten clutch rotor to 140-150 in.-lb. (15.8-16.9 N•m).

REWIND STARTER. Refer to Fig. ID15 for an exploded view of typical rewind starter. To service starter, first remove the upper handle and the clutch assembly as previously outlined. Unbolt and remove starter housing from engine.

Remove the rope handle and allow the rope to wind into the starter. Remove the two screws (14—Fig. ID15) and retainers (13). Removing starter pulley (11). Use caution when removing rewind spring (10) as the spring may unwind uncontrollably causing injury. Wear appropriate safety eye wear and

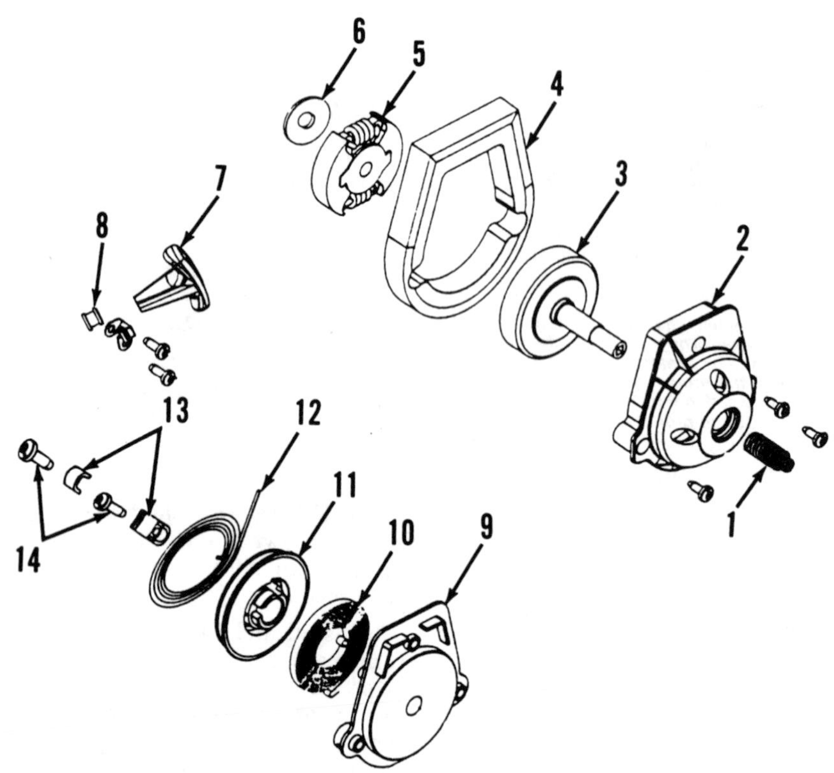

Fig. TO15—Exploded view of clutch assembly and rewind starter.

1. Spring
2. Clutch housing
3. Clutch drum
4. Isolator
5. Clutch rotor
6. Spacer
7. Rope handle
8. Guide eyelet
9. Starter housing
10. Rewind spring
11. Starter pulley
12. Rope
13. Retainers
14. Screws

gloves before removing the recoil spring from the housing. Drop the starter housing in a trash container or on the floor to release the spring from the housing. A replacement rewind spring comes prewound and contained in a spring retainer.

When installing new rewind spring, be sure that spring windings are clockwise (open end of spring inner hook is to the left). Grasp spring with needle nose pliers and remove spring retainer. Position spring in starter housing with spring hook installed into groove in housing, then release the needle nose pliers holding the spring. Lubricate the center post and spring side of pulley with small amount of grease.

If replacing starter rope, insert rope through hole in pulley and tie a single knot approximately 1/2 in. (12.7 mm) from end of rope. Pull the knot into pocket in the pulley. Hold pulley with pawl teeth towards you, then wrap rope around pulley in clockwise direction. Thread the rope through the guide eyelet (8), then attach the handle (7). Install the pulley over the center post of the housing while making sure the pulley engages the end of the rewind spring. Wind the pulley one full turn to preload the rewind spring. Install pulley retainers (13) and screws (14).

TWO-STROKE ENGINES

MIXING GASOLINE AND OIL

Most two-stroke engines are lubricated by oil mixed with the gasoline. The manufacturers carefully determine which type of oil and how much oil should be mixed with the gasoline to provide the most desirable operation, then list these mixing instructions. Often, two or more gasoline-to-oil ratios will be listed depending upon type of oil or severity of service.

You should always follow the manufacturer's recommended mixing instructions, because mixing the wrong amount of oil or using the wrong type of oil can cause extensive engine damage. Too much oil can cause lower power, spark plug fouling and excessive carbon buildup. Not enough oil will cause inadequate lubrication and will probably result in scuffing, seizure or other forms of engine damage.

Use only the gasoline type and octane rating recommended by manufacturer. Never use gasoline that has been stored for a long period of time.

Accurate measurement of gasoline and oil is necessary to assure correct lubrication. Proper quantities of gasoline and oil for some of the more common mixture ratios are shown in the accompanying chart.

When mixing, use a separate, approved, safety container that is large enough to hold the desired amount of fuel with additional space for mixing. Pour about half the required amount of gasoline into container, add the required amount of oil, then shake vigorously until completely mixed. Pour remaining amount of gasoline into container, then complete mixing by shaking. Serious engine damage can be caused by incomplete mixing. Never attempt to mix gasoline and oil in the unit's fuel tank.

Always observe safe handling practices when working with gasoline. Gasoline is extremely flammable. Do not smoke or allow sparks or open flame around fuel or in the presence of fuel vapors. Be sure area is well-ventilated. Observe fire prevention rules.

Ratio	Gasoline	Oil
14:1	0.9 Gal. (3.4 L)	8 oz. (235 mL)
16:1	1.0 Gal. (3.8 L)	8 oz. (235 mL)
20:1	1.25 Gal. (4.7 L)	8 oz. (235 mL)
25:1	1.5 Gal. (5.7 L)	8 oz. (235 mL)
30:1	1.9 Gal. (7.2 L)	8 oz. (235 mL)
32:1	2.0 Gal. (7.6 L)	8 oz. (235 mL)
40:1	2.5 Gal. (9.4 L)	8 oz. (235 mL)
50:1	3.1 Gal. (11.7 L)	8 oz. (235 mL)

Ratio	Gasoline	Oil
14:1	1 Gal. (3.8 L)	9.1 oz. (270 mL)
16:1	1 Gal. (3.8 L)	8.0 oz. (235 mL)
20:1	1 Gal. (3.8 L)	6.4 oz. (190 mL)
25:1	1 Gal. (3.8 L)	5.1 oz. (150 mL)
30:1	1 Gal. (3.8 L)	4.2 oz. (125 mL)
32:1	1 Gal. (3.8 L)	4.0 oz. (120 mL)
40:1	1 Gal. (3.8 L)	3.2 oz. (95 mL)
50:1	1 Gal. (3.8 L)	2.5 oz. (75 mL)

METRIC CONVERSION

Square centimeters	x .155	= Square inches
Square centimeters	= 6.4515	x Square inches
Square meters	x 10.7641	= Square feet
Square meters	= .0929	x Square feet
Cubic centimeters	x .061025	= Cubic inches
Cubic centimeters	= 16.387	x Cubic inches
Cubic meters	x 35.3156	= Cubic feet
Cubic meters	= .0283	x Cubic feet
Cubic meters	x 1.308	= Cubic yards
Cubic meters	= .765	x Cubic yards
Liters	x 61.023	= Cubic inches
Liters	= .0164	x Cubic inches
Liters	x .2642	= U.S. gallons
Liters	= 3.7854	x U.S. gallons
Grams	x 15.4324	= Grains
Grams	= .0648	x Grains
Grams	x .03527	= Ounces avoirdupois
Grams	= 28.3495	x Ounces avoirdupois
Kilograms	x 2.2046	= Pounds
Kilograms	= .4536	x Pounds
Kilograms per square centimeter	x 14.2231	= Pounds per square inch
Kilograms per square centimeter	= .0703	x Pounds per square inch
Kilograms per cubic meter	x .06243	= Pounds per cubic foot
Kilograms per cubic meter	= 16.0189	x Pounds per cubic foot
Metric tons (1000 kilograms)	x 1.1023	= Tons (2000 pounds)
Metric tons (1000 kilograms)	= .9072	x Tons (2000 pounds)
Kilowatts	= .746	x Horsepower
Kilowatts	x 1.3405	= Horsepower
Millimeters	x .03937	= Inches
Millimeters	= 25.4	x Inches
Meters	x 3.2809	= Feet
Meters	= .3048	x Feet
Kilometers	x .62138	= Miles
Kilometers	= 1.6093	x Miles

METRIC CONVERSION

MM.	INCHES		
1	0.0394	1/32	+
2	0.0787	3/32	–
3	0.1181	1/8	–
4	0.1575	5/32	+
5	0.1969	3/16	+
6	0.2362	1/4	–
7	0.2756	9/32	–
8	0.3150	5/16	+
9	0.3543	11/32	+
10	0.3937	13/32	–
11	0.4331	7/16	–
12	0.4724	15/32	+
13	0.5118	1/2	+
14	0.5512	9/16	–
15	0.5906	19/32	–
16	0.6299	5/8	+
17	0.6693	21/32	+
18	0.7087	23/32	–
19	0.7480	3/4	–
20	0.7874	25/32	+
21	0.8268	13/16	+
22	0.8661	7/8	–
23	0.9055	29/32	–
24	0.9449	15/16	+
25	0.9843	31/32	+
26	1.0236	1 1/32	–
27	1.0630	1 1/16	+
28	1.1024	1 3/32	+
29	1.1417	1 5/32	–
30	1.1811	1 3/16	–
31	1.2205	1 7/32	+
32	1.2598	1 1/4	+
33	1.2992	1 5/16	–
34	1.3386	1 11/32	–
35	1.3780	1 3/8	+
36	1.4173	1 13/32	+
37	1.4567	1 15/32	–
38	1.4961	1 1/2	–
39	1.5354	1 17/32	+
40	1.5748	1 9/16	+
41	1.6142	1 5/8	–
42	1.6535	1 21/32	–
43	1.6929	1 11/16	+
44	1.7323	1 23/32	+
45	1.7717	1 25/32	–
46	1.8110	1 13/16	–
47	1.8504	1 27/32	+
48	1.8898	1 7/8	+
49	1.9291	1 15/16	–
50	1.9685	1 31/32	–

MM.	INCHES		
51	2.0079	2.0	+
52	2.0472	2 1/16	–
53	2.0866	2 3/32	–
54	2.1260	2 1/8	+
55	2.1654	2 5/32	+
56	2.2047	2 7/32	–
57	2.2441	2 1/4	–
58	2.2835	2 9/32	+
59	2.3228	2 5/16	+
60	2.3622	2 3/8	–
61	2.4016	2 13/32	–
62	2.4409	2 7/16	+
63	2.4803	2 15/32	+
64	2.5197	2 17/32	–
65	2.5591	2 9/16	–
66	2.5984	2 19/32	+
67	2.6378	2 5/8	+
68	2.6772	2 11/16	–
69	2.7165	2 23/32	–
70	2.7559	2 3/4	+
71	2.7953	2 25/32	+
72	2.8346	2 27/32	–
73	2.8740	2 7/8	–
74	2.9134	2 29/32	+
75	2.9528	2 15/16	+
76	2.9921	3.0	–
77	3.0315	3 1/32	+
78	3.0709	3 1/16	+
79	3.1102	3 1/8	–
80	3.1496	3 5/32	–
81	3.1890	3 3/16	+
82	3.2283	3 7/32	+
83	3.2677	3 9/32	–
84	3.3071	3 5/16	–
85	3.3465	3 11/32	+
86	3.3858	3 3/8	+
87	3.4252	3 7/16	–
88	3.4646	3 15/32	–
89	3.5039	3 1/2	+
90	3.5433	3 17/32	+
91	3.5827	3 19/32	–
92	3.6220	3 5/8	–
93	3.6614	3 21/32	+
94	3.7008	3 11/16	+
95	3.7402	3 3/4	–
96	3.7795	3 25/32	–
97	3.8189	3 13/16	+
98	3.8583	3 27/32	+
99	3.8976	3 29/32	–
100	3.9370	3 15/16	–

MM.	INCHES		
101	3.9764	3 31/32	+
102	4.0157	4 1/32	–
103	4.0551	4 1/16	–
104	4.0945	4 3/32	+
105	4.1339	4 1/8	+
106	4.1732	4 3/16	–
107	4.2126	4 7/32	–
108	4.2520	4 1/4	+
109	4.2913	4 9/32	+
110	4.3307	4 11/32	–
111	4.3701	4 3/8	–
112	4.4094	4 13/32	+
113	4.4488	4 7/16	+
114	4.4882	4 1/2	–
115	4.5276	4 17/32	–
116	4.5669	4 9/16	+
117	4.6063	4 19/32	+
118	4.6457	4 21/32	–
119	4.6850	4 11/16	–
120	4.7244	4 23/32	+
121	4.7638	4 3/4	+
122	4.8031	4 13/16	–
123	4.8425	4 27/32	–
124	4.8819	4 7/8	+
125	4.9213	4 29/32	+
126	4.9606	4 31/32	–
127	5.0000	5.0	
128	5.0394	5 1/32	+
129	5.0787	5 3/32	–
130	5.1181	5 1/8	–
131	5.1575	5 5/32	+
132	5.1968	5 3/16	+
133	5.2362	5 1/4	–
134	5.2756	5 9/32	–
135	5.3150	5 5/16	+
136	5.3543	5 11/32	+
137	5.3937	5 13/32	–
138	5.4331	5 7/16	–
139	5.4724	5 15/32	+
140	5.5118	5 1/2	+
141	5.5512	5 9/16	–
142	5.5905	5 19/32	–
143	5.6299	5 5/8	+
144	5.6693	5 21/32	+
145	5.7087	5 23/32	–
146	5.7480	5 3/4	–
147	5.7874	5 25/32	+
148	5.8268	5 13/16	+
149	5.8661	5 7/8	–
150	5.9055	5 29/32	–

MM.	INCHES		
151	5.9449	5 15/16	+
152	5.9842	5 31/32	+
153	6.0236	6 1/32	–
154	6.0630	6 1/16	+
155	6.1024	6 3/32	+
156	6.1417	6 5/32	–
157	6.1811	6 3/16	–
158	6.2205	6 7/32	+
159	6.2598	6 1/4	+
160	6.2992	6 5/16	–
161	6.3386	6 11/32	–
162	6.3779	6 3/8	+
163	6.4173	6 13/32	+
164	6.4567	6 15/32	–
165	6.4961	6 1/2	–
166	6.5354	6 17/32	+
167	6.5748	6 9/16	+
168	6.6142	6 5/8	–
169	6.6535	6 21/32	–
170	6.6929	6 11/16	+
171	6.7323	6 23/32	+
172	6.7716	6 25/32	–
173	6.8110	6 13/16	–
174	6.8504	6 27/32	+
175	6.8898	6 7/8	+
176	6.9291	6 15/16	–
177	6.9685	6 31/32	–
178	7.0079	7.0	+
179	7.0472	7 1/16	–
180	7.0866	7 3/32	–
181	7.1260	7 1/8	+
182	7.1653	7 5/32	+
183	7.2047	7 7/32	–
184	7.2441	7 1/4	–
185	7.2835	7 9/32	+
186	7.3228	7 5/16	+
187	7.3622	7 3/8	–
188	7.4016	7 13/32	–
189	7.4409	7 7/16	+
190	7.4803	7 15/32	+
191	7.5197	7 17/32	–
192	7.5590	7 9/16	–
193	7.5984	7 19/32	+
194	7.6378	7 5/8	+
195	7.6772	7 11/16	–
196	7.7165	7 23/32	–
197	7.7559	7 3/4	+
198	7.7953	7 25/32	+
199	7.8346	7 27/32	–
200	7.8740	7 7/8	–

MM.	INCHES		
201	7.9134	7 29/32	+
202	7.9527	7 15/16	+
203	7.9921	8.0	–
204	8.0315	8 1/32	+
205	8.0709	8 1/16	+
206	8.1102	8 1/8	–
207	8.1496	8 5/32	–
208	8.1890	8 3/16	+
209	8.2283	8 7/32	+
210	8.2677	8 9/32	–
211	8.3071	8 5/16	–
212	8.3464	8 11/32	+
213	8.3858	8 3/8	+
214	8.4252	8 7/16	–
215	8.4646	8 15/32	–
216	8.5039	8 1/2	+
217	8.5433	8 17/32	+
218	8.5827	8 19/32	–
219	8.6220	8 5/8	–
220	8.6614	8 21/32	+
221	8.7008	8 11/16	+
222	8.7401	8 3/4	–
223	8.7795	8 25/32	–
224	8.8189	8 13/16	+
225	8.8583	8 27/32	+
226	8.8976	8 29/32	–
227	8.9370	8 15/16	–
228	8.9764	8 31/32	+
229	9.0157	9 1/32	–
230	9.0551	9 1/16	–
231	9.0945	9 3/32	+
232	9.1338	9 1/8	+
233	9.1732	9 3/16	–
234	9.2126	9 7/32	–
235	9.2520	9 1/4	+
236	9.2913	9 9/32	+
237	9.3307	9 11/32	–
238	9.3701	9 3/8	–
239	9.4094	9 13/32	+
240	9.4488	9 7/16	+
241	9.4882	9 1/2	–
242	9.5275	9 17/32	–
243	9.5669	9 9/16	+
244	9.6063	9 19/32	+
245	9.6457	9 21/32	–
246	9.6850	9 11/16	–
247	9.7244	9 23/32	+
248	9.7638	9 3/4	+
249	9.8031	9 13/16	–
250	9.8425	9 27/32	–

MM.	INCHES		
251	9.8819	9 7/8	+
252	9.9212	9 29/32	+
253	9.9606	9 31/32	–
254	10.0000	10.0	
255	10.0393	10 1/32	+
256	10.0787	10 3/32	–
257	10.1181	10 1/8	–
258	10.1575	10 5/32	+
259	10.1968	10 3/16	+
260	10.2362	10 1/4	–
261	10.2756	10 9/32	–
262	10.3149	10 5/16	+
263	10.3543	10 11/32	+
264	10.3937	10 13/32	–
265	10.4330	10 7/16	–
266	10.4724	10 15/32	+
267	10.5118	10 1/2	+
268	10.5512	10 9/16	–
269	10.5905	10 19/32	–
270	10.6299	10 5/8	+
271	10.6693	10 21/32	+
272	10.7086	10 23/32	–
273	10.7480	10 3/4	–
274	10.7874	10 25/32	+
275	10.8268	10 13/16	+
276	10.8661	10 7/8	–
277	10.9055	10 29/32	–
278	10.9449	10 15/16	+
279	10.9842	10 31/32	+
280	11.0236	11 1/32	–
281	11.0630	11 1/16	+
282	11.1023	11 3/32	+
283	11.1417	11 5/32	–
284	11.1811	11 3/16	–
285	11.2204	11 7/32	+
286	11.2598	11 1/4	+
287	11.2992	11 5/16	–
288	11.3386	11 11/32	–
289	11.3779	11 3/8	+
290	11.4173	11 13/32	+
291	11.4567	11 15/32	–
292	11.4960	11 1/2	–
293	11.5354	11 17/32	+
294	11.5748	11 9/16	+
295	11.6142	11 5/8	–
296	11.6535	11 21/32	–
297	11.6929	11 11/16	+
298	11.7323	11 23/32	+
299	11.7716	11 25/32	–
300	11.8110	11 13/16	–

NOTE: The + or – sign indicates that the decimal equivalent is larger or smaller than the fractional equivalent.

MAINTENANCE LOG

MAINTENANCE LOG

MAINTENANCE LOG